DEMOCRATIC ENLIGHTENMENT

Democratic Enlightenment

Philosophy, Revolution, and Human Rights 1750–1790

JONATHAN I. ISRAEL

OXFORD
UNIVERSITY PRESS

OXFORD

UNIVERSITY PRESS

Great Clarendon Street, Oxford OX2 6DP

Oxford University Press is a department of the University of Oxford.
It furthers the University's objective of excellence in research, scholarship,
and education by publishing worldwide in

Oxford New York

Auckland Cape Town Dar es Salaam Hong Kong Karachi
Kuala Lumpur Madrid Melbourne Mexico City Nairobi
New Delhi Shanghai Taipei Toronto

With offices in

Argentina Austria Brazil Chile Czech Republic France Greece
Guatemala Hungary Italy Japan Poland Portugal Singapore
South Korea Switzerland Thailand Turkey Ukraine Vietnam

Oxford is a registered trade mark of Oxford University Press
in the UK and in certain other countries

Published in the United States
by Oxford University Press Inc., New York

British Library Cataloguing in Publication Data

Data available

Library of Congress Cataloging in Publication Data

Data available

Typeset by SPI Publisher Services, Pondicherry, India
Printed in Great Britain
on acid-free paper by
Clays Ltd, St Ives plc

ISBN 978–0–19–954820–0

1 3 5 7 9 10 8 6 4 2

Acknowledgements

During the years I have spent working on this third volume of my Enlightenment series, I have benefited so extensively from discussion about the Enlightenment in its many aspects with colleagues—historians, philosophers, and social scientists— around the world that it would make little sense simply to present a long list of them here. To those who have helped me most to correct errors and advance my understanding of the numerous themes and aspects where I have profited from the expertise of others, I have repeatedly spoken of my sense of debt and obligation. I would simply like to add here that I am immensely grateful for all the stimulation and help that resulted from all this discussion and sing the praises, as many of them would wish to too, in particular of three splendid centres for research and debate where the largest amounts of this process of comparing notes went on. For training in informed as well as independent critical thinking about society, politics, the democratic freedoms, and the uses of knowledge, the humanities surpass everything else by far, and in this uncomprehending era when the humanities are in retreat in so many higher education systems around the world there is nothing to beat the international research institutes for advancing what is best in the humanities.

Without the immense advantage of having been based at the Institute for Advanced Study, Princeton, during the period on which I worked on this volume not only would it lack much of whatever strength it has but it would almost certainly never have been attempted at all. Neither the time, nor the scholarly resources, nor the debates, nor the cross-disciplinary stimulation would have been available to anything like the necessary extent. The several months that I spent at the NIAS (Netherlands Institute for Advanced Study), the Dutch equivalent of the Princeton Institute, were also invaluable in this respect as were the months I worked in Oxford based at Corpus Christi College. It is to these three centres, above all the Princeton Institute, that I owe my overriding debt. Further, I would like to add a hearty word of thanks to all the many librarians in libraries in Europe and both Americas that assisted with this vast task.

Contents

PART IV: SPINOZA CONTROVERSIES IN THE LATER ENLIGHTENMENT

List of Plates

List of Abbreviations

AHR	*American Historical Review*
AHRF	*Annales historiques de la Révolution française*
BJECS	*British Journal of Eighteenth-Century Studies*
BMGN	*Bijdragen en Mededelingen betreffende de Geschiedenis der Nederlanden (Low Countries Historical Review)*
BTLVNI	*Bijdragen tot de Taal-Land- en Volkenkunde van Nederlandsch-Indië*
CGdH	*Correspondance générale d'Helvétius,* ed. A. Dainard et al. (3 vols., Toronto, 1984)
CHEPh	Knud Haakonssen (ed.), *The Cambridge History of Eighteenth-Century Philosophy* (2 vols., Cambridge, 2006)
CHEPTh	M. Goldie and R. Wokler (eds.), *The Cambridge History of Eighteenth-Century Political Thought* (Cambridge, 2006)
Corpus	*Corpus: revue de philosophie* (Paris X—Nanterre)
DGV	R. Trousson and J. Vercruysse (eds.), *Dictionnaire général de Voltaire* (Paris, 2003)
DHS	*Dix-Huitième Siècle*
DJJR	R. Trousson and F. S. Eigeldinger (eds.), *Dictionnaire de Jean-Jacques Rousseau* (Paris, 2006)
ESB	*Études sur le XVIIIe siècle: Université libre de Bruxelles*
FHS	*French Historical Studies*
GCFI	*Giornale critico della filosofia italiana*
GWN	H. W. Blom, Wiep van Bunge, H. A. Krop, and M. Wielema (eds.), *Geschiedenis van de Wijsbegeerte in Nederland* (Rotterdam, 1990–2004)
HAHR	*Hispanic American Historical Review*
HEI	*History of European Ideas*
HPSGF	*Handbuch politisch-sozialer Grundbegriffe in Frankreich 1680–1820*
HPTh	*History of Political Thought*
IHR	*Intellectual History Review*
JES	*Journal for Eighteenth-Century Studies*
JHI	*Journal of the History of Ideas*
JHPh	*Journal of the History of Philosophy*
JMEH	*Journal of Modern European History*
JMH	*Journal of Modern History*

Kn.	W. P. C. Knuttel, *Catalogus van de Pamfletten-verzameling berustende in de Koninklijke Bibliotheek*
OHBE	R. Louis (ed.), *Oxford History of the British Empire* (5 vols., Oxford, 1998)
PAPS	*Proceedings of the American Philosophical Society*
RDE	*Recherches sur Diderot et sur l'Encyclopédie*
SECC	*Studies in Eighteenth-Century Culture*
SHPhSc	*Studies in History and Philosophy of Science*
SVEC	*Studies on Voltaire and the Eighteenth Century* (Geneva)
TJEAS	*Taiwan Journal of East Asian Studies*

Abbreviations of Libraries, Collections of Manuscripts and Collections of Official Printed Edicts and Prohibitions

AN Bolivia	Archivo y Biblioteca Nacionales de Bolivia, Sucre, departamento de manuscritos
ARH	The Hague, Algemeen Rijksarchief
ARH VOC	Algemeen Rijksarchief, The Hague, archives of the Vereenigde Oost-Indische Compagnie
AUB	Amsterdam: Universiteitsbibliotheek
BL	London: British Library
BN Lima	Biblioteca Nacional, Lima, departamento de manuscritos
GrUB	Greifswald: Universitätsbibliothek
GUB	Göttingen: Universitätsbibliothek
HKB	The Hague: Koninklijke Bibliotheek (Royal Library)
IAS	Institute for Advanced Study, Princeton
PBN	Paris: Bibliothèque Nationale
TUB	Tilburg: Universiteits Bibliotheek
VBM	Venice: Bibliotheca Marciana
WHA	Wolfenbuttel: Herzog August Bibliothek
WLC	Washington, Library of Congress
WUL	Wrocław (Breslau) University Library
YSL	Yale: Sterling Memorial Library

1

Introduction

1. DEFINING THE ENLIGHTENMENT

In recent decades the other major historical transitions towards modernity—the Renaissance and Reformation, and also the British Industrial Revolution—have receded somewhat from the commanding centrality they used to enjoy in the world of historical studies. Both the Renaissance and the Protestant–Catholic split have recently tended to lose something of their earlier importance in our society. The effect of this together with the growing clash between theological perspectives and secularism and the increasingly fraught question of universal human rights has been to push the Enlightenment increasingly to the fore as the single most important topic, internationally, in modern historical studies, and one of crucial significance also in our politics, cultural studies, and philosophy.

Meanwhile, a growing tendency, from the 1970s onwards, to contest the validity of the 'Enlightenment's' ideals and see its laying the intellectual foundations of modernity in a negative rather than a positive light has, at the same time, caused an escalating 'crisis of the Enlightenment' in historical and philosophical studies.[1] In particular, Postmodernist thinkers have argued that its abstract universalism was ultimately destructive, that the relentless rationalism, concern with perfecting humanity, and universalism of what they often disparagingly called 'the Enlightenment project' was responsible for the organized mass violence of the later French Revolution and the still greater horrors perpetrated by imperialism, Communism, Fascism, and Nazism in the late nineteenth and twentieth centuries. Many argued that the assumption that humanity is 'infinitely malleable', as James Schmidt put it, 'provided the intellectual inspiration for attempts by totalitarian states to eradicate every trace of individuality from their subjects'.[2] Others insisted that the Enlightenment reduced complex moral dilemmas to a superficial level using simplistic solutions to iron out long-existing and deeply felt community differences and values. This multi-faceted indictment was lent added philosophical coherence by Michel Foucault's overarching and powerful claim

---

[1] Schmidt, *What is Enlightenment?*, 1; Bartlett, *Idea of Enlightenment*, 7–11; Dupré, *Enlightenment*, 335–6, 338; Robertson, *Case*, 1–2; Withers, *Placing*, 4–5.

[2] Schmidt, *What is Enlightenment?*, 1.

that the Enlightenment's insistence on the primacy of reason was ultimately just a mask for the exercise of power. He maintained, often very convincingly, that Enlightenment was not just about liberation but even more about new forms of constraint. Postmodernist theorists urge us to forget the Enlightenment's quest for universal moral and political foundations, claiming different cultures should be left 'to determine their own priorities and goals without our discriminating politically or morally between them'.[3] In this way a new 'project' arose, replacing the intellectual foundations forged by the Enlightenment with a fresh set of criteria framing a postmodern world built on multiculturalism, moral relativism, and the indeterminacy of truth.

Given the overriding importance and vast scope of this global cultural-philosophical clash today any scholar discussing Enlightenment in broad terms has a clear responsibility to render as accurate, carefully delineated, and complete a picture of the phenomenon as possible. Except for those willing to yield to Postmodernism and concede the death of reason and moral universalism, it remains an ongoing, live, and vital issue. Moreover, even many of the Enlightenment's contemporary defenders appear to agree that this great movement in global thought, interpretation, and reform 'was flawed and one-sided'. But was it? Before we can answer we need scholarship to explore the issue thoroughly, and it is an astounding fact that many aspects of this great movement still remain remarkably little known.

In view of this, and since this present study has now grown into a trilogy of volumes and become too large for readers easily to obtain an overview of, it seems essential to begin here by providing a clear and concise résumé of the overall argument, to enable readers to grasp clearly what is being argued and how this volume connects with the previous two in the series. This is all the more essential in that numerous determined and sometimes sharply expressed critiques questioning my general interpretation of the Enlightenment have appeared in recent years, notably by Theo Verbeek, Paolo Casini, Margaret Jacob, Henry Chiswick, Antony La Vopa, Wiep van Bunge, Antoine Lilti, Sam Moyn, Dan Edelstein, and on one crucial point also Siep Stuurman—the latter insisting that there is no 'necessary connection' between one-substance metaphysics and Radical Enlightenment political and social reformism, a contention in which he as well as the others are most certainly mistaken—debunking efforts which raise important and relevant questions and objections that need answering, certainly,[4] but also include much that amounts

---

[3] Robertson, *Case*, 1.

[4] The closely argued thirty-nine-page critique (*Annales*, 64 (2009), 171–206) by Antoine Lilti is the most cogent and effective of these critiques so far despite the striking contradiction in his robustly defending the socio-cultural approach of Darnton, Chartier, and Roche against my criticism after having conclusively demonstrated in his main work, *Le Monde des salons* (2005), that their socio-cultural approach to the Enlightenment vastly overestimates the role of new eighteenth-century social spaces and practices, such as the salons, in generating Enlightenment ideas and is totally invalid as a method of explaining the Enlightenment phenomenon. His critique is entitled 'Comment écrit-on l'histoire intellectuelle des Lumières? Spinozisme, radicalisme et philosophie'. My reply is forthcoming in the journal *La Lettre clandestine* (*Annales* having refused to publish a response of matching length to Lilti's detailed argument). Stuurman's claim that 'there is no necessary linkage between metaphysics and politics',

to little more than failure to grasp the argument and inaccuracy in reporting what is actually being argued.

The Enlightenment, I maintain, was the most important and profound intellectual, social, and cultural transformation of the Western world since the Middle Ages and the most formative in shaping modernity. It must be understood both as an intellectual movement and as mainstream socio-economic and political history—for historiography a distinctly unfamiliar combination. It evolved on both sides of the Atlantic and began in the second half of the seventeenth century. The product of a particular era, it has profoundly affected every aspect of modernity. What was the Enlightenment? Historians have found it notoriously difficult to provide a fully adequate definition. Many definitions have been suggested and used which are correct and relevant up to a point and capture much of what historians and philosophers identify as the Enlightenment, but none seems altogether satisfactory. Peter Gay was right to claim that the 'men of the Enlightenment united on a vastly ambitious programme, a programme of secularism, humanity, cosmopolitanism, and freedom, above all, freedom in its many forms—freedom from arbitrary power, freedom of speech, freedom of trade, freedom to realize one's talents, freedom of aesthetic response, freedom, in a word, of moral man to make his own way in the world'.[5] Only his definition seriously overstates the secularism of the mainstream Enlightenment and the strength of the commitment of many enlighteners to free speech, free trade, and personal freedom. It is also largely valid to say that the Enlightenment 'began not as a definite "thing" or even as a chronological period, but as processes concerned with the central place of reason and of experience and experiment in understanding and improving human society'.[6] What distinguished the Enlightenment's particular emphasis on reason was indeed a belief that applying reason tempered by experiment and experience, not anything based on blind authority, would bring vast social benefits. It can also be justly defined as an era that pursued with greater consistency than any other the notion that things ought to be justified rather than 'blindly accepted from habit and custom'.[7]

But while true as far as they go such definitions crucially miss the social historical dimension: they fail to give a sense of the Enlightenment being a response to the dilemmas of a society standing at the confluence of the static, the traditional norms, with the rapid changes, fluidity, and pluralism so typical of modernity,[8] or a sense of the ideologically and politically embattled status of the Enlightenment, its being besieged by powerful forces from without while also being continually ravaged by disputes within. Like both the Renaissance and Reformation, in the Enlightenment intellectual and doctrinal changes came first but impacted on—and responded

---

expounded in his article 'Pathways' and elsewhere, is repeated in his published lecture 'Global Equality and Inequality in Enlightenment Thought', 1, 28, 31–2.

[5] Gay, *Enlightenment*, i. 3.   [6] Withers, *Placing*, 2.
[7] Dupré, *Enlightenment*, 358.   [8] Roche, 'Lumières concrètes', 94–7.

to—social, cultural, economic, and political context so profoundly that they changed everything. But unlike the Renaissance which revolved around the rediscovery of the texts of classical antiquity, or the Reformation which pivoted on a revolt against Catholic doctrine and ecclesiastical authority and forged several Protestant confessions, with the Enlightenment it has proven difficult even to agree as to which intellectual tendencies should chiefly be stressed. Even the notion that the Enlightenment placed a new and particular stress on 'reason' can be easily questioned by citing the examples of Hume and Burke, two of the Enlightenment's greatest thinkers. Given the notorious difficulty of providing a complete definition it is unlikely that there will be general agreement regarding the definition employed here. But it is important to begin by clearly formulating the definition used in these volumes and briefly explaining why this definition of the Enlightenment seems more adequate than other characterizations.

In defining the Enlightenment, we must bear in mind two particular difficulties hindering a satisfactory, historically accurate characterization: first, it is undoubtedly true that as a general cultural phenomenon the Anglo-American Enlightenment placed much less emphasis on the role of reason and philosophy as the agent of change than was the case in France, Italy, and Germany; secondly, it is necessary to remember that the very term 'Enlightenment' we use today and its French equivalent *Lumières*, or Spanish *Ilustración*, are to a large extent later nineteenth- and twentieth-century constructions—though the German *Aufklärung* was more widely used in the late eighteenth century; the term 'Enlightenment' therefore carries an ideological baggage and resonances often superimposed later and not part of the original phenomenon. Hence, a fully adequate historical and philosophical definition does not necessarily have to accommodate some of the things academics, politicians, social theorists, and others writing today mean by the term 'Enlightenment'. Especially alien to the eighteenth-century concept—and sometimes pernicious in our contemporary usage—is the today widespread assumption in some quarters that we in the Western world are 'enlightened' and need to defend and preserve a supposedly shared body of values.

Furthermore, a habit has developed in recent decades in historical studies of focusing much attention in Enlightenment studies on questions of sociability, *mondanité*, cultural spaces. The study of sociability and social practices is often interesting and important but has little directly to do with what contemporaries meant when they accounted innovations, recommendations, or changes 'enlightened', *éclairé*, or *aufgeklärt*, terms incessantly used at the time. No significant Enlightenment figure had sociability or social practices in mind when designating as 'enlightened', or the fruit of 'enlightened' attitudes, the great shifts, cultural, scientific, social, and political, they saw occurring, or as having recently occurred or as needing to occur. Therefore little attention is paid here to this aspect of eighteenth-century history and it is neither necessary nor advisable to find room for the cultural history of sociability and social practices in defining the Enlightenment. If the Parisian salons, for example, were an extremely important social space, their contribution to the

Enlightenment as such was practically zero except as a (very) marginal conduit of dissemination.[9] Sociability, in short, is just a gigantic red herring. But this most certainly does not mean that Enlightenment was a purely intellectual movement. There was a great deal of social grievance and legal archaism in the eighteenth century, and the Enlightenment precisely by establishing new principles, understood intellectually, set up a powerful process of social and political innovation, reformism, and change which profoundly affected the whole of society. The Enlightenment is not a story of ideas but a story of the interaction of ideas and social reality.[10]

John Robertson begins his important 2005 study by characterizing the Enlightenment as a shift commencing in the 1740s involving 'a new focus on betterment in this world, without regard for the existence or non-existence of the next'. The main intellectual effort, he argued, was 'concentrated on understanding the means of progress in human society, not on demolishing belief in a divine counterpart'.[11] His emphasis on there having been a core of original thinking to the Enlightenment 'that was not simply a matter of common aspirations and values' and within which 'the understanding of human betterment was pursued across a number of independent lines of enquiry' is in many ways excellent and, like earlier definitions, captures much of what is needed. Any workable definition of Enlightenment must focus on betterment in this world and get away from social practice and common values to stress especially new principles, concepts, and constitutional arrangements being introduced that are conceived to be transforming society for the better. But Robertson's characterization still has four considerable limitations. Both advocates and (the many) opponents of the Enlightenment typically saw the process as beginning in the mid and late seventeenth century so that the 1740s is simply too late a starting point; Robertson's formula insufficiently stresses the tendency to see human amelioration as something arising from a general transformation in men's thinking, attitudes, and ideas and by challenging accepted values, rather than stemming from other arguably useful forces for change such as economic processes, social practices, inherent national characteristics real or alleged, imperial expansion, religious revelations, rediscovering ancient texts or ancient constitutions; thirdly, it fails to capture the general consensus that what was needed and happening (or about to happen) was a giant leap forward, a vast revolutionary change, that the difference between enlightened attitudes and society and unenlightened attitudes and society is like light and darkness. At one point, Robertson criticizes Darnton for postulating too close a link between Enlightenment and the French and American revolutions; but here, arguably, Darnton was entirely correct.[12] Finally, missing here is any reference to the profoundly typical quest for universal solutions and recipes. Universalism was one of the quintessential characteristics of the Enlightenment.

---

[9] Lilti, *Les Salons*, 9–10, 107–9, 321–2, 413–15; Edelstein, *Enlightenment*, 10.
[10] Roche, 'Lumières concrètes', 92–3.
[11] Robertson, *Case*, 8.   [12] Ibid. 6.

Admittedly, other recent definitions have put more stress on pluralism and the national perspective within the Enlightenment than either Robertson or myself. But the concept of distinct 'national' enlightenments seems to me altogether invalid first because in most countries, including Russia, Scandinavia, the Austrian empire, Poland, Spain, Portugal, Greece, and post-1720 Netherlands, the United States, Canada, Brazil, and Spanish America, the primary intellectual influences were predominantly foreign—mostly French, British, or German, though before 1720 the Dutch factor was also crucial. Secondly, while there was never any basic unity to the local enlightenment in any given country, including Britain, America, and France where the Enlightenment was always divided between competing factions drawing inspiration from different sources both national and international, the rifts were characterized less by plurality than duality. Nowhere did these divisions point to a high level of fragmentation. Pocock holds that in studying the intellectual history of the late seventeenth and eighteenth century we encounter positions and lines of thought 'to which the term "Enlightenment" may usefully be applied, but the meanings of the term shift as we apply it. The things are connected, but not continuous; they cannot be reduced to a single narrative; and we find ourselves using the word "Enlightenment" in a family of ways and talking about a family of phenomena, resembling and related to one another in a variety of ways that permit various generalizations about them'. This seems to me far too vague and diffuse to be useful. There was a wide range of opinion, certainly, but it was not a spectrum but rather a set of rifts between closely interactive competitors readily classifiable as a single narrative. Indeed, with its two main contending streams—moderate and radical—the Enlightenment can only be understood as a single narrative.

The definition used here retains Robertson's emphasis on the unitary and fundamentally transforming character of the Enlightenment while avoiding the narrower, fragmented quality, and resort to national perspectives, of Pocock's definition. It also avoids the excessively unitary character of Gay's definition. Mainly, though, the definition proposed here attempts to be more complete than other definitions in particular by correcting Robertson's four gaps. That is it seeks to incorporate the full chronological span—the Enlightenment era runs from around 1680 to around 1800—to restore the centrality of 'philosophy' rather than other things as the primary agent of betterment, to reflect the close linkage of Enlightenment with fundamental transformation, challenging accepted values, and revolution, and, finally, to accommodate the quest for universality. Such a formula, one might suppose, at first glance, misses the essence of the British Enlightenment; but I do not think that it does. Even the most conservative of the Enlightenment's great philosophers, and the most inclined to restrict the scope of reason, Hume and Burke, clearly thought the principles and new (as they saw it) constitution produced by the Glorious Revolution of 1688–91, and the toleration, press freedom, and mixture of monarchy and republicanism issuing from it, had recently transformed England, Scotland, and North America fundamentally, and could transform other societies—Burke hoped to see this in India, Ireland, and France—comparably, and that philosophy and philosophical history played a large part as a critical tool, especially in revealing what the real nature of these salutary and transforming principles was and how to preserve and propagate them.

Enlightenment, then, is defined here as a partly unitary phenomenon operative on both sides of the Atlantic, and eventually everywhere, consciously committed to the notion of bettering humanity in this world through a fundamental, revolutionary transformation discarding the ideas, habits, and traditions of the past either wholly or partially, this last point being bitterly contested among enlighteners; Enlightenment operated usually by revolutionizing ideas and constitutional principles, first, and society afterwards, but sometimes by proceeding in reverse order, uncovering and making better known the principles of a great 'revolution' that had already happened. All Enlightenment by definition is closely linked to revolution. Here I think is an accurate, historically grounded, complete definition. This projected 'revolution'—this term was continually used in this connection at the time by Voltaire and other contemporaries—had either recently happened, as was often supposed in England, Scotland, and pre-1776 America, or was now happening, as Voltaire believed was the case in Germany, France, Switzerland, Scandinavia, Russia, and Italy, or would eventually happen, as was hoped by most radical *philosophes* and the first Spanish American *libertadores*, such political visionaries as Francisco de Miranda.

Enlightenment is, hence, best characterized as the quest for human amelioration occurring between 1680 and 1800, driven principally by 'philosophy', that is, what we would term philosophy, science, and political and social science including the new science of economics lumped together, leading to revolutions in ideas and attitudes first, and actual practical revolutions second, or else the other way around, both sets of revolutions seeking universal recipes for all mankind and, ultimately, in its radical manifestation, laying the foundations for modern basic human rights and freedoms and representative democracy. Certainly, there was a deep internal split between radical and moderate enlighteners. But both radical and moderate enlighteners sought general amelioration and both could readily accept Adam Smith's definition of 'philosophy' as the 'science of the connecting principles of nature'.[13] Both tendencies could agree that therefore nature and everything shaped by Nature is the sphere of philosophy and that 'philosophy' is the key debate with regard to everything. Of course, both sides adamantly insisted on their realism and practicality while assailing the opposition for being impractical, Burke rebuking Richard Price, for instance, for dealing in empty abstract propositions when speaking of inalienable rights.[14] But where moderate Enlightenment demonstrated its practical good sense by being able to compromise with the existing order, by disavowing reason's applicability in some areas and justifying existing constraints and circumstances in part, the radical wing claimed to be, and was, the more realistic in offering comprehensive solutions to

[13] Smith, *Essays*, 45.   [14] Thomas, 'Introduction', p. xix.

increasingly urgent unsolved social, legal, and political problems that the moderate Enlightenment proved unable to cope with.

2. INTERPRETING THE ENLIGHTENMENT: THE ARGUMENT

What caused the Enlightenment? As one would expect from so profound, far-ranging, and multi-faceted a phenomenon, its roots were numerous, complex, and very deep-seated. There were two main categories of causes that can be usefully classified as intellectual-scientific, on the one hand, and social-cultural on the other. The first group were essentially factors of destabilization undermining long-accepted scientific, theological, and philosophical premises. An obvious strand here was Copernicus' heliocentrism and the researches of Galileo rejecting all previously accepted notions about the relationship of the earth to the sun and other planets and changing the ways nature itself was conceived and science pursued. In other words, the impact of what today is commonly still called the 'Scientific Revolution', originally an idea forged by Fontenelle, d'Alembert, Voltaire, and others in the Enlightenment era, was a key cause of the Enlightenment.

But there were other major destabilizing initiatives such as the Renaissance's rediscovery of ancient Greek and Roman philosophy, especially the rediscovery of ancient scepticism which eventually introduced systematic doubt in every area of argument and belief, generating intense and long-lasting unease persisting well into the eighteenth century. Another strand was the tension between philosophical reason and theology associated with the advance of Western Averroism in the later Middle Ages and the inability of Aquinas' powerful synthesis of reason and faith to effect a fully satisfactory reconciliation. Another crucial cause and symptom of the underlying tension characteristic of intellectual life, especially in Italy and France, during the century and half prior to the Enlightenment proper, was the rise of a literary movement known as *libertinage érudit*, a tendency hinting at religiously and morally subversive ideas that operated in a hidden, veiled manner, especially by quoting disturbing and disorienting comments drawn from classical literature and encouraging readers to read between the lines. This trend helped generate what from the late seventeenth century evolved into an underground literature of clandestine manuscripts rejecting all the most basic and sacred suppositions of existing authority and religion.[15]

Among social-cultural and political causes of the Enlightenment the most crucial was the stalemate that ended the Wars of Religion and untidy compromises embodied in the Peace of Westphalia (1648), ending the Thirty Years War. God must be on one side or the other, men assumed, so how could the outcome of the struggle be absolute deadlock and totally inconclusive? The psychological shock of such a result

---

[15] Paganini, *Filosofie clandestine*, 3–13.

was tremendous, and the problems associated with organizing the many compromises that had to be hammered out forced a whole new culture of de facto toleration and acceptance of religious plurality which then had to be theorized and legitimized in complex ways. This unavoidable pressure to accommodate religious plurality peacefully had to be faced not just in Germany, France, Britain, and Ireland but also in the Netherlands, Czech lands, Switzerland, Poland, Russia, and Hungary-Transylvania. At the deepest level the dilemmas de facto toleration generated in a deeply traditional cultural world precipitated a weakening of theology's power to fix social norms and policy that arguably became noticeable in some areas of government policy earlier than in intellectual life. A prime example were the late seventeenth-century monarchies' willingness to give more emphasis to economic, and less to theological and legal, criteria than had been usual earlier, in widening de facto toleration and accommodating Christian dissenters and Jews.

Another social factor was the unprecedented expansion of the urban context especially in a few great capitals such as London, Paris, Vienna, Berlin, and Petersburg but also in the closely bunched Dutch towns, creating a new sphere of cultural cosmopolitanism fed by imported products and sometimes people from Asia, Africa, and the Americas and social and sexual fluidity and vagueness blurring traditional class distinctions. It is vital not to suppose, meanwhile, that anything like a socio-economic class shift of the sort Marxist historians tended to predicate was under way. Although it has been claimed that in North America the Enlightenment was the work of the 'landed gentry', in fact nowhere was the Enlightenment the work of any particular social group. Leading representatives of Enlightenment thought came from aristocratic, bourgeois, and artisan backgrounds and the Enlightenment movement itself always remained socially heterogeneous and non-class specific, in terms of its spokesmen, objectives, and socio-economic consequences.

Typically, when eighteenth-century authors referred to what we call Enlightenment they spoke of, 'ce siècle éclairé' [this enlightened century], 'ce siècle philosophique' [this philosophical century], the progress of reason, or invoked as Voltaire did writing to d'Alembert, on 4 June 1767, the 'triomphes de la raison' and this 'happy revolution occurring in the minds of all the well-intentioned over the last fifteen or twenty years'.[16]

Together, the long-term causes, intellectual-scientific and social-cultural, set in motion a philosophical 'revolution' which shattered all the major thought-structures and premises of the past causing an unprecedentedly sharp break in intellectual and academic life. Seven great philosophers were associated with this initial process of rupture—Bacon, Descartes, Hobbes, Spinoza, Locke, Bayle, and Leibniz—all of whom to a greater or lesser degree shared the 'revolutionary' tendency of all Enlightenment to sweep the past aside and lay down new premises. Within a very short space of time, these thinkers powerfully demonstrated that both the basic assumptions of centuries of previous thought and most men's prevailing beliefs

---

[16] Voltaire to d'Alembert, 4 June 1767, in Voltaire, *Corr.* xxxii. 138.

and ideas in existing society were fundamentally wrong and ill grounded. Were it possible, moreover, to improve men's thinking this would in itself greatly improve human life and institutions by rendering society safer, healthier, more tolerant, more effective in its use of science, and more orderly and equipped with better legislation and laws.

All seven, then, powerfully contributed to grounding the Enlightenment. However, the revolutionary tendency inherent in their innovations later developed along two distinct lines. On the one hand, there was an impulse to find ways to reconcile the new premises with reaffirming at least the most basic components of authority and faith drawn from the past in an adjusted, slimmed-down format. This strategy of compromise, allowing some of the theologians' claims and some validity to trad-itional sources of authority, was most explicit in Descartes with his two-substance metaphysics and the great German thinker Leibniz, but central also to Hobbes and Locke. The other embryonic tendency discernible among the seven great thinkers and many of their disciples deemed the new universal principles uncovered by philo-sophical reason the exclusive guide rather than the joint source of guidance and legitimacy and hence carried the revolutionary tendency further.

Bayle was pivotal in this process of polarization because his corrosive scepticism about everything and anything anyone believes served to sever moral thought and politics from theology altogether while his use of philosophical reason to legitimize toleration (in which respect he went further than Locke), and establish the social basis for moral, social, and political principles, had the effect also of separating social theory generally from theology and church doctrine.[17] However, Spinoza's contri-bution was arguably the most crucial in crystallizing what is here termed Radical Enlightenment, primarily because his thought goes further than that of the other six in undermining belief in revelation, divine providence, and miracles, and hence ecclesiastical authority, and also because he was the first major advocate of freedom of thought and the press as distinct from freedom of conscience and the first great democratic philosopher. Radical Enlightenment, the reader needs to bear in mind, remained a largely clandestine movement, generally denounced and decried, until the 1770s. It was everywhere a much weaker force, at least on the surface, than the moderate mainstream Enlightenment and before 1789 (with one or two very fleeting exceptions) never enjoyed the backing of any governments, commanders, or churches in the way moderate Enlightenment frequently did.

Many scholars contend that in the Enlightenment era 'Spinozism', a category fre-quently denounced and condemned, was not actually a coherent intellectual position but a vague, almost meaningless notion amounting to little more than a battle-cry useful for accusing enemies of being 'atheists'. Some even claim the term means substantially different things in different contexts. Doubtless there are isolated ex-amples of vague, loose usage. Much evidence can be cited, though, showing that this

[17] Bartlett, *Idea of Enlightenment*, 14–26; Mori, *Bayle philosophe*, 48–52, 266–71, 336; Israel, 'Bayle's Double Image', 135–51.

presumption of prevailing loose usage is wrong and that in all the major public controversies of the Enlightenment era from Spinoza's own time down to and after 1800, the term in fact designates a broadly coherent intellectual position. What is that position? In essence, it is the acceptance of a one-substance metaphysics ruling out all teleology, divine providence, miracles, and revelation, along with spirits separate from bodies and immortality of the soul, and denying that moral values are divinely delivered (with the corollary that therefore they have to be devised by men using terms relative to what is good or bad for society). Logically, 'Spinozism' always went together with the idea that this man-made morality should provide the basis for legal and political legitimacy—and hence that equality is the first principle of a truly legitimate politics. Always present also is Spinoza's concomitant advocacy of freedom of thought.

Wherever segments of governments, churches, universities, academies, and other learned bodies were pro-Enlightenment, prior to 1789, they invariably rejected radical ideas and preferred one or other variant of what is here termed 'moderate Enlightenment'. Even though all Enlightenment writers and thinkers, by definition, considered the philosophical and scientific assumptions of the past to be broadly wrong, in renewing science, thought, and culture, and introducing toleration and the legal, educational, and social reforms, many felt that reason is not and should not be the only guide and that a balanced compromise between reason and tradition, or reason and religious authority, is necessary. Some leading proponents of moderate enlightenment such as Voltaire and Hume accorded little or no validity to religious authority as such but nevertheless remained anxious to restrict the scope of reason and retain tradition and ecclesiastical authority, duly clipped, as the primary guides for most people. There was a marked tendency for the moderate Enlightenment to shy away from the idea that the whole of society needs enlightening, and some of its foremost practitioners, such as Voltaire and Frederick the Great, even insisted on not attempting to enlighten the great majority, seeing any such plan as ill advised and dangerous.

Both 'moderate' and 'radical' enlightenment, whether in France, Britain, Germany, or wherever, centre around the notion of 'revolution'. All enlighteners thought of the Enlightenment as something revolutionary in the sense of being a process wholly transforming our understanding of the human condition, effecting large changes in institutions and political life, and in the relationship of ideas to reality even if their field of specific action was limited, as with Wolff busily transforming German philosophy and the world of university studies or with the young Beccaria engaged in legal reform. The formerly widespread misconception among historians and philosophers that the modern usage of the term 'revolution' to mean fundamental, sweeping change was not in use before the French Revolution is, we have stressed throughout, totally wrong.[18] This assumption (still widespread among some scholars) has no basis in the evidence; on the contrary, nothing could be easier than to cite innumerable examples of such phrases as 'cette heureuse révolution' used by Voltaire to designate the Enlightenment as a transforming force as he did writing

---

[18] Israel, *Enlightenment Contested*, 3–14.

to d'Alembert in June 1767. Far from being unknown or rare, conceiving Enlightenment as a 'revolution' transforming everything either to a large extent or totally was wholly characteristic and, after 1750, became more and more so.

However, for Hume, Adam Smith, Ferguson, Franklin, John Adams, and Burke, the 'revolution' that counted was something that in Britain and North America had already happened in the first place with the Glorious Revolution, the perfecting of the British constitution, instituting a stable toleration and free press and the expansion of British prosperity and power. Crucial also, for them, was the recent rise of Newtonian science and Locke's empiricism which were also deemed to have profoundly changed Britain and the American colonies for the better and in principle to be a potential recipe for others. Nor were they alone in thinking so. Quite the contrary, British mixed monarchy, toleration, science, philosophical empiricism, and even English law were seen by a number of key figures on the Continent, most notably Voltaire and Montesquieu, as the best available example and package of values transforming society for the better, something to be emulated on all sides.

Considered philosophically, there were two varieties of moderate enlightenment, on the one hand the Lockian-Newtonian construct dominant in Britain, America, Spain, France, and Holland; and, on the other, the Leibnizian-Wolffian tradition dominant in Germany, central Europe, Scandinavia, and Russia. Both of these vigorous Enlightenment currents could find expression as a form of religious enlightenment (Protestant, Catholic, or Jewish), or alternatively flourish as a form of deism, atheism, or agnosticism. As regards the Radical Enlightenment, there was only one lasting philosophical basis—one-substance doctrine denying there is any divine governance of the world. Lots of thinkers shared or participated in such a vision, and helped shape it, but as Bayle, himself one of its leading heralds, emphasized, even though the rudiments of the system itself reached back to ancient times, and had flourished as an underground during the Middle Ages and the Renaissance, no other thinker had managed to lend so coherent a face to this way of thinking as Spinoza. Innumerable denunciations of one-substance doctrine and materialism in the eighteenth century commonly refer to these two (not quite identical) phenomena as 'Spinozism'.

By 1789, radical thought and its social and legal goals had indeed come to form a powerful rival 'package logic'—equality, democracy, freedom of the individual, freedom of thought and expression, and a comprehensive religious toleration—that could be proclaimed as a clearly formulated package of basic human rights. Only adherents of radical ideas embraced fundamental human rights as the veritable basis for social theory and political constitutions and enthusiastically welcomed this aspect of the Revolution. However, adherents of radical ideas did not have to be atheists and were almost never willing to admit (as Spinoza was not) to being atheists. There was undoubtedly some scope for reform-minded deists, Christians, Jews, and Muslims to join the one-substance Enlightenment. During the 1660s Spinoza had formed a close alliance with a group of Socinian Collegiants in Amsterdam, and subsequently, in Holland, Britain, and America, there existed significant groups of Unitarians, of whom Joseph Priestley (1733–1804) was the foremost publicist in the English-speaking world and Carl Friedrich Bahrdt (1740–92) in Germany, who not only rejected practically the entire apparatus of traditional theology, but steered their variant of Christianity as close to materialism as possible: Priestley actually claimed (not altogether coherently) to be a Christian materialist. Insofar as this religious fringe also called for a comprehensive toleration and full freedom of thought and the press and supported democratic initiatives, insisting the British constitution was very far from being the perfect thing most contemporary Englishmen believed it to be, and that there was an urgent need of far-reaching parliamentary, legal, social, ecclesiastical, and educational reform in Britain and the United States too, this group likewise belonged to the Radical Enlightenment. The Unitarian strand of the Radical Enlightenment, though, was always unstable intellectually and tended to fragment during the 1790s and, unlike the Unitarian churches more generally, disappeared during the early nineteenth century.[19]

During the late seventeenth and early eighteenth centuries, the Radical Enlightenment existed only in the form of tiny underground networks, atheist, radical deist, and Unitarian, in France, Holland, Germany, and England, propagating their ideas mainly in the form of clandestine manuscripts and a few illicit, anonymous publications that were vigorously suppressed by all authorities—monarchical, republican, ecclesiastical, and academic alike. Before 1750, the radical tradition was intellectually central to European civilization but socially and politically wholly marginal. From the great public controversy over the *Encyclopédie* of Diderot and d'Alembert, in France during the 1750s onwards, however, the position changed. This raises the question of how and why the radical tendency surged up from the underground to become briefly hegemonic in the 1780s and 1790s. Its advances in the 1780s and early 1790s was so impressive that Tom Paine and many others assumed Radical Enlightenment was on the verge of decisively transforming the political face and social and cultural norms of the entire Western world. Its successes in the years 1788–92, however, were very partial and its philosophical principles rapidly rejected and perverted by Robespierre and the Jacobins. As Paine, one of the giants of radical ideology, aptly expressed it a few years later: with Robespierre, 'the principles of the Revolution, which philosophy had first diffused' were 'departed from [and] philosophy rejected. The intolerant spirit of church persecution . . . transferred itself into politics; the tribunals, styled revolutionary, supplied the place of an inquisition; and the guillotine of the stake.'[20] And although the 'revolution of reason' was briefly reconstituted in the years 1795–1800, Napoleon (while incorporating some parts of it) shortly after 1800 definitively replaced its freedoms and democratic contours with a new kind of authoritarianism. Nevertheless, the Radical Enlightenment survived through the nineteenth century, especially in the minds of great artists and poets, like

---

[19] Israel, 'Meyer, Koerbagh', 197–8, 201–2, 207–8; Donnelly, 'Joseph Towers', 32–5; Van Bunge, *Nederlandse Republiek*, 73–4.
[20] Paine, *Age of Reason*, ii, preface.

Heine and George Eliot, as the hope for a free, just, equitable, democratic, and secular society in the future.

Some critics mistakenly suppose that I claim the Radical Enlightenment achieved its partial successes in the late eighteenth century through the power of ideas alone. This criticism has been repeated time and again but is completely misplaced. The principal reason for the partial successes of radical thought in the 1780s and 1790s was the almost total failure of the moderate Enlightenment to deliver reforms that much of enlightened society had for decades been pressing for. There were many religious minorities eager for a comprehensive toleration but except for France in 1789, no European country delivered a full toleration and in Britain the position of the Catholics and Unitarians remained especially unsatisfactory. Many publicists agitated for (more) freedom of thought and the press; yet no European country delivered full, formal freedom of the press and freedom of thought until Denmark did so, fleetingly, in 1770–2 and France during the years 1788–92. Serfdom still oppressed large numbers in central and eastern Europe; but nowhere were the serfs wholly emancipated before 1789. Black slavery marred the Americas; but only slowly and marginally were the slaves being emancipated. There were ceaseless (and all too justified) complaints about the archaic, inconsistent, and often highly inequitable character of Europe's legal systems (that of Britain included); yet, full equality before the law was nowhere delivered except by revolution in America first and then, in France, in 1789. Democratic ideas were nowhere respectable except to some degree in the nascent United States and, again, in France after 1789. Men tyrannized over women everywhere as they had for centuries. This remained the case after 1789; but in radical circles in France in 1789, some editors and spokesmen began calling for reforms to the marriage laws, seeing abolition of the dowry system and civil divorce as the key to less subjection of women as well as to generally diminishing the power of paternal family heads over individuals.

The official Enlightenment of the courts and churches broadly failed in their Enlightenment reform programmes extending from Chile to Russia and from Scandinavia to Naples, because moderate Enlightenment, dependent as it was on the backing of kings, aristocrats, and the ecclesiastical arm, was incapable of delivering the emancipatory reforms many others besides radical *philosophes* wanted (albeit even more people opposed them). It was because social grievance was widespread that radical ideas proved able to mobilize support and gain an important field of action, an opportunity widened by the fact that one-substance monism yielded a metaphysics and moral philosophy apparently more consistent and free of logical difficulties than any philosophical alternative—at least prior to the rise of Kantianism as a major cultural force in the late 1780s. Philosophies reconciling reason with religious authority, or, like Hobbes's naturalism, with absolutism, or, like Hume's scepticism, combining a pruned-back reason with tradition, inevitably incurred more difficulties than *la philosophie moderne* in looking consistent and in combining principles with sweeping reform. It may be true that most people remained wholly untroubled by inconsistency and 'bad arguments'. But there are always some at all social levels for whom intellectual consistency matters—and this applies especially to those aspiring to reform customs, laws, and institutions.

Briefly, one-substance metaphysics went hand in hand with sweeping reform. The whole point of the great *Pantheismusstreit* in Germany in the 1780s is that conservative thinkers like Jacobi and Rehberg concluded that no philosophy can withstand Spinoza using rational arguments as he is generally more consistent than any other thinker then available. From this they inferred the impossibility of blocking the materialism of Diderot, d'Holbach, and Helvétius intellectually and, consequently, the need, or duty, of true conservatives to abandon philosophy and Enlightenment altogether relying on faith and authority instead. Such arguments helped fuel the rise of the Counter-Enlightenment, rejecting reason and insisting that faith and authority are the sole true guides in human life, a key factor weakening mainstream Enlightenment. Spinoza's seemingly incomparable cogency (which greatly troubled Voltaire in his last years) cannot be dismissed, as many try to, as some sort of philosophical judgement on my part. Rather it is a historical fact that in the late eighteenth century, many people believed or feared (often much to their consternation) that one-substance monism, at least to all appearances, was much the most formidably coherent philosophy obtainable.

Finally, and integral to explaining why Radical Enlightenment eventually emerged so powerfully after 1770, is the evidence of the familiar mechanism of modern revolutions. Prior to the late eighteenth century, simmering discontent usually just kept on simmering. Institutionalized oppression persisted in pre-enlightened circumstances for centuries unaddressed or barely addressed. But this is not what happened between 1775 and 1810 when there were a truly astounding number of revolutions successful or unsuccessful in America, France, the Netherlands, Belgium, Switzerland, Ireland, Peru, New Granada (Colombia), Haiti, Italy, Spain, and the Rhineland. Study of these upheavals suggests the most crucial feature of their revolutionary mechanics is the introduction by an aggrieved but aspiring intellectual leadership of totalizing, all-renewing revolutionary ideologies the concepts of which the common people were not interested in and had little grasp of, but which could be successfully used (and manipulated) as channels for popular grievances and resentment.

Except for the American Revolution which followed a different pattern, all these revolutions were orchestrated by tiny batches of mostly strikingly unrepresentative editors, orators, pamphleteers, and professional agitators or renegade nobles, like Mirabeau and Volney—and practically never businessmen, lawyers, or office-holders. These entirely unrepresentative intellectuals captured a mass following by seizing on and amplifying popular protest arising from widespread discontent into a formidable political force. The leaders of the French Revolution of 1788–92 were socially completely marginal, and heterogeneous as well as unrepresentative; all they had in common was their ideological standpoint, and here the 'revolution of reason' was strikingly cohesive, especially after the pro-British, anti-*philosophique* moderate *monarchiens*—great devotees of moderate Enlightenment—were ousted from the

National Assembly in October 1789. This same pattern, a socially heterogeneous and unrepresentative tiny smattering taking the lead employing a coherent ideology, likewise recurred in Italy and characterizes the German radical *Aufklärung* and subsequent Mainz revolution of 1792–3.[21]

This cultural phenomenon—revolutionary leaderships ranging from Germany to Peru that are totally heterogeneous and unrepresentative socially but highly cohesive ideologically—is in many ways the key to understanding both the French Revolution and the saga of the Radical Enlightenment itself. A correct understanding of the Radical Enlightenment is impossible without overturning almost the whole current historiography of the French Revolution which puts far too much stress on alleged institutional and social factors not directly connected to the principles of the Revolution, thereby nurturing a quite incorrect notion of the three-way relationship between ideas, Revolution, and social grievance. One might object here that the interpretation I am proposing simply revives the accusations of those *anti-philosophes* of the late eighteenth and early nineteenth centuries who attributed the French Revolution to the supposedly malign influence of the *philosophes*. But what I am arguing is that the Radical Enlightenment—and not the Enlightenment as such—is the only important direct cause of the French Revolution understood as a total transformation of the political, legal, cultural, and educational framework of French life, administration, and society. Everything else, the financial difficulties that brought the French *ancien régime* monarchy crashing down, discontent of the peasantry, pre-1789 legal politics, and the French nobility's tenacious promotion of its power and privileges, however crucial to the mechanics of the historical process that made the Revolution possible, was entirely secondary, in fact tertiary, in shaping the revolutionary outcome. The countless contemporary commentators blaming the French Revolution on the *philosophes* were partly right, then, except they clouded the picture by conflating their greatest enemy, *la philosophie moderne*, or *philosophisme* as they often called it, to embrace the religious scepticism of Voltaire, Rousseau, Montesquieu, and Hume as well, in deference to the overriding priority given to religious concerns and ecclesiastical authority.

Failure to distinguish between the Enlightenment's two main rival factions not only played directly into the Counter-Enlightenment's hands but has badly confused modern scholarship. Failure to stress and explore the rift between radical and moderate tendencies has the especially grave disadvantage of making it impossible to explain why so many enlighteners and heirs to the *philosophes* vigorously opposed the Revolution. A major advantage of the classification proposed here, conversely, is that it affords a clear explanation as to why, even if it was not always automatic, ardent long-standing adherents of radical ideas, such as Gorani in Milan, Paine, Priestley, and Godwin in England, or Georg Forster in the Rhineland, instantly embraced the Revolution as the apotheosis of the Enlightenment whereas many other enlighteners, headed by Burke, Ferguson, and Gibbon, and in France by

---

[21] Blanning, *French Revolution*, 46, 255–9.

Mounier, Necker, and the *monarchiens*, and also Marmontel, were never willing to recognize the Revolution as anything of the sort.[22] The primary task of the historian of the French Revolution today is to refine, clarify, and deepen the late eighteenth-century insight that modern historiography has somehow lost much to its cost that *la philosophie* was the primary cause of the Revolution. It was indeed overwhelmingly the primary factor; but not quite in the way that the *anti-philosophes* envisaged it and to explain this is one of the central objectives of these volumes.

3. SOCIAL CONTEXT, CULTURAL PROCESS, IDEAS

Discussing political reform, law, and administration, at the close of his *Principles of Moral and Political Science* (Edinburgh, 1792), the eminent Scottish thinker and social theorist Adam Ferguson (1723–1816) beautifully summed up the difference between the sort of Enlightenment he endorsed and ardently supported, the empirically grounded path of moderation exalted by Montesquieu and subscribed to by most—but by no means all—British participants in the Enlightenment, and the kind he rejected.[23] Confident that the post-1688 British constitution was superior to 'any other constitution', as he put it in his tract denouncing the American Revolution in 1776, ' in the known world',[24] Ferguson compared the kind of Enlightenment he repudiated with an ambitious architect planning to tear down the entire edifice of existing institutions, lock, stock, and barrel, all at once, and then rebuild the house from scratch on purely rational principles. The intentions of such confident architects were not in themselves bad though they betrayed a distinct lack of respect for the divinely fashioned order of things, as he saw it, that anyone appreciative of the role of divine providence in history would not lack. But their method was catastrophically mistaken and the consequences of their recklessness would prove disastrous for men.

Like Hume, Adam Smith, Montesquieu, and Voltaire, Ferguson did not deny the need for improvements and to make society better. On the contrary, he too supported reform and was convinced God wants us to strive for improvement: even 'the walls', he remarked, 'may be renewed or rebuilt in parts successively'. He also saw the Glorious Revolution as a pivotal change of crucial world significance. But his Enlightenment sought to retain most of the existing foundations, walls, and roof in place at any one time, making only gradual, step-by-step, and carefully restricted changes without taking 'away so much of your supports at once as that the roof may fall in'.[25] If attitudes needed transforming extensively, the basic structure of government, law, and administration, as he saw it, and the main lines of social

---

[22] Blanning, *Reform*, 277, 279; Kontler, 'What is the (Historians') Enlightenment?', 363.
[23] Ferguson, *Principles*, ii. 496–7.
[24] Ferguson, *Remarks*, 13.   [25] Ferguson, *Principles*, ii. 497.

hierarchy, should remain in place. Most great figures of the Scots Enlightenment thought similarly. The one major exception was the republican-minded and remarkable John Millar (1735–1801), author of *The Origin of the Distinction of Ranks* (1771), an enlightener powerfully infused with a sense of the need to weaken aristocracy and push forward much more vigorously the emancipation of women, slaves, serfs, and the non-privileged generally.

Between these two consciously opposed and rival enlightenments, one wanting to tear the old house of *ancien régime* society down and put another in its place, the other seeking to modify and effect repairs on the old structure, given us by divine providence, and hence basically good, obviously, no compromise or half-way house was really possible. Equally, eighteenth-century science divided between those who saw the laws of physics, biology, and chemistry as divinely given, laws conceived, as Newton, and still more his disciples, had, within a framework of physico-theology, and those who saw no evidence of anything but the operation of purely physical forces. This fundamental rift could perhaps be bridged to some extent by personal friendships; but historians have hitherto not sufficiently stressed that it could not be bridged intellectually or in the practical consequences of so deep a philosophical rift. Thus, Condorcet has recently been accounted a 'close ally of Turgot'.[26] But while there were, indeed, practical issues, including questions of fiscal, judicial, and naval improvements, toleration, and widening freedom of expression, where they agreed,[27] when it came to basic philosophical questions the two were at odds and regularly, if politely, reverted to the same, unbridgeable disagreement. This, in essence, was exactly that differentiating moderate from Radical Enlightenment. Turgot espoused a basically Newtonian vision of the universe. He detested the ideas of Diderot, Helvétius, and d'Holbach.[28] Broaching his basic disagreement with Condorcet, in a letter of May 1774, Turgot invoked the principle of universal gravitation. Nature, held Turgot, like Newton, but unlike Spinoza, Diderot, and d'Holbach, requires an outside force to put it into movement; from this he inferred an external mover, and that all movement in the universe must be initiated by a higher cause working outside and beyond all known mechanical causes.[29] This 'first cause' must be both free and 'intelligent' like the soul of humans, and since 'freedom of the will' seemed to him equally undeniable, he rejected the arguments by which 'les philosophes irréligieux', that is Diderot, d'Holbach, and Helvétius, strove to demonstrate its 'impossibility'.

Minds, as Turgot formulated in his metaphysical dualism and Lockean psychology, are determined not by 'des moteurs' but by motives, not by mechanical causes but in pursuit of final causes. Beings that feel, think, and desire, he argued, have goals and choose means, and hence constitute a realm of things 'at least as real and as certain' as

---

[26] Williams, *Condorcet and Modernity*, 3.
[27] *Correspondance inédite de Condorcet*, 192.
[28] Poirier, *Turgot*, 266–7.
[29] Ibid.; d'Holbach, *Système de la nature*, i. 18–23.

that of beings deemed purely material and moved by purely mechanical causes.[30] Turgot, who, incidentally, possessed an immense personal library crammed with bibles and theology but containing comparatively little pure philosophy, adhered to a basically deist, more or less Voltairean standpoint. Condorcet, later to emerge as a prominent revolutionary leader, replied that he had examined his friend's 'reflections' on metaphysical questions with great pleasure but disliked his sliding from clear facts of physics to 'mythologie'.[31] Turgot's claim that the principle of an intelligent first cause, and the existence of minds that are free, is at least as consonant with what we know from science as mechanistic determinism struck Condorcet as wholly unproven and at odds with what we know, as incoherent philosophically and completely 'de mythologiques'.[32]

Throughout the history of the Enlightenment, whether we approach it from a scientific, religious, or political standpoint, this fundamental and irresolvable duality between the created and providential and non-created and non-providential schemes of reality was so important that it generally remained the chief factor shaping the Enlightenment's course. It is the starting point of the characteristically modern split between those who think in terms of science versus religion, as against the plea that science and religion do not conflict but stand in harmony, as well as the start of the equally basic modern split between 'right' and 'left' in politics and social theory.

Exactly as radical and moderate Enlightenment divided over the status of reason and tradition, and whether reality is governed by a knowing divine providence or by blind nature, so they diverged fundamentally over every basic issue. On one side was a body of thought maintaining that 'reason', meaning inference and argument based on physical and mathematical evidence only, is the sole criterion of truth, the exclusive guide in our affairs, and sole means of understanding the human condition. On the other stood the mainstream Enlightenment refusing this exclusive privileging of 'reason' and claiming two fundamental and distinct sources of truth, namely reason and religious authority (or alternatively tradition). True Enlightenment, held this camp, asserts the harmony between these. The religious main body of moderate Enlightenment, whether Catholic, Protestant, or Jewish, upheld formally dualist approaches, firmly separating spirit entities from physical ones, because this is essential for harmonizing reason with faith. In the case of essentially secular or deistic thinkers like Hume, Voltaire, and Montesquieu, Enlightenment moderation relied on forms of sceptical, de facto dualism of a sort restricting reason's scope and apt for explaining why the moral, social, and political order should not be primarily based on the dictates of reason.

Reason depending for its sway on reasoning, debate, and argument, Radical Enlightenment unreservedly endorsed freedom of expression, thought, and the press, seeing this as what best aids discussion and investigation, through debate,

---

[30] Poirier, *Turgot*, 150, 267; Turgot to Condorcet, Paris, 18 May 1774, in *Correspondance inédite de Condorcet*, 172–3.

[31] Condorcet to Turgot, undated May 1774, and Turgot to Condorcet, Paris, 24 May 1774, in *Correspondance inédite de Condorcet*, 177–8.

[32] Ibid. 178; Perrot, *Histoire*, 254.

law-making, and social amelioration, claiming 'we shall never experience how far human reason can reach in the sphere of general truths', as Diez, the first major German proponent of full freedom of the press, put it in 1781, 'if we restrict or wholly refuse freedom of thought'.[33] Against this, both moderate and still more the Counter-Enlightenment stream retained (or re-introduced) permanent elements of thought policing and censorship. For by proclaiming two separate sources of authority in human life—'reason' and religious knowledge (or else tradition)—both provided and also required greater scope for limiting debate, expression, the theatre, and the press. Where for Radical Enlightenment, truth ascertained by 'philosophy' (i.e. what today we would call science and philosophy) and the supposed 'truths' of theology and tradition stand in direct antithesis, theology being viewed by these thinkers as imposture, the mainstream subordinated human affairs, morality, marriage, and society generally to what was deemed the divinely created and revealed physical and moral order.

This divide, the key to any proper grasp of the Enlightenment, extends to practically everything of importance, even toleration, though both wings favoured toleration in general terms. The irreducible difference here concerned whether a full toleration, treating everyone equally, 'une tolérance universelle', was the proper aim along with full liberty of thought and expression, as materialists and Socinians (and also d'Argens's non-rabbinic Jews and liberated Muslims) maintained, or whether toleration should, as Locke argued, be delimited to exclude atheists, discriminate against some groups—in his case Catholics, Jews, and agnostics—and privilege others—in his case Protestants—while curbing 'dissolute' conduct. A full toleration moderate Enlightenment considered harmful to religion, morality, and social stability, while radical thinkers held that 'la tolérance universelle' and full freedom of thought and expression are 'les remèdes infaillibles', as d'Holbach put it, against the common people's prejudices.[34] Catholic apologists endorsing Locke and Newton were a very numerous segment of the moderate Enlightenment but one especially unwilling to countenance full toleration. According to the mid-eighteenth-century Catholic apologist the Abbé Hayer, *la tolérance universelle* is a pernicious concept originally introduced by Bayle, revived by La Beaumelle in his *L'Asiatique tolérant* (1748), and receiving its fullest form in the *Encyclopédie*. Quite different from true Christian tolerance, this *tolérance universelle* of the *encyclopédistes* was dressed up to sound very grand and positive but really amounts to 'une indifférence totale' for religious authority and tradition.[35]

All sweeping political and social reformism of a kind denying the basic legitimacy of *ancien régime* monarchism and institutions was, in principle, bound to be more logically anchored in radical metaphysics denying all teleology and divine providence than in moderate mainstream thought. Basic human rights defined as individual

---

[33] Diez, *Apologie*, 45; see also Laerke, 'Introduction', 6–7; Israel, 'French Royal Censorship', 66–7, 74.
[34] D'Holbach, *Essai*, 81–2.   [35] Ibid. 172; Lough, *Essays*, 395.

liberty, equality, freedom of thought and expression, and democracy were inextricably linked to radically monist philosophical positions during the Enlightenment era. Moderate thought, by contrast, of necessity postulated a strong providential dimension either explicitly, as a fundamental principle, as in Voltaire, Kames, Smith, Ferguson, Turgot, Wolff, and Mendelssohn, or else as an indispensable by-product and practical consequence, especially with regard to morality and legislation, as in Hume and Kant.[36] Proponents of far-reaching reform invariably found radical philosophy more amenable to their aims than systems more supportive of conventional and traditional standpoints.

Catholic, Protestant, deist, Stoic, and orthodox Jewish doctrines could easily explain individual corruption but not how human society overall, including the churches, had somehow managed to become comprehensively rotten, oppressive, malfunctioning, and corrupt. At the time, virtually all churches explicitly sanctioned *ancien régime* society's basic institutions on a daily basis—monarchy, aristocracy, and ecclesiastical authority, of course, but also, at least obliquely, serfdom, slavery, the impermissibility of civil divorce, and suppression by law of freethinking, homosexuality, and extra-marital 'fornication'. Intellectually, it was by no means impossible for a moderate enlightener angry about some perceived defect to cross the divide between non-providential and providential and join with radical voices in the political arena; but it was both rare and arguably also impossible to do coherently. Only Rousseau persistently combined a strong commitment to deism and divine providence with the complaint that all men are in chains and all societies and existing institutions fundamentally corrupt. But Rousseau, as we shall see, was a strange mixture of radical, moderate, and Counter-Enlightenment tendencies and on all sides continually accused of contradicting himself.

The fact that monist systems were far more readily adapted to radical politics than Christian, Jewish, or deist ones does not necessarily mean, though, that all those embracing a Spinozistic monism or Unitarian quasi-materialism in the style of the philosopher-scientist Priestley were automatically champions of democracy, equality, and individual freedom, rejecting the existing political and social order in its entirety, even if they often were. For there existed also other kinds of sweeping opposition to the status quo fuelled by one-substance doctrine. Boulainvilliers, a great foe of Louis XIV and monarchical absolutism, was a Spinozist but an aristocratic not democratic republican; and one can think of still more striking divergences from egalitarianism and democratic republicanism. Goethe was a passionate Spinozist in the 1780s and one resolved to reject all accepted opinions and traditions about the divinity, providence, nature, science, and the human condition; but he did so in a completely different way from the revolutionary democrats. He sought an inner transformation of himself and others on the basis of a new vision of things, a transformed perspective on nature and all reality rooted in the aesthetic of ancient Greece and what we would call the Italian Renaissance. His style of liberation from the status quo liberated not

---

[36] For Hume and Kant, see Hume, *Natural History*, 183; Kant, *Religion*, 140–5.

oppressed social groups but instead the higher individual, such as himself, seeking an inner revaluation of all values and release from everything conventional that ordinary men think and believe.

But everyone, democratic republican or not, rejecting divine providence, divinely delivered morality, and belief that God created the world, was implicitly a forward-looking revolutionary. This is because such a person refuses to acknowledge the existing order to be divinely intended or benevolent, even if, in Goethe's case, he was a revolutionary of an inward, distinctly peculiar kind. A philosophy excluding divine providence, and holding the existing order to have no divine sanction or preordained direction or benevolence, is inherently better suited to buttress claims that our world has been captured by self-seeking, oppressive elites and is fundamentally disordered than one holding that the moral, social, and political as well as the physical order *is* designed by a supreme intelligence. Philosophy denying the created, planned, and supervised character of the existing order, while simultaneously maintaining that reason can provide a better social and moral order, must therefore always be more appealing to outright opponents of 'priestcraft', intolerance, archaic laws, economic inequality, slavery, monarchy, religious, gender, and racial discrimination, and aristocracy than any theological or moderate Enlightenment system.

The point needs emphasizing because questioning the link between Spinozism and political radicality has recently become one plank of the growing literature devoted to attacking the concept of Radical enlightenment underpinning this series of volumes. However necessary the fuel of social discontent in making revolutions, monist systems were in fact indispensable to the rise of a generalized radical outlook which was, in turn, the principal cause of the French Revolution and the other revolutionary movements of the late eighteenth century. This thesis is rejected by Lilti, La Vopa, Moyn, Stuurman, and Chisick as a 'very reductive vision' not amenable to empirical verification. They see it as a form of anachronism projecting into the eighteenth-century cultural milieu a political configuration enabling one to locate authors as more or less 'radical'—that is more or less 'leftist' in the terms of a later era—in the 'name of an assumed homology between philosophical and political standpoints'.[37] To the extent that any effort is made 'to convert this philosophical logic into an analysis of historical process', avers La Vopa, 'it is by showing that complete rejection of theological and ecclesiastical authority led to rejection of other forms of authority'.[38] The obvious weakness of this criticism is that there is nothing whatever assumed in the linkage between radical philosophy and the politics of basic human rights politics in the late eighteenth century. On the contrary, all the evidence shows an inextricable and universal connection just as Paine states between 'philosophy', that is monist systems, and genuinely democratic (i.e. non-Robespierriste) radical politics, this being both inherent philosophically and clearly demonstrable factually in the French Revolution down to 1792.

---

[37] Lilti, 'Comment écrit-on', 197; Moyn, 'Mind the Enlightenment', 3–4.
[38] La Vopa, 'New Intellectual History', 723–4.

Lilti, La Vopa, etc. could not be more mistaken. There was always an inherent tendency during the Enlightenment for democratic and egalitarian revolutionary movements urging drastic change to justify their programmes via monist, materialist systems defining the moral order as something purely natural and properly constructed exclusively on the principles of equity and reciprocity in social relations. Conversely, it followed directly from their structures and value-systems that a comparable revolutionary and egalitarian tendency could not easily feed on Lockean empiricism, Hume's scepticism, Kantianism, mainstream Christianity, or de La Mettrie's atheistic epicureanism. Far more readers were convinced by moderate than by radical thought throughout the Enlightenment. But this embedded preference could not help the oppressed peasantries of Europe, religious minorities, serfs, slaves, tradesmen resenting monopolies and privileged businesses, imprisoned debtors, and other victims of an archaic legal system and penal code, and underprivileged colonists, including the Spanish American Creole; only radical ideas could. If it is true that many moderate as well as radical theorists wanted to reform the law and commercial regulation extensively and improve administration and social conditions, radical critics were right to say that without abolishing the existing order and changing political constitutions fundamentally none of this was attainable. As Turgot's failure in France and Beccaria's and Pietro Verri's in Milan showed, moderate approaches were basically impotent under *ancien régime* monarchy, aristocracy, magistracy, and ecclesiastical authority.

Political and socio-economic developments, then, are the real, the important social context that intellectual historians, no less than general historians, need to be relating ideas to and not the cultural spaces and trends identified by Chartier, Darnton, and their disciples, or the ambiguities and contradictions so beloved by the Postmodernists. The chief link between the historiography of Chartier, Darnton, and their followers and Foucault's thought is the latter's insistence that truth is not something that resides outside and separate from power and authority. It is not the outcome of protracted meditation in isolation of debate and control. Truth is not merely a thing of this world, maintains Foucault, but also something that takes multiple forms, being the outcome of many kinds of constraint and pressure. Each society, he contends, has its 'regime of truth', general politics of truth, and specific types of discourse underpinning its conception of truth as well as its own way of fixing the status of those it considers to be exponents of what is 'true'. Foucault's influence certainly spread far and wide and broadly infused discussion of the fundamental relationship of truth and power. But while such a philosophy is a splendid basis for multiculturalism, the coexistence of different sets of values, plainly anyone strongly committed to moral universalism and basic human rights predicated on the principle of equality must reject Foucault's philosophy as false. Anyone believing truth is universal, and that human rights imply a common code that it is the duty of everyone to defend, cannot avoid taking up cudgels not just against Foucault and Postmodernist philosophy but also against the exponents of historiographical theories and approaches focusing attention on sociability, ambiguities, and 'spaces' rather than basic ideas interacting with real social context, by which I mean socio-economic tensions and political clashes, the main lines, that is, of general history. I do not mean by this that the ambiguities and discontinuities of the Postmodernists are not genuinely parts of social context: of course they are. What I mean is that they represent a secondary sphere to be kept firmly subordinate to the main lines of social, economic, and political development. In other words, our diffusionists have a completely different conception of social and cultural context and how it intersects with ideas and politics from the one adopted here and, moreover, one difficult to relate coherently to either ideas or events.

Political revolutions, undoubtedly, are not made by philosophers but a collaboration of crowds with revolutionary leaders. Hence the chief bone of contention in this mounting historiographical quarrel is the question of diffusion of ideas outside narrow intellectual circles into society. At the close of the eighteenth century, radical ideas became what one contemporary called the 'torrent de l'esprit philosophique', a torrent so powerful that it swept aside and partially defeated the moderate Enlightenment, though it was itself in turn afterwards overwhelmed by contrary movements among the public, and especially Robespierre's (and later Napoleon's) authoritarianism and Counter-Enlightenment. This raises searching questions about the character of social and cultural history and especially the question of diffusion of Enlightenment ideas whether moderate or radical, a topic which has now become a regular battle ground between Chartier's and Darnton's many followers, on one side, and general historians holding that social and cultural context interacts with ideas very differently from how they envisage the process.

Diffusion of ideas, maintains Chartier, should not be considered a direct transfer, 'une simple imposition'; rather, reception of ideas is a form of appropriation that transforms, reformulates, and distorts what it receives. Opinion is never a mere receptacle or a soft wax to be shaped in any direction 'et la circulation des pensées ou des modèles culturels est toujours un processus dynamique et créateur'. Conversely, Enlightenment texts, he holds, have no stable, fixed 'signification stable et univoque', and their impact on the perceptions of a given society produces 'interprétations mobiles, plurielles, contradictoires'. Hence it is impossible to make any valid distinction between diffusion, conceived as a progressive adjusting and enlargement of socio-cultural contexts infused by new ideas, and a body of doctrines considered in isolation from this complex process of appropriation.[39] Chartier and Darnton are doubtless right that intellectual historians of the old type did either ignore or greatly oversimplify the process of diffusion. But their new conception of diffusion and public opinion, I maintain, must also be rejected as too simplistic. If *l'opinion publique* was never a passive receptacle of ideas, neither was it ever the actively responsive evolving receptacle postulated by Chartier either. The democratic republican Gerrit Paape (1752–1803) was surely far closer to the mark when he pronounced the public's reception of the democratic ideas set out in speeches, texts, and slogans in

---

[39] Chartier, *Origines culturelles*, 30–1.

the 1780s and 1790s a 'fantastic whirl', an utterly unstable mass of misrepresentation, contradictions, and wild, unexpected contortions that no one can express as a coherent whole.[40] This does not mean *l'opinion publique* is not worth studying. It is, precisely for its wild gyrations and obsessions. But such studies must be kept subordinate to the interaction of clearly and consistently articulated ideas expounded by representatives, leaders, and influential journalists with the political, socio-structural, and economic structures that chiefly determine social context. The revolutionary crowds, the cogent reasoning of some individuals from all backgrounds notwithstanding, mostly just followed their leaders and even that only sporadically, their grasp of ideological slogans and principles being always highly unstable, uncomprehending, volatile, and inconsistent.

One of Chartier's most curious arguments is that the Enlightenment and 'la philosophie' were to a large extent creations of the Revolution. 'En un sens, c'est donc bien la Révolution', he suggests, 'qui a "fait" les livres, et non l'inverse, puisque c'est elle qui a donné une signification prémonitoire et programmatique à certaines œuvres, constituées comme son origine.'[41] No doubt many enthuse over this stunning reversal of the once familiar order. But is anyone really inclined to imagine this could be literally true? It contradicts all the evidence. Conceiving the Enlightenment as a general reforming and regenerative force was well established by the 1760s and many pre-1789 texts refer to *la philosophie* as an engine powerful enough to cause a mighty political and social revolution. In the 1770s and 1780s there were numerous premonitions that a great 'revolution' would soon occur, with Albrecht von Haller's, Dom Deschamps's, and Louis Sebastien Mercier's, as we shall see, among the most emphatic, a circumstance historians have by no means sufficiently emphasized. The reason for the numerous pre-1789 predictions of a great revolution was the clear recognition that the growing 'torrent de l'esprit philosophique', as Sabatier de Castres put it, was such as to make any other outcome hard to imagine. A prior 'revolution of ideas', as Dominique-Joseph Garat, a lesser revolutionary leader, later expressed it, was essential, and such a revolution certainly occurred during the decades from the 1740s to 1789. It had to come first, Garat rightly insisted, before any revolution of fact could ensue, being the motor and shaping force behind the 'revolution of events'.[42]

Noticeable before 1788, expectation that a fundamental revolution was pending became positively commonplace in 1788 and early 1789 prior to the opening of the Estates-General. In the pamphlet *Lettre à Monsieur Raynal*, dated Marseille, 17 March 1789, for instance, a work issued before the Estates-General convened, we are assured of the expected vast transformation soon to occur, with France's pending 'new destiny' being something 'reason' had prepared and 'la philosophie dont vous [i.e. Raynal] êtes l'apôtre et le martyr' had shaped. The author asks why he

---

[40] Paape, *Onverbloemde geschiedenis*, 37, 45–6, 51; Israel, 'Gerrit Paape', 13–14.
[41] Chartier, *Origines culturelles*, 112–13.
[42] Garat, *Mémoires historiques*, ii. 230, 315.

should not state a truth known to all Europe: Raynal had 'prophesied' the great event about to take place by teaching the nation 'la justice de ses droits' and inspiring men with the hope of seeing themselves soon in possession of these rights. The people were thereby instilled with the courage and capacity for 'une heureuse révolution, que votre prédiction a préparée'.[43] There could be no clearer illustration of the close linkage of Radical Enlightenment with the process of revolution.

The common people's role, hence, was not just highly unstable and sporadic but also basically secondary, if not in providing the muscle that actually toppled the *ancien régime* then certainly in formulating the laws and forging the institutions that replaced it. One critic of the thesis that radical philosophy overthrew the *ancien régime*, apparently experiencing difficulty in understanding what is being argued, even asserts that 'neither *Radical Enlightenment* nor *Enlightenment Contested* seem able to make a case for the dissemination of Spinozistic ideas among the general European population'.[44] This is an absurd objection and one that betrays a complete failure to grasp not just the basic argument for *la philosophie* but the processes of diffusion and cultural reorientation we are dealing with. No sensible historian proposes a decisive spread of philosophical ideas among the general population. Philosophical ideas have never spread broadly among any population. But they do sometimes penetrate where it counts. The pre-1970 view that one would need to demonstrate the diffusion of Enlightenment ideas through society to show how Enlightenment ideas could activate revolutionary masses was never a cogent concept. The real question, if we are to construct a meaningful social history of ideas, is to ask from where did the revolutionary leaders most effectively voicing popular grievance and frustration before the Jacobin takeover—Mirabeau, Sieyès, Brissot, Volney, Condorcet, Bailly, Cloots, Forster, Roederer, Manuel, Gorani, and others, whether directing the Assemblée Nationale, the Paris municipality, the Mainz revolution, or the main revolutionary journals—derive their egalitarian and democratic concepts? What is the complexion of the ideas, proposals, and slogans enabling them to lead *l'opinion publique*? Not many coherent suggestions have been advanced; and there is only one convincing answer: the Radical Enlightenment.

It was the revolutionary leaders, then, or rather those who worked in a particular direction, egalitarian, democratic, and libertarian, whose minds were filled with radical philosophy, and for this, as we shall see, the evidence is overwhelming. Does this mean that if fundamental change was on the way, and philosophy shaped the great changes, that the Radical Enlightenment was responsible for what Deschamps called a 'révolution horrible' and for the Terror, as Samuel Moyn and many others maintain? Certainly not. As it veered towards briefly gaining the intellectual upper hand, in the 1770s, 1780s, and early 1790s, radical thought did not assert that the most essential changes would, should, or could take place violently or suddenly, in one go, in particular countries or regions. Before 1789, radical ideas

---

[43] [Bertrand], *Lettre* (Marseille, 17 Mar. 1789), 3, 22–3, 249.
[44] Chisick, 'Interpreting the Enlightenment', 49.

amply justified 'revolution' but also admonished that in politics as in medicine, violent remedies 'sont toujours dangereux' and should only be employed where 'l'excès des maux les rend absolument nécessaires'.[45] Spinoza and d'Holbach are both said to have disapproved of violent revolutions. Possibly they did but that hardly affects the issue. Radical Enlightenment consciously sought to revolutionize human existence by changing men's ideas, starting with those few capable of understanding philosophical arguments and then placing these in positions of influence; it never advocated or glorified violence or subversion for its own sake.

Diffusion and outreach was the challenge for all wings of the Enlightenment. Thinkers on both sides of the divide, Voltaire and Turgot no less than d'Holbach, Helvétius, and Priestley, agreed (at least in their more optimistic moments) that progress was not only occurring but accelerating thanks to books and printing. By the 1760s it appeared undeniable that a general 'revolution' in patterns of thought and social practice *was* indeed taking place. 'La révolution s'achève', intoned Delisle de Sales, in the early 1770s, 'et tout le monde devient philosophe.'[46] For Voltaire and Frederick, the 'revolution of the mind' happening before their eyes need not, should not, and could not involve the great mass of humanity. The principal task and objective of the 'revolution' which they endorsed was to weaken the influence of the churches and render governments and courts more secular, tolerant, and willing to concede individual liberty. But for their radical critics, culminating in Diderot, Helvétius, and d'Holbach, and their disciples, as well as Priestley, Price, Paine, and Godwin, moderate Enlightenment's partial liberation of man, based on a revolution in thinking confined to courts and social elites, was something restricted, reprehensible, and ultimately illogical and impossible. Those on the radical side of this schism considered it a great presumption to maintain, like Voltaire and Frederick, that most of humanity should be left permanently in the dark, condemned to live on for centuries in what they denounced as the most abject and crassest ignorance as well as endless degradation and exploitation. Enlightenment, held d'Holbach, who thought it impossible to ameliorate man's lot without attacking people's misconceptions and prejudices, means above all universal re-education since it is only by teaching men the truth that they will learn to understand their true interests 'et les motifs réels qui doivent les porter au bien'.[47]

What greater insult to the human race can there be than to claim reason is reserved for some while all the rest 'n'est pas fait pour la connaître'?[48] Those inclining to moderate positions saw no 'insult' and refused to agree that the existing status quo was as oppressive, and misery and injustice as all-pervasive, as the radicals contended. Moderate Enlightenment not only excluded the people from 'philosophical' debate on principle but also denied the common people's ignorance was

---

[45] Ibid. vi. 205.
[46] Delisle de Sales, *Philosophie de la nature*, v. 342.
[47] [D'Holbach], *Le Bons-Sens*, pp. vii–viii.
[48] D'Holbach, *Essai*, 65.

inherently detrimental to society. In this respect they were largely in line with the traditional attitude of the professional elites. Most statesmen and courtiers in the seventeenth and eighteenth centuries did not think politics should be followed and discussed by the common people, any more than most priests thought theology should or lawyers thought investigating and improving the law should. What the great mass of lawyers wanted, explained d'Holbach, was that the law should remain 'un mystère impénétrable', something like theology, adored at a distance by most as a sacred code while remaining shrouded in secrecy, and left in venerable silence.

If the good life depends on knowing the truth, held Diderot, Helvétius, and d'Holbach, then every human needs to become enlightened, 'la raison lui est nécessaire' as the latter put it, and he who enlightens his fellow man 'est un bon citoyen'.[49] Everyone needs to be enlightened because everyone has the same right to happiness and an equal share in society and the state, and hence to know 'the truth'; and also because the new secular, broadly utilitarian morality they strove to remake the foundations of society and politics on could not become sufficiently entrenched without first completely transforming attitudes moral, social, educational, and political in society. Hence, the people had to be taught to think about themselves and their connections with others and involve themselves in politics. But at the same time late eighteenth-century radical *philosophes* understood that the common people could not be the main agent of change. A dialectic was involved here of ideas and people that could only be driven by better laws and more enlightened government however this was achieved. 'Establish government universally on the individual wishes and collected wisdom of the people', held Joel Barlow, a leading spokesman of the American Radical Enlightenment and the ally who helped Paine smuggle his *Age of Reason* out of Paris after Robespierre had him imprisoned pending trial, in 1793, 'and it will give a spring to the moral faculties of every human creature; because every human creature must find an interest in its welfare'.[50]

Where the ignorance of the common people needed changing fundamentally, according to radical *philosophes*, their adversaries thought this impossible, something not to be attempted, and, if attempted, fearfully disruptive and dangerous politically and socially. Frederick denounced d'Holbach for proclaiming 'magisterially' that men in general are made to learn 'the truth'. On the contrary, retorted Frederick, experience shows plainly that the vast majority have always lived 'dans l'esclavage perpétuel de l'erreur' and that only someone hopelessly prey to the 'vanité de l'esprit philosophique' could imagine they could change this, or even reach anything near what Schiller called 'halbe Aufklärung' [half-Enlightenment]. This was not an argument about the limitations of diffusion and society's receptivity to philosophical ideas but rather about whether the rights, needs, and the interest of the majority 'est une loi générale' overriding every prejudice and superstition no matter how

---

[49] D'Holbach, *Essai*, 67.
[50] Barlow, *Advice*, ii. 57; Jacoby, *Freethinkers*, 41.

traditional and useful to particular interest groups, such as kings, priests, lawyers, ecclesiastics, and nobles within society.

Frederick even sought to quantify the sort of Enlightenment he thought practicable and would support. In France, seemingly the most crucial battle ground, 'philosophy' might perhaps sway the 200,000 or so most highly educated people, but of the sixteen millions he thought inhabited the country in his day, 'philosophy' would never reach the remaining 15,800,000. This prevailing ignorance, everywhere nourished by tradition, faith, and religious authorities, constituted a vast edifice best and most realistically left unchallenged.[51] It is not the business of the common people whose menfolk must work for their living and lack the time to study metaphysics, theology, and morality, or learn about philosophy, government, law, morality, international affairs, and statecraft. Consequently, to condemn monarchy and aristocracy, and advocate sweeping social reforms as d'Holbach, Diderot, Helvétius, and, later, Condorcet, Raynal, Brissot, Cloots, Mirabeau, Paine, Barlow, and many others did, in Frederick's opinion 'n'est ni sage ni philosophe'.[52] To urge that the state exists for the good of all and that subjects 'should possess the right of deposing when disgusted with their sovereigns' was to invite catastrophic social turmoil.[53] Citing the French Wars of Religion (1562–94), he reminded opponents of the horrors rebellion against legitimate kings can precipitate.[54] Nor was it just the style, scope, and practicability of the radical *philosophes'* programme the Prussian monarch, like his ally Voltaire, disputed but also their ultimate goals. Convinced, rightly, that the Radical Enlightenment— should it sufficiently gain ground—must entail the overthrow not just of kings but of the entire existing social order, that is of monarchy, aristocracy, existing laws, and church authority together, bringing about a universal revolution, the king reacted with fierce indignation and outright repression. Frederick did not just reject the radical *philosophes'* basic philosophical principles as mistaken, but lent his own hand to help discredit them, lambasting Diderot's and d'Holbach's views as dangerous and perfectly 'revolting'.

In all European countries, this impassioned reaction against the 'torrent de l'esprit philosophique' became more and more pronounced after 1770, and the defence of the existing social order more emphatic. At the same time, several prominent thinkers, such as d'Alembert in France, Burke in England, and Rehberg in Germany, became caught up in this counter-current, reverting from incipiently liberal positions in their earlier phases, as Enlightenment figures, to become pillars of conservatism, especially as regards political and social issues. In general, justification of monarchy, aristocracy, and empire on a moderate mainstream basis became more insistent and dogmatic even among those who could not altogether agree with Ferguson that rank and distinction in society were inherent in the divine order.[55] Whether they saw deference

---

[51] Frederick the Great, *Examen de l'Essai*, 17–19.
[52] Ibid. 26–8, 46, 64.
[53] Frederick the Great, 'A Critical Examination of the *System of Nature*', 171–2; Cassirer, *Philosophy*, 71.
[54] Cassirer, *Philosophy*, 52.
[55] Jen-Guo, 'Providence', 171, 180–6; Israel, *Revolution of the Mind*, 11–12, 130–1.

to aristocracy as grounded in the divine will or not, defence of aristocracy by 1789 had become more militant. 'It used to be thought necessary to flatter and deceive', commented Barlow, 'but here [in Burke's political philosophy] everything is open and candid. Mr Burke, in a frenzy of passion, has drawn away the veil; and aristocracy, like a decayed prostitute, whom painting and patching will no longer embellish, throws off her covering, to get a livelihood by displaying her ugliness.'[56]

The eventual failure, indeed progressive breakdown, of the previously always dominant moderate Enlightenment by the 1770s and 1780s—and its replacement by the Counter-Enlightenment as the mainstay of social conservatism—was thus as much a social and political as intellectual process. Prior to 1789, moderate Enlightenment did secure a few notable improvements. But its incapacity to address major unresolved problems was more striking. Throughout Europe, including Britain, the aristocracy and lower nobility remained overwhelmingly dominant in landowning, as well as socially and politically, while aristocratic legal and tax privilege remained everywhere largely intact. People without property scarcely enjoyed the protection of the law. Capital punishment remained mandatory theoretically and often in practice for many offences besides murder. Debtors were still being cast into prison and left to the mercy of their creditors. Jews had nowhere yet attained equality of status; persecution of homosexuals persisted. Even in Britain denial of the Trinity by Unitarians as well as atheists and Deists remained theoretically a 'crime' in law, and in most people's eyes, while dissenters and Jews refusing oaths of conformity remained excluded from Oxford and Cambridge and higher positions in society. Burke was rightly accused by Priestley of joining 'with a bigoted clergy' to ensure civil offices stayed confined 'to the members of the established church'.[57]

Hence, despite its intellectual dominance and some successes, moderate Enlightenment by 1789 found itself increasingly squeezed between the logic of revolution and its impotence to accomplish basic change. If, from a moderate standpoint, little could be done within the confines of *ancien régime* society, in Britain no less than continental Europe, to drive educational and law reform further, integrate Unitarians and Jews in society, or overcome the indissolubility of marriage and make divorce easier to obtain, owing to a powerful mix of social, political, and theological objections, neither could the press-gang be ended, serfs emancipated, or anything done about standing armies, great power jealousies, and the constant recurrence of appallingly bloody and destructive wars between rival dynasts. The ultimate meaning of 'moderation' was that the most pressing social problems could not be solved, and, as Barlow complained, nothing done to halt the growth in standing armies or curb great power rivalry, imperial expansion, and war.[58]

The much vaunted solid good sense and pragmatism of the mainstream, Barlow pointed out, also paralysed the Europe-wide efforts at judicial reform. If Beccaria's

[56] Barlow, *Advice*, ii. 21–2.
[57] Priestley, *Letters*, preface p. v.
[58] Barlow, *Advice*, i. 74.

celebrated treatise on judicial reform, *Dei delitti e delle pene* (1764), appeared in 'all languages' and outdid practically every other late Enlightenment work in fame, it inspired only a few superficial reforms here and there, he noted in 1792, despite that book being followed by other 'luminous' writings (those of Helvétius, d'Holbach, Mirabeau, and Brissot), authors who ventured 'much farther' than that 'benevolent philosopher, surrounded as he is by the united sabers of feudal and ecclesiastical tyranny, has dared to pursue it'.[59] Beccaria faltered, though moderate enlighteners opposed to the Revolution claimed he did open the gates to systematic legal reform.[60] A few law reforms were implemented but the crop was meagre. 'The publication, within the last half century of a great number of excellent treatises on the subject of penal laws,' averred Barlow, 'without producing the least effect, in any part of Europe, is a proof that no reform is to be expected in the general system of criminal jurisprudence, but from a radical change in the principle of government.'[61] This was substantially true.

From a radical perspective, fundamental revolution, that is revolution at once intellectual, social, political, and religious, was necessary and unavoidable for every segment of humanity if human potentiality was to be realized. Every nation, avowed Antoine-Marie Cerisier (1749–1828), an ardent supporter of the American Revolution and the Dutch democratic movement of the 1780s, and prominent in the latter, has a right to liberty because liberty is indispensable to its proper conservation and prosperity: to be free means to obey only laws tending 'au bonheur de la société et par elle approuvées'.[62] The radical tendency, accordingly, was revolutionary comprehensively, vesting no legitimacy in existing institutions, or in privilege and social hierarchy, or structures of education and moral thought, and altogether convinced, as Cerisier put it in 1781, that only reason can establish the 'véritables principes du gouvernement' and, hence, foster good government.[63] Moderate Enlightenment was also revolutionary but in a limited, partial fashion.

The secularizing, sceptical category of moderate thinkers found themselves bitterly rebuked by both the religious Enlightenment and the radicals. Hume, Voltaire, and Montesquieu, like their religious counterparts, strove to uphold much of the edifice of *ancien régime* institutions and social hierarchy, including traditional religion— at least for the majority. Not infrequently, the irreligion and scepticism of this sub-group led to their integrity and sincerity being questioned by both Christian apologists to their 'right' and the radical wing to their 'left'. Over time, these tensions engineered some dramatic shifts in the status of great thinkers. Thus, liberal Catholic apologists in France shifted from first attacking to later warmly appreciating Montesquieu whilst Montesquieu's reputation in radical circles, conversely, receded the more acceptable he became to enlightened Catholic sentiment. By 1790, Naigeon,

---

[59] Barlow, *Advice*, i. 93.
[60] Portalis, *De l'usage*, ii. 226.   [61] Barlow, *Advice*, i. 93.
[62] Cerisier, *Le Politique hollandois*, 6 (1783), 205.   [63] Ibid. 6 (1783), 179, 202–4.

one of Diderot's closest collaborators, publicly rebuked Montesquieu for being too
'frightened' of angering his contemporaries to express his real views about God,
religion, or the Church.[64] Society, even in France was predominantly religious in
the late eighteenth century, and the largest part of the Enlightenment overall religious.
The rest, however disrespectful privately, publicly evinced a healthy respect for religion's
power. The writings of the irreligious mainstream and radicals alike are full of gibes
aimed at popular belief. The frightful torments and martyrdoms suffered by Christ's
Apostles, remarks d'Holbach at one point, suggests they were less adept at working
miracles than the churches claimed.[65] But no one, radical or moderate, dared publicly
express such thoughts other than in anonymous, underground publications.

To understand the peculiar mix of coherence and dissonance constituting the
Enlightenment one must examine how different social groups and institutions, as
well as key rulers, employed, modified, and reacted to Enlightenment ideas. Attention must focus, as many have said, especially on the intersection between ideas and
society, philosophy and general context. What we learn from such an undertaking is
that intellectual debate is itself a social and cultural process reacting to the logic of
conditions no less than the play of ideas. The underlying divergence between the
competing impulses within the Enlightenment, we discover, arose first and foremost
from a dispute about the status of reason and this must be understood as a fact of
intellectual history but equally a fact of social and cultural history.

The methodology of this third volume of my Enlightenment survey continues that
employed in the preceding two. Our best chance of understanding the evolution of
Enlightenment ideas, thinking, and debate, in terms of their contemporary setting,
meaning, and relevance to society, is to focus primarily on major public controversies
and examine their broader context. 'This is hardly a novelty,' complains one critic;
'intellectual historians have been drawn to such debates since the discipline came
into being.'[66] This technique, holds another, has been widely adopted by others over
the last fifteen years and, moreover, many studies have produced analysis 'precise
and contextualized' of eighteenth-century controversies notably more attentive to
'literary strategies' and rhetorical devices as well as 'sociability' than I have been.[67]
Such criticism misses the point. In this study, 'context' means political events, social
tensions, legal processes, economic developments, material and aesthetic culture, and
educational institutions. By 'controversialist' method, I do not mean studying batches
of texts relating to controversies, something which indeed has been a method employed
by intellectual history since the outset (though such study is an indispensable part of
the procedure). Rather I mean a procedure, starting from the vantage point of general
history, to determine what the political, social, and cultural context of a given controversy is and how the controversy's course is shaped by political, legal, ecclesiastical,

---

[64] Naigeon, *Adresse à l'Assemblée Nationale* (1790), 27–9.
[65] [D'Holbach], *Le Bon-Sens*, 139.
[66] Chisick, 'Interpreting the Enlightenment', 35.
[67] Lilty, 'Comment écrit-on', 190.

academic, and popular interventions, most of which are not recorded in literary or philosophical texts but in other kinds of records. An equivalent approach would be to study economic history by placing economic developments within a general framework of politics, culture, and institutional change; something economic historians, who are notoriously apt to isolate economic factors from other kinds of factors—much as the old intellectual history abstracted and isolated ideas—almost never do.

The method of starting from the general conjuncture of a given controversy and asking how the various pressures involved shaped the outcome seems to me to be a procedure that far from being widely practised is something intellectual and cultural historians have rarely experimented with. What such a methodology amounts to is general history, political, economic, legal, and social, employing intellectual controversies as its material. This trilogy is a gathering of data and evidence making possible the formulation of explanatory categories, an essentially empirical study. If it was first suggested by indications that the quest for basic human rights based on democracy and equality that later became formative for modernity appeared to originate in a certain type of materialist, determinist, and atheistic (or, alternatively, radical Socinian) ontology, what it was that cemented this primary link between radical social and political positions and materialist, anti-religious systems, philosophically, can now be said to have emerged clearly—but only through research. It was because the evidence pointed to it that it became the object of the study to explain how and why the Enlightenment split into rival tendencies, generating what Voltaire called a 'guerre civile entre les incrédules', and how this rift throws light on the rise of libertarian and revolutionary ideas, democratic republican ideology, and basic human rights as corner-stones of 'modernity'.

Of course, it would be absurd to suggest that all moderate thinkers came down clearly on one side of key questions and radical thinkers always on the other. Some hardy spirits, most obviously Voltaire, forthrightly crossed the lines on some issues, alternately attracting hostility and applause from both camps. But this was relatively rare as most major philosophical questions in dispute, such as whether or not morality is divinely delivered, whether or not the Bible is divine revelation, whether or not the soul is immortal, whether or not prophecy is imposture, whether or not miracles are possible (where Voltaire took the opposite view to most other moderates), were basically either/or issues. These and comparable metaphysical questions automatically generated an overarching duality polarizing all scientific and philosophical debate leaving little room for in-between positions. For these are all questions to which thinkers (and everybody else) broadly have to answer yes or no, or else lapse into pure scepticism.

A chapter on earthquakes follows immediately on this introduction because, I believe, it illustrates with particular clarity why the Enlightenment could not be a simple spectrum of positions with infinite gradations and nuances between the most conservative and most radical standpoints. In the case of earthquakes, floods, droughts, and volcanic eruptions, there were, unalterably, only three positions possible: either all earthquakes and other natural disasters arise from purely natural causes and none from divine intervention; or, all natural disasters are divinely ordained and none arise from purely natural causes; or, finally, some result from natural causes and others from divine intervention, leaving those adopting this dominant standpoint with the ticklish problem of explaining how we account for the difference. These three standpoints corresponded exactly to Radical Enlightenment, Counter-Enlightenment, and moderate Enlightenment with the last being everywhere the most favoured overall but the thorniest philosophically. It was hard reality itself, the reader will realize from the example of earthquakes, that ensured there was no tenable intermediate ground between radical and moderate Enlightenment, or Enlightenment and Counter-Enlightenment positions. Lovers of compromise and gradualism, as always, abounded; but that could not prevent a general polarization driven by reality and metaphysical positions locking thinkers into lines of thought allowing no spectrum of intermediate views.

However scornful of the existing order and mere piecemeal improvements, radical thinkers were not especially optimistic and avoided short-term forecasts when explaining its notions of and plans for human improvement. Unlike Marxism, in the next century, it issued no guarantees even for the long term. Yet, it saw something inevitable about what it considered its rightness in philosophy. Despite the slowness of our steps, the evidence shows without question, remarks d'Holbach concluding his *Système social* (1773), that there is a gradual progress of 'la raison humaine'. If several ancient and modern philosophers dared embrace reason and experience alone, rejecting all theology, as the basis of their philosophy, breaking free of the 'chains of superstition', it was Leucippus, Democritus, Epicurus, and Strato who first began to lift the veil of prejudice and rescue 'la philosophie des entraves théologiques'. If their systems were too deficient in mystery and marvels for most men and everything slid back into the 'conjectures fabuleuses des Platons, des Socrates, des Zénons', Epicureanism, thanks to Lucretius, was never wholly forgotten and man's progress resumed in the seventeenth century with Hobbes, Spinoza, and Bayle.[68]

During the vast gap before and after the ancient Greeks, there were a few enlightened men, but such is the sway of ignorance and superstition that even 'les hommes les plus éclairés' could do no more than speak in veiled terms and by a 'lâche complaisance' shamefully mix lies with truth. What d'Holbach calls 'the universal prejudices' ['les préjugés universels'] impose themselves so powerfully over such long spans, even over the best minds, that many give up, despairing of mankind. Few are brave enough full-frontally to combat 'les erreurs universelles'. Far from being overly optimistic as their twentieth-century critics have frequently charged, or treating human beings as 'quasi-divine',[69] radical thinkers and mostly also the Enlightenment's moderate thinkers frequently tended, in fact, to be rather pessimistic.

Yet, the ultimate emancipation of man, and life in a free society according protection to all on an equal basis, under elected government ruling in the interest of society

---

[68] [D'Holbach], *Le Bon-Sens*, 247–8.
[69] As argued in particular by Gillespie, *Theological Origins*, 275.

as a whole, is not an impossible dream despite being continually obstructed and thwarted. Part of the proof that a general revolution defeating credulity and 'le pouvoir arbitraire' is not just thinkable but possible, even if only just, held d'Holbach, lies in the fact that particular local revolutions in history had already achieved significant things. During the Reformation, did not the English and Dutch throw off the papacy's yoke and later, after tremendous struggle, that of monarchical tyranny also?[70] Travellers to China, he adds, report that morality and courtesy towards others is general there, something taught even to the lowest of the citizenry. Would it not become possible one day to teach the common man to think in terms of uprightness, reason, and justice? 'If error and ignorance have forged the chains of peoples, if prejudice perpetuates them, science, reason and truth will one day be able to break them.'[71] A noble and beautiful thought, no doubt, but was he right? That was and remains today the unresolved challenge of the Radical Enlightenment.

---

[70] D'Holbach, *Le Bon-Sens*, 561.
[71] D'Holbach, *Essai*, 92; d'Holbach, *Système social*, 558–9.

Part I

The Radical Challenge

2

Nature and Providence

Earthquakes and the Human Condition

1. THE GREAT ENLIGHTENMENT EARTHQUAKE
CONTROVERSY (1750–1757)

The great Enlightenment controversy about earthquakes, volcanic eruptions, tsunamis, and related disasters in the 1750s, and later, was a prolonged, divisive, and
lively affair of great importance that is extremely revealing about the structure and
character of Enlightenment debate. Commencing well before the great Lisbon earthquake of 1755 and continuing long after, assessing the great Lisbon earthquake
became, so to speak, its hub. A controversy that attracted much public attention
over many years, the debate helps us grasp more fully the depth of the fundamental
split in Enlightenment thought and general consequences of this rift.

Catastrophic natural disasters raise difficult questions. The 'fearful earthquake'
that destroyed Jamaica's capital, Port Royal, on 7 June 1692, a bright, 'very clear' day
that earlier 'afforded no suspicion of the least evil', not only demolished the town
within minutes but after it was 'shaken to pieces' buried it in the sea, drowning
thousands, obliterating the cemetery, and 'dashing to pieces the tombs', sweeping the
'carcasses of those who had been buried out of their graves'. Sickness afterwards
carried 'off some thousands more'.[1] The devastation of Guatemala City, and collapse
of virtually all the city's churches, on 29 September 1717, resulted in the old town
being abandoned and the capital refounded at a new location.[2] The great Lima
earthquake of 28 October 1746, the thirteenth there since 1582, convulsed the middle
coastal zone of Peru, a region particularly prone to disasters, d'Holbach notes, in his
Encyclopédie article on earthquakes, leaving everything in ruins including most
houses and all Lima's seventy-four churches and fourteen convents besides the
famous harbour fortress subsequently replaced by the great *Real Felipe* fortress
commanding Callao today.[3] The university and the holy Inquisition's three buildings,

---

[1] Franklin, *Papers*, iii. 447–8.
[2] Roche, *Relación y observaciones*, 12, 31.
[3] Llano Zapata, *Memorias*, 338; *Histoire philosophique* (1780), iv. 217–18; Fisher, *Bourbon Peru*, 20.

including its magnificent chapel, all collapsed, and if this was unaccountable in the eyes of the devout how could God also destroy the cathedral, his temple?

Both the viceregal palace and regional high court were demolished, though due to the prevalence of low, lightly constructed housing, Lima's initial death toll, at only around 1,300 persons reportedly, was surprisingly light. Some were already construing their deliverance as a great 'miracle' owed to the beneficent 'protection of the Blessed Virgin' when, a few hours later, a huge tidal wave swept in from the sea, completing the destruction of Callao and, according to José Eusebio Llano Zapata (1721–80), Peru's foremost naturalist at the time, drowning a further 9,000 inhabitants mostly outside the city proper.[4] In all, calculated Llano Zapata, the quake and its aftermath cost around 13,000 lives.[5]

None of this, of course, prevented the status of several saints as protectors against earthquakes and their effects rising impressively. Callao's destruction and that of Lima, the aftershocks of which lingered for two years, also set the scene in another sense, fixing the terms in which the wider question of how to purge society of the devastating sins that were held to have caused the calamity was debated. There were reportedly a few sceptics in Peru who regarded the whole business in a philosophical light. But what the Lima aftermath chiefly showed was that the slightest unwillingness to defer to how the common people and clergy understood matters, in public, meant crushing retribution, since most believed that dissenters, deists, and freethinkers endangered everybody's safety. This theme infuses Diderot's short heroic tale of *Don Pablo*, a literary re-enactment of the real Don Pablo de Olavide, a Lima administrative official and the foremost Peruvian enlightener. Diderot's 'Olavide', likewise a native of Lima whose mother, father, and a sister all died in the catastrophe, judged it right to use the money left unclaimed by the dead and bereaved for defraying reconstruction costs, and built a theatre where the citizenry could dissipate the melancholy impression of the catastrophe they survived.[6] The clergy, though, disapproved and, as Diderot put it, blighted Olavide's career by reporting him to Madrid as a public malefactor.

An official account of the Peruvian disaster published on the viceroy's orders, at Lima, was reissued, later in 1746, in Mexico City and then at Madrid and Lisbon, and subsequently reissued in French and in English, the latter at London, in 1748, and then Philadelphia.[7] Such publications reflected not just the transatlantic public's fascination with these awesome occurrences but also the mounting disputes over their significance. Protestants saw the calamity as the hand of divine vengeance exacting retribution for the profligacy and idolatry of the Catholic Church. Peru's inhabitants, loyal Catholics terrified by the catastrophe, acknowledged that such a terrible occurrence must be divine retribution. From the outset, they responded with

---

[4] Diderot, *Don Pablo Olavidès*, 467; *Histoire philosophique* (1780), iv. 156–7; Walker, 'Shaking', 115–16.
[5] Llano Zapata, *Memorias*, 338–9.
[6] Diderot, *Don Pablo Olavidès*, 467–8; Walker, *Shaky Colonialism*; Imbruglia, 'Diderot storico', 233.
[7] Imbruglia, 'Diderot storico', 136, 144.

fervent religious processions and displays of faith. Preachers redoubled their efforts to bring the people to repentance and submission to God's will. The people's awe was further heightened, five years later, by news, relayed to Madrid and throughout Spain's empire by the viceroy in Peru, that all the towns in Chile—Santiago, Valparaiso, and La Concepción—had been decimated by violent earth tremors on the night of 24 May 1751, followed by a massive tsunami. All the churches, monasteries, and other buildings of La Concepción collapsed, with scarcely a house left standing.[8] This city too was refounded at a site several miles away in a more protected position, in January 1752.

Never before in mankind's history had there been anything like so wide a transatlantic awareness and response to a string of such terrible catastrophes, and this helped prepare the public psychologically, theologically, and philosophically for the still vaster catastrophe, in November 1755, of the Lisbon earthquake. Many eyewitnesses of the latter, when caught in the first tremors, instantly recalled reading of 'the miserable fate of Callao in the Spanish West Indies'.[9] In Peru, news of the great Lisbon earthquake evoked terrible memories and also, despite the doubters, recharged the people's deep emotional response and religious trust. In a pastoral letter to his archdiocese of 20 September 1756, Lima's archbishop, Don Antonio de Barroeta, pronounced the Lisbon catastrophe, which wrought spectacular damage along the entire Portuguese coast and in the Bay of Cadiz, to be wholly due to 'divine justice' and punishment for men's sins, albeit retribution administered with 'gran misericordia' [great merciful loving kindness].[10] Earthquakes occurred more frequently in Upper and Lower Peru than in Spain or Portugal, he admitted, but this was because Peru's sins outweighed those of Iberia. Peru would suffer less were it less prone to concupiscence and immodesty (especially in women's dress).[11]

The archbishop's main aim in issuing his edict was to 'confound those who, esteemed by philosophers, attribute earthquakes to subterranean volcanic eruptions and fires', bitterly rebuking all who alleged purely natural causes for such disasters.[12] By the 1740s, the Spanish American Church had begun to feel seriously troubled by Enlightenment ideas, although the Church could still count on undeviating support from the great mass of loyal Catholics who were expressly commanded not to heed 'the philosophers'. The chief culprit was Llano Zapata, Lima's leading bibliophile, a naturalist prone to scorn popular credulity and regarded by some as of an impious disposition. The illegitimate son of a priest, he was in any case an enlightener and, in particular, a defender of Buffon's theory of earthquakes as due to subterranean conflagrations.[13] But only a handful were susceptible to Llano Zapata's views, most Peruvians being far more impressed by the visions of a renowned local abbess,

---

[8] AGI Chile 275 'Certificación al duque de San Carlos', fo. 5ᵛ.
[9] *O terremoto de 1755*, 86.
[10] BN Lima Miscelánea Zegarra T 125/7 'Carta pastoral of the Archbishop de Los Reyes', 4, 18.
[11] Ibid. 10, 14; Walker, *Shaky Colonialism*, 23, 133, 149.
[12] BN Lima Miscelánea Zegarra T 125/7 'Carta pastoral', 18, 46.
[13] Llano Zapata, *Memorias*, 27, 340; Walker, *Shaky Colonialism*, 2, 11, 21–2, 44.

Mother Theresa de Jesus, who since the 1730s had regularly prophesied that Lima's lewdness would provoke divine devastation on a terrifying scale.

'The true subterranean fire', decreed the archbishop, 'is the lasciviousness burning in men's hearts; the true volcano is concupiscence.'[14] Only by building an edifice of true Catholic virtue could further such terrible calamities be prevented. Denunciation of 'the philosophers' for rebelling against God and Church by denying that earthquakes were necessarily intended by divine providence may have been one of the discouragements along with lack of books, scientific discussion, and publishing opportunities that induced Llano Zapata, in 1750, to leave his native Peru and start out on an arduous migration via Chile, Buenos Aires, and Brazil to Cadiz where he arrived just after the earthquake there. In Spain, he hoped, he would at last be able to publish his hugely detailed account of the flora, fauna, and minerals of Ibero-America, as well as benefit from the recently founded royal observatory, college of surgery, and other royal institutions recently established in Cadiz to promote Enlightenment science. A man of moderation, Llano Zapata sought to reconcile up-to-date science with faith, promoting Enlightenment and knowledge of the New World on both sides of the Atlantic. But his hopes were dashed and his magnum opus remained unpublished not only during his lifetime but, in its full version, until the twenty-first century. Meanwhile, he did not forget Peru; but his attempt, beginning in 1758, to institute a public library in Lima to counter the ignorance and indolence of the city's Spanish youth by which many 'very fine minds are being lost' also came to nothing.[15]

Not long after Lima's archbishop issued his decree, John Wesley (1703–91), organizational genius of the Methodist movement in Britain and America, published his *Serious Thoughts Occasioned by the Late Earthquake at Lisbon* (1756), composed in the autumn of 1755 at the urging of several followers. He too viewed the Lisbon catastrophe as a sign of divine displeasure, albeit in his opinion, unlike the archbishop's, God was angry with Portugal for its intolerance towards Protestants and hosting the Inquisition. Like the archbishop, though, Wesley saw no particular reason to single out earthquakes: all catastrophes without exception, including the wars of the age, were evident signs of divine anger. To Wesley, admonitory signs abounded everywhere. For example, a series of minor tremors had been felt in February 1750, throughout Britain and Ireland: the earth 'shook and reeled to and fro like a drunken man'—clear warnings to the godless to repent. 'Why should we not now, before London is as Lisbon, Lima, or Catania [where an earthquake buried tens of thousands in 1693], acknowledge the hand of the Almighty arising to maintain his own cause?'[16] 'Many thousands', he reminded readers, 'went quick into the pit, at Callao and Lima.' The 1750 seismological reverberations indicated that divine anger was focusing on English no less than Peruvian and Portuguese

[14] BN Lima Miscelánea Zegarra T 125/7 'Carta pastoral', 46–7.
[15] Peralta Ruiz, 'Tribulaciones', 62.
[16] Wesley, *Serious Thoughts*, 4, 11; Withers, *Placing*, 126.

depravity so that London and other cities could scarcely expect that further 'marks of God's displeasure' would be long in coming. Earthquakes for Wesley were explicable only as divine punishment of some and admonition summoning the rest to submit and humble themselves before it was too late.

An immensely popular preacher and theologian, Wesley, though sometimes claimed to be 'a man of the Enlightenment', was actually a leading precursor of Counter-Enlightenment in the transatlantic, English-speaking world. A fervent believer in miraculous healings as well as providence, visions, witchcraft, and ghosts, the *philosophes* he considered enemies of God. If he admired Locke's thought, especially his religiosity and Englishness, he roundly repudiated every other great Enlightenment thinker, reviling Voltaire, considering Montesquieu 'dry, dull, unaffecting and unentertaining: at least to all but Frenchmen', and dismissing Buffon's natural history as 'atheism barefaced', ranking the great naturalist well below Hume who at least, or so he supposed (by no means unreasonably), acknowledged the being of a God.[17] Yet in Britain too there were 'philosophers' out to subvert accepted thinking. Exactly the opposite view to his had earlier been expressed by the Scots republican Thomas Gordon in his *A Letter of Consolation and Counsel to the Good People of England Occasioned by the Late Earthquake* (1750).[18]

Many had been terrified by the tremors and preachers had built on this fear in their sermons; Gordon, a publicist inspired in particular by Bayle and Collins, strove to calm such apprehensions. No one was being punished by the Almighty or was destined to be cast into the pit.[19] Far from being indications of divine wrath or pending doom, the tremors were the outcome of purely natural causes. Do not earthquakes sweep the guilty and innocent alike, he insisted, echoing Spinoza, to destruction? They cannot be divine vengeance because they are indiscriminate and preceded by no clear admonitions. 'Divine warnings against particular places and particular sins cannot be dumb and unintelligible; cannot be sent by God to men, yet not be understood by men, like a law made not to be understood, therefore impossible to be observed, yet fraught with penalties, and worthy not only of a tyrant, but of the worst, the most cruel tyrant. Would it not be blasphemy to father such a diabolical ordinance upon the merciful God?'[20]

By 1750, the three irreconcilable positions of Counter-Enlightenment, moderate mainstream, and Radical Enlightenment with respect to earthquakes, volcanic eruptions, epidemics, and tsunamis were already clearly staked out. For the first, they were always directed by divine providence for a purpose—to admonish and chastise; for the second, they were sometimes purely natural and sometimes divinely directed; for the third, they were always due to natural causes alone. Between these

---

[17] Semmel, *Methodist Revolution*, 87; Shaw, *Miracles*, 178.
[18] This reference I owe to Giovanni Tarantino who discusses it in his paper (given at IAS in April 2009) 'Thomas Gordon and his "Republican" Catechism, or Le Symbole d'un Laïque'; see also Tarantino, *Lo Scrittoio*, 35–6, 41–2, 53–4.
[19] Tarantino, 'Thomas Gordon and his "Republican" Catechism'.
[20] [Gordon], *A Letter*, 9.

three irreconcilable positions no compromise was possible, philosophically, theologically, or scientifically. There was no spectrum of intermediate positions; and of
the three, the moderate mainstream certainly had to work hardest to sound coherent.
But if 'l'affreuse catastrophe de la capitale du Portugal', of November 1755, did not
change the terms of the transatlantic debate, it greatly amplified it, transforming the
post-1755 earthquake controversy into a transatlantic scientific theologico-philosophical furore of an intensity that eclipsed anything of the sort seen before. Not only
did it prompt more printed discourses than any other calamity of the age but, as
Jaucourt states in the *Encyclopédie*, it inspired on all sides diverse 'reasonings' among
the scientifically inclined.[21]

It was at 9.30 on All Saints' Day morning, 1 November 1755, with Lisbon's streets
thronged with people and 'all the altars in the churches lighted up with many wax
candles' and 'just at the time that they were fullest of people',[22] that disaster struck.
The initial shock brought down most of the city's fifty monasteries and convents as
well as other large buildings ecclesiastical and secular. The Spanish ambassador was
crushed to death amid the ruins of his embassy. 'The populace, it seems', recorded an
English eyewitness, 'were all full of the notion that it was the Judgement-Day; and
willing therefore to be employed in good works, loaded themselves with crucifixes
and saints; men and women, without distinction, during the intervals between the
shocks, were either singing litanies, or with a fervour of zeal stood harassing the
dying with religious ceremonies; and whenever the earth trembled, all on their knees
ejaculated, 'Misericordia!' in the most doleful accents imaginable.' Apprehensive that
being a Protestant might spell danger, this bystander dreaded 'the approach of every
person'.[23]

The violent tremors also started fires that inflicted more damage than the quake
itself, consuming the newly finished opera house along with many luxurious noble
palaces barely damaged by the shocks. Most people, having fled into the streets, 'lifted
up their suppliant hands to heaven, invoking the blessed Virgin', all expressing
'revulsion at the sins of their past life', confessing to the priests, begging 'pardon of
the incensed Deity, and ran from place to place trembling with fear, and making
the air resound with their mournful cries'.[24] The young Oratorian priest Pereira
de Figueiredo, in his *Commentario sobre o terremoto e incendio de Lisboa* (1756), an
account later published in London also in an English version, intermixed with
reporting the grim facts fulsome praise of the authorities' efficiency and the aristocracy's magnanimity in helping restore the shattered city and reports of several
heartening miracles, especially wondrous escapes of sacred relics.[25]

The conflagration lasted a week, consuming the merchants' warehouses and whole
libraries as well as most of the city's ecclesiastical and aristocratic art treasures and

---

[21] Jaucourt, art. 'Lisbonne' in Diderot, *Encyclopédie*, ix. 572–3; Haechler, *Encyclopédie de Diderot*, 571–2.
[22] *O terremoto de 1755*, 116; Gorani, *Memorie*, ii. 229; Poirier, *Tremblement*, 15.
[23] Poirier, *Tremblement*, 96–8; Poirier, '1755 Lisbon Disaster', 171.
[24] Pereira de Figuereido, *A Narrative*, 5.
[25] Kendrick, *Lisbon Earthquake*, 91.

the royal palace. 'All the heart of the city, the richest part of it,' recorded an English eyewitness, 'was burnt.'[26] Worse than the tremors and the flames was the horrendous tsunami with seismic tidal waves twenty feet high racing in from the sea, an hour afterwards, engulfing the city from the south-west, sweeping many of the already injured to their deaths against walls or in the sea. Many survivors fled inland seeking shelter in more elevated terrain. As far west as the Azores the seas were violently agitated. Paralysed with shock, many were greatly consoled, though, that all the royal family including the princes of the blood and leading nobles were unharmed.[27] What better proof that divine providence was at work? Next followed chronic food and water shortage and epidemics, causing a breakdown of normality and degree of demoralization barely conceivable. Some accounts later placed the total number of dead as high as 70,000, though Jaucourt, in his *Encyclopédie* article, avers the conservative figure, accepted today, of between 15,000 and 20,000.[28]

Days later, the first harrowing accounts appeared in Europe's press, graphically depicting catastrophe and spiritual anguish alike. The *Berlinische Nachrichten* carried the story already on 11 November. Once newspaper reports spread, the catastrophe became the talk of the cafés in all the capitals. Not the least commented on feature of the disaster was that some 40 million *cruzados* of merchandise, belonging to English merchants, had gone up in flames in Lisbon's warehouses, a circumstance that deepened London's sense of involvement and spurred dispatch of a relief fleet carrying money, grain, clothes, shoes, blankets, and 6,000 barrels of salt meat that reached Lisbon early in January 1756.

Besides Portugal, the disaster caused heavy damage in Andalusia and, as both Voltaire and d'Holbach noted, Morocco.[29] At Seville, some 6 per cent of all buildings were destroyed and most larger buildings damaged. In the Bay of Cadiz, recorded the authorities' investigating team, the ensuing tsunami crushed or drowned about 1,200 persons (including a grandson of the great tragedian Racine).[30] In the city of Cadiz, the raging sea breached the formidable fortifications and began flooding the streets, the spot where a great 'miracle' occurred when a priest holding an image of the Virgin and crucifix barred the water's path and reversed the flood being commemorated to this day. Beyond Cadiz, the coastline was lashed by the tsunami which, in Morocco, wrecked buildings at Tangiers, Larache, and Salé. Meknes, Fez, and Tetuan too suffered the deaths of thousands. But here again there were unmistakable signs of divine providence at work, the Franciscan friars at Meknes being greatly consoled to see that while many mosques and synagogues collapsed all Christian buildings survived intact. Equally, while nearly all Catholics, thankfully, were saved by 'divine

[26] Ibid. 17; *O terremoto de 1755*, 120.

[27] Gorani, *Memorie*, ii. 234–6; Poirier, '1755 Lisbon Disaster', 171–2.

[28] Jaucourt, 'Lisbonne', 573; Kendrick, *Lisbon Earthquake*, 34.

[29] Voltaire, 'Poème sur le désastre', 393; d'Holbach, art. 'Tremblemens de terre', in Diderot, *Encyclopédie*, xvi. 583; Kendrick, *Lisbon Earthquake*, 25.

[30] Saavedra, *Memorias*, 29; Téllez Alarcia, 'Spanish Interpretations', 51; Braun, 'Voltaitre and Le Franc', 147, 149.

providence', 'infinite' numbers of Muslims were crushed. 'Divine justice' was especially evident, enthused one friar writing from Meknes, in the heavy losses inflicted
on the 'infamous' Jews.[31]

The tremors were also felt, albeit much less strongly, in Catalonia, and parts of
southern France.[32] The canals of Holland and lakes of Switzerland, as well as Loch
Lomond, in Scotland, quivered dramatically, with the seas around western Spain,
Morocco, and Ireland being whipped up all almost simultaneously, and around
Jamaica some nine hours later.[33] In Portugal, the psychological scars long lingered.
Visiting Lisbon in the mid 1760s, the Milanese radical *philosophe* Gorani devoted a
chapter of his memoirs to the Lisbon catastrophe; Alfieri, the pre-eminent Italian
poet of the age, in 1770 described how his initial joy over the city's impressive setting
'quickly turned into melancholy and sorrow' on glimpsing from closer by heaps of
rubble still disfiguring many streets, 'particularly in the lower part of the city'.[34]

Much was hard to explain. 'The greatest shock to pious souls on this occasion',
observed Pereira de Figueiredo, 'was the matter of the sacred images, some of which
were completely torn to pieces, others buried in the ruins and others consumed by
the flames,' including some of the holiest in the city.[35] Yet, for most, the Lisbon
disaster conclusively proved both divine retribution for sins and miraculous intercession and hugely stimulated interest in wonder workings and miraculous rescue as
well as cult rivalries in Portugal, Peru, and Spain alike between competing saints as
protectors. As rescuers of earthquake victims, and spiritual pillars of endangered
buildings, San Egmidio gained ground as, among female saints, did Santa Justa and
Santa Rufina, locally reputed in Seville to have propped up the famous Giralda tower
on this, as on previous occasions.[36] The Jesuits sponsored a saint of their order,
Francisco Borja, as the 'perfect advocate' of those beseeching help, while the Oratorians proclaimed the unique capacities of San Felipe Neri. Non-Catholics were equally
convinced of the directing hand of providence. 'A remarkable providence seems to
have distinguished the Protestants,' enthused an English eyewitness, in November
1755, for among numerous foreign Protestants 'settled in Lisbon, only about 12 or 14
are missing, some of whom were saved in a miraculous manner, beyond all hope or
expectation of escaping'.[37]

Doubtless, all this was only to be expected. For earthquakes, like storms and
epidemics, as Spinoza explains, in the first part of his *Ethics*, have always been
thought to happen 'because the gods (whom men judge to be of the same nature
as themselves) are angry due to wrongs done to them by men, or sins committed in

---

[31] Harvard Afr 555 17.10 *Copia de huma carta escrita pelo Padre Guardiam do real Convento de Maquinés*, 4–5, 7–8; Poirier, *Tremblement*, 72–5.

[32] Cevallos, *Respuesta*, 85; d'Holbach, 'Tremblemens', 583; Bassnett, 'Faith, Doubt', 321.

[33] Bertrand, *Mémoires historiques*, 326; Withers, *Placing*, 125–6.

[34] Alfieri, *Memoirs*, 131.

[35] Pereira de Figueiredo, *A Narrative*, 7.

[36] Téllez Alarcia, 'Spanish Interpretations', 54–5.

[37] *O terremoto de 1755*, 152.

their worship. And though their daily experience contradicted this, and infinitely many examples showed that fortunate and unfortunate things happen indiscriminately to the pious and impious alike, men do not on that account abandon their long-standing prejudice. It is easier for them to put this among the other unknown things whose purpose they are ignorant of, and so remain in the state of ignorance in which they were born, rather than cancel that whole construction and think up a new one.'[38] Nature for Spinoza, as afterwards for Diderot, d'Holbach, and their many other disciples, is something blind that lacks conscious purpose. In a cosmos governed by a blind nature, human morality is transformed into something very different from what it is when based on theology. From commands divinely imposed under the threat of vengeance, morality in their hands became a set of rules, entailing the surrender of part of each individual's natural freedom in exchange for greater discipline, collaboration, and solidarity, and hence capacity to survive, for both the individual and the group.[39]

How could science and philosophy intervene without violating the terms in which the clergy and people understood matters? Among the first Iberian writers to modify conventional notions was a Catalan scholar, Juan Luis Roche (1718–94), at Puerto de Santa Maria in the Bay of Cadiz. A naturalist interested in earthquakes as natural phenomena, Roche published an open letter to the learned academies of which there were now several in Spain. By stressing the role of divine providence in protecting the port of Santa Maria and adducing natural factors to explain only the physical mechanics of earthquakes, carefully distinguishing this from the issue of why, when, and where they strike,[40] he more or less plausibly reconciled science with the popular and theological standpoint. For him too divine providence directed the basic course of the catastrophe. The 350-foot-high Giralda, the most famous medieval Moorish monument surviving in Seville, adjoining the cathedral, remained intact, he agreed, when the city's other towers collapsed, precisely due to Santa Rufina and divine intercession.

Two main scientific explanations were available at the time for those admitting exclusively natural causes together with those deeming the intention supernatural but the process natural. Roche promoted one of these, expounding the reasoning of Spain's most venerable Enlightenment savant, the Benedictine of Oviedo, Benito Jerónimo Feijóo (1676–1764). Based on letters from Feijóo of December 1755, Roche publicized the latter's opinions under the title *Nuevo systema sobre la causa physica de los terremotos* (Puerto de Santa Maria, 1756), attributing earthquakes to electricity. The first to introduce electricity into the Iberian debate, Feijóo had broadly adopted the hypothesis of the Italians Andrea Bina and Father Giambattista Beccaria (1716–81), a Turin-based naturalist internationally renowned for ingenuity in devising electrical contraptions and experiments, not to be confused with the still more celebrated

---

[38] Spinoza, *Ethics*, 441.
[39] Goggi, 'Spinoza contro Rousseau', 134, 144–6; Ballstadt, *Diderot*, 152.
[40] Roche, *Relación y observaciones*, 11–12, 21.

Beccaria of Milan. According to Beccaria's and Feijóo's theory of earthquakes, it was 'electric matter', as Priestley put it, 'which occasioned them'.[41]

This *materia eléctrica*, held Feijóo, 'lodged deep in the bowels of the earth' seeking outlets to the surface through networks of underground caverns where it was prone to explode pockets of combustible gases connected by subterranean but geographically far removed passages, a concept linked, especially by Beccaria, to theories of volcanic eruptions and to Franklin's and his hypothesis that lightning emanates from electrically charged atmospheric states in clouds.[42] Only electricity, contended Feijóo, could explain the simultaneous occurrence of earthquake tremors at far distant points, in 1755 at Cadiz and Oviedo, for example, towns 500 miles apart. The rival theory, that of spontaneous gaseous conflagrations igniting explosions under the earth's surface, seemed incapable of explaining this simultaneity of tremors at widely disparate points.[43]

If for some 'all these things are purely natural and accidental, the result of natural causes', in Wesley's disapproving words,[44] scarcely anyone dared publicly proclaim this position. Even the midway stance, balancing science and theology, encountered massive opposition in Iberia. In two detailed letters from Spain, of April and July 1756, sent to the *Journal encyclopédique* of Liège—a journal banned in Spain—one commentator, praising Spain's Bourbon monarchy for energetically promoting the Enlightenment, emphasized the difficulties men of science still confronted. Spain had made impressive progress in recent decades, granted this correspondent. The royal library in Madrid was now open to the public daily. After founding a public school of anatomy and a botanical garden, the crown had added a museum of natural history and other facilities for science.[45] Innumerable admirers of Locke and Newton daily plied churchmen with assurances that science and philosophy properly conceived constitute a separate sphere in no way conflicting with faith and revelation but in harmony with them. But Spain still lagged behind other lands in the pace of her Enlightenment, and the country's many out-and-out defenders of church authority still replied that such thinking 'conduit au matérialisme', threatening their adherents with the arm of the Inquisition.[46] Several scientific treatises discussing the earthquake had already appeared. But their authors, reported the *Journal encyclopédique*—Francisco Moreana, Fernando Amenda, and the Salamanca professor Tomas Moreno—had all been as apprehensive as Anaxagoras, offering their views only tentatively, as a hypothesis, to avoid persecution continually emphasizing the providential aspects of the catastrophe.[47] Yet, despite expressly asserting that

[41] Bertrand, *Mémoires historiques*, 203–4; Larsen, 'Lisbon Earthquake', 320.

[42] Larsen, 'Lisbon Earthquake', 368–9; Priestley, *History and Present State*, 359–60, 368; Pancaldi, *Volta*, 120.

[43] Kendrick, *Lisbon Earthquake*, 65, 100–2; Téllez Alarcia, 'Spanish Interpretations', 55.

[44] Wesley, *Serious Thoughts*, 11.

[45] Ibid. 125.

[46] [P. Rousseau], *Journal encyclopédique*, 5 (1756), 116–18.

[47] Ibid. 124–5.

earthquakes are divine providence in action, all three had been denounced as 'impies'. Men of science in Spain, though growing in number, were more intimidated than elsewhere and, hence, more guarded in their explanations, most of their countrymen refusing to see anything in earthquakes but the hand of God operating 'd'une manière miraculeuse' and ultimately one consoling to men.[48]

Private resentment at and opposition to the sway of ordinary men's thinking, consequently, was welling up within the Iberian Peninsula just as elsewhere. Indeed, much of the interest of the European-wide controversy during the years 1755–9 derived precisely from this growing theologico-philosophical split between the 'philosophers' and the people. Here was an issue in which the common people were greatly concerned, that could be decided, according to the enlightened, only by way of science and 'philosophy'; but everywhere most disagreed. A leading participant in the Spanish debate was Don Joseph Cevallos (1726–76), a future rector of Seville university and member of the Madrid Real Academia de la Historia, a naturalist who collaborated with Roche in publishing the *Nuevo systema*. An admirer of Feijóo eager to explain the mechanics of earthquakes in natural terms, Cevallos too sought to combine science with divine intervention albeit remaining sceptical about Feijóo's electricity theory. In February 1757, Cevallos published a ninety-six-page treatise professing great respect for the purely theological interpretation proclaimed by the bishop of Guadix and other church leaders, but insisting, with a discreet mix of deference and firmness, theology could by no means dispense with the assistance of science when evaluating earthquakes. For in part earthquakes *were* natural events as was proved by the indications of underwater upheaval far from the coast, the tidal wave's striking Lisbon an hour after the tremors, and widely dispersed tectonic repercussions registered huge distances away, besides prolonged aftershocks spreading in a regular pattern in all directions, demonstrating an interlinked chain of natural movements in space and time. Such phenomena plainly conform more to a mechanistic chain of physical cause and effect than a providential sequence.[49]

Cevallos advanced his scientific hypothesis cogently while continuously combining naturalistic, philosophical explanation with prevailing religious notions, scrupulously avoiding any appearance of challenging the received framework of theological and popular sentiment. A mid-way position between that of the *materialistas* and non-providential *Deistas* falsely contending that earthquakes are never supernatural events, on the one hand, and the dogma that they are always supernatural events, on the other, and sharply differentiated from both, is certainly tenable, contended Cevallos. It was precisely by denouncing in the most categorical terms the Spinozistic thesis that no earthquake or other natural disaster can be supernaturally intended by any deity as retribution for men's sins that this enlightener won the narrow space enabling him to state the moderate Enlightenment's viewpoint.[50] Cevallos, like

---

[48] Ibid. 123–4; Taylor, *Secular Age*, 654.
[49] Cevallos, *Respuesta*, 2, 44–5, 49–50.
[50] Ibid. 75; Walker, *Shaky Colonialism*, 23.

Feijóo, continually reminded readers that *philosophia experimental* was expressly sanctioned in Spain by the Church, universities, and the Inquisition. The most exacting religious orthodoxy conceivable had no objection to the doctrines of Locke and Newton.

The theological evidence, all relevant passages in Scripture and the Church Fathers, likewise prove, held Cevallos, that an earthquake 'is not always produced as *una especial providencia* [as a special providence] to express God's anger nor always caused by sins'.[51] If some earthquakes are supernatural in character and intended by God to punish men, others, including that of 1755, were not supernatural events, though admittedly this creates a practical problem for clergy needing to know how to interpret particular earthquakes for their congregations.[52] How were scholars to differentiate natural from supernatural earthquakes? The distinguishing mark of the purely natural quake, he proposed, is absence of theologically charged preliminaries such as prophetic predictions by known holy men or saints. When determining whether a quake is natural or preternatural, philosophers and theologians must ascertain whether prior predictions of divine retribution for specific actions occurred or a people or ruler had been warned against some particular profanation. It was also necessary to ascertain whether purely natural circumstances might have caused the quake and for this theologians *must* consult *físicos*, experts in natural history.[53]

2. PHILOSOPHY AND INTERPRETING DISASTER

Maintaining that some earthquakes are natural and other supernatural, however, the stance of the moderate mainstream, was fraught with the thorniest philosophical difficulties. If some earthquakes are not preternatural does that not prove that God could have created a better world? Surely a world without earthquakes, objects the Baron Van-Hesden, echoing Diderot's views in the *anti-philosophique* novel of that name targeting Bayle and Diderot in particular, by the French Minim prior Michelange Marin, would be better than the world we have?[54] Cevallos intervened valiantly on behalf of science; but it still seemed more consistent and clearer to keep to a Counter-Enlightenment framework insisting all earthquakes are God's work and all natural catastrophes evidence of divine anger, the wide incidence of earthquakes proving only that divine displeasure and retribution reach far and wide.

The most impressive presentation of the mainstream standpoint were the *Mémoires historiques et physiques sur les tremblemens de terre* (The Hague, 1757) by the

---

[51] Cevallos, *Respuesta*, 17–18, 39.
[52] Ibid. 80–1.
[53] Ibid. 89–91.
[54] Marin, *Baron Van-Hesden*, ii. 146–7.

head pastor of Berne's Huguenot church, Élie Bertrand (1712–90), theologian-scientist, expert on mineralogy and fossils, and member of the Royal Academy of Berlin. Bertrand assembled an impressive body of data about all the recent earthquakes, the latest devastating Quito in April 1756, compiling a true empirical analysis comparing recorded facts, dates, times, and other observations. Bertrand virtually established the science of seismology by systematically cataloguing quantitative data while carefully reviewing all the 'causes probables et possibles' of earthquakes, ranging from spontaneous underground combustion to electric discharges. But he also stressed that scientists did not actually know what causes earthquakes and the need for modesty in admitting the limits to our scientific knowledge.

Newton's true disciple, Bertrand strongly asserted the role of divine providence, condemning as 'un-philosophical' those 'proud spirits' who seek to know the reasons and define the cause of everything that is, explaining 'these terrifying phenomena' as if they were independent of divine action.[55] He admonishes readers not to doubt that divine providence operates via earthquakes for reasons linked not only to the moral sphere but also because these must have their 'physical uses' even if these are unknown to us. Bertrand's overarching physico-theology is reflected in his assuming the earth must require earthquakes for its well-being just as violent fevers are needed, occasionally, to correct the functions of the human body. Perhaps there is a need for the depths of the seas to be regularly stirred, to improve circulation and prevent corruption of the waters, and for the elements of the earth's interior to be periodically shaken together afresh to sustain and improve the soil's fertility.[56]

D'Holbach, like Diderot, followed Spinoza in offering exclusively scientific explanations for physical and human disasters of whatever kind. In his entry on earthquakes, in the *Encyclopédie*'s sixteenth volume, definable physical causes are the only admissible form of explanation for earthquakes as for volcanic eruptions and floods. But within this frame, he stood open to every hypothesis, reflecting the latest expertise in geology, mineralogy, water flows, electricity, gas chemistry, and mining practices and citing several recent scientific papers, including the report on inflammable vapours published in the French Royal Academy of Sciences' proceedings for 1763.[57] To Beccaria's electricity thesis d'Holbach preferred the 'chemical' theory widely current since the 1740s, attributing earthquakes to non-electrical underground conflagrations. Between the fiery centre of the world and the surface layers of combustible material, compounds bituminous and aluminous are constantly liable to ignite when inflammable vapours encounter volatile or vitriolic materials, as when coal presses on pyrite. Spontaneous subterranean conflagrations are then fed by vapours or ordinary air trapped in crevices, shafts, and grottoes, or by underground streams and water pockets. Fires encountering vapour, air, and water rapidly produce more vapour, a gaseous build-up that then inexorably expands

---

[55] Bertrand, *Mémoires historiques*, 3, 5–6; Cristani, *D'Holbach*, 143–4.
[56] Bertrand, *Mémoires historiques*, 19; Kafker and Kafker, *Encyclopedists*, 35.
[57] *Histoire de l'Académie Royale des Sciences* (1763), 229–40.

except where volcanic eruptions (phenomena intimately related to earthquakes in his view too) release pressure. In this way, gases accumulate until, finding no sufficient outlet in the rocky formations where they are trapped, irresistible pressure sets off violent underground movements and explosions of a sort bound to produce the most prodigious effects on the earth's surface both on land and under the sea.[58]

Against this controversial background, many wrestled inwardly with their doubts, using the public controversy to help clarify their own private views. Besides a host of preachers, theologians, academics, and lesser thinkers, three great names participated in the great Lisbon earthquake controversy—Voltaire, Rousseau, and Kant, the latter doing so first. Kant was indeed among the most original participants in the 'earthquake' controversy. He had published his *Allgemeine Naturgeschichte und Geschichte des Himmels*, a cosmology in which the young and as yet little known Königsberg professor attempted to characterize nature in its entirety in March 1755, shortly before the Lisbon calamity. There he stresses the overall purposefulness of nature as something emanating directly from God's will and thus from the highest, most beneficent reason. The Lisbon cataclysm led to two further short but emotionally and intellectually significant articles and a longer treatise, all composed early in 1756.[59] Here, all appeals to divine providence and teleology are set aside and Kant confines himself to empirical findings and seeking causal explanations. Like Cevallos, he was much struck by the complex after-effects, recording numerous empirical details such as the suddenly unfamiliar movements of currents and tides in Baltic ports. Partly scientific, his concern was no less moral and philosophical. Concentrating on analysing what had happened as a physico-chemical process, he suspends without rejecting all suggestion of a divine teleology at work in nature.[60] Nature, he was beginning to think, must be envisaged as an unknown enigmatic reality which nevertheless shapes human life, a reality men cannot know philosophically, but the consequences of which we must face with a clear sense of moral and intellectual responsibility: we cannot show divine providence is at work but must think and act as if it is.

The clash between Voltaire and Rousseau over the great Lisbon earthquake of 1755 developed into the eighteenth century's most famous public encounter over the meaning of such disasters. Rousseau had for some years before 1755 been striving to resolve his inner uncertainties over the question of good and evil in the world and the problem of divine providence. His response was partly prompted by the impact of the earthquake but perhaps more by the literary eruption that followed and his pending rupture with the *coterie d'Holbachique*. His long letter to Voltaire about the Lisbon catastrophe, effectively a dissertation on providence, was composed in August 1756. If nature follows a providential order there has to be some ulterior harmony and balance, unknown to us, explaining the necessity of earthquakes and

---

[58] D'Holbach, 'Tremblemens de terre', 581–3.
[59] Larsen, 'Lisbon Earthquake', 361.
[60] Ibid. 364–5; Kant, *Theoretical Philosophy, 1755–1770*, 147–8.

floods. The same is true up to a point in the case of man-made disasters and calamities, but here the moral and social implications are significantly different.

Voltaire had been deeply shocked, even scandalized, by the scale of the Lisbon calamity. It tore at his innermost convictions, forcing him to postulate dual levels of causality in the universe—the basic laws set by divine providence and a secondary layer of non-providential indirect causes, potentially causing immense physical and moral damage for which no one is responsible.[61] The preface to his celebrated 'Poème sur le désastre de Lisbonne' begins by referring to previous such disasters, including the devastating 'earthquake of Lima and Callao', noting how difficult it is for us to reconcile such calamities with any truly providential conception of the cosmos or notion of divine loving kindness. Deeply troubled by this problem, it lingered unresolved in his mind down to his last years. Why, he asks, in his *Lettres de Memmius à Cicéron* (1771), are there so many atheists? Because of the disasters and troubles, he answered, continually visited on humanity everywhere. The atheists, though, were mistaken. God exists and since it is impossible to conceive God as being anything but just, the axiom that God has ordained everything for the best must be embraced. Yet such a conclusion, he states in his poem, is hard to square with God's free will and responsibility for his actions and seemingly adds insult to the pain and suffering of human life.[62] Men continually suffer terrible setbacks. Animals are 'encore plus misérables que nous', for besides devouring each other, afflicted by diseases, and constantly attacked, they are hunted or exploited by men. In a world where big fish eat little fish, there is no species without its foes and tormenters. How can one reconcile such a terrifying reality, the lot of man and beast alike, with an all-powerful God who regulates the world and is surpassingly wise, just, and good? Where is divine justice? Why Lisbon and not Paris? He thus conveyed his anguish at the harsh character of divine governance and inscrutability of a divinity insensible seemingly to the immensity of human suffering. The general tone shocked many pious readers and disgusted Rousseau.[63] In closing, though, Voltaire reaffirms his confidence in divine providence and hopes of a future life.

While this text appeared at Geneva only in May 1756, copies circulated in Paris as early as January. The copy that reached him Rousseau assumed to have been deliberately sent by its renowned author, a celebrity heaped with good fortune and every comfort pronouncing everything 'bad' while he, Rousseau, dwelling humbly, acknowledged everything to be 'good'. He considered Voltaire's stance 'revolting'. In his reply, while recognizing that Voltaire expressly directs readers not so to construe the poem, he charged him with virtually doing away with divine providence, thereby contradicting himself and depriving man of his chief consolation amid the world's miseries.[64] It was the streak of scepticism in Voltaire's attitude that

---

[61] Martin-Haag, *Voltaire*, 70–2; Pomeau, *Religion de Voltaire*, 289.
[62] Voltaire, *Lettres de Memmius*, 445–6; Braun, 'Voltaire and Le Franc', 146, 151.
[63] Braun, 'Voltaire and Le Franc', 287–91; Poirier, *Tremblement*, 216–18.
[64] Voltaire, 'Poème sur le désastre', 397; Rousseau, 'Lettre à Voltaire' (1756), 310–11, 327.

troubled Rousseau. While acknowledging that he and Voltaire concurred in principle about divine providence, both repudiating the atheistic *philosophes modernes* whose views had earlier greatly unsettled him and which he now categorically rejected,[65] he insisted on what in his *Confessions* he calls 'the absurdity of this doctrine' of Voltaire, and here, indeed, he was right. If God exists, he is perfect, just, benevolent, and wise, and if he is almighty and just, then, ineluctably, 'tout est bien', at least if we look at the whole. Assuredly, the Almighty does not intervene in the course of individual lives, or particular events. But he does ensure the intended and beneficial course of the cosmos: divine providence does not concern individuals but 'est seulement universelle'.[66]

Voltaire's chief difficulty in combating Rousseau, as in fighting Counter-Enlightenment to the right and Radical Enlightenment to the left, was that his position was indeed hard to render cogent intellectually. How does one express agonizing pessimism and scepticism and yet emphasize the role of divine creation, justice, and providence? Here, radical thought had an obvious advantage. When casting his eye over humanity, remarked d'Holbach in 1772, both primitive and civilized men seemed helplessly trapped in a perpetual struggle with providence, compelled at every turn to parry the blows providence deals with its hurricanes, tempests, freezing conditions, hail storms, floods, droughts, and calamities of all kinds continually wrecking and paralysing mankind's efforts and destroying the fruits of man's labour. Men stubbornly attribute this ravaging of human existence, even earthquakes, to God's justice and mercy although everything that passes in the world proves in the clearest fashion that the universe is not governed by an intelligent being.[67] Another who rejected both Voltaire's and Rousseau's, as well as Kant's, approach was the German radical thinker Herder. Voltaire's crying out to the heavens in the wake of the Lisbon earthquake of 1755, he observed, in 1784, makes little sense to anyone sharing the Spinozistic view of nature he—and by that time a great many others in Germany—explicitly adhered to.[68]

Both Spinoza and Voltaire were wrong, held Rousseau, who, with great force and originality, alone forged a form of deism that could (just) be combined with the claim that human society everywhere was corrupt and in need of sweeping change. Misery and oppression, agreed Rousseau, are found everywhere. But this stems from the failings and corruption of human nature; it does not mean the world is not guided by the divine will. On this ground, he divided the world's evils into two kinds, physical and moral, the latter resulting exclusively from human failings. The former are indeed inevitable; but their more destructive effects on humans are mostly due to human misjudgement and folly. The Lisbon disaster proved this: 'nature' did not

---

[65] Rousseau, 'Lettre à Voltaire' (1756), 327–8; Rousseau, *Rêveries*, 83; Gouhier, *Rousseau et Voltaire*, 79–80, 86, 89.

[66] Rousseau, 'Lettre à Voltaire' (1756), 311–12; Rousseau, *Confessions*, 360–1; Gourevitch, 'Religious Thought', 200–1.

[67] [D'Holbach], *Le Bon-Sens*, 41–3, 66; Sandrier, *Style philosophique*, 278.

[68] Herder, *Ideen*, i. 23.

gather 20,000 households in six- and seven-storey blocks; had the city's inhabitants lived more naturally and been more evenly dispersed, the loss of life would have been vastly less, and perhaps minimal.[69] Rousseau concludes by reformulating Voltaire's discarded maxim 'tout est bien' [all is well], which in any case misrepresented, he thought, Pope's and Leibniz's optimism, as: 'le tout est bien' [the whole is well]. This, our moral anchor, we must embrace through faith. For it is not demonstrable by reason.[70]

It was Rousseau's drastic separation between natural man conceived as an isolated being, God's creation, and one endowed through natural conscience with innate moral ideas, and a society altogether unnatural, that enabled him to accomplish what no other eighteenth-century writer does, portray contemporary society as almost entirely corrupt and oppressive, much as Diderot and d'Holbach do, while simultaneously insisting, as they did not, that none of this compromises divine benevolence, justice, or responsibility. If one accepts Rousseau's absolute distinction between nature and society, the very thing that seemed most impossible, paradoxical, and self-contradictory to Voltaire, Diderot, d'Holbach, and Helvétius, the rest of Rousseau's construction acquires a certain logic and cogency. In any case, it was a system spectacularly apt for combining received notions, the ordinary person's insistence on creation, divine benevolence, and morality, with a powerful, active republicanism truly radical in its egalitarianism and republican thrust, a combination unique and potent. Its great weakness, viewed as a component of the Radical Enlightenment, was that it was a radicalism largely confined to the political sphere. Rousseau's moral philosophy, relying on the ordinary person's feelings, remained broadly traditional, most obviously in his conservative standpoint on questions of gender and sexuality. However much idealized, virtue in Rousseau remains inseparably tied to popular sentiment and popular cults. This opened up a vast gap between him, on the one hand, and Diderot, d'Holbach, and Helvétius on the other.

Not intended for publication at the time, Rousseau's text appeared in an unauthorized version, at Berlin, only in 1759, annotated by the Huguenot Wolffian and foe of Voltaire Formey. A copy reached Voltaire who replied to Rousseau, saying he was ill but would write back later. He never did; but his real answer, according to the latter, was *Candide*, the most renowned and vivid of all the great Frenchman's philosophical *contes*, though there is no particular reason to think Voltaire really had him in mind rather than Leibniz and Pope when composing it. As for its effectiveness as a reply Rousseau felt unable to judge since he never troubled, or so he claimed, to read Voltaire's story.[71]

---

[69] Rousseau, 'Lettre à Voltaire' (1756), 311–12; Poirier, *Tremblement*, 222–4; Damrosch, *Jean-Jacques Rousseau*, 296–7.

[70] Damrosch, *Jean-Jacques Rousseau*, 223; Parker, *Souveraineté*, 25–7; O'Hagan, *Rousseau*, 245–6.

[71] Rousseau, *Confessions*, 361; Gouhier, *Rousseau et Voltaire*, 96; Taylor, *Secular Age*, 317, 342.

3

The *Encylopédie* Suppressed (1752–1760)

1. FIGHTING 'LA PHILOSOPHIE MODERNE'

The incompatibility of radical ideas with moderate Enlightenment first became obvious and a matter of public concern during the battle over the *Encyclopédie*. Mired in controversy, from the outset, 'ce grand et utile livre', as an acute observer, the Marquis d'Argenson, called it, struck many contemporaries as neither 'useful' nor acceptable much like the *philosophes* directing it.[1] If what Burke later termed 'the vast undertaking of the Encyclopaedia, carried on by a society of these gentlemen' eventually became the biggest, most useful enterprise the human spirit had ever conceived, as Condorcet grandly expressed it, during its first three years (1750–2) it underwent a turbulent, embattled infancy.[2] After initial fanfares surrounding its launch, it ran into immediate trouble. By December 1751, d'Argenson spoke of a 'great storm' whipped up against the *Encyclopédie*, especially by the Jesuits, with an extraordinary fuss about it being made in Louis XV's presence.[3] The initial battles (1751–2) subsided, though, and the *Encyclopédie* survived its first years intact. From 1752 until 1757, more than half a decade, the 'society of great men' admirers saw behind it seemed, if not to have beaten their adversaries, at least to have weathered the worst.

The third volume appeared in October 1753 and, from then on, another complete volume appeared each year until volume vii, in 1757. The furore, seemingly, was dying down. Criticism and opposition abounded but at levels which in the mid 1750s looked promisingly manageable. By early 1753, the *Encyclopédie*'s editors may indeed have grown somewhat too confident for their own good. The third volume's hard-hitting preface and especially d'Alembert's provocative entry 'Collège' turned into what one pamphleteer called a regular 'battlefield': the editors, propagators of a false and irreligious 'esprit philosophique', according to their foes, here poured out their 'venom', deriding the established French, Spanish, Italian, and Austrian system of (especially Jesuit) higher education.[4] Youths allegedly emerged from Jesuit colleges with an imperfect knowledge of a dead language (Latin), health ruined by abstinence

---

[1] D'Argenson, *Journal*, vii. 56, 63.
[2] Condorcet, *Éloge de M. d'Alembert*, in Condorcet, *Œuvres complètes*, iii, preface p. viii.
[3] D'Argenson, *Journal*, vii. 56–8, 63.
[4] *Avis au public sur le troisième volume de l'*Encyclopédie (n.p., n.d.), 161–7; Adams, *Coyer*, 112.

and excessive prayer, obsolete notions of rhetoric and philosophy they should forget immediately, and religious knowledge too frail to survive the first encounter with a sceptic.[5] Such remarks were bitterly resented. But the teaching orders lacked the leverage to counter-attack effectively either at court or in society more generally. Father Berthier, editor of the Jesuit *Journal de Trévoux*, foremost earlier among the *Encyclopédie*'s critics, from November 1753 lapsed into virtual silence concerning the *Encyclopédie*, the Jesuits taking little part in the subsequent climactic battle.[6]

Meanwhile, lay interest in the project grew, subscriptions rising, despite the high cost, from 1,367 sets, in 1751, to 3,931, by the mid 1750s, so that the print-run for volumes v to vii was fixed at 4,550, for such large and costly tomes an impressive achievement for the mid eighteenth century.[7] Hundreds of workmen, typesetters, printers, correctors, binders, and others laboured on what was both culturally and financially now the first publishing project of the day in France and all Europe. Many subscriptions emanated from abroad, reinforcing the *Encyclopédie*'s role as a landmark not just in publishing but in the international progress and propagation of knowledge.[8] The editors' prestige rose accordingly. In January 1755, d'Alembert was inducted into the Académie Française, high honour for him personally and one that further enhanced the *Encyclopédie*'s standing. His friends regretted, though, that d'Alembert, always timid in public, said nothing of the benefits for mankind of *l'esprit philosophique* or anything challenging in his induction address, a show of reticence that disgusted Grimm.[9]

The quiet years of the mid 1750s, however, proved a mere lull intervening between a middle-sized and a massive controversy. From 1757, the project was again plunged in uproar and recrimination, indeed faced a fiercer, more widely concerted onslaught from then on than before. In 1751–2, the *Encyclopédie*'s foes had come close to aborting it by showing it contained veins of religious and political subversion concealed among much else. They had failed to make the most of their case, though, eventually losing the fight through spreading their attack too widely thereby distracting attention from irreligion and political subversion to less compromising issues, losing the initiative to Diderot's skilful defence. In terms of public image this proved a costly setback that considerably strengthened those under assault, so that after 1752, the chances of resuming the attack on a more effective basis without first changing the reading public's perception of the *encyclopédistes* and securing high-level support at court, in the *parlements* and universities as well the Church and the press, for several years seemed remote.

During the five-year lull following the court's restoring of the *Encyclopédie*'s licence in 1752, the foes of *la philosophie nouvelle* did not desist but made little or no headway. Neither royal ministers nor the high judiciary nor the (now bitterly divided

---

[5] D'Alembert, 'Collège', in Diderot and d'Alembert, *Encyclopédie*, iii. 635.
[6] Palmer, *Catholics and Unbelievers*, 18–20; Pappas, *Berthier's Journal*.
[7] Voltaire, *Questions*, i. 2; Darnton, *Business*, 11; Zabuesnig, *Historische und kritische*, ii. 196.
[8] Zabuesnig, *Historische und kritische*, ii. 198.
[9] Monty, *Critique littéraire*, 114.

and weakened) Sorbonne were eager to repeat the earlier embarrassing fiasco. A few publications, like the *Réflexions d'un Franciscain sur les trois volumes de l'*Encyclopédie, of 1754, reaffirmed the earlier charges of subversion, this tract pointing out that in entries such as 'Conscience, liberté de', the *Encyclopédie* improperly deploys Montesquieu's prestige to smuggle in a sweeping, unrestricted doctrine of toleration, misleading the reader by turning Montesquieu's moderate stance into something far more comprehensive. But for the moment such isolated attacks had little effect either in Catholic France or Italy, or predominantly Protestant Holland and Switzerland, or Germany.[10] While temporarily in Geneva, in 1754, and then still an active, core *encyclopédiste*, Rousseau encountered little difficulty in persuading the municipal Bibliothèque de Genève to subscribe to the *Encyclopédie*.[11]

In Switzerland too, men of moderation, including some indubitably pious ones, were by no means ready to accept that the *Encyclopédie*'s subversive tendency was so harmful that the whole vast enterprise should be scrapped, especially since much of it was patently useful and its contributors included some reliably Catholic and Protestant enlighteners. Unique among these was Edmé-François Mallet (1713–55), a Sorbonne theology professor and apologist for intolerance whose article 'Enfer' [Hell] was so orthodox it revolted Voltaire who complained about it to d'Alembert.[12] It was Diderot, not himself, explained d'Alembert, who exercised final editorial responsibility for everything outside mathematics and the exact sciences and, anyhow, they could not exert much pressure in such cases as they would find themselves totally alone if they tried to 'tyrannize' over their contributors.[13] An eminent Protestant participant was the Berlin Huguenot Wolffian theologian Jean Henri Samuel Formey (1711–97), whose widely consulted article 'Athéisme' declares that under natural law, rulers could justly execute atheists. What would be the fate of the *Encyclopédie*'s editors, inquired Father Jean-Nicolas-Hubert Hayer (1708–80), a leading opponent of the *Encyclopédie*, were Formey's opinion adopted in France?[14]

Not only were royal ministers and many clergy disinclined to be too readily swayed by the arguments of out-and-out *dévôts* but king and ministers needed to bear in mind that the contest was unfolding not just in France but before the eyes of the 'civilized' world, and that in Protestant lands opinion was even less willing to be swayed by Jansenist obscurantism and reactionary clergy than Louis XV's ministers. A leading man of science and medicine in both Germany and Switzerland, Albrecht von Haller (1708–77), a Protestant of impeccable piety and pillar of moderate Enlightenment as well as a leading light at Göttingen, typically commented in his review of the *Encyclopédie*'s second volume, in the *Göttingische Zeitungen von gelehrten Sachen*, in July 1752, that while impieties abounded scattered about the *Encyclopédie* these were so adroitly dispersed among much else that was frequently extremely

---

[10] *Réflexions d'un Franciscain*, 117–18, 124–5.
[11] Guyot, *Rayonnement*, 19.
[12] Kafker and Kafker, *Encyclopedists*, 240–1; Burson, *Rise*, 159.
[13] D'Alembert to Voltaire, Paris, 8 Feb. 1758, in d'Alembert, *Œuvres complètes*, v. 57–8.
[14] Hayer, *La Religion vengée*, xi. 340; Onfray, *Les Ultras*, 34–5.

useful (though he had many reservations about the scientific entries) that most lay Christian readers would find it hard to accept that the whole project should be scrapped.[15] Haller and his friend, the equally 'moderate' and correct Genevan biologist Charles Bonnet (1720–93), were later pointedly to change their minds.

During 1753–5, the *Encyclopédie*'s enhanced standing and improved prospects were reflected in its editors' growing success in recruiting an impressive array of new contributors, including such illustrious figures as Montesquieu and Voltaire. The latter, invited to contribute by d'Alembert (with whom he had been friendly for several years) in May 1754, that summer penned his initial entries, 'Élégance', 'Éloquence', and 'Esprit' for the fifth volume due the following October, covering the letter 'E'; d'Alembert subsequently commissioned more than a dozen further articles from him for the volume covering the letter 'F', including 'Faintaisie', 'Formaliste', and 'Fierté'. Crucially, though, none of Voltaire's entries concerned major social, philosophical, scientific, religious, or political issues.[16] The same pattern recurred with the letter 'G' for which, among other pieces, he wrote 'Gazette' and 'Gens de lettres'. Voltaire's assignments for the *Encyclopédie* were, invariably—undoubtedly at Diderot's insistence—wholly uncontroversial and unconnected with key controversies.

But if, during the mid 1750s, Diderot's and d'Alembert's team grew larger and more impressive, and their international profile more robust, it slowly became apparent that their adversaries were also gathering fresh support and preparing more effective lines of attack. Despite the deep and irresolvable split between Jansenists and Jesuits debilitating the French episcopacy and Church generally at this time, the irreligion and secularism of the radical *philosophes* appeared sufficiently alarming to both sides for a measure of cooperation on this issue to be possible. Indeed, accusing the *Encyclopédie* of being a massive new threat not just to ecclesiastical authority and religion but also monarchy and the social order promised to become the best available opportunity for rallying the church factions and persuading them to collaborate in a unifying common enterprise.[17] Meanwhile, there were also lay professional elements, especially academic and judicial, with a strong vested interest in encouraging the rival factions within the Church to join forces.

Suppressing the *Encyclopédie*, in any case, was now obviously completely impossible without precipitating a major new public controversy mobilizing a much broader phalanx of opinion than earlier and deploying arguments capable of persuading the now numerous moderately tolerant and liberal-minded magistrates, ministers, and crown officials, as well as university professors and the more progressive-minded clergy, that the *Encyclopédie* really was a clandestine vehicle for systematically materialist, atheistic, and anti-royalist doctrine. Accordingly, French *anti-philosophie* at this point noticeably modified its tone, emphatically inclining more to the Lockean mainstream than Counter-Enlightenment. Henceforth, down to the

---

[15] Haller, *Tagebuch*, i. 100, 102–3; Saada, *Inventer Diderot*, 110–12.
[16] Condorcet, *Vie de Voltaire*, 147; Naves, *Voltaire*, 15–17; Blom, *Encyclopédie*, 217.
[17] Condorcet, *Vie de Voltaire*, 148; Condorcet, 'Éloge de d'Alembert', p. xvii.

1790s, *anti-philosophie* argued its case against the *encyclopédistes* less by theological denunciation than by continually reaffirming the Church's respect for empiricism, up-to-date ideas, and the 'sublime' Newton as the *anti-philosophes* took to calling him and embracing the conclusions of recent science.

No revived campaign could make headway, though, without bringing much greater focus and clarity to the charge that the *Encyclopédie* was dangerous and subversive. Here, the *Encyclopédie*'s foes faced a formidable challenge in their target's skilfully camouflaged façade. For Diderot understood his business and the subtleties of veiling the clandestine propagation of radical ideas only too well. To most readers, Catholic or Protestant, even highly erudite ones, it was far from obvious what the real philosophical agenda of the *Encyclopédie* was. Clearly differentiating unacceptable radical strata from unobjectionable moderate Enlightenment layers of the *Encyclopédie* turned out to be an intricate, laborious, and unrewarding intellectual undertaking. The *Encyclopédie*'s foremost adversary during the early and mid 1750s, until his death in 1755, was the bishop of Mirepoix, Jean-François Boyer (1675–1755), former tutor to Louis XV, an anti-Jansenist prelate influential at court who railed so fiercely against the *Encyclopédie* in the king's presence that Malesherbes, the director of the royal censorship, was commanded to find some way, as he later recounted in his memoirs, to placate him.[18] The lay censors assigned to examine the scientific articles, complained Mirepoix, had been systematically duped by the editors' ruse of slipping 'des erreurs' of a sort identifiable only by trained theologians into articles about medicine, physics, and other profane sciences. Malesherbes mollified him by offering three additional theological censors of his choice authorized to oversee all the articles in the forthcoming volumes irrespective of ostensible subject matter.

The bishop chose the Abbé Millet, a veteran of the de Prades affair recollected by Voltaire from his schooldays, Father Tamponnet, a Sorbonne academic also sourly recollected by Voltaire, and Cotterel, three priest-*érudits* as eager to uncover 'error' as could be found. They set to work with such ardour, affirms Malesherbes, that scarcely a paragraph of volumes iii to vii was left intact by their red pens,[19] though this is hardly exact as the publishers did not, in practice, submit everything that they were supposed to to the censors. But the deletions were extensive. The Abbé Morellet later recalled how his article 'Gomariste' had whole paragraphs crossed through by Tamponnet massacring his plea for broadening toleration.[20] Nevertheless, so immense was the task and so adroit the editors in clandestine tactics, that even these professional guardians of orthodoxy proved quite unequal to uncovering innumerable seditious passages that they themselves, observed Malesherbes, later confessed to scarcely knowing how they could have permitted to pass at the time.

Yet the basic charge was not misplaced. The *Encyclopédie* really was a 'répertoire d'impiétés', its core philosophical, theological, social, and political articles really

---

[18] Venturi, *Le origini*, 76; Haechler, *L'Encyclopédie de Diderot*, 177; Burson, 'Crystallization', 974 n., 981.
[19] Malesherbes, *Mémoires*, 267–8; Grosclaude, *Malesherbes*, 106–9, 112; Burson, *Rise*, 150, 242.
[20] Morellet, *Mémoires*, i. 43.

constituting a camouflaged 'Spinosiste' engine of war or what an *anti-philosophique* journal, in 1802, called a bottomless pit of 'scepticism, materialism and atheism'.[21] The problem was that it was a cleverly concealed pit. Diderot's and d'Alembert's elusive tactics (and Malesherbes's discreet support) rendered their vast enterprise exceedingly hard to counter head-on without appearing unreasonably biased and censorious. With even the bishop of Mirepoix's hand-picked inquisitors being continually thwarted, it was far from clear how the *parti anti-philosophique* could ever mobilize a powerful enough outcry or sufficiently damning indictment to stop the *Encyclopédie*. Merely demonstrating that a few provocatively irreligious passages had slipped through the net here and there and could be found scattered inconspicuously through the text was not enough to overthrow it.

The tide began to turn with the changing international situation and political environment in France after 1756. It was also in 1756 that a leading *anti-philosophe*, Thomas-Jean Pichon (1731–1812), a senior ecclesiastic at Le Mans, *historiographe* to Monsieur, the king's brother, and a prominent *dévôt* at court, broadened the attack with his *La Raison triomphante des nouveautés ou Essai sur les mœurs et l'incrédulité* (Paris, 1756), the most comprehensive critique of the *Encyclopédie* thus far. Pichon portrayed the *beaux esprits* of his day as feeble imitators of their predecessors—the Lucretiuses, Hobbeses, and Bayles—but yet a manifestation of a deep social malaise fomenting freethinking even in such remote regions as Provence. Paris, contended Pichon, was the social source of the contagion. The capital had become a place of unbridled individuality where anyone could conceal his real identity among the throng, evading traditional morality and proper Christian constraints, the city of *la liberté*.[22] A new emphasis on intellectual attainment and old zest for pleasure-seeking were fusing insidiously, he thought, under the auspices of the 'philosophy' inspiring the *Encyclopédie*, a vehicle accelerating corruption of morals and causing the court aristocracy to abandon their pride in nobility's hereditary character.[23]

In Paris, practically anyone with a few *louis d'or* capable of affecting a polished tone and finding an appropriate outfit could pass himself off as a 'gentleman' or even a 'duke' or 'marquis' and yet genuine nobles flocked there, oblivious to the perils of moral depravity and lineage pollution. Worst of all, Paris had given birth to an extremely pernicious new social category—the café idlers and loungers in the Luxembourg gardens and Palais Royal, self-proclaimed *philosophes* and 'politiques universels' posturing ridiculously as well-informed connoisseurs, men who do nothing useful but sit uttering witticisms and talking interminably all day, issuing pretentious judgements on every topic, even the king's foreign policy.[24] These fatuous types had created a new public forum where they regaled passers-by with an unending stream of comment contrary to 'nos loix' and 'nos coûtumes les plus

---

[21] McMahon, *Enemies*, 126–7; Quintili, *Pensée critique*, 164, 185–90, 257–62, 264–76.
[22] Pichon, *La Raison triomphante*, 2–3, 6–9.
[23] Ibid. 10; Monod, *Pascal à Chateaubriand*, 395, 398–9.
[24] Pichon, *La Raison triomphante*, 57, 61–2, 64.

sacrées'.[25] One of these idlers, Morellet, later remarked in his *Mémoires* that the *encyclopédistes* indeed spent much of their time lounging in the cafés and public gardens often convening informal discussion groups. Apparently, it was in the gardens principally that one then heard the most acerbic criticism of the court.

Pichon's book initiated a sequence of attacks encouraging readers to identify the *philosophes* as the prime cause of the national moral malaise supposedly causing the monarchy's mounting humiliation and failure in war. It is no coincidence that the 'war' over the *Encyclopédie* culminated during the Seven Years War (1756–63), a particularly catastrophic period for France's fortunes, trade, empire, and monarchy. The connections between the general worsening state of affairs, financial crisis, and book censorship emerged clearly with a royal edict of April 1757, for the better regulation of 'la librairie', an accompanying document explaining that the king would no longer tolerate the licentiousness of the many writings circulating in the kingdom seeking to erode religion 'et à donner atteinte à son autorité'.[26] That Frederick the Great, renowned as prime royal patron of 'la philosophie' whose support had helped to rescue the *Encyclopédie* earlier, in 1751–2, was now openly France's enemy, allied to Britain, in the vast global conflict under way, did not help. So rife was this mood of suspicion and denunciation in France during the war years, Helvétius later recalled, in his posthumous *De l'homme* (1773), that much of the public seemed willing to believe the disastrous defeats, including the loss of most of the French empire in North America and India, was due to 'l'esprit philosophique'. The *encyclopédistes*, allegedly, had sapped the nobility's time-honoured military ethic, debased the troops' morality, even disordered the country's finances.[27]

From 1756, the *Encyclopédie*'s prospects darkened. Denouncing the *Encyclopédie* and its editors ceased to be solely the business of churchmen. While the fiercest diatribes from lay quarters assailed Diderot's personality and conduct rather than his philosophy, they also drew attention to his propagating forbidden doctrine. This offensive was led by the journalist Élie-Catherine Fréron, a foe especially of François Veron de Forbonnais (1722–1800), responsible for several economic entries in the *Encyclopédie*, and Alexandre Deleyre (1726–96), one of Diderot's close assistants, author of the article 'Fanatisme', in volume vi, depicting the entire history of the world as the history of ferocious superstition in action in the Indies as in Europe.[28] Fréron began by attacking Diderot's first play, *Le Fils naturel*, published in February 1757, an attempt to stage his conception of virtue as based on self-love. Accusing Diderot of plagiarizing the piece from a play by Goldoni, *Il vero amico*, Fréron went so far as to divulge a bogus 'letter' from Goldoni, supposedly sent from Venice, in July 1757, thanking a Parisian friend for sending a French 'translation' of his play under the curious title *Le Fils naturel*. The furore seriously harmed Diderot's reputation at the time, reinforcing the wider charge of plagiarism his adversaries

[25] Ibid., preface pp. xxiii and 15.
[26] Royal edict, Versailles, 16 Apr. 1757, in Malesherbes, *Mémoires*, 385; Haechler, *L'Encyclopédie*, 236.
[27] Helvétius, *De l'homme*, i. 449.
[28] Toscano, *Fanaticism*, 102–7.

continually laid at his door.[29] More damaging still were the *Petites Lettres sur de grands philosophes* (1757) by Charles Palissot de Montenoy (1730–1814), member of the Academy of Nancy and a long-standing ally of Fréron recently arrived from Avignon. Striking a chord with the public the *Petites Lettres*, according to Malesherbes, dealt the *encyclopédistes* a harsher blow than any royal decree.[30]

Reflecting the *anti-philosophique* backlash among the laity, Palissot's smear mostly pilloried Diderot and his accomplices' alleged hypocrisy, plagiarism, self-congratulatory airs, and obsession with dominating public opinion, together with their supposedly abysmal judgement in literary and artistic matters. Despite having principally quarrelled with d'Alembert, Palissot, wary of his social standing (and closeness to Voltaire), nevertheless aimed his barbs chiefly against Diderot. Self-appointed champions of toleration, the *encyclopédistes* were really heralds of intolerance. Joining the chorus decrying Diderot's plagiarism, Palissot commiserated with Goldoni, designated Diderot's *Essai sur le mérite et sur la vertu* just a translation 'servile et fautive de Milord Shaftesbury' and the *Pensées philosophiques* (1746) and *L'Interprétation de la nature* (1751) as impious and virtually stolen word for word, the text being 'toute entière dans Bacon'.[31]

In this way, a lay literary mythology of *anti-philosophie* pervaded the Paris cafés depicting the *encyclopédistes* as a dishonest and sinister clique conspiring to manipulate the Parisian intellectual and literary scene that appealed to many readers and theatre-goers.[32] Fréron and Palissot succeeded, from 1757, in damaging Diderot's and d'Alembert's reputations by depicting them as ineptly trying to usurp the role of chief arbiters of taste, the arts, theatre, and the public conscience. It was a polemic differing markedly from the Christian apologetic backlash with its predominantly theological concerns but one that did not lack a certain philosophical edge. Expressly exempting Montesquieu and Voltaire from their indictment,[33] in assailing Diderot's circle as fraudulent *usurpateurs*, a league of insolent *philosophes* seeking to pull the wool over the eyes of the reading public they were charged with secretly scorning, Palissot and Fréron did not forget to remind their readers, mostly officials, professionals, and courtiers, also of their 'atheism' and anti-monarchism.[34]

Likewise highly damaging both among the reading public and at court was a series of three satires pillorying the *philosophes* as 'Cacouacs'. Widely read for their witty style, the first of these diatribes appeared in October 1757, its anonymous author being either the Abbé Odet de Saint-Cyr (1694–1761), tutor to the dauphin's children, or else the lawyer Jacob-Nicolas Moreau (1711–1803).[35] The derisive epithet 'Cacouacs', echoing the Greek word for 'bad men' or mischief-makers, enjoyed a sensational vogue as a means of ridiculing the *philosophes modernes* as

[29] Almodóvar, *Década*, 97–8; Haechler, *L'Encyclopédie*, 233–5; Lepape, *Diderot*, 210–11.
[30] Malesherbes, *Mémoires*, 385; Freud, 'Palissot', 87; Saada, *Inventer Diderot*, 125.
[31] Palissot de Montenoy, *Petites Lettres*, 315–16; Balcou, *Fréron*, 128–32, 136.
[32] Balcou, *Fréron*, 133–5; Freud, 'Palissot', 83, 89.
[33] Fréron, *L'Année littéraire* (1759/1), 55, 63–4; La Harpe, *L'Aléthophile*, 10.
[34] Palissot, *Petites Lettres*, 129–30.
[35] Morellet, *Mémoires*, i. 4, 14; Lalande, 'Second Supplément', 45; Stenger, *L'Affaire des Cacouacs*, 10.

moral and cultural savages wreaking havoc on all sides that remained popular in some quarters until the Revolution.[36] Among those delighted by this new mode of attack was Father Hayer. He entirely concurred that the *encyclopédistes* were 'bad men' whose malicious principles tended to the ruin of altar and throne.[37] The success of the first 'Cacouac' lampoon elicited a sequel, the *Nouveau Mémoire pour servir à l'histoire des Cacouacs* ([Paris], 1757), this time definitely by Moreau, a writer dismissed by Morellet as a veteran tool of despotism and government hack who was also the queen's librarian. He had been incited to plunge the dagger in further, d'Alembert informed Voltaire, by Cardinal Bernis and possibly Madame de Pompadour herself.

While Moreau assailed Diderot in particular, labelling his *L'Interprétation de la nature* atheistic, he was no *dévôt* and probably had no need to be incited by anyone, being just a conservative monarchist lampooning the *philosophes* for his own reasons.[38] He was delighted his salvo enraged the entire philosophic party, though lambasting Voltaire and Montesquieu along with the rest was deemed poor judgement by Palissot and Fréron, despite the latter's aversion to Voltaire.[39] The Cacouac lampoons culminated with Saint-Cyr's *Catéchisme des Cacouacs* (1758). Again, heavy stress was laid on the atheistic intent of Bayle's thought and its close relationship to Diderot's, and on the *Encyclopédie*'s affinities with d'Argens, La Mettrie, Rousseau's essay on inequality, and Helvétius's *De l'esprit*, a newly published work frequently cited in Saint-Cyr's footnotes.[40] Saint-Cyr's style was to quote—and often misquote rendering his foes' utterances even more brazenly materialist than they were already—the more audacious sentiments in the *Encyclopédie*'s published volumes, connecting these with the more overtly anti-Christian declamations found in the *Pensées philosophiques* and savagely deriding the hylozoic doctrine embedded in *L'Interprétation* and Diderot's other early works.[41] Also fiercely denounced by both Saint-Cyr and Moreau were Diderot's political doctrines in his *Encyclopédie* article 'Autorité politique' and in the entry 'Gouvernement' by his— since September 1751—close ally Jaucourt, entries intimating republican doctrines altogether incompatible, contended Saint-Cyr, with the biblical injunction that power comes from God and hence with the true principles of society and monarchy.[42]

2. DIDEROT LOSES HIS CONTRIBUTORS

When volume vii of the *Encyclopédie* appeared, with its impressive list of contributors (and seventeen articles by Voltaire),[43] in November 1757, it again enjoyed the same

---

[36] Paulian, *Véritable Système*, ii. 136–9.   [37] Hayer, *La Religion vengée*, vii. 74.
[38] Stenger, *L'Affaire des Cacouacs*, 15.
[39] Morellet, *Mémoires*, i. 44; Moreau, *Nouveau Mémoire*, 34–5, 77–8; La Harpe, *L'Aléthophile*, 10–11, 13.
[40] Saint-Cyr, *Catéchisme*, preface p. xi, 4–5.   [41] Ibid. 11–18.
[42] Ibid.; Haechler, *L'Encyclopédie*, 165, 262–72, 481.   [43] Naves, *Voltaire*, 34.

triumphant success as the earlier volumes. But it was a text that also further exacerbated the battle in France and neighbouring countries and curiously compli-cated the editors' relationship with their leading contributors, especially Voltaire. While there was never any real intellectual dialogue between Diderot and Voltaire, each being acutely aware of the irreconcilability of their divergent world-views, a lasting collaboration had arisen between the latter and d'Alembert. Commencing in Berlin and consolidated in Geneva where, in January 1755, Voltaire purchased his residence Les Délices, beginning a more settled phase in his career, their collusion was to have far-reaching consequences for them all. It was during this first 'Genevan epoch', lasting until 1760, that Voltaire completed his *Essai sur les mœurs*, his most substantial 'philosophical' work, as well as his most celebrated story, *Candide* (1759), and major poems *Sur le désastre de Lisbonne* and *La Religion naturelle*, featuring the first public profession of his militant deism and repudiation of Christianity.

During the early months of his Genevan period, Voltaire, delighted by the beau-tiful scenery and flattering attention he received, lapsed into an uncharacteristically optimistic mood. So profound and obvious was the Enlightenment's impact on Geneva that he briefly imagined the former Calvinist republic to have become a model republic based exclusively on tolerance, philosophy, and reason inspired by the accommodating spirit of Socinianism. Numerous local dignitaries came to pay court to him at his new residence, conducting themselves, sneered Bonnet, like people impatient to see 'un animal très rare'. A leading figure of the Swiss Enlight-enment who loathed Diderot's materialism and Voltaire's deism alike, for a time Bonnet deliberately avoided dropping by, considering he had little in common with the famous newcomer. Eventually, though, prevailed on by friends, he too visited Les Délices, to pay his respects, and, finding Voltaire engrossed in reading Condillac, was forced, despite himself, to admire the great writer's ability to discuss that philosopher on the spot with evident expertise and discernment.[44]

Geneva was no longer Calvin's Geneva but a true republic, concluded Voltaire, 'rempli de vrais philosophes'. The Genevan *libraires* willingly convened reading groups, attended by 'les chefs du Conseil et de l'Église' at which Voltaire's two recent long philosophical poems were read out aloud. During these Genevan soirées, he was much gratified to find Locke being praised infinitely by everyone and his own sentiments 'universellement approuvés dans tous les points'. He himself attributed his emerging at this juncture as a publicly avowed deist, at odds with Christianity, to his arrival in Geneva and delight in discovering the republic had become a thoroughly enlightened place. But in his initial enthusiasm he misconstrued his audience's elaborate courtesies and discreet private Socinianism for intellectual assent. The Socinians, or Unitarians as they came to be called in the French- and English-speaking worlds, were a religious group whom he and other *philosophes* considered to be a sect of virtual *philosophes*, and a rapidly growing one, men who in

---

[44] Bonnet, *Mémoires autobiographiques*, 178–9.

order not to shock commonly received opinion too brutally did not openly reject all aspects of revelation and Christian tradition but virtually did so privately.[45]

Voltaire was right that the intellectual atmosphere in Switzerland had changed hugely in recent years, but greatly overestimated its anti-theological tendency, even though his erroneous notion seemed confirmed that very year by his being able to publish his *Essai sur les mœurs*, with its disparagement of Calvin, at Geneva. 'Le christianisme raisonnable de Locke', he inferred, is the religion of the preachers and adoration of an 'Être suprême, jointe à la morale' that of nearly all the magistrates.[46] This was not entirely wrong. The Genevan theologians did avow themselves men of the Enlightenment, readily acknowledging 'Newton, Leibnitz et Wolff', as one of them assured d'Alembert in print, in 1759, as 'nos maîtres en philosophie'.[47] The intellectually most eminent Genevan pastor at the time, Jacob Vernet, was enlightened and did harbour Socinian leanings.[48] But while Socinianism was always the most honoured strand of Christianity in the *philosophes'* eyes, even if in Voltaire's case, unlike Diderot's, Unitarianism was also reckoned the decisive step on the path to providential deism, to Swiss Protestant theologians Socianism remained, at least officially, a forbidden creed and a term used in public only disapprovingly.

In 1756, d'Alembert made a trip, via Lyon, to Geneva where he spent a month conferring with Voltaire and imbibing impressions, largely inspired by the latter, that he subsequently articulated in what proved the most explosive of all the *Encyclopédie*'s articles, the entry 'Genève'.[49] This article, though far from being as misleading and inaccurate as historians have sometimes claimed, was certainly grossly injudicious and not only according to the *Encyclopédie*'s foes but also Diderot and Grimm, who both disapproved of such openly offensive tactics. Appearing in the seventh volume, in 1757, d'Alembert's piece provided instant ammunition, especially in Switzerland, Holland, and Germany, for those claiming the *Encyclopédie* was dishonest as well as subversive.[50] Though Voltaire had no part in composing the piece, its publication ignited a long-running feud between him (and d'Alembert), on one side, and the Genevan senate and pastors, on the other.

The Genevan authorities were appalled to read in the *Encyclopédie* that theirs was now a *ville philosophe*, that their pastors' religion 'n'est autre chose qu'un Socinianisme parfait', and that their theologians reckoned it an injustice to the divinity to suppose he punishes our sins with eternal torments in Hell, although, in fact, this is exactly what Vernet did think.[51] The Genevan Reformed ministry established a nine-man commission to draft a crushing public retort, vehemently repudiating the

---

[45] Naigeon, art. 'Unitaires', in Diderot, *Encyclopédie*, xvii. 387–8.

[46] Palissot, *Petites Lettres*, 39; Gouhier, *Rousseau et Voltaire*, 130–2.

[47] *Lettre d'un professeur*, 14.

[48] Pomeau, *Religion de Voltaire*, 294–5; Gargett, 'Jacob Vernet', 37–8.

[49] Venturi, *Le origini*, 84–5, 105; Gouhier, *Rousseau et Voltaire*, 130–1; Pappas, *Voltaire and d'Alembert*, 9.

[50] Hayer, *La Religion vengée*, xi. 358–9; Vernet, *Lettres critiques*, i, preface pp. v–vii and ii. 287; Gouhier, *Rousseau et Voltaire*, 110–11; Pappas, 'Diderot, d'Alembert', 202–3.

[51] *Lettres de Genève*, 474–5; Pomeau, *Religion de Voltaire*, 305–6; Gargett, 'Jacob Vernet', 35–6, 39, 43, 47.

Encyclopédie's characterization of Geneva and its pastors, and demanding d'Alembert publicly retract his 'misleading' and defamatory statements, a text Fréron promptly publicized in France. D'Alembert, insisting on the accuracy of his depiction, emboldened by Voltaire, and backed by Diderot, showed little willingness to retract; rather, he adopted a defiant air, reprinting the article unchanged, a year later, in his collected essays published at Amsterdam.[52] The quarrel rumbled on in the background for years, with Voltaire repeatedly savaging Vernet and accusing him of hypocrisy and Vernet denouncing this dark conspiracy against Christianity of a few 'beaux esprits' pretending to be deists but actually veering 'au spinosisme et au matérialisme'.[53]

Voltaire had had practically nothing to do with the early stages of the *Encyclopédie* and never agreed with the core principles of *encyclopédisme* as expounded by Diderot. In fact, he always opposed the *Encyclopédie*'s underlying philosophical and political orientation. But while privately highly critical and, like many other contributors, deploring its marked unevenness in quality, he felt compelled to re-enter the public fray, having already before intervened as the *Encyclopédie*'s chief public champion, in 1751, the moment the venture again became the principal object of 'persecution' by Jansenists, Jesuits, Calvinists, the papacy, and all other 'inquisitors' and 'fanatics'. Given that by 1757 the *Encyclopédie* had become the prime ideological target of all the *anti-philosophes* in France, Holland, and Switzerland, including Fréron whom Voltaire especially loathed and the incensed Vernet, it was unthinkable for him to view the *Encyclopédie* in any other light at this stage than as a cause to be fought for.

If he was ever to become the presiding intellectual and moral leader of the *parti philosophique*, moulding it into a more unified movement, something Voltaire had by no means abandoned hope of achieving, there was no better path, since he no longer resided on French soil, than that of publicly championing the *Encyclopédie*. Thus, for a time, he viewed not the actual *Encyclopédie*, but the battle over its survival, as a crucial arena for promoting Locke's philosophy, deism, and his version of Enlightenment. The now again rapidly escalating struggle afforded him a golden opportunity not only to unify under his leadership and lend more *esprit de corps* to the *philosophes* but also, he hoped, to further their influence at Versailles and ensure, as he explained to Helvétius, that the *philosophes* as a group would henceforth manifest only an irreproachable loyalty to crown and court. Enlightening Europe's courts and uppermost social elites always seemed to Voltaire the only realistic way to redeem mankind from bigotry and superstition and, hence, the supreme good that 'nous puissions faire à la société'.[54]

The so-called 'Damiens affair', the attempted assassination of Louis XV by a fanatical defender of the *parlements* (regional high courts) in 1757, which, as Voltaire feared from the first, the *anti-philosophes* construed as further 'evidence' that the *philosophes* were stirring sedition in the country, only strengthened his conviction

---

[52] Diderot, *Corr.* ii. 26–8; *Lettre d'un professeur*, 4–5; Vernet, *Lettres critiques*, i, preface pp. iv, vi.
[53] *Lettres de Genève*, 475.
[54] Voltaire to Helvétius, 13 Aug. 1760, *CGdH* ii. 289.

that they had to show beyond any doubt that the *philosophes* would never conspire, 'ne formeront jamais de cabale', against the court and monarchy. During these years, Voltaire more and more adopted the habit of using the term *philosophes* to designate what he wished to see the *parti philosophique* become—namely a single, undivided faction influential at Versailles and firmly under his own direction, hence *Voltairiens*. He continually urged the others to drop their internecine differences (except regarding Rousseau) and pool their efforts, as he advised, on targets chosen by him: 'o philosophes, philosophes', as he was later to put it, writing to Helvétius, be united against the enemies of human reason. 'Écrasez l'infâme tout doucement.'[55]

Instead of unity with himself presiding, what he actually found, though, was an internecine philosophical civil war in Paris, still largely hidden from the public but no less real for that, dividing the *parti philosophique* into opposing blocs with differences too considerable ever to be bridged. Worse still, from his standpoint, more and more entries appeared in the *Encyclopédie* that were obviously—for the philosophically discerning—aimed nearly as much at his own system and 'la philosophie angloise' as against intolerance, obscurantism, and the *anti-philosophes*. If Voltaire scorned the Jesuit *Dictionnaire de Trévoux*'s short entry about Locke, Diderot's insultingly brief four-column article on Locke was so perfunctory that it continued to baffle readers as late as the 1790s, being much the shortest allocated to any of the great philosophers, aside from Malebranche (see Table 1). Far from concurring that Locke was the 'Hercule de la métaphysique', and subordinating everything to Lockean perspectives as promised in d'Alembert's (highly misleading) *Discours préliminaire*, Diderot, who never rated Locke highly, assigned Locke only the scantiest role in the *Encyclopédie*'s world-view.[56] Such brevity was bound to look like a deliberate snub.

Would to God, complained Voltaire later, writing to d'Alembert, in 1766, that the entire *Encyclopédie* had really been built on the philosophical lines promised in d'Alembert's *Discours* where Bacon, Locke, Newton, and English empiricism are throughout lauded to the skies.[57] Voltaire was undoubtedly right to insist that if

Table 1. Number of columns assigned by the *Encyclopédie* to early modern Western philosophers and philosophies

Spinoza	22
Leibniz	20
Cartesianism	20
Hobbes	18.5
Newtonianism	13
Locke, philosophie de	4
Malebranche	3

[55] Voltaire to Helvétius, around 25 Mar. 1761, *CGdH* iii. 12.
[56] Naigeon, *Philosophie*, iii. 127–30; Israel, 'French Royal Censorship', 72.
[57] Voltaire to d'Alembert, 5 Apr. 1766, in Voltaire, *Corr.* xxx. 159.

Locke, Newton, and English empiricism had really infused the enterprise through-out, as originally advertised, the *Encyclopédie* would never have got into any trouble at all, let alone been suppressed by Church and state.

But it was Diderot not Voltaire or d'Alembert who fixed the *Encyclopédie*'s intellectual agenda. Besides marginalizing Locke and the English approach more generally, it was bound to look distinctly odd to many that Diderot should allot Spinoza the largest amount of space (following Bayle's example, earlier) of any philosopher of modern times. Admittedly, this long and rambling article mostly purports to denounce Spinoza, as the editors could scarcely avoid ostensibly doing. But the entry sets about this task in such a strange fashion, recycling wholly out-of-date, irrelevant, and feeble theological arguments dredged up from the end of the last century, that to the discerning it was bound to look like yet another seditious ploy transmitting a half-concealed message to the aware.

The fact the *Encyclopédie* was a philosophical engine of war directed not only against Christianity but also against the providential deism and Creationism of Voltaire, Turgot, Réaumur, and the like, against Newtonian physico-theology and Locke's version of empiricism, emerges especially clearly from its approach to the creation of the universe and of animal and plant species and the question of the soul. The *Encyclopédie* article on the 'formation du monde' is clearly designed to suggest the intellectual precariousness of every transcendental metaphysical or theological doctrine concerning the origins of things, especially the idea of the prior existence of God's power to that of matter and assumptions that the organizing principle behind the cosmos must be intelligent, morally conscious, and hence benevolent. For Jesuits and Voltaireans alike man is no animal but a being of a different and higher order, possessing a unique God-given status. Plainly under fire here is what Diderot considered the untenable basis of Voltaire's deistic system, Diderot slighting both the theologians and Newtonians simultaneously. Likewise, the *Encyclopédie*'s entry 'Chinois', again penned by Diderot in person, not only attacks Christian sensibilities but also the deistic character Voltaire imputed to classical Chinese thought and culture.[58] All Voltaire's views were either directly or indirectly contradicted. The *Encyclopédie*'s long article on the Jews offers a wholly sympathetic analysis obviously aimed against Christian views and church authority, but equally contradicting the unyieldingly anti-Semitic depiction of this people and their traditions typical of Voltaire's Enlightenment.

Everywhere in the *Encyclopédie*, Voltaire found himself opposed on Locke, Newton, morality, providence, species, race, and creation. Not surprisingly, he became intensely exasperated, notwithstanding his willingness to help defend the enterprise from its enemies. It also dawned on him that if lay elements, particularly at court, and among the high magistracy, were out to condemn the *Encyclopédie* as anti-royalist and subversive, he needed to consider whether he could any longer afford to be associated with the venture. Only a few months after the appearance of the seventh

[58] Morin, '*L'Encyclopédie*', 90–1.

volume, tired of being relegated to marginal status, he suddenly performed a volte-face, resolving to dissociate himself from all further involvement. Late in 1757, he asked Diderot to return all his drafts and accompanying letters.[59] Having earlier advised d'Alembert, who had scant appetite for such combat, Condorcet later remarked,[60] not to abandon the fight, he now abruptly reversed his position, recommending that the struggle *should* now be abandoned; or at least, following d'Alembert's suggestion, that all the *encyclopédistes* should, in a dignified manner, publicly abstain *en bloc* from further work on the venture while waiting for public sympathy to swing back in their favour, enabling them to re-enter the arena later, in triumph.[61]

With the appearance of the again successful seventh volume, in 1757, few can have expected that the *Encyclopédie* was on the verge of being aborted. However, it proved to be the last to appear until 1765 (and last to appear legally at all), its publication being followed, as the novelist-*philosophe* Marmontel later recalled, by a complete change in the situation. Those who, from the public's point of view, were the foremost contributors, like Voltaire, seeing the shift in mood among the public and at court and the risks the *Encyclopédie* now exposed them to, at this point withdrew from the whole business. For months, Diderot made no answer to Voltaire's demand for the return of his drafts. Indignant at his silence despite renewed requests, he complained to d'Alembert, in February 1758, that nothing could justify his refusal 'de me restituer mes papiers' and of Diderot's 'impertinence'.[62] Eventually, he was persuaded to let Diderot retain and publish those pieces he had already submitted. Nevertheless Voltaire played no further role in compiling the *Encyclopédie* and, in June 1758, as the struggle neared its bitter climax, amid the mounting uproar surrounding Helvétius's *De l'esprit*, he definitively cut all links, a decision to which he subsequently adhered despite Diderot's several times urging him to reconsider.[63]

Voltaire's withdrawal clinched matters also for d'Alembert. Vain and ambitious, he too resented Diderot's editorial primacy and the growing influence behind the scenes of d'Holbach, Deleyre, and other unrelenting radicals, and especially loathed the defamatory attacks to which he and Diderot were daily subjected. There was now, he too realized, an orchestrated movement to destroy the *Encyclopédie* extending from Rome and Geneva to Paris, reaching to the upper echelons at Versailles, so that suppression had recently become much likelier than even a year earlier. In the new circumstances, the group driving the *Encyclopédie* must soon either suspend work, as he now urged, or be crushed.[64] Suppression, moreover, would certainly gravely compromise the social standing and careers in France of those involved. He by no means relished the thought of being shunned at Versailles or, in the worst case scenario, dispatched to the Bastille with Diderot.

[59] Ibid. 214–18; Pomeau, *Religion de Voltaire*, 301, 307–8.
[60] Condorcet, 'Éloge de d'Alembert', p. xiv.
[61] Naves, *Voltaire*, 54–5.
[62] Ibid. 56; Diderot, *Corr.* ii. 35; Pomeau, *Religion de Voltaire*, 307–8.
[63] Naves, *Voltaire*, 62–3; Pappas, 'Diderot, d'Alembert', 201; Burson, 'Crystallization', 991–2.
[64] Pappas, 'Diderot, d'Alembert', 195, 197–201; Mortier, *Le Cœur*, 44–6.

Meanwhile, d'Alembert was increasingly coming under Voltaire's spell, hence being drawn into the latter's court strategy.[65] By acquiescing in Voltaire's leadership, d'Alembert could aspire to become Parisian leader of a reconfigured *parti philosophique*. But while admiring Voltaire more than Diderot, he was nevertheless markedly less confident than the former that there really existed a powerful countervailing influence, in high places, capable of being mobilized to support a reconfigured, more royalist *parti philosophique*. In any case, after months of agonizing over the matter, fearing for his own position in the Académie Française and high society, early in 1758 he suddenly resigned as joint editor: 'adieu, mon cher et grand philosophe', he wrote to Voltaire, in February, 'je suis aussi dégoûté de la France que de l'*Encyclopédie*.'[66] Harshly criticized afterwards for cowardice, publicly disavowing his real opinions, and abandoning the fight at the crucial moment, he was still being vehemently rebuked for abandoning his colleagues, by Naigeon in an address before the National Assembly in 1790.[67]

Diderot, though wary of d'Alembert's proximity to Voltaire, repeatedly tried to draw him back to his side while also showing his resentment at d'Alembert's abandoning him with the battle at its fiercest.[68] The foes of the *philosophes*, he complained to Voltaire, were openly exulting in d'Alembert's resignation as if it were a great victory, viewing it as a triumph heralding the *Encyclopédie*'s certain pending doom. The crisis in the *Encyclopédie*'s fortunes caused by the withdrawal of Voltaire and d'Alembert, meanwhile, was greatly intensified by the impact of the furore erupting, early in 1758, over Helvétius's *De l'esprit*. This was a book published legally but that had been mistakenly authorized by the censor, provoking a public scandal that finally enabled the *Encyclopédie*'s adversaries to gain the upper hand in the struggle. The uproar was rather ironic in that Helvétius was not himself a contributor to the *Encyclopédie* and only subsequently became friendly with Diderot and d'Holbach, after publishing his bombshell.[69] *De l'esprit*, an (almost) openly materialist and atheistic work practically untouched by any influence of his early mentors, Montesquieu and Voltaire, the fruit of many years' painstaking labour, was assumed by some to be just a re-hash of Diderot's ideas. It was immediately condemned in the strongest terms by the Sorbonne at the instigation, notes Helvétius, of the archbishop of Paris.[70] On 22 November 1758, the archbishop, Christophe de Beaumont, directly intervened, adding a twenty-eight-page *mandement* denouncing *De l'esprit*'s moral doctrine, its materialism deriving, he held, from Hobbes, and designing 'to subjugate by force the empire of Jesus Christ and on its ruins establish laws that are purely human, the passions, and profane philosophy'.[71] Where Celsus

---

[65] Vernet, *Lettres critiques*, i. 14; Gay, *Voltaire's Politics*, 207.
[66] D'Alembert, *Œuvres complètes*, v. 60–1; Venturi, *Le origini*, 84; Trousson, *Denis Diderot*, 251–2.
[67] Naigeon, *Adresse à l'Assemblée Nationale*, 102–4.
[68] Balcou, *Fréron*, 142; Blom, *Enlightening the World*, 213–17.
[69] Diderot, *Réfutation*, 341; Smith, *Helvétius*, 149.
[70] Helvétius, *De l'homme*, ii. 958; La Harpe, *Philosophie*, i. 311; Desné, 'Voltaire et Helvétius', 406–8.
[71] Beaumont, *Mandement*, 10–12, 14; Cottret, *Jansénismes*, 84.

openly combats Christianity and Hobbes 'disguised his abominable system', *De l'esprit* employs 'by turns both boldness and artifice against the holy religion we profess'.[72] On the papal Index from January 1759, the work was banned by Church and state for irreligion but also for deprecating monarchy and insinuatingly exalting republican ideas besides introducing the principle, sharply condemned by the Sorbonne, that it is by good laws that men are made virtuous.[73] Over the winter of 1758–9, it seemed likely Helvétius would be imprisoned, a prospect filling him and his friends with dread.[74]

All this inevitably rebounded on the *Encyclopédie*. Helvétius's text not only outraged churchmen, professors, court, and judiciary but also annoyed mainstream Enlightenment thinkers like Voltaire, Hume, and Turgot. That his former protégé wholly ignored Locke and said not a word about himself appalled Voltaire.[75] Turgot scorned Helvétius even more than Diderot, dismissing him as a mediocrity whose seditious politics and materialism would prove disastrous.[76] Even the radical-minded berated this 'good-hearted man with more wit than his book', as Casanova put it, blaming him for his reckless, untimely intervention, endangering them all by casting the entire *encyclopédiste* movement in a flagrantly subversive light. Yet, by no means everyone despised *De l'esprit*. If 'no effort was spared to ruin Helvétius' by clergy and *parlement*, many readers were interested in its arguments. The answer to the vicious vituperation heaped on this benevolent author, declared his wife, Anne-Catherine, Madame Helvétius, a leading *salonnière* in her own right and a renowned beauty, was *De l'esprit's* impressive sales record.[77] In France alone, estimated the Abbé Gabriel Gauchat (1709–74), commenting later in 1758, over 10,000 copies sold in just a few months.[78] The radical editor of Boulanger's *Recherches* (probably d'Holbach) in 1762 likewise stressed *De l'esprit's* enormous success: 'the Apostles of error and fable, might fulminate as much as they please' but no less than thirteen editions had appeared by late 1759 'in all the great cities of Europe'.[79] But staggering sales success or not, the political repercussions, Turgot, like Voltaire, immediately grasped, must be ominous for all varieties of *philosophe*. The author of *De l'esprit*, labelled 'l'ennemi de tout gouvernement', at a moment of severe crisis in the French monarchy's fortunes, inevitably drew down fresh persecution on the *philosophes*' heads, especially menacing those without Helvétius's high social status and wealth.[80]

Adversaries of *la philosophie moderne* pounced from all sides, portraying *De l'esprit* as the work unveiling the veritable countenance of a movement its advocates had, hitherto, artfully concealed. Gauchat, postponing his rebuttal of Bayle's

---

[72] Beaumont, *Mandement*, 5; Burson, 'Crystallization', 992–3.
[73] Hayer, *La Religion vengée*, vii. 179–80; Naigeon, *Philosophie*, ii. 663; Wootton, 'Helvétius', 313.
[74] Smith, *Helvétius*, 153; Cottret, *Jansénismes*, 83–5.
[75] Desné, 'Voltaire et Helvétius', 408; *Correspondance inédite de Condorcet*, 140–5.
[76] Morellet, *Mémoires*, i. 7.
[77] *CGdH* ii. 265–7; Casanova, *Memoirs*, iii. 279–80; Goodman, *Republic*, 75, 258.
[78] Gauchat, *Lettres critiques*, xi, 'avant-propos' and preface p. xii.
[79] [Boulanger-d'Holbach], *Recherches sur l'origine*, i, preface p. vi.
[80] *Correspondance inédite de Condorcet*, 145; Smith, *Helvétius*, 159, 161–2, 167.

toleration, the planned eleventh part of his monumental *Lettres critiques, ou Analyse et réfutation de divers écrits modernes contre la religion* (19 vols., Paris, 1755–63), instead devoted his next volume to responding to the general outcry *De l'esprit* had aroused, seeking to counter the 'ravages d'un écrit si pernicieux'. While bracketing all the materialists together as addicts of *l'Hobbésisme*, the 'germ' of Helvétius's intellectual system he traced to Diderot's *Pensées philosophiques*. Identifying severe contradictions in Helvétius's purely secular morality detached from theology, an ethics fusing self-interest with the general interest, or 'l'intérêt public', Gauchat proclaimed Christianity the only truly 'enlightened' morality. 'La morale philosophique' rooted in the 'système de nos Hobbésistes' by contrast was wholly blind.[81] Helvétius he hesitated to pronounce an outright atheist but did point out, given the book was being read by so many and admired by some, that conclusions flow from it revealing the closest affinities with 'ce système horrible' [le Spinosisme] destroying the essence of 'l'Être suprême, et conséquement son existence'.[82]

Reports that *anti-encyclopédique* sentiment was triumphing at Versailles dismayed Voltaire, d'Alembert, and many others. Emphatic that in this crisis the *philosophes* must more than ever show unity and purposeful discipline, Voltaire, having advised Diderot from Lausanne in January 1758 to suspend work on the *Encyclopédie*, in February went so far as to summon all the *encyclopédistes* to follow his example and resign together *en masse*.[83] Hence, precisely when the accusations they were undermining religion, morality, and monarchy began to look more plausible, the rift between the two enlightenments, moderate and radical, became more obvious and open.[84] Feeling threatened, the more prominent remaining contributors did indeed at this point practically all abandon the project, as Voltaire urged, publicly distancing themselves during the next months from 'le parti encyclopédiste' and especially Diderot whose determination to soldier on, though courageous, struck many as hopeless in the changed circumstances.

Buffon, with the royal gardens and *cabinet* to supervise, quietly withdrew, confining himself henceforth to court circles.[85] François Quesnay, *économiste*, leading surgeon, and man of letters, unwilling to prejudice his status as personal physician to Madame Pompadour at court or be associated with Diderot's materialism, resigned, demanding the return of the draft articles he had already submitted, including key pieces on taxation and interest on loans and investments.[86] Turgot, equally familiar at court, cut all ties with the *Encyclopédie*, despite repeated efforts on Diderot's part to get him to reconsider.[87] Marmontel, a literary figure who had eagerly cultivated Diderot earlier, now felt obliged to consider his own position

---

[81] Gauchat, *Lettres critiques*, xi. 53-6, 111, 175, 177.

[82] Ibid. xii. 4, 61–2; McMahon, *Enemies*, 24.

[83] Voltaire to Diderot, 5 or 6 Jan. 1758, in Diderot, *Corr.* ii. 29; Naves, *Voltaire*, 55.

[84] Hayer, *La Religion vengée*, vii. 178–80; Proust, *Diderot*, 261.

[85] Marmontel, *Mémoires*, ii. 240–1.

[86] Kafker and Kafker, *Encyclopedists*, 323.

[87] Diderot to Turgot, 21 Jan. 1759, in Diderot, *Corr.* ii. 110; Manuel, *Prophets*, 25; Gillispie, *Science*, 6.

and withdrew.[88] Another defector was Charles Pinot Duclos (1704–72), wit and habitué of the Café Procope and the Café Gradot, author of several best-selling novels who, humble birth notwithstanding, boasted numerous aristocratic connections. Although his three or four entries on literary topics were of scant importance in themselves, his departure added further to the gloom now shrouding Diderot's enterprise. Did he see that this vile troop of *encyclopédistes*, Fréron asked Palissot, in January 1758, exulting over these successive setbacks to the *Encyclopédie*, was at last on the verge 'd'être exterminé?'[89]

Another notable defector was the young Abbé André Morellet (1727–1819), 'une nouvelle et excellente acquisition', according to d'Alembert, who, like de Prades earlier, possessed the valuable asset of recent theological training at the Sorbonne. Friendly with d'Alembert and Diderot (with whom he later quarrelled) since the de Prades affair, Morellet was neither an atheist nor a materialist but rather regularly defended theism and God's beneficence in debates with Diderot and d'Holbach. Recruited originally to write such theological articles as 'Fils de Dieu', 'Foi', 'Fatalité', and 'Gomariste' from a neutral, strictly historical perspective, he particularly admired Turgot under whose influence, from the mid 1750s, he developed a passion for economics. A pugnacious polemicist, Morellet proved a useful ally at first but not in the longer run. Returning from Italy, in March 1759, he felt someone in his impecunious position should not risk falling into official disfavour by 'attacking government and religion'. He too abruptly terminated his involvement.[90] During the next years, he focused mainly on economics, commencing a slow, general estrangement culminating decades later in his publicly renouncing the legacy of Diderot and Helvétius, early in the Revolution, in 1790. At that point, he definitively quarrelled with Madame Helvétius's circle and various disciples of Helvétius and d'Holbach with some of whom he had been close friends for thirty years but who, unlike himself, all supported the Revolution.

The outcry against *De l'esprit* sealed the fate of the *Encyclopédie*. Irretrievably floundering, seemingly, the project became deeply mired in personal recrimination. The resignations of all the more illustrious contributors together with the public scandal drastically changed the culture and working methods of Diderot and his few remaining accomplices, forcing them to take the whole project underground. The *anti-philosophes*' attacks intensified. With the two sides 'having exploded against each other with the highest degree of rage', as Rousseau expressed it later, in his *Confessions*, 'the two parties resembled rabid wolves, desperate to tear each other to pieces rather than Christians and philosophers who reciprocally wish to enlighten, convince and restore each other to the path of truth'.[91] It was only perhaps 'lack of turbulent leaders with influence on either side' that was missing for the situation 'to

---

[88] Diderot, *Corr.* ii. 74; Haechler, *L'Encyclopédie: Les Combats*, 237.
[89] Balcou, *Fréron*, 142, 194; Stenger, *L'Affaire des Cacouacs*, 10.
[90] Morellet, *Mémoires*, i. 41–2, 84, 88.
[91] Rousseau, *Confessions*, 366.

degenerate into a civil war, and God knows what a civil war of religion might bring about when the cruellest intolerance was at bottom the same on both sides.'[92]

Who exactly was being intolerant, though, and who were the 'aggressors' was a question constantly posed in the polemical exchanges. Diderot and his friends championed *tolérantisme*, calling their opponents 'fanatics'; yet it was they, retorted the *anti-philosophe* Guyon, like Rousseau soon afterwards, who were the 'real fanatics'. 'Born enemy of all partisan spirit' and intolerance, as Rousseau thought of himself, he too now judged the moment right to abandon the sinking ship. Deeply shocked by the scale of the attacks, Rousseau, in March 1758, followed Voltaire and d'Alembert in imploring Diderot to give up the *Encyclopédie*; the latter disdained to reply.[93] Their friendship was not yet quite finished but was almost. To the amazement of his former comrades, Rousseau, invoking his Calvinist origins, chose this moment to add his voice to the general denunciation of the *encyclopédistes*, much to Vernet's satisfaction publishing his *Lettre à M. d'Alembert sur les spectacles*, a resounding piece, dated March 1758, agreeing with those depicting the *encyclopédistes* as disreputable mischief-makers. Though very short on logic, in Grimm's opinion, this text effectively savaged not just d'Alembert's views on the theatre but also his claim that the Genevan preachers were Socinians in his article 'Genève'.[94] Moral uprightness without religion, held Rousseau, is scarcely plausible.[95] Although more directly aimed at d'Alembert than Diderot, the latter too was attacked, having devoted his own efforts to the theatre of late and being alluded to in the preface as a betrayer of friendship. Henceforth, Diderot and Rousseau stood for sharply contrasting views on art, theatre, and morality, as of everything else.[96]

With his active circle of contributors shrinking, the burden of research and writing more than ever fell on Diderot's own shoulders and those of d'Holbach and the diligent Jaucourt who, unlike the other *philosophes*, maintained close ties with the austere but ardent republican theorist Mably. But Diderot alone bore the brunt of the polemical attacks on the *Encyclopédie* as the other two remained unknown to the public. Of texts appearing in the wake of *De l'esprit*, the most comprehensive assault on the *Encyclopédie*'s core concepts—and that which most damagingly linked the *Encyclopédie* with *De l'esprit*—was the first two volumes of the eventually eight-volume *Préjugés légitimes et réfutation de l'*Encyclopédie (1758–9) published in August 1758, by the Jansenist *anti-philosophe* Abraham-Joseph Chaumeix (1730–90). Chaumeix's salvoes, lengthy extracts from which quickly reappeared in the Jansenist *Nouvelles ecclésiastiques*, brought the intensity of the public controversy to new levels.[97] Dubbed 'un ardent convulsionnaire' by Voltaire, Chaumeix's entire career during these years was devoted to assailing the *Encyclopédie*, *Le Censeur hebdomadaire*, the

[92] Ibid.; Guehenno, *Jean-Jacques Rousseau*, i. 419, 428.
[93] Rousseau to Diderot, 2 Mar. 1758, in Diderot, *Corr.* ii. 36, 44–6.
[94] Rousseau, *Lettre à d'Alembert*, 56–63; Trousson, *Jean-Jacques Rousseau*, 372–5.
[95] Monty, *Critique littéraire*, 44–6; Freud, 'Palissot', 111.
[96] Freud, 'Palissot', 111; Cherni, *Diderot*, 166–7.
[97] Havinga, *Nouvelles ecclésiastiques*, 77; Cottret, *Jansénismes*, 82–3.

new Jansenist journal he helped set up at Utrecht, inciting a campaign against the *encyclopédistes* also in the Dutch Republic where, again, his censures found strong support.

The *encyclopédistes*, held Chaumeix, are *matérialistes* who, attaching the faculty of thinking to all beings, plants and stones included, perceive little difference between men and animals and conflate body and mind into one.[98] 'I will leave it to Monsieur d'Alembert', he added derisively, to calculate what degree 'de connoissance une pierre a de son existence'.[99] Diderot was an unmitigated foe of religion who denies free will and for whom man is simply 'un corps organique, susceptible de sensations'.[100] Behind a charade of presenting a wide spectrum of opinion penned by dozens of contributors, including numerous topics of purely practical interest, Diderot had cunningly smuggled, Chaumeix showed in relentless detail, a camouflaged but highly coherent doctrine permeating the entire compilation and altogether destructive of religion, Christian morality, and monarchy. With their skilful and devious cross-referencing, the *encyclopédistes* had found an effective means of appearing to respect religion 'en la renversant en effet'.[101] Unsuspecting readers might suppose Locke and Buffon are 'honoured' in the *Encyclopédie* when actually both are mercilessly twisted and dragged into the *Encyclopédie*'s hidden agenda which is unreservedly 'sensualiste et matérialiste'. Diderot's scientific outlook indeed particularly diverged from Buffon's— whose biology he otherwise much preferred to that of Réaumur and Linnaeus—in rejecting his broad division between organic and inorganic matter, in favour of an unyielding monism.[102]

What is Diderot's moral system? Instead of drawing on Christianity, he thinks 'la volonté générale est le droit naturel' and that from society's 'volonté générale' all ideas of justice and morality derive. The *Encyclopédie*'s underlying message, Chaumeix correctly grasped, is coherent, prevalent throughout the *Encyclopédie*, and mostly presented 'à couvert', hence was a forbidden, clandestine philosophy, and its essence is that reason is man's exclusive guide in this world, and this life the only life there is, so that all the religious mysteries 'ne sont que des ténèbres'. Of course, by no means every contributor, grants Chaumeix, like Gauchat, and Hayer, was party to the conspiracy. But at its core, the project *is* a concerted conspiracy intended to undermine religion, political authority, and morality and the chief conspirator indisputably is the undertaking's *directeur*, 'M. Did....'.[103] In 1759, Chaumeix tacked on to his now eight-volume work a vigorous *critique* of Helvétius's *De l'esprit* arguing that essentially the same philosophical 'errors' inspired both the *Encyclopédie* and that work, the two being closely linked.[104]

---

[98] Chaumeix, *Préjugés légitimes*, i. 200–2, 209; Lough, *Essays*, 291–2.
[99] Chaumeix, *Préjugés légitimes*, i. 212.
[100] Ibid. i. 213–14, 222–3.
[101] Lough, *Essays*, 288; Proust, *Diderot*, 259–60; Haechler, *L'Encyclopédie*, 177.
[102] Mortier, *Le Cœur*, 255–6; Israel, *Enlightenment Contested*, 749; Ballstadt, *Diderot*, 155–7.
[103] Hayer, *La Religion vengée*, x. 305; Israel, 'French Royal Censorship', 67.
[104] Chaumeix, *Préjugés légitimes*, i. 137; Smith, *Helvétius*, 150.

Another massive assault was Hayer's *La Religion vengée*. Hayer, derisively styled 'lieutenant général de l'armée *anti-Encyclopédiste*' by Morellet but often shrewder than Chaumeix, was a Franciscan recollect friar and editor of this vast nineteen-volume attack on *la philosophie moderne* together with those Morellet calls his 'aides-de-camp'—Moreau, Jean Soret, a Paris magistrate,[105] and the Abbé Charles Batteaux (1713–80), a professor at the Collège de France and authority on aesthetics.[106] Unmasking the *Encyclopédie*'s methods, they announced their aims with an illustrated title page triumphantly showing 'true philosophy', hailed by the Church, submitting a copy of their work to an approving dauphin while 'Christian wisdom' tramples 'false philosophy' under foot. These 'persécuteurs des philosophes' as Voltaire called them, seeing the *Encyclopédie*'s key ideas derived from far back in the past,[107] devoted most of the first five volumes to crushing Bayle, whom Hayer, Gauchat, and Guyon all considered the *Encyclopédie*'s spiritual forefather albeit they also thought Diderot and his allies had gone well beyond his impieties.[108]

The backlash against Helvétius intensified the assault on the (radical) *philosophes* as a group, creating a viable basis for the judiciary's and court's intervention against the *Encyclopédie* as the emblem of the entire subversive movement. Now they had the upper hand, different segments of the Church vied with each other in whipping up public outrage while still pursuing their quarrels with each other. Refusing to allow the episcopate or Jesuits to usurp what they considered their primacy in the offensive against *l'esprit philosophique*, the Jansenist clergy decried the Jesuits' efforts, the *Nouvelles ecclésiastiques* roundly blaming them for making far too many concessions to the new philosophy and science in the past. It was precisely the Jesuits who had opened 'la route aux partisans de l'irreligion'.[109] As for the archbishop of Paris's *mandement* of 22 November 1758, condemning *De l'esprit*, this, though forceful, was dismissed by the *Nouvelles ecclésiastiques*, in January 1759, as too little too late, the archbishop, in their view, failing to cast the net widely enough.

The cumulatively devastating indictment amassed in layers by Chaumeix, Hayer, Moreau, Soret, Gauchat, Guyon, Fréron, Palissot, Saint-Cyr, and other *anti-philosophes* who followed laid the platform for the *Encyclopédie*'s formal condemnation, of January 1759, by the Paris *Parlement*. The *Parlement*'s proceedings against 'l'esprit d'irreligion à la mode, qui est aussi contraire à l'estat qu'à l'église', as a leading architect of the *anti-philosophique* campaign, the Cardinal de Bernis, styled the foe being fought, was headed by Jean-Omer Joly de Fleury (1715–1810), a senior and long-experienced member of the magistracy, mentioned always scornfully by Voltaire and d'Alembert but *avocat général* to the *Parlement* since 1746 and in 1768 to become its *président à mortier*. An out-and-out reactionary, he reviled all talk of toleration and liberty of thought. His *réquisitoire*, or formal indictment of *De l'esprit*

---

[105] Lough, *Essays*, 390–7; McMahon, *Enemies*, 22–3.
[106] Morellet, *Mémoires* i. 4, 14.
[107] Diderot, *Corr.* ii. 29–30; Masseau, *Ennemis*, 140; Proust, *Diderot*, 261–2.
[108] [Guyon], *L'Oracle*, 104–9.
[109] Masseau, *Ennemis*, 132, 136; Burson, 'Crystallization', 992–3.

and the *Encyclopédie*, of 23 January, deliberately bracketed the two, styling the former an abstract of the *Encyclopédie*'s core ideas and prime source of its *principes*.[110]

His object, explains Joly de Fleury in his preamble, was not to suppress this or that publication but rather indict the whole subversive movement, 'le sistème d'incrédulité' in general. Like Hayer, he stresses the *Encyclopédie*'s relationship to Bayle, accusing the editors with reviving his spirit and devious techniques. Just as Bayle's *Dictionnaire* employs an alphabetical layout and, in the major articles, a bewildering array of arguments both for and against, to disorient the reader and disguise his sedition when discussing religion, morality, or authority, so, Joly convincingly demonstrates, citing the *Encyclopédie* articles 'Âme', 'Aius Locutius', 'Autorité politique', 'Athée', 'Adorer', 'Conscience (Liberté de)', 'Christianisme', 'Dimanche', and 'Encyclopédie', 'le contre' always emerges clearly while orthodoxy is rendered obscure and unconvincing.[111] The compilers' insidious aim, like Bayle's, is to present God's existence 'comme problématique'.[112] The contributors diverged markedly among themselves, some championing natural religion, others materialism, atheism, deism, Protestantism, or Catholicism. But the compendium as a whole had a firm doctrinal core. According to this, there is no distinction between humans and animals, man is composed solely of matter, 'les sensations sont le principe de tout', thought is common to all creatures, and matter the necessary cause of thought and volitions, freedom of the will being just a *préjugé*. No Natural Law exists while human happiness consists in agreeable sensations prompted by exterior objects. The universe creates itself, creation is unproven, Scripture fiction, and faith useless, Christ for the *encyclopédistes* being no more than a 'simple législateur'. Dogma is a man-made contrivance, Christianity's rise a natural phenomenon, and religion and *fanatisme* synonymous terms, Christianity being just 'une fureur insensée' eroding society's foundations.[113] Finally, while professing impeccable probity, and to be restorers of true science, general benefactors of mankind, promoters of the nation's glory, and 'des génies du premier ordre', the editors advocate 'la tolérance universelle' which would fatally plunge revelation and miracles in doubt, foment libertinage, and heighten efforts to overthrow religion, morality, and church authority.

Endorsing this, and informed action was pending also in Rome where the Holy Office accelerated its own investigation of the *Encyclopédie* following Benedict XIV's death in May 1758, the magistrates pronounced *De l'esprit* an 'apologie du matérialisme', banning it together with several other radical works. *De l'esprit* they declared the *Encyclopédie*'s outline, or *abrégé*, a work articulating 'les détestables conséquences' more guardedly propounded in the *Encyclopédie* itself. Advertised as a great monument of learning, the *Encyclopédie* had become instead a badge of national dishonour, less the depot of all knowledge than repository of 'toutes les

---

[110] Joly de Fleury, 'Arrests de la Cour de Parlement portant condamnation de plusieurs livres et autres ouvrages imprimés' (23 Jan. 1759), in *CGdH* ii. 364; McMahon, *Enemies*, 21, 209 n. 10.

[111] McMahon, *Enemies*, 21, 209 n. 10; Negroni, *Lectures*, 208; Lough, *Essays*, 300–1.

[112] Hayer, *La Religion vengée*, x. 247, 304.

[113] Joly de Fleury, 'Arrests de la Cour de Parlement', 364–5.

erreurs'.[114] Especially pernicious, added their public condemnation, was the entry 'Éthiopiens' where the 'system of these authors' regarding generation and the primitive formation of men and animals is expressed especially brazenly.[115] The most ancient of peoples, the 'Ethiopians' are there insinuated to have been 'athées par système' conceiving of animals as products of the earth 'mise en fermentation par la chaleur du soleil, etc.'[116] Without disguise, 'Éthiopiens' presents the *encyclopédistes'* core doctrine that the universe 's'est formé de lui-même', evolving out of itself through the power of nature.

At the core of *la philosophie moderne*, as the decree styles the thought of Diderot and his allies,[117] lay a 'conspiracy' to attack 'les fondemens' of religion and the state, a conspiracy proclaimed to the world not just by Jansenists whose journal, the *Nouvelles ecclésiastiques*, enthusiastically reported Joly de Fleury's assault, but likewise the papacy.[118] From 1759 onwards, the Counter-Enlightenment *idée fixe* that there existed a clandestine philosophical plot to overthrow the existing political and religious order flourished in France and Italy nurtured by radical thought's most committed foes. It was a conspiracy thesis forging a new rhetoric of political motivation, denunciation, and suspicion projected for political and ideological reasons onto something that really existed but so far only intellectually, in the minds of a few thinkers, that was to have unforeseen consequences. For while, before 1759, there was no real organized conspiracy to foment an underground philosophical network to undermine the intellectual foundations of the existing order, outside Diderot's head, *la philosophie moderne* subsequently evolved into a real conspiracy in France and internationally—precisely owing to the *Encyclopédie*'s vigorous suppression.

Acknowledging the large sums invested by the publishers and their need to work in concert with the court, however, the *parlementaires* hesitated to declare an outright ban. *De l'esprit* was condemned outright with seven other 'ouvrages subversifs' cited in Joly's text—the 1755 reprint of d'Argens's *La Philosophie du bon sens* (The Hague, 1747), Voltaire's *La Religion naturelle* (1756), the 1757 reprint of Diderot's *Pensées philosophiques*, the *Lettres semi-philosophiques du chevalier de*** au comte de**** (Amsterdam, 1757), *Le Pyrrhonisme du sage* (Berlin, 1754), and the *Lettre au R. P. Berthier sur le matérialisme* (Geneva, 1759).[119] *De l'esprit* and the seven other writings were publicly lacerated and burnt in the courtyard of the Palais de Justice on 10 February. But the *Encyclopédie* itself was only relegated for further examination by a commission of nine consisting of three jurists, three theologians, and three philosophy professors.[120] The publishers were provisionally forbidden, though, by edict

---

[114] Oxford Bodleian, Mason 11/142 no. 70: *Arrests de la Cour du Parlement* (23 Jan. 1759) (Paris, 1759), 9–16.

[115] Ibid. 171–8.

[116] Ibid. 18.

[117] Ibid. 16.

[118] Birn, 'French-Language Press', 211; for Rome, see pp. 332–3 below.

[119] Joly de Fleury, 'Arrests de la Cour de Parlement', 369; Negroni, *Lectures*, 207.

[120] Oxford Bodleian, Mason 11/142 no. 70: *Arrests de la Cour du Parlement*, 30.

of 6 February 1759, to sell copies of the existing first seven volumes.[121] The *Encyclopédie* was now suspended but not yet definitively prohibited.

The anonymous *Lettre au R. P. Berthier sur le matérialisme* (Geneva, 1759) was a scathing riposte to the *Encyclopédie*'s adversaries, parodying the *dévôt* party's favourite tactic of scaremongering, loudly trumpeting the menace of materialism as a contagion permeating society's every cranny, even artists' studios.[122] Pretending to be an espionage agent operating from within *philosophique* circles scandalized that many women were now infected by *l'esprit philosophique*, the author offers his services as a spy to the editor of the *Journal de Trévoux*, Father Berthier, derisively dubbed 'Général de l'armée anti-matérialiste'.[123] The Jansenists, he reminds Berthier, hinting at the Jesuits' use of paid hacks, bitterly accused him of being harsher toward themselves than the *matérialistes*.

But still Diderot refused to give up. Diderot persists 'à vouloir faire *l'Encyclopédie*', d'Alembert advised Voltaire in late February 1759, predicting his co-editor would succeed only in ruining himself, the latest reports from Versailles indicating that the crown's chief legal officer, the chancellor, was daily expected finally to abort the project.[124] D'Alembert's information was correct. Anxious lest the *Parlement*'s unwieldy procedure might yet enable their prey to slip from their grasp, and encouraged by queen and dauphin, the *dévôts* now exerted their maximum lobbying power at court. All remaining doubt was dispelled when the royal Conseil d'État, on 8 March 1759, announced that the king considered the *Encyclopédie* a vehicle for disseminating *pernicieuses maximes* damaging to religion and morality. By royal decree its privilege was revoked and the publishers forbidden to bring out further volumes or sell existing stock of the first seven.[125]

With the *Encyclopédie* officially condemned in France and also Italy where Pope Clement XIII banned it provisionally in January 1759 and definitively in September,[126] work on the compendium apparently ceased. The *Encyclopédie* disappeared from French and Italian bookshops and shortly afterwards from the entire Spanish empire by decree of the Inquisition *Suprema* dated Madrid, 9 October 1759.[127] The hundreds involved in preparing the volumes and in binding and distribution dispersed to other work. But Diderot, by turns frenetic and then stoical, still refused to give in. Rather, under threat of arrest and renewed imprisonment, he persisted with his furtive scheme. He and his collaborators laboured on, only now wholly clandestinely. It was at this point that the director of the *librairie*, Malesherbes, made his later famous gesture of permitting transfer of the papers and drafts relating to the unpublished volumes to his own house as no one would think of

---

[121] Ibid. 372; Grosclaude, *Malesherbes*, 127.
[122] Salaün, *L'Ordre des mœurs*, 156–60.
[123] *Lettre au R. P. Berthier sur le Matérialisme*, 1, 5; Burson, 'Crystallization', 995.
[124] D'Alembert to Voltaire, Paris, 24 Feb. 1759, in d'Alembert, *Œuvres complètes*, v. 62.
[125] Darnton, *Business*, 12; Negroni, *Lectures*, 334.
[126] Negroni, *Lectures*, 209, 335.
[127] *Indice ultimo*, 76, 88.

searching for them there. With that, the whole undertaking slipped from public view. Very few knew that the project had not in fact been totally suppressed but gone underground. After the noisy crisis in its fortunes, records Marmontel, no more work was done on the *Encyclopédie* except 'en silence et entre un petit nombre de coopérateurs', to which he himself did not belong.[128]

The gloom enveloping the *encyclopédistes* thickened further in May 1759, with publication of the Sorbonne's formal condemnation of Helvétius's *De l'esprit*.[129] This additional denunciation mattered because its findings offered a detailed analysis of Helvétius's 'errors' demonstrating precisely how they paralleled equivalent tenets in the *Encyclopédie*. Among concepts highlighted in this way was Helvétius's thesis that the example of the Turks, Chinese materialists, Sadducaeans, Gymnosophistes, and others devoid of Christian notions of God and piety proves men can live morally, happily, and meaningfully without organized religion and that hope of pleasure and fear of temporal punishments better serves in making men virtuous than threatening eternal torment. The theology faculty had also taken pains to uncover the intellectual genesis of Helvétius's impiety. For besides irreligion and subversion, Helvétius was condemned for seeking celebrity by re-hashing arguments taken from others, a useful device for further linking *De l'esprit* with Diderot and the *Encyclopédie* and both with other banned texts. Helvétius's moral philosophy derived, declared the Sorbonne, from Spinoza, the *Code de la nature*, La Mettrie (especially in *L'Anti-Sénèque*), Mandeville, Diderot (*Pensées philosophiques*), and Montesquieu and its materialist doctrine of the soul from the *Encyclopédie*, Hobbes, Mandeville, d'Argens, La Mettrie, especially in his *L'Homme machine*, Collins, Hume, and Locke's *Essay* as well as the *Code de la nature* (of Morelly). Helvétius's crypto-republican political thought was held to stem from the *Code de la nature*, Diderot's article 'Autorité' in volume i of the *Encyclopédie*, La Mettrie, and Spinoza's *Tractatus Theologico-Politicus*.[130] The new materialism, added the Sorbonne doctors, had now reached the proportions of an *épidémie* whose effects were visible even in the remotest provinces. Here again, the public was assured, the *philosophes* constituted a 'conjuration formée' against the Christian faith and morality and the obedience 'due à l'autorité souveraine'. It was a charge altogether justified with respect to the radical *philosophes*, but complete calumny regarding Montesquieu, Voltaire, Turgot, and the moderate mainstream.[131]

Despite this implication in some quarters that the entire corpus of the *philosophes* was complicit in Diderot's double sedition against altar and throne, the interlinked suppression of the *Encyclopédie* in France, Italy, Spain, and the Austrian Netherlands represented a comprehensive ban on radical thought that directly benefited the moderate Enlightenment. The 1759 prohibition in fact constituted a major landmark in the cultural and intellectual history of western Europe and Spanish America, the

---

[128] Marmontel, *Mémoires*, ii. 364.
[129] Cottret, *Jansénismes*, 85; Burson, 'Crystallization', 994–5.
[130] 'Censure de la Faculté de Théologie de Paris', in *CGdH* ii. 211–12, 393–400.
[131] Ibid. ii. 389–422, here p. 391.

broad significance of which historians have in the past considerably underestimated. It aided the mainstream but also endorsed the theses of the *anti-philosophes* and, in addition, helped prepare the ground for the rise of the Counter-Enlightenment by legitimizing in Paris, Rome, Brussels, and Madrid the new rhetoric of 'conspiracy'. The great drama of the Enlightenment had reached a major turning point.

3. THE 'WAR' OF THE *ENCYCLOPÉDIE* AFTER 1759

However, as Morellet remarks in his *Mémoires*, the royal ban by no means ended the 'war of the *Encyclopédie*. *Anti-philosophie*'s triumph was grounded on an impressive edifice of documentation. Undoubtedly, it had wide-ranging implications for culture, intellectual life, and politics throughout Europe and the New World; but it was not an accurately enough directed blow. Although the ban was enthusiastically supported by numerous churchmen, jurists, and commentators, there were also some more circumspect spirits, including cardinals at Rome, who doubted the wisdom of proceeding on so broad a front. One obvious drawback was that condemning the *Encyclopédie in toto* implied the Church's hostility to much that was not subversive but manifestly useful. While much of the impetus behind the *Encyclopédie*'s suppression came, we have seen, from the Catholic and Protestant moderate Enlightenment which by the 1740s and 1750s had consolidated in France, Switzerland, and Holland as a movement unrelentingly Lockean and Newtonian in character, the Counter-Enlightenment too profited from the ban, some clergy seizing with alacrity the opportunity to condemn all strands of Enlightenment indiscriminately and put pressure on more liberal colleagues. Hard-line bishops in provincial France had their own local condemnations read out in their cathedrals. A diocesan circular issued on 21 November 1759 by Bishop de Fumel, of Lodève, for instance, pronounced all the *philosophes* collectively guilty of conspiring to destroy religion and morality by denying God's existence, works, and the marvels and hidden ways of divine providence. The bishop forbade the faithful to read not only the *Encyclopédie*, *De l'esprit*, Bayle, d'Argens, Diderot, La Mettrie, and de Maillet, but also Montesquieu, Voltaire, and Rousseau.[132]

At Liège, a clash over censorship powers and the *Encyclopédie* pitted the cathedral canons against the *Journal encyclopédique*, edited by Pierre Rousseau, an expatriate French playwright allied to the *philosophes*. The only European journal consistently defending the *Encyclopédie*, it was condemned as 'très dangereux' by the Louvain theology faculty in a fifty-two-page brochure addressed to the papal nuncio in Brussels and priesthood of Liège, resulting in the cardinal prince-bishop revoking the special licence granted four years before exempting it from ecclesiastical supervision, and ordering its suppression. Since the Austrian authorities refused permission for its

---

[132] Smith, *Helvétius*, 51–2.

transfer to Brussels, Rousseau moved his print-shop, late in 1758, to the small autonomous Walloon jurisdiction of Bouillon.[133] Resuming publication there, he solemnly undertook to promote 'l'esprit philosophique' with the most 'scrupulous circumspection' only moderately. The French royal ban and the now close linkage of 'philosophy' with impiety among the public, he acknowledged, had seriously harmed 'philosophy', so prejudicing most 'contre cette science' that *philosophe* and *impie* had become practically synonymous.[134]

In Switzerland too the religious moderate Enlightenment while fully endorsing the *Encyclopédie*'s condemnation strove to fence off all such prohibited, pernicious enlightenment from 'true' Enlightenment. Both Haller and Bonnet, the foremost figures of the Swiss mainstream, had by 1759 changed their minds about Diderot's *Encyclopédie* and now publicly endorsed its suppression. Disgusted by Buffon's hegemony over the natural history in the Paris *Encyclopédie*, Haller expressly endorsed the Paris *Parlement*'s ban, agreeing it was a pernicious 'conspiracy' aspiring to establish what Bonnet called 'le Grand Système' (i.e. Spinozism), but a conspiracy which he and Bonnet judged to be aimed as much against their Enlightenment as against orthodoxy and tradition.[135] It was hardly surprising thunderbolts had descended on the *Encyclopédie*, Bonnet assured the (atheist) astronomer Lalande in Paris, in April 1759. Just as Jupiter humbled the titans defying his supremacy, so Diderot and his accomplices could expect to be utterly crushed for their impiety: men daring to substitute the universe for God and publicly preach 'le Spinozisme' can scarcely imagine they will be left undisturbed by the authorities.[136]

Haller endorsed suppression but at this point fully expected to see the great venture migrate to Berlin, Petersburg, or Holland where, he hoped, it would be revised as well as completed on a changed and now reliably Christian basis. In the Dutch Republic, equally, Elie Luzac's *Nederlandsche Letter-Courant*, at Leiden, staunchly moderate in orientation, categorically condemned the *Encyclopédie* and approved its suppression, refusing to accept that it was in any way promoting enlightened attitudes. Admirer of Montesquieu and Wolff, Luzac, like Formey, Bonnet, and Haller, was a veteran champion of toleration, modern science, and freedom of expression, convinced the philosophy of Diderot, Helvétius, and their circle assaulted not just religion but reason itself, harming scholarship and society alike.[137] There is no Locke or authentic Newton in the *Encyclopédie*'s doctrines. Where is the 'English' perspective d'Alembert promised? He protested especially at how Condillac's sensationalist psychology enters under the cloak of Locke and is deployed in a way Condillac disowned to assert that all human ideas derive directly from sensation, eliminating Locke's non-material faculties of the mind. What the

---

[133] Fréron, *L'Année littéraire* (1759/6), 164; Birn, 'French-Language Press', 279, 282–3; Charlier and Mortier, *Journal encyclopédique*, 19–21, 96–9.

[134] [Rousseau], *Journal encyclopédique* (Bouillon, 1760), i. 10, 13.

[135] Guyot, *Rayonnement*, 33–4, 37.

[136] Quoted ibid. 34.

[137] Velema, *Enlightenment and Conservatism*, 57.

Encyclopédie propagated was nothing remotely resembling Locke's deference to Scripture and religion but rather the idea that nature creates society, politics, and morality.

Voltaire, meanwhile, alarmed by the ferocity of the assault on the *Encyclopédie* and seething with contempt for Joly de Fleury, Fréron, Vernet, and the *Parlement* together with the censors of Paris, Rome, Liège, Leiden, Berne, and Geneva, soon again changed tack. A personality very unlike d'Alembert, temperamentally incapable of staying out of a battle seizing universal attention, he saw no point in further cold-shouldering the *encyclopédistes* at this low point in their fortunes. As both Counter-Enlightenment hard-liners and moderate Catholic and Protestant apologists were exploiting the *Encyclopédie*'s downfall to widen the attack on *la philosophie* and include himself in their indictment, he saw little alternative but to renew his working alliance with Diderot and try to revive the spirits of the thoroughly battered and depressed Helvétius, who was now banished from the court and the queen's presence and whose recent humiliating forced recantation had left a 'certain savagery in his soul'.[138] The 'persecution' he had been subjected to was 'abominable', agreed Voltaire, who advised him, in January 1759, to emigrate to Geneva.[139]

Philosophically, Voltaire aligned with Turgot, Buffon, Hume, and other sceptics, deists, and social conservatives rather than the clandestine underground in Paris. But much more was at stake, he also saw, than the status of Locke and Newton, and following the Paris, Rome, Liège, and Madrid decrees, he could neither stay out of the fight nor escape unscathed should final victory go to the 'fanatics'. While continuing to resent Diderot's editorial and general strategy, and approving d'Alembert's withdrawal, as well as privately reviling both Helvétius's book and Diderot's ideas, he nevertheless judged it apposite, from his own standpoint and that of *la philosophie* generally, to side publicly with the *encyclopédistes*. What chiefly mattered in his eyes, as always, was less the philosophical debate as such than the publicity, public consequences, and politics of the growing tripartite rift in western European culture and how this affected his own position. Helvétius, d'Alembert, he himself, and Diderot, he urged, must be patient 'sages' and, above all, remain unified. There was, despite everything, perhaps a positive side to the mounting 'persecution': it was so appallingly bigoted it must surely generate a backlash of sympathy for 'philosophy's wounded martyrs', thereby creating more and more *philosophes*. If they would only remain 'moderate', loyal to the throne, and unified, the *philosophes* would assuredly win in the end (or at least win the kind of battle Voltaire was committed to). The light was spreading in France, England, Holland, Switzerland, and 'en Italie même; oui, en Italie'. Slowly but surely a 'multitude de *philosophes*' were emerging even in that land of darkness and beginning to challenge the supremacy of the papacy, clergy, scholastics, and Holy Office.

Meanwhile, the *Encyclopédie*'s remaining contributors, driven to conspire against the law, crown, judiciary, Sorbonne, Paris journals, and Church, sought ways to build

---

[138] *CGdH* ii. 259, Helvétius to Hume, 12 July 1759.
[139] *CGdH* ii. 195, Voltaire to Helvétius, Aux Délices, 19 Jan. 1759.

their organization on clandestine lines. Discreetly communicating to Malesherbes the offers Frederick the Great and Catharine the Great had both made to host the *Encyclopédie*'s completion in their capitals, should all doors remained closed in France, Diderot extracted from the *directeur* of the *Librairie* an unwritten and unannounced 'tacit' permission permitting the editing of the *Encyclopédie* to proceed. Nothing existed on paper. Maleherbes took some personal risk in conceding even this much. Inevitably under the circumstances, there was no commitment that publication in France would ever be allowed.[140] Officially, the whole business lacked legality, so that the few remaining accomplices had to trust only in each other's loyalty and discretion. But the work went on.

At a strategy meeting over dinner at the house of one of the publishers, Le Breton, in April 1759 erupted a fierce quarrel provoked by d'Alembert who at this point cut all links with the project. Continuing with the *Encyclopédie* was madness, he declared, blaming Diderot for the debacle and petulantly treating the *libraires* like 'valets' with d'Holbach looking on, seething with indignation, Diderot reported to Grimm afterwards, and Jaucourt shaking his head in silence.[141] The others agreed on a strategy of silent defiance, completing the *Encyclopédie* in a projected further seven volumes within two years, promoting the same principles as before, and relying on d'Holbach's extensive library for research, to avoid attracting unwelcome attention. The plan was to have the remaining volumes, secretly printed together, in Holland, brought out in one go, to minimize risk of suppression before completion. D'Alembert walked out, finally breaking with Diderot and d'Holbach. 'Il est sûr', commented Diderot, 'que l'Encyclopédie n'a point d'ennemi plus décidé que cet homme-là.'[142] By this point he also regarded Turgot and Morellet as committed opponents along with d'Alembert.

The key accomplices henceforth were Le Breton, Jaucourt, Saint-Lambert who took responsibility for a large batch of articles, and especially d'Holbach, whose money, library of 3,000 books including all up-to-date science and virtually all the Dutch, English, and French radical works of the late seventeenth and early eighteenth century,[143] and weekly dinner circle became the mainstay of the enterprise. From 1759 onwards, d'Holbach was pivotal through his unbending commitment, close collaboration with Diderot, and also his friendship with Malesherbes and other powerful men.[144] Meanwhile, Voltaire lent moral support from Geneva while continuing to oppose their ideas, constantly urging moderation and unity. Diderot responded by keeping him partially informed about his plans, through Grimm, while also requesting him not to divulge details to d'Alembert. Voltaire also received information from other contacts in Paris, notably Nicolas-Claude Thieriot, a regular correspondent who also helped him procure prohibited books. Diderot was the real

[140] Naigeon, *Mémoires historiques*, 181; Blom, *Encyclopédie*, 233, 238.
[141] Diderot, *Corr.* ii. 118–19, 272; Pappas, 'Diderot, d'Alembert', 202; Haechler, *L'Encyclopédie*, 395–6.
[142] Diderot to Grimm, c.1 May 1750, in Diderot, *Corr.* ii. 120; Lepape, *Diderot*, 217.
[143] Diderot, *Corr.* ii. 173; Eames, 'Baron d'Holbach's Library', 249; Pecharroman, *Morals*, 6.
[144] Haechler, *L'Encyclopédie de Diderot*, 477.

target of the proceedings against Helvétius at the Sorbonne and in the *Parlement*, reported Thieriot, in February 1759; the Jesuits intended to destroy Diderot 'et les honnêtes gens tremblent pour lui'.[145] In refusing to move the *Encyclopédie* abroad, as Voltaire, Turgot, and others urged, Diderot displayed courage but also hard-headed wariness not just of Voltaire but also of Frederick's repeated offers. He and d'Holbach knew they controlled the *Encyclopédie*'s contents for only so long as it remained in Paris. Moving abroad would automatically transfer control to new patrons, first and foremost Voltaire, d'Alembert, and Frederick, something Diderot had no intention of acquiescing in. By October 1759, he had completed nearly all the philosophical articles.[146]

In partial compensation for their losses, meanwhile, royal officials promised the publishers they could separately publish the *Encyclopédie*'s prepared plates illustrating the mechanical arts. The unfortunate course this affair took afforded the cabal 'contre les *Encyclopédistes*' a splendid fresh opportunity to defame the *Encyclopédie*.[147] To save time and money, the publishers had purchased, cheaply, from persons in the engraving business, illustrations that were unauthorized duplicates, or copies, lifted from designs prepared earlier, over many years, by the naturalist Réaumur, under the auspices of the Académie des Sciences. Before his death, in October 1757, Réaumur had discovered that his designs were being pilfered. Details of the theft were passed to Fréron by a disgruntled architect named Pierre Patte.[148] Having at every turn slighted the worthy Réaumur whilst alive, announced Fréron, Diderot had now suborned his plates, dishonestly procuring copies for money.[149] The accusations published in Fréron's journal, the *Année littéraire*, obliged the Académie Royale des Sciences to investigate. Diderot, denying any wrongdoing, published an announcement inviting all subscribers so desiring to visit the print works to inspect the 200 plates so far prepared. The Académie, despite finding the publishers had dubiously appropriated at least forty of Réaumur's plates, nevertheless exonerated all concerned to minimize the damage its own reputation, and that of members, including d'Alembert, linked to the *Encyclopédie*.[150]

The publishers, claimed Fréron, renewing his accusations in his *L'Année littéraire* in January 1760, had tricked the Académie's commission by presenting only some of the dishonestly procured plates. He also now more closely collated the theft to the *Encyclopédie*'s entries, pointing out details in the illustrations to entries such as 'Aiguillerie' and 'Épinglier' exactly matching features on Réaumur's plates.[151] Such was the outcry that Diderot had to publish another reply in Grimm's *Correspondance littéraire* while the publishers delayed publication, investing in some costly

---

[145] Thieriot to Voltaire, Paris, 23 Feb. 1759, *CGdH* ii. 223.
[146] Diderot to Sophie Volland, 14 Oct. 1759, in Diderot, *Corr.* ii. 272.
[147] La Harpe, *L'Aléthophile*, 11.
[148] Lepape, *Diderot*, 239; Trousson, *Denis Diderot*, 297–8; Balcou, *Fréron*, 182–3.
[149] Fréron, *L'Année littéraire* (1759/7), 341–55; Mortier, *Le Cœur*, 256.
[150] Fréron, *L'Année littéraire* (1760/1), 246–8, 250–2.
[151] Balcou, *Fréron*, 183–4, 244–5; Proust, *Diderot*, 228.

last-minute changes to make their plates correspond to his sanitized account, albeit without fully erasing the impression that the *encyclopédistes* had shamelessly pillaged Réaumur's work. Meanwhile, Fréron persisted in attacking the *Encyclopédie*'s existing seven volumes. An erudite critic, many of his accusations contained more than a grain of truth, though he usually exaggerated. Diderot's philosophical articles were plagiarized mostly without acknowledgement straight from Brucker's history of philosophy. Diderot's French style was 'obscur', 'amphibologique', and full of tiresome Latinisms and similes.[152] Constrained by the censorship, he could not fully express his contempt in print but, from a surviving letter to Malesherbes, we know that the Diderot circle to him were 'des coquins, des fripons, des faquins et des scélérats', with 'ce Tartuffe de Diderot' the most hypocritical and d'Alembert 'plus coquin que les autres, parce qu'il est plus adroit'.[153]

Hayer's *anti-encyclopédiste* drive also culminated in 1760, with volumes x, xi, and xii of *La Religion vengée*. Volume xi demonstrates in detail how a web of articles composed by 'le chef de l'*Encyclopédie*', using devious camouflage, constructed an entire system of interlocking doctrines contrary to religion, monarchy, and morality. It was a deliberate, systematic 'conspiracy' if not on the part of all the *encyclopédistes* then certainly Diderot, d'Alembert, and 'quelques associés ou plutôt accomplices'.[154] The entries 'Fatalité' (by Morellet), 'Fortuit', and 'Futur contingent' expound a philosophical necessitarianism wholly incompatible with free will and human liberty.[155] Diderot's long article 'Le Christianisme', supplemented by others, plainly insinuates Christianity is prejudicial to the well-being of society due to its intolerance, dogmatism, and cult of celibacy.[156] Identifying Christianity and 'fanaticism' is the point of (Deleyre's) article 'Fanaticisme'. Meanwhile, Diderot's political thought, culminating in outright justification of armed rebellion, is not just 'anti-monarchique mais encore anarchique'.[157] As to the conspiracy's objectives, Diderot aimed to replace Christianity with a 'tolérance universelle', 'complete freedom of thought and a general refusal by the educated henceforth to accept anything as true other than on the evidence of their own experience'.[158] Blind fatality was to replace divine providence, governing 'non-seulement l'espèce humaine, mais toute la nature'.[159] Diderot's articles 'Âme' and 'Animal' and entire treatment of the mind–body relation and the nature of man is a 'nouveau galimathias trop favorable au Spinosisme', abolishing the soul's spirituality and immortality, turning men into animals and both into physical machines.[160] The principal target throughout was 'M. Did...'.

[152] Balcou, *Fréron*, 198–200.
[153] Fréron to Malesherbes, 31 July 1760, in Voltaire, *Corr.* xxi. 508.
[154] Hayer, *La Religion vengée*, xii. 198.
[155] Ibid. xi. 43, 47, 49, 55, 63.
[156] Ibid. xi. 128, 133, 141, 172–3, 178, 196.
[157] Ibid. x. 244.
[158] Ibid. xi. 257–8, 267–9, 297, 328, 332–3.
[159] Ibid. xii. 199.
[160] Ibid. x. 347–52 and xii. 149, 162–3; Mortier, *Combats*, 219.

As far as the literary and fashionable Parisian public was concerned, much the most sensational part of the entire affair, and the *coup de grâce* that finally discredited the *Encyclopédie*, was *Les Philosophes*, a farcical comedy dramatizing the 'war', composed by Palissot helped by Fréron.[161] The spectacle opened on 2 May 1760, at the Comédie-Française, to a full house amid an unheard-of commotion, and not only carried the fight between the *parti philosophique* and their opponents onto the stage and deeper than ever into literary culture, cafés, and public arena, as well as at court, but turned the whole business into a form of popular entertainment. All Paris had been alive with excitement for weeks. As usual with Palissot, the play is pithily written, in a style judged 'charmant' by Fréron, but utterly shallow, though this did nothing to prevent its being a huge success. Widely deemed a hilarious satire of the maxims of the *encyclopédistes*, it drew immense applause, the 'comedy' rendering the *philosophes*, in the eyes of many, even more ludicrous and odious than before. But it had a deadly serious purpose. 'Diderot' appears as a duplicitous but incompetent hypocrite named Dortidius, and, as in Palissot's earlier *Petites Lettres*, is the personage chiefly derided. Pursuing a sordid ascendancy over opinion, Diderot, Rousseau, and Helvétius as 'Valère' all appear on stage as ridiculous intriguers cynically betraying every standard of decency.[162] Its buffoonery was designed finally to bury the *philosophes* in opprobrium and contempt while simultaneously driving a wedge between Diderot and Voltaire.[163]

Such savage ridicule was justified, argued some, being directed less at persons than reprehensible unChristian philosophy.[164] The *philosophes* were truly a danger to society, usurping the title of 'philosophers', undermining morality, and portraying men as the product of nature, 'alongside the reptiles'. No satire could be too cruel towards such conspirators, suggested one commentator, or elicit too much scorn from theatre-goers. But not everyone rejoiced over the theatre-going public's enthusiasm. There was also a certain backlash against the play's extreme maliciousness. The absence on the opening night of Palissot's literary patron, the duke of Choiseul, the most powerful minister at Versailles at the time, enabled Voltaire to hope that the duke had permitted the play's staging merely as tepid gesture to a long-standing protégé (which Palissot was) rather than to signal high-level approval for all-out rejection of the *parti philosophique*. Diderot made no attempt to respond, judging it beneath a philosopher's dignity to answer such a farcical caricature. Unsurprisingly, this was a time of considerable despondency in his life in which he fought to stem doubts about whether he really had the stamina and creative power to achieve the kind of impact he had hoped through philosophy and literature.

His seething inner rancour he sublimated for the moment by pouring his bitterness into one of his most brilliant dialogues, *Le Neveu de Rameau*, a devastating

---

[161] Morellet, *Préface*, 12, 19; Balcou, *Fréron*, 194–5.
[162] Masseau, *Ennemis*, 144–5; Trousson, *Jean-Jacques Rousseau*, 422–3.
[163] Fréron, *L'Année littéraire* (1760/4), 200, 231, 239; [Coste d'Arnobat], *Philosophe ami*, 16.
[164] [Coste d'Arnobat], *Philosophe ami*, 30–1; Lilti, *Le Monde*, 193–4.

exposure of the cynical unscrupulousness he attributed to the psychological syndrome surrounding Palissot and his circle. Set near the cafés and public gardens that were his habitual milieu, this text is a dialogue between a MOI (Diderot) and a LUI representing a profoundly cynical, atheistic *immoralisme* that contradicts everything Diderot held as his ethical ideal. Though transposed into an ageless encounter between two different strains of materialism seen as eternally in conflict, Diderot vividly conveys the collision of MOI and LUI conceived as the encounter of his radical Spinozist philosophy with its exalted ideals of man and society with the unscrupulous immoralism of lay *anti-philosophes* and the 'nephew' who in part represents Palissot. But powerful literary and philosophical *tour de force* though it was, it was an ethereal form of vengeance, this text remaining unpublished until the next century.[165] His real revenge on his jubilant foes was his pressing on in secret with the 'grande besogne', the mass of remaining work to be done to complete the *Encyclopédie*.

Diderot retreated into a silent underworld, though this did not prevent his being suspected of penning an anonymous libel tapping into the backlash entitled *Préface de la Comédie des philosophes* (actually by Morellet), accusing Palissot of designing to force all the *philosophes* to flee to Holland or Prussia. Styling Palissot a purveyor of *friponneries* combining the 'eloquence' of Chaumeix with Fréron's 'depth', this text denounces him as an ambitious intriguer who, not content with turning the title 'philosophe' into an insult, strove to turn France into a land where nothing was publishable without the permission of inquisitor-theologians, preferably from Coimbra or Salamanca.[166] Diderot, Palissot assured Voltaire, had written the libel; Diderot assured Malesherbes he had not, nor even seen or read Palissot's play.[167] A second riposte by Morellet, *La Vision de Charles Palissot*, was not just hard-hitting but highly indiscreet; casting aspersions on several eminent noble ladies, including Madame de Robecq, Choiseul's mistress, and Mesdames de Villeroi and du Deffand, both also belonging to Choiseul's entourage. These prominent society ladies, styled by d'Alembert 'des p...en fonctions' and 'de p...honoraires', openly scorned Diderot's circle but approved of Voltaire. An illicit book pedlar, or *colporteur*, arrested for carrying copies divulged the name of the *libraire* who printed it, and his interrogation led to Morellet's arrest under a *lettre de cachet* and imprisonment in the Bastille.[168] Justice for aristocrats and justice for others, it was no secret, were quite different things. Nevertheless, if defamation was the issue, complained Madame de Helvétius, writing to the elderly Lévesque de Burigny (who remained close to Helvétius and his wife throughout), why should Palissot remain free while poor Morellet rotted in prison.[169]

Voltaire had no personal reason to feel aggrieved by Palissot's play. Both Palissot and Fréron treated him (and Montesquieu) quite differently than they did Diderot

---

[165] [Coste d'Arnobat], *Philosophe ami*, 24–5.
[166] *Préface de la Comédie*, 6, 9–11; [Coste d'Arnobat], *Philosophe ami*, 13–14.
[167] Diderot to Malesherbes, 1 June 1760, in Diderot, *Corr.* iii. 33–5.
[168] Ibid. iii. 35.   [169] *CGdH* ii. 283–5; Trousson, *Denis Diderot*, 303.

and the *encyclopédistes*. To them, Voltaire's philosophy was something entirely distinct from the materialism they were lampooning. Palissot's comedy pointedly spared him the gibes heaped on Diderot, in an obvious effort to detach him from the *encyclopédistes*.[170] Nevertheless, he found himself in a delicate position. D'Alembert sent several frantic appeals, imploring Voltaire, as the sole *philosophe* able to intercede at Versailles, to act and in particular publicly blast Palissot, Fréron, and the prelates. It was all very well for Voltaire, at Geneva, constantly to urge the *philosophes* to remain united, reminding them that there were whole armies of *fanatiques* and *fripons* out there but very few *philosophes* and that their prospects would be nil if they remained at each other's throats, but what benefits did his royalism yield? The man the public saw as the head of the *parti philosophique* and who himself aspired to be their leader, in this fraught situation, needed to display decisive leadership. The freethinking Choiseul, interested in Voltaire's correspondence with Frederick, was not unwilling to cultivate his friendship. But Madame du Deffand and the others detested Diderot and his circle, so that Choiseul refused to do anything for him, or rescue Morellet, which meant that Voltaire, who constantly prized Choiseul as an ally in letters to d'Alembert, could not do so either. What this whole episode proved was that the only effective check on aristocratic power was other high aristocratic power. D'Alembert could only rescue Morellet, after two months' incarceration, through the intervention of the Maréchale de Luxembourg, a noble lady holding Rousseau in high esteem mobilized by the latter in what proved to be his last act of solidarity with the *parti philosophique*.[171]

Amidst the tangled high-society, philosophico-literary-sexual imbroglio created by Palissot's play, Voltaire proved unable to mobilize Choiseul, free Morellet, or crush Palissot with whom, much to their surprise, the other *philosophes* discovered he was in fact still continuing a personal correspondence. The man who in literary circles and high society was now the *encyclopédistes'* foremost adversary was at the same time a professed disciple of Voltaire's (in philosophical as well as literary matters) and regular correspondent who had stayed with him, at his invitation (in 1755). Voltaire, realizing he could not permit the younger playwright to define his relationship to the *encyclopédistes* or get away with sullying the name of *philosophe*, wrote reprimanding him politely but firmly despite Palissot's ties with Choiseul, albeit also not without considerable embarrassment. He was carrying raillery too far and unjustly dishonouring Diderot, Duclos, and Helvétius who were not in the least scoundrels. Indeed, Voltaire—ever ready to damn with faint praise—wondered whether 'leur probité n'est pas encore supérieure à leur philosophie'.[172] Subsequently, he further rebuked Palissot for allying with the likes of Chaumeix and Gauchat, and the poet Jean-Jacques Le Franc de Pompignan (1709–84), a Montauban magistrate (and brother of the bishop of that name) abhorred by Voltaire who in his recent induction address at

---

[170] Diderot, *Corr.* iii. 32; Balcou, *Fréron*, 197; Pearson, *Voltaire Almighty*, 277–8; Freud, 'Palissot', 32–3.
[171] Guehenno, *Jean-Jacques Rousseau*, ii. 47.
[172] [Rousseau], *Journal encyclopédique* (1760/5), 105–7; Naves, *Voltaire*, 75; Freud, 'Palissot', 181–3.

the Académie Française had fulminated against 'cette monstrueuse philosophie' in books teeming in all the aristocratic libraries of France, undermining 'virtue', denying the soul's immortality, and attacking altar and crown.[173]

Palissot's publishing his exchange of letters with Voltaire about his play, in July 1760, made sensational reading. He had tried and failed, the public learnt, to detach Voltaire from the *encyclopédistes*. But what the public did not learn was that the episode further widened the rift among the *philosophes* not just on the stage but in reality, albeit not in the way Palissot had hoped. Voltaire's aim, as ever, was to reconcile the *philosophes* 'avec le pouvoir' both royal or aristocratic, and especially Choiseul, and lend greater unity to the *philosophes* under his own leadership, supported by court favour.[174] But his proceedings in this instance served only to heighten Diderot's long-standing distrust of his ambitious, eccentric, high-handed behaviour and especially his much vaunted alliance with the court aristocracy and attempts to arbitrate the collective future of the *parti philosophique*. In November 1760, Diderot assured Voltaire (who bitterly criticized his failure to take up his pen in his own defence) that in the end lofty detachment from such crass behaviour as Palissot's would serve their cause best.[175]

What, finally, should the historian and philosopher conclude from the astounding twists of the 'guerre de l'*Encyclopédie*' down to 1760? First, it is obviously untrue that the *Encyclopédie* acknowledges its core doctrines 'openly', as some scholars maintain, or that it is 'reasonably typical of the general current' of Enlightenment thought, or that it represents some sort of 'consensus' of core Enlightenment ideas.[176] One critic recently claimed that the *Encyclopédie* predominantly reflects the mainstream Enlightenment views of Voltaire, Montesquieu, Maupertuis, and Turgot; one could scarcely be more mistaken.[177] Secondly, the thesis scholars today still regularly repeat, that the *Encyclopédie*'s central message represents a more or less common approach based on Locke and Newton that can usefully be called 'French Newtonianism', a 'unified' philosophical movement shaped by the writing and thinking of Voltaire who was promoted as head of the 'philosophic' movement precisely by the *Encyclopédie*, is fundamentally incorrect.[178] Finally, while it is usual to suggest that the royal suppression of the *Encyclopédie* was a fairly minor setback not widely supported and not a major episode in cultural history, this too is seriously misleading.

All these positions are widely held but completely untenable. In reality, the *Encyclopédie* always advances its core doctrines 'à couvert', acknowledging they are illicit by half concealing them, core doctrines wholly irreconcilable with mainstream Enlightenment thought. Secondly, without carefully distinguishing between a

---

[173] Le Franc de Pompignan, 'Discours', 46, 55, 59; Voltaire to Palissot, 12 July and 24 Sept. 1760, in Voltaire, *Corr.* xxi. 460 and xxii. 150–2.

[174] Pappas, *Voltaire and d'Alembert*, 20–1; Naves, *Voltaire*, 80; Trousson, *Denis Diderot*, 300–1.

[175] Trousson, *Denis Diderot*, 303–4; Freud, 'Palissot', 196.

[176] Hampson, *Enlightenment*, 86; Doyle, *Old European Order*, 192.

[177] Edelstein, *Enlightenment*, 95, 97.

[178] See, for instance, Shank, *Newton Wars*, 489, 495, 497–8, 502–3, 506.

moderate Voltairean Enlightenment based on Locke and Newton and a radical clandestine philosophical tradition chiefly rooted in Spinoza and Bayle, it is not just difficult but totally impossible to make any sense of this convoluted, protracted, and deeply significant struggle at all. For the *Guerre de l'Encyclopédie* was a tortuous contest in which opposed wings of the Enlightenment fought each other as well as the common foe even if, to an extent, they also huddled together for mutual defence against a combination of cultural forces which, among the public if not at court, proved stronger than either—the combined forces of Catholic moderate Enlightenment and the Counter-Enlightenment of the *dévôts* and Jansenists. Finally, the royal suppression of the *Encyclopédie* was a lasting setback of great cultural and intellectual importance and, as we shall see, in the Italian, Swiss, Belgian, Dutch, Spanish, Spanish American, and Austrian contexts as well as the French.

4

Rousseau against the *Philosophes*

1. BREAKING WITH THE *ENCYCLOPÉDISTES*

We must not date Rousseau's final, bitter break with his closest friends too early; for he was still powerfully drawn to these men by bonds of admiration, sympathy, dependence, and allegiance, as well as troubled by the growing discord between himself and them, over the question of God's governance of the world, right through the middle 1750s. His original plan to relocate to Geneva, in 1754, came to nothing, and he soon reverted to the cafés, salons, and philosophic repasts of Paris, though even then, recalled Morellet, the century's most eloquent writer remained bafflingly 'insociable'.[1] Thoroughly awkward, he was never a good talker, confirmed Louis Sebastien Mercier (1740–1814), a key commentator, best-selling utopian writer, and later journalist of the Revolution who knew and admired Rousseau personally and conversed with him often.[2] But as yet, there was no obvious, let alone irreparable, intellectual break. His key article 'Économie politique' of November 1755, in the *Encyclopédie*'s fifth volume (republished as a separate booklet, unrevised, in 1758), echoes much of Diderot's argumentation in his article 'Droit naturel', in the same volume. Even though in part criticism of Diderot's idea of *volonté générale*, Rousseau's article shows the two men still remained ideologically close, discussing questions of social theory together, and still allied in the public arena as committed *encyclopédistes*.[3]

Diderot, who first adapted the term *volonté générale* as an instrument of radical political thought, stresses the great importance of the concept, as does Rousseau who, in his entry, employs the term for the first time in his own work, cross-referencing the reader to Diderot, albeit giving the term a significantly different twist.[4] Having debated the idea a good deal together, they agreed that it is only in accordance with the *volonté générale* that the dutiful, well-meaning individual should regulate his conduct regarding individuals and society and that the *volonté générale*, defined as the secular, worldly well-being of the whole society and all its members, is the basis of morality and of legal and political legitimacy. Diderot, Rousseau, and d'Holbach all concurred,

---

[1] Morellet, *Mémoires*, i. 113; Garrard, *Rousseau's Counter-Enlightenment*, 34.
[2] Mercier, *De J. J. Rousseau considéré*, i. 246, 249.
[3] Trousson, *Jean-Jacques Rousseau*, 295; Hulliung, *Autocritique*, 27.
[4] Hulliung, *Autocritique*, 27; Wokler, *Social Thought*, 57–64; Roche, 'Encyclopedias', 191–2.

at this time and subsequently, that every statesman's first duty, as Rousseau puts it, is to 'conformer les lois à la volonté générale'. Diderot, however, invoking 'la volonté générale de l'espèce', already here emphasized far more than Rousseau the universality, moral absoluteness, and 'l'infaillibilité de la volonté générale'.[5] It may be Rousseau who here spells out the main consequence of *volonté générale*, namely that whatever previous political writers have claimed concerning different forms of government, actually there are only two kinds—those that conform to *volonté générale*, which Rousseau designates 'populaire', and those that do not, deemed 'tyrannique', but both thinkers shared this standpoint and continued to do so later. For Rousseau, Diderot, Helvétius, and d'Holbach alike these are the sole two possibilities. Only government having 'le bien du peuple' for its goal can be legitimate and all government that is legitimate truly pursues the public benefit and is 'légitime et populaire'.[6] There is no other kind of legitimate government and all absolutist and oligarchic rule is by implication illicit.

A turning point was reached in April 1756 when Rousseau left Paris for a rural retreat, a few miles to the north, on a property owned by Madame d'Épinay, L'Hermitage, at Montmorency. This answered an intense longing for solitude at a time when Rousseau was painstakingly rethinking his views, a personal need he later felt more and more intensely. By abandoning the *coterie d'Holbachique*—for the moment only socially—and retreating to the country, Rousseau crossed a line dividing his adult life in two and which he himself called 'la grande révolution de ma destinée'. When later contemplating this change retrospectively, he always assumed he was breaking free from something that had constrained him, thereby recovering his true self.[7] But 'la grande révolution' consisted of two elements— seeking his true self in isolation, and his rupture with the 'd'Holbachians'.[8] Life at Montmorency over the next five years formed the creative climax to his career, a time when he meditated and wrote with immense fervour. However, rural retreat at such a juncture inevitably struck the others as desertion from the battle at the crucial moment. For the 'storm excited by the *Encyclopédie*', as he himself remarks, was then 'at its greatest strength'. If, psychologically, detaching himself from the *encyclopédistes* began earlier and at this point was bound up with his love for Madame d'Houdetot, outwardly it resembled the defection from the *Encyclopédie* of d'Alembert, Morellet, Quesnay, Turgot, Buffon, Duclos, and Marmontel.[9] By 1756, Rousseau had abandoned the group but not yet broken definitively with Diderot. Rather, he proceeded slowly in detaching himself, moving step by step.[10] If he resented d'Holbach's patronizing attitude, he remained close to Grimm and especially Diderot: 'I loved

---

[5] Diderot, 'Droit naturel', *Encyclopédie*, v. 116; Rousseau, 'Économie morale et politique', *Encyclopédie*, v. 340; d'Holbach, *Politique naturelle*, 92; R. Wokler, *Rousseau and Liberty* (Manchester, 1995), 66–7.

[6] Rousseau, 'Économie morale et politique', *Encyclopédie*, v. 338–9.

[7] Rousseau, *Confessions*, 337; Damrosch, *Jean-Jacques Rousseau*, 256, 260–2; Gauthier, *Rousseau*, 153.

[8] Rousseau, *Confessions*, 332–4, 338, 351.

[9] Ibid. 366; Guehenno, *Jean-Jacques Rousseau*, i. 340; Trousson, *Jean-Jacques Rousseau*, 317–19, 321–2.

[10] Rousseau, *Confessions*, 386–7, 504; Wokler, *Rousseau and Liberty*, 60.

Diderot tenderly', he records, 'and esteemed him sincerely, and counted on the same feelings on his part with a complete confidence.'[11] Briefly their old comradeship continued, Diderot writing in a friendly fashion and only gently rebuking him over his withdrawal.

Near breaking point was reached in March 1757, however, when Rousseau received his copy of Diderot's play *Le Fils naturel*, a venture by which the latter set great store. Here Rousseau encountered the maxim 'l'homme de bien' lives in society, and only the badly intentioned, 'le méchant', lives alone.[12] Not unreasonably, he took this as an allusion to his own thirst for solitude. Less reasonably, he considered it an unpardonable insult. Recrimination converted recent strains into an open quarrel which, however, ended in reconciliation during a short visit to Paris.[13] Diderot tried hard to consolidate the reconciliation and restore their alliance, Rousseau admits, sending numerous messengers and messages after Rousseau left again, albeit, being preoccupied with battling the *Encyclopédie*'s foes, without fulfilling his pledge to return in person to the Hermitage. Rousseau alternately wrote that he did, and then did not, want him to come.[14] Finally, a renewed and this time irreparable quarrel erupted over the winter of 1757–8.[15]

Both thinkers were deeply and permanently injured by the break. It was afterwards impossible, records Mercier, who continued seeing both men, to mention Rousseau to Diderot without provoking a bitter, furious tirade, or Diderot to Rousseau without eliciting a long, agonized groan followed by silence.[16] Rousseau, Diderot later maintained, was never a consistent thinker but always a player with words, exercising a seductive spell on the public, being in this respect, as others, the opposite to Helvétius. Rousseau was more concerned 'd'être éloquent que vrai'.[17] Yet, he envied him his 'eloquence' and continued to consider him formidable. Indeed, the issue of Rousseau obsessed him even into his old age, and 'haunts' his last published work, the *Essai sur les règnes de Claude et de Néron* (1778).[18] In old age, Rousseau viewed himself as the victim of a decades-old conspiracy first concocted by Diderot and Grimm that had gradually swelled and eventually became virtually universal.[19]

After the public breach, about which he later claimed to feel few regrets apart from losing his closest companion, followed open war between Rousseau and his former comrades. This began, we have seen, with Rousseau's *Lettre à M. d'Alembert sur les spectacles* (1758), which created a great sensation in Switzerland and Germany as well as France.[20] As it happened, Diderot had discussed precisely d'Alembert's explosive

[11] Rousseau, *Confessions*, 382; Gauthier, *Rousseau*, 155–7.

[12] Rousseau, *Confessions*, 382; Rousseau, *Rousseau Judge*, 99–100, 264.

[13] Rousseau, *Confessions*, 386–7, 399, 406–7.

[14] Trousson, *Jean-Jacques Rousseau*, 328, 334, 336.

[15] Monty, *Critique littéraire*, 44; Zaretsky and Scott, *Philosophers' Quarrel*, 27, 186.

[16] Mercier, *De J. J. Rousseau considéré*, i. 245–6 and ii. 138–9; Guehenno, *Jean-Jacques Rousseau*, ii. 4, 148.

[17] Diderot, *Réfutation*, 292, 317.   [18] Hope Mason, 'Portrait', 53–4, 59.

[19] Rousseau, *Rousseau Judge*, 181–2, 267 n. 78.   [20] Naigeon, *Philosophie*, iii. 778.

article about Geneva with Rousseau before its publication during his sole visit to Montmorency and at that crucial moment Rousseau had raised no objection, a fact that afterwards amazed Diderot, smacking, to him, of blatant deviousness and betrayal. Saint-Lambert too was shocked by the unannounced attack and at this point broke with Rousseau. At Berlin, Formey jubilantly approved Rousseau's open rupture with the *philosophes modernes*. To the future author of the *Anti-Émile* (1763) and *Émile Chrétien* (1764), Rousseau was now the least distant of the *philosophes* 'from the truth', albeit still a foe of Christianity unable to draw the proper conclusions from the Lisbon disaster and his now public feud with Diderot.[21]

In France, Rousseau's *Lettre à M. d'Alembert*, with its full-scale assault on the theatre (after himself composing a comedy and opera), enjoyed a 'prodigious success', recalled Condorcet later, especially among the *gens du monde* who thronged the theatres most.[22] With this, Rousseau unleashed an unrelenting polemic against the 'philosophes modernes' without warning and precisely when the *armée anti-encyclopédiste* was inflicting on Diderot, d'Holbach, d'Alembert, and Helvétius their heaviest reverses.[23] Philosophically, it marked a turning point that had a certain logic and inevitability about it, given Rousseau's antipathy to the idea of human betterment via philosophy, reason, and knowledge, and the incompatibility of his newly thrashed-out opinions and those of the radical thinkers regarding religion, faith, morality, sexuality, and not least 'enlightening' the masses, a goal the Genevan henceforth totally repudiated. It was a polemic that continued through all his subsequent works including *Rousseau Juge de Jean-Jacques* (1772) down to his last text, the *Rêveries du promeneur solitaire* (1776–8).

For his in some respects traditionalist views on 'virtue', Rousseau expected only the derision of 'cette philosophie d'un jour' thriving, he claimed, only in Paris and flattering itself that it could stifle Nature's cry and the 'unanimous voice of the human race' regarding female chastity and confining women to the home.[24] Anticipating their censure for peddling 'préjugés populaires', he accused the *encyclopédistes* of callous presumption. He scorned their dismissing feminine modesty as a mere social device invented to buttress fathers' and husbands' control. The revolution in gender relations and sexual mores they proposed, he roundly rejected, declaring himself the standard-bearer of a wholly traditional view of woman's place, urging women's exclusion from all debate and public life.[25] After marriage, women should remain within four walls and not be seen by the outside world. 'Women do wrong', he argues, 'to complain of the inequality of man-made laws; this inequality is not of man's making, or at any rate not the result of mere prejudice, but of reason.'[26] 'Nature has decreed that woman, both for herself and her children, should be at the

---

[21] Gouhier, *Rousseau et Voltaire*, 108.
[22] Condorcet, *Œuvres*, iii. 124–5.
[23] Rousseau, *Rêveries*, 30–9; Garrard, *Rousseau's Counter-Enlightenment*, 34–5.
[24] Rousseau, *Lettre à d'Alembert*, 168–9.
[25] Ibid.; Rousseau, *Émile*, 325; Mercier, *De J. J. Rousseau considéré*, i. 34–6; O'Hagan, *Rousseau*, 188–90.
[26] Rousseau, *Émile*, 324, 330; de Staël, *Letters*, 13–18.

mercy of man's judgment.'[27] Intellectually, Rousseau's growing antagonism was partly driven by his fanatical streak, what Cloots later termed his 'esprit religieux', but also, and no less, the *Lettre* demonstrates, by a rather austerely traditional, classical republican 'Roman' notion of 'virtue', and a sentimental adherence to segregation of the sexes and confining women to the home, set in opposition to Diderot's family, marriage, and sexual libertarianism.[28] After 1758, Rousseau routinely assailed the core values of 'ces grands scrutateurs des conseils de Dieu'. Diderot and his circle, for their part, all dismissed as incoherent nonsense Rousseau's opposition of heart versus intellect, 'nature' versus reason, 'feeling' versus rational thought.[29]

Altogether more bizarre was Rousseau's simultaneous rupture with Voltaire. Voltaire and Rousseau apparently met only once, around 1750, and then only briefly, without anything noteworthy transpiring. Aside from their exchange over the Lisbon earthquake, in 1756, almost no correspondence passed between them. Rousseau detested Voltaire's egocentricity and prickly sensitivity while abundantly sharing the disdain for Voltaire's philosophical writings common to all Diderot's circle. He ignored not only *Candide* but, astoundingly, practically all Voltaire's published œuvre aside from *Zadig*, the *Dictionnaire philosophique*, the poem on the Lisbon earthquake, and the fiercely anti-Christian *Sermon des cinquante* which the latest research suggests was not by Voltaire in any case and which Voltaire always disowned but which Rousseau later publicly declared (much to Voltaire's indignation) was by him.[30] Nowhere does Rousseau discuss Voltaire's *Essai sur les mœurs*, metaphysical texts, or histories, any more than Diderot's, d'Holbach's, or Hume's writings.[31] Rousseau scorned Voltaire together with all the other *philosophes* and Hume, believing there was little to be gained by erudition and wide reading.

Voltaire, equally characteristically, read everything by Rousseau but found nothing to admire. Rousseau, he declared in 1765, 'n'est bon qu'à être oublié'.[32] But if Voltaire scorned Rousseau, neither, before 1758, did he yet consider him a menace, or someone to be publicly pilloried. Their open feud began simultaneously with that between Rousseau and Diderot but had far less general cultural and intellectual significance. Philosophically, the two contexts differed markedly since Voltaire had nothing against Rousseau's deism or advocacy of divine providence and agreed with his polemic against materialism. It was not Rousseau's ideas he detested but his conduct and attitude towards himself. Conversely, Rousseau held Voltaire responsible for the moral 'corruption' of Geneva and his native republic's political alienation from himself. Literary disagreements also contributed.

[27] Rousseau, *Émile*, 328, 346; Cherni, *Diderot*, 167–9.
[28] Toscano, *Fanaticism*, 109–11; Garrard, *Rousseau's Counter-Enlightenment*, 64–7, 89.
[29] Diderot, *Réfutation*, 292, 317; Mauzi, *L'Idée du bonheur*, 138–9; Goggi, 'Spinoza contro Rousseau', 151.
[30] Pomeau, *Religion de Voltaire*, 182; DGV, 1114–15; DJJR, 932.
[31] Rousseau, *Confessions*, 361; Zaretsky and Scott, *Philosophers' Quarrel*, 206; Gouhier, *Rousseau et Voltaire*, 8.
[32] Gouhier, *Rousseau et Voltaire*, 10; Davidson, *Voltaire in Exile*, 180.

Rousseau's clash with Voltaire was personal, political, and literary rather than philosophical, whereas his battles with Diderot, d'Holbach, and Helvétius were deeply ideological as well as personal. Even so, there was a notable point of convergence between these titanic feuds. For many of Voltaire's greatest successes were on the stage and it was he who had encouraged d'Alembert to eulogize Geneva as a haven of Enlightenment.[33] Hence Rousseau's efforts to mobilize Geneva's populace against Voltaire's plans for a theatre there could be construed as part of a wider war against Voltaire *and* the *Encyclopédie*.[34] Admittedly, Voltaire too resigned from the *Encyclopédie*. But as the struggle further intensified, he continually urged the *philosophes* to stick together in a common fight fought in an increasingly hostile environment. Showing solidarity with the others and defending a common cause, however, was the last thing Rousseau had in mind. As one scholar has accurately summed it up: 'the differences between radical and moderate philosophes in the second half of the eighteenth century were differences within the Enlightenment, whereas their differences with Rousseau were differences between the Enlightenment and someone who came to reject its fundamental assumptions and goals.'[35] This is broadly true.

After 1758, Jean-Jacques was just a 'vain déclamateur' in Voltaire's eyes, a nuisance impeding the cause of *la philosophie*. By the late 1750s, the two greatest literary masters of the French eighteenth century held each other in total mutual contempt. Several years after Rousseau's three most celebrated works, *La Nouvelle Héloïse*, *Émile*, and the *Contrat social*, had appeared, Voltaire, in 1767, answered someone styling him this 'grand homme' by protesting: how can you call a charlatan known only 'par des paradoxes et une conduite coupable' a 'grand homme'?[36] *La Nouvelle Héloïse* he dismissed as a third-rate imitation of Richardson's *Pamela. Émile*, savaged also by Grimm, he admired neither for its style, sentiment, nor ideas. He was scandalized when, in 1766, the poet Dorat publicly coupled his and Rousseau's names, in his poem 'Avis aux sages du Siècle, M.M. Voltaire et Rousseau', urging the two great *maîtres* to cease their unseemly bickering for the sake of their own future glory and 'l'honneur de l'humanité'.[37] Coupling their names, first as 'Voltaire and Rousseau' but soon reversing this order, became a feature of the literary scene.

Rousseau's defection shocked Diderot and Voltaire, and also Helvétius, who attributed his break with his former 'friends' to his love of paradox and contrariness, impulses overpowering his reason and typical not of a *philosophe* but a poetic writer better suited to 'seduce' than instruct readers.[38] Renouncing the (Spinozist) doctrine that virtue does not exist in the state of nature but is a social construct arising with

---

[33] Vernet, *Lettres critiques*, i, preface pp. vii, 13–17, and ii. 287.
[34] Rousseau, *Lettre à d'Alembert*, 129–33, 141, 154.
[35] Garrard, *Rousseau's Counter-Enlightenment*, 26–7.
[36] Zaretsky and Scott, *Philosophers' Quarrel*, 70–1; Gouhier, *Rousseau et Voltaire*, 10.
[37] Gouhier, *Rousseau et Voltaire*, 10; Dorat, 'Avis aux sages', 1–10.
[38] Helvétius, *De l'homme*, i. 76–7, 123, 453, 459; Rousseau, *Confessions*, 420–1; Gouhier, *Rousseau et Voltaire*, 125.

society, Rousseau, not only grounded his 'virtue' in sentiment rather than reason, objects Helvétius, a procedure aligning him with the British 'moral sense' school which he, d'Holbach, and Diderot all rejected, but in *La Nouvelle Héloïse* and *Émile* led him continually to contradict himself. 'Virtue' he sometimes declares innate in man and sometimes a sentiment acquired through experience and education.[39] If Helvétius rejected Rousseau's ethics, Rousseau undertook to refute Helvétius's *De l'esprit*, but never did so, admirers attributing this to his compassion on seeing Helvétius persecuted. Diderot and Helvétius broadly concurred about Rousseau but about one point, Diderot and Rousseau concurred in criticizing Helvétius: namely, the latter's failure to distinguish between simple impressions and emotional responses or 'sentiments' expressed by the whole person and hence determined by the personality.[40]

Another contemporary perspective on Rousseau's rupture with the *encyclopédistes* was that of Marmontel whose *Contes moraux* (1755–65) served as a vehicle for the popular diffusion of various of the *philosophes'* ethical concepts as, still more resoundingly, some years later, did his novel *Bélisaire* (1767). This thinly veiled satire of French society triggered one of the celebrated literary battles of the age. In his *Mémoires*, Marmontel describes d'Holbach's salon as the supreme *école philosophique* with Diderot's eloquence and face shining with inspiration 'diffusing his light in all our minds and warmth in all our souls', and d'Holbach who read everything and forgot nothing continually pouring forth 'les richesses de sa mémoire'.[41] After his two highly successful discourses, remaining in Diderot's and d'Holbach's shadow, the outshone, socially incompetent acolyte of this *école philosophique*, for Rousseau held little attraction. Rather, success aroused in him the ambition of founding a 'secte' and acquiring a following of his own. But despite impassioned monologues, affected poses, and eccentric dress and behaviour, he utterly failed to attract followers around the cafés, public gardens, and opera, a rebuff prompting him to look elsewhere and consider the ranks of his former allies' adversaries as a potential audience.

Seeing that by publicly repudiating Diderot, d'Alembert, and Voltaire, he was gratefully applauded by an immense throng, he broke with the *philosophes*, declaring war on Diderot as a way of becoming a hero to a large public. Deprecating reason, eulogizing popular simplicity, and denouncing the *philosophes* appealed widely, he discovered, especially to the religious and the more ordinary.[42] Disparaging reason, learning, and the sciences while championing feeling, *consensus gentium*, and divine providence appealed also to several priests who flattered themselves that Rousseau's espousal of faith could not be far off. Marmontel's analysis did not lack a certain plausibility especially as, at the time of the rupture, Rousseau did in fact fraternize with the editor of the Jesuit *Journal de Trévoux*, the same Father Berthier with whom Diderot, d'Alembert, and also Voltaire had bitterly quarrelled. A long-standing opponent of the theatre, Berthier warmly applauded Rousseau's defection

---

[39] Mercier, *De J. J. Rousseau considéré*, i. 65; Goldmann, *Philosophy*, 31.
[40] Mercier, *De J. J. Rousseau considéré*, i. 66–7.
[41] Marmontel, *Mémoires*, ii. 242–3.
[42] Helvétius, *De l'homme*, i. 523.

from the *Encyclopédie*, remaining over the next several years among his staunchest supporters.[43]

Paranoia culminating in *Rousseau Judge of Jean-Jacques* (1772) inspired Rousseau to treat the philosophical controversies of his age as a giant stage with himself as the central figure, the perennial victim of the conspiracy organized against him by the *philosophes modernes*, a plot afterwards joined by kings, prelates, and republics.[44] A corrupt society's sacrificial victim hounded relentlessly for telling the truth, he responded with alacrity to the first signs of real persecution, the *Parlement*'s ban on *Émile*, though, in reality, this was mild stuff compared to the treatment meted out earlier to Diderot and, in 1758–9, to Helvétius. The measures against *Émile*, observed Turgot, no friend of Diderot and the *encyclopédistes*, could easily have been avoided either by absenting himself for two or three months or by not placing his name on the title page in the first place.[45] Rousseau, agreed Mercier, hugely exaggerated the tepid persecution he underwent in France for self-dramatizing purposes.

Emigrating in June 1761, 'imagining' the royal authorities had forbidden him to write, he then migrated in succession, entirely perversely, to precisely those Swiss cantons, Geneva and Berne, where the ruling councils felt most threatened by his criticism of the aristocratic oligarchies controlling those republics. If there was no way, in the circumstances, public condemnation of *Émile* and the *Contrat social* could be avoided at Geneva in 1762, the order for Rousseau's arrest issued by the Genevan *Petit Conseil* and his subsequent banishment first from Geneva, then Berne, and finally the principality of Neuchâtel (followed by his sojourn in England), only occurred due to his obstinacy in staying precisely where his writings were most likely to stir up 'troubles intérieurs'. All this heightened suspicions that he purposely courted persecution, much as his quest for solitude was accompanied by an obvious thirst for the public's attention.[46]

2. VIRTUE RESTORED

Rousseau's post-1758 battle with the *coterie d'Holbachique* developed in four principal areas. These were the ethical-philosophical, religious, political, and aesthetic, corresponding respectively to (1) his rebellion against reason and the primacy of philosophy, (2) his assault on materialism and atheism, (3) the rift between his and Diderot's rival conceptions of *volonté générale*, and (4) his challenging Diderot's efforts to elevate the arts, claiming nature is the only genuine beauty of which art is but a feeble perversion.

---

[43] Pappas, *Berthier's Journal*, 152–8; Hulliung, *Autocritique*, 218.
[44] Rousseau, *Rousseau Judge*, 219; Rousseau, *Rêveries*, 39; Dent, *Rousseau*, 198–9; Gauthier, *Rousseau*, 38.
[45] Turgot to Condorcet, undated Dec. 1773, in *Correspondance inédite de Condorcet*, 146.
[46] Ibid. 146; Mercier, *De J. J. Rousseau considéré*, i. 245–6; Zaretsky and Scott, *Philosophers' Quarrel*, 124.

Where, for Rousseau, fully formed virtue is a sentiment detached from self-interest that readily prompts the individual to sacrifice his or her own interest for the common good, such a notion struck Diderot, d'Holbach, and Helvétius as far-fetched and illogical, stemming from what they saw as the false concept of 'moral sense' propounded by Shaftesbury, Hutcheson, and Smith.[47] In *Émile*, which he commenced at Montmorency in 1758 and completed in July 1761, and considered his greatest work, Rousseau seemed especially intent on establishing that 'virtue' is a feeling before becoming a set of ideas and something innate in man. But the ethical battle was not just between Rousseau and the *coterie*; for the clash soon became part of a much wider struggle. The *philosophes'* enemies, observed Turgot, focused on what attracted them in *Émile*, especially Rousseau's disparaging reason and eulogy of ordinary men's feelings, not on what they disliked.

Christian apologists could not easily forgive the *Contrat social's* sallies against Christianity, its holding the early Church to have destroyed the unity of cult and politics characteristic, according to Rousseau (and Boulanger), of pre-Christian Greece and Rome. Rousseau's contention that Christianity is incompatible with republicanism, 'preaches only servitude and dependence', and has a 'spirit so favourable to tyranny that it always profits from such a regime' was indignantly dismissed as were his assaults on priestcraft and thesis that 'Jesus came to set up on earth a spiritual kingdom, which by separating the theological from the political system, made the state no longer one, causing the internal divisions that have never ceased to trouble Christian peoples'.[48] Nor could Rousseau's reaffirming Spinoza's charge that the Christianity of the historical Jesus is something quite different from that of the Apostles propagated in the Gospels and Church Fathers[49] be simply laid aside any more than his denial of miracles in the *Lettres de la montagne*. According to Sabatier de Castres (who claimed to have discussed this with Rousseau at length in July 1770), Rousseau derived his critique of Christianity almost entirely from the *Tractatus Theologico-Politicus*.[50] Rousseau's debt to Spinoza was undoubtedly much greater than modern scholarship has tended to acknowledge—but also more fragmentary than Diderot's.

Most un-Spinozistic and welcome to the *anti-philosophes* was Rousseau's post-1757 commitment to a providential God ruling the course of nature who rewards and punishes men. Applauded too was his claiming atheism encourages immoralism, that the radical *philosophes* were 'apologistes du crime', and that their universal toleration needed drastic pruning especially by refusing toleration to atheists and repressing unseemly behaviour.[51] All this, together with his genuine admiration of Christ as a moral teacher and insistence that materialism is repugnant to reason, delighted the *Encyclopédie's* enemies. In this way Rousseau came to be praised by

[47] Helvétius, *De l'homme*, i. 457–8, 470–1; Cherni, *Diderot*, 433–6.
[48] Rousseau, *Social Contract*, 300, 306.
[49] Ibid. 304; Goldmann, *Philosophy*, 69–71.
[50] Sabatier de Castres, *Apologie*, 110; Vernière, *Spinoza*, 687.
[51] Nonnotte, *Dictionnaire*, 664; Brooke, 'Revisiting', 76–7.

veterans of the unremitting campaign against 'la fureur philosophique', like Bergier and Chaudon. In Rousseau, Catholic apologists felt they had identified a useful ally.[52] Where Diderot, d'Holbach, and Helvétius, following Bayle and Spinoza, wished the new secular morality, or *morale naturelle*, to be based on reason alone, Rousseau, whose *Émile* both Bergier and Jamin quote approvingly in this connection, contends that virtue cannot be built on reason but only sensibility and faith.[53] The fullest statement of his deist creed Rousseau expounds in the section of *Émile* entitled 'the Profession of Faith of the Savoyard Vicar'. Here, he sweepingly rejects his former allies' views on providence, reason, and morality as also on creation, free will, and the soul's immortality.[54]

Conceiving 'virtue' possible only for those heeding the pleas of the soul, and especially conscience and remorse, the threads linking man to God, Rousseau resoundingly condemned 'atheism'.[55] Affirming the inertness and inactivity of matter, he espouses a strict dualism of active and inactive substances coupled with a Lockean conception of mind.[56] Our consciences buttress the moral order and 'at the bottom of our hearts' one finds 'an innate principle of justice and virtue'.[57] Rousseau not only espouses the soul's immortality and the majesty of Scripture, enthused Jamin, but proclaims louder than anyone that the *encyclopédistes* are dogmatic, intolerant, arrogant, and dangerous.[58] Bergier gladly repeats Rousseau's remark that 'the only error' the *philosophes* proved to him was the foolishness of his former veneration for them, their conduct proving their principles delusions from which he was happy to have freed himself. Rousseau's change of heart Bergier applauded but, ever gentlemanly in combat, he felt obliged to add that while Diderot's and his friends' personal morals were above reproach this was considerably more, unfortunately, than he could say for Rousseau.[59]

The Diderot circle, by contrast, claimed morality has nothing to do with metaphysical entities man knows nothing about. Where 'virtue', Rousseau insists, is best fostered in primitive societies, radical thought envisaged the progress of *l'esprit humain*, knowledge and reason, to be the engine of mankind's moral improvement and education. Moral and political progress advances via philosophy and science lessening ignorance and increasing knowledge lessening misery. Consequently, there is always conflict between despotism allied to ignorance, on the one hand, and cultivation of the sciences producing moral and political amelioration, on the other. Since Rousseau adamantly denied this, privileging, rather, simplicity of heart and *sensibilité*, he repeatedly clashed with his former allies over all these basic

---

[52] Rousseau, *Social Contract*, 307–8; Rousseau, *Émile*, 239–40; Domenech, *L'Éthique*, 91.
[53] Bergier, *Apologie*, ii. 11, 22–3; Rousseau, *Émile*, 254–7; Kennedy, *Secularism*, 130.
[54] Rousseau, *Émile*, 237–48; Rousseau, *Lettre à Voltaire*, 309–10, 328; Belaval, *Études*, 150.
[55] Rousseau, *Émile*, 243–4.
[56] Ibid. 233–7.
[57] Ibid. 250–4; Domenech, 'Éthique et révolution', 38, 42.
[58] Jamin, *Pensées théologiques*, 88, 351, 353, 356.
[59] Bergier, *Apologie*, ii. 49–50; Rousseau, *Rêveries*, 38–9.

elements of his and their philosophy, prompted them to dub him 'l'apologiste de l'ignorance', a false prophet urging men to revert to their original state of misery, stupidity, and unreason.[60] What considerations, asks Helvétius, led Rousseau 'à prendre si hautement part pour l'ignorance'?[61] 'Disgusted with artificial manners and virtues', commented Mary Wollstonecraft later, 'the citizen of Geneva instead of properly sifting the subject, threw away the wheat with the chaff, without waiting to inquire whether the evils which his ardent soul turned from indignantly, were the consequence of civilization or the vestiges of barbarism.'[62] Much of this was simply reversing views he himself had earlier concurred with.

It was Diderot who first awoke and stirred the genius of Rousseau, observed Mercier.[63] During the late 1740s, when the great project of the *Encyclopédie* commenced, and during the early 1750s, when his political ideas decisively took shape, Rousseau was Diderot's closest friend and ally, and many of his ideas were undeniably aligned closely with his comrade's, however dramatically this changed after 1756–7. A well-known story, related both by him and Diderot, recalls how he first conceived the idea for his prize-winning essay the *Discours sur les sciences et les arts* (1750), during fierce summer heat, in 1749, whilst walking out from Paris to Vincennes to visit Diderot, at the time imprisoned there for publishing subversive writings. Diderot urged, half in jest, that to win, he must argue the unexpected, the very opposite to the other competitors, advice Rousseau took to heart. He later claimed this fixed the whole future course of his life. But who else would take such a deliberately perverse suggestion so seriously, commented Diderot later, as to ground his whole system on an imaginary, fantastic, completely false opposition between natural man and man in society, claiming the arts and sciences, like society generally, had exerted a mostly negative and corrupting effect on men?[64]

Adopting a position so contrary to that of everyone else, accusing the arts and sciences of compounding man's corruption, rather than enhancing humanity, in a prize competition arranged by the Académie of Dijon, 'among the most learned bodies of Europe', was a deep paradox which, Rousseau expected, would incur the disapproval of all.[65] The essay duly caused a stir, though Diderot had no high opinion of it and Rousseau himself later dismissed it as a mediocre piece, of all his works 'the weakest in reasoning'.[66] All the same, it remained typical of Rousseau to denounce modern man's unnaturalness, luxury, dissoluteness, and 'slavery', and the dissolution of natural human bonds, speaking of alienation as punishment for our efforts to forsake the happy ignorance 'où la sagesse éternelle nous avait placés'.[67] Philosophy

---

[60] Edelstein, *Terror*, 89.
[61] Helvétius, *De l'homme*, i. 497; Zaretsky and Scott, *Philosophers' Quarrel*, 6, 24.
[62] Wollstonecraft, *Vindication of the Rights of Woman*, 85, 88.
[63] Mercier, *De J. J. Rousseau considéré*, 245; Darnton, *Forbidden Best-Sellers*, 117.
[64] Diderot, *Réfutation*, 285–7, 292; Trousson, *Denis Diderot*, 143–4.
[65] Rousseau, *Discours sur les sciences*, 27, 29.
[66] Diderot, *Réfutation*, 287; Rousseau, *Confessions*, 295.
[67] Rousseau, *Discours sur les sciences*, 40; Starobinski, *Remède*, 167–9.

and science weaken liberty, he argued also later, by creating artificial needs that would not encumber 'natural man' and by diluting religion and 'virtue'.[68] Education should focus more on allowing a child's natural goodness to emerge freely than instilling knowledge, discipline, or moral notions.[69]

Deeply committed to science and erudition, d'Holbach, in his *La Morale universelle*, roundly rejects Rousseau's disparagement of the sciences. The latter conceived the sciences as negative in their origins, motives, and moral effects. Where, for Rousseau, science lures adepts into forgetting their basic duties in life and exploring false paths, true knowledge, holds d'Holbach, brings us to our duties. Where geometry, for Rousseau, stems from avarice, d'Holbach identified a primitive need among men to mark off possessions, to fix distinctions without which everything lapses into confusion. Where Rousseau dismisses history as a useless enquiry concerning princes and wars, diverting us from more edifying topics and stifling 'notre liberté naturelle', fostering a false *politesse* and a thousand vices, to d'Holbach history seemed eminently useful for demonstrating the effects of tyranny, oppression, conspiracies, and war and inspiring our search for ways to escape the man-made evils 'dont le genre humain fut si souvent affligé'.[70] Where the sciences, for Rousseau, encourage luxury and an urge to excel, fomenting arrogance, contempt for the ordinary, moral decay, and 'la corruption du goût et la mollesse', for d'Holbach only praise attaches to those nurturing the sciences and braving the dangerous pitfalls the quest for the truth exposes researchers to. What is truly criminal, avers d'Holbach, is to disavow learning, malign the arts, and seek to deprive humanity of knowledge, thereby obstructing the quest for the truth.[71] Unless dedicated to vague speculation and objects inaccessible to experience, philosophy and science, far from diverting men from genuine integrity, are never other than helpful to man's *bonheur*.

Far from extinguishing feelings nurtured by our natural liberty, reason and knowledge only strengthen liberty by demonstrating the wretchedness arising from slavery and tyranny. Far from spreading innumerable vices, the quest for knowledge rescues men from idleness, frivolity, and time-wasting, the usual companions of ignorance. As for Rousseau's thesis that the criterion of truth is uncertain, this Diderot and d'Holbach dismissed as utterly wrong-headed. Rather the criterion of truth *is* certain when one considers only objects verifiable via the test of experience, rigorously ruling out whatever no one can experience or has only fearful fantasies about. Far from being the offspring of idleness, the sciences and arts flow from Man's true needs and lead to finding whatever can contribute to his conservation 'et rendre son existence heureuse'.[72] In short, for his radical critics Rousseau's 'paradoxes' all

[68] Deneys-Tunney, *Un autre Jean-Jacques*, 43.
[69] Rousseau, *Émile*, 84, 89–90, 134, 141; d'Holbach, *Morale universelle*, i. 477–82 and ii. 937.
[70] d'Holbach, *Morale universelle*, ii. 202–3; Borghero, 'Sparta', 286–96; Starobinski, *Remède*, 166–70.
[71] D'Holbach, *Morale universelle*, ii. 203.
[72] Ibid. ii. 204–5; Dent, *Rousseau*, 51–2.

proceed from confusion, love of contrariness, or madness, and destroy virtue. To denounce reason and the sciences is to ensure men have no means to distinguish what enhances their existence from what curtails and diminishes it. The 'natural man' conjured up by the 'eloquent sophist' would be a contemptible creature lacking all means to procure his own well-being and avoid the perils ceaselessly menacing him.

Rousseau's eulogies of the 'virtue', physical prowess, and austerity of the pristine, unsophisticated Romans,[73] d'Holbach no less than Bergier considered absurd, the early Romans being a people as ferocious, aggressive, and intolerable to their neighbours as any recorded in history, being foes of everyone else's liberty, a race regarding the entire world as their prey.[74] As for Rousseau's argument that *politesse* undermines true friendship, it seemed to d'Holbach that Rousseau was hardly qualified to judge questions of friendship of any sort. Later radical voices were equally scathing about Rousseau's praise of archaic virtue. Wollstonecraft, who reproached Rousseau for far more than just his views on women, and not least for celebrating 'barbarism', remarked that 'he forgets that, in conquering the world, the Romans never dreamed of establishing their own liberty on a firm basis, or of extending the reign of virtue. Eager to support his system, [Rousseau] stigmatizes as vicious, every effort of genius; and uttering the apotheosis of savage virtues, he exalts those to demi-gods, who were scarcely human—the brutal Spartans, who, in defiance of justice and gratitude, sacrificed, in cold blood, the slaves who had shewn themselves heroes to rescue their oppressors.'[75]

The *Contrat social*, appearing just a month after *Émile*, reaffirms Rousseau's thesis that our heart not our reason governs our consciences and further developed Rousseau's strange fixation with ancient cults. The chapter on 'civil religion', restating his conviction that the cosmos is governed by a conscious, beneficent deity, recommends banishing whoever disavows this, natural religion's most basic dogma. It also recommends abbreviating toleration in other respects and even putting to death anyone who professes belief in divine providence and then afterwards repudiates this doctrine.[76] Sparta and pristine Rome were superbly adapted to uphold the *volonté générale* with their vibrant civic cults, sense of public virtue, and intimate linking of these with war, martial discipline, and xenophobia. They lacked only the principle of equality, a defect Rousseau set out to rectify.[77] What Boulanger deemed the worst feature of the ancient republics—fusing their republican politics with their religious cults—is precisely what Rousseau (and Mably) considered the very backbone of the republicanism of virtue they so vigorously opposed to the purely secular polity based on reason of Boulanger, Diderot, and d'Holbach.

---

[73] Rousseau, *Social Contract*, 298–309; Rousseau, *Émile*, 276–7.
[74] Bergier, *Apologie*, ii. 11; Rousseau, *Lettre à d'Alembert*, 196–9; d'Holbach, *Le Bon-Sens*, 177–8.
[75] Wollstonecraft, *Vindication of the Rights of Woman*, 84–5.
[76] Rousseau, *Social Contract*, 307; Garrard, *Rousseau's Counter-Enlightenment*, 71–2.
[77] Lafrance, 'Idée rousseauiste', 28; Riley, 'Rousseau's General Will', 130; Borghero, 'Sparta', 307–10.

3. DEISM AND THE ROOTS OF POLITICAL RADICALISM

Another clash arose over the question of legislation and the concept of the 'legislator'. For Rousseau the primal 'legislator', like Lycurgus, Numa, Moses, or Muhammad, must be a quasi-divine figure who, via special inspiration, alters human nature by removing men from their natural isolation into society, imparting to the group a new collective character specific to them.[78] For Rousseau, differently from Diderot, the 'legislator' transferring men from their pristine independence and solitariness, constructs a shared legacy of law, the principles of which they cannot grasp although these profoundly alter their human traits so that they must be powerfully exhorted and roused to embrace them. Rousseau's political thought, then, and perhaps especially his *Social Contract*, represents a strange mixture of Radical Enlightenment elements with strands of deism, cultism, eulogy of the ordinary, and intolerant censorship, and a strongly authoritarian and particularist aspect pertaining to his particular conception of *volonté générale*. His republican political radicalism was close to that of the Radical Enlightenment in some respects (but not all) but came to be grounded on a completely different metaphysics and moral philosophy.

How is this curious juxtaposition to be explained? Rousseau's second great success, the *Discours sur l'inégalité* of 1755, dates from before his break with Diderot and shows how closely the political and social radicalism Rousseau later grafted onto his deism and *anti-philosophique* moral philosophy originally converged with the thought world of the Radical Enlightenment. In the mid 1750s, his second discourse was often seen as a materialist and atheist work. There is little in it suggesting the deistic views that, according to the *Confessions* (1770), *Rêveries* (1782), and other later testimony, he then privately already professed.[79] At that time, he records, he continued frequenting the *coterie d'Holbachique* and publicly aligned with Diderot and Grimm, remaining their intimate collaborator and friend, esteeming them as honest men of good faith, without answering their sweeping denials of divine omnipotence, wisdom, and providence.[80] Christianity, he agreed then, is 'unintelligible dogma'. His friendship with them and commitment to 'philosophy' had, by his own admission, left him highly antagonistic to 'that farrago of little formulas with which men have obfuscated [what is essential in religion]'.[81]

For identifying Rousseau's characteristic positions during his close collaboration with the Diderot circle when he was, with them, an exponent of radical thought, the *Discours sur l'inégalité* seems crucial. The thesis he advances there, that man, morality, and society must all be considered products of nature, like other products of nature, was a position held in common with the others. His ardent wish to live as a free man, expressed in the work's dedication to the Genevan republic, along with his

---

[78] Garrard, *Rousseau's Counter-Enlightenment*, 57–8; Dent, *Rousseau*, 140–1, 153.
[79] Dent, *Rousseau*, 35–7, 85–6; Gouhier, *Rousseau et Voltaire*, 80; Emmet, *Secularism*, 116–17.
[80] Rousseau, *Confessions*, 329; Trousson, *Jean-Jacques Rousseau*, 275.
[81] Rousseau, *Confessions*, 329.

preference for 'un gouvernement démocratique, sagement tempéré' over other types of regime, cohered with his conviction—again shared with Diderot and d'Holbach—that rule by kings and oligarchies accustoms peoples to succumb submissively to oppression and slavery.[82] He yearned for a democratic republic without ambitions to conquer others and embraced the idea that men in the state of nature were originally entirely equal, flatly denying that the different orders and classes of men that evolved historically later, differences between rich and poor, privileged and unprivileged, powerful and weak, had any basis in a divinely intended, ordained scheme or possessed any legitimacy whatever.

Rousseau there treats institutionalized inequality as a purely human phenomenon and a harmful one. His arguments are 'conjectures', he states, drawn exclusively from the 'nature de l'homme', theories based on nature, devoid of any suggestion that divine providence guides the course of history, or man's destiny. His situating his enquiry in the context of the ancient Athenian philosophy schools highlights the fact that here 'philosophy' is his sole search engine.[83] 'Tout animal', man included, Rousseau depicts as 'une machine ingénieuse', equipped with awareness and senses for its own conservation, though here already he contends that man profoundly differs from animals in being an 'agent libre'.[84] It has been claimed that during this formative early period, as later, Rousseau was 'an outsider' among the *encyclopédistes*, 'a religious believer among religious skeptics, an egalitarian among elitists';[85] but there is scant evidence to support such a thesis. Rather the evidence suggests Rousseau changed from being more or less fully within Diderot's circle to becoming its greatest foe.

Combining deism, cultism, and a stress on creation of the universe by a benevolent God, with political and (some degree of) social radicalism rooted, as the latter must be, in the claim that existing human society, law, and institutions are fundamentally corrupt, was extremely unusual during the Enlightenment. Rousseau alone among important thinkers managed to combine these disparate elements. But he could do so only via the uncompromising separation he postulates between natural man and man in society. It was by limiting the scope of divine providence so that it has no role in the forming of human institutions, and his thesis that man is close to nature only outside of society, that enabled him to weld deism and a radical republican stance together. This crucial separation was roundly rejected by Diderot and d'Holbach, of course, who saw man in society as the natural state. They espoused rather Spinoza's idea that nothing is more useful to man than man and more apt to afford protection. The savage state or 'state of nature' to which certain 'speculateurs chagrins' (i.e. Rousseau) seek to revert is actually, retorts d'Holbach, nothing but a condition of misery, imbecility, and *déraison*.[86]

---

[82] Rousseau, *Essai sur l'origine*, 148–9; Domenech, 'Éthique et révolution', 38–40.

[83] Rousseau, *Essai sur l'origine*, 169, 172.

[84] Ibid. 182; Linton, *Politics*, 84–6; Garrard, *Rousseau's Counter-Enlightenment*, 2–6.

[85] O'Hagan, *Rousseau*, 3; Rosenblatt, *Rousseau*, 70–1; Garrard, *Rousseau's Counter-Enlightenment*, 2–6.

[86] Diderot, *Réfutation*, 316–17; d'Holbach, *Système social*, 213; Goggi, 'Spinoza contro Rousseau', 134–6.

Was Rousseau's deistic radicalism entirely unique? There were some others, it seems, who occasionally combined deism with radical thought in a similar way, by drastically restricting the omniscience and omnipotence of God. This was exemplified by a German noble in Danish service, Woldemar Hermann von Schmettau (1719–85), who published several deistic works anonymously, notably his *Auch Fragmente* ('Philadelphia' [Altona], 1783). Von Schmettau viewed contemporary society as fundamentally disordered and chaotic in many respects, urging fundamental changes, summoning the rulers of Prussia and Austria, for instance, to halt the appalling process of dynastic wars caused by monarchs.[87] He was authorized to do so by the far-reaching limits he places on God's power. In basic metaphysics, he asserts, there are only three tenable positions: (1) that there is no God, 'under which I include the atheistic view of Spinoza'; (2) that there is a God existing for all eternity who is perfect and from whom all other beings receive their being—hence, the God of the theologians; and (3) a limited God who is not the ground of everything that exists but rather the *Weltordner*, the bringer of order, the rational principle gradually reducing cosmic chaos to rationality. Both Spinoza's God and the God of the theologians, held von Schmettau, are impossible. Only by postulating a restricted non-omnipotent God can one simultaneously invoke a divine providence slowly ordering the world, and human destiny, and explain how the world can be severely disfigured by unreason, disorder, and the dreadful nonsense of theology.[88]

Rousseau, as has often been noted, belongs to the Enlightenment in some respects but, at the same time, was (or rather, became) its critic and foe. It is a conclusion about which there can be little dispute. However, it is arguable that insufficient attention has been paid in previous Enlightenment surveys to the crucial question of when and in what context Rousseau became the Enlightenment's most eloquent and impassioned adversary and to what precise degree he remained a representative of revolutionary Enlightenment, on the one hand, and the moderate mainstream, on the other. In particular, insufficient attention has been given to the shifting, chronological aspect of Rousseau's criticism and rejection of radical ideas and how his legacy was subsequently tailored by the Revolution.

Years after the death of the two protagonists, the quarrel between Diderot and Rousseau still resounded in the public arena, albeit only later, during the Revolution, did the real significance of their unresolved encounter fully emerge. Their dispute remained of interest, observed Wekhrlin, in 1785, 'because it contributes much to bringing to light the characters of two philosophers who uplifted their century'. Rousseau became the idol of his age acquiring vast numbers of admirers, while Diderot had far less of a following but nevertheless stood out as one of the 'most enlightened, humanity-loving and creative geniuses of his age'. Wekhrlin disavowed any intention to deflate the delirium surrounding Rousseau. But he at least preferred Diderot and the *Histoire philosophique*. It must give pause for thought that an

---

[87] Von Schmettau, *Auch Fragmente*, 19–20.
[88] Ibid. 31–4; Loche, 'Motivi politici', 236, 243, 247.

impressive list of honourable men denounced Rousseau's hypocrisy, contrariness, paradoxes, and bad nature, headed by d'Alembert, Hume, Voltaire, Helvétius, and Diderot, whilst no one of comparable stature ever championed Rousseau's integrity. Rousseau had finally looked to posterity to vindicate him as did Diderot and his circle to vindicate them. Is it 'philosophy' or the uneducated man's unspoiled nature that is democracy's ultimate true guide?[89] After their deaths, the tussle continued in the revolutionary public sphere, turning into a truly ferocious contest.

---

[89] Wekhrlin, *Graue Ungeheuer*, 4 (1785), 173–4, 179–80, 184; Hulliung, *Autocritique*, 238–40.

5

Voltaire, Enlightenment, and the European Courts

1. MODERATE ENLIGHTENMENT DOMINANT?

To turn the tables on the *philosophes'* foes, Voltaire in 1760 planned a sensational coup to remind everyone that he was their chief spokesman and defender and alone commanded the political weight to thwart France's episcopate, universities, and magistracy. Success would raise even Helvétius's spirits and decidedly rub the shine off the *dévôts'* recent victory in suppressing the *Encyclopédie*. The right way to advance toleration, freedom of expression, and his deist creed, Voltaire always maintained, was to sway the uppermost echelons of society by winning over its most influential figures. What counted was to win credit and 'reputation' at the top and sway the courts. In France, as before, the key figure, to his mind, was the Duc de Choiseul, whom he continued to cultivate assiduously while also grooming other prospective allies, including Louis XV's new lieutenant-general of police for Paris, Antoine-Raymond de Sartine (1729–1801), Comte d'Alby, a man who was to prove, in fact, a remarkably good friend to the *philosophes*.[1] The winning strategy, held Voltaire, was to use such ties to score telling, spectacular victories over their enemies.

If *l'infâme* had the advantage of mass support, he had the advantage, or so he believed, of discernment, wit, and influence where it counted. To achieve the effect he sought nothing would be better, it struck him, in 1760, than to eclipse the elevation to the Académie Française of the reactionary poet Le Franc de Pompignan by securing the election of none other than Diderot. If a bare majority had backed *anti-philosophie* by electing Le Franc, it was a fragile majority a little finesse could overturn. The Académie, now a crucial theatre of conflict between *la philosophie* and its adversaries, had a fixed number of forty members and, though deeply divided, included several *philosophes*, d'Alembert and Voltaire himself among them, and some sympathizers. The more Voltaire pondered the scheme, the more it appealed. It is astounding how often in his letters of these months he broaches his cherished plot to install Diderot in the Académie. In short, Voltaire assured d'Alembert, in early July

---

[1] Haechler, *L'Encyclopédie: Les Combats*, 298; Davidson, *Voltaire in Exile*, 110–11.

1760, Diderot's election to the Académie would be the perfect vengeance on Le Franc, Palissot, Joly de Fleury, the Jesuits, Jansenists, and court *dévôts*.[2]

Should his plan succeed, he would rejoice in the Alps with a giant bonfire and the first papers to be hurled on the flames would be Joly de Fleury's *réquisitoire* followed by Le Franc's academy address *déclamatoire*.[3] He implored the Comte d'Argental, one of his closest allies at court, to help to foment a 'cabale' capable of staging this little drama. He promised to come in person to cast his vote. Neither Choiseul nor Madame de Pompadour could fail to back such a scheme, this being the finest coup imaginable in reason's war against 'le fanatisme et la sottise'.[4] Victory would permanently demoralize the *dévôt* party. But d'Argental declined to help, deeming the plot hopeless, while d'Alembert, who prided himself on possessing a more discerning grasp of what passed at court than Voltaire, was equally adamant that in present circumstances inducting Diderot was impossible.[5]

While backing Voltaire's courtly, 'aristocratic' approach and just as eager to flatter Frederick and Catherine, d'Alembert shared none of his faith in Choiseul (who regularly had the letters between Voltaire and d'Alembert examined before having them sent on).[6] The Pompadour, d'Alembert realized, preferred not to be dragged into such intrigues.[7] It was in vain that Voltaire urged d'Alembert to join with Duclos, an expert connoisseur of the salons, a man of *sociabilité* if ever there was one,[8] but whom d'Alembert disliked, to form a cabal with another academician, Dortous de Mairan, who, however, scorned d'Alembert. Seeing his calls for concerted action yield no result, Voltaire became intensely frustrated. The *philosophes* were driving him to distraction, having no idea how to do things, he assured d'Argental; he would prefer to deal with the Paris opera's choir girls: 'elles entendraient mieux raison.'[9] He again implored d'Argental to help strike this great blow for 'reason'. Nothing would more unnerve the foe than to see the *encyclopédiste* commander-in-chief installed in the Académie. The only coup to surpass it, he jested, would be to get Spinoza elected ('il n'y a que Spinoza que je puisse luy préférer')![10]

Voltaire failed to deliver the shattering psychological blow he fantasized over precisely because the sensational effect of such a *coup de théâtre* rendered it exceedingly unlikely to happen. Even had Choiseul and the Pompadour backed his scheme, d'Alembert explained in August 1760 (in the same letter reporting Morellet's release), their combined influence would still not suffice. The bishops would run straight to the king and convince him Diderot's election must be blocked. Duclos deemed the

---

[2] Diderot, *Corr.* iii. 36; Voltaire to d'Alembert, 9 July 1760, in Voltaire, *Corr.* xxi. 449.

[3] Voltaire, *Corr.* xxi. 446; Haechler, *L'Encyclopédie: Les Combats*, 324.

[4] Voltaire to d'Argental, 9 and 11 July 1760, in Voltaire, *Corr.* xxi. 449; Pappas, *Voltaire and d'Alembert*, 24.

[5] D'Alembert to Voltaire, 18 July 1760, in d'Alembert, *Œuvres complètes*, v. 128.

[6] Davidson, *Voltaire in Exile*, 136.

[7] Pappas, 'Voltaire et la guerre', 532.

[8] Lilti, 'Sociabilité', 430.

[9] Voltaire to d'Argental, 14 July 1760, in Voltaire, *Corr.* xxi. 464.

[10] Voltaire to d'Argental, 25 July 1760, ibid. xxi. 494.

attempt worth undertaking nevertheless, since the initiative would at least ignite 'une petite guerre civile' in the Académie, something useful in itself to their cause.[11] But d'Alembert, while granting a 'guerre civile' can be useful, hardly thought it would be if it led straight to 'Pompey' (i.e. Diderot) being slaughtered.[12]

But none of this altered the wider perspective. Since it was the *philosophes* who cultivated 'reason' and prized orderly government, and the *anti-encyclopédistes*, especially the clergy, magistracy, and censorship police, who were bent on making trouble, to Voltaire it seemed irrefutable that Versailles must in the end alter course and support the *philosophes*. No doubt, the 'fanatics' would raise a fearful clamour and burn some books while retaining their grip over the credulous multitude. But the *dévôts'* present high standing at court could and would be overturned, leaving them crushed, 'sans crédit dans la bonne compagnie', by which Voltaire meant discredited in aristocratic circles, the salons, and among the more enlightened sections of the high judiciary. This, he believed, would suffice to triumph across the board, since 'c'est la bonne compagnie seule qui gouverne les opinions des hommes'.[13]

Louis XV well knew in his heart, Voltaire assured Diderot in December 1760, the distinction he must draw between reliable supporters of the crown, like the *philosophes* who would always remain loyal, and *les séditieux*, as he labels their adversaries, namely the churchmen, *anti-philosophes*, and Jansenist magistrates, inflaming popular opinion and stoking unrest.[14] The common people's credulity and bigotry, grants Voltaire, in his *Traité de la tolérance* (1763), might well be ineradicable. But this was of no consequence so far as rule of law, spreading toleration, and upholding civilized values are concerned provided the ruling elite themselves are tolerant, swayed by 'philosophy', and free of superstition.[15] Fortunately, reason was gaining the upper hand over popular notions at Paris, it seemed, though it was indeed shocking that this was by no means always the case in provincial cities. What chiefly appalled Voltaire about the Pierre Calas affair of 1762, when, at Toulouse, a Protestant was unjustly executed for a crime he did not commit, was less the crass, inhuman bigotry displayed by the populace than the fact the Toulouse magistrates chose to endorse it.[16]

In the great empire of China, he urges in his *Traité*, the ruling class had never resorted to intolerance while the common people's superstitious beliefs were never a danger to the state essentially because the Confucianist mandarins had always thoroughly disdained popular notions.[17] In Japan, the same was true: 'les Japonais étaient les plus tolérants de tous les hommes', having tolerated a dozen different religions. They had only expelled the Jesuits and other missionaries in the early seventeenth century, as the Chinese emperor had later, because Christianity's rise threatened both Japan and China with massive internal unrest and instability.[18] In the Americas, much else might be

---

[11] Voltaire to d'Alembert, 13 Aug. 1760, ibid. xxii. 44; Linton, *Politics*, 113.
[12] D'Alembert to Voltaire, 2 Sept. 1760, in Voltaire, *Corr.* xxii. 87–8.
[13] Voltaire to Helvétius, 12 Dec. 1760, ibid. xxii. 372; Pappas, *Voltaire et d'Alembert*, 36–8.
[14] Voltaire to Diderot, undated, Dec. 1760 in Voltaire, *Corr.* xxii. 368.
[15] Voltaire, *Traité de la tolérance*, 40; Martin-Haag, *Voltaire*, 132–3.
[16] Martin-Haag, *Voltaire*, 133; Voltaire, *Traité de la tolérance*, 38–40.
[17] Voltaire, *Traité de la tolérance*, 51, 126–7; Voltaire, *Philosophe ignorant*, 87.
[18] Voltaire, *Traité de la tolérance*, 51–2.

different but this basic principle was the same. Had not 'le sage Locke' in his statutes for the Carolinas allowed even the tiniest groups to set up their own churches and done so without causing the slightest social instability?[19]

The *Encyclopédie*'s suppression, Helvétius's humiliation, and the eclipse of the Diderot circle elevated Voltaire's star and that of the moderate mainstream. D'Alembert's and Turgot's stock rose steadily and from 1763 Hume conquered Paris. *Anglicisme* triumphed in the Paris salons scarcely less than in the Dutch and Swiss enlightenments. In 1763, 'at the close of a successful war', recalled Gibbon later, 'the British name was respected on the continent'. 'Our opinions, our fashions, even our games, were adopted in France; a ray of national glory illuminated each individual, and every Englishman was supposed to be born a patriot and a philosopher.'[20] For the time being, the philosophy wars of the age were broadly settled. Victory belonged to Locke and Newton combined with Hume's allure and Voltaire's deism (in the salons) along with such moderate Catholic Enlightenment as was sanctioned by progressive spirits in the Sorbonne, some magistrates and bishops, and the recently deceased Benedict XIV. If Voltaire publicly lent support to the radical *philosophes*, he also continually urged moderation, royalism, and unity, demanding they change course toward the goals he preferred for the Enlightenment as a whole. But it was no easy matter acquiring a clear view of what was happening amid the intellectual underground and cafés of Paris. It particularly frustrated him that Diderot remained unresponsive to his offers of help and calls for joint action, and with Diderot silent, how was the *parti philosophique* to regroup and move forward? He must have been more than a little astounded when Diderot, finally responding to a whole series of missives, in September 1762, announced he was moving neither to Petersburg nor Berlin, nor emigrating to Holland, having secured tacit permission to publish the *Encyclopédie* in Paris. Already he held the complete proofs in his hands.

The struggle was not one, in Diderot's opinion, the *philosophes* could easily run away from: it was not enough simply to publish the *Encyclopédie* somewhere and show the *philosophes* understood truth better than their adversaries. There was also a moral and political war to be waged. The *philosophes* had to demonstrate that they were also morally in the right, better than their adversaries, and that 'la philosophie' creates more 'gens de bien' than Christian theology.[21] Deep down, all this raised the question of whether Voltaire had really secured the leadership, displacing the hylozoic *matérialistes* from the helm. The underlying antagonism between the competing Enlightenment streams in Paris, Geneva, Berlin, and Amsterdam, in any case, had certainly not ended. For a time it was sufficiently muffled for the impression to arise that Voltaire's vision had no real rival. But to consolidate such a victory, internationally, much more was needed than merely the effective silencing of Diderot and Helvétius by the French courts and censors and even that was now in doubt.

---

[19] Ibid. 52; Zagorin, *How the Idea*, 296.   [20] Gibbon, *Memoirs*, 148.
[21] Diderot to Voltaire, Paris, 29 Sept. 1762, in Voltaire, *Corr.* xxv. 247–8.

He was convinced *la philosophie* could not succeed pursuing Diderot's strategy and could triumph in the only sort of war against bigotry and tradition he thought winnable, and worth winning, only if it adopted a 'courtly' strategy. Accordingly, he insisted on the need for the *philosophes* to prove their royalism. Only an emphatic pro-court strategy could disarm *anti-philosophie*, he admonished Helvétius, one of the principal offenders against his political strategy in the past, and convince Louis XV that it was in his interest to permit both the influence of the *philosophes* in his kingdom to grow, and that of the 'fanatics' to shrink. The *philosophes* must convince king and court aristocracy that they were his loyal, peace-loving subjects whereas their adversaries—'tous ces gens-là', as he put it, in October 1760—'sont des pertur-bateurs'; that we are 'citoyens, et ils sont séditieux', a theme central also to his *Traité de la tolérance* where (following Bayle without citing him) he accuses the clergy of nurturing the perfidious idea that peoples have the right to depose monarchs when these are proven heretics, as a way of subordinating politics to theology.[22] Loyalty to the monarchy, he urged Helvétius, in December 1760, was the *philosophes*' most essential priority.[23]

In the complex, two-front war he was committed to, Helvétius was always apt to be less of an ally than d'Alembert. Eager to revive his spirits, and lure him from the 'boutique' (of Diderot and d'Holbach), Voltaire continually exhorted him not to be cowed by 'his persecutors'.[24] But Helvétius, deeply affected by the humiliating re-tractions into which he had been forced,[25] lapsed into profound pessimism. His secret vengeance on the French establishment (his last book project) he brooded over endlessly but refrained from confiding to Voltaire. In his letters, he spoke only of his dread that the *parti philosophique* stared total defeat in the face, that, in France, 'reason' itself verged on extinction. With the judicial and ecclesiastical authorities stifling 'toute espèce d'esprit', intent on crushing the *philosophes* finally and eradicating all independent thinking, the court, he assured Voltaire despondently, in the spring of 1761, was merely standing by. The *philosophes* remained unpopular and hardly anyone beyond their own circles seemed to grasp the harm their being crushed would inflict on society. Would the French end up like the Portuguese sunk in backwardness and credulity, needing the English to supply the very clothes they wore?[26]

Helvétius must pull himself together, urged Voltaire; despite everything the *philo-sophes* would win in the end and their century would mark 'le triomphe de la raison'.[27] In the last twelve years, an astonishing 'revolution dans les esprits' had been set in motion and already the struggle was practically won in Prussia and Russia. Eventually, 'les lâches fanatiques' of France and Italy too, he confidently assured him

---

[22] Voltaire to Helvétius, 27 Oct. 1760, in Voltaire, *Corr.* xxii. 248; Voltaire, *Traité de la tolérance*, 84.
[23] Voltaire to Helvétius, 12 Dec. 1760, in Voltaire, *Corr.* xxii. 371–2.
[24] Naigeon, *Philosophie*, ii. 673; Naves, *Voltaire*, 88–9.
[25] Naigeon, *Philosophie*, ii. 671.
[26] Helvétius to Voltaire, Mar./Apr. 1761, in Voltaire, *Corr.* xxiii. 135–6.
[27] Voltaire to Helvétius, 26 June 1765, ibid. xxviii. 139–40.

in June 1765, would be beaten. However unrelenting the strife, freedom of thought and toleration would emerge victorious and be proclaimed indispensable to mankind while the names of Joly de Fleury and Fréron would be despised for ever. In corresponding with him, Voltaire urged his own philosophical agenda and disparaged Fontenelle, the figure he held responsible for disastrously steering Helvétius towards materialism, atheism, and utilitarianism.[28]

Voltaire could count on active allies and admirers in Paris, Berlin, Petersburg, Geneva, and Rome. If d'Alembert was Hume's favourite among the Paris *philosophes*, on account of his intellectual sobriety,[29] d'Alembert looked to the patriarch of Ferney as the *philosophes'* chief hope, strategist, and presiding figure.[30] D'Alembert, though privately an atheist and materialist, presented the respectable public face of *la philosophie* in the French capital while remaining henceforth uninterruptedly aligned with Voltaire. If he confidentially admitted his atheistic leanings on occasion, he made no public profession of such views, preferring not to do so, commented Naigeon later, either through personal weakness, ambition, or both.[31] Having broken with Diderot and d'Holbach, he refused to back their strategy and ambitions in any way. Publicly, he remained always circumspect and continually anxious about his standing at court. In this respect, his outlook stood in dramatic contrast to the attitude 'libre et hardie', as Naigeon called it, of Diderot.

As Voltaire's chief ally, d'Alembert was delighted by the flattering attention he received, from the Prussian, Russian, and many lesser courts. Visiting Prussia to confer with Frederick in 1763, he was treated, he assured his intimate lady friend (Julie de Lespinasse) in Paris, by generals, nobles, and princesses alike as someone of the highest consequence.[32] At Wolfenbüttel everyone addressed him as 'marquis'. At the Sans Souci palace, in Potsdam, he was lodged in 'la plus belle chambre du monde', while in the salon Frederick himself performed on the flute in his honour, after which he and the king strolled alone in the gardens.[33] Julie should not suppose all this had gone to his head; but plainly it had. Invited to become the new head of the Berlin Academy by the king, there was not a single member, reported d'Alembert, who did not ardently wish for this outcome.[34] Almost simultaneously, the British ambassador, less charmed by his personality than Hume, advised London of the visit of M. d'Alembert, 'author of several very ingenious books, in which he has shown great talents and still greater self conceit, with a most thorough contempt for the rest of mankind'. The Academy's members, he added, were all terrified lest Maupertuis be replaced with this dreadfully vain and dictatorial man.

[28] Ibid.; Mortier, *Le Cœur*, 28–9, 339; Mortier, *Combats*, 163–5.
[29] Hume to Walpole, Edinburgh, 20 Nov. 1766, in Hume, *Letters*, ii. 109–10.
[30] D'Alembert to Voltaire, 6 May 1760, in d'Alembert, *Œuvres complètes*, v. 67.
[31] Naigeon, *Mémoires*, 168; Belaval, *Études*, 187.
[32] Henry, 'Frédéric le Grand', 67–70, 92; Venturi, *Le origini*, 94.
[33] D'Alembert to Mlle de Lespinasse, Sans-Souci, 22 June and 2 July 1763, in Henry, 'Frédéric le Grand', 70, 76–7.
[34] Ibid. 66–7.

Frederick enjoyed discussing French literature and philosophy and did so, often with d'Argens, the court chamberlain, present, 'à merveille'. These evening discussions spanned the entire Enlightenment spectrum but dragged on interminably, forcing d'Alembert to stay up far later than he liked. With the king's views, fortunately, he found himself continually agreeing. When news arrived that the Sorbonne felt unable to pronounce on the thorny question of inoculation, he was delighted by Frederick's gibe that this was its first reasonable statement since its foundation.[35] Voltaire's œuvre Frederick knew intimately, d'Alembert concurring with his fulsome praise, even though he himself was then reading Voltaire's *Essai sur l'histoire générale*, in his rooms, and assuring Julie it was a work 'à faire vomir par la bassesse et la platitude de ses éloges'.[36] Rousseau's writings the king judged highly eloquent but devoid of logic and truth.[37] The Academy was frequently touched on.[38] D'Alembert refused to become its president but willingly advised the king on practical matters such as the need to boost the stipend of the mathematician Euler, then contemplating returning to Petersburg, whom d'Alembert judged the best of the Berlin *académiciens*. Curiously, their talks seem always to have skirted around the topic of the *Encyclopédie* and Diderot.

Voltaire intended to establish the ascendancy of his moderate Enlightenment by capturing the courts. The *dévôt* faction in France, despite everything, would not succeed in dominating Versailles. Rather, it was he who would do so, Louis XV's chief minister, Choiseul, being truly 'une âme noble et éclairée' who would not in the end permit a full-scale reaction against *la philosophie* in the highest corridors of power. But this was not a strategy easy to render cogent at a time when the French royal censorship remained unrelenting and all packages containing printed matter passing from the Swiss border into France, including his own, were opened by the authorities and everything judged impious confiscated. Distressingly, his own *Traité de la tolérance*, published at Geneva in November 1763, even if privately approved by Choiseul and other principal figures at court, was publicly boycotted by them. This was doubly disillusioning as Voltaire had scrupulously sent packets of copies for distribution at Versailles, via his friend Sartine, in Paris, prior to the book's general release and one of his treatise's chief points was that society, over the last half century, had become more stable and crowns stronger owing precisely to the spread of toleration. Yet despite his adopting a vigorously pro-monarchical stance and, in this case venturing (otherwise highly unusual) expressions of admiration for Christ, and greatly restraining his disdain for the Church, France's ministers joined the papacy in publicly condemning the work.[39]

Such rebuffs inevitably implied an element of contradiction in his position. Since the crack-down on *philosophique* literature was totally unacceptable to him, he could

[35] D'Alembert to Mlle de Lespinasse, Sans-Souci, 22 June and 2 July 1763, in Henry, 'Frédéric le Grand', 82.
[36] Ibid. 83.   [37] Ibid. 75, 81.   [38] Ibid. 87.
[39] Voltaire, *Traité de la tolérance*, 47–9, 101–7; Pomeau, *Religion de Voltaire*, 377–8; Davidson, *Voltaire in Exile*, 109–11.

not avoid practising, if not preaching, a double strategy that was to a degree duplicitous. Generally speaking, the *philosophes* must be known for unstinting loyalty to
the crown and acceptance of the social order. But as far as the royal censorship and
border inspections of packages were concerned, he could not avoid becoming vigorously subversive. Voltaire aspired to be the public champion of the *philosophes.* Yet,
neither Choiseul, on the one hand, nor the radical *philosophes*, on the other, would
follow his advice. Like Diderot, Helvétius simply refused to accept that the French
court would ever relent. 'Reason' must lose the current contest in France, he insisted,
because reason is powerless 'contre la puissance' and vested interests, and these were
powerfully stacked against them.[40] Thus, those Voltaire most aspired to lead ignored
his recommendations. Meanwhile, he complained through d'Alembert, Grimm, and
others, Diderot remained too reticent and had even failed in the elementary courtesy
of thanking him for his unstinting public support.

Diderot and d'Holbach liked neither the deism Voltaire everywhere promoted
through both publicly acknowledged and clandestine writings, nor his pro-monarchical leanings. Furthermore, his role as prime advocate of their cause grated even
though, at this stage, they could not vent their annoyance publicly. Privately, Diderot
expressed his irritation to his intimate friend Sophie Volland: 'who' on earth had
asked Voltaire to plead his cause and 'qui diable lui a dit qu'il l'avoit plaidée comme
il me convenoit'![41] Diderot and his circle considered Voltaire's philosophical poems
of the late 1750s proclaiming his deism, and recent philosophical essays, facile
and misconceived.[42] Especially exasperating was Voltaire's relegating them to the
margins, philosophically, while powerfully countering their programme of clandestine general subversion with an astonishingly vigorous and polemical undercover
campaign of his own, energetically stepped up from around 1760.[43] Now that he saw
that the royal censorship had to be massively subverted, this was designed not just to
propagate his top-down deist reformism but to suborn their ideas and dominate the
now indispensable underground stage.

Voltaire knew that Diderot's and d'Holbach's attitude towards his claims to
leadership was grudging at best and this was also something others continually
drew his attention to. Intellectually, there neither was nor could be any meaningful
alignment between him and the inner group of *encyclopédistes.* Palissot, writing to
Voltaire in December 1760, professed to have purposely spared d'Alembert's reputation out of regard for Voltaire who was his friend: 'mais Did***, D**** [Duclos ?],
mais H****[elvétius?]', those he had so savagely pilloried in his play, he demanded,
'sont-ils vos amis?' If Voltaire imagined these men would follow his lead, he was
greatly mistaken. Where Voltaire defended belief in a God who rewards and punishes
and the idea of a divinely created and ordained natural and human order as well as a

---

[40] Voltaire, *Corr.* xxii. 135–6.
[41] Ibid. xxii. 257; Pappas, *Voltaire and d'Alembert*, 25.
[42] Monty, *Critique littéraire*, 103–6, 109.
[43] Naves, *Voltaire*, 87; Mortier, *Le Cœur*, 214.

divinely given morality, the *philosophes modernes* rejected 'ces notions fondamentales et sacrées', elaborating the same 'revolting' positions disfiguring La Mettrie's writings.[44] In response to Voltaire's chiding him, in the summer of 1764, for having performed the singular feat of quarrelling publicly with both the *philosophes* and the *anti-philosophes*, the younger playwright denied having quarrelled with any 'vrais philosophes'. He had always praised and honoured Voltaire, Montesquieu, and d'Alembert, he reminded him, and that should suffice, he contended, not to be regarded 'comme l'ennemi des philosophes'.[45]

Intellectually, argued Palissot, Voltaire's continuing public alignment with Diderot and his circle made little sense. Voltaire, of course, knew this perfectly well but, as before, turned a deaf ear to all exhortations to break with the *philosophes modernes*. He denied there was a general split among the *parti philosophique* and, from his standpoint, with good reason. This was the only movement he could lead and it was plainly impossible for him to do so without proclaiming the unity of the cult of reason, toleration, freedom of thought, and *la philosophie*. The difficulty here was that he could only retain the confidence of Catherine and Frederick, and courtiers like Choiseul and d'Argental whose backing underpinned his now apparently commanding position, by constantly reaffirming the underlying conservatism of his political, social, and ecclesiastical stance, which inevitably eroded his appeal to those demanding more profound social, legal, and political structural changes.

It might be pointless to labour his conservative politics, providential metaphysics, natural theology, and deistic moral philosophy among his currently cowed and beaten Parisian colleagues, as he could not sway them and did not try. But neither could he promote the kind of Enlightenment he aspired to lead without projecting his views vigorously in society and establishing a solid following in France and the rest of Europe. If he could seize the initiative, intellectually, among the public and remain the *philosophes*' chief publicist, wit and *littérateur*, as well as foremost champion of toleration and general ambassador abroad, he would have won the contest even without carrying the Diderot circle with him. Due to the censorship in France, Italy, Germany, and Switzerland, though, such a programme was feasible only by means of a vigorous underground operating in competition, so to speak, with that of the radical underground. Voltaire needed to demonstrate that he was the movement's philosopher-in-chief, principal strategist, and political leader, and in the circumstances of the 1760s, this involved walking a precarious communicative as well as intellectual tight-rope.

Quantitatively, his performance was astounding, generating a mass of spectacularly successful clandestine publications which appeared in an unbroken stream through the 1760s. Briefly, he succeeded in seizing the initiative while his radical rivals in Paris found themselves both more tightly hemmed in by authority than he was, on the Franco-Swiss border, and heavily burdened with the work of completing

---

[44] Palissot to Voltaire, 1 Dec. 1760, in Voltaire, *Corr.* xxii. 349.
[45] Voltaire to Palissot, 26 July, and Palissot to Voltaire, 9 Aug. 1764, ibid. xxvii. 47, 64.

the *Encyclopédie*. During these years Voltaire came as close as was perhaps possible to reconfiguring the Enlightenment into a true unity and to dominating the Enlightenment as a whole.

Among his various clandestine manoeuvres of the early 1760s, Voltaire, in 1762, anonymously published, in Holland, a small compilation of extracts from the *Testament* of Jean Meslier (1664–1729), whose materialist philosophy, among the major radical systems of the early eighteenth century, happened to be a particular favourite of d'Holbach's and Naigeon's.[46] Voltaire recommended his 'Meslier' in numerous letters of the period, plying d'Alembert and Marmontel with copies and asking them to help draw attention to this text. There were more copies of 'Meslier's' *Testament* circulating in the mountains around Geneva, he assured d'Alembert in September 1762, than in Paris.[47] 'Meslier' was being read just as avidly in Switzerland as the *Sermon des cinquante*, he assured Helvétius, some months later; more and more 'souls' were being won by the *philosophes*. 'Meslier's' *Testament* and the clandestine *Sermon des cinquante* were proving especially powerful instruments for converting Christians to deism. 'Quelle réponse', he remarked, to the dreary commonplaces of the 'fanatiques'.[48]

However, the real Meslier was an atheist and unforgiving foe of nobility who dreamt of liberating the peasantry from their sway. What Voltaire had done was commit a literary assassination, fabricating a 'Meslier' in no sense anti-aristocratic, atheistic, or a social rebel but rather a providential deist loyal to monarchy who prayed for forgiveness for having taught his parishioners Christianity.[49] D'Alembert, typically, objected less to Voltaire's total falsification of Meslier's thought than the risks he expected friends to expose themselves to distributing copies. His acolytes Voltaire urged to be bolder and, in particular, help arrange the reprinting of 5,000 copies of 'Meslier' for distribution in Paris. D'Alembert refused, finding this too risky. The human race had become gradually more enlightened only because philosophers had taken care thus far 'de ne l'éclairer que peu à peu'.[50] Voltaire's manipulated 'Meslier' remained current for some years. But the ploy eventually misfired. A decade later, d'Holbach, Diderot, and Naigeon trumped his fabrication of a bogus 'Meslier' by reinstating the real Meslier in their even more successful *Le Bon-Sens* of 1772.

Such underground rivalry between two enlightenments during the 1760s required good and extensive intelligence and a reliable international network ensuring speedy distribution of one's own clandestine output and news of the competition. Here, d'Alembert proved but a mediocre asset. Informed a fresh edition of a major clandestine manuscript—the *Examen de la religion*, which Voltaire was perhaps the first to attribute to Du Marsais—had appeared and by early 1763 was causing a stir, Voltaire and d'Alembert both proved unable to procure their own copies for months.

[46] Israel, *Enlightenment Contested*, 716–28; Pellerin, 'Naigeon', 37.
[47] Voltaire to d'Alembert, 15 Sept. 1762, in Voltaire, *Corr.* xxv. 218.
[48] Ibid. xxvi. 199, 373; Mortier, *Le Cœur*, 100.
[49] Pellerin, 'Diderot, Voltaire', 54–5; Pearson, *Voltaire Almighty*, 306–7; Onfray, *Les Ultras*, 95–6.
[50] D'Alembert to Voltaire, 31 July 1762, in Voltaire, *Corr.* xxv. 140–1.

Though Voltaire had liked Du Marsais personally, he viewed him with suspicion because, like Meslier, he was a materialist and republican. Du Marsais, observed Grimm, in 1764, in his *Correspondance littéraire philosophique et critique*, a court journal of limited circulation, read mainly among the German princely courts, was 'un excellent esprit' and his text rather formidable. He stressed the cogency of Du Marsais's attack on the concept of revelation, reminding readers he had also been 'le premier grammairien du siècle'. Voltaire agreed it was an effective work 'plein de raison' but deplored Du Marsais's atheism and written style.[51] On finally obtaining his own copy, he could not resist chiding d'Alembert, in January 1764, for still not having his when the text had reportedly been surreptitiously circulating in Paris for some time. When he eventually managed to borrow a copy, d'Alembert assured Voltaire that Du Marsais's text seemed decidedly inferior to the 'Meslier' volume, a gratified Voltaire answering that 'Meslier' should indeed be in the pockets of all 'les honnêtes gens'.[52]

In June 1764, after labouring on it for three years amid considerable secrecy, scarcely mentioning it to anyone, Voltaire produced his great coup of the decade, anonymously publishing at Geneva (giving the false location 'à Londres') his *Dictionnaire philosophique portatif*. This was widely suppressed across Europe, publicly burnt at Geneva, condemned in December 1764 by the High Court at The Hague, and in March 1765 by the *Parlement* of Paris.[53] Since Voltaire had publicly declared the *Encyclopédie*'s suspension a grave disappointment to all right-minded men, many, Vernet among them, assumed this work's purpose was to fill the gap by providing a surrogate *Encyclopédie*. Many thought Voltaire's text a distillation of the *Encyclopédie*'s essential *esprit*. From Diderot's vantage point, though, the venture more resembled an attempt to suborn the *Encyclopédie* itself. Suspicions were strengthened by Voltaire's not only publicly denying his authorship but long pretending the *Portatif* represented the labours of the whole philosophic fraternity. While he later acknowledged composing some articles, he still insisted these were originally intended for the *Encyclopédie*, as indeed at least one major article, on 'idolâtrie', had been. Hence, it was not unnatural to suppose Voltaire's object was to supplant the *Encyclopédie*, on which unceasing labour continued in silence but which to the public looked moribund, plying a quite different philosophical outlook, one that was monarchical, anti-materialist, and anti-atheistic.[54]

The most distressing reverse, though, intellectually and psychologically, for Diderot and his colleagues, was a discovery made by Diderot himself in November 1764, when the printing of the remaining unpublished volumes of the *Encyclopédie*, at Le Breton's workshop, was almost complete. Checking the text of his highly subversive entry 'Sarrasins', Diderot happened to visit the print-shop after being absent for some time. He was deeply shocked to find this entry had been grossly mutilated after his 'final' correction of the printed proofs, without his knowledge,

[51] Voltaire to d'Alembert, 8 Jan. 1764, ibid. xxvii. 158.
[52] Voltaire to d'Alembert, 9 July 1764, ibid. xxviii. 25.
[53] Chaudon, *Dictionnaire anti-philosophique*, i, preface pp. xxvii–xxix.
[54] Naves, *Voltaire*, 89–90; Mortier, *Le Cœur*, 379.

by the publisher, in an effort to remove everything of an openly subversive character aimed against state or Church. On examining other major articles, he discovered these too had been mutilated in a similar manner, as had numerous other key articles by his co-contributors. Overwhelmed by shock, fury, indignation, and despair, he briefly contemplated washing his hands of the now mangled *Encyclopédie* entirely, but was dissuaded with difficulty, partly at Grimm's urging.

There survives a long letter of 12 November 1764 to Le Breton expressing the depth of Diderot's rage at this 'treason'.[55] The deletions had rendered the *Encyclopédie* something flat and miserable that would sell slowly and most of which would be pulped. 'The cries of MM. Diderot, Saint-Lambert, Turgot, d'Holbach, de Jaucourt and others all so respectable and so little respected by you will be repeated by the multitude.' Actually, the cuts did not constitute, overall, as severe a disfigurement as Diderot feared at first. Only a relatively small number of entries, like 'Sarrasins', 'Théologie scholastique', 'Théologie positive', 'Tolérance', and 'Pyrrhonienne, philosophie', in the latter case with whole paragraphs of Diderot's fervent praise of Bayle and his achievement removed,[56] were so heavily cut as to be effectively ruined. Otherwise, only a comparatively limited number of articles were altered in a significant way. Although some of the excised text was lost for ever, much of what was deleted by Le Breton has been recovered by modern research.

Voltaire, meanwhile, also clandestinely published his *Philosophie de l'histoire*, under the pseudonym 'the Abbé Bazin', powerfully restating his universal morality, anti-Christianity, providential conception of history, racial theories, and views about China, India, and Persia. Banned by Holland's provincial high court in July 1765, the Genevan authorities in August, and as 'très dangereux' by the Paris *Parlement*, it was prohibited by the papacy in 1768.[57] A rebuke came also from Choiseul's friend Marie, Marquise Du Deffand, who ranked among the principal salon hostesses of Paris, and hence *connoisseuses* of the Enlightenment's progress, and figured among his regular correspondents. She prided herself on having trained d'Alembert's 'mistress' (he was homosexual), Julie, in the art of running salons and was the first *salonnière* to fête Hume, who was amazed to see that in Paris such 'ladies are, in a manner the sovereigns of the learned world as well as of the conversible'.[58] Having regularly visited her salon during the early part of his stay, though, Hume subsequently, much to her chagrin, defected to her protégée and now rival, Mademoiselle de Lespinasse, who set up on her own in 1764. This and her break with d'Alembert only heightened her reverence, she explained, for the 'Abbé Bazin'. But she had become extremely uneasy over the intensity of Voltaire's clandestine campaign against religion.

Surely, she objected, in a long letter of January 1766, despite his protestations, he was, after all, undermining the ignorant notions of the common people.

[55] Gordon and Torrey, *Censoring*, 23, 30, 63; Blom, *Enlightening the World*, 283–5.
[56] Gordon and Torrey, *Censoring*, 49–51.
[57] Voltaire, *Corr.* xxviii. 488–9, 491; Knuttel, *Verboden boeken*, 36; de Bujando, *Index*, 931.
[58] Mossner, *Life of David Hume*, 452–4; Goodman, *Republic*, 75, 124; Lilti, *Le Monde*, 360.

Had 'Bazin's' philosophy (and his *Dictionnaire*) not been composed with an eye on a comparatively wide audience? Voltaire could be confident of her continuing support. But she totally repudiated 'vos philosophes modernes' as she called Diderot, Helvétius, and d'Holbach. No one was 'moins philosophes' than these presumptuous men trampling on all who 'ne se prosternent pas devant eux'.[59] Most people, even at court, would never grasp philosophic truth, nor become genuinely tolerant or moral in a philosophic sense, or capable of abandoning their prejudices. Nor should they, for it is faith and prejudice, not reason, that enable men to cope with life's complexities and sufferings. Credulity remained indispensable, society's rock, and Voltaire must scrupulously ensure he was not, by design or negligence, disturbing popular prejudices or aiding *philosophes modernes*.

Voltaire hastened to reassure the marquise of his infinite respect for the people's crassness and the vast distance between himself and the *philosophes modernes*. He particularly stressed how utterly remote he felt from those denying 'une intelligence Suprême productrice de tous les mondes'. He could not conceive 'comment de si habiles mathématiciens [as d'Alembert]' could possibly deny 'un mathématicien éternel'. Newton and Plato, anyhow, emphatically insisted on this Creator-God. For his part, he had never compromised the tenets of Newton's philosophy and never would.[60] Enlightenment, he concurred wholeheartedly with her, is not for the majority. The truth is something, he agreed, reserved for the few, or, as he put it two years previously, writing to Étienne-Noel Damilaville (1723–68),[61] an *encyclopédiste* who had become the chief intermediary between Voltaire and the Diderot circle, 'le gros du genre humain en est indigne'.[62]

But precisely because enlightenment was not for most, Voltaire could not abandon the underground text war in progress or cease printing anonymous and falsely attributed irreligious texts, for this was crucial to the outcome of the contest for the sophisticated reading public. How could he surrender the sphere of clandestine literature when anything even remotely daring was immediately subject to seizure by the French censorship and when the opposing faction of the *parti philosophique* were forging an entire pan-European network functioning parallel to and against his own, propagating republican, materialist, and atheistic thought in opposition to his tolerationist, deist, and monarchical system? How could the 'philosophes modernes' be defeated without countervailing enlightened efforts?

Fighting for the illicit arena of clandestine thought, Voltaire knew he could win in the long run only by lending more coherence and depth to his own philosophical system. Among other texts powerfully restating his philosophy (and resuming his war against Spinoza and Bayle) was his *Le Philosophe ignorant* (1766). Reason, he reiterates, reaffirming his objections to Spinozism and all one-substance materialism,

---

[59] Du Deffand to Voltaire, Paris, 14 Jan. 1766, in Voltaire, *Corr.* xxx. 40–1.
[60] Voltaire to Marquise Du Deffand, 20 Jan. 1766, ibid. xxx. 56.
[61] Morellet, *Mémoires*, i. 152; Davidson, *Voltaire in Exile*, 140–4.
[62] Pellerin, 'Diderot, Voltaire', 56 ; Mortier, *Le Cœur*, 96.

entails belief in God as creator of the universe and source of the universal moral code.[63] Again, he declares his passionate attachment to Locke, the philosopher who never feigned to know what he did not and reduced metaphysics to just six or seven basic truths. What he stressed most was that he and Locke did not argue that it is matter that thinks but only that it is impossible for us to say God cannot impart to matter the power to think.[64] Acknowledging our ignorance is indeed the height of wisdom. Curiously, Voltaire combines this stance with his dogmatic insistence that Locke was unquestionably right in pivoting his thought on a Creator God. Spinoza's basic mistake lay precisely in his not seeing the goals for which natural things are intended, that eyes are for seeing and ears for hearing and that all this is unthinkable without a Creator God who is the supreme intelligence and created the universe delivering morality to men.[65]

A frequent charge levelled at Voltaire by both *anti-philosophes* and radical writers was the claim that his scientific principles were out of date and unsound and that this undermined his entire deistic standpoint. Among several instances of this de facto convergence against Voltaire was the Abbé François's sally against his racial doctrine that the whites, blacks, Hottentots, Chinese, and Amerindians constitute 'des races entièrement différentes'.[66] Both Catholic *anti-philosophes* and radical *philosophes* had an interest in overturning Voltaire's racial hierarchy and reaffirming mankind's essential unity.[67] Not only was Voltaire vulnerable in disputed areas of biology but both *anti-philosophes* and radical *philosophes* tended to suggest that his deism was a sham façade, or incoherent rigmarole, behind which stood the sturdier logic of Spinoza, materialism, and atheism. Questioning Voltaire's wider philosophical coherence was a speciality not least of the Jesuit *anti-philosophe* Griffet, an author Fréron considered particularly effective in this area. One of Griffet's most telling objections, made quoting Voltaire's exact words, was that his assault on miracles in the *Dictionnaire portatif* merely repeats the arguments about the impossibility of God contradicting himself formulated by Spinoza in the sixth chapter of the *Tractatus Theologico-Politicus* and in his *Ethics*. Accusing Voltaire of not mentioning the source of his main armoury for attacking miracles and revelation out of fear that Spinoza's reputation for atheism would destroy confidence in his deistic system, Griffet further suggests that for all his deistic rhetoric, Voltaire might actually be a disguised 'atheist'. In any case, he was a philosopher secretly reliant on and unable to refute Spinozism.[68]

Such trenchant recrimination inevitably strengthened the suspicions of those who, encouraged by Rousseau's retort, construed Voltaire's poem on the Lisbon earthquake as a work of bogus deism actually sowing the seeds of atheism.[69] By asserting a

[63] Voltaire, *Philosophe ignorant*, 73, 76–7.   [64] Ibid. 74–6; Mortier, *Combats*, 195.
[65] Voltaire, *Philosophe ignorant*, 63–7.
[66] François, *Observations*, i. 4, 37–8; Voltaire, *Philosophie de l'histoire*, 6–7.
[67] François, *Observations*, i. 4, 37–8.
[68] Griffet, *L'Insuffisance*, i. 207–9.
[69] Ibid.; Le Masson des Granges, *Philosophe moderne*, 134.

God separate from his creation, Voltaire and his allies seemed confident that they would not be accused of being 'Spinosistes'. But even if one grants that Voltaire uses the term 'God' more sincerely than Spinoza, argued Griffet, to that extent he presents a manifestly incoherent argument—that God cannot change the laws of which he is the omnipotent author.[70] With such objections *anti-philosophie* helped inflict appreciable damage on Voltaire's Enlightenment but at the cost of weakening him in his confrontation with the radical fraternity.

2. REGROUPING AT CLEVES

Three significant reverses dented both wings of the Enlightenment in France in the mid 1760s: the renewed royal ban on the *Encyclopédie* of 1765, reaffirmed by the crown in 1766; the trial—for sacrilege supposedly inspired by the *philosophes* (especially Voltaire)—judicial torture, and execution of the Chevalier de La Barre; and the public furore against *la philosophie* during 1766–7 provoked by Marmontel and his novel *Bélisaire*. What these three episodes all demonstrated was that the irreligious Enlightenment generally remained unpopular as well as officially banned and, for the moment, a cause wholly on the defensive.

The completion and unexpected, illegal, appearance, in September 1765, a few months before the dauphin's death, of the *Encyclopédie*'s remaining volumes all at once, after six years of silent, underground planning, redaction, and correcting of proofs, inevitably caused a great sensation in France and abroad. The secretly printed volumes, though produced at Le Breton's printing works in Paris where over many months some fifty workers, sworn to secrecy, toiled at the task, appeared under the false address of 'Samuel Fauche à Neuchâtel', suggesting they had been produced in Switzerland, a ploy that would, it was hoped, enable the French authorities to turn the earnestly hoped-for blind eye.[71] This was a major event in Enlightenment history. At Geneva, on receiving the concluding volumes in the spring of 1766, Bonnet immediately threw himself into reading his set and sharing his reactions and indignation (not least against the Protestant Jaucourt) with Haller.[72] Receiving his set at the same moment, Voltaire rejoiced that Diderot and the *libraires* had, after all, surmounted the obstacles and carried the great project to fruition and similarly threw himself into reading great swaths of text, though, like Bonnet and Haller, he had decidedly mixed feelings about the outcome. Impressed by some articles— especially 'Hobbes', by Diderot, and the powerful piece 'Unitaires' demonstrating close linkage between Socinianism and radical thought, by Naigeon—he judged the general level to have fallen well below that achieved down to the eighth volume.

---

[70] Griffet, *L'Insuffisance*, i. 210 and ii. 55–7; Balcou, *Fréron*, 314 n.
[71] Trousson, *Denis Diderot*, 406.
[72] Guyot, *Rayonnement*, 40–1; Rey, 'Diderot à travers', 113, 116–17, 121.

Voltaire was amazed to see how much (over 40 per cent of each of the last four volumes) had been penned by Jaucourt himself.[73] What disappointed him most, though, was the overall philosophical message: the philosophical role of Locke, Newton, and Clarke was again minimal. Diderot persisted in viewing Locke as a thinker for mediocre minds whose principal point, that there are no ideas in the mind that have not come from the senses, is too simplistic and had in any case already been clearly formulated by Aristotle and Hobbes earlier.[74] He was extremely dissatisfied. 'Plût à Dieu', he enjoined d'Alembert, stressing the discrepancy between what had been promised and what had been delivered, that the *Encyclopédie* had really been based on Bacon, Locke, and Newton, proceeding 'comme votre *Discours préliminaire*'.[75] Even so, Voltaire exulted that the *Encyclopédie* 'en général' had appeared: it was a massive blow to 'fanaticism'; 'une grande révolution dans les esprits s'annonce de tous côtés'.[76]

Voltaire did not expect the court's negative reaction to be more than *pro forma* despite talk of a renewed ban. But here he was mistaken and soon greatly disillusioned. For this further challenge to royal, judicial, and ecclesiastical authority prompted a fresh and far from perfunctory crack-down. At first, Voltaire hoped Choiseul and the ministry were merely letting off steam, in anticipation of the pending annual assembly of the French clergy. In May 1766, he still spoke hopefully of the 'sagesse du ministère'. But the situation turned out to be much graver than he and the others had grasped at first. Certain political articles, such as Jaucourt's entry 'Peuple', turned out to have gravely offended the king's ministers. The royal authorities, urged on by the archbishop of Paris and court *dévôts*, began enforcing their prohibition in earnest. In April 1766, for disobeying the prohibition on distribution in the capital, the principal publisher, Le Breton, was thrown into the Bastille for three weeks. Hearing copies had been spotted at Versailles, the king issued an order, in July 1766, that everyone at court possessing the banned volumes must surrender them to the police. After a first brief flurry of sales, the publishers quickly retrenched. Copies ceased reaching subscribers in Paris and, by late 1766, the booksellers had virtually abandoned all effort to distribute the sets in France.

Voltaire was both astounded and outraged by the unexpected ferocity of the crack-down, quite unable to see what the king's ministers were so afraid of. Privately, he fiercely denounced the authorities' refusal to permit delivery to subscribers as 'unjust' and a theft: 'je voudrais bien savoir', he demanded, what harm can be done by a publication costing a hundred *écus*? Had the Gospels cost twelve hundred sesterces, Christianity would never have been established anywhere. Twenty volumes in folio are surely never going to engineer a 'revolution': it is those small portable books 'à trente sous qui sont à craindre'.[77] After all his assiduous cultivation of the court, and

---

[73] Haechler, *L'Encyclopédie: Les Combats*, 366, 369.
[74] Diderot, *Réfutation*, 295–6; Kaitaro, *Diderot's Holism*, 62–3.
[75] Voltaire to d'Alembert, 5 Apr. 1766, in Voltaire, *Corr.* xxx. 159.
[76] Ibid.
[77] Voltaire to d'Alembert, 5 Apr. 1766, in Voltaire, *Corr.* xxx. 159.

the private assurances from Choiseul and others, he also felt once again personally let down. From 1766, he no longer spoke of the 'wisdom' of the king's ministers. It also annoyed him that Diderot, d'Holbach, and the others remained mysteriously quiet about it all and that he heard nothing of retaliation with hard-hitting, caustic replies. Everywhere, he lamented, 'les fanatiques triomphent'.[78] Again there was talk of Diderot being in danger of being imprisoned, and, among his foes, of his shortly receiving his just deserts.

The decapitation on 1 July 1766, after judicial mutilation, by order of the *Parlement* of Paris, of the 19-year-old Jean-François Le Fèvre, Chevalier de La Barre, followed by the burning of his remains and some books, was a horrific event that intimidated some of the public but also, noted Voltaire, himself deeply shaken, profoundly shocked a great many others.[79] De la Barre had been accused, in August 1765, of desecrating, under the influence of *la philosophie*, a crucifix erected for a religious procession on the Pont Neuf bridge at Abbeville and, together with several friends, committing desecration and insulting the procession by ostentatiously walking past, singing blasphemous songs while keeping their hats on. The affair implicated Voltaire and deeply disturbed 'tous les amis de la raison et de l'humanité'. For Voltaire's *Dictionnaire philosophique*, *Épître à Uranie*, and other works had been found in de La Barre's rooms and were cited both at the trial and subsequent execution during which his *Dictionnaire* was thrown on the flames.

But in a different way the affair also implicated the entire French judiciary. Early on, the bishop of Amiens publicly declared that de La Barre and his co-accused should suffer the ultimate penalty. The Amiens judges provisionally sentenced de La Barre and the Chevalier d'Étallonde (who was later pardoned) to have their tongues excised and right hands cut off at the cathedral entrance and be burnt at the stake.[80] The seneschal of Abbeville then appealed to the Paris *Parlement* to determine whether these sentences should be carried out. The transfer of the prisoners to Paris where they stayed for three months precipitated a national sensation, the case developing into one of the most celebrated legal battles of the century. The twenty-five magistrates assigned to the case divided, several well-known Parisian *avocats* declaring the proceedings illegal. Nevertheless, in June, under pressure from the court and the bishops, the *Parlement*, presided over by Joly de Fleury, eventually confirmed the original sentence. De La Barre returned to Abbeville under heavy guard, for execution. On 1 July 1766, he went to his death with a calm, dignified demeanour, the Dominican assigned as his confessor openly weeping at his side.

The psychological shock to the entire Abbeville populace caused by this gruesome spectacle was such that it proved impossible to proceed with the other executions. These were deferred but never actually carried out. The whole 'atroce et absurde affaire' horrified Voltaire, d'Alembert, and Hume as well as Beccaria, who arrived in

---

[78] Voltaire to Damilaville, 18 Aug. 1766, in Voltaire, *Corr.* xxx. 386–7.
[79] Voltaire, *Histoire du parlement*, 555–6; Condorcet, *Vie de Voltaire*, 174–8.
[80] Morellet, *Lettres*, i. 57–8, 66 n. 20; Lascoumes, 'Beccaria', 109–10.

Paris for his ill-fated visit shortly afterwards. To them the execution was judicial murder perpetrated by fanatics, obscurantists, and Jansenists. 'It is strange, that such cruelty should be found among a people so celebrated for humanity', remarked Hume, 'and so much bigotry amid so much knowledge and philosophy. I am pleased to hear, that the indignation was as general in Paris [he was then in London] as it is in all foreign countries.'[81] Voltaire reacted in mid July, anonymously publishing an acerbic *Relation de la mort du Chevalier de La Barre*, to further heighten the dismaying effect—after which he took a trip for a month to a nearby Swiss spa, Rolle, lest the royal authorities order a search for him. The episode significantly damaged the French judiciary's reputation and that of the law as well as the *parlements*—indeed the entire French legal tradition and profession—in the eyes of many besides the *philosophes*.[82]

And the *philosophes* had some reason to be alarmed. For they had been instrumental in stirring up a public outcry against an execution ordered by the *Parlement* of Paris, the episcopacy, and the court. The bishops' pronouncements on the matter and other documents cited the *philosophes*, Voltaire assured Morellet, expressly naming several as *corrupteurs* of the young.[83] In Voltaire's fertile mind, the threatening atmosphere gave birth to a new scheme for advancing *his* Enlightenment. Feeling insecure under the shadow of the de La Barre execution and with the suppression of the recently completed *Encyclopédie* in full swing, at Paris, and reports of police raids on bookshops also in the provinces, Voltaire wrote solemnly summoning the *philosophes* in Paris to escape finally from such intolerable tyranny and evacuate France for the present, establishing a permanent colony of free, like-thinking *philosophes* under Frederick's royal protection, at Cleves, on the Rhine.

Frederick, meanwhile, displeased by the *philosophes'* stirring up a public outcry over official legal proceedings, reminded Voltaire that the Abbeville miscreants had defied the law. Inciting protest violated his, and Voltaire's, guiding principle that 'le vulgaire ne mérite pas d'être éclairé' [the common people do not merit being enlightened].[84] The judges were only carrying out what the law prescribed. All citizens, Voltaire doubtless concurred, must obey the laws. 'Crimes' of religious fanaticism every enlightened person loathes, but 'fanatisme dans la philosophie' and the harmful tendency to carry philosophic principles too far must also be eschewed. The young man's execution was regrettable. But it was the law; and it was vital the *philosophes* neither encourage such acts nor decry judges who could not lawfully proceed otherwise than they did. Socrates may not have believed in the gods but yet participated in prescribed sacrifices. This is philosophy's true path. Their Enlightenment, admonished Frederick, from Potsdam, on 11 August 1766, must always exude 'la douceur et la modération'. Their toleration guaranteed liberty of conscience but never sanctioned law-breaking or licensed youths to affront 'audacieusement à ce que le peuple révère'.

[81] Hume to Marquise de Barbentane, 29 Aug. 1766, in Hume, *Letters*, ii. 85.
[82] *Correspondance inédite de Condorcet*, 38, 184, 202, 205; Claverie, 'L'Affaire', 194–5, 252.
[83] Voltaire to Morellet, 7 July 1766, in Voltaire, *Corr.* xxx. 301; Gay, *Voltaire's Politics*, 280.
[84] Frederick to Voltaire, Potsdam, 7 Aug. 1766, ibid. xxx. 369–70.

Only an undeviating 'moderation' ensures liberty (for elites) with stability and tranquillity, the 'premier objet de toute législation'.[85]

Voltaire must be 'realistic' about what was attainable. Should the *philosophes* succeed in carrying out 'une révolution' in humanity's thinking, the resulting 'sect' could never be very numerous because one must be able to think to belong it and few indeed, held Frederick, are capable of that. Most do not wish to think critically or independently; and, furthermore, there are innumerable hypocrites concealing their turpitude behind what is commonly believed, besides princes persuaded they rule for only so long as the people remain deep in superstition. This may sometimes confront the *philosophe* with dilemmas but Enlightenment must never unsettle the majority, a boundary that will forever block those urging a general 'religion simple et raisonnable'.[86] Voltaire's satisfaction in the progress of ideas and the undoubted 'revolution' since 1740 in the way humanity thinks Frederick shared. He too wished society's elites to enjoy freedom of thought and expression. But he remained altogether averse to the radical reformism of Diderot and d'Holbach as he demonstrated at this point with his response to Voltaire's call for the *philosophes* to regroup at Cleves, in Prussia's westernmost corner.

Voltaire urged all the *philosophes* to join him under the king's protection. For months, he endeavoured to persuade d'Alembert, Helvétius, Marmontel, Diderot, Damilaville, and the entire *coterie d'Holbachique* to abandon Paris and reassemble under his leadership across the Rhine.[87] Only Rousseau with his 'orgueil ridicule' was omitted from the invitation.[88] 'Vous me parlez d'une colonie de philosophes', replied Frederick in August 1766, settled at Cleves. He was not unwilling to grant the *philosophes* asylum in Prussia, but only under the strict proviso they remain as tranquil as the title 'philosopher' predicates. The *philosophes* were welcome 'provided they remained moderate and pacific' [pourvu qu'ils soient modérés et paisibles].[89] The king agreed; but the scheme fell through. The attempt to regroup the *parti philosophique* at Cleves came to nothing. Unpleasant for the *philosophes* though the atmosphere in France was, Diderot, once again, refused to leave as did Marmontel, d'Holbach, and d'Alembert. Frederick too was at best lukewarm. When, two years later, in July 1769, the king wrote enquiring why he had received no letters from him in many months, Voltaire confessed to feeling so humiliated by the fiasco of 'la transmigration de Cleves' that ever since he had not dared offer His Majesty any ideas. To think a total 'imbecile' like Ignatius Loyola recruited a dozen loyal disciples with ease whereas he could not find even three *philosophes* to join him in Cleves made him wonder whether *la raison* was good for anything at all.[90]

---

[85] Frederick to Voltaire, Potsdam, 11 Aug. 1766, ibid. xxx. 381–2.

[86] Frederick to Voltaire, 20 Aug. 1766, ibid. xxx. 394–5.

[87] Naigeon, *Mémoires historiques*, 196–7; Pappas, *Voltaire et d'Alembert*, 62–4; Davidson, *Voltaire in Exile*, 174–6.

[88] Voltaire to Palissot, 16 Mar. 1767, in Voltaire, *Corr.* xxxi. 444; Burson, 'Crystallization', 999.

[89] Frederick to Voltaire, Sans-Souci, 13 Sept. 1766, in Voltaire, *Corr.* xxx. 434–5.

[90] Voltaire to Frederick, 31 Oct. 1769, and Frederick to Voltaire, 2 July 1769, ibid. xxxv. 59–60, 314; Trousson, *Denis Diderot*, 418.

Next came the *Bélisaire* affair which further intensified the intimidating atmosphere. A tailor's son among the best-known literary names in Europe, recently inducted into the Académie Française, Jean-François Marmontel (1723–99), was one of those lesser *philosophes* scorned by Mably as morally flippant lightweights. If he briefly emerged in 1767–70 as a central figure in the literary wars of the time, his renown also left him urgently in need of rescue. This was less because he was publicly charged by Palissot with plagiarizing much of *Bélisaire* (1767) from Mably's *Phocion*,[91] than because its fifteenth chapter vigorously reaffirms the universality of true morality and capacity of non-Christians to attain the highest ethical standards without Christian inspiration. This instantly rendered him a target of the *anti-philosophes*, triggering a new round of attacks on *tolérantisme* and *la philosophie*.[92] While Archbishop de Beaumont, Marmontel was relieved to find, adopted a relatively conciliatory stance, the outraged attacks in the Jansenist press not only on himself and the *philosophes* but also, he assured Voltaire, in March 1767, the archbishop and all the 'moderate' churchmen accused of shielding unbelievers while persecuting the truly devout, was unrelenting.[93] Besides the combined forces of the Jansenist clergy, jurists, and *canaille sorbonique*, noted d'Alembert, the *philosophes* were again facing an actively hostile faction at court.[94] But the Jansenists were the hard-core 'persécuteurs de la raison et de la philosophie' and would repeal reason itself, as Marmontel expressed it, if they could. They had the ear of some of the episcopate and the papacy. *Bélisaire* appeared on the papal *Index* as early as May 1767.[95]

If Marmontel was widely criticized by the *philosophes* for his spinelessness in agreeing to negotiate with the Sorbonne over retractions before the theology faculty which was preparing a detailed censure of the thirty-seven 'errors' it detected in *Bélisaire*, what especially troubled Marmontel, d'Alembert, and Helvétius was the predominantly hostile attitude of public opinion and the press guided by the crown. Royal authorities were permitting the 'canaille' of the Sorbonne to denounce *Bélisaire* in the journals and to compile their indictment while keeping Marmontel and his sympathizers tightly muzzled. All this, agreed Voltaire, was flagrantly unjust. But *Bélisaire*'s condemnation in France and Italy also struck him as untypical of developments more generally. Elsewhere, the revolution in ideas still seemed to be succeeding, indeed surpassing his hopes. During Catherine's recent tour of part of her empire, in July, she had occupied her leisure moments discussing *Bélisaire* with her ministers and was personally helping translate it into Russian.[96] In Vienna and Berlin too reaction was favourable in court circles. Marmontel should not be downhearted. 'Bénissons', he urged the others, 'cette hereuse révolution qui s'est

[91] Galliani, 'Mably', 183.
[92] Almodóvar, *Década*, 100; Cottret, *Jansénismes*, 42, 326.
[93] Marmontel to Voltaire, Paris, 8 Mar. 1767, in Voltaire, *Corr.* xxxi. 420.
[94] D'Alembert to Voltaire, 11 Mar. 1767, ibid. xxxi. 426.
[95] *Index Librorum Prohibitorum* (1786), 185; de Bujando, *Index*, 590.
[96] Voltaire to Marmontel, 25 July 1767, in Voltaire, *Corr.* xxxii. 228–9.

faite dans l'esprit de tous les honnêtes gens depuis 15 ou 20 années.'[97] He had no wish to die before again visiting Paris, he assured Marmontel, in November 1769, or without warmly embracing him in person along with Messrs d'Alembert, Duclos, Diderot, Saint-Lambert, and all the 'petit nombre de ceux' who with the fifteenth chapter of *Bélisaire* defend 'la gloire de la France'.[98]

3. A FALTERING MAINSTREAM

Yet, between 1765 and 1767, Voltaire lost something of his earlier confidence that his moderation was steering the Enlightenment with the aid of 'le pouvoir' and triumphing over radical ideas as well as bigotry and intolerance. Rather, like Frederick and d'Alembert, he was becoming increasingly uneasy about the advancing Counter-Enlightenment, on the one side, and radical challenge, on the other. In one of his letters to the despondent Marmontel, reaffirming his conviction that *la raison* was progressing despite the latest setbacks, he expresses his great indignation over the 'cloudy nonsense' diffused in the *Antiquité dévoilée*, the latest illicit materialist publication issuing from d'Holbach's 'boutique'. This highly subversive text, originally by Nicolas-Antoine Boulanger (1722–59), the civil engineer and *philosophe* whom Diderot had befriended but who died prematurely, soon after the *Encyclopédie*'s suppression, in 1759, was published, heavily edited (though Voltaire did not know this), by d'Holbach, together with an account of Boulanger's life by d'Holbach (or Diderot), in Holland in 1765. Printed by d'Holbach's accomplice the Amsterdam publisher Marc-Michel Rey, the book unequivocally restates the central radical thesis that kings and priests continued to perpetrate an age-old alliance at the expense of the people.[99]

Only later would it emerge that, for all his apparent ascendancy during the 1760s, and the reports of the Enlightenment's advances in Russia, Prussia, and Scandinavia, Voltaire in reality had failed to dominate the intellectual arena as he had hoped. Until the year 1770 when both the *Système de la nature* and the *Histoire philosophie*, the two most widely diffused works of the Radical Enlightenment, appeared, the true extent of his (and Catherine's and Frederick's) defeat in their drive for a hegemonic court Enlightenment remained hidden by the fraught circumstances of the *Encyclopédie*'s suppression and continuing crack-down in France and the rest of Europe on all anti-Christian literature. But beneath the surface a full-scale attack on Voltaire's and Frederick's Enlightenment no less than on the existing order had been gathering momentum since the early 1760s.

Since 1759, the real debates affecting the Enlightenment's course and prospects, in France as in Holland, Italy, Switzerland, and Germany, had unfolded underground,

---

[97] Voltaire to d'Alembert, 4 June 1767, in Voltaire, *Corr.* xxxii. 138; Mortier, *Combats*, 170–1.
[98] Voltaire to Marmontel, 1 Nov. 1769, in Voltaire, *Corr.* xxxv. 319.
[99] Voltaire to Marmontel, 23 Apr. 1766, ibid. xxx. 189; Sandrier, *Style philosophique*, 31–5.

largely unnoticed by most readers, behind closed shutters. Diderot, d'Holbach, and Helvétius, without explaining their strategy to Voltaire or d'Alembert, had withdrawn into a silent twilight world with their remaining disciples where, partly together and partly independently, the three heads employed small teams of dedicated assistants through the 1760s, to widen, refine, and complete their grand revolutionary project. In this way, they prepared and silently launched a soon resurgent and this time powerfully concerted and wide-ranging clandestine assault on established authority, convention, and not least the relativism and vaunted 'moderation' of Montesquieu, Frederick, Hume, and Turgot. This was their real response political, literary, and psychological to official suppression of their ideas and activity. Using the clandestine printing press and underground networks to propagate illicit literature on a far larger scale than before, intellectually they mounted the most comprehensively subversive and profoundly oppositional campaign the world had thus far (and has perhaps ever) seen.

This enlarged web of radical intellectual subversion in the 1760s was organized in three major interconnected but distinct initiatives. The first focused—with unstinting service from Jaucourt and d'Holbach—on completing the *Encyclopédie*; the second on reviving, codifying, and propagating the texts of all the French, Dutch, and British radical clandestine philosophic literature of the century hitherto down to 1760 in new editions, sometimes creatively edited and reconfigured as well as distributed more widely than earlier; the third, involving all three leaders, was the boldest and most innovative part of the conspiracy. It comprised a series of summing-up, culminating books headed by the *Histoire philosophique*, the *Système*, and Helvétius's long-brooded-over, posthumous reply to his persecutors, his *De l'homme* (1773), presenting a systematic materialist agenda so wide-ranging, innovative, and unsettling as to constitute a truly universal revolution of the mind and re-evaluation of all values.

Diderot and d'Holbach developed a close, at times almost daily, collaboration, each carefully refining his system in relation to the other and also to Helvétius. The latter, having had virtually no contact with these men before 1759, became, despite Voltaire's efforts to lure him away, a regular participant in the *coterie d'Holbachique* during the early 1760s, before leaving for his European tour (1764–5), his interaction with Diderot being significant precisely in the years the *Encyclopédie* was being secretly completed, and then again in the late 1760s.[100] Though simpler, shallower, and cruder, Helvétius's reformism remained broadly in line with theirs and was in some ways more systematic, readily communicated, and innovative—as well as no less contrary to Voltaire's project.

Initial signs that the real struggle between the limited reformism of Voltaire, Frederick, Montesquieu, and Turgot, and the radical 'revolution of the mind', had gone underground and that, far from ending, it was intensifying and spreading onto the international stage, came with the appearance of *Le Christianisme dévoilé*, under the false date '1756', supposedly published at 'Londres' and with Boulanger's name on the title page, but with place, author's name, and date all false. Antedating a work

---

[100] Smith, *Helvétius*, 188–9.

on the title page was a typical ruse of printers of illicit writings. The book was actually printed around 1761 at Nancy where furtive publication was arranged for d'Holbach by Saint-Lambert, an officer in the garrison there.[101] Variously attributed in the 1760s to Diderot, Voltaire, Bolingbroke, Saint-Lambert, Boulanger, and Fréret, it was actually d'Holbach's first major independent text. Originally, the work circulated in Paris in the pockets and baggage of army officers on leave. It argued that Christianity aids only princes devoid of virtue ruling over slaves whom they pillage and tyrannize over 'impunément' in league with priests whose function had always been to deceive men in the name of heaven.[102] Organized religion, asserts *Le Christianisme dévoilé*, is what sustains 'les despotes et les tyrans' in forging the malicious laws underpinning aristocracy and perverting morality and society. Denounced by Voltaire as deeply subversive and politically counter-productive, it reappeared in five underground editions, in 1765, when it began to be widely noticed, and again in 1766 in Holland, and, in 1767, several more times.[103]

Next, also in 1761, supposedly in Holland, but actually at Geneva, followed the *Recherches sur l'origine du despotisme oriental*. This work, published by Gabriel Cramer (Voltaire's publisher), composed originally around 1755, its title page designating its author as Mr. B.I.D.P.E.C., was another major posthumous text by Boulanger. His entire posthumous legacy was edited and supplemented by Diderot's team together with d'Holbach who was not only Boulanger's literary executor but that of virtually the entire pre-1750 radical tradition.[104] The book's exceptionally hard-hitting preface, *Lettre de l'auteur à M.****, addressed to Helvétius, which Voltaire believed (probably correctly) was written by Diderot, was so radical politically as to be expurgated by Cramer from many of the published copies at the request of certain worried 'brothers' in Paris, presumably Helvétius and his wife.[105] The most comprehensively subversive underground publication to appear yet, its publication spurred the Paris police, Diderot noted, to unprecedented efforts at suppression.

Its chief author, the authorities soon discovered, was the deceased Boulanger, a personage 'fort lié avec Mrs Diderot, d'Alembert et Helvétius', the last possessing a manuscript copy in his library.[106] Helvétius was highly nervous for a time lest he be accused of stage-managing its appearance; but the police were soon satisfied that he was not responsible. Conceived by Boulanger as a corrective to Montesquieu, the *Recherches* makes crystal clear that the coming *triomphe de la philosophie*, should the underground Enlightenment prevail, would overturn not just the Church and intolerance but the existing order politically, socially, and in all respects; and not just in Europe, for Boulanger introduced something that soon became a permanent

---

[101] Naville, *Paul Thiry d'Holbach*, 94, 411.

[102] Ibid. 94; d'Holbach, *Christianisme dévoilé*, 162.

[103] D'Holbach, *Christianisme dévoilé*, 7–8; Vercruysse, *Bibliographie* (unpag.); Pappas, *Voltaire and d'Alembert*, 100, 102–3.

[104] Venturi, *L'antichità svelata*, 6–7, 125; Wickwar, *Baron d'Holbach*, 58–9.

[105] Venturi, 'Postille', 233; Pappas, 'Voltaire et la guerre', 534; Israel, *Radical Enlightenment*, 702.

[106] Hampton, *Nicolas-Antoine Boulanger*, 43–4; Venturi, 'Postille', 232.

feature of the post-1770 Radical Enlightenment—its concerted assault also on the imperial structures of Asia and the Americas.[107] The book's notoriety spread rapidly. A clandestine German version appeared at Greifswald in 1767. Abhorred by Voltaire, it was sympathetically received by Herder, who judged the work's openly materialist conception of ancient history intriguing but rejected its denunciation of the great religious leaders as 'swindlers and scoundrels' as too dismissive.[108]

This affair greatly perturbed Voltaire who at once realized the book's divisive effect on the *parti philosophique*. Nothing could more emphatically contradict his strategy of allying with kings and aristocracy against the churches. It depicted kings and priests as eternal accomplices in an ancient, still continuing conspiracy to deceive mankind.[109] The first after Vico and Genovesi to represent human history as a purely natural process, Boulanger envisaged history as a succession of psychological and cultural stages. In the first stage, primitive human government by theocracy predominates and creates despotic systems built on dread of nature's destructive forces whose creator is conceived as an invisible 'sultan' and whose priests are 'les vizirs et les ministres, c'est-à-dire, les despotes réels'.[110] Of all the faults of ancient theocracy, the worst, held Boulanger, was its paving the way for 'oriental despotism' and 'l'horrible servitude qui en fût la suite'.[111] Theocracy not only lies at the origin of despotism but remained indispensable to it, force alone being insufficient for a stable, lasting tyranny. Lasting despotism requires foundations buttressed by priestly sanction.

Nothing could be more insidious nor 'plus maladroit', wrote an alarmed Voltaire to Damilaville, in January 1762, hoping the book would not have the impact he feared.[112] In fact, the work achieved a remarkable penetration for a clandestine text, appearing in six illicit editions between 1761 and 1764 with a further four prior to 1789. Dismissing Boulanger's thesis as mythical and unhistorical, Voltaire, knowing he would pass this on to Diderot and d'Holbach, assured Damilaville that it was vital to eschew all such rhetoric and prove, on the contrary, that priests have always been 'les ennemis des rois', a thesis he shared with Frederick and had often repeated, not least in his *Traité* where he claims over fifty theologians had pronounced it permissible to overthrow or kill sovereigns who defy church doctrines.[113] But here Voltaire fought a losing battle. Not only did Boulanger's argument gain wide exposure but the *anti-philosophes*—and also Hume, observed Bergier—loudly confirmed the radical view. For the *anti-philosophes* too insisted that the clergy is 'plus attaché au gouvernement monarchique' than any other segment of society, while only heretics, innovators, and fanatics of various kinds champion popular sovereignty.[114] Perfectly rightly,

---

[107] Boulanger, *Recherches sur l'origine*, preface pp. vi, ix, xiv.
[108] Herder, *Another Philosophy*, 10.
[109] Ibid. 231; Pappas, 'Voltaire et la guerre', 533–4.
[110] Boulanger, *Recherches sur l'origine*, 150; Venturi, *L'Antichità svelata*, 125–7.
[111] Boulanger, *Recherches sur l'origine*, 151.
[112] Hampton, *Nicolas-Antoine Boulanger*, 46.
[113] Voltaire, *Traité de la tolérance*, 84.
[114] Bergier, *Apologie*, ii. 184.

Boulanger later came to be celebrated as one of the founding prophets of the Revolution. The *Œuvres de Boulanger* were first legally published in two editions in 1791 and 1794.

In 1764 appeared a curious English rendering of Boulanger under the title *The Origin and Progress of Despotism in the Oriental and Other Empires of Africa, Europe and America*, the translator being none other than the English radical John Wilkes (1725–97). Wilkes, who retained Boulanger's teasing sub-title 'this theologico-political research is calculated for an introduction and key to Montesquieu's *Spirit of the Laws*', had known d'Holbach when the two were students together at Leiden, in 1744–6. When Wilkes had to flee to the Continent on being expelled from Parliament and having proceedings for libel opened against him, in 1763, he naturally sought refuge with the 'synagogue d'Holbachique', in Paris.[115] There, he studied radical ideas, met Diderot, and discovered Boulanger, whose work he undertook to translate, little of which passed unnoticed at the British embassy. Wilkes was the sole Englishman 'of rank and condition in this place to the number of seventy persons', noted Hume, now acting secretary responsible for organizing official receptions, not invited to the embassy dinner on 4 June 1764 to mark George III's birthday.[116]

No less than in the 1720s, 1730s, and 1740s, the clandestine character of such works remained fundamental. However, the mechanics of diffusion and social significance of this new wave of clandestine philosophical literature differed considerably from those of the early eighteenth century. Underground Enlightenment had ceased to be just a matter of circulating tiny quantities of manuscripts and a few printed copies. Legal and open methods of expression encountering only repression and humiliation as soon as any hint of criticism or opposition to the existing order was expressed, publishing anonymous works clandestinely and distributing them 'under the cloak' had become the only viable alternative and something highly effective in propagating reformist and critical notions. The most paradoxical aspect of this process of radical subversion during the 1760s was that this type of Enlightenment needed to be and remained illicit and clandestine and yet, owing to improved distribution techniques, the growth in oppositional sentiment, and the wide impact of *anti-philosophie*, as well as the futility of open criticism, nevertheless produced works that came to be very widely read and publicized.

Compared with the pre-1759 phenomenon, the intellectual underground of the 1760s was, therefore, an incomparably larger and socially broader process. Far greater numbers of pedlars, *colporteurs*, and petty dealers were involved, even if they were not necessarily taking fewer risks than in the past or exposed to less danger. Bookshop owners in France during the 1760s and 1770s did not dare to stock prohibited works 'under the counter', or anywhere on their premises. There were too many searches and too much police surveillance for that. Stocks of clandestine literature were kept in special caches and distributed through Paris (as also Amsterdam) in the streets and

---

[115] Naville, *Paul Thiry d'Holbach*, 90; Trousson, *Denis Diderot*, 379, 488.
[116] Mossner, *Life of David Hume*, 491.

taverns literally 'under the cloak' by *colporteurs*.[117] What had changed was the scale of the operation, the quantities involved, its geographical spread, and the much greater penetration of forbidden texts and ideas feeding into general debate.

A connected phenomenon is that opponents of the radical underground now abandoned their former policy of ignoring clandestine writings as if they did not exist, or were so shocking to respectable opinion that they need not be addressed. A growing realization that the strategy of silence could not prevent such writings being increasingly diffused, and greater awareness of the cultural consequences of allowing radical concepts to penetrate unopposed, led to the abandonment of the older practice. Diderot's anonymously published *Pensées philosophiques* seems to have triggered this transition to an open, public one-sided contest, with the underground remaining gagged and the condemnation being public. From the late 1740s, opponents began reacting to the challenge frequently and explicitly in print. Unlike earlier clandestine texts, and despite the booklet having been publicly condemned and hard to find, this text provoked a prolonged public debate continuing through the 1750s. This was because it proved useful to the *anti-philosophes* as ammunition with which to combat the *Encyclopédie*, but also partly due to a feeling that its exceptional eloquence had to be countered publicly.

Among the first refutations, the anonymously published 251-page *Pensées chrétiennes mises en parallèle, ou en opposition avec les* Pensées philosophiques (Rouen, 1747) went so far as to reproduce virtually the entire forbidden text, its author, Georges Polier de Bottens, justifying this by noting that such works were being read with much 'empressement et quelque sorte d'approbation de plusieurs personnes'. His adversary's text was 'vif, energétique et enjoué' and from the same pen, seemingly, as rendered Shaftesbury's thought into excellent French 'mais d'une manière très-inexacte et fort libre'.[118] Another *anti-philosophe*, Daniel Le Masson des Granges (1706–66), dedicating his work to the dauphin, denounced the *Pensées'* author— without citing Diderot's name—as 'le Déiste le plus audacieux de nos jours'.[119] Multiple printed refutations, often far larger than the original, reproducing major chunks of his text, and thus totally negating the aim of the ban, appeared in Holland, France, and Switzerland. A hidden psychological motive, undoubtedly, was a growing need among key intellectuals and churchmen to convince themselves of the truth, silencing inner doubts and embarrassment at being drawn into such a debate.

By the 1760s, the radical *philosophes'* foes felt there were no longer any grounds for ignoring clandestine writings whether new or dating from the pre-1750 era. Rather, since these texts were constantly reappearing in multiple clandestine formats and editions, there were now more and more cogent reasons to pillory them. Chaudon's *Dictionnaire anti-philosophique* (2 vols., Avignon, 1769), discussing the *Lettre de Thrasybule* and the *Examen critique des apologistes*, both attributed to Fréret,

---

[117] Belin, *Commerce des livres*, 78.
[118] [Polier de Bottens], *Pensées chrétiennes*, preface pp. A3, 4ᵛ, and 32.
[119] Le Masson des Granges, *Philosophe moderne*, 14, 29–30.

acknowledges they had previously circulated over many years without attracting much attention, doing so, though, only in tiny quantity, unknown mostly even to experts. Now they had become familiar; and of all the books written against religion today 'en si grand nombre', the *Examen*, published in 1766 (with 1767 on the title page), was among the likeliest to sway readers, a judgement Voltaire endorsed, noting that in the French provinces it was circulating fairly freely.[120]

A new cultural mechanics was at work stimulating both production of texts and growth of readership to the point that, by the mid 1760s, large-scale proliferation in print in rapid sequences of multiple editions had become commercially feasible. It was almost as if, starting, tentatively at first, soon after the *Encyclopédie*'s suppression, in 1759, this clandestinely concerted operation was a psychologically conscious retaliation against a system intent on eradicating thinking inherent in any thoughtful opposition. The result was a powerful surge in clandestine editions of forbidden texts and their distribution followed by a steep further escalation in the 1770s, especially in France, Holland, Germany, and Switzerland. Just as much as the shockingly impious libels ceaselessly produced, another well-known *anti-philosophe*, Dom Nicolas Jamin (1711–82), writing in 1768, decried the 'avidity' with which on all sides they were being sought and read.[121]

Perceptions of what was 'illicit' were shifting. Books one would have hesitated to confide to friends, in manuscript, forty years ago, commented Voltaire in October 1765, were now almost commonplace, continually cropping up on all sides, sometimes in six editions in eighteen months. Their messages, consequently, were far more directly and widely expounded than in the past, the old circumlocutions, allusion, and evasion going distinctly out of fashion. Bayle, remarked Voltaire, seems today 'beaucoup trop timide'.[122] Overall, the phenomenon reflected a marked shift from manuscript to printed, furtively private to virtually public, and from a hinted, semi-concealed to an openly proclaimed subversion. The burgeoning market for illicit books well supplied with printed texts previously long circulating in manuscript increasingly also offered new productions (sometimes including older material) by authors concealing their identities, both categories appearing under false names, intriguing initials, or no author's name at all, usually giving false places and, often, wrong publication dates.

The sheer quantity of illicit literature flooding the market was breathtaking. In 1764 appeared the *Dissertation sur Élie et Énoch*, a work attributed to Boulanger but probably touched up by d'Holbach, in four illicit editions, followed by the *Examen important de Mylord Bolingbroke* printed together with the *Analyse de la religion chrétienne*—attributed by Voltaire to Du Marsais—in a collection entitled *Recueil nécessaire* ('à Leipsik', 1765), actually published in Geneva. Next came *L'Antiquité*

---

[120] Chaudon, *Dictionnaire anti-philosophique*, 182; Voltaire to Comte and Comtesse d'Argental, 22 June 1766, in Voltaire, *Corr.* xxx. 277.

[121] Jamin, *Pensées théologiques*, preface p. xviii.

[122] Voltaire to d'Alembert, 16 Oct. 1765, in Voltaire, *Corr.* xxviii. 345.

dévoilée (1765–6), another item attributed to Boulanger but enhanced by d'Holbach, and the *Examen critique des apologistes de la religion chrétienne* (1766), today thought to be by Jean Lévesque de Burigny, stressing the divisions among the early Christians, 'un excellent livre', noted Voltaire, full of 'recherches curieuses et de raisonnements vigoureux'.[123] Scarcely a month passes, he noted in September 1766, when there does not appear in Holland either some 'excellent work' of Fréret or a less fine but still good one by Boulanger, or another 'éloquent et terrible de Bolingbroke', or something by de Maillet.[124]

Next appeared a fresh edition of the *Le Christianisme dévoilé* (1767), followed by the *De l'imposture sacerdotale ou recueil de pièces sur le clergé* ('Londres' [Amsterdam], 1767) and *L'Esprit du clergé* (1767), all by d'Holbach, and *L'Analyse du Traité théologico-politique de Spinosa* (1767) by Boulainvilliers, a work, we know from Diderot, that had exerted a particularly powerful impact on the young d'Holbach.[125] This was followed by Boulanger's *Dissertation sur saint Pierre* (1767), and *Les Prêtres démasqués* printed supposedly 'à Londres' but actually, like many of these texts, by Marc-Michel Rey, in Amsterdam, and the *Théologie portative, ou Dictionnaire abrégé de la religion chrétienne* (1767), reviewing the major Christian dogmas using a system of cross-referencing attributing everything to the interest of the clergy, sarcastically attributed to the 'Abbé Bernier', followed by d'Holbach's *Lettres à Eugénie ou Préservatif contre les préjugés* ('à Londres', 1768), a blistering attack on traditional female piety, pleading for 'la morale de la raison' to be embraced as the true 'natural religion'.[126] Next came the *Lettre de Thrasybule à Leucippe* (1768), edited by d'Holbach with Naigeon, announced as an 'ouvrage posthume de M.F.' and today mostly assigned to Fréret; a fresh edition of the *Traité des trois imposteurs* (1768), *La Contagion sacrée ou histoire naturelle de la superstition* ('Londres', 1768), again by d'Holbach, and a fragment of Collins entitled *Examen des prophéties qui servent de fondement à la religion* (1768).

The bombardment continued with *La Vie de David* (1768), a reworked 'translation' of an obscure English text based on Bayle's notorious *Dictionnaire* entry about David, styling him the 'Nero of the Hebrews' and worst of rulers whom 'priests' have the effrontery to present as a model prince,[127] and the notorious *Le Militaire philosophe* (1768), an early eighteenth-century tract by Robert Challe extensively reworked by Naigeon, among the most widely read of all these productions. It is the Baron d'Holbach, wrote Voltaire to Damilaville in April 1768, who brings all these *rogatons* [scraps] from Holland. A regular member of d'Holbach's dinner circle and one of both Voltaire's and Diderot's intimate friends, until he died of cancer in 1769, Damilaville was Voltaire's most regular link to the Paris underground in the 1760s. On several occasions Voltaire asked him to ensure none of the conspirators attributed

[123] Voltaire to Thieriot, 31 July 1766, ibid. xxx. 356; Laulannier, *Essais*, 162–3.
[124] Voltaire to d'Argental, 26 Sept. 1766, in Voltaire, *Corr.* xx. 466.
[125] Pecharroman, *Morals*, 12.
[126] D'Holbach, *Lettres à Eugénie*, 188–9, 216–20; Wickwar, *Baron d'Holbach*, 78.
[127] *David, ou l'histoire de l'homme*, 70, 76; Pecharroman, *Morals*, 131.

any of their productions to him.[128] After his death, sorely missed by Voltaire and Diderot alike, Damilaville was fondly recalled by a lady friend whom he converted to a 'philosophique' outlook whilst she was still very young as 'vraiment philosophe, et grand ennemi du fanatisme'.[129]

Confusingly for librarians and bibliographers still today, many of these offerings entered circulation either after, or prior to, the stated dates on their title pages. It rains texts 'sans nombre contre l'infâme', exclaimed d'Alembert in September 1767, listing *L'Esprit du clergé*, *Les Prêtres démasqués*, the *Théologie portative*, and *Le Militaire philosophe*, the last of which, however, gives '1768' on its title page.[130] Every week, remarked Voltaire in January 1769, surfaces another work of this sort, printed in Holland.[131] It was indeed not Switzerland (as is often claimed) but the Netherlands that remained the prime centre of production, Switzerland's role being secondary. The torrent continued with the *L'Enfer détruit, ou Examen raisonné du dogme de l'éternité des peines* ('à Londres' [Amsterdam], 1769), a work congratulating the Unitarians for discrediting belief in Hell, recommending Naigeon's scintillating article 'Unitaires' in the *Encyclopédie*, and proclaiming the ineffectiveness of threatening punishment in another life, even among the faithful.[132] These were followed by the *Examen critique de la vie et des écrits de saint Paul* (1770), attributed on its title page to Boulanger but actually by d'Holbach, and *L'Esprit du judaïsme* (1770), attributed to Collins but revised by d'Holbach. Another extremely seditious text was the *Histoire critique de Jésus-Christ*, banned at the request of the *consistoire* at Geneva on 26 March 1772, dating from 1770. While the world is full of professed 'Christians', claimed this text, scarcely any, paradoxically, possess even the slightest knowledge of their religion's origins, texts, key concepts, or early history.[133]

By the late 1760s, the outpouring of irreligious texts swelled to such levels that even Voltaire and d'Alembert could no longer keep up. It is raining bombs 'dans la maison du Seigneur', exclaimed Diderot in November 1768, listing the recently appeared *Lettres à Eugénie*, *La Contagion sacrée*, *L'Examen des prophéties*, and *Vie de David* and expressing concern lest one or more of the intrepid 'artillery-men' responsible for this magnificent bombardment fall into the authorities' hands.[134] Plainly, there was a dialectical connection between the 'intolérance du gouvernement', as Diderot put it, increasing from day to day, and the rising tide of illicit literature and its high status in the Paris cafés where speculation as to who was behind it all became an ever livelier topic. All this made Voltaire increasingly anxious. His chief concern, he assured Marc-Michel Rey in February 1769, was to prevent his

---

[128] Voltaire to Damilaville, 11 Apr. 1768, in Voltaire, *Corr.* xxxiii. 245–6; Sandrier, *Style philosophique*, 88.
[129] Madame Le Glaive Duclos to Voltaire, 26 Jan. 1769, in Voltaire, *Corr.* xxxv. 264.
[130] Pappas, *Voltaire et d'Alembert*, 103.
[131] Voltaire to d'Alembert, 13 Jan. 1769, in Voltaire, *Corr.* xxxiv. 243.
[132] *L'Enfer détruit*, 64–7, 84; Naville, *Paul Thiry d'Holbach*, 416.
[133] [D'Holbach], *Histoire critique*, preface p. 1; Voltaire, *Corr.* xxxviii. 484.
[134] Naville, *Paul Thiry d'Holbach*, 96; Trousson, *Denis Diderot*, 419.

name figuring in the ceaseless talk as to who the principal perpetrators of the conspiracy were.[135]

What occurred was a quantitative and also ideological shift. *Voltaireanisme* by the late 1760s, or what Fréron called 'les spécieux systèmes du déisme', was fast becoming marginalized. Despite the ban on the *Encyclopédie*, and stepped-up activities of the Paris police, Voltaire found himself being eclipsed by a 'silent revolution' driving a sea-change in the intellectual climate. His deism, deference to courts, veneration of Locke, and 'English ideas', partly thwarted by French royal policy, were being simultaneously rebuffed also by atheism, materialism, anti-absolutism, and one-substance doctrine. Here was a 'revolution of the mind' engineered by two active agents on the surface entirely opposing each other: a radical underground, on one side, and on the other a veritable army of royally backed *anti-philosophes* eager to overwhelm what they too now judged the primary threat to the existing order.

---

[135] Voltaire to Marc-Michel Rey, 7 Feb. 1769, in Voltaire, *Corr.* xxxiv. 285.

6

Anti-philosophes

1. *ANTI-PHILOSOPHIE* AS A CULTURAL FORCE

Anti-philosophie so-called was a powerful cultural movement of the eighteenth century, albeit one remarkably neglected by modern historians. A broad social and cultural response, emotional and psychological as much as intellectual, to the non-religious Enlightenment—deism, scepticism, and atheism (whether moderate or radical)—this was a phenomenon that spread right across both Catholic and Protestant Europe. Although rooted chiefly in French Catholic apologetics and primarily appearing in French to begin with, the rapidity with which its main titles reappeared in Italian, Spanish, German, and English translation, and eventually sometimes also Russian and Polish, rendered it, however problematic its effectiveness as an antidote to irreligion, pivotal as an agent of diffusion of key Enlightenment debates.[1]

Anti-philosophie generated an impressive phalanx of writers. Originally, in the 1750s, according to the Spanish enlightener Almodóvar, Thomas-Jean Pichon, a canon of the royal chapel at Le Mans, sarcastically dubbed by Morellet 'general' of the 'armée anti-Encyclopédiste', and his 'lieutenant-general', Jean-Nicolas-Hubert Hayer (1708–80), a Franciscan recollect from Saarlouis, figured 'among the most fervent defenders of the true religion' in France.[2] Later, Pichon and Hayer receded and new names came to the fore. Among the best-known *anti-philosophes*, remarked Condorcet, writing to Turgot in May 1774, were Nonnotte, Patouillet—compiler of a dictionary of Jansenist books—Bergier, Boscovich, and Caveirac.[3] The last was a notorious hard-liner for whom the Revocation of the Edict of Nantes (1685) did no harm to French society, a Counter-Enlightenment ideologue who considered toleration intrinsically harmful.[4] But such militantly anti-Enlightenment voices were very much in the background at this time and uncharacteristic of mainstream *anti-philosophie*.[5] Mostly its spokesmen were either genuinely men of the religious Enlightenment or at least, like the author of *Les*

---

[1] Butterwick, 'Provincial Preachers', 205.
[2] *La France littéraire*, i. 364; Almodóvar, *Década*, 135–6; Condorcet, *Œuvres*, x. 39.
[3] *Correspondance inédite de Condorcet*, 174.
[4] Caveirac, *L'Accord de la religion*, 60, 97; Almodóvar, *Década*, 127; Condorcet, *Lettre à M. l'Abbé* in *Œuvres*, i. 315; Masseau, *Ennemis*, 253.
[5] Voltaire, *Questions*, iii. 225 and ix. 210.

Erreurs de Voltaire (1762), the Jesuit polemicist Claude-François Nonnotte (1711–93), publicists prepared to dispute mainly in terms of philosophical arguments.

The personages cited by Morellet and Condorcet, though, were just a small sprinkling. A reasonably comprehensive list of the more eminent *anti-philosophes* would include, besides these, at the very least also François, Guyon, Pluquet, Soret, Marin, Maleville, Gauchat, Camuset, Jamin, Chaudon, Crillon, Le Masson des Granges, Sabatier de Castres, Barruel, Paulian, Lamourette, the Jesuits Henri Griffet and Francois-Xavier Feller, Caraccioli, and Madame de Genlis, besides François Marie Coger, another Jesuit roughly handled by Voltaire, author of the *Dictionnaire antiphilosophique* of 1767. Coger, who led the assault on Marmontel's *Bélisaire*, was professor of eloquence at the Collège Mazarin in Paris.[6] Stéphanie-Félicité, Comtesse de Genlis (1746–1830), the largely self-taught author of *La Religion considérée comme l'unique base de bonheur et de la véritable philosophie* (Paris, 1787), figured among the century's foremost female writers and was a leading *salonnière*.[7] Gauchat wrote the *Lettres critiques*, an undertaking, claimed his publisher in 1759, eclipsing in scale all other *anti-philosophique* projects: for while Hayer's *La Religion vengée*, published at the rate of three volumes yearly in instalments from 1757 to 1763, totalling twenty-one volumes, surpassed Gauchat's nineteen volumes in size, it was produced by a veritable *société de gens de lettres* whereas Gauchat composed his all on his own.[8]

Laurent François (1698–1782) figured among the few *anti-philosophes* active in the 1750s still prominent in the 1770s. A Lazarist priest who wrote the *Preuves de la religion de Jésus-Christ contre les Spinosistes et les Déistes* (4 vols., 1751), a major work reissued a quarter of a century later in 1784, and an attack on Voltaire, the *Observations sur la* Philosophie de l'histoire *et le* Dictionnaire philosophique (2 vols., Paris, 1770), he also published a rebuttal of Rousseau in 1764, and a general three-volume work assailing *les athées, les matérialistes et les fatalistes* (1767).[9] While several ancient philosophers stood behind the basic concepts of *la philosophie nouvelle*, especially the idea there is no God other than the universe, the principal modern thinker inspiring the post-1750 tidal wave of incredulity and irreligion, he thought, was Spinoza.[10] In effect, Spinoza's system had become the creed of the *impies* of his time. Since the *philosophes* were constantly proclaiming 'le tout', 'le grand tout', 'la nécessité naturelle', 'la nature', 'l'ordre de la nature', they were rightly designated *naturalistes*. But Spinoza, he contends, provided their main metaphysical frame.[11] He encountered difficulty, though, in plausibly connecting Voltaire with such naturalism. Readers should not be misled by the seemingly substantial differences between deism and materialism, he urges, for it is not their positive doctrines that chiefly distinguish the irreligious thinkers. Rather they were all united in opposing faith, piety, and eccle-

---

[6] [Sabatier de Castres], *Tableau philosophique*, 235; Everdell, *Christian Apologetics*, 45–6.
[7] Goodman, *Republic*, 77–8, 104; de Poortere, *Idées philosophiques*, 11–13.
[8] *Lettre au R. P. Berthier sur le matérialisme*, 31–2.
[9] Almodovar, *Década*, 128.   [10] François, *Preuves*, pp. i, 28.   [11] Ibid.

siastical authority. 'Le plan de la secte est un: c'est de tout détruire sans rien édifier.'[12] This would be a theme loudly echoed in 1786 by Adrien Lamourette (1742–94), an *anti-philosophe* especially insistent on the revolutionary implications of *la philosophie*: 'le vrai dessein de la philosophie est de tout bouleverser.'[13]

A Protestant as well as a Catholic movement, *anti-philosophie* included Swiss and German as well as French writers, and where purely Catholic showed an impressive willingness to acknowledge and utilize Protestant authorities. It drew extensively on Locke, Clarke, Abbadie, and Le Clerc. Chaudon declared his own intellectual lineage to reach back to Grotius and Abbadie as well as Locke while the Abbé Nicolas-Sylvestre Bergier (1718–90), who has been termed the 'most prominent champion of Catholicism in the latter half of the century',[14] praises Le Clerc with a warmth inconceivable even a few years earlier.[15] Among Reformed *anti-philosophique* authors writing in French were Geneva's presiding theologian mauled by Voltaire and d'Alembert in 1757–9, Jacob Vernet (1698–1789), and also Jacob Vernes, editor of the Genevan journal *Choix littéraire* (24 vols., 1755–60). Vernet, a pillar of Swiss 'enlightened orthodoxy' and author of the *Lettres critiques d'un voyageur anglois* (1766), was no less ardent an Anglophile and disciple of Locke and Newton than Voltaire though this did not prevent the latter styling him a 'hypocrite' and 'magot' [a kind of ape].

Locke's conception of the mind as something separate from the body, a passive, basically empty slate, was adopted by the *anti-philosophes* as the most vital barrier to theories that the soul, and human understanding, can be deemed material. Locke's philosophy, they contend, is always 'diamétricalement opposée' to that of our 'philosophes modernes'.[16] Locke judged it as much beyond the capacity of movement in matter to produce thought or knowledge, explained Nonnotte, whose *Erreurs* enjoyed considerable success with eight French editions by 1787, and several translations, including by 1780 Polish, as it is beyond the capacity of nothingness to produce matter.[17] Not all commentators today agree that Locke's empiricism, correctly understood, does actually block materialism and 'thinking matter' but this was certainly the general view at the time (and Voltaire's opinion), and the *anti-philosophes* continually deployed this argument against the *incrédules*. Despite his Catholic bias, Nonnotte was judged by the Protestant enlightener Haller to be fully justified in his account of Locke and assaults on Voltaire. *Anti-philosophes* ceaselessly praised Locke and Newton, proclaiming these great figures implacable adversaries of Diderot, Voltaire, Helvétius, and the *Système de la nature*.[18]

---

[12] François, *Observations*, 120–1.
[13] Lamourette, *Pensées*, 92.
[14] Palmer, *Catholics and Unbelievers*, 46.
[15] Bergier, *Grands Hommes vengés*, ii. 84.
[16] Maleville, *Religion naturelle*, iii. 292; [Crillon], *Mémoires philosophiques*, ii. 49.
[17] Nonnotte, *Dictionnaire philosophique*, 364; Haller, *Tagebuch*, i. 271.
[18] Marin, *Baron Van-Hesden*, iii. 47, 54–6, 308, 377–8, 384, 394; Maleville, *Religion naturelle*, i, preface pp. xlviii and iii. 292–3; Chaudon, *Dictionnaire anti-philosophique*, i. 259 and iv. 21; Barruel, *Les Helviennes*, ii. 205, 269–70; Nonnotte, *Dictionnaire philosophique*, 352, 364.

An admirer also of Samuel Clarke, Vernet advocated an enlightened and rational Christianity, grounded on the toleration of the 'judicieux Locke', that is a toleration truly bounded by and based on Christian principles and supporting Christian values. This was something he rigorously differentiated from the *tolérantisme universel* of the *encyclopédistes* based on *principes philosophiques* or what he too disparagingly calls *philosophisme*, an argument in which he was followed by others.[19] Among the most insidious strategies employed by philosophical subversion to undermine the social order, held Hayer, is 'l'esprit de Tolérantisme' championing a comprehensive toleration (not like that of Locke but like that of Bayle), a technique enabling the *encyclopédistes* to blacken upholders of religious values as 'perturbateurs du repos public', as Diderot and d'Holbach did routinely.[20] 'Voltaire', protested Madame de Genlis, in her best-selling attack on 'modern philosophy' of 1787, issued also in English the same year entitled *Religion Considered as the Only Basis of Happiness and True Philosophy* (2 vols., Dublin, 1787), falsely attributes to Locke 'opinions upon universal tolerance, absolutely contrary to those of that philosopher'.[21] Locke's epistemology and toleration was vital to the *anti-philosophes* and so was his endorsement of miracles and revelation. The *anti-philosophes* claimed to be more faithful guardians of Locke's legacy than their *philosophe* adversaries and in a way they were. The key to an *anti-philosophique* victory on an enlightened basis was a restricted reason and toleration inseparably linked to faith. Locke's epistemology and toleration was their corner-stone.

Neither Voltaire nor the radical stream considered Vernet's stance coherent or honest. That Vernet's toleration and Vernes's was false and hypocritical, contends Naigeon, in the *Encyclopédie*, emerges plainly from the lack of charity in their remarks about Socinians, the most hounded but also most rational of the Christian sects (with whom secretly they agreed).[22] Vernet's Enlightenment typified the moderate mainstream in venerating Locke, limited toleration, and also in seeking to avoid suggesting Geneva's republicanism was in any way a destabilizing, non-subservient factor in the political world of their day. There is no inherent, built-in tendency towards republicanism in Calvin's theology or the Reformed Church, insists Vernet, and especially not of the subversive kind pervading *la philosophie nouvelle*. Rather, Calvinist preachers always teach unquestioning deference to authority whether monarchical or oligarchic.[23] Reformed doctrine teaches submission and had always sanctioned the conservative pro-patrician, anti-democratic stance in Geneva's fraught local politics.[24] Calvinist pastors were equally deferential to oligarchy in the neighbouring patrician republics of Zurich and Berne.

[19] Vernet, *Lettres critiques*, i. 128, 146, 161–6.
[20] Hayer, *La Religion vengée*, v. 57, 98–102, 116.
[21] Ibid. ii. 14, 113, 116.
[22] Naigeon, 'Unitaires', 387–8.
[23] Hayer, *La Religion vengée*, ii. 160.
[24] Rosenblatt, *Rousseau*, 155–7.

Another typical feature of both the Catholic and Protestant wings of *anti-philosophie* was a tendency to eulogize the English for having found the true path in philosophy and science. Bacon, Locke, and Newton being the figures from whom the *anti-philosophes* drew their best arguments against the *nouveaux philosophes*, the background from which they came was also eulogized. The *nouveaux philosophes*, objected Bergier, claimed to be empiricists, basing their arguments on experience and observation, but yet entirely forsook that intellectual caution and modesty so characteristic of Locke and Newton, adopting instead a confident *hubris* typical of Spinoza, believing reason could penetrate to the first principles of things.[25] Strange and paradoxical though unbounded *anglomanie* might seem on the lips of French Catholic theologians, *anti-philosophes* frequently expressed intense admiration for the English as a people. Were not the English less prone than the French to be lured into atheism, materialism, and *l'esprit philosophique*? The Provençal Benedictine Dom Mayeul Chaudon (1737–1817) lauded English good sense to the skies. Englishmen were a more sensible, sounder people than the French and their Lockean philosophy and Newtonian science were the proof.[26]

Anti-philosophie synthesized Catholic and Protestant theological and scientific-philosophical arguments and also collated the literary efforts of the clergy and laity in new ways, the lay category comprising several of the ablest *anti-philosophique* writers, among them Soret, Fréron, Palissot, Caraccioli, Madame de Genlis, and the Montauban magistrate Le Franc de Pompignan. Le Franc sought an accommodation between piety and the increasingly secular world of French theatre and literature,[27] a quest lauded in Chaudon's *Grands Hommes vengés* (2 vols., Paris, 1769), a compendium rescuing the reputations of various writers and scholars ruthlessly mauled by the *philosophes* but considered praiseworthy by the clergy. In championing Le Franc against Voltaire's gibes, Chaudon styles him a fine French *littérateur* and poet, who courageously defended the 'cause of God' in his celebrated address before France's most august literary body, the Académie Française. On that occasion, citing Maupertuis's reversion to Catholic piety in his last years, and claiming only the 'virtuous and Christian sage' truly merits being called a *philosophe*, Le Franc denounced the *Encyclopédie* as a 'fausse philosophie' replete with infamous teachings 'qui frappe également le trône et l'autel', a 'monstrueuse philosophie', propagating among men not happiness but only strife, the ugliness of its maxims being abundantly illustrated by the immorality of its spokesmen.[28]

If Le Franc was the most eloquent, the most prolific lay *anti-philosophe* was Marquis Louis-Antoine Caraccioli (1719–1803), an impoverished purported 'noble' who earned his keep producing an astounding number of works of pious polemic. Among the most widely read of the *anti-philosophes* in French, Italian, and

---

[25] Citton, *L'Envers*, 248–50, 259.

[26] Chaudon, *Dictionnaire anti-philosophique*, i. 43, 47.

[27] Le Franc de Pompignan, 'Discours', 45, 55, 61; Almodóvar, *Década*, 131–2; McManners, *Church and Society*, ii. 328–9.

[28] Bergier, *Grands Hommes vengés*, i. 106, 110–13.

Spanish alike, Caraccioli especially stressed the Catholic Enlightenment's need to prevent the *philosophes* wholly appropriating the principles of toleration and reason.[29] It was the affectation of our 'beaux esprits' continually to exalt 'reason', he observes in the preface of his *Le Langage de la raison* (Paris, 1764). His aim in that work was to prove one cannot be 'vraiment raisonnable' without being a Christian.[30] Even if not properly a nobleman himself, he was simultaneously the *ancien régime's* most adamant 'philosophical' defender of nobility as a fundamental component of society.

Anti-philosophes lay and clerical, Catholic and Protestant, male and female, were adamant as to the basically rational character of Christianity and constantly emphasized the need to rest their claims on the most up-to-date science and philosophy. Newton's authority was constantly invoked not least by Bergier in his *Examen du matérialisme* (1771), where he explains Newton's conception of gravity as a non-mechanistic, supernatural force and the Newtonian thesis that movement cannot be innate in matter, deeming the author of the *Système de la nature's* attempt to argue against these principles a veritable affront to reason. According to that seditious author (d'Holbach), there cannot be anything in nature other than 'des causes et effets naturels', a view, holds Bergier, not just ungodly but totally un-Newtonian and out of line with recent discoveries in science.[31] When assailing the libertines and *matérialistes*, Bergier, Caraccioli, Chaudon, and the others continually stress the need for a moderate path harmonizing theology with philosophy, science, and toleration, to turn reason's instruments against 'ces Aretins insolens', expounding *la philosophie nouvelle*.[32]

Materialism to the *anti-philosophes* was a dogma as false as it was dangerous.[33] Chaudon's primary aim, he explains, was to unite the efforts of Protestants and Catholics with Locke's empiricism and Newton's physics to ground the most cogent, up-to-date defence of religion possible and especially of belief in creation, revelation, miracles, prophecy, Heaven and Hell, angels, spirits, demonology, exorcism, and other notions fundamental to Christianity. These were indispensable tenets not just for Christians but all adherents of all organized religions, being espoused likewise by Muslims, Jews, and the ancient pagans. One could dispute perhaps whether *anti-philosophes* were as up to date as they claimed to be. Bergier was scorned by Naigeon as a mere transcriber of Grotius, Abbadie, Clarke, Jaquelot, Bernard, Le Clerc, Mauduit, and Sherlock, echoing platitudes an 'infinity of other theologians' had uttered before.[34] But none could question his resolve to reconcile theology with enlightened philosophy and forge a true path of moderation.

---

[29] Palmer, *Catholics and Unbelievers*, 181; Masseau, *Ennemis*, 278; Sánchez-Blanco, *Absolutismo*, 123.
[30] Caraccioli, *Langage*, avant-propos, p. vi.
[31] Bergier, *Examen du matérialisme*, i. 27–8, 70; Cristani, *D'Holbach*, 149–51.
[32] Chaudon, *Dictionnaire anti-philosophique*, i, pp. iv–vi; Pascal, 'Diderot', 100.
[33] Caraccioli, *Langage*, 10.
[34] Naigeon, *Adresse à l'Assemblée Nationale*, 96–7.

The *anti-philosophes'* purpose was not to marginalize 'reason' in favour of simplicity of heart and sentiment, like the Counter-Enlightenment, but capture 'reason' for their camp. This tactic is adopted by François, Maleveille, Pichon, Marin, Bergier, Lamourette, Genlis, indeed nearly all these writers. Remote from Counter-Enlightenment especially in claiming theirs is adequate, consequent philosophical reason while that of the *philosophes* is not, *anti-philosophes* denied the so-called 'reason' of the *philosophes modernes* is truly 'reason' at all. In this way, they helped solidify the religious Enlightenment. To them, it was the *encyclopédistes* who violate 'reason': 'mais le fanatisme philosophique', exclaims Bergier, is blind, 'incapable de raisonner'.[35] The *anti-philosophes* saw themselves as the true party of 'reason' and the *philosophes*, for all their talk of reason, as that of unreason. Christianity's 'mysteries', claim the 'sect of the *philosophes modernes*', contradict 'reason' and the *anti-philosophes* affront 'reason'. What we reject, retorts Jamin, is only the arrogant, overarching 'reason' of Bayle, Voltaire, and Rousseau. We do not deprecate 'reason' or what is reasonable considered in itself.[36] This sounded all the more plausible in that the erudite journals published in France, like the *Journal des sçavans*, before 1788–9 mostly backed the *anti-philosophes* against the 'la secte des incrédules'. Locke and Newton were, for them, the supreme arbiters showing how to 'reason' correctly and that reason is not man's sole guide. Is our reason 'un si bon guide qu'elle seule nous suffise toujours'?[37] Assuredly not, answers Marin; but reason provides a useful guide for examining the *matérialistes'* philosophical claims. Diderot's tirades against faith and the Church he tests by Diderot's own criteria. What emerges from examining the *Pensées philosophiques* is that their author could not coherently order his thoughts. Doubtless, he knew the loose format he chose helps hide the contradictions and 'absurdities' of which his writings are full.[38]

The 'reason' of 'true philosophers'—whom Stéphanie-Felicité refused to confound 'with those perverse men, who have written with so much audacity against religion, government and morals'—is balanced, sensible, and, unlike that of *la philosphie moderne*, fully keeps abreast of the sciences. 'Philosophers, struck with the harmony of the universe, and the admirable laws of providence, have maintained, that nothing could be better and more perfect than the order of things which exist.'[39] Amongst these 'virtuous philosophers, who made the maxims of the gospel the basis of their morality', she lists her heroes—'Fénelon, Nicole, Pascal, Abbadie, Massillon, Addison, Clarke, Richardson, etc.'[40] Scornful that Voltaire, 'in order to give more weight to his opinions', should falsely, as she saw it, include among those justifying his ideas 'the learned Le Clerc', she, on the contrary, maintained that Le Clerc was foremost

---

[35] Bergier, *Examen du matérialisme*, ii. 424; Nonnotte, *Dictionnaire philosophique*, 522–36; Paulian, *Véritable Système*, ii. 95.
[36] Jamin, *Pensées théologiques*, 219; Chopelin-Blanc, *De l'apologétique*, 219–21.
[37] Bergier, *Examen du matérialisme*, i, preface p. xv.
[38] Ibid. i, preface pp. xvi–xviii, xxii–xxiii; Trousson, 'Michel-Ange Marin', 52–3.
[39] Genlis, *Religion*, i, preface, pp. xii and 5.
[40] Ibid. ii. 3–4.

among those who defend 'the good cause'. Still more crucial, it is always 'the wise Locke', a great hero of hers, who one should adhere to. *Anti-philosophes*, in emphatically embracing 'reason', defined reason's scope with greater rigour than the Huguenot *rationaux* who were their nearest predecessors and in so doing, as we have seen, continually employed Locke's empiricism to delimit reason and defend revelation, Christian salvation, and miracles in particular.[41]

Connected with their stress on 'true reason' was *anti-philosophie*'s disputing with the *philosophes* the true character of 'fanaticism'. In the quarrel between *philosophes* and *anti-philosophes* over toleration and intolerance, Christian apologists were continually (and often unfairly) accused of being dangerous 'fanatics'. The charge of 'fanaticism' was now vigorously thrown back in the *philosophes*' faces. If in his *Questions sur l'Encyclopédie* (1771–4) Voltaire justifiably labels Caveirac a bigoted 'fanatic' and had some reason for linking Patouillet, Chaudon, Nonnotte, Feller, and Guyon to 'fanaticism', he grotesquely exaggerated in suggesting they were capable, were there ever another St Bartholomew's Day, of perpetrating 'de grandes choses' of the most hideous and bloodthirsty nature.[42] Such talk, replied the *anti-philosophes*, was nonsense. 'Les nouveaux philosophes', averred the anti-Jansenist Benedictine Jamin, in his *Pensées théologiques* (1768), yet another successful work republished several times during the 1770s, continually preach toleration and yet are so intolerant themselves they refuse to tolerate the religion of their own country! 'Quelle inconséquence!'[43] They profess to be standard-bearers of reasonableness, modern science, freedom of thought, and tolerance, but the character of their 'moderation', remarks Chaudon caustically, emerges from Rousseau's feud with Hume and other such unseemly and atrocious *querelles philosophiques*.[44]

Chaudon, in his *Dictionnaire anti-philosophique*, gleefully cites the *philosophes*' turning against Rousseau. Whilst their 'friend', collaborating on the *Encyclopédie*, Rousseau counted among the acutest of intellects and most virtuous of men. No sooner had he broken with them, though, than they everywhere denounced him as a madman, 'charlatan méprisable', and 'critique insolent' hypocritically receiving support while pretending to refuse offers of help.[45] Fanaticism may be reprehensible but the 'most sure means of destroying fanaticism', retorted Madame de Genlis, 'is to demonstrate that it is reprobated by religion; it is with the Gospel particularly that it will be victoriously combated.' But no form of intolerance seemed more pernicious to the *anti-philosophes* than 'philosophic fanaticism', something 'infinitely more dangerous' than any religious fanaticism, a real threat, they urged, to social stability and the moral order.

The aim of 'philosophic fanaticism', avers Stéphanie-Félicité, is that of 'ruling over the minds of men'. The *Histoire philosophique* in particular she, like the Abbé

---

[41] Israel, *Enlightenment Contested*, 63–93.

[42] Voltaire, *Questions*, vi. 20.

[43] Jamin, *Pensées théologiques*, 43; Chopelin-Blanc, *De l'apologétique*, 154; Monod, *Pascal à Chateaubriand*, 454 n., 569.

[44] Chaudon, *Dictionnaire anti-philosophique*, ii. 101–4. [45] Ibid. ii. 102–4.

Lamourette, condemned for propagating 'philosophic fanaticism' and even summoning before the 'tribunal of reason' kings, princes, and everyone else supposedly blocking 'equality, equity, sociability and truth' while exhorting 'people of every nation to destroy temples and worship, massacre kings and potentates, and suffer no authority except that of philosophers'![46] The *philosophes* wanted to make all the laws and impose a complete equality. Historically, the charge levelled against the *philosophes* that they were the true 'fanatics' was to have a long and prosperous career, abundantly fomenting Counter-Enlightenment before, during, and after the Revolution.

Indeed, though genuinely part of the religious Enlightenment, *anti-philosophie* undoubtedly helped prepare the way, intellectually and psychologically, for the post-1789 resurgence of Counter-Enlightenment thought as the principal opponent of secular, anti-monarchical, egalitarian, and democratic ideas. Another thread connecting *anti-philosophie* and Counter-Enlightenment was the frequent appeals both to ordinary men's feelings and to simple faith as the ultimate criterion of truth and firmest foundation of monarchy and the social order. But it was especially by appealing to the widest possible readership and constantly dramatizing and vilifying radical thought, projecting its books authors, and organization as a vast and monstrous conspiracy endangering religion, the Church, morality, government, and the social order itself, that *anti-philosophie* prepared the way for Counter-Enlightenment. The novel entitled *Mémoires philosophiques du Baron de...* (1777) by Crillon, for example, paints a truly lurid picture of *philosophisme* as a high-society conspiracy insidiously subverting the aristocracy, doing so especially by means of an insidious network of tutors and governors of aristocratic sons, often 'atheists' reputedly mentored by *philosophes. Philosophisme* was accounted a conspiratorial movement with its own leaders and *consistoires* and a key base in the Paris café scene. Lamourette, who was to be guillotined in 1794, was no less emphatic in his *Pensées sur la philosophie de l'incrédulité* (1786) that *philosophisme* was not just an underground 'sect' but also an explicitly revolutionary conspiracy.[47]

Above all this conspiracy was comprehensive and exceedingly dangerous morally, socially, and politically. If the political and social *révolution* was still to come, what Lamourette called *la révolution déplorable* that *la philosophie* engineered in men's minds and morality had already penetrated all social levels.[48] To make themselves masters of the world, the Romans, remarked Crillon, had needed centuries; whereas to achieve the same thing, 'la philosophie had needed only thirty years' [pour remplir le même objet, trente ans ont suffi à la philosophie] that is, since the start of the *Encyclopédie*.[49] In this way, the tremendous upsurge of *anti-philosophique* discourse in Europe from the mid 1750s onwards, initially in reply to the *Encyclopédie*, had a most paradoxical cultural result. Its geographical and linguistic cultural impact was not just formidable but unprecedented. Not only in France but in Italy, Spain,

[46] Genlis, *Religion*, i. 126–7, 130, 133; Lamourette, *Pensées*, 83–5; McMahon, *Enemies*, 45.
[47] Lamourette, *Pensées*, 14, 90, 204.
[48] Ibid. 246.
[49] Crillon, *Mémoires philosophiques*, i. 132–3.

Ibero-America, Hungary, Poland, and the other Slavonic countries, translations from French *anti-philosophie* became a major and perhaps the major route by which detailed knowledge of the principal philosophical controversies percolated and parishioners received guidance as to how they should respond to key Enlightenment debates. Above all, *anti-philosophie* by focusing less and less on Voltaire and Rousseau and increasingly on 'ces esprits orgueilleux et pervers' accepting neither altars nor sceptres, nor social hierarchy in our world, did more in the end than most other socio-cultural factors to drag Radical Enlightenment to centre stage and draw readers' attention to its arguments and claims. By highlighting radical doctrines and ceaselessly emphasizing the peril, these resolute ideologues were in effect generating a self-fulfilling prophecy. Many readers first discovered radical ideas from reading the admonishing, deeply embattled tomes of *anti-philosophie* rather than from underground literature itself.[50]

Anti-philosophique literature, hence, is crucial not just for understanding the Enlightenment but, no less, the revolutionary era after 1770. It helps explain how the radical tendency surged up from the underground to win world-transforming successes over mainstream ideas after 1770 and how and why Counter-Enlightenment eventually eclipsed the religious Enlightenment as the main opponent of radical thought. It explains the mechanics of moderate Enlightenment's becoming trapped by 1788, and then being rapidly pulverized between Counter-Enlightenment, on the one side, and radical ideas, on the other. Voltaire scorned the *anti-philosophes* for the mediocrity of their writing and possessing the sort of minds one finds on every street corner, ridiculing them for selling their immense output at low prices, a troupe of famished writers boasting of defending religion 'à quinze sols par tome'. Guyon, an author extolled by the Jansenist *Nouvelles ecclésiastiques*,[51] he derided for selling more cheaply than the rest. But the very cheapness and ubiquity of their editions proves their vast and pervasive impact.[52]

For rhetorical and polemical effect, *anti-philosophie* conjured up a universal, overarching revolutionary antagonist expressly negating its own premises and, in constructing this confrontation, projecting a truly cosmic conflict of world-views. To thoroughly alarm readers and authorities alike, *anti-philosophes* required from the outset an overbearing, menacing foe with which no compromise was possible and that direly threatened the entire existing order.[53] Consequently, radical thought was always bound to be more relevant and useful to *anti-philosophie* than criticizing the relativism and moderation of Montesquieu, Voltaire, Turgot, or Hume. Needing a fully-fledged political and intellectual adversary that was really conspiring to overthrow kings, aristocracy, tradition, and empire, as well as capsize all sexual norms and overturn churches, aristocracies, and morality, there was little point in highlighting the challenge posed by Voltaire. For neither Voltaire nor any *philosophe*

---

[50] Mortier, *Anarcharsis Cloots*, 42–3.
[51] Cottret, *Jansénismes*, 49; Monod, *Pascal à Chateaubriand*, 389.
[52] Voltaire, *Questions*, vi. 20, vii. 122; [Sabatier de Castres], *Tableau philosophique*, 181–2.
[53] Citton, *L'Envers*, 49–50.

combating radical ideas, not even Rousseau, could convincingly be held to be trying to overturn the existing political, social, and religious order to anything like the same extent. Thus *anti-philosophie* simultaneously paved the way for the Counter-Enlightenment myth of a world masonic and philosophical revolutionary conspiracy and helped prepare the ground for the advance of *la philosophie nouvelle*.

Anti-philosophes felt compelled to address the common people as well as the intellectually sophisticated. Backed by the bishops, they resolved to 'enlighten' the faithful about what the radical thinkers were planning and prove that far from being 'useful' to society, 'la philosophie moderne' undermines, as an article in the *Journal des sçavans* put it in 1771, true morality, dissolves social bonds, and ruins the foundations 'de la subordination et de la tranquillité publique'.[54] Although the subject matter of *anti-philosophie* was primarily philosophical, its sphere of action was broadly educational, cultural, social, and moral. As one of the acutest *anti-philosophes*, Guillaume Maleville (1699–1771), remarked, *anti-philosophie* was a movement intervening in a struggle between thinkers and writers about key philosophical and scientific questions but mainly a movement seeking to sway the minds and consciences of ordinary folk, including France's artisans and labourers, indeed even the peasantry.[55]

Accordingly, a major difference between *anti-philosophie* and Counter-Enlightenment is that the veritable *anti-philosophe* attitude, while respecting simple piety, thoroughly disdained plain, anti-intellectual common sense attitudes. Praise of traditional piety implying there was little need to intervene in philosophical debates as the ordinary folk's simple devotion could be relied on as a bulwark, *anti-philosophie* rejected as a disastrous mistake. Many of France's provincial curates seemed to imagine, warned Maleville, writing in a remote rural area of western France, that the prevailing ignorance, illiteracy, and simplicity is the surest means of defending faith. How wrong they are![56] Inquiring, intellectually audacious men are found among all classes of society so that 'the truth' can be truly fortified only through spreading knowledge and awareness of cogent argument.

Christian philosophy must outmatch the *incrédules* intellectually or lose the people's allegiance, in the end even of the most ignorant. The quarrel in progress about creation, divine governance of the universe, and the overall architecture of reality was an intellectual fight. *Anti-philosophie* waged war on *la philosophie moderne*, and other explicitly anti-Christian strands of Enlightenment thought, such as the deism of Voltaire and Rousseau, Montesquieu's moral relativism, and Hume's scepticism, using the weapons of philosophy and science. But it undertook this new crusade for reasons ultimately less philosophical than pastoral, educational, and social and to a not inconsiderable extent also political. Popular instruction was hence basic to its mission. *La Religion vengée* appeared in short, cheaply purchased, regular monthly instalments, through 1757–63, in a format expressly chosen to expand

---

[54] *Journal des sçavans*, 53 (July 1771), 511.
[55] Maleville, *Religion naturelle*, v. 31–4, 36–8.
[56] Ibid. v. 34–5.

readership and sustain polemical impact through a crucial period of controversy and intellectual polemic.[57] Its purpose was not just to persuade but mobilize opinion and stir indignation against the irreligious *philosophes* as a faction, a *parti*, in French culture and society. As Hayer expressed his goals in dedicating *La Religion vengée* to the dauphin in 1757, he and his co-contributors championing religion and morality against the *encyclopédistes* aimed to revive an older conception of philosophy as something subsidiary to theology. Equally, they sought to champion Europe's thrones and the principle of monarchy itself.[58] A new phenomenon and one deeply charac-teristic of its age, *anti-philosophie* nevertheless also saw itself as engaged in an ancient war in progress since the first Christian centuries. In their books, admits Fréron, always the same arguments recur, the same reasoning. But this was because the *esprits forts* ceaselessly deploy the same 'paralogisms', sophisms, and sleights of hand to assail religion and monarchy, arguments their opponents must therefore ceaselessly rebut. What, after all, had today's foes of the Church brought to the debating table not already served up long before by Celsus, Porphyry, and Julian the Apostate?[59]

The unoriginality, obscurity, and emptiness of *la philosophie* was continually alleged, though Madame de Genlis introduced a new note with her notion that the eighteenth century was a lamentably superficial age compared to the seventeenth. Beside Racine, Pascal, and other great writers of the classic age, the *philosophes* were trivial men, shamelessly borrowing their tired 'sophismes' against religion from predecessors like 'Montaigne, Hobbes, Spinosa, Bayle, Collins, Tindal or Shaftesbury', these having, in turn, derived their ideas from ancient pagan philosophers.[60] Perceiving what the Abbé François termed the 'système monstrueux' formed 'dans ces derniers temps, d'un Spinosa, ou d'un Fréret sous le nom de *Thrasibule*', as having deep and ancient roots, seeping up over the centuries from the systems of Epicurus, Strato, and Lucretius, was widespread.[61] Yet the *anti-philosophes* did not doubt that the real challenge had begun only late in the previous century with Spinoza and Bayle, the latter's *Dictionnaire* of 1697, according to Chaudon, being 'un des plus pernicieux livres qui ait jamais paru', a work equally reviled, he points out, by Protestants and Catholics alike.[62]

2. CATHOLIC ENLIGHTENMENT AGAINST RADICAL THOUGHT

No part of the battle ground was more crucial than the fight over divine providence. The more one studies nature, the more science progresses, the more, held Bergier,

[57] Hayer, *La Religion vengée*, i. 9; Monod, *Pascal à Chateaubriand*, 378 n., 559.
[58] Hayer, *La Religion vengée*, i, preface p. iii; *La France littéraire*, i. 292, 407; Proust, *Diderot*, 261; McMahon, *Enemies*, 22.
[59] Trublet, *Correspondence*, 313–14.
[60] Genlis, *Religion*, ii. 80, 84–7.
[61] François, *Observations*, ii. 157, 159.
[62] Ibid. i. 53; Bergier, *Examen du matérialisme*, ii. 281.

one's awareness grows of the infinite empire exercised over it by the sovereign master who created it. Are they seriously proposing—with Epicurus, Lucretius, and Spinoza—that eyes were not given to us by a divine creator for seeing and ears not for hearing? Those philosophers who examine nature with the greatest care, Descartes, Leibniz, and Newton, are precisely those most welcomed and cherished by up-to-date church apologists such as himself, and precisely these figures were the most thoroughly persuaded of God's existence, beneficence, and divine providence.[63] No truly great philosophers, urged Nonnotte, were materialists: 'Pythagorus, Plato, Aristotle, Zeno, Descartes, Leibniz, Malebranche' all reckoned materialism 'la honte de l'esprit humain', and the death of virtue.[64] Has any people ever adopted atheism and materialism? Even the author of the *Pensées philosophiques* whose testimony is suspect to no *incrédule* frankly confesses, observes Malveille, that 'experimental philosophy' and Newtonian-ism have strengthened belief in a divine creator and regulator of the world and hence work against 'atheism'.[65] Although the 'modern pretended philosophers' regularly cite the researches of modern scientists, they allegedly misrepresented them, just as they did Locke, for their vile self-serving purposes. Buffon, a scientist admired by Stéphanie-Félicité, was allegedly grotesquely twisted by Helvétius in his *De l'esprit* and by Diderot who represents him as classifying men and animals very differently from how he actually does. It is the Christian 'argument from design', she argues, echoing earlier *anti-philosophes*, that is endorsed by all sensible and competent astronomers, natural-ists, botanists, and anatomists. 'Therefore the abominable system of materialism is so extravagant that there has never been a people who adopted it.'[66]

If men are as given to senseless veneration of wonders as the *philosophes* maintain, assert both Bergier and Jamin, materialism would have long been generally adopted as the hypothesis most conformable to men's beliefs. Most peoples would be materi-alist as no other creed offers so many unbelievable and unscientific mysteries, or such ridiculous contradictions contrary to reason. 'Matter', as the *matérialistes* represent it, is totally inconceivable, far more so than 'un Dieu spirituel'.[67] The 'mysteries' presented by the *Système de la nature* (of d'Holbach), protests Crillon, are not just 'inconcevables; ils sont évidemment impossibles'.[68] Spinoza's system is far more replete with mysteries than Christianity, held Chaudon, indeed altogether 'bizarre, 'monstrueux' and 'extravagant'.[69] If no competent philosophers are materialists, neither do competent thinkers deny miracles. If deists are hesitant or reject their possibility, as Voltaire does in his article 'Miracles', in his *Dictionnaire philosophique*, Locke and Newton whom Voltaire claims to venerate always champion revelation and miracles. At the opposite pole are those who attack belief in miracles with the

[63] Bergier, *Examen du matérialisme*, ii. 44; Genlis, *Religion*, ii. 72.
[64] Nonnotte, *Dictionnaire philosophique*, 368.
[65] Maleville, *Religion naturelle*, i. 2 and ii. 4, 26, 28.
[66] Ibid. i, 5–6, 12–15, 66; Poortere, *Idées philosophiques*, 13, 95–6.
[67] Bergier, *Examen du matérialisme*, ii. 232; Nonnotte, *Dictionnaire philosophique*, 351–3.
[68] [Crillon], *Mémoires philosophiques*, i. 211; Citton, *L'Envers*, 105, 123.
[69] Chaudon, *Dictionnaire anti-philosophique*, i. 268–9 and ii. 390.

greatest 'wickedness and fury', namely Spinoza, the 'Genevan deist' (Rousseau), Voltaire, the authors of *Le Christianisme dévoilé* (Boulanger and d'Holbach), and *Le Militaire philosophe* (Naigeon), the last deemed by Nonnotte a complete 'fanatic' resolved to destroy religion.[70] In denying miracles, none of these employs logic any more than countless other now forgotten names. Such nonsense is only found 'dans les Spinosa, les Bayle, les Voltaire', and the authors of *Émile*, the *Militaire philosophe*, the clandestine text he cites repeatedly, and *De l'analyse de la religion*, attributed by him to Du Marsais. These writers resembled the fumbling giants of fable, aspiring to climb the heavens to fetch God down to earth.[71]

Rousseau, though frequently denounced at first, came to be more and more often defended by *anti-philosophes* from the early 1770s onwards, or at least rated only a 'confrère timide' of the Church's real enemies, someone who wrote much, remarks Condorcet, useful to theologians.[72] 'The clergy and the devout', concurred Madame de Genlis, 'have all pardoned him, from the bottom of their souls, for what he wrote against religion, in favour of the repeated homages which he has rendered the Gospel.'[73] Especially lauded were Rousseau's praise of Scripture, unrelenting stress on 'virtue', and detestation of the *philosophes* 'comme des empoisonneurs'. 'No man ever said more against philosophy,' notes Madame de Genlis, 'nor spoke with more contempt of modern philosophers.'[74] 'Rousseau was the only man of genius of his time', she suggested, 'who respected the religious principles of which we stand so much in need', meaning for society, the individual, and for politics.[75] Does not *Émile*, for all its obvious faults, categorically assert separation of body and soul, showing materialism is repugnant to both reason and experience?[76] Hence, if the list of approved thinkers was headed by Locke and Newton, by the 1780s one could add if not the whole, then certainly strands of a carefully tailored Rousseau. *Anti-philosophes* loved his vehemence against his former friends and insistence that reason is not man's sole guide, God's existence being proved by our feelings not reason. His upholding divine providence and fixity of species,[77] points likewise keenly appreciated by Kant, also helped restore him to favour. 'The insurmountable barrier raised by nature between the various species', asserts Rousseau, in *Émile*, 'so that they should not mix with one another, is the clearest proof of her intention.' The Rousseau the *anti-philosophes* extol claims that 'nature content to have established her order, has taken adequate measures to prevent the disturbance of that order'.[78]

---

[70] Ibid. ii. 61; Nonnotte, *Dictionnaire philosophique*, 318, 368, 386, 393.

[71] Jamin, *Pensées théologiques*, 530, 581–2.

[72] Condorcet, *Lettre à M. l'Abbé*, in *Œuvres*, i. 307; Trousson, *Jean-Jacques Rousseau*, 524.

[73] Genlis, *Religion*, ii. 58–9, 111–12; Jamin, *Pensées théologiques*, 88; Albertan-Coppola, *L'Abbé*, 83, 86.

[74] Albertan-Coppola, *L'Abbé*, 353, 356; Genlis, *Religion*, ii. 8, 58–9, 111; de Staël, *Letters*, 77; Masseau, *Ennemis*, 304–6.

[75] De Staël, *Letters*, 77; Bergier, *Apologie*, ii. 133–4; Lamourette, *Pensées*, 113–15.

[76] Genlis, *Religion*, ii. 116; Rousseau, *Émile*, 236, 239, 252–3; Nonnotte, *Dictionnaire philosophique*, 352; Paulian, *Véritable Système*, i. 69–70, 72–7, 70.

[77] Rousseau, *Émile*, 238–9; Gourevitch, 'Religious Thought', 193, 199–200.

[78] Rousseau, *Émile*, 238.

Montesquieu too acquired an increasingly favourable image among the *anti-philosophes* as time went on, partly due to his well-publicized reconciliation with the Church, on his death-bed, but especially to the *Esprit des loix*'s claim that Christian states and society exhibit a general moral superiority over, and greater moderation than, other societies due to the gospel's exhorting charity and love for one's neighbour.[79] His well-publicized refutation of Bayle's claim that a truly Christian society could not long maintain itself likewise counted in his favour, though Bergier thought Rousseau, in his *Émile*, had eclipsed him in this respect.[80] Like Descartes, Montesquieu struck Condorcet as a prime instance of a thinker whose writings provoked intense opposition among theologians and all those ruled by 'prejudice' when they first appeared, but for later generations, on the contrary, became an arsenal where 'prejudice' found its most formidable weapons against reason.[81] Voltaire was never 'pardoned' to the extent Montesquieu and Rousseau were, his post-1755 attack on Christianity being too fierce and sustained for that. Yet, he too could be forgiven up to a point and sometimes quoted approvingly for championing God's existence, divine creation and regulation of the world, the divinely given character of morality, inertness of matter, and the ordering and separation of species. These contradictory responses of censure and approval were reconciled by stressing Voltaire's alleged incoherence. To illustrate this Nonnotte derides Voltaire's eulogy of Chinese wisdom and the supposed vast antiquity of their empire, complaining he offers no proof Chinese history really stretches back over 4,000 years, something that seemed incredible to him.[82]

While Nonnotte, Guyon, and Countess de Genlis discuss Voltaire at length, this was uncharacteristic of *anti-philosophie* overall. Indeed, some major works of *anti-philosophie*, like the six volumes of Maleville's *La Religion naturelle et la révélée établie sur les principes de la vraie philosophie* (6 vols., Paris, 1756), scarcely mention Voltaire, Rousseau, or Montesquieu at all. Although some *anti-philosophes*, like Madame de Genlis, pronounced Voltaire the founder of the 'philosophic sect', from an *anti-philosophique* standpoint choosing him entailed appreciable disadvantages. For one thing it meant playing down the political aspects of the movement: for stressing Voltaire's role at once removed the alleged threat to society and lessened emphasis on the atheism and necessitarianism of *la philosophie moderne* as Voltaire invariably affirms providence, free will, and the soul's immortality. Indeed, the only way to make Voltaire patriarch of the *philosophique* sect with some show of cogency was chiefly to stress the sect's incoherence, contending that *philosophisme* 'enrolled indifferently atheists and deists'. 'The sect formed by M. de Voltaire', asserts Genlis, 'having no fixed principles, could not have a plan; but it had an aim, that of persuading men and of domineering and reigning over their minds; and the means

---

[79] Chaudon, *Dictionnaire anti-philosophique*, i, p. xxxviii; Lamourette, *Pensées*, 203; Shackleton, *Montesquieu*, 392–8.
[80] Bergier, *Apologie*, i. 10–11, 161–7, 405 and ii. 127–8, 132.
[81] Condorcet, 'Essai sur la constitution', in *Œuvres*, viii. 186–7.
[82] Nonnotte, *Dictionnaire*, 77–91; Genlis, *Religion*, ii. 16; Pomeau, *Religion de Voltaire*, 344.

contrived to attain this were certainly dexterous and well-concerted.'[83] But the only concrete goal she alleged, apart from promoting the 'passions', was 'to attack religion and to preach unlimited tolerance'. Since Voltaire is also wholly unoriginal borrowing his ideas, she claims, entirely from Collins, Tindal, and Bolingbroke and was no longer esteemed in England, her approach not only risked emptying the conspiracy of real philosophical significance but also weakened the accusation that 'modern philosophy' posed a grave and immediate threat to society.

Voltaire, therefore, *had* to be deposed from leadership of the 'sect' to clear the way for the most effective argument against him, namely that his thought is not only inchoate but far from being the reliable barrier to atheism and materialism he claimed it to be. Here was a tactic apt seriously to damage Voltaire's reputation but one utilized at the cost of according greater cohesion to *la philosophie moderne*. *Anti-philosophie*, in short, lowered Voltaire's standing by elevating radical thought, turning it into the main menace, and publicizing the superiority of its arguments to Voltaire's. Diderot, d'Holbach, and Naigeon dismissed Voltaire's and Rousseau's deist creed as 'une religion inconséquente', something riddled with contradiction, and here Bergier and other leading *anti-philosophes* agreed.[84] The late Voltaire proved vulnerable too to the charge that he secretly diluted his anti-materialism and commitment to providence for tactical reasons. If he was successfully to dominate 'l'esprit philosophique' he had somehow—by finessing his own standpoint—to accommodate diverse views among the *incrédules* who consisted predominantly of materialists, atheists, and 'fatalistes'. To consolidate his position as 'maître', 'le grand oracle des impies', while maintaining the unity of 'la secte nouvelle', he needed to promote a de facto reconciliation of providential deism with materialism and naturalism.[85] Thus, Voltaire, whatever his own principles, having so often deprecated revealed religion, held Barruel, was bound to end up materialism's champion rather than opponent.[86] Hence, even in Madame de Genlis who does not really press her assault on him, Voltaire was less and less the effective head of *la philosophie moderne* after 1770, *anti-philosophie* increasingly focusing on the materialism of Diderot, Helvétius, and d'Holbach.

Superficially coherent, intellectually, held the *anti-philosophes*, *la philosophie nouvelle* inspired only completely inconsistent conduct. Always irresolute in their atheism and materialism, *nouveaux philosophes* mostly wavered, abandoning their impiety when on the point of expiring. François-Xavier de Feller (1735–1802), a Liège-based Jesuit, from Luxembourg, an erudite, hard-hitting polemicist with wide international connections who later squarely attributed the French Revolution—worst of all catastrophes in his view—to *la philosophie moderne*, even claimed Boulainvilliers, La Mettrie, and the author of *Le Christianisme dévoilé* (d'Holbach)

[83] Genlis, *Religion*, ii. 7, 16, 21–2, 107.
[84] Naigeon, 'Unitaires', 400.
[85] Genlis, *Religion*, ii. 160–1; [Guyon], *L'Oracle*, 125, 338.
[86] Barruel, *Les Helviennes*, ii. 38–44.

also all panicked at the end, contritely jettisoning their false principles for faith, Maupertuis 'entre les bras de deux Capucins'.[87]

It was Bergier, from the Vosges, principal of the college of Besançon and member of Besançon's Academy of Sciences, who was held to have most effectively demonstrated the materialists' inconsistencies. Thereby, he became the foremost spokesman of a philosophically oriented, up-to-date Catholic moderate Enlightenment.[88] Much praised by Fréron in his *L'Année littéraire*, Bergier enjoyed enduring success in French cultural life and high society, becoming the most prestigious, widely read *anti-philosophe* of his time, part of his reward being a canonate in Paris at Notre Dame. He set a high standard for the whole movement by attacking *la philosophie moderne* exclusively from the standpoint of 'reason', insisting on a high intellectual level, and eschewing the vituperation other *anti-philosophes* were not infrequently given to.[89] He first achieved renown in 1765 with his *Déisme réfuté par lui-même* against Rousseau which passed through five editions in three years, reappearing in Italian, Spanish (1777), and German, under the title *Der Deist, widerlegt durch sich selbst* (Vienna, 1779).[90] Grimm judged it the best, most thorough refutation of Rousseau available.[91] Having shown reason is too frail a guide for men, demonstrating the soul's workings and reality of spirituality, Rousseau, contended Bergier, destroys his own argument by complaining Christianity's 'mysteries' are 'obscure' and 'contradictory', in effect returning to the foe his weapons, reversing all he has previously said about our needing faith in natural religion.[92] And if his deism was totally self-contradictory, so is his toleration, for he holds materialists, atheists, and sceptics resisting 'dogmes essentiels' like divine creation, providence, and the soul's immortality should be punished.[93]

Applauded too were Bergier's *La Certitude des preuves du christianisme* (2 vols., 1768) and *Apologie de la religion chrétienne contre l'auteur du* Christianisme dévoilé (2 vols., 1769), direct encounters with radical thought. The first rebuts in detail a then notorious clandestine manuscript, *L'Examen critique des apologistes de la religion chrétienne*, today attributed to Lévesque de Burigny but then thought by Bergier and Feller to be by Fréret, a text circulating previously for decades but in tiny quantity which had lately gained prominence through being printed, at Amsterdam, in 1767. Being too late to prevent the public hearing about it, the next best thing, he thought, was to refute it thoroughly even if his critique, systematic and precise, also helped broadcast Lévesque's anti-Christian arguments more widely than the clandestine book trade on its own could have done.[94] Against *La Certitude*, the young

---

[87] Feller, *Catéchisme philosophique*, 12–13; McMahon, *Enemies*, 65–6.
[88] Almodóvar, *Década*, 128; McManners, *Church and Society*, i. 18.
[89] Balcou, *Fréron*, 314; Mortier, *Anarcharsis Cloots*, 42.
[90] Fromm, *Bibliographie*, i. 240; Masseau, *Ennemis*, 166; Sánchez-Blanco, *Absolutismo*, 177.
[91] Bingham, 'Abbé Bergier', 341 n.
[92] Bergier, *Déisme réfuté*, i. 226, 233–6; Rousseau, *Émile*, 253–60; Wokler, *Rousseau and Liberty*, 23, 65.
[93] Bergier, *Déisme réfuté*, i. 43–5; Bergier, *Apologie*, i. 210.
[94] Feller, *Catéchisme philosophique*, 252; McKenna, 'Recherches', 9–10.

Anarcharsis Cloots (1755–94), an affluent young *érudit* and admirer of Fréret, steeped in early eighteenth-century clandestine materialist texts, satirically inverted Bergier's arguments in his *La Certitude des preuves du Mahométanisme* ('à Londres' [Amsterdam], 1780), using the same logic to confirm the undeniable 'truth' of Islam.[95]

In the *Apologie*, Bergier provides a wider critique of 'la philosophie moderne', claiming *Le Christianisme dévoilé* derived from a long underground chain of tradition, offering no new arguments, and that its author had not needed to search far for his material. He locates his core ideas in Hobbes's system and in part Bayle.[96] Christianity the anonymous author pronounces harmful 'au Bonheur de l'état', opposed to the progress of 'l'esprit humain', and contrary to true morality, the latter being infused with society's real interests and the state.[97] A favourite maxim of his, as well as of Helvétius, Voltaire, and Rousseau, is that the truth can cause no harm.[98] But exactly this proves materialism, given the incendiary content of this text, 'n'est pas la vérité'.[99] The *Christianisme dévoilé* was doubly dangerous, for while ordinary folk cannot understand most philosophical works, this one is cunningly couched in simple, straightforward terms designed to seduce with its simplistic but pernicious maxims and incite them to rise up against priests and princes, and 'détruire le sacerdoce et la royauté'.[100] Here, Voltaire concurred with Bergier. The *Christianisme dévoilé* greatly disturbed him too and he filled the margins of his own copy, today preserved in Petersburg, with numerous protests and criticisms, contradicting d'Holbach's thesis that religion is not essential to men.[101]

Warmly congratulated at the French Assemblée Générale du Clergé, in June 1770, by the politically influential archbishop of Toulouse, Loménie de Brienne, Bergier's help was requested in composing the French Church's official *Avis aux fidèles sur les dangers de l'incrédulité* which appeared soon afterwards under the signatures of Brienne and two other prelates.[102] Congratulated by the pope and the grand dauphin as well as the court *dévot* faction, Bergier received his canonry at Notre Dame, in Paris, and, soon afterwards, following his culminating work of *anti-philosophie*, his *Examen critique* of the *Système de la nature*, was assigned permanent quarters at Versailles, becoming, in effect, resident court *anti-philosophe* as well as confessor to Mesdames, the king's daughters, the later countesses of Artois and Provence, and, in time, holder of yet more revenues to support his writing. Yet, not all of the *philosophes*' enemies were impressed. A writer propagating a deeply felt Catholic moderate Enlightenment that was liberal and relatively tolerant and included a stern critique of

[95] Bingham, 'Abbé Bergier', 340; Mortier, *Anarcharsis Cloots*, 42–5.
[96] Bergier, *Apologie*, i. 437–8.
[97] D'Holbach, *Christianisme dévoilé*, 17.
[98] Ibid. 6, 17.
[99] Bergier, *Apologie*, i. 8–9, 11, 24.
[100] Ibid. i. 23–4.
[101] Venturi, 'Postille', 238–9.
[102] Everdell, *Christian Apologetics*, 17; Masseau, *Ennemis*, 166; Albertan-Coppola, *L'Abbé*, 31–3.

Jansenism as well as of the *philosophes*, Bergier incurred the lasting enmity of the Jansenist journal the *Nouvelles ecclésiastiques* which, when not ignoring his publications, dismissed him as far too polite towards the enemy, too accommodating of certain *philosophique* notions, and too inclined towards Jesuit and Pelagian theology.[103] Feller likewise considered him altogether too conciliatory toward *la philosophie*.[104] Such was his respect for intellectual and moral integrity that some theologians suspected Bergier of harbouring the heresy that virtuous, upright heretics and infidels might be saved.

3. PHILOSOPHY, RELIGION, AND THE SOCIAL ORDER

Bergier, fat, affable, and temperamentally among the mildest *anti-philosophes*, humorously styled by Diderot 'le grand réfutateur des Celses modernes', reportedly met and—despite his literary war with them—held entertaining conversations with Diderot and d'Holbach, explaining this as an attempt to 'convert' them.[105] But only until 1770; after that he broke off all relations, seeing the conflict had now reached such proportions that all further friendly interaction had become impossible. Much more typical was his alarmism, deliberate attempt to unsettle the authorities, and depicting materialism in the most lurid light possible, insisting the threat was not just to religion but monarchy, the social order, and the common people as well. The philosophical *incrédule* is not just a rebel against God but a disturber of the public peace, a *séditieux* inciting social and moral instability, using philosophy as his tool. In truth, they were planning the revolution the *anti-philosophes* conjured up—even if more in men's minds than in fact.

Madame de Genlis blamed the *Système de la nature* and *Le Militaire philosophe* especially for fomenting a politically revolutionary stance exhorting 'philosophers of every nation' to go out and 'teach the people that government derives its power from society alone; and that, being established for its welfare, the people can revoke this power when its interest requires it, change the form of government, extend or limit the power which it delegated to its chiefs, over whom it always reserves a supreme authority'.[106] *Philosophisme* was seeding rebellion throughout society; but the most insidious aspect of their subversion, held Madame de Genlis, was their influence on servants. 'Servants, be subject to your masters with all fear', she quoted, from the Epistle of Peter chapter 2, 'not only to the good and gentle, but also to the froward'. For my part', she declared, 'if I saw in the hands of my servants the *Pensées philosophiques* [Diderot]—*Dictionnaire philosophique* [Voltaire]—*Discours sur la vie*

---

[103] Bingham, 'Abbé Bergier', 340–1; Van Kley, *Religious Origins*, 265; Cottret, *Jansénismes*, 108–9.

[104] Bingham, 'Abbé Bergier', 348; Albertan-Coppola, *L'Abbé*, 36; Masseau, *Ennemis*, 289.

[105] Masseau, *Ennemis*, 167–9; Diderot, *Corr.* x. 62; Bingham, 'Abbé Bergier', 343; Albertan-Coppola, *L'Abbé*, 161.

[106] Genlis, *Religion*, i. 132.

heureuse—Sur l'origine de l'égalité parmi les hommes [Rousseau]—*Les Mœurs* [Toussaint]—the *Confessions de J. J. Rousseau—Tableau philosophique de l'établissement dans les Indes* [Raynal]—*De l'esprit* [Helvétius]—*Le Code de la nature* [Morelly] etc. etc. I should be much alarmed, and I should not at all think myself safe in my house.'[107]

The *Essai sur les préjugés* (1770), today attributed to d'Holbach but then often attributed to Du Marsais, fiercely contested the depicting of the freethinkers as *séditieux* in this way, deeming this another instance of priestly hypocrisy and imposture. To be an *incrédule* means one rejects what everyone else believes, scorns conventional received thinking in the society in which one lives. Surely history demonstrates that to be an opponent and subversive when there is much that is wrong with society is an obligation not a crime. How can Christians dispute the necessity and validity of 'freethinking' wherever overturning the existing order is morally or socially justified? Were not the New Testament Apostles at Jerusalem 'incrédules et des perturbateurs du repos public'? Is their work then to be declared illicit? And what of Christian missionaries in the Indies? Are they not 'séditieux' proclaiming wholly new beliefs, unhesitatingly condemning whole societies to uproar, rebellion, and unrest?[108]

The *anti-philosophes* broadly succeeded in persuading 'l'opinion publique' that the word 'philosophe' was a synonym for 'libertine' and agitator, an *incrédule* without morals, foe of God, society, and the ordinary person, '*un séditieux* rejecting what everyone believes'. In this way, the 'modern philosopher' became not just someone whose arguments must be totally rejected but someone whose activities must be suppressed and severely punished. Convinced their antagonism toward the *philosophes*, and philosophy, was approved by God and Church, remarks the *Essai* (d'Holbach), those denouncing 'l'esprit philosophique' (since men always give free rein to their passions when they believe the gods approve of their aims) not only adopted a pitiless, inhuman vengefulness toward their adversaries but deliberately stirred up popular indignation against them.[109] This was clearly the aim of writers like Lamourette and the Abbé Joseph Nicolas Camuset (1746–1810) in identifying 'la philosophie' with materialist atheism, even if in doing so they unconsciously reinforced the radical *philosophes'* efforts to redefine and reconfigure 'philosophy' itself.[110] Condemnation of the clandestine philosophical literature by the *anti-philosophes* was thus an indictment, wake-up call, and demand for retribution.

Catholic Enlightenment meant explaining in enlightened terms why other forms of Enlightenment should be rejected. Aware Christians, contends Maleville, must know how to combat the *Lettres juives, Mémoires secrets de la République des Lettres,* and the *Philosophie du bon sens,* all by d'Argens, and answer Basnage, Bayle, Bekker,

---

[107] Ibid. i. 121.
[108] D'Holbach, *Essai,* 148–9.
[109] Ibid. 305–6.
[110] Rousseau, *Journal encyclopédique* (Oct. 1771), 186.

Boulainvilliers, Buffon, Collins, Bolingbroke, Bourlamaqui, Clarke, de Prades, Fontenelle, Jurieu, Leibniz, Mandeville, Maupertuis, Hobbes, Spinoza, Diderot, and Voltaire.[111] Aware, properly equipped defenders of the faith must also familiarize themselves with the earlier and often still unpublished clandestine literature since this raises many crucial questions and was the prime source of the contagion. Although, by the 1760s, the new attitude had ousted the old practice of trying to marginalize the clandestine manuscripts by ignoring their existence there was still much anxiety about broadcasting titles, editions, authors, and other concrete details about subversive texts.

Far from being unwilling to inform the public about underground texts, or the less-known subversive writers, the *anti-philosophes* seemed positively to relish every opportunity to emphasize the depth and extent of the challenge society faced. Some undertook extensive research in their quest to unmask more secret texts, uncovering as much of this subversive underground as they could, developing a new kind of intellectual connoisseurship, highlighting ideas and passages which hardly anyone would or could have known about previously. It all added to the spectre of dark, menacing, and ubiquitous conspiracy they sought to project. Maleville, for many years curé of Domme in the Périgord and besides his main work against 'la philosophie' author also of a two-volume *Histoire critique de l'éclecticisme* ('Londres' [Paris], 1766), was one who recognized the great extent to which *la philosophie nouvelle* of Diderot and the *Encyclopédie* stemmed from the clandestine manuscript philosophical literature of the late seventeenth and early eighteenth centuries. Griffet, before the Jesuit expulsion from France a well-known preacher in Bourges and Rennes, was another who discussed in print several little-known clandestine manuscripts.[112] Discussing and closely examining texts such as the *Réfutation des erreurs de Spinosa* (1731), really a defence of Spinoza, by Boulainvilliers, the *Nouvelles Libertés de penser* (1743), and de Maillet's *Telliamed*, Maleville judged such research essential for combating contemporary naturalism.[113] Among the most active in unveiling the world of clandestine thought in both printed and manuscript versions in the French provinces, Maleville was an author who combined scholarship with an ardent Jansenist piety.[114] His books were viewed with amused condescension by his adversaries. Noting his critique of the *Encyclopédie's* 'errors', in 1766, d'Alembert jocularly invited him to Paris where the *philosophes* would teach him how to write and 'vous nous apprendrez à penser'.[115]

Despite qualms, Maleville felt obliged to inform the public about still unpublished manuscript clandestine texts, including Boulainvilliers's *Abrégé de l'histoire universelle*,[116] albeit he tried to combat radical ideas without stimulating undue interest in

[111] Rousseau, *Journal encyclopédique* (Oct. 1771), 527.
[112] Griffet, *L'Insuffisance*, i. 98–119; Mori, 'Du Marsais philosophe', 190; Benítez, *Face cachée*, 258.
[113] Maleville, *Religion naturelle*, i. 273–4, 310–15, and iv. 25, 65, 132.
[114] Mothu, 'Un curé "Janséniste"', 25–7.
[115] Ibid. 27; Barrière, *Vie intellectuelle*, 525.
[116] Maleville, *Religion naturelle*, v. 300.

the manuscripts by refuting the arguments advanced in unpublished manuscripts, highlighting what he saw as their intellectual failings while withholding precise details about the texts themselves. He hoped in this way to avoid drawing unwelcome attention to particular manuscripts and minimizing the risk of their eventual publication.[117] But the cumulative effect of his efforts, inevitably, was the exact opposite. By defining the contagion they were combating, inflating its scope, and stimulating public anxiety, while also deploying radical ideas against the irreligious middle ground, the *anti-philosophes* could scarcely avoid heightening a sense of the pervasiveness, force, and coherence of the philosophical challenge they faced. In effect, they walked into a trap of their own making. The favourite technique of the pre-1789 *anti-philosophes* for countering *la philosophie moderne*, namely dismissing the radicals' pretension to be the voice of 'reason', urging their own superior claims to speak for true 'reason', relied on focusing attention on their opponents' alleged inconsistencies, moral failings, and logical fallacies. But in focusing on arguments they considered mortally dangerous, *anti-philosophes* faced an insoluble dilemma: they could not avoid themselves becoming one of the most effective agents of diffusion of radical ideas or stimulating intellectual curiosity about the sources of the contagion they did so much to dramatize.

Another unavoidable snag was the difficulty of identifying exactly who was behind the burgeoning flow of new subversive philosophical literature. If society faced a dangerous conspiracy threatening to undermine religion, government, and morals whoever was responsible should be arraigned before the highest courts figuratively and actually. But who exactly was responsible? Diderot had published nothing directly illicit since 1749, rendering him a somewhat remote target, especially as *anti-philosophique* literature often styles him 'l'auteur des *Pensées philosophiques*' or some other such circumlocution, thereby clouding matters further as it remained unclear who actually wrote that work, Diderot or La Mettrie. Meanwhile, d'Holbach, the single most prolific writer of materialist philosophy in France in the 1760s and 1770s, and prime redactor and editor of earlier clandestine texts penned by others, the writer who, together with Diderot, was the chief strategist of the *matérialiste* surge into print, remained completely unknown to the public and was never referred to by name by the *anti-philosophes* though Bergier, Crillon, Deschamps, and others presumably had some inkling of his real role.[118]

The elusiveness of those responsible for the great conspiracy was compounded by the more widely read examples of underground subversive radical literature composed earlier, in the 1730s and 1740s, being constantly reissued and recycled. Chaudon's *Dictionnaire anti-philosophique* (2 vols., Avignon, 1769), a compilation renamed the *Anti-dictionnaire philosophique* from its enlarged fourth edition, in 1775 onwards,[119] allocates d'Argens considerable space since fresh editions of his writings,

---

[117] Mothu, 'Un curé "Janséniste"', 31–2; Schwarzbach, 'Clandestins du Père', 169, 179.
[118] [Crillon], *Mémoires philosophiques*, i. 127–8; Robinet, *Dom Deschamps*, 71.
[119] Masseau, *Ennemis*, 286 n.

long in print though these now were, were continually resurfacing. His seven-volume *Mémoires secrets de la République des Lettres*, a compendium satirizing prevailing prejudices by interpolating them into absurd eulogies of generally venerated teachers and writers, published at Amsterdam in 1737, reappeared at The Hague and Amsterdam in 1743, 1744, 1747, and 1753, and then at Berlin in 1765–8, and 'à Londres' in 1784.[120] In unmasking the chief architects of the 'revolution of the mind', those responsible for orchestrating the clandestine Enlightenment's expansion after 1750, *anti-philosophie* encountered a perplexing quandary profoundly affecting its entire strategy. Church apologists conjured up a massively intimidating threat in terms of publications, manuscripts, and arguments advanced by an army of *esprits forts*, warning of catastrophic consequences while combining this with only the vaguest information as to who was actually heading this, the greatest conspiracy in history. The menace was pronounced immediate, dangerous, and revolutionary while the chief agents of subversion and diffusion, paradoxically, remained clouded in mystery, the only figures confidently identified as main conspirators having all been silent or dead for decades. The *Christianisme dévoilé*, new, widely diffused, and outrageously seditious, drew its inspiration, according to Bergier, from Bayle, Fréret (who died in 1749), and, still more elusive, 'd'une infinité d'autres écrivains'. Such an analysis might excite the curiosity of scholars but could only baffle most readers.

The mystery was further compounded by *la philosophie moderne*'s growing dynamism, social power, and force. Since ancient times, there had actually been very few philosophers of note whom the *encyclopédistes* could draw on, held the *anti-philosophes*, to support their overthrow of God, natural religion, and man's immortal soul. Only Spinoza, Servetus, Vanini, Socinus, Bayle, Hobbes, Toland, Collins, and, possibly, a few strands of Locke could be plausibly mobilized in support of the *encyclopédistes*' campaign against received ideas, contended Le Masson des Granges who, according to Fréron, victoriously refuted all the arguments of the *encyclopédistes*, and, among these names, most could not be said to provide more than minor components of the world's greatest conspiracy.[121] With so few credible progenitors for the *anti-philosophes* to choose from, Spinoza and Bayle were practically bound to eclipse everyone else as *anti-philosophie*'s twin chief culprits, the archpriests of the radical tradition.

4. *ANTI-PHILOSOPHIE* VERSUS SPINOZA AND BAYLE

Several key *anti-philosophes*, Hayer and the Jesuits, Berthier, Gauchat, and Feller, focused on Bayle rather than Spinoza as the original malign founder of the conspiracy threatening society and religion in late eighteenth-century Europe. But this was

---

[120] D'Argens, *Mémoires secrets*, i, preface p. 2.
[121] Le Masson des Granges, *Philosophe moderne*; Fréron, *L'Année littéraire* (1759/60), 68–9.

perhaps just a difference of emphasis as these writers too discerned a close alignment of Bayle's thought with Spinoza's.[122] Bayle's *Dictionnaire*, held Le Masson des Granges, was the arsenal from where 'ils ont tous pris leurs armes'.[123] Hayer devotes almost the whole of the first five volumes of the massive twenty-one-volume *La Religion vengée* to rebutting every thesis of Bayle, 'cet écrivain si célèbre, l'idole de la nation incrédule', lending him an overwhelming primacy in the profile of what was being opposed.[124] The emphasis on Bayle in Gauchat's *Lettres critiques* is also astounding. For Hayer and Gauchat, Bayle was the evil genius who perversely denied any difference between 'above reason' and 'contrary to reason', 'le Héros de la nation incrédule', 'notre ennemi capital'.[125] By denying anything can be above without being contrary to reason, Bayle transformed reason into a light opposing 'la lumière de la Révélation', his malign project later being continued by Diderot and the *Encyclopédie*.[126] Bayle, whom Hayer pronounced the 'prototype of our *beaux esprits*', and who according to Gauchat wrought 'plus de mal parmi les Chrétiens que tous les Incrédules ensemble',[127] tragically for the entire Christian world, had put his incomparable learning, prodigious memory, and profound judgement to work to undermine everything sacred.[128]

The earlier anti-Bayle campaign of the pre-1730 Huguenot intelligentsia, lamented Hayer, was actually a disaster for philosophy and religion. For Le Clerc, Jaquelot, Bernard, Crousaz, and the other *rationaux*, though rightly identifying Bayle as the prime foe, chose a catastrophically wrong tactic in countering him, disastrously contradicting themselves in attacking Bayle for his 'contradictions'.[129] Bayle rightly demonstrates 'invinciblement contre Jaquelot' that to attempt to show in what precisely the conformity of the mysteries of the faith with reason consists 'c'est anéantir la foi'.[130] The principle of above but not contrary to reason, Christians must embrace as a matter of faith, not philosophical demonstration. Only later did the full implications become clear of Bayle's thesis that we can only be certain something is true when it conforms 'avec cette lumière primitive et universelle que Dieu répand' in all men's souls, that is philosophical reason. Jaquelot, like Crousaz afterwards, floundered trying to combat this monster by claiming too much for reason. When Bayle and Jaquelot accused each other of being 'enemies of religion', both were correct.[131] The Christian philosopher's task, insisted Hayer rebuking Le Clerc and Jaquelot, is to employ reason to champion faith not reason.

---

[122] Pappas, *Berthier's Journal*, 203–4; Lough, *Essays*, 255.
[123] Le Masson des Granges, *Philosophe moderne*, 131.
[124] Hayer, *La Religion vengée*, i. 8.
[125] Ibid. i. 341, 345; Lough, *Essays*, 391–2, 394, 397.
[126] Hayer, *La Religion vengée*, iii. 9, 71; Proust, *Diderot*, 262.
[127] Gauchat, *Lettres critiques*, xiii, preface p. ix.
[128] Hayer, *La Religion vengée*, i. 75, 234; Feller, *Catéchisme philosophique*, 118.
[129] Hayer, *La Religion vengée*, i. 345.
[130] Ibid. iii. 225–32, 273–4.
[131] Ibid. iii. 225–32, 273–4.

Hobbes is also sometimes accorded a major role, notably by Bergier and Guyon.[132] Guyon, Gauchat, and Camuset all cite Hobbes as a main source of the materialism of the *Système de la nature*. 'Hobbes et ses sectateurs' Camuset associates especially with the tendency to view 'la matière comme le seul Être, comme la Nature universelle'.[133] But where all *anti-philosophes* considered the *Spinosistes* central to the story, only Guyon and Gauchat label the materialists 'nos Hobbésistes' or designate their philosophy *l'Hobbésisme*, and then only in passing, though this is not to deny that Hobbes actually was a powerful strand in the fabric vilified by *anti-philosophie*. No *anti-philosophes*, meanwhile, settled alternatively on Machiavelli or the clandestine thought world suggestively described in his *Dictionnaire* by Bayle of what we would call Renaissance Italy. Nor was any connection alleged, strikingly, between the new subversion and freemasonry or, indeed, Protestantism in any of its varieties apart from Socinianism which was, in any case, reckoned a separate phenomenon, more aligned with Islam and Judaism. In short, first-rank perpetrators and architects of 'the revolution of the mind' according to nearly all these polemicists amounted to just two: Spinoza and Bayle. This helped to lend a certain unity to the clandestine literature as an intellectual phenomenon but also aggravated the problem of identification confronting Catholic and Protestant apologists. For in the context of the 1760s, 1770s, and 1780s, if Spinoza and Bayle were the only names *anti-philosophie* could produce as chief inspirers of the movement to undermine religion and the existing social order and as perpetrators of a universal *tolérantisme* anchored in philosophical determinism and materialism, who exactly was directing their followers and heirs?

The city of Rotterdam had erected no statue to Bayle yet (it still has not done so today). However, if ever 'la nation impie' should wrest control over any country and inspire its legislation, warned Hayer, statues of Bayle and 'altars' dedicated to him will proliferate. For to the *philosophes modernes* Bayle is the universal inspiration; 'un philosophe sublime, un esprit transcendant'.[134] The crux of his thought and what makes it so harmful, holds Hayer, is the cunning methods he uses to reverse the true relationship between reason and theology, always making the latter the subordinate partner. If we examine Bayle's arguments, Hayer urges the dauphin, we discern throughout the absurdity and perfidy characterizing his entire oeuvre. For Bayle progressively extends toleration 'indifféremment à tout'.[135] The imposture inherent in his urging full toleration flagrantly emerges in the passage of the *Commentaire philosophique* where he impudently states that his system need not involve tolerating atheists if rulers prefer not to while offering no plausible argument for excluding them.[136] Bayle Hayer considers an 'atheist' but an 'athée fourbe et secret' [crafty and

---

[132] [Guyon], *L'Oracle*, 44, 57–9.
[133] Gauchat, *Lettres critiques*, xi. 249–51; Camuset, *Principes*, 250.
[134] Hayer, *La Religion vengée*, ii. 64.
[135] Ibid. v. 198.
[136] Ibid. v. 203–5; Israel, *Enlightenment Contested*, 149–51.

secret atheist] all the more insidious for masquerading as a fideist.[137] For Hayer, Bayle was the supreme impostor stifling truth itself under his pretence of philosophical reason.[138]

But Bayle could not be detached from Spinoza. *Anti-philosophes* all broadly agreed that Bayle surreptitiously advances a veiled *Spinosisme* while pretending to refute that miscreant. Bayle renders God's existence and beneficence problematic and if this is not a 'Spinosisme dogmatique, c'est du moins un Spinosisme Pyrrhonien'.[139] By this Hayer meant Bayle was a relentless sceptic regarding everything connected with faith, belief, doctrine, and authority, anything that anyone believes, while dogmatically espousing reason for all moral and social principles even to the point of claiming that 'la nécessité d'agir' which Spinoza postulates 'dans la divinité, est démontrée géométriquement'.[140] To stress reason and conceive of the universe as Bayle does, as governed by blind fatality, is *Spinosisme*. 'Donc le voilà convaincu d'Athéisme', declared Hayer, 'par ses propres principes'.[141] To render God's liberty problematic 'c'est Spinosisme', he insists, urging the dauphin to intervene. His *La Religion vengée* was dedicated to the dauphin and it was the latter's premature death, in 1765, that dashed the *anti-philosophes'* hopes for a more vigorous and energetic royal crackdown on *la philosophie moderne*. One can only conclude, repeats Hayer, further illustrating his point by citing Bayle's *Dictionnaire* article 'Xenophanes', that while Xenophanes, Spinoza, and Bayle were all 'atheists', Bayle was the most insidious being 'le plus fourbe et le plus hypocrite'.[142]

Bayle, though, was of limited use for condemning radical ideas and mobilizing public indignation against current foes. No utterance of Bayle could be quoted without entangling readers in a host of difficulties as to his meaning and the *incrédules* themselves no longer needed his evasion and elaborate stratagems. In style and method Bayle was now far too remote. A firmer target was indispensable. An *anti-philosophe* conscious of the difficulty was the head of the French Minim Friars, Michel-Ange Marin (1697–1767), an erudite monk, resident mainly at Avignon, who, like Bergier, strove to show separating morality from religion can never work; and that religion alone grounds true morality.[143] An austere moralist reflecting his order's reputation for humility by declining the post of 'General' of the Minims in Rome, in 1758, Marin robustly championed what to him was the true moral order, urging youth to shun the 'nouveaux philosophes' and their freethinking texts as moral plague. Seeking to mobilize a wide public, he launched his heaviest assault on the *encyclopédistes* in a five-volume philosophical novel, *Le Baron Van-Hesden, ou La République des incrédules* (5 vols., Toulouse, 1762), targeting Diderot in particular,

---

[137] Hayer, *La Religion vengée*, vi. 141; Smith, *Helvétius*, 76–7.
[138] Hayer, *La Religion vengée*, iii. 23.
[139] Ibid. vi. 177; McMahon, *Enemies*, 22.
[140] Hayer, *La Religion vengée*, vi. 177; Lough, *Essays*, 391.
[141] Hayer, *La Religion vengée*, vi. 141, 161–2, 170, 174.
[142] Ibid. vi. 195–215.
[143] Marin, *Baron Van-Hesden*, v. 196–8; Bergier, *Apologie*, ii. 213; Trousson, 'Michel-Ange Marin', 54–5.

dramatizing a philosophical debate on a passenger barge, sailing from Lyon to Avignon down the Rhône.

Here, Marin accords Bayle a prominent place in the rise of modern philosophical subversion. But, like François, Maleville, Genlis, and the Abbé François-André Pluquet (1716–90), he assigns the leading role to Spinoza, conceiving the entire edifice of modern incredulity to derive from Spinozism.[144] In his novel, Marin's fictional spokesman for the *esprits forts* is a young Dutch aristocrat, a good-natured Diderot-like figure of around 25, descended from Huguenot refugees. To pass the time, Van-Hesden enters into debate with an erudite hermit (representing Marin) and a small crowd of passengers gathers round, among them the boat captain, an uneducated man of the people who having 'heard so much talk about Spinoza and his system' wants to hear the truth, finally, about 'philosophy' and what the furore surrounding Spinoza is about. One gathered from his conversation that Van-Hesden was familiar with 'bad books' and especially 'les ouvrages de Bayle, qu'il estimoit infiniment'.[145] Van-Hesden in fact admires and defends Bayle rather than Spinoza and is stupefied when Marin's hermit proves he is a 'spinosiste sans le savoir'.[146] Spinoza's system is such a heap of contradiction, Van-Hesden, the boat captain, and the rest of the party learn, that his apologists, Boulainvilliers especially,[147] are reduced to charging Bayle with not understanding him correctly, an absurd charge, contends Marin, proving Spinoza is totally unintelligible even to disciples; for how can the vastly learned Bayle be accused of not reading him carefully enough? 'En un mot, ce n'est pas Spinosa qu'on n'entend pas, c'est Spinosa qui ne s'entend pas lui-même.'[148] Feller is equally adamant that even the most systematic form of atheism, Spinozism, is a mere 'tissu d'extravagances et de contradictions ridicules'. Voltaire, he notes, identified Spinoza as the thinker chiefly responsible for the ideas in the *Système de la nature*, a work so replete with contradiction even Bergier fails to uncover all its non sequiturs.[149]

Ultimately Spinoza was the only candidate who could be drummed up as prime instigator of the materialist moral and social theories developed in Diderot's *Lettre sur les aveugles*, the *Militaire philosophe*, the *Histoire philosophique*, the *Système*, and the new atheistic materialism's other foundational texts. Notorious everywhere, more even than Hobbes or Machiavelli, he was the only modern atheistic philosopher the meaning of whose writings presented relatively few problems. Furthermore, unlike Hobbes or Bayle, he remained entirely topical, someone continually cited in contemporary debate, a thinker who still in 1769, according to Henri Griffet (1698–1771), author of *L'Insuffisance de la religion naturelle* (2 vols., Liège, 1770), a major work warmly applauded in October 1769 by the *Journal des sçavans* in Paris for

---

[144] Israel, *Radical Enlightenment*, 80, 339.
[145] Marin, *Baron Van-Hesden*, i. 2.
[146] Ibid. ii. 27, 89–90, 102.
[147] Maleville, *Religion naturelle*, iv. 124.
[148] Marin, *Baron Van-Hesden*, i. 44.
[149] Feller, *Catéchisme philosophique*, 4–5, 26, 118.

its acuteness in combating 'la philosophie moderne',[150] still possessed, unfortunately for religion, 'un trop grand nombre de Disciples'.[151] 'Ce monstrueux système', averred Le Masson des Granges, *le Spinosisme* was the doctrine everywhere regarded as underpinning the clandestine ideology of the *encyclopédistes* as providing the 'sect' with its creed and lending it its unity and intellectual cohesion.[152] Despite his system being nearly a century old by 1770, Spinoza was continually highlighted by the *anti-philosophes* and the only real contender for the status of supreme patriarch of the sect.

Spinoza Maleville sees as the chief source of philosophical subversion and someone who reasons seductively and *admirablement* well. He is also a thinker who must be studied closely given the considerable effort needed to identify his weak points, effort necessary for every Christian priest capable of serious thought, precisely because so much clandestine literature is anchored philosophically in Spinozism.[153] Close scrutiny, however, was bound further to draw the public's attention to Spinozism, a quandary from which there seemed no escape. In his *Religion naturelle* Maleville apologizes for citing Spinoza's texts more frequently and at greater length than those of any other thinker. His justifies his doing so by saying that Christian apologists had all too often in the past failed adequately to confront what was unquestionably the most formidable challenge they faced. If one once affects to believe nature's works 'n'ont point Dieu pour auteur', as Maleville expresses it, 'Spinosa raisonne admirablement bien'. Were the cosmos after all not created by an intelligent workman, no one could explain more convincingly how mankind's preoccupation with final causes originally arose.[154] Disadvantage there might be in according Spinoza further prominence and pre-eminence. But the Christian apologist's first responsibility is to defeat not hide this writer's arguments.[155]

When each thread of atheistic materialism is examined, it soon emerges, held Marin, much like Maleville, François, Pluquet, Jamin, and Le Masson des Granges, that these more or less all originate in Spinoza's ideas and, in that guise, assume the appearance of coherence. These writers all agreed with Bayle that Spinoza denies divine creation of the world and species more cogently than anyone else and comes closest among anti-Scripturalists to proving we cannot find in Scripture 'la connoissance des choses naturelles et spirituelles',[156] as Maleville puts it, and was also the first thinker to dare 'réduire l'incrédulité en système'. In his chapters on miracles, creation, final causes, and Bible criticism, Maleville's principal target is invariably Spinoza and those he reckons his direct disciples, Boulainvilliers, Collins, and d'Argens. Many readers, observes Maleville, were curious to know whether Spinoza

---

[150] *Journal des sçavans*, 53 (July 1771), 494–5, 507.
[151] Griffet, *L'Insuffisance*, i. 5.
[152] Le Masson des Granges, *Philosophe moderne*, 20–5.
[153] Maleville, *Religion naturelle*, i. 30, ii. 46–8, 51–2, 115–31, iii. 323–8, iv. 107–80, 206–14, 254, v. 36–8, 141–63, and vi. 127–9.
[154] Maleville, *Religion naturelle*, ii. 48; Vernière, *Spinoza*, 427–30.
[155] Maleville, *Religion naturelle*, iv. 154.
[156] Ibid. iv. 144.

was everywhere daily accused of overthrowing the authority of the sacred books with reason and if so, to know the causes of his impact and how it happens he is so incisive, cogent, and skilful in arranging his arguments. Thus, when defending religion against the *incrédules*, the serious champion of faith and morality cannot dispense with explaining the arguments 'de cet homme fameux' in all their force.

The great advantage of squarely facing this challenge is that it must end in final defeat for the great conspiracy and the destruction of the foe's weapons. What a blow to the *incrédules*, and triumph for revelation, should it transpire that, after all, Spinoza's chief theses 'ne sont que la foiblesse même'![157] Maleville was unique, though, in stressing Spinoza's overall cogency. The centrality of Spinoza and Spinozism in the world-view propagated by *anti-philosophie* more typically led to odd, distinctly paradoxical, formulations awkwardly stressing both his seeming coherence and actual incoherence. In dedicating his book to the primate of the Catholic Low Countries, the archbishop of Mechelen, Count Franckenberg, Griffet portrays Spinoza as someone who had won a vast name for himself 'par la hardiesse et par la singularité de ses idées', despite not being, properly speaking, the inventor of his system at all. Spinoza's thought is really just a rehash of Lucretius and Pliny the Naturalist who, in turn, held Griffet, derived their ideas from older Greek predecessors. Likewise, with his geometric method of presentation, Spinoza impresses only 'esprits légers et superficiels' imagining his 'demonstrations' possess the rigour of mathematical explanations. Deeper minds see through his 'ridiculous sophisms'.

For *anti-philosophes*, Spinoza's system is built on 'contradiction'. In this way, a vast paradox arose, the very sophistry of this 'écrivain très-peu lumineux' rendering him 'respectable' in the eyes of a vast mass of the intellectually less acute.[158] Spinoza, argues Le Masson des Granges, postulates an infinite substance comprising a collection of bodies none of which is itself infinite within a single framework when, in fact, these two concepts, the infinite and the finite, are wholly incompatible, the one excluding the other.[159] This he thought typified Spinoza's logical errors. All Spinoza really accomplishes, held Le Masson, François, Pluquet, Marin, and Jamin, in contrast to Maleville, is to present a misleading rigmarole resembling a coherent system of thought but actually composed of non sequiturs and absurdities—as Bayle affirms.[160] Spinoza merely combines the concepts of some ancient 'atheists' and oriental thinkers that he had then further 'deformed' with diverse 'novelties' of his own.

Spinoza, then, for the *anti-philosophes*, was a unique specimen of impostor, self-contradictory and 'sans jugement' but yet, unlike Lucretius or Hobbes, a current menace, someone who had 'bien de sectateurs'.[161] Hence, Marin, like Houtteville, François, Pluquet, and other eighteenth-century French writers, broadcast Spinoza's theses at great length, affirming their impact and incisiveness while simultaneously

---

[157] Maleville, *Religion naturelle*, iv. 155.
[158] Griffet, *L'Insuffisance*, i. 5–6.
[159] Le Masson des Granges, *Philosophe moderne*, 24–5.
[160] Marin, *Baron Van-Hesden*, i, preface p. viii; Jamin, *Pensées théologiques*, preface p. xiii and pp. 345–6.
[161] Griffet, *L'Insuffisance*, i. 7.

pronouncing them rife with inconsistency. His Bible criticism, including his claim the Pentateuch was not written by Moses but Ezra, is dismissed as worthless chicanery by François.[162] But deception or not, Spinoza's holding there are no basic truths in Scripture other than moral truths was proving a seductive doctrine with undeniable revolutionary reverberations which *anti-philosophes* felt compelled to counter. For the core of their Enlightenment was that theology, science, and philosophy form a harmonious whole explained by reason and precisely this rationally based harmony Spinozism fundamentally challenges. Spinoza ends the fourteenth chapter of *Tractatus Theologico-Politicus* by restating why no one can demonstrate theology contains any truth at all, and why all men of goodwill must acquiesce in this whether they like it or not, urging that it is only through the thoroughgoing separation of philosophy from theology, and our accepting theology cannot provide universal truths, that a more compelling basis for society's moral and legal order can be found and promoted. Only by marginalizing theology can the disputes over religion, doctrine, and ecclesiastical authority, tearing European society apart during the Middle Ages, Reformation, and Wars of Religion, be transcended. Spinoza invites readers to 'take the trouble repeatedly to reflect [on these observations], and understand that he had not written them simply to make novel remarks, but to correct abuses, and indeed hoped one day to see them corrected'.[163]

Despite the weakness of his demonstrations, holds François, Spinoza says everything that can be said 'contre les prophètes' and the *esprits forts* of our day are nothing but 'ses misérables échos'.[164] Spinozism, finally, remained *anti-philosophie*'s principal philosophical target throughout because there were countless *incrédules* like Marin's Van-Hesden, unaware their core ideas derived from, and depended on, this source and were urgently in need of being rescued from the path of 'error'. Most *esprits forts*, stresses Marin, never consciously designed to embrace Spinoza's principles and mostly failed to realize their freethinking stemmed from and relied on such a universally condemned thinker.[165] Were all the vast mass of *incrédules* today corrupting France, Marin's hermit assures the boat captain and passengers, magically to be rolled up into a single roll of cloth, Spinoza would be the original pattern and sample of this universal textile.[166]

Here was indeed a striking paradox. Presenting Spinoza as supreme spokesman of modern incredulity, materialism, secularism, and political subversion was, from the standpoint of French, Italian, Spanish, and German *anti-philosophie*, indispensable but also a decidedly risky procedure, being in itself incoherent. Spinoza's leadership of the philosophical army undermining religion, morality, and the social order was affirmed to lend continuity, coherence, unity, and a clear profile to the seditious, atheistic, revolutionary philosophy *anti-philosophes* vowed to crush. Spinoza served

---

[162] François, *Preuves*, i. 452–526; Marin, *Baron Van-Hesden*, iv. 3–156 and v. 1–196.
[163] Spinoza, *Tractatus-Theologico Politicus*, 185.
[164] François, *Preuves*, ii. 42.
[165] Marin, *Baron Van-Hesden*, i, preface p. iv and ii. 25, 75.
[166] Ibid. i. 67–70.

as the unifying thread and a device for denying Meslier's and Fréret's originality and that of Boulainvilliers—'le commentateur de Spinosa', as Maleville calls him—as well as of Du Marsais, d'Argens, Boulanger, Diderot, Helvétius, Naigeon, Saint-Lambert, Deleyre, Delisle, and latterly d'Holbach and Naigeon. Yet, equally, the *anti-philosophes* insisted on Spinoza's 'obscurity', unoriginality, and lack of cogency, citing and inviting readers to consider his propositions.

In effect, *anti-philosophie* contended that no one can grasp what is happening without grappling with Spinoza. By assigning a unique centrality to Spinoza, many readers were bound to be drawn, in the privacy of their cabinets, to a philosophy they might otherwise have been happy to ignore. Officially, Spinoza was banned, unmentionable except in the terms of the most strenuous disapproval. Behind shutters, though, the picture was different. Voltaire in his last years was merely the most prominent of those obsessively seeking the cracks in Spinoza's seeming cogency. Madame de Genlis, champion of Locke, Newton, and Clarke, in listing the main subversive sources from which the irreligious *philosophes* borrowed their 'sophismes', mostly lists Spinoza first, in one place naming the chief subversive authors of modernity as 'Spinoza, Montaigne, Hobbes, Bayle, Collins and Shaftesbury'. Although Spinoza post-dates Montaigne and Hobbes, she explains, his role is more important than theirs: 'he attacked religion with fury. Ingenious as he was daring, he confounded and overturned all the principles of morality, and formed his frightful system of atheism, with much art, wit, and subtlety. The age he lived in was not far enough advanced for him: he seduced nobody; his incoherence and wickedness were exclaimed against, and his errors appeared equally odious and contemptible.' Yet, despite this, his 'errors' eventually came to 'rise from a long oblivion, and propagate themselves: they have been given to us [by Diderot, d'Holbach and Helvétius] as new and profound reasonings; as lights useful to mankind.'[167]

From the appearance of Helvétius's *De l'esprit*, in 1758, onwards, *la philosophie nouvelle* was portrayed by the *anti-philosophes* as opposed to monarchy, aristocracy, existing morality, and all social subordination and patriotism as well as religion.[168] Hayer firmly attributes such views to *De l'esprit*, a work Madame de Genlis still considered, in 1787, among the most seditious of all the *philosophes'* writings. Helvétius vowed to sweep away those (the clergy and princes) in whose interest it was to keep the people in ignorance, 'ces protecteurs de la stupidité, les plus cruels ennemis de l'humanité'.[169] Helvétius, complains Hayer, supposes the republican citizen's involvement in public affairs elevates him into a more elevated being than the subjects of kings, someone with the freedom 'de tout penser et de tout dire' and hence able to pursue higher ideals. Men submit to a less worthwhile life under monarchy than they could have in a republic, holds Helvétius, due to 'prejudices',

---

[167] Genlis, *Religion*, ii. 80.
[168] Helvétius, *De l'esprit*, 81–3, 350–75; Hayer, *La Religion vengée*, vii. 178–88; Wootton, 'Helvétius', 322–7.
[169] Helvétius, *De l'esprit*, 212, 218; Genlis, *Religion*, i. 30, 106–7.

'superstition' about royalty, like 'superstition' in religion, being instilled into them by priests. This 'philosophie insolente', protests Hayer, usurping the right 'de tout dire', even dares attribute to religion 'les troubles des États'.[170] The monarchical form, insists Chaudon, is unquestionably the best system of government for mankind being 'le plus naturel et le plus ancien' and the most durable. That monarchy provides the firmest government and the authority best suited to counter faction and internal strife, the worst of afflictions besetting mankind, is proved by experience.[171] Since political no less than religious sedition was the *philosophes'* undisguised aim, and given the progress made by this 'esprit de sédition, de révolte, de ligue universelle contre les souverains qui régissent le monde', all monarchs, admonished Dom Richard, must now tremble for their thrones.[172]

Basically true as far as the radical wing was concerned, this charge was bound to turn much or most of society against the *philosophes* generally. For it was not easily countered. Credulity, comments d'Holbach, imprisons 'l'esprit humain' to such a degree that for the unthinking majority everyone spurning 'superstition' is an unnatural 'de-natured' being lacking the right to the normal protection afforded by society. Everywhere, 'la philosophie' is persecuted, excluded from public discourse and education, from the favour and presence of kings and the nobility. Philosophy everywhere cowers in hounded isolation languishing 'dans le mépris'.[173] Intoxicated by the prejudices inculcated into them, most react with furious indignation to all and everything not 'aussi stupides que lui'.[174] Even among peoples priding themselves on being 'les plus libres', like those of England, Holland, and Sweden, superstition retains the power to crush all opposing received opinion.

---

[170] Hayer, *La Religion vengée*, vii. 187.
[171] Chaudon, *Dictionnaire anti-philosophique*, i. 155–6.
[172] Ibid. 210.
[173] D'Holbach, *Essai*, 309.
[174] Ibid. 310; Blom, *Wicked Company*, 96.

7

Central Europe

Aufklärung *Divided*

1. THE LEGACY OF LEIBNIZ AND WOLFF

In central Europe, by contrast, the main declared opponent of radical thought was the Leibnizian-Wolffian system. The 'war of the philosophers' that began in 1723 in central Europe with the expulsion of Christian Wolff (1679–1754) and banning of Wolff's philosophy by the Prussian crown developed, we have seen,[1] into perhaps the most prolonged intellectual battle of the century. It spread through Germany to reach also Switzerland, Austria, Bohemia-Moravia, Scandinavia, and Russia. Formal suppression of Wolff's philosophy at Prussia's four universities—Halle, Frankfurt an der Oder, Königsberg, and Duisburg—in the early 1720s was followed by public condemnations at Wittenberg, Rostock, and Tübingen, and finally Jena, one of the largest and most prestigious German universities, in 1724, with a ruling by the presiding theologian there, Johann Franz Buddeus (1667–1729). Buddeus pronounced Leibniz's and Wolff's most renowned doctrine, the 'pre-established harmony', 'highly damaging and dangerous' to belief in divine providence, free will, and reward and punishment in the hereafter.

However, the sustained onslaught launched by the Pietists and their supporters had also a marked contrary effect. Christian Thomasius (1655–1728) had already, earlier, struggled long and hard to weaken the grip of theological criteria and confessional thinking on the Protestant universities and intellectual arena; and his legacy had entrenched, as one of the foremost objectives of enlightened thinking in early eighteenth-century Germany, the need to restrain the impulse to confessional strife by further propagating his secularizing, non-theological, tolerationist outlook in state, society, and the universities.[2] Within a short time, Wolff's many disciples succeeded in concerting a movement of opposition that steadily grew in scope. If Wolff's foremost adherent in southern Germany, Georg Bernhard Bilfinger (1693–1750), had to leave Tübingen and transfer to Petersburg, the result was that Wolffianism became ensconced in the Russian capital. If the Swiss philosopher Niklaus Engelhard (1696–1765), professor at Duisburg from 1723, had to conceal

---

[1] Israel, *Radical Enlightenment*, 541–62.   [2] Hunter, *Secularisation*, 162–7.

his crypto-Wolffianism for five years before moving on, in 1728, to the freer atmosphere of Groningen, his teaching brought Wolffianism to primacy in the north-east Netherlands. Meanwhile, Wolff himself secured a chair and honoured position at Marburg, in Hesse-Cassel, the university that from the mid 1720s became the new headquarters of what Bilfinger was the first to call the 'Leibnizian-Wolffian system'. Between 1720 and 1740, Wolffianism gradually grew in strength in central Europe, Scandinavia, and Russia alike until by the 1740s it had emerged to a position more hegemonic across a wide area than any other eighteenth-century system.

With Frederick's accession to the throne, in 1740, Wolff was rehabilitated in Prussia with full honours, but not without massive controversy and debate. The contested rise of Leibnizio-Wolffian philosophy to dominance in Protestant central Europe by the early 1740s and Austria (and generally in Catholic central Europe by the 1750s) then in turn decisively influenced the entire further course of the Enlightenment in much of Europe. 'The triumph of the Wolffian philosophy', noted the Göttingen philosopher Johann Georg Heinrich Feder in 1767, was such that 'for a time all those who did not adhere to it were not, in the eyes of many, true philosophers at all'. This Wolffian hegemony brought with it the prevalence of Leibniz's view that God rules the universe through eternal laws but does not intervene in particular cases, which likewise meant rejecting the central principle of Newtonianism that God intervenes constantly and directly to regulate the government of the world and constitutes the motive force that drives it.[3] In Germany and much of northern Europe, Newtonianism and Leibnizio-Wolffianism were systems continually at odds through the 1740s, 1750s, and 1760s, especially in the Berlin and Petersburg academies. Thankfully, 'this prejudice', as Feder called Leibnizio-Wolffianism, had receded somewhat by the 1760s, allowing more room for alternative perspectives.[4]

Leibnizio-Wolffianism was challenged from both Newtonian and Pietist standpoints, both traditions accusing Leibniz and Wolff of embracing fatalism without saying so, as well as by radical thinkers. Yet its broad ascendancy continued at least until around 1780. The Berlin Jewish philosopher Mendelssohn, like many adherents of the Leibnizio-Wolffian system, still seemed confident, as late as 1774, that training students in Wolffian philosophy not only fortifies the kind of Enlightenment that combines with the core of tradition and religion (whether Christianity or Judaism), but likewise strengthens young readers' resistance to the 'writings of the paradoxical philosophers', that is 'Spinoza's posthumous works [*Opera Posthuma*]', the *Système de la nature*, and books of other well-known *esprits forts* representing the main intellectual challenge from the radical side, texts he thought well-educated young persons nevertheless should study 'to help with training the mind'.[5] A decade later, however, during old age, in the mid 1780s, a now deeply alarmed Mendelssohn seemed

---

[3] Israel, *Radical Enlightenment*, 558–62; Ahnert, 'Newtonianism', 474–5.

[4] Ahnert, 'Newtonianism', 483, 488; Feder, *Grundriss*, 43, 341; Heydenreich, *Encyclopädische Einleitung*, 162.

[5] Quoted in Altmann, *Moses Mendelssohn*, 284–5.

distinctly shaken by materialism's accelerating advance over the last thirty or forty years. The Leibnizian-Wolffian philosophy, he recalled, had been so dominant in the 1740s, 1750s, and 1760s that while the assaults of naturalists and freethinkers were noted and discussed, and refutations appeared regularly, their standpoint had been generally scorned. By the early 1780s, by contrast, while the arguments of Leibnizian-Wolffian physico-theology no longer commanded such widespread acceptance, a book like the *Système de la nature* could not only itself appear in German but found many readers and could penetrate deep into the German cultural world.

Wolffianism's success was attributable above all to its systematic quality, combining old and new, its confessional and political neutrality, and overarching comprehensiveness—a satisfyingly unified approach to theology, science, and philosophy. In lands where a legacy of harsh confessional strife that many princes, as well as others, sought to transcend and where rooted institutional and legal archaism blocked organizational reforms, the attraction of a confessionally neutral common culture of training, uniting Germany's patchwork of principalities and thirty universities intellectually while reinforcing submission to princely authority and state approved forms of religion, was huge. Wolffianism was a doctrine prizing order and orderliness above everything, justifying reform through bureaucratic rationalization and innovation, while simultaneously urging acquiescence in the existing religious, political, and social order. Central Europe, a cultural world of confessional disparity and fragmentation rooted in a pervasive dynasticism and courtly ethos, found stability in a system tailored to current needs in the legal, scientific, economic, fiscal, and educational spheres while remaining politically unchallenging and confessionally unproblematic but yet apt for weakening theology's general cultural role.

Does this mean that its early eighteenth-century Pietist foes were mistaken in denouncing Leibnizio-Wolffian doctrine as 'dangerous'? Buddeus and Wolff's leading adversary in Prussia, Joachim Lange (d. 1744), had accused Wolff not of veiled adherence to Spinozistic doctrines as such—for he acknowledged that Leibniz and Wolff genuinely conceived of God and the world as separate entities, and endorsed divine providence—but rather of indirectly opening the gate to Spinozistic naturalism, fatalism, and atheism through muddled thinking. Leibniz's view of the cosmos as ruled by mathematically defined general laws operating mechanistically once God has selected his 'pre-established harmony', or the best possible combination of natural laws, implies, they alleged, an immutable order of cause and effect that for all practical purposes, argued Lange in his *Causa Dei et Religionis Naturalis Adversus Atheismum* (1723) and other polemical writings, renders miracles problematic and ultimately, for those employing reason alone, differs little from *necessitas Spinozistica*. Moreover, contended Lange, Leibniz's thought effectively conflates body and soul. Of course, Leibniz and Wolff vigorously denied this, claiming their *harmonia praestabilita* fully affirms body and soul to be separate substances albeit operating through divine decree, in perfect synchrony, so as to appear to us to function as one.[6]

From the 1740s, the underlying struggle between Wolffianism and radical thought was complicated by the fact that conservative opponents of the emerging Leibnizian-Wolffian ascendancy, Pietists and philosophical eclectics, were by no means finally defeated. Even though their position had weakened by 1740, efforts to condemn Wolff's philosophy stemming from both Pietist and orthodox Lutheran standpoints still exerted a lingering impact. The battle went on even though anti-Wolffian eclectics and traditionalists, and Wolffians, found themselves fully united in one respect: Spinoza's system appeared to them more threatening than any other free-thinking or illicit doctrine because the world, as Feder expressed it, is to eclectics and Wolffians alike, and nearly all mankind, the principal proof of God's goodness, intentions, and perfections, and precisely this truth, the foundation of all Christian systems, Spinozism denies.[7]

An indispensable element in Wolff's success, both before and after 1740, therefore, was his unrelenting campaign, following Leibniz and culminating in his *Theologia Naturalis* (1736), to highlight the principal differences between the Leibnizian-Wolffian system and Spinozism. If Spinozism denies all possibility of miracles, final causes, and divine providence and Spinoza's 'unalterable necessity' undermines all religion, detaching morality completely from religious teaching, his own philosophy, far from disseminating 'fatalism', was the best available antidote to Spinozism.[8] Where Spinoza conflates body and soul, these remain entirely distinct substances in Leibniz and Wolff, except that where Descartes failed to explain the synchronization of the two, Leibniz's pre-established harmony splendidly resolves the problem. Where Spinoza's laws of motion are inherent and immutable, Wolffianism saw the laws of motion as not inherent in the nature of bodies themselves but deriving from the 'wisdom of God'.[9] Where Spinoza's determinism renders the course of nature fixed and unalterable, Leibniz and Wolff taught that 'plures mundos esse possibiles et ex iis Deum liberrime elegisse' [many words are possible and from them God freely chooses], so that general laws operate mechanistically only after God's free choice of the best. Leibniz and Wolff held God's power to extend to innumerable things that have never existed and never will, but could exist provided they are not in logic inherently impossible.[10]

Where Spinozists proclaim an 'absoluta et bruta necessitas', Wolffians theoretically at least were *contingentarii*, claiming God can suspend the order of nature whenever he wishes. Another vital distinction was that where Spinoza's system rules out creation from nothing, the Leibnizian-Wolffian system safeguards creation and

---

[6] Garber, *Leibniz*, 79–81, 263–4; Israel, *Radical Enlightenment*, 548.
[7] Feder, *Grundriss*, 132–4, 149.
[8] Wolff, *De Differentia Nexus*, 14–17, 28–31, 68–9; Laerke, *Leibniz*, 49–50.
[9] Wolff, *Natürliche Gottesgelahrtheit* [Theologia Naturalis], ii. 31; Wolff, *Vernünfftigen Gedancken von Gott*, 274; Bilfinger, *De Harmonia Animi et Corporis*, 113–14.
[10] Wolff, *Natürliche Gottesgelahrtheit* [Theologia Naturalis], ii. 31, 37.

everything the Bible implies about men and species. Through his books and teaching, Wolff continually drew attention to this basic rift in German intellectual life between the Leibnizian-Wolffian system and Spinozism. He did so successfully but at the price of entrenching academic refutation of Spinoza as a regular and absolutely central feature of university training and disputations. If the eighty pages devoted to refuting Spinozism in the *Theologia Naturalis* are largely free of the crude deprecation that had characterized earlier debate about Spinoza, they also helped transform Spinozism into standard fare in German academic discourse. If Wolff held that *Spinozisten* and *Naturalisten*, being universalists and fatalists, 'have no religion', he also declared the need for the philosopher to dispense with theological judgements and demonstrate with purely philosophical and scientific arguments that 'Spinoza did not prove the unalterable necessity of all things and nor could he have.'[11]

Carl Gunter Ludovici (1707–78), Wolff's chief ally at Leipzig, identified the years 1736–7 as the decisive turning point leading to Wolff's ascendancy and the eventual marginalizing of his conservative critics, Pietist traditionalists, and also the Thomasians with their looser, juristic, and eclectic philosophical legacy. Re-installed at Halle, Wolff, in 1743, became rector of the very university from whence he was banished twenty years earlier. It was also from the late 1730s that Wolffianism gained the upper hand in Sweden-Finland, first at Uppsala, then at Finland's university, Åbo (Turku), and, finally, in the mid 1740s, at Lund.[12] If the new king, Frederick, like many German courtiers, preferred French philosophical writings to his own works (much to Wolff's disappointment), and the recently revived Prussian Royal Academy of Sciences, in Berlin, became a battle ground between Wolffians and Newtonians with the latter being locally preponderant, he had the satisfaction at least of seeing his philosophy predominate in all the German and Scandinavian universities, nearly all chairs of philosophy (and many others) by the early 1740s being filled by his followers.

Though well known to specialists, Wolffianism's far-reaching, enduring hegemony in central and northern Europe is rarely stressed sufficiently in general accounts of the Enlightenment. Many historians seem baffled by the obvious fact that neither British nor French influences played any part in its emergence or composition, a reaction rooted in a long-prevailing but unfortunate tendency to overstate the centrality of British and French ideas in the overall make-up of the Western Enlightenment. But the Leibnizian-Wolffian system was not just exceptionally suited as a tool for reorganizing academic knowledge in a post-Aristotelian era, it was an Enlightenment vehicle in every respect. In Habsburg central Europe, the Enlightenment was never directly encouraged by the state during Maria Theresa's reign. Its gradual but eventually impressive advances in Austria and the Czech lands were essentially a localized, bottom-up phenomenon of which the Prague Enlightenment was a classic instance, stemming as it did principally from universities, local reading

---

[11] Wolff, *Natürliche Gottesgelahrtheit* [Theologia Naturalis], iii. 11–13, 22 and vi. 107, 112–13; Israel, *Radical Enlightenment*, 549–50.
[12] Israel, *Radical Enlightenment*, 560–1; Frångsmyr, *Wolffianismens genombrott*, 235.

groups, masonic lodges, and scientific societies as well as a few noble households.[13] At Prague, where Wolffianism's hegemony began in the 1750s with the revolt among the teaching professors, especially a group of Jesuit scholars, led by the mathematician Joseph Stepling (1716–78), against the vestiges of an Aristotelian past that had become discredited, it was, once again, the systematic quality of Wolffianism, its secularizing tendency and ability to bridge the Catholic and Protestant divide, that counted.[14] No other teaching tool could so effectively free philosophy and science from tutelage to theology while plausibly demonstrating why there is no inherent tension between theological truth and science.

From the 1750s, the essential framework of the Bohemian-Moravian Enlightenment was Leibnizian-Wolffian, but it was never just an outgrowth of the German *Aufklärung*. Rather it was an international Catholic synthesis in which Wolffianism, the primary ingredient, was fused with other typically moderate tendencies, most notably Muratori, whose *Della pubblica felicità oggetto dei buoni principi* (1749) envisaged a new balance between faith and society, laying greater stress on social well-being, lay morality, and practical improvements than figured in traditional Catholic doctrine and also on the need in a Catholic context for promoting the advance of letters, science, and medicine.[15] As in Germany, Locke and especially Newtonianism were also active influences. Another characteristic feature was a heavy stress on administrative and technological improvement.

In Germany, Austria, and the Czech lands during the Enlightenment, there was never any significant clash between German and foreign ideas, or between different national influences. Some scholars have tried to bring in the notion of deep-seated national differences; but this is not just unconvincing but highly misleading. The two principal splits within the *Aufklärung* were always between the Wolffian and anti-Wolffian currents vying for dominance of the mainstream, currents of thought officially sponsored and promoted, and, secondly, the divide between these and a rich underground of forbidden ideas, reading, and practices. Interaction between these three main blocs was constant, tense, and ubiquitous but not always characterized by uncompromising antagonism. The ideas of Leibniz and Wolff were also by far the foremost harmonizing and synthesizing engine in Enlightenment central Europe. Wolff's unswerving insistence on a perfect fit between reason and faith, and a problem-free harmony of reason with religious teaching, helped accommodate the new to the old with minimal friction and also, sometimes, compromise with its rivals. And yet the orthodox were right to be suspicious. For precisely in its unyielding insistence on harmonization and the rationality of religion and religious truth lay concealed the seeds of a deep-seated destabilizing tendency.[16]

[13] Israel, *Radical Enlightenment*, 422–6; Schüttler, *Mitglieder*, 222.
[14] Teich, 'Bohemia', 151; Shek Brnardić, 'Enlightenment', 423.
[15] Continisio, 'Governing the Passions', 383–4.
[16] Cassirer, *Philosophy*, 120–1, 175–6; Goldenbaum, 'Der "Berolinismus"', 344–5.

Radical Enlightenment had been firmly rooted in Germany since the 1660s. But during the late seventeenth and early eighteenth century, it succeeded in entrenching itself only clandestinely and in the face of overwhelming repression. A remarkable string of writers, scholars, and publicists, of whom Knutzen, Stosch, Lau, Wachter, Wagner, Edelmann, Hatzfeld, Fischer, and Johann Lorenz Schmidt were foremost, consolidated this entrenched radical tradition composed of illicitly published and manuscript clandestine writings mainly in German but also in Latin and French. Its dissident thinkers operated by establishing tiny informal networks, mostly shirking the limelight and largely inconspicuous but distributed across a strikingly wide territorial span. Unlike France, England, and Scandinavia, German-speaking central Europe comprised a large area disunited to an exceptional degree religiously, culturally, and academically as well as politically. Consequently, there existed no one centre of naturalist and freethinking trends any more than there existed a single centre of mainstream enlightened intellectual activity. Rather there was a growing network of nuclei with Hamburg, Berlin, Halle, Jena, Göttingen, Copenhagen, Königsberg, Leipzig, Vienna, and Prague, and before long also several small courts, such as Weimar and Gotha, at the forefront. If Berlin was the centre of the French-language press, Hamburg-Altona remained the capital of international commerce and epicentre especially of organized religious plurality, heterodox printing, and a broad toleration. Halle, meanwhile, was the chief centre of academic, text-critical scholarship, Göttingen of scientific debate and of intellectual contact with Britain, and Leipzig the unchallenged capital of German publishing and translation.

Leipzig, home to one of Germany's largest universities, also evolved during the 1720s, 1730s, and 1740s into a leading focus of the clandestine radical tendency.[17] It was there since the mid 1720s that the Spinozist librarian and scholar Johann Georg Wachter (1673–1757) resided until his death in 1757, and during the 1720s and 1730s that the anti-Newtonian and fierce critic of the German courts Konrad von Hatzfeld (c.1685–c.1751) tutored extramurally, instructing (his trial records show) numerous students in radical ideas as well as in English. Hatzfeld insisted that the root of all social and political evil in Germany, a 'pays d'esclaves' in his view, was the stifling character of princely government and lack of freedom of expression. He greatly deplored his countrymen's unreasoning deference to court authority and 'thinking that they must let themselves be flayed alive, and stripped of everything, rather than think of resisting their princes'.[18] At his trial for irreligion and blasphemy, at The Hague, in 1745, he freely admitted that, during his years in Leipzig and Berlin, until the early 1740s he regularly inculcated irreligious ideas into the students to whom he taught English.[19]

Also active in Leipzig during the last decades of their lives were Theodor Ludwig Lau (1670–1740) and Christian Gabriel Fischer (c.1690–1751), the latter an exiled

---

[17] Mulsow, *Freigeister*, 11–12.
[18] [Hatzfeld], *Découverte de la vérité*, pp. xl–xli, xlv, and 50; Israel, *Enlightenment Contested*, 338.
[19] ARH Hof van Holland MS 5454/13/I art. 29 and art. 343.

former Königsberg professor dismissed from his chair in 1725 for defiantly championing Wolff. Fischer, a fierce critic of the universities' conservative establishment, like the others, was often accused of fomenting Spinozist ideas.[20] Admittedly, the writings of these figures were not easy to come by. But it would be entirely wrong to infer from this that pre-1750 German materialism, naturalism, atheism, and pantheism were therefore little known. For the most striking feature of the German intellectual scene around 1750 was precisely that the general profile and bibliographical details of the Radical Enlightenment were widely known, indeed more so than anywhere else.

One reason for this greater penetration of 'Spinozism', and wider perception of the radical challenge, in Germany was simply the greater scale of academic culture itself, the sheer number of large libraries, librarians, and bibliographical surveys. Another was the culturally and socially uniquely widespread, developed, and published phenomenon of academic disputation. A further factor was the greater prominence assigned to 'history of philosophy' as an academic discipline than was the case in Britain or France. But the chief reason for the universal awareness of the Spinozist challenge was simply the overwhelming legacy of the Wolffian controversies of the 1720s and 1730s and the continuing hegemony of the Leibnizio-Wolffian system itself. For Wolff's was a system which defined itself—or had been compelled to identify itself—in opposition to Spinoza more than any other and one that prided itself on countering Spinozism with clear, systematic arguments rather than theological denunciation. Students were routinely trained in explaining how the arguments of philosophical atheism and naturalism were ill conceived, how Spinoza had couched his hermeneutics wrongly, how and why Spinoza and Collins 'had pushed die Freiheit zu denken [freedom of thought] too far', as one theologian put it,[21] and why their ideas amount to falling into the trap of 'necessity'. All this conferred on Spinoza a formalized status as presiding chief enemy of received truth and thinking that neither Hobbes nor other thinkers even began to rival.

Consequently, the underground challenge was impressively well publicized and delineated. Several remarkably detailed mid-eighteenth-century general surveys existed, composed by leading mainstream luminaries, most notably Siegmund Jakob Baumgarten (1706–57), a prominent figure at Halle where he was a full professor from 1734 and leading advocate of religious and intellectual toleration, anxious to fend off the challenge by drawing attention to every aspect of what he considered a serious and immediate peril. Laying aside the indignant fulminations of the orthodox, such works insisted on accurately reporting and refuting the 'errors' they fought, not just frankly acknowledging the difficulty of refuting Spinoza, Bayle, and their disciples but also here and there acknowledging positive elements in the views of the radical-minded. The Wolffians in this way enthroned the Radical Enlightenment at the very heart of the mainstream *Aufklärung*.

[20] Mulsow, *Freigeister*, 12–13.
[21] Löwe, *Dogmatische und moralische*, 7.

An ardent Wolffian since around 1730, and a highly effective lecturer who knew how to fill the lecture room, Baumgarten possessed an exceptionally wide knowledge of the theological and philosophical literature of his age which he employed in his campaign to reconcile the factions within Lutheranism and reconcile Lutheranism with Wolffianism, and hence with the Enlightenment generally.[22] He has aptly been called 'the preeminent representative of "theological Wolffianism"', and as such stood foremost among moderate mainstream German academic theologians striving to establish a limited toleration banishing confessional strife in favour of what he hoped would prove a lasting harmonization of reason and faith.[23] His entire intellectual strategy aimed to reconcile philosophy with theology, Lutheran orthodoxy with Pietism, toleration with coherence, and reason with faith as well as broadening Leibniz's concept of divine providence as regulating only the general lines with a providence guiding the particular lives of individuals.[24]

Especially striking is his bibliographical panorama of radical literature occupying a large portion of his eight-volume *Nachrichten von einer Hallischen Bibliothek* (1748–51), one of his best-known works. Here he provides all known details of Spinoza's works, everything related to Spinoza and the Dutch 'Spinozists', such as Lodewijk Meyer (1629–81), Abraham Johannes Cuffeler (*c.*1634–97),[25] and Johannes Bredenburg (1643–91), explaining the significance of this legacy for contemporary society. Maximilien Lucas figures as a devoted disciple of Spinoza and probable author of the 'godless' manuscript 'L'Esprit de Spinoza'. Meyer's *De Jure Ecclesiasticorum* (1665) was, he believed, neither by Meyer nor Spinoza. Meyer's *Philosophia Scripturae Interpres* (1666) is discussed from every angle with everything ascertainable about editions and translations recounted. One after the other, all the French and British as well as German naturalists, atheists, and anti-Scripturalists are examined for the benefit of scholars and students, one of his passages supplying the first detailed account of Radicati's thought and writings in German.[26] In fact, in Baumgarten, radical thought receives more space and greater eminence than any other challenge to the Wolffian ascendancy, strikingly eclipsing recent philosophical developments in England, for instance, a tradition which by and large Wolffians felt little need to address, not regarding the Leibnizian-Wolffian legacy as particularly at risk from this direction.

A declared enemy of all naturalism, freethinking, and Spinozism, Baumgarten, who built up one of the most impressive private libraries in Germany, was nevertheless sufficiently fascinated and preoccupied with these trends to become himself one of the most avid collectors of its illicit texts in Dutch and English as well as Latin, French, and German. Familiar with the *Cérémonies et coutumes religieuses de tous les*

[22] Löwe, *Dogmatische und moralische*, 128–9; *Nouvelle Bibliothèque germanique*, 24 (Jan.–Mar. 1759), 336, 340; Bordoli, *L'Illuminismo*, 39–40, 173–4.
[23] Lehner, *Kants Vorsehungskonzept*, 159–61, 168, 171; Sorkin, *Religious Enlightenment*, 115.
[24] Lehner, *Kants Vorsehungskonzept*, 161, 165–6.
[25] Baumgarten, *Nachrichten*, i. 141–8; Bordoli, *L'Illuminismo*, 16 n.
[26] Baumgarten, *Nachrichten*, ii. 527–43.

peuples du monde,[27] he was aware (as many were not) that it was edited by the adroit and wide-ranging Jean-Frédéric Bernard and relied for its subversive impact on incorporating passages of Boulainvilliers, Lahontan, and a range of Socinians.[28] Boulainvilliers's *Essai de métaphysique* he rightly deems a reworking of Spinoza's *Ethics* containing the 'most zealous defense of the grossest errors of Spinoza', and his *Vie de Mahomed* a full-scale attack on Christianity as a moral and social system.[29] Tyssot de Patot emerges in full detail,[30] as do Toland, Collins, Du Marsais's *Nouvelles Libertés de penser*, La Mettrie, and Diderot's *Pensées philosophiques*, along with the German response to the latter published at Halle in 1748.[31]

Another of Baumgarten's principal works presenting a not dissimilar picture was his *Geschichte der Religionspartheyen* [History of the Religious Parties] (1754), a compendium originating as a series of lectures delivered at Halle in the early 1750s. Edited by his best student, Semler, and published at Halle in 1766, it again demonstrated immense erudition. Baumgarten, in short, not only provided the most comprehensive tableau then available of the Radical Enlightenment, and its secret texts, but demonstrates in detail how all this was ramifying as an underground culture in Germany. His research underpinned a typically Wolffian refusal to be satisfied with merely denouncing the Spinozists and materialists as was usual among more traditional theologians. Engaging in an argued debate he strives to vanquish materialism and Spinozism in part via the risky strategy of trying to narrow the scope of the danger to be repelled, through hiving off and retrieving supposedly less objectionable strands and deliberately absorbing these into the wider philosophical synthesis he and other Wolffians strove to establish, continuing a project initiated by Leibniz that typified the Wolffian *Aufklärung* more generally.

At pains accurately to classify and evaluate even the more minor freethinkers' positions, Baumgarten was keenly aware of the need to differentiate between *eigentlichen Spinozisten*, or real Spinozists, such as (in his opinion) Meyer, Lucas, Boulainvilliers, and Hendrik Wyermars, whose *Den Ingebeelde Chaos* directly contradicts the doctrine of creation and presents the entire structure and organization of reality from an unmitigated Spinozistic perspective,[32] and writers synthesizing strands of *Spinozismus* with less sophisticated forms of atheism and materialism. He was especially anxious clearly to differentiate newer strands of radical thought from older types of atheism and materialism. Of course, there had been all manner of heterodox, sceptical, non-dogmatic, and unsystematic atheists in the world since the rise of philosophy, he reminds readers, but this was largely irrelevant in the modern context. What mattered now were the systematic philosophical atheists and materialists classifiable either as *eigentlichen Spinozisten* or approximate Spinozists, thinkers

---

[27] Baumgarten, *Nachrichten*, viii (1751), 31–45.
[28] Hunt, Jacob, and Mijnhardt, *Book*, 119, 222–4, 261; Israel, *Enlightenment Contested*, 377–80.
[29] Baumgarten, *Nachrichten*, i (1748), 26–33, 132–40; Bordoli, *L'Illuminismo*, 16 n.
[30] Baumgarten, *Nachrichten*, iii. 124–40.
[31] Ibid. ii. 476.
[32] Baumgarten, *Geschichte*, 39, 44.

characterized especially by their making no distinction between God and the world. Only via Spinozism, he insists, can modern philosophical materialism, naturalism, and anti-Scripturalism derive real force, direction, and serious coherence, the capability to drive a powerful plea for comprehensive toleration and freedom of thought. Hence, a prime task of the truly enlightened scholar is to block—but also retrieve elements from—the philosophical conception of the universe, based on reason alone, that Spinoza introduced into the world.

Baumgarten provided vivid accounts of all the German freethinkers, among them Johann Christian Edelmann (1698–1767), the best remembered of the early eighteenth-century German radicals in the later eighteenth century who, as we have seen, stirred up a hornets' nest with his widely banned *Moses mit aufgedeckten Angesichte* [The Revealed Face of Moses], in 1740, a work styling Scripture a purely human book, rejecting divine providence and original sin and calling for full freedom of thought, drawing on Toland and Collins besides Spinoza.[33] This book provoked dozens of published refutations, rendering Edelmann one of the most decried writers of the age. Much of the response, though, showed little inclination to take Edelmann's arguments seriously. According to the Gotha preacher Johann Caspar Löwe in 1751, Edelmann was a leading 'naturalist' and pantheist along with Spinoza, Toland, Collins, and Tindal but one who, like the others, was totally mistaken and just an 'ignorant' slanderer of Scripture.[34] The Wolffian intellectual elite, by contrast, felt the need to demonstrate that his arguments were erroneous. By 1748 Germany's foremost radical dissident had become the focus of a full-scale investigation by the Imperial Book Commission in Frankfurt, and concerted persecution on all sides. Having earlier been forced to flee from the principality of Neuwied, his home for many years, he found a precarious refuge, in 1746, at Altona, but, after his publications were publicly burned by the Frankfurt city government in May 1750, felt insecure there and was reduced to seeking protection from Frederick the Great, a monarch he professed to despise. Frederick permitted him to live unmolested in Berlin where, under an assumed name, he anxiously eked out the remainder of his days, but only on condition that he publish nothing more and remain henceforth completely silent.[35] A lifelong foe of radical thought, Frederick preferred not to permit publication of anything apt to disturb the prejudices and received beliefs of the common people.

Prolific and provocative Edelmann was no systematic thinker. On this ground, modern scholars maintain that he was not really a 'Spinozist'. But the pedantic habit of approaching Edelmann (as Stosch and Lau), as if the issue was whether they would pass a test before a modern analytical philosopher as consistent 'Spinozists', is quite unhistorical and from an intellectual historical point of view distinctly misleading.[36]

---

[33] Baumgarten, *Geschichte*, 5, 7; Edelmann, *Moses*, i. 131 and ii. 54, 60, 118–62.
[34] Löwe, *Dogmatische und moralische*, 5, 394, 444; Otto, *Studien*, 109 n.
[35] Mirabeau, *De la monarchie*, v. 40; Israel, *Radical Enlightenment*, 663.
[36] Schröder, *Spinoza*, 25–7; Otto, *Studien*, 108.

Whether or not Edelmann's formulations hang together coherently, whether or not the Spinozist strands in his thought precisely replicate Spinoza's argument, is scarcely relevant to what chiefly marks him out in cultural history. The real point, perfectly grasped by contemporary critics like Baumgarten and Semler, is that his religious and philosophical standpoint was steeped in Spinoza and closely tied to religious *tolérantisme*, political subversion, and sexual reformism. Edelmann mattered not because of philosophical coherence, or lack of it, but owing to his unconcealed desire to be a 'world reformer', as one opponent derisively put it.[37] He counted because of his unusually tenacious, and strongly subversive, anti-theological and revolutionary thrust.

Contemporary critics, however appalled, responded to his *Moses, Glaubensbekentniss*, and other writings, because they had a wide impact and categorically deny a separate, personal God, creation, miracles, revelation, free will, and the Christian religion as normally understood, denouncing the clergy as 'deceivers' and purveying doctrines directly opposed to ecclesiastical and princely authority. It is this combination of holding the world to be God and rejecting revealed religion and the miraculous, together with the stress on emancipating men socially, religiously, and sexually, and his plainly stated opposition to all existing political and social norms, that makes Edelmann fundamental in the story of the German Radical Enlightenment and places him firmly under the rubric of what was then meant by 'Spinozism'. By constantly bracketing Edelmann with Spinoza, contemporaries were not suggesting his system was absolutely identical to Spinoza's or that Spinoza was his sole guide. Far from it, as we see from Johann Christoph Harenberg (1696–1774), general school inspector of Brunswick-Lüneburg and an ardent champion of Locke's limited toleration, as well as, from 1738, member of the Berlin Academy of Sciences, whose two-volume 834-page assault on Edelmann was published at Brunswick in 1747–8. The 'doctrine Edelmann reiterates', he explains, 'is no different from the self-contradictory teaching of Spinoza', his predecessors being the 'Pantheists of the ancient world and include, besides the said Benedict Spinoza, also John Toland, Anthony Collins, Matthew Arnold, Thomas Woolstson, Theodor Ludwig Lau, and other such confused riff-raff'.[38] Edelmann's system is mostly already present, he remarks, in Lau's *Meditationes* of 1717.[39] Yet, where Collins and Lau are only referred to in passing and Toland to a modest extent, the whole weight of Harenberg's polemic rests on the thesis that 'Spinozism' is manifestly wrong, evil, and execrable as it overthrows religion, political obedience, and society's accepted norms, and because, in Germany, Spinoza succeeded in establishing a sect that directly menaces the religious, social, and political order.[40]

In his second volume, Harenberg launches into lengthy digressions about Wachter and La Mettrie, and (very) briefly discusses Hobbes. But again the whole burden of

---

[37] Hanssen, *Anmerckungen*, 43–4, 161, 244, 297.
[38] Harenberg, *Gerettete Religion*, i, preface pp. A5–A7; [I.L.V.M.C.E,] *Neue Offenbahrung*, 16–20, 52–7, 85.
[39] Harenberg, *Gerettete Religion*, i. 336–7.
[40] Ibid. ii. 648; Hanssen, *Anmerckungen*, 274–80, 281, 285.

the discussion revolves around Spinoza and, to a lesser extent, Toland. 'Everything created and propagated in the world is, following the pantheistic teaching, brought about through an inner working, *per actionem immanentem*.'[41] Here was the crucial issue: Edelmann, for Harenberg, is just part of a wider pantheistic threat to society, like Toland, a mere aide-de-camp trailing after Spinoza, carrying his heavy weapons, as he puts it,[42] an adherent of a Pantheistic movement revolving around Spinoza for whom 'Creation is nothing but procreation and propagation', miracles are impossible, and 'the New Testament an ancient, defective and purely human book'.[43] 'Edelmannische Freigeisterey' [Edelemanian freethinking], insists Harenberg, belongs to an underground threatening to destroy religion, piety, and society with one-substance doctrine. Advocates of one substance deny a personal God who rewards and punishes in the hereafter, maintaining that 'the World is God' and that 'when dogs bite each other, God bites himself'.[44] The kind of *Freigeisterei* stemming from Spinoza and Toland, moreover, Harenberg held to lead directly to sexual freedom.[45] Moreover, 'Spinozistische Lehre' [Spinozistic doctrines] try to show that kings are not knowingly placed over men by God and that the 'unalterable *Zusammenhang der Natur* [order of nature] abolishes morality'.[46] Among 'Spinozists', oaths and fear of divine retribution have no meaning. This is why Pantheism and 'Spinozism' are not tolerated in Germany, he asserts, reminding readers of Locke's view that atheists should not be permitted in any Christian society.[47]

Baumgarten, by contrast, offers arguments and yearns for the 'light of reason' to enlighten all men, including the editors of the underground literature he strove to combat, though this does not mean that he, any more than Edelmann's less liberal opponents, approved of a fully free press or free expression in Spinoza's or Collins's sense. While attempting to be coolly impartial in broaching the Edelmann controversies, he remained strikingly less worried by what he concedes was the excessive harshness of most of Edelmann's critics than by the, to him, disturbing signs of tacit, anonymous support for Edelmann in contemporary society. An anonymous pamphlet he reviewed at length in 1748, that in his opinion had been rightly banned, was the *Freye doch unmassgebliche Gedancken und Erinnerungen über die bisherigen Streitschriften wider den herrn Edelmann* [Free but Humbly Offered Thoughts and Recollections of the Polemical Writings against Herr Edelmann thus far] (1747). Uncharacteristically indignant, Baumgarten rebukes its author for pretending to adopt a tone of calm reasonableness while actually showing no 'upright and grounded impartiality' or love of truth.[48] For besides digressing 'in praise of the

---

[41] Harenberg, *Gerettete Religion*, ii. 441; [I.L.V.M.C.E,] *Neue Offenbahrung*, 4–6, 19–20.
[42] Harenberg, *Gerettete Religion*, ii. 642, 648.
[43] Ibid. i. 36–7, 49; Otto, *Studien*, 107–8.
[44] Harenberg, *Gerettete Religion*, i. 31–2, 191, 305–6, 320–7.
[45] [I.L.V.M.C.E,] *Neue Offenbahrung*, 84.
[46] Harenberg, *Gerettete Religion*, i. 59–60.
[47] Ibid. i. 72; [I.L.V.M.C.E,] *Neue Offenbahrung*, 113–14.
[48] Baumgarten, *Nachrichten*, i. 263.

infamous Spinoza and his errors', the author states that 'history shows that the theologians of most nations have been deceivers, and that it is not easy to be confident the clergy of today's religions are free from the same accusation'.[49]

More than perhaps any other clandestine production of around 1750, this text was symptomatic of the growing scale of the rift between moderate and Radical Enlightenment in mid-eighteenth-century Germany. Edelmann's writings, explains its author, had 'startled' and shaken a great many minds. Having seen all the publications *pro et contra* relevant to this furore, the anonymous author censures the way not only theologians but recent professional philosophers unhesitatingly decry Spinoza as the 'most abominable atheist, indeed more harmful than all other atheists'.[50] To call an 'atheist' someone who speaks so much of God, and so earnestly champions true morality, is un-philosophical, reprehensible, and absurd. Furthermore, this is only part of a more general 'deception' theologians have foisted on mankind 'in order to put themselves in authority, satisfy their avarice, ambition and licentiousness, and keep the common people in slavery, and often even to keep the secular authorities under their sway'.[51]

The Reformation, he argues, had begun clearing away 'superstition' but dismally failed to complete the job. One is ashamed at how widespread crass confessional thinking remains in Protestant Germany. Belief in the damnation of un-baptized infants and talk of goblins and fairies along with sorcery and witchcraft abounded. No reasonable Jew, Turk, or heathen ever believed neighbours of other faiths are destined for eternal damnation. Being steeped in intolerance, how utterly inferior present-day Christianity—not to mention the even more barbaric faith of Charlemagne and the Crusades—is in this respect as in others to the authentic, original teaching of Christ based on 'universal love'. If conventional religion requires censorship and compulsion to sustain it, the 'pure truth' based on reason needs no such unworthy foundation. The first step to a true reformation of religion, morality, and society is grasping that Christ cannot possibly be the sole path to salvation. The next is to grasp that Scripture is both imperfect and obscure; and the next that reason is the only sure and infallible guide in human life.[52] Anyone who truly follows reason will be 'no enemy of the true Christian morality'.[53] All those who have any feeling for mankind's 'misery', who know how often wretched circumstances have led to depravity, and see how much incomprehension contributes to failure to control our passions, and how much stems from good or bad upbringing and example, will realize that it is no fault of ordinary folk that they have come into life in conditions of such abject slavery, and that morality has so direly decayed.

In Leipzig, Berlin, Halle, and Hamburg-Altona, then, an indigenous Radical Enlightenment compounded of a mixture of Spinozism with Socinianism, Baylisme, and 'left' Wolffianism furthered by academic text-critical scholarship, and from the

---

[49] Ibid. i. 252–7.   [50] *Freye doch unmassgebliche Gedancken*, 3.
[51] Ibid. 10.   [52] Ibid. 16–19.   [53] Ibid. 41.

1740s also French materialism, had taken firm root and was spreading widely in German culture. Stosch, Lau, Wachter, Edelmann, and Schmidt were generally considered an integral part of a Spinozistic tendency heavily infiltrating the general culture of central Europe. It is doubtless true that key intellectual figures of the post-1750 era, like Lessing and Herder, found their own way to Spinoza directly and not via German radical writers, rather the reverse. Lessing was already engrossed in Spinoza by the early 1750s while Herder first became immersed in Spinoza from 1768 or 1769. Yet we should not underestimate the impact and pervasiveness of the clandestine tradition Baumgarten and others went to such pains to delineate. If Lessing and Herder only subsequently took an interest in Wachter, Lau, and Edelmann, their involvement with these writers nevertheless eventually grew: Herder had no less than five works by Edelmann in his library by the time of his death in 1803.[54]

Baumgarten showed his irenic side to better advantage with respect to Johann Lorenz Schmidt (1702–49), the translator—or as some preferred 'author'—of the notorious 'Wertheim Bible' of 1733 who, he thought, had been shamefully mistreated by those who persecuted him in the 1730s. For all his daring challenges to conventional thinking and assault on miracles, Schmidt wrote 'with too much respect and regard for the Bible', and for morality, to be deemed a mocker of religion.[55] Having escaped from his persecutors in southern Germany, Schmidt took refuge in Altona in 1738 under an assumed name 'Johann Ludwig Schroeter', surreptitiously continuing his career in illicitly published books. A Socinian steeped in Wolff, Schmidt claimed to be, and was, countering Spinozism and materialism from a 'left' Wolffian standpoint. Yet he was also an active propagator of Spinozism and materialism. It was at Altona that he translated Spinoza's *Ethics* into German (the only vernacular translation of the work to appear anywhere in Europe during the eighteenth century), an undertaking begun in 1742, using the copy and with the help of an Altona Sephardic Jewish doctor, David Gerson, reputed to be a passionate Spinozist.[56]

Moreover, this translation and the accompanying refutation, by Wolff, appearing under the title *B.v.S. Sittenlehre, widerleget von dem berümten Weltweisen unserer Zeit, Herrn Christian Wolff* (1744) [BdS. Ethics Refuted by the Famous Philosopher of our Time Herr Christian Wolff], Baumgarten pronounced highly competent but also, from a religious and moral standpoint, profoundly ill advised. Schmidt's stated justification for 'making this dangerous text known in our mother tongue', in his translator's preface, namely his desire to make Wolff's response better known, he found distinctly 'weak' since Wolff's refutation does not deal with remotely all the dangerous propositions in the *Ethics* but only its first premises, the rest being left unanswered or dealt with only by complex inference. Therefore, Schmidt was in fact publishing Spinoza without any adequate antidote. Unfortunately, in Germany there

---

[54] Bell, *Spinoza in Germany*, 40, 42, 54.
[55] Baumgarten, *Geschichte*, 152; Baumgarten, *Nachrichten*, viii. 2–18.
[56] Winkler, *Heimlichen Spinozisten*, 32–3.

was no lack of readers 'who with the greatest avidity' soak up Spinoza's arguments 'without bothering themselves with the refutations of these'.[57] He was willing to believe, though, this was just a regrettable lapse of judgement on Schmidt's part rather than deliberate subversion.

Schmidt, however, also translated other key radical works. At Leipzig in 1747 there appeared, without the name of either the author, translator, or publisher on the title page, his German translation of Du Marsais's *Examen de la religion*, among the most flagrantly irreligious of all the clandestine philosophical manuscripts of the eighteenth century, under the title *Die wahre Religion, oder die Religionsprüfung*. Prior to 1745, judging from the absence of surviving early copies in Germany, this text had spread mostly in France and exclusively in manuscript. But after being clandestinely printed in French, at Amsterdam in 1745, it began circulating in the German courts as did two reissues of this edition, in 1747 and 1749, these two latter editions probably produced at Potsdam.[58] The German translation of this 'poisonous libel', as the Gotha pastor Löwe called it in 1747, closely followed the arrival of the French version in German cultural life and notably contributed to the public controversy that now ensued. Some dozen publications appeared between 1745 and 1750 in Germany debating this text.[59]

Among those discussing Du Marsais's *Examen* in its German version were two leading Halle professors, Georg Friedrich Meier and, again, Baumgarten. With the diffusion of Du Marsais's *Examen* in French and German, the atheistic challenge, urged Baumgarten, had taken on in Germany a distinctly more threatening aspect. In his *Evangelischen Glaubenslehre* published posthumously in 1759–60, edited once more by Semler, Baumgarten pronounces reason the essential test of the truth of religious dogmas and the basic tool for studying Scripture. As a Wolffian, he deemed the world to be created by God and conserved in its proper order by divine providence while nothing inconsistent with reason can be part of divine revelation or result from properly grounded Bible hermeneutics.[60] But in Du Marsais's *Examen*, one finds the same stress on reason except expressed now with undisguised anti-Christian intent. Edelmann and Schmidt in some respects converged with Du Marsais's criticism of religion, attacks on religious authority, and priestcraft, but neither had finally relinquished a certain residual deistic religiosity and both repudiated Du Marsais's undisguised materialism and atheism. French materialism was fast becoming the core of the threat but this was just a shift of emphasis not a change of direction.[61] It was simply a more exact and accurate reworking of Spinoza's legacy.

---

[57] Baumgarten, *Nachrichten*, i. 115.
[58] Mori, 'Einleitung', pp. xxiii–xxiv.
[59] Ibid., p. xxiv; Löwe, *Dogmatische und moralische*, 7–8.
[60] Mori, 'Einleitung', 134–7, 142–3.
[61] Baumgarten, *Geschichte*, 37, 39, 44, 135, 142; Mori, 'Einleitung', pp. xxviii–xxix.

2. BERLIN AND ITS ROYAL ACADEMY

The encounter of French and German thought was nowhere more likely to yield dramatic results than in Berlin where Frederick the Great's recently revived Berlin Academy was among the foremost international mediators of the Enlightenment, albeit one with a peculiarly Frederician court slant. For it was a body that as late as 1774 remained heavily dominated by Huguenots, Swiss, and Frenchmen, Frederick purposely minimizing the presence of Germans and debarring Jews, the leading Jewish philosopher of the age, Moses Mendelssohn (1729–86) (who was several times proposed for the Academy by the academicians), being expressly rejected.[62] The Academy sought to mediate between Prussia and Europe but was also mediated in another sense. For while Frederick has often been credited with introducing freedom of the press and freedom of thought—and while he invited d'Argens, La Mettrie, and Voltaire to his court[63]—he quickly clawed back the press freedom he allowed initially, and by no means only with respect to Edelmann. Rather than allowing press freedom what he really aimed at was to remodel the Prussian censorship by vastly reducing the influence of theologians over the process and assigning control to a board of censors presided over by the high bureaucracy together with the Academy to which most of the board belonged. He never proclaimed any general principle of freedom of expression and the press or sought to enshrine any such principle in law.[64] The Berlin Academy also embodied Frederick's characteristic notion that the best exponents of science and philosophy could and should be raised to world eminence and influence by royal authority rather than left to emerge by elections or canvassing opinion among the Academy's thinkers and scientists themselves.

Under the freedom of the press decree of 1749, the basic function of the new Prussian censorship was to preserve public order and the interests of the state and crown while ensuring prevailing conventional religious and moral notions were not affronted or disturbed. Though more extensive than press freedom in most of the rest of Germany, Frederick's press 'freedom' was still powerfully constrained. It was with some reason, then, that Radical Enlightenment writers working in Prussia, like the erudite official (and Spinozist) Heinrich Friedrich Diez (1751–1817), who published the first major plea for comprehensive freedom of thought and the press in central Europe in 1781, while praising Frederick, could consider Germany a country where the life of the mind languished in fetters. Germany was a slavish land where philosophy remained distinctly backward by comparison with France, Diderot, Helvétius, and Voltaire, to him, being his century's greatest thinkers. German philosophy was 'slavish' because its socially and politically imposed function hitherto had been 'to prove the truth of Christianity' rather than seek the truth as such.[65]

---

[62] Pilati, *Lettere*, 70; [Mirabeau], *De la monarchie*, i. 214–15.
[63] Blanning, *Culture of Power*, 224.
[64] Ibid. 223–4; [Mirabeau], *De la monarchie*, i. 144; Tortarolo, *Ragione interpretata*, 157–8.
[65] Diez, *Apologie*, 47–9, 62.

The first president of Frederick's Academy, Maupertuis, a veteran Newtonian, had all along striven to diminish the standing of the Leibnizio-Wolffian philosophy in Germany. Seeing its prime task as being to counter the 'tyranny' of Wolffianism over the German philosophical mind,[66] he established an enduring tradition at the Academy that survived almost down to the great philosophical drama of the 1780s. His antipathy to Leibniz and Wolff was apparent not least from his *Essai de cosmologie* (1750), a work rendered into German by Lessing's cousin, ally, and early mentor, the naturalist, mathematician, and journalist Christlob Mylius (1722–54). Here Maupertuis unveiled his soon celebrated 'principe de la moindre action' [principle of least action], a theistic thesis according to which 'la quantité d'action' in the universe is always 'la plus petite qu'il soit possible', the least possible for its purpose, a physico-theological principle Kant, among others, expressly embraced until the 1760s.[67] What Kant, in 1763, called 'this important new insight' extremely useful for countering the dogma of 'blind necessity', Maupertuis deemed his crowning accomplishment, a thesis vital for grasping the nature of the cosmos and the most economical and straightforward proof of God's existence.[68]

Maupertuis also considered it a potent weapon (which it hardly was) against the dominant Leibnizio-Wolffians. Meanwhile, in 1751, a Swiss Wolffian mathematician resident in Holland, Samuel König (1712–57), former science tutor to Voltaire's lover Madame Du Châtelet, published at Berlin a forceful refutation of Maupertuis's theorem which he pronounced in part 'absolument faux' and for the rest true but already formulated, decades earlier, by Leibniz. While it was not his intention to accuse the Berlin Academy's president of deliberate plagiarism,[69] his objections precipitated a major furore, termed the 'affaire König', possibly the worst-tempered controversy to mar Berlin intellectual life in the eighteenth century. Had Leibniz really preceded Maupertuis in formulating the 'principle of least action'? Having examined König's objections, the Academy's mainly French-speaking fellows, prodded by Maupertuis and another Swiss mathematician, Leonhard Euler, one of their most eminent members, denounced König's conduct in the harshest terms, though a minority dissociated themselves from this judgement, albeit saying nothing publicly.[70] In June 1752 was published an official *jugement*, in the royal name, composed by the ardent anti-Wolffian Euler, declaring König guilty of disreputably adducing a forged copy of a non-existent Leibniz letter to malign the Academy's president.

Maupertuis's aim was to blight König's reputation and rebuff Leibnizism. Resigning his associate membership, König retaliated in collusion with Lessing's cousin Mylius, who since the mid 1740s had been active as a journalist, in the years 1745–7 publishing a weekly called *Der Freygeist*. Mylius, a young man of crypto-materialist tendencies acquired studying at Leipzig where Gottsched was one of his favourite

[66] Rehberg, *Sämmtliche Schriften*, i. 5–6.
[67] Beeson, *Maupertuis*, 243; Kant, *Einzig mögliche Beweisgrund*, 142.
[68] Kant, *Einzig mögliche Beweisgrund*, 142–3; Holland, *Réflexions*, ii. 81–2.
[69] Goldenbaum, 'Bedeutung', 389; Beeson, *Maupertuis*, 243.
[70] Beeson, *Maupertuis*, 244; [Rousseau], *Journal encyclopédique* (Bouillon, 1760), iv. 128–9.

teachers, was to die prematurely, at the age of only 31, in 1754. His writings were published shortly afterwards by his cousin Lessing,[71] on whose early development he exerted a considerable influence, but were banned in several states, including the Austrian monarchy, along with Lessing's early writings. Mylius' support enabled König to react by publishing an 'Appel au Public', an interesting example of the growing role of the general reading public in intellectual controversy. No learned academy, insisted König and Mylius, can be judge and jury concerning matters of mathematical and philosophical truth. Everyone is equal in the quest for knowledge as only demonstration through evidence and clear argument can be the criteria of what is true. As news of the scandal spread to the non-Prussian German and Dutch journals, the uproar not only exasperated Maupertuis but caused Frederick to worry that his Academy's international reputation was at stake.[72]

Although no printed criticism of the royal Academy was permitted inside Prussia, much criticism was expressed elsewhere, privately, even in Berlin. Mylius' scathing account of the Academy's procedures appeared in Hamburg.[73] The Leipzig *Neuen Zeitungen von gelehrten Sachen*, in Saxony, openly questioned the propriety of the Academy's *jugement*. At this point, Voltaire, then at Potsdam as Frederick's special guest but who disliked Maupertuis, also intervened on König's side, notably in the September 1752 issue of the Amsterdam journal *La Bibliothèque raisonnée* where he attacks Maupertuis's argument devastatingly, echoing Mylius' objections while also noting the unjust manner in which Maupertuis had abused his position as Academy president to condemn König's objections to his theorem officially and so peremptorily. Annoyed to find his president and Academy being belittled in this fashion, Frederick rebuked Voltaire who, mightily offended by this rebuke, next proceeded to publish his *Diatribe du docteur Akakia*, a satirical piece devastatingly deriding Maupertuis's writings and pretensions and, by implication, also the royal assault on the impartiality of reason.[74] Frederick replied by having nearly the entire stock of copies seized and burned, prompting Voltaire to resign his court sinecures and request leave to depart.

Just prior to Voltaire's departure, in April 1753, there appeared in London a volume entitled *Maupertuisiana*, containing interventions in the affair by various authors and also two pieces by Frederick himself, his eulogies of La Mettrie and of Charles-Étienne Jordan, where he explicitly espouses freedom of thought, texts plainly added in a subversive spirit to underline Frederick's despotic and blatant hypocrisy in this case. Their quarrel over Maupertuis long rankled with both Frederick and Voltaire despite repeated mutual efforts afterwards to repair the split. As late as 1771, after approving the statue to Voltaire that d'Alembert planned to have erected in the 'Athènes moderne' (Paris), Frederick was riled to find in

[71] *Catalogus Librorum Rejectorum, Continuatio* (1755); Mulsow, *Freigeister*, 57, 78.
[72] [Rousseau], *Journal encyclopédique*, 4: 121; Goldenbaum, 'Friedrich II', 124.
[73] Goldenbaum, 'Bedeutung', 402; Goldenbaum, 'Beziehungen', 90–1.
[74] Gay, *Voltaire's Politics*, 155–6; Pearson, *Voltaire Almighty*, 228–9; Goldenbaum (ed.), *Appell an das Publikum*, ii. 515–23.

Voltaire's *Questions sur l'Encyclopédie* yet another unrestrained attack on the long-dead Maupertuis, revealing a thirst for vengeance 'so atrocious that I almost repent of my contributing to the statue'. 'Bon dieu! Comment tant de génie se peut il allier avec tant de perversité!'[75]

Maupertuis in his last years, gloomy and deeply shaken, shifted from deism to openly professed belief in Christianity, though some discounted this as a tactic for public consumption rather than a genuine conversion.[76] It was against this background that the Royal Academy's prize competition committee, in 1753, invited essays, to be submitted by 1 January 1755, comparing the claim 'All is good' in Alexander Pope's *An Essay on Man* with Leibniz's 'system of optimism', his doctrine that this world is the best of all possible worlds, and that if God had not chosen the best world order from the possibilities available he would have chosen none. Discerning observers, Kant, Lessing, and Mendelssohn among them, at once recognized in the choice of prize topic of 'this acute and learned man', as Kant styled Maupertuis, a continuation of his feud with König, posing yet again the question of Leibniz's and Wolff's legacy. Kant considered competing but decided not to out of regard for Maupertuis and the Academy which he deeply respected.[77] He did, though, pen some fragments on Leibniz's optimism, criticizing him for excusing the world's evils and irregularities on the assumption God exists, and that he therefore must have done the best he could; Leibniz should have proceeded without making such assumptions, arguing by demonstration that the 'universal agreement and arrangements of the world, if they can be acknowledged to exist in and for themselves, furnish the most beautiful proof of God's existence and the universal dependency of all things on Him'.[78]

Lessing, highly critical of the Academy, did compete, persuading Mendelssohn to join him in satirizing the whole business as a piece of ridiculous posturing presenting a poet as if he were a philosopher comparable with Leibniz. Entitling their essay *Pope ein Metaphysiker!* [Pope a Metaphysician!], they highlighted the absurdity of confusing poetry with philosophy—'what is a poet doing among the metaphysicians?'—and defending Leibniz by clearly differentiating the two kinds of optimism Leibniz and Pope represented.[79] They also alluded ironically to features of Leibniz's thought supposed according to the Academy's *jugement* not to belong to his thought. Eulogizing Leibniz's *Theodicy*, Lessing and Mendelssohn reaffirmed the power and centrality of the Leibnizian-Wolffian legacy. For the moment, Lessing was happy to pose as a Wolffian, though probably already then Mendelssohn remained much closer to the Leibnizian-Wolffian legacy than he.[80] Lessing's championing

[75] Frederick to d'Alembert, 25 July 1771, in Voltaire, *Corr.* xxxviii. 36.
[76] Beeson, *Maupertuis*, 249.
[77] Kant, *Theoretical Philosophy, 1755–70*, 77; Zammito, *Kant, Herder*, 58–9.
[78] Kant, *Theoretical Philosophy, 1755–70*, 82.
[79] Mendelssohn, *Gesammelte Schriften*, ii. 47–9; Altmann, *Moses Mendelssohn*, 46–7; Goldenbaum, 'Einführung', 10–11.
[80] Cassirer, *Philosophy*, 192–4.

Leibnizio-Wolffianism was only partly genuine, as already then his own thought was fused with marked Spinozistic tendencies as emerges plainly from his then unpublished *Das Christentum der Vernunft* [The Christianity of Reason] (*c.*1753), a brief fragment saturated with Leibnizian notions of the harmony of the universe which, however, fails to view the universe as a matter of conscious choice, in the manner of Leibniz and Wolff, conceiving it rather as the necessary emanation of the godhead.[81] Views such as he and his cousin Mylius had cultivated in private could not, of course, at that time be openly propagated anywhere in Germany.

What became Lessing's general philosophical strategy, fusing Leibnizio-Wolffianism with strands of Spinozism to produce a synthesis of Leibniz and Spinoza, and his campaign to locate this at the very heart of German intellectual culture, doubtless partly originated in discussions with Mylius,[82] though the idea was actually first formulated in print, anonymously and in a decidedly veiled manner, as we saw earlier, in the *Philosophische Gespräche* (1755) of his friend Mendelssohn.[83] 'Spinoza', asserts Mendelssohn, 'had come to his important doctrine [that the order and connection of concepts is one and the same with the order and connection of things] not through what is false and absurd in his system, but rather through that in it which is true.' While Spinoza's system is often false, held Mendelssohn, it was via what is sound in it that he could discover important truths and interweave these with his less valid inferences. This interaction Mendelssohn pronounced crucial for the formation of Leibniz's thought but also something Leibniz could not acknowledge, since 'if Leibniz had openly confessed he borrowed the essential part of his harmony from Spinoza', the public would have decided 'from the outset that they had found in the reference to Spinoza's name grounds for refuting his doctrine'.[84]

But where Mendelssohn never proceeded beyond this, for Lessing this was just a starting point. A brilliant intellectual strategist, Lessing sought to reform society by a general process of re-education according to the values and criteria of what he thought of as useful philosophy. His ultimate goal was to ameliorate human life by creating a culture of investigation, criticism, and debate fired by 'reason', robust enough eventually to purge humanity of prejudicial older ideas via the force of public criticism and controversy. Such a goal meant espousing much of the Radical Enlightenment's intellectual and cultural programme which he, more than any other German writer of the age, aspired to absorb into the mainstream of cultural life. It was his lifelong task and one he pursued with inexhaustible wit, elegance, and determination. His strategy was to direct attacks on strongly entrenched prejudice and superstition, things that could be resoundingly and openly assailed, while simultaneously hinting at a much wider field of social criticism and subversion by suggestion and insinuation.

---

[81] Nisbet, 'Introduction', 2; Lessing, *Philosophical and Theological Writings*, 25–9.
[82] Goetschel, *Spinoza's Modernity*, 184, 301.
[83] Israel, *Radical Enlightenment*, 658–9; Laerke, *Leibniz*, 51.
[84] Mendelssohn, *Philosophical Writings*, 103–4.

His drive for cultural and social reform first manifested itself in his outspoken stance on toleration. From the moment, in 1754, that his early drama *Die Juden* [The Jews] (1749), a play representing a Jew as a model of moral rectitude, provoked his first public dispute, Lessing emerged as Germany's foremost champion of full toleration and freedom of thought. His exchange in the press with the well-known Göttingen professor of theology and eastern languages Johann David Michaelis (1717–91), who reviewed the play disparagingly, provoked a controversy deliberately stirred up by Lessing. In his review, Michaelis (who had a high opinion of Lessing) had offered some conventionally negative remarks about Jews, claiming they instinctively hate Christians and were debased by their lives as traders. Responding in a friendly, tactful fashion, Lessing seized the opportunity, after conferring at length with Mendelssohn and Aaron Gumpertz, the latter the same 'enlightened' Jew who had been, for a time, d'Argens's secretary, to focus the public's attention on the prevalence of anti-Semitic prejudice in German society.

Lessing did so by persuading Mendelssohn to write a long letter to Gumperz, discussing the question from various angles and severely criticizing Michaelis. In this 'letter', which Lessing then published anonymously in his *Theatralische Bibliothek*, Mendelssohn complains of the Christians' 'most bitter hatred' and 'the humiliation of our hard-pressed nation' on seeing it asserted in the press that their entire people probably could not produce 'a single honest man'.[85] Against this, Mendelssohn cited the Jews' zeal for charity towards others as well as towards their own. In a personal note to Michaelis, of October 1754, Lessing vouched for the letter's authenticity, assuring him it had really been written by one Jew to another, adding that the author's uprightness and 'philosophischer Geist' [philosophical spirit] 'lead me to expect him to become a second Spinoza, who in fully equaling the first will lack only the latter's errors'.[86] The idea that Spinoza offered besides well-known 'errors' valuable insights, in origin a Wolffian trait, had become a standard feature of Lessing's and Mendelssohn's rhetorical strategy.

Lessing was helped by the context in which he then worked, Berlin, heart of a changing world. Frederick, though more of a warmonger and authoritarian than a truly enlightened ruler, could not wholly escape the consequences of his much vaunted espousal of the Enlightenment. What had especially contributed to nurturing a more open and liberal atmosphere was the influx, thanks to Frederick's personal inclinations and tastes, of French writers, books, and conversation through the 1740s and 1750s. For this cultural transfusion, especially via the works of d'Argens and Voltaire (whose stylistic practices Lessing studied closely), fomented within the Prussian court and bureaucracy an incisive new culture of criticism, tolerance, and rejection of ecclesiastical authority, and the seeds of materialism as expounded by La Mettrie, Diderot, d'Argens, and (later) Helvétius and d'Holbach. Berlin was now the

---

[85] Feiner, *Jewish Enlightenment*, 115; Goetschel, *Spinoza's Modernity*, 186–7.
[86] Lessing, *Werke und Briefe*, 11/i. 58. Lessing to Michaelis, Berlin, 16 Oct. 1754; Altmann, *Moses Mendelssohn*, 40–4.

second major centre, after Holland, from which French-language publications and culture permeated northern Europe, projecting both *voltaireanisme* and *matérialisme*. Lessing was just the creative genius to grasp and build on the new possibilities of a dynamic cultural scene changing in part under the impact of recent French and British developments. A highly accomplished philologist and translation theorist, he knew French, Latin, Greek, Italian, Spanish, and—unusually—even English, sufficiently well to translate from all these.

Though never keen on Voltaire (with whom he seems to have had some sort of disagreeable encounter, in 1751), Lessing was intensely interested in the other *philosophes*. Bayle was as fundamental to his early development as to Hume's.[87] He also took a keen interest in d'Argens, La Mettrie, and Diderot.[88] The connection between Lessing's comments in 1751 about the author of the *Lettres juives* (i.e. d'Argens) having frequently enough declared himself a foe of religion 'but never an enemy of virtue' and his plays, *Die Juden*, and *Der Freigeist* (1749–50), the latter featuring a freethinker 'without religion but full of moral inclinations', is obvious.[89] Holding both Mendelssohn and Gumperz in high regard, Lessing early on adopted d'Argens's pronounced and at the time highly unusual philosemitism as a central strand of his own radical critique of German society. His interaction with d'Argens and Gumperz, and with the French and Jewish presence in Berlin more broadly, infused the whole of his quintessentially cosmopolitan and radical literary outlook typifying his deliberate use of public controversy, literary criticism, and wit to assail rooted prejudices and heavy-handed authority.

During his first period in Berlin (1748–51), Lessing regularly contributed reviews to the *Berlinische privilegierte Zeitung*, one of which, in June 1749, penned when Lessing was only 20, discusses Diderot's *Pensées philosophiques*.[90] It was also Lessing, by the early 1750s already famous in his own right as a trenchant, highly independent journalist and reviewer, who was the first (and apparently only) critic in Germany to review Diderot's anonymously published *Lettre sur les sourds et les muets*. There he deduces simply from the style that this too must be by Diderot.[91] He was also the first German writer to review Rousseau's *Discourse on the Arts and Sciences* (1750), and the only one to judge it with any sympathy. Indeed, he then translated the text and, in 1752, published it in German.[92] Later, in 1756, Mendelssohn translated and published, together with a shrewd critique of Rousseau's arguments, a German rendering of Rousseau's second discourse which he addressed to Lessing.[93] Within a few years, Lessing had become Germany's leading critic of contemporary literature, social theory, and taste as well as theatre. He was thus ideally equipped to become a general

[87] Nisbet, 'Introduction', 1–2.
[88] Goldenbaum, 'Beziehungen', 79–82.
[89] Lessing, *Werke und Briefe*, iii. 341; Zammito, 'Most Hidden', 346–8; Niewöhner, *Veritas sive Varietas*, 40.
[90] Albrecht, *Gotthold Ephraim Lessing*, 12; Saada, *Inventer Diderot*, 74, 80.
[91] Saada, *Inventer Diderot*, 98–9; Goldenbaum, 'Friedrich II', 132.
[92] Goldenbaum, 'Einführung', 16–17; Zammito, *Kant, Herder*, 92.
[93] Goldenbaum, 'Einführung', 32–9.

strategist of social and cultural renewal, being wide-ranging, adroit, and by turns studious, a brilliant talker, and a polished writer.[94]

Meanwhile, Lessing was also busy translating Diderot's plays into German and in 1760 published these—albeit without putting his name on the title page—as *Das Theater des Herrn Diderot*. Later he was instrumental in having the German versions of Diderot's *Fils naturel* and *Père de famille* performed at Hamburg and then at Vienna, where the latter was staged some twenty-six times between 1770 and 1774, as well as Gotha—a noted centre for German theatre at this time, Breslau, Augsburg, and Nuremberg. Diderot he pronounced the foremost philosopher since Aristotle to contemplate the stage and the critic who, beyond all others, had shown 'how far from nature and truth' France's poets and playwrights had drifted.[95] Lessing had embraced several of Diderot's core theses long before becoming chief promoter of his reputation in Germany, in particular proclaiming the ancient distinction between tragedy and comedy dissolved and the concerns of everyday life rather than the mythological and courtly fantasies of the nobility the theatre's proper sphere.[96] This 'ideological' shift helped generate from the late 1760s onwards an unprecedented enthusiasm for the theatre and interest in theatre journals in Germany.

3. KANT: SEARCHING FOR THE MIDDLE PASSAGE

Perhaps the most powerful critic of Wolffianism before Kant was Christian August Crusius (1715–75), a true bastion of the religious Enlightenment. In his first major intervention in the philosophical arena, his *Nova Dilucidatio* [New Elucidation] on the principles of cognition, published shortly after receiving the degree of *Magister*, at Königsberg early in 1755, Kant acknowledges the pervasive influence on his thought, in the 1750s, of this remarkable Leipzig professor described by one of his students, the later radical Bahrdt, as 'undeniably the greatest philosopher of his time'.[97] He was a philosopher the young Kant deemed 'celeberrimus' and 'among the most penetrating of our age'.[98] To Kant, Crusius seemed formidable not just as a thinker in his own right but as a general critic setting out the true scope and role of philosophy. Invoking the divine will as the origin of morality, Crusius also defended belief in spirits and demonology. Like Lange and Buddeus earlier, he considered the Leibnizian-Wolffian system objectionable because it detracts from God's freedom and majesty, casts doubt on the Trinity, and problematizes all *supernaturalia*.[99] Opposing Leibniz and Wolff, Crusius (and Kant) also rejected the ideas of Baumgarten

---

[94] Lessing, *Werke und Briefe*, 11/i. 38. Mylius to Lessing, Berlin, undated, Jan. 1752.
[95] Lessing, *Werke und Briefe*, iii. 44; Saada, *Inventer Diderot*, 242–3, 254–6, 267–8.
[96] Saada, *Inventer Diderot*, 242–3, 254–6, 267–8; Martinson, 'Lessing', 51, 54.
[97] Bahrdt, *Geschichte*, i. 118–19; Bahrdt, *Kirchen- und Ketzer-Almanach*, 43.
[98] Kant, *Nova Dilucidatio*, 17; Lehner, *Kants Vorsehungskonzept*, 91–2.
[99] Crusius, *Anweisung*, 64–5; Bahrdt, *Geschichte*, i. 179, 202, 224.

and his brother Alexander Gottlieb Baumgarten (1714–62), the latter primarily known today as the founder of philosophical aesthetics but then renowned as a leading Wolffian metaphysician and moral thinker. While agreeing that reason can demonstrate parts of the basic scheme of the cosmos, Crusius held that in Germany 'many', in particular the Wolffians, 'ascribe too much scope to reason and praise it in a Pelagian manner'.[100] His aim was to undo the separation between theology and philosophy engineered by Leibniz and Wolff and strengthen the first by more tightly subordinating the latter.

Urging tighter limits on the scope of 'reason' and a stronger role for theology in moral philosophy, Crusius during the 1740s developed both a rigorous epistemology and categorical moral philosophy that deeply impressed the young Kant.[101] Morality, being the guidelines the divinity decreed to men, is determined, held Crusius, not by the dictates of reason but by God's Will, so that 'the worldly philosophers' err greatly in assuming morality's object is worldly happiness. Ethics is simply the fulfilment of divinely imposed duty. Our conscience is the 'ground of recognition' by which we know the law of God and morality and hence the true foundation of philosophy. Since nothing in 'true philosophy and history' can diverge in the least from truth as delivered to us by revelation and morality—here he agreed with the Baumgartens and other Wolffians—everything in Christian morality accords with reason, though it may not seem so at times. Hence, apparent difficulties in rationally explaining a moral law based on revelation and conscience must always be discounted and never permitted to impede obedience to that law.[102] While Crusius, like Kant later, prioritizes duty in place of the radical thinker's pursuit of human happiness, he conceded some latitude to reason in grounding morality and legislation, acknowledging that moral laws, even if more definitely known from revelation, are deducible from reason. Cultivating reason and obeying God, he thought, go together.[103] That Christian morality demonstrably constitutes a more perfect moral edifice than the ancient pagan philosophers could construct struck Crusius as crucial to proving Scripture's divine character.

Opposing a general toleration, Crusius denied that individuals possess the right to examine fundamental questions for themselves or express their views freely where this means denying miracles, creation, revelation, or biblical authority. Neither in Prussia nor anywhere else was morality's autonomy from theology then officially recognized or individual autonomy of lifestyle endorsed. Under the laws of the confessional state it was not permitted publicly to deny the God-ordained character of the social hierarchy, challenge ecclesiastical authority, reject accepted moral norms, or openly question princely government. Tougher censorship in philosophy was needed, urged Crusius, especially a stronger ban on denying 'free will'. For God

---

[100] Crusius, *Kurzer Begriff*, 30; Bahrdt, *Kirchen- und Ketzer-Almanach*, 44–5.
[101] Beck, 'From Leibniz to Kant', 16.
[102] Crusius, *Einleitung*, 28–9; Crusius, *Anweisung*, 480–2.
[103] Crusius, *Anweisung*, Vorrede pp. A4–A7, 478; Crusius, *Kurzer Begriff*, 32–3.

gave men 'free-will' as the primary instrument of morality, to manage our passions and desires, so that refusing this doctrine undermines both religion and morality.[104] 'Bad' philosophical literature, by which he meant texts embracing determinism or fatalism, must also be prohibited.[105] Freedom of thought and freedom generally needed curbing. Dancing and theatre were two further areas where the degree of licence permitted was excessive and stricter regulation urgently required.[106]

Crusius' assault on the Leibnizian-Wolffian edifice pivots on the principle of 'sufficient reason', Kant being especially impressed by his critique of Leibniz's 'sufficient ground', the proposition that nothing can be true or exist for which there is not a sufficient reason or ground as to why it is true, or exists.[107] 'No fact can be real or existing and no proposition can be true', as Leibniz formulates the principle in his *Monodology*, unless there is a sufficient reason 'why it should be so and not otherwise'.[108] Crusius and, following him, Kant demurred, claiming men can only perceive 'possibility' after first apprehending existing things. He further objected (like Clarke earlier) that Leibniz's 'sufficient reason', implying the overall intelligibility of the world, cannot stand without a prior assumption that a benevolent Creator had created the universe on rational principles in the first place. Hence, employing 'that great principle', as Leibniz calls it, to demonstrate God's existence involves a purely circular argument that actually proves nothing.

Leibniz's principle, furthermore, implies that things exist by an absolute necessity, as Crusius had pointed out in a treatise of 1743. Even if Leibniz 'quibbles about the difference between moral necessity and absolute necessity', he still can be said to undermine the all-important principle of 'freedom of the will' and God's autonomy, thrusting everything back into the 'immutable necessity of all things', precisely the abyss in which the Stoics (and following them Spinoza) had cast mankind.[109] Most Leibnizio-Wolffians in his time seemed unaware, complained Crusius, that with the principle of 'sufficient reason' Leibniz removes God's freedom.[110] Kant agreed and, in his *Nova Dilucidatio*, adopts this argument while also rebuking Alexander Baumgarten, whom he cited frequently in his lectures during the 1750s, for relying on precisely this premiss.

Alexander Baumgarten, whom he ironically styled 'chief of the metaphysicians', besides further adorning the Leibnizian-Wolffian edifice with other additional Latin categories, had supplemented sufficient reason with 'the principle of consequence'. Nothing exists, according to Baumgarten's 'principle of consequence', which does not have something grounded in it: in other words whatever is has its inherent consequence. This conflicted, though, with Kant's pre-1770 doctrine of substances and

---

[104] Crusius, *Anweisung*, 60–1; Schneewind, 'Active Powers', 589–90, 592.
[105] Crusius, *Kurzer Begriff*, 362–5.
[106] Ibid. 118–20, 126–35, 362–5.
[107] Kant, *Nova Dilucidatio*, 17; Wessell, *G. E. Lessing's Theology*, 81–2; Zammito, *Genesis*, 18.
[108] Parkinson, 'Philosophy and Logic', 207.
[109] Crusius, *Anweisung*, 62–4; Kant, *Nova Dilucidatio*, 21.
[110] Crusius, *Anweisung*, 64–5, 67 n.

idea that the state of any substance having 'no connection with other substances, will be free from all change'.[111] As Baumgarten grounds his Leibnizian principle of consequence, objects Kant, 'in the same way he demonstrates the principle of sufficient reason', the former necessarily shared in the difficulties of the latter. All who lend 'the Wolffian philosophy its renown' Kant accused of flagrantly ignoring the contradiction—and the dangers—in maintaining 'that a simple substance is subject to constant change in virtue of an inner principle of activity'.[112] For this would mean a single substance can evolve and, as Wolff's Pietist critics maintained, inevitably savours of veiled Spinozism.

His demonstration that substances change only through interaction with other substances or *dependentia reciproca*, that non-interacting substances cannot change, and that 'if the human soul were free from real connection with external things, the internal state of the soul would be completely devoid of changes', contended Kant in 1755, 'overthrows utterly the Leibnizian pre-established harmony'.[113] Agreeing God's will must be conceived of as untrammelled by necessity, he also endorsed Crusius' demolition of Leibniz's distinction between absolute and moral necessity. In this way, Kant first rose to prominence as one of those striving to overthrow the Leibnizio-Wolffian hegemony.[114] But if the 'Supreme Divinity is completely free from all dependency whatever' and the Leibnizian-Wolffian-Baumgartenian edifice was shown to stand on false foundations, he also needed, as one of Germany's leading professional philosophers, to demonstrate—without falling back, like Crusius, on proclaiming theology the sole valid foundation of morality, law, and social theory—how exactly reason blocks Spinoza.

Kant's philosophy converged with that of Crusius in three respects and not only in his pre-critical (i.e. pre-1781) thought, but also later: (1) by insisting on the urgent need to restrict the scope of philosophical reason; (2) in demanding complete separation of spirit and matter and the apartness of humanity (or at the least the higher races) distinguished by 'reason' from the rest of the animal realm (he always remained hostile to the proto-evolutionist idea that men had grown out of organic nature);[115] and (3) in holding that in moral philosophy the main work cannot be done by reason, the vital mechanism being each person's conscience and feelings. Kant's approach to proving God's existence and governance of the universe, though, sharply diverged from those of Leibniz and Crusius, by starting with an emphatic refusal to accept the prior premiss of divine 'design'. Declaring it impossible 'that nothing at all should exist' and that existence is something 'absolutely necessary', he argued that 'it is not possible for several things to be absolutely necessary', hence the absolutely 'necessary being is unique' and also 'immutable and eternal'.[116]

---

[111] Kant, *Nova Dilucidatio*, 34, 37–8; Lehner, *Kants Vorsehungskonzept*, 261.
[112] Kant, *Nova Dilucidatio*, 38.
[113] Ibid. 39; Lehner, *Kants Vorsehungskonzept*, 261.
[114] Kant, *Nova Dilucidatio*, 21–2.
[115] Zammito, *Genesis*, 199.
[116] Ibid. 124–9.

This argument possessed greater logical rigour, in his judgement, and was ultimately of greater scientific value than those offered by Leibniz, Wolff, Crusius, or by the physico-theology of the Newtonians (and Reimarus). Dismissing Descartes's proof of God's existence and those of the empiricists as 'both false and utterly impossible', he concludes that 'either no strict proof of God's existence is possible at all, or the proof must be based upon the argument I have adduced'.[117] However, proving 'the necessary being is a simple substance' and immutable and eternal is insufficient by itself to escape what Kant too acknowledged to be philosophy's most pressing challenge: how to avoid the trap of Spinozism. Further steps were requisite for his line of reasoning fully to succeed. To plug the gap in his proof of God's existence and providence, Kant tried to adapt the thesis that the mind's properties, understanding, and will are indubitable realities that nonetheless only figure among the possible properties of things. Mind, will, and understanding must hence be possible in some things but not in others 'through the necessary being as a ground'.[118] This must be true for otherwise what is consequent would be greater than the ground itself. Nevertheless, there remains a problem. To evade Spinozism, Kant also had to establish that 'God is not the only substance that exists'. This he attempted to do by showing that 'in the world conflict, deficiency, changeability' are encountered 'all of which are the opposites of the determinations found in a divinity'.[119] But does such reasoning really prove the cosmos is governed by a single 'Intelligent Author' external to that cosmos and that Spinozism stands refuted? The last step seemed to amount to nothing more than Bayle's (apparent) refutation.

Thus, it was by no means clear that Kant's 'only possible proof' succeeds and that he had triumphantly built on Crusius to curb Wolffianism and destroy Spinozism. Herder, a fellow East Prussian and a born controversialist, dared at the age of 20, in 1764, to take issue with his teacher, Kant, on this point. He disputed his reasoning on the ground that 'being is indivisible' so that one cannot proceed, as Kant does, by dividing being into absolutely necessary being as distinct from contingent being.[120] Herder had a point and Kant was not pleased to thus be taken to task by his student. 'Kant seems to have become wholly withdrawn towards me,' complained Herder to his friend Hamann in August 1764.[121] But if Kant's 'only possible' proof was defective, then there exists no conclusive demonstration that the world is governed by a wise Creator. Realizing before long that his reasoning here was indeed insufficient, Kant returned to the drawing board.

One way to fight materialism, defend free will, and separate the *Immaterialisten* from the *Materialisten* (while also discrediting Wolff) was to fall back on Locke with his 'immaterial' faculties of the mind. This solution was favoured by several prominent academic figures, including Feder and Meiners, at Göttingen where the political

---

[117] Kant, *Einzig mögliche Beweisgrund*, 201.
[118] Ibid. 132; Guyer, *Kant's System*, 89.
[119] Kant, *Einzig mögliche Beweisgrund*, 134; Lehner, *Kants Vorsehungskonzept*, 283–5.
[120] Herder, *Selected Early Works*, 6.
[121] Zammito, *Kant, Herder*, 149–50.

link with the British crown encouraged an Anglophile orientation, though both these erudite philosophers also knew their French philosophical literature well. When we assert that all our ideas derive from sense impressions we should not define the latter as deriving only from 'outward' sense impressions, warned Feder, but also from the 'inner' sense impressions of the soul which are not material in character, a stance he defended against the materialists by tenaciously championing Locke's faculties of the mind.[122] This position also enabled him to provide a non-materialist defence of Condillac.

A similar approach characterized Johan Niklaus Tetens (1736–1807), from 1776, at Kiel. While Leibniz and Kant also considered the Enlightenment a general joint, European venture involving philosophers of all nations, no other German thinker proved so eclectic, and positive towards Locke and British empiricism while also appreciating Reid, Beattie, and the Scots Common Sense school, as Tetens.[123] Partly agreeing with Condillac and Bonnet, and embracing their principle of 'association', in his principal work, *Philosophische Versuche über die menschliche Natur* (1777), Tetens also strongly criticized them for failing to erect a sufficiently robust barrier against deriving thought entirely from outer feeling and perception in the manner of Helvé-tius. It is here that Locke's faculties of the mind provide invaluable fortifications on which to fall back.[124] Among the first to draw attention to Kant's concept of an a priori framework of the mind defining the space in which the mind orders the perceptions it receives, Tetens believed this, a stance Kant had first begun to publicize in his dissertation *De Mundi Sensibilis atque Intelligibilis Forma et Principiis* (1770), was indeed a reliable defence against materialist positions.[125] Tetens's tripartite division of mental activities into thinking (cognition), willing (desire and volition), and feeling was an original contribution to philosophy of the mind which, in turn, had some impact on Kant during the years he worked towards his *Critique of Pure Reason*.[126]

4. REIMARUS: EROSION FROM THE CENTRE

Besides Leibnizio-Wolffianism and radical thought, the *Aufklärung* was heavily suffused with Newtonian physico-theology. Germany's leading advocate of phy-sico-theology as a device to solve the general philosophic-scientific impasse, and refute Spinoza, was the remarkable philologist, philosopher, and professor of Hebrew and oriental languages and (private) deist Herman Samuel Reimarus (1694–1768). Pre-eminent at Hamburg, he was among the most formidably erudite men in Germany. Kant, surveying the scene in the early 1760s and knowing only Reimarus'

---

[122] Feder, *Logik und Metaphysik*, 52, 215.
[123] Tetens, *Philosophische versuche*, i. 45–6; Kuehn, *Scottish Common Sense*, 119.
[124] Tetens, *Philosophische versuche*, i. 7, 68, 108, 193, 336–8 and ii. 242–6, 254–7, 258–60.
[125] Ibid. i. 359–60, 398; Winkler, 'Perception', 255–6.
[126] Winkler, 'Perception', 255–6; Kuehn, *Kant*, 251.

publicly stated philosophy, expressly concedes, in his most important pre-critical publication *Der einzig mögliche Beweisgrund zu einer Demonstration des Daseins Gottes* (1763), the superior usefulness of arguments 'such as those Reimarus offers in his book on natural religion' to his own, for nurturing the ordinary German public with a readily accessible 'exposition of the important knowledge of God and his qualities'.[127] Undeniably, no one else in the *Aufklärung* so beautifully demonstrated the harmony of religion, science, politics, erudition, and philosophy from a Newtonian standpoint.

In Germany no less than France, the greatest intellectual impediment to the emergence of a stable and viable moderate mainstream consensus was the religious Enlightenment's vulnerability to a corrosive deism, fiercely hostile to the churches and their claims, like that of Voltaire. A moderate Enlightenment seeking to undermine Christian belief and attitudes, however problematically in the end, without challenging the rest of the political and social order was a dangerous rival for the middle ground. Reimarus, though no Voltaire, in private figured among the most hostile to the clergy's claims and—although few realized it during his lifetime— during the century's third quarter was Germany's foremost Enlightenment deist. Eventually, he was to prove a more dangerous destabilizing factor and threat to received thinking than almost anyone else, being caught in an agonizing trap, lifelong contradiction from which he could never escape and which ended by heavily damaging the theological establishment.

Reimarus began examining the foundations of Christian belief in a hidden, secret manuscript, a massive work begun around 1735—the complete text of which remained unpublished until 1972! From the outset, his lifelong quest seemed both inescapable intellectually at a private level, and yet, equally, something highly unsuitable for public exposure. He could evade neither the quest nor the trap of its implications. The early sections of his *Apology of the Reasonable Adorer of God* were composed during the Wertheim controversy, partly prompted by Schmidt's interventions. But the text was mostly written later and further expanded and thoroughly revised in the 1750s.[128] His estrangement from ordinary notions of religion, Bible authority, and morality Reimarus himself describes as a slow process of private doubt and questioning, driven chiefly by textual and philological evidence. His undertaking had unfettered autonomous reason as its foundation and reason he both extols and closely links to the general progress of philosophy and humanity. The only guide the honest searcher after truth can acknowledge, he concurred with the radical *philosophes*, is philosophical reason. Yet there was a crucial point where he parted company with them: he did not accept that reason is hence also humanity's chief guide more generally, insisting rather that society was not yet ready to face 'the truth' and would not be for generations.

Reimarus shared with radical thought the principle that everything is either according or contrary to reason and that nothing is 'above reason' as Locke, Le

[127] Kant, *Einzig mögliche Beweisgrund*, 200.
[128] Schmidt-Biggemann, *Theodizee*, 75, 77.

Clerc, Leibniz, and Wolff had argued. But in his case this failed to produce a radical outcome as, for him, reason can only be privately embraced as the overriding guiding criterion and not publicly.[129] Despite this strange bifurcation into respectable public 'Christian' and private 'anti-Christian' segments, and the irresolvable contradiction it drove him into, Reimarus' overall system nevertheless constitutes an impressively integrated whole, a high-point of the *Aufklärung*. A fervent crypto-deist, Reimarus pre-eminently exemplified the Enlightenment author radical in some respects and moderate in others; and while his 'moderation' in some respects is precisely what enabled him to be subversive in others, his radical tendency was confined to his unseen polemic against revealed religion and ecclesiastical authority. Beyond his silent plea for full toleration, and diminished church authority, his system evinced little of a radical character. Rather in most respects he shared the moderation of Challe, Wollaston, and Voltaire, his fierce aversion to Spinozism forming part of a broader antagonism towards all materialist, one-substance, and pantheistic positions.

Early in his career, in the summer of 1721, Reimarus undertook a five-month study trip to England.[130] But his stay there was much shorter than his stay in Holland and there is little basis for claiming, as some have, that Reimarus embraced hetero-doxy under English influence.[131] Rather, his few references to British deists in the footnotes and references of the *Apologie* are far eclipsed in importance by those to Grotius, Le Clerc, Bayle, Bekker, Van Dale,[132] and Spinoza. If there is one place where Reimarus mentions Toland's essay *Hodegus*, or the Pillar of Cloud, as something 'I used with benefit',[133] he otherwise dismisses Toland as just another 'Spinozist', rebuking him expressly for representing Pythagoras, Anaxagoras, Socrates, and Plato as 'pantheists'. To Reimarus, these were 'certainly no Pantheists but conceived God as an immaterial spirit quite distinct from the material world that he had created'; and even if some of them did envisage God as a life-giving force permeating Nature, 'yet they were still infinitely far removed from Spinozism'—an essential point for him.[134]

In the philosophical—as distinct from the text-critical—sections of his *Apologie*, Reimarus cites Hobbes only in passing, in reference to Rousseau's 'state of nature', and wholly ignores Locke. His undeviating aim philosophically—actually, in all three of his major works—is to refute materialism, mechanistic systems, and especially 'Spinozism'. In his two non-clandestine, published works, Spinoza is repeatedly cited as the principal example, indeed the general *princeps*, of all systematic atheistic and materialist thinking.[135] Spinoza's *Tractatus Theologico-Politicus* is also, of course, one source of Reimarus' Bible criticism.[136] But Reimarus the Bible critic does

---

[129] Von Kempski, 'Spinoza, Reimarus', 106–7; Schmidt-Biggemann, *Theodizee*, 73–4.
[130] Schmidt-Biggemann, 'Einleitung' to Reimarus, *Kleine gelehrten Schriften*, 9–65, here, 17–20.
[131] De Lange, 'John Toland', 6.
[132] Reimarus, *Apologie*, i. 480 n.d., 908, 914–15, and ii. 388.
[133] Ibid. i. 434; de Lange, 'John Toland', 7; Reventlow, 'Arsenal', 55.
[134] Reimarus, *Apologie*, ii. 658.
[135] Reimarus, *Vornehmsten Wahrheiten*, i. 6–7, 113, 188–91, and ii. 722, 734.
[136] Ibid. i. 857b.

not follow Spinoza in seeking to rescue shreds of moral worth from Scripture. Rather all the books the Jews presented as divine revelation, he avers, actually contain only very inferior 'concepts of God and his attributes, manifestations, wonders, Commandments and statutes'. In the Old Testament, one finds 'no trace of the immortality of the soul or of a future life', doctrines the fiercely anti-Jewish Reimarus wholeheartedly embraced.[137] His philological technique and New Testament hermeneutics actually derived chiefly from his famous Hamburg teacher (and father-in-law) Johan Albert Fabricius (1668–1736).[138] Besides Fabricius, Grotius was a key mentor, Reimarus commenting at one point in his biblical commentaries that Grotius had 'accurately discovered the literal and historical sense of most of the Scriptural text'.[139] Also vital for his general conception of *critique* was Le Clerc whom he met during his stay in Holland between the spring of 1720 and early 1722 and accounted someone who 'judges and criticizes very freely about everyone'.[140] His devastating anti-Scripturalism owed much also to Bayle's acerbic comments about the Old Testament and Schmidt's rejection of original sin.[141]

Reimarus' scathing New Testament criticism owed something also to the arguments of Socinus, Crell, and other Socinians,[142] and to Jewish or partly Jewish sources such as the *Hizzuk Emunah* of Rabbi Isaac of Troki, Manesseh ben Israel, and Van Limborch's colloquium with Orobio de Castro. Commenting on what he considered the New Testament's blatant fabrication of its pretended continuity with the Old Testament, a pretension fundamental to Christian claims but totally rejected by Reimarus, he calls Isaac of Troki the 'most thorough and strongest adversary of Christianity'. In the end, though, the most distinctive features of Reimarus' anti-Scripturalism, his denial of New Testament claims to be a continuation of Old Testament prophecies on textual grounds and construing such pretensions as a camouflage for political-eschatological ambition, were original with Reimarus himself.[143] Applying the most exacting philology, and alive to every discrepancy, he was relentless in uncovering inconsistencies between the four New Testament Gospels: 'nothing better or more thorough', commented Lessing, 'had yet been written.' 'The frequent contradictions of the evangelists... had never on any occasion been brought to light so circumstantially and deliberately as in [Reimarus' account] of the Resurrection.'[144]

It is 'Spinozism' (and materialism), not Spinoza himself, though, that was the undeviating target of Reimarus' efforts. His principal publicly acknowledged work, *Die vornehmsten Wahrheiten der natürlichen Religion* (Hamburg, 1754), a book

---

[137] Reimarus, *Apologie*, i. 721; Reimarus, 'Vorerrinerung', 6–7.
[138] Reimarus, *Apologie*, ii. 529, 578b.
[139] Ibid. i. 728 and ii. 270.
[140] Reimarus, *Apologie*, i. 314, 323, 325, 480, 509 n., 777, 857, and ii. 270–1, 387; Boehart, 'Hermann Samuel Reimarus', 127–40.
[141] Reimarus, *Apologie*, i. 233–6; Cassirer, *Philosophy*, 159–60; Reventlow, 'Arsenal', 53.
[142] Reventlow, 'Arsenal', 77–8; Reimarus, *Apologie*, ii. 269–70.
[143] Reimarus, *Apologie*, ii. 268; Schmidt-Biggemann, *Theodizee*, 81.
[144] Lessing, *Philosophical and Theological Writings*, 99.

rendered into Dutch (1758), French (Berlin, 1768), and English, as *The Principal Truths of Natural Religion* (1766), like his remarkable treatise on animals of 1760, chiefly cites as representatives of 'Spinozism' La Mettrie and Buffon. Buffon he accuses of expounding a simplistic *Mechanismus* of animal bodies and the doctrine that nature blindly forms life and creates species without the intervention of a divine Creator.[145] La Mettrie is pilloried not as an important figure in his own right but, as Reimarus himself states, as a way of attacking 'Spinozism' as a general intellectual-cultural phenomenon and proof 'Spinozism', like all 'atheism', undermines the existing moral order.[146]

Author of one of the most interesting treatises on animals of the age, entitled *Allgemeine Betrachtungen über die Triebe der Thiere, hauptsächlich über ihre Kunsttriebe* (1760), published when he was 66, Reimarus here vigorously reaffirms his physico-theology. If men and animals are constructed in essentially the same way, according to La Mettrie, Reimarus viewed mankind as something qualitatively quite distinct from the animal realm. Man's nature was specially created, he maintained, explicitly contradicting Spinoza,[147] to enable him to populate all the earth, rule over the animal world, and direct everything to his own uses and satisfaction. While the human body, like any animal's, may be a machine in terms of physical make-up, a human amounts to far more than a 'machine' since man's soul consists of quite a different substance from our bodies.[148] That the divine Creator in his wisdom would have bestowed such a noble capacity as our spirit, a spirit based on reason, the tool enabling men to unearth the deepest truths, and leading them to morality and religion, merely to be animal-like, so that our spirit and reason should satisfy base desires like hunger, thirst, and sensual needs, to him seemed totally implausible.[149]

All his life Reimarus remained deeply fascinated by animal behaviour, staking much on his physico-theological differentiation between men and other creatures and, in doing so, composed one of his century's most brilliant accounts of animals. Where all animal life is oriented towards the here and now, satisfying immediate drives, men, holds Reimarus, are designed by their very constitution, and hence the Creator, to reflect, develop their 'reason', and pursue a higher, purer, and more lasting perfection.[150] This uplifting rationality and spirituality seemed such a powerful argument to him as to constitute a convincing proof of the soul's immortality in itself. Dealing one by one with the ideas on animals of Descartes, Leibniz, Malebranche, Buffon, La Mettrie, and Condillac but ignoring Locke whose views about animals were also widely influential and who had undoubtedly introduced a philosophically novel way of distinguishing between animals and humans, Reimarus refutes all the earlier theorists. Observation had been inadequate, he urged, and

---

[145] Reimarus, *Vornehmsten Wahrheiten*, i. 273–6, 314–18, 346, 353, 360, 598–9.
[146] Ibid. ii. 734–43.
[147] Ibid. ii. 676.
[148] Ibid. ii. 475–7, 489–91.
[149] Ibid. i. 334.
[150] Ibid. ii. 704–9; Tetens, *Philosophische Versuche*, i. 744–5; Schmidt-Biggemann, 'Einleitung', 41, 46–7.

crucial facts missed. While his sections on Buffon and La Mettrie are substantial, he gives most attention to Condillac's *Traité des animaux*, refuting it in sixteen pages.[151]

Basically, his treatise develops the same argument as *Die vornehmsten Wahrheiten*, combating French materialism or what Reimarus terms 'Spinozism', a body of doctrine whose modern representatives, in Reimarus' eyes, were Buffon and La Mettrie. Animals have souls, certainly, as Condillac (and Locke) maintain, but not the ability to compare or associate ideas or images, remember or draw conclusions, or the capacity to change their notions or improve their knowledge or behaviour (a position placing him close to Locke).[152] Between the ape and the dumbest human, holds Reimarus, there is a greater gulf than between the stupidest human and a Leibniz or Newton. Here he was at his furthest from the *encyclopédistes*.

Basically an elaboration of Réaumur's doctrine of divinely given, inborn instincts, Reimarus saw animals' drives not as abilities they develop out of their own capacities but inborn, complete capabilities implanted by a transcendent power beyond nature.[153] Animals naturally neither invent nor develop nor improve. Each species is fixed, eternal, always behaves in precisely the same way. Animals are everything they should be and do everything they should do shortly after arriving in the world; and this is clear proof, he thought, of the divine *Werkmeister* not just imparting to Nature all mechanical laws, rules, and order but infusing life and motion into living creatures, imparting to souls all regular skills and abilities.[154] Animals' drives in this way became the best weapon available against Spinoza.

But how solid was Reimarus' argument? Is it altogether beyond doubt, enquired Tetens, that all animals lack man's power to reflect?[155] One of the acutest late Enlightenment discussions of the relationship between nature and animals is found in Herder's *Ideen zur Philosophie der Geschichte der Menschheit* (1785). Reimarus, grants Herder, had reflected on animals' habits and activities with greater care than almost anyone before him. But his argument only really seems plausible regarding insects, fish, and other lower forms of animal life.[156] The further up the chain of animal life one proceeds towards apes and men, the clearer it is that animals do in fact hesitate, make choices, learn, and develop their skills. But if Reimarus' physico-theology was rejected by Herder and received only lukewarm praise from Mendelssohn, many were impressed. Kant in 1763 termed it the best and most convincing exposition of its kind available in Germany. As late as 1790, he judged his books the most cogent elaboration of physico-theology in German.[157] Especially the *Vornehmsten Wahrheiten*, with its relentless attacks on materialists and non-providential deists, long remained the pre-eminent exposition of natural religion

---

[151] Reimarus, *Allgemeine Betrachtungen*, i. 13–14, 67, 319–20, 324–6.

[152] Ibid. i. 327–30, 333–4, 444; Reimarus, *Apologie*, ii. 501.

[153] Reimarus, *Vornehmsten Wahrheiten*, i. 448.

[154] Holland, *Réflexions*, 133; Jaynes and Woodward, 'In the Shadow', 147.

[155] Tetens, *Philosophische Versuche*, i. 745–6; Platner, *Philosophische Aphorismen*, i. 138, 144–6.

[156] Herder, *Ideen*, i. 155–6, 162.

[157] Kant, *Einzig mögliche Beweisgrund*, 200; Kant, *Critique of Judgment*, 329–30.

in central Europe and (rather ironically) was frequently used to bolster the religious Enlightenment. When the young Jewish philosopher Solomon Maimon attended a conference with Mendelssohn and several other Jews in Berlin in or around 1783, to consider what books representative of the *Aufklärung* should be rendered by Maimon into Hebrew for the improvement of Polish Jewry, some present (though not Mendelssohn) suggested the *Vornehmsten Wahrheiten* should top the list given its incomparably fine advocacy of 'natural religion and rational morality', the 'aim of all Enlightenment'.[158]

Unlike Wolff, Baumgarten, and Crusius, Reimarus does not accommodate miracles, indeed regards miracles as inconceivable to the philosophical mind and totally at variance with authentic Newtonianism, physico-theology, and morality.[159] But the divergences between him and the materialists far outweighed such convergences. The ultimate origin of men and animals cannot lie in the world, contended Reimarus, 'or in nature' as there is no 'natural', convincing way of explaining how the advent of the first men or first animals could emanate directly from nature or the world. Spinozists suppose the sun's warmth somehow animated inanimate matter bringing forth creatures and eventually men. But such proto-evolutionary notions he deemed utterly implausible precisely when viewed from a naturalistic perspective. The physical world of matter lacks movement and is wholly lifeless and hence in no way an active agent.[160] 'Thus, the world is brought to its reality, shaped and created, by a self-sufficient active cause which is external to it,'[161] a 'truth', insisted Reimarus, that directly contradicts Spinoza's definition of substance in his *Ethics* and doctrine that the physical universe is the only substance that can be called 'God'.

Reimarus accepted, as Leibniz, Wolff, Crusius, and Kant did not, that everything that happens in nature of a physical character in our world functions exclusively mechanistically and naturally.[162] But he denied one can base a cogent world-view on this insight. If he echoed Spinoza and Bayle in claiming that in philosophy there is no such thing as 'above reason', he more than anyone showed how vast was the gulf between all providential deism and the 'Spinozists'. To him it seemed clear that Spinoza and his followers had failed to grasp the basic laws of nature as Newton and all recent science had demonstrated them to us: 'they would not have made Nature their god had they grasped its laws.'[163] Spinoza's system, based on false definitions and faulty science, 'contradicts experience and the real world',[164] and with his errors in science, collapses his conception of the necessity and the determined character of all that is.

---

[158] Mendelssohn, *Gesammelte Schriften*, xxii: *Dokumente* 1, 184–5.
[159] Lehner, *Kants Vorsehungskonzept*, 139–41.
[160] Reimarus, *Vornehmsten Wahrheiten*, i. 83–4, 127.
[161] Ibid. i. 158, 167.
[162] Ibid. i. 196–7.
[163] Ibid. i. 127–48; von Kempski, 'Hermann Samuel Reimarus', 24–5.
[164] Reimarus, *Vornehmsten Wahrheiten*, i. 188.

Part II

Rationalizing the *Ancien Régime*

8

Hume, Scepticism, and Moderation

1. HUME'S ENLIGHTENMENT

There were competing moderate and radical strands of Enlightenment in Britain just as elsewhere and a crucial element in their clash were their rival conceptions of 'reason'. Perhaps the only way a purely secular philosophy, detached from theology and making no appeal to any theological claims, but firmly conservative in social, moral, and political orientation, could check the logic of radical arguments, anchoring not just philosophy but men's hopes and schemes for reform, was by combining a vigorous new scepticism about reason's scope with a fresh insistence on experience, experimental philosophy, and the advantages of the status quo. Precisely this, first from a philosophical and then an economic, moral, political, and historical standpoint, was Hume's towering achievement as an Enlightenment thinker and commentator.

The most powerful philosophical genius of the mid eighteenth century, David Hume (1711–76) acquired on both sides of the Atlantic a mixed but (despite his reputation for irreligion and incredulity) ultimately splendid standing. Almost single-handedly, he can be seen in retrospect to have punctured the epistemological perspectives of Locke and Berkeley, on the one hand, and the wider schemes of the continental moderate reformers, on the other, developing an alternative conception of society and human nature, on the basis of his sceptical epistemology, a construction powerful enough if not to undermine the Radical Enlightenment altogether, then certainly to cast a giant question mark over it and seriously impede its progress both as a set of philosophical propositions and political goals. Philosophers and reformers reacting against the recipes of Helvétius, Diderot, and d'Holbach, like Alessandro Verri in Italy, and in Germany Rehberg, turned as a matter of course to Hume. Unmoved by the radical coterie's philosophy, morality, and equality, he challenged all their premises, including their relatively optimistic conception of history as the maturing of human reason and their democratic republicanism, though he had a soft spot for aristocratic republics in small states like Venice and Geneva.

An inexhaustible fund of insights and ideas to those opposing radical notions, Hume posed an intellectual challenge, the formidable character of which some radical thinkers felt obliged to acknowledge. At the same time, though, he unwittingly refocused and helped sharpen aspects of the radical critique of existing conditions through the very acuteness of his objections. Richard Price, for instance, readily acknowledged that in early life he was much influenced by Samuel Clarke and, 'strange though it may seem', Hume. 'Though an enemy to his skepticism, I have profited by it. By attacking, with great ability, every principle of truth and reason, he put me upon examining the ground upon which I stood and taught me not hastily to take anything for granted.'[1] Condorcet too tried to absorb strands of Hume's epistemology into his system.[2]

Among leaders of the Milanese Enlightenment, the *encyclopédistes'* most vehement critic, Alessandro Verri, was powerfully attracted by Hume's insight, modesty, and quiet style, which suggested to him that by 'making less noise than other philosophers', he was gaining more followers. By contrast, the 'pompous, intolerant, bold and sneering airs of some philosophers [i.e. the *encyclopédistes*] have provoked unbounded indignation'.[3] In Paris, there was, indeed, too much militancy in the air, in Hume's view, and excessive personal animus in debate. Voltaire was someone, he assured Hugh Blair in April 1764, 'who never forgives and never thinks any enemy below his notice'.[4] To his brother's enthusiasm Pietro Verri responded, in March 1768: 'you are very British and cannot stand the enthusiasm of the French. I agree with you.'[5] He reminded him, though, that even if less attractive to them, and more prone to error, the French thinkers' very outspokenness and aggressiveness had reaped major benefits for mankind. Hume's calm tone and general style, indeed, differed markedly from those of the *coterie d'Holbachique*; but the gulf separating him from the *encyclopédistes* stretched far beyond mere differences of style. British Enlightenment, Alessandro's 'philosophical pilgrimage' of 1766–7 to Paris and London convinced him, was superior in every way to the French; and Britain's higher form of Enlightenment, as he conceived it, directly related to what he judged to be England's overall superiority as a society, constitution, and imperial power. Although he never met Hume, he entirely concurred with him that Diderot and his circle were simply not good thinkers. Rather they were drawing droves onto the wrong path through reasoning imprecisely and too boldly.

Much like Bayle, to whom the young Hume owed a greater debt than to anyone else—a debt Anglo-American historians have traditionally greatly underestimated—Hume 'degrades reason in appearance' but exalts her in reality.[6] It filled Alessandro with indignation that just because Hume refrained from emulating the likes of Diderot in openly attacking religion and did not categorically embrace atheism, Diderot, d'Holbach, and their disciples considered him and his philosophy flabby and weak-minded. They gravely misjudged both the subtlety and power of his

[1] Price, *Political Writings*, 142.
[2] Baker, *Condorcet*, 139–40; Williams, *Condorcet and Modernity*, 97 n.
[3] Mazza, 'Hume's "Meek" Philosophy', 216.
[4] Quoted in Gay, *Voltaire's Politics*, 81.
[5] Mazza, 'Hume's "Meek" Philosophy', 219.
[6] Ibid. 216, 225, 230; Buckle, *Hume's Enlightenment Tract*, 328–9; on the Bayle factor, see Paganini, 'Hume, Bayle', 236–46, 248, 263.

scepticism. It was not just the discreet tone of Hume's irreligion that counted here but also its implications for moral philosophy. Despite his questioning of miracles and revelation, and religious truth more widely, Hume's thought does not finally exclude miracles as Spinoza does and nor attack—indeed, in a way it actually reinforces— acquiescence in divine governance of the world. The key point for Hume was that it seems so obvious to men that the world must have an intelligent Creator and supervisor, that our sense of morality in significant ways depends on this commonly shared perception. 'The whole frame of nature bespeaks an intelligent author; and no rational enquirer can, after serious reflection', affirms his *Natural History of Religion* (1757), 'suspend his belief a moment with regard to the primary principles of genuine Theism and Religion.'[7] Here, Kant was to follow in his footsteps.

Read and admired throughout Europe, Hume's *Essays* (despite being banned by the papacy in 1761) and *History* became classic fare. Hume won a 'great reputation for himself in France', notes Rousseau, especially 'among the *encyclopédistes*, with his treatises on commerce and politics'.[8] Characteristically, though much involved with him personally during 1765–7, Rousseau neither read his books nor took any interest in his philosophy. Others in France, though, were more willing to study his work but generally, noted Verri, remained more impressed with Hume the historical, political, and economic thinker than Hume the philosopher, a statement that holds equally true, as it happens, for the American colonies before the Revolution.[9] Grimm expressly stated in 1759 that he thought Hume lacked the 'depth of genius of M. Diderot', a perception few today would agree with but widespread at the time.[10] Hume's six- volume *History of England* published between 1754 and 1762 was especially admired and long remained a standard work in French as in English. It impressed above all for its calm objectivity and reasonableness: 'Mr Hume, in his *History*, seems neither a parlia- mentarian, nor a royalist', commented Voltaire in 1764, 'nor an Anglican, nor Presby- terian; in him we find only the fair-minded man.'[11] But while Voltaire ranked Hume high among his preferred writers, he nowhere seriously engages with his thought.

While Hume's philosophy as such was neither understood nor often cited in France, at least before the 1780s,[12] the Scottish thinker had a potent battery of social, moral, and political arguments on his side and made adept use of them during his Paris years not least at the Baron d'Holbach's table and other salons. He and they had a common starting point in one respect: 'the general societies of men', held Hume, 'are absolutely requisite for the subsistence of the species; and the public conve- niency, which regulates morals, is inviolably established in the nature of man, and of

---

[7] Hume, *Natural History*, 134; Gaskin, *Hume's Philosophy*, 120–31; Fogelin, *Defense*, 29, 62; Robert- son, *Case*, 310.

[8] Rousseau, *Confessions*, 527; Baldi, *David Hume*, 63; de Bujando, *Index*, 452.

[9] May, *Enlightenment*, 38.

[10] Naigeon, *Philosophie*, ii. 748–9; Mossner, *Life of David Hume*, 479; Bongie, *David Hume*, 27.

[11] Quoted in Bongie, *David Hume*, 13; Pomeau, *Religion de Voltaire*, 194, 388.

[12] Forsyth, *Reason*, 40.

the world in which he lives.'[13] He too dismissed the 'useless austerities and rigours, suffering and self-denial' of the theologians.[14] But from there on, he and they diverged totally. Yet, such was his easy-going, good-natured temperament that there was little real tension between him and the *philosophes*, albeit neither was there any significant debate, just tacit mutual non-understanding—or perhaps worse. Hume in any case regarded what he considered the shortcomings of the Parisian radical *philosophes* as many and considerable, Helvétius in particular, one of the Parisian colleagues, besides d'Alembert, Marmontel, and Duclos whose company he found most congenial, striking him as superficial and lacking in proper rigour. But, equally, according to an Irish army officer in French service, Daniel O'Connor of Belenagare, writing in 1764, Helvétius (with whom he had just been conversing) judged Hume's ideas 'ill connected', convinced 'he never studied the all of anything, and that his treatise on the passions is a very superficial work'.[15] Gibbon, describing his visit to Paris in early 1763, met Diderot, d'Holbach, and d'Alembert but later recalled mainly their 'intolerant zeal'. Although he enjoyed the baron's 'excellent dinners' which were given 'with great frequency', he was shocked to find the *philosophes* 'laughed at the skepticism of Hume, preached the tenets of atheism with the bigotry of dogmatists, and damned all believers with ridicule and contempt'.[16]

The differences of substance in social theory and moral thought were in fact vast. More amenable to enlightened despotism than Diderot and d'Holbach, Helvétius was no less scornful of the nobility's notion of themselves as a different species from other men. That all men are a single category means they belong to a single family and that there is no such thing as an elite elevated by birth: 'tous par conséquent sont nobles.'[17] Hume's philosophy, he notes, equally demolishes the essence of nobility, the prejudice underpinning it; but Hume, as a conservative sceptic, neither could nor wished to push his critique further and assail also the de facto dominance of aristocracy in society. Reason has nothing to do 'with the regard paid to the rich and powerful', grants Hume, but this does not mean pretensions based on rank are fraudulent. Although we can expect no advantage from deference, and self-interest here is absent, 'the images of prosperity, happiness, ease, plenty, authority, and the gratification of every appetite' still have the effect that 'we naturally respect the rich, even before they discover any such favourable disposition towards us'. Proof of this is found in the fact that 'in all civilized nations' nobles are treated with a regard suited to their birth, condition, and riches. This is sheer prejudice and has no basis in reason or justice. Yet, insists Hume, it is powerful social reality. 'For what is it we call a man of birth, but one who is descended from a long succession of rich and powerful ancestors, and who acquires our esteem by his connection with persons whom we esteem?'[18] Nobility presides over us both inwardly and outwardly.

---

[13] Hume, *Enquiry Concerning the Principles*, 102–3.   [14] Ibid. 153.
[15] Helvétius, *CGdH* iii. 108; Mossner, *Life of David Hume*, 474, 480; Bongie, *David Hume*, 34.
[16] Gibbon, *Autobiographies*, 204, 262, 301; Himmelfarb, *Roads*, 40.
[17] Helvétius, *De l'homme*, ii. 821; Lough, 'Helvétius and d'Holbach', 377.
[18] Hume, *Enquiry Concerning the Principles*, 129; Hume, *Essays*, 17–18, 95, 528; Stewart, *Opinion*, 290–301.

Just as 'regard or contempt' for others, contends Hume, is the 'natural consequence of those different situations in life', of possessing wealth or languishing in poverty, so it works with all moral distinctions—our natural feelings of esteem or aversion, sentiment, is what guides us in shaping our responses and social relations.[19] Sentiment, held Hume, Ferguson, and Smith alike, is the true basis of morality in society and one must accept the consequences of this regarding the social order: 'upon this disposition of mankind to go along with all the passions of the rich and powerful, is founded the distinction of ranks, and the order of society.'[20] Nothing could be further removed from the radical outlook which contended, on the contrary, that reason displaces all other criteria, that men are equal and noble birth nothing, and that mitigating in some way the hegemony of rank, that is, better integrating the masses into society, law, and politics, is the philosopher's duty.

Hence, criticism of nobility in Helvétius, Diderot, d'Holbach, and their followers emerges as something entirely different from in Hume, Smith, Kames, and Ferguson. Furthermore, here again, the radical materialists' views were echoed by the radical Socinian fringe. One of the three chief perils threatening the nascent United States at its birth, admonished Price, in 1785, much like Brissot and the younger Mirabeau, was granting hereditary honours and titles of nobility. 'Persons thus distinguished though perhaps meaner than the meanest of their dependents, are apt to consider themselves as belonging to a higher order of beings, and made for power and government.'[21] Where, for most, the poor summon up, comments Hume, 'disagreeable images of want, penury, hard labour, dirty furniture, coarse or ragged clothes, nauseous meat and distasteful liquor',[22] in radical eyes, the downcast deserve the same respect and protection from oppression and brigandage (whether popular, aristocratic, or state-organized), and same right to be happy, as anyone else. The humblest of citizens possesses the same birthright, proportionate to his position, merit, and talents, as the most eminent of the citizenry, indeed the monarch himself. Consequently, a wise and equitable government will strive to protect those with little who work and assist those with nothing.[23] By 1770, the split between moderate and radical enlighteners over deference to aristocracy had indeed become one of the key strands dividing the two enlightenments.

Britain led the world in the eighteenth century in wealth, power, and dynamism. Envied by many, she was feared by all. Her growing world predominance in terms of cultural influence as well as diplomacy, wealth, and power was to an extent the direct result of profound structural changes associated with the Glorious Revolution, an event fondly and deeply cherished among most Englishmen and Americans, many Scots, and some Irishmen. Since the 1690s, the deep tensions arising from the

---

[19] Hume, *Enquiry Concerning the Principles*, 128–9.
[20] Smith, *Theory*, 52.
[21] Price, *Observations*, 71.
[22] Hume, *Enquiry Concerning the Principles*, 129.
[23] Helvétius, *De l'homme*, ii. 659–60; d'Holbach, *Éthocratie*, 654; d'Holbach, *Politique naturelle*, 75, 165–6.

strength of religious Dissent and the contested status and powers of the Anglican Church were resolved through the Revolution settlement, the Toleration Act (1689), and William III's policy of separating the Church of Scotland from the Anglican Church and reconfiguring it, all of which served to widen religious plurality on a stable basis and establish a broader framework for freedom of conscience and toleration than was found anywhere else in Europe or the New World at the time. After 1688 there was no longer any question that Parliament and its committees constituted the guiding force in government, though the influence of the crown remained considerable, and this not only set clear limits on the crown's prerogatives and secured the elevation and relative independence of the judiciary and courts, but also enabled the dominant aristocracy and gentry to wield a wider spectrum of political, imperial, military, and cultural as well as agrarian influence than was found in probably any other European land.

Many economic, political, and strategic factors contributed to Britain's greatness. But none carried more weight with Hume than her commerce. His reflections on 'commerce' had indeed a special place in the reception of this thought. For no other writer of the age aside from Adam Smith so emphasized the benefits of trade, and government support for trade, for spreading prosperity and as the key to furthering the well-being and happiness of men. 'The greatness of a state and the happiness of its subjects', he affirms, in the third part of his *Essays*, published in 1752, 'how independent soever they may be supposed in some respects, are commonly allowed to be inseparable with regard to commerce; and as private men receive greater security, in the possession of their trade and riches, from the power of the public, so the public becomes powerful in proportion to the opulence and extensive commerce of private men.'[24] This maxim he pronounces 'true in general'. Hume stressed the benefits of commerce across the board, commerce being something that stimulates industry and the crafts and ensures low interest rates and a plentiful supply of credit and funds. Like Turgot, Diderot, and Raynal, he thought it absurd to begrudge the growth of neighbouring countries' trade and shipping, as Europeans habitually then still did.

'In opposition to this narrow and malignant opinion, I will venture to assert, that the increase of riches and commerce in any one nation, instead of hurting, commonly promotes the riches and commerce of all its neighbours; and that a state can scarcely carry its trade and industry very far, where all the surrounding states are buried in ignorance, sloth, and barbarism.'[25] Here he concurred with his Parisian friends. Where he diverged from their analysis was in inferring that the benefits extend far beyond commerce's contribution to the wealth of merchants, manufacturers, and the middling strata's economic well-being. Commerce, for him, is also the chief stimulant to agriculture and lever for minimizing unemployment.[26] It is

---

[24] Hume, *Essays*, 255, 301–2.
[25] Ibid. 328–9; Skinner, 'David Hume: Principles', 232.
[26] Skinner, 'David Hume: Principles', 234; Hume, *Essays*, 277, 300, 303, 329.

through commerce and manufactures that agriculture is chiefly stimulated and the peasant encouraged to labour and produce more than he needs simply to subsist. Hence, he identified vigorous commercial growth as undoubtedly the chief factor behind Britain's astounding success, that is her achieving greater prosperity than other lands (aside from Holland) and a freer, more stable and orderly constitution.

With the expansion of trade, every nation will advance also in its political arrangements. 'As the ambition of the sovereign must entrench on the luxury of individuals; so the luxury of individuals must diminish the force, and check the ambition of sovereigns.'[27] 'Nor is this reasoning merely chimerical', he adds characteristically, 'but is founded on history and experience.'[28] Where merchants and tradesmen acquire a share of the prosperity and property formerly held by the privileged alone, they 'draw authority and consideration to that middling rank of men, who are the best and firmest basis of public liberty. These submit not to slavery, like the peasants, from poverty and meanness of spirit; and, having no hopes of tyrannizing over others, like the barons, they are not tempted, for the sake of that gratification, to submit to the tyranny of their sovereign. They covet equal laws, which may secure their property, and preserve them from monarchical, as well as aristocratical tyranny.'[29] Despite his broadly conservative views on British politics and admiration for the Italian republics, Hume was no supporter of aristocratic dominance per se; on the contrary, he favoured the rise of the middling sort, merchants and prosperous citizens, and believed that it was trade and prosperity that had made the House of Commons the constitution's dominant arm.[30]

Commerce was also, in Hume's view, the main stimulus behind the advance of the liberal arts, science, literature, and sociability. Growing sociability then in turn exerts a positive moral effect on society, since for Hume morality, as he reaffirmed in what he considered his best work, *An Enquiry Concerning the Principles of Morals* (1751), is something based chiefly on interaction, sensibility, and custom rather than reason. 'So that, beside the improvements which [men] receive from knowledge and the liberal arts, it is impossible but they must feel an increase in humanity, from the very habit of conversing together, and contributing to each other's pleasure and entertainment.'[31] Nothing more decisively separates Hume from radical thought than his insisting that 'reason' and moral philosophy cannot inspire action, moral improvement, or fulfilment of moral obligation and that we should look rather to habits, accepted mores, and social circumstances for the motives that do perform this work. That moral sensibilities move men to act in particular ways proves, he concluded already in his first major work, the *Treatise of Human Nature* (1739), that the 'rules of morality' are not 'conclusions of our reason' but of our sensibilities. As he further developed his moral theory, Hume constantly stressed that it is 'founded on uniform

---

27 Hume, *Essays*, 257.
28 Ibid.
29 Ibid. 277–8; Robertson, *Case*, 300, 319.
30 Hume, *Essays*, 278; Stewart, *Opinion*, 297–8.
31 Hume, *Essays*, 271; Norton, 'Hume, Human Nature', 162, 170; Porter, *Enlightenment*, 245–6.

experience and observation'. 'Utility' to society, or rather to particular societies, is what grounds justice, fidelity, honour, allegiance, and chastity as well as generosity and charity, affecting others positively and eliciting their praise. 'The intercourse of sentiments, therefore, in society and conversation, makes us form some general unalterable standard, by which we may approve or disapprove of characters and manners.'[32] 'Morality, therefore, is more properly felt than judg'd of.'[33] Curtailment of reason and hence moral philosophy as an agent of individual and social improvement in this way became central to his ethics.

Not only are trade, manufactures, and the mechanical arts crucial in determining the refinement, political condition, scientific status, and general health of states but the more labour is employed beyond that needed for subsistence, the more powerful as well as cultured is that state, as the excess can then be drawn off for recruiting into the army and navy, domestic service, or for colonizing abroad. 'Thus the greatness of the sovereign and the happiness of the state are, in a great measure, united with regard to trade and manufactures.'[34] 'In short', he summed up his case, 'a kingdom that has a large import and export, must abound more with industry, and that employed upon delicacies and luxuries, than a kingdom which rests contented with its native commodities. It is therefore, more powerful, as well as richer and happier.'[35]

That excessive inequality weakens any society Hume accepted as he did the claim that spreading prosperity in the direction of equality strengthens both society and the state. 'Where the riches are in few hands these must enjoy all the power, and will readily conspire to lay the whole burthen [of taxation and effort] on the poor, and oppress them still further, to the discouragement of all industry.' That 'every person, if possible, ought to enjoy the fruits of his labour, in a full possession of all the necessaries, and many of the conveniencies of life', he did not doubt. Indeed, precisely here 'consists the great advantage of England', he argued, 'above any nation at present in the world, or that appears in the records of any story'. The prosperity of her artisans 'as well as the plenty of money' were decisive assets. 'And if there were no more to endear to them that free government under which they live, this alone were sufficient. The poverty of the common people is a natural, if not infallible effect of absolute monarchy; though I doubt, whether it be always true, on the other hand, that their riches are an infallible result of liberty. Liberty must be attended with particular accidents, and a certain turn of thinking, in order to produce that effect.'[36] This led him to view the development of civil society as something driven, primarily, by economic need and desires, and hence to regard justice as in origin a prop to the requirements of the economic process, hence of the market. 'The motive that led people' to begin respecting property and contract, avers Hume, was 'enlightened

---

[32] Hume, *Enquiry Concerning the Principles*, 115–17.
[33] Hume, *Treatise*, 457, 470; Moore, 'Montesquieu', 181; Harris, 'Epicurean', 178–9.
[34] Hume, *Essays*, 262, 272.
[35] Ibid. 263, 270–1; Robertson, *Case*, 364.
[36] Hume, *Essays*, 265.

self-interest'.[37] In Hume's theory of justice and law, like Adam Smith's, there stands a built-in, inherent emphasis on justice being primarily a mechanism for the protection of private property and commercial contract.[38]

Always 'a friend to moderation', as he himself put it, Hume supplied enlightened 'moderation' with its most compelling and incisive intellectual armoury. Both his general method and stress on 'history and experience' as the ground of all sound social theory follow directly, he claimed, from Newton's discoveries in science. Newton, in whom Britain, he wrote, 'may boast of having produced the greatest and rarest genius that ever arose for the ornament and instruction of the species', had made truly epoch-making discoveries and 'seemed to draw off the veil from some of the mysteries of nature' while at the same time fully revealing the imperfections of the 'mechanical philosophy' and all the overarching, rationalistic systems and had thereby restored nature's 'ultimate secrets to that obscurity, in which they ever did and ever will remain'.[39] Hume envisaged Newton as a natural philosopher 'cautious in admitting no principles but such as were founded on experiment; but resolute to adopt every such principle, however new or unusual'. For Hume no less than Newton, only evidence drawn from experience and experiment is valid.

Politics, like ethics and political economy, is 'a science', grants Hume, but an experimental science, based on 'experience and observation' not abstract principles.[40] His philosophical scepticism conclusively proved, he believed, that our moral and political ideas rest on no basic premises established by reason; reasoning remains an indispensable tool, but only reasoning demonstrative from experience, or about probabilities, is valid. In principle, Diderot and d'Holbach agreed with this. But the consequences he draws from his empiricism are entirely different from theirs; in particular he believed they were extrapolating dangerously beyond the connections confirmed by experience.[41] This produced in him a particular and highly original brand of 'moderation' in every sphere. While he saw no evidence of the truth of any religious claim, he equally emphasized the naturalness, once reason has advanced beyond a primitive level, of believing in 'that perfect Being, who bestowed order on the whole frame of nature'.[42] Equally, a key result of Hume's 'science' of experimental, observed politics was the unquestioned superiority of 'moderation' as a political, moral, and general guiding principle, 'moderation not just in practice' but also in formulating the guiding principles of action and reform.

The value of 'moderation' Hume claimed to have learnt in part by studying the excesses of the two English political factions in Parliament—the Whigs and Tories. They dominated the British political scene but with both, to his mind, wildly exaggerating in their attacks on the other. 'But extremes of all kinds are to be avoided;

---

[37] Stewart, *Opinion*, 166.
[38] Ibid. 160–2; Zarone, *Cesare Beccaria*, 68–75.
[39] Hume, *History*, vi. 542; Hume, *Enquiry Concerning the Principles*, 98, 206.
[40] Fogelin, 'Hume's Scepticism', 95; Skinner, 'David Hume: Principles', 226, 229.
[41] Buckle, *Hume's Enlightenment Tract*, 325–6.
[42] Hume, *Natural History*, 136.

and though no one will ever please either faction by moderate opinions, it is there we are most likely to meet with truth and certainty.'[43] Another crucial premiss of political, social, and moral science, he thought, was that subjects should strive their utmost 'in every free state' to defend 'those forms and institutions, by which liberty is secure, the public good consulted, and the avarice or ambition of particular men restrained and punished'.[44] However, such endeavours are effective only while the constitution does its proper job. Men should endorse all government that affords liberty and good order. But these are the only justifying criteria; there is no other reason for supporting a government. No constitution can be legitimized by any abstract or supernatural principle of religion, creed, dynastic claims, or any charter or other principle no matter how ancient or venerated. 'A constitution is only so far good, as it provides a remedy against mal-administration; and if the British, when in its greatest vigour, and repaired by two such remarkable events as the Revolution [of 1688] and Accession, by which our ancient royal family was sacrificed to it; if our constitution, I say, with so great advantages, does not, in fact provide any such remedy, we are rather beholden to any minister who undermines it, and affords us an opportunity of erecting a better in its place.'[45]

For Hume, the British constitution's superiority lay solely in its practical achievements and had no other basis, certainly not in 'general principles', a term with distinctly negative connotations in his terminology. Both Locke and committed republicans like Toland, Trenchard, or Gordon had interpreted the Revolution of 1688–91 as grounded in some way in 'contract' or on popular sovereignty. Hume, by contrast, denied that anything like popular sovereignty was a factor in the Glorious Revolution. The people played no part in it, he stressed, while the change of dynasty was decided on in England and Scotland solely by majorities of the two parliaments. He did not doubt that the 'bulk of those ten millions [of Britain's inhabitants] acquiesced willingly in the determination: But was the latter left, in the least, to their choice?' Absolutely not. The aristocracy decided everything to the smallest detail. In the Revolution of 1688–91, there was not the least trace of a democratic tendency. Nor did he desire to see 'Revolution-principles' adopted as a general measure to make other governments appear in some way illegitimate. 'Let not the establishment at the Revolution deceive us, or make us so much in love with a philosophical origin to government, as to imagine all others monstrous and irregular.'[46]

While calmly conceding that the constitution had its imperfections, Hume insisted on its being a delicate balance of differently useful but imperfect principles that worked uncommonly well. The king's ministers, he allows, were to an extent corrupting Parliament and, by so doing, infringing 'liberty'. But he did not think corrupt practices could be simply cleared away any more than he agreed that parliamentary

[43] Hume, *History,* vi. 534; Ward, *Politics,* 313–14.
[44] Hume, *Essays,* 26.
[45] Ibid. 29–30; Haakonssen, 'Hume's Political Theory', 203–4.
[46] Hume, *Essays,* 472–3.

elections should be more frequent. Properly maintaining the 'monarchical' element in the British constitution, he argued, crucially depended on the infrequency of elections to the House of Commons. 'It is true the crown has great influence over the collective body in the election of members; but were this influence, which at present is only exerted once in seven years, to be employed in bringing over the people to every vote, it would soon be wasted; and no skill, popularity or revenue, could support it. I must, therefore, be of opinion, that an alteration in this particular would introduce a total alteration in our government, and would soon reduce it to a pure republic.' Such 'a pure republic', he conceded, might not necessarily be a step backwards in terms of liberty and good government; but he feared it would be and, in any case, preferred to avoid 'such dangerous novelties'.[47]

The crown's influence in elections and distributing favours and offices was accepted by most and positively argued for by some. Students of politics may 'give to this influence what name we please', held Hume, 'we may call it by the invidious appellations of corruption and dependence; but some degree and some kind of it are inseparable from the very nature of the constitution, and necessary to the preservation of our mixed government.'[48] Balancing arms of government might be more regular and defined in pure republics where the composition and procedures of each body can be more precisely formulated. 'But a limited monarchy admits not of any such stability; nor is it possible to assign to the crown such a determinate degree of power, as will, in every hand, form a proper counterbalance to the other parts of the constitution', a rather rare disadvantage, he believed, in the British constitution.[49] On one occasion, he even declared that 'though liberty be preferable to slavery, in almost every case, yet I should rather wish to see an absolute monarch than a republic in this island'.[50] But it was hard to be swayed by such arguments and from the 1770s increasingly so. 'The disproportion in the representation of this country', affirmed John Jebb, in a speech in 1782, 'the length of our parliaments, and the depredations committed, in various periods of our history, upon the right of suffrage, have utterly destroyed the ancient constitutional connection between the House of Commons and the people. The majority of that House are no longer the representatives of the Commons; they are the dependents of the nobles, the creatures of the crown.'[51] Here, was an indigenous resonance, and becoming distinctly louder, of the prime accusation brought by Diderot and the *Histoire philosophique* against the so celebrated British constitution: it leaves excessive influence in the hands of the crown and aristocracy.[52]

That government is illegitimate and 'tyrannical' when it does not further the interests of the majority, the central political principle of the hard-core philosophical republicans Meslier, Du Marsais, Boulanger, and the later radical *philosophes*, Hume

[47] Ibid. 36; Pocock, *Barbarism*, ii. 186, 220; Pocock, *Virtue, Commerce*, 135.
[48] Hume, *Essays*, 45, 277; Haakonssen, 'Hume's Political Theory', 209.
[49] Hume, *Essays*, 46; Stewart, *Opinion*, 282–3, 307.
[50] Hume, *Essays*, 17, 24, 52, 524; Stewart, *Opinion*, 282; Emerson, *Essays*, 151–2.
[51] Jebb, *The Works*, iii. 306–7; Gascoigne, 'Anglican Latitudinarianism', 232–3.
[52] *Histoire philosophique* (1780), ix. 208; Paine, *Rights of Man*, 192–202.

firmly denies. Likewise, he rejected the notion that government should rest on the people's consent. 'It is in vain to say that all governments are or should be, at first founded on popular consent, as much as the necessity of human affairs will admit. This favours entirely my pretension. I maintain, that human affairs will never admit of this consent; seldom of the appearance of it. But that conquest or usurpation, that is, in plain terms, force, by dissolving the ancient governments, is the origin of almost all the new ones, which were ever established in the world. And that in the few cases, where consent may seem to have taken place, it was commonly so irregular, so confined, or so much intermixed either with fraud or violence, that it cannot have any great authority.'[53] Moreover, in his last years, Hume became increasingly alarmed by the rise of populist movements in England and responded by stressing still more the pivotal role of nobility and gentry as the great political stabilizer.[54]

The people's inclinations, Hume acknowledges, statesmen often reckon with; but this is far more likely to occur in settled constitutions than 'during the fury of revolutions, conquests, and public convulsions' when military force or political manipulation decide everything. The case was similar regarding the alleged 'contract' grounded by some in the early Capetian phase of the French monarchy. Boulainvilliers 'was a noted republican; but being a man of learning, and very conversant in history, he knew that the people were never almost consulted in these revolutions and new establishments, and that time alone bestowed right and authority on what was commonly at first founded on force and violence.'[55] Denying 'contract', Hume was equally disinclined to see the stability and other chief advantages of Britain's constitution as stemming from ancient precedents, charters, and statutes. He frequently notes the bogus character of efforts to invoke precedent. 'Under what pretence can the popular party now speak of recovering ancient constitutions? The former control over the kings was not placed in the Commons, but in the barons: The people had no authority, and even little or no liberty; till the crown, by suppressing these factious tyrants, enforced the execution of the laws, and obliged all the subjects equally to respect each others rights, privileges, and properties.'[56] He judged ridiculous 'to hear the [House of] Commons, while they are assuming by usurpation, the whole power of government, talk of reviving ancient institutions.'[57] Here was a further rare point of convergence with radical ideas.

2. HUME, ARISTOCRACY, AND THE BRITISH EMPIRE

For most late eighteenth-century observers and most of the moderate Enlightenment, Britain was much the most successful nation of the age and the worthiest of

---

[53] Hume, *Essays*, 474; May, *Enlightenment*, 112.
[54] Pocock, *Virtue, Commerce*, 138.
[55] Hume, *Essays*, 486.
[56] Ibid. 497; Pocock, *Machiavellian Moment*, 493.
[57] Hume, *Essays*, 498; Pocock, *Barbarism*, ii. 255, 259.

admiration and emulation. Britain also possessed the most extensive and powerful world empire since Roman times, economically, politically, at sea, and militarily. Ever since the Glorious Revolution and the Union with Scotland (1707), Britain had experienced imperial success, great power status, and by 1713 also overwhelming financial superiority over others no less than greater general prosperity, dynamism, press freedom, and political stability. Even its sternest critics, while cautioning that the British constitution was less perfect than conventional notions would have it, granted that it was nevertheless the best actually existing.[58]

By the mid eighteenth century, a sense of—and belief in—British superiority over others was natural for most Englishmen, something taken for granted, almost an article of faith and badge of national identity. However, in Hume's philosophy it remained more a matter of cool demonstration and evidence, a project in which his own nation, the Scots, could take pride in sharing and also one shared in by the Irish, the Americans, the Canadians, and in some degree all men. The great changes introduced by the 1688 Revolution had been followed by a batch of additional new freedoms lending a particular allure and grandeur to the British state and the transatlantic society it fostered. 'And it may justly be affirmed', notes Hume, in his *History of England*, 'without any danger of exaggeration, that we, in this island, have ever since [the Revolution of 1688] enjoyed, if not the best system of government, at least the most entire system of liberty, that ever was known amongst mankind.'[59] Liberty flourished as never before. Liberty of the press, and newspapers in particular, established as an acknowledged 'freedom' since the lapsing of the Licensing Act in 1695, to a degree previously unknown, could justly be considered the safeguard of all the other freedoms (albeit the theatre in eighteenth-century England remained under rigorous censorship).[60] It was typical of Hume's experimental method of reasoning to stress the uniqueness of the context in which press freedom flourished and then explain it in terms of particular circumstances, preferring not to regard press freedom as an absolute principle. 'As this liberty is not indulged in any other government', he notes, 'in Holland and Venice, more than in France and Spain; it may very naturally give occasion to a question. How it happens that Great Britain alone enjoys this peculiar privilege?' His answer, given in characteristically qualified manner, is that it 'seems to be derived from our mixed form of government, which is neither wholly monarchical, nor wholly republican'. Above all, it was a particular, peculiar outcome not part of an inherent tendency.[61]

Typical also of Hume is his seeing English press liberty, indeed all her liberties, as something not just highly specific to context but so remote from principle as actually to stem from the contradictions and lack of consistency enshrined at the heart of Britain's constitution. 'As long, therefore, as the republican part of our government

---

[58] *Histoire philosophique* (1780), x. 74–5, 83–6.
[59] Hume, *History*, vi. 531.
[60] Colley, *Britons*, 40, 42; Worrall, *Theatric Revolution*, 1, 18, 36.
[61] Hume, *Essays*, 9–10; Pocock, *Barbarism*, ii. 260–1.

can maintain itself against the monarchical, it will naturally be careful to keep the press open, as of importance to its own preservation.'[62] He was not optimistic, though, that this inherently precarious balance between contradictory principles could be sustained indefinitely. Rather he thought the British constitution, mostly to its advantage, was so incoherent as to be ultimately unstable and bound to unravel, perhaps in the not too distant future. 'The just balance between the republican and monarchical part of our constitution is really, in itself, so extremely delicate and uncertain, that, when joined to men's passions and prejudices, it is impossible but different opinions must arise concerning it, even among persons of the best understanding.'[63] But when sooner or later Britain's parliamentary system did disintegrate through the force of its own triumphant practicality and incoherence, besides rising debt, too many wars, and populist notions, he was certain it would be best to avoid any shift to popular sovereignty. To avoid future 'convulsions and civil wars', absolute monarchy, he maintained, would be far preferable to moving in a republican or democratic direction. 'Absolute monarchy, therefore, is the easiest death, the true Euthanasia of the British constitution.'[64]

With liberty of the press came a degree of flexibility in enquiry and individual autonomy in the sciences, scholarship, artisanship, and the arts that contrasted strikingly with the constraints of the past and restrictions applying in most of Europe and non-British America. Meanwhile, the unprecedented growth of London fostered a degree of freedom in matters of dress, lifestyle, and personal freedom matched only by Paris. Mid- and late eighteenth-century Britain constituted a novel and exciting scenario characterized by a host of innovative new features, among the more unexpected and remarkable of which during the post-1688 era was the rise among most of the population of the prestige not just of Parliament, the constitution, navy, army, and English law, but also of the crown, aristocracy, empire, and the British state generally.[65] Even in Scotland and, to a lesser extent, Ireland, sections of the population felt reconciled to the Union and absorption into England's maritime empire. Englishmen being by and large intensely proud of their country's unparalleled success since 1688, the Anglican clergy found little difficulty in advancing the notion that God had distributed his blessings with particular liberality on Britain and that crown, constitution, and empire were divinely sanctioned and favoured institutions.

A particular problem for philosophers was the sheer extent of Britain's success overseas and in arms encouraging not just pride and feelings of superiority over others but intensification at least in England, among both the upper and lower strata, of an older proneness to cultural xenophobia that distinctly jarred on the Enlightenment's cosmopolitan ideals and, for some, clouded Englishmen's understanding of the real basis of Britain's success. Certainly, the more sophisticated, and Hume more

---

[62] Hume, *Essays*, 12–13; Stewart, *Opinion*, 240, 306–7.
[63] Hume, *Essays*, 64.
[64] Ibid. 53; Pocock, *Barbarism*, ii. 187; Hont, *Jealousy*, 347; Emerson, *Essays*, 153.
[65] Hume, *Essays*, 51.

than most, disdained simplistic claims about divinely given greatness and innate superiority. Hume thoroughly scorned the prevailing Gallophobia and xenophobia, a reaction bolstered by his own sometimes barely suppressed Anglophobia. 'Our jealousy and our hatred of France are without bounds' but only the former was 'reasonable and well-grounded'.[66] Elite as well as popular culture seemed hopelessly prone to narrow and prejudiced assumptions. Hence, partly in reaction to a general mood with which some felt scant sympathy, thoughtful conservatives searched for a more sober and secular doctrine justifying broad endorsement of the status quo, existing social hierarchy, and pre-eminence of the Anglican Church, and precisely this Hume's thought triumphantly provided. Hume's human nature was a mass of contradiction following no logically consistent course but exhibiting consistent patterns and basically unalterable, buttressing a profoundly undemocratic view of politics.[67]

The reading public's attitudes, insular by tradition and conviction, fastened on the domestic context alone and, for this too, Hume's thought afforded ample legitimization despite his aversion to xenophobia. In Britain, it was generally assumed, and with Hume's texts could be cogently argued, that the Enlightenment's principal aims—as formulated by Locke, Newton, Hume, Montesquieu, and Voltaire— empiricism in science, religious toleration, freedom of thought and the press, personal liberty, and security of person, had all been accomplished already. The revolution was complete. Hence, there was little need, it was confidently supposed, for any further Enlightenment in Britain. Meanwhile, the final defeat of Jacobitism in 1745, and receding of English 'deism' after the demise of Toland (1722), Collins (1729), and Gordon (1750), further heightened the feeling of England being *par excellence* the land of stability and consensus political and intellectual. This removed all sense of urgency in combating radical ideas and subversive anti-Scripturalism of the sort that had spurred Newtonian ideologues of an earlier generation like Clarke, Richard Bentley (1662–1742), and William Whiston (1667–1752). If some still cultivated determinist, naturalist, and materialist positions in private, questioned the authority and privileges of the crown and Anglican Church, and deplored shortcomings in the law and at Oxford and Cambridge, all this had become decidedly muted by 1750.

By the mid eighteenth century, British consensus had consolidated while the radical tendency had been marginalized. For the moment, England was no longer a country agitated by the challenge of freethinking which, to all appearances, was now causing far more disturbance elsewhere. 'France abounds with free-thinkers', commented Thomas Gordon, in 1750, 'no kingdom in Europe more, nor so much; Holland, above all countries, abounds with printing-presses, with free-thinking and obnoxious books, which are from thence dispersed all over the world. France

---

[66] Ibid. 315; Robertson, *Case*, 367–8, 370.

[67] Norton, 'Hume, Human Nature', 159; Buckle, *Hume's Enlightenment Tract*, 276; Harris, 'Epicurean', 180.

and Holland are not alarmed with Earthquakes, at least more than we are. Yet Amsterdam far exceeds (or perhaps it will sound more arch and satirical to say "beats") all the world, beats "even London", in the traffic of infidelity.'[68] It was inherent in the national consensus that Britain, unlike the rest, needed no further Enlightenment. But if English society, governance, law, and empire were no longer a problem for (most of) her own people, Britain was increasingly a problem for others. Having humiliated France in North America, the Caribbean, India, and the Mediterranean during the Seven Years War (1756–63) and since 1713 rapidly outstripped the United Provinces at sea and in commerce, including in Asian waters where the Dutch had previously presided since the early seventeenth century, by 1763 Britain no longer had any rival for world commercial, financial, technological, land, and maritime primacy. Her global hegemony, though, spelt decline and retreat for her defeated competitors—the Dutch, Danes, Russians, and Portuguese as well as France and Spain—and fears of further setbacks. Her world ascendancy also disturbed not a few philosophers. England, declared the *Histoire philosophique*, had created a wholly new form of 'monarchie universelle', subjecting all the world to her uncompromising sway in commerce, colonies and sea power.[69] Of all the imperial powers of his century, remarked Chastellux in 1772, undoubtedly the British were the most enveloped in a mania for domination, self-aggrandizement, and economic advantage.[70]

Britain's *monarchie universelle*, argued the *Histoire*, was something 'Europe' should wrest back from her and re-assign more equitably, in the interest of the common good and 'l'équité naturelle', returning to every maritime people the autonomy and freedom each had a right to exercise over the waters surrounding them.[71] There was no sympathy for this standpoint in Britain, of course; but in America and also Ireland, a land more rigorously subjected than the American colonies, there was some and it grew with time. Something, Hume acknowledged, was indeed seriously wrong: 'were our narrow and malignant [trade] politics to meet success, we should reduce all our neighbouring nations to the same state of sloth and ignorance that prevails in Morocco and the coast of Barbary. But what would be the consequence? They could send us no commodities: They could take none from us. Our domestic commerce itself would languish for want of emulation, example, and instruction: And we ourselves should soon fall into the same abject condition, to which we had reduced them.' He urged the English to revise their chauvinistic notions of international trade and relations. They and their European neighbours should cultivate 'enlarged and benevolent sentiments towards each other'.[72] A like injunction, more radical writers thought, ought to apply more generally. 'A total reformation', exclaimed Thomas Paine in 1782, 'is wanted in England. She wants an expanded mind—a heart that embraces the universe. Instead of shutting herself up in an island,

---

[68] Gordon, *A Letter*, 20.
[69] *Histoire philosophique* (1780), x. 170.
[70] Chastellux, *De la félicité publique*, ii. 161, 191.
[71] *Histoire philosophique* (1780), x. 170.
[72] Hume, *Essays*, 330–1; Hont, *Jealousy*, 6, 36–7, 115, 292.

and quarrelling with the world, she would derive more lasting happiness, and acquire more real riches, by generously mixing with it, and bravely saying, I am the enemy of none.'[73]

No such response was to be expected from public opinion, Parliament, or from Hume. What was best for Britain, indeed any polity, in his view, was more a question of custom, honesty, tact, and good sense than adhering to any grand plan proposed by philosophy. Nothing further separated his thought from Radical Enlightenment than his refusal to consider 'philosophy' the key to the general amelioration of mankind, his conceiving it as something that by its nature can have no guiding significance in human affairs. Since it is not reason that establishes and authenticates our trust and confidence in the basic realities dictating our daily calculations in normal life, our decisions, and views on moral issues and politics, must stem from experience, habit, and custom alone.[74] The value of philosophizing for society Hume sees in refining 'the temper' and pointing 'out to us those dispositions which we should endeavour to attain' by habit and intellectual activity. In this respect 'philosophy' can do some good politically. But 'beyond this I cannot acknowledge it to have great influence; and I must entertain doubts concerning all those exhortations and consolations, which are in such vogue among speculative reasoners'.[75]

Not only did Britain's radical tendency wane between the 1730s and the outbreak of the American Revolution in 1775–6, there was in English society and culture, well before as well as after 1775, a growing emphasis on hierarchy, monarchy, empire, and the interdependence of Church and crown, fed by the domestic impact of recent wars and the new configuration in domestic politics bringing the Tory country squires into alliance with the faction known as the 'Court Whigs', the Whig aristocratic leadership in Parliament. Vaunting the basic institutions of the British 'confessional state', hardened by rivalry with France and, after 1763, growing difficulties in America, came to be more and more insisted on in high society, the universities, and popular culture alike. The consequence was a further narrowing of attitudes that reinforced the prevailing consensus, deterred criticism, and was rarely stimulating intellectually. When it was, it mostly assumed a conservative cast. Gibbon acknowledged 'the philosophic Hume' as one of 'my masters', opposed the Swiss democratic tendency, liked all of Burke's anti-revolutionary creed except for his adoring 'church establishments', and later recalled whilst sitting as a member of the Commons, on the outbreak of the American Revolution, supporting 'with many a sincere and silent vote, the rights, though not, perhaps, the interest of the mother-country'.[76]

Aside from Burke, Gibbon, and William Jones and, of course, radicals rejecting the national consensus and the loyalist chauvinism that buttressed it—Paine, Priestley, Price, Jebb, Bentham, Godwin, and Wollstonecraft—later eighteenth-century English

---

[73] Paine, *Letter Addressed to the Abbé Raynal*, 69.
[74] Fogelin, 'Hume's Scepticism', 99; Robertson, *Case*, 299–300.
[75] Hume, *Essays*, 171, 180; Buruma, *Taming*, 27; Harris, 'Hume's Four Essays', 234–5.
[76] Gibbon, *Memoirs*, 53, 184.

Enlightenment, as distinct from the Scottish, produced few figures of international stature. Scotland, by contrast, remained a land of deep divisions rather than consensus. In the Lowlands, there prevailed since 1688 a somewhat harsh, constricting Calvinism that in the mid and late eighteenth century battled to retain its hold, while Catholic and Episcopalian Jacobitism, with their uncompromising legitimism, traditionalism, and hostility to the 1688 Revolution Settlement, remained a powerful force emotionally, also after 1745, especially but by no means only in the Highlands. All this rendered toleration, constitutional monarchy, and personal liberty locally highly contested issues. In Scotland, an exceptionally literate society had suddenly to adjust to new realities that fundamentally altered basic elements of Scottish identity. All at once the Scots needed to accept loss of separate nationhood and absorption into a world empire wholly dominated by England and become a collection of religious minorities embedded within an Anglican greater society, reorganizing their political, legal, and educational institutions accordingly. Scotland had entered a new era of expansion and reorientation with all their attendant problems and amid these challenges had no greater apologist for Union and political Anglicization, or foe of dogmatic legitimism and narrow confessionalism, than Hume.

'The true rule of government', held Hume, 'is the present established practice of the age.'[77] The whole tenor of his social and cultural thought, moreover, privileged precisely this rule also in the moral, educational, and legal spheres. Hume exalted 'moderation'; but his was a 'moderation' apt only to underpin prevailing usage. It was Hume's great strength but also no small weakness. Regarding the American crisis, his own personal perspective may have been even-handed and original. Privately, his benevolent pragmatism collided with both sides since he had no sympathy for the points of principle raised by either the Americans or Parliament in their quarrels about consent, sovereignty, and the right to tax the colonists. But publicly stated his principles were really useful only to one side—the Tory loyalists. Hume's overriding principle, 'moderation' clashed fundamentally not just with radical thought but also with the American Revolution and later, in the 1780s, the Dutch and French revolutions. In practical politics, this was unavoidable given the special usefulness of his approach to defenders of existing usage, empire, monarchy, aristocracy, and privileged state churches.

Less hostile to the American cause than Ferguson and other Scots enlighteners, in the years prior to his death, the year the Revolution began, Hume felt the whole business had been so incompetently handled by the British ministry that the colonies' secession had become inevitable. This was something Britain, in his opinion, should simply accept with the best grace possible without going to war. In a private letter of October 1775 he went so far as to declare: 'I am an American in my principles, and wish we would let them alone to govern or misgovern themselves as they think proper.'[78] But he was no eulogist of the Revolution as such and still less its principles;

---

[77] Hume, *Essays*, 498.
[78] Hume to Baron Mure of Caldwell, 27 Oct. 1775, in Hume, *Letters*, ii. 303; Wootton, 'David Hume', 297; Amoh, 'Ferguson's Views', 73.

and despite engaging in intense discussion with Benjamin Franklin, who spent a whole month with him in Edinburgh, in the autumn of 1771 when the American also met with other 'Brother Philosophers', notably Ferguson and Kames, felt scant sympathy for the man or his cause.[79] Where the radical thinkers supported the Revolution but also criticized it for not pushing equality, democracy, and toleration far enough, and not freeing the slaves, Scots Enlightenment was divided but on balance strongly opposed American independence.[80]

Ferguson, who in 1778 was appointed secretary to a British government commission sent to America to negotiate a settlement, roundly accused democratic pro-American British publicists, such as Price, of slighting the British constitution and wilfully ignoring Montesquieu's 'wisely' framed doctrine that 'Democracy and Aristocracy are not by their nature free governments.' Democracy no less than aristocracy is inferior, held Ferguson, to certain 'species of monarchy, where law is more fixed and the abuses of power are better restrained'.[81] 'Notwithstanding the disdain of our author [i.e. Price]', the British constitution, he maintained, bestows 'upon its subjects higher degrees of liberty than any other people are known to enjoy'.[82] Price, Priestley, and other supporters of the Revolution he lambasted for being too fond, with their talk of representation and democracy, of abstract principles. By displacing charters and precedent in favour of theoretical principles, they were ill-advisedly striving for ideal perfection 'which is apt to make us despise what is attainable and obtained, for the sake of something impracticable and sometimes absurd'.[83]

It was both despite and because of Hume's scant enthusiasm for the British cause in the pending struggle that his ideas continued to appeal to conservatives on both sides of the Atlantic and were widely seized on everywhere as a particularly effective politico-philosophical tool for combating democracy, egalitarianism, and anti-aristocratic sentiment irrespective of whether deployed for or against the colonists' stated principles and rhetoric. Hume's thought was warmly approved of on the conservative wing of the revolutionary leadership, by figures such as John Adams (1735–1826), then a young Massachusetts lawyer with strong 'classical republican' and socially and politically conservative views. Elected to the First Continental Congress, in 1774, Adams made no secret of his loathing of Paine and the entire radical ideology, and long continued to find Hume's philosophy highly congenial.

Yet, Hume's most outspoken admirers in America also included 'Tory' pamphleteers staunchly opposing the Revolution. One of these, writing under the pseudonym 'Candidus' in 1776, rejoiced that 'this beautiful system (according to Montesquieu), our constitution is a compound of monarchy, aristocracy and democracy', a system of ranks and hierarchy under which Britain ruled the Atlantic and commerce of the entire world. Convinced the colonies would lose greatly through independence,

---

[79] Mossner, *Life of David Hume*, 572–3, 595; Stewart, *Opinion*, 308–9.
[80] Berry, *Social Theory*, 107–9; Amoh, 'Ferguson's Views', 74.
[81] Ferguson, *Remarks*, 9.
[82] Ibid. 13.
[83] Ibid. 11–14.

'independence and slavery' he declared 'synonymous terms'. Against the 'demagogues' striving to 'seduce the people into their criminal designs' and break with Britain, he invoked not only Montesquieu but also 'the profound and elegant Hume'.[84] Such usage of his ideas became a regular feature of a wider tendency ranging Hume alongside Montesquieu as a pillar not just of monarchy and empire but also noble privilege and ecclesiastical rights, the existing status quo in Ireland, and so on, a tendency noticeable in Britain, America, Ireland, Italy, and even in Poland-Lithuania, a kingdom Hume despised and considered a failed society, but where his ideas were eagerly utilized by champions of nobility and by no means unreasonably. For if Hume did not agree with Montesquieu that nobility is indispensable as a bulwark against tyranny, he did think it often was, and considered republican stress on popular sovereignty and the right to resistance insidious. In describing England's crisis on the eve of the Civil War in 1642, around 1758, he located the gravest flaw in seventeenth-century English political culture in the notion that the people 'are permitted, at their pleasure, to overthrow and subvert an existing government.'[85]

Popular sovereignty, for Hume, was just part of a wider pernicious threat to order, established usage, and good sense. Britain's peculiar freedoms were inseparably linked in his mind to the dominance of the landed gentry and nobility. But precisely this class were being debilitated by current developments such as mania for empire, the growing national debt, and the rise of Whig populism, trends that would, he predicted, undermine the constitution.[86] 'An established government has an infinite advantage, by that very circumstance of its being established; the bulk of mankind being governed by authority, not reason, and never attributing authority to any thing that has not the recommendation of antiquity. To tamper, therefore, in this affair, or try experiments merely on the credit of supposed argument and philosophy, can never be the part of a wise magistrate, who will bear a reverence to what carried the marks of age; and though he may attempt some improvements for the public good, yet will he adjust his innovations, as much as possible, to the ancient fabric, and preserve entire the chief pillars and supports of the constitution.'[87] Ageing but still effective forms of government, for Hume, are not like obsolete machines to be cast aside for apparatus that looks more up to date and better designed.

A towering figure in eighteenth-century thought, for all his reasonableness, Hume was a deeply reticent voice regarding social, legal, and political reform. His philosophy placed the whole question of theory and precedent in the common law in a new light. Enlightenment and case law were not always in collision; but the harsh and antiquated realities of eighteenth-century legal practice rendered the kind of emphatic 'anti-philosophical' moral and legal conservatism promoted in Britain by writers like Hume, Blackstone, Ferguson, and Burke, as well as the public's

---

[84] 'Candidus' [William Smith], *Plain Truth: Addressed to the Inhabitants of America, Containing Remarks on a Late Pamphlet Intitled* Common Sense [i.e. by Tom Paine] (Philadelphia, 1776), 2–3, 37.
[85] Hume, *Essays*, 499–501; Moore, 'Montesquieu', 183.
[86] Hont, *Jealousy*, 345–6.
[87] Hume, *Essays*, 512–13; Haakonssen, 'Hume's Political Theory', 196, 201–2.

chauvinistic, almost mystical veneration for the law, deeply problematic. There was in Britain, complained Bentham in 1776, a prevailing but highly undesirable tendency to 'yield the same abject and indiscriminating homage to the Laws [as] is paid to the despot elsewhere'.[88] For those agreeing with this there was little in Hume or indeed the other major Scots enlighteners (aside from Millar) capable of bolstering pleas for reform. Thus, the existing edifice of case law abounded with anomalies and obsolete practices, providing a splendid handle for radical reformers like Bentham, Paine, Price, Priestley, and, later, Wollstonecraft to dismiss Hume's stance as a refusal to acknowledge the justice of rational objections and encouragement to popular prejudice.

Regarding religion, moral thought, social theory, and issues of gender and race, the Scots Enlightenment, like the English and American, tended predominantly towards that conservative 'moderation' Hume so ardently lauded. Mostly, the Scots opposed the radical tendencies driving the Western world toward fundamental human rights, democracy, and equality. However, one major figure, John Millar, professor of civil law at Glasgow from 1761 to 1801, did urge wide-ranging social reforms based on a broadly framed set of 'natural rights' carried over from the state of nature into the state of society, becoming in the process inalienable 'fundamental rights'. Millar conceived rank very differently from Hume, Smith, or Ferguson, subordinating social hierarchy to the idea of society as existing for the 'utility' and benefit of the majority with all of society's members being deemed equivalent in status and interests. His approach thus aligns with the basic argument for democracy in Spinoza and Rousseau.

Author of the *Origin of the Distinction of Ranks* (1771), a Presbyterian minister's son, and former pupil of Smith, Millar not only enthusiastically supported the American Revolution but later went so far as to justify Irish armed rebellion and their 'asserting their natural rights' against English imperial control while (again unlike the others) also bitterly criticizing the Americans' failure to free their slaves.[89] In December 1775, Hume warned his nephew against Millar's opinions at a time when he was carefully revising his own views. Millar might be right in principle that 'the republican form' of government is 'by far the best'. But in conceding this much Hume had in mind not democratic regimes but aristocratic republics. All the modern [aristocratic] republics in Europe—Venice, Lucca, Genoa, Berne, and Geneva—seemed to him 'so well governed, that one is at a loss to which we should give the preference'. 'But what', he asked, 'is this general subject of speculation to our purpose?' To him, republicanism was 'only fitted for a small state' and irrelevant to the British case. Any attempt to introduce the republican mode in Britain would 'produce only anarchy, which is the immediate forerunner of despotism'.[90] By the early 1770s Hume was disillusioned with key aspects of Britain's mixed monarchy, especially the House of Commons under Whig leadership, but yet could see no alternative.

---

[88] Bentham, *Fragment on Government*, 12.
[89] Millar, *Observations*, 223, 237, 241–2; Berry, *Social Theory*, 107.
[90] Mossner, *Life of David Hume*, 575; Stewart, *Opinion*, 282–3; Hume to David Hume the Younger, Edinburgh, 8 Dec. 1775, in Hume, *Letters*, ii. 306.

Increasingly gloomy in his last months, Hume supposed that one clear advantage of a republic 'over our mixt Monarchy, is' that it would 'considerably abridge our Liberty, which is growing to such an extreme, as to be incompatible with all government; such fools are they, who perpetually cry out Liberty: [and think to] augment it, by shaking off the monarchy.'[91] Where Millar aspired to curb monarchy and aristocratic sway, and saw history as a natural not a providential progression gradually emancipating the lower orders, Hume, like Gibbon, intensely disliked the democratic tendency he discerned on all sides.[92] The great limitation of his philosophy as a practical aid to civil society's advancement in the later eighteenth century was that his premisses afforded no theoretical ground not just for democratic republicanism but any broad reorganization of justice, politics, or morality, his philosophy assessing the validity of legal and moral systems on the basis of tradition and experience alone. The inconsistencies inherent in human life, and all moral and political systems, held Hume, are necessary to society.

Occasionally, his philosophy prompted Hume to defend usages scarcely any other Enlightenment theorist would support. The continuing use of the press-gang to supply men to the British navy was considered infamous in France and Holland and bitterly resented by some in England. But the practice remained deeply entrenched: 'this notorious infringement on the dearest rights of men, and... infernal blot on the very face of our immaculate constitution', as Wollstonecraft put it in 1790,[93] illustrated the tendency to prop up archaic, outmoded, and unjust structures with both popular support and the aid of Hume. With the pressing of seamen 'we continue a practice', admits Hume, 'seemingly the most absurd and unaccountable'; nevertheless, what matters, he reiterated, is not reason or principle but tradition, practice, and popular agreement. 'While this power is exercised to no other end than to man the navy, men willingly submit to it, from a sense of its use and necessity; and the sailors, who are alone affected by it, find nobody to support them, in claiming the rights and privileges, which the law grants, without distinction, to all English subjects.'[94] The press-gang violated the established liberties of Englishmen; yet here again principle must bow to what is in use, accepted, and popularly endorsed.

The *Histoire philosophique*, the most widely distributed of all radical texts in the late eighteenth century, a work well known in English translation, in Britain, Ireland, and America, pronounced English law the most irrational, entangled, contradictory, and chaotic corpus of law known to man.[95] Few in Britain would listen to such talk with anything other than furious indignation and loyalist scorn. But among the intellectually aware, here was a philosophical challenge, as Paine, Price, Priestley, Jebb, Bentham, Godwin, and Wollstonecraft well knew, impossible to ignore. Yet, Hume's thought created difficulty wherever fundamental legal reform was called for

---

[91] Hume, *Letters*, ii. 306.
[92] Ibid.; Sher, *Enlightenment*, 397; Garrett, 'Anthropology', 80–1, 86.
[93] Wollstonecraft, *Vindication of the Rights of Men*, 14; Mounier, *Considerations*, 47.
[94] Hume, *Essays*, 374–6.
[95] *Histoire philosophique* (1780), ix. 209.

since his philosophy inherently reinforces rather than questions the validity of actual usage. This stance, which led him to sanction the existing laws of marriage and approve of expectations of chastity being 'much stricter' regarding women than men,[96] ultimately could only aggravate the clash between moderate and radical positions with respect to all social, moral, political, educational, and legal issues. Despite their profound respect for each other as philosophers and each other's personalities, d'Holbach styling Hume 'a great man, whose friendship, I know to value as it deserves', the intellectual divide between Hume and his Parisian philosophical friends involved not just irresolvable disagreement but, at a certain level, lack of respect for the other's viewpoints.

Certainly, Hume was not always unwilling to oppose prevailing sentiment born of habit and existing usage in practical and moral affairs. There were exceptions, especially with regard to religious attitudes. His *Essay on Suicide* was to a slight degree 'daring', as it has been called despite remaining unpublished during his lifetime, so as not to cause offence, appearing only after his death under a codicil to his will releasing it for publication.[97] His text, suggesting suicide 'be no crime' and that 'both prudence and courage should engage us to rid ourselves at once of existence, when it becomes a burthen',[98] that is when pain and misery exceed any benefit life confers, provoked furious public as well as ecclesiastical indignation, beyond even his other writings questioning traditional religious views. Yet, here too, he conspicuously avoids explicit criticism of the existing law and social attitudes. Nor does he deplore the stigma, legal penalties, and disabilities with which sentiment and the law burdened the corpses, relatives, and financial estates of suicides. This lack of any wider reforming impulse amounts in fact to a profound theoretical difficulty anchored in the philosophical dilemmas implicit in Hume's attempt to explain how virtue can be in everyone's interest, and a public utility, when in his as in Smith's and Ferguson's thought, in essence virtue is conformity to a system of feelings, practice, and law centred on protecting property and prevailing notions.[99]

Modern historical surveys of the Enlightenment often seem to suggest that Europe's judicial systems could be and were swiftly and almost painlessly reformed in the eighteenth century, as if this was just a question of ending judicial torture, modifying the harsh treatment of debtors and unmarried mothers, and a few other widely acknowledged defects, and as if there was widespread support for the proposed changes in society and among the legal profession. But the evidence strongly suggests otherwise. Significant sections of the Enlightenment, and Hume in particular, systematically undermined every overall approach to rationalizing the law, thereby drastically limiting the scope for legal reform. In the legal and moral sphere, it was neither public opinion, nor economic pressure, nor governments, and

---

[96] Hume, *Enquiry Concerning the Principles*, 100, 216; Dabhoiwala, 'Lust', 152.
[97] Hume, *Essays*, 577–8 n.; Langford, *Polite and Commercial*, 479.
[98] Hume, *Essays*, 588.
[99] Stewart, *Opinion*, 122, 176–7.

especially not—Foucault could not have been more mistaken here[100]—magistrates or lawyers that acted as agents of change. The legal profession in fact contributed practically nothing to the reform programme anywhere in Europe. Rather it was philosophy itself—and especially *la philosophie moderne*—helped by the sheer accumulation of social difficulties and pressures (as distinct from public attitudes), that spread awareness of deficiencies and urged root and branch reform. This growing scope for action philosophy gained not owing to widespread support, for by and large this was scant, but rather because the legal systems of the age were so disfigured by outmoded usages and discredited intellectually that many government officials felt obliged to intervene if only on grounds of efficiency.

All sweeping legal reform programmes of the Enlightenment era stemmed from proposals drawn up by high-level officials, often acting in relative isolation and adopting solutions urged by 'philosophy' in response to long-standing social problems. This is plainly the case of Austria under Sonnenfels's and von Martini's guidance and also Prussia where there occurred, especially during the century's middle decades, perhaps the most concrete, sustained progress towards recasting the law, modernizing the penal code, and detaching ecclesiastical authority from ordinary justice. In Prussia, the key architects, apart from the king himself, were figures such as Samuel, Freiherr von Cocceji (1679–1755), one of Europe's leading voices urging abolition of judicial torture, son of a professor of politics and himself a professor and leading expert in natural law, and Philippe Joseph de Jariges (1706–70), the Huguenot *philosophe*, member of the Berlin Academy, and Spinoza and Bayle expert, who succeeded Cocceji as Prussian *Grosskanzler* [high chancellor], in 1754.[101] The men of legal practice and long experience simply had nothing to do with it.

There may have been few regions where both judiciary and general public were so obdurately opposed to 'enlightened' reform as in the Austrian Netherlands and Habsburg Hungary,[102] but the rejectionist reactions of the Belgian and Hungarian peoples in the late 1780s were really just extreme instances of the general response. Magistrates sometimes helped dismantle what 'philosophy' condemned as the most extreme aberrations. Thus, executions for witchcraft finally ended in those areas, notably Denmark, north-eastern Italy, and Bavaria, where they still occurred, because magistrates refused any longer to handle such cases. But here old-established practice was quashed because it had already been discarded in most countries and no one of any standing still defended the practice. Far more difficult and problematic was to reform entails, seigneurial rights, imprisonment for debt, civil divorce, the press-gang, laws of fornication, suppression of homosexuality, slavery, serfdom, and disabilities for religious minorities where powerful support for existing usages continued among the educated as well as the illiterate.

[100] Foucault, *Discipline and Punish*, 80–1.
[101] Hubatsch, *Frederick the Great*, 194–6, 212–14.
[102] Rousseaux, 'Doctrines criminelles', 230–5.

9

Scottish Enlightenment and Man's 'Progress'

1. SMITH, FERGUSON, AND CIVIL SOCIETY

A great philosopher, Hume was also part of a wider phenomenon. Scotland developed in the eighteenth century culturally and intellectually, as well as economically, with a vigour that nurtured a distinctive, local Enlightenment movement destined to exert a wide impact on both sides of the Atlantic and beyond. Geographically on Europe's fringe but central to the eighteenth-century transatlantic maritime system, the major cities—Edinburgh, Glasgow, and Aberdeen—of eighteenth-century Scotland and the universities had, by the century's second quarter, acquired an impressive network of reading societies, libraries, periodicals, lecture halls, museums, science cabinets, masonic lodges, and clubs. Together these formed a social and institutional basis for an enlightenment predominantly liberal Calvinist, Newtonian, and 'design' oriented in character which played a major role in the further development of the transatlantic Enlightenment overall.

The phenomenon was nothing if not part of a wider cultural adjustment and opening out of Scots society through a process of general reorientation towards the wider world. The Union (1707) with England proved a decisive catalyst politically and economically, in particular by enabling the Scots to share in every aspect of Britain's imperial expansion and trading system. This encouraged a rapid widening of horizons and, as Adam Smith and many others since emphasized, a vigorous expansion of commerce and industry.[1] Meanwhile, ending the Scots nobility's direct control of local politics and the processes of taxation and law lent at least a show of plausibility to what became a potent, abiding national myth, part truth, part fiction, that 'by the union with England, the middling and inferior ranks of people in Scotland gained a complete deliverance', as Smith expressed it, 'from the power of an aristocracy which had always before oppressed them'.[2] The betterment of society in this world was, in its main guidelines, more the precondition, frame, and accompanying context than goal of the Enlightenment in Scotland.

Scots thinkers generally repudiated Hume's universal scepticism but welcomed his delimiting of reason, applauding his adoption of commonly received sentiment as

---

[1] Smith, *Wealth of Nations*, i. 296–7.   [2] Ibid. ii. 547.

the foundation of moral sense. 'What pity is it', exclaimed George Campbell (1719–96), principal and professor of divinity of Marischal College, at Aberdeen, 'that this reputation should have been sullied by attempts to undermine the foundations both of natural religion, and of reveal'd.' Besides his critique of reason, Hume's Scots critics greatly esteemed what Campbell styled the 'many useful volumes he hath published of history, and on criticism, politics, and trade'.[3] Campbell was a local pastor but an unusually broad-minded one who respected Voltaire and deemed Montesquieu 'the most piercing and comprehensive genius, which hath appear'd in this age'.[4] Adhering to the so-called Common Sense school, and equally opposed to impiety, on the one hand, and superstition and 'enthusiasm', on the other, he fervently championed the goal of improvement through 'Christian Enlightenment' and, like other members of the Common Sense school, such as Oswald and Beattie, was widely read and admired in his time.

Campbell's *A Dissertation on Miracles* (Edinburgh, 1762) charges Hume with conflating and confusing under the umbrella 'experience', which he left insufficiently defined, both individual, personal experience and collective experience or testimony. Given its centrality in his philosophy, Hume's conception of 'experience' he held to be unwarrantably confined to the bounds of individual findings. To Campbell, it seemed essential to distinguish between individual and collective 'experience', and pay greater attention to the latter, since the 'merest clown or peasant derives incomparably more knowledge from testimony, and the communicated experience of others, than in the longest life he could have amassed out of the treasure of his own memory.'[5] Hume had failed to grasp the solidity of Christian tradition.

But Hume was just one basic challenge and source of inspiration. The Scots Enlightenment as a whole constituted a dramatic but complex intellectual response to two wider challenges—the strains of Scotland's own transition to its new status within the post-1688 British empire and, intellectually, to Montesquieu, Voltaire, Rousseau, and the *Encyclopédie*. The Scots enlighteners' deep preoccupation with these sources and also Bayle, Buffon, Turgot, Quesnay, and other French *économistes* and Mably, arose from an immediate practical need to grapple with the question of the origins of institutions, moral structures, and ranks as well as issues of status, law, and race. Kames's and Adam Smith's perspectives, like those also of Ferguson's *Essay on the History of Civil Society* (1767) and Robertson's 'View of the Progress of Society in Europe' (1769), bear witness to the considerable impact of contemporary French social, political, and biological thought on all the Scots enlighteners. While French epistemology, moral philosophy, and materialism exercised little persuasive power in Scotland, Montesquieu's *L'Esprit des loix*, which Kames, Campbell, and Ferguson praised hugely, figured prominently as did Buffon's natural history, Voltaire's *Essai*

---

[3] Campbell, *Dissertation on Miracles*, preface p. vi.   [4] Ibid. 139.
[5] Campbell, *Dissertation on Miracles*, 39; Stewart, 'Religion', 50.

sur les mœurs, parts of the *Encyclopédie*, and Rousseau's *Sur l'origine de l'inégalité*, all of which Ferguson cites in his great work.[6]

Hume may have disdained the ideas of the *encyclopédistes* but his early writings and notes were profoundly pervaded by Bayle. At every stage, French thought helped stimulate and shape major dimensions of the Scottish Enlightenment, especially its scepticism, enquiries into the historical process, economics, and social development. These same stimuli, in other circumstances, might also have fomented radical intellectual tendencies as well, as in Germany, Holland, and Italy and eventually also England, Russia, Scandinavia, and Ibero-America. But Scotland's religious, cultural, and political context militated powerfully against this so that Scots Enlightenment generally adhered to conservative positions, refusing grand schemes of amelioration in politics, law, economics, and constitutional legislation. All the Scots, despite their wariness of Hume (and the 'Common Sense' school's suspicion of Locke), fostered an austerely empirical approach, warmly embracing the concept of progress but predominantly preferring further social amelioration beyond what was gained in 1688–91 only via 'piecemeal, incremental reform' of the law and institutions through debate, the lecture hall, parliamentary procedure, and law courts.

Above all, Scots Enlightenment sought reconciliation (even in Hume) of philosophy and theology and nature with divine providence via a shrewd attuning of moral and legal thought to existing social norms. One of its towering figures, Ferguson, gave vivid expression to this distinctive mix of innovation and tradition in his 1773 lecture course on moral philosophy, a subject he taught at Edinburgh for twenty years. His starting point was that 'belief of the existence of God has been universal. The cavils of skeptics do not derogate from the universality of this belief, no more than like cavils derogate from the universality of the perception men have of the existence of matter; for this likewise has been questioned.'[7] Claiming that 'our knowledge in every subject is founded in some such [unquestionable] natural perception', he explains this by relying on the argument from design: 'in the nature of man, there is a perception of causes from the appearance of the effects, and of design from the concurrence of means to an end.' Refusing any possibility of seriously questioning the 'argument for design', his students were assured that 'no one can refrain from believing, that the eye was made to see, the ear to hear; that the wing was made for the air, the fin for the water, the foot for the ground; and so forth'.[8] In the Scots tradition, it seemed clear without further demonstration that 'nature presents final causes wherever our knowledge extends' and final causes are the 'language in which the existence of God is revealed to man'.[9] It was impossible to pitch tents any further from the world of the *nouveaux Spinosistes*.

---

[6] Ferguson, *Essay on the History*, 126, 130, 132, 135, 140, 143; Moore, 'Montesquieu', 179, 184, 190, 192; Rahe, *Montesquieu*, 173–4, 179.

[7] Ferguson, *Institutes of Moral Philosophy*, 114–15.

[8] Ibid. 116–17; Ferguson, *Principles*, i. 165; Stewart, 'Religion', 52.

[9] Ferguson, *Institutes of Moral Philosophy*, 118.

What the Scots thinkers strove for, in conscious response to Bayle, Montesquieu, Voltaire, and Rousseau, was to comprehend society's evolution from its original primitive and barbarous contexts, by stages, to what authors such as Hume, Kames, Ferguson, Robertson, Smith, and Millar all conceived as modern civil society—liberty, productivity, civility, toleration, 'refinement', and prosperity, exploring the social and political implications as well as searching for the economic and other causes. Here was an intellectual approach opening a great many new avenues. Smith, like Hume, Robertson, Kames, and Ferguson, was as deeply persuaded as the radical thinkers of the vital, indispensable role of an immense change in society, of 'a revolution of the greatest importance to the public happiness'. They too built their thought around the premiss that mankind generally positively requires this ' revolution' liberating all from the intellectual, social, moral, religious, political, and educational shackles of the past.

However, where radical thinkers viewed this general 'revolution' as something that had not yet happened but was needed, and involved prior planning by philosophers and legislators, for Smith, Ferguson, Kames, and Robertson, as for Hume, this 'revolution' had largely already happened and rather than being engineered by men with plans for ameliorating the human condition had been 'brought about by two different orders of people, who had not the least intention to serve the public'. If the political revolution had been wrought by the English aristocracy, and the intellectual revolution by Locke and Newton, the economic 'revolution' had a different origin, namely in a mix of the great proprietors who in their 'most childish vanity' had stimulated commerce with their demand for luxury goods and, on the other, the merchants and manufacturers who, though 'much less ridiculous, acted merely from a view to their own interest, and in pursuit of their own pedlar principle of turning a penny wherever a penny was to be got. Neither of them had either knowledge or foresight of that great revolution which the folly of the one and the industry of the other was gradually bringing about.'[10] Wonderfully, though, this revolution had nevertheless occurred transforming England, Scotland, North America, and, potentially, the entire world.

For the Scots (other than Millar) the 'revolution' that counted lay in the past and was devised not by humans but by an 'invisible hand'.[11] Most emphasized the political, legal, and institutional aspects of this 'revolution' rather than the economic; and it was precisely Adam Smith's role to focus attention on the latter. What his great 'revolution' really amounts to was the rise of commerce as a balancing element within a still noble-dominated, *ancien régime* society. 'Commerce and manufactures gradually introduced order and good government', he like Hume was convinced, 'and with them, the liberty and security of individuals, among the inhabitants of the country, who had before lived in a continual state of war with their neighbours, and

---

[10] Smith, *Wealth of Nations*, i. 418; Dupré, *Enlightenment*, 177–9.
[11] Taylor, *Secular Age*, 183, 201, 229; Winch, 'Scottish Political Economy', 449.

of servile dependency upon their superiors.'[12] Providence not philosophy engineered man's 'deliverance' from such deplorable conditions and dependence. Most commentators, though, French, English, or Scottish, seemed peculiarly unconscious of the economic dimension of the transformation. Indeed, 'Mr Hume', avers Smith, 'is the only writer who, so far as I know, has hitherto taken notice of it.'

The general liberating effect of the 'revolution' had proven vast. The institutions and moral structures carried over from the past had been successfully integrated into a wholly new context and now required further adjustment only at the edges. This was entirely characteristic of the Scots Enlightenment. Even Smith was no reformer of basic social structures, having no desire to change the political, legal, or cultural status of the capitalist elite or the labouring class in relation to the aristocratic ruling class. While rejecting Hume's scepticism (at least in public), Smith nevertheless shared his recognition of conventional norms and sentiment as the true basis of the moral and social order. Here, indeed, Hume can be deemed to speak for Scots Enlightenment virtually in its entirety. Where Ferguson justifies rank and aristocracy without qualification, Smith, in his *Theory of Moral Sentiments* (1759), admits the French thinkers were right to hold that the 'natural sympathy and affection for high rank' most men avow has no rational basis, but, like Hume, Kames, and Ferguson, judged veneration for rank nonetheless solidly grounded, being fixed in sentiment.

Smith, following Montesquieu, first formulated his later famous concept of 'human development' in 1762, in a series of lectures on jurisprudence, curiously paralleling Genovesi, as a process evolving through four stages, his 'four-stage theory'. Through each of these—first, the age of hunters; second, the age of shepherds; third, the age of settled agriculture; and fourth, the age of commerce—human society, following nature's law, grows more 'opulent' and closer to civility while developing a complex hierarchy of ranks.[13] Something roughly along these lines was a topos common to Ferguson, Millar, Robertson, and others of the Scots as well as Smith.[14] A society dominated by a warlike nobility—still a vivid, living memory in post-Culloden Scotland—under benign circumstances should and will yield to a society where individuals seek their betterment in a commercial, non-warlike milieu but still under the auspices of the aristocratic elite. This four-stage theory, as is often noted, underlies Smith's conception of the historical process. But while Smith is widely celebrated as a champion of commerce and the middle classes, it seriously distorts his views to separate his emphasis on the benefits of commerce as a civilizing agent from the wider social and political context in which he actually embeds his entrepreneurial middle class. For he is scarcely less a champion of the existing hierarchical order than Hume or Ferguson, something rarely given sufficient emphasis.

---

[12] Winch, 'Scottish Political Economy', 454; Smith, *Wealth of Nations*, i. 411.
[13] Rahe, *Montesquieu*, 172–3; Pittock, 'Historiography', 262; Berry, *Social Theory*, 123–6; Hont, *Jealousy*, 101–2.
[14] O'Neill, *Burke–Wollstonecraft Debate*, 36–46.

'Our obsequiousness to our superiors', he explains, 'more frequently arises from our admiration for the advantages of their situation, than from any private expectations of benefits from their good-will.'[15] Natural deference underpins the social order: 'upon this disposition of mankind to go along with all the passions of the rich and powerful, is founded the distinction of ranks, and the order of society.'[16] Smith's contention that men are naturally 'eager to assist' the rich and powerful 'in completing a system of happiness that approaches so near to perfection', as he puts it,[17] and 'desire to serve them for their own sake, without any other recompense but the vanity or the honour of obliging them', underpins much of his social theory. Nothing, we have seen, could have been further removed from the radical stance.

Smith began developing his (partially) free market doctrines, demonstrating the interaction between capital flows, in 1765–6.[18] Like Turgot and his predecessor, Vincent de Gournay, and later Condorcet, he sought to show how an environment encouraging individual effort and improving collective efficiency by removing obstacles physical, administrative, religious, and judicial to economic activity enhances society generally, an argument warmly seconded by Ferguson.[19] Smith did indeed display a highly critical attitude to many economic institutions and practices of his time and, like Hume, also worried about the 'expensive and unnecessary wars' typical of his age.[20] Betterment of society was central to his thinking. Certainly, he also hoped to see the labouring classes lifted from poverty and it has been claimed he was sometimes represented as a 'friend of the poor'.[21] 'No society can surely be flourishing and happy,' he grants, 'of which the far greater part of the members are poor and miserable. It is but equity, besides, that they who feed clothe and lodge the whole body of the people, should have such a share of the produce of their own labour as to be themselves tolerably well fed, clothed, and lodged.'[22]

However, his occasional remarks expressing indignation at how law and institutions are manipulated by the rich at the expense of the poor mostly occur in unpublished papers and remained marginal to his thought.[23] Mostly, he was disinclined to question the continuing dominance of the Scottish and English countryside by the nobility or the emphatically hierarchical character of British society. By 1776 when he published *The Wealth of Nations*, he does not appear to have moved far from the stance adopted in his *Theory of Moral Sentiments* where he maintains that success in business, like aristocratic birth, should be regarded as a sign of divine favour and that men should assume that 'wealth and external honours' are the proper

---

[15] Helvétius, *De l'homme*, ii. 821.   [16] Smith, *Theory*, 52.
[17] Ibid. 51–4.
[18] Poirier, *Turgot*, 150; Groenewegen, *Eighteenth-Century Economics*, 364, 373; Phillipson, *Adam Smith*, 188, 193–9, 204–5.
[19] Ferguson, *Principles*, ii. 426–30.
[20] Hont, *Jealousy*, 79, 111–13; Rothschild, *Economic Sentiments*, 68–9.
[21] Rothschild, *Economic Sentiments*, 61–2; Himmelfarb, *Roads*, 59–61.
[22] Smith, *Wealth of Nations*, i. 83; Winch, 'Scottish Political Economy', 452.
[23] Rothschild, *Economic Sentiments*, 69–70.

recompense of a life of virtue 'and the recompense which they can seldom fail of acquiring'.[24] This kind of 'sympathy', he still argued, has a definite social utility.

Smith both admired and criticized Quesnay and whilst in Paris in 1764–5, a decade after Quesnay and the older Mirabeau first introduced the new science of economics, studied *économistes* such as Dupont (who was not overly impressed with him initially) and Turgot.[25] As his magnum opus appeared only in 1776, two decades after the 'turn' to economics, it is understandable that Condorcet and other French contemporaries mistook his great work for a tardy reworking of theories crafted by earlier *économistes*, especially Turgot. But this was certainly to underestimate the comprehensiveness and breadth of Smith's vision. Smith stood close to the physio-crats and especially to Turgot. But his economic theory differed from theirs both in his aversion for their *esprit de système* and appetite for vigorous policies of political economy based on comprehensive grand plans for society, stemming from his ingrained preference for gradualism and epistemological modesty and from his different vision of the role of commerce and towns. For him, as for Hume, commerce not only drove modern prosperity but grounds modern liberty.[26]

In the age of Pitt and later, Smith's *Wealth of Nations* was always deemed the surpassing masterpiece of classical economics in the English-speaking world, and warmly endorsed by the governing elite. Still, his work was not only posterior to but, in some respects, also less internally consistent than Turgot's. Unlike Turgot, Smith was not actually a pure laissez-faire economist despite his attacks on Britain's protectionism and strictures against colonial trade and (in part) the Navigation Acts. Admittedly, he advocated free trade in agricultural products. But one of his main arguments for this was that foreign competition seemed unlikely ever to harm British producers, given the high cost of shipping grain and cattle.[27] Protection of national interests, especially manufacturing and shipping, against foreign competi-tion he largely endorsed. Even the monopoly of trade with British America under the Navigation Act, despite being styled despotic, misconceived, and damaging by him, had, he thought, been wise to begin with and was not something that could be discarded either quickly or altogether.[28] 'To open the colony trade all at once to all nations' risked provoking 'a great permanent loss to the greater part of those whose industry or capital is at present engaged in it'. And colonial trade Smith considered an immense benefit for Britain. 'The natural good effects of the colony trade... more than counterbalance to Great Britain the bad effects of the monopoly, so that, monopoly and all together, that trade, even as it is carried on at present, is not only advantageous, but greatly advantageous.'[29]

---

[24] Smith, *Theory*, 50–4, 61–4; Leddy, 'Adam Smith's Critique', 196; Robertson, *Case*, 394.
[25] Smith, *Essays*, 301–2, 304; Mossner, *Life of David Hume*, 486; Roche, 'Anglais à Paris', 502–3.
[26] Hume, *Essays*, 88-92; Phillipson, *Adam Smith*, 137, 141-4.
[27] Smith, *Wealth of Nations*, ii. 31–4.
[28] Ibid. ii. 35–8, 44, 78, 177–9; Winch, 'Scottish Political Economy', 460.
[29] Smith, *Wealth of Nations*, ii. 188–90.

Smith was only partly the laissez-faire economist he is so often claimed to be. Debating as a hypothetical question whether Britain should voluntarily emancipate all her colonies, something which, on his theoretical principles, might be supposed to benefit commerce, industry, and agriculture, he holds such a thing would never happen. This was not just due to national pride but also because such a scheme would be 'always contrary to the private interest' of the governing class 'who would thereby be deprived of the disposal of many places of trust and profit, of many opportunities of acquiring wealth and distinction, which the possession of the most turbulent, and, to the great body of the people, the most unprofitable province seldom fails to afford. The most visionary enthusiast would scarce be capable of proposing such a measure, with any serious hopes at least of its ever being adopted.'[30] Rather than advocating pure free-trade market forces, Smith was really a promoter of internal and international free trade within a liberal but still uncompromisingly imperial framework governed by an aristocratic ruling class whose own interest he was in many cases willing to see come first. His was thus a vision deferring in large part to the interests of a politically, militarily, and agriculturally dominant nobility. By no means does this feature separate his conception of economics fundamentally from Turgot's, or that of the *philosophes économistes*, but it does signify that he was much more of an apologist for empire, aristocracy, and the *ancien régime* social hierarchy generally than he has often been taken to be.

This applies to all aspects of *ancien régime* social hierarchy. While it may be true that Smith regarded slavery with moral distaste, it is far from evident that his 'abolitionist credentials were', as has been claimed, 'impeccable'.[31] On the contrary, emancipating enslaved blacks is simply not an issue that figures at all substantially in his perspective. Rather, his perfunctory remarks about the abolitionist movement in Pennsylvania are to a modern reader distinctly startling. 'The late resolution of the Quakers in Pennsylvania to set at liberty all their negro slaves, may satisfy us that their number cannot be very great. Had they made any considerable part of their property, such a resolution could never have been agreed to.'[32] In general, he offers no real moral objection to the continued use of slavery in the sugar and tobacco colonies where at the time their use seemed the only practicable option. His argument against slavery, such as it is, mainly pivots on the economic inefficiency of the institution.

All economic proposals emanating from capitalist merchants and manufacturers, averred Smith, need to be 'examined, not only with the most scrupulous, but with the most suspicious attention'. For the proposals of merchants and manufacturers (which the English, Scottish, and Irish aristocracy, in his view, needed to be far more on their guard against than they were) emanate 'from an order of men whose interest is never exactly the same as that of the public, who have generally an interest to deceive and even to oppress the public, and who accordingly have, upon many

---

[30] Smith, *Wealth of Nations*, ii. 198–9; Phillipson, *Adam Smith*, 229–31, 265–6.
[31] Broadie, *Scottish Enlightenment*, 96.   [32] Smith, *Wealth of Nations*, i. 391.

occasions, both deceived and oppressed it'.[33] This key feature, far too little stressed by modern commentators, was a major component of the markedly aristocratic orientation of Smith's thought and politics, an orientation he shared with all the Scots enlighteners apart from Millar.

Millar alone, deeply indebted, like Ferguson, to Montesquieu and Hume, and likewise espousing a theory of human progress encompassing four main stages, culminating in modern commercial society, refused to countenance the nobility's primacy, retention of traditional family values, persistence of slavery, and the 'servile condition of the fair sex, in barbarous countries'. The 'progress of a people in civilization and refinement' exerts a 'natural tendency to restrain' the 'primitive jurisdiction' of strong 'paternal authority' and the tyranny of heads of families. Here was a process, urged Millar, which needed pushing much further. Democratic-egalitarian republican in tendency, he admired neither modern aristocratic nor ancient Greek republics, all also to his mind steeped in slavery. A fierce critic of men's oppression of women and opponent of aristocratic primogeniture in Britain, to him it was abhorrent that serfdom should persist in 'Russia, Poland, in Hungary and several parts of Germany' and that slavery 'is at present admitted, without limitation, in the colonies which belong to any of the European nations, whether in Asia, Africa or America'.[34]

Impressed by the *Histoire philosophique*, Millar also later supported the ideals of the French Revolution. Of course, he also warmly endorsed the American Revolution but only up to a point, refusing to tolerate the Americans' failure to suppress slavery. Emancipation should have followed as the logical outgrowth of the revolution. 'It affords a curious spectacle', he regretted, 'to observe that the same people who talk in so high a strain of political liberty, and who consider the privilege of imposing their own taxes as one of the unalienable rights of mankind, should make no scruple of reducing a great proportion of the inhabitants into circumstances by which are not only deprived of property, but almost of every right whatsoever. Fortune perhaps never produced a situation more calculated to ridicule a grave, and even a liberal hypothesis, or to show how little the conduct of men is at bottom directed by any philosophical principle.'[35] Ultimately, the core difference between Millar and the main Scots Enlightenment tradition was that he found all this unacceptable and in consequence embraced 'philosophical principle' in a way the rest did not.

Very different were Smith's and Ferguson's perspectives. Like Robertson, Ferguson, and Kames, Smith celebrated the lapsing of 'feudalism' as a triumph for modernity. But neither he nor they were at all troubled by what replaced archaic baronial pretensions. For besides broadening horizons, the Union also opened a rich vein of military and colonial careers to the Scots nobility and substantially raised the value of

---

[33] Ibid. i. 264–5; Winch, 'Scottish Political Economy', 446–7; Phillipson, *Adam Smith*, 12–30.
[34] Millar, *Observations*, 224–5; Porter, *Enlightenment*, 253–4; Hampsher-Monk, 'On not Inventing', 139–40.
[35] Millar, *Observations*, 241–2; O'Neill, *Burke–Wollstonecraft Debate*, 35, 45–6.

landed estates and their revenues, both in the 'low country of Scotland' and remoter upland areas. 'The Union', notes Smith, 'opened the market of England to the Highland cattle. Their ordinary price is at present [i.e. in 1776] about three times greater than at the beginning of the century, and the rents of many Highland estates have been tripled and quadrupled in the same time.'[36] The Scots nobility had surrendered local power and tight control of social relations, certainly, but only in exchange for greater prosperity and a share in Britain's power and empire. His was a stance intended not just to promote the expansion of commercial and industrial capital by freeing trade from hindrances and restrictions, though it was partly that, but also to justify the continued dominance of the countryside, politics, and the empire of the nobility in England, Scotland, and Ireland alike and expressly with a view to keeping the commercial interest and the multitude politically within bounds.[37]

Up to a point, Smith opposed aristocratic primogeniture and entail laws designed to preserve noble estates. Entails, he acknowledges, 'are founded upon the most absurd of all suppositions, the supposition that every successive generation of men have not an equal right to the earth, and all that it possesses; but that the property of the present generation should be restrained and regulated according to the fancy of those who died perhaps five hundred years ago'. The 'exclusive privilege of the nobility to the great offices and honours of their country' in Europe, the pretext generally given for retaining entails, is, Smith grants, an 'unjust advantage over the rest of their fellow-citizens' that nobilities have 'usurped'. His critique of entails, however, offers scant scope for curbing aristocratic usurpation and had nothing in common with the wider critique offered by radical voices holding that primogeniture and entails constituted 'an everlasting rampart', as Wollstonecraft expressed it in 1790, 'in consequence of a barbarous feudal institution, that enables the elder son to overpower talents and depress virtue', fostering dependence and an 'unmanly servility' throughout society.[38]

Smith questions entails not on moral or social grounds, or because they reinforce dependence, but because their restrictive functions had become obsolete and they tied the hands of present and future generations excessively, hampering buying, selling, and long-term leasing.[39] Otherwise, he is content to leave the great proprietors and their dominance of society in place provided they buy and sell land more flexibly than before and assign longer leases of a sort, as he puts it, that render their tenants 'independent',[40] though even this, he acknowledges, was happening in Scotland only very patchily. Although he praises England for retaining fewer entails than other countries, actually well over than half the land of late eighteenth-century England remained in 'strict settlement', as aristocratic entails were called.[41]

---

[36] Millar, *Observations*, 158, 231–3, 246.   [37] Winch, 'Scottish Political Economy', 456.

[38] Wollstonecraft, *Vindication of the Rights of Men*, 23–4.

[39] Smith, *Wealth of Nations*, i. 395; Winch, 'Scottish Political Economy', 463.

[40] Smith, *Wealth of Nations*, i. 416–17.   [41] Habakkuk, *Marriage, Debt*, 47–8.

In Scotland, Smith urged only marginally more flexibility along English lines, without opposing the still overwhelming domination of the land by the nobility as such. In a passage acknowledging the nobility's unbroken grip over the land, he accepts that 'in Scotland more than one-fifth, perhaps more than one-third part of the whole lands of the country, are at present supposed to be under strict entail'.[42]

As a socio-economic theorist, Smith divides society into three distinct categories or classes, those that live by rent, those living by wages, and those living by investing their capital and by profit. 'These are the three great original and constituent orders of every civilized society, from whose revenue that of every other order is ultimately derived.' He envisages the interest of the landowning nobility, 'the first of those three great orders', as being 'strictly and inseparably connected with the general interest of society'. Insofar as landowners have any knowledge of their own interest, argues Smith, they can never mislead the public in political disputes over which economic policy to choose, 'with a view to promote the interest of their own particular order'. This was a crucial difference in his eyes between the landed nobility who are also the most refined and educated class, and the capitalist merchants and manufacturers. Rule by landowning aristocrats is not always ideal. The proper harmony of interest between the landowning class and the rest of society might falter, typically, Smith suggests, due to 'that indolence which is the natural effect of the ease and security of their situation' rendering much of the gentry 'not only ignorant, but incapable of that application of mind which is necessary in order to foresee and understand the consequences of any public regulation'.[43]

Smith by no means meant to suggest, though, that the merchants and manufacturers comprising his third order pursue the common interest better or more energetically than the nobility. On the contrary, merchants and manufacturers are not only mostly more ignorant than noblemen but, more crucially, always seek to widen markets and 'narrow the competition'; and while the first is usually in society's interest, 'to narrow the competition must always be against it, and can serve only to enable the dealers, by raising their profits above what they naturally would be, to levy, for their own benefit, an absurd tax upon the rest of their fellow-citizens'. Over 'the country gentleman', the merchant or manufacturer of Glasgow or anywhere else has no superior knowledge of the public interest. Rather it is through possessing superior knowledge of their own interest that merchants have 'frequently imposed upon [the landed gentleman's] generosity, and persuaded him to give up both his own interest and that of the public, from a very simple but honest conviction, that their interest, and not his, was the interest of the public'. In Britain, modern commercial society had now reached a point where the populace lived in 'liberty and independency'. Smith advocated no further significant changes in the structure of society whether in Scotland, England, the rest of Europe, or the colonial world. Neither did he seek to change economic organization other than by eliminating obstructions to free

[42] Smith, *Wealth of Nations*, i. 388–90; Porter, *Enlightenment*, 391–3; Berry, *Social Theory*, 102, 105.
[43] Smith, *Wealth of Nations*, i. 262–3; Phillipson, 'Adam Smith', 191–2, 197.

commerce. Again there has been a tendency among scholars greatly to overstate his reforming instincts (as some have also Hume's). Far from needing to plan vast changes, Smith's legislator has little further to do but steer a neutral course between society's three basic 'classes'—landed proprietors, capitalist, and wage-earners—while striving for internal free trade within the nation's borders, though even that, he thought, should be only gradually worked towards.[44]

In commercial society, the lower orders, averred Smith, are freer and more equal with those higher up the social scale, as well as more prosperous, than was the case when the feudal baronage dominated everything. This greater freedom, independence, and prosperity then in turn renders attainable a higher level of moral achievement and happiness than was feasible earlier or possible elsewhere. It is because the common people of England were 'altogether free and independent' that they were 'the honestest of their rank anywhere to be met with'.[45] Yet, what Smith called 'altogether free and independent' was actually a commercially oriented society based on empire and imperial tariffs, evolving within a context of overwhelming noble dominance of politics, the armed forces, the law, social debate, and the land and, in some integral fashion, since the sugar and tobacco colonies remained indispensable to the whole, entailing slavery. His 'causes or circumstances which naturally introduce subordination, or which naturally, and antecedent to any civil situation, give some men some superiority over the greater part of their brethren' were integral to his social and moral as much as his economic thought. 'Birth and fortune are evidently the two circumstances which principally set one man above another. They are the two great sources of personal distinction, and therefore the principal causes which naturally establish authority and subordination among men.' If Smith sometimes showed sympathy for the plight of the poor, he is far more concerned to agree that the nobility's 'natural' domination of society inevitably entails noble domination of the processes of law, politics, and military and property relations. He was perfectly aware that 'civil government, so far as it is instituted for the security of property, is in reality instituted for the defense of the rich against the poor, or of those who have some property against those who have none at all'.[46] But this he regarded as simply a general law of society the consequences of which must be accepted.

In adopting such a stance, Smith hardly differed from Hume, Kames, Ferguson, or the mainstream Enlightenment more generally. Ferguson assumed a more or less natural division in all societies other than the most primitive between 'the superior orders of the people', men of rank, and the 'promiscuous multitude', a division accepted and buttressed by 'Common Sense'. The great defect of Smith's and Ferguson's standpoints in an age of inexorably growing pressure for reform was that it provided no grounds for challenging the general principles of empire, aristocracy, slavery, and ecclesiastical power. Rather, it tended to reinforce assumptions that rank

---

[44] Smith, *Wealth of Nations*, i. 450, 456. [45] Quoted in Phillipson, 'Adam Smith', 188.
[46] Smith, *Wealth of Nations*, ii. 295–8; Buchan, *Adam Smith*, 3.

and inequality are innately part of the divine plan and 'absolute equality', as Smith put it, 'altogether visionary and unknown in nature'.[47] Slavery may have been mildly unpalatable to the Scottish thinkers, but in general they did much to reinforce existing hierarchies with their theories about stages of development, cultural property, and race.

As an analyst of rank, social classes, and of class relations and interaction, Ferguson was indeed highly original. His work long continued to arouse interest among philosophers, including Kant, Hegel, and Marx. As a philosophy of civil society, his *Essay* was more balanced, thoughtful, and subtle than the productions of Kames and Robertson. But he has relatively little to say about the clashes and tensions social, moral, and political created by the class divisions he was the first to highlight in a broad comparative context. His stress, rather, was always on the intricacy and delicacy of the relationship of law and institutions to social groups and conditions. His principal criticism of the radical *philosophes* as social theorists, significantly, was that they were apt greatly to exaggerate the evils of present and past society. He urged great caution in trying to build for the future on a 'supposed derangement in the only scenes with which we are acquainted'.[48] In fact, he viewed nobility as a desirable component of society to an even greater degree than Smith or Hume, considering it an essential safeguard against the 'corruption' and the supine quality he associated with the merchant class and commercial society itself. Ferguson, whose work is tinged with a marked republican concern with preserving public spiritedness and participation in public affairs, conceived the nobility as an antidote to commercial society's shortcomings. He does not deny that nobilities began as a specialized warrior class or that precisely this potentially threatens the rest of society with subordination to its power and interests:

In the progress of arts and of policy, the members of every state are divided into classes; and in the commencement of this distribution, there is no distinction more serious than that of the warrior and the pacific inhabitant; no more is required to place men in the relation of master and slave. Even when the rigours of an established slavery abate, as they have done in modern Europe, in consequence of a protection, and a property, allowed to the mechanic and labourer, this distinction serves still to separate the noble from the base, and to point out that class of men who are destined to reign and domineer in their country.[49]

A degree of subordination and exploitation were inevitable. But any regrets on that score were outweighed in Ferguson's mind by the need to cultivate political awareness, the moral qualities, and 'cultivation of arts on which [society's and the state's] real felicity and strength depend'. Society cannot be well led and balanced without 'cultivating in the higher ranks those talents for the council and the field, which cannot, without great disadvantage, be separated; and in the body of a people, that zeal for their country, and that military character, which enable them to take a share', under the leadership of the nobility, 'in defending its rights'.[50] It may be true that

[47] Smith, *Wealth of Nations*, i. 262.   [48] Ferguson, *Principles*, i. 317.   [49] Ibid. i. 230.
[50] Ibid. i. 348; Berry, *Social Theory*, 135–6; Geuna, 'Republicanism', 185–7.

under monarchy and mixed government, 'superior fortune is, indeed, one mark by which the different orders of men are distinguished; but there are some other ingredients, without which wealth is not admitted as a foundation of precedency, and in favour of which it is often despised and lavished away. Such are birth and titles, the reputation of courage, courtly manners, and a certain elevation of mind.'[51] It is precisely these aristocratic virtues, 'elevation of mind' especially, that cannot, without peril of 'corruption' and immanent decay, be dispensed with in large states, monarchies, empires, and mixed monarchies like Britain.

'Ambition, the love of personal eminence, and the desire of fame, although they sometimes lead to the commission of crimes, yet always engage men in pursuits that require to be supported by some of the greatest of the human soul; and if eminence is the principal object of pursuit, there is, at least, a probability, that those qualities may be studied on which a real elevation of the mind is raised.' When military challenges to the state cease, arises the greatest danger of internal decay because commercial pursuits take precedence 'and contempt of glory is recommended as an article of wisdom'. Mercantile habits breed what Ferguson called 'a general indifference to national objects', the greatest risk to which a predominantly commercial state is exposed. Trade, he concurred with Smith, almost inevitably undermines the noble ethic. But for him commercial society nurtures to a far greater extent than for Smith disadvantages as well as gains, tending to undermine nobility and the martial spirit, 'those principles from which communities derive their hopes of preservation, and their strength'.[52]

The nobility's responsibilities, in Ferguson's, even more than Smith's, schema, then, were weighty ones, vital to society's well-being. 'But the higher orders of men, if they relinquish the state, if they cease to possess that courage and elevation of mind, and to exercise those talents which are employed in its defense, and its government, are, in reality, by the seeming advantages of their station, become the refuse of that society of which they were once the ornament; and from being the most respectable, and the most happy, of its members, are become the most wretched and corrupt.'[53] Hence, the indispensability of the noble order in any modern mixed monarchical, commercial, and imperial society such as Britain is tenaciously defended by Ferguson. 'Nature seems to have ordered that, in proportion as men shall depart from their original poverty, they shall depart also from that original state of equality, in which it was necessary for every individual to labour for himself.'[54] 'Everyone has a right', he argued, 'to the condition in which, by the ordinary course of human nature, he is fairly placed'; hence, it followed 'that liberty, in every particular instance, must consist in securing the fairly acquired conditions of men, however unequal'.[55]

[51] Ferguson, *Essay on the History*, 385–6.
[52] Ibid. 396; Porter, *Enlightenment*, 394–5; Geuna, 'Republicanism', 186.
[53] Ferguson, *Essay on the History*, 399.
[54] Ferguson, *Principles*, ii. 422–3; Berry, *Social Theory*.
[55] Ferguson, *Principles*, ii. 464; Grenby, *Anti-Jacobin Novel*, 129–30.

Here, liberty and nature together underpin basic inequality. On appearing, Ferguson's *Essay* was a work warmly welcomed, unsurprisingly, among persons of 'reputation and rank'. The archbishop of York thought 'that in many things it surpasses Montesquieu' while others lauded its elegance of style and 'great purity of language'.[56] Even Hume, unimpressed though he was (presumably partly at least due to Ferguson's obtrusive physico-theology), was struck by the 'unexpected' huge success Ferguson enjoyed. Confident as he was that should Ferguson learn of his disliking the *Essay* this would be as unlikely to cost him his regard as Helvétius's criticism of the *L'Esprit des loix* cost him 'anything of Montesquieu's friendship', given Ferguson's character, he still preferred not to put the matter 'to a trial', swearing his correspondent, Hugh Blair, to 'secrecy towards every person, except Robertson' concerning his low opinion of the work.[57]

Ferguson stood out above all for his willingness to defend nobility, proclaim divine providence, and underline the political implications of an enlightened naturalist-evolutionist conception of society prizing sentiment as the basis of morality and social awareness. Many commentators have stressed the classical republican aspect of Ferguson's worries about growing division of labour in modern society and plea for a more active and dynamic politics.[58] He accepted that the nobility's origins, viewed as part of the historical process, must be judged haphazard since men 'arrive at unequal conditions by chance', but this made no difference to the nobility's elevated character and indispensability.[59] Having, like Robertson, Blair, and most Scots, publicly opposed the American Revolution, denouncing Price's (wholly unLockean) thesis that government is for and by the people, from a very early stage, Ferguson likewise condemned the French Revolution. Early reports merely confirmed his belief that the 'violence of popular assemblies' must be restrained no less than monarchical tyranny and the 'unrestrained prevalence of aristocratic authority'. There is no 'species of tyranny', he insisted, under which 'individuals are less safe than under that of a majority or prevailing faction of a corrupted people'.[60]

Choosing between different forms of government, any 'fortunate people' will adopt a mixture of monarchy, aristocracy, or democracy rather than any simple form. Between British mixed monarchy and the nascent democracy lately established by the French, he wrote, before the Terror, in 1792, it is not difficult to decide which to prefer: 'under one species of establishment, we observe the persons and possessions of men to be secure, and their genius to prosper', while under the other, 'prevalent disorder, insult and wrong, with a continual degradation or suppression of all the talents of men, we cannot be at a loss on which to bestow the preference'.[61]

---

[56] Hume, *Letters*, ii. 125, 136.   [57] Hume to Hugh Blair, 1 Apr. 1767, ibid. ii. 133.
[58] Berry, *Social Theory*, 135; Hont, *Jealousy*, 296–7.   [59] Berry, *Social Theory*, 101.
[60] Ibid. 107–8; Ferguson, *Principles*, ii. 464–5.
[61] Ferguson, *Principles*, ii. 499; Amoh, 'Ferguson's Views', 83–4.

2. KAMES, RACE, AND PROVIDENCE

Among the Scots, indeed among all enlighteners, Henry Home, Lord Kames (1696–1782), was one of the first to analyse and explore the stages of history, to view human development as a complex process and attempt through studying history and society to widen our understanding of what humanity is. An assiduous and original intellect in many ways, he was a classic exemplar of Enlightenment in his central preoccupation with—and very broad conception of—human improvement. He was at the forefront in Scotland as a key interlocutor and intermediary being closely involved in every debate and development and, after a time, almost every notable academic appointment (despite never having attended university himself), and was a pioneer of what came to be known as the 'common sense' approach to moral philosophy. In 1785, three years after his death, the greatest of the 'Common Sense' philosophers, Thomas Reid (1710–96), gratefully referred to their lively philosophical exchanges, warmly praising 'his zeal to encourage and promote everything that tended to the improvement of his country, in laws, literature, commerce, manufactures, and agriculture'.[62]

Kames also had closer relations with Franklin than the other Scots from even before 1759 when the latter spent two weeks in his company on his Berwickshire estate, an intimate friendship that continued down to Kames's death.[63] While opposing American Independence, calling the rebels 'ungrateful', on the eve of the Revolution he corresponded with Franklin in a most conciliatory manner and certainly objected to the exploitative fiscal and commercial policies Britain pursued in North America even more strongly than Hume, a distant relative and ally of his, or Smith.[64] Furthermore, he was one of the most studied and best-known of European thinkers in the American Enlightenment, more so than almost any of the other Scots apart from Hume, being the strongest influence, for example, on Jefferson's 'Common Sense' notion of morality and aesthetics and a key source of his concept of equality.[65] But Kames is especially important for his remarkable grasp of the interconnectedness of the different dimensions of human activity, being passionately interested in everything from poetry to implements and having much to say about betterment in agriculture, trade, and the arts (indeed our aesthetic sense generally) as well as about technological innovations, the history of law, a speciality of his, and moral development.

Scotland now shared in Britain's constitution and empire and this meant that her social theorists needed to consider her society as an imperial as well as domestic entity and the social functions of empire, trade, ethnic subordination, slavery, and race. Together with Hume, and to an extent paralleling Vico, Genovesi, and Montesquieu, Kames developed his abiding and profound insight that human

---

[62] Kames, *Elements*, i. 1–3; Sher, *Enlightenment*, 143; Lehmann, *Henry Home*, 76–7.
[63] Lehmann, *Henry Home*, 76–7.
[64] Ibid. 123–4.   [65] May, *Enlightenment*, 293, 343, 346, 356.

history, and hence human betterment, evolve simultaneously in many spheres of activity, through institutional, legal, and socio-economic stages, being well advanced in this study by the 1750s. Law 'becomes then a rational study', he explained in his *Historical Law-Tracts* (1758), 'when it is traced from its first rudiments among savages through successive changes to its highest improvement in a civilized society'.[66] A keen advocate, together with Smith and Robertson, of the idea that the Scottish feudal baronage's withering away was the crucial step towards Scotland's recent flowering and modernity, at the heart of his concern was an effort to uncover the mechanics of the processes that lead to modern civil society with its 'civilized' sociability, liberties, and amenities.

So fervent indeed was Kames about Scotland's release from the recent horrors of feudalism, baronial arrogance, and noble domination that this formed a corner-stone of his entire philosophy of man. It made him highly conscious of the hierarchical and oppressive character of most societies and the complexity of social and political emancipation. He was a much more vigorous and active enemy of primogeniture, and that 'unnatural and ruinous' policy of entails of land as a device for noble dominance of society, than Hume or Smith.[67] Release from bondage and a slow gradual emancipation of humanity as a whole from crude forms of subordination was certainly one of the central threads of his philosophy of man and yet it was a vision curiously focused on the past and willing to accept that in Britain the process was virtually complete. Kames had no wide-ranging proposals for changes in the future and few or no suggestions for further political reform not even with respect to slavery or serfdom areas where his general theory led him to adopt a definite moral stand against in passing but not to develop an extended critique.

Kames continued with this path-breaking endeavour over a longer span than anyone else: for decades. In his *Sketches of the History of Man*, the culmination of thirty years of collecting 'materials for a natural history of man', anonymously published in Edinburgh in 1774, he tried to uncover the underlying logic of the 'progress toward maturity' as he calls it, among different peoples. Like Montesquieu and Genovesi, he examined social, institutional, and economic development against the backdrop of morality, law, manners, education, learning, and the arts. Incorporating the earlier French idea of the *histoire de l'esprit humain*, Kames contributed prominently to building a new kind of theoretical history that has been aptly termed 'evolutionistic naturalism', albeit a naturalism vigorously adapted to a broadly Christian-deist providential metaphysical framework.[68] The *Sketches* sold respectably and, in May 1775, calls were issued in the Philadelphia press summoning 'those gentlemen who choose to promote science in America' to support an American edition by subscription.[69] With the Revolution erupting at that point, the timing was unfortunate, though, and the subscriptions stretched only to a much abridged version that appeared in 1776.

[66] Quoted ibid. 183.   [67] Lehmann, *Henry Home*, 126–7.   [68] Ibid. 178–80.
[69] Sher, *Enlightenment*, 528–30.

What is human betterment? What is society? And what is the meaning and the direction of the progress Kames discerned in human history? At every point his naturalism was blended with elements of natural theology and especially a concern with providence and final ends; and if providence is everywhere manifest so is its general direction and significance. A supporter of Hume's quest to restrict reason's scope, he too was extremely critical of abstract reasoning, ruling out whatever oversteps direct sense experience. Not much of natural theology, he insisted, can be established by philosophy construed as abstract reasoning.[70] Nevertheless, reason is man's greatest possession and its proper use has as complex a social and cultural history as any aspect of culture. 'Rude ages exhibit the triumph of authority over reason.' 'In later times, happily, reason hath attained the ascendant: men now assert their native privilege of thinking for themselves; and disdain to be ranked in any sect, whatever be the science.'[71] The answers come not from authority or speculative reason but from a long, careful, intricate, and essentially empirical study, one of the most original aspects of which in his case was a detailed discussion of the history and varieties of matrimony and the social role of sexuality among humans. He was quite clear that the position of women had been especially bad among 'savages' among whom matrimony, 'having no object but propagation and slavery, is a very humbling state for the female sex', but that women's position had vastly improved with social progress.[72]

Basic to Kames's research was the question of racial differentiation and whether humanity forms a single entity: 'whether there be different races of men, or whether all men be of one race, without any difference but what proceeds from climate or other accident, is a profound question of natural history, which remains still un-determined after all that has been said upon it.'[73] Attacking Buffon for his 'very artificial rule for ascertaining the different species of animals', namely that any two animals that mate, producing issue that can also procreate, 'are of the same species', Kames firmly rejected his 'holding all men to be of one race or species', simply because a man and woman 'however different in size, shape, in complexion, can procreate together without end'. Buffon, holds Kames, cannot deny 'there are different races of men' and 'that, certain tribes differ apparently from each other, not less than the lama and pacos from the camel or from the sheep, not less than the true tiger from the American animals of that name'.[74] Despite the Bible's declaring a single origin of humanity in Adam and Eve, or monogenism, Kames espoused polygenism, convinced different races have separate origins and lineages. This he adapted to Christian doctrine to a degree by maintaining a fundamental distinction between bodily characteristics and the soul: the soul is one thing, the body quite another. The unity of all men of whatever species is certain spiritually but is chiefly a matter of spiritual redemption, though there is certainly also such a thing as equality before

[70] Stewart, 'Arguments', 721.   [71] Kames, *Elements*, i. 17.
[72] Berry, *Social Theory*, 109–11; Lehmann, *Henry Home*, 247.
[73] Kames, *Six Sketches*, 1.   [74] Ibid. 7–8; Carhart, *Science*, 231–2.

the law.[75] Regarding capabilities, social organization, culture, and politics, however, men and women are far from being equal so that when discussing history, law, and social questions one should not assume the oneness of humanity in the style of the *encyclopédistes*.[76]

Countering Buffon's, Diderot's, and d'Holbach's view 'that all men are of one race or species', Kames held 'that there are different races of men fitted by nature for different climates'. This he combined with a theory of racial degeneracy operative wherever races are transplanted to what he considered the wrong climatic and geographical milieu, one of his most notable doctrines. Thus Spaniards settled on the Caribbean littoral of South America, held Kames, 'lose their vigour and colour in a few months' and move only languidly, an explanation for the notorious indolence of the Spanish Americans very different from that of Diderot who believed racial characteristics had nothing to do with the languid tendencies of the Creoles. Equally, Europeans born in Batavia, contended Kames, 'soon degenerate. Scarce one of them has talents sufficient to bear a part in the administration. There is not an office of trust or figure but what is filled with native Europeans. Some Portuguese, who have been for ages settled on the sea-coast of Congo, retain scarce the appearance of men.'[77] The degeneracy of whites in the Indies Kames took to be a proof of the God-given, providential character of racial difference (as of all fundamental character-istics): God had created different races of men to accommodate the variety of the world's climates and conditions.[78] This left many outside Europe innately inferior physically and intellectually and provided a splendid justification for European colonial empires in the tropics, though he does not say so explicitly. What his schema does not justify, though, are systems of imperial subordination in temperate climes such as that of North America.

Kames's polygenetic racial theory has been claimed to be 'particularly benign',[79] and it was clearly a way of including all men and women in the history of society and improvement while accounting for the vast disparities in the levels achieved, though it was also an intellectual device for ensuring white men born in the tropics, as well as non-Europeans, should, as a matter of course, stay subordinate to Europeans sent out from northern climes.[80] Empirical observation persuaded Kames that climate can-not, however, be the decisive factor in generating basic racial differences as such. For these often coexist in the same or similar climes. It is a mistake to assert climate has a 'commanding influence' on skin colour and ethnic typology. Man, holds Buffon, 'white in Europe, black in Africa, yellow in Asia, and red in America, is still the same animal, tinged only with the colour of climate'.[81] He is 'totally silent', complains Kames, 'upon a fact that singly overturns his whole system of colour, viz. that all Americans [i.e. Amerindians] without exception are of a copper-colour, though in

---

[75] Lehmann, *Henry Home*, 253; Garrett, 'Human Nature', 199.
[76] Kames, *Six Sketches*, 6; Berry, *Social Theory*, 81.
[77] Kames, *Six Sketches*, 12–13.   [78] Garrett, 'Human Nature', 199–200.
[79] Ibid. 200.   [80] Kames, *Six Sketches*, 13.   [81] Ibid. 15; Lehmann, *Henry Home*, 253–4.

that vast continent there is every variety of climate'.[82] Equally, 'there have been four complete generations of negroes in Pennsylvania, without any visible change of colour: they continue jet black as originally'.[83]

Blacks, held Kames, are undeniably 'a different race from the whites'. They are innately different but one should not infer from this (as he admitted he had formerly) innate 'inferiority in their understanding'.[84] His researches showed that the actual 'inferiority of their understanding' is really 'occasioned by their condition', meaning their social, economic, and technological as well as climatic circumstances. Men ripen in judgement through challenges and fulfilling their potential. But in Africa blacks had little reason to exercise judgement or prudence, subsisting 'upon fruits and roots which grow without culture: they need little cloathing; and they erect houses without trouble or art.' Among the peoples 'on the east coast of Africa, who are directed purely by nature, the officers of state are, with respect to rank, distinguished by the length of the batoon each carries in his hand'.[85] Equally, in the New World, the blacks 'are miserable slaves, having no encouragement either to think or to act. Who can say how far they might improve in a state of freedom, were they obliged, like Europeans, to procure bread by the sweat of their brows?' Some African kingdoms, especially Whidah, he notes, 'have made great improvements in government, in police and in manners'.[86]

Everywhere intellectual and moral as well as technical and economic progress is occurring but at different speeds and very different levels. 'There are different races of men', he insisted, knowing his thesis faced 'strenuous opposition' from those seeing humanity as one entity and 'who hold every distinguishing mark, internal as well as external, to be the [subsequent] effect of soil and climate'.[87] Many follow Buffon and 'Montesquieu, who is a great champion for the climate' and a philosopher of whom Kames was highly critical, but were mistaken.[88] For race was one of the key components, he was convinced, in explaining the vastly different levels of human existence attained in the world together with climate, specific challenges, and actual conditions, and the stage of 'civil society' reached. Races as differently constituted creations help explain the simultaneous universality and yet disparate character of human progress.

'Moral sense is born with us', he argued, as also is 'taste'. Both are key fields of sensibility but 'require much cultivation': 'among savages', he asserts, revealing both his anti-Rousseauism and distinctly negative view of primitive men, 'the moral sense is faint and obscure; and taste still more so. Thus, taste goes hand in hand with the moral sense in their progress toward maturity, and ripen fully only under the right conditions. Want, a barren soil, cramps the growth of both; sensuality, a soil too fat,

---

[82] Kames, *Six Sketches*, 15.
[83] Ibid. 16; O'Neill, *Burke–Wollstonecraft Debate*, 117–18.
[84] Kames, *Six Sketches*, 37–8; Garrett, 'Human Nature', 200.
[85] Kames, *Elements*, i. 160.   [86] Kames, *Six Sketches*, 38.
[87] Ibid. 31.   [88] Ibid. 36–7; Berry, *Social Theory*, 82–3.

corrupts both; the middle state, equally distant from dispiriting poverty and luxurious sensuality, is the soil in which both of them flourish.'[89] Hence external conditions of different kinds counted most but race and gender were crucial factors too.

Kames's racial polygenism, theory of degeneracy, and stress on moral sense led him to spurn theories of the state of nature, and man's early development, like those of Rousseau, Ferguson, Robertson, and Millar, envisaging all societies as having a common character in the initial stages.[90] However, while different races have different tendencies and capabilities, and less developed (or degenerated) peoples are best supervised by civilized ones, nevertheless within Kames's schema the technical and economic and especially the legal, moral, and aesthetic progress of man in general are universal because moral and aesthetic criteria of judgement, and the development of common notions based on these, are the same for all men, being rooted in the soul, that is in Common Sense, the primal knowledge vested in the soul.[91] Just as he did not doubt that social progress brings a progressive easing in the originally brutal subordination of women to men, he had no doubts about the 'progress of the female sex' also intellectually, morally, and aesthetically, albeit only in due proportion, in a subordinate role to men. 'The man', he points out, 'as a protector, is directed by nature to govern: the woman, conscious of inferiority, is disposed to obedience. The intellectual powers correspond to the destination of nature: men have penetration and solid judgment to fit them for governing; women have sufficient understanding to make a decent figure under good government; a greater proportion would excite dangerous rivalship.'[92] Like most ethnic groupings, women, in Kames's schema, are innately inferior to European men despite their sharing in moral and intellectual progress.

For Kames, the Glorious Revolution and the links with England and North America were fundamental. A distinctive feature of the Scots Enlightenment's approach to history and civil society was a reconfiguring of Scottish patriotism and rejection of its traditional format. Like Hume and William Robertson (1721–93), Kames proved an eager literary, cultural, legal, and constitutional Anglophile and they all consciously constructed their widely read histories 'for English readers'; and he too, like Smith, assumed readers shared his conviction that Britain's imperial dominance was a positive force in the world as well as in Scotland.[93] Hume's and Robertson's historiographical model was one, it has been observed, in which the barbarities of Scottish and Irish history are deemed normative but those of the English past exceptional. Basic to this perspective was a willingness actively to promote an imperial 'moderate Enlightenment' system of values, based on toleration, freedom of expression, and civil liberty in which 'England represents

---

[89] Kames, *Six Sketches*, 121; Carhart, *Science*, 159; Gibbons, *Edmund Burke*, 214.
[90] Garrett, 'Human Nature', 200.
[91] Makreel, 'Aesthetics', 548–9.
[92] Kames, *Six Sketches*, 194–5; Lehmann, *Henry Home*, 230; O'Neill, *Burke–Wollstonecraft Debate*, 89–90.
[93] Mossner, *Life of David Hume*, 278, 352; Broadie, *Scottish Enlightenment*, 32, 50.

modernity' and her political traditions and institutions are landmarks of progress in the world's history. Eager supporters of the Act of Union, they envisaged the link with England as part of the great emancipating event, freeing Scotland from the darkness and burdens of an unhappy past dominated by baronage, confessional strife, and wretched economic backwardness. Hume agreed despite his *anglicisme* being curiously tinged with barely suppressed Anglophobia.[94] Kames, like Robertson, departs from a pure historical naturalism, views Hume could endorse, only when explicitly characterizing history as a triumph of justice and the good directed by general providence, though he never suggests, as Robertson did in the case of the defeat of Spanish Armada of 1588, that there are also instances of particular divine intervention.[95]

On such issues as the being of God, divine creation of the world, free will, immortality of the soul, providential superintendence, and the absurdity of 'fatalism', few of the Scots were willing to prevaricate. Ferguson adhered to a typical Common Sense position, much indebted to Reid,[96] championing the principle of *consensus gentium* (so demeaned by Bayle) as a support for the notions of a benevolent deity and the workings of providence. In Ferguson, more even than most other Scots thinkers, all stages and types of human development are parts of a divinely created and programmed nature. His researches taught him, as they taught Kames, to study man anthropologically and historically, in concrete societies using properly documented facts, rather than as an abstract individual, and to see the true nature of man emerging more from the history of groups, and from types rather than from studying individuals.[97] His schema for what he called 'the General History of the Human Species', and the workings of divine providence which he too believed he discerned in it, tended though in his case, in contrast to Kames, to render the 'varieties of the human race', and inequality, aspects of a finally harmonious, intended whole.

Divine design, for Ferguson, 'this fabric of nature, so fitly organized in the frame of every individual is organized also in the assemblage of many individuals into one system, whether of the earth which they inhabit, or of the sun and planets of which this earth itself is but a part: so that the same character of design, which the most ignorant may read in the first aspect of things that most nearly concerns them, the learned may read also throughout the whole system or volume of nature.'[98] It was natural for Ferguson to extend this principle to the successive stages of civil society itself, eliminating the idea of essentially defective, wrongly constituted, and unhappy societies of the sort that loomed so large in the thought of the radical *philosphes*. 'Throughout the whole of every kingdom', there was a certain 'analogy to the kingdom of mineral, vegetable and animal with its continual diversity of kind, species, and individual', creating 'a chain of connection and mutual subserviency,

---

[94] Pocock, *Virtue, Commerce*, 127, 138.
[95] Berry, *Social Theory*, 40, 47, 162, 173; Broadie, *Scottish Enlightenment*, 57.
[96] Ferguson, *Principles*, i. 75, 154–6, 322–4, 330.
[97] Pocock, *Virtue, Commerce*, 130.   [98] Ferguson, *Principles*, i. 165–6.

which renders the vestige of intelligent power the more evident, that parts are so various, while they are so happily ranged and connected'.[99] Smith evoked providence less emphatically, leaving some question (still disputed today) as to how seriously to take his appeals to a benevolent deity guiding both nature and human history. When it came to the public arena, though, he was even more 'prudent' than Hume, neither his lack of Christian belief nor indifference to ecclesiastical authority being at all obvious.[100]

Yet, if divine providence—whether invoked sincerely or merely prudentially—had ordained the prevailing social hierarchy in Europe, retorted the radical *philosophes*, only 'a very small number of men', providence decided, should live comfortably and at ease, enjoying the means to be happy while a 'foule immense d'infortunés', objected d'Holbach, groan under oppression, 'languissent dans la misère'.[101] Among the first radical *philosophes* to follow Rousseau in focusing on inequality was Helvétius in his *De l'esprit* (1758). Helvétius stressed what to him was the undeniable truth that beyond a certain level of luxury (which in itself he regarded as morally neutral) possessions cannot significantly enhance any individual's happiness. By contrast, excessive 'inégalité de richesses entre les citoyens' most certainly creates and spreads the unhappiness, or lack of contentment, of by far the greatest number and, simultaneously, multiplies the incidence of robbery and theft.[102]

Entirely different was the approach of the Scots. Deeply influenced as he was by Montesquieu, especially in his support 'for propriety of manners adapted to the constitution of the state',[103] and the necessity of aristocracy and rank in a mixed monarchy like Britain, Ferguson thought different institutions, social systems, and moral emphases appropriate to different societies: 'human nature no where exists in the abstract, and human virtue is attached, in every particular instance, to the use of particular materials, or to the application of given materials to particular ends.'[104] Like the others, he developed a complex typology of stages beginning with primitive societies and ending in civilized societies, 'the polished state', after passing through the stage of the 'barbarous state', characterized by crude forms of social subordination like feudalism, and then further intermediate stages.[105] Human history is a progression and, in some respects, a progress; but there is nothing automatic about it. 'When we say that the Author of nature, has projected a scene of discipline and progression for men; it is not meant to affirm any rate of actual attainment for this versatile being. The faculties are given to him, and the materials are presented for his use: but the effect is optional to him.'[106] The history of civil society, as he envisaged it, represented a form of progress, but one involving much less that could be designated

---

[99] Ibid. i. 173.

[100] Mossner, *Life of David Hume*, 53, 323; Robertson, *Case*, 396; Leddy, 'Adam Smith's Critique', 201–4.

[101] [D'Holbach], *Le Bon-Sens*, 36–7.

[102] Helvétius, *De l'esprit*, 34–5; Helvétius, *Notes*, 1; Vergani, *Traité*, 113; Wootton, 'Helvétius', 324.

[103] Ferguson, *Principles*, ii. 416–17.   [104] Ibid. ii. 418–19.

[105] Perinetti, 'Philosophical Reflection', 1131–3.   [106] Ferguson, *Principles*, i. 314–15.

moral or political progress than in Smith's social theory, being driven essentially (as in Rousseau) by changes in the character of property relations and growing inequality. Why should modern man look with disdain upon the primitive savage? 'The savage who performs, however rudely, the several tasks of human life for himself, though greatly inferior to the scientific performer, may in fact be as much superior to the mere labourer, who is no more than a tool in the hand of a master artist?'[107] Equally, many features of 'polished societies', in Ferguson's view, had a distinctly ambivalent character or were undesirable with a dangerous potential for harm. In particular, after the Seven Years War, he warned against 'the ruinous progress of empire' and condemned 'admiration of boundless dominion', a real danger in Britain at the time, as a 'ruinous error'.[108]

Feudalism and slavery may have been discredited for the most part, but Scots Enlightenment did much to erect potent new hierarchies based on stages of development, sentiment, cultural properties, as well as tentative racial theories. In response to criticism, Hume did later soften, in the 1777 edition of his essay 'On National Characters', his remarks about race found in the original 1753 version, removing what he had said earlier about different races being different species, qualifying his statement about negroes being 'naturally inferior to the whites', and deleting his assertion that 'there scarcely ever was a civilized nation of any other complexion than white', but his reworking of the passage merely confirms his belief in the reality of racial hierarchy and the innate inferiority of blacks.[109] In 1777, he retained his remark that in Jamaica 'they talk of one negroe as a man of parts and learning, but it is likely he is admired for slender accomplishments, like a parrot, who speaks a few words plainly.'

3. REID AND 'COMMON SENSE'

Where Hume thought our sense of justice is acquired, Kames thought this a weak basis for man's sense of justice and postulated rather that divine providence had implanted the sense of justice in us, that it is a 'native' sense that social and historical processes then refine, just as he believed providence had instilled modesty and the inclination to sexual chastity in women.[110] This difference corresponded to a basic rift in the Scots Enlightenment between the 'moral sense' thinkers developing Hutcheson's idea that 'moral sense' begins as an inbuilt sensibility but acquires most of its content from outside, from society, and the 'Common Sense' thinkers like Kames and Reid for whom the basic content of morality, like our sense of justice

---

[107] Ferguson, *Principles*, i. 251.
[108] Ibid. ii. 500–1; Pittock, 'Historiography', 275.
[109] Hume, *Essays*, 208; Brown, 'Social Sciences', 1078–9; O'Neill, *Burke–Wollstonecraft Debate*, 118; Mankin, 'Hume', 86.
[110] O'Neill, *Burke–Wollstonecraft Debate*, 30–1.

and women's modesty, is there from the outset but needs to be refined by social circumstances. This was not perhaps as crucial a divide as that separating those Enlightenment thinkers ascribing moral ideas among men to an 'an original power or faculty in man', as Reid expresses it, on the one hand, which some call 'the Moral Sense, the Moral Faculty, Conscience', and on the other those who 'think that our moral sentiments may be accounted for without supposing any original sense or faculty appropriated to that purpose'.[111] The latter were the materialists and Spinozists who believed that morality was entirely a social construct that builds on the individual's sense of self-interest and instinct for self-preservation, having nothing to do with any providence or with inbuilt sensibilities. But the difference between Scots 'moral sense' and 'common sense' had significant implications too.

'Moral Sense thinkers' deemed 'moral sense' a natural sentiment that grows, like Rousseau's, in every human at a certain point, much like puberty, and renders acts of benevolence and unselfish behaviour as natural as selfish acts are. This tradition derived originally, its chief exponents acknowledged, from Shaftesbury's critique of Hobbes's purely egocentric conception of human nature. Together with the Common Sense group, Moral Sense thinkers scorned what Kames called the 'blindness of some philosophers, who by dark and confused notions, are led to deny all motives to action but what arise from self-love'.[112] Linked also to Hutcheson's feud with Mandeville, it was an approach disdained by radical *philosophes* for its dependence on the idea of soul as a separate substance or entity from the body, and one with guiding impulses, and (usually at least) reliance on divine providence. The 'moral sense', they thought, was impossible because it lacked any identifiable physical foundation.[113] For Helvétius, Diderot, and d'Holbach, any 'sense' must be something 'physical' and this the benevolent sensibility ascribed to humans by their adversaries plainly was not. Consequently, they dismissed 'les Shaftesburistes' as Helvétius terms the Moral Sense philosophers as virtual theologians, confused thinkers proceeding without any real empirical basis, illegitimately mixing philosophy with theology. Yet, 'absurd' or not, both 'moral sense', and soon also 'Common Sense', were due for long and glorious careers. The Scots 'moral sense' philosophers were a group assailed by Helvétius in his *De l'homme*, d'Holbach, in his *Système social*, and Delisle de Sales, in his *De la philosophie de la nature*, as relying on murky foundations, amounting in Hutcheson's case to an incoherent anti-Hobbesian 'galimathias' that is neither a 'system' nor 'philosophy', just an endless assertion of the notion of moral instinct.[114]

The alternative to 'moral sense' was the 'Common Sense', the chief representatives of which were Kames, Reid, Campbell, Ferguson, James Beattie (1735–1803), and James Oswald (1703–93), who all believed our chief conclusions in natural theology

---

[111] Reid, *Works*, ii. 589.

[112] Kames, *Elements*, i. 41.

[113] Berry, *Social Theory*, 158; Himmelfarb, *Roads*, 31–3.

[114] D'Holbach, *Système social*, 64, 66, 107, 114, 168 n.; Delisle de Sales, *Philosophie de la nature*, i. 8, 272–3, 466.

derive not from reason but our inbuilt moral faculty, the inner light of intuition. For Hume and Smith, tradition and actual usages is the only sound basis for developing our moral doctrines; for Kames and Reid, very differently, common sense is the unique source of first principles and the authentic impulses of our human nature and hence both the starting point and boundary of all sound philosophy. Both Moral Sense and Common Sense thinkers readily spoke of 'moral sense' as something separately developed in man, purposely ingrained by divine providence and quite distinct from the dictates of reason. But in the one case it is the capacity that is there at the outset, the content is acquired; in the other it is mostly bestowed beforehand. 'The God of nature', explained Kames, 'in all things essential to our happiness, hath observed one uniform method: to keep us steady in our conduct, he hath fortified us with natural laws and principles, preventive of many aberrations, which would daily happen were we totally surrendered to so fallible a guide as is human reason.'[115]

If Hume typified Scots Enlightenment in any respect it was in his central premiss that philosophical reason cannot be the guiding principle in morality and that tradition, sentiment, religion, and schooling always count for more. In denying reason any great role, Reid and the Common Sense school stood close to the Humean legacy. Reason does not show the way, agrees Reid, and neither do human aspirations in any shape or form. But the Common Sense group were hostile not just to Hume's scepticism and moral compatibilism, his doctrine that there is no contradiction between considering man's will free and yet determined by natural causes, but also had reservations about the cogency of the concept of 'moral sense' itself since its stress on sentiment and men's responsiveness to convention and society's rules imply that certain actions are not intrinsically immoral but only so because a particular society happens to disapprove.[116] Where the Moral Sense and Common Sense schools especially clashed was in epistemology and over the question of how knowledge of moral rules reaches our 'moral sense'. For the latter group, moral sense being more directly implanted in men by providence, particular moral qualities, like fidelity, propriety, gratitude, and our 'sense of justice' and especially women's chastity are already converted into duties precisely by our 'moral sense'.

Where the Moral Sense philosophers understood 'moral sense' as a learning faculty mainly determining our specific duties through experience, through external interaction with other men and through individual responsiveness to society's rules of morality, cultivation by society, and by the individual in him- or herself of virtue, for Common Sense philosophy moral awareness is fully implanted from the first. 'The first principles of morals', held Reid, are in every adult and sane person, they 'are the immediate dictates of the moral faculty'.[117] 'The road of duty is so plain', he maintained, 'that the man who seeks it with an upright heart cannot greatly err from it.' By contrast, the road to happiness, the prime goal not just of the French materialists but

---

[115] Kames, *Elements*, i. 242; Ahnert, 'Soul', 247.
[116] Ahnert, 'Soul', 246; Stalley, 'Reid's Defense', 34–6; Russell, *Freedom*, 182.
[117] Reid, *Works*, ii. 590–1; Stewart, 'Arguments', 721.

also the 'moral sense' school, is not obvious to us but rather 'dark and intricate, full of snares and dangers', and hence to be trodden only with apprehension and fear. 'The happy man, therefore,' held Reid, 'is not he whose happiness is his only care, but he who, with perfect resignation, leaves the care of happiness to him who made him, while he pursues with ardour the road of his duty,' a pursuit which involves sentiment combined with judgement.[118]

In Common Sense, divine providence (real or prudentially invoked) operates more through the individual than the collective, while, with 'moral sense', the case is the reverse and society is the primary agent. 'This moral sense', wrote Witherspoon, who dominated Princeton philosophy at the time of the American Revolution, 'is precisely the same thing with what in Scripture and common language, we call conscience. It is the law which our Maker has written upon our hearts, and both intimates and enforces duty, previous to all reasoning.'[119] When someone acts unjustly, held Kames, their own shame and remorse supplemented by the 'indignation united with hatred in the hearts of others, are the punishments provided by nature'. Our conscience both informs us when we are being unjust and punishes us for it. 'Stupid and insensible', concludes Kames, 'must he be, who, in a contrivance so exquisite, perceives not the benevolent hand of our Creator.'[120] The Creator in short has provided a faculty that shapes and disciplines the individual, albeit providing for some more liberally than others. This was a Christian but could also be a deist position. Though the first and one of the most vigorous exponents of Scottish Common Sense, and one of the most preoccupied with the notion of divine providence working through human history, law, and institutions, the 'finger of God' steering everything in its proper direction, not least 'in the provision of animal food for man',[121] Kames nevertheless stood slightly apart from the rest of the school. Beattie, despite granting that he 'professes to honour' Christianity, was one among many who found his thought in some sense suspect. For not only was the Bible much less central for him, he sometimes seems to be denying 'free will' in favour of necessitarianism and even expressing doubt about the soul's immortality.[122]

'Conviction, and steadiness of principle', held Beattie, professor of moral philosophy at Marischal College, Aberdeen, a writer who enjoyed vast success far beyond Scotland, 'is that which gives dignity, uniformity and spirit, to human conduct, and without which our happiness can neither be lasting nor sincere'. Where solid conviction 'constitutes, as it were, the vital stamina of a great and manly character', for Common Sense philosophers, and especially Ferguson, scepticism or a hesitant commitment to socially accepted values, like Hume's, betrays a faltering from what is nevertheless still faintly present, 'a weak and sickly understanding, and a levity of

---

[118] Reid, *Works*, ii. 586; Russell, *Freedom*, 93 n.; Cuneo, 'Reid's Moral Philosophy', 248–9.
[119] Witherspoon, *Lectures*, 17–18.
[120] Kames, *Elements*, i. 244.
[121] Kames, *Six Sketches*, 54.
[122] Ibid. 234, 241, 246; Broadie, *Scottish Enlightenment*, 141–2.

mind, from which nothing can be expected but inconsistency and folly'.[123] Moral flabbiness abounds. But for the Common Sense no less than the moral sense group, the guarantee that 'a great and manly character' is right in his undeviating convictions lies precisely in his adhering to convention, what society considers respectable, the Almighty's direction of society.

For the 'moral sense' philosophers, society both shapes the individual conscience initially and remains decisive as a controlling mechanism throughout. 'This natural disposition to accommodate and to assimilate, as much as we can, our own sentiments, principles, and feelings, to those which we see fixed and rooted in the persons whom we are obliged to live and converse a great deal with', argued Smith, 'is the cause of the contagious effects of both good and bad company.'[124] Morality's rules are ultimately founded upon experience of what in particular cases our moral sense approves or disapproves of. Smith's starting point in his *Theory of Moral Sentiments* is Shaftesbury and that 'ingenious philosopher' Hutcheson, the first 'who distinguished with any degree of precision in what respect all moral distinctions may be said to arise from reason, and in what respect they are founded upon immediate sense and feeling'.[125] Endorsing Hutcheson's insistence that moral judgement and moral action are disinterested and that both depend on natural feelings rather than 'reason', Smith wholly rejects the notion that we consider particular actions praiseworthy or blamable because they seem to us to conform to, or be inconsistent with, general principles of morality as the Common Sense school as well as Lockeans and materialists maintained. 'The general rule, on the contrary', is formed by finding from experience that 'all actions of a certain kind, or circumstanced in a certain manner, are approved or disapproved of'.[126] Inwardly situated but externally cultivated feeling, and the effects on sentiment of social pressure and convention are, hence, the chief factors constructing 'the general rules of morality' in Smith's as in Hume's eyes.

For both currents (apart from Hume), the role of divine providence remained decisive. For Smith, there could be no question of error, ignorance, or prejudice interfering with the learning process or debasing the moral content of society's rules. The morally upright and worthy person, the person to be relied on, can only be he or she who evinces what he calls a 'sacred regard' for society's rules. How can it be that there really exists no risk of being misled by following convention and reverencing society's rules? The guarantee lies, in Smith's doctrine, in what is ultimately no less a conjectural and theological stance than that of the Common Sense school. Since 'no other end seems worthy of that supreme wisdom and divine benignity which we necessarily ascribe' to God, the philosopher merging belief and reason by stressing 'moral sense' readily grants the 'happiness of mankind, as well as of other rational

---

[123] Beattie, *An Essay*, 147; Sher, *Enlightenment*, 146.

[124] Smith, *Theory*, 224.

[125] Ibid. 320.

[126] Ibid. 266, 457–63; Norton and Kuehn, 'Foundations', 941–2, 978; Seigel, *Idea of the Self*, 146–7.

creatures, seems to have been the original purpose intended by the Author of Nature when he brought them into existence'. In both Smith and Hume the cultivation of virtue is indeed anchored in the pursuit of happiness.[127]

The close entwining of Smith's moral philosophy (and system of economics) with 'the idea of that divine Being, whose benevolence and wisdom have, from all eternity, contrived and conducted the immense machine of the universe, so as at all times to produce the greatest possible quantity of happiness' underpins his moral philosophy: 'when the general rules which determine the merit and demerit of actions come thus to be regarded, as the laws of an All-Powerful Being, who watches over our conduct and who, in a life to come, will reward the observance and punish the breach of them; they necessarily acquire a new sacredness from this consideration.'[128] The general direction of society can be assumed to be the right one precisely because social progress is guided by providence. 'The administration of the great system of the universe, however, the care of the universal happiness of all rational and sensible beings, is the business of God and not of man.' The great difficulty here, as also with Reid's Common Sense, is that it was only a short step further to considering those inclined to rebel against established moral rules, since these are 'the scheme which the Author of Nature has established for the happiness and perfection of the world', to be 'in some measure the enemies of God'.

Any doctrine supposing that the human mind gravitates naturally to a God-given 'conformity of thought' inherently threatens to relegate intellectual dissent, or 'the exceptions' as Ferguson calls dissidents, to a category of deviation, accounted both antisocial and opposed to the divine design. Of course, not all intellectual deviation from the commonly held view of things necessarily conflicts with the conceptual framework developed by Hume and Smith, or that of Reid and Ferguson; some provision is made for higher minds deriving valid 'conceptions from a better source than vulgar opinion'. But those whom Ferguson calls 'less fortunate in their character', meaning freethinkers, libertines, French materialists, and atheists, 'by whom singularity is mistaken for eminence, and is entertained as an object of ambition affect to dissent from the multitude, and work themselves into singular notions of things, taken up at first from affectation, and continued through time into habit'.[129] Such men deserve only contempt as they reject both Moral Sense and Common Sense and repudiate received opinion more generally—by basing their conclusions on philosophical 'reason' and stretching reason beyond its legitimate bounds. Here, Priestley was entirely at one with Bentham, Paine, and Godwin in repudiating the positions of Hutcheson, Hume, and Smith alike with those of Reid, Kames, Beattie, and Ferguson.[130]

Mid-eighteenth-century Scotland was certainly more tolerant than a few decades previously, and many prided themselves on their country's (partial) escape from

---

[127] Seigel, *Idea of the Self*, 147; Smith, *Theory*, 283–4.
[128] Smith, *Theory*, 236–7, 294; Ahnert, 'Soul', 248–50.
[129] Ferguson, *Principles*, i. 135.   [130] Himmelfarb, *Roads*, 93.

bigotry. But the Scots public did not fully embrace toleration any more (and arguably somewhat less) than those of the Netherlands, Scandinavia, or England. Deism, freethinking, agnosticism, and thoroughgoing scepticism, as well as atheism, remained highly unwelcome, positions one could not admit to openly without suffering serious consequences for one's standing and career. To Hume's (discreetly veiled) atheism and scepticism there was more hostility in Scotland than in England or France even though Hume always scrupulously avoided libertine talk of the kind usual among the Parisian *philosophes* and was regularly teased by Helvétius for his 'narrow way of thinking in these particulars'.[131] His failure to secure a chair in philosophy at Glasgow in 1752, followed by the attempt to organize his expulsion from the Church of Scotland in 1755–7 and suppression of his projected volume of *Five Dissertations* in London under pressure, civil and ecclesiastical, in 1756, were all signs of a cloud of disapproval the effects of which on his position would have been graver had he not been personally well liked and regarded among various liberal Scottish Presbyterians for his affability, discretion, and obvious virtues.[132] Robertson, prominent in and, in 1766, moderator of the General Assembly of the Church of Scotland, was often more Hume's protector than his critic. In the General Assembly, he laboured, especially in 1756–7, to avoid Hume's formal condemnation and expulsion from the Church.

With Scots intolerance formidable, the appeal of both powerful philosophical traditions was enhanced by their emphatic social and political conservatism and explicit balancing if not of faith and theology then of the accepted rules of society against philosophical reason. Common Sense identified a positive role for philosophy as an aid to both the individual and society, but did not envisage 'philosophy' as a discipline in the way most ancient and modern philosophers conceived it. It is through the 'discernment peculiar to rational beings called common sense', insisted the Common Sense school, that 'we perceive all primary truths' about God, the soul, and morality 'in the same manner as we perceive objects of sense by our bodily organs'.[133] The evidence of Common Sense, so much more persuasive according to these authors than Locke's or Hume's arguments, was in part simply a popularized version of early eighteenth-century English Newtonian physico-theology: 'if the most ignorant, thoughtless and stupid of the human race, who is not an idiot, will peruse, with moderate attention, the works of Derham, Ray, or the display of Nature by the Abbé de Pluche, he will have not only a perception, but a feeling both of the being and perfections of God.'[134] 'That the world is upheld and conducted by a being of absolute perfection', averred Oswald, 'is a truth to which all nature bears testimony; that this supreme being is our rightful sovereign and judge, cannot be doubted; that it is our wisdom, as it is our duty, to conduct ourselves so as we may be able to give

---

[131] Hume to Sir John Pringle, 10 Feb. 1773, in Hume, *Letters*, ii. 274; Stewart, 'Hume's Intellectual', 55.
[132] Mossner, *Life of David Hume*, 230–1, 347–8; Broadie, *Scottish Enlightenment*, 118.
[133] [Oswald], *Appeal to Common Sense*, i. 190; Kuehn, *Scottish Common Sense*, 33.
[134] [Oswald], *Appeal to Common Sense*, ii. 84; Sher, *Enlightenment*, 148, 310.

him an account of all our actions; and, that as he has a right to call us to account, at what time and in what manner he sees fit, so it is our business, without further inquiry, to hold ourselves in readiness, can as little be doubted. These are truths which philosophers ought and might have inculcated on mankind with great success. But they were diverted from it by that intemperate love of reasoning which is the foible of the human mind.'[135] Oswald, preacher and prominent member of the Scots Church's General Assembly, accorded philosophy a place but thought philosophers had neglected their real task.

Thomas Reid, professor of philosophy at King's College, Aberdeen, from 1751 and, from 1764, Smith's successor as professor of moral philosophy at Glasgow, was the foremost exponent of 'Common Sense' principles and the man, according to Ferguson, who stripped the philosophy of mind of 'the mist of hypothesis and metaphor with which the subject had become enveloped' by Locke, Berkeley, and Hume.[136] Reid achieved a remarkably high standing in both the Scottish and the American Enlightenment. He accepted Hume's argument for scepticism on the basis of modern philosophy's claim that we know nothing about things except by way of our perceptions and ideas, but then countered the effect of this by denying, as Priestley put it, that 'there is any resemblance between objects and ideas' or that the one can be produced by the other.[137] Most things we would like to know we can never know with any objective philosophical precision or certainty.[138] This is true also of what we need to know, but the latter we nevertheless know with full and unquestionable certainty being men made by the Creator. Reid believed it was precisely Hume who had most consistently and devastatingly demonstrated the implications of what he calls the 'ideal' system, interpreting the sceptical conclusions Hume arrives at as evidence of the basic error of his, Locke's, and Descartes's first premiss. For Reid, the sceptics had unwarrantably undermined common sense's authority with a false epistemology,[139] where, in reality, the dictates of common sense are inevitably the first principles of all thinking and cannot be proved or disproved. Mere 'vulgar prejudice' masquerading as common sense can, of course, be refuted by self-evident reasoning; but true 'common sense' principles require no proof and cannot be disproved being the indispensable and inescapable basis of our perceptions and ideas.

A pious believer and active, churchgoing Presbyterian, Reid was relentless and incisive in his attack on Locke, Berkeley, and Hume alike. His teacher at Marischal College, Aberdeen, George Turnbull (1698–1748), had ruled in his *Principles of Moral and Christian Philosophy* (1740) that nature and nature's products exist by divine will and that therefore minds, as part of nature, are undoubtedly created for a divinely ordained purpose; our basic ideas are not arbitrary. Viewing Hume as a second

---

[135] Sher, *Enlightenment*, 51; [Oswald], *Appeal to Common Sense*, i. 47–8.

[136] Ferguson, *Principles*, i. 75.

[137] Priestley, *An Examination*, 26, 28–9, 62–3.

[138] Reid, *Works*, i. 126–33; Klemme, 'Skepticism', 132; Wolterstorff, 'God and Darkness', 82–3, 87, 91–3.

[139] Klemme, 'Skepticism', 128.

Berkeley but this time lacking God, Reid deemed his sceptical conclusions, rooted in Locke, clear evidence of the basic error of Berkeley's, Hume's, Locke's, and Descartes's first premiss, namely 'the common theory of ideas, or images of things in the mind, being the only objects of thought'.[140] 'All the arguments urged by Berkeley and Hume, against the existence of the material world', concludes Reid, 'are grounded upon this principle—that we do not perceive external objects themselves, but certain images or ideas in our own minds.'[141] Berkeley, having 'proved, beyond the possibility of reply, that we cannot by reasoning infer the existence of matter from our sensations', had begun a drift to absurdity completed by Hume.[142] 'Nay, if I admit Berkeley's and Hume's theory, of the non-existence of matter, I must believe that what my senses declare to be true, is not only not truth, but directly contrary to it.'[143]

Reid grants the internal coherence of Hume's philosophy, acknowledging that 'it is justly deduced from principles commonly received among philosophers'. 'The modern skepticism, I mean that of Mr Hume, is built upon principles which were very generally maintained by philosophers', observed Reid, 'though they did not see that they led to skepticism.'[144] Hume, 'upon the principles of Locke, who was no sceptic, hath built a system of scepticism, which leaves no ground to believe any one thing rather than its contrary.'[145] To assail Locke's account of the mind, Reid reaffirmed that the mind is essentially active and matter passive. Locke, he urged, is neither sufficiently empirical nor consistent in his account of the mind's operations, those active powers of the mind which he acknowledges are not acquired habits but the mind's original equipment termed by both Reid and Locke 'faculties'.[146] The first step in bypassing Locke, evading Hume, and generally correcting error in epistemology, holds Reid, is to demolish Locke's thesis that we have no ideas other than those deriving from sense impressions made on our organs of sense and processed by the mind's faculties. The competent philosopher must reject this because it reduces the authority of Common Sense to nothing and allows scepticism a free rein concerning all truths, including those of theology which are never the immediate objects of sense.[147] Human rationality and what makes rational men fundamentally different from the insane and from animals is not, urges Reid, the power of the mind's faculties to abstract from sense impressions, as Locke holds, but the guidance provided by Common Sense in determining the true relations between qualities and powers, a knowledge of truth altogether prior to sense which is the real touchstone of human rationality. Men are distinguished from animals by a prior system of knowledge and ideas acquired quite independently of sense impressions. Common Sense's dictates,

---

[140] Reid, *Works*, i. 88, 91, 98–9, 103, 306; Stewart, 'Rational Religion', 152.
[141] Reid, *Works*, i. 446.
[142] Ibid. i. 129, 207, 286–7, 293, 439.
[143] Beattie, *An Essay*,133; Tetens, *Philosophische Versuche*, i. 392–3.
[144] Reid, *Works*, i. 438.
[145] Quoted in Mossner, *Life of David Hume*, 299; Wolterstorff, *Thomas Reid*, 192, 256–7.
[146] Wolterstorff, 'God and Darkness', 80–1; Stalley, 'Reid's Defence', 29–30.
[147] Reid, *Works*, i. 215–16; Wolterstorff, *Thomas Reid*, 36–7.

the first principles of all thinking, are neither provable nor disprovable, being unconnected with our physical senses and hence reasoning. This argument Reid deemed entirely convincing when supported by examples.

The first example exemplifying Locke's errors is our knowledge of the being and attributes of God, something we know for certain from Common Sense but which, held Common Sense philosophers, cannot be demonstrated by reason or the senses. (Here we perceive Scottish Common Sense's tacit, underlying kinship with Hume.) Equally, from Common Sense we know of our future life in the hereafter though this too is not fully susceptible to rational demonstration. Another vital example is our instinctive knowledge of what our moral duty is in relation to our fellows, to our country, and to God. Free will is another basic premiss of Common Sense immediately rescued by Reid's procedure. There can be no other basis for asserting 'free will' than Common Sense. Reid, always a vigorous champion of Newtonian physico-theology, as well as differentiation of mind and matter, flatly repudiated not only Hume but likewise the radical necessitarianism and materialism of Priestley, Helvétius, and other materialists.[148] Other incontrovertible instances of first principles restored by rejecting Locke's, Berkeley's, and Hume's epistemology, according to Reid, are trust in the existence of material objects, belief in our own existence, and acceptance of the reliability of our faculties. Just as no human ingenuity can create a particle of matter and the whole extent of men's power over the material world, as Locke observes, consists of combining, disjoining, and mixing the matter at our disposal, so 'in the world of thought the materials are all made by nature and can only be variously combined and disjoined by us'.[149]

Consequently, no philosophical system can produce any concept or impression that is 'not the work of nature, and the result of our constitution'. We cannot reason soundly from objects to ideas. 'But are we', asked Reid, 'to accept nothing but what can be proved by reasoning?' Locke's, Hume's, and the generally prevailing doctrine of the mind is especially objectionable, held Reid, because it authorizes the 'votaries' of philosophy to 'extend her jurisdiction beyond its just limits and to call to her bar the dictates of Common Sense'. The whole tradition of modern philosophy from Descartes to Hume had unwarrantably undermined Common Sense's authority by embracing a false epistemology built on confusing 'sensations which can have no existence but when they are felt' with 'the things suggested by them'.[150] Locke's and Hume's misjudgements had generated a meaningless war of Common Sense versus philosophy in which the latter 'will always come off both with dishonour and loss; nor can she ever thrive till this rivalship is dropt, and a cordial friendship restored', for while Common Sense has no intrinsic need of Philosophy, philosophy 'has no other root than the principles of Common Sense'.[151]

---

[148] Reid, *Works*, i. 52, 82, 87; Stalley, 'Reid's Defense', 31–2, 41; Wood, 'Hume, Reid', 127.
[149] Wood, 'Hume, Reid', 130–2; Reid, *Works*, i. 128.
[150] Reid, *Works*, i. 129–31; Klemme, 'Skepticism', 128.   [151] Reid, *Works*, i. 101.

Locke's uniquely high standing among philosophers had indeed so widely permeated general culture and society in Britain, America, France, Italy, and Spain, by 1750,
that disparagement of his thought had become equivalent to disrespect for the
ordinary, regular, established, and hence to criticize him had become generally
objectionable, even immoral. In France, complains Hayer in his *La Religion vengée*,
the 'blind respect' and unquestioning reverence generations of scholastics reserved
for Aristotle during the Middle Ages had now been so entirely transferred to Locke as
the measure of everything usual, conventional, and proper that it was no longer
acceptable in ordinary society to question his special genius and primacy.[152] Yet 'if, as
[Locke] represents, we can have no ideas besides those arising immediately from
impressions made on our organs of sense, or our own reflection upon these', objected
Oswald, 'then the authority of common sense [as prior to sense impressions] must go
for nothing, and a free scope is given to skepticism, with respect to all truths that are
not the immediate objects of sense'.[153] Locke was incompatible with Common Sense
and, as Shaftesbury maintained, also with 'moral sense'.

Was Locke really a safe redoubt for established morals and conventional thinking?
No one doubts, granted Oswald, that Locke 'seriously believed the great truths of
religion and was sincerely attached to them'. Without that, he could not have won the
uniquely high status he enjoyed. But the philosophical evidence he offers for the
truths of religion is wholly inadequate for 'the bulk of mankind' and ultimately an
invitation to Hume's scepticism. The evidence 'for the being and perfections of God'
Locke categorically asserts 'to be equal to mathematical certainty'. But if it requires a
highly sophisticated process of 'deduction' by means of our reason 'or else we shall be
as uncertain and ignorant of this as of other propositions which are in themselves
capable of clear demonstration', it is 'easy from hence to foresee the fate of those who
are incapable of the attention and application of thought necessary even for mathematical, and still more necessary for pursuing a thread of metaphysical demonstration'.[154] Unphilosophical persons must then be wholly lost in uncertainty and
obscurity. It was therefore open to doubt whether Locke's empiricism was a useful
philosophy to propagate in the colleges and in society. 'Mr Locke, with justice,
resolves the source of moral obligation into the will of God; but, revelation apart,
hath left us no criterion to be depended on for discovering the divine will.'[155] Locke,
ominously, had in many countries from Spain and Italy to America triumphantly
become the basis for conventional thinking; but his thought is not a reliable basis for
the conventional and what is ordinarily thought.

Critics of Common Sense tended to dismiss its arguments as a feeble response to
Locke's empiricism. Priestley prided himself on having more effectively combated
Hume and defended Christianity in his *Institutes* than any exponent 'of this new
common sense' and was especially scornful of Oswald: 'the disgust his writings gave
me was so great that I could not possibly show him more respect.'[156] Equally, Beattie's

---

[152] Hayer, *La Religion vengée*, vi. 244.   [153] [Oswald], *Appeal to Common Sense*, i. 70–1.
[154] Ibid. i. 75.   [155] Ibid. i. 89; Kuehn, *Scottish Common Sense*, 32–3.
[156] Priestley, *An Examination*, preface pp. xvi, xxvii; Porter, *Enlightenment*, 410.

An Essay on the Immutability and Nature of Truth (1770) was fiercely critical of Locke and especially the latter's epistemological individualism, prompting Hume, in 1775, to account Beattie a 'bigoted silly fellow'.[157] But Beattie had a point. 'It is a favourite maxim with Locke, as it was with some ancient philosophers, that the human soul, previous to education, is like a piece of white paper, or *tabula rasa*; and this simile, harmless as it may appear, betrays our great modern into several important mistakes.'[158] Locke was 'no sceptic', and sincerely endeavoured to promote virtue, but the first book of Locke's *Essay*—which he calls 'the worst' and most misleading—propagates the 'dangerous doctrine, that the human mind, previous to education and habit, is as susceptible of any one impression as of any other: a doctrine which, if true, would go near to prove, that truth and virtue are no better than human contrivances; or, at least, that they have nothing permanent in their nature, but may be as changeable as the inclinations and capacities of men; and that, as we understand the term, there is no such thing as common sense'.[159]

Reid countered Hume's scepticism by denying, as Priestley put it, that 'there is any resemblance between objects and ideas' or that the one can be produced by the other.[160] Fundamental to his epistemology is the assumption we can trust our faculties being God's creatures. 'The mind of man is the noblest work of God which reason discovers to us and, therefore, on account of its dignity, deserves our study.'[161] The basis of virtue is found neither in the benevolent prudence and utility underpinning Hume's morality, nor in attuning conduct to the feelings of others and reacting on the basis of 'moral sense'. It resides rather 'in living in all good conscience—that is, in using the best means in our power to know our duty, and acting accordingly'.[162] The diverse moral codes found among men since ancient times demonstrate sufficient convergence, despite differences, for us to conclude with certainty that much is clear and definite in our knowledge of good and evil, just and unjust, integrity and lack of integrity. Quite different is the question of how we distinguish good from bad, just from unjust, in purely theoretical terms. This is far less certain, as Hume claimed, but also much less significant, having little to do with our actual knowledge, daily lives, and performance of our duties. For Reid, we know first 'by our moral faculty' what is right and what is wrong, and acquire feelings of sympathy, approbation, or disapprobation only afterwards, not the other way round as the moral sense theorists contended. While sensations precede judgement in the case of the outer senses, it is exactly the reverse for Reid with respect to moral perception: feeling results from judgement and is regulated by it. His stance and that of his followers, crucially, was also a form of revolt against the general Enlightenment's assumption that the unreasoning attitudes of ordinary folk are irrational or

---

[157] Kuehn, *Scottish Common Sense*, 32–3; Berry, *Social Theory*, 81.
[158] Beattie, *An Essay*, 149–50; Stewart, 'Religion', 54.
[159] Beattie, *An Essay*, 238–9.
[160] Reid, *Works*, i. 293–5; Priestley, *An Examination*, 26, 28–9, 62–3; Stewart, 'Hume's Intellectual', 50.
[161] Reid, *Works*, i. 217.
[162] Turco, 'Moral Sense', 150; Cuneo, 'Reid's Moral Philosophy', 247.

not a function of reason. Men simply do not need skill in reasoning to hold rational views.[163]

A crucial political and cultural consequence of Reid's, Oswald's, Beattie's, and Ferguson's approach was the obligatory, compulsory character of the new criterion when examining or recommending possible proposed changes in law, social practice, or education. Society should be improved and laws refined not by applying any set of general principles derived from philosophy or reason but rather from Common Sense premises, grounding conclusions on the basic orientation of existing practice, laws, and institutions. A disturbing feature of this approach was an inevitable pressure to condemn those who, dissenting from the rest to scandalize the public, justify vice, play the fool, or ape the mad, refusing to embrace principles definitely known from Common Sense through being securely anchored in what ordinary folk believe. Anyone opposing the main principles concerning God, the soul, our afterlife, and right and wrong commonly accepted in society might then be constrained, observed Priestley to silence, 'better' behaviour, or more discretion with the aid of the magistracy.[164] This notably illiberal implication ensues directly from believing our knowledge of the most vital truths we know with a quick, clear, and indubitable certainty 'given to us by our Maker to serve an almost infallible direction', as Priestley described it, 'in the whole conduct of life and especially in matters of religion'. This he pronounced a ridiculous and detestable doctrine. Especially unacceptable to him was the way 'Common Sense' served 'to supersede all rational inquiry into the subject of religion'.[165]

The huge prestige of Scots Common Sense won numerous adherents in the embryonic intellectual life of the American colonies. The new president at Princeton, appointed in 1766, Witherspoon, convinced man has an innate sense of good and evil and that only revelation can correct the distortions of unaided reason, admired Hutcheson up to a point but was particularly an enthusiast for Common Sense, especially Reid.[166] To help combine study, faith, duty, and reason in the new style at Princeton, he brought with him a working library of over 300 books, including works by almost all the recent Scottish enlighteners, Hume, Hutcheson, Kames, Reid, and Ferguson prominent among them. Witherspoon's *Lectures on Moral Philosophy* adopts Scottish Common Sense as a better instrument than Locke's empiricism for defending Protestant principles against such threatening novelties as Berkeley's idealism, Hume's scepticism, and French materialism.[167] But however popular in the nascent United States, Scots Enlightenment was simply not an obvious basis from which to develop a purely secular morality, or a social egalitarianism based on the principle of equality, or democratic theories, rather it was resolutely committed to a more or less natural division in all societies other than the most primitive between 'the superior orders of the people' and the 'promiscuous multitude'.

---

[163] Woltorstorff, *Thomas Reid*, 220.   [164] Priestley, *An Examination*, 230.
[165] Ibid. 232–3; Priestley, *Autobiography*, 113.
[166] Sloan, *Scottish Enlightenment*, 110–12.   [167] Kuklick, *History*, 47–9, 59–60.

The overriding defect of both Scottish Common Sense and Hume's and Smith's 'moral sense' in an age of far-reaching reform was that neither provided any viable grounds for challenging aristocracy, monarchy, empire, race distinction, or ecclesiastical authority. Rather both 'moral sense' and 'Common Sense' cohered with a social theory proclaiming rank and inequality integral to the divine plan, rendering 'absolute equality', as Ferguson expresses it, something 'altogether visionary and unknown in nature'.[168]

[168] Ferguson, *Principles*, i. 262.

10

Enlightened Despotism

1. RADICAL ENLIGHTENMENT AGAINST 'ENLIGHTENED DESPOTISM'

'Enlightened despotism', endorsed by Voltaire, Turgot, Grimm, and Beccaria as a key tool of enlightened social and legal reformism, was yet another issue splitting the Enlightenment into opposed blocs. Moderate enlighteners supported 'enlightened despotism' for itself, or as with Hume, the best solution in most cases (i.e. outside Britain), while radical thinkers, with their republican instincts, were unenthusiastic in principle and, eventually, despite lingering support where circumstances seemed to necessitate this outcome, as with Joseph II, did so with growing reluctance. Error and untruth, including enlightened despotism, have their moments of utility for men, acknowledged Sylvain Maréchal, a hardened materialist, in 1790: they act as a brake on the rampant emotions of 'un peuple esclave et ignorant'; but, from the moment a nation becomes *éclairée* [enlightened], and therefore free, it should not be governed other than by its own laws.[1]

Gradually there emerged a generalized radical critique of enlightened despotism. The enlightened man, urged Helvétius in his *De l'esprit* (1758), senses that in countries with despotic governments all alterations, including attempts at reform, end up becoming merely 'un nouveau malheur', as despotic government corrupts everyone and everything.[2] In unenlightened lands, everyone being ignorant 'du bien public', reformers are mostly either impostors promoting their own interests or mediocrities feebly instructed in what is required. In Russia, the only plausible course was little by little to change the form of government. Failing to understand this, Peter had not truly accomplished anything 'pour le Bonheur de sa nation'.[3] A great ruler rarely follows another on the throne. He should have foreseen, having done nothing to improve the empire's constitution or power structure, that the Russian people would simply relapse into the barbarism from which he attempted to drag them.

Radical thought increasingly hardened towards 'enlightened despotism', especially during the 1770s and 1780s. Without doubting Peter's great impact, some

---

[1] [Maréchal], *Catéchisme du Curé Meslier*, 3.
[2] Helvétius, *De l'esprit*, 350.   [3] Ibid.

enlighteners began asking whether any 'enlightened despot' can truly benefit their peoples or humanity. Diderot, no less than Rousseau, albeit in a notably different fashion, disputed Voltaire's notion of Peter as a surpassingly great and enlightened reformer, in his *Histoire de l'empire de Russie sous Pierre le Grand* (1759), the legislator who almost single-handedly pulled Russia from the Middle Ages into the Enlightenment era. If Rousseau deplored his dragging the Russians from their own authentic traditions, to Diderot he pursued glory and vain splendour only for himself rather than advanced the general interest, something that would entail tackling serfdom and raising Russia's cultural level by combating the ignorance, barbarity, and credulity for which Rousseau, in Diderot's eyes, was little more than an apologist.[4]

In the Enlightenment debate about 'enlightened despotism', Russia remained pivotal, being the first and, arguably, most dramatic instance of enlightened despotism's ability to transform society. Many eighteenth-century foreign writers, and Voltaire most of all, lavished extravagant praise on Peter and Catherine, creating an air of expectancy which, however, often proved disillusioning to the relatively few Western writers, thinkers, and educationalists who actually saw that country. The Italian poet Alfieri, visiting Petersburg in 'an extraordinary pitch of eager expectation' in 1770, immediately experienced bitter disillusionment. 'I had read Voltaire's history of Peter the Great, met several Russians at the Turin Academy, and heard their developing nation much praised.'[5] Assured that Catherine had 'no other object in assuming the reins of government than to repair the evils committed by her [murdered] husband, give the country a constitution, and restore some of the rights of which Russians had been deprived by serfdom, he was appalled to find 'una servitù così intera dopo cinque o sei anni di regno di codesta Clitemenestra filosofessa' [a servitude almost total after five or six years of rule by this philosophic Clytemnestra].[6] Despite having already frequented several European courts, he preferred not to be presented to the 'celebrated female autocrat, Catherine, so that I never beheld the countenance of a sovereign who, in our days, has become so famous'. Detesting 'tyranny' and aghast at what he saw at Petersburg, he refused to continue to Moscow as originally planned and 'ardently longed to return to Europe'.[7]

After the mid 1760s, it became axiomatic for Diderot and his circle, increasingly veering towards (a publicly disguised) republicanism, to consider 'enlightened despotism' illegitimate, detrimental, and contrary to the 'volonté générale'—in short, an evil to be opposed. By the early 1770s, Diderot held that 'le gouvernement arbitraire d'un prince juste et éclairé' is always pernicious and even the rule of a wholly well-intentioned absolute monarch something harmful to be resisted.[8] Many (including his friend Grimm) considered government by a 'despote juste, ferme, éclairé' the best

---

[4] Goggi, 'Diderot et le concept', 357–9; Wolff, *Inventing Eastern Europe*, 199–200.
[5] Alfieri, *Memoirs*, 102.
[6] Ibid. 103.
[7] Ibid. 103.
[8] Diderot, *Réfutation*, 381; *Histoire philosophique* (1780), x. 39, 41–2; Imbruglia, 'Two Principles', 490.

kind.[9] 'Quelle extravagance!', retorts Diderot in the *Histoire philosophique*. However virtuous, any prince doing 'good contrary to the general will is a criminal, for the simple reason that he exceeded his rights'. However enlightened, by acting against the 'general will', such a prince treats his subjects as a herd of sheep, driving them by violence to what he thinks is for their own good and building foundations for a less scrupulous despotism in the future, since his successors will inherit his power but probably not his enlightened attitude.[10] Here, as elsewhere, Diderot proved an advanced thinker. Other radical writers remained more equivocal for a time, ready to extol at least the most promising exceptions, especially Catherine's reformism during the first decade of her reign (1762–96) and Joseph's until his ruinous failures of the late 1780s. Complete rejection ensued only after 1787–9. Earlier, despite glaring deficiencies, enlightened despotism often seemed the best or only corrective available in the prevailing harsh and oppressive circumstances. Until around 1785, Joseph symbolized the promise of more enlightened times ahead for central Europe in the eyes of Herder, Lessing, and many other *Aufklärer*.[11] Only the enlightened despots, furthermore, could halt the fatal spiral of crushingly costly and destructive European wars. Wilhelm Ludwig Wekhrlin (1739–92), the German radical journalist who edited a remarkable series of periodicals published at Nuremberg during the 1780s (but whose *Das graue Ungeheuer* was banned in Habsburg Austria from 1788),[12] appealed in 1786 to both Frederick and Joseph to promote human 'happiness' by giving men the peace that only they, seemingly, could deliver.[13]

The disagreement concerned not just 'enlightened despotism' itself but also the virtues of monarchy more generally and entailed profoundly conflicting evaluations of the practical improvements that the Enlightenment had accomplished and could be expected to accomplish, in Russia, Prussia, Austria, many lesser German states, Spain, Portugal, Denmark-Norway, parts of Italy, and (after 1773) Sweden, all of which found themselves under enlightened despots. The split also involved conflicting assessments of the cultural values emanating from Europe's enlightened courts. Grimm, Catherine's chief cultural policy adviser abroad, and among the first to employ the term *despote éclairé*, viewed the enlightened courts with special enthusiasm: 'moi aussi', he wrote at one point, 'j'aime de tels despotes à la passion.'[14] For the Enlightenment of Voltaire, Turgot, and Hume—and in politics also d'Alembert and Goethe—it remained axiomatic that 'enlightened despotism' was the only sensible option for most countries. Only enlightened despotism, held the brothers Verri, could sweep away the centuries-old abuse of vested interests powerfully entrenched in the higher echelons of society, the so-called 'corpi intermedi' so decried by the

⁹ Diderot, *Political Writings*, 207; Diderot, *Fragments échappés*, 448; Diderot, *Réfutation*, 381–2; Beales, 'Was Joseph II an Enlightened Despot?', 4–5.
¹⁰ Diderot, *Political Writings*, 208; *Histoire philosophique* (1780), x. 39, 42; [Deleyre], *Gemälde von Europa*, 32.
¹¹ Lessing, *Anti-Goeze*, 204.
¹² Böhm, *Ludwig Wekhrlin*, 59.
¹³ Wekhrlin, *Graue Ungeheuer*, 6 (1786), 163–4.
¹⁴ Beales, 'Was Joseph II an Enlightened Despot?', 4.

Milanese enlighteners.[15] Many believed such rulers embodying the new principles of law, justice, toleration, and the responsibilities of the state had already virtually banished the old unthinking despotism and intolerance holding 'sous le joug d'une servitude absolue nos ancêtres', as one moderate enlightener expressed it, and that 'la philosophie' had thereby gained impressive ground. But equally others demurred, disliking royal courts and seeing the vaunted improvements as hardly measuring up to what circumstances demanded.[16]

By the 1770s, it had become a commonplace of radical ideology that unenlightened people, where sufficiently brutalized and imposed on, readily submit to 'slavery' and that, in this matter, Montesquieu was fundamentally mistaken, Europeans being generally little different from Asia's subservient masses. It was a thesis, objected the Dominican professor Richard, directly contradicting 'the atheists' claim' that Man is so constituted that he desires liberty necessarily.[17] But oppression, replied Diderot, d'Holbach, and their sympathizers, subservience, and unreflecting resignation render men insensible to the injustice blighting their lives. Imperceptibly, the oppressor comes to appear justified. Thus the Franco-Dutch publicist and promoter of human rights Cerisier in November 1783 offered in his journal a powerful retort to the widespread claim that the enlightened despots were everywhere successfully freeing men from unenlightened rule. If most Europeans consider themselves freer than in earlier centuries, this stemmed from an abject willingness to taste freedom 'très-superficiellement', enlightened despotism blinding men to their real condition and accustoming them to many curbs 'on their natural rights' so that, generally, they were far less resentful of oppression than they should be.

The great advantages and wealth enjoyed by high nobles habituate other men to assume aristocrats are permitted everything while even the faintest protest is forbidden to them. No one should be surprised, then, if Europeans just like 'les Asiatiques' become accustomed to bearing the yoke and different levels of deprivation.[18] Do not the circumstances in which most Europeans dwell amply testify 'contre leur liberté prétendue'? Is one free groaning under an excessive workload, the pay for which is insufficient to satisfy one's most basic needs? How many labourers in both town and country display on their faces the imprint of utter misery? If one surveys Europe's regions, does one see a flourishing population? Mostly, Europe's inhabitants hesitate to have children through dread of transmitting to a new generation the relentless drudgery weighing them down. Is it freedom to be loaded, like the French peasant farmer, with imposts and *corvées* so onerous, one either abandons one's parents' legacy or leaves one's plot partly uncultivated? Is liberty lack of adequate clothing in harsh weather? Are men 'free' where commerce is everywhere encumbered with royal monopolies, exemptions, privileges, and hindrances?

---

[15] Venturi, *Riformatori Lombardi*, 484; Beales, 'Was Joseph II an Enlightened Despot?', 5. Tortarolo, *L'Illuminismo*, 161–2.

[16] Cerisier, *Le Politique hollandois*, 6 (1783), 'Lettre à l'auteur', 195–6.

[17] Richard, *Défense de la religion*, 169–70.   [18] Cerisier, *Le Politique hollandois*, 6 (1783), 196.

In practically all European countries most commoners were anything but prosperous. I would have said 'in all', adds Cerisier, but one must except Holland where a greater degree of ease is found 'pour toutes les classes de la société', even the very poorest, than anywhere else.[19] That is a great achievement; but everywhere else, the fate of most was distressing. If 'la liberté et le bonheur' distinguish Europe from Asia, as many suppose, following Montesquieu, how is it we do not find impartial laws applying 'également aux grands comme aux petits?' Why are innocence and weakness usually worsted by status and favour? How is it that a poor man rarely obtains justice against so-called persons of quality? How does a powerful man's whim, or even that of his mistress or valet, instantly hurl the humbly born upright man into prison? 'Enfin, une heureuse tolérance', does it permit every citizen to think as he pleases provided he obeys the law? Plainly not. With so much blighting their happiness, Europeans were poorly placed to boast of imagined advantages over Asians when the latter languish under only marginally more onerous conditions. Montesquieu's vaunted 'advantages' utterly fail to impress those few generous souls aware of 'les véritables droits de l'homme'.[20]

Among the growing band of hardened adversaries decrying Prussian oppression was the first South American fighter for independence, Francisco de Miranda, who, in September 1785, visited Potsdam, met the king, and attended Frederick's last review of his troops.[21] Circumstances combined with radical thought generated a powerful emotional revulsion not just against traditional ideas and authority but also 'enlightened despotism' and forms of absolutism professing a veneer of enlightened ideas. The contradiction between Frederick's pretensions to be *un roi philosophe* and reality or what key radical writers such as Diderot, d'Holbach, Mirabeau, Alfieri, Lessing, Herder, Cerisier, Brissot, Paine, Miranda, and Wekhrlin considered a mean, exacting, and appalling tyranny had become all too manifest. Frederick especially attracted this kind of hostility, most trenchantly in Diderot's (at the time) unpublished and often highly sarcastic *Principes de politique des souverains* (1774), where the Prussian monarch emerges as a cynical militarist and warmonger systematically despoiling his own people.[22] His reign did more than anything else to convince Diderot, Lessing, and Herder that Enlightenment and 'enlightened despotism' are in reality totally contradictory principles.[23] Plainly, Frederick did not believe in treating his subjects as independent-minded, mature individuals, commented later Christian Wilhelm Dohm (1751–1820), a Prussian official with private radical leanings much concerned with contemporary social issues. His aim, rather, was to forge a hierarchical, noble-dominated, and heavily dependent society, unremittingly subject to crown and army, discriminating in favour of the nobility being for him a paramount political maxim.[24]

[19] Ibid. 197.   [20] Ibid. 198.
[21] Rodríguez de Alonso, *Siècle*, 132–7; Zeuske, *Francisco de Miranda*, 88–91.
[22] Diderot, *Principes*, 477–8.
[23] Del Negro, 'Rappresentazioni', 148–9, 153 n.; Blanning, *Culture of Power*, 215–16, 225.
[24] Dohm, *Denkwürdigkeiten*, iv. 381–2; Blanning, 'Frederick the Great', 268–9.

Aside from his wars and militarism, the worst feature of Frederick's rule from a radical perspective was his neglect of the common people's education, a deficiency especially marked in rural areas. This stemmed from the royal conviction that popular ignorance, credulity, and prejudices were best left undisturbed. Frederick had no sympathy for the thesis (so cherished by Helvétius) that education could be used to forge a more moral, civilized, and decent society. A particularly unfortunate aspect of his education policy, according to Dohm, was his decision, after the Seven Years War (1756–63), to assign large numbers of invalid soldiers, especially at 'under-officer' level, to teaching posts in village schools. This was a useful means of simultaneously pensioning them off and instilling discipline into children. But compensating veterans in this way, a method continued until the end of Frederick's reign, meant fusing the crassest ignorance with an undeviatingly authoritarian attitude, thereby ruining Prussian elementary education as an 'enlightened' project, as his education minister, Von Zedlitz, himself admitted.[25]

Nor were Prussia's failures in the educational sphere limited to primary education. Like Voltaire, Frederick revered Locke and desired to promote his thought.[26] But he made little effort to encourage science or widen academic debate and had no real notion how universities and secondary schools enhance a society based on secular values. For someone with so close an interest in literature and philosophy—and arranging the activities of his Academy of Sciences, and its choices of essay prize titles—it astounded some how little he sought to apply 'philosophy' in the eighteenth-century sense to social reform and how little he did for advancement of the sciences.[27] The assiduity he showed in drawing the foremost French *philosophes* to his court only heightened the contrast between an elaborate charade of courting 'philosophy' and the militarism and harsh authoritarianism of his rule. Assuredly, Maupertuis, Voltaire, and d'Alembert remained Frederick's staunch allies. But none of these sought fundamental legal, social, or political reform.

Radical *Aufklärer* scarcely minded the Academy's conducting its proceedings in French; for this encouraged participation in the general Enlightenment and rendered its activities international. What they reviled was its being deployed chiefly to acclaim the ruler while doing nothing to advance and purify German as a language of science, philosophy, literature, and education.[28] Frederick was also much criticized for forbidding Prussia's students to study abroad as if useful knowledge is not infinitely more advantageous for a country, objected Mirabeau, than the money a youth spends in two years' studying abroad.[29] Frederick's university policy, dismissed by Mirabeau as 'absurde', reflected the same narrow, oppressive fiscalism and mercantilism pervading the whole of the king's social policy, the very thing credited by Mirabeau,

---

[25] Dohm, *Denkwürdigkeiten*, iv. 446, 452; Goldenbaum, 'Der "Berolinismus"', 316.
[26] Dohm, *Denkwürdigkeiten*, iv. 447–50.
[27] Ibid. iv. 450–2; Beales, *Enlightenment and Reform*, 37.
[28] Herder, *Philosophical Writings*, 354–5; Dohm, *Denkwürdigkeiten*, iv. 456; [Mirabeau], *De la monarchie*, i. 214–15.
[29] [Mirabeau], *De la monarchie*, i. 225–6.

Dohm, and others with stifling enterprise and blighting Prussia's exports (aside from Silesian linen), the factors underlying her economic stagnation and sluggish population growth.[30]

Nor did the comparative freedom of speech and the press permitted by Frederick at all impress radical critics. Liberty to speak and write freely, observes Diderot, either marks 'l'extrême bonté du prince, ou le profond esclavage du peuple'. Mostly such freedom is allowed only 'à celui qui ne peut rien'. Prussia's population, Frederick's press freedom proved, was simply too cowed to oppose tyranny in any way.[31] Unusually tolerant regarding religion and philosophy though he was, noted Mirabeau, the king made no move to institute freedom of thought as a general principle 'par une loi claire et précise'. Rather, he permitted archaic, highly intolerant laws to remain formally on the statute books while lapsing into (potentially temporary) disuse.[32] His failure to abolish press censorship in principle confirms, argued Mirabeau, how extremely hard it is for kings, with even Frederick unwilling to concede it, to institute formal freedom of expression or recognize toleration not just as benefits but basic human rights.[33]

Helvétius, admittedly, was thoroughly charmed by Frederick, as he repeatedly assured his wife, whilst staying several months at Berlin in 1765. Everything about the king's manner and conversation pleased him, recalling the inspiration he found in Voltaire's company. The negative evaluation circulating among Diderot's circle he considered incorrect and unjust. Contrary to their view, the king was 'plein d'humanité'.[34] The king has treated me 'on ne peut pas mieux', he added, on departing Potsdam.[35] He was grandly fêted also, on both his outward and return journey, at the equally 'enlightened' and Francophile court of Gotha,[36] further reinforcing his impression that enlightened despotism was, after all, a viable path to comprehensive improvement and a happier humanity. But if Frederick put time and effort in charming Helvétius—as he had, earlier, Voltaire and d'Alembert—the founder of utilitarianism was known for his *naïveté* in such matters and afterwards rebuked by Diderot for being so easily swayed by the 'tyrant'.[37] He remained blissfully unaware that Frederick, writing to d'Alembert, a few weeks before his visit, scornfully dismissed *De l'esprit.*[38] Frederick liked conversing with such men; but his chief object in cultivating Helvétius, observed Dohm, was to profit from his expertise in fiscal organization and taxation.[39]

---

[30] [Mirabeau], *De la monarchie*, ii. 38–40, 46–7, and iii. 392, 412, 422, 428, 467, 472–3.
[31] Diderot, *Principes*, 501.
[32] [Mirabeau], *De la monarchie*, i. 144–5.
[33] Ibid. i. 144–5, 230, 232, 357.
[34] Helvétius to Madame Helvétius, Potsdam, 5 and 11 Apr., in Helvétius, *CGdH* iii. 169–70, 172.
[35] Helvétius to Madame Helvétius, Berlin, 28 May 1765, in Helvétius, *CGdH* iii. 190.
[36] Klüpfel to Grimm, Gotha, 20 Apr. 1765, and Helvétius to Madame Helvétius, Potsdam, 28 Apr. 1765, ibid. iii. 175–6, 178.
[37] Diderot, *Réfutation*, 381–2, 412, 444–5; Helvétius, *CGdH* iii. 171.
[38] See the notes to Helvétius, *CGdH* iii. 169.
[39] Dohm, *Denkwürdigkeiten*, iv. 507–8.

Everywhere proclaimed an 'enlightened' monarch, Frederick *was* 'enlightened' in terms of moderate Enlightenment values. His very real efforts to counter 'l'oppression théologique' and advance toleration earned universal acclaim. But even his religious toleration looked distinctly problematic to radical minds.[40] His church policy caused unease because by largely withdrawing from regulating outward religion, he left the churches in Prussia to fragment into competing blocks. If Socinianism positively flourished within the public Reformed and Lutheran churches, so did every other current.[41] The crown simply stood back, permitting the Lutheran Church to become a contested arena with little to hinder even the most reactionary preachers. Neologist theologians, Semler, Eberhard, and the rest, tirelessly laboured to wean the public from what all the enlightened deemed credulity and superstition. But their only real support from the monarch in Prussia was the same freedom of expression accorded to hard-line conservative preachers. Such indifferentism introduced new and severe strains into society. There were good radical as well as Protestant grounds for doubting, for instance, whether it made sense to leave education and moral instruction in Catholic Silesia largely in Jesuit hands.

A glaringly unenlightened aspect of Frederick's rule completely at odds with his vaunted toleration that bothered some, notably Diderot, Dohm, Brissot, Mirabeau, Cloots, and Miranda, was his marked aversion toward the Jews. Their religion and traditions, in Frederick's opinion, rendered them so deficient in the qualities he desired to foster in Prussian society, especially loyalty to state, discipline, and military valour, that he thought it impossible usefully to integrate them into society or remove discriminatory barriers against them.[42] He granted toleration and residence rights to a small wealthy elite capable of contributing to state coffers, or in some other capacity, including eminent Enlightenment figures like Moses Mendelssohn, Gumperz, and Markus Herz, whilst simultaneously enforcing strict work and residence curbs on the majority and drastically restricting Jewish immigration into Berlin, Königsberg, Breslau, and other main cities. If centuries of what Dohm called 'Christian oppression' had cut the Jews off from virtually all honest ways of earning their living other than trade, Frederick's policy simply aggravated this 'oppression' and the growing problem of Jewish vagrancy and criminality in central Europe.[43] Here, though, Frederick's prejudices accorded with the general feeling: while the small Berlin Jewish community were already strikingly 'affranchis' [emancipated], remarked Mirabeau in 1787, remarkably few non-Jews showed any willingness to plead the cause of the Jews.[44] In Berlin, as everywhere else, prejudice, ignorance, and fanaticism, he adds, were the chief features of ordinary thinking.

---

[40] Ibid. iv. 466–8; Raeff, *Well-Ordered Police State*, 67–8.

[41] Dohm, *Denkwürdigkeiten*, i. 232; Mirabeau, *De la monarchie*, v. 29–32.

[42] *Archivo Miranda*, i. 388; Mirabeau, *De la monarchie*, v. 45; Dohm, *Denkwürdigkeiten*, iv. 482–3.

[43] Dohm, *Denkwürdigkeiten*, iv. 484–7; Feiner, *Jewish Enlightenment*, 108, 120–1.

[44] Mirabeau, *De la monarchie*, v. 46, 55–8.

Worst of all was Frederick's reluctance to move towards emancipating the serfs whether in Pomerania, East Prussia, or Silesia. He would do nothing against the interests of the nobility whom the king was always at pains to support as far as he could, systematically discriminating in their favour in the army and bureaucracy. He rigorously defended existing entail restrictions: noble lands could generally be sold only to other nobles.[45] He biased the fiscal system in their favour. In Silesia, he fully confirmed noble sway over the serfs along with the tithes and privileges of the Catholic clergy.[46] Without the nobility's strong support, the military character of the kingdom would have been unsustainable. 'On entering the states of the great Frederick' which appeared to me like a vast guard-house', remarked Alfieri, in 1769, 'my hatred was still more increased of the infamous trade of soldier, the sole basis of all arbitrary authority, which must always rely on so many thousand hired minions. On being presented to His Majesty [i.e. Frederick], I experienced not the slightest emotion either of surprise or respect, but on the contrary, a rising feeling of indignation which became daily strengthened in my mind on beholding oppression and despotism assuming the mask of virtue.'[47]

2. THE GERMAN SMALL STATES

Could radical enlighteners hope for more from the small states? Loathing of Frederick, Maria Theresa, and Catherine, and, from 1787, growing doubts about Joseph, not infrequently encouraged radical minds to view the small German states with a more positive eye, a proclivity with a certain logic, despite being distinctly problematic given the ingrained conservatism of most of these. Many princely courts were in fact havens of Enlightenment.

Arriving in Berlin in December 1785, shortly before Frederick's death, Mirabeau stayed with interruptions for nearly two years, forming an alliance with the reforming circle around Dohm.[48] Used to expressing himself discreetly (being in Frederick's service) Dohm and his friends quietly sympathized with the American Revolution against the British crown and colluded with Mirabeau, briefing him on German topics, including Jewish emancipation, in which both men were keenly interested and about which Dohm, a few years earlier, had published the pre-eminent text in German *On the Civic Improvement of the Jews* (1781). Prominent in this group, cautiously criticizing Prussian state policies, and Mirabeau's closest ally in Berlin, was Struensee's younger brother Carl August who, after being expelled from Denmark in 1772, had become a financial official in the Prussian bureaucracy.[49] Another of

---

[45] Mirabeau, *De la monarchie*, i. 148–9, 153–4, 268–9, 302–3, 352.   [46] Ibid. i. 354.
[47] Alfieri, *Memoirs*, 97; D'Ancona, 'Federico il Grande', 13–14.
[48] Luttrell, *Mirabeau*, 80–1; Heinrich, 'Debatte', 829, 884; Weber, 'Mirabeau', 177.
[49] Weber, 'Mirabeau', 172.

Dohm's allies, Diez, also a prominent advocate of Jewish emancipation and general reform, was, however, absent during 1784–90, as Prussian envoy in Constantinople where he became Germany's foremost expert in Turkish, Persian, and Arabic.[50]

Mirabeau remained in Prussia until early 1787 compiling, together with Jakob Mauvillon (while also dispatching secret reports to royal officials in Paris), a massive six-volume study of that kingdom published in 1788, a book Gibbon read early in 1789 and pronounced a 'great work' but that did not, however, appear in German and never became widely known.[51] Having been ignored by Frederick, Mirabeau made himself unpopular from the start with the new king, Friedrich Wilhelm II, by presenting a petition—doubtless in collusion with Dohm, Struensee, and others (but later pronounced 'foolish' by moderate enlighteners, like Biester)—in 1786, appealing for greater press freedom, toleration, and civil liberty and a pruning of aristocratic privilege.[52] Extracts of Mirabeau's work did, however, appear in German translation in 1789 in one of central Europe's most important enlightened periodicals, Biester's *Berlinische Monatsschrift*, extracts stressing the German small states' particular advantages for promoting *Aufklärung*. Later, in 1789–92, this intervention attracted the attention of reactionary commentators eager to prove sinister subversion had been rife not just in France but also among the Berlin 'Aufklärungssynagoge' [Enlightenment synagogue] where 'wild' spirits allied with Mirabeau had supposedly contemplated 'cutting off some heads'.[53]

The German small states had a common interest in banding together as far as they could to curb Prussia's and Austria's relentless expansionism. Several small courts, notably Weimar, Dessau, and Gotha, the latter being the court with which Grimm was most connected, were internationally renowned centres of modern thought, literature, and high culture. Voltaire spent over a month at Gotha lavishly fêted by the duke and duchess, in 1753, before settling on Lake Geneva, and considered returning there subsequently.[54] Duke Ernst-Ludwig of Saxe-Gotha (1745–1804), who succeeded his father in 1772, had lived in Paris as a young man where, in 1768, Helvétius presented him with the copy of *De l'esprit* still gracing the splendid Gotha ducal library today.[55] Where Gotha chiefly cultivated French, and Weimar German, culture, the Calvinist court of Dessau, under Leopold III Friedrich-Franz of Anhalt-Dessau who ruled for a staggering fifty-nine years (1758–1817), during which he undertook no less than four trips to Britain, unyieldingly preferred English notions, gardens, architecture, philosophy, imperialism, and aristocratic manners.[56] The small German courts between 1750 and 1789 were havens of Enlightenment in varying styles. But were they suited to promoting Enlightenment in the sense of human betterment, driven by 'philosophy' in this world?

---

[50] Heinrich, 'Debatte', 828–9; Tortarolo, *Ragione sulla Sprea*, 182; Hess, *Germans, Jews*, 35.

[51] Gibbon, *Memoirs*, 225; Luttrell, *Mirabeau*, 87.

[52] Luttrell, *Mirabeau*, 82–3; Weber, 'Mirabeau', 171, 174; Weber, 'Publizistische Strategien', 828, 884.

[53] Weber, 'Mirabeau', 170; Tortarolo, *Ragione sulla Sprea*, 184–5.

[54] Davidson, *Voltaire in Exile*, 9, 11, 18.

[55] Helvétius, *CGdH* iii. 176.   [56] Umbach, *Federalism*, 17–22.

The enclosed, confined stuffy atmosphere of the small states had serious draw-backs. *Kleinstaaterei*, the system of small states, hampered all efforts to remove local dues and tolls and improve long-distance road travel which in much of Germany was greatly inferior to France, as Helvétius discovered to his dismay. Wherever princes and Imperial Free Cities presided, it was also much harder than in large states to propose plans for major canals such as would link the Rhine and Weser, or the Weser and Elbe, and for standardizing coinage, weights, and measures,[57] though the tradition-bound, intensely legalistic, and privilege-oriented Imperial Free Cities, in this respect as in others, struck Mirabeau and Wekhrlin, as being even worse than the principalities. But the small principalities did offer some tangible advantages when compared with large, powerful monarchies, especially with respect to freedom of movement, thought, and the press. Amidst a multiplicity of small principalities, princes unwittingly acted as a check on each other. If one grew more despotic, individuals could easily transfer to another nearby without being prevented.[58] Publishers and booksellers could play off one petty prince against another when seeking to evade restraints on publishing. The arts and sciences as well as publishing were more widely diffused through being cultivated by many small courts rather than just one great enlightened despot such as Frederick, Catherine, or Joseph.

Consequently, *Aufklärung* was found to have spread more extensively through the upper strata of society in small-state Germany than in the great despotisms.[59] In fact, Mirabeau, Dohm, and their friends found proof of what they thought were the much greater advances achieved by the *Aufklärung* in small- than in big-state central Europe, in the far higher levels of literacy one encountered in the small states than in Austria, Bohemia, and Hungary as well as Pomerania, Silesia, and East Prussia. It was differences in religion, assumed most people, observed Mirabeau, that explain why, in literacy, reading, and general *Aufklärung,* Austria, Bohemia-Moravia, and Hungary lagged behind Germany proper. But that most of Germany consisted of small fragments while Austria remained a large 'enlightened despotism', he suggested, could well be of greater significance. '*Aufklärung* spreads steadily, at least through society's upper levels, infinitely more', experience seemed to prove, 'in small states than in great monarchies'.[60]

Above all, where great monarchies maintained vast armies and were forever striving to become stronger and gear for war, small-state Germany directed by the league of princes or *Fürstenbund* had in recent years done an exemplary job of preserving the peace.[61] These were grounds for preferring the small states. Yet, radical enlighteners had little real reason for pride in the pace of reform in either small or large states. Serious hindrances abounded as was amply admitted in the writings of Justus Möser (1720–94), the most prominent *Aufklärer* associated with the small

---

[57] *Berlinische Monatsschrift,* 13 (1789), 140–1, 152.   [58] Ibid. 143–5, 147.

[59] Ibid. 148–9, 151–2.

[60] Ibid. 151–2; Blanning, *Culture of Power,* 114, 132–5.

[61] *Berlinische Monatsschrift,* 13 (1789), 161.

states system. Pre-eminent in the north-western prince-bishopric of Osnabrück, no one more fully aired the inner contradictions of German small-state Enlightenment than he. Until the late 1780s a staunch moderate enlightener, in the end the growing difficulties and his intensifying antagonism to egalitarian ideas estranged him (not untypically among high-level moderately enlightened bureaucrats at the time) from all Enlightenment, bringing him over to the Counter-Enlightenment.[62]

As a regular contributor to the *Berlinische Monatsschrift* and—until 1789—a leading German reformer, Möser's thought exhibited the typical hallmarks of a court official's distaste for radical ideas. The *Berlinische Monatsschrift* (founded 1783), edited by Johann Erich Biester and Friedrich Gedike, aimed to heighten awareness of key issues, report significant advances in knowledge, encourage cultivation of German literature, and offer extracts from foreign journals as well as biographies of notable personalities.[63] With moderate conservative reformers, like Biester, Möser shared much. But his overriding concern was to highlight the dangers to existing legal structures and traditions posed by 'our philosophical times', which he did by underlining the difference between the theoretical justice of the *philosophes* and positive law. Philosophers, like kings, stand too high, he admonished readers, to see the reality of things exactly enough, something achieved only through long experience.[64] Most *Aufklärer* aspired to extend what they considered true and just by 'power' and suppress error by 'power'. But precisely here he detected great peril of subversion, anarchy, and irreligion.

As prime administrator of Osnabrück, Möser's responsibility was to mediate between the nobility, towns, and bishop and regulate the principality's legal affairs. Like Montesquieu, Voltaire, Hume, Smith, and Burke, he supported a particular view of society, rejecting 'reason' wherever used to revolutionize social, political, and moral theory. In the German small states, like Britain and France, Enlightenment often involved strong attachment to the basic forms of *ancien régime* hierarchy and restricting reason's scope as part of a wider defence of princely authority, constitutional tradition, aristocracy, confessional allegiance, and ecclesiastical privilege. Ardent for Locke, Newton, and British empiricism, Möser loathed the social reformism of Helvétius, Diderot, and their German disciples. Here was a rift, moreover, that could hardly remain on a purely intellectual level: for Möser, one of Germany's most eminent historians, journalists, and political memorialists, faced an insoluble dilemma. He was genuinely dismayed by his country's archaic legal structure and juridical system, religious intolerance, administrative inefficiency, and the entangling of jurisdictions so characteristic of the Holy Roman Empire, not to mention the stagnant state of agriculture and inadequate roads and communications. Germany needed a wider religious toleration and many other improvements. But the overriding problem to his mind was how to attain a limited, British-style purely pragmatic

---

[62] Tortarolo, *Ragione sulla Sprea*, 176; Knudsen, *Justus Möser*, 2.
[63] Knudsen, *Justus Möser*, 22, 167, 172; *Berlinische Monatsschrift*, 1, 'Vorrede'.
[64] *Berlinische Monatsschrift*, 1, 506–12; Schmidt, *What is Enlightenment?*, 192–3.

Enlightenment (while admiring much in French aristocratic values and taste) in the face of the onslaught, as he saw it, from the 'shallow rationalism' of the materialists. Möser greatly prided himself on being free (as he imagined) from purely intellectual influences. No one could be more practical-minded in his estimation. But what his pragmatism amounted to in practice was safeguarding existing corporatist traditions especially courts and aristocracy—and, hence, retaining serfdom.[65]

Serfdom, still a widespread institution in much of central Europe, posed a particular difficulty. As syndic (secretary) of the Osnabrück nobility and the principality's chief administrative officer, upholding serf obligations and dues owed to the landowning nobility and Church formed part of his professional responsibilities. Here, he showed in his memorandum on the Osnabrück peasantry, submitted to Joseph II's officials in 1779, Möser was a genuine reformer. But his aim was to retain the principle of 'dependency' and trappings of legal bondage while mitigating the fiscal and legal scope of serfdom.[66] Seigneurial rights needed curbing but at the same time had to be maintained. They could best be pruned back, he thought, by stressing the double character of serfdom in the principality: 'the serf exists in a two-fold bond, the first rooted in the state, the second in the lease contract between him and the lord.' Episcopal jurisdiction could be used to curb arbitrary seigneurial sway, permanently resolving the whole question of *Bauernbefreiung* (peasant emancipation), by leaving the peasantry legally still subject to lord and Church but less oppressed.

Another small-state pragmatist (and eventual anti-Enlightenment ideologue) was August Wilhelm Rehberg (1757–1836). Eager to marshal Hume, Reid, and Kant for the conservative cause, Rehberg emerged as a still greater foe of materialism and deprecator of the French Revolution.[67] Heir to a Hanoverian administrative dynasty, trained at Göttingen, he too found employment (from 1783) in Osnabrück partly under Möser's direction and prided himself on his pragmatism,[68] but was far more deeply immersed in philosophy. Spinozism, he had concluded by the late 1770s, is irrefutable on paper. Yet, religion and Spinozism, commanding separate spheres, can coexist.[69] Around 1790, he embraced Kantianism and, like some other conservatives, began claiming that system to be especially suited to counter Spinozism, materialism, and revolution. Initially, Kant himself had recognized and respected the tendency of his own philosophy to form a barrier to republicanism, equality, freedom of thought, and democracy. But then, held Rehberg, he betrayed his own principles by shamelessly speaking out, through the 1790s, in favour of a revolution most German commentators increasingly repudiated.[70]

---

[65] Knudsen, *Justus Möser*, 26–7, 30, 61–4.
[66] Ibid. 133–6.
[67] Otto, *Studien*, 300; Tavoillot, *Crépuscule*, pp. xxix–xxx.
[68] Knudsen, *Justus Möser*, 184; Tortarolo, *Ragione sulla Sprea*, 334, 348.
[69] Otto, *Studien*, 308–9.
[70] Kuehn, *Kant*, 376.

3. JOSEPH II, 'JOSEPHISM', AND THE AUSTRIAN MONARCHY

Joseph II of Austria, co-ruler of the Austrian Habsburg empire with his mother Maria Theresa from 1765 to 1780 and sole monarch from 1780 until his death in 1790, pushed through more reforms and with greater vigour than any other enlightened despot. To no other 'enlightened despot' accrued so much (albeit often qualified) praise from the radical constituency. Although the way was prepared for him by the many initiatives of his most renowned 'enlightened' minister, Prince Wenzel Anton Kaunitz (1711–94), state chancellor from 1753 to 1792, and while Maria Theresa had already sanctioned many of the epoch-making reforms he implemented, usually she did so (except where of Jansenist inspiration), unwillingly or belatedly whereas Joseph embraced the cause of reform with unprecedented energy and resolve.

Maria Theresa was undeniably popular but decidedly 'unenlightened'. Famous for her piety and intolerance alike, and refusal to appoint Protestants to positions of responsibility in Austria,[71] she sought to continue the traditional Habsburg assault on Calvinism, Lutheranism, Judaism, and Orthodoxy, as well as Islam and the Socinians, especially in Hungary but also in Bohemia, Moravia, Croatia, and in Austria itself.[72] Her *Religionspatent* (1778) reaffirmed a quite remarkable spectrum of restrictions and disabilities on Protestants, Jews, and Orthodox with especially harsh treatment, including flogging, forced labour, and transportation to Transylvania, reserved for Catholic apostates and anyone attempting to convert Catholics to other faiths.[73] Excluding non-Catholics from the administration remained a principal goal of Habsburg policy. Personally deeply unsympathetic to Enlightenment ideals as such, the empress long resisted yielding ground to the principle of toleration. Proposals for an Academy of Sciences at Vienna were shelved at her insistence. She did, however, support the Austrian Jansenist ecclesiastical reform programme and, since some of its goals overlapped with those of the *Aufklärer*, she and the eight Austrian archbishops and thirty-six bishops, all drawn from the high nobility and disposing of immense influence and revenues (only part of which Joseph later aspired to transfer to other uses),[74] were from early on receptive to the kind of Catholic moderate reformism advocated by writers like Muratori and Genovesi. When it came to strengthening parish organization and shifting resources from the regular to the 'secular' clergy, there was a certain convergence of enlightened and Jansenist priorities reaching back to the 1750s. A series of measures promoted by Kaunitz and sanctioned by the empress, culminating in 1772, and implemented in Hungary as well as the core Austrian lands, trimmed ecclesiastical jurisdiction and privilege, reorganized training of priests, placed curbs on the expansion of monastic property and leaving of legacies to the Church, reduced the number of saints' days

[71] Lessing to Eva König, Wolfenbüttel, 1 May 1772, in Lessing, *Gesammelte Werke*, ix. 525.
[72] Evans, 'Maria Theresa', 195; Till, *Mozart*, 125–8; Scott, 'Reform', 167.
[73] Beales, *Joseph II. Against*, 169, 172, 174–5.
[74] Scott, 'Reform', 164, 166–7; Beales, *Enlightenment and Reform*, 20; Evans, 'Maria Theresa', 195–6.

celebrated as public holidays, and reorganized the censorship, removing this from ecclesiastical hands.

Transferring the Austrian censorship from Jesuit hands, as we have seen, followed protests arising from the ban imposed on Montesquieu's *L'Esprit des loix*, in 1753, prompting creation of a state censorship commission under a Dutch Jansenist protégé of Kaunitz, Gerard van Swieten (1700–72). This did not, though, prevent Maria Theresa's reconfigured censorship from remaining uncommonly rigorous. Not just obvious radical works, such as those of Spinoza, Tyssot de Patot, d'Argens, Morelly, and La Mettrie, were banned but so were numerous far less obviously subversive writings including Holberg, La Beaumelle, Hume's *Essays* in German, Bekker (in German), Schmauss, and even Thomasius' *Monats-Gespräche* of 1688.[75] Maria Theresa also espoused a vigorous programme of elementary education, again implemented in Hungary besides the core Austrian lands, that was closely linked to the ecclesiastical reforms and figured eventually among the most striking features of 'Josephism'.[76] The educational reforms, though partly also inspired by enlightened ideas in the minds of a few key officials like Kaunitz, likewise reached back to the 1750s, drawing much momentum from Jansenist efforts to weaken the Jesuit role in society and a perceived need to render popular Catholicism more a faith of inculcated doctrine and points of belief than practices and rituals.

Maria Theresa was readily persuaded of her obligation to provide state-supported Catholic elementary education on a monarchy-wide basis. As the purpose of both ecclesiastical and educational reforms was to extend the state's grip over the population, the measures had the effect of widening and standardizing, not least in the schools, use of Czech, Slovak, Hungarian, and the empire's other vernacular languages, a cultural consequence partially counterbalancing use of German as the language of administration, the army, and high culture.[77] Exclusively using German also—except in Austrian Italy—were the main universities, including Prague, Olomouc, and Lvov, institutions increasingly absorbed into a highly integrated plan to churn out future bureaucrats, and officials to govern the empire. Under Joseph, the crown strove to concentrate higher education in the largest universities, Vienna, Prague, Pavia, and Lvov, and lower the status or close smaller universities like Innsbruck, Brünn, and Cracow and colleges intended solely for nobles like the Vienna Theresianum, founded 1749 but closed by Joseph in 1773. Expanding the main universities, neither Kaunitz nor Joseph desired to stimulate research, debate, or intellectual excellence for their own sake. The point, for them, was strictly pragmatic: to use universities as a tool to centralize the empire and improve its administration. For this, the emperor needed professors and textbooks focused on

---

[75] *Catalogus Librorum Rejectorum* (1754) and Continuatio (1755 and 1757); Trampus, *I Gesuiti*, 18; Israel, *Radical Enlightenment*, 108, 115.

[76] Evans, 'Maria Theresa', 197; Scott, 'Reform', 164, 172, 174–6; Beales, *Enlightenment and Reform*, 20, 22–3.

[77] Evans, 'Joseph II and Nationality', 210–11.

expounding and inculcating social, moral, and economic approaches approved by the crown.[78]

The differences in outlook between Maria Theresa and Joseph were great. Nevertheless, one must avoid exaggerating, as has often happened in the past, the extent to which Joseph actually differed from his mother in being an 'enlightened' ruler inspired by Enlightenment ideas. Except for Spain, Portugal, and the Papal States, nowhere else in Europe did there exist a monarchy where prevailing social norms and culture contrasted more strikingly with Enlightenment goals and values—moderate or radical—than the Habsburg monarchy. Prior to Joseph, Austria's administration and institutions continued to be suffused with Catholic Counter-Reformation longer and more unrelentingly than anywhere else on the Continent outside the Iberian peninsula. By 1765, Austria's ruling house had been focused on reinforcing ecclesiastical direction of society, supremacy of theology in education, censorship of reading, and fomenting neo-scholastic anti-intellectualism, anti-Protestantism, and anti-Semitism besides antagonism to all forms of libertinism, for two centuries. Vienna, according to Pilati in 1774, remained Europe's very headquarters of intellectual backwardness and obscurantism, a capital where the lists of forbidden literature were 'more extensive' than in Rome.[79] Another detractor, Wekhrlin, looked back on Vienna in the empress's last years (he lived there in 1766–76) as truly Rome's rival as the European capital least willing to accept 'new truths' and discoveries.[80]

Yet, successive military defeats, in the War of the Austrian Succession (1740–8) and Seven Years War (1756–63), lent a sense of urgency to pressure for reform among the higher echelons of the court bureaucracy and army further intensified by a growing realization that Austria and Bohemia, like Bavaria and the rest of Catholic Germany, were failing to match Protestant Europe's economic and technical progress. Such anxieties induced a psychological and administrative atmosphere in which an unusually vigorous and reform-minded emperor could push through a string of far-reaching changes quickly.[81] But officials and Enlightenment writers aspiring to influence the process had to adapt their proposals and ideas to the requirements and realities of an expanding Catholic and militarist absolutist imperial state,[82] pressures generating a fundamental antithesis between Radical Enlightenment and 'Josephinism' which came to be sharply voiced before, as well as more widely after, 1789.

In the 1760s and 1770s, Van Swieten personally listed hundreds of works as 'damnatur' in his register of prohibited titles. Joseph urged greater freedom of the press; but it was never his intention to permit the free circulation of Enlightenment literature. The real battle in the 1760s and 1770s was over whether a reforming moderate Enlightenment should be allowed. For several years from 1767, Cardinal-Archbishop Christoph Anton von Migazzi, a stern Jansenist and admirer of Muratori, led a briefly successful even if ultimately defeated campaign to block the

---

[78] Woolf, *History of Italy*, 103; Trampus, *I Gesuiti*, 80, 109. [79] Pilati, *Lettere*, 23.
[80] Wekhrlin, *Graue Ungeheuer*, 1 (1784), 329–30; Böhm, *Ludwig Wekhrlin*, 19, 23; Wilke, 'Spion', 325.
[81] Scott, 'Reform', 150. [82] Bernard, *Limits*, 3.

progress of a wider moderate Enlightenment and, especially, stifle *Der Mann ohne Vorurtheil* [The Man without Prejudice], edited by Joseph von Sonnenfels (1732–1817), a journal designed to inculcate the habit of reading good German prose and spreading enlightened ideas among the Viennese middle class, on the ground the journal was tolerationist, 'irreligious', and harmful to church authority.[83] Sonnenfels tentatively attacked prevailing 'prejudices' much like other enlightened authors while also insisting that prejudices strengthening religion, monarchy, and a state's capacity for war are essentially good.[84] Defended by Kaunitz who, like Joseph and others, pointed out the drawbacks of strong censorship, Sonnenfels fought on tenaciously.[85] It was not before 1780, however, that Kaunitz and Joseph could finally introduce a markedly more liberal press regime, though even then all deistic and naturalistic literature, including Voltaire, as well as materialism remained strictly prohibited.

Sonnenfels, converted son of a Moravian rabbi from Nikolsburg and a formidable Hebraist who became professor of politics (*Polizei- und Cameral-Wissenschaften*) at Vienna university in 1763, was for several decades the leading Enlightenment spokesman in the Austrian capital and, generally, the guiding figure in the development of mainstream Enlightenment attitudes in Austria and the Czech lands. He was unyielding in defence of aristocracy, monarchy, ecclesiastical authority, and censorship, and in his hostility to radical ideas. He praised Hume's notion of society as a social pyramid and Montesquieu for demonstrating the interdependence of monarchy with aristocracy and a society of orders, maintaining that 'man beklagt sich unbillig über die Ungleichheit der Stände' [one complains unjustly about the inequality of classes].[86] But this still left scope for a wide-ranging reform agenda. His *Politische Abhandlungen* (Vienna, 1777) was a key work less for theoretical innovation than its passionate advocacy of the need for a proper balance between the different social orders, demonstrating the wide gap between a balanced ideal of social hierarchy headed by aristocracy, on the one hand, and, on the other, permitting privileged elites to engross an excessive portion of society's wealth and resources.

While every citizen's duty is to submit to the position in society to which he was born, for Sonnenfels, Johann von Justi (1720–71), a writer and official who served enlightened despotism in both Vienna and Berlin, and Karl Anton von Martini (1726–1800), another key academic inspirer of governmental reforms, it is equally every citizen's right to further his own prosperity and interests within the limits set by his status and social position; and the state's duty to assist this process.[87] Like Justi and Martini, Sonnenfels was a champion of status, inequality, aristocracy, and subordinating morality to the clergy. He roundly denounced Bayle for claiming a society of atheists could be viable.[88] But he opposed what he saw as 'excessive

---

[83] Trampus, *I Gesuiti*, 159, 280; Beales, *Enlightenment and Reform*, 216.
[84] Sonnenfels, *Der Mann ohne Vorurtheil*, 3 (1773), A2–7.
[85] Kann, *A Study*, 185, 187; Szabo, *Kaunitz*, 187–8.
[86] Sonnenfels, *Politische Abhandlungen*, 122–3.
[87] Ibid. 91–2; Tribe, 'Cameralism', 539–40.   [88] Sonnenfels, *Der Mann ohne Vorurtheil*, 6: 48–57.

inequality'. Privileged elites, like the nobility and clergy, rightfully preside over society, its resources, and goals. But they do not possess the right to do this to the extent some among them might deem appropriate and it is the enlightened ruler's duty not just to subordinate society to aristocracy and the Church and fight irreligion but also curb the excessive aspirations of nobles and clergy, in the latter case including their usurped 'right' to grant ecclesiastical sanctuary to wrongdoers. The privileged elites should be strongly supported but also kept in bounds in the interests of what Sonnenfels deemed a healthy social balance under monarchy.[89]

Under his social theory, which stood closer to German cameralism, especially Justi, than the economic theories of the French *économistes*, it followed that the nearer to the monarch a given social elite found itself the more restricted in size it should be. It was the monarch's responsibility to ensure that the nobility did not grow by much and also that privileged strata while rightfully differentiating themselves from others with appropriate grandeur did not become excessively grand.[90] Among the middle strata of Viennese society he detected an unhealthy thirst for noble status that he thought (despite his own elevation by the empress to the status of 'baron') needed curbing. Upward social mobility rulers should discourage. Equally, monarchs needed to check the clergy's growth and the growth of its property, ensuring the Church focused on disciplining the laity without acquiring too many possessions.[91] In the same spirit, he warned against excessive growth of learning, erudition, and the arts, the ruler's duty being to prevent the emergence of too many colleges and academies as also too many theatres and artists. The good ruler strives to maximize population levels as much as possible while furthering the prosperity of society as a whole.[92] Sonnenfels regularly stressed the role of divine providence in fixing social and demographic realities, maintaining that the European colonial empires outside Europe no less than the Habsburg monarchy in central Europe formed parts of the divine scheme and were specially ordered by the divine will.[93]

A general re-codification of law and reorganization of the administration and state finances were urgently needed, urged Sonnenfels and his backers, not just to integrate the empire's disparate regions but to promote the *Algemeine Wohlfahrt* ['general welfare'] of the population, an emphasis lending his theories a decided economic thrust. Promoting the 'general welfare', for Sonnenfels, included promoting prosperity and economic efficiency, an aspect of his doctrine Joseph took particularly seriously.[94] Promoting Enlightenment in Austria-Bohemia-Hungary, though, proved arduous and between 1765 and 1780 involved a constant tussle of wills between Joseph and his mother.[95] While there were points where their intentions

[89] Ibid. 4 (1773), 30–8; Sonnenfels, *Politische Abhandlungen*, 92, 101.
[90] Sonnenfels, *Politische Abhandlungen*, 101–3, 107–8, 126–7.
[91] Ibid. 135–7, 143–4.
[92] Ibid. 94–5, 99, 123.
[93] Ibid. 96–9.
[94] Tribe, 'Cameralism', 543; Sonnenfels, *Politische Abhandlungen*, 91, 164.
[95] Beales, *Enlightenment and Reform*, 182–6.

and aspirations converged, most notably in their common receptiveness to Muratori's plea for a simplified, rationalized, more socially and practically engaged Catholicism shorn of superfluous popular 'superstition',[96] there was far more that divided them. If both sought to damp down upsurges of popular fervour like Johann Joseph Gassner's astoundingly successful exorcist movement in southern Germany, the empress and her son acting together to engineer Gassner's expulsion from Regensburg in 1775, their disagreements were yet more striking.[97] Between 1765 and 1780 every step forward required unrelenting pressure on the empress and her advisers from enlightened officials and reformers backed by Joseph.

Despite his Jewish birth, Sonnenfels emerged as a highly influential intellectual and cultural guiding figure in the Austria of the 1770s but exclusively as the mouthpiece of a moderate Enlightenment entrenched at court and firmly allied to enlightened despotism. The Theresian code revising and regulating judicial procedure in criminal cases, the *Constitutio Criminalis Maria Theresiana*, issued in 1769, originally made few concessions to Beccaria or any enlightened ideas, indeed endorsed the use of judicial torture, including, Kaunitz noted scornfully, in cases of 'witchcraft'. State centralization and cutting back local and customary justice was the code's aim rather than any programme of enlightened reform. Severely criticized in the press and his lectures by Sonnenfels, the code underwent revision in stages. Yet however deferential to authority and the Church, significant reforms including the abolition of judicial torture in Austria, in December 1775, were achieved by dint of tenacious lobbying, though the simultaneous campaign to persuade Maria Theresa to abolish the death penalty failed, this measure being implemented only later.[98] The greater part of the work of demolishing local customary and traditional law and eliminating noble privilege from the penal law had to wait until Joseph's accession to the throne.

Carrying forward the rationalization, standardization, and simplification of justice culminated in Joseph's *Allgemeine Gerichtsordnung* of 1781. Sonnenfels, while acknowledging that much of the inspiration for reforming the penal code emanated from Montesquieu and Beccaria, needed, being heavily dependent on Kaunitz's and Joseph's backing (and bitterly criticized by church leaders), to take particular care to assure court, nobility, army leadership, and bureaucracy that in promoting an agenda influenced by such writers, he and his disciples were by no means motivated by 'philosophy' or any equalizing considerations but were exclusively concerned to promote the welfare of the state, administration, army, good morals, and religion.[99] Stripped of control of theatre censorship in 1770, but shielded by Kaunitz from the archbishop's further attempts to bridle him, Sonnenfels continued propagating a broad programme of administrative, legal, and economic reformism from within the university especially among higher officialdom.[100]

[96] Scott, 'Reform', 162–3; Till, *Mozart*, 126–7, 167.   [97] Middelfort, *Exorcism*, 44–50.
[98] Bernard, *Limits*, 14–15; Vocelka, 'Enlightenment', 199–200.
[99] Sonnenfels, *Über die Abschaffung*, 91, 102; Kann, *A Study*, 185–8.
[100] Szabo, *Kaunitz*, 186–8; Lessing, *Gesammelte Werke*, ix. 391; Tribe, 'Cameralism', 543–5.

For a time, Joseph's reformism earned him the unstinting support of radical thinkers no less than that of zealous advocates of enlightened despotism like Sonnenfels. In the late 1770s and early 1780s, Diderot, Raynal, and many others entertained high hopes of the emperor.[101] Herder too initially expected much. Only after the emperor's catastrophic failures, late in his reign, added to his earlier disillusionments with Frederick and Catherine, did Herder become entirely disgusted with all 'enlightened despotism'.[102] Until 1790, out-and-out radical publicists like Weishaupt, Wekhrlin, Paape, and many others, besides quieter, more discreet exponents of radical ideas like Dohm, though often highly critical of some aspects, continued supporting 'Josephism' even while abjuring 'enlightened despotism' more broadly. For them, Joseph remained, as Dohm put it, 'one of the noblest benefactors of mankind ever to have sat on a throne'.[103] By 1790, however, his reform plans had manifestly failed and, in retrospect, looked bound to fail, averred the radical-minded jurist Knoblauch, not having been well thought out or formulated and being vitiated by Joseph's 'pride, avarice and impulse to despotism, the three chief defects of his character'.[104] Worst of all was his self-destructive militarism and rivalry with Prussia together, in Mirabeau's view, with his failure sufficiently to prune back ecclesiastical power and privilege. Meanwhile, many 'moderate' enlighteners, especially in the Austrian Netherlands and Hungary where practically all the enlightened were nobles, staunchly opposed all and any whittling down of noble privilege, fiscal exemptions, or serfdom. Their estrangement from Joseph had already set in much earlier, from around 1784–5.[105]

Joseph's approach, while partly shaped by and sometimes formulated in terms of Enlightenment ideas, and readily dressed up by officials to look 'enlightened', was not really that of either wing of the Enlightenment properly understood. The more closely one scrutinized his reforms, the plainer were the contradictions and less evident any coherent conception. Scholars anxious to downplay the role of Enlightenment ideas might well infer that books had scant effect on Joseph.[106] But while he was basically uninterested in metaphysical questions so were many *Aufklärer*, and Joseph undoubtedly was familiar with the writings of Martini, Sonnenfels, and the physiocrats.[107] If he avoided meeting Voltaire in 1777, his readiness to dine with Raynal at Spa in 1781 was widely publicized and greatly offended many clergy in the southern Netherlands. If personally far less interested in French thought than Frederick or Catherine, unlike them, he had 'correct ideas', averred Dohm, 'of the rights of peoples'.[108] 'The progress of the reformation in Austria happening before our eyes', enlighteners assumed, 'is obviously an effect of philosophy', as Wekhrlin

[101] Mortier, *Le Cœur*, 234.   [102] Barnard, *Herder's Social and Political Thought*, 59, 72–3.
[103] Dohm, *Denkwürdigkeiten*, ii. 244.
[104] [Knoblauch], *Taschenbuch*, 8–9, 20–1; Mirabeau, *De la monarchie*, i. 361–4.
[105] Evans, 'Maria Theresa', 205.
[106] Beales, *Enlightenment and Reform*, 117; Beales, 'Was Joseph II an Enlightened Despot?', 11.
[107] Dohm, *Denkwürdigkeiten*, ii. 244–6; Kann, *A Study*, 184–5.
[108] Dohm, *Denkwürdigkeiten*, ii. 244; Altmann, *Moses Mendelssohn*, 452.

put it, 'and belongs only in the history of the latter'.[109] Joseph eschewed metaphysics; yet enlighteners were not wrong to construe his work as 'philosophy' in action. Only 'philosophy' in action could have produced a comprehensive package of far-reaching reform amid such a densely tangled mass of tradition, privilege, and overlapping jurisdiction as the Habsburg monarchy. The contradictions lay rather in the social context and kind of 'philosophy' he embraced.

Joseph brought a formidable array of 'enlightened' officials, professors, and ministers to the fore. Yet, the monarchy continued to be governed primarily by the high aristocracy, like the Kaunitz with their core lands in Moravia, the Liechtenstein, Lobkowitz, Kinsky, Waldstein, Esterhazy, and the rest, and this inevitably imposed appreciable constraints on what could be accomplished in administration, education, the army, or the Church. A few dozen great families directly owned roughly one third of the monarchy, headed in Bohemia by fifty-one princely families and seventy-nine counts. In Hungary, the Esterhazy owned approximately ten million acres, including forty small towns and thirty palaces or castles not to mention hundreds of villages. If the *Hochadel* [high nobility] predominated at court, at local level, the peasantry was notoriously defenceless throughout the monarchy in the face of the many hundreds of lesser lords and their agents. Money dues, labour dues, legal subjection, and formal inferiority inescapably shaped the lives of the rural population. Except in a few Alpine regions, social, economic, and legal subjection to the landowning elite so pervaded at every level that noble privilege can fairly be said to have been, alongside Catholicism, the empire's overriding principle.

Buoyed by his sense of justice and 'philosophy', the emperor ventured into uncharted waters. He tried to abolish the centuries-old and widely onerous institution of serfdom in stages, with heroic tenacity proceeding well beyond the series of piecemeal marginal decrees designed to restrain noble oppression instigated by Kaunitz and promulgated over the previous fifteen years, limited, piecemeal measures like the Silesian *robot* patent of 1768, following an armed rising in Austrian Silesia in 1767—and which merely stipulated how labour services were to be exacted without limiting them—and the Bohemian patent, following the peasant rising of 1775, restricting labour services to three days per week.[110] Yet here again, partly in response to further peasant unrest, change came chiefly due to Joseph's being convinced, as were some of the great Bohemian lords, that serfdom was simply not an efficient labour system. It was never his intention, at any stage, to attack noble privilege or noble dominance of society, administration, and the military as such. Rather, in seeking to subordinate the nobility's interests to those of the state overall, he strove to curb its despotic sway over the peasantry by encouraging voluntary commutation of labour dues into money rents, much as he also did by introducing strands of egalitarianism into the penal code.[111]

---

[109] Wekhrlin, *Graue Ungeheuer*, 6 (1786), 157; Beales, *Enlightenment and Reform*, 74.
[110] Wekhrlin, *Graue Ungeheuer*, 6 (1786), 165–6; Van Horn Melton, 'Nobility', 198.
[111] Beales, *Joseph II. Against*, 469, 486.

Joseph's unparalleled efforts to combat serfdom and prune back noble power and privilege made it impossible for the Radical Enlightenment not to eulogize his rule for a time. First, in 1781, serfdom attached to persons, or *Leibeigenschaft*, requiring the lord's permission for serfs who wished to move, marry, or leave the land, was abolished in Bohemia, Moravia, and Austrian Silesia, in the face of vehement noble opposition, abolition extending the following year to Austria and, in 1785, to Hungary where the nobility was even more hostile. Other measures restricted the lords' rights of jurisdiction and power to regulate peasant inheritances, marriages, and movements. The legal rights of lords to exact forced labour remained in force until 1789 when these were abolished in theory, but replaced by monetary exactions specified by the crown, leaving the nobility's agrarian and social superiority still largely intact. Some progress towards eradicating the most onerous and degrading aspects of serfdom and enhancing freedom of movement was achieved but many nobles successfully continued obstructing emancipation and exacting labour dues in the old manner down to 1848.[112] The peasantry's subservience to nobility and Church remained fundamentally unchanged in many areas owing to tenacious resistance and the ultimately limited character of Joseph's goals in reforming the nobility.

The Habsburg monarchy, 'Josephism' notwithstanding, remained a land of social hierarchy based on monarchy, nobility, and ecclesiastical privilege, though not all social structures bequeathed by the past proved equally resilient. In the urban economic sphere change proved easier to accomplish. Combining the recommendations of French physiocracy with cameralism, Joseph removed many local internal road and river tolls and regulations and demolished much of the guild structure, establishing free trade within the empire which operated alongside an imperial tariff wall around her borders. In 1784, a general barrier involving heavy tariffs designed to shut out foreign manufactures was established around the core Habsburg lands with the explicit aim of stimulating industries at Vienna—an architecturally imposing, fast-growing metropolis of 180,000 inhabitants at this time—and in Bohemia and Moravia, and met with some success.

Besides aristocratic and ecclesiastical privilege, further basic limitations on the progress of the Austrian Enlightenment lay in Joseph's proneness to view everything from the perspective of the state and little from that of the individual. Abolishing the death penalty (in practice though not in name), the new Austrian code substituted not just rigorous penal labour and harsh imprisonment but degrading penalties supposedly for the public benefit which the emperor demanded from the outset, penalties criticized as inhuman, even 'atrocious', by radical critics in the later 1780s. Brissot was among those appalled by stories of huge gangs of chained prisoners put to work dragging barges up stretches of the Danube against the current, penal forced labour so harsh practically all those assigned to these work-gangs reportedly died in under a year, among them Count Podstatsky-Liechtenstein who, after gambling

---

[112] Van Horn Melton, 'Nobility', 198; Doyle, *Old European Order*, 101–2.

away his inheritance, had forged banknotes.[113] This new system of forced labour devised by the emperor allegedly in the public interest, far from being a concession to Beccaria was really just another form of death penalty, only a slow death by overwork and undernourishment. Especially deplorable, held Brissot, was the branding of these criminals on the cheeks. Whatever a person has done, argued radical critics, one should never banish entirely from their hearts the hope of one day returning to society. Otherwise what motive can there be to improve and reform?

Substituting forced labour and imprisonment for the death penalty meant more prisons and guards and a general strengthening of the police service that featured among the most notable changes under Joseph. Kaunitz had taken a close interest in the organization of the Paris police since at least 1770, and from 1780 not only Vienna but also other main cities witnessed a marked expansion of police powers, personnel, and surveillance, and recruiting of informers. Under the command of Count Anton Pergen, earlier involved in the educational reforms, the police became a major factor in central European life.[114] Eager to curb corruption and render the bureaucracy more responsive to his requirements and those of the army, Joseph set secret police spies to work reporting on what bureaucrats were doing at every level of the administration. One effect of this expansion of police activity, noted Wekhrlin, was that in Vienna prostitutes soliciting men became subject to a degree of harassment and frequency of imprisonment never witnessed before. This campaign, highly unusual in Enlightenment Europe, was linked not just to the Jansenist and Muratorian roots of Maria Theresa's and Joseph's reforms but possibly also the emperor's suspected venereal disease. In 1784 followed renewal of older regulations closing the city's brothels, an enactment rigorously enforced.[115] Reform was perhaps needed in this sphere too, commented Wekhrlin, who applauded most of Joseph's policies, but the police drive against Vienna's 'nymphs of the night is too inhuman'.[116] Joseph's police proved unbending also in other respects, acquiring a splendid reputation among noblemen for disciplining impertinent or insufficiently deferential coachmen and servants. The state was assuming the role of enforcing unquestioning deference to the nobility and the Church's rigid sexual code.

Joseph's famous *Toleration Edict* (1781), severely criticized in conservative Catholic circles in Austria and Bohemia and in the Austrian Netherlands, was another measure bound to be greeted enthusiastically by the enlightened. Yet, not just to the radically inclined but also to moderate enlighteners and spokesmen for Austria's religious minorities, it seemed disturbingly grudging and restrictive. Radical thinkers conceived of toleration as more than just incorporating the main Protestant churches and Orthodox into society at the level of private worship, or removing the harshest

---

[113] [Brissot], *Lettre à l'Empereur*, 10, 13; Kann, *A Study*, 189; Beales, *Joseph II. Against*, 551; Bernard, *Limits*, 15, 18–19, 32–4, 47.

[114] Bernard, *Limits*, 26–30; Beales, *Enlightenment and Reform*, 22, 138, 213.

[115] Hull, *Sexuality, State*, 258; Bernard, *Limits*, 40, 45.

[116] Wekhrlin, *Graue Ungeheuer*, 10 (1787), 83–6; Mondot, *Wilhelm Ludwig Wekhrlin*, i. 406–9.

restrictions from the Jews of which, Dohm and others estimated, there were around half a million in the monarchy. To dismantle Jewish disabilities a whole series of additional edicts abolishing or changing all manner of long-standing regulations varyingly in force all over the empire had to be adopted, the edict for the Bohemian Jews appearing in November 1781 and for Hungarian Jews in March 1783. In Vienna, the atmosphere under Joseph, as afterwards, was by no means especially tolerant, however. Although the old ghetto restrictions were abolished under the edict on the Jews of Lower Austria, of January 1782, for which Sonnenfels was partly responsible, and Jews could now live anywhere in the city, restrictions on their numbers continued and they were permitted only small synagogues concealed from the street, inside private homes.[117]

Freeing the Jews, Dohm remarked, was far too contrary to the deeply prejudiced attitude of most people to be implemented without countless opponents and critics raising an outcry. In many places it could not be implemented without allowing the Jews entry into areas of economic activity, crafts, and retailing from which they had previously always been excluded, hence at the expense of Christian neighbours, a 'disadvantage' the emperor only belatedly grasped and subsequently tried to counter by reintroducing disabilities of various kinds. Above all, it was never Joseph's intention to increase the number of Jews in Vienna or the monarchy as a whole by encouraging Jewish migration from elsewhere.[118] Thus his own legislation obliged him to introduce fresh restrictions forbidding Jews without special permission living in places they had not lived in before. Even where they had dwelt in sizeable numbers for centuries some of the special taxes and occupational restrictions applying to Jews specifically remained or were reinstated. Yet, despite all the defects and inconsistencies of the legislation, Joseph treated the Jews, as Dohm put it, 'as the Jews had thus far never been treated in any Christian state'.[119] He created a model for emancipating the Jews, followed as yet nowhere else, introducing a change which, in Dohm's view, needed to be adopted everywhere.[120]

Toleration undoubtedly had a huge impact on central Europe, especially in Vienna, Trieste, Hungary, Bohemia-Moravia, where crypto-Protestantism among the serfs was by no means entirely dead, and Galicia, regions with substantial numbers of Calvinists, Lutherans, Jews, and Orthodox. But it also established new forms of religious hierarchy. Protestant and orthodox churches were not permitted to acquire handsome façades, spires, or entrances facing directly on the street.[121] In the Czech lands fringe Protestant sects remained excluded altogether from the terms of the *Toleranzpatent*, Socinianism continuing to be persecuted and the so-called 'Bohemian deists' and Bohemian Brethren to be repressed as before. No sectarian

---

[117] Scott, 'Reform', 170; Heinrich, 'Debatte', 830.

[118] Heinrich, 'Debatte', 264–5; Beales, *Joseph II. Against*, 203–7.

[119] Heinrich, 'Debatte', 261–2; Altmann, *Moses Mendelssohn*, 452; Sorkin, *Religious Enlightenment*, 197, 237.

[120] Dohm, *Denkwürdigkeiten*, ii. 265.

[121] Teich, 'Bohemia', 144–5; Vocelka, 'Enlightenment', 202–3; Hebeis, *Karl Anton von Martini*, 79.

creeds descending from the Hussite or other movements were allowed; non-Catholic Christians had to choose between Lutheranism or Calvinism. As 'philosophical' critics objected, this was hardly comprehensive toleration in the sense of instituting genuine freedom of thought, belief, and practice, especially as controls on expression remained stringent. Atheism remained a serious crime and the works of materialist *philosophes* rigorously banned.[122]

Indeed, keeping religious minorities in their place and enforcing book censorship gained new impetus from the strengthening of the police. It was not toleration, observed Wekhrlin, in 1785, that explained the recent influx of Protestant skilled artisans, professionals, and booksellers to Vienna, but backwardness of the crafts and the ingrained 'idleness' of the Viennese. If some easing of book censorship for serious academic and critical works ensued, curbs remained extensive and were better enforced than earlier. So remote was Joseph from proclaiming an 'unrestricted press freedom', the new rigour fomented a rapidly growing, well-organized traffic in forbidden books.[123] Sonnenfels himself later joined the state censorship commission which might be construed as a sign of growing liberalization. Certainly his membership of the Illuminati reminds us of the need to differentiate between the court official and Sonnenfels's private views. Yet he seems to have fully accepted the need for strict political, moral, and religious controls and state support for the supremacy of the Catholic Church. The marked puritanical streak in his and Joseph's outlook ensured the continued prohibition of libertine as well as irreligious and politically subversive publications.

In the Austria, Bohemia, and Hungary of the 1780s, lands where confessional thinking, prejudice, and discrimination were deeply ingrained at all levels, genuine toleration was not really possible without a long period of preparation. However broadly framed, any toleration edict could only have been implemented in a grudging, mutilated, and perverted fashion, especially outside Vienna.[124] Nor was a full toleration the emperor's aim. Throughout his life and reign Joseph remained quite devout. In the ecclesiastical sphere his goal was to purify and strengthen the Church's sway, despite signs of lack of sympathy for Jansenism which in Habsburg lands reached the zenith of its prestige around the end of Maria Theresa's reign but rapidly lost ground thereafter.[125] The by the 1770s fairly noticeable advance of scepticism and irreligion among sections of the nobility and the Vienna urban elite was not something Joseph contemplated with favour. It was his purpose neither to weaken the hold of the Catholic Church over the population, nor preside over an unbelieving court. Rather, his aim was to reform the Church and render it more effective by lessening the role of the contemplative orders and switching resources to active

[122] Dohm, *Denkwürdigkeiten*, ii. 255–8; Beales, *Joseph II. Against*, 191.
[123] Wekhrlin, *Graue Ungeheuer*, 5 (1785), 148, 188; Beales, *Joseph II. Against*, 90–1.
[124] Dohm, *Denkwürdigkeiten*, ii. 248, 255–6, 258; Mirabeau, *De la monarchie*, i. 361, 364.
[125] Ward, 'Late Jansenism', 180–2.

pastoral work, and also building on the already substantial universal Catholic primary education established by the general school ordinance, or *Algemeine Schulordnung*, of 1774.[126] Many interpreted his actions as an attack on the Church, and there was fierce opposition from among some clergy. But Catholicism's dominant role in Austrian society was vigorously remodelled rather than reduced.

Joseph undertook the most drastic, far-reaching monastic reforms attempted in *ancien régime* Europe, suppressing around a third of all the male and female cloisters in the Habsburg lands. He 'secularized' their resources, transferring their revenues to support new parishes serviced by curates who were often former regular clergy, created three new bishoprics, and both raised the number and improved the standards of seminaries training priests. Following Sonnenfels and Von Martini, the ecclesiastical commission created in 1782 to carry out these changes targeted only monasteries performing no obvious social function whether of a welfare or educational character.[127] Over 700 monasteries and priories were closed, setting in motion one of the greatest social and cultural shifts of late eighteenth-century Europe. The regular clergy fell from a level of around 53 per cent of all ecclesiastics in the core Austrian lands to only 29 per cent by 1790.[128] The result was a substantial lowering of the ratio of parishioners to parish priests, in Bohemia from 903 to 791, the total number of secular priests in the core Austrian lands rising from 22,000 to 27,000.[129] There was a steep drop in numbers of nuns. In short, greater resources were now allocated to the laity's spiritual direction rather than less.

Joseph differed less in outlook from his younger brother and successor Leopold, who ruled as grand duke of Tuscany from 1765 until 1790, when he, in turn, became Austrian emperor, than has sometimes been supposed. Familiar with the work of the Verri brothers and Beccaria in Austrian Milan, and an admirer of the French *économistes*, Leopold too was committed to comprehensive change on the basis of enlightened ideas, and in a few cases he may have been the more enlightened. Leopold's new criminal code, introduced in 1786, abolishing both judicial torture and the death penalty, was noticeably influenced in its key provisions by Beccaria.[130] More generally, though, much the same qualifications apply here as with Joseph. Leopold's attitudes were rooted in a modified Jansenism more than the Enlightenment, and while occasionally Jansenists and *Aufklärer* saw eye to eye, 'at bottom, their premises were different'.[131] Beyond Jansenist ideas on reforming and strengthening the Church, it was especially the ideas of the French *économistes* and German cameralists that appealed to these Habsburg rulers. During the 1770s and 1780s a considerable number of Tuscan and Milanese monasteries, deemed superfluous by

[126] Dickson, 'Joseph II', 97.

[127] Hebeis, *Karl Anton von Martini*, 77; Beales, *Prosperity and Plunder*, 193.

[128] Beales, *Prosperity and Plunder*, 194–5; Beales, *Enlightenment and Reform*, 248–50; Dickson, 'Joseph II', 98–101.

[129] Dickson, 'Joseph II', 103–6; Beales, *Prosperity and Plunder*, 194; Sorkin, *Religious Enlightenment*, 237–8.

[130] Anderson, 'Italian Reformers', 66.   [131] Ward, 'Late Jansenism', 177.

the court, were suppressed. The grain trade was freed from restrictions, from 1767, and the Florentine guilds abolished in 1779, both measures designed to free trade from local and internal hindrances.

In Habsburg Tuscany, as in Milan, there was no real freedom of thought or comprehensive toleration. While Leopold received the applause of leading spokesmen of the Italian moderate Enlightenment, like Piettro Verri and Beccaria, from the moment he became grand duke of Tuscany he promoted Jansenists to chairs in theological faculties and bishoprics and backed their programmes and publications. If he permitted publication of some Enlightenment works, in general he was more interested in reorganizing and extending Catholic elementary education and reforming parish administration and the spiritual direction of the laity, eradicating superstitious practices and credulous legends from sermons, liturgy, breviaries, and so forth, than in secularizing education and society.[132]

But the greatest and most damning criticism of Joseph and Josephism from within the central European Radical Enlightenment was that the emperor ultimately undermined his own reformism, sacrificing his efforts to improve Austria's internal 'economy', society, and organization through his unrelenting rivalry with Prussia and obsessive militarism. By building up his armies, seeking alliances, seeking to expand his territory, and preparing for war, Joseph exhausted the empire's treasure, threw his territories into turmoil, and blighted his own achievements; or, as Wekhrlin put it, metaphorically Joseph 'lost Silesia twice'.[133]

4. MUSIC, LITERATURE, AND THE FINE ARTS

Besides issues of power, constitutionality and law, and militarism and war, enlightened despotism also raised far-reaching questions concerning the arts and cultural development. In an age in which music, opera, painting, architecture, and theatre all took on an astounding new breadth and vitality, and noticeably began to widen their involvement with the realities of contemporary society, as well as receive growing support from connoisseurs and enthusiasts at different levels of society, especially among the professional and administrative elites, students, and the nobility, the relationships of the arts to national attitudes, social questions, moral issues, politics, and religion were all becoming increasingly important.

'Enlightened despotism' tended to steer expanding artistic and musical activity, however, increasingly towards the court and also major noble residences such as the palace of Prince Nicholas Esterhazy, at Eisenstadt, in western Hungary, where Haydn, dressed in his prince's livery, routinely conducted concerts on days and at times fixed for him, and from where, as a household official, he needed princely permission to

---

[132] Ward, 'Late Jansenism', 177–9.   [133] Wekhrlin, *Graue Ungeheuer*, 11 (1787), 174–7.

travel. Court direction, as some saw it, seriously distorted music's, opera's, and literature's relationship to the wider public. Equally, enlightened despotism could be regarded as having a broadly negative effect on the sciences, since under its sway everything was directed towards court priorities and state institutions, depriving men of learning, no less than great artists, of the independence and freedom of research devoted to science for science's sake, essential to the progress of their endeavours in a more balanced, truer, more fundamental way.[134]

Enlightened despotism magnificently fostered the arts but simultaneously had a distorting, alienating effect on high culture as the despot's personal taste and political priorities inevitably determined the direction of cultural policy. In Anhalt-Dessau, architecture, gardens, and design had to be in the English style; in Gotha, French. In Weimar, under Goethe's supervision, a severe classicism harking back to antiquity, and later Italian models, prevailed. At Petersburg, it was especially colossal architecture signalling imperial grandeur that set the tone and for this purpose Catherine preferred neoclassicist rationality and calm orderliness, a tendency marking her era off sharply, architecturally as in other respects, from the previous four decades in Russia.

'Enlightened' cultural policy in Catherine's case was less a matter of redirecting trends within the country than superimposing, from above, something largely alien to Russia's past. Petersburg especially was transformed by a 'storm' of large-scale construction work. While several Russians trained abroad were employed both by her, and the Russian high nobility, as architects, the general tone was set by Frenchmen, notably Jean-Baptiste Vallin de La Mothe (1729–1800), the most active importer of French influences into the empire, and especially Italians such as Antonio Rinaldi (*c*.1710–94) and Giacomo Quarenghi (1744–1817), from Bergamo. Quarenghi, a former assistant of Mengs, admirer of Palladio, even greater enthusiast for antiquity than most of the others,[135] and connoisseur of Florence, Verona, Mantua, Vicenza, and Venice, was the greatest architect of her reign. He arrived in Russia in 1780, on Grimm's recommendation, the empress having assured the latter in August 1779 that she preferred Italian architects to the French as they were less 'academic' in approach, the French, knowing too much, she thought, being uninspired.

Neoclassicism, the predominant European architectural style of the period, was adopted in Petersburg in a particular way. First, there was a preponderance of commissions issuing from the court causing an abrupt switch from previous styles; for Catherine disliked the grandeur of Bartolomeo Rastrelli's recently completed Winter Palace and detested the Baroque and Rococo buildings of the recent past in general.[136] She demanded dramatic changes both in architectural style and the scale of operations, commissioning buildings that were astoundingly large for their ostensible purpose, among them the Petersburg Academy of Arts (1765–89), parts

---

[134] D'Holbach, *Politique naturelle*, 241–2; Ferrone, *I profeti*, 179.
[135] Hamilton, *Art and Architecture*, 213–14.   [136] Ibid. 199.

of which were not finished until many years after her death, and Rinaldi's vast, regimented Gatchina Palace (1766–81), fifty kilometres south of Petersburg, originally built for Catherine's favourite Count Grigory Grigorievich Orlov, the man who engineered the coup of 1762 that brought her to the throne (and who arranged her husband's murder). Rinaldi also designed another palace for Orlov, the so-called Marble palace (1768–85), today among the finest older buildings in Petersburg. Such buildings combined impressive size with exterior simplicity conveying a sense of solidity, strength, and imperial grandeur recalling the greatness of the Roman imperium.[137] Also in 1768, plans were drawn up for reconstructing the Moscow Kremlin which, had they been implemented, would have totally erased the whole complex of what today are considered priceless late medieval and sixteenth-century monuments, substituting a vast system of squares and neoclassical palaces, within an immense four-storey façade stretching along the Moscow River. Demolition had already begun and a solemn dedicatory ceremony been held in 1773 when, due to the vast cost of her Turkish war, Catherine cancelled the project. At the ceremony, the architect chiefly responsible, Vasilii Bazhenov (1737–99), a former assistant to Rastrelli, son of an Orthodox priest and a product of the new academy in Petersburg, declared his goal to be to turn Moscow into a new Constantinople, his massive construction to be the acropolis of this third 'Rome', or Tsarograd.

This grandiose imperial impulse within enlightened despotism mostly operated, experience proved, in a different and incompatible direction from that characterizing the most creative, transforming tendencies in society. Enlightened despotism seemed destined always to generate a basic contradiction in the artistic sphere, between court taste and aspirations and the wider cultivated public. Against this, Herder in particular reacted with distaste and impressive insight. Opposing the dominant aristocratic culture of the courts and noble residences, he did more than any other central European Enlightenment writer to foster a sense of language, literature, and poetry, and also art, being the possession and special legacy of peoples, cultural assets that must be nurtured in the interest of those cultural traditions to which they belong.[138]

His critique focused on the cultural policies of the lesser princes, Joseph and especially Frederick. There was no better illustration of what he and also Lessing, so deplored, in the theatre, concert hall, and opera house alike, than Frederick's court. Although the king's liking for recitals and skill on the flute (warmly praised by d'Alembert, in 1763) were legendary, Frederick studiously ignored German theatre and literature, patronizing only composers and musicians cultivating the 'Italian' style, all of whom are totally forgotten today. He studiously ignored all the Bachs, knew practically nothing of Mozart, and scorned the compositions of Haydn.[139] In fact there was no aspect of contemporary music or theatre in the German-speaking world that he supported at any stage of his long reign. Well versed in French literature

---

[137] Hamilton, *Art and Architecture*, 201–5; Brumfield, *History of Russian Architecture*, 262–3.
[138] Herder, *Philosophical Writings*, 322–3; Blanning, *Culture of Power*, 258–61.
[139] Blanning, *Culture of Power*, 216–17.

to a degree that astounded d'Alembert and Helvétius, his contempt for the German language and German philosophy was notorious even before he found it necessary to broadcast his prejudices by slighting the country's language, theatre, and even its greatest writer, Goethe, in his pamphlet *Concerning German Literature* (1780), which he penned in French and had translated by Dohm.

If Frederick scorned German culture, Joseph, ruling the most polyglot monarchy in Europe, patronized German as both an administrative and cultural tool. He played a vigorous role in cultural life, deeming the theatre an important instrument of moral guidance, and initiated or accelerated many new trends in Austrian high culture. Vienna Sonnenfels aspired to make the artistic and educational capital not just of Catholic central Europe but of German high culture generally. To the joy of German writers, if against Kaunitz's Francophile preferences, Joseph strongly supported Sonnenfels's project for replacing French with modern German drama and transforming the Vienna Court Theatre into what became the *Deutsches National-Theater* [German National Theatre].[140] These ideas for a national theatre advanced in the 1770s with the backing of Goethe and also Lessing, who initially rejoiced at the prospect of Sonnenfels achieving in Vienna what he had failed to accomplish in Hamburg.[141] In this way, Vienna emerged as the best, most professional theatrical milieu in central Europe, but also one curiously suspended between the court and public. For a time Lessing hoped to be appointed director there and actively angled for the position, initially, at least, with Sonnenfels's backing. The latter had often praised his plays in the past. But while this was never likely to happen in any case whilst Maria Theresa was empress, as she resisted appointing any Protestant to such a position, Lessing soon came to believe it was especially Sonnenfels himself who, for his own reasons, blocked his appointment. Where Sonnenfels considered Lessing a mere man of letters and himself the leading voice of social, cultural, and economic reform, Lessing, from late 1772, spoke of him only in the bitterest terms, motivated partly by pique but also aversion to what he considered the latter's opportunism and hypocrisy and his turning hopes of a true German cultural capital into what Lessing came to consider a farce.[142]

Joseph and Kaunitz disagreed about theatre, but concurred regarding music. Kaunitz had long been a keen patron of opera and concerts and especially the efforts of Christoph Willibald Gluck (1714–87) since the early 1760s to reform the Vienna opera by integrating music, text, action, and dance along new lines. Gluck was thus a frequent guest at Kaunitz's palace while Kaunitz regularly attended Gluck's performances.[143] From the outset Kaunitz was also an enthusiastic patron of Mozart—who was also personally well acquainted with Sonnenfels and Van Swieten, and who, during his mature years, in Vienna, staged a number of concerts at the great

[140] Lessing, *Gesammelte Werke*, ix. 391–2; Till, *Mozart*, 46–7, 49, 95–6.
[141] Lessing to Eva König, Wolfenbüttel, 25 Oct. 1770, in Lessing, *Gesammelte Werke*, ix. 383.
[142] Ibid. ix. 411, 584–5, 604; Kann, *A Study*, 239–41.
[143] Szabo, *Kaunitz*, 26–8.

nobleman's palace. In the wake of these developments in the 1760s and 1770s, Joseph actively emulated what by the 1770s had become a tradition of staunch encouragement of fine music, theatre, and opera at the Habsburg court. On occasion, Joseph, who had considerable respect for Mozart, would even back his projects to the extent of compromising slightly his otherwise unswerving support for social hierarchy, though theatre and opera censorship remained strict. Having banned Beaumarchais's *Marriage of Figaro* for its unflattering portrayal of aristocratic arrogance, tyranny, and abuse, the emperor also proposed banning Mozart's opera on the same subject, despite both the social criticism and eroticism being here considerably moderated. After a lengthy discussion with the composer at the palace in 1786, in which Mozart insisted it included some of his best music and that nearly everything 'objectionable' had been excised, however, Joseph relented, despite its still plainly being an opera where human worth bears no relation to social station.[144] The emperor permitted the opera first in Vienna and afterwards, no less triumphantly, in Prague, but only after ensuring ticket prices were set so high virtually only nobility could attend the performances.

Mozart figured among those in Joseph's Austria who most loudly railed against aristocratic and episcopal philistinism. He did so in letters to his family expressing the many frustrations of his career at Salzburg and Vienna.[145] Certain aspects of Enlightenment thought seem to have affected him deeply and Mendelssohn's books had a prominent place in his personal library.[146] While it is impossible to know for sure whether his three-month stay in Paris, in 1778, with Grimm and Madame d'Épinay, when he met members of Grimm's circle, probably including Diderot and d'Alembert,[147] in any way influenced his interest in the topic of sexual liberation and other aspects of what some have perceived as a radical edge to his thinking, and while Grimm (who had no understanding whatever of Mozart's character and greatness) afterwards quarrelled with him, it is certain at any rate that his life and music, and in particular several of his operas, reflect core Enlightenment ideals.[148] Clearly, he also remained broadly sympathetic to the aims of both Joseph and Leopold. Resentful at his treatment at the hands of the prince-archbishop of Salzburg, from 1784 he became a keen freemason in a part of Europe where freemasonry was permeated with Illuminism, a movement which, as we shall see, was to a degree a vehicle for radical ideas. Mozart became, at least in a general way, supportive of the ideals of equality, fraternity, and anti-aristocracy, themes central not only to *Così fan tutte* and *Figaro* but also, albeit in a more mystical vein, *Die Zauberflöte* [*The Magic Flute*] of 1791, the year of Mozart's death. To what extent the latter, in which reconciliation among nations and the unity of mankind are prominent themes, is pervaded by Illuminist ideology remains disputed, as does the question of how far its central figure Sarastro is modelled on the leading

---

[144] Beales, *Joseph II. Against*, 166–8; Bramani, *Mozart massone*, 27, 98–101.
[145] Bramani, *Mozart massone*, 24. [146] Ibid. 144–5; Till, *Mozart*, 194, 197.
[147] Bramani, *Mozart massone*, 27, 44, 87. [148] Ibid. 28, 87, 215–16; Till, *Mozart*, 238–9.

Austrian Illuminist Ignaz von Born, who died whilst the work was being composed. But Mozart undoubtedly admired Born and most experts think the opera is in some way linked to Illuminism. The parable of Tamino and Papageno, starting out on their journey blinded by superstition and ignorance but stumbling towards the light guided by the 'Egyptian priests' who provide the moral education they lacked, savours strongly of Born's system and outlook.[149]

Joseph's patronage of the arts had exceptionally fruitful effects in Austria itself. But outside the monarchy's German-speaking areas its consequences were quite different. Here, once again, his reforms raised searching questions about the relationship of enlightened despotism to peoples and their culture: if the 'enlightened despot' sought only to impose his or her own cultural preferences as the cultural policy of the state, he or she was also apt to impose their own preferred language and where several languages were spoken to subordinate the rest to whichever was thus privileged. In the Habsburg monarchy, this meant an increasing subordination of administration, army, Church, higher education, and the arts to the German language. Herder expressly took Joseph to task for defying what he considered manifestly the law of nature. As language is the expression of the character, the 'soul', of a people, to disregard the empire's other languages was tantamount to enslaving and oppressing them unjustly. Rejecting Joseph's approach led Herder to envisage a general shift to nation-states as the way to respect the natural diversity and linguistic variety of peoples.[150]

---

[149] Till, *Mozart*, 123, 281–3; Reinalter, 'Ignaz von Born', 376; Bramani, *Mozart massone*, 73–4, 246.
[150] Barnard, *Herder's Social and Political Thought*, 58–9.

11

Aufklärung and the Fracturing of German Protestant Culture

1. DEISM BESIEGED

For all his bottled-up resentment which occasionally pushed him to express himself in the bitterest terms, Reimarus' repressed indignation at the way mankind are defrauded and exploited by priests never found any public expression during his lifetime. Though acutely conscious of the injustice and irrationality of much of the contemporary world, Reimarus was no foe of physical, social, or racial hierarchies as such, not even colonial subordination or Man's exploitation of animals. Rather his relentless stress on a providential Creator, and on physico-theology, served—as with physico-theology was generally the case—to justify in principle existing political, family, racial, and other forms of social hierarchy, much as with Wollaston and Voltaire. Dividing his thought into rigidly separate public and private realms, on one level he strove for and attained a coherent as well as broadly conceived, all-embracing *Weltanschauung*. Yet, at the same time his physico-theology nurtured within itself a kernel of incoherence that has a special significance for the modern scholar exploring the cultural and intellectual predicament of Germany in the later eighteenth century: the key element of inner discord was the repressive silence Reimarus imposes on himself. The implications of his thought were vast but unspoken and internalized.

Where Johann Lorenz Schmidt hurled himself into public controversy, forcefully as well as publicly lambasting critics of his Wertheim Bible (1735), Reimarus, though privately equally antagonistic to conventional thinking, remained altogether reticent and inactive. Where Schmidt, while living in difficult circumstances at Altona, actively strove to undermine existing religious, intellectual, and moral premises, not least by translating Tindal, Du Marsais, Boulainvilliers, and Spinoza, Reimarus asks in the *Vorbericht* of his manuscript *Apologie* that his lifelong research, something that had cost so much scholarly and emotional effort over many years, should remain concealed from the public view, available only to a few 'understanding friends', as it was contrary to his wishes that the results of his striving should become generally accessible through publication 'bevor sich die Zeiten mehr aufklären' [before the times become more enlightened]. Better the common mass of men should remain steeped in ignorance and error yet awhile than that he, 'even if it was not through his fault that it happened, should antagonize the people, throwing them into a zealous rage, by stating the truth'.[1] All too familiar with the prevailing religious intolerance and what to him was the narrow vindictiveness of Lutheran society, he dreaded the reaction he foresaw, a backlash ruinous to his reputation, peace of mind, and position that would hurl society into turmoil.[2] He shrank above all from being hounded like Stosch, Schmidt, Wachter, Lau, and Edelmann. It was decidedly ironic that Reimarus' clandestine œuvre should in the end prove Lessing's aptest tool for forcing some of the age's most urgent questions out from the shadows.

It is best for the wise man to remain patient under the prevailing superstition, bigotry, and crassness and keep silent rather than that he should make himself and others wretched by declaring 'truths' the public is not yet ready to hear. But how could the age become more 'enlightened' if the most 'enlightened' fail to challenge common errors and prejudices or express their views publicly? Schmidt's, Lessing's, and Herder's view was diametrically opposite to that of Reimarus: if the philosophers 'have treasures', declared Herder in 1765, in a text expressing profound disillusionment with the state of contemporary German philosophy, 'well then, these must become common property; if they do not have them, if they are themselves useless to the state, then let their caves be destroyed and let the night-owls of Minerva be taught to look at the sun'.[3] Having proved himself a brilliant teacher, since 1762, at the Collegium Friedericianum in Königsberg and then latterly at Riga, and immersed himself in the literary critical writings of Lessing which exerted a powerful influence on him at this time,[4] Herder by 1765 had developed a marked aversion toward traditional academic culture and attitudes and a certain resentment also towards his prime mentor, Kant. From this, arose an ingrained antagonism to all easy, conventional Enlightenment and especially that of Montesquieu and Voltaire. Under Kant's stimulus, he had studied Rousseau and come to share Rousseau's idea that civilized mankind was in a thoroughly disordered and corrupted condition. But he did not agree with Kant's response.

The only viable remedy, urged Herder, was fundamental reform of philosophy and its functioning in the public space. 'Only philosophy can be an antidote for all the evil into which philosophical curiosity has plunged us.'[5] But then 'philosophy' has to do its proper job. From an early stage, Herder grasped that advancing 'freedom, sociability and equality' by themselves, without 'virtue' and the legal underpinning to go with it, is not enough and could easily wreak vast havoc.[6] Sterile and useless metaphysics must be replaced with a philosophy of the 'healthy understanding', something 'immediately useful for the people'.[7] This deeper, more real Enlightenment, one transforming everyday life, would be both the product and interpreter of human history: 'history of mankind in the noblest sense—you shall be!'[8] Herder's

---

[1] Reimarus, *Apologie*, i. 41.   [2] Boehart, 'Hermann Samuel Reimarus', 134–5.
[3] Herder, 'How Philosophy', 7.   [4] Zammito, *Kant, Herder*, 146.
[5] Herder, 'How Philosophy', 18.   [6] Ibid. 88.   [7] Ibid. 19.
[8] Herder, *Another Philosophy*, 79.

aspirations in philosophy, literature, and politics during the 1760s and 1770s were in many ways closer to the reforming spirit of Diderot and Lessing than that of Kant, Hume, Montesquieu, or Voltaire. He demanded public debate with big consequences ignoring churches and princes, a vigorous broadening of Enlightenment, an altogether new kind of philosophy, using an accessible literary and rhetorical style such as had been recently perfected by Lessing, though Lessing had not yet accomplished all that he thought him capable of.[9]

Around 1760, following a short period back in Berlin (1758–60), in which he again saw much of his friend Mendelssohn, began a new phase in Lessing's engagement with philosophy and in particular Spinoza and Spinozism, as well as Leibniz and Wolff. His intellectual growth during these years must be considered against the backdrop of the culminating battle over the *Encyclopédie* in France and further advance of the ideas of Diderot, Helvétius, and the *encyclopédistes* more generally in Germany, together with the entrenched, persistent reticence of such commanding figures ruling contemporary thought, literary judgement, and taste as Wolff, Reimarus, and Johann Christoph Gottsched (1700–66), professor of philosophy and poetry (and state censor) at Leipzig. A celebrated foe of the fantastic, pompous, and 'unnatural' in the theatre, Gottsched was also the chief promoter of Bayle's reputation and literary œuvre in Germany, his translation of Bayle's *Pensées diverses* (1741) appearing among the works banned by several states including the reformed censorship in the Austrian monarchy in the 1750s.[10] A private deist, he proceeded quietly, gingerly, and with gentle hints only.

The path to a comprehensive reform programme for German society, religion, politics, and culture was not yet open. But it was being clearly enough pointed out to the intellectually adventurous, and Gottsched as Germany's leading academic commentator on the French literary scene was beginning to pile on more hints. The radical work that played so decisive a role in France and Italy in 1758–9, Helvétius's *De l'esprit*, appeared in German, at Leipzig, in 1760, under the title *Discurs über den Geist des Menschen*, accompanied by a long, relatively audacious subversive preface by Gottsched who by this point was increasingly unmasking his deism and corrosively critical and sceptical attitude, even if one that remained distinctly guarded. Helvétius's *Discurs* was among the promptest, most widely noticed renderings into German of the major French Radical Enlightenment writings and demands scholarly attention especially owing to its exceptional effect in the 1760s and 1770s in the German universities. Noting the huge controversy surrounding the book in France and lively interest it elicited in Germany, the translator, Johann Gabriel Forkert, a Berlin official, worked quickly, dedicating his translation to a higher Berlin financial official, Carl Sarrn.[11] In his preface, Forkert commented on the readiness of the common people to hurl the epithet 'atheist' in all directions and appealed to scholars

---

[9] Herder, *Selected Early Works*, 154–5.   [10] *Catalogus Librorum Rejectorum*, Continuatio (1755).
[11] Forkert, dedication to Carl Sarrn; Smith, *Bibliography*, 186.

to take greater care before accusing anyone of 'atheism'. Emphasizing Helvétius's novelty and the usefulness of his ideas, he defended him, insisting on the 'truth' of many of his conclusions and their importance for social and cultural reform. What was 'useful' in the book in his eyes amply justified translating and propagating it.[12]

Gottsched's public excuse for associating himself with such a subversive text was that it had already been translated and was about to be published before he became involved. Seeing that it was about to appear in any case, he had felt it was his duty to compose a lengthy introduction to assist readers in differentiating the excellent things it contained from its malicious and impious strands. He had earlier read the book in French with the utmost care and immediately grasped its central importance but would not himself have translated it or encouraged anyone else to, or so he claimed, because much of its argument was indeed irreligious, 'erroneous', and definitely dangerous in the hands of inexperienced readers. With the translation ready for the press, he had been asked to check the text and issue a loud warning to readers against irreligion against which everyone must be on their guard.

Even in his later deist phase in the 1750s and 1760s, Gottsched remained a man of the radical fringe only in a tentative, cautious way. But his intellectual curiosity and natural liberality of mind led him subtly to help stimulate discussion of such subversive writings, just as earlier, he had initiated the German debate about Bayle. It was precisely this gently probing, liberal attitude that had already nurtured at Leipzig such vigorously enquiring young acolytes as Mylius and Carl August Gebhardi who had subsequently, during the 1730s and 1740s, veered to radical positions.[13] Gottsched's flirting with radical ideas, and assisting their propagation, made him, to a degree more than Reimarus, an ally of Lessing's and Herder's subversive strategies. His irony and relative political audaciousness showed itself particularly in his forty-two-page preface to the Helvétius translation. Helvétius's *De l'esprit*, impious though it was, undoubtedly raised vital questions, setting many 'truths' in a new light. Its analysis of human motivation and action, argued Gottsched, is more thorough than any other since Locke.[14] However, it was above all Helvétius's boldness in criticizing Montesquieu that impressed him and especially his thesis that it is not climate, or geographical context, that determines the moral and legal context of societies but rather the legal apparatus devised for regulating men's behaviour and desires.[15] Helvétius's book had been suppressed by the Paris *Parlement*, noted Gottsched, because it abounds in propositions offensive to the Catholic Church and the French monarchy. But this ought to create no difficulties in Protestant Germany as it was mostly, or so Gottsched assured readers, Helvétius's mockery of monks, superstition, and papal dogma and his ridiculing the Catholic Church's ban on Copernicus and treatment of Galileo—something wholly unproblematic for Lutherans—that had produced *De l'esprit*'s condemnation.

---

[12] Forkert, 'Vorbericht des Übersetzers', 3. [13] Mulsow, *Freigeister*, 13–14, 80–1.
[14] Gottsched, 'Vorrede', A4ᵛ; Krebs, *Helvétius*, 45. [15] Gottsched, 'Vorrede', A4ᵛ.

Why should a book burnt in Paris because it violently offends the pope, Catholicism, and the French state be forbidden in Germany? Pressure to ban the book in German Protestant lands would be senseless, he urged, highly implausibly, in the present religious and political context. Where Helvétius denigrates the French royal establishment and court, affixing the 'hated names' *Despotismus* and 'Despoterey' to the French monarchy, this was amply justified there given the reality of French 'despotism' which sells high offices for money rather than awards them on merit, manifesting all the wretched consequences that ensue when princes sacrifice the public interest to their own concerns and pleasures. But in Germany where the situation differed completely such disparaging epithets had no place. In the Holy Roman Empire, unlike absolutist France, thankfully, there was no sway of 'sultans' and 'viziers', only rule by pious, upright princes and expert councillors.[16] Stressing the admirable qualities of 'deutsche Freyheit' [German freedom], Gottsched praised the wisdom and sense of responsibility of the representative estates of the principalities which, he says, when making laws and regulating government, seek only the generally desired, beneficial effect, or 'at least would do so if they consisted of good patriots'.[17] 'Warum sollte man nun in Deutschland ein Buch, wie dieses vom *Geiste des Menschen* ist, scheuen und verbiethen?' [Why, then, in Germany, should such a book as *De l'esprit* be dreaded and forbidden?] This preface was noticed by d'Holbach's ally Chastellux, on passing through Frankfurt; he wrote to Helvétius, praising and undertaking to translate it into French (if he did, his rendering is lost).[18]

The translator had been encouraged by someone in Berlin who preferred not to be named but whose character and writings were well known and who amply deserved the title of 'true philosopher'.[19] This, presumably, was Lessing who had frequently been the first in Germany to notice the significance of recently published illicit French works in the past. During his last two-year stay in Berlin (1758–60), much closeted with his friends Mendelssohn and Nicolai, Lessing initiated and edited the *Briefe die Neueste Litteratur Betreffend* [Letters Concerning the Most Recent Literature] (1759–65), a critical periodical in which he famously applied Diderot's theories about how to reform the theatre, rejecting Gottsched's plea for French literature's neoclassical models, and discusses translation theory and the role of translation in the development of German culture.[20] More than Gottsched, Reimarus, or Mendelssohn, who as a Jew needed to be doubly cautious, Lessing nurtured a subversive agenda that was religious, philosophical, and cultural in the first place but undoubtedly also political. In Berlin he had widely intimated his dislike of Prussia's role in the Seven Years War (1756–63) and antipathy both to the Prussian militarist state and nobility, especially the high nobility, from which, Mendelssohn noted later, he always felt estranged. The antipathy between him and the Prussian monarch appears to have

---

[16] Gottsched, 'Vorrede', B2ᵛ; Naigeon, *Philosophie*, ii. 673; Krebs, *Helvétius*, 42.
[17] Gottsched, 'Vorrede', B3ᵛ.
[18] Krebs, *Helvétius*, 46–7.
[19] Forkert, 'Vorbericht des Übersetzers', 3.
[20] Berghahn, 'Lessing', 68–72; Mortier, *Combats*, 53–4; Saada, *Inventer Diderot*, 74, 80, 98–9.

been entirely mutual since Frederick blocked a proposal in 1760 to confer on him membership of the Berlin Academy.[21]

During his Breslau years (1760–5), holding the post of secretary to the garrison commander, Lessing, eager further to refine his conception of philosophy's useful-ness as a reforming tool, undertook a closer study of key philosophical texts. It was at this time that he studied Spinoza's *Ethics* intensively and took up anew the issue of the relation of Leibnizio-Wolffianism to Spinozism with Mendelssohn. Mendelssohn had portrayed Spinoza as a precursor of the Leibnizian-Wolffian system who first formulated the 'pre-established harmony'. Reviewing Mendelssohn's book in March 1755, Lessing had agreed Leibniz was not the 'inventor' of the pre-established harmony, Spinoza having preceded him in this all-important step by eighteen years.[22] But where Mendelssohn subsequently always adhered to this position which fitted his own commitment to natural theology and the harmony of Judaism with reason,[23] Lessing by the early 1760s was striking out in a different direction.

In his essay *Durch Spinoza ist Leibniz nur auf die Spur der vorherbestimmten Harmonie gekommen*, composed around the same time he wrote to Mendelssohn, in April 1763, reopening the question of the Spinoza–Leibniz relationship, he again concurred with Mendelssohn 'that it was Spinoza who led Leibniz to the *vorherbes-timmte Harmonie* [pre-established Harmony]'.[24] But he now also claimed Spinoza's conception of body and mind, as distinct manifestations of the same single reality, obviates all need for a theory of pre-existing harmony to explain the order and connections of the real world. It was precisely the separation of body and spirit in Leibniz that obliged him to introduce such a master-plan, to explain how God's intentions infuse physical reality, synchronizing body and mind: 'Leibniz seeks by means of his harmony, to solve the puzzle of how two such different things as body and soul can be unified; Spinoza, as against this, sees no distinction between them; he therefore sees no union and no puzzle requiring solution.'[25] The difference between Leibniz's and Spinoza's opposed conceptions he vividly illustrated using the simile of two primitive savages gazing at their reflections in a mirror for the first time. Once over their initial astonishment, they try to explain the phenomenon. As the image in the mirror makes exactly the same movements as a real body, and in the same order, both grasp that the sequence in the mirror and in reality share an identical cause. But where one infers the two things are different but somehow synchronized, the other concludes body and image are one and the same.[26]

Lessing's intention here was plainly to marginalize pre-established harmony and imply the intrinsic superiority of Spinoza's solution to the mind–body problem, potentially opening up a large gap between himself and Mendelssohn. Shortly

---

[21] Goldenbaum, 'Der "Berolinismus" ', 350 n.   [22] Lessing, *Gesammelte Werke*, iii. 142–3.
[23] Israel, *Radical Enlightenment*, 658; Goetschel, *Spinoza's Modernity*, 191–5.
[24] Lessing, *Werke und Briefe*, ii. 245; Stiening, 'Zur Bedeutung', 205, 212–13.
[25] Lessing, *Werke und Briefe*, ii. 245–6; Herder, *Gott*, 95; Pätzold, *Spinoza, Aufklärung*, 28–9.
[26] Lessing, *Werke und Briefe*, ii. 246–7; Lessing, *Philosophical and Theological Writings*, 33–4.

afterwards Mendelssohn, who had earlier read Helvétius's *De l'esprit* in 1762, at Lessing's urging, but, unlike his friend, found it thoroughly superficial, composed his most famous work, *Phaedon* (1767), an undertaking he had since 1760 discussed repeatedly with Lessing in Berlin. It was the text that secured his reputation as a leading European philosopher. Building on Leibniz, Wolff, Alexander Baumgarten, and Reimarus, in particular,[27] Mendelssohn here upholds precisely the reverse of Spinoza's and Helvétius's thesis—namely, the incorruptibility and immortality of the soul. Especially for this reason, it was a work that received exceptionally high praise not only in published reviews but also in the private comments of his friend Nicolai—an equally staunch foe of Helvétius and French materialism[28]—and of such leading intellectual celebrities as Isaak Iselin (1728–82), a leading Enlightenment figure in Switzerland, and, initially, Herder. Reprinted many times, it appeared in Dutch in 1769, French in 1772, and Danish in 1779.

Lessing, though, was now set on a wholly divergent path. With Mendelssohn striving to vanquish Spinoza, La Mettrie, Diderot, and Helvétius by showing that 'a thinking whole' cannot arise from 'unthinking parts' and that the moral order is indissolubly linked to the soul's immortality, his closest friend and ally placed Leibniz's doctrine of the soul under a large question mark together with the entire Leibnizian-Wolffian scheme of natural theology.[29] *Phaedon* was not just a major work of the *Aufklärung* but a key marker to its internal divisions. Having initially reacted enthusiastically, Herder (who had both of Helvétius's main works in his library in both French and German) was soon full of doubt as to its cogency. 'With you and most philosophers and theologians', as he put it, writing to Mendelssohn early in 1769, the soul 'is liberation from sensual perceptions and entire spiritual perfection from which the rewards of the future condition derive in the first place', and yet 'what is a soul liberated from all sensual perceptions, and what is a purely spiritual perfection in a human soul? I must confess: I do not know.'[30] Herder who also found Helvétius superficial at the same time categorically rejected Mendelssohn's idea that a de-sensualized soul is a meaningful idea or that it can help advance human happiness.

A fragment penned by Lessing in 1763, his *Über die Wirklichkeit der Dinge ausser Gott* [On the Reality of Things outside God], is a further indication that, like another ex-Wolffian, Christian Gabriel Fischer, before him, he had now embraced Spinoza's monism as his own philosophy. 'If in the concept God has of the reality of a thing, everything is present that is found in its reality outside him, then the two realities are one, and everything supposed to exist outside God exists in God.'[31] There can be nothing in reality outside God's thoughts. Rejecting dualistic conceptions of the God–world relationship, Lessing though still speaking of 'natural religion' seems to

---

27 Altmann, *Moses Mendelssohn*, 149, 151.   28 Krebs, *Helvétius*, 54–5, 157.
29 Goetschel, *Spinoza's Modernity*, 194 -5; Pätzold, *Spinoza, Aufklärung*, 99–100.
30 Altmann, *Moses Mendelssohn*, 170–4; Markworth, *Unsterblichkeit*, 39–44.
31 Lessing, *Werke und Briefe*, ii. 243; Stiening, 'Zur Bedeutung', 206–7.

have no longer been a positive deist, in any meaningful sense; unlike Voltaire, Turgot, Mendelssohn, or Reimarus, he no longer conceived 'natural religion' as a divinely bequeathed or imposed universal system of morality. Rather morality and natural theology was now for him something universal but anchored in the unalterable and eternal laws of the nature of things. Another private fragment Lessing penned in Breslau, in or around 1763, and which, of necessity, he left unpublished, was his *Über die Entstehung der geoffenbaren Religion* [On the Origin of Revealed Religion].[32] Here again the radical stance characterizing his orientation from the late 1750s plainly emerges. This text is a list of eleven basic propositions, of which one is that 'Alle positiven und geoffenbarten Religionen sind folglich gleich wahr und gleich falsch' [all positive and revealed religions are hence equally true and equally false].[33] However, they are all equally true, he adds, merely in that it had everywhere been 'necessary to reach agreement on various things in order to obtain unanimity and accord in the public religion'. By contrast, they are all 'equally false', in that organized religion secures agreement in a way that 'does not simply coexist with the essential elements [of natural religion], but weakens and suppresses them'. The best revealed or positive religion is hence that which contains the fewest conventional additions to natural religion, imposing the fewest limitations on the good effects of natural religion.

Traditional metaphysics, Herder agreed with Lessing (and Kant), should be abandoned and the centre of gravity shift from metaphysics to moral philosophy. Herder, though, did not believe Kant had drawn the correct conclusions from his penetrating analysis and close engagement with the works of Hume and Rousseau. 'If philosophy is to become useful for human beings then let it make the human being its center.'[34] Revolutionizing philosophy in this way would cause a convergence and merging of philosophical debate with anthropology, politics, and the public sphere. 'All philosophy', he says in *How Philosophy Can Become More Universal*, of 1765, 'which is supposed to belong to the people must make the people its central focus, and if philosophy's viewpoint is changed in the manner in which, out of the Ptolemaic system, the Copernican system developed', that is should 'our whole philosophy become anthropology', then 'new fruitful developments' will assuredly follow.'[35]

It was during his last year in Riga (1768–9) that Herder most intensively engaged with Leibniz and also began his subsequently unremitting preoccupation with Spinoza. Equally, it was from around this time that he became an admirer of Diderot whom he met when, after resigning from his post in Riga, he travelled to France during the latter part of 1769, before visiting Holland. Writing to Hamann, from Paris, he proclaimed Diderot the leading philosopher in France.[36] Not unlike Lessing earlier, Herder was attempting to modify Leibniz's thought by adjusting it, in the direction of hylozoism, and absorbing elements of Spinoza. By reworking and

---

[32] Lessing, *Philosophical and Theological Writings*, 35–6.   [33] Lessing, *Werke und Briefe*, ii. 241.
[34] Herder, *Philosophical Writings*, 21; Herder, *Selected Early Works*, 117.
[35] Herder, *Philosophical Writings*, 29.   [36] Zammito, *Kant, Herder*, 330.

blending elements from Leibniz, Spinoza, and Diderot in this manner, Herder forged an eloquent, poetic philosophy of nature conceived as a force inherently mobile, self-creating, and immanent with constant potentiality.[37] Hylozoism was the concrete link between Diderot and Spinoza, and the fervently embraced principle rendering Spinoza central to Herder's conception of nature, God, man, society, and morality.

In September 1770 began the friendship between the now highly erudite Herder and five-year younger vastly talented aspiring poet Goethe. Their meeting in Strasbourg was to prove a key formative experience for both. Over the winter of 1770–1, whilst the invalid Herder remained confined to a darkened room, Goethe visited him on an almost daily basis, becoming (and cheerfully designating himself) Herder's acolyte.[38] The experience helped shape Goethe's general intellectual outlook, conception of his role and aims in German literature, and self-emancipation through a rapid retreat from his earlier Christian commitment. Herder, perhaps the best-equipped tutor in criticism, literature, and philosophy he could conceivably have found, put the young poet through an intensive crash course in general Enlightenment thought and it was at this time—though only some years later did he embark on a close reading of Spinoza's texts—that Goethe's awareness of the latter's special relevance to his own development, creativity, and concerns began.

A few years later, in 1775, Goethe became tutor to the then 18-year-old Duke Carl August, and arrived in Weimar where he soon rose to the ranks of the duchy's governing council and from the late 1770s figured as one of the duke's most active and trusted administrators. At Weimar, he developed a particular kind of secular small-state paternalism, loyally supporting the interests of the duke and his court. At Weimar too, where Herder also settled in 1776, debate about the *Aufklärung* was to reach one of its great peaks.

2. BAHRDT AND FREEDOM OF EXPRESSION

Goethe consciously divested himself of received notions through discussion with Herder and his literary endeavours. A more common route to auto-emancipation and a radical standpoint in *Aufklärung* Germany, though, was by following the public debate in Protestant theology, especially by diverging from orthodoxy via the path of Socinianism leading to the psychologically difficult wrench of rejection of miracles, of the soul's immortality, mysteries, belief in spirits, the Trinity, and other central dogmas. This was the classic path to radical thought of Johann Lorenz Schmidt, Lessing, Herder, Bahrdt, and doubtless many other prominent figures of the mid and later *Aufklärung*. Carl Friedrich Bahrdt (1740–92) was a pre-eminent figure of German radical thought and, after Struensee and Diez, the next German writer

---

[37] Zammito, *Kant, Herder*, 316–18.   [38] Boyle, *Goethe*, i. 94–9.

resoundingly to proclaim press freedom a precious and universal benefit for humanity. He stands out as one of the later Radical Enlightenment's most interesting figures for this reason and especially because his tortuous intellectual trajectory is closely documented in his voluminous autobiography, completed in 1790, mostly composed at Magdeburg after his imprisonment there by Frederick's successor for writing a satirical play, *Das Religions-Edikt*, attacking Prussian authoritarianism and the 1788 edict on religion.[39] The inner path by which Bahrdt reached his radical conclusions, step by step discarding all 'superstition', intolerance, and credulity, he described as the 'steps of my *Aufklärung*'.[40]

It was as a follower of Crusius, under whom he studied at Leipzig in the years 1756–61, and fervent Pietist that Bahrdt began his career. His long spiritual trek away from Pietism and the world of Crusius began in the early 1760s and by 1768 his heterodoxy had already become sufficiently obtrusive to cause his removal from his first university chair, in biblical philology, at Leipzig (held in the years 1766–8), though his dismissal also involved a scandal over a prostitute. Two years later, in 1771, he had to resign his second chair, this time at Erfurt. After years of teaching theology, it was whilst holding his third chair, at Giessen (1771–5), a position he owed to the support of his mentor during the middle stage of his progression from conservative to radical, the great Halle theologian Johann Salomo Semler (1725–91), that he finally abandoned belief in the doctrines of the Trinity, resurrection, original sin, atonement, repentance, supernatural grace, and eternal damnation as well as study of Hebrew and other ancient languages, and finally broke all ties with Christianity as conventionally understood. Semler figured among the leaders of the most daring and innovative reform group in the Lutheran Church at the time, the so-called Neologist movement, and was then rated by Bahrdt one of the foremost promotors of *Aufklärung* in Germany and especially a towering champion 'der algemeinen Denkfreiheit' [of universal freedom of thought].[41]

Bahrdt's conversion to a Unitarian standpoint, rejection of miracles and (practically) all supernatural agency, was sufficiently reflected in his 1773 rendering of the New Testament into everyday language to provoke fierce opposition at Giessen. His many adversaries there, led by the 'other Möser', the Pietist Friedrich Karl von Möser (1723–98), an enlightened critic of the military policies of the small states who also greatly deplored anything irreligious, denounced Bahrdt's New Testament version as blasphemous before the local church consistory and laboured to eject him from his third chair.[42] Faced with a choice between humiliating retraction or formal condemnation, Bahrdt again preferred to resign: 'lieber mit Weib und Kind betteln, als Priestern und Theologen einen solchen Triumpf lassen!' [Rather beg with wife and child in the streets than give the priests and theologians such a triumph].[43] Besides

---

[39] Bahrdt, *Geschichte*, ii. 200–1, 221, 223, and iii. 46; Goldenbaum, *Appell*, ii. 911.
[40] Bahrdt, *Geschichte*, ii. 199, iii. 58, and iv. 107, 116–17; Laursen and Van der Zande, 'Introduction', 91–2. [41] [Bahrdt], *Kirchen- und Ketzer-Almanach*, 160–5; Bordoli, *L'Illuminismo*, 243.
[42] Bahrdt, *Geschichte*, ii. 261, 264–6; Flygt, *Notorious Dr Bahrdt*, 70, 114; Schmidt, *What is Enlightenment?*, 8. [43] Bahrdt, *Geschichte*, ii. 266.

numerous detractors, he left behind a circle of friends that developed later into an enduring local radical network centering around two professors, August Friedrich Wilhelm Crome (1753–1833) and Johann Wilhelm Hezel, and also the Dillenburg jurist and Spinozist Knoblauch, who spent much time in Giessen.

At the time, Bahrdt was still a Unitarian. There are no miracles and God does not interrupt the eternal and unalterable laws of nature, he held, but the world is governed by divine providence. Although he now considered reason and 'philosophy' the chief guide in human life, he also maintained that it is precisely 'philosophy' that assures men of God's existence and divine guidance of the world.[44] To his congregants, he explained his views in cautiously Leibnizian terms, proclaiming that God had preordained everything in the best possible way. After 1775, he dedicated himself to a life of religious and educational reform while facing huge obstacles to achieving his goals. During his stay in Switzerland in 1775–6, he also began to develop pronounced republican sympathies.[45] On visiting Amsterdam, in 1777, he found his reputation as a freethinker had preceded him and that no one would permit him to preach, local Lutherans and Reformed being equally set on boycotting his ideas and educational schemes.[46] Fear lest he introduce children to godlessness blocked his educational efforts at every turn. Eager to establish networks, he proceeded from Holland to England armed with introductions supplied by an old friend, the father of the anthropologist Georg Forster.[47] In England, he at once contacted Joseph Priestley (with whom he conversed in Latin), whose 'philosophical head' in no way disappointed him, albeit Priestley was clearly no exegete or man of languages. 'I spent many hours with him in which I gushed forth, mocking both the German theologians and the English Thirty-Six Articles [of the established Church].'[48]

Back in Germany, Bahrdt resumed subversive activity while battling obstacles of every sort. Fighting a wall of prejudice with only a handful of allies he found to be no easy matter. He was openly shunned, he records, by passers-by on the street. Early in 1779 he published his deistic *Glaubensbekentnnis* [Confession of Faith], openly denying original sin, salvation through grace, and Christ's divinity.[49] With this, he came under attack not only from the entire body of conservative and moderate theologians but now too from the Neologists, especially Semler. Many regarded the Neologists' boycotting Bahrdt rather cynically, notes Mirabeau, in his work on Prussia's monarchy, as the latter were scarcely less 'Socinian' than he. Semler who henceforth labelled Bahrdt a 'naturalist' rather than 'Christian' was suspected by some of acting from jealousy or self-serving motives.[50] Probably, though, Semler felt driven to condemn not so much Bahrdt's paring his faith down to something as sparse as Priestley's, but rather his publicly presenting himself as a fearless and outspoken Unitarian. For Bahrdt, Jesus remained central but now as humanity's great moral philosopher—and man's redeemer from superstition, credulity,

[44] Bahrdt, *Geschichte*, ii. 49, 51; Bahrdt, *System*, 50–3.   [45] Mühlpfordt, 'Europarepublik', 323–4.
[46] Bahrdt, *Geschichte*, iii. 269–70.   [47] Mühlpfordt, 'Europarepublik', 327.
[48] Bahrdt, *Geschichte*, iii. 270.   [49] Bordoli, *L'Illuminismo*, 51–3.   [50] Ibid. 245–54.

and priestcraft.[51] In March 1779, the imperial court imposed a general ban on his writings, ordering his expulsion from the empire should he refuse to retract his denial of the core dogmas. The ban was enforced in some states, including Hesse-Darmstadt, where the court was spurred by the Giessen consistory, headed by Ludwig Adolf Christian von Grolmann, later to emerge as among the most relentless Counter-Enlightenment spokesmen in Germany.[52] Like Edelmann earlier, Bahrdt found himself with no other alternative but to seek refuge in Prussia, where he was welcomed by Frederick's 'enlightened' education minister Von Zedlitz, and began seeking yet another university position.

Halle needless to say refused him a chair. Too radical for Semler, the latter publicly labelled him a 'naturalist' and indifferentist whose teaching was inimical to Christianity's core teachings.[53] Semler also tried to dissuade him from settling in Halle and refused all help when he came nevertheless, interceding with Zedlitz in an unsuccessful attempt to prevent his being allowed to teach in any capacity, even as an unsalaried private *docent*. Bahrdt's opinions, contended Semler, would be detrimental to the students placed in the university's charge.[54] The university's other leading light, Johann August Eberhard (1739–1809), a former Lutheran preacher in Berlin, close friend of Mendelssohn, and Halle professor of philosophy since 1778, proved more amenable for a time. He figured among the most liberal, learned, and Judaeophile in tendency among the *Aufklärung's* leaders, as well as, in Bahrdt's opinion, one of Germany's best philosophers.[55] But later he too withdrew his friendship. Who would have thought, asked Mirabeau, that in a university dominated by Semler and Eberhard 'Bahrdt pût être reçu autrement que comme un martyr de la liberté de penser'?[56]

Despite not being permitted to teach theological topics or metaphysics, Bahrdt taught at Halle for nearly a decade, drawing large student audiences until crossed emphatically off the lecture list, at the commencement of the new reign, in 1788. He lectured on rhetoric and history, including a course on Tacitus, supplementing his meagre income with numerous articles for the press. His personal trajectory, however, was not yet quite complete. The preface to the third edition of his rendering of the New Testament published at Berlin at this time comprehensively rejected all the specifically Christian doctrines. He now accepted only that 'Moses and Jesus, like Confucius, Socrates, Luther and Semler, and he himself, were all tools of divine Providence by which it seeks to advance goodness among men'.[57] Among the many who rebuked him in print over subsequent years was Kant who was particularly

---

[51] Bahrdt, *System*, i. 53–4.
[52] Haaser, 'Sonderfall oder Paradigma', 257.
[53] Bahrdt, *Geschichte*, iii. 393 and iv. 24–5; Jacob, 'Karl Friedrich Bahrdt', 422–3; Bordoli, *L'Illuminismo*, 21, 56, 254.
[54] Bahrdt, *Geschichte*, iv. 61, 65–6, 73; Semler, *Lebensbeschreibung*, i. 10–12; Sauter, *Visions*, 56, 80.
[55] Bahrdt, *Kirchen- und Ketzer-Almanach*, 51; Bourel, *Moses Mendelssohn*, 74.
[56] Mirabeau, *De la monarchie*, v. 36–7; Flygt, *Notorious Dr Bahrdt*, 210–11.
[57] Bahrdt, *Geschichte*, iv. 120.

repelled by his 'fanciful fiction that [Christ] sought death in order to promote a worthy purpose through a shining and sensational example', in effect, postulating Christ's 'suicide'.[58]

Divine providence he continued to endorse, albeit, like Priestley, espousing a providence of a strikingly vague, very generalized kind. What is bad and defective in the world, he argued, is less essential than what was 'good' and causes less 'pain' than the positive things bring joy.[59] Bahrdt's mature thought combined this deistic-Socinian conception of providence with philosophy and an increasingly strident advocacy of *Aufklärung* as the basis of human happiness and hence (whether or not they know it) the veritable goal of all men.[60] 'Reason' he proclaimed the exclusive criterion of truth, and those philosophers who embrace 'reason' as their sole criterion, the only ones venerating Christian teaching as one should. He proposed a general reform of society but held that 'philosophy' is never rebellious or subversive. Any trouble or disturbance arising from reform efforts stems from popular bigotry, a dangerous force that had overthrown many a prince but is never the fault of the philosophers.[61]

While Bahrdt vaunted the progress of 'reason', it was this same progress that had fomented the rise of atheism and Spinozism, something occurring, he explained, because the very brightness of the light emitted by reason blinds some so that they can no longer see properly. Though deeply influenced by Spinoza, he argued that by denying God, divine providence, and the soul's immortality, Spinozism leaves the heart 'cold'. Even so, for Bahrdt, atheism and Spinozism were not intrinsically evil or damaging as the priesthood maintained. Rather, 'atheists' deserved respect and acceptance. Everyone believing in a 'rational morality' even if they deny God, he taught his followers, is 'your brother' and should be loved just as Muslims, Jews, and anyone else of a different belief deserve love and respect, a standpoint inseparable from his championing a full toleration and freedom of the press.[62] The error of the *Spinozisten* is simply a failure to perceive God's hand in the processes of creation, the world's design, and the profusion of species. Distinct traces of physico-theology lingered in his thought.

By his own account, Bahrdt's spiritual odyssey, virtually secularizing his thought altogether, finally removing residual notions of the supernatural character of revelation and Jesus' mission among men, ended in the late 1770s. What more than anything else completed the long transition from theologian to Radical Enlightenment activist was the *Fragmentenstreit*, and, rather ironically, Lessing's accompanying attack on Semler. This was less unusual than is sometimes assumed. Indeed, many scholars and students shifted their ground at this point, much of Germany's intelligentsia becoming distinctly unsettled by the uproar. In embracing what seemed to him the only conclusions to be drawn from the *Fragmentenstreit*, Bahrdt felt as if he

---

[58] Kant, *Religion within the Boundaries*, 96.   [59] Ibid. 121, 135, 158, 236.
[60] Bahrdt, *System*, i. 72.   [61] Ibid. i. 84; Bahrdt, *Geschichte*, iv. 123.
[62] Bahrdt, *System*, i. 135, 224, 239, and ii. 114–15, 353–4.

was finally finding himself and being awakened from a deep, stultifying sleep.[63] After three decades of wrestling with texts and his conscience, he could finally announce that Scripture is *not* divine revelation.[64]

3. LESSING AND THE *FRAGMENTENSTREIT*

Pivotal likewise in the personal development of Herder, Semler, Eberhard, Mendelssohn, Jacobi, and Lessing himself, the *Fragmentenstreit* of the mid 1770s constituted one of the later Enlightenment's greatest, most decisive controversies. Publishing key fragments from Reimarus' unpublished secret *Apologie oder Schutzschrift für die vernünftigen Verehrer Gottes* [Apology, or Defence of the Rational Worshippers of God], in stages, between 1774 and 1778, was from the outset intended by Lessing to provoke a major furore. He aimed to demonstrate the problematic character of revelation so incontrovertibly as to clear Germany's confessional air by weakening all orthodoxy definitively and discrediting all untenable beliefs. Censorship and ecclesiastical authority would be decisively undercut, he hoped, with the expected consequence that the constant need everywhere for concealment and hypocrisy in intellectual life and debate would finally abate. Success would clear the way for a true toleration and genuine liberty of thought. Based at the ducal library at Wolfenbüttel, near Brunswick, where he became director, after leaving Hamburg, in May 1770, Lessing launched a venture that he foresaw would incur great difficulties for himself but that he judged urgently necessary.

It was plain enough from the outset that publishing sections of Reimarus' text would antagonize the public and provoke an unprecedented outcry and by no means only among the orthodox. The 'anonymous author' had, after all, in Lessing's words, 'mounted nothing less than a total onslaught on the Christian religion. There is not a single aspect, not a single angle, however well concealed which he has not attacked with his scaling ladders.'[65] His own aims, however, were different. He too sought the 'downfall', as he privately expressed it, 'of the most detestable edifice of nonsense', meaning not just orthodox religion of the traditional, dogmatic, prejudiced, and overbearing kind but, equally, what he considered its intellectually diluted and emotionally shallow 'Neological' successor.[66] He and Reimarus would leave nothing standing of Christian dogma or ecclesiastical authority; but he aimed to leave the ultimate moral significance of Christianity intact, even perhaps strengthened.

Spinoza's Bible criticism, indeed, was tact itself compared to this critique. At one point Reimarus remarks that Celsus and Porphyry could scarcely have gone further in assailing Christianity.[67] His assault was textual but buttressed by physico-theology.

---

[63] Bahrdt, *Geschichte*, iv. 111.   [64] Ibid.; Flygt, *Notorious Dr Bahrdt*, 223–9.
[65] Lessing, *Philosophical and Theological Writings*, 96.   [66] Alexander, 'Einleitung', 254.
[67] Reimarus, *Apologie*, i. 61.

Divine revelation of any kind seemed to him inconceivable since for him (as for Spinoza and Lessing) the divine must be universal and absolute and cannot be made manifest in the particular and historical.[68] The image of Judaism and the Old Testament was certainly damaged too. In October 1770, Lessing had lent Mendelssohn a copy of the Reimarus manuscript to study at his leisure, in Berlin, and, since then, the two had exchanged letters on the subject. To Mendelssohn's objection that Reimarus' diatribe against the Old Testament prophets makes no allowance for the circumstances of their time, Lessing answered, in January 1771, that historical conditions are relevant for judging ordinary men but not 'patriarchs or prophets'. Those designated the highest models of virtue by society constitute a different case and Reimarus was right to decry them for their defective morality.[69] But the main thrust of the attack throughout, unprecedentedly, was against the New Testament.

The initial batch of *Fragmente eines Ungenannten* [Fragments of an Unknown Man] or 'Wolfenbüttler Fragmente' appeared, at Brunswick, in 1774, published in Lessing's house journal *Zur Geschichte und Literatur* 'from the treasures of the ducal library at Wolfenbüttel'. They supposedly came from a manuscript 'by an unknown author', possibly the Wertheim editor (i.e. Schmidt), recently discovered among the ducal library treasures, spurious details added to deflect attention from the recently deceased Reimarus and his family. A Gotha publisher offered to bring out the unknown author's complete text. Lessing was dissuaded, though, from accepting by Reimarus' daughter Elise, a freethinking lady for whom he had the greatest regard and who was anxious, together with her brother, to protect their father's reputation. Despite commencing with one of the milder portions and letting a healthy interval transpire before resuming, the furore was immense and afterwards only grew in intensity. At Halle, the shock among the theology students was palpable, some, reportedly, so deeply shaken as openly to waver in their faith and propose abandoning careers in the Church, deeming the *Fragmentarist*'s objections unanswerable.[70]

There was much speculation as to who the *Ungenannte* could be, and while there were other suspects, including Mendelssohn, and some who without mentioning Mendelssohn did think it must be a Jewish plot,[71] slowly the secret of the 'unknown's' identity partially emerged.[72] Sworn to silence, Lessing's Berlin friends probably knew it was Reimarus even beforehand, and so, after a certain point, did Herder, at Weimar, and Hamann, at Königsberg, and there were lively rumours afoot citing Reimarus also in Hamburg, though it is true that some discerning onlookers, like Lichtenberg at Göttingen, were unaware it was he as much as five years later.

---

[68] Wessell, *G. E. Lessing's Theology*, 77; Schilson, 'Lessing and Theology', 164.

[69] Lessing to Mendelssohn, Wolfenbüttel, 9 Jan. 1771, Lessing, *Gesammelte Werke*, ix. 407; Altmann, *Moses Mendelssohn*, 255.

[70] Semler, *Beantwortung*, 'Vorrede', A2; Bordoli, *L'Illuminismo*, 268.

[71] Altmann, *Moses Mendelssohn*, 252–4, 566.

[72] Lessing to Johann Albert Heinrich Reimarus, Wolfenbüttel, 6 Apr. 1778, in Lessing, *Werke und Briefe*, iii. 142–3; Lichtenberg, *Schriften*, iv. 363.

Despite Lessing's assurances that he had not disclosed their father's authorship to anyone, Reimarus' son and daughters soon took offence, accusing him of besmirching their father's memory.[73] Yet, curiously, throughout the public controversy, the half-concealed author continued always to be publicly referred to, even in the 1790s, as the *Ungennante*, *Unbekannter* [unknown], or simply the 'Wolfenbüttel fragmentarist'. Though Diez, in 1781, lists Reimarus together with Tindal and Collins as a notorious freethinker and Bahrdt mentions Reimarus as the *Fragmentarist*, the case remained like d'Holbach's authorship of the *Système*: connoisseurs knew the culprit's identity but practically no one mentioned his deeply embattled name in public.[74]

In his editorial commentary on five fragments published together, in 1777, Lessing pronounced them to be around thirty years old and however destructive of the letter of Scripture not corrosive of religion's true spirit. Not unlike Semler, Lessing thought Reimarus mistaken in arguing that because the historical and textual proofs of Christianity's truth are altogether deficient, the Christian religion as such is therefore fraudulent and morally corrupt. If her founding texts are suspect, held Lessing, this does not mean Christianity does not possess an inner core of moral truth that remains inspiring and beneficial especially as much of mankind trusts deeply in it.[75] Reimarus had his facts right but had drawn the wrong conclusions and ultimately been short-sighted. 'Christianity existed before the Evangelists and Apostles wrote about it', so that 'however much may depend on these writings, it is impossible for the whole truth of religion to be based on them'.[76] Few failed to note, though, that Lessing, like Spinoza, Edelmann, Priestley, and Bahrdt, was implying 'true Christianity' is a body of moral doctrine imperfectly expressed in the Gospels and totally perverted by churchmen.

Lessing was sincere in partially dissociating himself from Reimarus' views which he truly considered too dogmatic, polemical, and divisive to serve any ultimately constructive purpose. Throughout his career, his chief 'practical philosophical' objective had been to avoid turning the *Aufklärung* into the kind of unedifying slanging match raging in France. There was a better, and socially more harmonious, way to disarm theologians, he believed, despite being himself a formidable polemicist, than relentlessly battering them head-on, namely, steer matters gently forward through 'enlightened' examination and free enquiry, thereby bridging the gap between conventional religion and unfettered philosophy and gradually emancipating the warring parties from blinkered dogmatism. His aim was to reconfigure German culture with a minimum of strife on the basis of reason, toleration, anti-confessional universality, and freedom of thought generating mutual respect between the competing theologico-philosophical cultural blocs.

---

[73] Alexander, 'Einleitung', 17.

[74] Diez, *Apologie*, 66; Bahrdt, *Kirchen- und Ketzer-Almanach*, 141–2.

[75] Schmidt-Biggemann, *Theodizee*, 97; Forst, *Toleranz*, 403–4.

[76] Forst, *Toleranz*, 400–1; Lessing, *Philosophical and Theological Writings*, 62–3; Schilson, 'Lessing and Theology', 166.

The orthodox clergy, headed by Johann Melchior Goeze (1717–86), at Hamburg, the Lutheran Church's leading opponent of Enlightenment, toleration, and Jewish emancipation, led the outcry, denouncing Lessing for abysmal judgement and abominable effrontery in publishing such blasphemies and for the 'frivolousness' of his 'objections' to the *Unbekannter*'s theses. To Goeze it seemed obvious Lessing besides withholding his name was flagrantly championing the *Ungenannter*'s erudition and arguments while feebly pretending otherwise.[77] All possible objections to Christian theology had long since been stated, in ancient and modern times, and comprehensively refuted. This Lessing flatly denied. 'A great many at least of [these objections], have been answered as deplorably as they were stated. To the superficiality and ridicule of the one side, the other has not infrequently replied with pride and disdain. Vast offence was taken if one side equated religion with superstition; but the other has not scrupled to denounce doubt as irreligion, and belief in the adequacy of reason as infamy.' The dismal outcome of one side deprecating 'every clergyman as a scheming priest, while the other disparages every philosopher as an atheist' was that each 'turned its adversary into a monster' and, unable to defeat him, pronounced him beyond the law.[78]

The *Ungennanter*'s views, answered Lessing, in his *Anti-Goeze* (1778), were neither groundless nor blasphemous and there was nothing insidious in publishing them. If misguided in his conclusions, his text was impressively learned and could on no account be ignored. According to Goeze, these 'poisonous' fragments should not have been published. But the manuscript was extant in multiple copies and could not have been long kept secret. 'Or, do you think', he challenged him, 'that it does not matter what a few intelligent men believe in secret' provided the common people are kept on the proper track and that 'only the clergy should guide them in that'?[79] Had the author destroyed his manuscript there would be no problem. The 'unknown' was 'such a prudent man' that he did 'not wish to annoy anyone with the truth'. But he, Lessing, did not believe at all in reticence in such things 'being completely convinced that no truths advanced for consideration only' cause trouble and that only false, alleged 'truths adopted into general use set the common crowd into a zealous religious fury'. The *Ungenannte* had no desire to make anyone unhappy through premature disclosure 'whereas I, like a madman hazard my own peace of mind because I think disclosures with some basis to them cannot be made early enough to the human race'. Truth comes first and emerges only from free discussion. It was Goeze not Lessing who was guilty of misconduct by perverting what should be calm intellectual debate into a deafening public furore.[80]

Times must first become 'more enlightened', affirmed the *Ungenannte*, before the truth can be published. But how can men become more enlightened without greater readiness to consider whether what some insist is true is really so?[81] Despite the

---

[77] Lessing, *Anti-Goeze*, 529.   [78] Lessing, *Philosophical and Theological Writings*, 63–4.
[79] Lessing, *Anti-Goeze*, 521; Whaley, *Religious Toleration*, 151–68.
[80] Lessing, *Anti-Goeze*, 478, 494–5, 529.   [81] Ibid. 520; Reimarus, *Apologie*, i. 41.

misgivings of his friends, in May 1778 an undeterred Lessing published the most challenging and, for most, repulsive of the *Fragmente*, 'Vom Zwecke Jesu und seine Jünger' [About Jesus' Aims and his Followers]. Here Reimarus, highlighting crucial discrepancies in the Gospel text, denies the resurrection, claiming the disciples must have secretly removed the corpse from the tomb. Far from being God, Jesus was just an ambitious political insurgent with no thought of founding a new religion, someone who wagered, as Kant disapprovingly summarized his conclusion, 'his life for merely a political and illegal purpose'.[82] The Apostles were subversives who, having unexpectedly lost their leader, devised a desperate plan to keep up their adherents' spirits and 'sustain the momentum of the movement he initiated'.[83] This appealed to freethinkers. 'What would we be without freethinking?', enthused Wekhrlin, a warm admirer of Lessing, in his journal, at Nuremberg, in 1787: was Jesus not the most radical of all the radical thinkers? 'Had Christ not been a freethinker where would religion be today?' Surely 'the Vaninis, Spinozas and Mirabeaus were nowhere near so audacious as the philosopher of Nazareth, the most daring freethinker of all time'.[84]

This fragment, where Reimarus tries to undermine Christianity's foundations, styling the resurrection a shoddy deception and those who based the structure of belief and authority later elaborated by the Church on Christ's divinity and resurrection total impostors who were not following Jesus' teaching at all but resorting to a silly stratagem, provoked outrage on every side. Jesus' mission had never been designed to establish a new religion or system of belief, or introduce the Christian sacraments, contended Reimarus, nor was it accompanied by supernatural signs, wonders, or miraculous cures, nor did it have any universal aims, being intended merely to rouse the Jews to penitence and political action.[85] This must be a Jewish conspiracy, persisted Goeze, with Lessing the accomplice of the Jews.[86] Mendelssohn wrote assuring Herder he had nothing to do with its composition or publication.[87] Postulating a complete disjunction between Jesus' intentions and the Apostles' claims with its Spinozistic reverberations greatly appealed to Lessing.[88] But he disapproved of Reimarus' disparagement of Christ as such. His belittling depiction of Jesus in fact contrasted dramatically with the moral greatness and universalism Lessing himself, much like Spinoza, Herder, Semler, Eberhard, Goethe, and Bahrdt, attributed to the Christ figure.

All along, Lessing had striven to engage less the dogmatic guardians of orthodoxy (who were already sufficiently compromised in the eyes of the enlightened, and plainly incapable of debating the issues on the basis of reason and evidence) than

[82] Kant, *Religion within the Boundaries*, 96.
[83] Reimarus, *Apologie*, ii. 183–4, 305; Lessing, *Anti-Goeze*, 504–5.
[84] Wekhrlin, *Graue Ungeheuer*, 11 (1787), 224.
[85] Freund, 'Ein Trojaner', 140; Reimarus, *Apologie*, ii. 179–450.
[86] Hess, *Germans, Jews*, 117–18.
[87] Mendelssohn, *Gesammelte Schriften*, xxii: *Dokumente*, i. 172; Altmann, *Moses Mendelssohn*, 565–6.
[88] Schmidt-Biggemann, *Theodizee*, 81–2.

the far more tolerant, flexible, and intellectually engaged Neologists—Semler, Eberhard, Steinbart, Teller, Sack, Spalding, and Johann Friedrich Jerusalem—and in this he eventually succeeded. Much indebted to Baumgarten's philosophical theology, these theologians were committed to a serious re-conceptualizing of Christianity and to basic reform. They were leaders of a powerful liberal movement among the Lutheran clergy strong at Hanover, Brunswick, and particularly in Prussia where Frederick made no move to oppose their growing dominance in the Berlin upper consistory (*Oberconsistorium*) and universities. The foremost Lutheran theologians of the later Enlightenment, Semler and his allies were renowned for their revisionist Bible criticism and philological expertise. Committed to reforming Christianity on the basis of reason and a historico-critical approach to Scripture and theology, they constituted a towering branch of the mainstream Enlightenment.

Lessing designed to bring into the open what he considered the blatant inconsistencies and hypocrisy in their position. Their chief aim, according to Gotthelf Samuel Steinbart (1738–1809), writing in 1778, a leading Neologist philosopher-theologian at Frankfurt an der Oder, admired by Bahrdt, was to reform the religious notions and attitudes of the common people combating the conservative (but also Frederick's and Voltaire's) notion that popular superstition is best left undisturbed.[89] For Steinbart too Christ was the world's moral inspiration. With Semler, Steinbart, and the others Lessing could agree that the 'pure, true Christian religion cannot be attacked, despised or mocked'.[90] None of the theological disputes that had ever divided the world's churches, Steinbart agreed with Lessing, has any relevance to the genuine Christian doctrine of salvation at all.[91] The Neologists were vigorous reformers who only dominated for the moment because an unbelieving philosopher-king sat on Prussia's throne, tacit crypto-Socinians silently abolishing the Church's ancient dogmas from within, especially by showing these to be later accretions inessential to true Christianity.

But while claiming this superfluous accretion of 'mysteries' and dogma harms true Christianity more than Judaism or heathendom,[92] the Neologists nevertheless remained firmly within the Church, seeking a broad compromise between reason and tradition especially but not only on an institutional level. They claimed to eschew the old 'spirit of persecution' and preach enlightenment, toleration, freedom of thought, earnest enquiry, and moral fervour; but Lessing and Bahrdt found them in many ways too deferential to authority, confessional categories, and Lutheran ecclesiastical tradition, which Semler sought to lessen but not eliminate, and too ready to seek privileged influence and status for themselves, in short too allied to church institutions and the Prussian state. The essence of the radical charge was that they secretly agreed with most of the Fragmentarist's theses but were insufficiently

---

[89] Steinbart, *Philosophische Unterhaltungen*, 100–1; [Bahrdt], *Kirchen- und Ketzer-Almanach*, 171–2.
[90] Semler, *Beantwortung*, 'Vorrede', B3ᵛ; Bordoli, *L'Illuminismo*, 275.
[91] Bordoli, *L'Illuminismo*, 12–13.
[92] Semler, *Beantwortung*, 'Vorrede', B4ᵛ and 65.

committed to the truth, intellectual freedom, and a free press, and, hence, to a degree, hypercritical.[93]

Among the most fervent advocates of *Aufklärung*, the Neologs castigated deists, naturalists, and Bahrdt for demeaning the institutional structures and religious legacy of the past, unjustly deprecating Church, clergy, and tradition. Among their goals was to counter the wave of materialist publications and effectively reassure the common people in their faith, obviating what they feared would otherwise become a silent mass drift away.[94] Above all, they aimed to establish a stable ecclesiastical authority over society, morality, universities, and students. Crypto-Socinians, considered crypto-deists by many orthodox, they nevertheless worked specifically within the Church's institutional bodies and universities and were, therefore, frequently rather inhibited when it came to politics, toleration, and censorship, indeed could be distinctly slow to act in accord with their stated principles. They vigorously supported toleration, explained Semler, but opposed indifference and *Leichtsinnigkeit* [frivolousness].[95] In particular, they resisted a fully free press. Lessing thought them hypocrites also because of their proneness, inherent in their situation, to profess one thing but act (as with Bahrdt) rather differently. Given that Semler later defended the reactionary Prussian decree for the protection of religion, of 1788, under which Bahrdt was imprisoned, Lessing's stance was subsequently abundantly vindicated.[96] Especially irritating to Lessing was Semler's insistence that there remained an appreciable gap between the moral outlook of a truly reformed Christianity of the kind he advocated and the views of *Naturalisten* (like Lessing and Bahrdt), the *Naturalisten* considering only their stomachs whereas Christians cultivate a higher morality.[97]

Lessing scorned highly skilled exegetes like Semler, Eberhard, Jerusalem, Steinbart, and Sack who publicly eschewed denying the reality of revelation and the resurrection, as Reimarus, Bahrdt, and he himself did, while in their study groups openly questioning whether the churches' stated doctrines had any basis in the biblical texts.[98] They were mincing words. At least the orthodox did not spuriously try to adjust their absurd beliefs to the latest textual scholarship and historical reality. Semler and his colleagues simultaneously sought to champion revelation while yet, it seemed to him, dissolving it, knowing perfectly well it had no textual basis, but refusing to admit this. Such shoring up of traditional belief and ecclesiastical authority via ever more sophisticated historical-critical research and nuance he pronounced misguided, self-defeating, slightly fraudulent, and beside the point.

The war over 'the Fragments' was certainly not one the Neologs had any appetite for. Of course, they rejected Reimarus' contention that Christ and the Apostles were

[93] Bordoli, *L'Illuminismo*, 21, 265–6.

[94] Steinbart, *Philosophische Unterhaltungen*, 106–7.

[95] Semler, *Lebensbeschreibung*, ii. 11–12; Cassirer, *Philosophy*, 176; Sorkin, *Religious Enlightenment*, 158–61.

[96] Sorkin, *Religious Enlightenment*, 22; Sauter, *Visions*, 56, 80.

[97] Semler, *Beantwortung*, 'Vorrede', A6ᵛ, B3ᵛ; Semler, *Lebensbeschreibung*, ii, 'Vorrede', 12–13.

[98] Gerrish, 'Natural and Revealed Religion', 659.

'malicious deceivers'; but much of his textual analysis they could only endorse. They too aimed to widen toleration. They had no wish to enter the arena against Lessing whose literary work and plays they admired—though some of them disapproved of his *Emilia Galeotti* (1758), a drama set in a petty principality where the Machiavellian Gonzaga prince is a ruthless despot fired by lust, as undesirably anti-monarchical and subversive.[99] Yet they also felt they had little choice but to counter the Fragments' denouncing the Apostles as 'deceivers', something Semler considered 'dangerous for many people' that ought to have been left unpublished. The Neologists also detected a hint of mockery in Lessing's tone and of imposture in his claim to be bringing the fragments into the open only to allow 'the fire' to burn out as the conflagration could not otherwise 'be extinguished', given that the manuscript had long circulated before 1774.[100] After long hesitation, with friends seeking to dissuade him, Semler eventually answered Lessing's challenge with his *Beantwortung der Fragmente eines Ungenannten* (1779), citing 'errors' in the *Ungenannte*'s critique. By answering the *Unbekannte* as he did, Semler was not so much taking issue with Reimarus, Bahrdt, and Lessing as seeking to check the growing indifference to and even mockery of religion in certain quarters, calm deep public consternation arising from Lessing's initiative, and meet fears that the *Fragmente*, left unchallenged, would hopelessly 'poison' the minds of students.

Even among society's lowest strata, reportedly, many had begun depicting and despising Christ like the *Ungenannte*.[101] They were supposedly emulating some among their betters. The Neologist goal was not to mobilize popular indignation and anti-Semitic sentiment, in the style of the orthodox, but demonstrate the *Fragmentarist*'s anti-Scripturalism to be exaggerated and vulnerable to detailed criticism, rejecting Reimarus' close linkage of Christ with Second Temple Judaism. They sought to uncover just enough errors in his scholarship to leave room for qualified rejection of his main thesis while leaving much of his critique of Christian tradition, the churches, and the New Testament text intact and, something important for them, driving the whole community of Lutheran theologians to unite and agree finally what Christianity's core ingredients really were.[102]

Whatever the *Naturalisten* gained through the Fragments, Semler strove to show, neither their anti-Scripturalism nor other arguments detract from Christianity's core meaning and justification.[103] The reality of Jesus may have been remote from how the Gospels and the Church depict these but this matters far less than Christ's transcendent spiritual significance. The Apostles had two different sets of teachings, one brimming with miracles and wonders for the ignorant majority, the other a religion of reason for the enlightened few. Against the *Fragmentarist* Semler's strategy was to prove the new current, Neologist theology better met the growing challenge

[99] Semler, *Beantwortung*, 'Anhang', 8–9, 14.
[100] Ibid. 9, 13; Semler, *Lebensbeschreibung*, 'Anhang', 9, 14.
[101] Semler, *Beantwortung*, 'Vorrede', A3 and 66; Bordoli, *L'Illuminismo*, 268.
[102] Semler, *Lebensbeschreibung*, ii, 'Vorrede', A3; [Bahrdt], *Kirchen- und Ketzer-Almanach*, 163.
[103] Semler, *Beantwortung*, 'Vorrede', A6ᵛ and B3ᵛ.

posed by scholarship and philosophy than orthodoxy.[104] Traditional orthodoxy to him was indeed the crassest dogmatism and *Antichristentum* 'much worse than Judaism or heathendom',[105] something demolished partly by historicizing its dogmas, like Baumgarten, partly by historicizing Scripture itself to meet Spinoza, on textual grounds, half way, and partly by rehabilitating and praising heterodox fringe Christians of the past, known for veering towards philosophy and naturalistic positions, notably Lodewijk Meyer whose *Philosophia S. Scripturae Interpres* Semler republished at Halle in 1776, accompanied by a remarkably positive commentary, and Balthasar Bekker, whose *Betoverde Weereld* of 1691–3 he brought out in an improved German translation in 1781.[106]

Semler's *Beantwortung*, of course, was merely one among over thirty books and pamphlets beside reviews and shorter pieces comprising the 'Fragment controversy'. But it was the most generally respected rejoinder although there were also many who complained that he gave too much away. Among Semler's critics was Johann Bernhard Basedow (1723–90), a leading pedagogue (and admirer of Rousseau), director of the famous experimental school founded in 1774 and surviving until 1793 at Dessau, known as the *Philanthropin*, a educational novelty characterized by stress on experimental science and eliminating Latin. Like Bahrdt (who taught there for a time), Basedow had studied under Crusius and long opposed the Wolffian ascendancy and the Baumgartens whose legacy Semler so vigorously embodied. Avowing a sceptical, practical stance closely aligned with Hume and Scottish Common Sense (much scorned by Bahrdt), Basedow was a pillar of the Anglophile moderate current, proclaiming, like Kant but on a less theoretical level, belief in God, providence, and the soul's immortality essential from a 'pragmatic' standpoint for human happiness.

Despite his hostility to rigid orthodoxy and theological control of education,[107] Basedow judged Semler's 'defence' a disaster likely to wreak nearly as much havoc as the 'Fragmentist' himself.[108] Men, he argued, have a 'duty to believe'. But Semler's general stance he, like Lessing and Bahrdt, considered 'two-tongued' and hypocritical as it differed hardly from Bahrdt's standpoint except in supporting state regulation of public debate about religion to safeguard the rudiments of orthodoxy.[109] An enlightener keen to expand toleration (up to a point) and minimize confessional differences by basing Christianity on 'reason', Basedow nevertheless rejected the more forthright 'philosophical spirit' of his time, insisting on reason's limits and the need to protect belief in Christ's divinity, the soul's immortality, original sin, and salvation by supernatural intercession.[110]

---

[104] Ibid. B7.   [105] Ibid. B–B4^v, B6.

[106] Van der Wall, 'Religie en verlichting', 31; Bordoli, *L'Illuminismo*, 39, 41, 91, 439.

[107] Altmann, *Moses Mendelssohn*, 567, 678; Kuehn, *Scottish Common Sense*, 270–1; Umbach, *Federalism*, 46–9.

[108] [Basedow], *Urkunde des Jahrs 1780*, 22–3.

[109] Ibid. 29–30, 37, 134–5, 137–8.

[110] Ibid. 123, 130–2; [Bahrdt], *Kirchen- und Ketzer-Almanach*, 18–20.

One thing the controversy proved beyond question, at least to the likes of Lessing, Herder, and Bahrdt, was the need for full freedom of thought, conscience, and of the press. How can any theologian be confident that he has the answers, asked Lessing, and how can his flock know he has, if it is not permissible to state freely and plainly every reasonable objection? Both Bahrdt and Herder who likewise took Lessing's side in the quarrel heartily agreed with this. Semler, though, dismissed such rhetoric as a ploy to confuse the public regarding Lessing's own private stance. Throughout the controversy Lessing professed to repudiate the Wolfenbüttel Fragments and remain a loyal Christian while largely concurring with Reimarus about the gospel and its historical background, proclaiming the 'inner truths 'of faith something quite distinct from the veracity and historicity of particular events or of reported miracles like the resurrection. He obviously did not believe in the resurrection or miracles. Neither did he think Christianity's true moral core should be directed by church consistories or any clergy. 'The theologians think you are a freethinker', wrote Nicolai to Lessing, in April 1777, 'and the freethinkers that you have become a theologian.'[111]

Official Lutheranism, insisted Semler, was not so hostile to reason or socially harmful as the *Fragmentist* and Bahrdt claimed and Lessing hinted. Bahrdt to his mind carried his campaign against theology much too far.[112] Especially, he rejected Bahrdt's public denial of Christ's divinity and the Trinity, accusing him of wanting to impose a new universal 'religion' on the world and abrogate the laws of the state.[113] It was precisely Semler's efforts to reconcile reason with faith, forging a liberal Christian synthesis by bringing Christ's divinity into question in a muffled manner without directly acknowledging the weakness of the grounds for belief, that struck Lessing as the heart of the quarrel. In highlighting Semler's inconsistencies, lack of openness, and sidelining of textual evidence, Lessing hoped to reveal what he saw as the hypocrisy at the heart of the Neologist undertaking.[114] Meanwhile, Bahrdt joined in scathingly dismissing such theologians as Georg Friedrich Seiler at Erlangen, a master trimmer who one moment compliments 'our heretics' on their love of truth, to show how tolerant he is, while the next 'whining' about the advance of 'dangerous principles' and feebly defending the Trinity. Semler he accused of betraying his own earlier path-breaking enlightening efforts, the *Fragmentenstreit* inaugurating his 'second epoch'—a time of shameful retreat and budding intolerance that 'darkened half his earlier renown'.[115]

Lessing, though, never fully replied to Semler. The church consistories, dismissing his claim to be strengthening Christianity by facing up to difficulties the Neologists refused to confront, redoubled their protests and not without success. If Frederick remained indifferent, the duke of Brunswick, long uneasy and now besieged by his

---

[111] Nicolai to Lessing, Leipzig, 24 Apr. 1777, in Lessing, *Werke und Briefe*, iii. 69; Altmann, *Moses Mendelssohn*, 559.

[112] Bahrdt, *Geschichte*, iv. 131.

[113] Ibid. iv. 70–2.

[114] Nisbet, 'Introduction', 10–11; Schilson, 'Lessing and Theology', 161.

[115] [Bahrdt], *Kirchen- und Ketzer-Almanach*, 158–9, 162; Flygt, *Notorious Dr Bahrdt*, 234.

local consistory, became thoroughly alarmed. In July 1778, he forbade Lessing to publish any more of Reimarus' manuscript which he confiscated along with other papers, permanently cancelling his prized ex officio exemption from ecclesiastical censorship.[116] He was forbidden to publish anything more on the controversy without ecclesiastical permission. To the relief of most, princely and ecclesiastical authority had finally intervened to abort Reimarus' subversion and forbid Lessing's use of it. Yet it had never been a genuinely open public debate at any stage as the main text and facts surrounding it had all along been withheld. No more than the rest of Europe was Germany ready for a truly open public debate on such matters. The clamp-down was followed by rumours that Lessing was leaving Wolfenbüttel for Vienna, which in the event were not borne out. Deeply frustrated Lessing tried to reverse the decision to withdraw his censorship exemption; but with his position now gravely weakened, and dogged by ill health, he found himself hampered on all sides especially in being gagged from answering his opponents' sallies,[117] an outcome Mendelssohn, worried from the start, had long predicted.

The controversy was thus shelved, so to speak, by ducal authority. Herder was among those disappointed that Reimarus' full text remained unpublished and that the authorities chose to render the whole business inconclusive.[118] Lessing himself, by the autumn of 1778, was increasingly given to feelings of depression and defeat. But he worked on, striving, notably with the full version in 1780 of his *The Education of the Human Race*, a tract betraying unmistakable signs of the impact on him of Fontenelle and Diderot as well as Spinoza, boldly to transform men's notion of revelation from a glorious divine intervention into the progressive unfolding of collective human reason. He sought to redefine revelation, converting it from a miraculous event into a development understood only non-miraculously and historically as a long-term process, the progressive emergence of the rationality and moral consciousness of man in society.

Hence, Lessing substituted for a philosophical 'reason' that is static, analytical, and lodged in the individual, a collective social 'reason' dynamic, historical, and synthetic and driven by freedom of thought and debate.[119] Revelation and religious truth were reconfigured as natural phenomena essential to balancing individual interest and freedom against collective need and social order. Lessing validated the core of Moses' and Jesus' teaching while relegating Judaism—in a manner that disappointed Mendelssohn—to the status of an obsolete vestige of a primitive past. Theology, through the marginalizing of the biblical account, in this way came to be disarmed and subordinated to philosophy, critique, and history of thought.

---

[116] Duke of Brunswick to Lessing, 13 July 1778, Lessing, *Werke und Briefe*, iii. 163–4; Freund, 'Ein Trojaner', 137; Elise Reimarus to Lessing, Hamburg, 29 July 1778, in Lessing, *Werke und Briefe*, iii. 174–5.

[117] Karl Lessing to Lessing, Berlin, July 1778, in Lessing, *Werke und Briefe*, iii. 164; Engel, 'Von "Relativ wahr?" ', 229.

[118] Herder to Lessing, Weimar, 25 Dec. 1778, in Lessing, *Werke und Briefe*, iii. 218.

[119] Cassirer, *Philosophy*, 194–5.

12

Catholic Enlightenment

The Papacy's Retreat

1. MODERATE VERSUS RADICAL ENLIGHTENMENT IN ITALY

The philosophical drama of the 1760s and 1770s in Germany was paralleled by a no less profound and far-reaching philosophical crisis touching every aspect of culture and society in Italy. Anyone keen for a rapid harmonization of Enlightenment and recent science with the teachings of the Church and the best of tradition might well have supposed there was little to prevent the prompt realization of their hopes in the years around 1740: by 1760, though, the picture had changed completely. In the 1740s, Catholic Enlightenment seemed to be emerging as a reconciling, hopeful, and concrete possibility. Heresy trials were a thing of the past. Advocates of conservatism antagonistic to Enlightenment ideas were for the moment marginalized. Sections of the clergy and episcopate, headed by the new pope himself, Benedict XIV (pope: 1740–58), took an active interest in the implications of science and the new ideas. The papacy clearly preferred a guarded reception of the new ideas as far as they could be espoused without compromising the Church's teachings and authority to any alternative and also a conciliatory stance towards those Italian princes intent on curtailing ecclesiastical immunities and fiscal privileges.

Many within the priesthood as well as lay society were receptive to the new philosophies and Newton, Locke, Leibniz, and Linnaeus were all widely embraced. All of Italy's seven principal universities—Padua, Pavia, Bologna, Pisa, Rome, Naples, and Turin—had found themselves in a distinctly decayed state at the end of the War of the Spanish Succession in 1713. But thereafter, beginning with the Academy of Sciences founded at Bologna in 1714, a series of reform initiatives, helped by Italy's long interval of relative peace in the eighteenth century, transformed most of these centres, raising academic standards and furnishing them with an impressive array of astronomical observatories, physics cabinets, botanical gardens, better anatomical theatres, and cabinets of rarities. Modern science and philosophy were very much in the air. Catholic enlighteners also proved receptive to much of Montesquieu and the pre-1755, essentially Lockean-Newtonian (and still ostensibly Christian) stance of

Voltaire.[1] During this period, Italy's several science academies became thoroughly imbued with the physico-theology of the Newtonians and botany of Linnaeus, and eagerly debated the latest electrical theories and experiments.[2]

There was considerable enthusiasm for such consciously innovative books as Voltaire's *Lettres philosophiques* of 1733 (not banned by the papacy until 1752) and Montesquieu's *Lettres persanes* of 1722 (not banned until 1762).[3] A few Enlightenment texts had appeared on the Index, and one or two, notably Giannone's *Civil History of the Kingdom of Naples* (1723), were vigorously suppressed, but always under traditional categories anathematized by the Church, not for introducing broadly innovative social, educational, legal, or epistemological ideas. Banned texts were condemned for 'heresy', 'judaizing', 'Socinianism', 'Pyrrhonism', or obscenity or else questioning ecclesiastical privilege, or, as with d'Argens's *Lettres juives*, because the author was deemed an outright 'enemy of revealed religion'. During the 1740s and early 1750s, the Inquisition interfered relatively rarely and the pressure of censorship generally eased. The first great prophet of cautious, step-by-step, ecclesiastical and social reform, the Modenese Ludovico Antonio Muratori (1672–1750), one of the prime architects of Catholic Enlightenment, previously embroiled in difficulties with the Holy Office, found himself in calmer waters from 1740, now directly under the pope's special protection.[4]

The Italy of the 1740s and 1750s was indeed a land marked by an eager, widespread enthusiasm for Enlightenment science and for Locke, Newton, Montesquieu, and the early Voltaire. Likewise, the indigenous flowering of early Enlightenment thought and erudition seemed destined to be officially endorsed, largely adopted, and accommodated. The outstanding figures—Muratori, Genovesi, Vico, Maffei, Giannone, and Gravina—all reflected a powerful impulse towards intellectual renewal, reform, and improvement, and reviving the investigative and critical apparatus of Italian scholarship combined with cautious accommodation of new philosophies and approaches entering from England, France, Holland, and Germany. The quest to reconcile Catholic teaching and Enlightenment so as to produce a more open and flexible intellectual culture capable of absorbing new philosophical systems and scientific findings and easing restrictions on thought without jeopardizing theology's primacy or the Church's dominance in social theory, and moral, educational, and cultural life was most powerfully represented by Muratori and Antonio Genovesi (1712–69), both men, especially the former, leading voices in Austria and Spain as well as Italy.

Everywhere signs of renewal abounded. The curriculum at Rome's Sapienza university was extensively revised, following the arrival at the Collegio Romano, in 1740, of the dynamic Ragusan Jesuit Ruggiero Boscovich (1711–87). Newtonianism

[1] Israel, *Radical Enlightenment*, 513–20.
[2] Rotta, 'Voltaire in Italia', 420–1; Findlen, 'Forgotten Newtonian', 317–21.
[3] Maire, 'L'Entrée des "Lumières" ', 114; Delpiano, *Governo*, 86; de Bujando, *Index*, 632.
[4] Bertelli, *Erudizione*, 172, 414–15, 417–19; Tortarolo, *L'Illuminismo*, 37.

became the officially approved path in natural philosophy there and at Bologna where Voltaire's *Éléments de la philosophie de Newton* figured prominently in teaching by the mid 1740s.[5] Doctrinally, none of this involved real difficulties as no Newtonian works had been placed on the Index. But it involved a considerable adjustment in terms of scientific outlook and intellectual attitudes especially regarding Copernicus, Galileo, and heliocentrism. There were to be no more proceedings, ruled Benedict, against writers expressing heliocentric views. Meanwhile, just as 'filosofia newtoni-ana' became entrenched as the veritable basis of Italian scientific thought under papal sanction by the early 1740s, so many Italian academics and clergy had become ardent *Locchisti*, as Locke's disciples were known, Locke's thought rapidly becoming a basic component of Catholic Enlightenment. Locke's empiricism, held Tomaso Vincenzio Moniglia (d. 1787), a Dominican and professor of Scripture and ecclesiastical history at Pisa, in his *Dissertazione contro i fatalisti* (2 vols., Lucca, 1744), and especially his emphasis on God's transcendence and 'proof' that matter at rest is wholly inert and cannot move of itself, constituted the most up-to-date basis for reconciling reason and faith and grounding a sophisticated modern epistemology without endangering belief in miracles and revelation. By separating the sphere of sense-experience from that of spiritual entities emphatically, Locke's empiricism could justifiably be viewed as the best barrier available against the *Spinosisti*, those representing the most virulent and dangerous intellectual threat to Catholic belief and thought in the eyes of Moniglia and Genovesi.[6]

Yet, it is also necessary to avoid following a certain strand of historiography extolling Benedict XIV as the herald of a truly modern liberal turn within the Church. For his and his cardinals' adoption of a moderate enlightened stance and firm espousal of Locke and Newton involved only a very limited retreat from the past in what were bound to be the most heavily contested domains—religious toleration and freedom of conscience and thought—and, generally speaking, the programmes of institutional, legal, and cultural as distinct from educational renewal the papacy endorsed were not very far-reaching. Benedict's Enlightenment opposed all questioning of the Church's still extensive powers and privileges, and denied all right to individual freedom of conscience, routinely obstructing attempts to extend toleration. When, in 1740, the Bourbon ruler of Naples, the future king of Spain, Carlos III, officially readmitted the Jews into Naples and Sicily (whence they had been expelled in 1492 and from the city of Naples in 1533) on an experimental basis, the attempt to promote this limited re-entry, mainly with an eye to stimulating commerce, was fiercely resisted by local preachers who stirred up the populace against the few who responded, opposition the papacy backed. The plague epidemic afflicting Messina in 1743 was among the malign occurrences ascribed to divine

[5] Rotta, 'Voltaire in Italia', 389, 420; Gross, *Rome*, 51–5; Pepe, 'Milieux savants', 223.
[6] Moniglia, *Dissertazione contro i fatalisti*, i. 41–2, 53, 143, 167; Moniglia, *Dissertazione contro i materialisti*, i. 47, 239, and ii. 231–2, 235.

displeasure over the return of the Jews. By the time Jewish readmission was formally rescinded, in 1746, it was already a dead letter.[7]

Benedict's real goal, reflected in his educational and science policies, attitude to Voltaire, championing of ecclesiastical privilege, and unbending adherence to the sixteenth-century ghetto regulations tightly confining the cultural and economic activities of Rome's large Jewish community,[8] was to adjust the ecclesiastical culture and attitudes of the past so as the better to entrench them, to adopt as realistic and effective a defensive posture as possible, yielding ground only at the edges the better to defend the core. The compromises he made he was mostly forced to make and for this reason they were rarely revoked subsequently even by his most emphatically Counter-Enlightenment successors.

Meanwhile, the most erudite of Italy's philosophers, Antonio Genovesi (1712–69), based at Naples, having scrutinized the entire European philosophical scenario of the 1740s, published two grand surveys, his *Elementa metaphysicae* (1743) and *Elementorum artis logicocriticae libri* V (1745), identifying disturbing fault-lines in all the acceptable modern philosophical blocs—Cartesianism, the Leibnizian-Wolffian system, and Locke's 'way of ideas', all of which he found more problematic than they appeared at first as regards durably harmonizing reason and faith.[9] What worried him most was what he considered the lack of real internal coherence in all three main modern moderate traditions, serious lacunae leaving room for the advance of what he deemed the false coherence of the anti-Christian underground of the *fatalisti* and *Spinosisti*, that is atheistic materialism. Much of the first part of his *Elementa* is devoted to systematic attack on Spinoza's *Ethics* and *Tractatus Theologico-Politicus* and on Spinoza's disciples Cuffeler and Boulainvilliers.[10]

Equally, there was acute anxiety about the destabilizing implications of even the most minimal *tolerantismo*. It was to warn students and the academic community against this principle, as well as against deism and materialism, that Moniglia published his *Dissertazione contro i materialisti ed altri increduli*, in two volumes, at Padua in 1750. A huge work with much to say about the subversive impact of Bayle and Spinoza, it stresses the close relationship between Spinozism and materialism. From a strictly philosophical standpoint Spinoza is arguably not a materialist since his parallelism of mind and body postulates two separate orders of causation and explanation with no causal interaction between them, the two dimensions being the same thing conceived under different aspects. But for the eighteenth century what mattered far more was that Spinoza rules out spiritual entities existing separately from bodies, holding that mind is always an aspect of body, so that anything spiritual must be material with no exceptions. Spinozism was hence invariably identified with materialism and very frequently considered the chief root of modern materialism, as

---

[7] Chadwick, *Popes*, 18–19.
[8] Ibid.; Caffiero, 'Gli ebrei', 111.
[9] Genovesi, *Elementa metaphysicae*, i. 26–33, and ii. 63, 98; Venturi, *Illuministici italiani*, v. 7–8.
[10] Genovesi, *Elementa metaphysicae*, i. 41, 50–6, 98–100.

was entirely logical given that Spinoza provides the most systematic denial of creation and final ends and most coherent doctrine of substance monism. Only if the *Spinosisti* are justified in their theory of substance and God, emphasized Moniglia, do the *materialisti* have a foot to stand on;[11] and this was quite true. In the Italy of 1750 as throughout Europe, there was no disputing that Spinoza 'e totalmente materialista' [is totally a materialist]. 'Spinozism is a repugnant, insolent and furious materialism and consists in not acknowledging any other substance than the divine substance, or any other divine substance, or other god, than uncreated and thinking matter.'[12] In Moniglia as in Genovesi this counted as the supreme threat. In Italy, Spinozism was the generic name of what was already a clearly conceptualized philosophical repressed underground challenging the very core of authority, theology, tradition, and belief, just as Locke's thought was the acknowledged bridge between faith and Enlightenment among those seeking an intellectually coherent Catholic Enlightenment.

By the 1740s, the public ascendancy of a Catholic Enlightenment acceptable to both Church and princes looked unchallengeable. But Catholic Enlightenment was in reality only very precariously dominant; and among the clergy as well as in the princely courts, universities, and science academies, it soon proved to lack sufficient support and sufficiently robust foundations to perform the work its adherents advocated. Both the post-1748 intellectual crisis and Counter-Enlightenment reaction that followed were already inherent in what became an arduous and complex three-way struggle. The long-standing tension between conservative theologians and the Enlightenment broadly defined culminated during 1749–51 in a highly significant and protracted initial battle in the papal Congregation of the Faith, at Rome, over what was undoubtedly the single most influential Enlightenment text in Italy during the century's third quarter, Montesquieu's *L'Esprit des loix* (1748). This episode also represented one of the most significant defeats for Pope Benedict's flexibility and reformism.

The clashes concerned *L'Esprit*'s moral naturalism and relativism and alleged underlying 'Spinozism', features being counterbalanced by Montesquieu's stress on Christianity as the moral inspiration of the best and most moderate forms of government. The dispute, carried on at the highest levels in Rome, stimulated a brisk sale of copies mostly supplied by Genevan publishers. Rome's incipient Counter-Enlightenment was headed by Cardinal Ganganelli, the future Clement XIV (pope: 1769–74).[13] In the end, Montesquieu's more provocative comments, such as his saying that no prince since Julian the Apostate had been worthier to govern men, or that Montezuma had been 'sensible' to say that if the Spaniards' religion was good for their country, Aztec cults were good for his, tipped the balance against him.[14]

---

[11] Moniglia, *Dissertazione contro i materialisti*, 302.

[12] Ibid. 309–10; Delpiano, *Governo*, 40, 223.

[13] *Index Librorum Prohibitorum* (1786), 101; Shackleton, *Montesquieu*, 370–7; Godman, *Geheime Inquisition*, 239–47; de Mas, *Montesquieu*, 16–17.

[14] *Propositiones Extractae ex Libro cui Titulus,* De l'esprit des loix (Geneva, 1750), nos. ix and xiii.

Following a long debate, Ganganelli and the conservatives triumphed. In November 1751, *L'Esprit des loix* was formally banned by the papacy, much to the distress of Montesquieu himself who had repeatedly implored the French ambassador in Rome to help avert it.

L'Esprit des loix was banned, however, only *donec corrigatur*. This was a clausule much used by the Congregation before 1750, consonant with a traditional procedure soon to be discarded along with the other changes of the 1750s. Mild terminology, the formula meant that much of the book was sound and that it was prohibited only provisionally until particular impieties were deleted, in theory leaving open the prospect of its legally appearing in a revised version later.[15] Montesquieu as such, accordingly, was not especially stigmatized by the prohibition, and even in ecclesiastical circles continued to enjoy great renown. Nevertheless, the edict exerted a negative effect on the status of *L'Esprit* in Italy and proved a turning point in the wider history of the Enlightenment. As confirmed in March 1752, the ban also comprehended the Italian translation,[16] prepared by the pro-Bourbon Florentine abbot Giuseppe Maria Mecatti, archivist of the last Medici grand duke, two volumes of which had appeared at Naples in 1750. By this point, the translation—itself a major project—was abandoned half finished, the two latter volumes never appearing.[17] Not until 1774 was a complete Italian version available, clandestinely printed at 'Amsterdam' (i.e. Venice).[18]

If Catholic Enlightenment was powerless even to ensure the unrestricted diffusion of Montesquieu, how could it resolve the many and intractable problems arising from the overlapping of Church–state jurisdiction, law reform, the problem of toleration, and alignment with the religiously and politically cautious Enlightenment? The new situation, after 1751, like Genovesi's thought, reflected not just the dilemmas of philosophical enquiry in mid-eighteenth-century Italy, but also the wider and deeper crisis of the Italian reality itself—the extreme difficulty of solving the country's chronic administrative and judicial as well as economic and social structural problems within the framework of Catholic moderate Enlightenment. If, philosophically, the main lines of Italy's emerging intellectual and cultural crisis were evident by 1750, by the late 1750s it was fast becoming obvious that the country was caught in a tight political-intellectual impasse from which there was no easy exit. Benedict XIV's tentative Enlightenment, the phase of cultural stability of the 1740s, circumstances proved, was ultimately illusory—a wholly insufficient basis for freedom of thought, toleration, wide-ranging Enlightenment, or significant moral and institutional reform.

Admittedly, neither the ban on *L'Esprit des loix* nor suppression of the Italian translation prevented the broad diffusion of Montesquieu's influence in Italy. But

---

[15] Gross, *Rome*, 261–2; Maire, 'L'Entrée', 114–16.
[16] *Index Librorum Prohibitorum* (1786), 101, 277; de Bujando, *Index*, 632.
[17] Davidson, 'Toleration', 231; de Mas, *Montesquieu*, 28–9, 36, 187.
[18] *L'Europa letteraria. Giornale*, 1 (1772/3), 102–3.

much of this was *sotto voce*.[19] After 1750, commentators felt obliged to exercise discretion when discussing his ideas. While most prominent Enlightenment figures during the century's third quarter, including Genovesi and Beccaria, were manifestly indebted to the great Frenchman, they were also wary of his naturalism. Of particular relevance here are Genovesi's notes on Montesquieu, included after his death in the third Italian edition of *L'Esprit des loix* published at Naples, in 1777. Montesquieu Genovesi admired for many reasons, above all his zeal for *moderazione*, but he remained suspicious of the libertine dimension of his work, such as his thesis that climate had powerfully contributed to Christianity's prevalence in particular regions. As for his suggesting religious offences perpetrated in private should not be punished by the ecclesiastical or secular authorities, this Genovesi felt obliged to reject explicitly and outright.[20]

Genovesi's and Muratori's desires for a flourishing Catholic Enlightenment were partly dashed by Benedict's failures and death but not wholly. For if Benedict failed altogether to get his way, so did his Venetian successor, Carlo Rezzonico (son of the noble who completed the Ca' Rezzonico, on the Grand Canal), Clement XIII (pope: 1758–69). Enlightenment undoubtedly suffered setbacks under this austere supreme pontiff.[21] Suppression of enlightened works intensified; priests were banned from attending theatres; tighter restrictions, destined to remain in force for over a century, were placed on access to the Biblioteca Vaticana.[22] Clement, like his successor Clement XIV, abhorred and waged war on 'l'esprit philosophique', his denouncing the atheistic fringe being as unrelenting as his rampant nepotism. Following his election, in November 1758, the papal nuncio in Paris was alerted that the new pope planned to combat pernicious ideas far more vigorously than his predecessor, being horrified by reports of a 'scuola d'ateismo' [school of atheism], headed by 'd'Alembert, Buffon, Diderot, de Maillet [who had died in 1738], Yvon, Crebillon, La Touche, Rousseau, Helvétius and others'.[23] If some of his data were obsolete, there was no doubting the gravity with which Clement viewed the threat posed by the philosophical movement to religion, clerical privilege, and ecclesiastical authority. The new pope's campaign against 'pernicious philosophy' was announced as a special feature of his pontificate in the published announcements to their dioceses, or *mandements*, issued by the archbishop of Paris and other French bishops in 1759.

In this context, the papal ban of 1759 on the *Encyclopédie* represents, as many have noted, a turning point in the wider cultural mechanics of the Italian Enlightenment and one destined to have even wider effects than suppressing the *Esprit des loix*. The ban materialized only after years of bitter internal strife within the Vatican.[24] The question unresolved at Benedict's death, in 1758, prior to the royal suppression in

---

[19] Imbruglia, 'Due opposte letture', 191, 193.
[20] Genovesi, *Note* to the *Spirito delle leggi*, ii. 9–11 and iii. 89; Berselli Ambri, *L'opera*, 147–9.
[21] Berselli Ambri, *L'opera*, 56, 60, 63.
[22] Gross, *Rome*, 272; Pepe, 'Milieux savants', 223–4.
[23] Cardinal Torrigiani to Nuncio Luigi Gualtieri, Rome, 15 Nov. 1758, *CGdH* ii. 148.
[24] Delpiano, *Governo*, 94–7; Maire, 'L'Entrée', 108, 122, 132, 134.

France, was whether the papacy should impose a limited form of censure, as one might expect under Benedict, or more forthright terminology, comprehensively suppressing the *Encyclopédie*. If the latter's scathing remarks about the Inquisition, Crusades, papal authority, and priestly celibacy were unacceptable and its eulogy of Montesquieu problematic, proponents of Catholic Enlightenment argued that such imperfections could be expunged. Moderate enlighteners were thwarted, though, by a growing realization in the Vatican of the real character and pervasiveness of the work's core theses.

As the *Encyclopédie* was neither a work of theology nor concerned doctrine Benedict had assigned the business to the Congregation of the Index. The Congregation's committee split, but with even the most hostile member, Giovanni Luigi Mingarelli, a leading Hellenist and orientalist at Bologna, recommending only deletion of a long list of unacceptable statements, such as those concerning life and matter in Diderot's article 'Animal'. Even Mingarelli urged no more than a *donec corrigatur* edict, pinpointing 'errors' for removal while implying the work as a whole was acceptable and, if revised, publishable.[25] A draft papal statute along these lines was actually drawn up. However, this outcome failed to satisfy the new pope and the whole affair was transferred to the Holy Office. The Inquisition's twenty-seven-page report written by a Jansenist history professor at Bologna, Mauro Sarti, saw no possibility of satisfactorily revising the *Encyclopédie*. If especially outraged by the editors' diatribe, in their preface to volume iii, against Jansenism, he considered the whole work infused with atheistic and dangerous concepts.[26] Claiming Helvétius's *De l'esprit* reveals the *Encyclopédie*'s true doctrinal position, echoing recent French attacks on the *Encyclopédie* in the *Nouvelles ecclésiastiques* and *Préjugés légitimes* of Chaumeix whom the new pope had personally congratulated in writing, Sarti, like Chaumeix, firmly brackets the *Encyclopédie* with *De l'esprit*, a work lately prohibited in the most stringent terms (and in every language) by papal edict of January 1759.[27]

Endorsing Sarti's view, the pope banned the *Encyclopédie in toto* together with eleven other works on 5 March 1759.[28] But this still left open the question of the revised version being prepared at Lucca; and here the Inquisition committee themselves split. Based on the original French text, the Lucca edition (28 vols., Lucca, 1758–76), styling itself the 'seconde édition enrichie de notes', began appearing in 1758, distributed by the publishing house of Vincenzo Giuntini. The chief editor, Ottaviano Diodati (1716–86), was a Lucchese nobleman who had already produced an Italian version of the Liège *Journal encyclopédique*.[29] A year before the 1758 papal prohibition, he dedicated the first of the eventually seventeen volumes of his 'corrected' *Encyclopédie* to the Lucca senate, meeting with 'universal approbation'. An

---

[25] Maire, 'L'Entrée', 122–4.   [26] Ibid. 127–31; Delpiano, *Governo*, 96.

[27] *Index Librorum Prohibitorum* (1786), 101; Morellet, *Mémoires*, i. 72; Venturi, *Settecento riformatore*, ii. 252, 255–6; Maire, 'L'Entrée', 135.

[28] *Damnatio et Prohibitio Operis in Plures Tomos Distributi, Cujus est Titulus: Encylopédie* (Rome, 1759), 2; *Bibliothèque des sciences*, 12 (1759), 1st part, 234–5; Godman, *Geheime Inquisition*, 258–60.

[29] Arato, 'Savants, philosophes', 76–7.

enormous mass of Italian notes and 'corrections' designed to counter the *Encyclopédie*'s sweeping critique of Catholic theology, papal jurisdiction, and Christianity generally had been compiled over several years by a team headed by a future archbishop of Lucca and himself.[30]

Furthermore, much of this vast labour of deleting unacceptable passages and adding footnotes to render the new version acceptable to Catholic opinion had, even though most volumes had not yet appeared, already been approved by the Congregation and was being prepared for the press.[31] Thus, the edition with the 'Lucca corrections' was already an authorized as well as in part a published reality, with some 1,500 subscribers and the first seven volumes, published in the years 1758–60, proving a considerable success. Not even all the Inquisitors, let alone the Congregation, believed such 'errors' as remained sufficed to justify prohibiting such a costly, large-scale, and internationally known compilation that undoubtedly contained a prodigious amount of useful practical information. Thanks to scrupulous editing, the Lucca version had already won a reputation for orthodoxy and piety and become a veritable pillar of Catholic Enlightenment not just in Italy but also Spain and Spanish America where it was being warmly recommended to the public.[32]

As the definitive papal condemnation of the *Encyclopédie* in all versions, of 3 September 1759, admits, several highly placed churchmen felt that a purged version could have been useful to society, scholarship, 'and even Christianity' if accompanied by extensive notes to sensitive articles erasing all 'danger' and everything 'harmful'. Some were inclined to consider Chaumeix's accusations rather exaggerated; and then there was the risk a definitive ban might prompt an Italian or French edition printed in Geneva without the Lucca 'antidote' and hence subject to no ecclesiastical censorship at all.[33] Against this, Cardinal Agostino Orsi, a Dominican and active opponent of Catholic Enlightenment and all *materialismo, fatalismo,* and *indifferentismo,* urged that a comprehensive ban rigorously enforced in Italy and France would sufficiently deter the Genevan publishers from risking such a costly venture.[34]

Six months after banning the original, the pope's select committee reached agreement to suppress the Lucca edition too. The Church could not avoid quashing this version also, as 'the poison spread throughout the work is not of such a nature as to be capable of being eradicated by deletions and explanatory notes', though the decree also betrays a note of embarrassment that those labouring for years on the Lucca revised text had now 'lost their time and labour'.[35] Thus the *Encyclopédie* was condemned outright in all versions as 'continens doctrinam atque propositiones falsas, perniciosas et scandalosas, ad incredulitatem et religionis contemptum inducentes', besides endangering morals.[36] Posted in the Campo dei Fiori where Bruno

[30] Arato, 'Savants, philosophes', 77; Delpiano, *Governo*, 95–6.   [31] Maire, 'L'Entrée', 133.
[32] Almodóvar, *Década*, 96.
[33] *Estratto della letteratura europea* (Berne, Oct.–Dec. 1759), 44, 66–7.
[34] Godman, *Geheime Inquisition*, 260–1; Maire, 'L'Entrée', 132.
[35] *Damnatio, et prohibitio*, 2; Delpiano, *Governo*, 97.
[36] Maire, 'L'Entrée', 128, 131.

was burnt at the stake in 1600 and on the exterior walls of major churches, the edict summoned loyal Catholics, under pain of excommunication, to surrender all private copies of the *Encyclopédie*'s existing volumes to be burnt by their parish priest.[37]

These developments further changed Italy's intellectual climate. Not the least significant result was that the Jansenist accusation that the *nouveaux philosophes* were an active conspiracy formed by Diderot, d'Alembert, and Helvétius, an underground potentially fatal to faith, morals, and the Church, became integral to papal policy and thinking. A significant force during the 1740s and 1750s, Italian moderate Enlightenment had now pervaded Spain, Spanish America, Portugal, Brazil, and Austria as well as Italy itself. But it also remained a fragile, closely besieged construct. A few months after the definitive papal condemnation, of 1759, all work on the Lucca version ceased due to the ban (initially ignored by the Lucca senate) and to marketing difficulties, the papal decree severely depressing sales. Italy's largest Enlightenment project thus came to be suspended for years, only resuming in the late 1760s—the twelfth volume appearing in 1769. The project was not completed until 1776.

Censuring Voltaire, meanwhile, now a publicly declared deist and foe of Christianity, also gathered momentum while works such as Montesquieu's *Lettres persanes* previously deemed not especially threatening were now prohibited.[38] Generally, all this had the effect of negating the Church's prior willingness to tolerate aspects of Montesquieu and Voltaire, pruning the Italian moderate Enlightenment back and further aggravating the friction between Counter- and Catholic Enlightenment, as well as between the mainstream and Radical Enlightenment. Catholic Enlightenment had lost its former hegemony in the Vatican; but, of course, could not so easily be driven from the Church, universities, and society generally. It sought refuge, in particular, in a doggedly unphilosophical pragmatism. After 1750, Genovesi abandoned his former eclectic search for a coherent metaphysics and ethics to concentrate on political economy, especially after being appointed, in 1754, to the new chair in political economy at Naples, among the first of its kind established in Europe. He nevertheless remained defensively engaged in philosophical debate, persisting with his polemic against Spinozism into his last years as well as with denouncing Bayle's impieties, especially the latter's insinuating thesis that 'superstition' is worse than 'atheism'.[39] Meanwhile, the quest for human betterment remained central to his thought, his staunch defence of religious orthodoxy, aristocracy, and enlightened monarchy by no means precluding his ambition to reform all three in various respects. The nobility he urged to engage more with the rest of society, invest in industry, and help introduce useful improvements.[40]

To fortify an impregnable bridge between reason and faith, progress and tradition, definitively blocking Spinozism, Genovesi drew up five basic propositions together

---

[37] *Index Librorum Prohibitorum* (1786), 95; Negroni, *Lectures*, 202, 209.
[38] Maire, 'L'Entrée', 107–16.
[39] Zambelli, *Formazione filosofica*, 603–12; Villlari, 'Antonio Genovesi', 605–7.
[40] Imbruglia, 'Enlightenment', 79–80; Robertson, *Case*, 354.

constituting what he called *teologia filosofica*, a core of natural theology designed securely to weld philosophy and theology together. These were: (1), that there exists an eternal and omniscient intelligence; (2), that the universe is the creation of this intelligence and something ordained to be conserved under immutable laws; (3), that men are ruled by divine providence from whom we derive the basic rules of what is just and virtuous, rules that are immutable, being the will of God; (4), that no virtue remains without reward, nor vice without punishment in the hereafter; and (5), that the soul departs its body to be eternally happy, or wretched, depending on whether it had been virtuous or sinful.[41] Theology and philosophy could in this way unite and their union be held to characterize all truly enlightened education, ethics, politics, legislation, scholarship, and social policy.

Genovesi's and Muratori's Catholic Enlightenment combined defence of Christianity with championing monarchy, aristocracy, and the existing social and moral order, all resting on the principles of physico-theology and the beneficence of divine providence. Yet, Genovesi's legacy was not altogether a harmonizing and moderating one. His 'philosophical theology', tying reason and faith together, was designed to buttress a specifically Catholic Enlightenment. 'Reason', if based on Newtonian physico-theology, as he held it must be, leads undeviatingly, he maintained, to the truths of Christianity.[42] Yet these avowals could not hide the fact that his basic propositions were potentially compatible also with deism, Socinianism, and other forms of monotheism so that, to an extent, his philosophy too was a factor of instability even if Genovesi himself always rejected deistic arguments. His teaching attracted numerous able and influential students not all of whom adopted his unreservedly conservative social, political, and religious stance. Among the latter were the anticlerical Giuseppe Maria Galanti and still more radical-minded thinker Francesco Longano di Ripalimosani (1729–96), author of a work on 'natural man' published at Naples in 1767 that showed a distinct unwillingness to accept Rousseau's vision of the noble savage.[43]

2. BECCARIA AND LEGAL REFORM

Politically, Catholic Enlightenment aligned with 'enlightened despotism'. Genovesi knew the chronic backwardness of Neapolitan society and difficulty of framing adequate social reforms, but sought the solution in enlightening princely authority.[44] He flatly disagreed with Montesquieu that division of powers enhances 'moderation' in monarchies and that ambition and honour is monarchy's moral foundation while

[41] Genovesi, *Delle scienze metafisiche*, 168, 173.
[42] Ibid. 20–3, 180–2, 236–8, 268–9, 282.
[43] Zambelli, *Formazione filosofica*, 431, 435; Ricuperati, *Frontiere*, 292; Imbruglia, 'Enlightenment', 87–8; Ferrone, 'Il problema', 164.
[44] Imbruglia, 'Enlightenment', 74–6; Imbruglia, 'Due opposte letture', 203.

'virtue' is the moral basis of republics, a proposition he dismisses as a crude sophism neither cogent nor useful.[45] How can a Christian monarchy's laws possess their required force if 'virtue' is not their basis? Montesquieu in his book on the Roman empire's decline sees moral corruption as the cause of the ruin of great states. Does this not altogether contradict his claim about monarchy in *L'Esprit*?

Discussion of such philosophical, political, legal, and social issues aroused keen interest throughout Italy not least in *Il caffè*, the celebrated if short-lived journal produced at Milan in the years 1764–6 by Pietro and Alessandro Verri, Beccaria, and the group of ten or twelve leading enlighteners gathered around them. Pietro Verri (1728–97), an army officer who rose to become a high functionary in Milan, active in economic affairs, and the personage at the centre of the Enlightenment group dubbed the *coterie de Milan* in Paris, began his intellectual career by closely studying *L'Esprit des loix* in the years 1759–60.[46] Montesquieu was deeply admired by the architects of Milanese enlightened despotism. But like Genovesi, they highlighted his 'errors' as well as his 'wise reflections',[47] albeit unlike him, they did not especially look to the Church to promote Enlightenment in Italy and were less than emphatic in declaring their Catholic orientation. While anxious not to give offence, they looked primarily to 'enlightened despotism' to take the initiative and engineer the improvements Italy needed.

Nothing better illustrates the besieged, tightly constrained, precarious character of Italy's Enlightenment than the career of the Italian who made the greatest impact on the wider European scene—Beccaria—and the closely entwined lives of his friends Pietro and Alessandro Verri. Studying first at the Jesuit Collegio Farnesiano, in Parma, where he underwent what he later called 'eight years of fanatical and servile education',[48] and, then, the university of Pavia (1754–8), Beccaria graduated in law in September 1758. Soon after, in 1761, he was won over, he later informed Morellet, his French translator, to what he called 'sentiments of humanity', that is an enlightened outlook. This happened, he explained, via reading Montesquieu's *Lettres persanes* followed by other 'excellent' books of the *philosophes*.[49] But it was especially the 'second book [of philosophy] I read that wrought a revolution in me', he records, and this 'was by M. Helvétius'. 'It was he who pushed me powerfully in the direction of the truth and first awoke my attention to the blindness and misfortunes of mankind. I owe a large portion of my ideas to the reading of *De l'esprit*.'[50]

Beccaria's career as an enlightener began in Milanese literary society, especially among a select group he helped to found, the Accademia dei Pugni (1761–4).

[45] Imbruglia, 'Due opposte letture', 204; Genovesi, *Note* to the *Spirito delle leggi*, i. 316–17; de Mas, *Montesquieu*, 73–4, 112–15, 118.
[46] De Mas, *Montesquieu*, 51–2; Capra, *I progressi*, 157, 160, 162.
[47] *Il caffè, ossia Brevi e vari Discorsi*, i. 83, 110, 180.
[48] Helvétius, *CGdH* iii. 253.
[49] Venturi, *Settecento riformatore*, i. 677.
[50] Beccaria to Morellet, Milan, 26 Jan. 1766, in Helvétius, *CGdH* iii. 251–2; Venturi, *Riformatori Lombardi*, 3, 6; Imbruglia, 'Piacere', 176.

Doubtless it was his friend and mentor Pietro Verri who introduced him to Helvétius since *De l'esprit* was a book that had also greatly impressed Verri.[51] Though perhaps not a great thinker, Helvétius and *Helvétianisme* unquestionably exerted, noted Naigeon in 1791, a remarkable impact on the more intellectually inclined reform-minded in Italy,[52] much as Helvétius also did in Germany and Russia. The English utilitarian Bentham, a thinker willing, on occasion, to acknowledge Beccaria as 'my master', clearly recognized that also his philosophical inspiration and zeal for reform originated in Helvétius.[53] In addition, Beccaria imbibed Diderot, d'Alembert, Hume, and Buffon. Of Diderot he exclaimed, in 1765, 'what a wonderful man he must be!'[54] In aspiring to become a 'philosophe', Beccaria was motivated by his reading and by a quarrel with his family over his wishing to marry a girl he loved whom his parents deemed their social inferior. The Verris too had quarrelled with their father.[55]

Beccaria viewed himself and his friends as locked in a stupendous combat with the forces of superstition, ignorance, and fanaticism. In Milan, a city of 120,000 inhabitants, he assured Morellet, 'there are hardly twenty individuals desiring to instruct themselves and devote themselves to truth and virtue'. He offered to send Morellet copies of *Il caffè*, the journal of the *Pugni* that his 'dearest friend', Pietro Verri, edited with the permission of the Austrian imperial authorities, and to which they all contributed, 'my friends and I being convinced such journals are among the best ways to coax those incapable of serious application to read a little. We publish a sheet on the model of the *Spectator* which in England has done so much to add to the culture of the mind and progress of good sense.'[56] Discarding the format of the erudite journals, theirs being intended rather to penetrate Milanese aristocratic and upper bourgeois café society, a major object was to propagate in Italy ideas of French economic writers, especially Forbonnais, Verri's favourite *économiste*.

Beccaria's *Delle delitti e delle pene*, the most famous eighteenth-century Italian work after Vico's *New Science*, completed in January 1764, was composed with the help of other leading Milanese enlighteners, especially Pietro Verri and his brother.[57] Between them, the brothers Verri and Beccaria formulated a 'utilitarian' theory of penal law, much influenced by Helvétius and, to a lesser extent, Rousseau, whose *Contrat social* Verri and Beccaria both got to know in 1762.[58] Beccaria's masterpiece was hence the fruit of intensive group dialogue much like Rousseau's initial two *Discours*.[59] Expounded, noted Bentham later, with the 'precision and clearness and

---

[51] Verri, *Meditazioni*, 13, 58; Capra, *I progressi*, 160.
[52] Naigeon, *Philosophie*, ii. 673.
[53] Halévy, *Growth*, 52, 56–9; Zarone, *Cesare Beccaria*, 42; Blamires, 'Beccaria', 74.
[54] Venturi (ed.), 'Storia e dibattiti', 365; Venturi, *Settecento riformatore*, i. 677.
[55] Venturi, *Settecento riformatore*, i. 647–8; Venturi, *Riformatori Lombardi*, 3.
[56] Venturi (ed.), 'Storia e dibattiti', 365–6; Morellet, *Memoires*, i. 167; Capra, *I progressi*, 189–91, 220; Dioguardi, *Attualità*, 20, 28.
[57] Venturi, *Settecento riformatore*, i. 704–5; Venturi, 'Storia e dibattiti', 116, 122, 186.
[58] Wokler, *Rousseau*, 169; Capra, *I progressi*, 192–3.
[59] Venturi, *Riformatori Lombardi*, 6, 386–7.

incontestableness of mathematical calculations',[60] Beccaria's theses aspired to be universally applicable and, as his disciple Gorani stressed in 1770, were a powerful stimulus to social reform.[61] The object of legislation, held Beccaria, like Verri, Helvétius, and later Bentham, should be 'the greatest happiness of the greatest number', though Bentham, in 1776, reformulated the maxim to read: 'it is the greatest happiness of the greatest number that is the measure of right and wrong.'[62] Beccaria capped his quest for fairness, proportionality, and precision in the penal law with pleas for an end to judicial torture and the death penalty.

The renown of Beccaria's *Delle delitti*, a landmark of Enlightenment literature, spread swiftly. Hailed everywhere, its penetration was aided by the author's 'seductive' style.[63] Though banned by the papacy in February 1766, Italian commentators were frequently positive, especially in private. Filippo Maria Renazzi, professor at the Sapienza, in Rome, a keen disciple of Locke and Montesquieu, welcomed the treatise albeit dissenting strongly—as had Genovesi from Montesquieu—from what Beccaria says about religious 'offences', insisting Italy's laws must punish impiety and religious irreverence.[64] In Naples it was especially among Genovesi's pupils and disciples that it resonated.[65] An international best-seller, d'Alembert read it in September 1765, Turgot, acquiring both the Italian and French versions, soon after, and Hume, 'with great care', in 1766.[66] Appearing in two different French editions, the book was immediately banned in France, though, by the Paris *Parlement*, due to its scorning all existing law.[67] Published in English in 1767, it appeared in an influential Spanish version by Juan Antonio de las Casas in 1774 (this edition banned by the Inquisition three years later), and in German, at Ulm, in 1778, under the title *Des herrn Marquis von Beccaria unsterbliches Werk von Verbrechen und Strafen*.

Beccaria proposed to reform the penal law according to what is good or bad for society. Until a defendant is pronounced guilty, he is entitled to the state's protection just like other citizens, so that it betrays the state's own true functions, when investigating crimes, to subject accused persons or unwilling witnesses to judicial torture or any intimidation.[68] 'Torture has been abolished in Sweden', he observed, 'and by one of the wisest monarchs of Europe [i.e. Frederick], who, bringing philosophy to the throne and legislating as the friend of his subjects, has made them equal and free under the law which is the only equality and freedom reasonable men could demand in the present state of things.'[69] Rather than execution, over in a moment, sentencing to hard labour is more lasting and effective as a deterrent. His denunciation of judicial torture fitted with the tenor of the age. Ended in Sweden in

---

[60] Rosen, 'Utilitarianism', 551.   [61] Gorani, *Vero dispotismo*, i. 38 and ii. 272.

[62] Bentham, *Fragment on Government*, 3; Verri, *Meditazioni*, 61, 82.

[63] Spiriti, *Riflessioni economico-politiche*, 32–5; Imbruglia, 'Piacere', 176; Pasta, 'Dei delitti', 146–7.

[64] Pasta, 'Dei delitti', 129–30; de Bujando, *Index*, 116.

[65] Pasta, 'Dei delitti', 139.

[66] Ibid. 14; Mazza, 'Hume's "Meek" Philosophy', 214.

[67] Venturi, *Riformatori Lombardi*, 18, 24–5.

[68] Beccaria, *On Crimes*, 39; Globig and Huster, *Abhandlung*, 67.

[69] Beccaria, *On Crimes*, 42; Hubatsch, *Frederick the Great*, 41, 211; Blom, *Wicked Company*, 223.

1734 and Prussia in 1740, it was abolished after Beccaria's book appeared in Baden in 1767, Saxony in 1770, Denmark in 1771, Austria in 1776, and in France in August 1780.[70]

Among the most sensational literary successes of the age, the book was eloquent and effective. In one swoop Beccaria discredited the entire legal culture of the Western world as archaic, barbaric, violent, and irrational. But while the work's reception was broadly enthusiastic, it was also fiercely criticized by conservative and some reform-minded jurists several of whom discerned, as most admirers did not, that Beccaria's system was rooted in the 'suppositions' of the *philosophes modernes*. Especially objected to were Beccaria's references to equality which critics assumed he took from Rousseau.[71] The Neapolitan jurist Giandonato Rogadeo, commissioned by the Maltese grand master to reform Malta's laws along Catholic enlightened lines, a reformer operating in Malta with undeniable zeal and energy, immediately grasped that from a specifically Catholic viewpoint Beccaria's book was highly pernicious and, in 1777, demanded it be generally banned.[72]

Many of Beccaria's admirers indeed had little understanding of the implications of his philosophical premises. 'It is better', held Beccaria, 'to prevent crimes than punish them.' Conceiving each person to have joined with every other to form the state solely to protect themselves from insecurity, intruders, and marauders, he inferred from this purely protective-utilitarian role that the sovereign is never justified in taking anyone's life. Inspired by Helvétius, Montesquieu, and Rousseau, Beccaria held that the essential aim of all good legislation is the 'art of guiding men to their greatest happiness, or the least unhappiness possible, taking into account all the blessings and evils of life'. This meant that all the legal arrangements hitherto employed for this end had been woefully misconceived 'or contrary to the proposed goal'.[73] Like the *encyclopédistes*, Beccaria did not doubt that philosophy, of the sort he had acquired from Helvétius, was the principal agent of change. If government and society as well as individuals wished to see crime and degradation curbed then they must accept that 'enlightenment and freedom go hand in hand'.[74] His treatise ends with the striking general axiom: 'in order that punishment should not be an act of violence perpetrated by one or many upon a private citizen, it is essential that it be public, speedy, necessary, the minimum possible in the given circumstances, *proporzionata ai' delitti* [proportionate to the offences], and determined by the law.' This principle is both rational and just but, he added, 'poco conforme all'uso, legislatore il piú ordinario delle nazioni' [little conforms to present usage—the most common legislator among nations].[75]

---

[70] Lardizábal y Uribe, *Discurso*, 284; Doyle, *Old European Order*, 212.
[71] Venturi, 'Storia e dibattiti', 173, 187.
[72] Vergani, *Traité*, introduction pp. xxv, xxxiv–xxxvi; Ciappara, *Enlightenment and Reform in Malta*, 64.
[73] Beccaria, *On Crimes*, 103; Jonard, *L'Italie*, 188.
[74] Beccaria, *On Crimes*, 105; Vergani, *Traité*, introduction p. xxxiv.
[75] Beccaria, *On Crimes*, 113.

'Assaults upon persons', argues Beccaria, 'as distinct from thefts without violence (better punished by monetary fines), should always entail corporal punishment or imprisonment rather than monetary fines' so that 'the rich and powerful should not be able to put a lowly price on assaulting the weak and poor'.[76] Otherwise, the wealthy or powerful man will readily expatiate his crime with a sum that may seem substantial to a destitute victim but is trifling to the miscreant and without proportion to the penalty he would wish to see exacted on whoever did the like to him. Concerning the nobility, Beccaria argued that 'punishments ought to be the equivalent for the highest as for the lowest of citizens'. 'The criterion of punishment', he answered those deeming it unjust to punish nobles alike with commoners, given the difference in upbringing and shame brought on an illustrious house, 'is not the culprit's sensitivity but the harm to the public which is all the greater when perpetrated by the more privileged'.[77]

A chief category of crimes in his system consists of those infringing the well-being, security, and freedom of individuals. Conceiving the 'true definition' of crime to be 'harm to society'[78] must thus here be understood in terms of Helvétius's and Beccaria's central principle that society consists of individuals of equal worth and rights. Hence there are no religious crimes. Violating another individual's right to security that each citizen earns by surrendering part of his natural freedom should incur the heaviest punishments society's laws prescribe, whoever is responsible.[79] If murders and thefts by ordinary folk are reckoned grave crimes so, equally, should be such crimes perpetrated by rulers, nobles, and magistrates against those under their power, as they are causing equivalent damage and since inequality of treatment destroys faith in the law's commitment to justice. The law must always be an equal and 'calm modifier of individual passions' and hence must not itself be swayed by passions or award favours, or seek vengeance. The penal code must be designed only to 'deter the offender from doing fresh harm to his fellows and others from doing likewise'.[80] Hence, chastisement and methods of imposing it should conform to a carefully calculated scheme of proportionality, ranging upwards from light retribution for brawling and rowdiness in the streets, fixed to make the most appropriate impression while minimizing pain inflicted on the condemned.[81] Unlike Bentham and Filangieri later, though, Beccaria did not think proportionality in punishing crimes was fixable with geometric precision.[82]

The deplorable state of Europe's current legal systems arose, he held, from the indefensible tradition of treating society as an agglomeration of families rather than individuals. Recognizing the primacy of families, leaving husbands to exercise an unchecked ascendancy over their wives and children, means turning a society of

[76] Ibid. 50.   [77] Ibid. 52.   [78] Beccaria, *On Crimes*, 24.
[79] Ibid. 25; Filangieri, *Scienza della legislazione*, iv. 14.
[80] Filangieri, *Scienza della legislazione*, iv. 16; Beccaria, *On Crimes*, 31.
[81] Beccaria, *On Crimes*, 31.
[82] Filangieri, *Scienza della legislazione*, iv. 140; Rosen, 'Utilitarianism', 553, 557.

100,000 individuals into one with 20,000 autonomous persons and 80,000 slaves.[83] This fundamental error, he urged, served to justify the ruinous practice of confiscating convicted criminals' property irrespective of the effect on children and female dependants. According excessive weight to family bonds and not enough to individual rights generates huge conflicts and distortion within society over fundamental loyalties and morality. Likewise, existing practice stigmatizing families of suicides,[84] and imprisonment of debtors where no culpable fraud has been proved beyond default owing to misfortune or the wrongdoing of others, was altogether unsatisfactory.[85] He was scathing also about the draconian punishments for smugglers when states themselves foster smuggling by heaping duties on commodities the public wants, something all the more undesirable in that most people do not think smugglers do harm to society.[86]

Beccaria's reform proposals called in question not just existing practice but the whole basis of privilege legal, fiscal, and ecclesiastical. All this was flatly contrary to Hume and broadly in line with Diderot and d'Holbach, as was Beccaria's theory of human progress with his insistence that man's natural right in the state of nature carries over into society and his optimism that mankind could look forward to a future 'state of equality and happiness', even though still very distant, based on true justice and natural feelings.[87] Beccaria's legal principles, in short, sprang from a concept of equality before the law (without which Helvétius's utilitarian moral philosophy made no sense and had no application to law reform) that some recognized to be incompatible not just with nobility, ecclesiastical authority, and theology's supremacy, but also prevailing notions of family.[88] Much crime, suggested Beccaria, is really the fault of an intrinsically unequal society that foments it, though he was less forthright here than d'Holbach in his *Système social* (1773).[89]

Beccaria's reformist vision clashed fundamentally with the essentials of the *ancien régime*. Yet, at the same time, he belonged to the reforming clique at the Austrian Habsburg court in Milan and, like Pietro Verri in his *Meditazioni sulla felicità* (Livorno, 1763), relied on the principle of enlightened princely absolutism to carry through his agenda. There were also other elements in Beccaria that contradicted the principles of Helvétius, Diderot, and d'Holbach, though initially this was readily smoothed over. His explicit deference to the Church Beccaria urged his allies in Paris to ignore as purely discretionary and insincere. When writing his book he had had the unfortunate experiences of Machiavelli, Galileo, and Giannone in mind, he explained, and could hear 'the rattling chains of superstition and howls of fanaticism stifling the faint moans of truth' outside his door, thoughts that 'caused me—forced me—sometimes to veil the light of truth in a pious shroud'. He planned to defend

---

[83] Beccaria, *On Crimes*, 60; Pii, 'Republicanism', 269–71.   [84] Beccaria, *On Crimes*, 83–6.
[85] Ibid. 89–90.   [86] Ibid. 87–8.
[87] Beccaria, 'Pensieri', 106–12; Venturi, *Riformatori Lombardi*, 15; Jonard, *L'Italie*, 211.
[88] Tortarolo, *L'Illuminismo*, 162; Ferrone, *Società giusta*, 115.
[89] D'Holbach, *Système social*, 437–8.

humanity with passion but 'without becoming a martyr to it'.[90] Initially, Beccaria was hailed in d'Holbach's salon as a welcome recruit to their ranks. However, his constant hesitation when writing, pliability, readiness to please, and excessive vanity suggested a certain spinelessness that, before long, made the *encyclopédistes* suspicious of his utilitarian radicalism. So did what Grimm called his timidity in publicly thanking Morellet who translated his text into one of its two French versions for 'disfiguring' his book whilst privately being furious about it.[91]

Beccaria was opposed by those realizing his legal philosophy leaves no room for crimes of heresy, sacrilege, blasphemy, or sorcery and none for 'fornication' or homosexuality or scope for policing and coercion to support religion and officially supported moral standpoints.[92] In Beccaria and Pietro Verri, theological criteria have no role in defining offences or determining punishment, something tacitly undermining the very foundation of the Inquisition.[93] While there was no explicit attack on religion, it slowly became clearer that in Beccaria one encounters a complete desacralizing of the law and penal code, a separation of legal thought from theology that later culminated in Bentham's justification of a whole range of irregular sexual practices from sodomy and lesbianism to female adultery.[94]

Briefly, Beccaria and his friends had embraced the radical principles at the heart of Helvétius's utilitarian conception, that the benefit of society is the ultimate criterion in law as in philosophy and that, in every state, the principle most conducive to virtue is exactitude in punishing and rewarding actions useful or damaging to society.[95] Verri's *Meditazioni*, published two years before Beccaria's treatise and later praised by d'Holbach for its concept of 'justice', and, owing to similarity of arguments, sometimes thought to be from the same pen as 'Delle delitti e delle pene', likewise argues that the 'goal of the social contract is the well-being of each of the individuals joining together to form society', so that this well-being becomes absorbed into the 'public happiness or rather the greatest possible happiness distributed with the greatest equality possible'.[96] Gabrielle Verri, Pietro's father, had led the efforts in the Milanese to resist fiscal reform opposing Habsburg state policy on behalf of noble privilege. His sons, Pietro and Alessandro, rebelling against his particularism and conservatism, became the most eloquent local supporters of Habsburg imperial enlightened reform.[97]

Beccaria and Verri sought to use their conception of the penal code to guide men, via their reason and passions, to the progressive advancement of the public happi-

[90] Venturi (ed.), 'Storia e dibattiti', 363; Manuel and Manuel, *Utopian Thought*, 234.
[91] Venturi, *Riformatori Lombardi*, 24; Capra, *I progressi*, 204–8.
[92] Venturi, 'Storia e dibattiti', 174–5; Lascoumes,'Beccaria', 110–12.
[93] [Verri], *Il caffè*, 1: 84–5; Verri, *Meditazioni*, 60–1; [Palmieri], *Riflessioni*, 27, 31–2.
[94] Pasta, 'Dei delitti', 125–7; Dabhoiwala, 'Lust', 172.
[95] Helvétius, *De l'homme*, ii. 571.
[96] Verri, *Meditazioni*, 60–1; d'Holbach, *Système social*, 121, 168 n.; Venturi, *Settecento riformatore*, i. 714–15.
[97] Bellamy, 'Introduction', pp. x–xii, xiv; Capra, 'L'opinione', 112.

ness.[98] Happiness in Beccaria is conceived as the rational pursuit of men's interests facilitated by freedom to pursue them, and measures maximizing the collective wealth, guaranteed by the state on the basis of equal protection for all. Like Diderot and d'Holbach who likewise dismissed the whole of existing European jurisprudence as a 'barbaric and brutal' remnant of ancient practice, Beccaria saw the wrongheadedness and archaism of the existing legal system as rooted in its giving priority to protecting the property, interests, and advantages of the privileged. Beccaria and Verri were not, however, opposing the principle of nobility as such, merely anxious to curtail privilege, impose one system of justice for all, and improve the nobility's moral calibre, making nobles more active and useful to society.[99] Nobles should be encouraged to participate in commerce, urged *Il caffè*, echoing the Neapolitan reformers.

There was, then, a definite radical edge to the stance originally adopted by Beccaria. If, instead of being equitably allocated, the legal system's benefits actually favour aristocratic exemption and privileges and those of the clergy and magistrates so that the law, instead of providing an equalized benefit for all, promotes advantages for some at the expense of the rest, then it may be said to promote disorder and crime. Beccaria's particular blend of enlightened individualism with utilitarian social-collective thinking produced a theory obliging government to promote not just the greatest possible collective advantage but public happiness by protecting every individual's interests on an equal basis, under what he deemed an implied social contract.[100] This notional 'contract' served to prevent the state's conception of the common good being employed to marginalize the interests of less favoured individuals, hence was potentially a device for subordinating constitutions to the radical *volonté générale*.

Aware he had been read with approval by d'Alembert, Diderot, and Voltaire, Beccaria visited Paris in October 1766, accompanied by Alessandro Verri, who like his brother Pietro was then also a passionate reformer. Full of eager expectation, Beccaria and Verri arrived for an extended stay.[101] Their reformism was warmly applauded. D'Holbach and the others went out of their way to welcome and encourage them. Beccaria, though, shy and uneasy, was taciturn and made a poor impression. Diderot, having read his book in the original with great pleasure (while reprehending Morellet's mutilated translation), and liking Beccaria personally, had no wish to offend him.[102] But neither was he overly impressed. In remarks later published in the *Correspondance littéraire*, in 1771, he suggested the reaction to Beccaria's book had been overblown and rather perverse. While acknowledging his eager 'humanity', he was not persuaded his book was 'aussi important, ni le fond des idées aussi vrai, qu'on le prétend'.[103]

---

[98] [Verri], *Il caffè*, 1: p. xv.   [99] D'Holbach, *Essai*, 117; Capra, *I progressi*, 224–5.
[100] Zarone, *Cesare Beccaria*, 78–9; Bellamy, 'Introduction', pp. xx–xxi.
[101] Morellet, *Lettres*, i. 56. Morellet to Beccaria, Paris, July 1766.
[102] Naigeon, *Philosophie*, ii. 222.   [103] Ibid. 210.

Meanwhile, according to Alessandro, the effusive praise he received turned Beccaria's head, provoking a bitter quarrel that permanently soured their relationship. Disgusted by the Parisian *encyclopédistes'* irreligion, Verri concluded he and his Milanese circle had erred and that it was not *la philosophie moderne* but 'English ideas' that pointed the way forward.[104] While not yet breaking outright with the Parisian coterie,[105] by early 1768 he scorned what seemed to him their fanatical attitude to religion, morality, and society.[106] Once realizing what was really at stake, he recoiled from attacking privilege and elites, becoming pessimistic about prospects for accomplishing any serious reform in Italy.[107] Pursuing his quarrel with Beccaria, before long emerging as one of his fiercest critics, he declared himself an ardent admirer of Hume whose *Essays* had been widely known in Italy since the mid 1750s, despite being placed with the rest of Hume's œuvre on the papal Index in 1761.[108] But Beccaria too was taken aback by what he saw and heard in Paris and, despite coming to stay for six months, abruptly returned to Milan early in December. He had no complaint against the 'amis' in Paris, he assured them, but, back in Milan, lapsed first into isolation and his habitual indolence, failing to send the copies of Vico's *Scienza nuova* promised to d'Holbach and Morellet, and then a prolonged melancholy alienating him from all former friends and further writing.[109]

Whatever the precise intellectual and psychological explanation of his and Alessandro's revulsion from radical ideas and each other, the social and religious aspects of the rupture were clearly central. Aristocrats championing enlightened despotism and unwilling to break with the Church, Beccaria and the brothers Verri realized they could not ally with Diderot's circle and abandoned the radical stance they had initially adopted. What Alessandro and Pietro found especially wrong-headed in d'Holbach's and Diderot's attitude was their believing a theological view of the world necessarily involves deception and contempt for mankind and that *l'esprit théologique* is inherently contrary to sound moral ideas. Breaking with the *encyclopédistes*, Alessandro took to continually denouncing the 'arrogance of Gallic philosophy' and urging the advantages of Hume, though he focused mainly on the sceptical dimension of his thought, construing his stance as further from atheism than it actually was.[110] He was also quickly won over also by other aspects of the British Enlightenment. Spending the winter of 1766–7 in London, he became so enthusiastic he would have liked to relocate all the *Caffetisti* there. With Hume he agreed entirely that the Parisian *philosophes* were too emotional and insufficiently precise to be good philosophers. Both brothers henceforth regularly disparaged the *encyclopédistes'* 'enthusiasm' and 'fanaticism', praising what they saw as the superior reasoning and modesty of the British. Meanwhile, both Pietro and Alessandro accused Beccaria of ingrati-

[104] Mortier, 'Diderot and Penal Law', 204; Capra, *I progressi*, 267–8.
[105] Helvétius, *CGdH* iii. 268.
[106] Venturi, *Settecento riformatore*, i. 745.
[107] Morellet, *Mémoires*, i. 168, 170.
[108] [Verri], *Il caffè*, 1: 85, 110; Mossner, *Life of David Hume*, 228–9; Ricuperati, 'Cultura italiana', 39.
[109] Morellet, *Lettres*, i. 88–9.   [110] Mazza, 'Hume's "Meek" Philosophy', 233–5.

tude and 'enthusiasm', comparing his estrangement from former comrades with Rousseau's betrayal of his. It was a rift never to be healed.

Alessandro's switch from French to British sympathies, though, proved merely a half-way house in his retreat from radical thought. Eventually, he became an outright foe of all Enlightenment, a champion of Counter-Enlightenment, leading among other things to quarrels with his brother. Pietro Verri, looking back in 1792, took pride in remaining loyal to the same enlightened principles over three decades, a moderation urging a thorough reform of the law and fiscal system while endorsing enlightened despotism, aristocracy, and the Church.[111] Neither brother, or Beccaria, ever broke with 'enlightened despotism' or religion.[112] Yet, briefly, at their most creative, all three had regarded Helvétius, Diderot, and d'Alembert as their true mentors. It was a contradiction Beccaria especially could not inwardly resolve. He remained deeply troubled by it for many years after his Parisian visit. After discontinuing his correspondence with Diderot's circle around 1772, he abandoned *la philosophie* altogether, believing it could not help resolve Italy's predicament as he understood it. In 1777, he went so far as to sell the more 'philosophical' part of his personal library, completing his abandonment of radical ideas and reversal of his conversion of 1761.[113]

But his famous book could not be so easily be negated. Certainly, not only devotees of radical thought admired and used it. A striking feature of Beccaria's impact in Italy, noted the Marquese Giuseppe Spiriti (1757–99), a leading Neapolitan reformer, in 1793, was the long-fashionable tendency among government ministers to pick out one or two particularly celebrated features, his critique of the death penalty or judicial torture, for instance, and then apply this out of context, often with manifestly negative results, leaving the rest of Italy's generally ramshackle judicial system in place. The campaign against the death penalty eloquently exemplified this. By the 1780s, use of the death penalty was much reduced in practice, almost in disuse in Naples and Tuscany even before the Tuscan penal reform of 1786 abolishing capital punishment together with judicial torture. Threat of execution no longer served to deter and the already alarmingly high murder rate in the Neapolitan countryside soared further along with the rising numbers sentenced to forced labour. In the Neapolitan realm, in 1779, attested official records, there were 11,000 prisoners assigned to forced labour—equivalent to half the 22,000 nuns in Naples' convents. This compared with only 15,000 penal labourers in France, observed Spiriti, a country with over three times Naples' population.[114] Inadequate or corrupt supervision of the penal gangs, meanwhile, enabled many prisoners to escape, encouraging malefactors to view robbery and murder as crimes one was apt to get away with scot free. Such remarks underlined not just the problematic character of Beccaria's

---

[111] Venturi, *Pagine repubblicane*, 168; Capra, 'L'opinione', 111–12; Ghibaudi, *Fortuna*, 164.
[112] Mazza, 'Hume's "Meek" Philosophy', 236; Dioguardi, 'Attualità', 35.
[113] Pasta, 'Dei delitti', 122–3.
[114] Spiriti, *Riflessioni economico-politiche*, 24, 32; Gorani, *Mémoires secrets*, i. 34, 53–4, 79.

reception but, more broadly, the inherent insufficiency in the *ancien régime* context of moderate Enlightenment itself.

One text rejecting radical *philosophisme* from a moderate standpoint, eulogizing Montesquieu and Hume while accusing Beccaria of disastrously fomenting egalitarian ideas in Italy, was the *Trattato sulla pena di morte* (1778) by the Milanese jurist Paolo Vergani (1753–1820). The reason Beccaria's ideas penetrated widely, and the impetus for reform gathered a dangerous impetus, protested Vergani, was that in the supposedly enlightened atmosphere of the day nothing from the past was venerated any longer, an insidious outcome resulting from the idea that sovereign authority stems from the free consent of individuals. The crux of Italy's problem, he thought, was a fatal weakening of the principle that sovereignty and society are ordained by divine providence.[115] The popular sovereignty propounded by the materialists and Beccaria, complained Vergani, was totally incompatible, philosophically, with Newtonian physics and all doctrine stressing the divinely constituted and regulated order of things in nature and society, besides the God-given character of morality and law. *Les philosophes modernes*, by idealizing individual autonomy, had fallen into the trap of envisaging individuals as independent in the state of nature instead of being placed there, by their Creator, in relations of subordination and dependence, in families and social ranks. They championed freedom and independence on the basis of equality as the true human condition, employing false principles, ruinously eroding Christianity (and providential deism), indeed all theism proclaiming hierarchy, rank, and aristocracy.

A central contradiction lay at the heart of the Milanese Enlightenment that could never be resolved: Beccaria and the brothers Verri had adopted Helvétius's utilitarianism as a starting point and then rejected his conclusions. But there was a second basic contradiction on a more political level. For their reformism aligned with an enlightened despotism and, hence, entrenched nobility that in the end rendered it unviable. Beccaria's political objective in Milan was to prune privilege drastically and remove the impediment of intermediary bodies like the clergy and 'senate', a legal *parlement* claiming extensive powers over the administration and justice. He sought to supersede these intermediary bodies by simultaneously reinforcing the 'rights' of the individual and the enlightened monarch's authority. His combining these aims explains the curious procedure, characteristic also of Pietro Verri, of coupling Helvétius's utilitarianism with a contract theory of politics, designed less to limit the sovereign's authority than invalidate intervening layers of power claimed by the nobility, clergy, and magistrates (*togati*).[116] Trapped between intermediary powers and enlightened despotism, and the urgent need for social and institutional reform, Beccaria's and the Verris' moderation, by stripping radical social theory of its anti-Catholicism and republicanism, effectively undermined itself.

---

[115] Vergani, *Traité*, 8–11.
[116] Lalande, *Voyage*, i. 446; Young, 'Despotism and the Road', 271, 273–6.

During the middle third of the eighteenth century Italy's Enlightenment presented a impressive flowering of philosophical enquiry, scholarly innovation, and scientific research and, at the same time, a sporadic drive initiated by the princely courts to strengthen the machinery and secular authority of princely government and improve the states' finances and economic resources. The latter yielded a batch of initiatives designed to cut back aspects of ecclesiastical power and privilege. Both processes, however, led to long-standing tensions and a full-scale intellectual crisis in which the Church retreated from its relatively liberal stance of the 1740s, creating a chronic disparity and imbalance between intellectual endeavour and institutional and ecclesiastical reform that proved formative for the Italian Enlightenment.

As awareness of the archaism of Italy's legal systems and administration and institutionalized inequalities grew, there was little sign of any weakening of the resistance to far-ranging reform. Rather there was a complete impasse. Reviving Italy's decaying industries, crafts, and commerce and stagnant agriculture remained blocked by a vast array of custom, privilege, exemption, and vested interests, especially 'rights' of nobles, clergy, and legal elites and noble entails, privileges of cities, localities, guilds, and urban patrician oligarchies. As reform initiatives in the circumstances of the 1760s and 1770s were bound to multiply and intensify, while defence of privilege showed no sign of abating, serious friction seemed unavoidable should anything more than the most modest package of the reforms be attempted.

13

Society and the Rise of the Italian Revolutionary Enlightenment

1. THE 'REFORM OF ITALY' CONTROVERSY

Beccaria and the Verris were not the only admirers of Helvétius and Diderot in Italy forced by circumstances or inner estrangement to retreat. Other incipient radicals existed including the ex-Franciscan Fortunato Bartolomeo de Felice (1723–89), a former professorial colleague of Genovesi who wrote the introduction to the eight-volume edition of Burlamaqui's *Principes* (1766–68) and edited the mainstay of the Swiss Protestant Enlightenment—the great Yverdon revised version of the *Encyclopédie*.[1] This *Encyclopédie* was to emerge, from 1770, as Protestant Switzerland's answer to the irreligious *Encyclopédie* of Diderot. A Protestant convert, in 1756 de Felice established his journal *Estratto della litteratura europea* in Berne. In 1762 he moved to Yverdon, near Neuchâtel. On first settling in Switzerland, as a renegade Neapolitan monk fleeing the ecclesiastical authorities in Italy, however, building on a reputation for anticlericalism and defiance of Rome, he had aligned with the most forthright enlighteners north of the Alps, Diderot and Helvétius.

Nevertheless Italian readers abroad were too few to keep the *Estratto* afloat and the papal ban condemning *De l'esprit* issued just when De Felice's favourable review appeared, placed him in difficulties. Faced with either retracting or seeing his journal banned in Italy, he chose the former, explaining to readers that he had been unaware the Church forbade Helvétius's ideas whilst composing his laudatory pieces.[2] Having bended once, de Felice became increasingly amenable to ecclesiastical pressure. Despite privately loathing Chaumeix's tirades, he even praised Chaumeix's *Préjugés légitimes*, a work widely admired in Italy.[3] Subsequently, he threw in his lot with Haller and Bonnet, declaring unrelenting war on the *encyclopédistes*. As general editor of the Yverdon version, he purged Diderot's subversive input, composing numerous 'corrections' and 'improvements' besides fresh articles of a very different stamp assembled with the help of the Lausanne academy and the Economic Society of

---

[1] Watts, 'Swiss Editions', 220; Rotta, 'Voltaire in Italia', 395; Ricuperati, 'Cultura italiana', 41; Ferrone, *I profeti*, 112, 389 n. 27, 418.
[2] Donato, 'Réfutation ou réconciliation?', 106–8, 110.   [3] Ibid. 108–9.

Berne. The publishers had planned to produce his (originally) thirty-four volumes in five or six years starting in the mid 1760s, but by 1772 had still only progressed to volume viii.[4] Delays apart, though, de Felice, Bonnet, and Haller eventually scored a considerable success, conclusively entrenching moderate Enlightenment at the heart of Swiss Reformed society.

But banning books and purging Diderot's *Encyclopédie* could not change the fact that Italy was a country beset with social problems and economic and political difficulties that looked insoluble, and increasingly so, in terms of moderate solutions. The discreet reformism of Genovesi, Beccaria, and the Verris scarcely even began to tackle the immense edifice of ecclesiastical power, noble privilege, legal archaism, judicial oligarchies, defective administration, rejection of religious toleration, stagnant economic conditions, fiscal inefficiency, and relentless inequality. Doubtless, the prescriptions of *moderazione* looked infinitely preferable to radical ones to most. But *moderazione* proved powerless to engineer substantial reform or ease deprivation made worse by an appalling famine in Naples in 1764. The reason mainstream Enlightenment, as elsewhere, signally failed in Italy in the 1770s and 1780s was simply that enlightened *moderazione* under the auspices of princely absolutism, aristocracy, and the Church was unable, by and large, to tackle her chronic difficulties.

Hereditary power, institutional inertia, and entrenched ecclesiastical authority amid deteriorating conditions in an age of professed enlightenment and new ideas must inevitably generate a frustrated, angry reaction in the minds of some critics, scholars, and publicists. It was during the mid and later 1760s, in the wake of the battle over the *Encyclopédie* and over Helvétius, and the appearance of Rousseau's principal works, that a renewed and broadened current of Radical Enlightenment emerged within Italian culture and one that was by no means limited to Naples, as has been suggested.[5] Manifested most forcefully in the writings of Pilati, Gorani, Alfieri, Longano, Dragonetti, Filangieri, and Pagano, this new widening current of radical thought, without losing either its sense of indebtedness to Giannone and Vico and fondness for other Italian intellectual sources, notably Machiavelli, Sarpi, Genovesi, and Beccaria, or a robust universalism receptive to foreign philosophy, was chiefly remarkable for its preoccupation with Italy's economic and social problems and its wide-ranging critique of the Church. This wave issued a general call for sweeping action to correct abuses, justifying doing so using perspectives unmistakably pregnant with revolutionary potential for the future.

The most explosive Enlightenment controversy in pre-1789 Italy—and the furore that caused the most stir elsewhere in Europe—was triggered by *Di una riforma d'Italia*, a book clandestinely printed at Villafranca (i.e. Venice) early in 1767, and

---

[4] It appeared in the event in forty-two volumes with six of supplements in the years 1770–6; Watts, 'Swiss Editions', 220; *L'Europa letteraria. Giornale*, 4/2 (Venice, Apr. 1769), 108; Darnton, *Business*, 19–21, 36.

[5] Ricuperati, *Frontiere*, 34.

forbidden with unusual promptness by the local archbishop and then, by emergency edict of papacy and Inquisition, in July.[6] Its author, Carlantonio Pilati da Tassulo (1733–1802), was a civil law professor and noble from the Val di Non, near the German–Italian language border in the Trentino, trained at Leipzig, Göttingen, and in Holland, a country with which his life became much entwined. Pilati, with his unmistakably crypto-Protestant leanings, fully embraced the worlds of German and Dutch as well as Italian Enlightenment.[7] His prior work, *L'esistenza della legge naturale impugnata, e sostenuta* (Venice, 1764), attacking the current influence of Roman law, case law, and 'natural law' concepts, criticizing Italy's legal culture as a needlessly complex, arcane construct accessible only to specialist jurists, had already been banned earlier.[8]

Many had in the past sharply criticized one or another aspect of Italian society and proposed changes. But Pilati was the first reformer to pronounce everything highly defective. Verri's and Beccaria's reformism envisaging a wide-ranging programme of improvements paled in comparison with Pilati's call for a total transformation of Italy's institutional, legal, moral, educational, and religious framework.[9] The impact of *Di una riforma d'Italia* (1767) was sensational. It burst like a bombshell, a second part appearing in 1769 with German editions issuing at 'Freyburg' (i.e. Zurich) in 1768 and 1775, a French abridgement at Paris, and a full French version, at Amsterdam, in 1769. A sequel, *Riflessioni di un italiano sopra la chiesa in generale* (1768), declaring 'Borgo Francone' its place of publication, was followed by *Italia riformata* (1769), a fragment illicitly printed at 'Rimini'. A second full edition appeared at 'Villafranca' (i.e. Coira, in Switzerland), in 1770, and a third, after the author visited southern Italy, in 1776. Radical concepts had long percolated in Italy as a hidden anti-ecclesiastical and anti-papal underground. But Pilati's assault, while certainly echoing some themes expounded decades earlier by Giannone and Radicati, and subsequently by Beccaria, went considerably further than any predecessor in generalizing grievances and complaints into a comprehensive, interlocking critique and creating a national public furore.

On the papal Index from July 1766,[10] Pilati's book was also prohibited by state governments in Tuscany, Venice, Milan, and elsewhere. Inevitably, there was much lively speculation as to who this bold subversive could be, de Felice being among those suspected.[11] Voltaire asked d'Alembert, in a letter of October 1768, whether he had yet read it, observing that this book had had 'un prodigieux effet en Italie'; he praised but also deplored it for condemning everything while failing to offer

---

[6] *Index Librorum Prohibitorum* (1786), 249–50; Delpiano, *Governo*, 106–7; de Bujando, *Index*, 712.

[7] Pilati, *Lettere*, 43; Venturi, *Riformatori Lombardi*, 563; Tortarolo, *Ragione interpretata*, 29–31.

[8] Pilati, *Ragionamenti*, 65, 106, 109–10; Venturi, *Settecento riformatore*, ii. 255–6; Ferrone, *Società giusta*, 18.

[9] Venturi, *Riformatori Lombardi*, 566–7; Venturi, *Settecento riformatore*, ii. 263–4.

[10] *Index Librorum Prohibitorum* (1786), 27; Ferrone, *Società giusta*, 18.

[11] Zambelli, *Formazione filosofica*, 699.

concrete solutions.[12] Actually, Pilati purposely attacked neither Catholic doctrine, nor the princes, nor the existing social and political order directly.[13] Rather his book stresses the severe economic and social predicament confronting Italy, highlighting the multiple chronic deficiencies he identifies and portraying these as chiefly the fault of the clergy and wrongly grounded legal and educational systems. At the same time, though, he subtly implicated all the peninsula's elites and governments in the staggering list of ills he analyses. He declared himself a disciple of Machiavelli, the 'divine Newton', and 'incomparable Montesquieu'. Opponents protested that while his text was indeed full of *Machiavellismo,* it was plainly inspired also by 'other impious writers'. Among his favourite authors, we know, was d'Holbach.[14] Italy Pilati portrays as a land of degradation and decay debased principally by 'the clergy badly directed and regulated', their relentless drive to foment credulity being everywhere buttressed by superstition, ignorance, and the Church's continual denunciation of the *filosofi* as the scourge of the world.[15]

Additional causes of the parlous state of the country's agriculture, industries, crafts, and commerce were corrupt administration, absence of toleration, antiquated higher education, and poor judicial procedures rooted in a legal culture Pilati pronounces the worst in Europe.[16] Italy's truly lamentable condition was solemnly sanctioned by churchmen by whom he expected to be pitilessly denounced to the 'credulous and ignorant vulgar' in 'accordance with their Christian habit', as a dreadful 'heretic' seduced by false philosophy.[17] Persecution and a blighted reputation awaited whoever spoke out about the country's chronic difficulties. But is that grounds to stay silent and 'tolerate with resignation the calamities caused by the clergy'?

Whether princes would be justified in reducing or abolishing the clergy's 'privilegi temporali e civili' was a question raised also by others, notably Paolo Frisi (1728–84), another of the Milanese coterie, who did so in an unpublished memorandum on princely temporal power composed at Kaunitz's request, in Vienna, in 1768.[18] But Pilati alone aired the issue publicly and abrasively. The Church's privileges and tax exemptions originated from the current princes' ancestors. But given the clergy had proved ungrateful to the civil power, why should such privileges continue? It was for the 'august' princes to decide about this as also whether the prevailing system of intolerance served their principalities' best interests. But since obviously neither the one nor the other did, Pilati summons them to curb ecclesiastical privilege drastically and proclaim toleration for the Protestants and Jews (he does

[12] Voltaire to d'Alembert, 15 Oct. 1768, and Voltaire to d'Alembert, 13 Jan. 1769, in Voltaire, *Corr.* xxxiv. 85–6, 243; Venturi, *Riformatori Lombardi,* 565.

[13] Venturi, *Settecento riformatore,* ii. 263–5.

[14] [Graffini], *Brevi riflessioni,* 21; *L'Europa letteraria. Giornale,* 5 (May 1769), 103–4; Pilati, *Lettere,* 120; Carpanetto and Ricuperati, *Italy,* 278.

[15] Pilati, *Lettere,* 125; Venturi, *Settecento riformatore,* ii. 31–2, 447, 451.

[16] Pilati, *Riforma d'Italia,* i. 3–4.

[17] Ibid. i. 4–5.   [18] Venturi, *Riformatori Lombardi,* 323.

not mention deists) while forbidding inter-confessional polemics. Pilati was actually the only Italian author of the age publicly to advocate a 'tolleranza absoluta', as opponents called it, accompanied by freedom of thought, expression, and the press. Toleration he pronounced an indubitable benefit for society generally and invaluable device for restraining theological zeal. Diversity of religions produces indifference to theological distinctions and there is nothing more precious to men than this. For indifference to theological differences fosters reason, peace, and love of one's neighbours while simultaneously stimulating the arts and crafts and benefiting the state.[19]

Popular credulity Pilati deplores in the most vehement terms. Practically every reform attempted so far failed due to popular resistance mobilized by clergy, most spectacularly against Giannone. The Jesuit expulsion from Naples had had to be postponed, due to an eruption of Vesuvius, officials immediately realizing the populace would link the two, crassly avowing divine displeasure.[20] Pilati's claiming Italy faced a profound crisis caused by religious orthodoxy, the clergy, and intolerance predictably provoked outrage as did his denouncing 'false piety' and suggesting the Church Fathers were mainly motivated by a spirit of rivalry and faction.[21] On bigotry, he brought his sarcastically erudite humour eloquently to bear. Boyle founded a famous lectureship in London for whoever lectured most powerfully against unbelievers and Jews. Much better in Italy would be prizes for whoever lectures best against hypocrites, zealots, and false *dévôts* as these harm religion most by persuading intelligent onlookers that any faith affording such scope for the most bigoted to be hailed as the wisest of men cannot conceivably be the true one.[22]

Other enlighteners, like Frisi, agreed with much of this, but only privately.[23] What was unprecedented about Pilati was the uncompromising tone, the outspoken public protest. Reducing the clergy's numbers and confiscating church lands he pronounced essential, as was curbing ecclesiastical tax privileges. Clerical numbers and property in Italy at the time indeed far surpassed those elsewhere in the Catholic world. The Venetian Republic, according to the 1766–7 census, boasted one priest, monk, or nun for every 133 inhabitants.[24] In the Neapolitan realm, with around four and a half million inhabitants, without Sicily, in 1740, resided 50,000 secular priests and 31,000 regulars, roughly a priest for every sixty inhabitants, dramatically more than Austria, for example.[25] From Sicily alone were banished 786 Jesuits, in 1767, around one eighth of those expelled from the entire Hispanic world. Reducing the clergy, though, was just a first step. Equally essential, for Pilati, was introducing freedom of thought and expression and curbing theology's role in education, along with theology's and

[19] Pilati, *Riforma d'Italia*, i. 46–7; Venturi, *Settecento riformatore*, ii. 265; Berselli Ambri, *L'opera*, 190–1; Chadwick, *Popes*, 436.

[20] Chadwick, *Popes*, 363; Baldi, *David Hume*, 230–2.

[21] Pilati, *Riforma d'Italia*, i. 6, 242; [Graffini], *Brevi riflessioni*, 33, 162–4.

[22] Pilati, *Riforma d'Italia*, i. 194–5.

[23] Venturi, *Riformatori Lombardi*, 293–5, 309, 322–8.

[24] Chadwick, *Popes*, 97.   [25] Ibid. 96, 363; Gorani, *Mémoires secrets*, i. 78–9, 415.

canon law's sway over moral attitudes and the law. Priestly celibacy and asceticism inspiring countless books about saints and holy hermits likewise needed discrediting.[26] The cult of saints was both ignorance and an obstacle to developing a sound political consciousness, being contrary to the welfare of the state and hence true religion.[27] Urging Italy's youth to discard the countless texts composed by monks 'che ammorbano il mondo' [that make the world stink], he recommended a wholesome new moral culture replacing that of the friars supplied by the *filosofi*. To assist this moral and cultural transformation, Italy's youth needed to learn French, English, and, possibly, German; for only by reading better books could they acquire sufficient insight to reject the old 'scholastic tyrants' and attain genuine maturity and liberty.[28] Only when colleges had been drastically reformed and seminaries made state-controlled institutions would Italy's remodelled nobility and clergy begin to think more rationally and responsibly.

In assuming that only 'philosophy' can produce a general moral and intellectual reform, and that this alone could cure Italy's ills, Pilati's enlightenment was typically radical. Even reformers highly sympathetic to segments of his programme, like Frisi among the enlighteners most committed to the idea of a general regeneration of Italy, institutional, scientific, and educational, resented his tone. Frisi, who had visited Paris and knew Diderot, d'Holbach, and d'Alembert (to whom, as a mathematician, he was particularly drawn), objected that his sweeping proposals were impracticable and would never sway Italy's princes who were all too 'pious' and 'moderate' to contemplate such an agenda.[29] It was a chimera to imagine anyone could cure Italy's deficiencies all at once, under a single programme. To proclaim the necessity of a veritable mountain of reform and stir public opinion to support such a campaign was an 'imprudenza', placing the whole project beyond the bounds of what was justifiable or feasible.

A few princes were willing enough, though, to tackle aspects of ecclesiastical privilege and immunity, if only to enhance their own authority. Among them was a future son-in-law of Maria Theresa, Ferdinand, duke of Parma (1751–1802), who following his father's early death, in 1765, ruled from the age of 14. Parma, since Deleyre became court librarian there, in 1760, and Condillac Ferdinand's tutor, in 1763 (staying until 1767), emerged as the chief focus of French intellectual culture, including radical ideas, in the peninsula and this influenced the young duke's statecraft.[30] Capping a series of measures curbing ecclesiastical rights, in January 1768, Ferdinand's council forbade appeals to Rome by the duchy's clergy for pensions and offices without permission, and proclaimed papal bulls invalid unless endorsed by the ducal signature.[31] An outraged Clement XIII excommunicated the teenage

[26] Pilati, *Riforma d'Italia*, ii. 431–2, 459–60, 462–3; [Graffini], *Brevi riflessioni*, 163, 165.
[27] Venturi, *Settecento riformatore*, ii. 266.
[28] Pilati, *Riforma d'Italia*, ii. 451–2; de Booy, 'Traduction', 30.
[29] Pancaldi, *Volta*, 47–50; Venturi, *Riformatori Lombardi*, 290–2; Woolf, *History of Italy*, 117.
[30] Venturi, *Pagine repubblicane*, pp. xix, 169.
[31] AN Bolivia ALP Exp. Colon. no. 13, fo. 7ᵛ; Chadwick, *Popes*, 365–7.

duke, issuing a special bull proclaiming his decree null and void. This bull in turn provoked an international furore with Spain, France, and Naples all involved. Carlos III refused to accept the principle that the pope could outlaw princely edicts at will and, by decree of 16 March 1768, suppressed the bull throughout the Spanish world. Even in Upper Peru (Bolivia), officials were ordered to seize and burn all the copies of the papal document they could find.[32]

Frisi, who was familiar with Tuscany, having taught at Pisa from 1754 to 1764 (where he helped revive Galileo's reputation), and several other states, was right, of course, that no princes would endorse Pilati's recipe. Such sweeping change was inconceivable without first overcoming powerful vested interests. Pilati himself recognized it would take 'una grandissima rivoluzione' [a huge revolution] to execute his project, something that he thought should be brought about only gradually with a minimum of violence, though it would, he thought, mean burning an immense quantity of 'superstitious books'.[33] Such a prediction met with scant sympathy. Rejected by his family, abandoned by his wife, and persecuted by the authorities, he resigned his professorship and fled. Migrating first to Holland, where the publishing firm of Marc-Michel Rey offered to render his book into French, he continued on to Switzerland where, during the years of his greatest productivity (1767–71), operating under constant surveillance, he edited a short-lived journal, the *Corriere letterario* (1768–9), at Chur.[34] He briefly returned to Italy, staying for a time among the circle of Andrea Tron, the most reform-minded jurist of the Venetian senate, but was arrested by the Inquisition in December 1769 and deported by the Venetian senate. Banished permanently from the peninsula, this future ardent supporter of the French Revolution found himself condemned to decades of exile.

To render Pilati's *Riforma* into French, Rey commissioned a certain Jean Manzon (1740–98), a Piedmontese admirer of Diderot, residing since 1767 in Prussia's Low Countries enclave at Cleves where he edited the journal *Courrier du Bas-Rhin*. Manzon not only translated Pilati but provided an even more daring preface and notes heaping still fiercer epithets on Italy's churchmen than Pilati's.[35] He also criticized princes more forthrightly than Pilati and more directly indicted religion, besides generalizing his critique by suggesting all Europe suffered the same appalling ills afflicting Italy. To this he added a sarcastic challenge—following the recent burning of the German edition of Pilati by the court at Dillingen—defiantly inviting the princes to burn his translation too.[36] Rey's literary editor advised discarding Manzon's additions as being so inflammatory as to be bound to antagonize princes everywhere. The enterprising Rey opted instead for a double strategy—an official

[32] Exp. Colon no. 13, fos. 1–2^v, 11^v–13.

[33] Venturi, *Riformatori Lombardi*, 573; Tortarolo, *L'Illuminismo*, 195–6.

[34] Venturi, *Settecento riformatore*, ii. 288–9, 323; Carpanetto and Ricuperati, *Italy*, 278, 281.

[35] Venturi, *Settecento riformatore*, ii. 280–2; Venturi, *Pagine repubblicane*, 135; Beermann, *Zeitung*, 17, 28.

[36] Beermann, *Zeitung*, 29 n.; Venturi, *Settecento riformatore*, ii. 286–7; de Booy, 'Traduction', 36, 40.

edition lacking the new material and a clandestine variant, likewise of 1769, retaining Manzon's barbs.[37]

2. REFORMING AUSTRIAN MILAN

The controversies surrounding Montesquieu, Helvétius, Beccaria, and Pilati doubtless helped foment a widening critique of existing practice and institutions in administrative and court circles. This is certainly suggested by comments of Pietro Verri and Frisi. For the moment, though, the initiative remained firmly in the hands of those embracing Muratori's and Genovesi's Enlightenment, the approach Genovesi outlines in his *Delle scienze metafisiche per gli giovanetti* (Naples, 1766). Italy's ills could best be corrected by a combination of acceptance and pragmatism, smoothing the edges of the existing order and working with the princes. This was the path of realism, conflict avoidance, piety, and deference but also of true Enlightenment vaunting its *moderazione* and earnest reform, one that repudiated *la philosophie moderne* and had no reason to quarrel with political authority, Church, lawyers, or nobility. The new science of political economy together with better administration and Church–state relations would suffice to free scientific enquiry from scholastic restraints and commerce from hindrances as well as generally stimulate economic activity, renovate the law and fiscal system, revitalize the universities, most of which were still in a fairly stagnant condition, and also render the nobility more improvement-minded and the clergy less privileged and autonomous.

The new academic science of political economy developed by the *économistes* in France, Forbonnais especially, had as its basic goal to render society as populous, prosperous, and vigorous as possible within its existing framework.[38] Monarchy and aristocracy, held Genovesi, are not inherently contrary to the spirit of free commerce and economic growth. Citing Louis XIV's championing of France's great trade companies and Peter the Great's founding new industries in Russia, he celebrated the achievements of such rulers, especially Peter.[39] Growing inequality and social stratification he, much like Turgot, considered a natural, inevitable, consequence of economic expansion and, therefore, a positive thing. So was the increasing complexity of the law. Provided the *togati* were shorn of their archaic group political privileges and the worst outmoded 'feudal' legal vestiges were reformed, in itself proliferation of lawyers—viewed by him as professional guardians of law and hence of commerce—and their growing social prominence represented a benefit.[40] As for the endemic poverty of the largest productive class, the rural peasantry, the answer,

[37] De Booy, 'Traduction', 39–40; *L'Europa letteraria. Giornale,* 5 (May 1769), 104.

[38] Genovesi, *Lezioni di comercio,* i. 21; Robertson, *Case,* 353–5.

[39] Genovesi, *Lezioni di comercio,* i. 43, 240, 331; Zambelli, *Formazione filosofica,* 743; Imbruglia, 'Enlightenment', 74.

[40] Genovesi, *Lezioni di comercio,* i. 65–6, 159–61.

held Verri, was to lift restrictions on the grain trade, promoting a general 'libertà del comercio de' grani' as Turgot advocated in France.[41] He appreciated the serious nature of Naples' social problems and agreed it was philosophy's task to help resolve them but offered remedies altogether less confrontational and milder than Pilati's.[42]

Man's progress Genovesi conceived as the central theme of history, a guided, providential process slowly elevating humanity through four basic socio-economic stages. These four stages, a topos that became standard in both the Neapolitan and Scottish enlightenments,[43] he classified as the savage-nomadic phase prior to settled agriculture, 'barbaric' cultures based on sedentary agriculture but lacking the arts, sciences, and literature, stable 'cultivated' agricultural societies boasting the arts but lacking commerce, and, finally, modern cultivated societies sustained by commerce and luxury manufactures, the only kind, in his view, where learning, science, and the arts advance rapidly. Trade, free markets, and supervision by enlightened despotism offered the best path. This resort to liberal economic theory and practice was the mainstream's prime recipe and in parts of Italy—the Milanese, Parma, and Tuscany—their approach produced real improvements. The great weakness was that there were still greater difficulties and more of Italy where *moderazione* made little progress either towards overcoming the obstacles or alleviating social problems.

According to Frisi, in 1771, Italy's most impressive advances were being achieved in the Milanese.[44] This may well be correct even though Frisi himself was Milanese and inclined to praise the Austrian administration there both in Vienna—where he stayed at court, in 1768—and abroad, and despite Milan, now a city of 120,000 inhabitants, often being regarded by foreign visitors as backward compared to northern cities. The city was still not lit up at night, recorded the visiting French astronomer and atheist Lalande in 1769.[45] In the Milanese, the Austrian administration tended to rely on the best available local experts, Frisi, Beccaria, and Verri among them, striving to reform the law, fiscal system, and institutions, stimulate the economy, modernize higher education, and encourage science. In Vienna, Kaunitz and other ministers recognized that no such changes were achievable without breaking the local nobility's, Church's, and *togati*'s hold, and ministers were not shy in pushing for this outcome. A close working alliance between government and (moderate) Enlightenment evolved, as it did also in Naples, Tuscany, Modena, and Parma, and much was achieved.

The presiding figure at Milan was Carlo di Firmian (d. 1782), the statesman who for many years, from 1759, headed the group of reforming senior officials administering the duchy. He led efforts to renovate the fiscal system, register church properties, and reduce ecclesiastical fiscal immunities as well as, in 1768, transfer book censorship from the Inquisition (and Milanese senate) to an imperial

[41] Verri, *Discorsi*, 228–9, 237–8; Imbruglia, 'Enlightenment', 78–9.
[42] Villari, 'Antonio Genovesi', 614–15.
[43] Genovesi, *Lezioni di comercio*, i. 58–62; Pagano, *Saggi politici*, 172; Imbruglia, 'Enlightenment', 75–6.
[44] Venturi, *Riformatori Lombardi*, 292, 297; Pancaldi, *Volta*, 49, 51.
[45] Lalande, *Voyage*, i. 344, 438.

commission. During the 1770s, Firmian also reformed Pavia university, among other changes instituting Beccaria's chair in law despite the papacy's ban on his celebrated book.[46] A noble from the Trentino and ardent Anglophile, Firmian's Enlightenment revolved around Locke, Newton, and the quest for useful improvements. Greatly interested in current developments in physics, especially electricity, his large library included the publications of all the major electrical writers—Franklin, Nollet, Beccaria, Priestley, and Volta.[47] When the young Volta, by 1770 already figuring among Europe's foremost naturalists, returned from his first foreign trip, to Switzerland, Strasbourg, and Ferney (where the aged Voltaire granted him a half-hour interview, in 1777), Firmian warmly approved his follow-up plans, welcoming this strengthening of contacts with foreign enlighteners. He even promised state funds to help purchase apparatus in Geneva and Paris for Volta's celebrated physics cabinet in Como.[48]

Firmian's programme was a veritable show-piece for enlightened absolutism. He took pride in furthering science and orchestrating the drive for improved efficiency in the economic, fiscal, legal, and military spheres while insisting on maintaining the privileges and the special role in administration of the nobility. The overall result was a distinctive local version of the Enlightenment, officially backed and eminently respectable, reflected in Milan's several journals, cafés, and impressive libraries. Proof of its vitality lay in Volta's researches, a celebrated new astronomical observatory in Milan, the arrival from Modena of the leading biologist, Spallanzani, and especially the rapid emergence to international status of Pavia university. At Pavia, whence Boscovich had transferred from Rome, student numbers rose steeply from around 150 in 1750 to over 1,000 by 1788, at a time when Turin, Bologna, and most other Italian and European universities languished with lamentably low student enrolments. Further proof lay in the disaffection of much of the Milanese nobility and clergy.

Together with Naples and Tuscany, Austrian Milan produced what, for a time, was perhaps the most creative conjunction of Enlightenment and enlightened despotism in Europe. Whereas in Piedmont the intermediary power of obscurantist, conservative officials remained dominant, and Venice and Rome were gripped by inertia, in the Milanese, Tuscany, Modena, and Parma, a far-reaching transformation was under way. Major reforms, such as the elimination of tax-farmers and restoration of direct administration of the fiscal system in 1768–70, for which Pietro Verri as a member of the Lombard supreme council for the economy worked energetically, were implemented.[49] Noble fiscal privilege was trimmed, the old civic patrician elite were eliminated from the administration, a change carried through more completely in the Milanese from the 1760s than in Tuscany where local patricians, *togati*,

---

[46] Lalande, *Voyage*, i. 445–6; Szabo, *Kaunitz*, 184, 216; Carpanetto and Ricuperati, *Italy*, 165–6.
[47] Pancaldi, *Volta*, 63–4.
[48] Ibid. 154–5.
[49] Woolf, *History*, 100–1; Capra, 'Habsburg Italy', 228–9.

and nobles remained prominent.[50] Many monastic houses were suppressed; book censorship was brought under state control (1768). Was this not ample evidence of the correctness of Verri's and Beccaria's strategy?

Yet, in Milan too, despite the onslaught on the old system of law initiated by Beccaria, Verri, and the *Il caffè* circle, the judicial elite entrenched in the Milanese senate still obstructed or seriously delayed much of their programme,[51] while other deep-seated problems remained wholly untouched, with education remaining in clerical hands, censorship extensive, and religious toleration non-existent. In such a context, it is hardly surprising that a local strain of radical thought should emerge. If the respectable Enlightenment's criticism of the prevailing institutional and legal framework stayed muted, the inevitable consequence of its deference to princes, nobility, clergy, and lawyers was an upsurge, behind the scenes, of a more sweeping denunciation of prevailing usages and authority, more forcefully condemning noble and ecclesiastical privilege, fiscal inequality, and administrative and judicial corruption.

Historians have often claimed that in Italy very few were 'willing to follow Radicati, Giannone, or Pilati, in their progress from religious doubt to Protestantism, tolerance, or even deism or atheism'.[52] But the real extent of the underground of radical anticlericals, crypto-materialists, and opponents of Christianity is by definition quite unknowable today. Sometimes, we know the names of others who categorically rejected Italy's religion, intolerance, and ecclesiastical primacy over culture and science but little more. Volta, toiling in his laboratory at Como, is known to have been one such philosophical materialist but one who rarely spoke, even in private, of his rejection of everything conventionally accepted and believed.[53] Mostly, though, we are ignorant even of their names, making it impossible to prove the older view is wrong. Nevertheless, unmistakable signs of a movement of radically enlightened opposition inspired by Helvétius, Pilati, the pre-1767 Beccaria, and the *encyclopédistes* proliferated from the mid 1760s, suggesting that such radical commentators and opponents were, in fact, less rare than is assumed even if mostly obliged, by circumstances, to veil their views.

The most frustrated, outspoken, and closely linked to philosophical developments abroad among Milanese reformers was an adventurous, well-travelled nobleman, Giuseppe Gorani (1740–1819), author of *Il vero dispotismo* (2 vols., 'Londra' (i.e. Geneva), 1770). This was an incisive work of political thought composed in Milan, in 1769, and banned by the Inquisition with the full agreement of the forces of *moderazione* in August 1773. It was a work distinguishing between 'tyranny' as something always malign and 'despotism' that can be bad or good depending on whether or not it is infused by *l'esprit philosophique* and true 'virtue'.[54] This was less

[50] Capra, 'Habsburg Italy', 225–6; Szabo, *Kaunitz*, 184.
[51] Capra, 'Habsburg Italy', 227–8; Capra, *I progressi*, 342, 464–5.
[52] Woolf, *History*, 78–9.
[53] Pancaldi, *Volta*, 24–5.
[54] Gorani, *Vero dispotismo*, i. 35–6 and ii. 22; Delpiano, *Governo*, 255; de Bujando, *Index*, 396.

an affirmation of faith in 'enlightened despotism', though Gorani does eulogize Catherine and Leopold of Tuscany, than a call to 'enlightened despots' and 'despotic' republics to mount more vigorous programmes of principled, sweeping, and necessary change. His ideal revolutionary 'despot', aspiring to fulfil the 'general will', is called on to impose freedom of thought and a sweeping toleration, drastically curtail church property and privilege, and implement the legal and educational reforms projected by Pilati.

After years abroad as an officer in the Habsburg Austrian army, campaigning in Bohemia, Saxony, and Silesia, a spell as a prisoner in East Prussia, and having visited Petersburg, Riga, and Paris where he met several *philosophes*, Gorani returned in 1767 just when the 'Reform of Italy' furore erupted. He first gained prominence in 1767–9, among the circle associated with *Il caffè*. His principal mentor in 'philosophy' was Beccaria whom he venerated and who read his drafts, encouraging his ambitions as a political thinker. His original goal was to combine Austrian enlightened despotism, or Josephism, with more individual and collective freedom.[55] He decidedly shared Pietro Verri's scepticism about Montesquieu and resolve to eliminate all 'intermediary powers', especially the power of the nobility and ennobled magistracies.[56] Admiring Beccaria, 'cet homme extraordinaire', for his knowledge and insight, Gorani also, however, trenchantly criticized him for his timidity, irresolution, and lack of 'véritable grandeur d'âme'.[57]

Like Pilati, and more than Beccaria, Verri, and Frisi, or indeed Volta, Gorani loathed Italians' intolerance, superstition, and bigotry. Prevented from publishing in Italy, he left for Switzerland. On appearing, in two volumes at Geneva in January 1770, his book met with critical reactions ranging from qualified approval, as with Verri who noted its kinship with Beccaria's masterpiece, to outrage at what commentators considered undisguised sedition and irreligion. There was never any question *Il vero dispotismo* would be condemned by the Inquisition as impious, insulting to the Church, and intent on establishing deism, *tolerantismo*, and Beccaria's principles besides lauding Giannone.[58] In Switzerland, Gorani was briefly caught up in Voltaire's support for Catherine's war to liberate Greece (Voltaire urged him to go to Greece), but mainly he engaged in literary activity, first at Geneva and then, during 1771–4, at Noyon, working for an adviser of the court of Gotha, Georg-Ludwig Schmidt d'Auenstein (1720–1805), author of the *Principes de la législation universelle*, a figure with numerous connections in Paris.[59] In 1774, he returned to Milan where he dwelt quietly for some years; but in August 1787 he broke definitively with his relatives and class, and, after visiting Rome and Naples, went permanently into exile abroad. During the Revolution, he moved to Paris, becoming a French citizen and *révolutionnaire*, incurring confiscation of his property in Milan by the

---

[55] Carparetto and Ricuperati, *Italy,* 271; Ricuperati, 'Cultura italiana', 42.
[56] Gorani, *Vero dispotismo,* i. 18, 67–9; Capra, *I progressi,* 291–2.
[57] Venturi, *Riformatori Lombardi,* 484–5.
[58] Ibid. 484; Delpiano, *Governo,* 113.
[59] Chappuis, 'Joseph Gorani', 367–8.

Austrian authorities as well as harsh criticism from Verri. A leading propagandist of the Revolution for a time, Robespierre's dictatorship estranged him from that too and he returned, disillusioned, to Switzerland, where he spent the remainder of his long life.

A prolific writer, Gorani has hitherto been little cited in surveys of the Enlightenment and when he is mentioned is classified merely as a disciple of Rousseau.[60] Some features of his thought do reflect Rousseau's vision, especially his claiming the best government is 'un vero e legitimo dispotismo fondato sopra la virtu' [a true and legitimate despotism founded on virtue] and that it matters little how absolute and 'despotic' a government is provided it is imbued with 'virtue' and the 'general will'.[61] Also Rousseauist is his stressing sovereignty's indivisibility. Yet, it is quite wrong to classify him as a Rousseauist. First, the range of his intellectual sources was extremely impressive. *Il vero dispotismo* brims with references to Machiavelli, Sarpi, Giannone, and Beccaria, besides Helvétius and Diderot, both of whom he warmly praises besides Rousseau. He also liberally cites Mably, Voltaire, Montesquieu, Marmontel, Buffon, Duclos, Vauvenargues, and d'Alembert (with whom he corresponded). Diderot he calls a 'vero filsosofo', quoting his remark in the *Pensées philosophiques* that 'superstition' harms God more than atheism.[62] British thought was altogether less central; but Gorani knew Hume and also cites Locke with respect to education, a major interest of his.

Especially unlike Rousseau is Gorani's zeal for 'philosophy' as the true source of all Enlightenment, emancipation, freedom, and progress: 'O filosofia, sostegno de troni, conservatore della libertà, felicità delle nazioni' [Oh philosophy, buttress of thrones, preserver of liberty, happiness of nations]! Still more important, *Il vero dispotismo* contends that the 'general will' is something universal and explicable exclusively in terms of what is in the interest of the majority according to reason, especially the principle of *l'utilité générale*, an orientation plainly aligning him with Helvétius, Diderot, and Beccaria rather than Rousseau.[63] It is because *volonté générale* based on *l'utilité générale* is, for him, the overriding criterion characterizing government anchored in 'virtue' that Gorani insists, as he continued to do, on the indispensability of toleration and 'libertà di parlare e di scrivere reguardo alle religione ed alle leggi' [freedom of speech and writing about religions and about the laws].[64] 'Despotism of virtue', for Gorani, bestows benefits equally on all so that it has no enemies. Everyone loves it and 'no one tries to destroy it because each loves himself'.[65] Gorani figured among the first to predict that the sway of privilege was generally so oppressive in Europe that a violent general revolution was the probable as well as logical outcome.[66]

---

[60] Ghibaudi, *Fortuna*, 179; Venturi, *Riformatori Lombardi*, 481–94; Ferrone, *I profeti*, 156–7.
[61] Gorani, *Vero dispotismo*, ii. 6, 42, 231; Tortarolo, *L'Illuminismo*, 161; Delpiano, *Governo*, 114.
[62] Ferrone, *I profeti*, i. 98.
[63] Gorani, *Vero dispotismo*, i. 50, 67, 98.
[64] Ibid. i. 105–12; Gorani, *Recherches*, i. 319–29; Ferrone, *I profeti*, 156.
[65] Gorani, *Vero dispotismo*, i. 224.
[66] Chappuis, 'Joseph Gorani', 376–8; Gorani, *Mémoires secrets*, i. 456; Venturi, *Riformatori Lombardi*, 491–2.

Crucial not just to Gorani's but to the general formation of Italian (and French and German) Radical Enlightenment during the 1770s and 1780s is the basic rift between Rousseauism and radical ideas that increasingly manifested itself. In Gorani's case, this emerged fully only with a work not published until 1792 in French, but originally composed in Italian, in 1786, entitled *Ricerche sulla scienza dei governi* [Researches on the Science of Government] (Lausanne, 1790).[67] Here, Gorani profusely regrets having being 'seduced' by Rousseau's eloquence during his 'youth', deplores the *Contrat social*, and admonishes readers against the Genevan's 'absurdes paradoxes' and 'errors'.[68] He repudiates Rousseau's political thought, stance on religion and censorship, and views on commerce.[69] By 1787, he had also rejected enlightened despotism. Becoming openly hostile to Joseph II, he put his faith now in representative democratic republicanism. After 1789, he summoned the Italian people to join the 'General Revolution' and throw off the yoke of their princes, courts, and the Church.

A sure sign that an underground Radical Enlightenment crystallized in Italy in the 1760s and 1770s was a shift, as in France some years earlier, to publicly issuing admonitions about forbidden radical texts. Various works, often translations of the French *anti-philosophes*, attacking 'les philosophes modernes', began announcing details of recent illicit publications. An original Italian contribution to the genre was the *Verità di teologia naturale contro gli atei, deisti e materialisti e specialmente contro l'opera intitolata* Le Bon-Sens (Padua, 1778) by Antonio Maria Gardini (1738–1800), a Venetian admirer of Moniglia and Bergier, later bishop of Crema. Gardini eulogizes his enlightened century for the vast intellectual and scientific advances achieved, warmly praising, besides Bacon and Newton, Redi, Musschenbroek, 's Gravesande, and other Newtonians and defenders of religion. Admirable progress had been made. But this progress was now menaced by a host of dangerous *fanatici*, an intellectual crisis stemming from an underground but widespread general attack on religion and ecclesiastical authority. The thinkers chiefly responsible for this crisis were Bayle, the great 'oracle' and master of the modern freethinkers, Spinoza with his pantheism, Helvétius with his materialism now being trumpeted through his posthumous work *De l'homme*, and 'Mirabaud' or whoever composed the execrable *Système de la nature*.[70] These were the chief culprits, though he warns against Boulanger, d'Argens, and Fréret as well.

The centrality of the *Système* and its sequels in Italian debate was widely manifested from at least 1771–2 when several Italian-language journals reviewed Voltaire's and Bergier's refutations in detail. That Voltaire, mobilizing Spallanzani's biology against Needham's, went all out to discredit the *Système* whose author, the most impudent *incrédule* ever to appear in print, appeared to be a follower of Hobbes and

---

[67] Venturi, *Riformatori Lombardi*, 491; Gorani, *Recherches*, i, translator's preface; Ghibudi, *Fortuna*, 177.

[68] Gorani, *Recherches*, i. 1–2, 100; Venturi, *Riformatori Lombardi*, 492.

[69] Gorani, *Recherches*, i. 100 and ii. 101; Venturi, *Riformatori Lombardi*, 492.

[70] Gardini, *Verità di teologia*, preface pp. xx and 11, 21–3, 54–5.

Helvétius and dared assail Clarke, Descartes, Malebranche, and even Newton, was widely noted.[71] Bergier had, in the eyes of many, triumphed by definitively demonstrating the static quality of matter against the Spinozists and author of the *Système*. Human misery, proved Bergier, stems not from ignorance and credulity as the *incrédules* contend but lack of religion. Yet, the *Morale universelle* (of d'Holbach), a remarkably detailed Italian review of 1777 went so far as to allow, is infused with genuine moral fervour and presents interesting educational ideas, grounding a cogent concept of 'reason' by closely aligning reason with experience.[72]

Where 'lo spirito filosofico' [l'esprit philosophique] was formerly practically unknown in Italy, commented the aristocratic Abbate Conte Jacopo Belgrado (1704–89), a Jesuit Newtonian naturalist who knew Bologna and the court at Parma intimately, in 1782, one now saw signs of it in its orderly new, 'cultivated' guise insinuating itself everywhere, including the princely courts and residences of the nobility.[73] Gardini's counter-attack focuses on the anonymous *Le Bon-Sens ou Idées naturelles opposées aux idées surnaturelles* ('Londres' [i.e. Amsterdam], 1772), today attributed to d'Holbach and Naigeon, banned by papal edict in August 1775. A text expounded in short enumerated paragraphs plainly addressed to the unsophisticated, it concludes by assuring readers religion has never done anything other than keep mankind in ignorance 'de ses vrais rapports, de ses vrais devoirs, de ses intérêts véritables'. Far from curing the world's ills, religion can only make them worse—'les aggraver, les multiplier et les rendre plus durables'.[74] *Le Bon-Sens*, admits Gardini, speaks in a manner capable of 'seducing' many readers,[75] reflecting a clear convergence of argument with the *Système* and the *Système social* (likewise by d'Holbach), drawing its main propositions, including its theory of motion in matter, from Spinoza. 'Many copies', he says, were turning up in Catholic cities.[76] Undoubtedly, some readers were being 'seduced' and the result was not just the spread of 'lo spirito filosofico' and growing denial of the sources and legitimacy of religious authority but a closely connected assault on the existing social, political, and educational order.

Gorani thought in terms of 'revolution' but how was the coming revolution to be achieved? It was owing to disillusionment with the enlightened reform programme in Milan (and the Austrian empire generally), that Gorani, by 1787, had switched from championing Josephism to seeing popular insurrection as the way to accomplish the structural changes Italy needed. In transferring his aspirations from enlightened despotism to the common people, Gorani was inspired less by any Rousseauist myth of primitive men being exempt from the corruption of civilization, than by a growing interest in actual examples of popular insurrection. Like Alfieri, he greatly admired Pasquale Paoli and the general uprising he led in Corsica against the

---

[71] *Giornale de' letterati* (Pisa), 7 (1772), 3–57; *L'Europa letteraria. Giornale*, 2/2 (Dec. 1771), 19–27.
[72] *Giornale de' letterati* (Pisa), 26 (1777), 86–123 and 27 (1777), 23–58.
[73] [Belgrado], *Dall'esistenza*, preface pp. 1–2.
[74] D'Holbach and Naigeon, *Le Bon-Sens*, 340.
[75] Ibid., preface pp. viii–ix.   [76] Gardini, *Verità di teologia*, preface, 54–5, 56 n.

Genoese aristocratic republic. When Genoa failed to pacify the island, its senate transferred it to France for a price, a negotiation chaired by Choiseul. Paoli had then led a heroic resistance to the French who pacified the island in 1768–70 but only with considerable difficulty. Gorani afterwards visited Corsica to gain direct knowledge of political conditions there.[77] Popular resentment and armed rebellion he began to see as the most promising method of toppling the *ancien régime*. One of the realms he specifically predicted (albeit wrongly) would soon explode in revolution, following Corsica's example, was Naples.

3. DEPRIVATION, REVOLUTION, AND THE 'TWO SICILIES'

No other part of Europe so clearly illustrates why Radical Enlightenment gained in both theoretical and practical momentum from the later 1760s as the 'Two Sicilies', as the kingdom of Naples was also known. There too one encountered many lay as well as ecclesiastical critics abominating the likes of Pilati and Gorani and accusing them of disgraceful impiety.[78] Yet it would be hard to find a land more exemplary of the radical claim that most men are unnecessarily oppressed, wretched, and deprived by badly framed laws and institutions, and 'priestcraft'. A naturally fertile land, the Two Sicilies were nevertheless, as Gorani and others pointed out, a country where most dwelt in distressing destitution.[79] Nowhere else was the primacy of privilege, Church, and nobility and consequent stagnation of towns and countryside to the majority's disadvantage so heavily entrenched. Equally, it was difficult to see by what respectable political means significant improvements could be secured.[80]

In this soil, the seeds planted by Giannone, Beccaria, and Pilati quickly germinated. An anonymously published booklet published at Naples in 1765 or 1766, under the title *Trattato delle virtù e dei premi* [Treatise of Virtues and Rewards], echoing both Helvétius and Beccaria, experienced a notable reception history of its own. 'It was received with an applause', commented its English editor, four years later, 'little inferior to that which had celebrated the name of Beccaria.'[81] Two Italian editions sold out quickly followed by a French edition. It then reappeared in London, in 1769, in a bilingual version in English and Italian attributed to the Neapolitan jurist Giacinto Dragonetti (1738–1818). Among the more radical-minded Neapolitan reformers (and among Tom Paine's sources), Dragonetti stands out especially for contending that the nobility constituted the chief obstacle to reforming Italian agriculture, law, and society. The work appeared also in Spanish, at Madrid in 1775, where it was promptly banned by the Inquisition.[82]

[77] Venturi, *Pagine repubblicane*, 170, 194, 219; Tortarolo, *L'Illuminismo*, 218.
[78] Pilati, *Lettere*, 111; Venturi, *Settecento riformatore*, ii. 301.
[79] Gorani, *Mémoires secrets*, i. 268, 380, 387; Mortier, *Le Cœur*, 392–3.
[80] Ferrone, *Una scienza per l'uomo*, 170–1.
[81] [Dragonetti], *Treatise*, preface.   [82] Sánchez Blanco, *Absolutismo*, 204.

'The rewards of virtue', holds Dragonetti, who, like his hero Helvétius, also recommended some redistribution of landed wealth from big landowners to peasantry to ease inequality, should 'be proportionate to its public utility and the sacrifice it costs its author'. While 'distinction of ranks' in society was originally meant to 'reward the good', government had continued favouring the nobility ever since, 'on the presumption that they would not degenerate'. Consequently, 'an implicit faith in noble virtue continues to ensure the distribution of considerable favours on the basis of birth alone'.[83] This is fundamentally wrong. 'To make peoples happy is the great obligation of rulers' and the way to do this, urged Dragonetti, who later, in 1799, figured in the Jacobin revolution in Naples, is to 'reward virtues according to their merits'.[84] Hereditary nobility lacks all legitimacy and should be eliminated from high position and its rewards.

Naples' economic malaise was rooted in long-entrenched legal, social, organizational, and moral structures. In mainland Naples with Sicily, according to estimates of the mid 1780s, roughly a third of the land belonged to the Church and was managed by the realm's twenty-two archbishops and 116 bishops and aristocratic abbots. The rest belonged mostly to *latifondisti* called 'the baronage'.[85] Virtually all olive presses belonged to either noble or ecclesiastical landlords. Social malaise combined with near universal illiteracy. Nearly all books belonged to the baronage, clergy, or lawyers. In Naples the man 'qui pense', commented Maréchal, must always be 'mal à son aise'.[86] Noble and ecclesiastical privileges and immunities were so extensive and entangled that it was hard even to ascertain their real extent. The countryside seethed with disputes about land tenure and property rights processed by an army of lawyers sworn to uphold justice but who, in practice, complained Gorani, lived more at the peasantry's and townsmen's expense than that of landowners in whose favour it was generally in their interest to resolve disputes.[87] Under the Sicilian 'constitution' of society, remarked Maréchal, in 1784, the island was fertile only 'pour le clergé et la noblesse'. The peasants were little disposed to work as this would benefit only their 'maîtres ingrats et souvent dangereux'.[88] Consequently, despite fertile soil and a favourable climate, Sicily's agriculture remained remarkably backward and unproductive.

Reform-minded ministers, mostly eager *illuministi*, struggled to revive Naples' economy and cure its worst deficiencies. Would-be reformers could at least condemn the scene of impoverishment and stagnation without impugning the current ruling dynasty (Bourbon), by throwing the blame on the pre-1713 Spanish Habsburg dynasty. Thus, Giuseppe Spiriti, in describing Calabria in 1793,[89] warmly praised

---

[83] [Dragonetti], *Treatise*, 33, 39–41; Wootton, 'Helvétius', 326.
[84] [Dragonetti], *Treatise*, 145, 151, 179; Rao, 'Feudal Question', 109.
[85] Gorani, *Mémoires secrets*, i. 84; Maréchal and Grasset, *Costumes civils*, ii. 15–16.
[86] Maréchal and Grasset, *Costumes civils*, ii. 44–5.
[87] Ibid.; Palmieri, *Riflessioni*, 28; Gorani, *Mémoires secrets*, i. 54–5.
[88] Maréchal and Grasset, *Costumes civils*, ii. 21.
[89] Spiriti, *Riflessioni economico-politiche*, preface and 1–7.

the crown's efforts while stressing the region's desperate condition and the hopeless state of its institutions. Calabria's archaic social structure and justice system and the common people's appalling *ignoranza*, debased morality, and *superstizione* were all symptoms of a desperate structural malaise,[90] ascribed by Spiriti to the overweening power and privileges of barons and office-holders. But the evil arose in the Middle Ages and was consolidated later by the negligence, fiscal errors, and reliance on venality of office of the Spanish Habsburgs.[91]

Among the most distinguished *illuministi* were several who wrote primarily on economic and administrative problems like Spiriti, Giuseppe Maria Galanti (1743–1806), a Genovesi disciple, and Giuseppe Palmieri, Marquese di Martignano (1721–94), an *économiste* likewise committed to liquidating the 'régime féodal'.[92] Palmieri, author of the *Riflessioni sulla pubblica felicità relativamente al regno di Napoli* [Reflections on the Public Happiness Relative to the Realm of Naples] (1787), in 1791 became chairman of the Supreme Council of Finance. These men strove to revive the economy by freeing commerce from hindrances, reforming the antiquated fiscal system, and improving the general administration, efforts encountering obstinate resistance from the privileged orders in general but supported by a small minority of enlightened nobles, office-holders, and churchmen. With the population approaching five million, and steadily increasing through the 1770s, the Neapolitan Bourbon court knew the problems were urgent and the situation chronic. In the 1790s, its efforts continued now with strong British backing in the context of the crown's bitter struggle against the ideas of the French Revolution and activism of local Jacobins. But the Bourbon court was never able to surmount the obstacles to reform, either before 1789 or after, and ultimately the whole effort collapsed. The land remained in the grip of a system that left the court simply too fragile and deprived of revenue to avoid massively spiralling debts. By 1806, these totalled over 100 million ducats, as against the kingdom's modest twelve million in annual revenues.[93]

To rescue the kingdom, Spiriti, like Gorani, Dragonetti, and Filangieri, looked to a combination of *la filosofia* and enlightened ministers. The continued growth of the capital during the late eighteenth century and steady expansion of international trade seemed to promise opportunities for agricultural expansion at least in the coastal regions of Calabria, Puglia, and Campania where investment in olive oil, silk, and wine production slowly increased. But the drive for improvements was everywhere impeded by the *régime féodal*, as the reformers termed the intricate system of land tenure, aggravated by the elusive status of much of the best land which was often held not in outright ownership by one landowner but a multiplicity of rights enjoyed by different interested parties, subject to overlapping claims and customary uses.[94]

[90] Spiriti, *Riflessioni economico-politiche*, 7, 10, 38, 51; Gorani, *Mémoires secrets*, i. 35.
[91] Spiriti, *Riflessioni economico-politiche*, 11, 38, 51.
[92] Gorani, *Mémoires secrets*, i. 128, 383.
[93] Davis, 'Napoleonic Era', 135–6. [94] Ibid. 136; Chorley, *Oil, Silk and Enlightenment*, 11–12.

The thickly layered disorder of what passed for the judicial and fiscal administration was really, held Spiriti and Gorani, a corrupt system of organized rapacity preying on the rural population.[95] Everywhere the *ancien régime* economy was plagued by lack of genuine justice.

Raising agricultural productivity required investment in enclosures, irrigation, and replanting and acquiring better implements but scope for such improvements remained limited whilst the complexities of the land-tenure system remained unresolved. Another difficulty was that most revenues raised by the state, like most of the nobility's revenues, were transferred from the provinces to the capital into the hands of the court, officials, ecclesiastics, merchants, and absentee landlords residing in Naples, continually draining the countryside of resources.[96] With a population approaching half a million, Naples, like Madrid, witnessed the growth of an immense service sector, subsisting by providing amenities to court aristocracy, magistrates, and Church, or on charity. By the 1780s, Naples evidently boasted more horse-drawn carriages than Paris and more liveried servants than any other capital.[97] Unlike Madrid, though, Naples also sucked population into its immediate hinterland so that practically half the kingdom's population dwelt within a sixty-mile radius, the capital being the only large city—aside from Palermo, in Sicily, with a population of 110,000. All other regional centres, like Lecce, capital of Puglia but home to only 15,000 inhabitants, remained economically stunted.[98] 'The capital', remarked Galanti, 'with its excessive size, and holding all the provinces under its yoke, is the permanent cause of that state of languor and misery in which we constantly see them.'[99]

The baronage, buoyed by the lawyers, clergy, and merchants, resided in urban idleness rather than on their estates, promoting agriculture, as in England: 'why, among us', asked Palmieri, were the English and French nobilities emulated only in matters of 'fashion and frivolous things'?[100] Naples' stifling dominance proved impregnable especially because its rich and poor alike had a vested interest in sustaining the oppressive land-tenure system and backward fiscal administration, two principal causes of the lack of opportunities for change and growth in the provinces.[101] The silk industry, even more burdened with antiquated forms of inspection and taxes than olive oil, seemed impervious to innovation, Palmieri mostly blaming ignorance and indolence for the mediocre quality of Neapolitan silks, olive oil, and wines.[102] All these problems were continually discussed by the Neapolitan *économistes* but being deeply embedded in ancient usage, law, and patronage proved exceedingly hard to tackle. Compared with these, straightforwardly

---

[95] Gorani, *Mémoires secrets*, i. 54, 354–5; Spiriti, *Riflessioni economico-politiche*, 6–18.
[96] Spiriti, *Riflessioni economico-politiche*, 78, 136–7.
[97] Gorani, *Mémoires secrets*, i. 402–3.   [98] Ibid. i. 399–401.
[99] Galanti, *Descrizione*, ii. 187–8; Gorani, *Mémoires secrets*, i. 399, 401, 404–5.
[100] Palmieri, *Riflessioni*, 32.
[101] Chorley, *Oil, Silk and Enlightenment*, 15; Villani, *Mezzogiorno*, 95, 103.
[102] Palmieri, *Riflessioni*, 61–3.

practical obstacles, like outmoded agricultural techniques and the dreadful state of the roads, seemed simplicity itself.

But while the Neapolitan Enlightenment was intensely preoccupied with local practical problems, it is wrong to suppose, as some have, that it was therefore characterized by a local and pragmatic attitude and eschewed philosophical debates. For Naples' economic problems were inseparable from the land-tenure system and privilege which in turn were inseparable from the administrative institutional tangle which, in turn, was not detachable from the legal morass or from ecclesiastical authority. In fact, even the most unrelenting pragmatism in the world was impotent on its own. The only way was a fundamental plan for sweeping changes, along with reasoned justifications for reducing noble and clerical privilege.[103] Practically all reformers accepted that 'la pubblica felicità' [the public good], meaning the well-being of society as a whole, could not be effectively pursued in Naples without profound changes in attitudes and institutions.[104] It was hard to contest Gorani's thesis that *la philosophie* was the only agent potent enough to rescue blighted Naples.[105]

Those confronting the Bourbon monarchy's structural problems were mostly enlightened officials or courtiers as there was no one else apart from clergy with the requisite educational level. There was much to suggest Gorani was right that Italians more readily acquiesced in lack of freedom of thought and expression than other Europeans and that tradition and credulity religious, social, and political reached further in Naples than elsewhere.[106] The reformers fell roughly into two groups—*économistes* and legal reformers, a particular foe of privilege and 'intermediary powers' among the latter being Naples' foremost political thinker Gaetano Filangieri (1752–88), a studious but also practical-minded young noble, a former army officer with a Hungarian wife, steeped in Vico, Montesquieu, and Beccaria.[107] During the years 1778–9, Filangieri completed and, in 1780, published the first two parts of his great work, the *Scienza della legislazione*, volumes reissued at Naples in 1781 and Venice in 1782 while the third and fourth parts appeared in 1783 and a fifth in 1791. Planned in seven volumes, his magnum opus, the foremost Enlightenment work produced in the Mediterranean world after Vico, remained incomplete. Filangieri's *Scienza*, like the works of Beccaria, Pilati, Gorani, and Dragonetti, opens a wide rift between existing circumstances and the dictates of reason, building a powerful plea for equality before the law and comprehensive legal reform as determined by 'philosophy'. Rejecting tradition outright, he urged abolition of privilege and primogeniture, laicization of education, freedom of the press, and some redistribution of landed wealth.[108]

---

[103] Chorley, *Oil, Silk and Enlightenment*, 9–10.   [104] Palmieri, *Riflessioni*, 26.
[105] Gorani, *Mémoires secrets*, i. 280.   [106] Gorani, *Recherches*, i. 327–9.
[107] Filangieri, *Scienza della legislazione*, iv. 19–20.
[108] Feola, *Dall'Illuminismo*, 16; Martino, *Tra legislatori*, 91, 99–100; Tortarolo, *L'Illuminismo*, 161.

Unsurprisingly, given his disrespect for revealed religion, vehement declamations against the clergy, terming ecclesiastical wealth 'exorbitant', call to reduce monastic numbers, and implied rejection of Christianity's basic values and morality, his work was banned outright by the papacy in December 1784, and referred for further investigation by the Inquisition.[109] Besides labelling Louis XIV's Revocation of the Edict of Nantes an act of 'fanaticism', his text, complained the Church, subverts authority and religion.[110] In Filangieri were fused the practical and theoretical Enlightenment, grasped Goethe, who met him in Naples in March 1784, in a most impressive manner. 'He is one of those noble-hearted young men to whom the happiness and freedom of mankind is a goal they never lose sight of.' A reformer of impassioned views who never wasted words on frivolities but loved discussing Montesquieu and Beccaria as well as 'his own writings—all in the same spirit of good will and sincere youthful desire to do good,' he expressed, Goethe also noted, a marked antipathy to the Emperor Joseph: the 'thought of a despot, even as a phantom possibility, is horrible to noble minds'. This remark is doubly noteworthy in that at Naples, observes Gorani, Joseph had become *the* key reforming model.[111]

It was Filangieri, Goethe also notes, who first introduced him (as he did others) to Vico, making him aware of the latter's high standing in Naples where 'they rank him above Montesquieu'. Along with Giannone, Vico was indeed resurrected in the 1780s as the hero of the Neapolitan *illuministi*.[112] Besides constantly warning against 'despotism', Filangieri, like Gorani, stressed the need for unified sovereignty and had many reservations about Montesquieu who was too focused, in his view, on explaining things as they were whereas what was needed in Italy was to explain how they should be.[113] His programme aimed at demolishing the baronage's and *togati*'s privileges and authority and could in no way be reconciled with Montesquieu's intermediary powers and championing of noble status. British mixed monarchy he roundly rejected. What attracted him, as with Beccaria, Gorani, Dragonetti, and his friend Francesco Mario Pagano (1748–99), professor of ethics at Naples university since 1770, was Helvétius's universalist anti-relativism.[114] Pagano rejected Montesquieu even more emphatically than Filangieri, insisting on one 'natural order of justice and equity' which is the same for all mankind.

The contradictions in Filangieri's position as a radical-minded official in a monarchical regime trapped between the ideals of enlightened despotism and a civic republicanism inspired partly by the American Revolution whose stress on personal liberty, toleration, and the pursuit of happiness he (unlike Pietro Verri) strongly

---

[109] Motta, 'Condanni inquisitoriali', 294–6, 323; Ferrone, *Lezioni*, 131, 142; Goggi, 'Ancora', 153–4.

[110] Motta, 'Condanni inquisitoriali', 297, 311–12; Delpiano, *Governo*, 116, 263, 299.

[111] Goethe, *Italian Journey*, 192; Verri, 'Legge, potere', 357; Gorani, *Mémoires secrets*, i. 450.

[112] Goethe, *Italian Journey*, 198, 202–3; Pagano, *Saggi politici*, i. 7, 17, 29, and ii. 16, 155, 163; Ricuperati, 'Cultura italiana', 43.

[113] Filangieri, *Scienza della legislazione*, i. 19; Verri, 'Legge, potere', 362–4.

[114] Feola, *Dall'Illuminismo*, 27; Ferrone, *Società giusta*, 38–9, 49, 61 n., 52, 194; Berti, 'Modello britannico', 19–20, 34–7.

sympathized with, infuse the whole of his great work. When condemning British policy in America, he follows Raynal.[115] His guiding philosophical principle was that 'la felicità pubblica non è altro che l'aggregato delle felicità private di tutti gl'individui che compongono la società' [the public happiness is nothing other than the aggregate of the private happinesses of all the individuals who compose a society].[116] This too located him alongside Diderot, d'Holbach, Helvétius, Dragonetti, Gorani, and the young Beccaria. It was a formula with egalitarian implications all too plainly anchored in Helvétius's *De l'esprit* and in the *Histoire philosophique*, two radical texts comprising two out of three of Filangieri's three (with Hume's *Essays*) chief and most frequently cited sources.[117] A key strand of his thought is his assault on noble and ecclesiastical fiscal privileges where he repeatedly echoes Raynal's and Diderot's *Histoire*.[118] Filangieri and his allies and adherents, Galanti, Cirillo, Pagano, and Donato Tommasi, the man who wrote the *Elogio* published in his honour, after his early death, were convinced the solution to Naples' predicament lay in a complete rupture with the laws, customs, and practices of the past.[119] Like Helvétius, they believed in a comprehensive reform of legislation following a single standard.

At the heart of their analysis was the notion that the kingdom's institutions and legal procedures had themselves become the instruments of interest, oppression and injustice. Thus, an 'anti-feudal', anti-baronial polemic gathered momentum in the 1770s and 1780s in the work of all the Neapolitan *illuministi* with Filangieri's *Scienza* as the culmination. As in Milan, these decades were a time of grand reforming projects, marking a decisive shift from the past, even if some figures at court, such as Ferdinando Galiani who negotiated a commercial treaty with Catherine the Great's Russia in 1787, remained more interested in stimulating commerce than social and institutional reform as such and disliked Filangieri's sweeping proposals.[120] A particularly energetic reformer was Domenico Caracciolo, who had had many contacts with the *philosophes* as a diplomat in Paris, and during his viceroyalty in Sicily (1781–6) initiated a string of practical improvements including abolition of Palermo's Inquisition tribunal and instituting the splendid botanical gardens (still a landmark of Palermo today), though his administration made less progress in land reform and trying to reform legal abuses.[121] At the heart of the conflict between reformers and conservatives lay the accusation propounded most forcefully by Filangieri, Gorani, and Pagano, that baronial privilege and landed property with ecclesiastical interests were the basic cause of the people's poverty and their society's oppressive constraints on freedom of thought and intellectual advancement.

---

[115] Goggi, 'Ancora', 126–7.
[116] Filangieri, *Scienza della legislazione*, ii. 235; Verri, 'Legge, potere', 374.
[117] Filangieri, *Scienza della legislazione*, i, p. xix; Goggi, 'Ancora', 112–13.
[118] Doyle, *Aristocracy*, 186; Goggi, 'Ancora', 140–1.
[119] Goggi, 'Ancora', 117–23; Pagano, *Saggi politici*, i, introduzione pp. xxi–xxii; Feola, *Dall'Illuminismo*, 26–7.
[120] Rao, *Regno di Napoli*, 120–1.   [121] Ibid. 116.

At court and in the press, the Neapolitan Enlightenment in its culminating phase became a full-blown political and social movement immersed in the problems of the kingdom's stagnant condition, poverty, and *ignoranza*, compounded by the state's chronic indebtedness and the Church's overwhelming ascendancy. Its most striking feature for the modern historian, philosopher, and political scientist is that it was a reform movement practically devoid of popular support. A great social project as well as classic Enlightenment undertaking, it had to be primarily intellectually driven. There was no way it could be powered by pressure to change emanating from broad-based opinion, cultural shifts, or conventional thinking.[122] For there was no broad-based opinion in favour of change. The Two Sicilies' twelve provinces, remarked Gorani, the most backward and oppressed part of Italy, languished under an aristocracy, 'ces monstres titrés', and clergy more exploitative than anywhere else; yet, scarcely any of the local populace were 'assez éclairés pour sentir leur état'.[123]

The social history of the Neapolitan Enlightenment was a social history of structures and beliefs that were intellectually, and politically, but not popularly contested. There was no tendency towards a shift of economic dominance from one group to another. There existed no growing commercial interest gradually wresting economic power away from older elites or acting as a solvent loosening the structure of *ancien régime* society.[124] There was no change in social practices. In Naples no more than Milan where Maria Theresa was a genuinely popular ruler, and much more so than Joseph, did the people demand or support sweeping reforms. Yet, despite the lack of support within society, Enlightenment and enlightened reform were central preoccupations in Neapolitan high culture in the 1770s and 1780s, the years Caracciolo was chief minister in Naples (1786–9), marking the high-point of the reforming tendency in the Mezzogiorno. In 1787, at a moment particularly favourable to the reformers, the Supremo Consiglio delle Finanze, erected by the crown to reform the fiscal system five years before, was bolstered by the appointment of Filangieri who thus joined Palmieri at the top and was briefly responsible for the efforts to reform taxation on olive oil exports. Intellectuals were the backbone of the reform movement because there was no other available backbone.

But the reforms ran into insuperable opposition, and to the profound distress of his friends and the reform party, the 'always dear, loved and immortal Filangieri' died prematurely just a year later, before exerting any real impact.[125] Ardent to rescue the people from poverty and deprivation,[126] Filangieri, like Helvétius and d'Holbach, or Pagano, Pilati, Gorani, and Dragonetti, did not seek exact equality of wealth. Rather they fought to counter excessive inequality through legislative means in the interests of society as a whole.[127]

---

[122] Villani, *Mezzogiorno*, 164–8.   [123] Gorani, *Mémoires secrets*, i. 452–3, 456.
[124] Chorley, *Oil, Silk and Enlightenment*, 58–9.
[125] Pagano, *Saggi politici*, i, introduzione p. x; Feola, *Dall'Illuminismo*, 20–2.
[126] Ferrone, *Società giusta*, 337–9.   [127] Filangieri, *Scienza della legislazione*, ii. 237–9.

Even though there was no question in the minds of Filangieri and his disciples (at least before 1789) that they had to work within the context of monarchy, the battle between monarchy and republicanism, inevitably, was under way in their thoughts. Foe of all despotism, Filangieri, transcending the discreet hints of his *Scienza*, referred explicitly, in a letter to Franklin of December 1782, to the inner torment he suffered from his sense of alienation from monarchy and the court.[128] But while radical thought infuses Filangieri's work more fundamentally than Beccaria's, yet radical ideas were only partially adopted by him. Political legitimacy in Filangieri, as in Gorani and Dragonetti, derives always from below, from society. But Filangieri was no revolutionist in the post-1789 sense and could not escape the logic of reform in a backward monarchy with an economy and administration dominated by aristocracy.[129] He was a thinker trapped, as has been aptly commented, in the dangerous space between reform and revolution.[130] But this did not prevent a moderate enlightened French opponent of the Revolution, Jean-Marie Portalis, claiming in the late 1790s that Filangieri's *Scienza* proved that enlightened despotism was not as powerless as some claimed and that, given more time, could have established basic human rights.[131]

Filangieri's dilemma was precisely the tragedy of the late Neapolitan Enlightenment more generally and especially of Pagano and, another member of Filangieri's circle, the kingdom's foremost naturalist and botanist, Domenico Cirillo (1739–99). A scientist much connected with Linnaeus in his early years, albeit a revisionist Linnaean who rejected the insistence on fixity of species and Creationism of most Italian naturalists at the time, Cirillo ardently supported the reform campaign. But from 1789, the Bourbon court, deeply alarmed by events in France, lurched within a few years from vigorous reformism to outright reaction in alliance with Britain. By 1793–4, it had broken altogether with 'philosophy' and basic reform.[132] This left committed reformers with little alternative but to turn to revolutionary agitation. Becoming one of the heads of the abortive Neapolitan Jacobin revolution of 1799, Cirillo ended his life as an out-and-out insurrectionist, on the gallows.[133]

Pagano, another admirer of Vico, Genovesi, and Beccaria,[134] also broke with the Bourbon *ancien régime* and conspired against it. His most substantial general work, the *Saggi politici* (1783–5), reissued in a far more radical version in 1791, speculated about the early history of humanity. A fervent admirer of the Enlightenment, and well aware that as yet there existed no wider reading public in Naples in any way likely to support a programme of systematic reform no matter how urgently needed, Pagano loathed the 'feudal spirit' of the past and was acutely aware of the realm's

[128] Martino, *Tra legislatori*, 158; Berti, 'Modello britannico', 22, 41–2.
[129] Ferrone, *Società giusta*, 63–5, 72.
[130] Feola, *Dall'Illuminismo*, 16, 23; Imbruglia, 'Gaetano Filangieri', in Kors (ed.), *Encyclopedia*, ii. 51.
[131] Portalis, *De l'usage*, 224.
[132] Rao, *Regno di Napoli*, 128–9.
[133] Feola, *Dall'Illuminismo*, 18, 22; di Mitri, 'History of Linnaeism', 271, 274.
[134] Pagano, *Saggi politici*, i, introduzione pp. ix–x and 7–8; Ferrone, *I profeti*, 279.

chronic difficulties. To him all humanity constituted a single 'universal society' but most of it needed to be awoken to its true situation by means of expanded programmes of public education and intensified efforts of academies, theatres, and societies and this, he thought, was especially true of Naples.[135] The chief theme of his studies, as with Vico and Genovesi, was mankind's history, a social and cultural process understandable, in his view, only by monist or pantheistic philosophers.[136] Nature being a single entity to him always manifested the same basic 'uniforme e costante legge' [uniform and constant laws], a fact rendering basic human rights universal and equivalent everywhere.

When the Neapolitan republic was declared, in January 1799, he became head of its legislative committee and in this capacity drafted the republic's new constitution, penal code, and decrees abolishing entails and feudal privilege. Naples' Jacobin republic collapsed, however, to the delight of the populace and clergy, as well as the court of St James in London, five months later. It was a defeat due, one of its leaders remarked, to overestimating the power of 'philosophy'. Among those who paid the price was Pagano. With the Jacobin surrender, he was seized, tried, and executed.

---

[135] Pagano, *Saggi politici*, i, introduzione, pp. ix, xxi, and ii. 168, 176; Jacobitti, *Revolutionary Humanism*, 24–6, 173 n. 58; Ricuperati, *Frontiere*, 34; Calaresu, 'Searching', 74–7.

[136] Pagano, *Saggi politici*, i, introduzione; Ferrone, *I profeti*, 280.

14

Spain and the Challenge of Reform

1. REMAKING A TRANSATLANTIC EMPIRE

The objectives of Carlos III (reigned: 1759–88) and the clique of reforming ministers he brought to the helm—Campomanes, Floridablanca, and Aranda—involved programmes of economic stimulation, imperial reorganization, and administrative and legal reform, profoundly altering Spain's relationship to the past, the Church, and its empire. Overall, the clergy lost some autonomy and some immunities were curbed. But it was certainly never the Spanish crown's goal to disrupt the traditionally close collaboration of Church and state and religious uniformity, characteristic of the country since the later Middle Ages, or indeed the social hierarchy, or firm subordination of the empire to the metropolis. Rather, reformers within the administration, Church, education, science, and the economy under Carlos III saw the crown as the engine with which to push through the organizational changes they considered essential, rendering the court the prime focus of moderate enlightened thinking and debate.

The best recent Spanish historiography, in particular the fundamentally revisionist work of Sánchez-Blanco, makes clear the extraordinary degree of distortion and misapprehension surrounding the Spanish Enlightenment permeating the traditional historiography. The notion that the Spanish Enlightenment overall had an essentially national, unitary, royal, and Catholic character and that the enlightened absolutism and ministers of Carlos III were the backbone of this wide-ranging, ambitious Enlightenment has today been altogether discarded and rightly so. The ministers of Carlos III did try to change Spain fundamentally; but in the main they were not committed to 'enlighten', secularize, introduce toleration, reduce the role of the clergy, institute freedom of thought and expression, reform society's legal basis, or soften the edge of social hierarchy. Only a few ministers and officials were seriously committed to enlightened aims. Most were first and foremost absolutists and their objective was always to reinforce monarchy, empire, aristocracy, as well as—within a somewhat changed format—adjust ecclesiastical authority and control over education. Carlos III, it is clear, in marked contrast to Frederick or Catherine, personally had no sympathy whatsoever for the Enlightenment, much preferring hunting.

The profoundly mistaken notions about the Spanish Enlightenment that have for so long distorted the picture have thankfully at last been thoroughly laid to rest, and this in itself involves a considerable revolution in historical thinking. In what follows I have broadly followed Sánchez-Blanco: Carlos III was no enlightener, his government was chiefly concerned to reinforce the main pillars of existing Spanish society, his much vaunted reform of the universities entirely failed to secularize or modernize them, and during his reign there was no toleration, secularism, or freedom of thought, expression, or the press in Spain and its empire; and it was never the royal intention that there should be. Equally important, the disillusion and estrangement this caused, given the extent of social inequalities and total lack of toleration, at least among a few administrators, nobles, professors, editors, and other highly educated, critically minded individuals, had by the 1780s provoked a profound intellectual and political rift between an oppositional and partly still underground Enlightenment and a regime that increasingly endorsed the country's numerous Catholic apologists, or *antifilósofos*. In other words the profound rift between conservative royalists and *afrancesados*, or French-oriented liberals, characteristic of the post-1789 era was already plainly evident in Spain well before 1789. The story of the Enlightenment in Spain is a story of bitter and tremendous conflict.

However, in the analysis that follows I depart from Sánchez-Blanco's assessment in two respects. First, in rejecting the older framework, forged in particular by Jean Sarrailh, Sánchez-Blanco arguably went too far in denying the enlightened credentials of some of Carlos's ministers and too far in denying the feasibility per se of a 'Catholic Enlightenment'.[1] There was a royal and Catholic Enlightenment in Spain, even if it never really gained the upper hand over the reactionary Counter-Enlightenment so deeply entrenched in the Spanish Church, universities, and law courts. It was an enlightenment that rightly venerated Father Benito Jerónimo Feijóo (1676–1764) as its founding father and eulogized Locke and Newton in particular but also embraced much in Montesquieu, Hume, and Robertson. It was also an enlightenment deeply fearful of the radical tendency. As Campomanes himself remarked of the French *Encyclopédie*, the latter was a work that needed to remain firmly banned in Spain owing to its subversive content: nevertheless, from the point of view of the Spanish crown this was a pity in some respects as this compendium undoubtedly contained a great deal of useful practical information about crafts, techniques, and economic processes.[2]

Sánchez-Blanco rightly argues that Carlos III's ministers supported the *antifilósofos* and were profoundly opposed to large tranches of enlightened thought and that it was never their intention to weaken the Spanish Church or secularize Spanish society. All notions of citizenship, equality, and the sovereignty of the people were anathema to them. But he fails to acknowledge that some of the Spanish *antifilósofos* were not exponents of Counter-Enlightenment but, rather, resembled Bergier and other *anti-philosophes* (whose writings were well known in Spanish translation) in continually eulogizing Locke and Newton, venerating Feijóo, and calling for reforms

---

[1] Sánchez Blanco, *Absolutismo*, 78, 223–4, 248–9, 443.   [2] Campomanes, *Discurso*, iv. 5.

in education and the sciences as well as government and the economy. Spanish royal and Catholic Enlightenment if much less of a dominant force than it has traditionally been represented as being was still a ubiquitous force: its insurmountable problem was that it was inherently incapable of tackling the main social, educational, and cultural difficulties facing the country, albeit in this respect Spain scarcely differed from France, Britain, Italy, Germany, or Russia except perhaps somewhat in degree. Sánchez-Blanco is right to insist that there was a basic and inherent conflict between the royal policies of Campomanes and Floridablanca, on the one hand, and the genuine enlightened tendency in Spain. But he missed the fact that this oppositional critique of Spanish society and culture welling up within sections of Spain's admittedly rather narrow reading public, generating a conflict between moderate and Radical Enlightenment, in many ways typified the more general predicament of the Enlightenment. In any case, one must begin with the split between moderate and radical wings of the Enlightenment: without starting there, nothing at all about the Spanish Enlightenment can be correctly grasped.

The exceptional power and prestige of Church and aristocracy far more readily combined ideologically with the intense conservatism of traditional Spanish culture and higher education than the ideals of much, or most, enlightened philosophy. In practice, this imposed huge constraints on mainstream Enlightenment in the Spanish world (and Portugal and Brazil), extending even beyond those applying elsewhere that had very far-reaching implications. If the comprehensive religious and intellectual toleration espoused by Frederick, Joseph, and Catherine was ruled out in Spain from the outset, press censorship too remained even more repressive and wider in scope than was usual in Austria and Germany. To this extent the anti-Spanish bias so much resented by chauvinists and Catholic apologists frequently pervading foreign perceptions of Iberia throughout the eighteenth century was far from ungrounded. French *philosophes* and Protestant enlighteners alike viewed Spain as intellectually the most bigoted, benighted, and isolated of lands, and most destitute, as Helvétius supposed, of men of genius and true virtue.[3] The fierce intolerance of Spain's Habsburg monarchs and the Inquisition's central role in earlier centuries, as well as the unparalleled standing, privileges, and authority of the Church and backwardness of the universities, often appeared to justify foreign observers in adopting an attitude of profound antipathy and disdain. 'Poor Spaniards! When will you shake off that fatal lethargy,' exclaimed Casanova when travelling in Valencia in 1769, and overcome 'your ignorance' and 'all the prejudices that degrade you'. What could bring about the transformation Spain needed? 'A furious revolution, a terrible shock, a conquest of regeneration; your case is past gentle methods, it needs the cautery and the fire.'[4]

Yet, Spain was less devoid of enlightened impulses than outsiders supposed. Even in the 1750s with the country still ruled by Fernando VI (reigned: 1746–59),

---

[3] Helvétius, *De l'homme*, i. 82; Cañizares-Esguerra, *Nature, Empire*, 24, 106.
[4] Casanova, *Memoirs*, vi. 194.

characterized by Diderot, in 1782, as a ruler over whose mind the clergy exercised 'un ascendant sans bornes',[5] awareness spread among observers of the wider European scene that encouraging new developments were occurring in Iberia. The *Journal étranger* in 1758 complimented Spain for being a country where, despite the difficulty in maintaining intellectual contact with the world outside, the sciences and arts 'sont maintenant fort cultivés' and Spain's contribution one which henceforth 'peut figurer avec distinction dans l'Europe sçavante'.[6] Particularly encouraging was the rise of scientific academies, growth of a lay reading public, and the noticeable expansion of publishing, especially in Madrid, Valencia, and Barcelona.[7]

Appreciation of Spain's role mounted through the 1760s and 1770s and, indeed, became a feature of enlightened thought itself. It afforded him particular consolation, remarks Diderot, in the *Histoire philosophique*, to recognize that reform, revival, and enlightenment had made considerable progress in Spain in recent years, and that 'la condition d'Espagne devient tous les jours meilleure'.[8] A more enlightened royal court was now making strenuous efforts to improve administration and revive the economy. Aristocratic birth was no longer the exclusive and only qualification for high office. The silk, woollen, and dyeing industries were reviving, trade between Spain and Spanish America expanding, and many new activities and crafts becoming established. Paper mills producing good paper, excellent print workshops producing attractive books, societies and academies devoted to advancing science, economic thought, and useful crafts were taking root all over the country. Both the fine arts and scientific research were gaining new momentum, a process bound sooner or later to stem prejudice, credulity, and ignorance.[9] Among the key institutions of Spain's Enlightenment were the royal academies and the later famous royal botanical gardens, or Jardín Real, established at Madrid by royal decree of Fernando VI in October 1755, and in 1779–80 transferred, under Floridablanca's auspices, to the Prado. Furnished with many plants from Spanish America, it was strictly arranged on the principles of Linnaeus and featured an attached lecture hall where, over the decades, a resident professor of botany expounded Linnaean concepts.[10]

In contrast to many Protestant writers, Diderot, Helvétius, and their allies were free of any prejudiced notion of Spaniards being innately cruel, superstitious, and credulous. Enlightenment, for Diderot, is intellectual and moral advancement arising from a wider process of cultural and social transformation. For radical, as opposed to the moderate enlightenment, the complex problems of Spain and Spanish America were just an extreme instance of the general human predicament, a case not of innate intolerance, religious corruption, and cruelty but of morally disfiguring institutions and a highly defective social structure bolstered by ignorance and wrongly organized educational institutions. Spain's chronic ills were perfectly curable but only by

---

[5] Diderot, 'Don Pablo Olavidès', 467.   [6] *Journal étranger* (Dec. 1758), 3.
[7] Enciso Recio, *Divulgación*, 313–31.
[8] *Histoire philosophique* (1770), iii. 298–9; *Histoire philosophique* (1780), iv. 402–3.
[9] Ibid. iv. 403–6.   [10] *Memorial literario, instructivo y curioso* (Apr. 1784), 28–41.

attacking privilege, ignorance, and credulity. Precisely the signs of change strengthened their thesis, central to the whole structure of radical thought, that Spain's manifold defects stemmed not from innate national deficiencies but rather exactly the same defective structures of authority, oppressive social hierarchies, systems of 'error', and popular acquiescence in oppression as blighted the human condition everywhere, Britain included.

Not only were Diderot and other radical voices right about the signs of change in Spain but, from a modern perspective, there is a further point arising from their analysis. While the Inquisition's continuing grip and the Church's immense prestige placed far-reaching constraints on the expression of new ideas, especially philosophical and scientific ideas with serious theological, moral, and social implications, there is a reverse side to this coin which historians have rightly of late come to recognize. For precisely these unusually repressive features lent an added edge to behind the scenes rebellion and clandestine 'philosophical' debate, something that had become a widely noticed feature of Spanish culture by the 1760s and 1770s. Hence, while it is true that moderate mainstream Enlightenment advanced more slowly and met more resistance in the Spanish world than in North America, for example, it is equally true that radical ideas tended to find more fertile ground than in North America or Britain. The very fact that moderate Enlightenment's prospects and room for manoeuvre were more tightly constrained than elsewhere guaranteed a richer underground seam of repressed aspirations, resentment, and frustration being expressed in terms of the new radical concepts.

For moderate enlighteners at court, among the supporters of Don Pedro Rodríguez Campomanes (1723–1802), Spain's chief economic reformer, and Floridablanca, there seemed for a time abundant reason for optimism. Enlightenment could surely succeed by working together with the other forces striving for reform, centralization, and economic improvement. If 'enlightened despotism' could achieve much in Italy, Germany, Russia, and Scandinavia, it could accomplish much in Spain and Spanish America too. Some leading figures in the administration not only considered themselves enlighteners but were convinced Carlos III's reforms amounted to a comprehensive, thoroughgoing, and successful 'revolution' that would open the gates to a full-blown Catholic Enlightenment. As Don Pedro Varela y Ulloa, a senior official under Floridablanca, put it, 'this revolution proclaims the re-establishment of our agriculture, crafts, navigation and commerce, and promises us a state of happiness and prosperity unknown hitherto'.[11] But no matter how energetic and focused on political economy and practical goals, Varela y Ulloa and the others soon proved to be fighting an unwinnable battle. They remained staunchly loyal to Muratori's and Genovesi's ideal of publicly avoiding the deeper metaphysical and social questions, while concentrating on practical reforms in alliance with liberal elements in the Church. They prided themselves on their pragmatism and good sense, and the viability of the path of political economy buttressed by legal and

---

[11] Varela y Ulloa, 'Discurso preliminar', pp. xxviii–xxxxix; Hauben, 'White Legend', 7.

educational reform eschewing 'philosophy'. But in the end their vaunted pragmatism proved wholly illusory, incapable of resolving the deep-seated socio-economic structural problems weighing on Spain and her empire.

Campomanes, Floridablanca, and their allies promoted an Enlightenment that exalted crown, aristocracy, empire, and religion offering what they thought were viable solutions to the country's economic backwardness, antiquated laws, and dysfunctional institutions. Their great problem was not lack of resolve or clear goals but the inherent inability of moderate Enlightenment in such a context to deliver. No matter how energetic, and zealous for moderation and intellectual *anglicisme*, virtually every major problem court reformers sought to address entailed intractable and insuperable difficulties stemming from Spain's rigid social hierarchy, institutions, religion, and culture or the interests of the clergy. Every important initiative raised questions about the scope and powers of monarchy, aristocracy, and the Church, or impinged on belief, religious uniformity, and royal censorship, or raised questions about the principle of empire. So dominant were the nobility and clergy, and pervasive the principles of closely supervised religious uniformity, and subordination of the colonies to the metropolis, that in Spain it was even plainer than elsewhere that 'moderate' Enlightenment solutions no matter how attractive to governments and most enlightened opinion could not overcome the structural difficulties or avoid generating a hugely divisive process of social, political, educational, and cultural debate and criticism which itself threatened to engulf existing authority and institutions, civil and ecclesiastical.

Not the least intractable difficulty was the over-regulated, thoroughly obsolete commercial relationship of Spain to its American empire and the Philippines. For it was impossible to address the problems of colonial trade and Spain's economic backwardness without raising basic questions about the empire's political subordination to Spain, the excessive numbers of monasteries and convents, the discouragingly large amount of land being underused or poorly used for agriculture through being legally 'entailed', that is tied to noble houses or ecclesiastical bodies, and so forth. Certainly, detailed discussion of economic and some social issues was encouraged by Campomanes first throughout Spain and then, later, in the empire. The introduction of the so-called 'Economic Societies of the Friends of the Country', around seventy of which were instituted through the length and breadth of the empire between 1763 and the early nineteenth century, constituted one of the foremost 'enlightened' changes introduced by the reforming ministers of Carlos III and were the centrepiece of Campomanes's policy.[12] Campomanes attributed Spain's economic decline to ignorance, misuse of resources, and failure to exploit the opportunities of empire, and in particular lack of interest in new techniques and excessive conservatism in popular modes of craft work.[13] The 'economic societies' were designed to revive economic life in the regions by recruiting the dominant elites, the nobility and clergy especially, directly into the process of debating and devising

---

[12] Schafer, *Economic Societies*, 48. [13] Campomanes, *Discurso*, i, 'advertencia', 1–11.

improvements in agriculture, mining, commerce, navigation, industry, and the crafts. They were bodies intended to create a public platform for debate, diffusing responsibility for analysing and resolving Spain's economic and social dilemmas through the upper strata of society. But precisely by so doing they also broadcast throughout the empire the formidable intractability and interrelatedness of the problems.

The first of these bodies was founded in the Basque country at the close of the Seven Years War by a noble who had studied in Toulouse, much devoted to Newton and the new physics (including 's Gravesande), the count of Peñaflorida (1729–85).[14] He conceived the idea together with Manuel Ignacio de Altuna (1722–62) who in the early 1740s had been a close friend of Rousseau in Venice. Altuna, recalled Rousseau later, read widely, venerated Locke, was unusually wise, and was as 'devout as a Spaniard' outwardly but inwardly cared not at all what his friends believed, even if atheists.[15] Originally framed as a 'Project and Plan of Agriculture, Sciences and Useful Arts for Guipuzcoa', the society held its first general annual meeting in Vergara in 1765.[16] Endorsed by the crown the same year, its 127-page statutes, approved by royal authority, were published in 1773. It was dominated from the outset, as Campomanes wanted, by aristocrats, officials, lawyers, and other locally prominent men. Originally a local society, it developed into a wide ranging Basque association which by 1773 boasted some 400 members, many based in Madrid, Seville, and Cadiz with a significant proportion (around 190, or nearly a quarter) in Spanish America.

Sister societies sprang up in rapid succession, including those established in Seville by Olavide in 1775, and in Asturias by Campomanes in 1780, both heavily dominated by nobles and clergy, the latter electing one of the foremost of the Spanish mainstream enlighteners, Don Gaspar Melchior de Jovellanos (1744–1811), a leading official and keen promoter of the exact sciences, its director in 1782. Nothing could have been more 'unphilosophical' in the radical sense than the statutes of these associations or more focused on political economy, or more supportive of the prerogatives of Church, aristocracy, or monarchy. Based in capital cities of provinces, often meeting in city halls under the chairmanship of a local royal or civic high official, and intended to be self-financing, they were designed to meet weekly, encourage inventions and improvements, establish libraries of economic literature so as to make technically useful foreign works translated from other languages into Spanish accessible, collect statistics, and offer prizes for the best discourses on economic issues and improvements. They were also entrusted with reorganizing, supervising, and promoting schools.

The economic societies devoted most of their efforts to scrutinizing new textile techniques, agricultural implements, promoting science locally, and the like. But they were permitted also, at least in theory and secondarily, to discuss more general issues

---

[14] Sarrailh, *L'Espagne éclairée*, 433–8.
[15] Rousseau, *Confessions*, 275–7; Guehenno, *Jean-Jacques Rousseau*, i. 143, 160, 162.
[16] Schafer, *Economic Societies*, 28–9.

of social policy. The 'economic societies' usually had four classes of members, that of the province of León, for example, calling these *honorarios, numerarios, natos,* and *professores.* The last category were the province's acknowledged technical experts in all the relevant fields, the men (women were excluded) made ex officio members without paying any subscription. *Numerarios* were the ordinary subscribing members, including a few prosperous merchants and financiers, each paying seventy *reales* a year, the fund accruing being allocated for the society's running costs, purchasing books, publishing, and offering prizes. The *natos* were chiefly the parish priests of the province, a group exempted from paying the subscription, while the first class, the *honorarios,* were such nobles and high-born persons, equally exempt from subscribing, deemed to reflect status and honour on the society.[17]

Five paramount obstacles obstructing general economic reform were the country's low level of consumption due to mass poverty, aristocratic entails (*mayorazgos*), ecclesiastical privilege and property, the heavy burden of military expenditure, and entrenched resistance to technological change. But in an empire dominated by crown, aristocracy, and clergy, lack of religious toleration, and the rigidity of the colonies' subordination to metropolitan Spain, it proved difficult to tackle any of these directly. Since the 'economic societies' could in no way challenge, indeed in their make-up strongly reflected, the nobility's and clergy's dominance of society, the only way they could raise the status of commerce and industry, besides vague calls to emulate economically more successful societies like Britain, was to summon the Castilian and Aragonese nobilies to transform themselves into commercially minded trading nobilities, like that of Venice, an ideal to which all the 'economic societies' subscribed. It was for this reason that the Royal Economic Society of Mallorca, for instance, in 1781 paid for and sponsored a translation of the Abbé Coyer's *Noblesse commerçante* (1756). The Abbé Gabriel-François Coyer (1707–82) had for some time figured among moderate *philosophes* approved of in Spain. An ardent Anglophile friendly with Voltaire (but scorned by Grimm), Coyer promoted reforms compatible with social hierarchy, his chief aim being to make France's nobility resemble the British gentry by persuading it to become commercial in spirit.[18] His book was rendered into Spanish by an *oidor,* or high magistrate of Mallorca's royal chancery, Jacobo Maria de Spinosa y Cantabrana, afterwards chief prosecuting magistrate of the royal *audiencia* (regional high court) of Catalonia. Powerfully stressing the decline of Spain's commerce,[19] this official argues in his preface that trade was so potent a factor in the modern world that it had enabled the Americans within a short time to amass resources sufficient to throw off the 'yoke and the pride of England'. Spain needed an equally vigorous expansion of commerce and for this the nobility must overcome their *repugnancia* for trade and assume the lead.[20]

---

[17] *Estatutos para la Sociedad Económica… de León* (Madrid, 1783), 5–7.
[18] Adams, *Coyer,* 31, 92–3; Chaussinand-Nogaret, *French Nobility,* 38, 107.
[19] Spinosa y Cantabrana, 'Discurso preliminar' to Coyer, *Nobleza commerciante,* pp. xxxviii–xxxix.
[20] Ibid., pp. iii, lix, lxi.

Crown and 'economic societies' aimed to render the Spanish nobility more commercial and the people more industrious; they also sought to involve the clergy in this process. Nor were either the nobility's lack of a commercial spirit or the clergy's relative detachment the only defects attributed to them. Also urgently needed in Spain, held Jovellanos, was a reform and purification of the very principle of nobility. He bitterly deplored the proliferation of 'pseudo-nobles' and nobles who thought their privileges were justified purely by birth alone rather than by attainments and personal virtues, besides corrupt officials who, for personal gain, fabricated coats of arms for those able to pay for social elevation but lacking genuine entitlement to nobility. But like Campomanes, he continued to uphold the principle of nobility as such and the separation of nobles from the rest, the *plebeyos*, as fundamental. As his highest social ideal, Jovellanos envisaged a balanced 'reciprocal *dependencia*' with both nobles and crown respecting the genuine, historic privileges rooted in the past with both enhancing the spiritual authority of the clergy which he aspired to see somewhat more under royal control, certainly, but also strengthened in their didactic, moral, and social roles.[21]

From the 1760s many important reforms were introduced in the economic and administrative spheres and nowhere with greater impact than in Spanish America. It is clear, however, that what really drove this imperial reorganization was less the 'economic societies', enlightened programmes, or Campomanes's reformism than Spain's heightened vulnerability following her humiliating defeats in 1761–3—and France's loss of her colonies in Canada and India—at British hands. Under the settlement of 1763, Spain had to cede Florida, Pensacola, and all her claims in North America east of the Mississippi to Britain, placing the latter in a potentially commanding position throughout the northern Gulf of Mexico. This in turn forced the Spanish crown to invest heavily in strengthening the fortifications of Havana and New Orleans (transferred by France to Spain in 1762, along with the rest of Louisiana, in compensation for Spain's losses in Florida) to create a surrogate bulwark against Britain's increasingly overbearing preponderance. Equally, the court was stung by military defeat into massively expanding and professionalizing the army and navy. This created an urgent need drastically to increase revenues, forcing the crown to launch an ambitious programme of major reforms on both sides of the Atlantic, in the Americas often supervised by Marqués Don José de Gálvez y Gallardo (1720–87), who presided over colonial affairs, to resolve the urgent problem of the empire's languishing trade and revenues.

Among other initiatives, from the mid 1760s a series of measures were enacted in the Consejo de Indias [Council of the Indies], in Madrid, designed to liberalize the trade regime in empire and stimulate commerce between the various colonies as well as between the Indies and the metropolis. The old monopoly of the American trade based on Cadiz, established in Habsburg times, ended officially in 1765 and,

---

[21] Jovellanos, *Obras en prosa*, 92, 99–100, 112; Campomanes, *Discurso*, i. 33; Anes, *Siglo de las Luces*, 38.

henceforth, trade with Cuba, Puerto Rico, and the whole Spanish Caribbean was thrown open also to Malaga, Alicante, La Coruña, Santander, Barcelona, Cartagena, and Gijón. The system of *comercio libre* [free trade], as it was called, was then extended first to Yucatan and Campeche, in July 1770, and eventually to all of Spanish America. Commercial seaborne contact between the Pacific ports of Peru and New Spain (Mexico and Guatemala), officially closed since 1634,[22] was reopened in 1774. Trade with the Philippines and the Far East was permitted to all investors in the empire, in Peru, New Granada, and Cuba as well as Mexico and Spain.[23] From 1778, the policy of internal 'free trade'—without any right for Spanish America to trade with foreign parts, a prohibition now more strictly imposed than ever—was in force throughout the empire. Steadily, between 1750 and the outbreak of the French Revolution, Spain's trade with her empire expanded, as did silver output in Mexico and yearly total bullion imports from America to the metropolis.

A major innovation in the New World, following Spain's defeat in the Seven Years War, was the setting up, in 1776, again on the initiative of Gálvez, of the viceroyalty of Río de la Plata with its capital at Buenos Aires and jurisdiction over parts of what had formerly been the viceroyalty of Peru besides what is now Argentina and the former Jesuit missions in Paraguay. In 1783, the new viceroyalty was divided into eight *intendencias* and, in 1785, a royal *audiencia*, or regional high court, was added. The intention was basically strategic, to turn the River Plate estuary into a meaningful barrier to British power (and French interloping) in the South Atlantic, where Britain had established a foothold in the Falkland Islands in 1766, as well as block the southwards expansion of Portuguese Brazil and improve communications and postal services between Spain and Upper Peru and between administrative bodies throughout southern South America. But it was a costly initiative requiring heavy spending on new military and naval installations the crown could ill afford. Although the new entity was originally meant also to reinforce the long-standing prohibition on importing textiles and other European products via Buenos Aires,[24] wider strategic, jurisdictional, and military considerations soon led to a re-routing of much of the transatlantic commerce between Spain and Peru from the Caribbean—and overland at Panamá—to the previously prohibited southern route via Tucumán and Buenos Aires, thereby unhinging the old, established system of regulating commerce in the Indies.

2. THE JESUITS AND CARLOS III'S CHURCH POLICY

If the cornerstone of the *comercio libre* policy in the Spanish Indies was the package of new laws enacted in Madrid from the mid 1760s, Bourbon *comercio libre* in Spain

---

[22] Israel, *Race, Class and Politics*, 100–1.
[23] AN Bolivia exp. Colon. 1786 no. 17, 10 May 1785, fos. 5ᵛ–6, 13.
[24] AGN Lima sup. gov. leg. 204, cuad. 1313, fo. 1, 26 Feb. 1778.

itself hinged on other decrees of the mid 1760s reaffirming edicts lifting the restrictions on the domestic grain trade and exporting cereals tentatively introduced in the previous reign, in August 1756 and November 1757. Thus far, these still had little effect, as officially fixed pricing to stabilize bread prices generally remained in force to deal with the inertia and administrative confusion in the grain market. But in 1761, a court-appointed *junta* of ministers and advisers, led by Campomanes, announced a policy of free trade in grain and minimal intervention in the grain market by local authorities, lifting the remaining restrictions, relying on laws against hoarding and profiteering to prevent serious instability in bread prices. Unfortunately for the crown, though, defeat in the Seven Years War was followed by several bad harvests in the mid 1760s, culminating in 1765.

The resulting sharp rise in grain prices in the interior had, by 1765, generated considerable unrest. The advisers Carlos III had brought with him from Naples, headed by the Marqués de Esquilache, were unpopular, and antipathy to the king's entourage combined with bread shortages in March and April 1766 precipitated some massive if relatively restrained riots in Madrid. The disturbances began with agitators stirring discontent in the taverns and rapidly developed into the biggest popular upheaval in eighteenth-century Spain, albeit featuring a distinct element of manipulation of the common people's distress by highly placed opponents of the regime.[25] An additional factor was the clergy's indignant opposition to pending government reforms affecting them, proposed by Campomanes and under review, in particular to prevent further bequests to the clergy designed to convert previously taxable lands into tax-free property covered by ecclesiastical privilege. After days of tumult in Madrid, on 26 March, swelling crowds, availing themselves of a store of arms, seized control of the capital, after which the rioting spread to Zaragoza, Seville, Cuenca, Granada, and other cities.

Helpless in this grave predicament, a furious monarch found himself left with no alternative but to make numerous concessions to the people that were then read out to the mob in Madrid's Plaza Mayor. These included reversion to price fixing, dismissal of unpopular ministers, notably Esquilache who returned to Sicily, and appointment of several new ministers, notably Don Pedro Abaca de Bolea, Conde de Aranda, a grandee with a wide diplomatic experience in Vienna, Dresden, Berlin, and Paris, known for his enlightened inclinations. Governor of Valencia at the time of the riots, he was now named *presidente* of the Consejo de Castilla, from which powerful position Aranda exerted considerable influence down to 1772. A rival of Floridablanca, Aranda stood at the hub of a reform-minded aristocratic network that included his son-in-law, the Marqués de Mora (d. 1774), who, in the years 1766–72, resided in Paris where he was an intimate of d'Alembert.[26]

---

[25] Rodriguez, 'Spanish Riots', 121–6.
[26] Condorcet to Turgot, 11 Aug. 1772. in Condorcet, *Correspondance inédite de Condorcet*, 96; Oltra and Samper, *Conde de Aranda*, 53.

In subsequently investigating and assessing the riots, king and ministers were especially shocked by reports that some clergy, including Jesuits, had been spotted among the crowds and, in several instances, were accused of complicity in the disturbances. While the Jesuits and other orders indignantly denied any involvement, Aranda and Campomanes seized the opportunity or, as some saw it, pretext to instigate a formal investigation into the Jesuits' practices more generally. It was not, however, Enlightenment ideology, as some supposed at that time, that drove this investigation, but rather the king's known dislike of the Jesuits' ultramontane attitudes and extensive privileges. Alarmed by the riots, impressed by the recent expulsion of the Jesuits from France, and conscious of the long-standing clash between the royal administration on the River Plate and the Jesuit missions in Paraguay, Aranda and his colleagues drew up a detailed indictment, stressing the order's autonomy, tight, corporate character, vast inventory of property, alleging abuse of popular piety, and incompatibility of its privileges and statutes with the crown's supremacy, especially in Paraguay. The king was advised to seize all the Jesuit colleges in Spain and expel them together with those of their novices who refused to leave the order, albeit 'with all decency' and respect for their persons.

The king needed little persuading and Aranda and Campomanes were entrusted with putting the expulsion into effect.[27] By decree of 27 February 1767, the Jesuits were banished from the entire empire, and their 134 *colegios* and establishments, on both sides of the Atlantic, and goods and lands appropriated by the crown. Aranda decreed that their books and buildings were not to be taken over by other orders but assigned to the universities. Everywhere, Jesuit investments were transferred, papers, books, and archives seized, and opportunities for protest or raising support for their cause among the laity blocked. In total, including those from the Philippines, between 5,000 and 6,000 Jesuits were expelled, most eventually transferring to the Papal States where Pope Clement XIII, much distressed by Spain's action, initially refused to admit them, but relented after they spent a year on Corsica (from whence they had to depart when the island was transferred to France). They were then admitted *en bloc* to the papal territories. Among the exiles was the leading intellectual figure in New Spain, Francisco Xavier Clavijero (1731–87), author of the *Historia antigua de México* and former professor of philosophy in the Jesuit colleges of Valladolid (Michoacán) and Guadalajara. A refugee for the rest of his life, Clavijero settled at Ferrara and later Bologna where he died.

Privately, Aranda and Campomanes were undoubtedly motivated by secularizing Enlightenment ideas. Publicly, though, in deference to Spanish circumstances and the king, they took scrupulous care not to try to explain or justify the Jesuits' expulsion in terms of enlightened thinking of any sort, indeed said as little as possible about the reasons for the Jesuits' banishment, merely referring vaguely in their published decrees to 'gravísimas causas' [very grave reasons] while insisting on the

---

[27] Anes, *Siglo de las Luces*, 251; Mestre Sanchis, *Ilustración española*, 42.

need to maintain public order and tranquillity. As with all key issues of the age, the grounds of the expulsion were treated as a royal secret that was in no way a public matter. Circular letters were dispatched reassuring the bishops that the king's trust in them remained unabated, albeit also forbidding any clergy to defend the Jesuits or criticize their expulsion. Significantly, the only public criticism of the Jesuits permitted was theological indictments that had swelled in recent years with the growing influx into the country of Jansenist books and ideas. Ministers gladly encouraged expression of this kind of criticism, including that of the long dead but virulently anti-Jesuit Aragonese bishop Juan de Palafox who had become locked in a famous battle with the Mexican Jesuits in the 1640s and whose works, suddenly freed from Inquisition disapproval at royal insistence, had been conspicuously reissued in 1762.[28]

Carlos's ministers never intended to assail ecclesiastical privilege, authority, or property or be drawn into a wider confrontation with the Church. Their goal rather was to place the clergy on a tighter rein, prevent more tax-exempt property coming into clerical hands, and, as in Austria and Habsburg Italy, involve the clergy more rather than less in regulation of society. They wished the clergy to conduct themselves almost as if they were state servants. The eight archbishops and forty-eight bishops who presided over the Church in Spain in the 1760s remained immensely powerful and privileged, receiving directly some 12 per cent of all ecclesiastical revenue, and these men saw little reason to disturb their close alignment with the crown.[29] More problematic was the popular reaction in the Indies and among Creole local elites. For the Jesuits had hitherto played the predominant role in higher education and had many friends. Ripples of murmured protest against royal policy developed, especially in New Spain where the disgruntlement led to several pro-Jesuit disturbances at San Luis Potosí, Guanajuato, and elsewhere.

While Gálvez, then serving as royal visitor-general in Mexico, relied on deploying troops and harsh prison sentences to restore order, Mexico City's archbishop, an anti-Jesuit traditionalist, Don Francisco Antonio Lorenzana y Buitron, issued an extraordinary archiepiscopal edict, in September 1768, condemning sedition and pronouncing the unrest chiefly rife—in the form of murmured protests, visions, and 'revelaciones fanáticas' about the pending return of the Jesuits—in the monasteries and convents. The worst subversion, declared the archbishop, was to be found in female convents, nuns being excessively susceptible to their spiritual directors, some of whom were 'followers of the maxims and doctrines of the expelled regulars' deliberately stirring resentment and 'divulging among the public ideas contrary to the public peace'. Such suspect confessors, charged the prelate, were 'not only disturbing the tranquillity of New Spain's nuns, dividing them into factions and encouraging them to discuss matters of government altogether inappropriate to the

[28] Israel, *Race, Class and Politics*, 217–33; Sánchez-Blanco, *Absolutismo*, 43, 64, 82.
[29] Barrio Gozalo, 'Iglesia y religiosidad', 248, 265.

weakness of their sex, but also to their monastic profession of withdrawal'. All New Spain's nuns, he commanded their spiritual directors, must be admonished that it is never legitimate to speak ill of the sovereign, prelates, or secular authorities, that 'it is no article of the faith that the order of the Jesuits or any other order has to continue until the end of the world', that it is forbidden to speak for or against any act of government, and that 'lo que debe executarse es obedecer, y callar' [that what should be put into effect is to obey and shut up].[30]

The immediate effect of the expulsion, an action supported by the (by this time) quite widespread Jansenist following in the Spanish Church, was to open the way, indeed necessitate, a general reform of secondary and higher education throughout the empire as the Jesuits had long provided most teachers in both local *colegios* and university teaching. Although the Dominicans, Augustinians, and other orders all profited from the Jesuits' departure, their expulsion opened up a massive gap that could not easily be filled. The vacuum created in the universities and *colegios* was precisely the kind of space in a heavily theologically oriented culture that rival religious orders and the Jansenist-minded higher clergy and professors were eager and sometimes also well equipped to fill. The drawback from the viewpoint of more advanced enlightened circles was that the situation provided no obvious route by which any fundamental transformation of the curriculum and philosophical foundations of education or any tilting of the balance away from theology and ecclesiastical control could be achieved. In effect, the crown proceeded quickly with a comprehensive programme of educational reform without at first introducing any plans or argued framework other than Jansenist critiques of the Jesuits to buttress it.[31]

At the same time there were genuinely enlightened impulses in Spanish society. Consequently, reforming higher education proved a challenging, highly complex business in theology and philosophy no less than medicine and law, involving dozens of battles all over Spain, New Spain, and Peru in which royal officials could often get things done only by forming alliances with local Jansenist prelates. These were often vehemently anti-Jesuit, anti-Dominican, and opposed to *Probabilismo* and other theological tendencies specifically associated with the Jesuits.[32] Such prelates willingly embraced a politics of deference to the crown, a strict *regalismo*. But they aimed chiefly at purifying and renewing religious piety in reaction to, rather than in alliance with, the Enlightenment and had no sympathy for secularizing tendencies as such. They stood fully behind the Inquisition's war on Enlightenment impiety generally as well as more specifically against the *materialistas*.[33] The now elderly but highly influential Gregorio Mayáns y Siscar (1699–1781), at Valencia, a keen reader of the

---

[30] Lorenzana, *Cartas pastorales y edictos* (Mexico City, 1770), 63–4.

[31] Mestre Sanchis, *Ilustración española*, 42–3; Alvares de Morales, *Ilustración*, 58–60; Schmidt, 'Contra "la falsa filosofia"', 244–6.

[32] Alvares de Morales, *Ilustración*, 59–60; Lorenzana, *Cartas pastorales*, 22–8; Castro, *Filosofía*, 49–50.

[33] Saugnieux, *Jansénisme*, 29, 38, 43, 46; Barrio Gozalo, 'Iglesia y religiosidad', 278; Mas Galvan, 'Jansenismo', 262–3.

French Jansenist journal *Nouvelles ecclésiastiques*, was a key adviser in educational reform, and his *Idea for the New Method which should be Practiced in Teaching in the Spanish Universities* (1767) typified the whole reforming effort in seeking only modest compromises between the scholasticism of the past and the new sciences and an essentially conservative outcome.[34] Jansenist influence was a real asset to the reformers in getting certain things done but more of a brake than help to any intellectual programme aspiring to a more far-reaching reform of the universities and colleges.

A key focus of reform were the episcopal seminaries for training ordinary parish clergy, for these were among the most entrenched strongholds of Aristotelian, Thomist, and scholasticist thought. When reform began in earnest, in 1774, at the episcopal seminary in Murcia, the initiative, typically, was taken by the new Jansenist bishop of Cartagena, D. Manuel Rubín de Celís (bishop of Cartagena: 1773–84), a prelate who had spent some time at Rome and was willing to alter the curriculum and combat Dominican zeal for Thomism in accord with the views of leading moderate mainstream intellectual figures like Mayáns and the physician Andres Piquer (1711–72). But whilst he did adopt new textbooks in philosophy, curbing scholasticism, Rubín de Celís authorized such changes chiefly with a view to smoothing the simultaneous adoption of Jansenist textbooks in the teaching of theology.[35]

It was impossible, however, to push in one direction in the seminaries and monasteries, in close alliance with the dominant faction among the prelates, while pushing philosophically and culturally in an opposite direction in the *colegios* and universities. Hence, the only solution was for ministers to find an intellectual basis for compromise between theology and science weighted in favour of the former. Certainly, this allowed for some expansion of teaching in mathematics, medicine, and science. At Salamanca, a government commission, highlighting the chaotic state of the medical faculty in 1766, noted that while Aristotle and Galen were no longer the staples of medical authority they had formerly been, there was little consensus about how to replace them. Under a reform 'plan de medicina' approved in Madrid, in 1771, the university was required, in line with Mayáns y Siscar's 1767 proposals for the universities, to establish a botanical garden, medical exhibition hall (museum), regular anatomical demonstrations, and an anatomical theatre, as well as adopt the texts of Boerhaave and commentaries of Van Swieten and Haller, supplemented with courses in chemistry and Newtonian physics based on the *Physica* of Petrus van Musschenbroek.[36] Overall, though, the reforms meant preserving the general supremacy of theology and control of philosophy and science by ecclesiastics.

The conspicuous reluctance of even the most committed representatives of enlightened, as distinct from Jansenist, ideas to express their views publicly, in and after

---

[34] Peset and Peset, *Gregorio Mayans*, 130, 153–5; Mestre Sanchis, *Ilustración española*, 42–4.
[35] Mas Galvan, 'Jansenismo', 266–7, 271–3.
[36] Mayáns y Siscar, *Idea del nuevo metodo*, 234–5; Addy, *Enlightenment*, 93–4, 97–8, 105.

1767, demonstrates how weakly rooted in society, below the court and the high aristocracy, moderate mainstream Enlightenment concepts really were. Enlightenment was everywhere strongly entrenched in Spain in certain circles but could not be broadly used for public justification and consumption. Spain, seemingly, was not ready for an open declaration of enlightened goals and offered ample scope for a strong counter-offensive against Enlightenment values, goals, and 'philosophy', and this was not long in coming. A target eminently suitable as a scapegoat and means of inflicting a stinging ecclesiastical rebuff on the Enlightenment clique presiding at court and its cultural and educational reform programmes was one of the most zealous acolytes of Aranda, the soon famous Peruvian Don Pablo de Olavide (1725–1803).

3. THE OLAVIDE AFFAIR

Olavide, wealthy and from a privileged family, left Peru for Spain, in 1751, in the aftermath of the great earthquake of 1746, accused of explaining it in purely natural terms and misappropriating funds belonging to some of the deceased. The years 1757–65 he spent abroad, mainly in Italy and France where, among others, he got to know Voltaire, spending a week at Les Délices in 1761.[37] He read voraciously and was enthusiastic about many enlightened authors. In 1766, after returning to Spain, his chief patron, Aranda, arranged for his appointment as royal *asistente* of Seville and *intendente* of Andalusia, the top administrative posts and key positions of influence in southern Spain. Casanova who met him in Madrid three years later together with Aranda and Campomanes described him and them as 'men of intellect and of a stamp very rare in Spain'; though not exactly learned 'they were above religious prejudices, and were not only fearless in throwing public scorn upon them but even laboured openly for their destruction'.[38]

Despite being furnished with a special dispensation from Benedict XIV to import and possess 'prohibited' books, he had a first brush with the Inquisition in 1768 when twenty-nine boxes of books he had purchased abroad arrived in Bilbao: they contained 2,400 volumes found to include not just numerous prohibited titles but also many works forbidden even to persons holding a special Inquisition exemption.[39] His library, including a complete set of the *Encyclopédie*, Diderot learnt later,[40] as well as the works of Bayle, Montesquieu, Voltaire, and Rousseau, he housed in the Seville Alcázar, the imposing royal quarters where he was rumoured also to have hung a portrait of Voltaire (for whom he felt a particular veneration).[41] The Seville

[37] Etienvre, 'Traducción', 106.   [38] Casanova, *Memoirs*, vi. 127.
[39] Sánchez Espinosa, 'An *ilustrado*', 184.
[40] Diderot, 'Don Pablo Olavidès', 472; Olavide, *Evangelio en triunfo*, iv. 286.
[41] González Feijóo, *Pensamiento*, 216.

Alcázar quickly became the meeting place of the Enlightenment in Andalusia. It featured a regular reading circle, to which belonged the young Jovellanos.

Olavide soon discovered that the social and cultural realities of Andalusia which he considered distinctly shocking constituted a formidable obstacle to all the reforms he wanted to introduce. What appalled him most was the peasantry's wretched condition and how completely noble status and ecclesiastical privilege dominated local society. In the province of Seville, 250 local noble lineages, he calculated, headed by the dukes of Medina Sidonia, Arcos, Osuna, Medinaceli, Alba, Sanlúcar, Béjar, and Veragua with seven counts, owned, or indirectly controlled, over 80 per cent of the land with seigneurial jurisdiction over most towns and villages. Medina Sidonia alone possessed 83,000 peasant 'vassals' in thirty villages. Also in Seville province, he assured Aranda, there were no less than 15,830 ecclesiastical personnel, including 2,588 Franciscans, 774 Dominicans, 732 Carmelites, 985 Mercedarians, 451 Augustinians, and, until he expelled them, 324 Jesuits. In the city of Seville alone, a provincial capital with 76,463 inhabitants according to the subsequent 1786 census, he found 3,500 (in fact there were around 4,500) ecclesiastical personnel, amounting to around 6 per cent of the total. With twenty-eight convents, eleven more than the larger city of Madrid, and forty-seven monasteries, Seville had seventy-five monastic houses, far outstripping Córdoba, Valencia, Granada, and Toledo, all notorious for high concentrations of clergy.[42] Seville was indeed 'the *imperium monachorum* [imperium of the monks]' more than any other Spanish city.[43]

Unlike Campomanes (who was nonetheless well aware of the chronic social problems of Andalusia) and Floridablanca, Olavide was an enlightener anxious to curtail clerical privilege and weaken the regular orders in both land ownership and the universities. With the Jesuit expulsion, he had, or so it seemed, an excellent opportunity to reorganize Seville's university on more secular lines. But his scorn for religious orders and scholasticism, and admiration for 'esta gran revolución' as he called the Scientific Revolution, encountered fierce resistance from the Dominicans who were particularly attached to the legacy of scholastic scholarship and had previously shared the teaching with the Jesuits. Here was a split replicated to a considerable extent everywhere in Spain and its empire but particularly acute in Seville.

Olavide's critique of the Spanish universities, admittedly, had been foreshadowed in Feijóo and Mayáns; but he went well beyond them and most other reformers, especially with respect to promoting science and seeking to secularize. His objective, unlike that of Mayáns, was to transform the academic curriculum root and branch and establish a wholly new order of studies, discarding Thomism and giving much greater emphasis to mathematics and the sciences following the doctrines of Wolff, Newton, Malpighi, Boerhaave, and Leibniz and in Natural Law Grotius, Pufendorf,

---

[42] Barrio Gozalo, 'Iglesia y religiosidad', 254; Aguilar Pinal, *Sevilla de Olavide*, 72–3.
[43] Aguilar Pinal, *Sevilla de Olavide*, 72.

and Barbeyrac.[44] Deeming the university a public establishment, instituted by the government to educate men to serve the state, it seemed to him there was scant room in it for the hegemony of the regular orders and their tenacious scholasticism.[45] Unlike the others, Olavide proposed to extirpate 'los dos espiritus, de partido y escolastico' [the two spirits, of faction and the scholastic] from 'our universities' and to act on this maxim. Aranda approved Olavide's plan for the thorough reorganization of Seville's university in 1769, although in the end the outcome differed little from reform plans adopted for Oviedo (1774), Zaragoza (1775), Granada (1776), and Valencia (1786).

Olavide's reform activities and general attitude offended the clergy as did his efforts to build a theatre to stage opera and plays. An ennobled man himself, he did not oppose aristocracy as such, nor was he a foe of religion. But in the Andalusia of his time, he found it impossible not to become enveloped in far-reaching schemes for attacking entrenched privilege and engineering a measure of land reform. Harshly critical of both clergy and nobility, he had become convinced Spain resembled 'a body without vigour or energy, being composed of parts which do not unite with each other but each one of which separates itself from the rest'.[46] The country's chronic plight was primarily due, he thought, to intellectual conservatism combined with institutional corporatism. Scholasticism was the evil blighting Spanish intellectual life and ruining its literature and theatre, and general ignorance the bane of the land. Although he had some supporters, he generally lacked support among both populace and elites. His efforts to reduce the city's 1,100 religious confraternities and proposals for financial reform and virtually everything else were opposed by the city council.[47]

Further inland, Olavide became the driving force behind the new rural colonies, the so-called 'Nuevas Poblaciones de Sierra Morena' established with Campomanes's support, communities free from aristocratic and ecclesiastical control, designed to develop a barren, largely deserted, mountainous stretch of Andalusia. Its principal settlement was named La Carolina, after the king. Nurtured by some hard-working Swiss, German, and Austrian Catholic colonists (among whom a few Protestants apparently slipped in) invited by Campomanes, who was generally keen to stimulate the arrival of skilled Catholic immigrants from abroad,[48] the villages throve during the four years, 1769–73, whilst Olavide spent much of his time there. Keen to curb the influence of the German Capuchin monks assigned to direct the spiritual life of these rural colonies (where hitherto there were no monasteries), Olavide lost no time in antagonizing these too, especially their leader, Fray Romualdo de Friburgo. According to information that later reached Diderot, the Capuchins were

---

[44] Ibid. 175, 188; Alvares de Morales, *Ilustración*, 46–7.
[45] Olavide, *Plan de reforma*, 156; Sánchez-Blanco, *Absolutismo*, 107.
[46] Sánchez-Blanco, *Absolutismo*, 50, 146–8, 175.
[47] Marchena Fernández, *Tiempo ilustrado*, 41–2.
[48] Campomanes, *Discurso*, i. 321–3, 344; Paquette, *Enlightenment*, 88.

particularly outraged by Olavide's influencing colonists against leaving donations to the Church in their wills. Among Olavide's admirers was a still more radically enlightened Creole, Francisco de Miranda, future first military leader of the movement for Spanish American independence, then a young captain in the Spanish army. Miranda penned a brief description of La Carolina, which he visited en route between Cadiz and Madrid in 1778 and which greatly impressed him with its orderly appearance and administration and flourishing condition. Like Casanova, he warmly praised Olavide as a benefactor of the whole region and an 'extraordinary man'.[49]

After 1772, Aranda lost influence and exerted less direct impact, though in his new role as Spanish ambassador in Paris, he remained well placed to continue stimulating intellectual interaction between Spain and France and promoting the reputations in Spain of his favourite authors, Voltaire, Raynal, and Rousseau.[50] His departure left Olavide dangerously exposed. By 1776, opposition to his reforms was so intense the Inquisition felt strong enough to confront him directly and, through him, challenge the entire Spanish Enlightenment and reform movement head on. The way appeared open for a spectacular coup of a kind that would restore the Inquisition's since the 1740s somewhat sagging prestige and sensationally check the progress of enlightened reformism. It was not hard to find charges. Olavide was arraigned before the Inquisition tribunal at Seville and also that of Córdoba, for denying miracles, attempting to restrict religious processions, calling the friars 'ignorantes', and saying the Church should be subordinate to the secular power.[51]

The Inquisition *Suprema* in Madrid began stage-managing the entire proceedings and secured the king's and Floridablanca's consent to their arresting the most senior royal official in Andalusia. Olavide was duly seized and, in November 1776, transferred along with his books and papers to Madrid for trial. Everyone with any knowledge of his activities, Campomanes included, was interrogated. No one dared speak out in Olavide's defence for fear of incriminating themselves. Asked about the discussion group in Seville, the salon where his own Enlightenment formation, including his early interest in Beccaria, was first stimulated, Jovellanos replied that he could remember nothing of what was discussed there.[52]

Olavide's imprisonment caused a sensation not only in Spain but also Paris and Geneva where a now fast declining Voltaire, unable exactly to recall the Peruvian's name, expressed outrage that 'M. Benavides, ou Olavides...un philosophe très instruit et très aimable', had been incarcerated by ghastly Inquisitors—and with royal consent!'[53] An acquaintance of Olavide's, Miguel Gijón, arrived in Paris, late in 1777, where, contacting Marmontel, he provided many additional details about the affair. Grimm published some notes about it in his journal, in January 1778.

---

[49] *Archivo del General Miranda:Viajes, Diarios (1750–1785)*, i. 124; Rodriguez de Alonso, *Siècle*, 36; Casanova, *Memoirs*, vi. 128–30.
[50] Spell, *Rousseau*, 49–51.
[51] Diderot, 'Don Pablo Olavidès', 470; Marchena Fernández, *Tiempo ilustrado*, 84.
[52] Marchena Fernández, *Tiempo ilustrado*, 91; Sánchez Espinosa, 'An *ilustrado*', 185.
[53] Marchena Fernández, *Tiempo ilustrado*, 26; Lafarga, *Voltaire en España*, 68.

By January 1780 Diderot who was especially fascinated by the case had got to know not only Gijón, but, through him or Raynal, also Eugenio de Izquierdo, an enlightened official at Spain's embassy in Paris.[54] If Olavide was a perfect target for the Inquisition, his trial was a weapon in the Radical Enlightenment's arsenal. The affair did much to stimulate the forming of a kind of running seminar on Hispanic affairs among Diderot's and Raynal's circle.

The king supported the Inquisition's well-publicized drive against the 'principal errors of the *Naturalistas* and *materialistas*' and in this instance did so, even though it infringed his authority, without sign of hesitation, apart from forbidding a major public *auto-da-fé* to impress the Madrid populace. Olavide's complete humiliation he permitted in a restricted *auto-da-fé* behind closed doors. On 24 November 1778, after two years of close confinement and interrogations, garbed in a yellow *sanbenito* and cape of shame, Don Pablo was led trembling to his ritual condemnation before a carefully selected audience of forty grandees and royal councillors, including Floridablanca and others of Carlos's principal ministers.[55] The list of all Olavide's 'errors', heresies, excesses, and offences against the Church, amounting to 140 articles, were intoned in an eight-hour ceremony in which Olavide collapsed and had to be revived with wine.[56] He was sentenced to confiscation of all his property, perpetual banishment from Madrid, Lima, and Seville, loss of noble status and all offices and titles, and eight years' strict confinement in a monastery where 'true' doctrine could be instilled into him. He was sent to a monastery of Sahagun, in León, and a year later the Capuchin monastery in Murcia, and afterwards a Dominican friary in the same city.

The trial of Olavide became a *cause célèbre* evoking incredulous scorn in Voltaire, d'Alembert, Diderot, and the 'philosophical' party that such a thing was still possible, but in Spain the impact of the *auto-de-fé* as a discouragement to Enlightenment was appreciable.[57] Thoroughly intimidated, Olavide retreated into piety and, as his later writing proves, subsequently repudiated 'philosophy'. The profound impression made by his solemn condemnation also powerfully affected others. Among the seventy-eight witnesses present, Don Felipe de Samaniego, archdeacon of Pamplona, afterwards made a full confession of his own lapses. Shortly after the *auto-da-fé*, he voluntarily confessed to having read Hobbes, Spinoza, Bayle, Voltaire, Montesquieu, d'Alembert, Diderot, and Rousseau and declared his willingness to disclose the names of those who had procured forbidden books for him and with whom he had discussed prohibited literature.[58] His list of names included those of Aranda, Campomanes, Floridablanca, and Almodóvar.

The Inquisition's coup narrowed the scope for an effective moderate reformism psychologically, intellectually, and politically, driving the intellectually aware either

---

[54] Lafarga, *Voltaire en España*, 93–4; Diderot, *Corr.* xv. 87; Trousson, *Denis Diderot*, 600–1.
[55] Diderot, 'Don Pablo Olavidès', 471–2; Marchena Fernández, *Tiempo ilustrado*, 93.
[56] *Mémoires secrets*, xii. 203, entry for 24 Dec. 1778.
[57] Diderot, 'Don Pablo Olavidès', 472.
[58] Sarrailh, *L'Espagne éclairée*, 302–3; Herr, *Eighteenth-Century Revolution*, 78.

into docile submission or privately adopting radical ideas. Olavide may have become a martyr for the cause of freedom of thought, conscience, and expression abroad, his fame spreading across Europe; but the real lesson of the story was the impossibility of tackling Spain's problems via Voltaire's or Turgot's Enlightenment in late eighteenth-century Spain. After over two years of confinement, Olavide was helped to escape. Reaching France, the fugitive was fêted as the pre-eminent Spanish enlightener of the age, among others, by Diderot, Grimm, Miranda, and John Adams. He remained in France, from 1781, for the next seventeen years, dwelling under the assumed name 'the comte de Pilo'. Diderot conferred with him early in 1781 and probably also subsequently.[59] But Olavide and Diderot by no means saw eye to eye and the heroic literary 'Olavide' created and subsumed into the Radical Enlightenment by Diderot, published by Grimm in his *Correspondance littéraire*, in February 1780, though good Enlightenment propaganda, proved a highly ironic concoction.[60]

For the real Olavide's reversion to faith proved all too real and became more pronounced in exile until, in 1797, he published, anonymously, in Madrid his four-volume *El Evangelio en triunfo, o historia de un filosofo desengañado* [The Gospel Triumphant, or the History of a Disillusioned Philosopher], one of the foremost texts by a Peruvian before the twentieth century. Here he recounts in detail his personal total disillusionment with modern philosophy, lightly veiled as an epistolary novel. In his monastic cells he had come definitively to reject the 'false philosophy' of the *materialistas*. It was neither unrelenting indoctrination nor any spiritual conversion that changed him, he later claimed, but rather cogent arguments, the arguments of 'true philosophy' as expounded by Bergier and other *anti-philosophique* writers.[61] He himself was disgusted with the 'false philosophy' and secretly, he maintained, so were all the leading *philosophes* even if they only revealed their disillusionment nearing death. Deep down the *philosophes* all longed for faith and reconciliation with the Church. Voltaire, too, in 1778 had desperately wanted to confess, receive the last rites, and die as a Christian, but the implacable *philosophes* 'who surrounded his death-bed in Paris had forced him to die' without solace, closing the door to all religious succour.[62]

This work became a pre-eminent Counter-Enlightenment text in the Spanish world, reaching its sixth edition by 1800. There had never been a age when 'philosophy' spoke more about improving things or gave so many lessons to humanity 'as in our century', acknowledged Olavide, but it talks deceitfully of eradicating superstition and correcting abuses, guided by pernicious doctrines that actually corrupt society.[63] Everyone 'knows or has heard tell of Voltaire, Rousseau, d'Alembert, Raynal, Diderot, Hume and other philosophers of our days'; but which of these really had such inspired thoughts as Fray Luis de Granada, Bossuet, Fénelon, Bourdalou, 'and many others of that sort'?[64] Were not the latter, preaching a higher

[59] Diderot to Madame de Vandeul, 28 July 1781, in Diderot, *Corr.* xv. 256–7.
[60] *Mémoires secrets*, xviii. 93, entry for 20 Oct. 1781; Diderot, *Corr.* xv. 87, 166.
[61] Olavide, *Evangelio en triunfo*, iv. 306–7.
[62] Ibid. ii. 162.   [63] Ibid. ii. 103, 148.   [64] Ibid. ii. 159–60, 162.

morality and pious submission, altogether more sublime? Religion is the power that truly corrects abuses and gives men the capacity to love and help each other, not falsely but with sincerity. One can feel compassion for those unable to grasp Christian truth but what is unpardonable and for which the *philosophes* deserve only condemnation and punishment is their trying to eradicate religion from the people's minds and deprive the poor of their consolation.[65] Even though he himself was its most celebrated victim, the post-conversion Olavide expressly supported the Inquisition's last great, sustained campaign as something urgently needed. If Inquisition trials of personages suspected of holding deistic, atheistic, or materialist views in Spain during the later eighteenth century were relatively few, these sufficed to exert a far-reaching cultural impact.

4. SPAIN AND THE RADICAL CHALLENGE

In Spain, as so often elsewhere, Locke and Newton presided throughout as chief champions of the harmonious conjunction of science and theology, of philosophy with revelation, and of rigorous methodology postulating separate spirits, miracles, and providence, hence symbolized intellectual respectability. In the revised edition of his *Lógica* (originally published in 1747) reissued in 1771, Piquer fervently praises Bacon, Locke, and Newton besides Muratori while simultaneously lambasting Voltaire and Rousseau. Using the 'famous' 1757 edition of Voltaire's works, he charged the former with subverting the most sacred principles of religion and secular society, 'deprecating the Christian religion', and abetting the progress of *el materialismo*, stressing what he called the 'defective logic prevailing generally in his works so that they should be viewed, as they merit, as almost always opposed to reason'.[66] Were Voltaire's maxims presented unadorned with clever literary flourishes, 'a cara descubierta' as Spaniards liked to say, probably no sensible person would embrace them. Only because they come dressed with wit and stimulate the imagination did they impress those with more sensibility than rationality. It is said Voltaire is a fine poet; what I affirm is that he is neither a logician nor a true philosopher.[67] In effect, in Spain the Inquisition and the religious factor relegated Voltaire to the status of de facto ally of radical thought and materialism.

Spain's young men, urged Piquer, should read Claude-Marie Guyon's *Oráculo de los nuevos philósophos* [*L'Oracle des nouveaux philósofes*] (1759), a work appearing in Spanish, translated by Fray Pedro Rodríguez Morzo, in 1769, where, in his view, Voltaire's errors and alliance with the *materialistas* were fully unmasked.[68] In recommending this book, significantly, Piquer was directing youth to a text where one also learns much about the *nuevos philósofos* looming behind Voltaire—Diderot,

---

[65] Ibid. ii. 153 and iv. 23.   [66] Piquer, *Lógica*, 142–3, 145.   [67] Ibid. 145.
[68] Ibid. 144–5; Lafarga, *Voltaire en España*, 81.

d'Holbach, Helvétius, and Raynal. Their epoch, lamented Piquer, had engendered a whole caste of insidious *semisabios* [half-wise] whose learning consists of a few short books written in a brilliant, sharply worded style. Such readers are deflected from piety and solidity due to lack of sound erudition and, once misled, think themselves justified in pronouncing on the most sacred matters![69] Seeking to 'introduce their errors throughout the Christian world', the false philosophers' approach was to offer 'bad logic' and sophisms. For by sound logic one must concede the truth of revelation, repudiating all arguments of 'los Socinianos, Atheistas, Deistas, Materialistas, Naturalistas, and other *sectarios* of this kind who multiply so much today'.

Like Feijóo and others, Piquer always viewed the Spanish Enlightenment as a battle ground where Christian moderation, based on Locke and English ideas, fights the *materialistas*, and this is indeed exactly how the crown, ministers, and the Church also viewed it. Sound logic convinces us, he insisted, that no matter how barbarous, there is no people that does not have a religion 'because the seeds of it are planted in the hearts of all men'.[70] If the Jesuit Father Acosta held the Aztecs and Maya of New Spain had no religion, he was totally mistaken as many English authors emphasize and as emerges from the *consensus gentium* argument that Piquer championed against Bayle.[71] Sound logic shows there is nothing that contradicts reason in the miracles and mysteries recounted in Holy Scripture. The rising *Naturalismo* may be 'el systema dominante de nuestros días' [the dominant system of our times] but the *nuevos philósofos*' claim there is nothing other than natural religion is utterly illogical. Naturalism is evil, more so perhaps even than atheism and materialism as the latter carry their errors openly, 'a cara descubierta', while the *Naturalistas* proceed by dissimulation, trapping the unwary with their talk of 'God' who, however, for them does not possess all his perfections but only those confirmed by reason.

Certainly, the holy mysteries of the Trinity and Incarnation, like other revealed truths, are beyond the grasp of our reason, grants Piquer, but 'we deny that they are contrary to it'. How is the perfect conformity of this with sound logic to be made clear to students? And how can we best refute Bayle's claim that reason cannot defeat the Manichaean thesis assigning the divinity responsibility for the moral and physical evils men suffer so masterfully countered by Leibniz in his *Theodicy*? No fundamental point of the Christian religion conflicts with reason properly understood. Piquer's strategy, like Feijóo's, hangs crucially on 'el celebre Locke'. Locke held that 'if Revelation proposed maxims evidently contrary to reason and destructive of it, we should be obliged not to embrace them'. But, crucially, he also taught that the doctrines faith teaches must be believed when merely above and not contrary to reason, as with the Fall of the Evil Angels, Resurrection of the Dead, and other miracles Locke proves are unconnected with reason. Locke's surpassing genius and crucial contribution to sound epistemology, concluded Piquer, was his correctly

---

[69] Piquer, *Lógica*, 225.
[70] Ibid. 238.   [71] Ibid.

placing overriding curbs on human reason, restricting it and demonstrating that nothing Christians believe in any way contradicts it.

Mainstream Enlightenment undeniably had deep intellectual roots in Spain and played an important part, even if a subsidiary one, in motivating and formulating Bourbon reformism. Nevertheless by the time of the Olavide trial, in 1778, it had not only failed but imploded, leaving a vacuum filled on the right by an extremely vigorous Counter-Enlightenment and, on the left, far more precariously, by the radical perspective. This happened because moderate Enlightenment in Spain, despite some successes in its efforts to revive commerce and economic life, proved entirely unable to tackle the main body of the country's problems. Even if one aimed well short of what was proposed by the *Histoire philosophique* and sought nothing more nor less than more freedom of thought and critical expression, some de facto religious toleration, secularized universities, and a modicum of legal reform, this was still completely unobtainable. The obstacles facing legal reformers vividly illustrate the general predicament. Among key texts appearing in Spanish were Beccaria's famous work on the principles of legal reform (1774), sponsored by Campomanes, albeit furnished with a notably cautious introduction. Beccaria was widely influential in the Spain of the 1770s among others on Jovellanos.[72] However, Beccaria's standing as part of the acceptable face of the Enlightenment in Spain was never secure and his principles were vehemently attacked by several authors, including Pedro de Castro, a professor of theology at Seville and apologist for tradition who also contested Feijóo's objections to judicial torture. He defended the practice as something legitimized by long usage. The Inquisition headed a campaign to have Beccaria prescribed that succeeded in 1777.[73] Henceforth, even legal reform explicitly following Beccaria was forced to join the underground radical opposition.

The only alternative available to leading legal reformers was to appear to condemn Helvétius and Beccaria when in fact not doing so. This was the technique of the empire's foremost legal reformer, Don Manuel Lardizábal y Uribe (1739–1820), a Mexican Creole and nephew of a bishop of Puebla who in the years 1785–7 headed a royal commission established by Campomanes and Floridablanca to plan a general revision of Spanish law. Lardizábal established the principal line of Enlightenment legal reformism in the Hispanic world, a tradition inspired chiefly by Beccaria and Filangieri, but steering a course rhetorically always moderate and cautious. In his *Discurso sobre las penas* (1782), the foremost Spanish work to appear in the wake of Beccaria, Lardizábal uses arguments taken from the former, and from Feijóo, against judicial torture, for instance, while simultaneously pretending broadly to reject Beccaria. Likewise, he deploys Filangieri but without citing him explicitly.[74] His repeatedly invoking the (in Spain, supposedly prohibited) *L'Esprit des loix* of

---

[72] Sánchez Espinosa, 'An *ilustrado*', 185.
[73] Risco, 'Présence de Beccaria', 149, 151; Astigarraga, 'Political Economy', 6; Tomas y Valiente, 'Humanitarianismo', 381–2.
[74] Tomas y Valiente, 'Humanitarianismo', 384, 386–7; González Feijóo, *Pensamiento*, 173.

Montesquieu, he justified like Almodóvar by stressing Montesquieu's veneration for Christianity, and attacks on Bayle. Montesquieu he praises for pulverizing 'la impia paradoxa de Bayle, y todas sus vanos sofismas' [impious paradox of Bayle and all his vain sophisms].[75]

Filangieri's *Scienza*, among the foremost of all Enlightenment works relating to law reform, in the early nineteenth century enjoyed considerable success in the Spanish world and, from the appearance of the first volumes in Italian, in 1781, met with the firm approval of certain high officials in Spain.[76] Rendered into Spanish by a Valencian jurist named Jaime Rubio during the years 1787–9, the first volume appeared in 1787. However, despite omitting many of the more daring passages of the original, and heavily stressing the work's piety and links to Montesquieu, as well as giving up his position as mayor of Vich to move to Madrid to try to prevent the Inquisition banning his work, his efforts failed and by decree of 7 March 1790, the Inquisition comprehensively banned Filangieri too in both Italian and Spanish.[77] Nevertheless, Lardizábal used his work extensively.

Iberian circumstances, then, created a vast gap between a timid, hesitant mainstream and radical ideas even wider and harder to bridge than elsewhere. Here Voltaire was deemed a outcast, a fellow-traveller of the *materialistas*. Equally implacably, radical thought labelled the entire religious, scholastic, and ecclesiastical culture of Spain 'tyranny' and 'oppression' presenting a contrary logic bound to appeal to some shut up within the stifling world of Spanish regalism and devotion. Mercier's utopian novel (in part echoing Raynal) *L'An 2440* (1771), a devastating assault on the *ancien régime* anonymously published with a false place of publication and no printer's name, reached Madrid in its 1776 French reissue in at least some copies, according to a Spanish royal edict of March 1778, and despite thoroughly scandalizing opinion there circulated in the hands of a few. Well it might. In Mercier's utopia, statues embodying the various European nations in postures of supplication, expiating their former crimes against humanity, would one day adorn Paris standing beside a great statue of long-suffering 'sacred humanity' near the temple of 'God'. But 'Spain, even more criminal than her sisters, would be represented remembering agonizingly, besides other unforgivable crimes, the Inquisition and covering the Indies with thirty-five million corpses': 'Spain may sigh and supplicate her fill, but never should she expect forgiveness.'[78]

For particularly condemned works, like Mercier's, crown and Church took special measures. Mercier's book, the royal decree explains, was not just a tissue of blasphemy against 'our sacred Catholic religion' but sought the overthrow of the entire system of existing civil and ecclesiastical government. Rooted in the 'new philosophy' and exceeding all the rest in impudence, it poured out 'horrendous invective against

---

[75] Lardizábal y Uribe, *Discurso*, 98–9; Almodóvar, *Década*, 91–2; Scandellari, 'Diffusion', 5, 8.
[76] Astigarraga, 'Traduttori', 239–41; Tomas y Valiente, 'Humanitarianismo', 387–8.
[77] *Suplemento al Índice*, 21; Astigarraga, 'Political Economy', 7–12; Scandellari, 'Diffusion', 3.
[78] BN Bolivia Exp. Colon. 1778, no. 20, fos. 1ᵛ–2; Mercier, *Memoirs of the Year*, 167.

sovereigns and temporal lords and their laws, ministers and magistrates', inciting readers to adopt an attitude of 'independencia y absoluta libertad' [independence and absolute liberty]. It marked the path to anarchy, showing the ways and means to bring it to effect. The Inquisitor-General's prohibition issued shortly before the royal ban likewise stresses its assault on monarchy as well as religion, stipulating that even those possessing Inquisition licences to own *libros prohibidos* [prohibited books] were not permitted to read this work.[79] The royal edict ordered searches for copies not just in Madrid 'but all the ports and frontiers', all copies found to be publicly burnt by the public hangman. The same procedure was followed in Spanish America. The royal *audiencia* of Charcas administering justice in Upper Peru, alerted by the Council of the Indies via Buenos Aires, had posters put up condemning the book even in the *plazas* of small Indian towns of the Upper Peruvian interior.[80]

Clandestine circulation of forbidden philosophical texts indeed comprised the very core of the sedition the Inquisition sought to extirpate and this is what especially requires the historian's attention. Some of this was manuscript material. Naigeon's *Le Militaire philosophe* reportedly circulated in manuscript in Spanish translation under the title 'El Filósofo militar; o dificultades sobre la religión propuestas al P. Malebranche', a version formally condemned by Inquisition edict of 20 June 1777.[81] Voltaire's *L'A,B,C, dialogue curieux*, originally published in French in 1768, circulated in Spanish in manuscript; although no copy of the late eighteenth-century translation, *Diálogos del A.B.C.*, appears to survive today, it circulated for a time especially in Salamanca. Its translator and chief propagator, witnesses subsequently testified to the Inquisition, was one of the professors, Don Ramón de Salas. During 1791, Salas apparently carried the manuscript around with him and enjoyed reading out passages to small groups of friends in intimate gatherings held at his home. He was duly arrested and tried.[82]

But clandestine printed literature was the main vehicle. Besides pronouncements of the Inquisition and the crown, there were also many additional signs that radical anti-Christian Enlightenment was spreading on both sides of the Atlantic in the Spanish world among small, widely dispersed hidden networks.[83] Individuals and groups were not merely reading but in some cases collecting and organizing what was certainly a considerable circulation of forbidden books. A consignment of 254 mostly French works seized by the Inquisition at Soria, in 1792, belonging to an ecclesiastic who happened to be a locally warmly recommended high-society tutor, included texts by d'Holbach, Helvétius, Mably, Volney, Filangieri, and Tom Paine.[84] Such evidence explains the intensity and high level of government support for the Inquisition's last great campaign: its vigorous censorship drive of the late eighteenth

[79] BL 4625 g 1/56. Edict of Inquisitor-General, Madrid, 6 Mar. 1778.
[80] BN Bolivia Exp. Colon. 1778, no. 20, fos. 3ᵛ–4; BL 4625 g 1/55 real cédula, 17 Mar. 1778.
[81] *Índice último*, 104.   [82] Lafarga, *Voltaire*, 185–6.
[83] Barrio Gozalo, 'Iglesia y religiosidad', 270.   [84] Rodríguez López-Brea, *Don Luis de Borbón*, 32.

century. Crown and universities helped establish a clear basis for suppressing those large segments of the Enlightenment judged irreligious and materialist, starting in October 1759 with the *Encyclopédie,* works condemned by both state and Church and fiercely suppressed for decades.[85] Book suppression in late eighteenth-century Spain was a truly massive exercise. Madrid booksellers had to submit annual inventories of their stock, listing authors, places of publication, and titles, declaring under oath and signature they stocked no *libros prohibidos* either on or off their advertised premises.[86] Book burnings were familiar occurrences. Rousseau received a letter, in April 1765, from a Lausanne bookseller recently travelling in Spain who personally witnessed the public burning of *Émile,* outside the main Dominican priory, in Madrid.[87] However, the drawback of such methods was that not everyone is persuaded or intimidated by them.

The highest aristocratic personages and government officials, moreover, remained exempt from the Inquisition's attentions. Aranda, Almodóvar, Roda, Muzquiz, and Don Nicolas de Azara, Spanish envoy in Rome, among the most audacious of all the Spanish *éclairés,* though all suspected by some, were left alone. At a certain level of Spanish society it was simply impossible to curb circulation of radical texts and ideas even though in some cases such men were encouraging a wider interest in forbidden books.[88] The Inquisition was obliged to concentrate its attention, as with Olavide, on levels prestigious but slightly lower down. Two celebrated trials were those of Tomas and Bernardo Iriarte, two brothers who were nephews of the royal librarian. Tomas de Iriarte (1750–91), author of several successful comedies, had translated two of Voltaire's plays and was suspected of sharing his views. Bernardo Iriarte (1735–1814), a member of the Royal Academy in Madrid, later to be a high official in the regime of Joseph Bonaparte during the French occupation of Spain, was also steeped in French philosophical literature, indeed a Francophile ideologue who ended his life in exile at Bordeaux. Another such trial was that of a secretary at the ministry of war, in Madrid, Bernardo Maria de Calzada, in 1790–1. Having developed a taste for philosophical literature, Calzada had translated some Condillac, Diderot's play *Le Fils naturel,* and Voltaire's *Alzire* into Spanish. Chiefly at issue was less his possession of prohibited books and discussing them, than evidence of his impiety and private hostility to the Church. Pronounced guilty, disgraced, and briefly imprisoned, he was permanently banished from Madrid, ending his career.[89]

Besides diplomats serving abroad and reporting and sending books and papers home, key Spanish networks propagating awareness of Radical Enlightenment clandestine literature existed also among university academics, and in reading circles connecting middle-ranking to senior army officers. Spanish Radical Enlightenment culture by the 1770s and 1780s was undoubtedly a more solid and extensive cultural

---

[85] *Índice último,* 76, 88; Defourneaux, *L'Inquisition espagnole,* 123, 152.
[86] BL 4625 g 1/49. Inquisition edict, Madrid, 2 June 1756.   [87] Spell, *Rousseau,* 39.
[88] Ibid. 142, 163.   [89] Ibid. 68–9; Defourneaux, *L'Inquisition espagnole,* 164.

phenomenon than historians once supposed, spreading principally via oral contacts, private letters, and furtively exchanged texts passing from hand to hand. During garrison duty at Melilla, in 1775, the Venezuelan Miranda shared with a fellow Creole officer, a Peruvian named Manuel Villalta, who had already earlier travelled in several parts of Europe, a large consignment of illicit books and manuscripts. Both Miranda and Villalta were subsequently reported to the Inquisition and, in the same month, November 1778, that Olavide was condemned in Madrid, Villalta was arrested in Seville for possessing forbidden books (and obscene pictures).

Reports of conversations involving both men held at Melilla and Cadiz specified impious discussions occurring in Miranda's own rooms. By 1779, Miranda, now in Madrid, is known to have possessed some 230 books, many in several volumes, including numerous works of the Radical Enlightenment prominent among them the *Histoire philosophique*, the *Système de la nature*, Helvétius's *De l'esprit*, works of Bolingbroke, Diderot's *Lettre sur les aveugles*, Beccaria, and *L'An 2440* of Mercier with its denunciation of despotism and electrifying prophecy of a future massive black slave revolt in the Indies leading to the liberation of all the slaves.[90] Miranda may perhaps not yet have been the hardened radical, republican, and opponent of the crown and Church he had become by 1783–4. But he had incontestably traversed part of that route intellectually by the mid 1770s and, more importantly, the evidence plainly suggests, it was radical literature that brought him to his militantly libertarian outlook.

Both royal censorship strategy and the intellectual grounds for it were plain enough in principle. The main snag, as with the contested status of Beccaria in Spain, was to draw a viable line between moderate and radical thought. For the precise dividing line proved elusive. One problem was that the wide-ranging ban imposed by Church and state on most of the Enlightenment turned out to be too sweeping to be practical. Not only were the *Encyclopédie*, Bayle's *Dictionnaire* (since 1747), Fontenelle's *Histoire des Ajaoiens*, and the works of d'Argens, Diderot, and Mably *prohibidos in totum* by the Spanish Inquisition Index, but so was Montesquieu's *L'Esprit des loix* banned in 1756 together with Adam Smith's *Wealth of Nations*, Beccaria, Voltaire's *Lettres philosophiques*, and Rousseau's *Discours sur les origines de l'inégalité*.[91] By a general Inquisition edict issued at Madrid on 18 August 1762, Voltaire was placed in the so-called 'primera clase' [first class], or *prima classis auctorum damnatae memoriae*, his entire œuvre now being comprehensively prohibited as inculcating 'el Deismo y Naturalismo'.[92] The ban encompassed everything already published and everything published by Voltaire in the future.

By Inquisition decree of 1771, several explicitly materialist works were condemned together—d'Holbach's *Système de la nature*, Robinet's *De la nature*, and Delisle de

[90] Rodríguez de Alonso, *Siècle*, 40–2.
[91] *Índice último*, 59, 105; Defourneaux, *L'Inquisition espagnole*, 106, 122.
[92] Defourneaux, *L'Inquisition espagnole*, 125; Carbonero y Sol, *Índice*, 452, 669; Lafarga, *Voltaire en España*, 51.

Sales, *Philosophie de la nature*, together with works of La Mettrie.[93] After this, Radical Enlightenment permanently replaced heresy and deism in the Inquisition's published decrees as the Spanish Church's principal target, though besides pure 'philosophy', numerous works of literature were included in the prohibited category on grounds of immorality. 'Lascivious' literary works were also often banned on the double grounds that they were lascivious and philosophically corrupting. Among several by Restif de La Bretonne forbidden in late eighteenth-century Spain was his exploration of Paris night life entitled *Les Nuits de Paris*, condemned by the Inquisition for combining eroticism with tacit propagation of the 'impious system of Spinoza'.[94]

The shock of the *philosophes'* assault on received religious, moral, and social beliefs created a degree of alarmism and Counter-Enlightenment militancy which henceforth itself served as the prime engine for propagating awareness of radical thought in the Iberian world. Mostly brief, indirect, and infrequent until around 1770, thereafter polemical attacks on the clandestine Enlightenment were frequent and direct. The Cistercian Father Antonio José Rodríguez, author of *El Philoteo* (Madrid, 1776), expressly states that the subversive new philosophy threatening to undermine society entering from abroad acquired new momentum in Spain during the early 1770s.[95] The pamphlet *España triunfante en el actual siglo filosófico* [Spain Triumphant in the Present Philosophic Century], published at Madrid in 1786, a popularly written, forty-seven-page satire, lampoons the underground 'philosophic religion' as something becoming widespread, even seeking to usurp the place of the Catholic religion in Spain, depicting this sedition as seeping in from all sides and forging not just new dogmas and a new morality but also its own rites. The new philosophy was a creed that 'in imitation of the Christian religion would soon also have its own Apostles, martyrs and confessors'.[96] This insolent sect was in urgent need, though, of summoning its first 'General Council of the Church' to resolve disputed points of dogma and 'arrange everything necessary to form and compose a new Bible, new body of church law, and new catechism' so that it should no longer reveal so blatantly that its chief Apostles continually contradict each other.

Compared to 'England, Prussia, Holland, and Geneva' Spain remained resistant and loyal Spaniards were more outraged and appalled than other nations by the freethinking libertinism undermining all that is best and most sacred. But while most of Spanish society comprised a firm bulwark against the all-ravaging army of 'philosophy' eroding European faith, morality, and society, 'la filosofía', supreme enemy of all honest and good men, had, nevertheless, made worrying inroads in Spain too. Consequently, the loyal and pious now needed to be better warned and armed against it. This pamphlet paints a lurid picture of a fight to the finish. A sceptic doubting that Radical Enlightenment succeeded in entrenching itself in Spain might object that this vision, however lurid, might be fantasy, sheer alarmism,

[93] Lafarga, *Voltaire en España*, 130.   [94] Defourneaux, *L'Inquisition espagnole*, 110.
[95] Herrero, *Orígenes*, 105–7; Sánchez-Blanco, *Absolutismo*, 225.
[96] [D.J.C.], *España triunfante*, 38–9.

not an account of reality. But even if it was, it proved a self-fulfilling prophecy, for there was so much of this literature by the 1780s that by itself it rendered radical thought an actual, urgent cultural reality in Spain. The *philosophes'* assault on religion, tradition, and morality, exclaims Josef de Palacio y Viana, writing in 1788, was the most formidable challenge Christianity had ever faced in its history despite the Roman emperors' ferocious persecution of the early Church before Constantine. Abolishing Christianity is the 'grand concept of the philosophical cabal' fired by 'libertinage and incredulity', the 'goal towards which these impious men who call themselves *filósofos*, evil-doers also assailing kings and monarchy, direct all their efforts'.[97]

True 'philosophy' seeks the stability of societies reinforcing morality and sovereign authority, false 'philosophy' pursues the opposite course: hence, 'true' philosophy is Christianity. Where Catholicism is unquestionably the faith 'most favourable to princes', the *filósofos* are 'the most envenomed enemies of sovereigns whom they depict in the blackest colours'. These evil men incite revolt, seeking to substitute 'philosophy' for Christianity.[98] No one, held Palacio—whose analysis relies extensively on Nonnotte, an author well known in Spain—could prevent the philosophical contagion that 'inundated Europe with impious and repugnant writings' from entering Spain. The situation was especially alarming because 'all those who have just come out of the colleges and universities' want to be authorities and think for themselves about religion. 'Even women whom God made for the delight of society, for delicacy and softness of sentiment, for modesty, reserve, and docility' were being corrupted by this perfidious new call for freedom of thought and the right to think for oneself. Palacio, significantly, was not writing for scholars: rather, he intended his book to be 'very useful' to all readers and especially 'ecclesiastics'.

For this reason it is significant that most of his tirade against 'philosophy' is not directed primarily against Voltaire and Rousseau but far more frequently against 'Fréret', 'Du Marsais', and 'Bolingbroke' whom he considers the evil geniuses lurking behind such clandestine texts as the *Essai sur les préjugés* (1770) 'par Mr. D.M.' (actually by d'Holbach) and the *Examen critique des apologistes de la religion chrétienne* (1766), then attributed to Fréret.[99] For claiming there were originally many more Gospel accounts than those sanctioned by the Church, and charging the early Church Fathers with selectively suppressing and manipulating the evidence, Palacio labels Du Marsais and Fréret the most odious of liars and impostors. Equally, the Spanish translators of Guyon, Nonnotte, Bergier, and Chaudon, while demonstrating how antithetical radical ideas were to prevailing structures of thought, authority, and belief, were simultaneously providing Spanish readers with detailed information about the clandestine Enlightenment's general critique of received belief.[100] From this we can see how erroneous it is to focus mainly on Voltaire and Rousseau when

---

[97] Palacio y Viana, *Defensa*, 4–5, 21.   [98] Ibid. 53–45, 58, 67–8.
[99] Ibid. 320–36.   [100] Sánchez-Blanco, *Absolutismo*, 228, 342.

considering the penetration of French thought into Enlightenment Spain as is usually done.

Indeed, Voltaire presented a particular difficulty, not just because he scarcely fitted the atheistic-materialist radical mould into which Spanish ecclesiastics squeezed him but also because he tirelessly recommends Locke and Newton. The problem was unsolvable given Voltaire's hostility towards Christianity, something that provoked overwhelming hostility towards him in Spain. But the result was continually to distort and misrepresent him so as to align his œuvre, quite wrongly, with the *materialistas*, something that also meant turning him into an ostensible but actually false and deceitful ally of Locke and Newton, misrepresentation that then generated further difficulties. Thus, another disciple of Nonnotte, the Jeronimite friar Fernando de Cevallos (or Zeballos) (1732–1802), in a work entitled *Juicio final de Voltaire* [Final Judgment about Voltaire], a bulky text originally drafted shortly after Voltaire's death, in 1778, but forbidden by the authorities, and not published until the start of the following century, firmly locates Voltaire in a line he himself would have definitely disavowed.

Inspired to write the book by the looming 'menace' of a cabal of false philosophers and fanatics, Cevallos accuses the latter of dishonestly seeking to build on Voltaire's prestige. This ubiquitous sect conspiring in Spain 'to canonize him and celebrate the apotheosis of this man', Cevallos attacks by tying Voltaire to the materialists exploiting his impact rather than seeking to explain his views as such.[101] Voltaire, urges Cevallos, master-minded a vast conspiracy of intellectual subversion, along with Beccaria and many other 'falsos filósofos' undermining society, religion, and morality in Spain, a plot deliberately seeking to replace Christianity and 'la profunda filosofía de Neuton [Newton]' with the venom of 'materialismo y fatalismo'.[102] Voltaire may have received fanfares of praise, inflating his reputation, but this could not hide the deeply pernicious character of his work. Thus, Mirabeau, Cevallos identifies, rather perversely, as an 'Apostle of Voltaire' and at the same time as 'la cabeza de los materialistas' [head of the materialists].[103]

After 1789, Cevallos, at Seville, was among the many in Spain convinced the 'horrible tempest' descending on the French royal family 'and the whole of that unhappy monarchy' was the work of the *philosophes*.[104] The element of distortion in his intensely political as well as philosophical Counter-Enlightenment ideology lies in the insistent linkage of the Revolution with Voltaire and even, lurking behind him, Protestantism. Here was a true package logic: it was characteristic of Spanish Counter-Enlightenment to view deism, atheism, Socinianism, materialism, and libertinism as all equally offspring of Enlightenment *falsa filosofía* and yet all ultimately stemming from Protestant inspiration.[105] This new ideology forged by writers like Cevallos and Palacio conjured up the spectre of a secretive, conspiratorial, but

[101] [Cevallos], *Juicio final*, i, 'prefacio', 5–7.
[102] Ibid. i. 363–4; Tomas y Valiente, 'Humanitarianismo', 379; Sánchez-Blanco, *Absolutismo*, 230–4.
[103] [Cevallos], *Juicio final*, ii. 58, 71, 104.   [104] Ibid. ii. 32.   [105] Herrero, *Los orígenes*, 94–5.

comprehensive antithesis to established thought. The radical *philosophes* were attempting to replace Christian metaphysics with *Naturalismo*, to 'put the *Tractatus Theoligico-Politicus* of Espinosa in place of the *Suma theologica* of Saint Thomas [Aquinas]', the *De Cive* and *Leviathan* of Hobbes in that of long-sanctioned political ideas, and the precepts of Helvétius's *De l'esprit*, the *Encyclopédie*, 'and the diction-naires' in place of true Christian morality.[106]

In this criminal plot to usurp and besmirch the glorious stature of 'los verdaderos filósofos' [the true philosophers], Locke, Newton, and Leibniz, substituting for their thought the poison of *filosofismo*, Voltaire allegedly took the lead. Hypocrisy, calumny, and twisting the facts were allegedly second nature to 'Voltaire' as were the 'cruel derision and strokes of mockery this Centaur heaped on the face of the weightiest philosopher there has been in this age', namely Newton. Envious of Newton, Voltaire 'resolved to rob him of his glory by turning himself into a Newtonian'. The young Voltaire had been a piratical adventurer.[107] His conspiracy to subvert the legacy of the 'true philosophers', contends Cevallos, is nowhere more manifest than when he pretends to defend them, 'for he mixes them together with a troop of abominable *confrères* whom he insidiously tries to shield from public condemnation'. It was perfidiously to promote the 'false philosophers' that 'Voltaire' included them in discussions about unobjectionable ones, such as Locke and Newton 'who have not been accused by anybody'. Voltaire's indiscriminately citing irreligious writers who should never be mentioned at all in the same breath as a Montaigne or Descartes was outrageous. Readers are urged to 'note the malignity in the following passage' where Voltaire, asking who are the writers most denounced by intolerant detractors for fomenting dissension in society, answers: 'Pomponazzi, Montaigne, La Mothe le Vayer, Descartes, Gassendi, Bayle, Spinoza, Hobbes, Lord Shaftesbury, Count Boulainvilliers, Maillet, Toland, Collins, Fludd, Woolston, Beguar [Bekker], the disguised author of Jacques Massé [Simon Tyssot de Patot], that of the *Espion turc*, that of the *Persian Letters* [Montesquieu] and of the *Pensées philosophiques* [Diderot].'[108] What could be more insidious and dishonest than fusing the innocent and malign like this?

Counter-Enlightenment rapidly gained ground in the Spanish world fusing with a partly Jansenist reaction against 'philosophy' and 'reason', not least among the Creole clergy in Mexico.[109] It succeeded in transforming the very meaning of the term 'philosophy' into something highly pejorative, equivalent to denoting opposition to religion, something widely reflected, remarks Olavide, in common parlance by the 1790s.[110] What this Counter-Enlightenment rhetoric envisaged was always war between 'philosophy' and religion, never science and religion as the nineteenth century came to think of it. All men must be constantly on their guard against the chief apostles of this world-threatening new *filosofía* opposing religion, authority,

---

[106] [Cevallos], *Juicio final*, i. 207–8.   [107] Ibid. i. 363.   [108] Ibid. i. 368–9.
[109] Sánchez-Blanco, *Absolutismo*, 224–36; Schmidt, 'Contra "la filosofía falsa"', 245–7.
[110] [Olavide], *Evangelio en triunfo*, ii. 151.

morality, and sovereigns. But who exactly were they? 'Philosophy', we learn, had four chief 'Evangelists' and the first of these prime spokesmen of *filosofía moderna*, proclaims *España triunfante*, was of course 'Espinosa' [Spinoza] who also always appears to be the most cogent and consistent of the four in his views though actually he contradicts himself continuously. Next comes the 'famous Bayle' who, despite belonging to the same philosophical party as Spinoza, attacks him saying 'his work is full of contradictions'.[111] The third 'Evangelist' of *materialismo* is 'Volter' [Voltaire] who, in turn, derides Bayle, denouncing him as an ignoramus, while the fourth is Rusó [Rousseau] who, in turn, assails Voltaire with epithets as generous as those Voltaire heaps on Bayle.[112] This whole *religión filosófica* [philosophic religion], of which Helvétius's *De l'esprit* is cited as a particularly noxious instance, is a perfect 'chaos of opinions'. This text too names several clandestine former manuscripts recently printed illicitly, in France, under their Spanish titles, including the *Análisis de la religión*.[113]

Vicente Fernández de Valcarce's *Desengaños filosóficos*, the first three volumes of which appeared between 1787 and 1790, was a further notable contribution to this literature. Dean of the cathedral of Palencia, a zealous scholastic, and defender of demonology, Fernández Valcarce not only summons readers to take up arms against 'Espinosa, Rousseau, Voltaire' and other self-appointed *filósofos* who despise 'true wisdom' which can only be based on faith and obedience to the Church but also denounces mainstream enlightened thought, charging Locke and Newton with 'incredible ignorance'.[114] But the foremost representative of the stark ideology of Spanish Counter-Enlightenment was a pugnacious Valencian, Juan Pablo Forner (1756–97), a prominent legal official. A pupil of both Piquer and Mayáns, Forner, whose character and literary efforts were scorned by Jovellanos, was a particularly skilful and knowledgeable Counter-Enlightenment polemicist.[115] His credentials as an out-and-out reactionary have recently been challenged and some have reclassified him as a thoroughgoing sceptic and Baconian who, in purely legal matters, was something of a reformer.[116] But this hardly alters the case. It is true that Forner venerated Bacon and Locke; but in late eighteenth-century Spain, fervour for Locke mostly indicates a fiercely conservative stance. Forner recommends the most rigorous empiricism but chiefly as a way to counteract Raynal's far-reaching critique of Spanish society. Raynal and Robertson might claim Spain's decline was due to religious intolerance, expelling Jews and Moriscos, hostility to new knowledge, and over-regulating imperial trade, but a truly rigorous empiricism proves them wrong on every count. Locke and his follower Condillac deserve praise for imposing strict and much needed limits on human reason.

---

[111] *España triunfante*, 40.   [112] Ibid.

[113] Ibid. 39–40; Herr, *Eighteenth-Century Revolution*, 218.

[114] Herr, *Eighteenth-Century Revolution*, 113–14; Spell, *Rousseau*, 95.

[115] Araujo Costa, 'Influencias de Huet', 307; Sánchez-Blanco, *Absolutismo*, 357–60.

[116] Cañizares-Esguerra, *Nature, Empire*, 106–9; Scandellari, 'Difusión', 3.

Even so, Forner's praise of Bacon, Locke, and Condillac is qualified. For they had not gone far enough with their sceptical empiricism, in his view, and, in any case, were unoriginal, Locke's epistemology being, supposedly, just an imitation of Aristotle's.[117] A law professor who in the 1790s rose to become *fiscal* of the royal *audiencia* of Seville, Forner represents an essentially new phenomenon—an enemy well acquainted with the Spanish (and general) Enlightenment from inside. In repudiating Enlightenment ideas and aspirations, Forner, more perhaps than any other contemporary writer, consciously tailored an ideology fitting the chauvinistic, strongly repressive wave in Spanish culture reacting against the Enlightenment. In his *Discursos filosóficos* (1787), he is partly echoing Jacobi's intervention against Spinozism published in Germany two years before. Philosophy cannot provide men with a secure route to truth or understanding of the essence of things. An admirer of the fideism and anti-Cartesianism of Bishop Huet, Forner locates in the Cartesian revolution the beginnings of 'modern philosophy's challenge to received ideas which he considers a disaster for mankind. Essentially a form of Christian neo-scepticism, his Counter-Enlightenment was infused with Huet's fideism, an aggressive anti-intellectualism, chauvinism, loyalism, willingness to espouse strict censorship, and explicit anti-Spinozism. All this he combined with a call to orient university reform towards purely vocational and practical subjects.[118]

Those *philosophes* declaring all religions, Christianity included, political inventions, seeing no more difference between Christ and Muhammad than between Confucius and Moses, Forner labels the 'Don-Quixotes de filosofía'.[119] These corrupters deeming themselves philosophers could best be discredited, held Forner, by turning philosophy itself against them. How absurd to call 'our century philosophical' when all the 'modern philosophers' really did was build on foundations laid by 'Espinosa' and rely excessively, like him, on reason, reaching the perfidious notion that there is no God, providence, or divine government of the universe. Never would they have stooped to such blasphemies had they not misguidedly idolized 'reason'.[120] The modern philosophers' errors are nothing new but merely repeat those of the Stoics, Epicureans, and others the Christian fathers long ago refuted. The atheistic determinism of Collins and the other *fatalistas modernos*, chaining the will and reducing man to a servile necessity, merely regurgitates the *fatalismo* of the Greek Stoics.[121] Leibniz tries to overturn Bayle's dangerous sophisms, using philosophy, but ultimately he and Wolff had merely embraced a 'fatalismo' scarcely better than Spinoza's.

Forner later resumed his polemic against the Enlightenment in his *Preservativo contra el atheismo* (Seville, 1795). Here even more hostile, sarcastic, and sweeping

[117] Sánchez-Blanco, *Absolutismo*, 354–64; Cañizares-Esguerra, *Nature, Empire*, 108–9.
[118] Araujo Costa, 'Influencias de Huet', 3–4; Alvares de Morelos, *Ilustración*, 154, 268.
[119] Forner, *Discursos filosóficos*, 2; Tomas y Valiente, 'Humanitarianismo', 389.
[120] Forner, *Discursos filosóficos*, 14–15; Matthey, 'L'Ombre', 424.
[121] Forner, *Discursos filosóficos*, 21–2.

than before, 'my aim', he declares, 'is not to cure the mad, deaf and blind but rather to preserve the healthy from the risk of becoming contaminated by the recent insanity of sophistry at work in much of Europe'.[122] 'Philosophy' was to blame for the French Revolution. Only through Catholic faith and values can society be well ordered, morally based, and stable. Forner here reveals himself to be even more comprehensively Counter-Enlightenment than Cevallos though he too differentiates two broadly incompatible Enlightenment categories that ought not to be confused. On the one hand were those who had not been wilfully blind or perverse, thinkers misled but ultimately well intentioned. These 'good' thinkers honestly tried to limit reason and champion 'mysteries' above reason together with spirits and miracles. These were 'Grotius, Pufendorf, Cumberland, Leibniz, Wolff, Locke, Clarke, Wollaston, and Crousaz' and others declaring 'moderation'.[123] Far more despicable and noxious was the age's materialist *filosofismo*. Than this nothing is blinder or more contrary to truth. Bayle is assailed for his sophistry to promote the idea of a viable and moral society of 'atheists'.[124]

Antifilósofos spoke of Spain's penetration by radical texts while simultaneously facilitating readers' entry into the world of clandestine thought and so did certain texts of a pro-Enlightenment character such as the *Memorias literarias de Paris*, by Don Ignacio de Luzán, secretary of the Spanish embassy in Paris, and the *Década epistolar de Paris* (1781) by the duke of Almodóvar. The latter, published under his pseudonym 'Francisco Maria de Silva', accords Rousseau a strikingly favourable write-up, rating him well above d'Alembert, while emphasizing the subversive character of Raynal's *Histoire*, a text Almodóvar himself translated.[125] Purporting to be doing nothing more than reporting developments in Paris, and to be shocked by such irreligion, Luzán and Almodóvar propagated awareness of radical literature while complaining of Spain's intellectual backwardness and yet, assuring readers that Spain nurtured more enlightenment and understanding 'than ordinarily is thought and than appears'.[126]

Almodóvar's text is noteworthy for the informative accounts it provides of various previously little-known French radical writers. It explains that Saint-Glain took refuge in Holland as a *Calvinista* 'but degenerated into an atheist by reading the famous Spinoza'. It was Saint-Glain who rendered into French the *Tractatus Theologico-Politicus*, 'the manual from which the philosophers of this century have drawn the arguments' with which they have declaimed against Moses and the Old Testament.[127] Fréret Almodóvar declares a man of great learning and insight despite the 'deplorable' fact he wrote such corrupting works as the *Lettre de Thrasibule à Leucippe* and the *Examen des apologistes de la religion chrétienne*, 'the very quintessence of the systems of Hobbes and Spinoza'.[128] Diderot he styles as the chief moving

---

[122] Forner, *Preservativo*, 27.   [123] Ibid.   [124] Ibid. 24, 131–7.
[125] Almodóvar, *Década*, 108–15.
[126] Ibid., 'al lector' and pp. 60–1; Defourneaux, *L'Inquisition espagnole*, 144; Spell, *Rousseau*, 63.
[127] Almodóvar, *Década*, 82.   [128] Ibid. 84.

force behind the *Encyclopédie*, a compendium about which opinion remained divided but one must acknowledge as 'an obra grande' [a great work]. Admittedly, Almodóvar recommends the 'corrected' edition of Lucca, this version eschewing impiety and containing excellent notes by orthodox Catholics.[129] Diderot and Robinet Almodóvar labels 'extravagantes' on account of their materialism but also styles erudite, influential men of importance in scientific matters.[130]

A further sign that behind the shutters social criticism, political opposition to the crown, and radical ideas were merging in the Spain of the 1780s was the rise of a new style of barely deferential journalism, embodied in such journals as *El censor* (1781–7) and *El correo (de los ciegos) de Madrid* (1786–91) that specialized in making caustically ironic and sarcastic remarks about the nobility, clergy, and royal administration.[131] Around the role of *El censor* in particular a considerable controversy developed. Published by two obscure officials, this journal aroused the ire of both government ministers and the clergy by claiming that nowhere else in Europe had a certain kind of theology and a certain sort of morality contributed so much to 'our ignorance and poverty'.[132] It could not be explicit and relied very heavily on innuendo. But the aware knew what this meant. It was hard to miss the sarcasm behind the suggestion that Spaniards took good care to stifle at birth sciences concerned with worldly happiness knowing better than others the specious vainglory of worldly things; or the complaint in the observation that the *apologistas* tirelessly vaunting Spain's glory were actually reinforcing the obstacles to the country's advancement.[133] The journal caused particular annoyance by suggesting that 'the seeds of ignorance' so plaguing contemporary Spain were planted in the age of Ferdinand and Isabella, implying without saying so that the expulsion of the Jews and Muslims and setting up of the Inquisition were the cause of Spain's backwardness.[134]

Olavide, Miranda, and other *materialistas* in the Spanish world of course urged an attitude to Church and state that no adherent of mainstream Enlightenment in or outside Spain could endorse. The full radical programme was totally out of the question. The Spanish crown, held the *Histoire philosophique*, should abolish the Inquisition, end the Church's overweening authority, and drastically reduce the number of clergy and their property.[135] Toleration should be introduced, the standing army cut by two-thirds, Spanish America opened to immigration of all kinds including Protestants, Muslims, and Jews. In the Indies, the slaves should be freed, the Indians relieved of onerous oppressive burdens, and American-born Creoles entrusted with high posts hitherto reserved for peninsulars. The remaining mercantilist restrictions on Spanish and Spanish American commerce should be removed.[136]

[129] Ibid. 95–9.   [130] Ibid. 97–8, 106–7; Defourneaux, *L'Inquisition espagnole*, 144–5.
[131] Sánchez-Blanco, *Absolutismo*, 328–40.   [132] Redondo, *En boca cerrada*, 22, 34–5, 51–2.
[133] Ibid. 39, 42, 56–7.   [134] Ibid. 35–8; Sánchez-Blanco, *Absolutismo*, 373.
[135] *Histoire philosophique* (1780), iv. 425–6.
[136] Ibid. iv. 297, 405–6, 408–9, 414–15, 426; *Histoire philosophique* (1770), iii. 297, 301.

Needless to say, there was no prospect any of these measures could be adopted in the Hispanic world at the time for the simple reason that it was impossible to do so without breaking the historic alliances between crown and Church, and crown and nobility, or without abandoning the unrelentingly Catholic, aristocratic, and military character of the empire. The price paid was a profound rift in Spain's intellectual culture.

Part III

Europe and the Remaking of the World

15

The *Histoire philosophique*, or Colonialism Overturned

1. THE BOOK THAT MADE A WORLD 'REVOLUTION'

If ever there were a book that met with general approval, the 'concours unanime' of the entire literary world, averred Linguet, in 1788, it was the *Histoire philosophique des deux Indes* by 'Raynal'.[1] There could be no doubt as to the work's massively best-selling status. Yet Linguet's remark nevertheless rang oddly as most contemporary observers viewed it far less positively, agreeing rather with Madame de Genlis that 'this monstrous work' ranked beside *Le Militaire philosophe* (Naigeon and d'Hol-bach) and Helvétius's *De l'esprit* and *De l'homme*, as among the most subversive of all works of *la philosophie moderne* and most harmful to government, religion, and morality.[2] Top best-seller among the writings of the Enlightenment, it was also one of the most radical and widely condemned.

The book's commanding but paradoxical impact, moreover, was by no means confined to France. Among major Enlightenment publications none provided a more challenging general outlook or had a greater effect on both sides of the Atlantic and the rest of the world.[3] The first prominent Russian radical writer, Alexander Radishchev (1749–1802), apologizing for incensing the Empress Catherine with his vehement critique of Russian society in 1790, offered as his excuse that he had been deluded by 'Raynal'.[4] Explaining how the *Histoire philosophique* became a destabilizing force everywhere is indeed indispensable for any general Enlightenment history and provides the focus of this present chapter. If in the 1750s and 1760s, the *Encyclopédie* effected the first great injection of radical thought into mainstream European intellectual and cultural life, and d'Holbach's mature works, commencing with the *Système de la nature* (1770), formed a second engine propelling the Democratic Enlightenment's advance, the culminating impulse from 1770 in terms of impact and general ramifications was the spectacular diffusion of the *Histoire* and its brood of daughter texts.

---

[1] Linguet, *Annales*, xv (1788), 399. [2] Genlis, *Religion*, i. 31, 107.
[3] Mondot, 'Réception', 204.
[4] McConnell, *Russian* Philosophe, 69–70, 87, 106, 113, 198; Bancarel and Goggi, *Raynal*, 495.

Together, the *Histoire*'s three primary editions, and the various polemical summaries and commentaries derived from them, comprise the Radical Enlightenment's—indeed the whole Enlightenment's—most devastating single blow to the existing order. The *Histoire* ramified not only through its own re-editions and literary offspring but spawned a whole new literary genre and style of journalism, summoning public opinion to stand and oppose every affront to 'les droits de l'humanité' everywhere.[5] Diderot's rhetoric of universal basic human rights universally violated, so starkly distinct from Rousseau's doctrine, became deeply embedded not only in French philosophical discourse in the 1770s and 1780s but also in Germany, through the writings of Dohm, Diez, and Wekhrlin and, still more resoundingly, in the radical republican strain in Italy with the many echoes of 'l'immortale Raynal' in Gorani, Filangieri, and Pagano. We have seen that together with Helvétius and the *Encyclopédie*, the *Histoire* comprised one of Filangieri's three chief intellectual sources.[6]

Oppression the *Histoire* envisaged not just as straightforward tyranny imposed by princes or other despots allied to priests, but rather as a multi-layered social, cultural, sexual, and psychological construct involving complicity and manipulation at every level. Tyranny is ultimately the work of peoples, not kings.[7] But how does that come about? Like the *Encyclopédie*, the *Histoire philosophique* was the fruit of arduous research, team-work, and complex editing, a compilation expressing the collective vision of the inner core of *encyclopédistes*, especially Diderot who devoted much time and effort to the project from 1766 onwards.[8] Like d'Holbach's culminating works, this compendium is remarkable, indeed path-breaking, for collating and integrating the Radical Enlightenment's critique of the existing order into a single, highly integrated, but comprehensive set of libertarian principles, recapitulating and consolidating as a tightly knit revolutionary core the entire tradition of radical thought, reconfiguring its complex legacy into a remarkably effective ideological *machine de guerre*.

It was from the *Encyclopédie* that the *Histoire* drew its underlying premises. 'This depot of all the errors and insights' of human kind, the *Histoire* proclaims a triumph that would have been less imperfect had it not been brought to fruition amidst repression and persecution. The *Encyclopédie* had its faults but nevertheless constitutes a supreme monument to human effort, organization, and knowledge that will remain for centuries the very emblem of one of human history's greatest turning points—the age of *la philosophie*.[9] By no means, though, does the *Histoire* merely restate positions set out earlier. Rather, shifting the emphasis in key areas, it represents a distinctively new phase in the Radical Enlightenment's evolution, in

[5] Mondot, 'Reception', 189–95; Pocock, *Barbarism*, iv. 229–37.
[6] Filangieri, *Scienza della legislazione*, i, pp. xix, 15 n., 28 n., 78–9, and ii, pp. v, vii; Goggi, 'Ancora', 112–13, 159.
[7] Imbruglia, 'Indignation', 169.
[8] Duchet, *Diderot et l'*Histoire', 31–2, 50, 52; Goggi, 'Diderot e l'Histoire', 38; Bancarel, *Raynal*, 24.
[9] *Histoire philosophique* (1780), x. 339–40; [Petit], *Observations*, 117–19.

particular attaining an ideological cogency that in significant ways transcends even d'Holbach's impressive synthesis. Above all, the *Histoire* widens the discussion of society to encompass all varieties of men, reversing, as it has been put, 'prior judgments about the Old World's political and moral superiority', and so did its various offshoots, including *L'Esprit des usages et des coutumes des différents peuples* (3 vols., 'Londres', 1776) by the future revolutionary Jean-Nicolas Démeunier (1751–1814).[10] The *Histoire*'s ostensible theme is Europe's expansion and trade from the founding of the Iberian colonies onwards; but this great 'revolution' in global history it deploys to depict the atrocities of colonial exploitation, rapacity, and barbarism of the 'civilized', global effects of superstition, and, throughout, the worldwide symbiosis of 'despotisme' and 'fanatisme'. All this is infused, moreover, with a more nuanced doctrine of liberty of commerce than that of the *Encyclopédie*, one conceiving of economic freedom as governed by social rules aiming to restrain excessive inequality of wealth.

The *Histoire* documents in detail how the 'revolution' in navigation, shipbuilding, and maritime commerce created a 'nouveau genre de puissance' subjecting the entire globe to Europe, so that a small segment of the world gained 'un empire absolu' over the rest despite the latter representing a far vaster proportion of the globe and its inhabitants and resources.[11] Non-Europeans came under the heel of Europeans. Yet, this 'empire' ruthlessly extended by Europeans over the 'two Indies' also, held Raynal's team, transformed our world for the first time into a single moral and political arena so that the same basic categories and moral values henceforth applied universally to all. For the European colonial empires exercised a supremacy that was purely military and technical, a tightly organized system of oppression, devoid of moral or legal legitimacy, pushing deprivation, misery, and exploitation as far as they would go and altogether contrary, as Gorani later echoed, to the true spirit of commerce. Hence, this same global process that forged such an unequal hierarchy of power and wealth also constructed a single world arena, or what the *Histoire* terms 'la société universelle', turning mankind into a single spectacle and inversely demonstrating the true universal morality founded on equality and the common identity of all men's aspirations, needs, and illusions.[12]

Weighed down by repressive structures of authority, tradition, and faith, mankind is nevertheless pregnant with revolutionary potential constituting a context capable of serving the common good and the reciprocal individual interest of all the humans who compose it. Out of this growing interaction of the world's regions, and steady advance of awareness and Enlightenment, will eventually emerge, albeit only with much agony and violence, a general improvement that may one day liberate every people. The present order is one of such relentless tyranny and oppression that it undermines itself. There is no iron law of history, no destined beginning, mid-point,

[10] Richter, 'Comparative Study', 166; Tarin, *Diderot*, 23; Nash. 'International Repercussions', 15.
[11] *Histoire philosophique* (1780), x. 222–3.
[12] Ibid. x. 471; Gorani, *Recherches*, ii. 105–6; Wilson, 'Enlightenment Philosopher', 417.

or end to this tightening oppression; but the basic logic of equity, philosophy, and also commerce defined as 'une communication libre et universelle' finally envisages all the peoples of the world as a single society in which all members share an equal right to participate in all the rights of each.[13] The glaring contradiction between present reality and the reality conceived by *la philosophie nouvelle* is the dialectic of the coming revolution.

This universalization of man's categories, understanding, activity, politics, and moral system, rendering Europe scarcely less oppressed and weighed down than Asia or Africa, was a change of capital significance. Despite a streak of deep pessimism and even despair at men's blindness to enlightened values and inhumanity to man, an all-encompassing ignorance prevailing everywhere, the changing world context shaped by the drama of the two Indies, that is the logic of the human condition, held out a distant but wonderful glimmer of hope—the hope that for all the world's wretchedness *la philosophie* would in the end conquer greed, credulity, zealotry, and crassness so that, finally, all the colonies established by the Europeans in the Indies would obtain their freedom, in the process forging a new more equal social order without monarchy, nobility, and slave-owners. Where Rousseau has virtually nothing to say about the black and brown peoples, not even ending the slave trade, the *Histoire philosophique* carries anti-slavery on to a new level of mobilization and combat.

Earlier Enlightenment critiques of black slavery, indeed, pale by comparison with the uncompromising assault in 'Raynal' which drew its power precisely from being merely a component of a much wider, more general rejection of the existing order—from being 'philosophical'.[14] It was from 'Raynal' that a whole generation of radical publicists—Brissot, Condorcet, Volney, Chastellux—derived the passionate intensity and terminology of their unrelenting hostility to slavery and ardent conviction that *la philosophie* would in the end destroy it. 'Others might be satisfied with saying what should be done', predicted Chastellux confidently, but he for his part was willing to assert without a shadow of doubt that *la philosophie*, whose voice is only heard when selfish interest is softened somewhat, would seize the opportunity presented by the change in economic perceptions questioning the efficiency and profitability of slavery to bring about a general emancipation of the blacks from servitude. 'Reason', he announced, in 1787, not only could but would destroy slavery.[15]

Composing key parts of this work, Diderot styled himself a historian composing the world's history by turns hopeful and grief-stricken 'almost always' with tears in his eyes.[16] World history is the arena of man's misery and cruelty but also of a growing awareness of the causes and nature of that wretchedness, the philosophical comprehension that is the liberating agent that one day, just possibly, can overcome it. However prejudicial the effect of habit, superstition, ignorance, and exhausting labour on oppressed populations, nothing can sufficiently brutalize men's minds as

---

[13] *Histoire philosophique* (1770), ii. 249–51; Démeunier, *L'Esprit*, ii. 96–7, 114, 148; Hope Mason, 'Materialism', 159–60.   [14] Sala-Molins, *Code noir*, 253; 257–8.
[15] Chastellux, *Discours sur les avantages*, 54–5, 58, 65, 68.   [16] *Histoire philosophique* (1780), iv. 2.

to erase entirely from their consciousness the flagrant injustice of the prevailing allocation of status, wealth, property, privilege, opportunities, and drudgery. Oppression and exploitation by their very nature breed revolt and finally, at least potentially, revolution. Through a mixture of cupidity, cruelty, and contempt, Europeans had become not just the conquerors and *usurpateurs* of the globe, but also a resented and justly hated class of oppressors. This violent state of subjection, held Diderot and Raynal's other collaborators, already filled most of Asia's peoples with burning resentment, making them ardently desire 'une heureuse révolution'. When will 'cette révolution' with all its consequences occur? No one knows: 'mais il faut qu'elle se fasse.'[17]

How often has one heard the man of the people raise up his hands imploringly to heaven and ask: what was his crime to have been born on earth plunged in a state of destitution 'et de dépendance extrême'?[18] In this work, Diderot's circle succeeded in formulating something like a new universal morality linked to a general social theory, aiming at the conservation 'et le bonheur commun de l'espèce humain'.[19] It was a vision, closely linked to their materialism and atheism, postulating a new kind of social science based on gathering information about all manner of usages and structures and then explaining these in a way designed to inspire a revolutionary impulse to reorganize human life on a new and better basis. Systematized oppression he pronounced an unavoidable ill and inherent part of a dialectic that inevitably ensures 'all arbitrary power rushes towards its own destruction, and that everywhere "revolutions"—quicker or slower, sooner or later—will bring back the reign of liberty', something he envisaged as unpredictable but the law of nature.[20]

This budding revolutionary ideology was then further developed in the later editions and various spin-off publications.[21] By pivoting its entire analysis of global misery and exploitation on the manifest defects of the colonial systems, the *Histoire* perfected a strategy that fully exploited the circumstance that the moderate mainstream shared parts of this critique and could only agree that much had gone woefully wrong in the Indies. No sooner had their colonies acquired any value, concludes Adam Smith, than each European mother country strove 'to secure to herself the monopoly of their market and to enlarge her own at their expense, and consequently, rather to damp and discourage than to quicken and forward the course of their prosperity'. Significant differences between colonial systems existed and Spain's might well have been the worst. But even 'the best of them all, that of England', admitted Smith, 'is only somewhat less illiberal and oppressive than that of any of the rest'.[22]

---

[17] Ibid. x. 470; *Histoire philosophique* (1770), ii. 271–2; Pagden, 'Effacement', 140–1.
[18] [Raynal-Hedouin], *Esprit et génie*, 48.
[19] *Réponse à la Censure de la Faculté*, 158–9; Deleyre, *Tableau*, 150–1; Bénot, 'Y a-t-il une morale matérialiste?', 86; Diderot, *Political Writings*, 210–11.
[20] Diderot, *Political Writings*, 174; Mortier, *Combats*, 243; Hope Mason, 'Materialism', 159; Shovlin, *Political Economy*, 135, 137; Ibrahim, *Diderot*, 187–8.
[21] Duchet, *Diderot et l'histoire*, 52–3.
[22] Smith, *Wealth of Nations*, ii. 170–3; Hampsher-Monk, 'Edmund Burke', 128–30.

For the first time, all sections of humanity were being drawn into the same discussion about the human condition and its basic characteristics, in a manner apt to transform men's views about government, empire, trade, the relationship between barbarism and civilization, and most crucial of all between the different races, religions, and genders. Not the least significant aspect of this broadening of the world's awareness, held Raynal and his team, was the Enlightenment's discovery of primitive peoples and the insights philosophy derives from studying these in relation to the 'civilized' nations. It is sometimes claimed the *Histoire philosophique*, and Diderot specifically, 'systematically' inverted conventional notions of the relation of primitive to civilized man, of *l'homme sauvage* to *l'homme policé*. But Diderot does not assert the 'superiority of savage peoples'.[23] Rather, as he himself put it, it is the ignorance 'des sauvages qui a éclairé, en quelque sorte, les peuples policés'.[24] Substituting a dynamic conception of the relation of developed human societies to primitive society, or the savage state, for Rousseau's opposition between the *état social* and the *état sauvage*, Diderot in this way developed a highly original perspective while simultaneously pursuing his lifelong polemic with Rousseau. In the *Histoire* Diderot denies the savage state possesses any special moral validity for us, utopian quality, or intrinsic superiority, or that it can sensibly be judged by the philosopher preferable to the civilized state. He asserts rather the necessary and unavoidable interactive relationship between the two, and for all its inequality, problems, and vastly higher crime rates, the potential superiority of developed society for human happiness and contentment.[25]

Diderot's concept emerges nowhere more clearly than in the *Histoire*'s discussion of the treatment of women in the 'état sauvage'. The female of the species is unjustly oppressed by men everywhere. Among the Amerindian tribes of the Orinoco basin, though, as in 'toutes les régions barbares' one finds women being oppressed in a particularly revolting manner. No worse 'tyrannie' over women exists anywhere in the New World.[26] Primitive men disdain their womenfolk and tyrannize over them more than civilized men because where strength and courage are the only virtues women remain totally abject and dependent. But just as we discern a progression social and political through stages in the evolution of civil society and *l'esprit humain* so this progression, holds the *Histoire*, slowly transforms men's treatment of women. Most overpowering among primitive men, contempt for the female is less brutal among nomads. Next, among sedentary agricultural peoples possessing a more developed sense of the domestic sphere relations between the sexes become still less unequal and better still in highly polished societies where woman receives a new-found status and importance through domestic refinement, arts, fashion, delicate crafts, and expansion of commerce.

---

[23] Richter, 'Comparative Study', 166–7; Imbruglia, *L'Invenzione*, 333–41.
[24] Diderot, *Political Writings*, 192–3; [Petit], *Observations*, 54; Dagen, *L'Histoire*, 563.
[25] Mauzi, *L'Idée du bonheur*, 564–5 n. 3; Goggi, 'Diderot e l'"Histoire"', 40–1.
[26] *Histoire philosophique* (1780), iv. 111–13.

To Diderot, Deleyre, and other authors of the *Histoire* this is not just a lesson of anthropology but a reality inherent in the basic progression of the human condition and reason itself, an anti-*Rousseauiste* conception of social development strongly endorsed in Britain, in 1771, by Millar, and Germany by Forster and then further elaborated in French, in 1776, by Démeunier, an author who repeatedly cites Millar (whom his friend Suard translated).[27] What Millar calls the 'servile condition of the fair sex, in barbarous countries' is central to his radicalism and stands wholly in accord with the *Histoire* and at odds with Rousseau. 'Among all savage nations, whether in Asia, Africa or America, the wife is commonly bought by the husband from her father' and it was this, argues Millar, that afforded complete authority over her. Only the 'progress of a people in civilization and refinement has a natural tendency to limit and restrain this primitive jurisdiction'.[28] Woman's liberation lies in the future.

Effectively integrating its vision of history and anthropology into a coherent and powerful new radical ideology depended on several crucial philosophical steps. The appalling oppression the *Histoire* holds to characterize the European presence in the Indies East and West was for the first time explained not as the innate faults of, or rapacity or cruelty inherent in, particular nations or religions, but as arising from conditions and structures of authority. Cruelty and oppression are made features not of individuals, nations, or types of men, but of men at a particular stage of development where defective institutions and corrupt states of mind, and ignorance, prevail. Credulity aggravated by priestcraft is routinely blamed throughout the *Histoire* for preparing the ground for tyranny and exploitation, and simultaneously for the passivity and abject submissiveness of the most downtrodden.[29]

The same philosophical formula extends to Diderot's analysis of the famed indolence of New World Creole Spaniards. Idleness and social decadence were not so ingrained as commonly supposed and by no means an insurmountable obstacle to their becoming enlightened and energetic.[30] Creole failings, vitiating though they were, he firmly attributes to the unparalleled influence of monks and nobles in Ibero-America, the rooted sway of error rather than the Spanish and Portuguese nations as such.[31] For ingrained indolence, like humanity's other disfigurements, derives, he argues, from bad institutions and intellectual deprivation, not national flaws or innate proneness to vice.[32] Under the new dispensation, political and social circumstances mould behaviour patterns, moral systems, individuals, and group identities alike. Under the right circumstances, most men, perhaps even the worst marauders, rogues, and pirates, can be reconfigured into honest, well-disciplined, reasonable

---

[27] Ibid. iv. 115–16; Démeunier, *L'Esprit,* i. 77–8, 101, 133; Beiser, *Enlightenment,* 165.
[28] Millar, *Observations,* 19–21, 24–5, 101–2; Muthu, *Enlightenment,* 63–5.
[29] Deleyre, *Tableau,* 56; Bénot, 'Y a-t-il une morale matérialiste?', 89.
[30] *Histoire philosophique* (1780), iv. 405–6.
[31] [Raynal-Hedouin], *Esprit et génie,* 310.   [32] Dagen, *L'Histoire,* 560–2.

people.[33] 'Les hommes', declares Deleyre in one of the spin-off publications, 'sont ce que le gouvernement les fait.'[34]

The *Histoire*, in other words, further heightened Radical Enlightenment's growing focus on systems of government, law, and subordination and the general problem of government's relationship to the common people's happiness. Here was a text more widely read than any other Enlightenment work, offering all men 'philosophy' stressing basic equality and the right to happiness of all, offering not solace or a path to resignation, or Rousseau's therapy for the world's ills—isolation, detachment, and indulging in solitary introspection[35]—but a means to unmasking the truth and discovering comprehensive solutions which by definition were realizable only via a great 'revolution'. Much in the *Histoire*'s vision is original, and although many of the hardest-hitting passages written by the now often weary and rapidly ageing Diderot appeared only for the first time in the 1780 edition when much fresh material was added, the core ideas guiding the enterprise as a whole already emerged clearly in the early drafts of the late 1760s and in the first (1770) edition.

Many readers, reactions suggest, grasped the work's revolutionary implications at the time and early on it was recognized as one of the most decisive publishing events in all history. Indeed, if book history has ever recorded a surpassing, ultimate climax, then the drama surrounding the *Histoire* was undoubtedly it. Despite a conspicuously slow start, these volumes eventually achieved an even greater penetration of European culture than the *Encyclopédie* or d'Holbach's chief works, circumventing all efforts of governments and churches to check their diffusion. Fifth on Darnton's list of clandestine best-sellers in France during the twenty years 1769–89, it sold far more extensively than many today more renowned works, including Rousseau's *Confessions* and the *Contrat social*.[36] Selling briskly also in inland provincial towns like Montpellier and Besançon, in maritime urban contexts like Bordeaux and Marseilles clandestine sales edged ahead, seemingly, even of the *Système de la nature*.[37] Beyond France, it had much the widest documented impact of any Enlightenment work, becoming well known and influential, as the Dutch writer Luzac put it in 1780, 'everywhere'.[38] Yet, for several decades it was not just one of the texts most openly inciting discontent with existing conditions but also, in much of Europe, one of those most frequently searched for and intercepted by the police.

'It was through philosophy of this kind', as has aptly been said, 'that the Enlightenment reached the general reading public', as, one might add, did its social criticism.[39] An uncompromising Anglophile, Luzac accused 'Raynal' of reckless disregard for factual accuracy which he thought typical (despite his own Huguenot

---

[33] Diderot, *Political Writings*, 179, 181.   [34] Deleyre, *Tableau*, 157.

[35] Starobinski, *Remède*, 166–83.

[36] Darnton, *Corpus*, 88–9, 194, 199, 253; Darnton, *Literary Underground*, 85, 140–1.

[37] Darnton, *Corpus*, 213, 219; Darnton, *Forbidden Best-Sellers*, 34, 48, 63.

[38] Luzac, *Hollands rijkdom*, i. 259.

[39] Darnton, *Forbidden Best-Sellers*, 73; Darnton, *Great Cat Massacre*, 221; Wilson, 'Enlightenment Philosopher', 420.

origin) of French writers.[40] The Dutch version, the *Wysgeerige en staatkundige geschiedenis van de bezittingen en de koophandel der Europeanen, in beide Indien* (Amsterdam, 1775), he accused of blatant misrepresentation of the Dutch East Indies.[41] Smith who calls Raynal 'the eloquent and sometimes well-informed author of the *Philosophical and Political History of the Establishment of the Europeans in the Two Indies*', also clearly had doubts about the book's factual reliability.[42] But nothing halted the *Histoire*'s advance. Banned by the papacy in 1774, this by then sensational best-seller appeared during its first eighteen years in over forty French editions and in at least forty-eight editions by 1795.[43] Over twenty editions appeared in English, including several in Ireland and America, along with two rival complete translations into German, both from the second edition albeit diminishing somewhat, regretted the radical-minded Diez, the strength and 'fire' of the original.

One of these, published at Hanover, was the work of Jakob Mauvillon (1743–94), professor of military engineering at the college Carolinum, in Cassel, a radical enlightener, ally of Dohm and Mirabeau, and from 1780 head of the cell of Illuminati there.[44] Versions appeared in Italian (1776) and also in Danish, Spanish, and Polish, the latter at Warsaw in 1783.[45] The rapid diffusion of the *Histoire* and polemics surrounding it marked a new stage also in that for the first time a key European Enlightenment debate was swiftly extended to both North America where the English translation figured among the few continental European works to find a wide readership before 1789, and the Caribbean, New Spain, and Central and South America.[46] It had a noticeable effect also in the by now substantial resident European communities in India and Indonesia. In short, the *Histoire philosophique* was a key component of the pre-1789 Western 'revolution of the mind'.

The first three of the first edition's six volumes were largely complete by early 1766 (i.e. before Diderot's involvement) with the fourth volume already well under way. Saint-Lambert who wrote the section on Siam, for the fourth volume, and doubtless other early sections on Asia, is the only other *encyclopédiste* definitely known to have worked on the project before Diderot joined but there were others.[47] The *Histoire*'s main editor, Guillaume-Thomas Raynal (1713–96), a lapsed Christian who quitted the Jesuit order in 1747, had long been friendly with Diderot, having figured among the original team of *encyclopédistes* and regular participants at d'Holbach's salon.[48] He also frequented Madame Helvétius's circle, the other Paris salon where radical thought chiefly flourished and where Helvétius debated 'philosophy' while continually refining (over fifteen years) the text of his *De l'homme*.[49] In the public's eyes,

[40] Luzac, *Hollands rijkdom*, i. 4.   [41] Ibid. i. 2, 4,259, 269, 274, 281, 286, and ii. 35–7, 136–41.
[42] Smith, *Wealth of Nations*, i. 219.
[43] Linguet, *Annales*, xv (1788), 400; Bancarel, 'Éléments', 121–2; Pagden, 'Effacement', 129.
[44] Dohm, *Geschichte*, 11; Schüttler, *Mitglieder*, 101; Fromm, *Bibliographie*, v. 251.
[45] [Deleyre], *Gemälde von Europa*, 'Vorbericht', p. iv; de Bujando, *Index*, 744.
[46] May, *Enlightenment*, 177, 193, 225, 235.
[47] Brot, 'Collaboration de Saint-Lambert', 101–3; Pagden, 'Effacement', 130.
[48] Morellet, *Mémoires*, i. 221–4.   [49] Goodman, *Republic*, 145.

Raynal's name became firmly attached to the *Histoire* as sole author and he did in fact conceive, collate, and manage the project, though his ostensible sole authorship was also a means of shielding Diderot and others from unpleasant consequences and garnering renown for himself.

Diderot worked on the project from around late 1766. Subsequently, other *ency-clopédistes* joined the team, notably Alexandre Deleyre (1726–96), the trusted disciple Diderot had sent carrying messages to Rousseau at the Hermitage, in 1756–7, an implacable radical (and critic of Rousseau) who also composed the *Tableau de l'Europe, pour servir de supplément à l'*Histoire philosophique... des Deux Indes ('Amsterdam' [Maastricht?], 1774), a supportive commentary on Raynal's volumes incisively reiterating many key theses of Diderot and d'Holbach.[50] A fellow atheist and materialist (and democratic republican), Deleyre too conceived liberty as something to be (re)born from the bosom of oppression.[51] He later became a deputy in the National Assembly, remaining a firm *philosophe* supporter of the Revolution until his death in 1796. Another participant was d'Holbach whose views on colonialism, like those of Condorcet and Volney, perfectly complemented Diderot's.[52] While much research and writing proceeded in solitary circumstances, farmed out as if a domestic cottage industry, its conceptualization mostly evolved in d'Holbach's salon where Raynal regularly delivered talks on the Indies, so that to an appreciable extent the work emerged from group discussion.[53]

Although Diderot's contribution commenced less than three years before the original version's completion, it was already substantial by 1770. The more than eighty fragments he penned for the 1770 edition mostly reappeared unchanged or revised in the 1774 edition, comprising over twice the number of fresh fragments he added then.[54] Of the forty-one passages by him concerning Spain and the Spanish Indies featuring in the 1780 version, twelve were already present in 1770 with five more appearing in 1774.[55] Nevertheless, both intellectually and quantitatively Diderot's contribution dramatically escalated with a climactic effort in 1777–8, for the 1780 edition, producing around three times as much text overall as in 1770. In 1780, he contributed roughly a third of the entire text—La Harpe, in 1797, even claims he wrote as much as half—ordering much detail as well as determining the work's general tone and argument.[56]

It was obvious from the outset that the *Histoire* was the work of 'une société de philosophes politiques', a group effort, and that much of the renown accruing to Raynal was not rightfully his.[57] Besides rumour, there were several reasons for

[50] Deleyre, *Tableau*, 150–59; Bénot, *Diderot*, 226 n.; Quintili, *Pensée critique*, 440–2; Trousson, *Jean-Jacques Rousseau*, 334, 336, 369.
[51] Deleyre, *Tableau*, 53; *Réponse à la Censure de la Faculté*, 176; Imbruglia, *L'Invenzione*, 329–31.
[52] *Correspondance inédite de Condorcet*, 95; Wickwar, *Baron d'Holbach*, 207–8, 246.
[53] Goodman, *Republic*, 145; Sandrier, *Style philosophique*, 506–7.
[54] Duchet, *Diderot et l'histoire*, 51–2.
[55] Tietz, 'Diderot', 279.
[56] La Harpe, *Philosophie*, ii. 159; Duchet, *Diderot et l'histoire*, 59; Trousson, *Denis Diderot*, 605.
[57] [Bernard], *Analyse*, 4–5; Hope Mason, 'Materialism', 152.

connoisseurs of the clandestine literary scene, like the editors of the radical *Mémoires secrets*, Matthieu François Pidsansat de Mairobert (1727–79) and his friends, to conclude from the anonymous first edition that a well-organized team must be involved. Besides the project's vast scope and store of data, featuring much statistical and other material about the Spanish, Portuguese, English, and Dutch colonies that could only have been supplied by highly placed personages abroad or in diplomatic posts, there were conspicuous variations in writing style. That this *société de gens de lettres* must also include at least one major *philosophe* seemed clear from the fact that the 'philosophical' digressions were too energetically expressed, compelling, and 'trop contraires à sa manière de penser' to stem from Raynal's mediocre brain.[58] His earlier writings had not been distinguished by any great depth and he was generally less esteemed, by the reading public, observed the *Mémoires*, in 1781, than by foreign diplomats whose society he cultivated at his weekly *déjeuner philosophique*, an event mainly attended by foreign residents.[59] Among the foreigners later reported to have assisted were Aranda, then Spanish ambassador in Paris, and his embassy secretary, Don Ignacio de Heredia, besides the Portuguese envoy, de Souza.[60]

According to the earliest reference in the *Mémoires secrets*, of April 1772, those concerting this new great philosophical venture were 'Duclos, Diderot and d'Alembert'.[61] This was probably just guesswork as subsequent reports in the *Mémoires* make no further mention of d'Alembert and Duclos, listing Raynal's main team rather as Deleyre, d'Holbach, Diderot, Paulze, and Pechméja. Pechméja left his mark. Others too, besides these, contributed. But whatever the exact list, the 'philosophical' inspiration derived from Diderot in constant discussion with Raynal, d'Holbach, Deleyre, Saint-Lambert, Pechméja, and others.[62]

Jean de Pechméja (1741–85) was a little known professor of eloquence at the royal college of La Flèche, accounted an 'habile homme' by Naigeon who dreamt of a future general rising of the oppressed and ultimate reconciliation of the exploited and their exploiters. During the Revolution, the by then deceased Pechméja's not inconsiderable role in the making of the *Histoire* was recalled by some.[63] In particular, he drafted the *Histoire's* unprecedentedly vigorous stance against slavery and was at least partly responsible for the wholly new note the *Histoire* introduced into the Enlightenment debate about slavery. Protesting against slavery was not new in 1770. Montesquieu and others had earlier condemned slavery as an institution. Yet Montesquieu, argues the *Histoire* already in 1770 in a segment penned seemingly by Pechméja,[64] was culpable for condemning slavery only tentatively and even being

---

[58] *Mémoires secrets*, vi. 142.   [59] Ibid. xvii. 199, 30 May 1781.
[60] Perronet, 'Censure', 283; Folkerts, *Bedeutung*, 163; Tietz, 'Diderot', 280.
[61] *Mémoires secrets*, vi. 118–19, 1 Apr. 1772.
[62] Sandrier, *Style philosophique*, 488–507.
[63] Deschamps, *Correspondance*, 810; Bénot, *Diderot*, 215–16; Strugnell, *Diderot's Politics*, 216, 226; Tarin, *Diderot*, 144; Pellerin, 'Naigeon', 28.   [64] Bénot, *Diderot*, 206, 210.

incapable of dealing with the question in a sufficiently earnest manner.[65] For it utterly degrades reason itself to employ philosophical argument to combat an abuse so totally contrary to reason without doing so with great indignation and vigour. In fact, Montesquieu had been somewhat inconsistent on this topic, his relativist, climactic approach to the world's moral and political systems leading him to suggest that in certain contexts and climactic conditions slavery was a natural and possibly appropriate institution like serfdom in eastern Europe.

Montesquieu's relativism and reservations could easily be used to qualify or deflect condemnation of slavery and the slave trade and some later moderate enlighteners did use his approach in this way, his social theory being regularly invoked in the late eighteenth century by defenders of slavery as a means of lending intellectual respectability to their claims.[66] In the French Caribbean, a form of pro-slavery conservative Enlightenment ideology emerged in particular in the writings of M. L. E. Moreau de Saint Méry (1750–1819), a lawyer who published several books about the Caribbean and in 1790 served as deputy for Martinique in the French Constituent Assembly. Few inflected Montesquieu's relativism in a pro-slavery direction to the extent that Saint-Méry did. But there was a still greater philosophical obstacle facing those seeking abolition than pro-slavery apologetics—the prevalence of a large in-between element, adopting a middle-of-the-road position, admiring Montesquieu, agreeing that black slavery is morally wrong and in principle indefensible, but yet, like Smith, considering it indispensable, in practice, for the foreseeable future, given the economics of plantation economies, the harsh realities of *raison d'état*, and international competition. These were the commentators the *Histoire* deplored for excusing 'par la politique, ce que reprouve la morale'.[67]

The *Histoire* was, in many ways, a devastating denunciation of violence, fanaticism, superstition, greed, and despotism; but it was certainly also more than that. For the work undertakes to defend oppressed peoples everywhere by summoning them first to understand the causes of their misery, poverty, and exploitation and then revolt.[68] Diderot believed he discerned something like an inevitable process of growing resentment leading to insight and comprehension followed by black revolt which would one day overturn the supremacy of the British, French, Dutch, and Danes alike throughout the Caribbean and adjoining areas. He believed it was a process that had already commenced in the hills of Jamaica, where escaped blacks had several times ambushed and defeated British planters and troops sent to suppress them, and also in the interior of Surinam. In Surinam, in 1780, the Dutch were calculated to possess 430 sugar, coffee, and other plantations operated by 60,000 black slaves subject to 2,824 slave owners.[69] Because of the relative ease of escaping into the interior, there as in Jamaica, plantation-owners there subjected their slaves,

---

[65] *Histoire philosophique* (1770), iv. 167; *Histoire philosophique* (1774), iv. 236; Rahe, *Montesquieu*, 157–8, 160.

[66] Ehrard, *L'Idée*, 735–6; Ghachem, 'Montesquieu in the Caribbean', 12–14.

[67] *Histoire philosophique* (1770), iv. 167.

[68] Duchet, *Diderot*, 170.   [69] *Histoire philosophique* (1780), vi. 402–3.

alleged the *Histoire*, to an even tighter, crueller captivity than on the Caribbean islands and in neighbouring lands. But this could not prevent the escape of substantial numbers 'de ces déplorables victimes d'une avarice infame'. Dutch raiding parties hunted them in the forests but without being able to suppress them. Already, to an extent, their 'independence' had had to be accepted. Some of these black fugitives now lived peacefully in their own villages; others formed armed bands which had taken to attacking and pillaging the Dutch.[70]

2. PHILOSOPHY AND THE INDIES

The *Histoire philosophique des deux Indes* first appeared, in 1770, in six volumes, without name of author, editor, or publisher on the title page and 'Amsterdam' given as place of publication, though, as Grimm remarks, it was certainly produced in France, at Paris or, he suggested, perhaps Nantes. Initially, it made little impression, failing to secure 'tacit permission' for sale in France and angering the royal chancellor who found in it passages 'contrary' to religion and monarchy. The *libraire* who published it, despairing of better sales, sold his stock to an Amsterdam *libraire* who tried to sell them elsewhere but with no better success.[71] Initially, hardly anyone noticed the work and its effect was negligible. It was already being ascribed to Raynal from early on and in France, as late as April 1772, remained 'very rare and extremely expensive', noted Grimm, who then had had the work in his hands for only a few days.[72]

Though only beginning to digest its contents, Grimm at once realized that here was a text of exceptional importance that could only have been composed in France and was extremely audacious, the work of a 'grand ennemi du despotisme'. So risky was this project for its authors (whose identity he must have known) that he thought the less said about its authorship the better. Personally, he disapproved of the whole business. He did not believe such audacious, provocative views were truly 'philosophic', nor that any careful student of human nature would judge them so. Diderot's and d'Holbach's friend Galiani, who read the *Histoire* at Naples in September 1772, and had his own doubts as to whether Raynal was the main author, reacted similarly. He liked Raynal and thought the book well written, but flatly disowned its political message which he found too utopian. Writing to Madame d'Épinay, avowing himself a hardened 'Machiavellian', he pronounced the whole notion that Europeans should halt their 'ravages' in the Indies far-fetched and even made light of the call to end the slave trade.[73]

---

[70] Ibid. vi. 421–2.
[71] [Bernard], *Analyse*, 2; Courtney, 'Métamorphoses', 111.
[72] Grimm, *Corr. littéraire*, vii. 460; [Bernard], *Analyse*, 1. Droixhe, 'Raynal à Liège', 210.
[73] Galiani to Madame d'Épinay, Naples, 5 Sept. 1772, in Galiani, *Correspondance*, ii. 113–15.

The early impact, then, was slight compared with what came later. There were no further editions in 1770 and 1771.[74] The informal embargo in France was soon likely to become an outright ban, commented the *Mémoires*, in May 1772, due to the growing stir created by the few copies circulating. One finds there 'des réflexions si fortes, si hardies, si vraies', explained this underground journal, and so contrary to the principles on which 'on voudroit établir le despotisme actuel', that it was scarcely imaginable diffusion would long be tolerated at any level.[75] Such initial reaction as there was was mostly unfavourable. Even so, Grimm at least recognized the *Histoire* as a work of capital importance, and also, he predicted, one that would prove an international 'sensation' eventually, a prediction rapidly born out.[76]

What rescued the *Histoire* from oblivion, some supposed, was the royal *arrêt de conseil* of 19 December 1772. This followed after a horrified courtier showed some of the more seditious passages to the king himself and Louis personally ordered the chancellor to ban the *Histoire* immediately. It contained numerous propositions, the chancellor informed the royal council, 'dangerous' to religion and the state.[77] For many at the time, and since, it was attractive and splendidly ironic to assume the royal ban was what caused the sudden rapid improvement in the book's fortunes and secured it a vast readership.[78] Other details, though, show the ban was not the cause but a response to the work's belated popularity, albeit formal repression doubtless added to making it a *cause célèbre*. Sales picked up noticeably earlier in 1772 and the work was reissued at least four times between May and December 1772, the fast rising sales precipitating the ban. In the months before the royal *arrêt* many read it, among them Turgot, then royal *intendant* at Limoges, who finished reading it in July. He too disapproved, though, firmly disagreeing with Condorcet's positive judgement. It was eloquent, he granted, but its ideas were paradoxical, self-contradictory, and as immoral as those of Helvétius which he detested.[79]

The pace quickened further with at least eleven more reprintings in 1773, none naming an editor or publisher, all specifying 'Amsterdam' as the place of publication, though several are known to have appeared at Liège and others were doubtless produced in Paris. In February 1773, the Sorbonne named a theological commission to conduct a thorough investigation.[80] By late 1773 the *Histoire* had become an international sensation and in England, despite disapproval of its impiety, profited from the spread of reports of the East India Company's misconduct in Bengal. Horace Walpole, one of many who read the *Histoire* that year, felt utterly despondent at the horrifying thought that in India, as he put it, writing to Sir Horace Mann, 'we have outdone the Spaniards in Peru!'[81]

---

[74] Courtney, 'Métamorphoses', 111–12.   [75] *Mémoires secrets*, vi. 142, 22 May 1772.

[76] Grimm, *Corr. littéraire*, vii. 461.

[77] *Mémoires secrets*, vi. 245; Bancarel, 'Éléments', 122; Folkerts, *Bedeutung*, 63; Negroni, *Lectures*, 350.

[78] [Bernard], *Analyse*, 2; Droixhe, 'Raynal à Liege', 205; Deschamps, *Correspondance*, 713.

[79] Turgot to Condorcet, 14 July 1772, in *Corr. inédite de Condorcet*, 172; Morellet, *Mémoires*, i. 222.

[80] *Mémoires secrets*, vi. 277.

[81] Irvine, 'Abbé Raynal', 567; Strugnell, 'Religion', 180.

The second revised edition was originally published by the well-known firm of Gosse, again in six volumes, at The Hague, in 1774.[82] Embellished with illustrations and maps, it included much fresh material, including a whole new concluding section raising many general issues, but also removed some passages from the original to fit changes of interpretation. It was the 1774 version that Filangieri utilized when composing his great work of political thought.[83] By the early 1770s, Diderot had sharpened his condemnation of all types of authoritarian government and tied this more closely to his critique of oppressive social forms and harmful popular beliefs. This new more radical phase in his thought commenced before his departure for Russia, with his scathing 'Pages contre un tyran' (1771), which like the new fragments for the *Histoire* first appeared separately, in Grimm's *Correspondance*, in 1772, under the title *Fragments échappés du portefeuille d'un philosophe* (1772).[84] Rather than changes in basic argument these represented shifts of emphasis, with more stress on the right to rebel, a further hardening of the *Histoire*'s tone, the novelty of which, Diderot remarks elsewhere, had forcefully struck many.[85] Another change was from the originally highly favourable account of the pre-Conquest Inca and Aztec civilizations, infused by the perspectives of the seventeenth-century Hispano-Inca chronicler Garcilaso de la Vega.[86] This gave way to a more nuanced and sombre, but still partly positive, assessment of the indigenous American empires.[87]

Again the names of the editor and contributors were withheld. However, the publisher prepared, for separate sale alongside the 1774 edition, a portrait of Raynal, who now decisively emerged as the internationally renowned 'author' of a sensational compilation. At least fourteen reprintings of the revised edition appeared between 1774 and 1778, principally at The Hague but also Amsterdam, Liège, Maastricht, and Paris with a Genevan variant, of 1775, including the material omitted from the 1774 version.[88] Unsurprisingly, the *Histoire* ranked high in the 'catalogue' of 'pernicious' works submitted by the national assembly of the clergy in August 1775 as evidence of subversion of religion in France and on the list of 'mauvais livres' presented by a delegation of prelates headed by Bishop Le Franc de Pompignan to Louis XVI, in person, shortly afterwards.[89] The *Histoire* had now joined the *Système de la nature*, *Le Bon-Sens*, and Helvétius's *De l'homme* (1773) as among the most notorious of all radical books. Louis promised to do everything in his power to clamp down.

---

[82] [Bernard], *Analyse*, 2.   [83] Goggi, 'Ancora', 112.

[84] Diderot, *Fragments échappés*, 447–8; Filangieri, *Scienza della legislazione*, i. 78–9; Bénot, *Diderot*, 150–1; Tarin, *Diderot*, 80.

[85] Diderot, *Supplément*, 167; Echeverría, *Maupeou Revolution*, 224.

[86] Cañizares-Esguerra, *How to Write the History*, 36–7.   [87] Ibid. 36–7.

[88] Courtney, 'Métamorphoses', 116.

[89] *Mémoires secrets*, viii. 141, 191–2, 289. 10 Aug., 25 Sept., and 19 Dec. 1775; Chopelin-Blanc, *De l'apologétique*, 123–4.

The outbreak of the American Revolution in 1776 drew further attention to the *Histoire*, leading, among other things, to separate publication in English of its sections concerning North America under the title *A Philosophical and Political History of the British Settlements and Trade in North America, from the French of the Abbé Raynal* (2 vols., 1776). Published first at Edinburgh this version included the *Histoire*'s remarkable eulogy of Pennsylvania, a segment with a pronounced utopian flavour exploiting a myth originally projected in a passage of Voltaire's *Lettres philosophiques* (1734).[90] Pennsylvania the *Histoire* extolled as proof that mankind can after all dwell in peace and prosperity without 'masters', 'priests', or 'slaves' and also, a point echoed by Filangieri, without prostitutes, men marrying when they wish.[91] Pennsylvania stood for a better world and a better life for humanity. 'If ever despotism, superstition, or war', states the translation, 'should plunge Europe again into that state of barbarism from whence philosophy and the arts have drawn it, the sacred fire will be kept alive in Philadelphia, and come from thence to enlighten the world'.[92]

By contrast, the *Histoire*'s coverage of still 'puritanical' New England and the southern colonies was much less favourable. The gentrified, hierarchical, slave societies of Virginia, Georgia, and Carolinas especially were scathingly criticized. While Locke is praised for promoting 'an unlimited toleration in matters of religion', the *Histoire* takes him to task for being much less 'favourable to civil liberty'. Whether Locke's failure to advance humanity's cause in his constitution for the Carolinas stemmed from those who commissioned it restraining 'his views', as happens with every writer employing his 'pen for great men or ministers; or whether Locke, being more of a metaphysician than a statesman, pursued philosophy only in those [areas] opened up by Descartes and Leibniz; the same man, who had dissipated and destroyed so many errors concerning the origin of ideas made but very feeble and uncertain advances in the path of legislation'.[93] Especially deplored was his allocating the 'eight proprietors who founded the settlement and their heirs, not only all the rights of a monarch, but all the powers of legislation'. The court composing this sovereign body, called the Palatine Court, Locke accorded the 'right of nominating to all employments and dignities, and even that of conferring nobility, but under new and unprecedented titles'.[94] More reprehensible still, the 'nobles' composing the projected legislature's upper house are assigned hereditary honours and 'their possessions made unalienable, a circumstance totally inconsistent with good policy'.[95]

By 1776, the *Histoire* was 'generally known and admired', as the English *Monthly Review* put it in November 1776, 'throughout Europe'.[96] Raynal still took care,

---

[90] Ansart, 'From Voltaire to Raynal', 73; Strugnell, 'Religion', 187.
[91] *Réponse à la Censure de la Faculté*, 165; Filangieri, *Scienza della legislazione*, ii. 80–1.
[92] Raynal, *A Philosophical and Political History*, i. 172–4; Bénot, *Diderot*, 234.
[93] *A Philosophical and Political History*, i. 206; Farr, 'Locke', 169–70, 179.
[94] *A Philosophical and Political History*, i. 206–8.
[95] Ansart, 'From Voltaire to Raynal', 83; Farr, 'Locke', 184; Buck-Morss, *Hegel and Haiti*, 28.
[96] Irvine, 'Abbé Raynal', 573.

though, not to acknowledge his authorship publicly as this would inevitably invite repression. In 1777, a Paris *libraire* published a clandestine abridgment (whether or not Raynal himself ever authorized it), entitled *Esprit et génie de l'Abbé Raynal, tirés de ses ouvrages*, edited by a certain Jean-Baptiste Hedouin. Highlighting the main work's most audacious statements, this text repeated Diderot's thesis that in the eyes of the 'tribunal de la philosophie et de la raison' morality is a science the object of which is the conservation and the 'bonheur commun de l'espèce humaine'.[97] What could be the 'motive of your jealous ambition', European sovereigns were berated, 'to acquire possessions in the Indies other than eternalize the misery of their inhabitants?'[98] Incensed by its tirades against empire, absolutism, Church, *ministres despotes*, and the social order,[99] the authorities seized the stock, caught the printer, and arrested the publishers. As a warning to others, the latter, heavily fined, were stripped of their licences to sell books.[100] The 'editor' was imprisoned, though the condemned person later turned out to be a cousin of the same name, already a prisoner for another offence, who generously took the blame.

At this point, Raynal, with a government expulsion order (to which Turgot was accessory) pending, departed for a lengthy trip abroad. Visiting Holland first and then England, he gathered much additional material about the empires for the third revised edition.[101] Meanwhile, over the winter of 1777–8, Diderot laboured for months over his extensive segments for the third edition, additions comprising some 700 pages of text, among the most subversive and eloquent of the entire compilation.[102] In late 1778, he toiled, at some cost to his health, sometimes as much as fourteen hours a day.[103] Whole sections were changed and enlarged, and the entire project rendered still more challenging as well as brought into closer alignment with the American Revolution now firmly under way. His contribution to the *Histoire*'s third edition was his last throw, a final denunciation of political oppression, obscurantism, and ecclesiastical authority everywhere, putting the finishing touches to an ideology summoning the world's peoples against what he and d'Holbach deemed the general system of world oppression. Indicting all the governments and churches of the globe, he devoted his last energies to the project, but again clandestinely, his role remaining as unnoticed by the outside world as with the previous two editions. Most readers had no inkling until reports of it began circulating during the Revolution.

Diderot had more and more come to appreciate the rich possibilities of this extraordinary undertaking as a vehicle for projecting radical ideas on all sides, to all men and all parts of the world. Unprecedented numbers were reading it. Admittedly, most read it not to imbibe radical ideas but because it was crammed with useful

[97] [Raynal-Hedouin], *Esprit et génie*, 12–13; Deleyre, *Tableau*, 150–1; [Petit], *Observations*, 122.
[98] [Raynal-Hedouin], *Esprit et génie*, 259.
[99] Ibid. 291–3.
[100] *Mémoires secrets*, x. 152, 16 June 1777; Conlon, *Siècle des Lumières*, xviii. 365.
[101] Goggi, 'Autour du voyage de Raynal', 374, 399, 403.
[102] Muthu, *Enlightenment*, 72–4.   [103] Trousson, *Denis Diderot*, 605.

facts about the wider world hard to find elsewhere and, as Linguet later observed, offered a more complete account of international trade and the European colonies than one could find at the time elsewhere, as well as because many readers supported its appeals to end mercantilist restrictions and monopolies and liberalize trade.[104] Many of its readers doubtless disliked the relentless sallies against religion, monarchy, aristocracy, as well as empire; but these were so skilfully interspersed among unobjectionable pages and so closely fused with sentiments moderate enlighteners often concurred with, concerning slavery and European serfdom, that some were bound to be drawn further into sympathizing also with the *Histoire*'s wider assault on the status quo. In this way, readers across a vast geographical span could scarcely avoid absorbing, both consciously and unconsciously, its basic message. More even than the *Encyclopédie*, the *Histoire* was unparalleled as a vehicle for infiltrating minds accustomed to think conventionally. Hints of support then in turn spurred Diderot and his colleagues on to new efforts. *La philosophie*, affirmed Deleyre, advances in part by the *philosophes* leading the people; but equally via the people encouraging the *philosophes*.[105]

By the time he visited Russia, in 1773, Diderot had long viewed autocracy and ignorance as universal plagues, chronic across the globe as well as characteristically Russian scourges. Subsequently, he closely followed the specific case of Russia as well as that of Spain,[106] a country and empire whose exceptional backwardness and fanaticism had been trumpeted to the whole world in 1777 with Olavide's arrest. The Inquisition 'ne souffre pas qu'on apprenne à penser', preferring everyone to believe blindly and remain ignorant about everything except its power and prerogatives.[107] But how does an entire people and empire come to languish under the sway of such tyranny? After Olavide escaped, we have seen, he lived in Paris under an assumed name, enabling Diderot, from the summer of 1781, to confer with him as he did also with another Spanish American enlightener, Miguel Gijón y León, already earlier, a still more valuable source of information about the Hispanic world generally.[108]

Not unconnected, perhaps, with Diderot's developing themes for his writing in discussion groups dedicated to particular topics, including his dinner circles devoted to Spain and Russia, were rumours circulating in Paris, prior to publication of the third edition, that a new enlarged edition was pending, rumours greeted with great displeasure, commented the *Mémoires secrets*, by the clergy and the 'partisans du despotisme'. Harsh preventive action might have ensued had police and official anxieties not been allayed at the crucial moment by a well-honed campaign of disinformation. Word spread that the new edition aimed to provide splendid new maps and illustrations, and lend the work greater respectability. This time Raynal would not only append his name and portrait but delete the more

---

[104] Linguet, *Annales*, xv (1788), 399–400.
[105] Deleyre, *Tableau*, 146; [Deleyre], *Gemälde von Europa*, 289.
[106] Diderot, *Fragments échappés*, 451–2; Tarin, *Diderot*, 31–3.
[107] Diderot, 'Don Pablo Olavidès', 472.
[108] *Mémoires secrets*, xviii. 93, 20 Oct. 1781; Bénot, *Diderot*, 311; Tietz, 'Diderot', 280.

scandalous passages.[109] By assigning earnings from previous sales for a 1,200-*livre* prize announced by the Academy of Lyon for the best essay on whether the discovery of the Americas was 'useful or damaging' to mankind, Raynal further encouraged the notion he sought rehabilitation.[110]

The third, augmented version poured from the presses in three simultaneous editions, during 1780, the largest at Geneva, for a consortium of Parisian *libraires*. There were to be at least eleven further French-language reissues between 1781 and 1786, at Geneva, Neuchâtel, Paris, and Liège.[111] The new version, readers soon realized, was even more remorseless and wide-ranging in its assault on religion, monarchy, and the empires than its predecessors, and the authorities reacted accordingly, even though, apparently, there was initially little distribution in France. By intervening forcefully at this late stage, royal ministers were taking a considerable, calculated risk. As Linguet later remarked, there were now well over 100,000 copies of the *Histoire* in circulation and it had been read throughout the world for over a decade with great reservation in some respects but also often with approbation. Imposing a new, comprehensive prohibition on such an exceptionally widely known work was bound to appear at best as bizarre and, at worst, incomprehensible and distinctly ridiculous.[112] The last thing ministers wanted was to look ridiculous. But within France, a rising tide of denunciation fed by deep anger among the clergy and countless complaints, as well as the king's own displeasure, forced the government's hand. Again, the king was shown some especially 'reprehensible' passages and, according to the *Mémoires secrets*, actively intervened behind the scenes, bitterly berating ministers for tacitly permitting such a work 'to penetrate into France'.[113] Louis was amazed to find that even his own war minister, the reactionary Vergennes, a known foe of the *philosophes*, and other courtiers, had subscribed to the new edition. The foreign minister was obliged to write at once to Geneva, at this time a French protectorate, demanding immediate banning of the new edition there.

The *Parlement* of Paris and Sorbonne, meanwhile, were bombarded with demands to condemn and suppress the work. On 25 May 1781, Séguier, the *avocat général*, presented the *Parlement* with a detailed *réquisitoire*, denouncing the new edition in the most vehement terms, especially the work's brazenness in claiming 'philosophy' had entered the world to cure men of their errors and vices, the latter being the chief cause of humanity's wretchedness, and that religion should be replaced by 'philosophy' as mankind's chief guide. Deemed infamous blasphemy and treason combined was its thesis that the 'chaîne funeste' oppressing humanity derives equally from throne and altar.[114] The 'tyrants' the *Histoire* declaims so violently against were

---

[109] *Mémoires secrets*, xv. 208–9, 2 July 1780.

[110] Ibid. xvi. 8; Raynal, *Révolution de l'Amérique*, avertissement, pp. ix–xi; Labbé, *Gazette littéraire*, 235.

[111] Courtney, 'Métamorphoses', 118.

[112] Linguet, *Annales*, xv (1788), 400.

[113] *Mémoires secrets*, xvii. 198, 30 May 1781.

[114] Oxford Bodleian, Mason 1.1 142/87: *Arrêt de la Cour du Parlement qui condamne un imprimé ayant pour titre* Histoire philosophique ... des deux Indes, 25 May 1781 (Paris, 1781), 6–7.

the Christian kings of Europe. When the *Histoire* condemns 'la tyrannie et l'impos-ture', it is the sovereignty of princes and the Christian faith against which it aims its barbs: it is the clergy of all lands in the eyes of the *Histoire* who are the *imposteurs*.[115] The work openly attacked kings and abjured the Church's teaching as false and barbaric, 'une morale abjecte'.

Overturning the fundamental principles 'de l'ordre civil', the *Histoire* sought to substitute for all accepted laws, principles, and religious doctrine 'une philosophie audacieuse et sacrilège'.[116] Recasting world history, its real message, observed Séguier's *réquisitoire*, was that 'philosophy' wishes to be 'God', that *la philosophie* should make the laws and provide society with its moral base, transforming the entire world. Could any insanity be more outrageous? The *Parlement*, labelling the work 'impie, blasphématoire, séditieux, tendant à soulever les peuples contre l'autorité souveraine', on 29 May 1781, ordered it to be publicly lacerated and burnt, issuing a warrant for Raynal's arrest. But ministers privately warned him in time and the author, just back from abroad, promptly departed afresh. Raynal's foes in France had to content themselves with intensifying the ban. Several bishops posted their own edicts, among the most vehement being the *mandement* of 3 August 1781 of Le Franc de Pompignan, now archbishop of Vienne, forbidding anyone to read the new—or any—version of the *Histoire* in his archdiocese. While his *mandement* also forbade reading Rousseau, it expressly states the latter's moral ideas to be 'less depraved' than those of other *incrédules*. Nothing is more 'odious' or contemptible, declared Le Franc, than an apostate priest [i.e. Raynal], such as had penned this conflation of sacrilege and treason; such a renegade is despised by all.[117]

Police raids on French booksellers were stepped up. In one raid, two provincial *libraires*, at Rochefort, near Poitiers, advertising themselves as suppliers of the *Histoire*, named Masseau and Bonhomme, had their entire stock seized by order of the council of state of 25 May 1781. Heavily fined, they too were stripped of their licences to sell books.[118] From Paris, in late July 1781, the young Jean-Pierre Brissot de Warville (1754–93), the future revolutionary leader, then immersed in the clandestine book trade, wrote warning the publishers at Neuchâtel that 'the strictest orders' had been issued to prevent the book arriving across the Swiss border and that police spies had been sent to 'inspect the printing and to discover what route the books will take'.[119] Many copies entered circulation, nevertheless; but this by no means signifies that efforts at suppression had no effect. In France, noted Deleyre, the ban made the book both rarer and costlier than it would otherwise have been.[120]

Raynal, meanwhile, arriving in Spa, a fashionable resort, in the southern Netherlands, celebrated as the 'café of Europe', lodged at the Hotel de Hollande, basking in

---

[115] Oxford Bodleain Mason 48/12: *Arrest de la Cour de Parlement qui condamne un imprimé en dix volumes* (Paris, 1781), 7–9 ; Cottret, *Jansénismes*, 110–11.

[116] *Mémoires secrets*, xvii. 192–3, 196, 28 and 29 May 1781.

[117] Ibid. xviii. 79; Perronet, 'Censure', 281–2.

[118] Oxford Bodleian Mason 1.1./142/86: *Arrêt du Conseil d'état du Roi, du 25 May 1781* (Paris, 1781), 1.

[119] Quoted in Darnton, *Literary Underground*, 64.   [120] *Réponse à la Censure de la Faculté*, p. iv.

celebrity, the eyes of all Europe fixed on him.[121] Authorized by the 'enlightened' prince-bishop, François-Charles de Velbruck, his Spa sojourn provoked heated debate in nearby towns. At Liège, the former Jesuit Father Feller reprinted the Paris *Parlement*'s condemnation and concerted a local protest campaign against the 'fanatique' Raynal being allowed to stay, in his *Journal historique et littéraire*.[122] Feller's strident anti-Jansenism had not endeared him to the prince-bishop, however, and for a while he was ignored. For weeks, the furore became fixated on the degree of acknowledgement accorded to Raynal by visiting princes. Prince Heinrich of Prussia, Frederick's younger brother, dined with him, announced Grimm (who was then also visiting Spa), and warmly praised him. *Le public chrétien* was much consoled, however, reported Feller, when the Austrian governess of the southern Netherlands, Marie-Christine de Lorraine, daughter of Maria Theresa, when visiting Spa publicly snubbed him. Much to Feller's dismay, this splendid 'humiliation pour toute la philosophie en corps' was negated, shortly afterwards, though, when the Emperor Joseph himself sat down with Grimm and their host, Prince Heinrich, to dine with the 'fanatique'. Where Joseph had once pointedly avoided Ferney, a few years earlier, snubbing Voltaire (causing Feller to rejoice), he now permitted Raynal to stay in the Austrian Netherlands (albeit while nevertheless continuing to ban the *Histoire* in Austria).[123] At this point, a visiting young Frenchman, another future revolutionary, Nicolas Bassenge, published a laudatory poem somewhere in the vicinity, entitled *La Nymphe de Spa*, eulogizing Raynal and also Joseph for meeting him, styling the latter 'le bon Joseph aux préjugés fatal'.[124]

Raynal meanwhile did not neglect his business affairs. In Liège, where several editions of the *Histoire* had appeared and local *libraires* helped organize the smuggling of this and other underground texts printed in Holland into France, he had much to discuss. In July 1781, he visited Maastricht, base of the publisher Jean-Edmé Dufour who in 1775 and 1777 several times reissued the 1774 version and who, in 1774, had also brought out Deleyre's incisive summary of the *Histoire*, the *Tableau de l'Europe*,[125] the latter was subsequently rendered into German by Heinrich Friedrich Diez, Spinoza's late eighteenth-century biographer, and published at Dessau in 1783, adding to the growing debate surrounding the *Histoire* in Germany. In the spring of 1782, Raynal visited Mainz, Gotha, and Weimar where he regaled Goethe and his circle with Parisian anecdotes.[126] In April, he reached Berlin where (despite the *Histoire*'s disparagement of Frederick's kingship) he enjoyed the monarch's protection and was further fêted. He was unable to return to France until 1787.

Condemnation of the *Histoire* culminated in the summer of 1781 with publication of Séguier's fourteen-page *réquisitoire* and, in August, the Sorbonne's detailed

---

[121] *Mémoires secrets*, xviii. 191; Bancarel, 'Éléments', 127.

[122] Droixhe, 'Raynal à Liège', 219; Froidcourt, *L'Abbé Raynal*, 22, 25–6.

[123] Froidcourt, *L'Abbé Raynal*, 91; Beales, *Joseph II. Against*, 153–4.

[124] *Réponse à la Censure de la Faculté*, 189–90; Froidcourt, *L'Abbé Raynal*, 41–3.

[125] Froidcourt, *L'Abbé Raynal*, 34.

[126] Fromm, *Bibliographie*, v. 252; Labbé, *Gazette littéraire*, 234; Bancarel and Goggi, *Raynal*, 25–6, 159.

114-page theological indictment. The latter, warmly applauded by Feller, and reprinted at Liège, identified in the text no less than eighty-four grave 'errors', dividing this mass of 'pernicious' doctrine into four categories.[127] The first comprised erroneous theses about natural law and mankind's history, the *Histoire*'s gravest fault here being denial of divine providence 'dans l'ordre moral'. Second came blasphemous statements about revealed religion, its 'horreurs' including the thesis that all religions 'indistinctement' are 'imaginées par des imposteurs' and that there is in the history of religions an inherent process of rationalization whereby Catholicism yields to Protestantism, Protestantism to Socinianism, Socinianism to deism, and deism to 'scepticism'.[128] Third followed infamous heresies about the origins of morality and nature of 'good' and 'bad'. The final category were the *Histoire*'s treasonable statements about monarchy and government.[129] Its author is labelled an 'écrivain incendiaire' openly kindling 'le flambeau de la sédition'.[130] Shortly afterwards, in view of its 'philosophie insensée', the synod of the prince-bishopric of Liège by *mandement* of 27 October 1781 prohibited the *Histoire* too; echoing the Paris *Parlement*, it too pronounced it 'impious, blasphemous, seditious and tending to raise peoples against sovereign authority'.[131]

Raynal was abroad; but in Paris Deleyre (and perhaps Diderot) replied for him, with the *Réponse à la Censure de la Faculté de Théologie de Paris contre l'*Histoire philosophique (1782), an incendiary text, celebrating *la sagacité sorbonnique* with withering sarcasm. The theologians are here styled enemies of reason blinded by prejudice and mired in intellectual and spiritual fraud: 'quelles insultes n'ont-ils pas faites à la raison humaine!'[132] What a contrast with *la philosophie*, a gentle and wise mother who never expresses herself other than through 'la voix de la douceur et de la persuasion'.[133] Reiterating Diderot's principle that before the 'tribunal of philosophy and of reason' morality is no business of theologians but a science whose aim is 'la conservation' and the 'Bonheur commun de l'espèce humaine', it pronounced the ancient distinction between temporal and spiritual spheres 'une absurdité palpable'.[134] Reason and the worldly good of the majority, constant and eternal, are the only rules that matter in the true moral order, *la morale universelle*.[135]

Radical *philosophes* denounced the 'collusion sacrilège entre l'autel et le trône'.[136] Opponents conjured up a lurid conspiracy of blasphemy, conspiracy, and betrayal, adopting the ideological frame announced by the assembly of the French clergy at their gatherings of 1770 and 1775, terminology highlighting the mutually dependent ties between religion and political power, throne and the altar, and irreligious

---

[127] Froidcourt, *L'Abbé Raynal*, 55.

[128] *Histoire philosophique* (1780), x. 14–15.

[129] Oxford Bodleian Mason 1.1/ 142: *Determinatio Sacrae Facultatis Parisiensis in Librum cui Titulus:* Histoire philosophique (Paris, 1781), 5–8; *Mémoires secrets*, xviii. 16, 35–6, 31 Aug. and 11 Sept. 1781; Droixhe, 'Raynal à Liège', 220–1.

[130] Oxford Bodleian Mason 1.1/ 142: *Determinatio Sacrae Facultatis*, 112–13.

[131] *Réponse à la Censure de la Faculté*, 189, 191–2.   [132] Ibid., preface pp. iv, ix–x.

[133] Ibid. 163; Lüsebrink, 'Zensur', 154–5.   [134] *Réponse à la Censure de la Faculté*, 158–9.

[135] Ibid. 160–2.   [136] Deleyre, *Tableau*, 154.

character of the plot they confronted.[137] Those attacking religion in a multitude of works, and again here, exclaims Séguier's preface, constitute a criminal 'conjuration' intent on undermining monarchy with the attested proofs of the Christian religion to substitute a 'senseless philosophy' in its place. There was indeed much of an incendiary nature in the *Histoire* as in the reprint of *Esprit et génie*, suppressed in 1777, but now expanded and republished (apparently at Geneva) in 1782, under the title *Esprit de Guillaume-Thomas Raynal, également nécessaire à ceux qui commandent et à ceux qui obéissent* (2 vols., 'Londres', 1782), restating the revolutionary challenge. The chapter 'du despotisme et de la tyrannie' proclaims all peoples are made for liberty and that historical circumstances alone explain why peoples are encumbered with oppressive governments. Even the English would be among the world's most slavish peoples were they ruled by three Queen Elizabeths in a row.[138] The *Esprit* adds as blunt a summons to revolt as is found anywhere in the 1780s. 'La révolte est une ressource terrible', it reaffirms, in Diderot's words, 'mais c'est la seule qui reste en faveur de l'humanité, dans les pays opprimés par le despotisme.'[139]

The *Esprit de Guillaume-Thomas Raynal* declares war on kings and priests. Monarchy renders peoples ignorant and superstitious because despotism cannot long sustain itself without the aid of 'la superstition'. Opponents reacted by bitterly decrying what they saw as overly zealous ardour for *la liberté*, prone uselessly to incite a *soulèvement général* of the world's nations, producing bloody chaos everywhere.[140] The *Histoire*, alleged its foes, threatens humanity with a general 'revolution' including in the Americas where it was totally unrealistic to imagine the Indians and blacks ever resuming control of what had been wrested from them and hence incitement serving only anarchic and no conceivably useful purposes. The *Histoire* assures the world's peoples that their rulers and priests are 'des despotes et des tyrans'. Was this not to unchain domestic animals, complained one critic, and turn them into ravaging beasts?[141]

Kings, held Diderot and the *Histoire*, are what keep society's different layers in a continual state of oppression and war, the legitimizing factor endorsing institutionalized theft, treason, and murder.[142] The ensuing state of subjection produces a kind of 'tranquillity' bequeathed to society by 'absolute power' a tranquillity freezing the mind, eradicating initiative, and reducing men to 'une léthargie universelle'.[143] As monarchs fear 'l'esprit républicain' and aspire to prevent its spread among their subjects (whose shackles they daily make heavier), they collude together in secret intrigue linking all monarchies in a common design to destroy 'les états libres', an allusion to the recent suppression of the democratic party in Geneva, earlier in 1782, an anti-democratic coup undertaken by the French court allied to the, at this time, anti-democratic oligarchic republic of Berne. The Genevan revolution had briefly

---

[137] Perronet, 'Censure', 277.   [138] [Raynal-Hédouin], *Esprit et génie*, 75.
[139] Ibid. 76; *Esprit de Guillaume-Thomas Raynal*, i. 112; Bancarel and Goggi, *Raynal*, 286.
[140] [Bernard], *Analyse*, 71–3.   [141] Ibid. 185–6, 215–16.
[142] *Esprit de Guillaume-Thomas Raynal*, i. 121, 123, 125.   [143] Ibid. i. 123.

raised spirits in the radical fraternity; its defeat for the moment had suppressed the voice of liberty. But the American Revolution remained in full swing and there would come a day when all men would comprehend finally how they are cheated and that liberty is from heaven and the first root of virtue: 'et le jour du réveil n'est pas loin.'[144]

More incisive even than the main work, the *Esprit de Guillaume-Thomas Raynal* excoriated the colonial empires. Europeans were all guilty of the worst excesses in the Indies not only toward their subject populations but also other Europeans. The Crusades were a horrible atrocity, mass ignorance triumphing alternately under the banner of the Cross and the Crescent.[145] Spain preferred to depopulate her own territory and turn the New World into a graveyard rather than equitably share her wealth with others. The Dutch, in the sixteenth century gallant republicans resisting kings, in the next resorted to every secret and public crime to prevent the rest of Europe and Asia sharing in the East Indies spice trade, hurling great stores of pepper and spices into the sea rather than sell them at reasonable prices.[146] The English, for their part, stripped the French in Acadie (Nova Scotia) of everything and ruthlessly drove them out, deliberately ruining them and causing many to perish to prevent their ever returning.[147]

All European nations, meanwhile, brutally tyrannized over the Jews. Will the Jews one day find refuge in Jamaica or another corner of the universe where arrogant and tyrannical Christians and Muslims will finally leave them in peace and they can be free?[148] But the sharpest denunciation is of Europeans' mistreatment of their non-European subjects. Perhaps no nation, charged Diderot, had ever turned their prejudices, ignorance, and superstition into such an idolatry as the Spaniards: never has unreason been 'plus décidée, plus ferme et plus subtile'.[149] Nevertheless the cruelty and other faults of the Spaniards were simply the defects of their time. Change the circumstances and Spain too will assume an entirely different character: 'ses qualités seront héroïques, sa mémoire sera sans reproche.' Spanish rapacity in the Americas will generate its own reaction in the human soul: 'les déprédations des espagnols dans toute l'Amérique ont éclairé le monde sur tous les excès du fanatisme'.[150]

3. TRANSATLANTIC IMPACT

The first full translation of the 1770 edition appeared in London in 1774, just as relations between Britain and her colonists were becoming seriously fraught. More English-language editions followed at Edinburgh and, later, Dublin (in 1784) as well as London. A translation of chapter twenty-eight of the eighteenth book, concerning

---

[144] *Esprit de Guillaume-Thomas Raynal*, i. 130; *Réponse à la Censure de la Faculté*, 176.
[145] *Esprit de Guillaume-Thomas Raynal*, i. 322.
[146] Ibid. i. 138; Bénot, *Diderot*, 175–6, 178–80.
[147] *Esprit de Guillaume-Thomas Raynal*, i. 137–8.   [148] Ibid. ii. 77.
[149] Ibid. ii. 139.   [150] Ibid. ii. 139–40.

the English colonies, reappeared in 1775, at Philadelphia, published by James Humphreys, under the title 'The Sentiments of a Foreigner on the *Disputes of Great Britain with America*', a fragment then reprinted in *Virginia Gazette*, in September 1775, with extracts resurfacing, in February 1776, in the *Maryland Gazette*. The *Histoire* clearly played a part in the literary ferment accompanying the opening moves of the American Revolution.[151] The heavily revised section dealing with recent events in North America in the *Histoire*'s third edition also reappeared separately, under the title *Révolution de l'Amérique*. This text was to boast a scarcely less remarkable history than the main work, or the *Esprit*, and similarly appeared in numerous editions, including a German version under the title *Geschichte der Revolution von Nordamerika* issued at Berlin, in 1786.[152]

This text begins by styling the *Histoire philosophique* 'certainly one of the finest works to appear since the revival of letters, and perhaps the most instructive of any that have been known'.[153] The *Révolution de l'Amérique* was at once banned in much of Germany as sympathizing with rebellion and casting aspersions on princes supporting Britain. Called a 'production monstrueuse' by Feller, it was prohibited also at Liège: yet, it was read there and in his native Luxembourg as well as Germany with avid interest. With remarkable prescience, Feller surmised that its notably favourable reception in Liège might presage dire consequences for the prince-bishop's regime.[154] Only a few years later it was seen that indeed it did.

Raynal and his collaborators not only endorsed the American Revolution but refused to sanction the idea cherished by most Americans that their Revolution arose from essentially local and specific circumstances anchored in particular rights and legal traditions. To Diderot and his radical colleagues, the American Revolution had nothing whatever to do with the cherished particular rights of Englishmen. Repeating Diderot's famous phrase 'that the history of civilized man is but the history of his misery' [l'histoire de l'homme civilisé n'est que l'histoire de sa misère], *The Revolution of America* endorses insurrection against 'tyrannical' monarchs by oppressed peoples, everywhere, while expressly disavowing that philosophers were responsible for the unrest. 'It is well known, that it is not the speculations of philosophers which provoke civil troubles. No subjects are more patient than we.'[155] Yet one of Diderot's most inflammatory remarks is reiterated here with unqualified approval: 'on se délivre de l'oppression d'un tyran ou par l'expulsion ou par la mort'.[156]

Britain calls the Americans 'rebels'. Why? Because 'they will not be your slaves'.[157] British complaints about colonial ingratitude, illegality, and rebellion are scathingly dismissed *in toto*. Diderot refuses even to discuss whether British fiscal oppression, trade restrictions, and general mismanagement were sufficiently oppressive to justify

[151] Benhamou, 'Diffusion', 302.   [152] Fromm, *Bibliographie*, v. 252.
[153] Raynal, *Revolution of America*, 'Advertisement', p. iii.
[154] Droixhe, 'Raynal à Liège', 217–18.
[155] Raynal, *Revolution of America*, 39; Raynal, *Révolution de l'Amérique*, 36.
[156] Raynal, *Révolution de l'Amérique*, 41.   [157] Raynal, *Revolution of America*, 43.

rebellion in terms of the legal rights and traditions the Americans went to such trouble to invoke, considering this completely irrelevant. 'All authority in this world has begun either by the consent of the subjects, or the power of the masters. In both one and the other case, it may justly end. There is no prescription in favour of tyranny against liberty.'[158]All colonies everywhere always possess an automatic right to repudiate any royal sovereignty wherever this is what the citizenry desire; no crown or mother country can ever be justified in opposing 'the general will' of a colonial society. Even suggesting a people has justified grounds for rebelling based on particular 'rights', privileges, or precedents is entirely to misunderstand the true nature of human society and politics. The *Histoire's* great principle—despite Raynal personally being rather equivocal about the Revolution—was that the American colonists, or rather all colonists everywhere, are always 'en droit de se séparer de leur métropole', independently of 'tout mécontentement'.[159]

The *Revolution of America*, first published in London, in 1781, became an immediate best-seller. Reprinted in New York by James Rivington that year, and the next year at Philadelphia and several other places, this work not only presents the Revolution as part of a process of general revolution but as a kind of centrepiece of world history. Stressing the crucial role of Tom Paine's famous pamphlet *Common Sense* which it describes at length it rightly pronounced this tract decisive in persuading Americans to take the plunge, in 1775–6, and fight for their independence.[160] Paine's subsequent *Letter to the Abbé Raynal on the Affairs of North America* (Philadelphia, 1782) corrects some inaccuracies and inconsistencies of detail but reinforces the general message, lending the text further publicity, enabling it to supplement Paine's own publications as a factor mobilizing opinion behind the Revolution.[161]

The *Histoire* backed the Revolution but also delivered Diderot's impassioned appeal to the insurgents, in making their new society, not to forget about equality, to shrink from a too unequal a division of wealth furthering the excessive opulence of a few and impoverishment of a multitude of citizens from which arises 'l'insolence des uns et l'avilissement des autres'. Americans, he urged, should also avoid all appetite for conquest or domination. Stability and tranquillity diminish as states expand. They should use arms to defend themselves but never to attack others.[162]

4. THE *HISTOIRE PHILOSOPHIQUE* AS A PROJECT OF WORLD REVOLUTION

The *Histoire* and the two general summaries of 1777 and 1782 clearly summoned the world's oppressed to rise against their rulers in the name of liberty: never will the

---

[158] Raynal, *Revolution of America*, 41; Strugnell, *Diderot's Politics*, 207–9; Imbruglia, 'Indignation', 175–6.
[159] Diderot, *Œuvres complètes*, xv. 535; Lamourette, *Pensées*, 204.
[160] Raynal, *Revolution of America*, 79–90; Raynal, *Révolution de l'Amérique*, 74–86.
[161] Benhamou, 'Diffusion', 302.　　[162] Diderot, *Œuvres complètes*, xv. 547.

tyrants freely consent 'à l'extinction de la servitude, et pour les amener à cet ordre de choses, il faudra les ruiner ou les exterminer'.[163] It was a view Diderot already plainly expounded by 1771.[164] And if the *Histoire* urged an end to servitude and removal of royal despots, it also declared war with equal emphasis on the social systems prevailing in Europe. 'Tyrants' can do nothing on their own, a tyrant is merely the moving force, the *Histoire* and its summaries maintained, the pivot of systems of social repression, the motor 'des efforts que font tous les sujets pour s'opprimer mutuellement'.[165] It was the entire social order based on monarchy, aristocracy, and ecclesiastical authority that needed to be swept away. This was not something everyone in Diderot's circle could endorse. Grimm was now more than somewhat perturbed. His long friendship with Diderot had come under strain ever since their visit to Russia, in 1772–3, when his old comrade's increasingly critical attitude towards Catherine's despotism had begun seriously to alarm him.[166] While Grimm's admiration of enlightened despots and Diderot's hostility had already grated on each by 1772,[167] the Russian visit brought the split to the surface. At Petersburg, Grimm showed distinct signs of placing his status as a courtier and agent of princes above other considerations and the two regularly disagreed about the appropriateness of Catherine's rule for Russia.[168] Grimm was also aware of Frederick's growing exasperation. While the Prussian monarch was more and more dissatisfied with the direction taken by *la philosophie*, Diderot was in no way willing to mollify him. With each passing year the latter's political and social radicalism became more pronounced, leading Grimm to retreat further from his former intimacy with him. Their amity, close and continuous for over three decades, neared breaking point in 1781.

If anyone had the suavity and cynical wit to bridge the gulf between Radical and moderate Enlightenment it was surely Grimm. But in the end this overly taxed even his ingenuity. As Catherine's agent in Paris and, since 1776, representative of the court of Saxe-Gotha, he found himself in a position where elegant *mondanité* and cosmopolitanism could no longer bridge the competing enlightened streams. Forced to choose, his ties with the courts, monarchy, and aristocracy in the end weighed more with him than the emancipatory vision of the *encyclopédistes*. With the new edition of Raynal raising a storm, and Raynal himself in exile, he began speaking in derogatory terms about him and his work at Parisian soirées, on one occasion, in March 1781, in the presence of Diderot's beloved daughter. Diderot gave vent to his indignation as if he were Raynal, composing his *Lettre apologétique de l'Abbé Raynal à Monsieur Grimm*, a manuscript written between March and May 1781.[169]

---

[163] *Histoire philosophique* (1780), x. 45; *Réponse à la Censure de la Faculté*, 177; *Esprit de Guillaume-Thomas Raynal*, i. 129. [164] Diderot, *Fragments échappés*, 451.
[165] *Esprit de Guillaume-Thomas Raynal*, i. 121.
[166] Diderot, *Lettre apologétique*, 192.
[167] See Grimm's footnotes to Diderot, *Fragments échappés*, 448, 451 n.
[168] Duchet, *Diderot et l'Histoire*, 40–1; Trousson, *Denis Diderot*, 608–9.
[169] Trousson, *Denis Diderot*, 609–10; Bénot, *Diderot*, 311; Lepape, *Diderot*, 410–11; Lilti, *Le Monde*, 207.

Diderot—though it is not known for sure whether he actually circulated it or not—here flatly denies Grimm's insistence that 'Raynal' had been either cowardly or reckless in attacking Europe's sovereigns. 'Raynal' surely knows, Grimm had protested, that the princes he assails either cannot exact revenge, in which case the *Histoire*'s assaults are cowardly, or else that a ruler can, in which case his outpourings are pointless and self-destructive. It is useless defiance to assail legitimate monarchs. Not at all, retorted Diderot: attacking someone unable to exact revenge is not necessarily cowardice: it suffices that he merits being attacked.[170] As for lambasting rulers well placed to retaliate, where this is done for the 'good cause', the common good, far from being madness it is an act of generosity. Every *philosophe* and 'homme éclairé' with Grimm's attitude must remain silent, unable to criticize government, legislation, or office-holders or denounce abuse, vice, and 'error', the sole topics 'dignes d'occuper un bon esprit'.[171] It was not Raynal's but Grimm's course, acquiescence in tyranny, that is the path of cowardice. A writer revealing his name on the title page of a work attacking authority may be rash but is no 'madman'. Ultimately, it makes no difference whether philosophy's enemy is powerful or weak, philosophy should assail every foe until he ceases being vicious. To seek praise, rewards, and general approbation is the conduct of a courtier and flatterer. The philosopher is not afraid of persecution. His responsibility is to tell the truth and be useful to mankind. 'Ah, mon ami', he ends this trenchant, bitter piece. I see that your soul is mortgaged to Petersburg, Potsdam [Frederick], and 'l'œil de bœuf' [Vergennes], to the antechambers of the great and their courts. 'I do not recognize you any more.' His friend had become 'un des plus cachés, mais un des plus dangereux antiphilosophes'.[172] You live among us 'mais vous nous haïssez'.[173] Tragically, the 'Demosthenes' of our world pass away while the abject Palissots, Linguets, and Frérons, scornful of *la philosophie*, base and subservient minds of the sort scathingly portrayed in his *Neveu de Rameau*, invariably flourish.[174]

Grimm's betrayal of their friendship and principles, as Diderot saw it, ranked with his rupture with Rousseau and Le Breton's 'treason' as one of the three surpassing upsets of his life. Grimm at this point sided definitively with Catherine, Frederick, and the 'enlightened despots', and later repudiated the Revolution, while the *Histoire* roundly denounced Frederick's Prussia, Catherine's Russia, and Gustavus' Sweden, as among the most obnoxious and repressive examples of 'gouvernement despotique' even though all three genuinely belonged to the (moderate) Enlightenment. The religious tolerance prevailing at Petersburg counted for something, grants Diderot, the only group formally excluded being the Jews. But the philosopher should not be deceived by this much vaunted tolerance of the Russian capital. It might be a fine achievement were not the remainder of the Russian empire dismally sunk in 'les plus

[170] Diderot, *Lettre apologétique*, 189–90; Hulliung, *Autocritique*, 109–10.
[171] Diderot, *Lettre apologétique*, 190.   [172] Ibid. 144; Strugnell, *Diderot's Politics*, 88.
[173] Diderot, *Lettre apologétique*, 191; Duflo, 'Diderot', 130.   [174] Diderot, *Lettre apologétique*, 194.

grossières superstitions', guided by an excessively numerous clergy plunged 'dans la crapule et dans l'ignorance'.[175]

The *Histoire* portrays mankind and the world in a sombre light. Humanity is one. There are no superior or inferior peoples for the radical *encyclopédistes*. The earth should be shared by all equally. Yet everywhere humanity is plunged in degradation, superstition, ignorance, and tyranny, and responsibility for this by no means rests with autocrats and priesthood alone, nor the colonizers and their missionaries, or courtiers and court eulogists. Human misery stems equally from the *avilissement* of the people, the savage, brutal character of men's ignorance, and superstitious vener-ation for monarchy and the prestige of rank. Resentment and rebellion are natural responses to exploitation but usually lead nowhere. If in western Europe the people escaped from 'la tyrannie féodale', remarked Deleyre, they did so only to succumb to the still greater despotism of kings: 'tant le genre humain semble né pour l'escla-vage.'[176] Diderot allows no exceptions to this uniformly dismal picture. It applies in Europe, Africa, and Asia and every stage of development. Whether under the heels of their emperors and priests, or pillaged and decimated by Spaniards, it applies equally to the Aztecs and Incas. The Peruvians illustrate this 'profond abrutissement, où la tyrannie peut plonger les hommes', all the Peruvians without exception having lapsed into an 'indifférence stupide et universelle'.[177]

Only radical thought maintained that 'le genre humain entier', as Diderot, Deleyre, Pechméja, and the other collaborators in the *Histoire philosophique* put it, form a single great society 'dont les nations diverses sont les membres répandus sur la face de la terre'. All men are warmed by the same sun, subject to the same needs, and prone to the same desires, all alike seeking 'le bien-être et d'écarter la douleur'.[178] The peoples of the world were thus linked together by the same ties and interests linking each individual in any particular society to his fellow citizens. This principle of univer-sality and unity, and the idea that the community of nations is a society like any human society only on a grander scale, the radical enlighteners conceived as the foundation of all true morality, morality for them being a set of rules governing relations between social classes and international relations as well as relations be-tween individuals. If the desire for happiness is common to all men, urged Helvétius, each nation should observe the same duties and rules with regard to other peoples that social life prescribes 'à chaque individu envers les membres d'une société particulière'.[179] With this Diderot and d'Holbach were in complete agreement. Diderot and d'Holbach fully accepted that true morality is one and must be identical

---

[175] Diderot, *Œuvres complètes*, xv. 550, 553–4; [Deleyre], *Gemälde von Europa*, 36–7.
[176] Deleyre, *Tableau*, 56.
[177] *Esprit de Guillaume-Thomas Raynal*, i. 119; Imbruglia, 'Indignation', 168.
[178] D'Holbach, *Morale universelle*, ii. 2; d'Holbach, *Système social*, 41, 75–6, 82; *Histoire philosophique* (1780), x. 444–8; Condorcet, *Esquisse*, 89, 91.
[179] Helvétius, *De l'esprit*, 254, 258; d'Holbach, *Morale universelle*, ii. 2; d'Holbach, *Éthocratie*, 704–5.

'pour tous les habitants de notre globe' and should everywhere underpin the system of laws and international relations.[180]

The *Histoire philosophique*, needless to say, was held in particularly high esteem by the leaders of the Revolution, after 1789, except that is for Robespierre and his allies who disparaged this work and others like it as irreligious, atheistic, and unRousseau-ist. In January 1790, Raynal was hailed in the National Assembly as 'l'apôtre et presque le martyr de la liberté'.[181] The final irony was that when it came to the test, it emerged, in 1791, that Raynal himself did not, or at least did not any longer, endorse the revolutionary ideals of the immense text published in his name. He had been pulled along, it transpired, by Diderot, Deleyre, and the rest in a direction that ran against his own personal temperament as this evolved during the 1780s, when he slowly edged back from positions his name was inextricably tied to. After sending an open letter, in May 1791, disavowing the Revolution by which the entire assembly was dumbfounded, he was denounced as a shameless renegade by revolutionary leaders of all shades, led by Cloots.[182] Raynal, it turned out, was scarcely a *philosophe* at all and had no genuine love for freedom or emancipation; neither was he really the author of the *Histoire*.

---

[180] D'Holbach, *Système social*, 71; Diderot, *Supplément*, 178.
[181] Mortier, *Le Cœur*, 456; Tarin, *Diderot*, 42, 56.
[182] Tarin, *Diderot*, 33, 40–1; Mortier, *Anarcharsis Cloots*, 169.

16

The American Revolution

1. ENLIGHTENMENT AND THE BIRTH OF THE UNITED STATES

One of the greatest, most formative events of modern history, the American Revolution has immense intrinsic significance in itself and is one of the most closely studied of all historical events. However, its very close, intimate relationship with the international Enlightenment, though often acknowledged, has rarely been explored. The American Revolution had a complex intellectual and ideological history that needs briefly to be outlined here both for its debt to enlightened ideas and the effect that it, in turn, exercised on them. We must take account of the fact that the American Revolution from the outset acted as a vast seismic shock, inspiration, and agent of change not only in North America and continental Europe but also within Britain itself as well as Ireland, the Caribbean, Ibero-America, Canada, and South Africa.

Before 1775, the common (white) man in the American colonies was unquestionably freer, held the *Histoire* and other contemporary accounts, more independent, and more prosperous than in Europe or anywhere else. Even those beginning as common craftsmen, notes Adam Smith, mostly set themselves up as independent farmers. 'From artificer he becomes planter, and neither the large wages nor the easy subsistence which that country affords its artificers, can bribe him rather to work for other people than for himself.' As a craftsmen, he feels he is 'the servant of his customers, from whom he derives his subsistence'. But as a farmer who cleared and prepared his own land, he is 'really a master, and independent of all the world'.[1] And precisely this spirit of individual endeavour the Enlightenment was well placed to nurture into a general ideology of liberty and independence. However, in its moderate format the American Enlightenment proved less well placed to build on the tendency to equality and democracy, qualities the *Histoire* and other texts deemed no less typical of the American context.[2]

To begin with, prior to and during the political crisis of the mid 1770s, what occurred was a clash between the fiscal and mercantilist exigencies of British imperial policy and a resurgent but traditional British popular Whig political rhetoric. It was a

---

[1] Smith, *Wealth of Nations*, i. 384.   [2] Dunn, *Setting the People Free*, 80–1.

struggle that produced a flood of conflicting discourse and positions starting towards the end of the Seven Years War (1756–63) and culminating in the revolutionary conflict of the mid and later 1770s. At the origin of the American Revolution stood a batch of long-standing political and ideological tensions rooted in the contradictions between the privileges and rights of Englishmen as defined by Whig tradition and the realities of mercantile and military control exerted by the British crown, Parliament, and imperial administration (justified by both Tory and moderate Whig interpretations of the Glorious Revolution). The ideological roots predominantly shaping the revolutionary creed in America extolled the Glorious Revolution of 1688 in a particular manner, venerated both republican and contractarian English writers such as Sidney, Harrington, and Locke, and assumed that—precisely by virtue of their being 'English'—Americans already had a 'constitution'—and that the best in the world. Here were the makings of a fundamental conflict that proved irresolvable without a rupture that many viewed as a kind of civil war.

But it is important to note from the outset that neither the gentry-republican Whig nor the Lockean strands chiefly powering the Revolution offered any real objection in principle to the British crown, aristocracy, legal system, or empire as such—either in relation to the colonists themselves, or anyone else. Americans, stressed Edmund Burke, in a warning speech to Parliament in March 1775, were 'not only devoted to Liberty, but to Liberty according to English ideas, and on English principles. Abstract liberty, like other mere abstractions, is not to be found.'[3] This broadly hegemonic moderate Enlightenment ideology that so profoundly shaped revolutionary America remained essentially silent on the subjects of monarchy, aristocracy, and empire and also on basic human rights, slavery, democracy, and law reform.

The fiscal, economic, and jurisdictional disputes souring the relationship between the colonies and Britain were already acute by the late 1760s, so much so indeed that the growing tension between America and Britain was already then a major topic of international comment. Some observers were already convinced that the American colonies, as Chastellux put it, in 1772, would soon witness a 'guerre civile' between the colonists and the British metropolis.[4] As early as March 1771, Hume took an exceptionally gloomy view of the situation, speaking of 'our Union with America' as something 'which, in the nature of things, cannot long subsist'.[5] Sam Adams of Massachusetts later assured Benjamin Rush that independence from Britain had been his chief goal and 'dearest wish' already 'seven years before the war', hence from the late 1760s.[6] But independence needed justifying and a thorough new constitutional and ideological grounding, and the intellectual furore surrounding its birth was intense. Consequently, there was never a point in the history of the American

---

[3] Burke, *Pre-Revolutionary Writings*, 222.
[4] Chastellux, *De la félicité publique*, ii. 163; Sonnenscher, *Before the Deluge*, 301.
[5] Hume to W. Strahan, Edinburgh, 11 Mar. 1771, in Hume, *Letters*, ii. 237.
[6] Rush, *Autobiography*, 139.

Enlightenment and the American Revolution when their disparate moderate and Radical Enlightenment tendencies did not clash and when this split, correctly defined, was not the chief factor shaping the Revolution. Equally, there was no stage when 'America' as an Enlightenment ideal was not a deeply contested image and set of values within the wider, transatlantic Enlightenment.

Assuredly, it was the British Moderate Enlightenment, not the democratic republicanism of Paine and the *Histoire philosophique*, that for most Americans expressed the core principles of the American Revolution. Nevertheless, there had long been a radical republican tinge to political culture in the colonies, also solidly British in origin, absorbed through Bolingbroke's ideas and, most importantly, *Cato's Letters*, a famous commentary on Parliament and government in England originally published in London between 1720 and 1724, composed by John Trenchard and Thomas Gordon. The latter were veteran critics of British institutions, sometimes dubbed neo-Harringtonians. A London-based freelance author of Scots origin, Gordon was an eager researcher, historian, and self-made man of erudition as well as journalist who had known Collins and Mandeville, and was certainly an out-and-out republican subversive enough when discussing early Christian history later to attract the attention of d'Holbach. His conception of toleration and the nature of morality, like his views on earthquakes, were strikingly radical, altogether divorced from traditional thinking and religious doctrine, and steeped in Bayle.[7] Through *Cato's Letters* (1720–4) and the even more anticlerical *The Independent Whig*, large collections of articles and pamphlets attacking corruption, place jobbing, ecclesiastical influence, and other shortcomings in the British parliamentary regime, colonial America incorporated a potentially radical Whig republican tinge to its Enlightenment already many years before the onset of the Revolution.[8] This is true despite the undoubted fact that *Cato's Letters* is more of an ideological hodge-podge than is often admitted and features large tranches of Lockean contractual liberalism as well as country Whig theory.[9] *Cato's Letters*, furthermore, was material evidently as—or more—familiar to readers than Locke's writings in mid-eighteenth-century America.[10]

It is perfectly correct, therefore, to envisage the American Revolution as a reflection of the ideological split between the moderate and 'radical' Whig legacies in late seventeenth- and eighteenth-century England, the first stressing parliamentary sovereignty and the second popular sovereignty. It also marked a split between Lockean contract theory and republican leanings although in reality these more often went hand in hand, mixed together, than has sometimes been assumed. But it is vital not to suppose the kind of Radical Enlightenment ideology that shaped Gordon formed

---

[7] On Gordon I am indebted to an unpublished paper given by Giovanni Tarantino at IAS; see also Pocock, *Barbarism*, iii. 316; Bailyn, *Ideological Origins*, 35–9.

[8] May, *Enlightenment*, 38; Pocock, *Machiavellian Moment*, 467–8, 476, 507; Pocock, *Virtue, Commerce*, 240, 248; Wood, *Radicalism*, 57, 101, 103, 240; Ferguson, *American Enlightenment*, 84.

[9] Ward, *Politics*, 289.

[10] Ibid. 17, 304; Pocock, *Machiavellian Moment*, 468; Kammen, *Colonial New York*, 207.

the ideological root of the Revolution.[11] For in America, the 'radical' Whig political legacy was largely reconfigured within a wider moderate Enlightenment framework. This left the fusion of popular sovereignty with radically enlightened thought more generally a real and active presence in the Revolution but a subsidiary, fringe phenomenon.

Typical of the intellectual make-up of American mainstream Enlightenment was the *Novanglus*, a series of letters penned in 1774–5, later republished many times, by John Adams (1735–1826), a young Massachusetts lawyer and future president with strong 'classical republican' and socially and politically conservative leanings, elected to the First Continental Congress in 1774. In this tract, Adams, while disavowing any intention of seeking American Independence, glories in 'revolution principles', meaning those of 1688 which he considers 'are the principles of Aristotle and Plato, of Livy and Cicero, and Sidney, Harrington and Locke'. He insists on Americans' 'attachment to their constitution' (even though this was long before there was any written 'constitution'), arguing in line with both Locke and *Cato's Letters* that defence of this 'constitution' would justify armed rebellion against the British crown. Since 'the nature of the encroachment upon the American constitution is such as to grow every day more and more encroaching', drastic steps were needed.[12] 'If we enjoy the British constitution in greater purity and perfection than they do in England, as is really the case, whose fault', he asks, 'is this? Not ours.'[13] For Adams, as for the British moderate Enlightenment, the 'revolution' that really mattered had already occurred in 1688 but needed to be fully realized and rightly interpreted.

Adams stressed Americans' aversion 'to the late innovations' by the British Parliament, 'horror of arbitrary power and the Romish religion', and willingness to defend their 'constitution' by force of arms if necessary.[14] If Americans like himself supporting the revolutionary cause were 'rebels' and 'traitors', as the American Tories alleged, then 'the Lords and Commons', states his *Novanglus*, 'and the whole nation [of England and America], were traitors at the revolution [of 1688]'.[15] Furthermore, Parliament was not Britain. For Adams it mattered greatly that the 'people of Great Britain are not united against us'. If king, ministry, Parliament, and the army and navy sought to tyrannize, 'we are assured by thousands of letters from persons of good intelligence, by the general strain of publications in public papers, pamphlets, and magazines, and by some larger works written for posterity, that the body of the people are friends to America, and wish us success in our struggle against the claims of Parliament and administration'.[16] Ardent for the existing 'constitution', Adams was a thoroughgoing traditionalist and anti-democrat who openly disliked the radical

[11] Ward, *Politics*, 17–18, 289, 291–5.
[12] Adams, *Novanglus*, 26–34; Pocock, *Machiavellian Moment*, 531, 546.
[13] Adams, *Novanglus*, 91; Bonwick, *American Revolution*, 2–4, 134; Grant, *John Adams*, 144–5.
[14] Adams, *Novanglus*, 12.
[15] Ibid. 27; Bailyn, *Ideological Origins*, 81, 83.   [16] Adams, *Novanglus*, 29.

republicanism, democratic tendency, and Anglophobia of Tom Paine's *Common Sense*.[17]

Like the ruling British gentry who were the chief heirs to the Revolution of 1688, Adams enthusiastically embraced aristocracy and empire and tacitly endorsed slavery. Nurturing marked anti-French and anti-Dutch sentiments, neither did he at all object that Britain should impose her imperial hegemony nearly everywhere else in the world. Even the fact that Britain 'has confined all our trade to herself' posed no difficulty; indeed, he says, 'we are willing that she should, as far as it can be for the good of the empire'.[18] He opposed neither Britain's world ascendancy nor her aggressive mercantilist policy, his objection to the imperial format as it evolved in the 1760s and early 1770s being simply that Britain refused to grant the colonists enough local autonomy when it came to issues of taxation in return for their economic subordination to the metropolis. The American Enlightenment, like the Enlightenment everywhere, had its radical wing that developed very different perspectives. But the dominant mainstream viewed English institutions, political ideas, and law mostly very favourably. What was ideologically awkward for revolutionary leaders such as Adams, Franklin, and Hamilton was that while there was significant support for the American cause in Britain and Adams and the others greatly stressed this sympathy, virtually the only spokesmen willing publicly to support the Americans against royal policy (aside from Burke) were radical reformers and democrats considered outrageous dissidents and outcasts by the British mainstream Enlightenment, men who repudiated traditional and moderate notions in favour of a more sweeping, radical stance.

Among those most active in England in publicly championing the American refusal to submit to Parliament's demands was Richard Price (1723–91), most notably in his key pamphlet *Observations on the Nature of Civil Liberty* (February 1776). Price and his friend Priestley, as Adams acknowledged, were useful allies up to a point and were widely read in America.[19] But their undisguised Socinianism and democratic tendencies also presented the Revolution with a problem. His political principles, claimed Price, 'are the same with those taught by Mr Locke'; but this was patently not the case. Rather, like Diderot, Helvétius, and also Rousseau, and the *Histoire philosophique*, Price held not just that the people were sovereign when setting up the original contract, as Locke argues, or in the style of the 'radical' Whig tradition, but, further, that government is just an agency for executing the will of the people in the interest of the majority, which is something very different. Such a basis rendered representative democracy central to Price's system.[20] His stance was actually completely incompatible with Locke's principle that the people must obey those to whom they entrust government as long as the latter abide by the terms of the

[17] Bailyn, *Ideological Origins*, 288–9; Foner, *Story*, 16–18; Nash, *Unknown American Revolution*, 190, 202–3.

[18] Adams, *Novanglus*, 37.

[19] Bonwick, *American Revolution*, 53.

[20] Price, *Political Writings*, 20; Thomas, 'Introduction', 20; Dickinson, 'Friends', 14.

entrustment or contract by which authority was originally delegated. Price's stand in favour of the American Revolution was therefore not authentically rooted in the main Anglo-American political thought tradition at all and this was reflected in his unusually negative attitude towards Britain's institutions.

Far from agreeing that the British constitution was the 'perfection of government', as the vast majority in both America and Britain insisted, Price, in his pamphlet of 1776, terms Britain 'a state so sunk that the majority of its representatives [in the House of Commons] are elected by a handful of the meanest persons in it', a mere few thousand out of a population of seven million, constituting an electorate far too restricted to be in any way representative, a monstrosity enabling the crown to manipulate the legislature. On this ground he deemed the British constitution illegitimate and corrupt.[21] He agreed with the American leadership that Britain sought to tyrannize over the American colonies but took this to lengths Adams and most of the others could not condone. If many Americans in and out of Congress disliked Parliament's recent 'Quebec Act' (1775) principally because it accorded equal rights to Catholics in Canada and extended Canadian jurisdiction over large tracts between the Ohio and the Mississippi coveted by some of the American leadership, Price, Jebb, and other English radicals opposed it on far more fundamental grounds because of its imperial pretensions, and because to them it implied collusion with a small, partly ecclesiastical elite and looked like a transparent attempt to make the English king also 'a despot over all that country'.[22]

Far more to Adams's taste were Hume's sentiments. The snag was that no one of a basically conservative disposition, in Britain, was likely to agitate publicly on the Americans' behalf. Even in private, few were as inclined to the American standpoint as Hume. Defending monarchy, aristocracy, a drastically restricted electorate, as well as the absolute sovereignty of Parliament over the entire empire, Ferguson, closer to the general feeling, expressed unshakable belief in 'the undoubted right of England, to require from America some share in the taxation necessary to support the Imperial Crown and the Empire of Great Britain'.[23] 'It is certainly true', he urged, 'that no nation ever planted colonies with so liberal or so noble a hand as England has done. But she has done so on the plan of those very charters, statutes and precedents which are now to be set aside.' The colonists boasted their English legacy of constitutional freedoms. But Britain 'having done so much for her colonies', countered Ferguson, was a most unfavourable basis 'from which to infer the right of her colonies to do nothing for her'.[24]

Ferguson urged the colonies to pull back from 'civil war' and work instead for 'reunion of the Empire'. He spoke of the American 'revolt'. But Adams and other American pro-Revolution conservatives wholly repudiated such terminology. They thought in terms of legitimate, justified 'rebellion', 'open, avowed resistance by arms,

[21] Price, *Political Writings*, 25, 43.
[22] Ibid. 43; O'Shaughnessy, *Empire Divided*, 124–5; Grant, *John Adams*, 128, 140, 168.
[23] Ferguson, *Remarks*, 31–2.   [24] Ibid. 27.

against usurpation and lawless violence'. According to Adams, only 'resistance to lawful authority makes rebellion'. 'Hampden, Russell, Sidney, Somers, Holt, Tillotson, Burnet, Hoadley, etc.', he insisted, 'were no tyrants nor rebels, although some of them were in arms [against the king] and others undoubtedly excited resistance against the Tories.'[25] A college-educated lawyer, Adams knew his Grotius, Pufendorf, and Barbeyrac, but Sidney and Locke were his favourites and it was these sources that shaped his doctrine of justified resistance. A theorist who detested Paine's influence on the American Revolution for the rest of his life, he sanctioned resistance not 'by the people, the vile populace or rabble of the country' but rather by the 'greater and more judicious part of the subjects of all ranks'. Justified resistance must be led by the higher ranks and the tyranny 'must be so notorious and evidently clear, as to leave nobody any room to doubt of it'.[26]

If Adams and the Virginia planter and polymath Thomas Jefferson (1743–1826) later quarrelled over many issues of Enlightenment, revolution, and the future of America, at this stage their standpoints were less far apart, though Jefferson was already a republican deist by the early 1770s.[27] In his *A Summary View of the Rights of British America*, a tract written in the July heat of 1774 at his plantation of Monticello, and anonymously published at Williamsburg, Virginia, the 31-year-old reacted strongly against the 'many unwarrantable encroachments and usurpations, attempted to be made by the legislature of one part of the empire, upon those rights which God and the laws have given equally and independently to all'.[28] King George III should reflect that he was 'no more than the chief officer of the people, appointed by the laws', a sentiment directly recalling *Cato's Letters*.[29] Armed resistance he too justified on the ground that there was evidently a 'systematical plan of reducing us to slavery'. As he saw it, the Revolution's legitimacy turned on those 'sacred and sovereign rights of punishment [of tyrannical kings] reserved in the hands of the people' exercised in 1688 and on the fact that 'our ancestors, before their emigration to America, were the free inhabitants of the British dominions in Europe', that is of England, Scotland, and Ireland, and that 'no circumstance has occurred to distinguish materially the British from the Saxon emigration [to America]'.[30]

Britain remained for most Americans, even those angriest about recent clashes of interest between Parliament and the colonists, pre-eminently the land of liberty, modernity, true religion, science, and enlightenment. But if Jefferson at this stage was just one among many claiming king and Parliament were acting tyrannically, that Parliament's claims were misjudged and the king the 'only mediatory power between the several states of the British empire',[31] a genuinely radical undercurrent was also

[25] Adams, *Novanglus*, 38; Grant, *John Adams*, 65, 67.
[26] Adams, *Novanglus*, 64–6; Nash, *Unknown American Revolution*, 424–5; Ward, *Politics*, 386, 410.
[27] Luebke, 'Origins', 344–5; Jayne, *Jefferson's Declaration*, 19.
[28] Jefferson, *A Summary View*, 5.
[29] Ibid. 5; Pocock, *Virtue, Commerce*, 84; Ward, *Politics*, 295–301.
[30] Jefferson, *A Summary View*, 6–8.   [31] Ibid. 16; Ward, *Politics*, 352.

present in America, particularly in Philadelphia. This alternative perspective found its most vigorous expression, we have seen, in what was certainly the most widely read, reprinted, and discussed of all the pamphlets of the American Revolution— Tom Paine's *Common Sense, Addressed to the Inhabitants of America*, composed in discussion with, and with the strong encouragement of, Benjamin Rush who also suggested the title and helped find a printer, a Scotsman, willing to print it, anonymously, in the spring of 1776.[32]

Tom Paine (1737–1809), who originally arrived in America late in 1774, observed, during his first months in Pennsylvania, that while most people thoroughly detested the ministry in London they continued to revere England as such. Their grievances 'operated without resentment, and their single object was reconciliation'.[33] Shocked by news of the 'battle' of Lexington, in April 1775, in Massachusetts, when British troops opened fire, killing some local militiamen, Paine began to suspect that resolving the conflict peacefully was unlikelier than he had at first supposed. During 1775, at Philadelphia, he became acquainted with several brilliant, well-read, politically aware young intellectuals such as Rush, and David Rittenhouse, scientist, democrat, and early enthusiast for a complete break, men who had both already made up their minds that war with Britain was unavoidable. He soon concluded that in confronting the foes of colonial liberties, violent resistance was the only way to compel this 'unprincipled enemy' to 'reason and moderation'.[34] But by publicly adopting this stance, already in the autumn of 1775, Paine, like Rush and Rittenhouse, placed themselves out on a limb, holding a distinctly firmer position than most other Americans were yet prepared to countenance.

Over the winter of 1775–6, most hesitated to declare for full independence and, later, when they finally took the plunge, did so with deeply divided feelings. Benjamin Franklin, in Europe then and long afterwards much the most famous American Enlightenment figure, found himself in England in the mid 1770s representing Congress, and as such proved far more conservative socially and politically than is usually admitted.[35] Reluctant to countenance a resort to arms, he 'took every method in his power', as Priestley who knew him well at that time later recalled, 'to prevent a rupture between the two countries'. Indeed, 'he urged so much the doctrine of forbearance, that for some time he was unpopular with the Americans on that account, as too much a friend of Great Britain'.[36] His view shifted dramatically, though, from late 1775, on hearing the terms in which the colonists were being denounced in Parliament.[37] Undoubtedly, there were many instances of moderates privately preferring not to have to choose between the British crown and the revolutionary Congress.

---

[32] Nelson, *Thomas Paine*, 79–80; Foner, *Tom Paine*, 74, 84.
[33] Paine, *Common Sense*, 39, 45; Keane, *Tom Paine*, 100.
[34] Keane, *Tom Paine*, 103; Foner, *Tom Paine*, 71–95.
[35] Walters, *Benjamin Franklin*, 107.
[36] Priestley, *Autobiography*, 116–17; Wood, *Americanization*, 123, 155.
[37] Wood, *Americanization*, 149–51.

Common Sense has been described as a 'radical masterpiece' and justifiably so.[38] The pamphlet, published in January 1776, engineered a decisive shift in sentiment. It passed through no less than seven editions in Philadelphia alone that year as well as others at Newport, Salem, Hartford, Lancaster, New York, Albany, and Providence and five printings in London, besides further editions at Edinburgh, Newcastle, and elsewhere. Paine himself later estimated that 'not short of 150,000' copies were sold in America.[39] *Common Sense* also rapidly became known in France and Holland, emerging as the best-known manifesto of the Revolution in Europe and America alike. What better illustration could there be, commented the *Histoire philosophique*, when opinion is divided, and different factions compete, with much of the public doubtful and irresolute, of the power of 'philosophy' to clarify matters and take the lead?[40]

According to a contemporary historian of the Revolution, William Gordon, Paine's pamphlet, impressive in style, manner, and language, was indeed superbly timed: it 'produced most astonishing effects' and was 'received with vast applause; read by almost every American; and recommended as a work' replete with truth.[41] Given the angry mood among much of the colonial public at the time it was generally read approvingly. Most Americans, observes Raynal's *Revolution of America*, had previously restricted themselves to opposing the British ministry within limits authorized by existing constitutional and legal procedures. Only after reading Paine's text could those seriously contemplating a bid for independence by force of arms, now led, according to the *Histoire*, by Hancock, Franklin, and the two Adamses, speak out freely, without reservation.[42] However, Paine's uncompromising republicanism and unprecedented forthrightness in denouncing British institutions and law, as well as British policy, Parliament, and crown, antagonized as well as swayed Americans. John Adams was far from being alone in disliking its radical tone. John Witherspoon (1723–94), the philosopher of Princeton and leader of the Scots Common Sense tendency in America, president and chief preacher of the College of New Jersey (today Princeton University), and one of the signatories to the Declaration of Independence, was another on the worst terms, both intellectually and personally, with Paine.[43]

Witherspoon did more than anyone to place moral philosophy high in the curriculum in the American colleges in the late eighteenth century. His *Lectures on Moral Philosophy*, the first widely known work of American philosophy, though not published until 1800, was penned in the late 1760s and early 1770s and began circulating as lecture notes at that time, introducing students to a programme of reading drawn especially, but not only, from the British mainstream Enlightenment.

---

[38] Ibid. 119–20; Rush, *Autobiography*, 114–15; May, *Enlightenment*, 162.
[39] Keane, *Tom Paine*, 109–10; Nash, *Unknown American Revolution*, 189.
[40] *Histoire philosophique* (1780), ix. 289–99.
[41] Gordon, *History*, ii. 275.
[42] Raynal, *Revolution of America*, 79–90.
[43] Foner, *Tom Paine*, 120–3; Ward, *Politics*, 386; Page, *John Jebb*, 179.

Acutely conscious of the troubled relationship of faith and reason arising from the study of Locke, Berkeley, deism, and Hume's atheistic scepticism (which he regularly attacked), on the one hand, and the danger of 'infidelity' and atheism, on the other, Witherspoon espoused the Scottish Common Sense movement as the best solution. Besides Hume, Collins, Leibniz's *Theodicy,* Wollaston's *Religion of Nature Delineated,* and Clarke's *Demonstration,* his course comprised Reid's *Inquiry,* Hutcheson, and Smith's *Theory of Moral Sentiments.*[44] At the same time, his lectures afforded students some grasp of the primary rift dividing the European thought as the two great classics of Clarke and Leibniz used by Witherspoon in his teaching are both chiefly directed against Spinoza (and in the latter case also Bayle).

So starkly divergent was Paine's viewpoint from the 'revolution principles' of most of the revolutionary leadership that *Common Sense* became deeply embattled on the revolutionary almost as much as on the Tory side. That Paine 'remains difficult to fit into any kind of category' familiar in eighteenth-century Britain and America has been rightly and strongly stressed, Paine having 'no real place', as one leading scholar has put it, 'in the club of Honest Whigs to which Franklin had introduced him in London'.[45] Little is known for certain about the intellectual sources of Paine's Radical Enlightenment universalism. He claimed never to have read Locke and, certainly, never resembles Locke in tone. However, it is definitely incorrect to say that '*Common Sense* does not consistently echo any established radical vocabulary'.[46] Paine's *Age of Reason* (1793–4), the work that later announced his rejection of Christianity and destroyed his reputation among most Americans, labelling him an 'atheist' in the eyes of society, is explicitly and heavily indebted to Spinoza;[47] and while there is no indication that he read Spinoza much before that late stage in his career, he was certainly familiar with other radical sources when he composed *Common Sense.* Such hints as *Common Sense* itself provides suggest that by the mid 1770s he knew a little Rousseau and Voltaire, was much impressed with 'Raynal', and also knew Priestley's *Essay on the First Principles of Government* (1768).[48]

Interestingly, among his proven sources at this stage was the *Trattato delle virtue e de' premi* (1765) of Giacinto Dragonetti (1738–1818), a 'wise observer on governments', Paine styles him, who, like Beccaria and Gorani, was a direct disciple of Helvétius. Dragonetti's treatise, we have seen, appeared in a bilingual, strongly republican version, in English and Italian, in 1769.[49] Dragonetti, like Filangieri and Gorani, was an anti-feudal, anti-aristocratic ideologue who was also anti-Rousseauist in his fervent enthusiasm for philosophy and science. Dragonetti's text expresses the

[44] Witherspoon, *Lectures,* 11, 24–6; Sloan, *Scottish Enlightenment,* 130, 133; May, *Enlightenment,* 63.

[45] Pocock, *Virtue, Commerce,* 276.

[46] Ibid.

[47] Robbins, 'Lifelong Education', 140–1.

[48] Paine, *Common Sense,* 54; Paine, *The American Crisis,* 1 to 3, 4; Keane, *Tom Paine,* 133; Carpanetto and Ricuperati, *Italy,* 257; Wootton, 'Republican Tradition', 36–9.

[49] Dragonetti, *Treatise on Virtues,* preface; Paine, *Political Writings,* 28; Robbins, 'Lifelong Education', 139; Wootton, 'Republican Tradition', 36–7.

same fierce complaints about improper distribution of posts, rewards, and wealth in society typical also of Helvétius and Paine.[50] But if Dragonetti was one source, Paine's uncompromising tone suggests that it was especially the *Histoire philosophique* that his revolutionary, universalist style of argument echoes. Since Priestley, like Dragonetti, likewise derived the radical utilitarian core of his argument partly from Beccaria (who borrowed his principles, we have seen, chiefly from Helvétius), it would seem Paine's uncompromising radicalism was not part of the Anglo-American 'commonwealth' and classical republican legacy at all (though it may owe something to Sidney) but rather a strand of a Radical Enlightenment which, as has been stated, 'sets him clearly in the Spinozist republican camp', albeit with roots in his case lying initially in the Franco-Italian sphere and only later directly in Spinoza's thought.[51]

In any case, what distinguishes Paine's discourse from that of mainstream American revolutionary ideology is its appeal to universal values and total refusal to invoke English tradition, precedents, and history. Indeed, the pamphlet launches into an even fiercer denunciation of the British constitution and empire, as well as of Parliament and the crown, than Price's, sweepingly rejecting all monarchy (like the English translation of Dragonetti), while brimming with republican and democratic fervour.[52] As Pocock notes, '*Common Sense* breathes an extraordinary hatred of English governing institutions.'[53] Claiming, in sharp contrast to Adams, that the Revolution was not local in character but something 'universal, through which the principles of all Lovers of Mankind are affected', Paine held that 'the cause of America is in a great measure the cause of all mankind', a claim paralleling Diderot's contention that the cause of the rebels, as it is put in the 1780 edition of the *Histoire*, is 'celle du genre humain tout entier'. Whatever his precise relationship to the *Histoire* in its English versions, Paine indubitably struck a note and appealed to principles dramatically different from those infusing the tracts of Adams, Jefferson, and the revolutionary leadership.[54]

'The so much boasted constitution of England' and the cult of 'balance of powers' surrounding it, concedes Paine, might once have been 'noble for the dark and slavish times in which it was erected' when the 'world was overrun with tyranny'. But in the centuries since, it had become highly 'imperfect, subject to convulsions, and incapable of producing what it seems to promise', namely 'freedom and security', the true aim and purpose of government. 'I know it is difficult to get over local or long standing prejudices', argues Paine, 'yet, if we will suffer ourselves to examine the component parts of the English constitution, we shall find them to be the base remains of two ancient tyrannies, compounded with some new republican materials.'[55]

[50] Wootton, 'Republican Tradition', 38; Dragonetti, *Treatise on Virtues*, 33, 39, 40–1; Robbins, 'Lifelong Education', 35.   [51] Wootton, 'Helvétius', 326–8; Ward, *Politics*, 391–2.
[52] Dragonetti, *Treatise on Virtues*, 179; Paine, *Common Sense*, 10–14; Taylor, 'Down with the Crown', 53.   [53] Pocock, *Virtue, Commerce*, 276; Ward, *Politics*, 383–4.
[54] Dragonetti, *Treatise on Virtues*, 2; *Histoire philosophique* (1780), ix. 374–5; May, *Enlightenment*, 162; Ferguson, *American Enlightenment*, 117; Nash, 'International Repercussions', 2; Page, *John Jebb*, 178.
[55] Paine, *Common Sense*, 10; Bailyn, *Ideological Origins*, 285–6; Ward, *Politics*, 176–7, 384–5.

These two lingering strands of 'ancient tyranny' were monarchy and 'the remains of aristocratical tyranny in the persons of the peers'. The unrelenting, almost universal 'prejudice of Englishmen, in favour of their own government by king, lords, and commons', he argues much like the *Histoire*, 'arises as much, or more, from national pride than reason'.[56]

Not content with this, Paine urges the impossibility of coming to just conclusions about the theories of others 'while we continue under the influence of some leading partiality', and the pressing need for further 'inquiry into the constitutional errors in the English form of government'. Veneration for the British constitution is just sheer ignorance. Nor could Americans taking up arms for their independence do justice 'to ourselves while we remain fettered by an obstinate prejudice. And as a man who is attached to a prostitute, is unfitted to chuse or judge of a wife, so any prepossession in favour of a rotten constitution of government will disable us from discerning a good one.' Unlike Adams, Paine roundly denied that the British empire and mercantilist trading system was either justified or good for anyone. Far better would be an open commerce with all countries. Here again are arguments strikingly reminiscent of Raynal, Diderot, Helvétius, Dragonetti, and later Filangieri. Such a plan, he argues, 'will secure us the peace and friendship of all Europe; because it is the interest of all Europe to have America as a free port'.[57]

With such arguments Paine offended many as he did also by claiming 'Europe, and not England, is the parent country of America,'[58] challenging even the 'warmest advocate for reconciliation to shew a single advantage, that this continent can reap, by being connected with Great Britain'.[59] Broaching many issues at the very heart of the split between Radical and moderate Enlightenment in Europe and America, he did not hesitate to 'reprobate the phrase of parent or mother country, applied to England only, as being false, selfish, narrow and ungenerous'.[60] Reminding readers that the first New England settlers had been fleeing Stuart despotism, he added: 'this new world hath been the asylum for the persecuted lovers of civil and religious liberty from every part of Europe.'[61] Men emigrated to America, fleeing not the 'tender embraces of the mother, but from the cruelty of the monster', that is monarchy, aristocracy, empire, British law, and national prejudice. Less than one-third of the population of the colonies, held Paine, 'are of English descent'.

Achieving independence and eliminating monarchy, aristocracy, and empire from the American scene was something that should go hand in hand, in Paine's view, with requisite changes to her domestic practices and procedures. 'Let the assemblies be annual', he urged, 'with a president only.' 'Representation' should become 'more equal' and all the colonies should elect their representatives in the same way, dividing their territory into electoral 'districts', each to 'send a proper number of delegates to

---

[56] Paine, *Common Sense*, 14; Keane, *Tom Paine*, 114–16; Nelson, *Thomas Paine*, 84–6.
[57] Paine, *Common Sense*, 37.
[58] Ibid. 34.   [59] Ibid. 37; Nelson, *Thomas Paine*, 87; Foner, *Tom Paine*, 75–7.
[60] Paine, *Common Sense*, 36.   [61] Ibid. 34–5.

Congress; so that each colony send at least thirty. The whole number in Congress will be at least 390.'[62] In short, he concludes, quoting Dragonetti—or constructing a quote from phrases drawn from him (though the sentiment itself stems from Helvétius), the 'science of the politician consists of fixing the true point of happiness and freedom'; the goal being 'a mode of government that contained the greatest sum of individual happiness, with the least national expense'.[63]

Those relatively few Americans who in the immediate post-revolutionary era expressed unbounded enthusiasm for Paine, among them the Connecticut-born Eliahu Palmer (1764–1806), leader of the American Illuminati who designated Paine 'one of the first and best of writers and probably the most useful man that ever existed upon the face of the earth', invariably embraced Radical Enlightenment unreservedly and were steeped in French *philosophie moderne*. Like Paine, 'Volney and Condorcet, Godwin and Barlow,' wrote Palmer, 'are justly entitled to the universal gratitude and applause of the human race; they have attacked error in its strong holds—they have pursued it with a powerful and discriminating intellect. It has already lost half of its force, and the philosophy that is denominated infidel, will ere long chase it out of existence. It is this philosophy that has developed the laws of the physical world, and exhibited the principles on which its systematic order depends—it is this philosophy that has unfolded the moral energies of human nature, which has become the object of calumny in the estimation of a cruel and persecuting superstition.'[64]

Assailing monarchy and the British empire, and calling for sovereignty of the people, Paine's pamphlet was fiercely denounced by anti-independence loyalists, like the Tory assistant rector of Trinity Anglican Church in New York, Charles Inglis, author of an anonymous reply, *The True Interest of America Impartially Stated*. Paine's tract Inglis styled 'an outrageous insult on the common sense of Americans, an insidious attempt to poison their minds, and seduce them from their loyalty and truest interest. Even Hobbes would blush to own the author for a disciple.' No one could doubt its author was an 'avowed, violent republican, utterly averse and unfriendly to the English constitution'.[65] Denounced as a 'rebel' by the Tories, Paine retorted early in 1777 'that the republic of letters is more ancient than monarchy, and of far higher character in the world than the vassal court of Britain. Only he that rebels against reason is a real rebel; who rebels against "tyranny" in defense of reason, has a better title to Defender of the Faith than George the Third.'[66] 'Britain, as a nation', he wrote in January 1777, 'is in my inmost belief the greatest and most ungrateful offender against God on the face of the whole earth: blessed with all the commerce she could wish for, and furnished by a vast extension of dominion with the means of civilizing both the eastern and western world, she has made no other use of both than proudly to idolize her own "Thunder" and rip up the bowels of

---

[62] Ibid. 51.   [63] Ibid. 54; Dragonetti, *Treatise on Virtues*, 17, 31, 33, 89.
[64] Palmer, *Principles*, 158.   [65] [Inglis], *True Interest of America*, p. vii.
[66] Paine, *The American Crisis*, pp. i–iii, 9.

whole countries for what she could get.' Britain, rather like Alexander the Great, he claimed, 'has made war her sport' and inflicted vast misery: 'the blood of India is not yet repaid, nor the wretchedness of Africa yet requited.'[67]

This was not the first time Paine invoked the further Indies in the American context. An article by him entitled 'A Serious Thought', in *The Pennsylvania Journal; and the Weekly Advertizer*, of 18 October 1775, not only referred to 'independence' and detaching America from Britain which very few Americans had thus far ventured to propose openly, but goes so far as to draw parallels between England's tyrannizing over the whites and murder of the native Americans in Canada and the American colonies and the 'horrid cruelties exercised by Britain in the East Indies', together with her despoiling the 'hapless shores of Africa, robbing it of its unoffending inhabitants to cultivate her stolen dominions in the West'.[68] The piece was obviously chiefly inspired by the *Histoire* and introduced a style of revolutionary rhetoric never heard before that American mainstream Enlightenment was never prepared to countenance in any way. *Common Sense* was something new and exciting in the American context of 1776 because it propagated outright radical sentiments that even a year before could hardly have been articulated with impunity, the expression of which in the colonies had suddenly become possible due to the wide rift opening up between the colonists and the crown. The real revolution of 1776, then, as Paine himself affirmed,[69] was an intellectual shift that preceded the *Declaration of Independence* though not by much and which cannot be understood without reference to Paine, the *Histoire philosophique*, and radical thought.

Only a few months after Paine's pamphlet appeared, and in its direct wake, Jefferson was commissioned by Congress to write the *Declaration of Independence* (1776). Although today there is still a remarkable degree of disagreement among scholars as to what the real intellectual theoretical hub was around which Jefferson's thinking evolved, even a mere glance at the *Declaration* suffices to show that the long-standing argument in American historiography about whether the text of the *Declaration* was primarily 'Lockean' or 'classical republican' is scarcely relevant. For while both Locke and 'classical republicanism' featured in Jefferson's prior reading, thinking, and conclusions, the spirit of his ideas and this text, and insistence that Britain's monarchy and Parliament had no claims over the American colonists at all and that it is only to secure men's 'unalienable Rights' to 'Life, Liberty and the pursuit of Happiness' that governments are instituted among men, is neither Lockean nor classical republican. Rather, the radical dimension is the key to Jefferson's thinking, the intellectual sources of the *Declaration* deriving, recent research suggests, from the early eighteenth-century republican writers like Bolingbroke and Gordon with perhaps a touch of Paine.[70] Later, as his thought developed, Jefferson shared the criticism of the French radical writers of Montesquieu whose *Esprit des loix* he

---

[67] Paine, *The American Crisis*, 17.   [68] Ibid. 16–18.   [69] Foner, *Story*, 16.
[70] Ward, *Politics*, 350, 398, 401; Albertone, 'Thomas Jefferson', 124–5.

came to see as 'emblematic' of exaltation of Britain 'in opposition to the American model'.[71]

Jefferson, when he commenced his studies at William and Mary College, in Virginia, in 1760, had encountered the Scottish professor William Small (1734–75) from whose conversation, he records, 'I got my first views of the expansion of science and of the system of things in which we are placed.'[72] What Jefferson acquired from Small was a trend of thinking that led him among other authors to Bolingbroke; and what he drew from him was not just a set of ideas incompatible with biblical religion and the idea of revelation but incompatible also with notions of divine providence diverging from the universal laws of nature. The exact extent to which Bolingbroke drew his outright rejection of miracles and theory of 'imposture' and priestcraft as well as his ideas about Bible, religion, and the relationship of politics to religion directly from Spinoza—and his questioning of the justice of the biblical God, from Bayle—rather than Toland and Collins, remains open to dispute. What is incontestable is that his system was broadly 'Spinozistic' in the eighteenth-century sense, not Lockean. The same applies to Bolingbroke's doctrine of the equal status of all men and peoples before 'Nature's God'.[73]

The Declaration of 4 July 1776 makes no mention of precedents or any contract, or charters, and departs wholly from hitherto hegemonic rhetoric of the special rights of Englishmen. This text had to be broadly acceptable and accommodating. Nevertheless, proclaiming all peoples to have an 'equal station', given to them by the 'laws of Nature and Nature's God', and that 'all men are created equal', offered concepts more broadly in line with radical than moderate Enlightenment principles. Jefferson admired Paine, and the strands of radical republicanism and egalitarianism in his thought were probably indebted to him as well as Gordon and Bolingbroke.[74] The Jeffersonian doctrine of fundamental equality, that all men are created equal by nature, crucial to the argument of the *Declaration*, from 1776 was fundamental to the Revolution. But it also served as a basic contradiction within the Revolution. Indeed, Jefferson, a Virginia planter and slave-owner—owning over a hundred slaves at the time he wrote the Declaration[75]—mirrored more than any other leading figure of the American Revolution the underlying tension between radical and 'moderate' principles within the Revolution.

The great political debate about liberty, constitution, and order that took place between 1763 and 1789 in America, in its more theoretical moments, was a debate about the nature of man and the best kind of society and, from this, the best political constitution. As such, it marked the culmination of the American Enlightenment and, simultaneously, a widening of the rift between the Enlightenment's moderate and radical tendencies. In three major respects—the steady growth of slavery, mainly in the south but to an extent also in New York, Pennsylvania, and in the state of New Jersey (where the number of slaves roughly doubled between 1770 and 1800), the

[71] Ibid. 133. [72] Jayne, *Jefferson's Declaration*, 19. [73] Ibid. 37–8, 40.
[74] Ibid. 21. [75] Foner, *Story*, 32–3.

marginal status accorded to the Indians, and the tendency toward religious and social segregation (and political neutralism) of the Quakers, Mennonites, Moravian Brethren—American social structure could be said to be have become actually more rather than less variegated and hierarchical than that of Britain.

From first to last the public debate focused on political rather than social issues. The leading figures in this debate—Franklin, John Adams, Madison, Jay, Hamilton, Dickinson, Jefferson, and Patrick Henry—were men of great experience and, often, considerable intellectual stature. The lawyer James Madison (1751–1836), another eloquent product of the Virginia gentry class later known as the 'Father of the Constitution', was by 1787 wholly convinced that the Americans had 'accomplished a revolution which has no parallel in the annals of human society'.[76] Having studied at Witherspoon's Princeton, he had become an outspoken opponent of ecclesiastical power and sectarian thinking, intent on ensuring a full toleration, while personally espousing a simplified, rationalized Christianity and, rather unusually, like Jefferson, was something of an intellectual Francophile. Frail in health but studious, he read widely in French, including Bayle, Leibniz, Voltaire, and even Diderot who was very little read (apart from unwittingly, in the *Histoire philosophique*) in Enlightenment America.

Madison, much interested in the history of republics, was partly indebted to Mably's *Observations sur les Grecs* (1749) for his idea that 'popular government' in small states is less 'tempestuous' when integrated into the authority and laws of a large confederacy.[77] He also liked Mably's argument that an indispensable stabilizing and energizing role in the otherwise allegedly anarchic Dutch Republic had been played by the stadholderate.[78] Some of Madison's ideas about the need 'to break and control the violence of faction', methods for countering factiousness, and the advantages of large republics, were doubtless indebted to Hume's political essays and history of Britain as well as the theories of Montesquieu and Mably.[79] Alexander Hamilton (1755–1804), by contrast, was born in the West Indies but trained in law at King's College, in New York. He proved a gifted officer in the revolutionary army and rose to the rank of colonel and eventually aide-de-camp to Washington. A leading critic of the Articles of Confederation, he early on urged the need for a strong federal government and, in 1787, served as one of the three delegates from New York to the Constitutional Convention in Philadelphia.

A convinced sceptic concerning philosophical reason, impressed by Hume, Hamilton followed Hume and Montesquieu in his suspicion of democracy and pessimistic view of human nature as well as of prospects for establishing a stable republic without a strong personal executive.[80] 'A dangerous ambition more often lurks behind the specious mask of zeal for the rights of the people', admonished Hamilton, in his first Federalist paper, dated 27 October 1787, 'than under the

---

[76] Hamilton, Madison, and Jay, *The Federalist*, 64.　　[77] Ibid. 82–3.　　[78] Ibid. 92.
[79] Ibid. 211–12, 214, 235–40.　　[80] Pocock, *Virtue, Commerce*, 140.

forbidding appearance of zeal for the firmness and efficacy of government.' The former, it seemed clear to him, 'has been found a much more certain road to the introduction of despotism, than the latter' while 'those men who have overturned the liberties of republics the greatest number have begun their career, by paying an obsequious court to the people, commencing demagogues and ending tyrants'.[81]

With its strong presidency and senatorial upper chamber representing states rather than voters, the American constitution has been aptly termed 'perhaps the greatest monument of the Moderate Enlightenment' in any country, and also the last,[82] though in time it proved more capable of being combined with democratic principles than originally seemed to be the case. In the 1790s, most onlookers, in any case, were mainly struck by its undemocratic features, the strong presidency being applauded by numerous enthusiasts for British constitutional practice and tradition as entirely in the spirit of Hume. The pro-British Irish Catholic propagandist Theobald McKenna, in a pamphlet published at Dublin in 1793, went so far as to claim that the new American constitution 'labours to palliate, what it cannot remedy, the mischiefs of democracy. So closely have the legislators of the new World adhered to the British system, that the omission of the king's name in public acts, is the only difference discernible. The American president, whilst in office is a limited monarch; the American senate, a temporary peerage.'[83]

Locke and Montesquieu were the political theorists the Founding Fathers—and their opponents—most often invoked, and while they also cast a sideways glance at the Dutch States General and Venice, republics esteemed by the Founding Fathers for retaining a formal aristocratic dominance of politics and the judiciary, the British constitution always remained their chief point of reference. Indeed, there were still a few prominent figures among them, such as the conservative Delaware delegate John Dickinson (1732–1808), who would have preferred a limited monarchy to the presidential system finally agreed upon. A strong presidency was conceived as a surrogate for the monarchy still regarded by many as a peculiar and indispensable strength of the British constitution. Generally in America, the new constitution was widely lauded as a way of institutionalizing the combination of monarchy, aristocracy, and democracy deemed the secret of Britain's greatness while retaining (a necessary compromise if South Carolina and Georgia were to ratify) the principle of slavery along with mechanisms for separating the branches of state power—executive, legislature, and judiciary—along the lines recommended by Montesquieu (strongly seconded by Jefferson).

Not all the Founding Fathers were equally pleased with the result. Thomas Jefferson, 'who was certainly a man of the Enlightenment', it has been aptly said, 'sometimes Moderate but sometimes Radical', was not in Philadelphia when the text was finalized, in 1787, but in Paris. When he studied the new constitution, he had

---

[81] Hamilton, Madison, and Jay, *The Federalist*, 3.
[82] May, *Enlightenment*, 100; Pocock, *Barbarism*, ii. 220–1.
[83] McKenna, *An Essay on Parliamentary Reform*, 37.

serious doubts, worrying in particular about what he thought might be the dangerous degree of power assigned to the powerful new president. But he acquiesced.
Madison did much to win him round.

2. COUNTER-ENLIGHTENMENT AND MODERNITY

Denominational differences had some bearing on the evolution of the American
Revolution considered as a set of attitudes and values, but only marginally. Just as
many Episcopalians and Quakers supported Britain in the coming trial of strength
'from a dread of the power of the country being transferred into the hands of the
Presbyterians', as Rush put it, so many of the latter, often of Scots background, were
eager 'Whig' supporters of the Revolution, being keen to engineer precisely such a
shift in the balance between the rival church blocs. Other denominational minorities
were also opposed to Anglican pretensions and tradition and, according to Rush, 'so
were the Jews in all the States'.[84] Patterns of allegiance also varied somewhat according to local conditions. In Virginia, possibly the most united as well as culturally
most Anglophile colony, most of the landowning gentry and their dependants,
including the Anglican clergy, first adopted a strongly Whig rhetoric of defiance
and then moved to support the Revolution. In South Carolina, the only socio-
economic division that decisively shaped politics was between established 'low-
country' coastal districts, politically dominated by gentry planters, on one side,
and recently arrived backcountry farmers, on the other, a deep and bitter enough
rift but one more likely to deter than encourage rebellion against the metropolis.

The Middle Colonies were more divided religiously, ethnically, and culturally as
well as socially than much of the South; but only in Pennsylvania did men divide
along lines that can to some extent be explained in socio-economic terms and also
religious alignments.[85] In New York, a colony well to the fore in protesting against
British policies, there were various bitter internecine class and community divisions,
so much so that New York was also the last and among the most hesitant of the
colonies actually to vote for independence, though the majority supported the war
against Britain resolutely enough after 1776.[86] Although proportions varied from
area to area, the Tory presence was considerable in all Thirteen Colonies. The
political rift and ensuing ejection of the Tories undoubtedly involved a major social
and cultural shift in one sense. In proportion to total population the number of Tory
loyalists removed or marginalized for refusing to repudiate the British crown was in
fact huge, in the Middle Colonies especially. Some Tories became Nicodemites,

[84] Rush, *Autobiography*, 117–19.
[85] Brunhouse, *Counter-Revolution*, 75–7, 89–90; Nadelhaft, *Disorders*, 8–14.
[86] Kammen, *Colonial New York*, 337–8.

withdrawing into local isolation, others departed voluntarily to Britain, Canada, or the Caribbean, others were imprisoned, killed, or forcibly expelled.

However, none of this was in any meaningful sense class-based or religiously or culturally structural. By and large, the vacuum left by the *émigrés* who fled was filled not by new and up-and-coming social strata, or newly arrived immigrants, or ethnic or religious minorities previously lower down the social scale, but by the same sort of people, sharing the same general outlook (aside from fleeing Anglican high-flyers) as those filling the revolutionary assemblies and officering the revolutionary armies.[87] As there were no specific social or religious groups that either supported or opposed the tendencies that culminated in the Revolution, such major large-scale social displacement and substitution in offices that the Revolution entailed possesses little explanatory significance in terms of social strata or religious affiliation. This was a great advantage in forging a new society on the basis of Enlightenment aims and values. Many scholars have noted that the Revolution produced in America a wider acceptance of the idea that men of different backgrounds could live together in harmony on the basis of equality and striving for the common good. What have been less explored are the politically, socially, and culturally extremely divisive and contested reverberations of this embracing of Enlightenment and the prolonged and bitter clashes arising from rival ideologies generated within the bosom of the American Revolution.

Adam Smith was doubtless right to assert that there was more equality 'among the English colonists than among the inhabitants of the mother country. Their manners are more republican, and their governments, those of three of the provinces of New England in particular, have hitherto been more republican too.'[88] The middle strata of society in America tended to be more mobile and fluid socially, culturally, and religiously than equivalent sections of the population in Europe. With about two-thirds of the adult male population able to read at some level, and a much higher proportion in New England, literacy levels surpassed those in Britain and possibly even those in Holland, the highest in Europe. But complex social hierarchies were still the rule and with their rapidly growing white population, growing underclass of slaves, increasing presence of usually chronically impoverished free blacks, the large German minority in Pennsylvania, and the Amerindian fringe, it was also obvious that the American colonies had by the time of the Revolution become a land of considerably greater ethnic and cultural diversity than Britain.

All this was to prove a substantial problem for American society in the revolutionary era. While the Indians and blacks were not acknowledged as fully human or entitled to have their rights recognized, America did still serve as a model Enlightenment society in certain respects. America abundantly proved that people of different extractions could live side by side in relative concord and harmony, by integrating different European religious and ethnic groups. In the state of New York,

---

[87] May, *Enlightenment*, 179; May, *Divided Heart*, 150–9.   [88] Smith, *Wealth of Nations*, ii. 166.

observed Paine, in 1790, 'about half' of the population were Dutch and the rest a mixture of English, Irish, and Scottish; in New Jersey again one found 'a mixture of English and Dutch, with some Scottish and Irish', while in Pennsylvania where fully one third of the population were German, the English amounted to no more than another third.[89] All the colonies featured considerable numbers of Irish and Scots with several having smaller but widely scattered communities of Huguenots and Jews. Like Raynal and Diderot, his intellectual forerunners, Paine rejoiced in this fast progressing ethnic-cultural transformation.

But in the eyes of radical writers, as we see from the burgeoning critique of the American Revolution in the 1780s, it quickly ceased to serve as anything like a fully exemplary case, being judged insufficiently inclusive, tolerant, democratic, or egalitarian.

Colonial society, including that of Virginia, the Carolinas, and the Caribbean, was doubtless more fluid than society in Britain and Ireland, and, at least in New England and the Middle Colonies, less aristocratic and sensitive to gradations in rank. Formal aristocracy was much weaker than in England or Scotland and so was established, state-supported ecclesiastical power. Locke's system for the Carolinas failed to survive beyond the early eighteenth century, and the principle of legally endowed aristocracy and an exclusively aristocratic 'upper house' in the colony's assembly lapsed after a certain point. Yet, entail laws restricting certain lands to particular families did take root in the south and remained in force in Virginia until these were abolished (with strong support from Jefferson) in the late eighteenth century.[90]

More importantly, informal gentry and a commitment to the principle of social hierarchy undoubtedly remained strong throughout the colonies. Adam Smith rightly insisted on this point. 'In none of the English colonies [in America] is there any hereditary nobility.'[91] Yet in all of them 'as in all other free countries, the descendant of an old colony family is more respected than an upstart of equal merit and fortune; but he is only more respected, and he has no privileges by which he can be troublesome to his neighbours.'[92] What survived and by no means only in the southern colonies was the idea of social hierarchy dominated by an elite envisaged as a solid gentry set by status and education above the mundane concerns of ordinary trade and manufacture.[93] For most of the American gentry, lawyers, officers, and upper-class contractors and professionals who took the lead in the American Revolution, free, enlightened, and limited government was and should continue to be based on the gentry-based parliamentary monarchy embodied in the British constitution, a supposedly age-old tradition originating with the Anglo-Saxons, mortally threatened by Stuart tyranny in the 1630s and again in the 1680s, and then, with the aid of divine providence, triumphantly restored and consolidated by the Glorious Revolution of 1688–91.

---

[89] Paine, *Rights of Man*, 166 n. [90] *A Philosophical and Political History*, i. 208–9.
[91] Smith, *Wealth of Nations*, ii. 165. [92] Ibid. ii. 165–6. [93] Wood, *Radicalism*, 28, 37, 157.

Precisely because there was barely any true aristocracy of lineage and breeding, the newly wealthy plutocracy of trade and the southern plantations were able to exploit the prevalent culture of 'distinction', 'pre-eminence', and 'dependency', and the political opportunities offered by the colonial legislatures, to create new forms of gentry and bestow fresh gradations of privilege and rank, bringing to the fore merchant and agrarian elites which, however lacking in polished credentials in Old World terms, commanded good prospects of dominating public life to a considerable degree in the New World. In the main, people of standing and wealth married each other and controlled the state assemblies, in New York, Pennsylvania, and New England no less than in Maryland, Virginia, and the Carolinas. Under Maryland's new constitution, some 70 per cent of white male property-owners were entitled to vote but only around 20 per cent were qualified to sit in the state legislature.[94]

Although his deism was highly untypical, Franklin, by far the best-known representative of the American Enlightenment in Britain and Europe, was emblematic of this dominant new political and social elite culture. A lifelong Lockean who rejected Christian belief whilst reading Shaftesbury and Collins as a young man, in the 1720s, he had long been a convinced deist (or atheist). But since the early 1730s he had ceased discussing issues of religion and morality except in private, out of discretion, and simply refused to discuss deism publicly. It is true that he continued propagating deism behind the scenes. 'It is much to be lamented', recalled Priestley, who had long and spirited discussions with Franklin, in London in 1775–6, 'that a man of Dr. Franklin's general good character, and great influence, should have been an unbeliever in Christianity, and also have done so much as he did to make others unbelievers.'[95] But for the evolution of the American mainstream Enlightenment, the distinction between Christianity and deism per se is of less importance than that, obvious from the contrast between Franklin and Jefferson (who developed into a very different kind of politician and reformer), between Humean deism and a potentially more egalitarian radical deism.

Renowned for his strong preference for scientific and intellectual activity with a strictly practical bent, Franklin strove to ameliorate the world by applying the results of experiment and experience on the basis of a scepticism of a strongly Humean kind. Like Hume, he was sceptical of the power of reason to transform the world, and even more than Hume, judged belief in and adherence to accepted religious notions essential for society and upholding the moral order; consequently, he was usually hesitant about the emancipatory, democratic tendency within the Revolution.[96] Not believing that reason can serve as the chief prop in human life, or establish the basic rules of morality, Franklin supported affiliation with the Anglican Church as part of a wider strategy of commitment to tradition and established religion, deeming this necessary for the social and moral regulation of men. Also like Hume, he feared the

---

[94] Bonwick, *American Revolution*, 131–2. [95] Priestley, *Autobiography*, 117.
[96] Pocock, *Barbarism*, ii. 226; Walters, *Benjamin Franklin*, 33, 86–7, 125.

disorder and demagoguery associated with the Wilkes and Liberty movement in England.

Although by 1770 he had moved to an antislavery standpoint, Franklin failed to free the several slaves he owned himself. In fact, he championed the ideal of a leisured and propertied gentry class (of which he was proud to have become a member) closely associated with Anglican and Newtonian conceptions of social order. Combined with Locke's philosophy, this mix of social conservatism and Newtonianism shaped a Moderate Enlightenment mainstream bloc that represented the strongest force among the elites of American society and those above a certain educational level.[97] It dominated in the colleges, among the Virginia gentry and the social elites more widely. The Enlightenment maturing in mid- and late eighteenth-century North America, then, was predominantly a Lockean-Newtonian construct formed within a religious culture, characterized by an unparalleled plurality of churches espousing a certain conception of toleration and insisting on 'balance' and 'moderation' as basic principles. It was a moderate Enlightenment predicated on the idea of the ultimate oneness of science and religion, the fusion of monarchism and republicanism, and a balance of tradition and reform. But it was a thought world of a somewhat parochial kind uncompromisingly Anglo-Scottish in tone, reading matter, and intellectual orientation. While educated colonials could often read French and authors like Pascal and Bayle were by no means unknown, the impact of French thought in pre-revolutionary America remained largely marginal except for Montesquieu and the *Histoire philosophique* in English.

Meanwhile, in the American colonies, as in Germany, Scandinavia, the Netherlands, and Britain, the main rival and critic of the Moderate Enlightenment as far as most people were concerned was not radical thought but an unyielding Counter-Enlightenment burgeoning up in America in two varieties—emotional evangelicism and conservative ultra-Protestantism. This challenge, especially powerful among the less educated, was based on a mixture of theological authoritarianism and biblical fundamentalism. Surging first among the German sects and the Dutch Reformed, the Great Awakening became a powerful force within American Presbyterianism, dogmatic, simplistic, and appealing especially to the barely literate. The early and mid-eighteenth-century Awakening clashed fundamentally with both mainstream and Radical Enlightenment. Above all, it was a form of reaction to what seemed to many the complacency of the long preoccupation with reason, balance, and compromise characterizing the Newtonian Enlightenment.[98] Through the 1740s and 1750s, moderate enlightened attitudes in all the colonies had been powerfully assailed by a wave of vehement religious zeal, New Light revivalism and anti-intellectualism especially attracting recently displaced and poor churchgoers. It was a movement comprehensively denying reason is or could be a leading guide in human life. Men are rightly guided, it insisted, only by the Bible, conscience, and religious authority.

---

[97] Walters, *Benjamin Franklin*, 125–6, 141, 145; Wood, *Radicalism*, 85–6, 119; Nash, *Unknown American Revolution*, 123, 156; Stewart, *Opinion*, 305.   [98] Stewart, *Opinion*, 44–5.

By the 1750s the Awakening had divided, though not weakened, American Prot-estantism and profoundly altered the relationship of the Enlightenment to American Society. All the leading pre-Revolution revivalists, Jonathan Edwards, George White-field, William Tennent, and his son Gilbert, who led the fiery New Jersey revival, put the burning inner faith of the individual, and assertive piety, above erudition or reason, insisting on divine sovereignty and judgement and stressing human depend-ence, in place of the balance, order, and regularity of the Newtonians.[99] Disciples of Locke, Tillotson, and Clarke, moderate enlighteners believed that order and ration-ality are as integral as faith to a godly world and that the revivalists' constant fomenting of internecine church quarrels, and denunciations of fornication, adul-tery, and gambling as well as of non-revivalist clergy, were divisive and apt to get out of hand.[100] The revivalists were of course even more negatively viewed by the deists and *indifferenti*.

As in Britain and elsewhere, the fervent revivalism characteristic of the Great Awakening gained considerable popular support but was socially intensely conser-vative and hostile to intellectual innovations aspiring to reconfigure social and moral institutions and practices. If Wesley was adamantly opposed to the Socinian radicalism of Priestley and Price, the same is true of his American counterparts. Jonathan Edwards (1703–58), the most learned of the revivalists, evinced a suspi-cious, antagonistic attitude towards Enlightenment deism, Newtonianism, and secu-larizing notions of history, and, linked to this, a mostly indifferent or neutral attitude towards slavery, science, economic reorganization, secular education, and politics.[101] Like French Jansenism, the Great Awakening was a deeply rooted parallel cultural movement with historical origins reaching far back into the past. Fiercely critical of the Anglican and 'Old' Presbyterian establishment, it surged up especially through Presbyterian, Congregationalist, and Baptist channels reaching as far south as Virginia and the Carolinas. In Massachusetts and Connecticut there were also a category of clergy, labelled the 'Old Calvinists', who consistently opposed both the Arminian rationalists of Boston and the New Divinity men inspired by the New Light, seeing the latter as rebels against the discipline, tradition, and sobriety of genuine Calvinism.

3. PRINCETON, HARVARD, YALE, AND COLUMBIA

Since the early eighteenth century, theology at Harvard and Yale had been thoroughly saturated and supplemented by the thought of Locke and Newton. The New Light, the Revolution, and the undercurrents of deism and radical ideas were the four great

[99] May, *Enlightenment*, 50–2; Kuklick, *History*, 13–15; Lambert, *Founding Fathers*, 138–5.
[100] May, *Enlightenment*, 55–60.
[101] Zakai, *Jonathan Edwards' Philosophy of History*, 215, 220, 223; Marsden, *Jonathan Edwards*, 256–8.

challenges galvanizing theology, philosophy, and debate generally, unsettling the relaxed Lockean-Newtonian ethos at the American higher education colleges during the later Enlightenment. These challenges turned these institutions into the key arena in North America for the playing out of the Enlightenment drama. The most crucial changes from the 1770s were the countering of the New Light, drastic weakening of the Anglican dimension (primarily in New York and Philadelphia), the rise of Unitarianism, and the perceived threat of 'infidelity'—deism, materialism, and radical ideas. Talk about the penetration of deism and atheism in the colleges, including William and Mary College, at Williamsburg, where many of the Virginia gentry studied and where the professor who set Jefferson on the road to radical deism, William Small (trained at Aberdeen), began teaching natural philosophy in 1758, reached back long before 1750 but significantly grew in intensity after the Revolution.[102] This important and partly hidden current, so crucial in the lives of Franklin and Jefferson, often originated in reading Collins and Bolingbroke, and about them, in the College libraries and professors' collections.

Until 1775, Anglicanism was a growing dimension in the colleges. Among the most interesting figures of the American Enlightenment, and one of the main spokesmen of British-style Moderate Enlightenment in America, was William Smith (1727–1803), yet another Scottish educationalist but in his case Episcopalian and much influenced by Tillotson. A declared foe of sectarianism, intolerance, and religious polemics he was no friend either of Presbyterians or Quakers. An educational reformer with 'modern' ideas, as some said, he retained a strong sense of social hierarchy and the naturalness of aristocracy. Appointed to head the Philadelphia academy under Anglican leadership, through Franklin's intervention, he formed it into an important centre of higher education under Anglican ascendancy, his recommended reading, predictably highlighting Bacon, Locke, Hutcheson, and Newtonian physico-theologians like Ray.[103] Exceptionally accommodating theologically, he typified the insistence on the cultural and political superiority of Britain so typical also of Franklin before 1775, always emphasizing the superiority of 'British liberty', laws, and institutions in his speeches and tracts.

Fiercely anti-French and like Franklin and most of the American gentry class strongly supporting Britain's imperial expansion during the Seven Years War, he helped establish schools to teach Pennsylvania Germans (of whom, like Franklin, he had a rather low opinion) the superior advantages of British government, traditions, and theology and the English language.[104] Judging by his oration to the American Philosophical Society, in 1773, Smith envisaged Britain's empire as a harmonious entity rightly destined to dominate the world and bring 'law and happiness' on the basis of the principles of 1688 to all the Americas, meaning French-speaking Canada and other captured French dependencies besides the English colonies.[105]

---

[102] Walters, *Benjamin Franklin*, 22–3, 40; Jayne, *Jefferson's Declaration*, 19–22.
[103] May, *Enlightenment*, 83.
[104] Frost, *Perfect Freedom*, 37.　　　　[105] Ibid. 49–50; Rhoden, 'William Smith', 63.

Together with Franklin, he took the lead in establishing what became the foremost American society for the promotion of natural science and philosophy, in 1766, reviving Franklin's earlier efforts to establish a Philadelphia philosophical society. A partly Quaker group, more interested in practical improvements than intellectual endeavour, had established a body which Smith successfully merged, in 1768, with the Philadelphia-based American Society for Promoting and Propagating Useful Knowledge. The latter was famous above all for its library which, though open to the public only one day a week, was warmly praised by the *Histoire philosophique* as the best in the New World and quite exceptional for its collection of scientific instruments and natural history museum.[106] The resulting American Philosophical Society backed now by a more Anglican and upper-class group of patrons, and the colony's governor and assembly, commenced under Franklin's presidency. Among other exploits that rapidly became known in Europe, the society, guided by one of Smith's and Franklin's ablest protégés, Rittenhouse, concerting with scientists in England, helped track the transit of the planet Venus across the sun, in 1769, an empire-wide scientific collaborative project intended to fix the distance and size of both bodies.

But Anglicanism was loyalist and the Revolution tended to blight the Anglican-dominated colleges, those of Philadelphia and New York. Smith opposed the Stamp Act and rejected the traditional Anglican high-flying doctrine of non-resistance. But he was also energetic in writing to England pleading for moderation and reconciliation.[107] From 1776 onwards, his lack of sympathy for the Revolution became sufficiently obvious that on the approach of General Howe, he was arrested together with other Tory suspects and removed from his position as head of the College in Philadelphia, and from his pulpit, for the duration of the war. In 1779, the Pennsylvania assembly revoked the college's charter, dismissed Smith, and reconstituted the college with a board consisting of a mixture of Presbyterian, Lutheran, Baptist, and other trustees.[108] From that point on, Smith was a partially discredited figure, living most of the 1780s in a rural area of Maryland.

Another from 1775 philosophically and theologically besieged seat of learning was the newly established King's College (the future Columbia University), in New York, an institution whose title along with some of its lecturers migrated during the Revolution, to Halifax, in Nova Scotia. King's College became a fiercely contested arena particularly after Samuel Johnson, another royalist and devotee of social hierarchy as well as New York's leading Anglican and one of the few enthusiasts for Berkeley's philosophy in America,[109] became first president, in 1753. Originally intended as the American colonies' Anglican reply to Princeton, Harvard, and Yale (all predominantly Presbyterian and Calvinist), King's College developed into a working compromise between Anglicanism and Calvinism through being governed

---

[106] [Petit], *Observations*, 64–9, 75; *Histoire philosophique* (1780), ix. 41.
[107] Frost, *Perfect Freedom*, 49–50, 57; Rhoden, 'William Smith', 69–70.
[108] Frost, *Perfect Freedom*, 66.   [109] May, *Enlightenment*, 78–80.

by a mixed board of Anglicans and Presbyterians albeit with an Anglican president. Johnson, remaining president there until 1763, presided over what remained, until it was disrupted in 1776, a very small and not particularly flourishing but notably tolerant, theologically eclectic, philosophically engaged, and socially conservative educational project showing marked affinities with the type of non-sectarian, moderate Enlightened Christianity entrenched at the College of Philadelphia.

More important centres for propagating enlightened ideas in the eighteenth century, as well as arenas for pursuing the quarrel between New Light and establishment enlightened Christianity, were the other higher education colleges. If the Arminians won the battle at Harvard, and Old Calvinists gained a precarious hegemony at Yale, at Princeton it was for a time the adherents of the New Light who were in the ascendant.[110] The College of New Jersey, later Princeton University, had come under the control of ardent admirers of Edwards, intent on reshaping American Presbyterianism to reflect his priorities and agenda. Located midway between Philadelphia and New York, this college for a time exerted a remarkable cultural influence opposing most aspects of the Enlightenment, especially in the Middle Colonies and Virginia and via Virginia throughout the south, eventually becoming the parent of numerous seminaries in Kentucky and Tennessee. The emphasis shifted to solidly moderate Enlightenment, though, from the late 1760s after the trustees turned to Scotland for a new president.

Seeking someone able to reconcile in some measure Princeton's warring New Light and Old Light theological factions, they appointed Witherspoon, formerly a stalwart champion of the popular Calvinist (anti-Enlightenment) wing of the Church of Scotland. Originally expected to combat the New Divinity men at Princeton more in the style of the New England 'Old Calvinists', urging not reason but Calvinist orthodoxy, discipline, and sober morality as the essence of religion, Witherspoon, who had latterly become a man of the Enlightenment, in fact introduced the Scots Common Sense school of philosophy with tact but great vigour and acumen. This outcome was partly the doing of Rush, a former student of the college now studying medicine in Scotland, whom the trustees had consulted and who, perhaps largely unknown to them, had also lately discarded the attitudes he had held previously, and adopted Enlightenment views and 'republican principles'.[111]

At Princeton, Witherspoon quickly ousted the admirers of Edwards from their former dominance. Since the early eighteenth century, Princeton, Harvard, Yale, like the colleges in New York and Philadelphia, were not just centres of intense Protestant theological debate but also motors for the propagation of Newtonian natural philosophy, Lockean epistemology, and now, after Witherspoon's arrival, Scots 'Common Sense'. Mid-eighteenth-century Harvard College has been aptly described as a 'post-Calvinist adaptation of the Moderate English Enlightenment'.[112] That

---

[110] May, *Enlightenment*, 61; Kuklick, *History*, 39, 47.
[111] Rush, *Autobiography*, 50–1, 109, 115.   [112] Ibid. 58.

college's discreet accommodation of liberal theological tendencies from the 1740s onwards sheltered the rise of a strong Arminian-Unitarian tendency which by the 1790s came near to establishing a local dominance.[113] This was the world, in the late 1750s, where the young John Adams absorbed his Locke and Newton and learnt to become theologically anti-Calvinist and rather neutral. Though subject to vehement criticism from conservative Calvinists who considered Harvard especially but to an extent all these institutions too lax in doctrine and discipline as well as from 'New Light' revivalists who strongly suspected their academic learning and philosophy hampered true piety, the colleges held their own as increasingly confident centres of Moderate Enlightenment in a strongly Protestant mode. In this respect, their activities were powerfully seconded by the reading societies, clubs, and bookshops of Boston and especially Philadelphia which by the 1760s had become the wealthiest, most flourishing, intellectually liveliest, best equipped with new crafts and machines, and most book-oriented city in the Americas.

Yale, at this time the largest of the colleges, remained the most solidly Calvinist on the surface where a ceaseless battle between old-style theology and Moderate Enlightenment loomed much larger than strife between moderate and radical tendencies. Ezra Stiles, president of Yale from 1777 to 1795, was an 'enlightened' Calvinist and ardent supporter of the Revolution who believed that higher education had an important role to play in making the Revolution succeed and in elevating American political culture to a higher level. Not unconnected with this, he counted as the foremost harmonizer and reconciler of not just Enlightenment and traditional religion in New England but also of the Enlightenment's moderate and radical tendencies (to the extent he found this possible).[114] He had read most of the French Enlightenment classics and, not unlike Franklin whom he greatly admired, had been drawn in his youth to deism. Later he reverted emphatically to religion, became a minister at Newport Rhode Island, and opposed deism, Anglicanism, and New Light zealous emotionalism all with equal vigour. Unlike most Connecticut ministers, he was also a declared democrat and much interested in comparative religion as well as generally unusually broad-minded. He remained an ardent supporter of the French Revolution from 1789 down to his death in 1795.

A far less accommodating presence at Yale, and bitter rival of Stiles, was the New Divinity theologian Timothy Dwight (1752–1817), a grandson of Edwards and Stiles's successor as president. Dwight shared Stiles's antipathy to atheism, deism, and French materialism, but unlike him, from early on, also strongly opposed democracy and the French Revolution, classifying all sympathizers with that revolution and, indeed, with Jeffersonian ideals as 'infidels'.[115] Dwight and his followers continually urged the primacy of theology and firmly repudiated enlightened ideas of all kinds, making no distinction between conservative deists and revolutionary

---

[113] Kuklick, *History*, 50; Grant, *John Adams*, 24, 34, 37.
[114] May, *Enlightenment*, 185–6; Nash, 'American Clergy', 395; Wood, *Radicalism*, 190, 251.
[115] Morgan, 'Ezra Stiles', 117.

materialists. In 1788, he anonymously published *The Triumph of Infidelity: A Poem* in which Satan recounts his successes and recruitment of disciples across the world, a text that has been called 'the first major American anti-deist work'.[116] The poem is ironically dedicated to Voltaire who, 'with a diligence and uniformity which would have adorned the most virtuous pursuits', obstinately 'opposed truth, religion, and their authors, with sophistry, contempt and obloquy; and taught, as far as [his] example or sentiments extended their influence, that the chief end of man was to slander his God and abuse him forever'.[117] Much of the poem focuses on Satan's older English recruits, flaying Hume as well as Satan's 'Tolands, Tindals, Collinses and Chubbs, Morgans and Woolstons, names of lighter worth'. But he also lambastes such contemporaries as 'pertest Priestley' who 'calls mankind, to see his own corruptions of Christianity'.[118] By the 1790s, Unitarianism was regarded as a new major threat at Yale, Harvard, and Princeton alike.

Another strand of the radical challenge in America, though, was to be found among a tiny handful in the colleges who proved susceptible to French materialism. The most notable American graduate in this group before 1789 was a future friend and close ally of Paine, the Connecticut-born Yale graduate and well-known poet Joel Barlow. In several writings and addresses of the late 1780s, Barlow expressed his view that society can be moulded and remade by ideas and that the 'present is an age of philosophy; and America, the empire of reason', terminology already unmistakably redolent of radical thought. In 1788 he left for Paris and during 1790–2 was in England where he formed a close relationship with Paine, Price, Godwin, and Wollstonecraft. He became an ardent supporter of the French Revolution but one who was little influenced by Rousseau. A hard-core radical and ally of Volney, he preferred the materialism of d'Holbach and Helvétius.[119]

The seepage of radical ideas into mainstream society in America, in any case, was, we have seen, nothing new. Rather it had all along provoked a widespread reaction in the American colleges and societies and among most of the veteran leaders of the American Revolution a certain edging towards the 'right' in ideological terms that expressed an acute awareness already prior to 1776 of the links between Christian moderate Enlightenment and social hierarchy, on the one hand, and radical tendencies and egalitarian social goals on the other. Social realities rendered this an inevitable situation and, after 1776, increasingly so.

4. UNDEMOCRATIC STATES

As in all revolutionary contexts, deep rifts had soon convulsed American politics and society. At Philadelphia, the dominant clique were irreconcilably split from the

---

[116] May, *Enlightenment*, 190.   [117] Dwight, *Triumph of Infidelity*, dedication p. iii.
[118] Ibid. 16, 18–19, 21.   [119] May, *Enlightenment*, 191, 239–42; St Clair, *The Godwins*, 159, 529.

outset. Early in 1776, Pennsylvania's assembly was still dominated by an alliance of moderate Tories and Whigs backed by loyalist Quakers, the Anglican establishment, and the locally important Swiss-German-Alsatian Mennonites and Moravian Brethren. Against this coalition were ranged the farmers of the colony's West together with the mostly disenfranchised Presbyterian lower class of the capital led by a remarkable group of locally nurtured artisan scientists, educators, and popular philosophers including Paine, Rush, Owen Biddle, Thomas Young, an Irish physician who was a militant deist, and the Presbyterian astronomer Rittenhouse who had read and commented on the manuscript of *Common Sense* prior to its publication, a declared foe of 'luxury' as well as tyranny.[120] The coup in the Pennsylvania assembly of 1776 occurred because supporters of Independence, alarmed by the Pennsylvania assembly's dragging its feet and persisting in hoping for reconciliation with the British crown long after the fighting began, resolved on drastic measures to change the assembly's policy.

It was the introduction into Congress of a resolution calling for each colony to adopt measures equal to the exigencies of the emergency, ironically by an avowed advocate of gentry oligarchy and opponent of democracy, John Adams, that provided the pretext and occasion for the Pennsylvania radicals opposing the Anglican–Quaker hegemony to engineer their coup. It was a local upset in which Paine actively participated on behalf of the anti-elite, anti-ecclesiastical, and democratic cause.[121] This unexpected upset in a key colony's politics led to the establishment of the famous supposedly democratic constitution of Pennsylvania of 1776 so admired by Diderot and Raynal's team, and vehemently denounced by Adams in his political writings. Endorsed by Paine—and much more hesitantly by Rush who afterwards turned against it and by Benjamin Franklin (1706–90) whose half-hearted backing sufficed to earn him Adams's permanent hostility[122]—the new Pennsylvania constitution was for several years the chief focus of American revolutionary democratic republicanism. Mably examined it closely and worried that it was too democratic for a society that he thought lacked the austere moral standards needed to make true democracy work. He agreed, though, that from a strictly theoretical standpoint, considering only human dignity and the common rights all men have from nature, Pennsylvania's constitution surpassed all the others.[123] All the other revised state constitutions retained power in the hands of the traditional elites.

In none of the colonies in 1776–7 were the new and in some cases extensively revised state constitutions submitted to the people for ratification.[124] Only the Pennsylvania revolutionary assembly removed property qualifications for voters, discarding most of the previous corpus of religious discrimination (notably tests for office-holders debarring Catholics and Jews), replacing these with a taxpaying

[120] May, *Enlightenment*, 123, 213, 245; Foner, *Tom Paine*, 109, 115–17.
[121] Foner, *Tom Paine*, 109, 116–17; Brunhouse, *Counter-Revolution*, 14–18, 80–1.
[122] Grant, *John Adams*, 234–5; Frost, *Perfect Freedom*, 65, 80.
[123] Mably, *Collection*, viii. 366–71, 385–6.   [124] Nadelhaft, *Disorders*, 34.

qualification which enfranchised practically the whole of the state's free male adult population barring only a few paupers and servants (as well as free blacks and slaves).[125] It was a change that brought reality distinctly closer to the glowing image of *Pennsylvania* presented in the *Histoire philosophique*,[126] but one that still left some considerable way to go, especially (but not only) through its failure to address the question of slavery.

A few idealistic Americans and those many European readers whose image of the American Revolution was shaped primarily by the *Histoire*—and subsequent radical commentators on America such as Millar, Brissot, and Volney—viewed the American Revolution as seriously defective in certain respects, its most flagrant shortcoming being its failure to address slavery. An impressive start had been made to generating an emancipationist, anti-slavery movement in America; but this had no direct connection with the Revolution and, still less, with the Lockean and classical republican roots of American mainstream Enlightenment. It was more than slightly ironic that the first major proponent of black emancipation, and ending slavery, in America, Anthony Benezet (1713–84), a Philadelphia Quaker schoolmaster and social critic, was of Huguenot background, born in France, at Saint-Quentin, who not only combined Quakerism with a broad Enlightenment culture, studying books—not least about Africa and black history—in German and Dutch as well as French and English, but was also one of the initiators of Quaker efforts to aid the French refugees driven out of Nova Scotia by the Anglo-American forces during the Seven Years War whose tragic plight was so graphically publicized by the *Histoire*. More ironic still, Benezet was one of those who opposed the Revolution and persisted indefatigably publishing anti-war pamphlets during the Revolution.[127]

The Quakers, of course, had a long tradition of incipient egalitarianism and philanthropy. Yet, even Quaker commitment to the abolition of black slavery, and especially their forming local associations in Pennsylvania and attempting to influence their neighbours against slavery, had been a remarkably late development— John Woolman's first major attack on slavery appeared only in 1754—far in the wake of the first Enlightenment attacks on the principle of slavery.[128] This does not mean of course, that religious inspiration had little to do with the—from the 1770s—growing Quaker commitment to abolishing slavery. Plainly, it did. But it is not correct to maintain, as many still do, that the Quaker conscience as such initiated the anti-slavery campaign. Rather the spread of enlightened ideas, including the religious Enlightenment, nurtured bold initiators, Benezet and Woolman principally, who prompted and nudged the Quakers and later other Christians into belatedly re-examining their consciences and their attitudes toward the blacks and slavery. American moderate Enlightenment, meanwhile, remained predominantly

[125] Foner, *Story*, 18; Wood, *Americanization*, 165–6; Frost, *Perfect Freedom*, 63–5.
[126] *Histoire philosophique* (1780), i. 16, 24, 28–30, 88.
[127] Jackson, 'Anthony Benezet', 9–10, 14; Thomas, *Slave Trade*, 470–1; Bonwick, *American Revolution*, 168.   [128] Davis, *Problem of Slavery*, 213–15.

indifferent to this issue (even among the Quakers) just as it was also silent with respect to general legal reform and the principle of democracy.

The slow-moving campaign against slavery begun in Pennsylvania and other northern states where slavery's economic role had always been marginal made only inconclusive, halting steps. A languid process in the north, especially in New Jersey and New York where substantial numbers of slaves were to be found, no move at all was made to end slavery from Maryland southwards. With Quaker help, the Pennsylvania assembly did pass an anti-slavery law in March 1780 but, owing to considerable opposition and hesitation, failed to free Pennsylvania's 6,000 black slaves outright (at the time New Jersey had some 10,000 slaves), or fix a time-frame for eventual outright abolition, or even stipulate emancipation from the age of 21 as an earlier draft had proposed; the new law stipulated only that children of slaves (many of whose owners were Presbyterian or Dutch Reformed Calvinists) would be declared free on reaching the age of 28, an age unlikely to be reached by many or most.[129]

Wekhrlin, writing in 1784, agreed that humanity's 'great project' of freeing the blacks was now thankfully at last under way, congratulating the Pennsylvania Quakers for initiating a process he hoped to see spread throughout the world. In emancipating the black peoples from oppression, it was 'philosophy' that was doing the main work, he—like Chastellux and others—stressed, adding that Christianity was greatly at fault for countenancing slavery over so many centuries and still, in most parts, serving to block emancipation.[130] Condorcet, writing in 1781, and Chastellux, Clavière and Brissot in 1787, fully expected that with the Revolution and the continued progress of Enlightenment in the New World as in the Old, the stain of black slavery would not long continue to sully the 'purity of American laws'. The Marquis de Chastellux, d'Holbach's and Diderot's friend, a writer fascinated by America who fought in the revolutionary war as an officer in the French forces, was convinced of the inevitability of prompt emancipation.[131] Price, while accepting that the 'emancipation of the Negroes must, I suppose, be left in some measure to be the effect of time and of manners', likewise held that 'nothing can excuse the United States if it is not done with as much speed, and at the same time with as much effect, as their particular circumstances and situation will allow'.[132] Much praise is due, averred Brissot, 'to the spirit of equity and liberty which inspired the Pennsylvania Assembly with the humanitarian principles expressed during the debates preceding the enactment' of the law of 1780 which permanently abolished slavery in principle, requiring slave-owners to register their slaves, acknowledging the rights of young slaves to be protected from despotic masters, and that 'declared the children of slaves free at the age of twenty-eight.'[133]

[129] Nash, *Unknown American Revolution*, 325; Bonwick, *American Revolution*, 169.
[130] Wekhrlin, *Graue Ungeheuer*, 1 (1784), 250–2, 255.
[131] Condorcet, *Réflexions sur l'esclavage*, 249; Chastellux, *Discours sur les avantages*, 54–8, 90–1; Clavière and Brissot, *De la France*, 324.
[132] Price, *Observations*, 83–4; Foner, *Story*, 32; Nash, 'International Repercussions', 6.
[133] Keane, *Tom Paine*, 196; Nash and Soderland, *Freedom*, 103.

Yet the limited character of the Pennsylvania statute due to compromises necessary to get the bill through gravely disappointed serious abolitionists. Paine had hoped at least for abolition from 21 and a statutory limit, rejected in the event, within which complete abolition would be declared. 'Why did this respectable assembly not go further? Why, for example, did it not grant freedom, or at least the hope of freedom, to Negroes who were slaves at the time of the enactment' of the 1780 law?' It seemed thoroughly unsatisfactory to radical *philosophes* that the child of a 'Negro slave in Pennsylvania', as Brissot put it, 'can hope to enjoy liberty some day and his master cannot withhold it from him when he has worked for him till the age of twenty-eight, yet the unhappy father of this child is forever deprived of his freedom'.[134] The only legal justification offered was that slaves were property and property is something sacred. To add insult to injury, the 1780 law stipulated that 'a slave may not bear witness against a free man'.

As far as fighting slavery and instituting education for blacks was concerned, Benezet had shown the way. 'What author, what great man, will ever be followed to his grave', wrote Brissot, commenting on Benezet's funeral, in 1784, 'by four hundred negroes, snatched by his own assiduity, his own generosity, from ignorance, wretchedness and slavery?'[135] But the fact remained that anti-slavery was not integral to or inherent in the American Revolution. After failure to oppose slavery, the next worst defect still disfiguring Pennsylvania, contended Raynal, Diderot, Brissot, Volney, and the other European radical critics of the Revolution, was the residually repressive religious legislation, depriving atheists of civil rights and involving the legal obligation for every person above 17 years of age to enrol under one religious communion or another, a measure reportedly designed to exclude deists and non-observant agnostics as well as atheists. 'Un déiste pouvoit-il se soumettre à cette condition?'[136] Clearly not. Office-holders, furthermore, had to acknowledge the divine inspiration of the Old and New Testaments, a stipulation expressly devised to exclude Jews and Muslims beside deists and atheists.[137] Those voted in as the state's legislators had to declare belief in 'one God, the Creator and Governour of the universe, the rewarder of the good and punisher of the wicked', and acknowledge Scripture 'to be given by divine inspiration'. Later in 1793, Paine deplored also the restrictive Sunday legislation instituted in Pennsylvania, as in the other states, to underpin Christian assumptions enlightened individuals might not share, a further unjustified infringement, as he saw it, of the state on individual liberty.[138]

Still, guaranteeing full freedom of worship, enfranchising Jews and Socinians, and not expressly excluding anyone from the electorate on grounds of belief, the new Pennsylvania constitution was a remarkable landmark. Supported by many of the

---

[134] Nash and Soderland, *Freedom*, 111; Brissot, *New Travels*, 229.
[135] Quoted in Jackson, 'Anthony Benezet', 13.
[136] *Histoire philosophique* (1780), ix. 89; Frost, *Perfect Freedom*, 65.
[137] Frost, *Perfect Freedom*, 74–5; Brunhouse, *Counter-Revolution*, 14–18, 78–9; Rush, *Autobiography*, 130, 148–9.   [138] Rush, *Autobiography*, 83; Paine, *Age of Reason*.

local Scots, Irish, and German immigrants, it provided for a single chamber legislature, executive administration by committee, annual elections, and popular election of militia officers. Other state institutions were refashioned accordingly. In 1779, the new state government reformed the College at Philadelphia, a known hotbed of Anglicanism and Toryism, turning it into a Presbyterian-dominated, republican-minded state university of Pennsylvania. To adherents of moderate Enlightenment, like the university's former rector, William Smith, such changes were dangerous innovations, unBritish and anti-Anglican, being explicitly egalitarian, contradicting Montesquieu by failing to provide for division of powers, and checks and balances, and in abrogating Pennsylvania's religious and educational traditions. However, Pennsylvania's democratic constitution remained a unique experiment, an isolated and precarious phenomenon in the newly born United States more generally, and one marred in the eyes of Paine, Rush, and other radicals by its dependence on an uncompromising Presbyterian intolerance that in 1778 extended to measures forbidding the production of grain-based whiskeys and other alcoholic beverages.

Yet for all that Pennsylvania remained a model. The state was more prosperous (for whites) than most of the rest of America and indeed the world, a place where poverty, Chastellux noted, had been virtually eliminated (for whites), standing in this respect in sharp contrast to Virginia and the other southern states and territories.[139] Why was Pennsylvania prosperous? Precisely because the state's much-vaunted religious toleration, averred the *Histoire*, drew in a wider mixture of faiths and nations—Dutch, Swedes, French, and Germans—than other states.[140] Glowingly eulogized by the 1770 edition of the *Histoire*, and afterwards by Helvétius, Pennsylvania was mankind's foremost haven of religious peace and tolerance, a place where traditional constraints had supposedly lapsed and slaves were on the verge of being emancipated.[141] 'In Pennsylvania', '(one of the happiest countries under heaven before we [the British] carried into it desolation and carnage)', averred Price, in 1778, 'all sects of Christians have been always perfectly on level, the legislature taking no part with one sect against others, but protecting all equally as far as they are peaceable.'[142] Deism though not rife was entrenched. Nearly every white man was independent and young persons were allegedly free to marry without parental interference.

In Radical Enlightenment mythology, Pennsylvania represented the ultimate model of freedom of conscience, simplicity, virtue, and equality, a topos, indeed a veritable 'Americanist' creed, strongly challenged from the outset, however, by moderate as well as fundamentalist critics protesting that the picture was utterly uncritical, utopian, deceptive, and false.[143] In Pennsylvania, Quakers, Presbyterians, Lutherans, Mennonites, and others had deeper roots than the Anglicans. But rapid

---

[139] *Histoire philosophique* (1780), x. 30; Nash, *Unknown American Revolution*, 387–8.
[140] *Histoire philosophique* (1780), ix. 24.
[141] Ibid. ix. 30–41; [Petit], *Observations*, 75–8; Helvétius, *De l'homme*, i. 135–6.
[142] Price, *Political Writings*, 18.
[143] Ansart, 'From Voltaire to Raynal', 76; Foner, *Tom Paine*, 235–6.

immigration and fierce theological polemics, as well as Pennsylvania's being the only state to have no establishment law regulating religion, had by the mid eighteenth century produced a situation in which a loose Latitudinarian and Newtonian Anglicanism was the current chiefly appealing to the now dominant non-Quaker political and commercial elite. If the *Histoire* eulogized the colony as the only country on earth with no official church and where, thanks to William Penn, no tiresome disputes about mere 'words' or mutual loathing stemming from quarrels about 'des objets incompréhensibles' disturbed the public sphere, the Anglican Enlightenment no less than the other church establishments took a dim view of this situation and strove to change it by introducing a more robust system of ecclesiastical authority through the state legislature.[144] Pennsylvanians did not live without Bible discipline or churches directing their lives, countered hostile critics, or without legal requirements firmly buttressing parental authority over offspring of marriageable age. Rather, Pennsylvania was in every way a respectable colony characterized by social strata and church discipline.[145]

During the late 1770s and through the 1780s, the only major figures articulating universalist egalitarian and republican ideas were Paine, Jefferson, and the 'universalist' Rush. In Edinburgh, Rush had switched to radical ideas because scepticism, having destroyed his confidence in conventional political notions, led him to suspect, as he put it, 'error in everything' he had previously learnt in America.[146] Back in America, he became a famous medical, religious, and political reformer, and from 1780, for some years, an advocate of 'Universalism', that is the doctrine of universal salvation of souls irrespective of belief or behaviour, the only theology he could see rendering all souls equal, and considering union between all the Christian denominations an urgent necessity if 'corrupted' Christianity is to be eradicated and mankind's interests promoted.[147] Having earlier helped to found the first anti-slavery society, Rush opposed capital punishment, and urged the extension of publicly supported education at all levels, especially the adoption of free primary school instruction. Like the Unitarians, to whom he was close, Rush stressed man's obligations to the entire human race, opposing all theology dividing Christians into separate denominations. Eager to unify reason with religion, he proposed stripping away practically all traditional theology.

When the War of Independence ended, Rush, deeply conscious of the contradiction between the Revolution's stated egalitarian ideals and the continuing subjection and marginalization of the blacks and native Americans, figured prominently among the few refusing to accept that the Revolution was now complete.[148] A reader of Locke, Sidney, Montesquieu, and Helvétius, and (like Priestley and Price) an admirer

---

[144] *Histoire philosophique* (1780), ix. 41; Lambert, *Founding Fathers*, 110–14, 141.
[145] Petit, *Observations*, 76–8.
[146] D'Elia, *Benjamin Rush*, 32–3, 66–7.
[147] Ibid. 88–90.
[148] Sloan, *Scottish Enlightenment*, 195; Nash, *Unknown American Revolution*, 121–2.

of David Hartley's philosophy, Rush sought to promote a worldly progress based on liberty, equality, and fraternity in which all men would share, though, like Price, he never accepted that unaided reason alone is the exclusive source of truth. Education was essential to harmonize 'the wills of the people', 'produce regularity and unison in government', and further propagate the true principles of the Revolution.[149] Americans in his view needed not just a new constitution but also 'to effect a revolution in our principles, opinions and manners so as to accommodate them to the forms of government we have adopted'.[150] It was not difficult to see what he meant.

Notable reforms pushing toward democratic republicanism accompanied the American Revolution here and there, but in a piecemeal fashion without any systematic embracing of democratic principles. If a partially democratic constitution was adopted 'on the authority of the people', in Pennsylvania, this proved only temporary and the suffrage was substantially widened only in five of the twelve other states, and in at least one of these, South Carolina, the state constitution was simultaneously altered in other ways so as to reinforce the dominance of the local landed 'aristocracy'—and hence also slavery.[151] In the other seven states, the electorate remained heavily restricted and effective power and influence confined to the hands of relatively small landed and commercial elites. Separation of Church and state, on the other hand, was widely embraced and, in Virginia, the Anglican Church was disestablished; but very little was done to further education or reform the chaotic legal apparatus.

The so-called 'radical revolution' of 1776 in Pennsylvania, only half-heartedly supported by Franklin, remained incomplete in many respects, and through the 1780s was gradually eroded, as an alliance of moderates and conservatives, carefully dissociating themselves from Toryism, gradually regained the upper hand. As proscription of Tories eased, after 1780, there was a general retreat from democratic standpoints in many sectors.[152] The College of Philadelphia (now the University of Pennsylvania) was restored to its old charter and first rector, the remarkable William Smith now recalled from Maryland to resume his rectorship. Although the Pennsylvania legislature remained nominally neutral regarding the different confessions (and in practice anti-Anglican), theological criteria were progressively re-introduced under a variety of amendments. In particular, the legislature in 1779 voted through an act for the 'Suppression of Vice and Immorality', not just stiffening Presbyterian notions of Sunday observance but instituting swingeing fines for blasphemous talk and swearing. Prohibiting all work as well as sport and gambling on the Lord's Day, the act also banned cards, dice, and other gambling from taverns, and theatrical performances.[153] Finally, in 1790, the democratic constitution of 1776 was replaced

---

[149] D'Elia, *Benjamin Rush*, 70–1, 75, 81; May, *Enlightenment*, 235–6.

[150] D'Elia, *Benjamin Rush*, 91–2, 101; Sloan, *Scottish Enlightenment*, 195; Ferguson, *American Enlightenment*, 153.

[151] Paine, *Rights of Man*, 186–7; Brunhouse, *Counter-Revolution*, 14–18; Nadelhaft, *Disorders*, 29–38.

[152] Brunhouse, *Counter-Revolution*, 80–1, 254.   [153] Frost, *Perfect Freedom*, 71–2.

with a constitution providing for a two-chamber legislature, a more restricted franchise, and other new checks and balances but also a more genuine religious toleration.[154]

5. AN INCONCLUSIVE LEGACY

On the many enquiring minds in Europe and elsewhere dissatisfied with the general state of the world around 1780, the American Revolution had an extremely stirring effect. While almost all European 'nations', commented Mably, in July 1783, regarded most of their citizens rather like the animals on farms to be governed for the particular advantage of the owner, some Europeans were greatly inspired by the thirteen American 'republics' demonstrating 'la dignité de l'homme'. According to Mably, the Revolution also showed that the uplifting principles by which such men wished to be governed are be found in 'philosophy'.[155] But there was a definite failure of convergence here. For 'philosophy' in Mably's—the radical *philosophes'*—sense had not inspired the Revolution while, in their eyes, the Revolution was not yet complete.

The slavery issue, Amerindian exclusion, and a defective toleration were three serious deficiencies in the American Revolution in radical eyes, but not the only ones. One of the most serious blemishes on American society and culture, according to the *Histoire* and the radical fringe, was what they considered—quite differently from most Americans—the dreadfully defective legal system America inherited from England: 'there is not in the whole world', as the English version of the *Histoire* puts it, 'a code so diffuse, so perplexed, as that of the civil law of Great Britain.' Unfortunately for American society and for the American model of Enlightenment, 'by their dependence and their ignorance, the colonies have blindly adopted that deformed and ill-digested mass' and from this 'immediately there sprang up a numerous body of lawyers to devour the lands and inhabitants of those new-settled-climates. The fortune and influence they have acquired in a short time have brought into subjection to their rapaciousness the valuable class of citizens employed in agriculture, commerce, in all the arts and toils most indispensably necessary for all society...'[156]

If radical enlighteners considered the American constitution defective in being insufficiently democratic, not building on the principle of equality, presiding over a ramshackle, illogical legal system, and retaining slavery, advocates of the new constitution during the late 1780s and 1790s increasingly feared and condemned radical ideas. The clash was political, social, religious, and philosophical and even-tually came to be expressed in terms of the numerous and obvious contrasts between

---

[154] Ibid. 74–5; Rush, *Autobiography*, 130, 158–9; Brunhouse, *Counter-Revolution*, 156–8, 221–6.
[155] Mably, *Collection*, viii. 340.   [156] *A Philosophical and Political History*, ii. 194.

the French and American revolutions, though this feature was by no means as ubiquitous in the American moderate–radical split before the late 1790s as many modern commentators have supposed. For contrary to what is often assumed (and in sharp contrast to Britain), most Americans, like Stiles, remained broadly sympathetic to the French Revolution from 1789 until the mid 1790s. Ideological hostility towards the French Revolution was by no means automatic or marked in the United States—where until around 1795 most tended to assume the French were simply emulating the American Revolution.

Initially practically all shades of American opinion supported the new revolution across the Atlantic with hardly any exceptions. Equally, most Protestant preachers not only rejoiced during the French Revolution's early stages but were by no means distressed by the early attacks on the property, jurisdiction, and sway of the Catholic Church, indeed remained broadly sympathetic also during the years 1792–4.[157] Even John Adams who since the 1780s loathed Diderot and the *encyclopédistes* and, from the outset, was distinctly suspicious—indeed later claimed to have been the first (in 1786) to convert Burke from enthusiasm to dread at the prospect of revolution in France[158]—was partly won over initially. He was encouraged by the new revolution, he assured Price, from New York, in April 1790, and hopeful, but had learnt from experience 'to rejoice with trembling. I know that encyclopedists and economists, Diderot and d'Alembert, Voltaire and Rousseau, have contributed to this great event more than Sidney, Locke or Hoadley, perhaps more than the American Revolution; and I own to you, I know not what to make of a republic of thirty million atheists.'[159]

Adams had little confidence, furthermore, in the French single-chamber new constitution. 'Too many Frenchmen', the problem was, 'after the example of too many Americans, pant for equality of persons and property. The impracticability of this, God Almighty has decreed, and the advocates for liberty, who attempt it, will surely suffer for it.'[160] Although in his growing aversion to French developments, after 1790, Adams remained close to Burke, whose antagonism to the Revolution in France was uncompromising from the first,[161] he differed from him in being less anchored in tradition and more concerned with general principles of politics and society and indeed here adopted a slightly more liberal view than Burke. 'I am a mortal and irreconcilable enemy to monarchy', he felt able to reassure Rush in April 1790, 'I am no friend to hereditary limited monarchy in America. This I know can never be admitted without a hereditary senate to control it, and a hereditary nobility or Senate in America I know to be unattainable and impracticable.'[162] Adams had nothing against hereditary nobility as such but in the United States realized that hierarchy and aristocracy had to be informal.

---

[157] Nash, 'American Clergy', 394; Sharp, 'France and the United States', 205–11, 214.
[158] Ripley, 'Adams, Burke', 220.
[159] Ibid. 221; May, *Enlightenment*, 285; Adams to Richard Price, New York, 19 Apr. 1790, in Adams, *Works*, ix. 563–4.　　　　[160] Adams, *Works*, ix. 564; Grant, *John Adams*, 169.
[161] Grant, *John Adams*, 166–7; Ripley, 'Adams, Burke', 221.
[162] Adams to Rush, New York, 18 Apr. 1790, Adam, *Works*, ix. 566.

17

Europe and the Amerindians

1. AZTECS AND INCAS RECONFIGURED

Had the Indians been successfully, rightly, and justly incorporated into the New World European empires and, from 1775, the nascent United States, or was their subjugation an ugly blot on humanity? Was the pre-1492 Indian past a gory cata-logue of oppression, barbarism, and superstition or a beacon of light in world history? Were the 'barbarous', unChristianized, and hostile Indian peoples, on the frontiers of empire, the Cherokee of Kentucky and Tennessee, the Apaches and Comanches agitating the northern frontier of New Spain, and the Araucanians of southern Chile, truly children of the Devil and of darkness who should be ruthlessly subdued militarily and have their lands taken? Or were they nobly resisting unjust encroachment?

The rising in response to the onset of the Revolution of major sections of the native American peoples, against white Americans, along virtually the entire border of white settlement in the nascent United States, in the mid and late 1770s was proof enough that neither the American Enlightenment nor the Revolution had succeeded in finding an adequate place for Amerindians in their scheme of things. In Tennessee and Kentucky, the Cherokee peoples split. By 1776–7, most of the established elders felt the struggle to defend their ancestral lands from white encroachments had become hopeless and acquiesced in 'peace treaties' with the United States, massive further land sales, and total subordination and marginalization. By 1783, the Cherokee had lost three-quarters of the land they had held before the Revolution; and yet, in retaliation for continuing attacks on white settlements by dissident hostile Cherokee, many of their villages were raided and devastated nonetheless.[1]

This collapse and the elders' surrender, however, also prompted a massive 'seces-sion' of younger warriors determined to defend their hunting grounds who moved westwards under a chieftain named Dragging Canoe (c.1732–92) and set up a new confederacy in lands to the north of what is now Chattanooga. In alliance with, and supplied with ammunition by, the British, the militants who withdrew to Chick-amauga Creek, the 'Chickamauga' Cherokee, unremittingly fought the Revolution,

---

[1] Parmenter, 'Dragging Canoe', 117, 125–6.

refusing to surrender for over a decade after 1783.[2] How to formulate, evaluate, and regulate the Amerindian relationship to the Revolution, colonial society, and to Europe inevitably figured among the most contested, perplexing, and controversial questions confronting *la philosophie*. For the late Enlightenment, the issue loomed all the more in that the Indians in Spanish America, continuously decreasing from the 1520s down to the early seventeenth century, had begun to recover demographically from the late seventeenth century, and increased slowly but steadily through the eighteenth.

In much of the New World occupied by Europeans during the late eighteenth century, including the vast majority of what is today the United States, the Amerindian population remained still the dominant segment demographically. According to royal statistics of the 1790s, some 58 per cent of the population of the viceroyalty of Peru (including what are today Bolivia and Ecuador) were classified as 'Indians', or around 650,000 out of approximately 1,100,000 people. Another 22 per cent (245,000) counted as half-castes or *mestizos*, some 7 per cent (81,000) as black, and around 13 per cent (131,000) as American-born 'Spaniards', or Creoles.[3] While Indians, according to viceregal figures, in 1790, numbered only 24 per cent of the population of Mexico City, New Spain's capital, in the largely Indian townships surrounding the capital, such as Texcoco, Coyoacan, and Xochimilco, Amerindians still represented over 80 per cent of the total.[4]

The most eloquent plea that the Indians had been nobly and impressively integrated, the *Tardes Americanas* (Mexico City, 1778), by the Andalusian ecclesiastic and Indian expert José Joaquín Granados y Gálvez (1734–94), took the form of a long, eloquent dialogue between an 'Indian' and a 'Spaniard', remarkable for the fervour of its praise for the 'American Spaniards' and insistence on a basic harmony between Indians and *Criollos* within the bosom of the Church. Dedicated to the reforming minister José Gálvez—who, ironically, was the strongest advocate in Madrid of harsh military methods against the unruly tribes around Spanish America's frontiers—it was a paean of praise also for the monarchy and Carlos III's enlightened ministers, Granados's dialogue being especially insistent that through the Catholic Church and faith, and also Spanish monarchical order and justice, all three main ethnic-cultural blocs—European Spaniards, *Criollos*, and Indians—or four, counting the *mestizos*—had learnt to dwell together in undisturbed, permanent harmony under king and pope, without hint of either Indian uprisings or the despicable sedition and unruliness of the rebel 'Bostonians'. The Indian masses may have been credulous and barbaric, but the Aztec nobility and priestly class had been admirable, pious, knowledgeable, and politically sophisticated.[5]

Yet, in their confidential reports from the New World, royal officials often expressed great unease about the fraught, chronically unstable relationship between

---

[2] Ibid. 117, 128–33. [3] Fisher, *Bourbon Peru*, 55. [4] Gibson, *Aztecs*, 145, 148.
[5] Granados y Gálvez, *Tardes Americanas*, 533; Cañizares-Esguerra, *How to Write the History*, 233–4.

Indian and 'Spanish' society. The Spanish monarchy's heightened feeling of insecurity and vulnerability after the Seven Years War (1756–63), and especially during Spain's war against Britain during the American Independence War, led to numerous military forays—and much talk of many more—against the Apaches, Comanches, and, in the Gulf of California, the Seris, on the northern, as well as against the Araucanians on the southern (Chilean) frontier, with the aim of strengthening Spain's grip on these frontier zones.[6] In the viceroyalty of New Granada (today Colombia), a detailed report of July 1779 stressed that Indian society since the sixteenth century had proven markedly less robust and orderly than in central Mexico or Peru and that the advance of *mestizaje*, that is of a mixed-blood population and disintegration of traditional native communities, was far advanced. Wherever in New Granada essentially 'Indian' towns and communities still existed, this was due only to their remoteness from Spanish and *mestizo* communities. This striking contrast with New Spain and Peru resulted primarily, according to the investigating magistrate, from the fact that the Indians' political and legal organization in those realms had been much more developed, prosperous, and 'civilized' before 1492 than in New Granada. This had helped the Aztecs and Incas adapt, after the Conquest, to the highly segregated legal and institutional framework imposed by the Spanish crown, replicating a system of nobility and local administration like that of the Spaniards while preserving their society and autonomy.[7]

Ever since the early eighteenth-century publications of Louis-Armand, the Baron de Lahontan (1666–1715), a radical writer still vividly remembered by Diderot and the late eighteenth century for his eulogy of the moral uprightness and sexually free attitudes of the Canadian Indians (whose supposedly nobler ethics he vividly contrasted with what he insinuated was the servile, crass, and perverted morality of the Europeans),[8] the makings of a Spinozistic, anti-Christian vision of the indigenous American peoples had pervaded radical thought. This strand of the radical tradition had afterwards been reinforced by the impressions of the French naturalist and explorer La Condamine in the 1730s and 1740s, an enthusiast for the Inca ruins of Cuzco who, despite his low opinion of the intellectual and moral stature of the Amerindians, helped seed the late eighteenth-century strikingly utopian vision of the Incas. While disdaining the Incas' moral qualities, La Condamine was astonished that a people lacking metal implements could construct such massive, impressive, and beautifully engineered palaces, temples, fortresses, roads, and bridges. The way was open creatively to combine the veneration for the remnants that so struck La Condamine with the radical perspective of Lahontan and of Bernard's *Cérémonies et coutumes religieuses*, in which the cults of the Incas, Aztecs, Iroquois, and Hurons are dispassionately compared with Catholicism, Protestantism, and other Old World religions and readers found numerous subversive allusions to naturalism

[6] Weber, *Bárbaros*, 143–5, 148–51.
[7] AGI Santa Fe 1084. Fiscal of audience of Bogotá to crown, Bogotá, 29 July 1779.
[8] Israel, *Radical Enlightenment*, 89, 580–2; Goldmann, *Philosophy*, 75; Pernety, *Dissertation*, 80–3, 118.

and pantheism as forces underlying all the world's religions, and even human sacrifice is represented in a more neutral, less condemnatory tone than was usual in Spanish accounts of the New World.[9]

It was actually one of eighteenth-century France's foremost female writers, the renowned *salonnière* Françoise de Graffigny (1695–1758), utilizing such (radical) authors as Lahontan, Bernard, and Vauvenargues, and also the detailed record amassed by the great Inca-Spanish half-caste chronicler Garcilaso de la Vega whose account of the Inca empire hostile critics dismissed as a 'roman insensé',[10] who with her *Lettres d'une Péruvienne* (1747) first powerfully concocted the potent late Enlightenment myth of the virtuous and heroic Incas. Her *Lettres* narrate the story of a young Peruvian woman, Zilia, ravaged and enslaved by Spaniards, dragged from her homeland and adrift in Paris, whose quiet heroism helps her transcend her terrible tribulations and eventually become a beacon of light to the Parisians. Banned by the Church in 1765, this unremitting attack on the cultural intolerance and moral myopia of the Europeans, with its erudite footnotes explaining the history of the Indians, figured among the eighteenth century's best-selling novels, appearing in some fifty editions between 1747 and 1800.[11] Raynal read and reviewed the book when it first appeared but at that time disdained it, complaining that Graffigny had created a heroine incompatible with woman's subordinate role. Such an uplifting, model personality, he suggested, would far more fittingly be represented as a man.[12] Crucially, Zilia discovers (somewhat to her own surprise) that books proved her single, greatest support, her path to salvation; books and the elevating philosophy they contain were the life-line that saved her, the redeeming force renewing the world, an enthusiasm for the morally redeeming role of reading like that encountered in Vauvenargues.[13]

The myth of the noble Incas and *la philosophie*'s power to elevate men was then sternly countered by the most famous late Enlightenment work concerning New World history, natural history, and ethnography, Cornelis de Pauw's *Recherches philosophiques sur les Américains* (2 vols., London, 1770). The Incas, held de Pauw, had no philosophy and scarcely any astronomy or mathematics; furthermore, their language, like that of all the indigenous American peoples, was incapable of expressing abstract ideas. The notion that the Inca, Aztec, and Maya architectural remains are impressive is a ridiculous tale. Actually, rather few Inca remains survived, and their impressiveness had been vastly exaggerated by Garcilaso and by Spanish writers aspiring to cover the *conquistadores* with a wholly undeserved glory for defeating such feeble, primitive, and precarious empires as those of the Incas, Mayas, and Aztecs, empires lacking metals, literacy, and all rudiments of philosophy.[14]

---

[9] Pernety, *Dissertation*, 19–20; Graffigny, *Lettres*, 222–3, 236–7; Mallinson, 'Introduction', 34; Hunt, Jacob, and Mijnhardt, *Book*, 8–10, 226.   [10] De Pauw, *Recherches*, ii. 176–7.
[11] Mallinson, 'Introduction', 1.   [12] Ibid. 62, 69.
[13] Graffigny, *Lettres*, 160, 237.   [14] De Pauw, *Recherches*, ii. 169–70.

De Pauw depicts the Spaniards in the New World as the 'indolent and fanatical possessors' of a territory they had devastated, concurring with the notion that Spain's and Portugal's American acquisitions were an unmitigated human disaster. But while scarcely less scathing about Spanish 'barbarism' than the *Histoire philosophique*, he judged the New World's discovery and colonization to be an irreversibly ruinous mistake, claiming human progress generally could not possibly benefit from integrating the New World and its peoples. The New World's climate, geography, and natural conditions were so unfavourable, contended de Pauw, that humans and all other species inevitably degenerate there subsisting only in inferior forms. He insisted on fundamental differences between the races, The Amerindians were a race of men replete with all the defects of children, 'une espèce dégénerée du genre humain', wretched, languid, and 'sans élévation dans l'esprit'.[15] Despite the fact that he had never visited the Americas and despite ecclesiastical disapproval of his pervasive racial ideology, de Pauw's treatise, widely read, commanded a surprising degree of prestige in the 1770s and 1780s.

New World fauna, flora, and men de Pauw all held in abysmally low esteem. Yet, this Dutch writer was also a distinctly useful prop to European colonial aspirations of every hue, less due to his disparagement of the Amerindians than his thesis that the American-born Spaniards, the Creoles, had inexorably degenerated in the American climate and become inherently inferior physically, mentally, and morally to Spaniards and any other officials, soldiers, administrators, and priests sent out from Europe.[16] On this point, de Pauw notably clashed with Benito Feijóo, Spain's first major Enlightenment figure and one with a splendid reputation in Ibero-America precisely because in his *Theatro crítico* he had consistently defended the Creoles against their Iberian detractors, praising their intellectual and scientific capabilities which he pronounced equal to those of Europeans.[17]

Of course, radical writers were by no means the only Enlightenment critics of the churches' social, political, and moral efforts in the New World. Reimarus, unlike Semler and Lessing, refused to accept that Christianity had been at all morally improving in the Indies any more than in Europe, its perverse belief structures, in his eyes, producing only ruinous moral and social outcomes. Deploring all systematic proselytizing and imposing revealed religion by edict, he maintained that Europe's New World empires were inherently illegitimate. What must the Amerindians think of the Europeans with their claims to religious and moral superiority? What they see are 'people who through abduction and deception reduce other men to slavery, depriving them of their lands and goods, people wholly given up to lechery and gluttony and set on ruining the simplicity of the savages' way of life with their alcohol and debauchery'.[18] But he kept his devastating critique of the whites' treatment of the Amerindians strictly to himself, saying nothing about this in public.

---

[15] De Pauw, *Recherches*, i, preface p. xiii ; Weber, *Bárbaros*, 45.
[16] De Pauw, *Recherches*, ii. 164–5; Imbruglia, *L'invenzione*, 317–19.
[17] De Pauw, *Recherches* ii. 165–6; Gonzalez Feijoo, *Feijóo*.   [18] Reimarus, *Apologie*, i. 154.

De Pauw was far less scathing about the missionaries and the effects of Christianity in the New World, but his work was nevertheless wholly unwelcome in ecclesiastical circles. For he not only rejected Montesquieu's thesis that the Amerindians had sincerely become attached to Christianity, but claimed no one can sincerely adhere to a religion if unable to grasp its teachings and dogmas. He acknowledged the missionaries' zeal was well meant, but deemed their 'labours a waste of time as no Indian ever understood a single word of the Gospels'.[19]

The prestige and prevalence of de Pauw's ideas in the 1770s obliged the radical current to go beyond mere eulogy of Indian moral capacities in the style of Lahontan and Graffigny and develop a broader, more formidable political and social thesis concerning the Incas, Maya, and Aztecs as well as the wilder Araucanians, Apaches, Iroquois, and Cherokee. The *Histoire philosophique* accomplished this by presenting a glowing and notably utopian vision of especially the Inca empire which it then powerfully contrasted, politically, culturally, morally, and psychologically, with the downtrodden, brutalized condition of the modern Peruvians, Mexicans, and Maya under Spanish rule since the sixteenth century. The *Histoire's* objective was less to convict Spain of appalling exploitation, cruelty, and barbarism than demonstrate that tyranny and brutal traumatization are the usual lot of man and despotic oppression a highly intricate psychological, cultural, and social process as well as a political phenomenon that altogether debases the perpetrators as well as the victims. Diderot and his colleagues rejoiced that Spain's condition was improving and her industries reviving, especially in Catalonia.[20] But to hasten the revival and generate new vitality across the Atlantic, they also urged a much wider freedom in the New World colonies than anyone was likely to countenance at court in Madrid. Diderot even suggests in one passage that the right way to revive Puerto Rico was to remove all trade and religious restrictions, and measures excluding foreigners, wholly devolving administrative and judicial control onto the island's citizens themselves.[21]

Magnificently, the Incas had brought neighbouring peoples and lands under effective control, doing so, according to the *Histoire*, for no other purpose than to ensure 'le Bonheur des hommes'. All three editions of the *Histoire* present an impossibly utopian tableau of the Inca empire as a rare haven from human corruption and a sphere without crime,[22] lacking inheritable private landed property and where the ruler collects no taxes but exists solely to ensure his subjects work diligently on collective building projects and cultivating their lands and remain uncorrupted. There was supposedly no indolence or leisured class living in luxury on the sweat of others. The Inca emperors descended from a great first legislator, Manco Capac, who, having convinced his subjects he was the son of the sun, had formulated his society's basic laws, including one abolishing human and animal sacrifice. All laws issuing from his legendary capital, Cuzco, commanded the Incas to support and love

---

[19] Ibid. i. 160–1.   [20] *Esprit de Guillaume-Thomas Raynal*, ii. 144.
[21] Diderot, *Œuvres complètes*, xv. 568–9.
[22] *Histoire philosophique* (1770), iii. 139; *Histoire philosophique* (1774), iii. 158.

each other.[23] Manco Capac might well have been remembered as the most eminent of all humanity's legislators had not Confucius surpassed him in discarding superstition 'pour faire recevoir et observer la morale et les loix'.[24]

But not only radical thinkers found reasons to elevate the image of the Indians. The Aztecs' standing was notably polished by the erudite Jesuit Francisco Xavier Clavijero (1731–87), author of the epoch-making history *La historia antigua de México*. Clavijero, having studied Descartes, Newton, and Leibniz as part of his higher education at Puebla de los Angeles, in the early 1750s, had began researching the pre-Columbian history of the indigenous civilizations in the mid 1750s. Besides Puebla and Mexico City, he taught also at Valladolid (now Morelia) in Michoacán. On the Jesuit expulsion from Spain's empire, in 1767, the foremost Mexican Enlightenment figure was exiled, settling in Italy where he discovered and was outraged by de Pauw's *Recherches*. His voluminous, handsomely illustrated study, describing ancient Mexico in unprecedented detail, partly a reply to de Pauw, unfortunately appeared, however, only after a lengthy delay, in 1780–1, and in Italian only.

Clavijero eulogized not just the Aztecs but, like Granados, also the Toltecs with their imposing capital at Tula, the first great builders and civilizers of central Mexico, and other pre-Aztec Mexican civilizations, stressing the antiquity, splendour, and number of their cities, their use of sign-writing and texts, showing they were the first to sow cotton and maize, and extolling the magnificence of their architecture and engineering as demonstrated by their aqueducts, streets, palaces, and general construction methods.[25] The *conquistadores* had been deeply impressed by what they saw, astonished not least by Aztec proficiency in music, dance, and astronomy. Like Granados, he praised the marriages and racial intermingling of the *conquistadores* with Aztec princesses and noble women, and wished miscegenation at aristocratic level had gone further.[26] However, this remarkable attempt to foment pride in Mexico's indigenous past and stress the splendour and authenticity of the pre-Conquest codices, Clavijero's striking neo-Aztecism, had only a limited impact at the time. Recognizing a subversive strain infusing his otherwise solidly ecclesiastical, monarchical, and aristocratic stance, the crown authorized publication in Spanish only under the proviso that extensive changes were made, removing most of the eulogy of the Aztecs. Clavijero refused to comply so that no Spanish version materialized until after the great independence struggle, in 1826.

The *conquistadores* had overthrown the indigenous civilizations, reducing their populations to subject status. The new emphasis on the intellectual, astronomical, and artistic skills of the pre-Colombian civilizations inevitably threw into starker relief their post-Conquest debasement and humiliation and, according to most

---

[23] *Histoire philosophique* (1770), iii. 114.
[24] Ibid. iii. 110–14; *Histoire philosophique* (1780), iv. 31, 34–43.
[25] Clavijero, *Storia antica*, ii. 198–205; Granados y Gálvez, *Tardes Americanas*, 8, 10–11, 14–16; Browning, 'Cornelis de Pauw', 297.
[26] Cañizares-Esguerra, *How to Write the History*, 246.

observers, the stupidity and incapacity in which they had lapsed since the 1520s. The submissiveness and wretched passivity into which the Indians had sunk had long helped facilitate and, for some, even justify the widespread forced labour drafts, debt-peonage, and other forms of institutionalized coercion imposed in the Indian villages under Spanish rule, to service the Spaniards' mines, haciendas, *obrajes* (textile workshops), and plantations.[27] The *Histoire* stressed that an acquiescent, relentlessly exploited population were being compelled but were also accustomed by their own previous practices and attitudes to perform exacting labour services often over great distances without payment. Theirs was an innocent as well as wretched docility which the *conquistadores* had ruthlessly exploited. Unlike earlier accounts, though, the *Histoire* used this dispiriting, appalling tableau as a weapon against empire, wholly repudiating both Spain's imperial claims and those of the Church, denying outright the Amerindians' intellectual and moral inferiority and any justification for reducing them to spiritual, political, and moral bondage. Contrasting this tableau with the past glories of the Incas, Maya, and Aztecs, the *Histoire*, furthermore, encouraged the Creoles to seek inspiration for their budding patriotism and identity in the ancient indigenous cultures.

Raynal and Diderot afforded the 'American Spaniards' a means of deepening their own local patriotism while promoting, contrary to the summons for *gachupín*–Creole solidarity in the *Tardes Americanas*, their uniquely sweeping critique of Spain's laws, empire, monarchy, Church, and institutions.[28] The *Histoire*'s argument clashed comprehensively, at every level, with the doctrines of de Pauw, the Church, and the Spanish Bourbon court. All royal courts ruling great global empires in the late eighteenth century faced a growing threat from radically enlightened ideas deliberately undermining justifications for European and Christian dominance of the Indies. Potential support for this ideological and intellectual challenge to empire lay in Creole dissatisfaction and hopes for more of the benefits of empire to be settled on them. Indeed, the intellectual and psychological levers making long-standing Creole grievances an actual and real threat to the Spanish and Portuguese empires arose chiefly from the arguments and perspectives forged by radical thought. For radical ideas provided the only available, clear, and systematic justification for overthrowing Spanish rule. Without Radical Enlightenment concepts, Creole consciousness had no way to become a fully-fledged opposition ideology denying the legitimacy and authority of Spain's crown, laws, and institutions. Neither traditional Spanish legal thought, nor university training, nor the Catholic Church provided the slightest grounds for a general anti-colonial, republican, tolerationist, economically liberal, egalitarian revolt.

Inquisition edicts issued in March 1776 declared the *Histoire* prohibited 'in whatever language', an illicit work forbidden even to university professors equipped

---

[27] Israel, *Race, Class and Politics*, 28–33; Gibson, *Aztecs*, 220–1; Cañizares-Esguerra, *Nature, Empire*, 84–5.

[28] Browning, 'Cornelis de Pauw', 297–8; Breña, *Primer liberalismo*, 257–8.

with special Inquisition licences enabling them to read other *libros prohibidos*, a work brimming with blasphemous and impious propositions deprecating sovereigns and trying to cast infamy on the Spanish nation, its rulers, and ministers.[29] However, the *Histoire* proved an ideological incursion difficult to check. A senior diplomat, Don Pedro Jiménez de Góngora y Luján (1727–96), duke of Almodóvar, among the most active and influential of the Spanish *éclairés*, a nobleman who had served Carlos III as his ambassador in London for some years and who later, in 1784, became director of the Royal Academy of History in Madrid, even undertook, we have seen, to translate the *Histoire* into Spanish.[30] Writing under the pseudonym 'Francisco Maria de Silva', Almodóvar urged the exceptional value and importance of Raynal's work while also admitting its subversive character.[31] He recommended close discussion of the *Histoire*'s merits and demerits in general terms, rather than focusing on its critique of Spain, deliberately drawing attention to Raynal's project as something debated everywhere and that enlightened men could hardly avoided discussing, in fact needed to discuss.

But how could a translation of the *Histoire* ever appear legally in Spain? Diderot's indictment of the Conquest and *conquistadores*, among the *Histoire*'s most graphic and horrifying sections, emphasizing the moral responsibility of the Spanish crown, viceroys, and Church in the general 'enslavement' and debasement of the Indies, helping organize and sanctioning what Raynal and his team declared oppression and royally authorized brutality on an unparalleled scale, permeated large parts of the work and was far more sweeping and systematic than the more traditional, partly religiously motivated critique of Spain in Robertson, or that in de Pauw or any moderate Enlightenment texts. Far from spreading any worthwhile light, the *conquistadores* and missionaries, arriving, as they did, in a century 'd'ignorance et de barbarie' when all true principles of political and social organization were unknown, or had been forgotten, brought only devastation, misery, exploitation, and death, totally disrupting the age-old harmony between nature and humanity in the New World previously prevailing over countless centuries.[32]

Given that much of Raynal's Spanish material accrued through the complicity of Spanish contributors, it is possible to discern in this collaboration and Almodóvar's efforts to promote the *Histoire*, together with Diderot's 'Spanish' seminars in Paris, the first seeds of an embryonic Spanish radical enlightenment clandestinely at work, retaliating against what some saw as the unparalleled crime wrought by bigotry, prejudice, imperial bureaucracy, ecclesiastical authority, and royal prerogative over three centuries throughout the Hispanic world, against the Jews and Muslims as well as the Amerindians and imported black slaves. In Spain, Portugal, and their colonies, the full unexpurgated version of the *Histoire* always remained strictly prohibited. Copies undoubtedly penetrated Ibero-America, but these must have been relatively

---

[29] BL 4625 g 1/53. Inquisition edict, Seville, 23 Mar. 1776.
[30] Defourneaux, *L'Inquisition espagnole*, 142, 163.
[31] Almodóvar, *Década*, 108–15.   [32] Folkerts, *Bedeutung*, 63–6.

few.[33] In preparing his Spanish version, once he had obtained his own copy of the 1780 edition (in October 1782) Almodóvar, of course, needed first of all to delete the harsh criticism of Spain and Catholicism which meant cutting out huge sections. 'It has been no little work', he remarks in the preface to his translation, to purge Raynal's text 'of its poisonous *effluvios*, correcting that pride and elation' so unseemly, all agreed, in a writer calling himself 'el defensor de la humanidad, de la verdad, de la libertad' [defender of humanity, the truth and liberty].[34]

Almodóvar also deleted many other sections especially relating to religion. But the *Histoire*'s devastating critique of British conduct in India and Dutch misrule in Indonesia he left intact along with much else likely to influence readers against colonial empires, in the hope of obtaining royal permission to publish while also still exerting a substantial influence on Spanish Enlightenment debate and society.[35] Eventually, he succeeded. Endorsed by Jovellanos, the first volumes of his sanitized rendering appeared around the time of Diderot's death, in 1784, under the title *Historia política de los establecimientos ultramarinos de las naciones europeas* (5 vols., Madrid, 1784–90). By dint of the most scrupulous self-censorship Almodóvar also managed to secure royal permission for several subsequent volumes, publication of a truncated *Histoire* in Spanish being halted only when the crown became seriously alarmed by the spectre of revolution, in 1790, by which time five volumes had appeared.

2. AMERINDIANS: SAVED OR TO BE SAVED?

There were many 'errors and impieties' in the *Histoire*, agrees Almodóvar, in his *Década epistolar*. Yet, the 'plan of this work is excellent'; indeed, it is a great accomplishment, being the most seductive, curious, and depraved, in short the 'best and worst' of all the recent philosophical works in French.[36] This was as close as he could get to justifying the book and his plan to propagate it in Spanish. For besides Raynal's 'disgraceful' attack on the Catholic religion and the fact that 'our church, nation and government' are the most insulted in the parts full of mistakes and lies, there were also other 'false principles' the public needed to be warned against. Still, there were extensive sections full of valuable insights, worthy of the closest consideration.[37] His venture was (eventually) allowed chiefly because prohibiting altogether such a widely acclaimed and influential work was no longer a feasible option for the Spanish crown. Nothing could prevent the *Histoire* becoming

---

[33] 'Malo de Luque' [Almodóvar], *Historia política*, i, 'prologo' p. viii.
[34] Ibid. i, p. v ; Folkerts, *Bedeutung*, 73; 77; Paquette, *Enlightenment*, 50–1.
[35] 'Malo de Luque' [Almodóvar], *Historia política*, i, 'prologo' p. v; Defourneaux, *L'Inquisition espagnole*, 156–7; Tietz, 'Diderot', 295.
[36] Almodóvar, *Década*, 109, 113.   [37] Ibid. 113–16.

a general talking point around the world. Their best course, Carlos III's ministers therefore resolved, was thoroughly to emasculate it. In allowing the Spanish version to circulate, ministers hoped to guide the ensuing debate by propagating—partly through Almodóvar's 'corrected' version but also other publications—a fundamentally different, an alternative enlightened narrative of Spain's role in the Americas, projecting a far more positive image of crown, nation, and Church, fully negating that advanced by the uncensored version. In this way, Almodóvar's rendering came to be aligned with other Spanish texts refuting the original *Histoire philosophique*, including that of Juan Nuix de Perpinyà (1740–83), a Catalan ex-Jesuit in exile in the Papal States. Appearing originally as *Riflessioni imparziali supra l'umanità degli spagnuoli nell'Indie* (Venice, 1780), his book, with a long preface by Varela y Ulloa, was published in Spanish under the title *Reflexiones imparciales sobre la humanidad de los españoles en las Indias, contra los pretendidos filósofos* (Madrid, 1782) with full royal endorsement.

The main target of Nuix's and Varela y Ulloa's polemics were the French radical *philosophes* though they also assail de Pauw and Robertson. Extolling the Enlightenment in its royalist, Catholic, and socially conservative mode, Varela fiercely rebukes Raynal and his accomplices for virulent anti-Spanish 'prejudice' and insidious philosophical principles. Though a Jesuit who had personally suffered from Spain's enlighteners, Nuix perfectly fitted the crown's requirements, (mostly) abiding as he did by his promise in his preface to combat the *flagrantes contradicciones* of the *Histoire*, a text causing unprecedented havoc in Spain and the Indies purely 'philosophically', without anger or theological judgements, employing only the *philosophes'* own criteria—reason, argument, and facts. On this basis, he denounced the *Histoire* as grossly misleading. The modern 'espíritu filosófico', grants Nuix, was indeed transforming the world and might accomplish something of universal value. Spain and its empire in any case could not escape its impact. His aim was to show how pure 'philosophical' argument could be used to shield Spain's record and exalt the Catholic Church.[38] It is as 'philosophers' not as his nation's foes that he assails Spain's detractors—self-styled *philosophes* whom he deplores as irreligious subversives, the greatest *perturbadores* of the age.

Setting aside the insult to Spain (keenly resented though this was by Nuix, Varela, and Granados), the real issue was the *Histoire*'s and *la nueva filosofía*'s open challenge to accepted morality, values, and faith. While Robertson is rebuked for depicting the *conquistadores* as 'cruel, greedy, ambitious and inhuman', the 'errors' of his *History of America* (2 vols., London, 1777) are considered minor compared with the *Histoire*'s. Indeed, Robertson's reputation in Spain was trimmed only marginally. Certainly, his history was being suppressed 'with the greatest rigour and vigilance' throughout the empire by special decree of December 1778, the ban being reissued in Buenos Aires in June 1779, and by the *Audiencia* of Charcas for Upper Peru and Potosí in July.[39]

---

[38] Nuix, *Reflexiones imparciales*, author's preface, pp. xxxiii, xxxviii.
[39] AN Bolivia ALP Exp. Colon. No. 264, fos. 1, 3ᵛ–5, ban on Robertson, Charcas, 22 July 1779.

But faced with the much greater threat from Raynal, Madrid's attitude to Robertson quickly softened. Banned owing to his anti-Catholic and anti-Spanish remarks, the book's basic views on politics, society, and economic life, resembling Hume's in stressing the importance of habit, what society is used to and established institutions, and the superiority of the civilized over the primitive, greatly appealed in particular to Campomanes, who prized Robertson's way of justifying social conservatism with appeals to divine providence. Neither did Campomanes or other Spanish ministers object to Robertson's insistence on Amerindian (and Creole) inferiority and natural subordination to Europeans.[40] In Robertson, Campomanes (who, together with his other posts, had, since 1764, directed the Royal Academy of History in Madrid), also found a congenial account of the economic factors behind the rise and fall of nations and apt justifications for his own economic and institutional reforming measures.[41]

By accommodating Robertson, Spain could also claim to have brought to the New World not just Christianity but also economic and technological betterment. For in his history the 'line by which nations proceed towards civilization, the discovery of the useful metals and acquisition of dominion over the animal creation' represent 'steps of capital importance in their progress'.[42] Robertson, not unlike de Pauw, considered the Aztecs and Incas primitives, their backwardness being especially evident, he thought, in their failure to discover iron and other metal-working and their domesticating only ducks, turkeys, rabbits, and a species of 'small dogs'.[43] Despite the ban on the original, Campomanes therefore arranged for a translation of Robertson prepared by his Academy, a sanitized version correcting 'errors' and deleting impious passages while promoting Robertson's views about economic progress, social 'maturity', Indians, Creoles, empires, and society which Campomanes and his colleagues broadly endorsed, though the translation in the end never appeared owing to continuing objections and doubts.

The point of reissuing Nuix and Robertson in official Spanish renderings was above all to reinforce the crown's counter-offensive against the *Histoire* and vindicate Spain's treatment of the Indians. Claiming 'Raynal' had not only demonstrably falsified the historical record and gratuitously insulted the Spanish monarchy and nation but introduced pernicious basic principles, Nuix contrasts Las Casas, writing in the sixteenth century, who accused the *conquistadores* of barbarously pillaging, mistreating, and decimating the indigenous population, with the *Histoire*'s very different approach. For Diderot and Raynal, followed later by Démeunier's *L'Esprit*, blame Mexico's and Peru's catastrophic depopulation, after 1520, on the 'slow oppression' initiated by the *conquistadores*, tyranny elaborated and sustained without being significantly mitigated, by crown and Church.[44] Diderot had no desire to

[40] Berry, *Social Theory*, 36–7, 46–7; Pittock, 'Historiography', 269–73.
[41] Cañizares-Esguerra, *How to Write the History*, 174–6; Mestre Sanchis, *Apología*, 64, 205.
[42] Robertson, *History of America*, 153.
[43] Ibid.; Hargraves, 'Beyond the Savage Character', 104–5; Pocock, *Barbarism*, iv. 208.
[44] *Histoire philosophique* (1770), iii. 44–6, 49; *Histoire philosophique* (1780), iv. 394–8; Démeunier, *L'Esprit*, ii. 114, 119–20, 131.

excuse the *conquistadores*. Cortes, conqueror of New Spain, he portrays as thoroughly 'despote et cruel', a mass murderer steeped in innocent blood whose undertakings were ruthless, barbaric, and unjustified. The Inca population's treatment by Pizarro, conqueror of Peru, was even more despicable. But the philosopher's job is to look beyond the surface and uncover the real reasons for things.[45] Cortes consequently emerges more as a representative of his age and a set of attitudes than any nation or faith, and his cruel deeds as part of a wider system of injustice and 'superstition' inherent in all colonial rule whether in the Americas, Africa, or Asia, even if in the Spanish world this fatal mix had produced the most extreme 'fanaticism' known to man.[46]

Among those contributing to this new ideology of fanaticism and cruelty produced by social and cultural factors applying in the main everywhere, and in all societies, another of Diderot's associates, Marmontel, should not pass unmentioned for his drama rendered into English as *The Incas: Or, The Destruction of the Empire of Peru* (2 vols., London, 1777), extolling what he calls the 'great wisdom and goodness of the Incas'. For this too caused a considerable stir internationally. Marmontel likewise propagates a completely naturalistic explanation for Spain's atrocities: 'we shall see', argues Marmontel, 'that among any other people, the same circumstances would have found men capable of running into the same excesses.' Europeans being incapable of hard manual exertion in the tropics they must, unless willing to abandon their conquests, either restrict themselves to mere peaceful trade or else compel Incas and other indigenous peoples 'by force into the necessary tasks of ransacking the bowels of the earth, and cultivating its surface'.[47]

The official Enlightenment was well placed to counter with some effect. Different though they are, the accounts of the demographic collapse of the Amerindians given by Las Casas and the *Histoire*, observes Nuix, are both profoundly mistaken. The veritable cause of the catastrophe, which the *Histoire* should have admitted, was the devastating epidemics that followed the Conquest and for which Spain bore no responsibility.[48] The *Histoire*, he argued, betrays inexcusable bias also in analysing Spain's economic misfortunes. The Spanish empire's decline stemmed, held the *Histoire*, from royal exactions, religious intolerance, enslaving Indians and blacks, sheer rapacity, and a barbaric resolve to exclude foreigners, along with the crown's ceaseless appetite for war, all exacerbated by over-regulation of trade designed to limit participation in transatlantic commerce to a handful of well-connected, readily managed merchants. Here, though, Diderot and Raynal had the better argument, their account not differing greatly from that which modern scholars offer for the decline of Spain's Atlantic shipping and commerce after 1600. Denying any grave

---

[45] Diderot, *Œuvres complètes*, xv. 467; Diderot, *Fragments échappés*, 451.

[46] Diderot, *Fragments échappés*, 451; [Raynal-Hedouin], *Esprit et génie*, 307–8; Hauben, 'White Legend', 11.

[47] Marmontel, *The Incas*, i, preface p. iii.

[48] Nuix, *Reflexiones imparciales*, 28–9, 81–5; Slicher van Bath, *Bevolking*, 205; Cañizares-Esguerra, *How to Write the History*, 183–4.

structural defects in the empire's commercial organization, or treatment of the Indians, was hardly convincing. The chief cause of Spain's lamentable economic decline, according to Nuix, was neither royal mismanagement, poor policies, nor religious intolerance, but the armed intrusions and piratical attacks of Spain's foreign rivals. Spanish shipping and commerce were ruthlessly disrupted and 'oppressed by foreigners', the Parisian *philosophes* ought to have acknowledged, and paralysed more and more, the incessant depredations perpetrated by the Protestant English and Dutch over many decades bringing poverty, ruin, and depopulation to Castile.

Nuix's calm and measured replies, even when dispelling gross exaggeration and the *encyclopédistes'* disparagement of the Ibero-American Church, including the charge that the entire monastic population of New Spain was ignorant and lazy, and superstitious oppressors of the Indians, exemplified the 'philosophic' tone and reasonableness of the Enlightenment.[49] Spanish atrocities, alleged Raynal, were such as to appal and 'enlighten' the entire world regarding the crimes of 'fanatisme'. By imposing their faith across the vast tracts whose population they devastated with fire and sword, the Spaniards rendered Christianity 'odieuse en Europe', their brutality discrediting both themselves and all they stood for, alienating far more Catholics from the Roman communion than the missionaries made new Christians among the Indians.[50] Total calumny, retorted Nuix, the real facts were quite otherwise, as the reasonable and impartial observer could judge from the passages of *L'Esprit des loix* where Montesquieu, a writer venerated by everyone participating in this controversy, affirms that it is Christianity that universally softens despotism's edge and first pointed the way towards abolishing slavery.[51]

Montesquieu's praise of Christianity, however, is brusquely dismissed by Diderot in the *Histoire* where the Catholic Church is stated always to have colluded in extending slavery and Indian forced labour in the Spanish Indies.[52] However unfairly, according to Christian critics who hastened to Montesquieu's defence, the *Histoire* flatly rejects Montesquieu's claim that throughout history the 'spirit' of Christianity worked to counter slavery.[53] Not only were the Amerindians abominably exploited—except by the Jesuits in Paraguay where political circumstances differed entirely—but Catholicism is so little disposed to curb servitude that in Bohemia, Poland, and Catholic Germany, 'pays très-catholiques', the people are enslaved still, with the German ecclesiastical princes not the least active in upholding serfdom.[54] The Church, countered Nuix, had long sought to 'soften' the harshness of slavery and uphold the political rights of the Amerindian indigenous population, as well as the law of the nations civilizing the waging of war, for which all humanity owed a debt of deep gratitude, not the insults of the *philosophes*. Where the English in North

---

[49] Diderot, *Œuvres complètes*, xv. 470-1; Nuix, *Reflexiones imparciales*, preface p. xxxviii.
[50] Deleyre, *Tableau*, 5.
[51] Nuix, *Reflexiones imparciales*, 174–5; Montesquieu, *Œuvres complètes*, 698.
[52] *Esprit de Guillaume-Thomas Raynal*, ii. 61–2.
[53] Ibid.; [Bernard], *Analyse*, 45; [Raynal-Hedouin], *Esprit et génie*, 268.
[54] [Raynal-Hedouin], *Esprit et génie*, 269.

America presumed Amerindian lands to be 'vacant', and available for appropriation by new settlers—Locke had indeed argued along these lines—allowing any Englishman to appropriate them, rendering the divide between colonist and Indian communities an essentially warlike, 'external' one, Spain, with greater humanity and justice, always acknowledged the Indians' rights to their land and maintained a system of land registration and protection for Indian property.[55] Moreover, where Robertson and other British authors portray the Amerindians as so primitive as to be virtually incapable of rational thought, almost a different species, Church and crown in Spanish America had always evinced a proper regard for the Indians.[56] It was indeed Robertson's view that 'if the comparison be made with the people of the ancient continent, the inferiority of America in improvement will be conspicuous, and neither the Mexicans nor Peruvians will be entitled to rank with those nations which merit the name of civilized'.[57]

Devil-worship and false gods, human sacrifice, and other horrific New World practices were all eradicated by Christianity displacing pre-Conquest idolatry. If one rolled all the philosophers of ancient and modern times into one with all their pretensions to wisdom and humanity, they still would not have bequeathed mankind so great a benefit as this.[58] Only deists or atheists, like the authors of the *Histoire*, would deny the glorious character of the Church's achievement among America's indigenous peoples. Certainly, the Church upholds monarchical authority, categorically refusing peoples any right to resist, or limit rulers' power by subversive means; and occasionally this might appear to condone unjust rule. But who is not horrified by the *Histoire*'s system—and that of other 'modern philosophers' who open the door wide to insurrection—expressly subordinating legitimate royal and ecclesiastical authority to the interest of the majority in society?[59] The *Histoire* flagrantly summons the Indians, and also the blacks, *mestizos*, and Creoles, to revolt. Varela y Ulloa's footnotes signal the most emphatic agreement here, remarking that 'la libertad immoderada, y la rebellion' [excessive liberty and rebellion] stem directly from the ideas of those termed *enciclopedistas*.[60]

Finally, Nuix deploys philosophical arguments to oppose the *Histoire*'s demands for a universal *tolerantismo* and *libertad en pensar, en hablar, y en escribir* [liberty of thought, speech, and of the press] which, protests Nuix, would mean the total ruin of Spain, the Americas, and indigenous Indian society, indeed all society. Here, Nuix's hitherto carefully tended reasonableness finally deserted him. How can the *philosophes* champion a general *tolerantismo*? Here Nuix launches into a vitriolic attack on the Jews whose perverseness and antisocial character, he says, undermine every society. The *encyclopédistes* he accused of perversely turning a blind eye to this appalling menace. The *Histoire* defends the Jews. 'Raynal's' *Esprit* in both the versions

---

[55] Nuix, *Reflexiones imparciales*, 278, 284; Elliott, *Empires*, 264–5.
[56] Nuix, *Reflexiones imparciales*, 278, 284–5.
[57] Robertson, *History of America*, 152.   [58] Nuix, *Reflexiones imparciales*, 298.
[59] Ibid. 176–8; Hauben, 'White Legend', 8–9.   [60] Nuix, *Reflexiones imparciales*, 177 n.–8 n.

of 1777 and 1782 even goes so far as to affirm that the Jews are 'our brothers' and should be freed from the abominable persecution and political and economic shackles they were everywhere subjected to in Christian lands—a typical radical theme subsequently echoed by Dohm, Cloots, and others, who all attributed the perverse stress on trade in Jewish society to the discrimination and disabilities heaped on them by Christian rulers. The *Histoire* even suggests the Jews should be allowed to live 'enfin libres, tranquilles et heureux dans un coin de l'univers', perhaps on their own Caribbean island.[61] The freedom of thought and expression the *enciclopedistas* proclaim would permit every religious and philosophical sect to express its views, no matter how contrary to Christianity. Not only would the Jews be freed to publicize their atrocious opinions about Christ but so would the atheists, *Hobbesianos*, and *materialistas* who would be able publicly to espouse *materialismo*. Equally, the *enciclopedistas* would be free to impugn royal authority, something that should always remain detached from the people and free of their criticism. Writers would freely emulate the *Histoire* in continually maligning authority royal and ecclesiastical as 'despotism', reducing all legitimate government and religion to 'monstrous anarchy'.[62]

Nuix's virulent anti-Semitism was by no means shared by everyone at court in Madrid. Carlos had attempted but failed to re-introduce a Jewish presence into Naples in the 1740s. In 1797, Varela himself formulated a proposal (last hinted at during the time of Olivares) that the Jews, or at least some Jewish merchants, should be readmitted into Spain to help stimulate commerce.[63] Though never implemented, this suggestion appears to have been approved in principle by the Godoy regime. But below the level of government ministers intolerance remained deeply entrenched and any such dramatic departure from the past few centuries unthinkable. In Iberian society, tolerating any religious minorities remained inconceivable. Far more typical was Nuix's view that the *tolerantismo* of the *enciclopedistas* is something unchristian, anti-Christian, and total anathema to Spaniards. *La tolerancia universal* is a doctrine that can only be conscionably upheld by men professing polytheism or atheism.[64] All monotheistic religions, he quoted Hume as declaring (while completely ignoring his ironic intent), are necessarily intolerant and cannot avoid so being, so that one cannot expect Christianity to be other than 'intolerant'.

The battle against the *Histoire* in the Spanish imperium continued for decades. Besides enlisting Nuix, royal officials commissioned the still more learned royal *cosmógrafo mayor de Indias*, Juan Bautista Muñoz (1745–99), a Valencian professor of philosophy, to compose a full-scale narrative of the Spanish conquests and empire in the New World. This project, initiated in July 1779, aimed at providing a solid documentary basis for rejecting all hostile claims regarding Spain's role in the Indies

---

[61] [Raynal-Hedouin], *Esprit et génie*, 278; [Cloots], *Lettre sur les juifs*, 45, 53–4.
[62] Nuix, *Reflexiones imparciales*, 186–9; Hauben, 'White Legend', 8.
[63] Hauben, 'White Legend', 7; Israel, *European Jewry*, 92.
[64] Nuix, *Reflexiones imparciales*, 190, 192–3.

and her treatment of the Indians.[65] This was a work of apologetics expressly undertaken to protect the reputations of the Spanish crown, Church, and nation. As such, Muñoz's enterprise was a quintessential manifestation of mainstream Enlightenment. Sworn to write only fully objective, unimpeachable documents-based history such as had never been written before, hoping to achieve in history 'what philosophers have practised in the various natural sciences and for which they have rightly been called *restauradores* [restorers]', Muñoz started work.[66] Truth only emerges from solid evidence properly evaluated. His guiding principle, he proclaimed, was to question everything previously written about the Indies, taking nothing for established, so as to expound only truth on the basis of incontestable documentary proof.[67] To enable him to carry out this project, first the archives of Madrid and then papers from other hitherto obsessively secret Habsburg and Bourbon archives were opened to his researchers. The ensuing collecting and filing of documents relating to the Indies resulted in 1784 in the setting up of the celebrated Archivo de Indias in Seville, today the world's single most important archive of Europe's colonial expansion.

Muñoz's great weakness in refuting the *Histoire* was that his novel and elevated method of writing enlightened history was too slow. Only after years in the archives and libraries did he take up his pen and write anything of significance. He powerfully enlisted enlightened historiography in the service of Spanish royalism and Catholicism but not quickly enough, the first volume only being presented and approved for publication by the committee of the Royal Academy of History, chaired by Almodóvar, in 1791. Demonstrating the legitimacy of the crown's acquisition of its New World possessions, the integrity of the crown's and Church's treatment of the Indians, and Spain's spreading the 'light of European culture and the religion of Christ among infinite barbarous and impious nations' needed vast research to be effective. Christianity alone, much late eighteenth-century opinion was willing to agree, was a benefit so great as to justify all Spain's New World wars and conquests. Yet, Muñoz had to admit that the conquests scarcely reflected Christianity's true spirit. Christianity's true 'arms', he agreed, are exhortation, gentleness, and patience.[68] History, though, ruled that ever since the Crusades, it had been the practice to consider fighting infidels something devout and sacred undertaken to remove obstacles to religion's spread. According to the lights of the age, whoever did not believe in Christ was truly a foe who might be justly dispossessed of his lands and goods. Those Christian princes who invested most in conquering territory from the infidels were considered the most pious and this was still so in the sixteenth century. No one had disputed the Spanish king's right to undertake such ventures

---

[65] Muñoz, *Historia*, i, 'prologo' p. II; Tietz, 'Diderot', 297; Cañizares-Esguerra, *How to Write the History*, 170–1.

[66] Muñoz, *Historia*, i, 'prologo' pp. iv–v.

[67] Ibid. i. 1; Mestre Sanchis, *Apología*, 205, 207.

[68] Muñoz, *Historia* i. 157; Cañizares-Esguerra, *How to Write the History*, 196; Paquette, *Enlightenment*, 48.

then, and no one in his day could dispute the legitimacy of Ferdinand and Isabella's and Charles V's conduct in terms of then prevailing ideas.[69]

2. THE TUPAC AMARU REBELLION

Immediately prior to the great Indian rebellion of 1780–3, in Peru, the crown had striven to extend the reach of the viceregal administration and the grip of Catholic allegiance in the Indian villages, mobilizing the Indian nobles, or *caciques*, and establishing village 'public schools', with teachers paid from local Indian tributes. This went together with a highly unpopular campaign of introducing new consumption taxes on the Indian population. At the heart of this programme which had fiscal, cultural, and religious aims all at the same time was a determined royal attempt to reduce the use of Quechua, Aymara, and other native languages in the two Perus in favour of Spanish.[70]

The *caciques*, denounced in the *Histoire* as a bogus nobility concocted by Spain[71]— a charge only partly correct since many did actually descend from pre-Conquest Aztec and Inca nobles—were used to dealing with the royal and church authorities in Spanish but often remained illiterate and unable to write Spanish, and sometimes even to sign their names. In central Mexico too, in the 1770s and 1780s, many or most *caciques* could not properly read or write Spanish, a serious hindrance to their fulfilling their legal and administrative functions.[72] The proposed schools would better integrate Indian societies into the empire, render the *caciques* better administrators, and those beneath them better subjects and Catholics. Implemented in some places with the help of the parish clergy, this initiative amounted to one of the most ambitious programmes of state-sponsored elementary education of the entire Enlightenment era and, though blighted by the subsequent risings, at least some of these schools continued to operate through the 1780s and later.[73] The effect was to expand use of Spanish and reduce the prevalence of indigenous languages, in Lower and Upper Peruvian society, principally Quechua and Aymara. Meanwhile, according to a detailed report from Santiago, dated January 1784, most Indians living on and around the missions of central and southern Chile, as far as the frontier with the still independent Araucanians, were effectively bilingual and had no difficulty in speaking Spanish.[74]

---

[69] Muñoz, *Historia*, ii. 158–9.
[70] AN Bolivia Exp. Colon. Ad. 1777 no. 27: 'Expediente sobre que se erijan escuelas y se prohiban los differentes idiomas que se usan (Carangas)'; AN Bolivia Exp. Colon. No. 15, 18 Jan. 1774 (provincia de Sicasica), fos. 2, 4–7.
[71] *Histoire philosophique* (1770), iii. 46–7.
[72] Gibson, *Aztecs*, 149.
[73] BN Lima X 349.1 B22A, Baquíjano, *Alegato* (1788), 12.
[74] AGI Chile 193 'Relacion general del estado de las Misiones' (31 Jan. 1784).

In scale, impact, and its subsequent resonance, the Tupac Amaru rising was much the greatest Amerindian revolt against colonial rule of early modern times. It began some ten months after an earlier rising, provoked by new taxes, in Arequipa, in southern Peru, in January 1780, a rising marked by close collusion between local Creoles, *mestizos*, and Indians as well as friction between the groups. The main insurrection began in November 1780 and was led by the *cacique* of Tinta, José Gabriel Tupac Amaru, a *cacique* who had spent a year in Cuzco, in 1777, involved in litigation, hoping to lighten the burdens on his people, an experience which reportedly 'opened his eyes'. The insurrection began with the capture and hanging in the town square of the royal district governor, or *corregidor*. Tupac Amaru proclaimed the end of forced Indian labour under the hated draft known as the *mita*, and the forced retail of goods and abolition of various consumption taxes as well as the office of *corregidor*. His leadership fanned the rising into a truly massive rebellion that shook the entire viceroyalty and one in which in some places (most notoriously at Oruro) Creoles—including some priests—and *mestizos*—again took part, though there are conflicting reports as to whether Creoles and *mestizos* continued colluding with Tupac Amaru's rebel army even after the Indians in some areas began (contrary to Tupac Amaru's wishes) slaughtering significant numbers of whites.[75] Some bands among the rebel Indians also stripped away the mask of Catholic piety and renounced Catholicism, attacking altars, images, and priests who had often proven unrelenting in exacting personal services from the Indians in their parishes. The slaughter of many Spaniards, and the sacking of churches and chapels in the Valley of Cochabamba and elsewhere, looked concerted and systematic.[76] Most insurgents, though, remained loyal to the Church.

Having unwittingly prodded the Indians to revolt, by piling fresh imposts on local produce, offices, and alcoholic beverages, as well as through ambitious schooling and language projects, the crown found itself facing a rebellion of unprecedented magnitude whilst simultaneously immersed in a bitter and costly colonial war with England. In this predicament the viceregal authorities further increased their reliance on peninsular administrators and troops out of a (well-justified) suspicion that there was a dangerous strand of Creole–Indian collusion in the insurrection. At the same time the crown sought to strengthen the standing of those *caciques* who loyally stood by crown and Church by taking up arms against the rebels. Often substantial landowners and traders, such *caciques*, already exerting a wide influence in some areas, were loaded with new titles, honours, and medallions bearing the bust of the king, all part of a mounting campaign to lever as many *caciques* as possible away from the mass of Indian villagers and *mestizos*, and bind them closer to the regime.[77] Indian levies raised against the rebels by loyal *caciques* indeed proved instrumental to defeating the rebellion in the culminating military encounters in the Andes. In this

---

[75] Robins, *Priest–Indian Conflict*, 27, 125–6, 158–9, 172–3, 183.   [76] Ibid. 72, 155, 178.
[77] Ibid. 124; Fisher, *Bourbon Peru*, 81, 84.

way, the Indian nobility came to seem crucial to the entire structure of Spanish rule in the Indies. After the rebellion was finally quashed, several *caciques*, such as Don Juan, son of Don Diego de Chuquihuanca, were formally proclaimed by the crown knights of the prestigious Spanish military order of Santiago.[78] For having opposed the rebellion, the Indian town of Jujuy (today in north-western Argentina) was awarded the title of 'Muy Leal y Constante' [very loyal and constant] and grandly fêted.[79] By the mid 1780s Spanish authorities were distributing silver medals in remarkable profusion to Indian chiefs from Louisiana and the New Mexican Comanche frontier in the north to Chile in the south.[80]

But suppressing the rebellion could not remove the basic contradiction undermining Spain's imperium in the Indies. The often high-handed administrative and fiscal reformism, and militarization of the empire, that had originally provoked the insurrection continued more or less uninterrupted after its suppression. What Carlos III and his ministers saw as the unavoidable need to militarize the empire, and strengthen its defences against both internal subversion and external threats (especially British power), and generate increased resources, was bound to provoke a complex, multi-layered reaction. In Chile alone, by the autumn of 1781, following a scare the previous year with reports sent from Spain announcing that a British squadron prepared in Bengal was about to attack Valdivia, the president of the *audiencia* in Santiago reported there were no less than fourteen garrisoned coastal forts equipped with artillery in the territory.[81]

The threat of Creole subversion was a constant worry. Reports of collusion of 'American Spaniards' in the uprising may have been exaggerated but it certainly occurred, not least in and around Cuzco where the whole town was made to watch when captured insurgent leaders, among them Lorenzo Farfán, *cacique* of Pisaq (a noted centre of Inca ruins), were publicly executed in the principal plaza.[82] Evidence collected by the viceregal authorities showed that a number of Spaniards had figured in Tupac Amaru's entourage, among them a church organist and a wealthy hacienda-owner, Don Antonio Molina, who was reported to be one of his principal advisers.[83] Distrust and fear of further such collusion then in turn became an additional factor exacerbating the growing estrangement between the royal administration and the Creoles.[84]

The Tupac Amaru revolt in Peru and that of Tupac Katari, further south in Upper Peru, not only administered a profound shock throughout Andean South America, but made a deep impression also elsewhere in the Americas and Europe as well and

---

[78] AN Bolivia ALP CaCh-1594, letter of the Viceroy of La Plata to Don Ignacio Flores, 13 Dec. 1783.
[79] AN Bolivia ALP CaCH-1616, letter of the Viceroy of La Plata to the *Audiencia* of Charcas, 23 July 1785.
[80] Weber, *Bárbaros*, 186–91.
[81] AGI Chile 192 pres. of *audiencia* to Gálvez, Santiago, 5 Nov. 1781.
[82] BN Lima MS C432 (1780), 'Expediente del proceso y sentencia de Lorenzo Farfan'.
[83] AN Bolivia Audiencia de Charcas, SGI-20, fos. 4ᵛ–6, 8.
[84] Fisher, *Bourbon Peru*, 80–1, 97–9; Robins, *Priest–Indian Conflict*, 125–6, 178–9, 183.

had a considerable impact on prominent Creole personalities. Fleury Mesplet, the subversive French printer active in Montreal, or someone in his circle, had earlier published a highly seditious text in Canada, in 1777, the *Apocalypse de Chiokoyhikoy*, summoning not just Canada's Indians to rise against the British (in support of the American rebels) but also the Indians of Spanish America to rise against the Spanish crown; this text with its alarming message was prohibited in Spain, in May 1778, and repeatedly banned in and around Peru and Chile by the viceregal authorities after the Tupac Amaru rising began, in 1780.[85] Eminent among early Creole critics and aspiring reformers of Bourbon reformism in the New World was Don José Baquíjano y Carrillo, Conde de Vistaflorida (1751–1818), a leading notable of Lima where he was born in 1751. He had been sent to establish himself at court in Spain, at the age of 22, in 1773, but been expelled from the metropolis for extravagant behaviour, and denied the position of high court judge (*oidor*) in Lima to which he and his family desired him to be appointed. Among his more formative experiences in Madrid, he later recalled, were talks with foreign diplomats through whom he had first gained his awareness of developments in enlightened Europe.[86] Returning, in 1776, he subsequently notably combined begrudging the way the court had treated him with philosophy by injecting a strong dose of subversive political consciousness into Lima Creole society, coloured emotionally by the Tupac Amaru rising.[87] Although never explicitly committing himself to the idea of Spanish American or Peruvian independence, he abundantly demonstrated how radical ideas could serve a transformed actively insurgent Creole political consciousness.

The strength of Baquíjano's commitment to Enlightenment ideas emerges from his writings of the 1780s, his footnotes showing familiarity with Feijóo, Leibniz, Fénelon, Montesquieu, and the *Encyclopédie*, as well as, more crucially, Raynal and Marmontel. It was precisely Baquíjano's reputation for up-to-date erudition that led to his being nominated to present the university of Lima's academic eulogy at the inauguration of a new viceroy, Don Agustín de Jáuregui y Aldecoa, in the presence of virtually every important personage of the viceregal capital, on 27 August 1781, an event that occurred whilst much of Peru was still engulfed in rebellion, and whilst a new rebellion raged in New Granada. The occasion triggered one of the most notorious acts of political defiance of the colonial era.[88] The *Elogio* Baquíjano delivered in the viceroy's presence, instead of effusing the obsequious flattery usual on such occasions, became a famous landmark in the history of Peru's liberation from colonial status. While reaffirming the 'love' of the 'españoles americanos' for the Bourbon dynasty, his speech publicly referred to Raynal and the *Histoire philosophique*, daringly depicting the Conquest not just in negative but horrific terms, a catalogue of 'tiranía y sangrienta politica' [tyranny and bloody policy]. In several

[85] *Apocalypse*, 1–5; Amunátegui, *Precursores*, 256–7.
[86] BN Lima X 349.1 B22A, Baquíjano, *Alegato* (1788), 3–5.
[87] Castro, *Filosofía*, 107–16.
[88] Maticorena Estrada, *Colección*, i/iii. 185–6; Castro, *Filosofía*, 106–16.

direct allusions to Raynal, he notes the likelihood of an oppressed people revenging itself 'on the imprudent hand that subjects and oppresses it', a reference which though not exactly the foreshadowing of Peruvian independence some nationalist historians later claimed it to be, unquestionably infused a heightened radical perspective on Peru's problems and deep questioning of the Bourbon regime's legitimacy into the cultural world of Lima's elite.[89]

Baquíjano, admittedly, was no egalitarian.[90] Like Miranda, Belgrano, San Jorge, and other Creole subversives of the period, he had his social position to protect. But he also had strong grudges and there was plainly something that powerfully attracted him in the destabilizing, profoundly subversive tendency pervading the radical works he quotes and, still more crucial, that he directly linked to the insurgency racking Peru. The *Histoire* in particular aroused in him a pronounced sympathy, evident also among the Creoles implicated in the Comunero rising in New Granada, for the historic plight and ravished basic rights, as Diderot and the radical *philosophes* expressed it, of the Incas and other Amerindians. Referring repeatedly to Raynal (using a version published in 1775), Baquíjano even dared cite the obviously incendiary passage, describing prompt dismissal of extortionate and oppressive mandarins in the Chinese empire whenever the people lodge complaints against them, to underline his claim that power stems from the people.[91]

If he defines the 'people' in the case of Peru ambiguously, he clearly meant by it something broader than just the Creole elite, affording, if not inclusion, then at least justice for the Indians.[92] The Tupac Amaru insurrection, insinuated Baquíjano, was a justified response to oppression, royal fiscalism, and intrusion. The condition of Peru's indigenous peoples under Spain he denounced as a form of 'slavery' based on 'avarice', a 'dominación tirana' (tyrannical domination) rooted in vested interests maintaining illegitimate exactions and tribute.[93] Indubitably, Baquíjano claims Raynal and other foreigners exaggerated the oppressive character of Spanish rule in the Indies. Yet exploitation and illegality, he says, characterized the recent colonial reality. Some years later, in 1788, he again affirmed in print his profound sympathy for the modern descendant of the Incas, 'that wretch who with the sweat of his brow purchases the feeble sustenance with which he prolongs his sad days in misery and nakedness' and whose 'cause', he suggests, viceregal and Creole society had unjustly 'abandoned'.[94]

At the ceremony itself, the stunned viceroy judged it best to take no public offence. Nor, on learning the text was being printed and distributed, did he try to prevent Baquíjano's *Elogio* circulating in the city. Lima's San Marcos university enjoyed autonomous privileges, including the right to print these inaugural orations, which

[89] Baquíjano, *Elogio*, 82–3, 88–9; Riva-Agüero, 'Don José Baquíjano', 477.
[90] Fisher, *Bourbon Peru*, 89–90; Carrion Caravedo, 'La Soberanía', 65, 67.
[91] Baquíjano, 'Elogio' (1781), 89; see also Maticorena Estrada, *Colección*, i/iii. 106; Castro, *Filosofía*, 111.
[92] Castro, *Filosofía*, 111, 114–15; Carrión Caravedo, 'La Soberanía', 68–9.
[93] Carrión Caravedo, 'La Soberanía', 11–12; Castro, *Filosofía*, 110–11.
[94] BN Lima X 349.1 B22A, Baquíjano, *Alegato* (1788), 11.

he hesitated to infringe. The university may have been in urgent need of a 'total reforma' [total reform], like practically everything else in the viceroyalty,[95] in Baquíjano's opinion, but in this instance, its being an archaic, privileged, autonomous structure worked in his favour. Ministers in Madrid, though, on learning of the incident, viewed Jáuregui's reticence less as prudence than abjectly failing to defend the royal interest.[96] Reprinted three times, the *Elogio* lost Baquíjano, now a marked subversive and *libertino*, all chance of further royal favour.[97] 'One of the most pernicious and subversive papers that have been spread about in that realm',[98] in Gálvez's opinion, the pamphlet was vigorously suppressed on orders from Madrid, copies already distributed being searched for and whenever possible seized.[99] Of 600 copies produced 312 copies of Baquíjano's text were retrieved and remitted to Spain.[100]

Baquíjano's rooms were searched and his papers and books seized. Among the latter were titles by Montesquieu, Marmontel, Raynal, Linguet, and Machiavelli besides the *Encyclopédie*, and copies of his *Elogio*. Ministers in Madrid were afterwards 'very surprised' to learn that Marmontel's *Bélisaire*, Raynal, and the *Encyclopédie* 'run freely' in Peru, these being books which 'beside being prohibited for all classes of person by the Inquisition are also banned by the state'.[101] The *Encyclopédie* had been outlawed in the Spanish Indies since January 1761. Renewed orders for the suppression of Raynal and Marmontel's *Bélisaire* had been issued in June 1780,[102] and the ban on Montesquieu reaffirmed in December 1781. The most notable items in Baquíjano's library were precisely the works emerging as chief targets in what was fast becoming a general campaign against subversive literature in Spanish America.[103] The viceroy was instructed to ensure strict suppression of all the banned works in close concert with the Inquisition. Baquíjano's books were publicly burnt by the authorities in Lima.

The third revision of the *Histoire* appeared too early, in 1780, to report the Tupac Amaru rebellion itself. But here as before resounds the thesis that all men are equal and equally capable of what is best and worst, the submissiveness and resignation of the Indian masses under unremitting oppression being deplored not as innate characteristics but the outcome of their debasement by crown, landowners, and the Church.[104] Being relentlessly downtrodden had reduced the Incas to 'une indifférence stupide et universelle'.[105] So servile and abject were they that the Indians made no effort to resist or escape, something no one could comprehend 'si on ne savait pas combien l'habitude et la superstition dénaturent l'espèce humaine'.[106] If the Incas' descendants, and those of the Aztecs and Maya, remained severely traumatized this

---

[95] BN Lima MS C1285 (1785), Baquíjano, 'Expediente', 15–16.
[96] Maticorena Estrada, *Colección*, i/iii. 185, 213–15.
[97] Riva-Agüero, 'Don José Baquíjano', 482; Schmidt, 'Against "False Philosophy" ', 151–6.
[98] Riva-Agüero, 'Don José Baquíjano', 481.   [99] Ibid.
[100] Maticorena Estrada, *Colección*, i/iii. 241, 251.   [101] Ibid. 254.
[102] Maticorena Estrada, *Colección*, i/iii. 265, 274.   [103] González Sánchez, 'Libros europeos', 349.
[104] *Histoire philosophique* (1770), iii. 49–51.   [105] Ibid. iii. 141–5.   [106] Ibid. iii. 51.

resulted from a repression so prolonged and severe it would lock any people in the same supine condition. The Indians' real capacities were hidden for the present but evident in the evolution of Indian society itself and even in a few places in contemporary society. The Maya of the Chiapas region, reports the *Histoire*, had preserved a clear 'superiority' in attitude over New Spain's other indigenous peoples due to their unique advantage in having been taught and protected by Las Casas, the great Dominican who fought oppression and tenaciously resisted when the *conquistadores* had tried to subject them. His teaching revived their virtues, their higher moral calibre infusing their language, arts, and crafts being evident especially in the elegance of their dress and their dignified bearing.

The general revolt in the Indies the *Histoire* so resoundingly predicts seemed already to be heralded by the Tupac Amaru insurrection. Both the *Histoire* and the Peruvian revolt helped foment the new ideology of militant, sweeping opposition and enlightened awareness among the Creoles, fanning their incipient cosmopolitanism and *panamericanismo*. Francisco de Miranda (1750–1816), the earliest leader of the Independence movement in Spanish America, having arrived in Spain, from Caracas, in 1771, was among the first on whom the *Histoire* has been known to have definitely had an impact, in his case as early as 1772 or 1773.[107] The *Histoire* was destined to play a vital part in the further evolution of both his own personal ideology and the wider Spanish American Radical Enlightenment. Years later, during his European tour of 1785–9, he visited Marseilles, to meet his hero, Raynal, who was then residing there. They met several times in December 1788 and February 1789, sipping Spanish American drinking chocolate sent by Raynal's friend Aranda from Spain. Miranda learnt how Heredia, secretary of the Spanish embassy in Paris, when Aranda was ambassador there, had supplied much of the detail relating to the Spanish Indies. Miranda was dismayed to find, though, that Raynal's appetite for emancipation through rebellion had cooled noticeably since publishing the great work.[108]

---

[107] Spell, *Rousseau*, 131.

[108] Rodriguez de Alonso, *Siècle*, 596–7, 615–16; Spell, *Rousseau*, 131–2; Racine, *Francisco de Miranda*, 101–2; Bancarel and Goggi, *Raynal*, 380–2.

18

Philosophy and Revolt in Ibero-America (1765–1792)

1. THE CREOLE–PENINSULAR RIFT

In recent decades it has become commonplace in the historiography of Spanish-America's Independence to minimize the role of Enlightenment ideas and portray the great rupture with Spain—and with monarchy generally—as something occurring, incidentally, suddenly, almost by accident without forethought or direct linkage with anyone's plans or schemes. The great rupture has come to be attributed by scholars to very short-term factors—essentially just the crisis of the Spanish monarchy precipitated by Napoleon's invasion of Spain, in 1808. Insofar as there was any doctrinal content, urge several recent writers, it was something traditional, locally driven, and patriotic rather than an outgrowth of the European or transatlantic Enlightenment.[1] This view has been accompanied by the claim that the impact of the examples of the American and French revolutions was generally secondary.

But the idea that great developments ensue from no particular cause other than an accident (i.e. Napoleon's invasion of Spain disrupting the Spanish court) and that the American Revolution presented no great spectacle or shock to Ibero-Americans is intrinsically highly implausible. First, such a view lacks explanatory force, providing no explanation of how the emancipation ideology that permeated both Spanish and Portuguese America by the 1780s first emerged onto the scene. Secondly, it fails to provide any explanation of why many key leaders of the Spanish American consciousness were so deeply, even fanatically steeped in a certain type of Enlightenment ideology. Thirdly and fourthly, it severely underrates the impact and novelty of the American and French revolutions against the backcloth of the unrelenting conservatism, monarchism, and religious subservience of traditional Spanish American culture and values. Finally, the revisionist view is impossible to square with contemporary opinion and much other late eighteenth-century evidence.

Where there has recently been a degree of interest in the impact of the Enlightenment on Spanish American Independence, the stress has been on the primacy of

---

[1] Rodríguez, *Independence*, 3, 65–74; Fisher, *Bourbon Peru*, 100–4; Chiaramonte, *Ilustración*, 46–8; Breña, *Primer liberalismo*, 218, 260.

British influences. But this too is something questionable both for the background period down to the 1790s and also for the initial movements, from 1808.[2] In what follows, I shall argue that Enlightenment developments before 1808 were crucial for setting the scene and subsequent direction of Spanish American Independence, that intellectual debates are not separable from the examples of the American and French revolutions, and also that before 1808 the primary intellectual influences were not in fact British but French and Italian.

Intellectually and ideologically no less than economically and militarily, Spain's hold on her New World empire was rendered altogether more precarious in the late eighteenth century, partly by global strategic developments and partly by the Enlightenment—both 'moderate' and radical. Her imperial role was then further brought into question by the American Revolution. The viceroy of New Granada (today Colombia), writing to Gálvez from Cartagena de Indias, in July 1781, at the height of the Comunero insurrection in the northern Andes, reported to Madrid his great apprehension due to the convergence of major rebellion in Spanish America with the widespread and intense awareness of the Revolution to the north; he was deeply fearful 'because the form of *independencia* won by the English colonies of the North is now on the lips of everyone [participating] in the rebellion'.[3] For these reasons and because it makes little sense to examine the causes of the Spanish American Independence movement without first properly evaluating the impact of the Enlightenment and the American and French revolutions on Spanish America more generally, the only sensible approach is to begin with the Spanish American Enlightenment's beginnings and evaluate its impact.

As in Spain itself, the public debate commenced with the penetration of the writings of Feijóo, the great enlightener to whom, as a Dominican opponent of Rousseau put it, writing in Mexico in 1763, 'the [Spanish] Americans owe a debt of eternal gratitude'.[4] Holding philosophy and science to have had a crucial role in reordering our world and that the American-born were the intellectual equals of European Spaniards, he was widely read in the Spanish dependencies during the 1740s and 1750s, enjoying as he did the seal of both royal and (during the pontificate of Benedict XIV) papal approval. In the Indies, an added point for the Creoles and those of *mestizo* extraction with education—a few of which did exist—was his criticism of the Conquest, in his view something more deserving of 'execration than applause', together with his condemning the *conquistadores'* rapacity and cruelty toward the Amerindians.[5]

From the 1740s, the Enlightenment exerted not just a profound but a profoundly disturbing impact throughout Spanish America culturally, economically, socially,

---

[2] Racine, 'British Cultural', 423–5.

[3] AGI Santa Fe 578/1 Viceroy Florez to Gálvez, Cartagena, 11 July 1781.

[4] De Pauw, *Recherches*, ii. 165; Mariano Coriche, *Oración*, 'Prologo' p. iii; Chiaramonte, *Ilustración*, 31–4.

[5] Gonzalez Feijóo, *Pensamiento*, 154–8; Mestre Sanchis, *Apología*, 62.

and politically. The greatest danger for the crown was the Enlightenment's capacity to intersect with the long-standing grievances and disaffection of the Creole elite, a social and political problem of the first order and in this period an increasingly unsettling factor of disturbance culturally, intellectually, and politically throughout Spanish America. The seeds of the far-reaching estrangement between American and peninsular-born Spaniards in the New World, already rightly highlighted by the *Histoire philosophique* as the most powerful factor of change and disturbance in Ibero-America, in 1770, reached all the way back to the mid sixteenth century and had originally been encouraged by certain decisions, or errors of policy, on the part of the Spanish crown which had never adequately tried to address or diminish this breach. Rather, both Habsburg and Bourbon royal policy had continually aggravated the festering split between *españoles americanos* and *españoles europeos* (European Spaniards) by heaping favours, trust, and the higher posts of the Americas on those newly arrived from Castile, known in New Spain as *gachupines* and in Peru (and to New Granada's Comunero rebels) as *chapetones*. Crown and viceroys adhered to this practice even though peninsula-born newcomers were frequently not genuinely of noble origin and rarely came prepared with much knowledge of local conditions.

Nearly all New World Spanish viceroys were peninsula-born nobles, usually of middling rather than grandee status, and these—and their military governors of the major fortresses—had then systematically discriminated against American-born Spaniards not only by filling their own entourages with relatives, subordinates, and countrymen but also by influencing royal appointments to the regional high courts (*audiencias*), district governorships, and command of frontier posts. The viceroys generally discriminated in this way partly to ensure their personal authority but also in deference to the crown's long-standing, justified fear that Creoles would prove more partial to their own locality's and region's interests than those of the metropolis. The depth of the rift, arguably much sharper and more deeply rooted than anything comparable in English-speaking America, stemmed from a complex past over several centuries and was continually aggravated by royal and viceregal policy. Of course, this was nothing new, quite the contrary. What proved to be the equivalent of political dynamite in Spain's New World Empire, however, was the convergence of ancient grievances with fundamentally new Enlightenment ideas.

So deep was the psychological, cultural, and historical split between Creoles and peninsulars which in New Spain had been a major factor in the turbulent politics of the 1620s and 1640s (the celebrated Palafox affair),[6] that it had long affected appointments at all the middling and higher levels in the administration, religious orders, and even the craft guilds. At the great silver-mining centre of Potosí, in Upper Peru, a rigid system of alternating civic offices between Creoles and 'Europeans' to try to stabilize a virulent rivalry reaching back to the mid sixteenth century was confirmed and formalized by the viceroy in 1759. From the crown's standpoint,

---

[6] Israel, *Race, Class and Politics*, 217–47.

introducing a strict *alternativa* enabled the viceroy to hold the balance between Creoles and peninsulars and hopefully effectively manage disputes and disturbances. But the *alternativa* accomplished this by further deepening and institutionalizing a now ineradicable social tension.[7] By thus hardening the division royal and viceregal policy estranged the Creoles further from the royal administration and eventually from the crown itself, from the instant a suitable legitimizing ideology became widely available. Much as civil society was divided in this way, so were the clergy. The religious orders in Spanish America had since the early seventeenth century devised extremely arcane and complex voting procedures, like the Dominican *alternativa* and, in New Spain, the Franciscan *ternativa*, designed to defuse tensions when electing their priors and provincial heads. These rules stipulated that Creoles and peninsulars hold key offices by turn, further formalizing a split which thereby became still more deeply embedded and capable of generating bouts of feuding of sometimes astounding virulence. Published histories of the religious orders in Spanish America teemed with accounts of extremely vehement quarrels between the two main rival cultural-ethnic factions.

As early as the early seventeenth century, then, an elaborate culture of Creole–peninsular rivalry fed into Spanish America's local politics.[8] This suffused socio-cultural war, for that is what it was, seriously affected even the retail, commercial, and artisan guilds. In Lima, for example, the sixteen Peruvian shoe-shop owners in the city in 1780 complained bitterly that the peninsula-born shoemakers, despite being only five in number and hence barely more than a quarter of the total, possessed the 'right', which in common justice seemed indefensible, to preside alternately and command a half share in its honours and offices under an *alternativa* instituted only recently, by viceregal edict of August 1777, supposedly to end a long history of commotion marring the guild. Rather than ensuring quiet, the edict's only function according to the Creole shoemakers was unjustly to render the 'maestros europeos' (European masters) pre-eminent.[9]

Don José de Gálvez, the *visitador-general* who inspected New Spain in 1765–71 and remained a key figure in the royal government of the Indies subsequently, famously scorned the Creoles' abilities and resolutely pushed for changes that provoked a further upsurge of resentful antagonistic *Criollismo*, especially among the privileged strata of locally born whites.[10] Gálvez was anything but untypical in this disdain: many 'European Spaniards' (and other Europeans) considered the Creoles unreliable, ignorant, indolent, and not up to performing higher responsibilities. Locally born New World writers in the late eighteenth century complained bitterly of this prejudice while praising Feijóo for trying to discredit it.[11] In the sphere of intellectual

---

[7] BN Bolivia EC Ad 1767, no. 43 'Del cavildo de Potosí sobre la alternativa'.

[8] *Histoire philosophique* (1770), iii. 297–8; *Histoire philosophique* (1780), iv. 325–7, 401–2; Israel, *Race, Class and Politics*, 102–9; Elliott, *Empires*, 200–1.

[9] AGN Lima Gob. Pol. Ad. Leg. 36/348, fos. 3–4, 5^v, 12^v, 17^v, 19^v.

[10] Schmidt, 'Against "False Philosophy"', 137–8.

[11] Mariano Coriche, *Oración*, 'Prologo' p. iii; de Pauw, *Recherches*, ii. 165–7.

debate, however, the Creoles' eighteenth-century detractors, headed by de Pauw, were quick to ridicule Feijóo's stance. His eulogizing 'l'esprit sublime des Américains' was derided as absurd by de Pauw who pointed out that the Spanish American universities were yet to produce a single Creole celebrated in medicine, botany, or philosophy.[12]

A few royal high officials, meanwhile, more sympathetic to the 'españoles americanos' than most, had by the 1770s begun worrying lest the New World's intricate culture of racial classification and social status was itself becoming a threat to the empire. Most newly arrived peninsulars were greatly 'mistaken about the true character of the Creoles', wrote one senior official, having just toured Mexico in 1781, 'considering them lazy' and failing to grasp that insofar as they were really indolent and corrupt 'it is the Europeans who have made them such, by proceeding with "un despotismo absoluta", everywhere enforcing oppression, graft and extortion and only sending out to the Indies men so inured to vice and effrontery as to be total misfits in Europe'. The Creoles were considered poorly educated and trained. 'But what are the Creoles going to apply themselves to if there are no crafts and if industry is prohibited by the crown?'[13]

Bourbon reformism in late eighteenth-century Spanish America was inspired by a style of Enlightenment thinking that was emphatically royalist, state oriented, Catholic, mercantilist, and deeply conservative in its views of social structure. Its general aim was to strengthen the empire as a whole viewed as a transatlantic system and consolidate the royal grip over Spanish America, by improving the effectiveness of its administration, fiscal apparatus, commercial ties, and military defences, not least by adopting a new administrative system in the provinces headed by *intendentes*, a system introduced in Cuba in 1765, Venezuela in 1776, Peru in 1784, and Mexico in 1786. Since these goals were attainable only with ecclesiastical support and that of local elites, it was also an educative movement, an ideology seeking to extend the grip of a particular kind of cultural system—royal, metropolitan, bureaucratic, mercantilist, aristocratic, and uncompromisingly Catholic.

The emphasis on aristocratic and ecclesiastical power, as well as monarchy and favouring the economic interests of the metropolis, was unrelenting. Psychologically, the effect of the great Indian rebellion of 1780–3 was further to intensify the dialectic of Creole–peninsular antagonism and increasingly authoritarian tenor of crown policies. By heightening suspicion further and making the *chapetones* feel still more insecure, the great rebellion further intensified the drift to militarization, bureaucratization, and heavier fiscal pressure. Meanwhile, other changes, especially after 1770, social, political, and intellectual, caused a marked shift in ways of articulating Creole–peninsular antagonism. During the century's third quarter, the *Histoire philosophique* rightly observes, there occurred a fundamental transformation in Creole education and culture. For the first time, a small but highly significant

---

smattering of the Creole landed elite began following up their basic education in Spanish America's local universities with fashionable tours and study periods in Spain and elsewhere in Europe. These European tours, a key Enlightenment development, led to their discarding, observed the *Histoire*, the traditionally narrow, pious, blinkered outlook nurtured in the Spanish American universities, developing wider horizons, and involving themselves in a range of new activities, and in particular espousing enlightened ideas, projects, and perspectives which further stimulated their quest for new opportunities.[14] Their quest then being firmly blocked by the expanding bureaucratic-military complex back in Spanish America produced a total reconfiguring of the political and cultural scene by transforming the old antagonism into a confrontation seething with a new ideological intensity that ultimately proved fatal to *ancien régime* Spanish America. This, we have seen, was exactly the trajectory of Baquíjano and Miranda. It was a decisive cultural development that eventually generated a full-fledged revolutionary consciousness and entire class of potential revolutionaries, a key factor in a wider veritable 'revolution of the mind' driven by intellectual and cultural change.

The entire orientation of royal policy served to intensify what by 1780 was a fully conscious ideological clash rooted in opposed Enlightenment perspectives. Defeat and humiliation in the Seven Years War (1756–63) nurtured a concerted campaign by the crown to exact more resources from its American dependencies, as well as rebuild and strengthen coastal fortifications, expand garrisons, tighten the royal grip over the northern, southern, and Caribbean frontiers, and generally militarize the empire, Spanish America's counterpart to the simultaneous intensification of fiscal pressure in British North America.[15] These efforts were accompanied by efforts to remodel many local institutions that in the past were havens of Creole oligarchic influence and local control, especially the city councils. At the same time, the new instituted so-called 'free trade' policy was often consciously used by the imperial administration to favour the interests of merchants based in metropolitan Spain to decimate and destroy local industries and established mercantile patterns in regions such as Peru, the former pre-eminence of Lima in particular being notably reduced by the reforms.[16] The viceroys also launched a drive to expel as many European foreigners—especially British, Irish, Portuguese, and French—as possible and, still more paranoid, supervise the rising number of foreign scientific experts assisting with specialist commercial, mining, and scientific projects so closely as to compromise their effectiveness.

Crown interference with civic governance proved particularly unsettling. The Creole-dominated city government of Mexico City, the *cabildo*, lodged an unprecedented passionate protest against this creeping encroachment in 1771. Occurring well before the immediate crisis preceding the American Revolution erupted, their verbal rebellion took the form of an explosive document published by them and

---

[14] *Histoire philosophique* (1780), iv. 223–4.   [15] Fisher, *Bourbon Peru*, 28.
[16] Marks, *Deconstructing Legitimacy*, 62–4, 85–6.

dramatically publicized among the Creole elites of Lima, Potosí, and Charcas, indeed throughout Spanish America. Insisting on the 'nobility' of the *conquistadores'* descendants, Mexico City loudly complained of the prejudice against Creoles and notion prevalent in Spain that they have many innate defects. It was a stand pregnant with implications for the future. While making no comparable plea for the *mestizos* whom de Pauw and others deemed innately 'inférieurs aux Créoles', let alone the peninsulars, it added a resounding warning: failure to overcome prevailing prejudice against Creoles and assign them more influential positions, and ill-advised policies promoting peninsulars to their exclusion, would not just heighten current discontent but could well result in the 'perdida de esta América' [the loss of this America].[17]

The double and in some ways contradictory impact of the Enlightenment in Spanish America, then, is the key to understanding the rise of the post-1770 Spanish American revolutionary consciousness. The impact of the Enlightenment was only noticeable among the administration, elites, higher professions, and the universities. It is true that it did not seep down far into society. But the hunt for professional, administrative, and ecclesiastical training status and rewards was crucial to Spanish America's local politics and by its very nature highly susceptible both to Enlightenment intellectual subversion and internal social divisions. From Chile to New Spain, higher education was thus simultaneously socially divisive and highly fragmented, an unremitting engine of conservatism and sedition. Numbering eighteen in 1700, there existed no less than twenty-eight Spanish American universities by 1790, practically as many as in the German empire.[18] Here was a cultural-ecclesiastical complex of truly massive proportions and daunting disarray. That the Creole elites were studying, developing social aspirations, and reading far more widely than in the past and with unprecedented zeal and simultaneously developing an intellectual awareness lending new intensity and depth to long-standing resentment and antagonism provided a wholly new backcloth to the complex interaction between rebellion and ideas in late colonial Hispano-America.

2. BOURBON ENLIGHTENMENT IN THE AMERICAS

Commencing in the early 1770s, then, surged up a highly articulate political dissent, consciously reacting to the efforts of Carlos III's ministers, Campomanes, Floridablanca, and Gálvez, to consolidate their control over local administration in the viceroyalties and exploit the Spanish New World's silver, cotton, cash crops, timbers, and other resources more efficiently.[19] The conception of Enlightenment driving

---

[17] Schmidt, 'Against "False Philosophy"', 142, 144; Meissner, *Elite im Umbruch*, 82, 219, 327.
[18] Soto Arango, 'Enseñanza ilustrada', 92; Arboleda and Soto Arango, 'Introducción' to D. Soto Arango et al. (eds.), *La Ilustración en América colonial* (Madrid, 1995), 1–46; Cañizares-Esguerra, *Nature, Empire*, 47–8.   [19] Campomanes, *Discurso*, i. 2, 8, and iii, pp. lii–liii, lix–lxi.

government reform throughout Spanish America and its colleges, as the viceroy of New Granada emphasized in a report sent to the Council of the Indies in Madrid in 1789, followed instructions sent from Spain and was wholly anodyne from a religious and philosophical standpoint, seeking to replace scholasticism less with new general concepts or approaches, despite an enhanced acceptance of Newtonianism, than an eclectic approach prioritizing 'utiles ciencias exactas' [useful exact sciences]. Royal policy, in line with Campomanes' relentless pragmatism, in principle heavily favoured specialized study of metallurgy, chemistry, mathematics, medicine, botany, and law.[20] Indeed, no reform movement was ever more insistent on 'practicality' and eclecticism combined with religious piety than the official Enlightenment diffused by the crown in Spanish America. The difficulty was that the universities were ill equipped to teach these disciplines and precisely this undeviatingly pragmatic stance proved intensely problematic.

Everywhere in the Spanish America of the 1760s and 1770s one encountered not just more administrators and soldiers sent from Europe than before the Seven Years War, but also new kinds of expertise and experts mobilized by the crown—military engineers, naval engineers, mining engineers, physicians, surgeons, mineralogists, and botanists. Most of these experts were products of the new specialized royal institutes in Spain; but others came from elsewhere. Altogether, between 1768 and 1810 the crown and its viceroys organized over sixty land survey, botanical, and exploratory expeditions, several in collaboration with French naturalists, to regions ranging from California to southern Chile, involving a massive outlay of administrative capacity, personnel, and expertise as well as funds.[21] Royal use of as well as support for science was indeed abundantly in evidence throughout the empire by the 1780s when newly designed fortresses and sophisticated artillery batteries rubbed shoulders with new medical facilities and newly founded botanical gardens modelled on the Madrid Real Jardín Botánico, notably those founded in 1788 at Chapeltepec, on Mexico City's edge, and in Lima, designed as show-places for the flora of the Indies. Lima's botanical garden arose partly on the initiative of a noted champion of Spanish America's scientific establishment and corps of Linnaean botanists, Hipólito Unanue (1755–1833), who was also to be an early supporter of Peru's independence.[22] Physician, botanist, and expert climatologist, Unanue in the years 1791–5, significantly, also edited Lima's first enlightened periodical, *El Mercurio peruano*.[23]

In Spanish America Enlightenment was a movement, a new social and reading culture, a fundamental change in the fabric of civilization itself. A royal Enlightenment, familiar from the pattern prevalent in Spain, based on Newton, espousing an ideology of physico-theology and eager to promote science, spread vigorously across the continent. A striking feature was the universal adoption of Linnaeus' orderly

[20] Viceregal reports on New Granada, in Posada and Ibañez, *Relaciones*, 152, 251, 334–5.
[21] Clément, 'Expedición botánica', 132, 142; Clément and Nozal, 'L'Espagne, apothicaire', 157.
[22] Cañizares-Esguerra, *How to Write the History*, 300; González Bueno, 'Plantas y luces', 112–15, 118–19. [23] González Bueno, 'Plantas y luces', 118; Castro, *Filosofía*, 98–105.

classification of plants, culminating in the establishment of regular public lectures in Linnaean botany in Mexico City in 1788, a trend reinforcing the royal vision of modern science as a projection of the political and social order harmoniously underpinned by religion and theology. It was an enlightenment enabling viceroys and scientific experts with their expeditions, projects, cabinets of curiosities, and gardens to project an image of the crown as the Divinity's agent supervising a harmonious transatlantic order extending throughout the natural and the cultural and social worlds. Since organized science on this scale was expensive, the expeditions, academic learning, and especially the scattering of relevant new university chairs established at this time, besides being a way of expanding the empire's natural resources and representing them in a visible form, everywhere reinforced the dependence of higher education, scholarship, and science on royal patronage. Reform proposals requiring more up-to-date science, medicine, legal concepts, and experimental philosophy were considered and in part adopted by the royal authorities successively in the universities of Santa Fé de Bogotá (1768), San Felipe de Chile (1768), Universidad de Río de la Plata (1771), San Marcos de Lima (1771), and Caracas (1786).[24]

In line with Campomanes' drive to widen exploitation of America's natural resources which led the royal authorities to investigate the timber qualities of the trees in many areas, in southern Chile even beyond the bounds of the settled area, the royal administration patronized natural history research on a considerable scale. If there was much in traditional culture and the prevailing ignorance obstructing the programme, the crown sought to overcome the obstacles especially to practically oriented research. When officials in America corresponding with the Madrid botanical gardens were hampered in remitting seeds and plants by the negligence and unresponsiveness of the royal postal services, stern reprimands were dispatched from the court in Madrid.[25] The chaotic style in which port officials in Callao, Veracruz, Havana, and Cartagena dispatched the growing quantities of natural history exhibits and specimens for museums, academies, and royal gardens in Spain, with items jumbled and unlabelled in unmarked boxes, prompted a royal edict issued from Aranjuez, in May 1789, requiring botanical, zoological, and mineral specimens to be systematically labelled before being remitted in future, boxed in clear categories, minerals separately, fish together, birds in separate chests, with everything clearly marked.[26]

Foremost among luminaries of this royally sponsored expansion of science, learning, and academies in Spanish America was Don José Celestino Mutis (1732–1808), a Seville-trained medical man, eclectic, naturalist, and expert botanist, originally from Cadiz, who arrived in the Americas as physician to a new viceroy, at Bogotá, in 1761. A transatlantic celebrity, sustaining a regular scholarly correspondence with

---

[24] Arboleda and Soto Arango, 'Introducción', 29, 46–7, 54–5.
[25] AN Bolivia CaCH-1653 carta circular, 16 July 1787.
[26] AN Bolivia RC adiciones 79 *royal cédula*, Aranjuez, 31 May 1789.

naturalists in Europe, notably with Linnaeus and his circle in Sweden, Mutis lectured, wrote, and collected botanical specimens and drawings—large quantities of which he remitted to the royal gardens in Madrid and Seville—and led a number of scientific expeditions. A philosopher and theorist, he also helped transplant and propagate numerous useful trees and shrubs, refining and improving a remarkable array of plant oils, resins, gums, dyes, beverages, and precious woods.

Among his most celebrated undertakings was his research into the properties, and methods of extraction and propagation, of quinine from trees found on New Granada's Andean slopes and 'tea of Bogotá', a tea-plant he discovered in 1761 and unsuccessfully attempted to establish, as a valuable cash crop supposedly rivalling Chinese tea in taste and quality.[27] Ministers were eager to learn of ways Spain might utilize newly discovered plants, hoping not least to erode the massive revenues the British, Dutch, and French derived from their sugar exports from the Caribbean and tea and coffee imports from the East. Quinine, an extract used to treat malaria and other virulent fevers in the New World, Mediterranean, Africa, and Asia, was one substance the Spanish crown did succeed in establishing a valuable commercial monopoly in, and in becoming guarantor of its quality, a success extended by new research. Quinine had earlier been considered of suitable quality only when extracted from Peruvian cinchona trees. Mutis's efforts to prove New Granada quinines, though slightly different, were equally efficacious against fevers sparked off a fierce feud over the respective qualities of Peruvian and New Granada quinines persisting well into the 1790s.[28]

In botany, an orthodox disciple of Linnaeus, Mutis, in 1784 was elected a foreign member of the Royal Swedish Academy of Sciences.[29] Expedition leaders and key professors were, of course always representatives of the mainstream, official Enlightenment. Pragmatism, empiricism, Newtonianism, and physico-theology were the order of the day. In New Granada, Creole students began being taught the elements of the Newtonian philosophy in the colleges of Bogotá, Popayán, Quito, and Caracas even before the expulsion of the Jesuits, often using Spanish translations of the physics textbooks of the Dutch naturalist Musschenbroek.[30] In 1764, Mutis delivered a public discourse in Bogotá entitled *Elementos de la filosofía natural*, celebrating the achievements of Newton; later he translated Newton's *Principia Mathematica* into Spanish. They were living in an 'enlightened' age, his Creole students were assured, experiencing a philosophical and scientific revolution driven primarily by 'experimental physics' together with zoology, the new astronomy, and Linnaeus' botany, in which every 'secret' of nature was being uncovered by scientific researchers whom he designates 'los Físicos'.[31] Like Feijóo, Piquer, and Verney, Mutis eulogized Bacon, Boyle, and 'el grande Newton' whose modesty, constancy, and caution, as well as

---

[27] Ibid. 156.   [28] Ibid. 149.

[29] Posada and Ibañez, *Relaciones*, 253, 338–9; Cañizares-Esguerra, *Nature, Empire*, 123; Clément and Nozal, 'L'Espagne, apothicaire', 147–9.

[30] Arboleda and Soto Arango, 'Introducción', 30.   [31] Mutis, *Elementos*, 44.

great insight and mathematical skills, underpinned rejection of all dangerous metaphysical systems.

Philosophy based on Bacon, Locke, and Newton Mutis dubbed 'la verdadera filosofía' [the true philosophy] and this was the system he championed at every opportunity. English empiricism and promoting the exact sciences, in his eyes, constituted the clear, legitimate, and justifiable path of Enlightenment. Newton's 'experimental philosophy' had not only eliminated Cartesianism, he explained, but blocked materialist atheism and swept it from the field.[32] 'Almost all the [non-materialist] French', he assured his students, 'are now today Newtonians.'[33] The goal of Newtonian science was to know 'the Author of Nature by his works', though the results, held Mutis, would undoubtedly also be of immense usefulness in other spheres, especially teaching natural religion and moral philosophy. Newtonian science, proclaimed Mutis, is the clearest proof the world is governed by a supreme Creator and agent, namely God.[34] Nothing, he urged, had so greatly advanced learning and love of experimental science as 'the academies and societies established in all the important cities of Europe, and the expeditions to exotic parts, frequent and repeated journeys, and the splendid prizes with which sovereigns had embellished the natural sciences and benefited the human race'.[35]

The Enlightenment of Celestino Mutis and others like him proclaimed the great harmony between science and religion and between crown and people. But Enlightenment, he informed his Creole audience, not only produces fresh knowledge, vistas, and benefits, it also generates new dangers, the latter from a social and especially religious perspective. 'Who does not see that false systems of physics may lead men into atheism or at least excite opinions about the divinity and the universe that are very dangerous to the human race.'[36] Studying science and applied philosophy, Mutis did not attempt to conceal, had led many moderns, including 'some modern philosophers of great reputation', to mechanistic and materialistic conceptions of the universe paralleling those of certain ancient philosophers. Hence, the principal challenge confronting royal Enlightenment in the Indies, as elsewhere, was to combine useful and exact sciences with religious orthodoxy, sound philosophy, and loyalty to the crown. Fortunately, it was precisely experimental science, he argued, especially 'the philosophy of Newton', that most effectively protects men against the evil of materialism. In a discourse delivered before the viceroy, in 1773, he went so far as to claim that Newtonian physico-theology not only firmly underpinned the Enlightenment in Spanish America but had in principle destroyed the 'sect of atheists' in Europe.[37]

If there was still considerable resistance to the Enlightenment in Spanish America, as in Spain, this did not prevent steady progress in experimental science, insisted Mutis, most impressively in Madrid, though compared to what was happening in the

---

[32] Ibid. 50–1; Arboleda and Soto Arango, 'Introducción', 42, 51–2.   [33] Mutis, *Elementos*, 59.
[34] Ibid. 66–7.   [35] Ibid. 44–5; Cañizares-Esguerra, *Nature, Empire*, 122–3.
[36] Mutis, *Elementos*, 46.   [37] Mutis, *Sustentación*, 71; Clément, 'Expedición botánica', 152–3.

Spanish world generally that was just a fragment of the true 'revolución acaecida en el corto espacio de diez años' [revolution brought about in the short space of ten years].[38] The 1760s were indeed decisive. In Madrid, Cadiz, Seville, and Barcelona alike, men of all classes now espoused the new philosophy, enthusiastically forming 'libraries and cabinets of natural history, dedicated to perform and repeat numerous observations and experiments'.[39] And this was as it should be, for if society and its educators in Spain and its empire were successfully to block the atheistic systems and materialism and reinforce faith, they must combat the obstinate credulity and superstition of the conservative-minded, like his foes, the Dominicans, opposed to reforming the universities.

When his Dominican critics objected that Mutis was being dangerously innovative and that the Copernican system he regularly taught was 'intolerable to Catholics', he replied, invoking Feijóo, that Copernican astronomy is integral to the Newtonian philosophy and that, at Rome, the Inquisition had lifted its ban on the teaching of such astronomy which, in any case, was basic to Newtonianism and, hence, the curricular reforms adopted in Spain's universities.[40] As long as Spain's imperial Enlightenment emulated the English model, basing everything on Locke and Newton, nothing was to be feared. Yet his Dominican critics were by no means entirely mistaken. Up-to-date expertise in medicine, mining, law, and military technology was being continually urged yet proved to be unattainable without being mixed with a more literate, book-oriented, open, questing intellectual culture. But this was intrinsically impossible without freeing the mind and equipping the intellect to enter new spheres, hence without introducing a considerable measure of freedom of thought and expression, and independence of judgement, and here there was much the crown proved unable to control, as the subsequent careers of Unanue and others directly involved in the royal Enlightenment plainly illustrated.

At the royal college in Popoyán, Mutis's colleague Professor Felix Restrepo lent his energies over many years to advancing the cause of Newtonianism, presiding during the period 1782–9 over no less than forty-seven philosophical disputations, of which more than half invoked Newtonian principles.[41] In June 1786, he presided when his most celebrated student, the astronomer and physicist Francisco José de Caldas (1768–1816), expounded Newton's theory of light. Caldas, intensely Enlightenment oriented and antagonistic to the old scholastic philosophy, joined Mutis on his forays, becoming a noted mathematician and botanist in his own right, and an important contributor to the science of explaining and mapping plant distribution in terms of geographical conditions.[42] Later, he worked as assistant to the famous Alexander von Humboldt, in Ecuador in 1802. Additionally, he was for years much involved in the enlightened literary societies flourishing everywhere in Ibero-America from the 1780s. But Restrepo corresponded with Franklin and was later

---

[38] Mutis, *Sustentación*, 71.   [39] Mutis, *Elementos*, 45.   [40] Mutis, *Sustentación*, 85–7, 89–91.
[41] Arboleda and Soto Arango, 'Introducción', 56–7; Escobar Villegas and Salazar, 'Otras "luces"', 107.
[42] Adelman, *Sovereignty*, 183–4; Cañizares-Esguerra, *Nature, Empire*, 113–16, 124–5.

among those who loudly invoked Filangieri as an inspirer of the Spanish American Revolution while Caldas emerged after 1808 as the very symbol of the symbiosis of Enlightenment and Spanish American revolution, serving the independence movement both as an ideologue and military engineer. In 1816, he was captured by royalist forces and shot.

3. RADICAL ENLIGHTENMENT DIFFUSED ACROSS THE ATLANTIC

Worrying contradictions inherent in the Enlightenment of Locke and Newton were compounded by the chronic state of disarray in which the Spanish American universities lapsed after 1767. Spanish American universities and colleges during the later eighteenth century, like the rest of Spanish American society, remained, of course, heavily regulated and theologically closely supervised. It was never the intention of Carlos III's reforming minister either to secularize the universities or deprive the clergy of their pre-eminent position in higher or lower education. Rather, the expulsion of the Jesuits from the universities had the effect of transferring responsibility in higher education teaching to the other orders. But if the crown made only hesitant, partial efforts to promote modern science and mathematics in the universities, it was at great pains to enhance royal control and diminish clerical autonomy by dividing up the chairs and responsibilities as much as possible between the different orders. At the university of San Felipe at Santiago, in Chile, in December 1783, there was a rector, vice-rector, and fifteen professors of whom no less than eight were ecclesiastics, some canons of the cathedral, others friars belonging to different orders.[43] The university possessed a professor each for medicine and mathematics and at least four chairs in 'philosophy'; but philosophy in late eighteenth-century Chile was still predominantly theological, Thomist, and scholastic. The crown profited from the changed situation by holding the balance between the orders and through needing to pay no salaries to the professorial majority living in monasteries. But there was a major drawback to this continuance of ecclesiastical domination after 1767—a growing and irresolvable underlying tension between the officially still dominant scholasticism and the incoming tide of new science and enlightened ideas.

Teaching in all of the Spanish American universities, then, remained predominantly under the control of the religious orders. Rather than any swift royal campaign fundamentally to reform the content of university teaching along broadly new lines, there was a slow royal and sporadic local efforts to do so patchily. The transition to modernity in university teaching was neither effectively concerted by the crown nor systematic but it slowly occurred nevertheless driven by the general priorities of the crown and the impact of the new academies and institutes in the peninsula.

---

[43] AGI Chile 192. Pres. of *audiencia* to Gálvez, Santiago, 11 Dec. 1783, section 'real universidad'.

Superficially, the hegemony of theology and Thomism lingered. But the coherence and stability of teaching and the curricula was badly affected by the post-1767 disarray and the impact of competing interests and demands, causing much interruption in courses and teaching personnel as well as chronic lack of funds. Worse, what on the surface resembled a compromise between modern science and intellectual conservatism steeped in scholasticism, prevailing throughout the entire expanse of territory from the northern fringes of New Spain (California, New Mexico, and Texas) to Chile and Argentina, was actually a disorderly, chaotic system attempting to function on an expanding scale while incorporating a large dosage of new science within a resistant, enveloping theological shell. Rather than coherently shaping the outlook of the continent's legal, medical, and local landowning Creole elite and more highly educated clergy, the universities had become engines spreading confusion, frustration, and dissatisfaction.

Intellectual subversion stemmed above all from the fact that Spanish American Creole young men were travelling further afield than in the past for the purpose of completing their education and preparing for their careers, a few, such as Lardizábal and Olavide, going on to impressive careers in Spain. At precisely the same time that the crown was promoting more officials with European training to positions in the Indies, Creole families began sending their sons to Spain (and sometimes elsewhere in Europe) in appreciably greater numbers than before, to acquire the higher education, finish, and connections, and also army commissions—since 1760 a much expanded opportunity—which the changing situation demanded. Among these young, ambitious, often intellectually inclined arrivals in Europe were several Venezuelans, including Miranda who became an army officer, several later famous Argentinians, the Chilean Alonso de Rojas, and able Peruvians such as Olavide, Unanue, and Baquíjano, men equipped with sophisticated book knowledge combining a degree of erudition with frustrated ambition. There was even the occasional woman, such as Olavide's sister Gracia, who participated prominently in his salon at Seville.

The key group of disseminators of the ideas of the radical *philosophes* in Spanish America prior to 1789, consequently, were young Spanish Americans travelling and studying in Spain, France, and elsewhere and then returning to the New World where they at once considered themselves natural leaders of opinion. Not a few returned completely converted to radical ideas of basic human equality, popular sovereignty, universal toleration, and also, burning with resentment at the oppression exercised by the Spanish crown and its viceroys, utterly convinced of the merits of armed revolution as the requisite way to obtain their elevated new goals. Raynal, Helvétius, Mably, the *enciclopedistas*, Beccaria, Filangieri, and Rousseau became the idols of a highly motivated contingent of enthusiasts for radical ideas, prominent among whom were Baquíjano, Miranda, Manuel Belgrano, an Argentinian who returned to Buenos Aires in 1793 after years of studying in Spain, and Simon Rodríguez.

Baquíjano, we have seen, was an outstanding representative of the new radicalized Creole political consciousness. His family, of Basque origin, had strong aristocratic pretensions but had only recently purchased their Peruvian title of 'counts of Vista-florida'. Whilst in Spain, he later recalled, he read widely, studied the sciences, learnt languages, became acquainted with Olavide and Jovellanos, in Seville, and also with Campomanes and Floridablanca in Madrid. He also visited Barcelona and Valencia, becoming he later recalled a totally new person intellectually, transformed above all by enlightened reading.[44] Enthusiastic especially for Bayle, Montesquieu, Voltaire, and the *Encyclopédie*, back in Peru he made sure others came to share his zeal.[45] A lecturer at Lima university, a friar denounced to the Inquisition, in 1789, for reading Bayle's *Dictionnaire*, was found to have borrowed the set of large volumes he was studying from Baquíjano. In 1790, he was instrumental in setting up the 'Sociedad económica de Amantes del País' in Peru and became the editor of its journal *El Mercurio peruano*.[46]

Manuel Belgrano (1770–1820), a Buenos Aires Creole whose father was Italian, was dispatched to Salamanca at 16. There from 1786 to 1793 he studied law, became passionately interested in political science, and read the *économistes*, Montesquieu, Rousseau, Genovesi, Filangieri, and many others, later, after returning in 1794, becoming a key figure in the movement of political subversion on the River Plate. Returning to Buenos Aires, he was not only fiercely resentful of the viceregal administration but disgusted by the traditionalism dominating the social and economic thought of the River Plate's social and intellectual elite.[47] Rodríguez, born in Venezuela in 1771 and sent at the age of 14 to study in Europe, lived and studied successively in Spain, Germany, and France, becoming familiar with many Enlightenment texts. After reading Rousseau's *Émile* he was inspired to take up pedagogy and, on returning to Caracas, wrote influential educational treaties. He was later the guardian and teacher of Simon Bolívar, *El Libertador*, who in turn was to prove a lifelong disciple of Enlightenment thought—albeit of Enlightenment thought in a particular vein. Recent research has revealed strong echoes of the Neapolitan constitution of 1799 drawn up by Filangieri's friend and disciple Pagano in Bolivar's constitution of Angostura (1819), a further reminder that the revolutionary republicanism agitating the Hispanic world as well as much of Europe between 1780 and 1820 drew mainly on the tradition of radical republican thought evolving after 1760 in Italy as well as France.[48] As a youth Bolívar not only studied Locke, Montesquieu, Voltaire, and Rousseau but also Helvétius, Mably, Filangieri, and Lalande.[49] The subversive Enlightenment in Latin America, generally speaking, owed as little to British ideas as the royal Enlightenment was predominantly rooted in British empiricism and Newtonianism.

Another prominent representative of this crucial group, forming the politicized Spanish American Radical Enlightenment, was Don Antonio Nariño y Álvarez

[44] BN Lima X349.1B22A, Baquíjano, *Alegato*, 5; Riva Agüero, 'Don José Baquíjano', 473–4.
[45] Spell, *Rousseau*, 135; Castro, *Filosofía*, 107.
[46] Riva Agüero, 'Don José Baquíjano', 78; Soto Arango, 'Enseñanza ilustrada',105.
[47] Adelman, *Sovereignty*, 149, 151–2; Paquette, *Enlightenment*, 137.
[48] Escobar Villegas and Leon Maya Salazar, 'Otras "luces"', 89.   [49] Ibid.

(1765–1824), son of a peninsular Spanish financial official, or *contador*, and Creole mother. Having acquired a wide knowledge of the Enlightenment by the 1780s, in 1789 he formed a famous reading and discussion circle, or *Círculo Literario*, in Bogotá which gathered regularly in his magnificent library.[50] In 1789 Nariño acclaimed the French Revolution, in the early 1790s he translated Paine's *Rights of Man* into Spanish, and, in 1794, he secretly arranged the printing of a translation of the 1789 French *Declaration of the Rights of Man* and, with co-conspirators, even dared distribute copies along the main routes to Bogotá, a clandestine operation jointly suppressed by the viceroys of New Granada and Peru. He was imprisoned, along with a score of other suspects, some students, his library of 1,800 volumes being sequestrated in August 1794.[51] Fear of the local 'conspirators' he inspired continued haunting the authorities in Bogotá through the 1790s. From the list of his confiscated books, Nariño's knowledge of radical as distinct from moderate Enlightenment can be seen to have been extensive, even if it often derived from the *Histoire philosophique* or translations of works like Nonnotte's *Dictionnaire*, Bergier's *Déisme réfuté*, and Bergier's *Apologie*, all of which figured among his collection.[52]

Nariño figured among several local Creoles, 'algunos espíritus inquietos' [some restless spirits], as the authorities called them, who became distinctly suspect in the eyes of the viceroys and *audiencias*. Among his intimates was Pedro Fermin de Vargas Sarmiento, a Creole administrative official also actively plotting rebellion against the viceregal regime by 1791 at the latest who afterwards composed the text of the secret *Los derechos del hombre y del ciudadano* [Rights of Man and of the Citizen], based on the French declaration of 1789, published in Madrid, in 1797. Another erudite subversive was the *mestizo* pedagogue Javier Eugenio de Santa Cruz y Espejo (1747–95), founder of the public library of Quito who subsequently died in prison, after being arrested for composing subversive pasquinades. Another was the Creole naturalist Dr Sebastian López Ruiz, educated at Panamá and Lima, who, after having had his sizeable collection of Enlightenment books sequestrated, departed for Spain in 1792. Another whose books and papers were seized when he was arrested at Lima in 1794, Joaquín Alzamora, a teacher of French and mathematics originally from Panamá, had also learnt his Enlightenment in Spain and later, at Lima, participated in seditious meetings.[53] These were all part of a continent-wide intellectual ferment of great political and cultural significance.[54]

References to prohibited Enlightenment literature in Spanish America proliferated from the 1770s onwards, unsurprisingly, and were strikingly more frequent than in English-speaking North America. The massive risings of the early 1780s in Peru and

[50] AGN Lima Go. Corresp. Leg. 207/ 2093, order of the Peruvian viceroy, 26 Nov. 1794; Spell, *Rousseau*, 131; Adelman, *Sovereignty*, 93, 149.
[51] Ruiz Martínez, *Librería*, 25, 140, 184, 209; McFarlane, 'Science and Sedition', 97, 104.
[52] Ibid. 184, 209; Adelman, 'Rites', 396, 399.
[53] AGN Lima, Real Audiencia cuad. 949, trial of Joaquín de Alzamora, fos, 21, 23, 29ᵛ–30.
[54] Ruiz Martínez, *Librería*, 114–15, 182–3, 189.

New Granada then further encouraged an atmosphere of republican subversion, intrigue, and conspiracy, as well as a marked degree of sympathy for the Indian risings among Creole intellectuals. These great rebellions came to be studied by leading members of the Creole elite in the light of the *Histoire philosophique* in particular, hence of Diderot and his circle. The 1778 Madrid royal edict banning *L'An 2440*, Mercier's utopian fantasy, predicting a general revolution in the Old and New World led by *la philosophie* and involving a violent slave insurrection,[55] in November 1773, mentions 'muy seguros y indubitables informes' [very certain and indubitable reports] that such subversive literature was penetrating Spain and its empire.[56]

Penetration of texts such as these unsettled the royal administration throughout the Indies causing royal officials to scrutinize the attitudes of the Creole elites with an increasingly worried eye. A most revealing document emanating from high administrative circles of these years is the diary of Don Francisco de Saavedra de Sangronis, a royal commissioner who toured parts of the Caribbean and Mexico between 1780 and 1783 and then became *intendante* of Caracas. Spain, he was convinced, must either lose its empire in the New World in a 'short time' or else consolidate its hold for centuries to come, depending principally on whether or not the crown proved able drastically to change its administrative, economic, and cultural policies.[57] If Spanish policy continued along existing lines, proceeding 'with tyranny and oppression', as he put it, and failing to secure a wholehearted change in attitude among peninsular Spaniards in positions of responsibility there, there was little prospect of long avoiding 'una fatal catástrofe'.[58] It was not the American Revolution, however, that he considered the principal destabilizing element in the situation but rather that the Creoles 'are today in a very different situation from that of a few years ago, having enlightened themselves a lot in a short time'. Crucial, he like the *Histoire* judged, was the change in the Creoles' cultural and intellectual orientation. In Spanish America, 'la nueva filosofía va haciendo allí mucho mas rápidos progresos que en España' [the new philosophy is there making much more rapid progress than in Spain itself], while faith and religious zeal, 'the most powerful restraint on them', had worryingly diminished in recent years. Growing trade with the Anglo-Americans aggravated the threat, by introducing more 'new ideas about the rights of men and sovereigns'. But the overriding menace was the influx of French books 'de que hay allí immensa copia, va haciendo una especie de revolución en su modo de pensar' [of which there is an immense quantity, literature that is making a kind of revolution in their way of thinking].[59]

'In our America', lamented Saavedra, thousands of copies 'of the works of Voltaire, Rousseau, Robertson, the Abbé Raynal and other modern philosophers which those

[55] Baker, 'Revolution', 52; Darnton, *Corpus*, 17–18; de Bujando, *Index*, 610.
[56] Ibid. Exp. Colon. 1778, no. 20, 1^v–2.
[57] Saavedra, *Memorias*, 134, 149, 202; Weber, *Bárbaros*, 159; Morales Padrón, 'México', 356–7.
[58] Morales Padrón, 'México', 357.
[59] Ibid.; Saavedra, *Memorias*, 134; Ruiz Martinez, *Librería*, 25–6.

natives [i.e. the Creoles] read with a special enthusiasm' were circulating.[60] Consequently, '[Spanish] Americans are generally persuaded that Spain has formed a project to extort all the resources she can from those possessions and keep them always in a position of weakness.' Only urgent reforms and good, prudent, and responsible officials, and especially a change of heart causing the dependencies to be treated like provinces of Spain rather than 'colonies', could reverse this menacing development. Reforming and improving the colleges in Spanish America, curbing their conservatism, scholasticism, and ecclesiasticism, was a particularly high priority, this being the only way to stop principal Creole sons being dispatched to France to finish their education.[61]

The first Creole consciously to devote himself to building a liberation movement, leader of a failed armed invasion of Venezuela from Curaçao, at Coro, in 1806, Miranda became a conscious revolutionary after abandoning his previous career as a Spanish army officer. But his Enlightenment odyssey commenced soon after arriving in Madrid, in 1771. A voracious reader and bibliophile, by 1774 Miranda already possessed an impressive collection of Enlightenment works, including the five volumes of d'Alembert's *Mélanges*, Helvétius, Voltaire, Madame Du Chatelet, Locke's *Essay*, and the underground novel *L'admirable don Iñigo de Loyala* by the Huguenot Spinozist Charles Levier, a text deriding the Jesuits published in Amsterdam in 1736.[62] By 1780, Miranda owned around 350 books, including many radical works, among them Bolingbroke and Raynal, and over the next years acquired more.[63] He defected in the Caribbean after serving in North Africa (1774–6) and Cuba (1780–3) following what he regarded as an unacceptable injustice perpetrated by a hated superior.

Miranda first openly announced his plans for liberating Spanish America in the immediate aftermath of American independence, in New York where, early in 1784, he met Paine among others. But by the close of the American war, his inner, psychological rebellion against the Spanish crown, documentary evidence shows, was already well advanced. In discussion with John Adams (who despised him), Miranda spoke ceaselessly of the 'independence of Spanish America', always stressing the South American colonies' 'impatience under the Spanish yoke'.[64] During 1785, he spent six months in London, elaborating his republican schemes and contacting Priestley and Bentham among others. The years 1785–9 he then spent travelling in continental Europe, including Russia where he resided for some time at Catherine's court, and Scandinavia where he showed considerable interest in the prisons and other public institutions, as well as the universities and statistics concerning university students. In Denmark, he was appalled by the wastefulness of the crown in maintaining no less than fifteen palaces in Sjaelland alone.[65] Republican-minded and

[60] Weber, *Bárbaros*, 35.   [61] Morales Padrón, 'México', 357.
[62] Rodríguez de Alonso, *Siècle*, 20, 23–4; Israel, *Radical Enlightenment*, 302.
[63] Racine, *Francisco de Miranda*, 21, 27.
[64] Ibid. 63–4.   [65] Barton, *Northern Arcadia*, 8, 30, 37–8, 48.

intensely anticlerical, Miranda was a man of the Enlightenment and specifically of the Radical Enlightenment.[66] If inspired by the American Revolution, the books he read were primarily of French provenance and undoubtedly shaped his vision of Spanish American Revolution in which women and mulattos would participate.[67] Helvétius, Raynal, and Rousseau were particular favourites, together with the *Philosophie de la nature* of Delisle de Sales.[68] If Miranda also found the latest daring French books useful for advancing his numerous love affairs with older, sophisticated women, this does not alter the fact that such literature crucially shaped his emerging liberation ideology.

During an interview with the aged Mendelssohn, in Berlin late in 1785, he positively harangued the old man 'with his ideas of liberty and independence' and anti-monarchism, his North American travelling companion recorded in his diary, ideas the Jewish philosopher, a declared foe of French materialism, tried to suggest were 'ideal and foolish'.[69] Like Adams, Mendelssohn rejected Miranda's revolutionary creed, realizing it was anchored principally in the Enlightenment of Diderot, Helvétius, d'Holbach, and aspects of Rousseau. Miranda's life and thought encapsulated a Spanish American 'revolution of the mind' beginning well prior to and independently of the Revolution of 1775–6 and complete in embryo by the 1780s.

4. THE AMERICAN REVOLUTION AND THE SPANISH AMERICAN REVOLUTION (1780–1809)

While the intellectual impact of North American revolutionary thought and writings on Spanish America was less important as a spur to Creole intellectual revolt than the *Histoire philosophique* and other French subversive and republican texts, it was nevertheless a stirring example and model of revolution for Ibero-America as well as in Europe and powerful stimulant to European philosophical debate about the Spanish New World's future. Like Europe's radical enlighteners, prominent Creoles took an eager interest in the revolt against British imperial sway in North America, while the dramatic spectacle of revolution in the New World was anything but reassuring for the royal courts at Madrid and Lisbon.

The outbreak of the North American Revolution sparked a lively debate in Ibero-America and Spain, paralleling the wider transatlantic debate as to whether it better served enlightened humanity generally, and other countries' interests, to aid the American rebels against Britain or boycott them. No one doubted, commented Almodóvar in 1783, in the prologue to his Spanish version of the *Histoire* published at Madrid the following year, that 'La rebolucion de la America Anglo-septentrional'

---

[66] Lynch, 'Francisco de Miranda', 24.   [67] Racine, 'British Cultural', 427.
[68] Racine, *Francisco de Miranda*, 40–1, 48; Racine, 'Love', 96–8.
[69] *Archivo Miranda*, i. 384; Rodríguez de Alonso, *Siècle*, 137.

[the revolution in English North America] was a subject worthy of the closest attention, indeed a topic 'not just essential but indispensable for our instruction, useful and pertinent'. He drew attention to this great event, or so he claimed, to 'benefit the patria and the public, offering my zeal to the common cause'.[70] There were many worrying ambiguities in the situation. Ferguson's claim that France, Spain, and Holland would gain nothing from helping the Americans gain their independence seemed persuasive to many. 'Will their own colonies', asked Ferguson, meaning those of the Dutch and French as much as those of Spain and Portugal, 'become more dutiful after this example of a supposed successful revolt?'[71] Indeed, in Europe considerable apprehension was felt lest France and Spain actively assist in 'erecting the colonies of North-America into a power independent of Britain' thereby unwittingly precipitating a chain reaction, a wider spirit of rebellion and independence in Peru, Mexico, the West Indies, Brazil, and the rest of Ibero-America.

This disturbing possibility featured regularly in high-level discussions among leading ministers both in the Indies and in Spain at the time, and was deliberately drummed up as an immanent threat by the Portuguese Jewish *philosophe* Isaac de Pinto (1717–87), who led a strongly pro-British, Orangist, and anti-American propaganda campaign in the Netherlands, intended to deter France and Spain as well as Dutch sympathizers from supporting the American cause.[72] Both the American Revolution's backers and opponents regarded a general uprising in the Caribbean and Ibero-America stemming from 'cette grande révolution' in North America as an immediate possibility to be carefully considered. Thus, the first news of the great revolts that shook the Spanish American viceroyalties in 1780–3 seemed to many an indication that the widely expected Spanish American Revolution was already beginning. Among the earliest texts discussing the dilemma posed by the American Declaration of Independence, for Spain, was a *discurso* on *comercio libre* [free trade] read by Count Francisco Cabarrús, an expert in financial matters and enthusiast for aspects of Rousseau adamantly opposed to admitting women to the economic societies, delivered before the 'economic society' of Madrid, in February 1778. A naturalized Frenchman and member of the Madrid salon headed by Campomanes, in which Jovellanos was also a regular after moving from Seville, in 1778, Cabarrús was later widely known for his *memoria* of 1781, urging creation of a Spanish national bank modelled on the Bank of England, an institution needed, he argued, to enable the Spanish crown to finance its military and naval operations more efficiently.[73] A supporter of Campomanes' and Floridablanca's policies, Cabarrús also endorsed their reformism in the Indies except that, being seriously alarmed by what he saw as the very real and immediate risk to Spain's empire, he urged extreme caution in dealing both with the North American rebels and the Spanish American Creoles.

---

[70] Almodóvar, *Historia política*, i, 'prólogo' pp. iii–iv.
[71] Ferguson, *Remarks*, 47; McDaniel, 'Enlightened History', 204.
[72] *Réplique au Second Discours* (Kn. 19248), 46–7; Morales Padrón, 'México', 356.
[73] Anes, *Siglo de las Luces*, 108–9.

Such anxieties undoubtedly disturbed all Carlos III's ministers even where more eager to intervene on the rebel side against Britain. Aranda, the most anti-British of Carlos III's ministers, then ambassador in Paris, and a familiar of Raynal, openly advocated assisting the Americans. But like Cabarrús, he was also acutely aware that the American Revolution posed a real risk of converting rapidly into an Ibero-American liberation movement or revolution, to his mind something to be avoided at any cost, being bound to have a devastating effect on Spain and destroy her status as a global power. The New World Spanish imperium had already, he believed, become extremely precarious due to Creole disaffection and subversion internally and British expansionism externally. If Spain's American empire, or large parts of it, were all too easy prey for the British, it was equally at risk he believed from the rising Creole consciousness, on the one hand, and a fast-growing, newly independent United States, on the other.

It would require the greatest vigilance, urged Aranda, as well as increased military effort and financial outlay, to secure Spain's hold on her empire. Pondering various schemes for constitutional and imperial reorganization, at the end of the American war, in 1783 he drew up a most remarkable secret plan intended for discussion in Madrid court circles. Spain could probably best prolong its standing and power, he urged, by initiating an orderly, planned devolution of power. The Spanish monarch had long regarded him as too full of grand schemes; but this one was prescient as well as grandiose. He proposed dividing the empire into four federated and allied but loosely connected, autonomous strategic zones—Spain, New Spain, Peru, and Venezuela-New Granada—each equal in status, and possessing its own ruler in the person of a different member of the existing royal family and its separate nobility, church hierarchy, and dependencies. Multiple sets of noble and court privileges would coexist but with Cuba, Santo Domingo, and Puerto Rico reserved for Spain's own particular direct sphere of jurisdiction and command.[74]

The prospect of revolution in the Spanish and Portuguese Indies was also conjured up by European supporters of the American cause intent on neutralizing alarmist warnings concocted by anti-American publicists like de Pinto. A prominent Franco-Dutch supporter of the Americans, Antoine Marie Cerisier (1749–1828), wishing to see Canada join the United States in rebelling against Britain, argued, in 1779, that the 'le spectacle de la liberté' supplemented by powerful help from the Americans, once free and independent, would probably rapidly transform the face of all the New World empires. A powerful movement shaking 'le joug de la dépendance' throughout all the Americas could be expected.[75] A disciple of Diderot and d'Holbach much taken with the *Histoire philosophique*, Cerisier in 1778 styled the American Revolution the happiest event 'qui pouvoit arriver à l'espèce humaine en géneral' and an outstanding opportunity to repair the great 'crime' the *conquistadores* perpetrated in

---

[74] Amunátegui, *Precursores*, iii, 259–61; Oltra and Samper, *Conde de Aranda*, 60, 84, 101; Elliott, *Empires*, 367.
[75] *Réplique au Second Discours* (Kn. 19248), 27–8.

depopulating the Spanish New World. The new United States' inhabitants would reach out to the rest of their hemisphere, extend their influence, and replenish with their offspring the indigenous population earlier so cruelly decimated.[76] France, having proved the reliable defender of 'la liberté helvétique, la liberté germanique, la liberté belgique', in Cerisier's opinion, and now also 'la liberté Américaine', would surely back this vast transatlantic revolutionary process, checking Britain and extending liberty deep into Canada as well as Ibero-America and the Caribbean.

Another factor evoking sympathy for Spanish American independence was the predominantly adverse image supposedly 'enlightened' northern Europe and the United States nurtured of Spain. Not entirely unfairly, Spain was widely viewed as an unenlightened, obdurate, and weak power, addicted to narrow selfish goals and resolved to maintain 'les colonies dans une dépendance la plus absolue de la métropole'. This deeply negative image was enhanced by the Olavide Inquisition trial in 1778. That affair generated so much adverse publicity in Paris, affirmed Heredia, at the Spanish embassy, that Spaniards were now considered even 'more barbarous than the savages of Canada'. Olavide was presented as an oppressed Peruvian Creole as well as supposedly a martyr to the true Enlightenment.[77] The supposed approaching end of the Spanish monarchy in the New World was thus being construed by some as a glorious liberation promising liberty and Enlightenment together for an entire subcontinent, overthrowing Inquisition, intolerance, royalty, and obscurantism all at once together with slavery, economic over-regulation, and rigid subordination to aristocratic values. South Americans, it was natural to assume, aspired 'to be free and independent' while the Spanish crown lacked sufficient military force in the Americas to suppress the 'revolutions' seemingly bound soon to materialize.

The Spanish crown, maintained the *Histoire philosophique*, had always tightly enclosed as well as repressed Spanish America, viewing contacts of any kind between Spanish America and Asia as well as Europe apart from Spain with blinkered suspicion. For over a century Madrid had sought to confine maritime traffic between Mexico (via Acapulco) and the Philippines, the so-called 'Manila galleons', to an absolute minimum in a misguided quest to prevent inroads into Spain's own textile exports to Spanish America.[78] For Spanish America and humanity generally, held the *Histoire*, it made far more sense to overthrow Spain's entire imperial economic and strategic stance. Destroying it would in every way benefit Spanish America's inhabitants. With Ibero-America henceforth clothed by Asia rather than Europe, clothing would become both cheaper and more suited to the Mexican and Peruvian climates.[79] By comparison, Madrid's efforts to reform the old restrictive regulations looked narrow and self-interested, the entire Spanish American empire remaining imperially centred and heavily regulated, one that continued to obstruct foreign participation in the continent's trade.[80] Indeed, it was not until 1785 that the crown,

---

[76] Cerisier, *Observations impartiales* (Kn. 19191) (1778), 15.
[77] Imbruglia, 'Diderot storico', 235, 252.
[78] *Histoire philosophique* (1770), iii. 90–1. [79] Ibid. iii. 92. [80] Ibid. iii. 79, 298.

on Gálvez's initiative, seriously attempted to regenerate commerce between Spanish America and the Far East. The royal plan was to create a 'powerful' new company 'for the commerce of the Philippines' with court financial backing and appeals to wealthy investors in Potosí, Lima, and Charcas to participate.[81]

The danger that, following the Revolution in the Thirteen Colonies, North American power would simply replace that of Spain, Portugal, Holland, and France in the Caribbean and Central and South America was frequently mooted by foes of the United States. Neither Cerisier nor other sympathizers of the American cause seemed unduly alarmed by the prospect of an overbearing new nation establishing its hegemony over the other New World empires. The American rebels' unbounded aggressiveness and greed, suggested pro-British propagandists in Holland and Germany, meant that, once fully independent, the United States would simply 'subjugate southern America' and by this means eventually come to dominate Europe too.[82] Against this, pro-American pamphleteers cited the vast distances involved and sheer logistical difficulty confronting Anglo-Americans attempting to expand into Spanish America, given the vastness of the deserts and other formidable geographical barriers separating the United States from Texas, New Mexico, and New Spain. While it might be in North Americans' interest to 'favoriser cette révolution' commencing in Spanish America, it would not serve their interests to dispatch armed forces to annex territory or direct the pending Spanish American revolution. Indeed, the new United States would probably prefer not to encourage the Spanish American Revolution at all as Anglo-Americans would assuredly prefer trading with Spanish Americans under the weak Spanish crown than with independent Creoles organized in free republics and locally stronger. Anglo-Americans would only be alarmed and inclined to intervene, suggested one pamphleteer, if they thought there was a real prospect that a single united, free republic might emerge. For this would constitute a major power rivalling the United States for domination of the New World's resources.[83]

To the radical *philosophes* of the 1770s it was plain Spanish America would be both freer and happier if rid of the Spanish crown, Spain's aristocrats, and her churchmen and Inquisition, and that some Creoles already desired to break away. In the wake of the American Revolution, not only did it look likely that the mooted Spanish American Revolution would soon follow but also that, having signalled the advent of liberty in the western hemisphere, it would initiate a powerful chain reaction throughout the French, British, Dutch, and Portuguese colonies as well which would then all rebel and rupture their chains of dependence on Europe. Cerisier, writing in *Le Politique hollandois*, judged this a good outcome for humanity and the world and one that could help build the transition to world peace that he and other radical publicists so strongly advocated.[84]

---

[81] AN Bolivia EC ad 1786 no. 17 cédula, 10 May 1785.
[82] *Réplique au Second Discours* (Kn. 19248), 31–3.
[83] Ibid.   [84] Cerisier, *Le Politique hollandois*, 5 (Mar. 1783), 52–3.

To moderate enlighteners this seemed neither an attractive nor a likely scenario. Softened by ease, and the opulence of their plantation lifestyle, Spanish America's Creoles surely remained too sunk in moral debauchery and an indolent lifestyle to devote themselves to any great struggle: 'car une révolution dans l'Amérique espagnole ne saurait être l'affaire d'un moment.' Such a struggle against the Spanish crown would be long and arduous, and one in which it would be difficult to concert rebel strategy and tactics linking Mexico, Peru, and Venezuela. Were Spaniards, whether born in Europe or the Indies, a people really suited to making, or sharing in, 'les grandes révolutions'? One pro-American pamphlet published in Holland claimed the English and their American brethren were surely altogether better suited to such enterprises, the Spaniards of the New World, being 'des sujets passifs, dont l'indolence et la paresse sont au plus haut point'.[85] If Creole society appeared sunk in inertia, provincialism, and the past, and most Creoles continued wasting their time playing cards, drinking, and in the arms of prostitutes, behind the scenes, held the *Histoire*, abounded many sophisticated young Creoles, including some who had completed their education in Europe, minds refashioned by enlightened teaching, reading, and discussion, often tutors, editors, and *littérateurs*, and all thinking in terms of fundamental change.[86]

5. PHILOSOPHY AND SELF-EMANCIPATION FROM SPAIN

The sedition confronting the viceregal authorities in Spanish America in the early 1780s was by no means confined to Upper and Lower Peru and New Granada. In 1781, the Spanish authorities unmasked a conspiracy in Chile headed by Don José Antonio Rojas, a young hacienda-owner who had plotted together with two recent French immigrants, Don Antonio Gramuset, a soldier, and Antonio Alejandro Berney (Vergne), a Latin teacher familiar with a wide range of Enlightenment philosophical texts,[87] who had arrived in Santiago from Buenos Aires in 1776 as a tutor in the train of a Spanish nobleman whose sons were entrusted to his care. Counting on popular resentment against royal fiscalism and reformism, the conspirators plotted a rising designed to detach Chile from the Spanish crown. To this end, they prepared a draft republican manifesto and constitution, a 'philosophique' tract proclaiming the abolition of slavery and all social hierarchy, and purporting to create a democratic republic in which even southern Chile's unsubdued Araucanian Indians would participate along with other citizens and under which, following Beccaria (and Mercier), the death penalty would be abolished.[88] A leading landowner, Rojas was afterwards released by the viceregal authorities and, later, again travelled in Europe

---

[85] *Réplique au Second Discours* (Kn. 19248), 28, 33.
[86] *Histoire philosophique* (1780), iv. 405–6.
[87] Amunátegui, *Precursores*, iii, 191–2, 194–6, 208.
[88] Ibid. 195; Spell, *Rousseau*, 133–4.

now rehabilitated into respectable society; the two Frenchmen, though, were deported to Spain for execution, one dying en route.

A 30-year-old at the time of the conspiracy, in 1780, employed as an aide to the presiding magistrate of the high court in Santiago, Rojas was highly educated, well connected, and considered a 'noble';[89] in short, he exemplified the political subversion generated by the Radical Enlightenment in Spanish America. A trained mathematician and naturalist with a collection of scientific instruments and an impressive library of French works, he too had travelled in France as well as Spain prior to returning to the same Chile he had left as a loyal vassal of the crown just a few years before, his head brimming with radical ideas. Among the books he shipped back to South America which the royal authorities afterwards seized was an entire set of Diderot's *Encyclopédie*.[90] To avoid problems, he had replaced the title pages of his more subversive books with false but innocent-sounding titles. It was during what was practically a research seminar held at Rojas's *hacienda*, at Polpaico, with Berney presiding, that the group debated and formulated the openly revolutionary manifesto of their Chilean conspiracy.

Rojas and his friends also drew inspiration from the great rising of Indians and *mestizos* under Tupac Amaru in Peru, an episode providing disaffected Creoles with a model and much food for thought. In the summer of 1782, the viceroy in Lima sent an investigating judge to discover how the rebellion had originally begun in Arequipa, today in southern Peru, one of the first centres of organized subversion. This official's report proved that whatever the role of Indians and *mestizos* subsequently, the Arequipa disturbances had begun with local Spanish trouble-makers and misfits posting up protest placards on church doors and in public squares, complaining against recent taxes and the arrogance of the *chapetones*, inciting attacks on guardhouses, jails, and customs houses. One such protest affixed to the cathedral's main door read: 'the king of England loves his subjects, unlike the king of Spain.'[91] This posting up of protest pasquinades had began in December 1779.[92] Overall, the great rebellion in Upper and Lower Peru was a general rising of Indians and the illiterate; but there could be no question that it began with certain literate people, Creoles and Indian nobles (*caciques*), manipulating the general resentment against recent royal tax increases. It was a rebellion in which at least some 'españoles Americanos' participated. In retrospect the entire episode served on both sides of the Atlantic to show how existing resentment and traditional ideas could be orchestrated by leaders using new ideas about liberty, citizenship, and popular sovereignty to overthrow oppression, monarchy, and *chapeton* disdain.

The Tupac Amaru uprising in Peru clearly also helped spur the 1781 'Comunero' revolt in New Granada. This massive insurrection, again provoked by recent tax rises, was predominantly a *mestizo* rebellion, half-castes forming the majority in that

---

[89] AGI Chile 192, Benavides to Gálvez, Santiago, 3 Jan. 1782.
[90] Amunátegui, *Precursores*, iii, 201–3.
[91] AGI Lima 661, fos. 470ᵛ, 472, 473ᵛ–475ᵛ, 479.   [92] Ibid., fos. 480, 496.

OFFICINA WITTIANA.

1b. The Amsterdam Book-Shop of Hermanus de Wit in 1763, engraving by Renier Vinkeles. (By courtesy of Roger-Viollet/The Image Works)

Etablissement de la nouvelle philosophie.
Notre Berceau fut un Caffe.

1a. The Birth-place of 'la nouvelle philosophie'. Diderot and his circle always regarded the 'nouvelle philosophie' as a group effort and the Paris cafes such as the Café Procope as its cradle. (By courtesy of the Musée Carnavalet, Paris/Roger-Viollet/The Image Works)

2. Denis Diderot (1713–84). Portrait by Dimitri Levitzky made in 1773. (By courtesy of the Musée d'art et d'histoire Ville de Genève)

3. The Paris Salon of Madamé Geoffrin: a reading of a play by Voltaire in 1755. Painting by Anicet Charles Gabriel Lemonnier. (By courtesy of the Réunion des Musées Nationaux/Art Resource, NY)

4b. Paul-Henri Thiry, Baron d'Holbach (1723–89). Portrait by Louis Carrogis Carmontelle (1717–1806). (By courtesy of the Réunion des Musées Nationaux/Art Resources, NY)

4a. Benedict de Spinoza (1632–77). Anonymous portrait. (By courtesy of the Herzog August Bibliothek, Wolfenbüttel)

5. David Hume (1711–76). Portrait by Allan Ramsey. (By courtesy of the Scottish National Portrait Gallery)

6a. Adam Ferguson (1723–1816). Portrait by Sir Joshua Reynolds. (By courtesy of the Scottish National Portrait Gallery)

6b. Adam Smith (1723–90). Portrait by unknown artist. (By courtesy of the Scottish National Portrait Gallery)

7. The 'Coterie' of Milan (1776) showing from left to right Alessandro Verri (seated), G.B. Biffi (standing), Cesare Beccaria (reading), L. Lambertnghi and Pietro Verri. Painting by Antonio Perego. (By courtesy of the Collezione Sormani Verri, Milan)

8. 'The Declaration of Independence, 4 July 1776'. Painting by John Trumbull. (By courtesy of the Yale University Art Gallery/ Art Resource, NY)

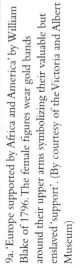

9b. 'The Negro Revenged' depicting black defiance, engraving by Henry Fuseli illustrating an abolitionist ballad by William Cowper composed in 1788. (By courtesy of the Victoria and Albert Museum)

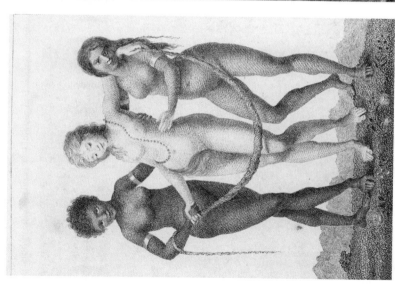

9a. 'Europe supported by Africa and America' by William Blake of 1796. The female figures wear gold bands around their upper arms symbolizing their valuable but enslaved 'support'. (By courtesy of the Victoria and Albert Museum)

10a. Claude-Adrien Helvétius (1715–71) portrait by Michel Vanloo. (By courtesy of a private collection)

10b. Anne-Catherine, Madame de Helvétius (1722–1800) portrait by Michel Vanloo. (By courtesy of a private collection)

11. Armed Clashes between Democrats and anti-Democrats in Rotterdam, 1784. (By courtesy of the Atlas van Stolk, Rotterdam)

12. Mary Wollstonecraft. Portrait by John Opie of *c.*1797. (By courtesy of the National Portrait Gallery, London)

CHARAVAY FRÈRES ÉDITEURS A PARIS

PHOT & IMP. LEMERCIER & Cᵉ

Mʳ. J.ᵉ A.Nᵉ de CARITAT Marquis de CONDORCET

Secretaire Perpetuel de l'Academie Royale des Sciences
de l'Academie Françoise, de l'Institut de Bologne, des Académies
de Petersbourg, de Turin, de Philadelphie et de Padoüe.

13a. Jacques-Pierre Brissot (de Warville) (1754–93). (By courtesy of Roger-Viollet/The Image Works)

13b. Marie-Jean-Antoine-Nicolas de Caritat, marquis de Condorcet (1743–94)

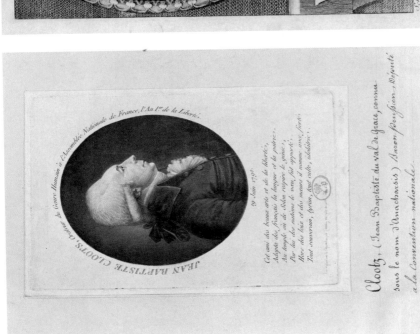

14a. Anarcharsis Cloots (1755–94). (By courtesy of the
Réunion des Musées Nationaux/Art Resources, NY)

14b. Ludwig Wekhrlin (1739–92), radical journalist.
Engraving by A.W. Küfner of 1788.

15. The French Revolution commences: The 'Tennis Court Oath' June 1789, Painting by Jacques-Louis David. (By courtesy of Erich Lessing/Art Resource, NY)

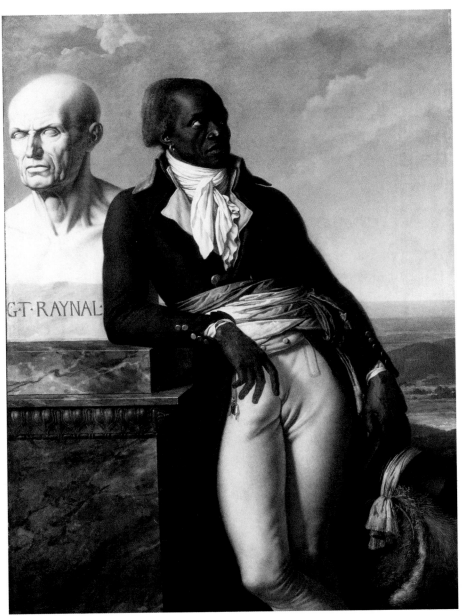

16. Jean-Baptiste Belley (1747–1805) next to a bust of Raynal, deputy from Saint-Domingue
to the National Convention in Paris. Portrait by Anne-Louis Girodet de Roussy-Trioson. (By
courtesy of the Réunion des Musées Nationaux/ Art Resource, NY)

viceroyalty, though Indians, blacks, and whites were also extensively involved. By May 1781, the New Granada insurgents, headed by Creoles, had overrun the areas of Tunja, Sopamosa, Cipaquita, Mariquita, and the environs of Bogotá. The rebels elected 'generales' and 'capitanes' to lead them who extended their authority to all the towns the insurgents controlled, dividing their supporters into *associones* and *companías*. Among the leading elements, reported the viceroy to Madrid, figured a number of *letrados*, military deserters, and renegade ecclesiastics.[93] Having captured the passes leading to Bogotá, the rebels also intercepted large quantities of incoming official correspondence from Lima, Quito, and Popayán, completely disrupting viceregal communications. Word of the insurrection swiftly reached British Jamaica, causing the viceroy to worry that even the landing of a small force sent from there could have incalculable consequences for Spanish authority and power in northern South America. Despite the war in the Caribbean, reinforcements had to be rushed from Cuba.

The *sediciosos* adopted as their general manifesto a verse pasquinade expressing fierce sarcasm about the royal government, administration, taxes, and clergy, and accusing some of the latter, especially the Capuchins, of being accessories to exploitation and robbery. The text expressed the rebels' clear consciousness of being inhabitants of a particular country, New Granada, with interests different from those of European Spaniards. Equally important, their manifesto strikingly contradicts the thesis in the conventional historiography that the rebellion was an essentially traditionalist upheaval, untouched by Enlightenment thinking.[94] The identity of the author of this *Pasquín General*, a text which surfaced mysteriously in Bogotá, in April 1781, remains uncertain. But while couched in terms readily accessible to the masses, it was plainly written by a highly literate person who, it is thought, either was, or was commissioned by, Don Jorge Miguel Lozano de Peralta, first marquis of San Jorge de Bogotá (1731–93), a Creole noble profoundly at odds with the royal regime. A major landowner and title-holder, Lozano was a veteran of several disputes with the royal *audiencia* of Bogotá and city *cabildo*. In May 1777, he had been punitively stripped of his title by the *audiencia* for refusing to pay a royal tax (*lanzas*) linked to noble status.

The massive rising with which they were grappling, the authorities grasped from the outset, was not spontaneous. Starting in the Tunja area, in the towns of Socorro and San Gil, trouble began in the former with a riot of some 2,000 women and children, armed with stones and chanting slogans, protesting about recent taxes and the royal tobacco monopoly. While in both places local priests exemplarily performed their duty over subsequent days, repeatedly mounting counter-demonstrations with large crucifixes and banners urging the masses 'in the name of Christ crucified and his most holy mother' to cease all agitation 'and bear with love the commands of our sovereign and not insult his representatives', the authorities

---

[93] AGI Santa Fe 58/1 Flórez to Gálvez, Cartagena, 11 July 1781.
[94] González, 'Introducción', 9–11; König, 'Rebelión', 259–61; Elliott, *Empires*, 365.

were extremely alarmed to hear the rioters responded by stoning the priests and driving them back into their churches.[95] But what chiefly shocked the viceregal authorities was the astounding speed with which the rebellion gripped a huge area. As the tumult gathered momentum during the spring of 1781, it was obvious the Creole militias in the towns, and Creoles generally, were supporting the royal authorities either half-heartedly or, in some places, not at all.[96] There was seditious talk not just about 'bad government' and removing new taxes but also of rising to gain an 'absoluta libertad' [absolute liberty]. In the viceroy's surviving correspondence, we find repeated and urgent references to the need to discover the 'true authors' [verdaderos autores] of the insurrection.[97]

Anti-royal collusion on this scale had never occurred before. Besides the *Pasquín General*, many other protest placards were posted up. One, affixed to the gate of the convent church of Santa Clara in Pamplona on 18 April 1781, presenting a list of eleven demands mostly about removal of new imposts, assured the authorities the people had no wish to live without a king to regulate their lives but whatever happened, cost what it may, even their lives, were determined to remove the insupportable burden oppressing them.[98] This text again dwells specifically on the split between *chapetones* and Creoles. Other pasquinades inveighed against 'tyranny', in general, suggested some monasteries be abolished, referring to the cruel oppression afflicting the Indians, invoking Tupac Amaru.[99] Robbery under a royal cloak, one poster urged the people, remains robbery, and rebellion in such a case is 'holy, is just in natural law'.[100]

Modern historiography has been extraordinarily unaware of the real character of the great New Granada rebellion. A royalist military commander facing the rebel army, Don Joaquín de Finestrad, was one who entertained few doubts about the source and inspiration of such unprecedented subversion. The author of the *Pasquín General* he dubbed 'the new philosopher' [el Nuevo Filósofo], defining him as a person guided 'by the system of reason' promoted by intellectual innovators and one designed to replace tradition, church doctrine, religion, and theology.[101] The common people, or what he terms 'el pueblo idiota' [the idiot people], might be credulous, ignorant, steeped in tradition, and untouched by new ideas, but clearly now posed a severe risk to crown, Church, and the colonial system alike. Recent experience plainly showed they could be easily roused and misled (as he thought of it) and directed by sophisticated Creoles infused by the ideas of 'the new

---

[95] AGI Santa Fe 663A 'Testimonio sobre la sublevación de las dos villas de San Gil y Socorro', fos. 16 , 35, 38, 42, 48–9, 50ᵛ, 146ᵛ.

[96] Ibid., fos. 65ᵛ–66, 88, 198, 202ᵛ.

[97] Ibid., fos. 10–11, 16ᵛ, 42ᵛ, 129.

[98] Ibid., fos. 180–1ᵛ.

[99] AGI Santa Fe 663A/2/26, fos. 254–6.

[100] AGI Santa Fe 663A 'Testimonio', fo. 258ᵛ.

[101] Finestrad, *Vasallo instruido*, 41–2, 363, 375–6; González, 'Introducción', 10; Cárdenas Acosta, *Movimiento*, i. 40–53.

philosophy'. 'The anonymous author's purpose, and the purpose of the new philosophy, more generally', averred Finestrad, was to convince the people the 'kings of Spain were not the legitimate lords of America, that their dominion is not by hereditary right, that their sovereignty is the result of a violent usurpation, that the natural and legitimate sovereignty resides in the people of the land: a monstrous proposition!'[102]

One might object that Finestrad was clearly someone who had become accustomed to thinking about the 'new philosophy' as a general instrument of subversion and was imposing his own prior assumptions. To an extent he was. But the fact that royalist commanders were filled with their own fixations depicting the entire system of colonial rule being undermined by the 'new philosophy' only further confirms how crucial this entire construct of 'new philosophy' destroying monarchy, Church, and social order was. By late May 1781, the 'Comunero' commander, Don Juan Francisco Berbeo, a Creole who had spent some time in Dutch Curaçao, controlled a large area and, according to royalist estimates, had an army of around 15,000 insurgents poised to advance on Bogotá. In the end, the crisis was resolved without a pitched battle, Berbeo opting to negotiate from strength whilst he could and while the royalist forces remained depleted and disorganized by the insurrections in Peru and the struggle in the Caribbean. On the royalist side, there was weakness, fear, and considerable alarm lest the capital be captured and sacked.

Accordingly, the so-called capitulations of Zipaquira (June 1781) were concluded, basically a package of fiscal alleviation couched in the terminology of traditional Habsburg royalism.[103] However, the twenty-second clause clearly echoes the terms of the 1771 Mexico City protest stipulating that henceforth 'nationals of this America' should be preferred to 'Europeans' in all the main administrative posts.[104] Needless to say, the agreement was never adhered to by the crown. Once the main rebel army dispersed, the authorities regained their assurance, though as late as October the situation remained very tense and it was not until the spring of 1782 that it was felt in Bogotá that the insurrection was truly over.[105] Nor did the authorities fail to act on their suspicions as to who was behind the rebellion. Far from receiving redress, the richest, most dissatisfied Creole in Nueva Granada, Don Jorge, found himself exiled soon afterwards to the coastal fortress of Cartagena.[106] Having recovered the upper hand, the authorities pursued a policy of amnesty under a royal 'general pardon' toward the common people combined with undiminished resolve to root out the 'principales motores' [principal movers] and 'true authors' of the sedition.[107]

A few years later, shortly before the Revolution in France, Finestrad published his apology for the New Granada viceregal government under the title *Vasallo instruido*

---

[102] Finestrad, *Vasallo instruido*, 363, 387; Phelan, *People*, 157–9; König, 'Rebelión', 263–5.
[103] Phelan, *People*, 70–2, 86.
[104] König, 'Rebelión', 263–4; Cardenas Acosta, *Movimiento*, ii. 26.
[105] AGI Santa Fe 578/1/23, Florez to Gálvez, Cartagena, 22 Oct. 1781.
[106] Phelan, *People*, 71.   [107] AGI Santa Fe 577a. Viceroy to Galveza, Cartagena, 10 Apr. 1782.

en el estado del Nuevo Reino de Granada (1789). 'In some countries of Europe', he wrote, 'there has taken shape the arrogance of writing with excessive liberty contrary to the respect due to religion and sovereigns.' The pernicious maxims resulting now posed a direct threat to religion and the crown in the Indies.[108] His main object in chronicling the revolt, he says, was to impress on the hearts of the people 'the true doctrine which secures thrones, supports fidelity, fortifies obedience and establishes peace in society'. The root of the trouble in New Granada, as in Peru, was that in 'these remote regions there had become ensconced secretly' the ideas expounded in Hobbes, Wolff, Gravina, Vatel, the Frenchman Raynal, and the Scotsman Robertson, the most famous of the foreigners who wrote without respect and with excessive insolence against religion and subordination. Some of their maxims and propositions had evidently been taken up by the author of the *Pasquín General* [i.e. the verse manifesto], and these Finestrad denounced as a contagious cancer menacing all of society, 'a black vapour that obscures everything'.[109]

Order and stability in Spanish America could not continue without crushing the arrogance and *fanatismo* of Raynal and others writing in Europe against Spain, its religion, and traditions. Only 'a false philosophy' tries to undermine the biblical and theological basis of royal authority in the New World, assuring the people the *conquistadores* were tyrants and usurpers.[110] The alleged misconduct of the '*conquistadores* is the cement of their new philosophy'.[111] 'Raynal', 'the declared enemy of the Spaniards', had proclaimed the 'tyranny of the Spaniards' in conquering the New World. What hypocrisy! Deriding the English and French claim that the lands they occupied in the Americas, unlike those conquered by the Spaniards, had been 'empty', Finestrad suggested it was the British and French who were the real tyrants and usurpers as their North American dominions had been unjustly seized from the Indians without any just title and without providing any compensation.[112] 'The new philosopher' tries to persuade the 'ignorant masses' sovereignty belongs to them.[113] They had arisen, the 'furious Raynals, Robertsons and other libertine philosophers, friends of the independence of every sovereign; but their fury will accomplish nothing'.[114]

The 'false philosophy of the libertines' destroys the basis of unquestioning submission to legitimate authority in both religion and politics especially by diffusing among American-born Spaniards the idea that God does not intervene in the historical process miraculously and did not, after all, speak through angels, but revealed himself only through clouds and sun-rays.[115] If among the Creole elite purely natural causes replace divine providence, all justification for Spanish dominion in Ibero-America was at an end. It was the 'most obstinate infidelity of the philosophers' that had fomented the idea that the conquest of the Indies stemmed

---

[108] Finestrad, *Vasallo instruido*, 35.   [109] Ibid. 41–2.   [110] Ibid. 380.   [111] Ibid. 404.
[112] Ibid. 384, 388–9.   [113] Ibid. 383; König, 'Rebelión', 268.
[114] Finestrad, *Vasallo instruido*, 45; Adelman, *Sovereignty*, 26.
[115] Finestrad, *Vasallo instruido*, 316–19.

from rapacity and greed and was not the outcome ordained by divine providence. Repeatedly denouncing Raynal and also Robertson, he strove to demolish their critique of the Spanish colonial administration employing ideas derived directly from the providential thought world of the mainstream Enlightenment.[116] Popular sovereignty Finestrad altogether repudiates, asserting the monarchy's absolute power in the Indies conceived of as a final, unending social contract. The vassal's duty is blindly to obey the commands of the divinely anointed sovereign.

The notion that the power wielded by sovereigns derives from the people, and that the sovereign's breaking the terms of the alleged contract implies they are absolved of their duty to obey, he considered a catastrophe destined to produce endless misery and disruption of the sort France experienced in the Wars of Religion. Such thinking derives directly from the *fanatismo* of arrogant philosophy.[117] The duty to obey sovereigns is never suspended and revolt never justified. How arrogant and harmful to base philosophical systems on idle speculation rather than 'certain experience' and the 'visible phenomena of nature', the true and beneficial providential ideas of Newton, Whiston, and other sound moderns. Fired by envy and bitterness, the 'new philosophy' brims with inconsistency and its abominable doctrine that 'right' and 'wrong' are not absolutes but merely human preoccupations, subject only to the laws of society, or what Finestrad calls 'arbitrary laws'. This was the claim of 'all the *materialistas*'.[118] But the *materialistas* were wrong and would learn from loyal writers that the Conquest was truly the 'fruit of Spanish valour', Spain's glory, not rapacity, and was supported by the 'natural law' theories of Grotius and Pufendorf.[119]

Expectations prevalent on both sides of the Atlantic that a general revolution in the Spanish New World was commencing remained widespread in the late 1780s and 1790s and were intensified by violent disturbances in Mexico in 1785–6, following harvest failure there, and by the onset of revolution in France. Jefferson wrote from Paris to a colleague in London in 1787, remarking, 'there are combustible materials' in Spanish America, 'they wait the torch only'.[120] The beginnings of 'liberty' manifest in Spanish America for some time now, declared Brissot, in his revolutionary journal *Le Patriote français*, in April 1790, after receiving news via New Orleans of more clashes in Mexico, the previous October, involving troops, whites, and Indians, were finally tending toward an explosion which he did not hesitate to label the 'révolution dans l'Amérique espagnole'.[121]

The final drama that led to the independence of most of Spanish America began with a series of risings in Upper Peru (Bolivia), Mexico, and on the River Plate (Argentina) in the years 1809–10 that, when compared with earlier revolts in colonial Spanish America, exhibit several common and typical features. Especially characteristic of the movement of 1809 was the prior plotting among university teachers and

---

[116] Phelan, *People*, 86, 214.   [117] Ibid. 247, 368–70.
[118] Finestrad, *Vasallo instruido*, 404–5.   [119] Ibid. 382.
[120] Elliott, *Empires*, 371.   [121] Brissot, *Patriote français*, 237 (2 Apr. 1790), 2.

other highly educated Creoles, and a sophisticated ideology of liberty, anti-monarchism, free expression, and individual emancipation infusing this conspira-torial-oppositional underground culture with philosophical content. Jaime de Zudañez and Bernardo de Monteagudo, the leaders who planned and led the rising in Charcas in 1809, were steeped in a Radical Enlightenment political rhetoric of republicanism, popular sovereignty, and the primacy of the interests of the majority, and had been infused with it for years, well before 1809. Raynal, Filangieri, Mably, and Rousseau were their ideological heroes. Where had they had acquired their new Radical Enlightenment culture? The answer lies in the intellectual ferment in motion in local universities, bookshops, and private parlours, and their ideology, far from something new, had become established from Chile to New Spain in the 1770s and 1780s.[122]

[122] Francovich, *Filosofía en Bolivia*, 57–61; Loayza Valda, 'Revolución de Charcas', 126–7; Rodríguez, *Independence*, 3; Breña, *Primer liberalismo*, 333–4.

19

Commercial Despotism

Dutch Colonialism in Asia

1. AN ASIAN EMPIRE

The Dutch colonial system in Asia the *Histoire philosophique* at one point describes as an overburdened ship, sailing low in the water and prevented from sinking only by furious labour at the pumps.[1] It was an image introduced in the 1750s by one of the reforming governors-general of the Dutch East Indies. In the mid eighteenth century, despite Britain now being stronger at sea and on land and with a total Asian trade, based on India, increasingly outstripping that of the Dutch, the Dutch-controlled enclaves still constituted geographically the most extensive and diverse, and organizationally most intricate, European colonial empire in Asia. The decline of their Asiatic imperium, more relative than absolute—but also absolute—seemed clear from the fact that both outgoing and returning Dutch fleets to Asia, having grown steadily in size from the early seventeenth century until the 1720s, then reached a plateau from which trade levels, shipping volume, and profitability afterwards fell back markedly, especially in the 1740s.[2]

Circumstances somewhat varied from region to region. But many high officials of the Dutch East India Company, or VOC (Verenigde Oost-Indische Compagnie), clearly grasped that it was the system itself that had ceased to function efficiently or at all adequately. The dismal state of the Malacca entrepôt captured from the Portuguese in 1641, formerly one of the most flourishing emporia of the East, typified the stagnation, failure, and dysfunctional character of the VOC's trading system in east Asia by the mid eighteenth century. Malacca had steadily decayed partly because neighbouring Malay princes could no longer be so easily intimidated as formerly and preferred selling their tin to the English who paid better and partly due to the Dutch authorities' reluctance to permit any diversion of the traffic purposely concentrated on Batavia (Jakarta).[3] Meanwhile, the ruinous effects of an 'unenlightened' blinkered

---

[1] *Histoire philosophique* (1774), i. 293.
[2] Bruijn and Lucassen, *Op de schepen*, 14, 21; Israel, *Dutch Republic*, 942–3.
[3] *Histoire philosophique* (1774), i. 163; Jacobs, *Koopman in Azië*, 155–7.

attachment to the past, outmoded, redundant practices, rigid bureaucracy and rules, and rampant corruption among the Company's employees at every level, typified Malacca as every part of its empire.

Yet, the political and military eclipse of the Dutch in Asia was very recent. In the foremost Dutch Enlightenment account of Asia, François Valentijn's *Oud en Nieuw Oostindien* (1724–6), a monumental work presenting a vast tableau of Asia under European domination in unparalleled detail, the Dutch could still be proudly represented as having no other real rivals in power and splendour beyond the Cape, the British as well as the French at that point still lagging considerably behind, even in Bengal as well as southern India and south-east Asia.[4] Dutch Asian commerce eclipsed all the rest until the 1730s; and if, by the 1770s, British returns from Asia exceeded Dutch returns overall by a ratio of around three to two, the Dutch Company continued to dwarf the commercial activity of the French, Swedes, Danes, and Portuguese, the four other European nations operating chartered East India companies. Commercially and still more politically and militarily, the Dutch remained pre-eminent throughout much of south and south-east Asia until the Fourth Anglo-Dutch War (1780–4). A Dutch report indicating relative positions in terms of annual returns of the six European powers with Asiatic operations shows that as late as 1780, Dutch gains from Asia were still approximately equivalent to all four of the lesser trading powers put together (see Table 2).

Since 1730, a process of rapid, inexorable decay had set in. Yet, as a colonial exploiter the VOC nevertheless actually extended its reach during the later eighteenth century in some areas, turning its establishment into more of a real empire and tightening its hold over subject populations. Despite the relative receding of its general Asian economic and military power, outside Bengal and Coromandel it still remained politically and culturally the European 'colonial' power in Asia *par excellence*. There were no less than ten senior VOC commanders with the rank of 'gouverneur' in the mid eighteenth century under the VOC's *gouverneur-generaal* based at Batavia, in Java, and his council, the Raad van Indië. These commanders, local political heads and heads of judiciary as well as military and naval commanders, presided over Ceylon, Negapatnam (headquarters of the Dutch (i.e. southern) Coromandel coast of south-east India), Cochin (presiding over the Dutch Malabar coast of south-west India), Malacca (the Singapore of early modern times), Makassar, eastern Java,

Table 2. The relative positions of the European powers trading with Asia around 1780 (million guilders)

British EIC	30	Denmark	5
Dutch VOC	20	Sweden	3.5
France	8	Portugal	3.5

Source: ARH VOC 4761, fo. 29.

[4] Fisch, *Hollands Ruhm*, 21–6; Chaudhuri and Israel, 'East India Companies', 428–9.

Amboina (controlling the nutmeg-producing Banda islands), Ternate (Fort Oranje), and South Africa. All of these had substantial civilian establishments, military garrisons, and shipping resources under their command.

The empire radiated out from Batavia in all directions over a vast expanse. The number of forts the Company still maintained in Asia in the later eighteenth century, despite its many reverses in India and steady decline as a trading power since 1730, remained impressive. Ceylon was overawed on all its sides by Dutch garrisons. Amboina and neighbouring islands featured no less than ten forts with the Company's headquarters at Casteel Victoria on the main island. The Banda Islands had three forts, the largest, Casteel Nassau, on Neijra. There were four or five small garrisons along the west coast of Sumatra. On the Malabar coast of south-west India, there remained substantial garrisons at Cochin, Cranganore, and Cananor with smaller garrisons at six or seven other places in between, while on the Coromandel coast where Dutch trade had long been integrally linked with their Java trade and the Moluccas, lingered, besides the major Dutch fortress at Negapatnam, some ten other forts and lodges, including Tegenapatnam and Fort Geldria at Paleacat.[5] Many of these, particularly in southern India where Britain and France had wholly replaced the Dutch as the leading European powers by the 1740s, had indeed become militarily and politically largely redundant. But the position seemed very different at Negapatnam and in regions like Ceylon, the Straits of Malacca, and the Indonesian archipelago where the Dutch remained locally dominant militarily and in naval power and where the directors in Holland, the so-called *Heren XVII*, felt they needed to retain a firm hand to fortify their grip on the spice and textile trades as well as their now increasingly fragile hegemony over local princes, taxes, trade routes, and navigation.

In Ceylon, in central Java where the VOC fought an inconclusive war of expansion in the years 1749–55 and around the Straits of Malacca (and what became Singapore), the Dutch continued expanding their territorial holdings until the 1780s, when they extended their establishment in the Straits in response to the growing challenge from the British and French and the growth of Malay and Chinese shipping bypassing the Company's ships and tolls. The sultanate of Johore's independence ended with an imposed treaty in 1784, and a Dutch garrison of 254 men was established in a fort in the harbour of Tanjung Pinang, controlling the island of Riau, close to where Singapore stands today. In western Borneo the Dutch dramatically extended their presence from 1779 in collusion with the local Muslim sultan of Pontianak, Syarif Yusuf, a usurper who had conquered the place and ousted the previous sultan signing an agreement to admit the Dutch and exclude other Europeans, confining his overseas trade to the former, in return for their recognizing and supporting him as sultan.[6] Such efforts continued the VOC's time-honoured

---

[5] Smith, *Wealth of Nations*, ii; Luzac, *Holland's rijkdom*, i. 286.
[6] Van Goor, 'Seapower, Trade', 88, 93, 96.

heavy-handed techniques of control even if they no longer worked at all efficiently. For the most part, the Dutch failed to achieve their local objectives in the Straits, managing neither to regulate the carrying trade between the China Sea and the Indian Ocean nor to control the Malay tin trade.[7] While there was some growth in Malacca's entrepôt traffic after 1750, this accounted for only a small portion of the total growth of the Malay Peninsula import–export business, most of which bypassed the Dutch settlements.

In terms of numbers of personnel, reach, image, and outward pomp, then, the Dutch Asian seaborne imperium remained the quintessential European colonial enterprise in the East during the later Enlightenment, certainly outside India, and a topic crucial to philosophical discussion of Europe's relationship to Asia. It was an indispensable case. The Dutch had a larger system of inter-Asian trade and shipping than the British until 1780, a more diverse set of Asian peoples under their rule, and a wider-reaching establishment of fortresses, trading posts, garrisons, and shipping. The Dutch were the only European nation in regular commercial contact with Japan and their deliveries of Japanese copper to Coromandel, Ceylon, Java, and Canton, passing mostly via Malacca, peaked in terms of quantity and profitability only around 1760.[8] Nor was it certain this decrepit but vast imperial system was beyond repair and condemned to inevitable further decay. Rather, observers frequently spoke of its revival and, as with Chastellux, still regarded the Dutch (until 1784), or an alliance between France and the Dutch, as offering the best and likeliest prospect for reversing British ambition in India and Asia generally.[9]

Batavia was Asia's most imposing colonial metropolis. 'The town is remarkably large and well built', noted the Swedish visitor Carl Peter Thunberg (1743–1822), the most important of Linnaeus' Swedish disciples, 'the houses are mostly of stone and are elegant, with spacious rooms, which are open to the free air, in order that they may be refreshing and cool in this burning climate.'[10] Most foreign visitors, remarked the *Histoire*, regarded the city as one of the 'plus belles villes du monde'.[11] By the early eighteenth century, with its population nearing 100,000, well-laid-out streets and canals, and elegant Dutch residences, the city dominated central Java and by the 1790s, with around 150,000 inhabitants, most recent Asian immigrants from else- where, was unique as a meeting point of West and East. 'Here just as in Amsterdam', wrote Thunberg, 'is to be found a mixture of all nations and languages.'[12] Owing to the Company's long-standing distrust of the Javanese, most of the Asian free population consisted of overseas immigrants, especially Makassarese, Balinese, and *mestizos*; but also numerous Chinese. The latter, noted Thunberg, 'like the Jews in Holland, carry on a very extensive trade and cultivate most of the arts and handicraft professions'.[13] Batavia also boasted easily the largest concentration of Europeans in

[7] Reid, 'A New Phase', 63, 65–7.   [8] Shimada, *Intra-Asian Trade*, 42–3, 91.
[9] Chastellux, *De la félicité publique*, ii. 164–5.   [10] Thunberg, *Travels*, ii. 217.
[11] *Histoire philosophique* (1770), i. 191–2.   [12] Thunberg, *Travels*, ii. 217.   [13] Ibid.

Asia of the Enlightenment era, around 10,000 according to the *Histoire* (actually around 6,000), over a third of all the Europeans in Asia.[14]

What the Cape of Good Hope is between Europe and every part of the East Indies, commented Adam Smith, 'Batavia is between the principal countries of the East Indies.' It lay upon the most frequented route between India and China and was the natural point of call for much of the traffic between the two main zones of southern Asia. In addition, 'it is, over and above all this, the centre and principal mart of what is called the country trade of the East Indies; not only of that part of it which is carried on by Europeans, but of that which is carried on by the native Indians; and vessels navigated by the inhabitants of China ... of Tonquin, Malacca, Cochin-China, and the Island of Celebes, are frequently to be seen in its port.' In terms of its commerce and role in Asian navigation, it had indeed become a kind of 'Amsterdam' of the East. However, it was very different in that its presiding role was political, military, and cultural as well as maritime and commercial. Like the Cape, averred Smith, its highly advantageous position had enabled Batavia to 'surmount all the obstacles which the oppressive genius of an exclusive company may have occasionally opposed to [its] growth'.[15]

The Dutch Asian empire after 1750 was remarkable, and for 'philosophy' pivotal, above all, for the large number of petty native princes and diverse peoples held by treaty arrangements in formal subjection nominal, partial, or total. To enforce their despotic system of restriction and monopoly, the VOC had long been accustomed to using its military establishment based in its east Asian 'castles', forts, and lodges,[16] together with a resident fleet which, in 1763, still consisted of eighty-seven ships and fifty-six armed barques and patrol vessels.[17] These were employed to enforce compliance with a batch of extremely one-sided treaties, often ruthlessly imposed on dependent or sufficiently intimidated local princes termed by the *Histoire* 'esclaves couronnés'. The treaties underpinning the VOC's imperium in the East were designed thoroughly to subordinate the interests of the small and weak principalities of south-east Asia and southern India to the Company's commercial interests and hegemony.

The sultan of Makassar and his successors accepted the indefinite presence of Dutch troops and the VOC's local headquarters at 'Casteel Rotterdam' besides other forts on his territory under a treaty of 1668, imposed by Cornelis Speelman (1628–84), Celebes's conqueror, and undertook both to prevent his own subjects trading with Europeans other than the Dutch and the Javanese, Sumatrans, Malays, Siamese, and 'Moors' from transporting goods to his territory or trading there.[18]

---

[14] *Histoire philosophique* (1770), i. 191–2; Troostenburg, *Hervormde Kerk*, 13–14; Gaastra, *Geschiedenis*, 73.
[15] Smith, *Wealth of Nations*, ii. 219; Van Goor, 'Seapower, Trade', 83, 104.
[16] *Histoire philosophique* (1770), i. 226, 228, 231.
[17] ARH VOC 4790 'Bedenckingen', 193.
[18] ARH VOC 4785, *Naerder Artyculen ende poincten* (Batavia, 1668), articles 7, 8, and 11.

He was also required to forbid his subjects to sail to any destinations other than Johore, Borneo, Bali, or Java and help suppress all other non-Dutch navigation sailing between Makassar and Bima, Timor, and Solor. In exchange for cloth, spirits, and opium, the last shipped regularly via Batavia from Bengal (where Clive became one of its addicts), the Dutch appropriated Makassar's rice surplus for distribution elsewhere in Asia. In the 1760s, the VOC's patrol vessels, according to the *Histoire*, still kept most foreign vessels away from Celebes, the Chinese alone being permitted to sail there, bringing silks worked and unworked, porcelains, and tobacco. From a purely commercial standpoint, the modest profits from the island's trade failed to justify the garrison's expense. But viewed strategically, to the Dutch these forts, in Malabar and Ceylon as in Celebes, 'the key' to the Spice Islands, still seemed essential.[19]

For similar reasons, a Dutch military presence remained on Timor. In fact, this was a pattern replicated on all sides. In 1669, Speelman had likewise imposed on the 'kings' of Bima and Dompo, islands to the south and opposite Makassar, lying between Java and Timor, even more oppressive treaties, proclaiming a total monopoly over their seaborne trade and suppressing all navigation in native proas between Makassar and those islands 'for ever'. These princes were supposed to exclude not only all non-Dutch Europeans but, again, also the Javanese, Malays, Siamese, and 'Moors'.[20] Bima too languished under a garrison. It was the same in the Moluccas where the VOC aimed to monopolize the entire spice output, the Company authorizing the size of the crop as well as paying for it at an imposed, low price, mainly with goods, especially Coromandel cotton cloth, shipped from within its Asian empire. The Company distributed all the Moluccas' output itself, in both Asia and Europe. The consequences for the local population were highly oppressive: especially in diminished activity, opportunity, and ruthless pricing. 'In the spice islands', noted Smith, 'the Dutch are said to burn all the spiceries which a fertile season produces beyond what they expect to dispose of in Europe with such profit as they think sufficient.'[21] 'By different arts of oppression, they have reduced the population of several of the Moluccas nearly to the number which is sufficient to supply with fresh provisions and other necessaries of life their own insignificant garrisons and such of their ships as occasionally come there for a cargo of spices.'[22]

On Amboina, the centre of cloves cultivation, the VOC likewise confined all commerce and navigation to its own ships and agents, rigorously controlling the quantity of cloves produced, fixing at 500,000, according to the *Histoire*, the number of cloves trees permitted.[23] In the Banda Islands, the Company was even more rigorous in dictating production levels and regulating seagoing traffic, insisting it

---

[19] *Histoire philosophique* (1770), i. 154, 158.
[20] ARH VOC 4785, *Vreede Articulen gemaeckt tussen de Generaele Nederlantse Geoctroyeerde Oost-Indische Compagnie ende de Coningen van Bima en Dompo* (Batavia, 1669), articles 3, 4, and 5.
[21] Smith, *Wealth of Nations*, ii. 219.
[22] Ibid. ii. 220.   [23] *Histoire philosophique* (1770), i. 149–51.

alone could store and export the nutmeg crop, excluding all other participation. Here too the Company directly owned the estates and had long been uncompromising in imposing its system of colonial subjection and 'armed trade' under enforced trade terms. With its dictated prices, captive labour force, and effective exclusion of all competition, it operated a system of armed monopoly reflecting aspirations pervading the whole of its vast operation from South Africa to the Moluccas.

Of all European colonial systems that of the VOC was the most reliant on fortresses, naval patrolling, and exorbitant treaties. Yet, at the same time it was also the most obviously inefficient, militarily overstretched, wasteful, and locally destructive, besides, for historical reasons, being the most resistant to the efforts at reform and reorganization initiated by enlighteners bent on raising standards, improving social conditions, and doing something for the 'happiness' of the people. It was the world's foremost example of a grandiose, once powerful, but utterly failed colonial system financed by distant vested interests, an empire that not only blighted larger areas and oppressed more diverse peoples than any other in Asia but also one that could plausibly be said to harm the prosperity of the Netherlands itself. 'If, without any exclusive company,' conjectured Smith, the Dutch East India trade 'would be greater than it actually is, that country must suffer a considerable loss by part of its capital being excluded from the employment most convenient for that part'.[24]

Presented to the world most forcefully, yet again, in the *Histoire philosophique*, the picture conveyed to the European reading public by radical writers of the rapacity, brutality, irrationality, and sheer destructiveness of European colonialism in its seventeenth- and eighteenth-century format in Asia was particularly exemplified by the case of the VOC's empire. The image of wasteful and destructive oppression that its very name conjured up was diffused on all sides. Herder is sometimes accused of attacking 'colonialism 'not on the basis of unjustified oppression and exploitation of other peoples' but because he thinks it will decimate the colonizing nation and damage national entities. But actually he was genuinely horrified, deploring the social and cultural effects of worldwide European expansion, in 1774, much like the *Histoire*, rating Dutch pillaging of the East Indies comparable culturally and morally with that of the *conquistadores* in the New World. 'Spaniards, Jesuits, and Dutchmen how much has the formation of humanity to be grateful to you for, already, in all parts of the world!'[25] Agreeing with Diderot, Raynal, and Chastellux in his *De la félicité publique* (1772), he urges historians and philosophers to focus more than they had on the most crucial of all 'philosophical' questions, the 'image of happy or unhappy, of declining or ascending humanity'.

Diderot's devastating critique, echoed in various subsequent works, including Christian Wilhelm Dohm's noteworthy history of the Europeans in the East Indies, was rendered especially appalling by the contradiction between the despotic sway the

[24] Smith, *Wealth of Nations*, ii. 216.
[25] Herder, *Philosophical Writings*, 325, 381; Young, *Colonial Desire*, 39; Pagden, 'Effacement', 141.

VOC had carved from the territories and islands it conquered or dominated and the Dutch Republic's core values, the constitutional principles underpinning the institutions and freedoms of Europe's most prosperous and freest society. This brutal discrepancy was something Diderot, Raynal, and likewise Dohm continually stressed. Diderot eulogized the Dutch Revolt against Philip II but in a particular way, fiercely criticized by Luzac, who felt the *Histoire*'s authors had deliberately minimized the role of what he considered the heroic, far-sighted princely leadership of William of Orange—and, later, that of the stadholderate generally—as well as of Protestant religious zeal.[26]

The *Histoire* did indeed understate the role of religion and princely authority in the Revolt, Diderot massaging the facts to maximize the tragic contrast between the Dutch fight for political and social freedom and their denying this same freedom and dignity, and the rights underpinning it, to the Asian peoples they dominated. At home, the Republic had afforded freedom, dignity, and a laudable prosperity to its citizens by eradicating monarchy and aristocracy and via their famed toleration, besides prompt, disinterested administration of justice and 'de très-belles loix', teaching everyone their duties providing 'des réglemens admirables pour les négocians'.[27] In Holland unlike England, there was no aristocratic sway, monarchical corruption, absurd legal system, or press-gang. How then was everything exactly the reverse in the Dutch Asiatic empire where the sailors and employees were wretchedly paid and the populace everywhere subjected to the most unrelenting exploitation?

The contradiction seemed a deeply ironic, tragic phenomenon but instructive. 'Republicans' who had shaken off the yoke of Philip II's despotism had not shrunk from imposing a comparable or worse tyranny on others not only in Asia but also South Africa, where the 'Hottentots' were despicably treated.[28] The Dutch heartily detested monarchy but needed 'slaves': 's'ils ont brisé des fers, c'est pour en forger.'[29] How can such a gross discrepancy be explained? The answer lay in ignorance and also, suggested Diderot, the gradual erosion of Dutch liberty itself, owing to the increasingly oligarchic character of their constitution after 1572 and especially since the—to his mind—entirely retrograde Orangist 'revolution' (ardently eulogized by Luzac) of 1747–8, a development shamefully strengthening, in his view, the courtly, monarchical, and aristocratic element in Dutch society at the expense of the country's uplifting genuine republican traditions and values. Interested in living conditions in the Dutch colonies, whilst at The Hague in the spring of 1774, Diderot took the opportunity to confer with persons returning from long stays in the East Indies to gather more facts and check as far as he could the accuracy of the claims set out in the 1770 and 1774 editions of the *Histoire*.[30]

---

[26] Luzac, *Hollands rijkdom*, ii. 40–1, 45, 47; Van Vliet, *Elie Luzac*, 333; McDaniel, 'Enlightened History', 213. [27] *Histoire philosophique* (1770), i. 231–3; Muthu, *Enlightenment*, 106.
[28] Muthu, *Enlightenment*, 110–12, 114; *Histoire philosophique* (1770), i. 138, 161.
[29] *Histoire philosophique* (1774), i. 229–30; Bénot, *Diderot*, 176.   [30] Diderot, *Corr.* xiv. 64.

Europeans might not degenerate physically in the Indies, granted Diderot and, later, Dohm who expressly acknowledges his inspiration in Raynal (and hence Diderot), but they undoubtedly had degenerated morally and politically. The Dutch, contended Dohm, exercised a cruel and despotic sway over the indigenous peoples they dominated acquired by emulating the tyrannical ways of the Asiatic potentates themselves. Lavishly attended, the governor-general at Batavia was more slavishly pampered and feared than most Asian princes. Among no other European nation in the Indies was this spirit of 'injustice and harshness', forsaking all standards of humanity and decency, more pronounced than among the Hollanders.[31] That senior officials of the Dutch colonies in the East were so often incompetent but ruthless men wholly 'without talent', according to the *Histoire*, allegedly resulted from the system of favouritism and patronage pervading the VOC since 1749 when the stadholder, proclaiming himself the Company's 'Chief Director' (*opperbewind-hebber*), had assumed direction of the Company's affairs.[32]

2. THE ENLIGHTENMENT RADIATING FROM BATAVIA

Yet, among the Company's senior employees, noted the *Histoire*, there were several who were 'enlightened' and motivated by an entirely new spirit. The *Histoire* cited in particular Baron Gustaaf Willem Van Imhoff, governor of Ceylon (1736–9) and governor-general at Batavia (1743–50), and Jacob Mossel (1704–61); later observers adding the name of Pieter van den Parra (governor-general: 1761–75).[33] Van Imhoff, the first professedly 'enlightened' and seriously reforming governor-general, was chiefly concerned to rescue and revive the Dutch commercial, political, and military position in India and Indonesia. Surveying the entire scenario of Asian trade and European organization in Asia, he judged the Company's recent decline, especially but by no means only in mainland India, 'certain and beyond all doubt'.[34] When contemplating the position, in a long analysis written in 1741, he adopted a much broader perspective than his predecessors and generally worked energetically not just for a general reorganization and amelioration of the system but a fundamental transformation of its character.

Those Asian territories remaining effectively under Dutch control, which he listed as Ceylon, the parts of Malabar and Coromandel where the Dutch remained locally dominant, Makassar, Ternate, Amboina, Banda, central Java, and the Malacca Straits, could realistically be called 'colonies', and here the Dutch presence neither should nor could be evaluated in purely commercial terms. Many interests and assets were

[31] Dohm, *Geschichte*, 50, 54–6, 65; Hess, *Germans, Jews*, 2.
[32] *Histoire philosophique* (1780), x. 97; Israel, *Dutch Republic*, 1079.
[33] *Deutsches Museum*, 1779/ii (July–Dec. 1779), 199–200; and 1781/ii (July–Dec. 1781), 106.
[34] Van Imhoff, *Consideratien*, 445.

involved. What was needed, he thought, was to extend control, rationalize administration, law, and health measures as well as trade, and overall ensure Dutch colonial
society expanded and grew more diversified rather than was pruned back, in particular
by encouraging private enterprise and bringing out more settlers from the Netherlands.
One of his and Van der Parra's favourite projects was to open trade between Batavia
and the Dutch enclaves in India and Malacca (and hence China) to private Dutch
merchants and ships based at Batavia, but here their plans met with scant success.[35]

The steady expansion of Dutch colonial society obliged the Company's directors in
Holland to accept that an increasing proportion of the cargo on their ships sailing to
Asia, and between different parts of Asia, was destined for different purposes from
commerce in the old manner. While the Company scarcely stood to profit from the
growing quantity of tools, manufactures, and materials shipped out each year to
Batavia, intended not for exchange for Asian products but simply for use in Asia,
little could be done to curb this expensive commitment as the materials were
essential for the upkeep of the fortresses and the workshops and businesses, and
general use and well-being, of Batavia's European inhabitants and for the other main
centres of Dutch settlement.[36] Much of the VOC's still considerable volume of
activity was thus dictated by the Company's role as a colonizer and ruler rather
than any quest for greater business efficiency and profitability. As for Batavia itself,
Van Imhoff, unlike some later 'enlightened' VOC planners, urged further enhancing
its role as a general Asian trade entrepôt and developing the city to become more
than ever a focus of Dutch power, commerce, and influence in Asia.[37]

Van Imhoff's and his successors' willingness to look beyond purely commercial
factors in appraising the garrisons and colonial settlements typified the Dutch
moderate reformers' efforts to re-conceptualize the aims and functions of their far-
flung empire. From the late seventeenth century, the Dutch headquarters at Batavia,
like Malacca, Colombo, and Negapatnam, on a smaller scale, was gradually transformed from being the hub of a pan-Asian maritime trading network into the
administrative and cultural focus of what was now increasingly a territorial colonial
state deriving much of its income from agricultural production, tributes, tolls, and
other exactions raised from the hinterland of Java, the Straits, Ceylon, Sumatra, and
the southern Coromandel coast. Van Imhoff, like his successors, an enthusiast for the
idea of reviving the Dutch colonial system through stimulating urban development
and intensive agriculture, tried to stabilize the Dutch enclaves' relations with neighbouring populations and territories as part of his plans to accelerate and systematize
this process. Hence, among the most urgent reforms, held Van Imhoff, was changing
the Company's attitude to its existing agreements with native princes, to sustain the
latter in their privileges in a more scrupulous and generous manner than in the past,
and try harder to cultivate their friendship.[38]

---

[35] Das Gupta, *Malabar*, 85–6; Gaastra, *Geschiedenis*, 101, 123–4; Reid, 'A New Phase', 63.
[36] Van Imhoff, *Consideratien*, 507.
[37] Ibid. 526–7.   [38] ARH VOC 4758 'Reedenkundig', 533–4.

It was 'extremely necessary', he stressed, 'that both the Company and its particular employees' learn to 'deal more reasonably with these princes than is the case now'.[39] Company officials failing to show proper respect or to be sufficiently sensitive to the princes' concerns should be punished as an example to others. He urged the Company to encourage its employees to put more effort into acquiring local languages especially before first being sent out to the Indies and learning the customs of the places where they were sent, showing those who did learn Asian languages they were more highly valued than employees who did not.[40] Meanwhile, he acknowledged the crucial importance of reducing overstretched military and naval commitments where possible if Dutch trade and influence in Asia was to revive and prosper.[41]

To develop Batavia and its hinterland, Van Imhoff, like Mossel later, encouraged Chinese settlement in the low-lying districts surrounding Batavia, offering parcels of land at low prices on which to grow foodstuffs and other crops.[42] Likewise at Malacca, Colombo, Negapatnam, Bantam, and other centres, both local Asian and European society became rapidly more diverse culturally and religiously as well as ethnically, and the number of *mestizos* increased appreciably, all of which presented a host of new social and cultural dilemmas. In his *Oud en Nieuw Oostindien* of 1726, Valentijn had propounded a typically early Enlightenment assessment of the religions and peoples of Asia and their moral systems and sexual practices, lamenting the confusion, disorder, and corruption that seemed to him to prevail on all sides. He strongly criticized the VOC for not doing enough to promote the expansion of Reformed Christianity in the East and for not imposing a more Christian conception of social order and discipline on society more generally.

In the Dutch empire of the Enlightenment era, as in British India later, one regularly encountered typically enlightened terminology urging reform in the name of humanity, the happiness of peoples, and reason being used by missionaries and others advocating expanding Christianization in the East as well as in the rhetoric of those opposing the missions and espousing deism or a secular version of Enlightenment.[43] Divine providence had manifestly placed much of southern Asia in Dutch hands. However, this had created what Valentijn and many others considered a burgeoning problem by stimulating migration to Dutch Batavia, Malacca, and the other main centres of large numbers of Confucianists, Buddhists, and Hindus, often over great distances. This confronted the VOC with the question of how to combine a degree of toleration with active Christianization. In the past the Dutch had imposed a particular system of religious semi-intolerance in Asia specially adapted to the Asian context. At Batavia the rule in the later seventeenth century was that all mosques and Chinese temples had to be located in the outskirts, while in the strictly demarcated inner city where most of the Dutch resided, the Reformed confession was the only religion whose observance was publicly permitted.

---

[39] Ibid. 534.   [40] Ibid. 534–5.   [41] Van Imhoff, *Consideratien*, 522–3.
[42] Ibid. 530; *Histoire philosophique* (1770), i. 190, 193.
[43] Fisch, *Hollands Ruhm*, 129–34; Carson, 'British Raj', 57.

In the inner city of Batavia, not only were no Asian religions practised outside private rooms but neither were Catholics, alternative Protestant confessions, or Jews permitted to erect houses of worship or organize charitable or educational institutions.[44] This aspect of the VOC's institutionalized intolerance particularly affected the substantial number of German and Scandinavian seamen and soldiers in the Company's service. Active intolerance in the Asiatic empire also infused the measures taken, most notably in Ceylon, to prevent indigenous populations earlier converted to Christianity by the Portuguese from receiving Catholic priests or continuing their Catholic allegiance. It was not until the British conquest of Ceylon, in 1795, that the intolerant policy pursued by the Dutch on the island was finally abandoned.[45] In the seventeenth century, Dutch Reformed Church preachers and their helpers had also made some progress in establishing an indigenous Asian Calvinist culture in Batavia, Amboina, and elsewhere especially among Portuguese- and Malay-speaking immigrants and *mestizos*, but devoted little effort to proselytizing among the Chinese, or beyond Batavia's outskirts among the Muslim Javanese.

Van Imhoff was a Lutheran albeit with wide intellectual interests and promoter of mainstream Enlightenment in many of its ramifications, including the Christianization programme. His governor-generalship marks the real commencement of an official Enlightenment in the East Indies, and although several of his projects, such as his 'Latin school' and Académie de Marine, failed, more generally his initiatives, including allowing Lutherans more leeway, had a certain impact throughout the network of Dutch settlements from Japan to South Africa. He initiated a fashionable reading circle among the senior Dutch administrators, in Java, that was the predecessor of the 'Society for Arts and Sciences' founded by the high administration there in 1778, a group that by the early 1780s was reported in Germany to gather regularly and display a keen interest in science and scientific experiments.[46] From the 1740s onwards, there was a steady growth, mainly among the Company's high officials, preachers, and surgeons, of interest in enlightened literature, debating, building libraries, collecting scientific data, and formulating schemes for improvement. In terms of intellectual content this Dutch Asiatic enlightenment, as one would expect, was mainly an outgrowth of the Dutch Enlightenment in Europe but with a considerable admixture of French and Lutheran German influences. By 1780, there were several impressive personal libraries in Batavia, including at least two reportedly well stocked with German philosophy.[47]

From the 1720s, mainstream Enlightenment was in the air at Batavia. But its progress especially in terms of practical and legal improvements and institutional changes, if by no means to be underrated, was slow and halting due to formidable difficulties and obstructions encountered on every side. Regarding religious

[44] Fisch, *Hollands Ruhm*, 115–17; Valentijn, *Zaken*, 5, 7.
[45] Schrikker, *British and Dutch*, 20, 96, 145.
[46] Ibid. 100, 120–1; Gaastra, *Geschiedenis*, 106; Israel, *Dutch Republic*, 1058; Withers, *Placing*, 68.
[47] *Deutsches Museum*, 1781/i (Jan.–June 1781), 501–4.

toleration for Lutherans, Catholics, Muslims, Confucianists, Buddhists, and Jews, mainstream Enlightenment in the Dutch Asiatic empire delivered conspicuously little and late. The close alignment of the Reformed Church with the VOC's direct-orate in Holland ensured a tenacious resistance to efforts to develop organized non-Reformed church communities and communal institutions at Batavia, Colombo, Malacca, Amboina, and also in South Africa where the governor still rejected requests from the sizeable local Lutheran community for their own churches as late as 1772 and 1773. A formal Lutheran church appeared in Cape Town only in 1780; and even after 1780, the drift towards religious toleration continued to be vigorously criticized by some Reformed preachers in the East and fiercely opposed in Holland by a growing Calvinist Counter-Enlightenment, one of the chief spokesmen of which, Petrus Hofstede (1716–1803), a preacher at Rotterdam, was a publicly declared foe of all Enlightenment values including any formalized toleration.[48]

Van Imhoff strove to establish churches and schools in the capital's surrounding area, the Ommelanden, to Christianize Batavia's immediate hinterland.[49] Hoping to see Batavia become the 'mother' of a tolerant 'enlightened Christianity' in the East, in which the Reformed and Lutheran churches would cooperate in a friendly fashion and also accept other Christians, he followed up Valentijn's earlier plea that more effort be put into Christianizing the Muslim population as well as the largely Chinese populace of the suburbs outside Batavia's walls. He urged the directors to be stricter than in the past in ensuring that Reformed preachers and *proponenten* (candidates) sent out from the Netherlands acquired one of the Asian languages before leaving, or else Portuguese, southern Asia's lingua franca, 'so as to make themselves compre-hensible to the inhabitants'. Malay, Malabar, and Portuguese he deemed the most useful languages in this respect.[50] The Company should establish printing presses, he advised, both at Batavia and in Ceylon to print texts in all the languages current in the areas under Dutch control, especially bibles in Asian languages and Portuguese.

The efforts to render Protestantism in Dutch colonial Asia more tolerant but also more expansive and dynamic, though partly a response to a traditional criticism of the VOC in the Netherlands where its failure to take its Christian missionary obligations seriously enough, cravenly bowing to Chinese and Japanese dislike of Christianity, was an old complaint, also reflected many aspects of the mid-eighteenth-century European 'religious enlightenment'. Differences of opinion about the merits and demerits of the missionary campaign and the bounds to which toleration should extend were by no means the only tensions besetting what developed into a basic rift within the Enlightenment in Asia. Those in the Nether-lands in the mid eighteenth century who believed in the VOC's legitimacy and importance to national interests, and they were many, broadly supported the pro-gramme of reform and innovation undertaken in Ceylon, South Africa, Amboina,

---

[48] [Bahrdt], *Kirchen- und Ketzer-Almanach*, 221–8; Israel, *Dutch Republic*, 1059.
[49] Israel, *Dutch Republic*, 539–40; *Deutsches Museum*, 1781/ii (July–Dec. 1781), 107.
[50] Israel, *Dutch Republic*, 540.

and the other colonies as well as at Batavia, but usually only to missionize and render the Dutch Company more viable commercially, militarily, and administratively. But in the Dutch Asiatic empire, as in British India, there was a constant tension between the quest for economic and military efficiency, and pressure to Christianize, on the one hand, and the unavoidable need to confront increasingly complex issues of law, community, and ethnic relations and racial questions, on the other.

After 1740, the governors-general at Batavia pursued a programme of general rationalization but had to order their priorities, placing the rescue of the Dutch political and military position in Asia first. In pursuing greater efficiency many social, moral, legal, and health problems they confronted there were either neglected or aggravated. Nothing could be done, seemingly, about the poor wages and conditions of the Company's lower employees, especially seamen and soldiers. By the 1760s, complaints about the Company and its high officials were more prevalent than ever among VOC shareholders and employees, with a continuing deterioration in remuneration and steepening decline in the Company's share price on the Amsterdam stock exchange, its stock falling particularly disastrously, by around half, during the twelve years 1762–73, a period when the Company's annual losses and indebtedness rose sharply and the stark reality of its basic unprofitability became more glaring.[51] A particularly worrying and complex social problem was the growing intermediary role of the Chinese between the Dutch and indigenous populations, a development that aggravated inequalities and greatly complicated ethnic, fiscal, and employment relations in the colonies.

Chinese immigrants had by the mid eighteenth century come to practise 'presque exclusivement' Batavia's crafts and manufacturing activities and those of many other Dutch bases. While large-scale Chinese immigration into Dutch Taiwan (until 1661) had been a notable phenomenon as early as the 1620s, elsewhere in the Dutch Asian empire this was a more recent phenomenon stimulated by the lifting of the Chinese emperor's ban on emigration, in 1684. Although the rapid increase in the Chinese population of Java, Sumatra, the Malay Straits, and Borneo in the period 1720–80 crucially contributed to a wide range of old and new activities, it also encouraged diversion of shipping, tin-mining, pepper and coffee production, and other activities away from areas under Dutch control.[52] Much as at Spanish Manila, another newly founded European colonial city with a sizeable Chinese immigrant community implanted within an ethnically different and mainly agrarian society, the Batavia Chinese constituted a relatively homogeneous, skilled, and well-educated ethnic group and fast became much the most skilled, industrious, and disciplined community. They had their own chief representative who, as also elsewhere in the

---

[51] ARH VOC 4758, 'Reedenkundig berigt wegens de ware oorsaake van het bederf mitsgaders de middelen van redres der Nederlandsche Oost Indische Compagnie' (May 1773), 4; *Deutsches Museum*, 1779/ii (July–Dec. 1779), 199; Gaastra, *Geschiedenis*, 132, 139.

[52] Van Imhoff, *Consideratien*, 198; Blussé, *Strange Company*, 73–4, 78; Trocki, 'Chinese Pioneering', 93–7.

Dutch colonies, was called the 'captain'. Chinese also controlled most local land-based trade in agricultural produce and leased and operated most farms owned by affluent Dutch burghers besides dominating fishing and the long-distance trade with China. Chinese tax-farmers, furthermore, collected most of Batavia's taxes and tolls on behalf of the Company, especially those on the city's markets, on (predominantly Chinese) gambling, a special poll-tax on the Chinese population—the only group which paid such a tax—and local land and water tolls.

The Company's increasing reliance in Java, Sumatra, and elsewhere, and that of many princes under its tutelage, on Chinese functionaries, skills, and artisans to collect taxes, operate the Malay tin mines, and generally serve as the key intermediary between the European and native populations they exploited in effect created an entirely new kind of tripartite society. But much as the governors-general consistently understated the role of official corruption and rapacity in the empire's decline, they seem also to have underestimated the problems caused by increasing use of Chinese as intermediaries in aggravating oppression of the rest of the population.[53] An anonymous observer who had spent thirty years in the Company's service was quoted in the *Deutsches Museum*, in 1781, after returning to Europe from the East Indies, as citing Cheribon, a small and weak sultanate on Java's north coast only recently brought under direct Dutch control, and eastern Java, as clear examples of territories formerly flourishing that had become completely impoverished and reduced to stagnation in recent decades owing to heavy tolls and tax-farms operated by Dutch officials employing Chinese intermediaries.[54]

Chinese also both organized and supplied labour for the sugar plantations that arose in the late seventeenth century in the Ommelanden, the directly administered districts close to Batavia. The sugar plantations yielded significant profits and provided much employment but also polluted local waterways and generated stagnant pools and fish-ponds, providing, although no one knew this at the time, perfect breeding grounds for the malaria-bearing mosquitoes now thought to have been the main cause of the terrible epidemic that afflicted Batavia in the years 1733–8 and continuing high sickness and mortality rates especially among newly arrived Europeans from the 1730s onwards.[55] The VOC and the Company's European critics were acutely conscious of the health problem if not of its precise cause;[56] though here too the Company looked culpably negligent to its critics, being accused of failing to allocate sufficient funds to provide adequate supplies of quinine and other relatively expensive medicines.[57] Supposing the city's chronic health problem was due to mud and residue in the city's canals, the authorities concentrated on deepening the canals and improving the flow of stagnant water. Considerable efforts were made to improve sanitation and the canals. But Batavia failed to revert to being the relatively healthy location it had been before 1733, indeed became increasingly notorious for

[53] *Deutsches Museum*, 1779/ii (July–Dec. 1779), 201–11.   [54] Ibid. 215–16.
[55] Van der Brug, *Malaria en malaise*, 63, 67, 114, 117.   [56] Ibid. 92, 99.
[57] ARH VOC 4790 'Bedenckingen', 54.

being an unhealthy place. Mortality rates among newly arrived European sailors and soldiers rose to unprecedented levels. In May 1763, there were reportedly no less than 863 Dutchmen lying sick in Batavia's two hospitals of whom 162 died that month.[58] Not the least disturbing aspect of the problem was the tendency for the military garrison to slump far below its appropriate strength, weakening the Dutch position throughout south-east Asia.

The relatively prosperous condition of the by 1710 eighty-four mostly Chinese-owned sugar plantations surrounding Batavia, with their large labour force operating 130 sugar mills, was decisively reversed in the 1730s due to a sharp drop in the purchase price for sugar. This resulted from a growing inability of Javanese sugar to compete with Bengal sugar, in Asia, and lowering of demand for Java sugar in Europe owing to rising imports from the Caribbean.[59] Falling incomes resulted in unemployment and unrest that fed an alarming upsurge of rural lawlessness and banditry around Batavia. An attempt, in the spring of 1740, to ship some of the excess Chinese labouring population to Ceylon heightened ethnic friction and led to one of the greatest and most terrible catastrophes of the age. Rumours that, once out to sea, the forced emigrants had been disposed of by being thrown overboard sparked a full-scale revolt in Ommelanden. The rebel leaders also attempted to raise the Chinese population within the city walls where 'so few Dutch and so many Chinese live', as their proclamation put it, 'and where nevertheless the Dutch dare treat the Chinese so harshly and oppress them so unjustly that it can no longer be tolerated'.[60]

In effect, the Chinese rebels in Java in 1740–1 declared war on the Company and the Dutch nation. Despite fielding an army of Dutch, Buginese, and other Indonesian troops, Van Imhoff, able commander though he was, failed to disperse the rebel force surrounding the city that increasingly encroached and even set fire to its southern suburbs. A sudden panic gripped the Dutch soldiers, sailors, and burghers that turned into a murderous frenzy. An indiscriminate massacre began of the Chinese within the walls. A truly appalling atrocity ensued that continued for three days and in which almost all the estimated 10,000 Chinese of the metropolis were slaughtered.[61] The massacre administered a tremendous shock throughout the Chinese trading diaspora in south-east Asia, deeply angered the Chinese court, and further blackened the VOC's reputation throughout Asia as well as significantly further harming its revenues and commercial prospects. It was doubtful, remarked Van Imhoff afterwards, whether the China trade carried in Chinese junks to Batavia, a key strand of the Dutch imperial system in Asia, would ever recover from this 'fatale revolutie'.[62]

Above all, the great massacre of 1741 seriously dislocated the local economy.[63] It was in the hope of reducing dependence on the Chinese that Van Inhoff urged the systematic settlement of poor Dutch and other European farmers on terrain close to

[58] ARH VOC 4790 'Bedenckingen', 55. [59] Van Imhoff, *Consideratien*, 510.
[60] Blussé, *Strange Company*, 94. [61] Ibid. 95–6; Trocki, 'Chinese Pioneering', 93.
[62] Van Imhoff, *Consideratien*, 500. [63] Ibid. 531; Arasaratnam, 'Monopoly', 11.

Batavia and providing them with small Company subsidies to buy farm equipment and feed themselves until their land became productive.[64] The best way to do this, he advised, was for the Company to recruit poor farmers in the Republic and send them out, ten or twelve on every outgoing East Indiaman, in this way creating a rural Dutch colony in central Java alongside a reduced number of Chinese, something like what had been achieved, albeit slowly, in South Africa.

Against this backcloth of ethnic friction, as well as disagreements about toleration and Christianization, enlightened attitudes and reform proposals were bound not just to diverge but split into two fundamentally different kinds of reform agenda. The context encouraged an official high-level Enlightenment mainly concerned with shoring up rather than abolishing the existing structure and rendering it viable and efficient. Equally, though, there arose a much more radical critique seeking to transform the Company's role more fundamentally. Without proposing total liquid- ation of the Company, the *Histoire* and the bolder Dutch and German critics proposed ending the difficulties and disruption the Company incurred in its colonies by completely transforming its relationship with its Asian subjects—by paying reasonable prices rather than the lowest possible they could extort, ending their tyrannical tax-farming practices, and acknowledging the basic humanity and right to a life of dignity, autonomy, and freedom of those over whom they ruled.[65]

However decayed the Dutch empire in Asia, it was still considered capable of being transformed into something useful to all and worthy of enlightened respect. Even the Malabar fortresses, arguably, were not altogether superfluous. 'Avec plus de lumière', avers the *Histoire*, 'on parviendroit peut-être à la rendre utile.'[66] What chiefly mattered was neither national interest nor ethnic status, nor missionizing. Dutch colonialism's defects were just a variant of the universal human predicament and proneness to tyranny and oppression. What mattered were the possibilities for improvement and furthering 'enlightenment' and here the Company offered distinct advantages compared with other empires, or the native princes. The VOC's empire had the largest organization and communications system and widest reach. If the Company could be reborn, changed into an instrument for advancing the 'bonheur' of the native populations under its sway, then it could, through contributing to human betterment, acquire the legitimacy and justification for its rule it presently lacked, indeed greater legitimacy and justification than the East Indies' native princes could boast or were ever likely to acquire.

Commercial jealousy, one of the greatest plagues afflicting humanity, according to the *Histoire*, had forged a system of oppression and regulation that was irrational and ultimately unworkable. Curbing corruption and despotic ways, and allowing native populations more freedom and advancing their prosperity, was the goal of the most radical critics.[67] The rival agendas offered did involve some overlap but overall the

---

[64] Van Imhoff, *Consideratien*, 530–1.   [65] *Histoire philosophique* (1770), i. 212–13.
[66] Ibid. i. 177.   [67] *Deutsches Museum*, 1779/ii (July–Dec. 1779), 202–17.

Histoire's recipe for saving the VOC from otherwise certain collapse and ruin centred around the need to abandon the mentality of 'armed trade' and dismantle the very colonial structures Van Imhoff and Mossel strove to rescue, structures defended by Luzac, claiming his opponents made insufficient allowances for local circumstances and the 'treacherous' character of the natives. But for the most part, their different approaches and goals pitted the two agendas against each other. The fundamental aim of the treaties the VOC had imposed on the princes, and still sought to enforce, was to buy their pepper, spices, and other commodities at dictated prices 15 or 20 per cent less than the English, French, and Danes were willing to pay on the open market. Seventeenth-century, ultra-mercantilist methods denounced by Raynal and Diderot for their inherent immorality were also counter-productive economically, they claimed, and only depressed Dutch trade wherever, from Malabar to Ternate, the VOC sought to enforce such infamous 'agreements'.[68]

At Batavia, all foreign nations were currently excluded from access except for the Chinese whose junks, mostly from Canton and Amoy, brought tea, silks, and porcelain, and Spaniards from Manila in quest of cinnamon for reshipment, via the Manila galleons, to Acapulco. How narrow-minded, mean, and absurd! The Company could be saved, argued both the *Histoire* and Adam Smith, only by abandoning such monopolizing, strong-armed strategies and opening up Dutch Asiatic commerce to private individuals trading under the Company's protection whether using her ships or not.[69] Batavia should be declared a general entrepôt open to all nations.[70] Such a measure would greatly enhance the traffic converging from all directions and dissolve the edifice of narrow regulations and bureaucratic corruption presently controlling but also stifling the traffic. Only such far-reaching reform could save the VOC and render the Dutch Asiatic colonies thriving and legitimate.

The VOC's contraction in its core zones of activity—southern India, Ceylon, and south-east Asia—was chiefly due, according to the Dutch themselves, as well as Adam Smith and the *Histoire*, less to foreign competition per se than outmoded restrictions, heavy-handed fiscalism, official corruption, and an obsessive compulsion with fixing prices, routes, and the terms of trade. Of the Company's chronic structural defects, the worst, according to one of its harshest critics who signed his long critique, addressed to the *Heren XVII*, of May 1773 simply as 'the East India Patriot', was the poor quality—due to abominable pay and conditions—of the Company's European employees in Asia; the next an inbuilt resistance to change and adherence to old commercial strategies of a highly oppressive kind; and third, a top-heavy, overly bureaucratic concentration of power at Batavia.[71] The true consequence of the Company's 'vile treatment' of its employees was a 'contagion' of corruption that betrayed the Company's affairs at every step and spelt the rapid

---

[68] *Histoire philosophique* (1770), i. 177; Luzac, *Hollands rijkdom*, i. 269, 285–6, 290.
[69] *Histoire philosophique* (1770), i. 220–1; *Histoire philosophique* (1774), i. 280, 312, 320.
[70] *Histoire philosophique* (1770), i. 221; *Histoire philosophique* (1774), i. 311–12.
[71] ARH VOC 4758, 'Reedenkundig berigt', 535–6.

deterioration of both garrisons and ships' crews. Better pay and conditions alone could cure this.[72]

Only a freer, more benign social and economic regime could preserve the VOC stronghold of Ceylon and other key footholds such as the Cape in the long run. At present, the Cape was a valuable base but one strictly reserved for the Company's own fleets and personnel. Current practice was for VOC officials to purchase fresh supplies and provisions for its ships at fixed, wretchedly low prices from white settlers over whom, according to the *Histoire* (and at least some colonists), the Company tyrannized abominably. The projected enlightened VOC of the future should turn the Cape into the very model of toleration and hospitality for all. Were ships of all nations admitted and South Africa's settlers permitted to trade also with North America, the colony would soon flourish and fresh colonists arrive from all parts. Not surprisingly, the first stirrings of concerted political opposition to the VOC in South Africa began shortly after the onset of the American Revolution, in 1778. VOC rule without any participation in running the colony by the white settlers had become intolerable to some. The direct connection between spreading Enlightenment concepts and organized opposition emerges clearly from the fact that the Cape's two leading instigators of protest were a native of Rostock, Joachim van Dessin, owner of a collection of around 4,000 books, and a Cape schoolmaster, J. H. Redelinghuys, who subsequently became an active 'Patriot' democrat, political propagandist, and, eventually, a hard-line Jacobin.[73] Colonial society bred its own Radical Enlightenment.

Nowhere were the Dutch forts properly maintained; nowhere did the Company deploy good-quality troops or possess up-to-date warships of the line able to resist the British successfully. Recent governors-general had tried to strengthen Batavia's fortifications but these remained ramshackle. Without completely dismantling the old system, and replacing it with a totally new conception, there was no way to save this 'colosse d'une apparence gigantesque' that was now highly vulnerable. The VOC's entire network of bases in the Moluccas and Amboina might well suddenly be overrun by a single large British or French expeditionary force. A great blow to the United Provinces, such an outcome would, paradoxically, also be a calamity for their native inhabitants too. For whether Britain or France acquired these colonies, either would have less reason than the Dutch to reform, improve, and exploit the indigenous populace less. The *Histoire*'s recommendations were philosophical and disinterested, announced its authors, offered purely out of devotion to 'le bien général des nations'.[74]

Central to Diderot's conception but of scant relevance according to Luzac and moderate reformers were the questions of social hierarchy and political tyranny.

---

[72] *Histoire philosophique* (1770), i. 215–16.
[73] Schutte, *Nederlandse Patriotten*, 61–4, 71, 75; Israel, *Dutch Republic*, 1060–1.
[74] *Histoire philosophique* (1774), i. 312–13.

Underpinning the system of treaties, forts, and garrisons was not just an over-burdened inefficient system of administration, logistics, and expenditures needed to sustain them but also a heavily complicit local political and social colonial system, part Dutch, part Chinese, part indigenous. A crude form of tyranny imposed on local populations over an immense area operating by 1795 for two centuries, the VOC's trading empire functioned only through collusion with the petty princes of south-east Asia and southern India. While the VOC compelled the inhabitants of Java, Sumatra, and other islands with varying degrees of success to surrender their pepper, rice, coffee, and cotton at dictated prices, and receive imports solely from the Company, this was only possible through their arrangements with the sultans.

The sultanate of Bantam in western Java having been forcibly reduced to tributary status, and the English, French, and Danish 'factories' ejected, in 1682, acquiesced without murmur in its subsequent subjection. A local revolt in 1755–6 was easily put down with the sultan's help. Cheribon seemed too docile ever to rise against the unjust prices received for their produce, a VOC garrison of a hundred men sufficing to ensure total subjection to the Dutch and their Chinese underlings.[75] The Madura islanders, off Java's north-east coast, were coerced by a garrison of just fifteen men unresistingly to surrender their rice 'à un prix très-foible'.[76] Minimizing competition pivoted throughout on tyrannical, exploitative princely authority, backed by over-whelming religious authority. The sultan of Palembang, like other Sumatran sultans, fully collaborated with the VOC, selling them his entire pepper crop at an imposed price and excluding foreigners, while keeping most of the proceeds for himself, paying to his wretched subjects in the fields toiling to produce the pepper virtually nothing.[77]

In Ceylon, where by 1750 the originally tiny colonial settlements of Colombo, Jaffna, and Galle had grown into real Dutch Asiatic towns, smaller models of Batavia, land available for cultivation belonged, to a much greater extent than in India, to the sovereign whether the Company around the coast, or the 'king' of Kandy inland. This 'destructive system', according to the *Histoire*, had the ruinous consequences inevit-able under so inequitable a regime: 'les peuples y vivent dans l'inaction la plus entière.'[78] Ceylon's cinnamon output, whether destined for Asia, Europe, or Spanish America (whither the largest part was shipped via Manila or Cadiz), was monopol-ized by the Company to the exclusion of all other bidders. In the expanding area under direct control, Sinhalese labourers working the fields were a totally servile labour force, paid practically nothing, toiling 'pour un livre de riz par jour'.[79] Until the 1760s, most of the annual crop came from further inland; and, for this, the VOC needed to pay higher prices. After the war of 1765–6, though, with the Dutch ruling

---

[75] *Histoire philosophique* (1770), i. 187–8; Gaastra, *Geschiedenis*, 63–4.
[76] *Histoire philosophique* (1770), i. 189.
[77] Ibid. i. 159–60; Démeunier, *L'Esprit*, i. 356; Jacobs, *Koopman in Azië*, 53–4.
[78] *Histoire philosophique* (1770), i. 173–4; *Histoire philosophique* (1774), i. 246–7.
[79] *Histoire philosophique* (1770), i. 172.

more of the island directly and the king of Kandy forced to submit to more onerous terms than before, the balance changed.[80]

'The interior, middle, and mountainous parts of the island', recorded Thunberg, pursuing scientific research in Ceylon in 1777–8, 'belong to the king of Kandy, who is now so completely hemmed in on every side, that he can neither smuggle nor sell any cinnamon to foreign nations.'[81] The war of 1765 provided more scope for cinnamon produced under direct Dutch rule but, more importantly, permanently changed production methods. From 1769, observed Thunberg, the Dutch began planting and cultivating cinnamon trees themselves. Planting and cultivation, as opposed to gathering from cinnamon trees in the wild, began under Governor Willem Van der Valck (1765–85), a Dutchman passionate about plants born in Ceylon who had studied in Utrecht and whom Thunberg considered 'very learned and affable' and 'at the same time the most disinterested of all the Company's officers I ever met with'; he genuinely sought amelioration and to improve relations with the population.[82] No one could doubt that the Enlightenment was an active force in the Ceylon of the 1770s and 1780s. But especially under the island's next reforming governor, Willem Jacob van der Graeff (1785–94), the Company not only greatly increased the numbers of labourers it employed directly but took to relying on what was virtually forced labour, for the lowest possible remuneration, mediated by local headmen who greatly enriched themselves in the process.[83]

After 1740, there were manifold signs of a Dutch enlightenment in Asia as in South Africa. But it was a top-down, hierarchical enlightenment akin to the enlightened despotism of central and eastern Europe. From the perspective of establishment reformers like Van der Valck and Van der Graeff, figures who had certainly read enlightened literature and, in the latter case, even claimed to be partly motivated in striving to improve order and hygiene in the towns as well as stimulate commerce and agriculture, by reading Raynal,[84] the new order was genuinely concerned with general amelioration and the people's welfare as well as extending the Company's colonial reach. But the good intentions of some notwithstanding, it is doubtful whether much genuine improvement was achieved. The appalling system prevailing in Ceylon, contends the *Histoire*, could not be mitigated simply by expanding Company control; it could be ended only by changing the system of institutionalized forced labour and redistributing the land, as private property, among those who cultivated it.

Village heads in Ceylon, like the sultans of Sumatra, Borneo, and the Malay Straits, were nothing, according to radical minds, but 'les vils instruments du despotisme de la Compagnie'.[85] If the Dutch could find the wisdom to alter course in their relations with the Ceylonese fundamentally, proposed the radical enligteners, the people

[80] Ibid. i. 172–3; Schrikker, *British and Dutch*, 52.   [81] Thunberg, *Travels*, iv. 184–5.
[82] Ibid. iv. 174; Schrikker, *British and Dutch*, 40, 44, 54.   [83] Schrikker, *British and Dutch*, 53–7.
[84] Ibid. 97.
[85] *Histoire philosophique* (1770), i. 189; *Histoire philosophique* (1774), i. 225, 266–7, 269.

would forget, even learn to 'detest', their former native sovereigns and adhere loyally 'au gouvernement qui s'occupera de leur bonheur'.[86] Equally, had the VOC been 'more just and more enlightened' in the Moluccas, it could have saved itself the expense of its forts and garrisons, ceased basing trade on compulsion and imposed conditions, and through more generously paying indigenous cultivators induced them to be less indolent and cultivate indigo and pepper as well as cloves.[87]

Among the ugliest blots on the Company's record, according to radical commentators, was institutionalized slavery. Many Makassars, Balinese, Timorese, and Muslim Malays, in Batavia, as in Manila, were slaves under law. Batavia was one of four main concentrations of organized slavery in the VOC's empire, the others being Amboina, the Banda islands, and the Cape.[88] In the Bandas, slaves—mostly from the islands east of Bali as far as Timor—toiled in the fields cultivating the spice trees. By contrast, at Batavia where they were mostly domestic servants, they generally received better treatment than in Banda or South Africa and were often seen, notes Valentijn, carrying the parasols and cushions of white ladies going to church. But slavery is slavery and as the VOC colonial code forbade ownership of slaves who were Christians, there was no alternative to creating ethnically mixed groups of non-Christian slaves idly awaiting masters and mistresses outside churches while services were in progress.

The Dutch Asiatic empire was a highly organized commercial tyranny interlocking with a system of native despotism previously already firmly in place among the native peoples and highly efficient in securing compliance. The VOC had always been a contradiction, combining as it did the roles of a once uniquely large commercial organization with the attributes of a virtual sovereign state possessing its own army, navy, coinage, legal code, and diplomatic service (albeit formally under the States General in The Hague). But expanding the Company's territorial and fiscal exploitation of Java, Sumatra, Ceylon, Moluccas, and other islands it controlled, during the later eighteenth century, both further swelled and complicated its organization and bureaucracy, multiplying the contradictions within the wide spectrum of its activities. This only aggravated relations between the two enlightenments, the one seeking to reform and improve the Company's existing institutional framework on a semi-tolerant but firmly Protestant basis, working from within, the other summoning the Company to transform itself into something emancipating, benevolent, and completely different. The final meaning of the rift between the two enlightenments in Asia was doubtless only dimly perceived by most but was certainly glimpsed by a few and made explicit in a passage of 'Raynal' almost certainly penned by Diderot himself where the reader is told no programme of reform, however comprehensive, could ever place the Dutch Asiatic empire on a sound basis or cure its ills whilst it remained

---

[86] *Histoire philosophique* (1770), i. 173–4.
[87] Ibid. i. 151.
[88] Démeunier, *L'Esprit*, ii. 124; *Deutsches Museum*, 1881/ii (July–Dec. 1781), 103–5; Knaap, 'Slavery', 196–7.

an instrument of vested interests in the United Provinces. For every organization exercising control in one part of the world but subject to political and financial control in another is inherently oppressive and exploitative, an 'établissement vicieux dans son principe'.[89]

Contemplating the Dutch colonial empire, moderate Enlightenment and those, like Kant, steering between the two enlightenments could mostly only bow before the mountain of incriminating evidence. In his essay on *Perpetual Peace* of 1795, Kant, echoing Bayle's observations of a century before, observed that the Chinese and Japanese, 'whom experience has taught to know the Europeans, had wisely refused them entry into their countries, though the former permit all the Europeans to approach and the latter permit access to one nation, the Dutch, while at the same time segregating them, like prisoners, from every communication with the inhabitants'.[90] The real tragedy, he added, was that the dreadful, truly shocking havoc the Europeans had wrought in the East served no real purpose since the brutal systems of exploitation devised and 'all the commercial companies guilty of them' had merely laid down the paths of their own eventual ruin. Just as the slave trade and the West Indian sugar plantations proved economically inefficient, the creaking Dutch colonial empire had become so despotic and entwined with Europe's rivalries and wars that it could no longer be viably maintained or kept apart from Europe's politics, conflicts, and philosophical debates. Discredited, besieged, and inefficient, the VOC seemed doomed to flounder and collapse.[91]

---

[89] *Histoire philosophique* (1780), i. 245; Bénot, *Diderot,* 179.
[90] Kant, *Perpetual Peace,* 83–4.   [91] Ibid. 84.

20

China, Japan, and the West

1. SINOPHILIA IN THE LATER ENLIGHTENMENT

A curious feature of early eighteenth-century Enlightenment debate about China and Japan, we have seen,[1] was the strange circumstance that the identical claim that the classical Confucianists were 'atheistic', virtual *Spinosistes* was routinely advanced by two diametrically opposed camps in the dispute. The same argument was incorporated into divergent, antagonistic strategies, creating a bizarre juxtaposition. Where Malebranche and the anti-Jesuit wing of the Church disparaged traditional China, Korea, and Japan (and, by implication, the Jesuits) by bracketing classical Chinese moral and philosophical tradition with Spinozism, the radicals identified Confucianism with Spinozism to insinuate that Spinozism was an ancient, venerable, wholly natural mode of thought, once conceivably that of most of mankind.[2] This subversive implication came to be widely propagated following Bayle's assertion that 'la plupart des nations orientales' shared Spinoza's 'sentiments'. D'Argens's literary device of having his Chinese visitor to Paris report back to China that numerous Europeans had latterly espoused a philosophy identical to that of the Chinese *literati* and that in Europe the originator of this mode of thought was a philosopher called 'Spinoza' built on the foundation Bayle laid.[3]

The (main) Jesuit standpoint, on the other hand, stressed the Chinese intellectual tradition's adherence to natural theology and a providential God, a position endorsed by Leibniz and later Voltaire. The quarrel between advocates of Bayle's thesis, including Collins and many other freethinkers, on the one hand, and the two opposed ecclesiastical traditions, Jesuit and anti-Jesuit, about Chinese classical thought was then further convoluted by the positions of Voltaire and Hume who, on the one hand, rejected the non-Jesuit Christian apologists' disparagement of Chinese thought as atheistic and materialist while simultaneously refusing to extol features of Chinese and Japanese culture, real or alleged, that radicals admired. Like Bayle, Collins, d'Argens, and other radical writers, Voltaire and Hume wrote enthusiastically of the complete toleration both the Chinese and Japanese had long

---

[1] Israel, *Enlightenment Contested*, ch. 25.   [2] Ibid. 645.
[3] Ibid.; d'Argens, *Lettres chinoises*, i. 106; Vernière, *Spinoza*, 352–3; Ehrard, *L'Idée*, 409.

enjoyed, of the educated elite's alleged disdain for popular religion, and that the Chinese mandarins 'have no priests', as Hume put it, 'or ecclesiastical establishment'.[4] But agreement ended there. What Voltaire and Hume could no more accept than the Jesuits, Leibniz, or Malebranche was the implication that Europe could be seen to be a manifestly defective society morally, socially, and politically as well as religiously when compared with the better-ordered societies of China and Japan. If radical writers enthused over the lack of hereditary nobility in the government and administration of China this feature held no attraction for them. Such differences of perspective injected a constant tension between the early radical standpoint and the views of Voltaire and Hume as well as between radical thinkers and Christian apologists. Hume, in his *Essays*, proposed that China, being 'one vast empire, speaking one language, governed by one law, and sympathizing with the same manners', was wholly conventional in its thinking, cultivating 'the greatest uniformity of character imaginable' so that in China 'posterity was not bold enough to dispute what had been universally received by their ancestors'.[5] Voltaire, in contrast to Hume and Montesquieu, stood almost alone on the moderate side in projecting an emphatic Sinophilia.

Christian values were profoundly challenged by the Sinophilia of radical thought and, in a more limited way, the sceptical moderate Enlightenment. But only the radical fraternity deployed the Chinese example as a weapon in a war against social hierarchies based on birth and lineage and exalted Chinese moral philosophy and attitudes for being supposedly independent of natural theology and a providential God who rewards and punishes. After 1750, Helvétius was one who remained within this tradition, lauding classical Chinese moral rectitude and refusal to acknowledge a guiding and omnipotent God who, were he to exist, must be unforgiving and unjust.[6] Only moderate Enlightenment (Christian and sceptical), on the other hand, assumed Europe's general superiority in science, crafts, economic life, and the arts as well (with Voltaire an exception here) as morality. Adam Smith starkly contrasted Europe's economic dynamism with the stagnation and poverty of China, and despite cultural barriers impeding the sale of Western goods in China, for both Smith and Hume the 'skill and ingenuity of Europe in general surpasses that of China, with regard to the manual arts and manufactures'.[7]

Anti-Jesuit theologians dismissed Chinese historiography as deceit, Chinese philosophy as nonsense, and Chinese astronomy as worthless. But both Jesuit and anti-Jesuit Christian apologists sternly condemned the freethinkers' approving that the mandarins, being Confucianists, identified God with Nature, teaching an oriental 'Spinozism' or what d'Holbach termed 'une espèce d'athéisme raffiné'.[8] The deistic and sceptical moderate mainstream disliked this thesis too but, in addition, backing the Jesuit position against Bayle and Malebranche, deemed it factually incorrect.

---

[4] Hume, *Essays*, 78.   [5] Ibid. 122, 204.   [6] Helvétius, *De l'homme*, ii. 810.
[7] Hume, *Essays*, 313; Berry, *Social Theory*, 121.
[8] Lough, *Essays*, 189; Israel, *Enlightenment Contested*, 640–52.

While sometimes willing to stress, as Voltaire frequently does, the peculiar wisdom of the Chinese sages, this strand of Enlightenment emphasized the deism of the mandarins, Hume accounting 'the *literati*, or the disciples of Confucius in China' the sole 'regular body of deists in the universe'.[9] The only point, then, where Voltaire and Hume really converge with radical thought regarding China and Japan is their agreeing about the lack of theocracy and the mandarins' much lauded disdain for priestly imposture, mysteries, and theology.[10] The reason Voltaire trumpeted the extraordinary *sagesse* of the Chinese, protested the *anti-philosophes*, was to promote deism. To advance deism and make the deists look triumphant, complained Nonnotte, 'Voltaire nous vante beaucoup les Lettrés Chinois', making the Chinese scholars deists.[11]

This great controversy about China's position in the history of global thought continued unabated through the second half of the eighteenth century. But the pattern of positions characteristic of the pre-1750 debate broke down and was fundamentally reconfigured. In particular, the pre-1750 radical tradition's Sinophilia was replaced by a harshly damning critique, a shift driven partly by Montesquieu's great impact but more by the growing stream of reports from the Far East spreading doubt about the reliability of earlier reports and hence also the constructions vying Enlightenment factions had placed on them. Another factor undermining the utopianism of earlier evaluations of China was the increasing emphasis of radical thought on the idea that the true criterion for evaluating moral systems is the effectiveness and benevolence (or reverse) of their social and political effects. Enthusiasm for China as a source of inspiration and a model haltingly receded after 1750, though many traces of the older articulation persisted.

The thesis that China was a shining paragon among the nations Diderot consistently doubted as we see from his article 'Chinois', in the *Encyclopédie*, and his becoming still more sceptical later. D'Holbach, on the other hand, originally an enthusiastic Sinophile like Helvétius, changed his views about Chinese society and politics, eventually becoming more disparaging even than Diderot. Yet, the intellectual, ideological, and polemical baggage attaching to the earlier positive image could be neither easily nor straightforwardly discarded. Indeed, in the years around 1760, whilst d'Holbach remained an enthusiast, disagreement about China and Japan posed a considerable problem for the two leading radical voices labouring to finalize the *Encyclopédie*. To resolve it, a remarkable symposium convened at Grandval, d'Holbach's country-house, twenty kilometres from Paris, in late September and October 1760 in which China headed the topics for debate. To help the discussion—Diderot arrived bringing quantities of books that amazed Madame d'Holbach—additional guests were invited including a Scots Catholic missionary,

---

[9] Hume, *Essays*, 78; Voltaire, *Philosophie de l'histoire*, 115–16; François, *Observations*, i. 93 and ii. 16.
[10] Voltaire, *Philosophie de l'histoire*, 53, 112, 115; Voltaire, *Fragmens*, 143–8; Pomeau, *Religion de Voltaire*, 159, 388.
[11] Nonnotte, *Dictionnaire philosophique*, 85–6; Bergier, *Apologie*, ii. 353.

Father Hoop (Hope?), who had spent many years in China, an expert on its religion, society, morality, manners, and philosophy whose expertise, it was hoped, would help resolve the difficulty. Like d'Holbach at this time, Hoop was an ardent Sinophile, positive about almost every aspect of China. If the picture of China projected at Grandval was reliable, there was indeed much to praise, Diderot reported to his mistress, Sophie Volland, and Chinese *sagesse* must be admirable: 'mais j'ai peu de foi aux nations sages.' The notion that there actually existed superior models in itself struck him as deeply problematic. It seemed far more likely that men are everywhere the same: that always 'il falloit s'attendre aux mêmes vices et aux mêmes vertus'.[12]

Kept indoors by incessant rain, the participants aired their contrasting views for weeks with the Scottish missionary still in attendance in early November. Depressed by the weather, Diderot talked, read, and overly consumed the baron's fine food and wine while continually pondering China. That all religions except for Christianity were tolerated there while among the ruling class no faith was respected or privileged greatly appealed to him too. Apart from Christianity, all religions are tolerated, 'entendez-vous', he exclaimed writing to Sophie, 'tolérées!'[13] But that the mandarins were as upright as he was assured, or the emperor's power as limited, or that China possessed 'les loix les plus sages de l'univers', he could hardly believe.[14]

With so much at stake, it was no simple thing to abandon tenaciously held earlier positions without leaving adversaries victorious in the field. The *Encyclopédie*'s editors and their close allies needed to discover and proclaim the truth if they could—and they needed to agree. This they failed to do fully at this stage, or later, so that one finds clear evidence of two distinctly different China interpretations in the later as well as earlier portions of the *Encyclopédie*. If Diderot lauded Chinese philosophy and toleration, he remained deeply sceptical about Chinese society, institutions, and politics. 'Le despotisme, mon amie', he assured Sophie, 'est la plus terrible des séductions; on n'y résiste pas.'[15] D'Holbach, for the moment, remained positive about both dimensions. In his article 'Ju-Kiau', the baron reaffirms the atheism of the Neo-Confucianism of 'Chu-tse and Ching tse', terming their philosophy a universal monism proclaiming the heavens, earth, elements, and all nature's productions one self-creating entity, adding that this formative nature is 'une cause aveugle et inanimée, qui ignore la cause de ses propres opérations'. Jesuit missionaries, he remarks, citing Father Du Halde, confirm that Chinese Neo-Confucianism acknowledges no supernatural cause and no other principle but a 'vertu insensible, unie et identifiée à la matière'.[16] But one finds also articles, such as 'Hing-Pu', in volume viii, where d'Holbach persists in extolling Chinese institutions and practice. No Chinese, he declares, could be put to death legally without the approval of the

---

[12] Diderot to Sophie Volland, Grandval, 25 Sept. 1760, in Diderot, *Corr.* iii. 87–8; Trousson, *Denis Diderot*, 327, 329.

[13] Diderot to Sophie Volland, Grandval, 27 Sept., in *Corr.* iii. 95.

[14] Diderot to Sophie Volland, Grandval, 27 Sept., 6 and 10 Oct., ibid. iii. 95–6, 144–5, 232–3.

[15] Diderot to Sophie Volland, Grandval, 1 Nov. 1760, ibid. iii. 212.

[16] D'Holbach, art. 'Ju-Kiau', in Diderot and d'Alembert, *Encyclopédie*, ix. 53; Lough, *Essays*, 185–6.

Hing-Pu, a supreme tribunal of mandarins, and the signature of the emperor himself, proving 'le cas que l'on fait à la Chine de la vie d'un homme'.[17] In the article 'Lettrés', in volume ix, he styles the mandarins a highly educated class of upright and tolerant scholars inspired by a form of atheistic materialism rejecting all supernatural entities and equating God with nature.

This view of China remained linked, as earlier in Bayle, to a related positive view of Japan. But, here again, already in the *Encyclopédie* we also encounter a markedly negative strand in the radical analysis. What the *Encyclopédie*'s editors especially disliked was the hierarchical character of Japanese society, the samurai military ethic, and primacy of the nobility.[18] Always more puritanical about such matters than Diderot, d'Holbach also deplored the Japanese cult of eroticism and tradition of the Geisha. At the same time, though, Japanese thought, religion, and morality were assumed to have been strongly penetrated, among some strata at least, by Chinese Confucianism, and here, both in Diderot's article 'Japonais' and d'Holbach's relevant entries, Japan shares the attractions of China. Japanese philosophers and meditators are warmly praised by Diderot in the article 'Siuto', for example, where the *sintoistes* are described as 'philosophes' with a profound veneration for Confucius, and by d'Holbach, in the article 'Xensux' lauding a sect of monks who deny the soul's immortality and Heaven and Hell, maintaining that all men's hopes should 'se borner aux avantages de la vie présente.'[19]

The older positive notions of China and Japan received new life, moreover, from Quesnay, Le Mercier, and other *économistes* writing in the 1760s who were deeply impressed by the stability and productivity of Chinese agriculture and, then, by Raynal and his team in the 1770 and 1774 editions of the *Histoire philosophique*. These developments further compounded the intellectual and ideological problem. Who is so indifferent to the happiness of a large portion of mankind, ask the *Histoire*'s authors, as not to hope the true condition of China should really conform to the picture presented in the 1770 edition?[20] But it is above all the truth that counts for *philosophes*, held the radical outlook, and the unresolved disagreement between Diderot and d'Holbach and growing body of empirical evidence compromising the positive image had to be confronted.

It proved difficult for Catholic publicists, meanwhile, to destroy the radical Sinophile myth of Chinese exceptionalism while simultaneously rejecting Voltaire's equally Sinophile insistence on Chinese deism, because attacking Voltaire's view of China meant agreeing with the radicals that Confucianism amounts to fatalism, materialism, and determinism. Some defenders of Chinese classical thought in the West, commented Bergier, might be right in classifying Confucianism as closer to

---

[17] Lough, *Essays*, 185; d'Holbach, art. 'Hing-Pu', in Diderot and d'Alembert, *Encyclopédie*, viii. 210.

[18] Lough, *Essays*, 177, 183.

[19] Ibid. 184; d'Holbach, art. 'Xenxus', in Diderot and d'Alembert, *Encyclopédie*, xvii. 654; Proust, *Diderot*, 135.

[20] *Histoire philosophique* (1780), i. 224.

natural theology and deism than Spinozism or atheism. But even if strict Confucianists are 'deists', as Voltaire claims, Chinese philosophy itself cannot be so easily absolved of Spinozism. The history of Chinese thought clearly illustrates the rule that deism inevitably degenerates, lacking the cohesion of true religion, so that later Confucianism or at least a branch of Confucian thought, so-called 'New Confucianism', unquestionably had evolved into materialism and 'atheism'. Due to this continuing linkage, radical thinkers could no more easily jettison Confucianism than deny that some articles in the *Encyclopédie*, as Bergier put it, vaunt 'les mœurs et le gouvernement des Chinois comme un prodige'.[21] To an extent, they were stuck with the legacy of the past.

One way to attack Voltaire and the radicals simultaneously in this context was to tarnish the antiquity of Chinese classical culture. Another was to overturn the myth of the integrity of the mandarin ruling class. In his *Anti-Dictionnaire philosophique*, Chaudon scorns veneration for the great antiquity of Chinese civilization, invoking the unreliability of Chinese chronicles and historiography. The *philosophes* were also misrepresenting, he claimed, the real character of the Chinese ruling class. In reality, the mandarins were idolatrous and superstitious. It is hence just as hard to discover 'la vérité et la sagesse chez les philosophes de la Chine que chez les Sophistes de France'. Vice and error prevail everywhere and to imagine otherwise is not to know human nature. Those with actual experience of China were providing evidence totally disproving the claims of Voltaire and other 'sophistes' who had never been there. 'Quelle étrange manie!' They disparage everything we see around us 'et on loue ce qui est à mille lieues'.[22]

As the reports from European visitors to China turned increasingly negative, radical thinkers found themselves in a thorny dilemma. If they continued praising Chinese society they risked being increasingly represented as deluded idealists defying reality. If they rejected the Chinese model, they would seem to be endorsing Christian insistence on the corrupt and vicious character of Chinese society and Spinozistic ideas. They could not in any case wholly disown Confucianism, now indelibly linked to Spinozism and its moral legacy. This predicament, unsurprisingly, caused much hesitation and, once changes in interpretation became unavoidable, disagreement as to how to justify abandoning previously strongly held standpoints. The 1780 edition of the *Histoire*, the most radical version, frankly confesses that this was all extremely embarrassing, an acute difficulty for the moment impossible to resolve. At the risk of appearing totally incoherent and paradoxical, the *Histoire* in its final format resorted to the extraordinary device—yet one typical of Diderot with his love of dialogue—of openly admitting that 'among thoughtful men' in the West there were two completely irreconcilable and rival opinions on the subject of China and Japan. The problem posed by this rift between China's *admirateurs* and *détracteurs*,

[21] Bergier, *Apologie*, ii. 16; Lough, *Essays*, 188–92.
[22] Chaudon, *Dictionnaire anti-philosophique*, i. 120–1.

declared the 1780 edition, had to be candidly faced and could only be dealt with empirically through extensive further research and more direct experience of the Chinese reality. The difficulty would only finally be resolved by careful sifting of facts by experienced researchers with a good knowledge of Chinese spending periods both at the imperial court in Peking and traversing the Chinese provinces, conversing freely with Chinese at all social levels.[23] In this way, the Enlightenment proved a sharper stimulus to thorough, systematic, and intensive study of other parts of the world than any other cultural flowering known in human history.

2. CHINESE SOCIETY: TWO INCOMPATIBLE RADICAL ACCOUNTS

The only honest course—a characteristically Diderotian procedure—was to explore the disagreement, present the dialogue between divergent viewpoints, lay out the evidence as we have it before the discerning reader, asking him or her to weigh and decide.[24] According not only to the 1770 and 1774 editions of the *Histoire*, therefore, but in part also to that of 1780, China's traditions, institutions, and laws are declared excellent and the reason that China was 'le pays de la terre où les hommes sont les plus humains'.[25] Chinese virtue is praised to the skies. All this was utopian and also outmoded. But the *Histoire*'s partial retention of the old positive depiction of China nevertheless has real significance for understanding the Enlightenment through clearly expressing what, according to the radical *philosophes*, an ideal society would look like.

Superstition 'est sans pouvoir à la Chine' (a claim vigorously contested by Christian authors), so that while Buddhist and other priests exert vast sway over the common folk, such priests altogether lacked authority among the administrative class.[26] The same applied to Japan. The benefits accruing from lacking institution-alized ecclesiastical authority were immense and are what had made China and Japan altogether more tolerant, tranquil, and rational than other lands. Furthermore, claimed the 1770 and 1774 editions, since ancient times China had lacked a heredi-tary nobility capable of forming factions in the state and fragmenting sovereignty, like that of Europe, by exploiting their families' wealth and connections and the dependence of those under their control. Early on in China's development, aristoc-racy had disappeared. Hence, there was neither 'servitude réelle ni servitude person-nelle' and none of the 'tyrannical abuses' sanctioned in European feudal laws, charters, and 'privileges'.[27] In the 1780 edition of the *Histoire*, a version that

---

[23] Bergier, *Apologie*, 225.   [24] Ibid. 224–5, 246; Muthu, *Enlightenment*, 82.
[25] *Histoire philosophique* (1770), i. 97; *Histoire philosophique* (1774), i. 137.
[26] Ibid. i. 135; *Histoire philosophique* (1770), i. 95; [Bernard], *Analyse*, 87, 89.
[27] *Histoire philosophique* (1770), i. 90.

sharpened the radical assault on hereditary nobility also in many other contexts, this key contention of the older positive interpretation was fully retained. Entirely unknown in China, urged Diderot and his colleagues, were the 'distinctions chimér-iques' attaching to birth and lineage that elsewhere obliterate the original equality nature establishes among men, equality that should never cede to anything except merit and virtue.[28] Happily for all mankind, China is a civilization uniquely eman-cipated from the insidious and irrational institution of aristocracy to which Europe owes so many incompetent statesmen, ignorant magistrates, and inept generals. In the Chinese empire, the first minister's son enjoyed no greater advantages at birth, holds the 1780 edition, than those received from nature. 'Une égalité si parfaite' allegedly afforded 'une éducation uniforme' inculcating into the Chinese corre-sponding, and hence thoroughly edifying, principles. Any Chinese discarding 'cette fraternité générale' would at once be consigned to being an isolated, wretched creature.

Instead of the 'distinctions frivoles' noble birth confers on men elsewhere, in China, and also Confucianist Korea, added Démeunier, personal merit establishes real distinctions ['le mérite personnel en établit de réelles à la Chine'].[29] Very different from the European nobility, the mandarins 'sont des philosophes' of the Confucian school of thought, hold the 1770 and 1774 editions, men who, far from relying on their families, lands, and connections, have no support other than the emperor's authority.[30] Raised on doctrines inspiring only 'humanity', love of order, respect for the laws, and philanthropy, the mandarins eclipsed Europe's ruling elites in every way. No one obtains high office in China, asserts d'Holbach, in his *Système social* of 1773, unless free of popular religious notions and aware that 'morality is the only religion of every reasonable man'.[31] The idea there was no distinction between nobility and commoners in China, merit not nobility determining promotion to the highest positions, lingered even in the 1780 version's negative alternative tableau. Magistrates, urges the *Histoire*, were often chosen from among families of mere labourers who, in China, usually possess enough to provide for their children's education.[32]

Morality drawn from Confucian philosophy was taught to children using didactic books explaining that 'happiness' stems from 'tranquillity'. This contrasted strikingly with the values inculcated into Japanese children. In Japan, unfortunately, boys were taught from heroic poems, exuding a highly charged, emotional military ethic that was anything but tranquil or beneficial to society.[33] But in China, the 'menu peuple', claimed the 1770 and 1774 editions, through Confucianism, civil service examin-ations, and the mandarins' integrity and the good order they cultivate, had in some degree absorbed 'enlightened' notions about government and its functions and the

---

[28] *Histoire philosophique* (1780), i. 211–12. [29] Ibid. i. 212; Démeunier, *L'Esprit*, i. 289.
[30] *Histoire philosophique* (1770), i. 94–5; *Histoire philosophique* (1774), i. 134.
[31] D'Holbach, *Système social*, 312.
[32] *Histoire philosophique* (1770), i. 90. [33] *Histoire philosophique* (1780), i. 263.

real character of their own interests and had thus acquired more political and moral good sense than other peoples. Diffusion downwards of enlightened concepts fomented both social justice and political stability. The people being 'plus éclairé', it was also more stable and tranquil than elsewhere.[34] Nowhere was agriculture more flourishing. Ordinary folk were sober and reasonable, living in accordance with nature to a greater degree than other peoples. Everything was used and re-used with nothing wasted.[35]

Consequently, China, held the 1770 and 1774 editions, remained the great exception, part of the world uniquely free of oppression, superstition, tyranny, and misery, the only land where these are not the normal lot of man and one showing that others do not have to remain oppressed. Among the Chinese, one encountered a reliance on 'reason and virtue' not found elsewhere.[36] Accustomed to justice and reasonable dealing, seeing crime punished with moderate and civilized penalties, the Chinese evince 'humanity' even where rigorous justice might be expected. Imprisonment for crime meant confinement in clean and comfortable cells and being properly treated until one's sentence was completed.[37] Understanding perfectly that sovereignty resides in the people, not the emperor, and loyal to the principles of justice rather than laws, emperor, or state, the people, averred the 1770 and 1774 editions, are never blindly submissive to anyone.

What it was that imposed effective curbs on despotism in China was readily discerned. The emperor knows he reigns over a people attached less to figureheads or the law than its own happiness. Seeing he must keep taxation moderate and that if he yields to the temptation to tyrannize, as rulers generally do elsewhere, violent resistance ensues and that he will be cast from his throne, he studiously avoids doing so.[38] Indeed, so convinced is he the people know their 'rights' and how to defend them that whenever they decry a district official, the latter is immediately recalled and investigated, for no other reason than having provoked discontent. If guilty, he is punished; but, if found innocent, he is not reinstated: 'c'est un crime en lui d'avoir pu déplaire au peuple.'[39] Frequent disturbances in times of shortage presuppose a people 'assez éclairé' to grasp that respect for the law and property rights is not something absolute but rather an obligation of the second order, subject to the 'absolute rights' nature establishes to satisfy the needs of all who compose society. When basic necessities are lacking, the Chinese no longer recognize the authority of those who fail to feed them, alleges the *Histoire*—to the indignation of many critics who could see nothing 'enlightened' here, and no 'religion' but only 'superstition'. They rebel. Neither religion, nor morality, held the *Histoire*, lay down other maxims in China. 'C'est le pouvoir de conserver qui fait le droit des rois.'[40]

---

[34] *Histoire philosophique* (1780), i. 95; Lough, *Essays*, 189.
[35] *Histoire philosophique* (1770), i. 88.
[36] Ibid. i. 98–9; *Histoire philosophique* (1780), i. 219.
[37] *Histoire philosophique* (1770), i. 97.
[38] Ibid. i. 93; *Histoire philosophique* (1774), i. 132; *Histoire philosophique* (1780), i. 205–6.
[39] *Histoire philosophique* (1770), i. 93.   [40] Ibid. i. 92–3; [Petit], *Observations*, 32–3.

Among the Chinese, 'ce peuple de sages', mature, and *raisonnable*, what binds men together and civilizes them is 'religion', but 'religion' in the Spinozistic sense meaning 'la pratique des vertus sociales', a definition horrifying to opponents but usual among the radical 'fraternity'.[41] In his political fragments, of 1792, Herder, wondering what kind of 'religion' the French Revolution would produce, automatically supposed it would be a 'European Chinamen's state, a type of Confucius-religion'.[42] Detaching morality from what was called 'religion' in the West, a separation anchored in Spinoza and Bayle, remained deeply ingrained in radical thought and this too continued in the later phases of the Radical Enlightenment. Despite his mounting critique of China by the 1770s, d'Holbach gladly acknowledges that China remained the only country known to man where politics, by virtue of the constitution itself, is intimately 'lié avec la morale' and soundly grounded morality understood as some-thing wholly distinct from theological rulings.[43] D'Holbach still thought the Chinese governing class and court scrupulously kept moral thought separate from the 'superstition' of conventional religion, while conventional religion lacked all credit among the elite: 'la science des mœurs en a rempli la place.'[44]

The generally enthusiastic view of China pervading the 1774 and 1770 versions of the *Histoire* explains the continuance of the older radical view of China in Filangieri and the late eighteenth-century Italian Radical Enlightenment. For Filangieri, we have seen, the *Histoire* was a prime source but specifically in its 1774 edition. In his *Scienza* the political and legal context shaping Chinese society remains vastly bene-ficial, bringing all men under the rule of law.[45] The sciences, arts, and crafts had long prospered on the back of a flourishing agriculture, pointing to another of China's particular merits. Since the pursuit of knowledge, science, and philosophy, held Filangieri like Diderot and d'Holbach, but very differently from Rousseau, drives moral and political progress, and humanity's general amelioration, and since the advance of knowledge depends on lessening superstition and credulity, the main props of oppression and human misery in their eyes, only a philosophy that respects learning, like Confucianism, can be a viable foundation for moral and political advancement and human freedom.

But were knowledge and the sciences being cultivated in China? Here there was room for doubt. Catholic apologists were especially dismissive. Even those *literati* disdaining the excesses of popular religion, contends Bergier, remained addicted to divination, superstitious belief in spirits, and ancestor-worship.[46] The Chinese, argued the *anti-philosophes*, had never cultivated physics, or accomplished anything of significance in medicine or astronomy, or developed 'true philosophy'. They were

[41] [Petit], *Observations*, 32–3; *Histoire philosophique* (1770), i. 88.
[42] Herder, *Philosophical Writings*, 367.
[43] D'Holbach, *Système social*, 312–15.
[44] Ibid. 312.
[45] Filangieri, *Scienza della legislazione*, i. 133, ii. 26 n. 100, 126, and iii. 211.
[46] Bergier, *Examen du matérialisme*, ii, 266.

devoid of modern geography, map-making, and cosmology before the Jesuit missionaries' arrival, knowing nothing, as Nonnotte puts it, 'about 'la statique, l'hydrostatique, l'optique, la nature de la lumière'. Never had they imagined the earth could be round; rather, they believed 'bêtement qu'elle étoit plate comme une table'.[47] If the Chinese boast no Descartes, Newton, Copernicus, or Kepler, neither in the fine arts do they possess a Raphael or Michelangelo. China's architecture they judged devoid of refinement and taste, let alone genius.

Disillusionment with what was increasingly recognized as Chinese ignorance, weakness in science, and obstinacy in adhering to credulous beliefs all helped turn the Radical Enlightenment against the Chinese model. D'Holbach, who changed his mind about China (as he did about Britain) in the mid 1760s, Diderot, Herder, and others now stressed the drawbacks of China's cultural isolation, though Diderot adds that it was perfectly understandable the Chinese preferred to avoid contact with Europeans given the danger the latter represented.[48] Chinese culture, with its isolation, immensely intricate and difficult script, veneration for tradition, adherence to ancient rites, was resistant to change and, unfortunately, singularly impervious to all innovation in the arts and progress in the sciences.[49] Worse than ignorance, though, was the mounting evidence of disturbing defects in Chinese morality, practices readily highlighted by *anti-philosophes* eager to demonstrate the viciousness of the anti-Christian critique. Moved by sheer prejudice toward Christianity, radical writers had grotesquely misrepresented China, claiming 'sans fondement' that the Chinese were wiser, better, and more just and benevolent than was really the case.[50] In reality, China was a sink of moral turpitude and disorder vitiating every aspect of administration, society, and family life.[51] Bergier, following Montesquieu (and Hume) in representing the Chinese as the most unreliable and deceitful of peoples, rebuts d'Holbach's *Christianisme dévoilé* (1769) in part by dismissing the entire radical eulogy of China. Whether or not Montesquieu really intended his depiction of Asia as an antidote to Voltaire's deistic eulogy of China and Persia, his designating China a moral, legal, and political despotism in every respect proved eminently useful to the *anti-philosophes* in combating both Voltaire's and the radicals' myths of China. Such was the mandarins' love of 'good order' and the 'law of the peoples', remarks Bergier sarcastically, that they prey on foreigners and Chinese alike, everywhere fomenting corruption and crime. Just as at Sparta men were permitted to steal, so in China, avowed Bergier citing the *Esprit des loix*, one is encouraged to deceive.[52]

The highly idealized view of Chinese political tradition and the Chinese administrative class projected in Voltaire and the earlier editions of the *Histoire* struck

---

[47] Nonnotte, *Dictionnaire philosophique*, 86–7; [Feller], *Journal historique* (1782), 236.
[48] Diderot, *Political Writings*, 101, 175; Herder, *Philosophical Writings*, 248, 255.
[49] *Histoire philosophique* (1770), i. 99; d'Holbach, *Morale universelle*, i. 222.
[50] Bergier, *Examen du matérialisme*, ii. 349–50, 354.
[51] Ibid. ii. 385; [Petit], *Observations*, 36.
[52] Montesquieu, *L'Esprit des loix*, xix, ch. 10; Bergier, *Examen du matérialisme*, ii. 350; Diderot, *Political Writings*, 100 n.; Krause, 'Despotism', 251.

Christian apologists as so perverse as to smack of deliberate, malicious imposture fired by 'philosophical' bias.[53] China's supposedly admirable stability they pronounced as much of a myth as the integrity of the mandarins. Actually, the country was both despotic and unstable, having been shaken to the core by at least twenty-two 'révolutions générales' leaving China's harassed emperors constantly on the verge of dethronement and being exterminated.[54] *Philosophes* offering false comparisons impudently vaunting infidels to the detriment of 'Christian nations' should be punished by being sent to live under the rule of those they so ridiculously praised.[55] The Chinese ruling elite might be suffused with deism; and many of their mandarins and philosophers were doubtless 'athées et matérialistes, comme chez nous'; but this proved only that Chinese philosophy was closely tied to immorality, total ignorance of science and nature, and a dismally failed society.[56]

The old radical eulogy of China was no longer viable. A drastically revised account was needed not just to fit better with recent reports but also to conform to the *Histoire*'s unrelentingly gloomy picture of the rest of the globe. The harsh reality was that in China and Japan, as throughout the globe, government was conducted by a religiously sanctioned monarch and mandarins chosen by the court to rule and who had rendered China a society steeped in tyranny, deception, and injustice. Justice in China in reality was disfigured by corruption, venality, and—as also in Korea and Japan—cruel, archaic punishments to a degree scarcely paralleled amongst even the world's most 'depraved' peoples.[57] China was a land where foreigners were regularly fleeced and opium addiction rife. All those who know the Chinese, claimed the alternative 1780 version, agree one cannot be too careful if one wishes to avoid being duped.[58] Far from being philosophical, the mandarins were servile, indolent, and ignorant. All this fitted the drive to persuade readers 'combien la servitude est naturelle', as Démeunier put it,[59] and that China and Korea were not exceptions in a world characterized by ignorance and oppression. Transforming Europeans' image of China's society, government, and administration went hand in hand with Diderot's, d'Holbach's, and Mably's new thesis that the ordinary Chinese was no more likely to be guided by reason than others. In fact the Chinese were even more 'slavish', credulous, morally depraved, and infused with ridiculous vanity and the famed examination system nothing but an empty ritual exercise.[60]

The grim reality was made still grimmer by the very immensity of China's population, demographic pressure having long been a curse forcing down incomes

[53] Voltaire, *Philosophie de l'histoire*, 109, 119; [Bernard], *Analyse*, 89–90; Bergier, *Apologie*, ii. 16, 352; Rahe, *Montesquieu*, 126–32.

[54] Bergier, *Apologie*, ii. 17–19, 144, 146.

[55] Ibid. ii. 19; Démeunier, *L'Esprit*, i. 367 and ii. 164.

[56] Bergier, *Apologie*, ii. 251–2, 391; Krause, 'Despotism', 251.

[57] *Histoire philosophique* (1780), i. 246; Mably, *Doutes*, 97–163; Démeunier, *L'Esprit*, iii. 194–6.

[58] *Histoire philosophique* (1780), i. 232, 240; and Feller citing Raynal, *Journal historique* (1782), 238–9.

[59] *Histoire philosophique* (1780), ii, 114.

[60] *Histoire philosophique* (1780), i. 232–44; Mably, *Doutes*, 133–6.

and instilling a mean, unthinking mechanical urge for survival, depriving men of time for repose and contemplation. Such grinding pressure excised from the soul all true feeling for humanity.[61] Basest of all was the hideous practice of infanticide, something that, after 1750, horrified all European commentators. 'China, the only country where this practice of exposing children prevails at present', remarked Hume, in 1754, 'is the most populous country we know of; and every man is married before he is twenty. Such early marriages could scarcely be general, had not men the prospect of so easy a method of getting rid of their children.'[62] 'Marriage is encouraged in China', agreed Adam Smith, 'not by the profitableness of children, but by the liberty of destroying them. In all great towns several are every night exposed in the street, or drowned like puppies in the water. The performance of this horrid office is even said to be the avowed business by which some people earn their subsistence.'[63] Reports that Chinese custom and law permit fathers to expose or stifle unwanted infants, grants the *Histoire*, like Millar, Démeunier, and d'Holbach, were all too justified: they kill their infants without inhibition; in the streets of Peking, children lie crushed 'sous les voitures ou dévorés par les bêtes.'[64]

The turn to a profoundly negative image engineered by Diderot, d'Holbach, and their disciples in the 1780 version of the *Histoire* applied to politics, social structure, morality, and science and also to the Confucian intellectual legacy. Chinese education, according to the earlier editions, was not only uniform across that vast land but based on Confucius' philosophy which ensured that it was excellent. Reason, held Confucius, is an emanation of the Divinity and the supreme law is the concordance of reason with nature: 'toute religion qui contredit ces deux guides de la vie humaine', Confucians instructed the people, 'ne vient point du ciel.'[65] Earlier, d'Holbach, whilst working on the *Encyclopédie*, warmly praised the Chinese for cultivating Confucius' memory and keeping alive, even under the Tartar and Manchu ascendancy, their reverence for ancient philosophy and science. How exemplary that to gain a place in the administration, one was obliged, also under the Manchus, to study Confucius intensively! However, Diderot and d'Holbach had subsequently concluded that the modern Chinese, despite their ostensible respect for philosophy, were 'sans mœurs', *misérables* basely adept through dwelling under a government 'despotique et barbare' at rendering useless 'les leçons de morale la plus sensée.'[66]

Far from being enlightened, as Isaac Vossius, Temple, Fréret, d'Argens, and other radical predecessors claimed, credulity and unshakable vanity were now held to

---

[61] *Histoire philosophique* (1780), i. 245; Mirabeau, *Lettres*, i. 164–6.

[62] Hume, *Essays*, 399; [Bernard], *Analyse*, 91–3; Millar, *Observations*, 111; [Feller], *Journal historique* (1782), 240–1.

[63] Smith, *Wealth of Nations*, i. 76; Ferguson, *Essay on the History*, 213; Naquin and Rawski, *Chinese Society*, 108, 110.

[64] *Histoire philosophique* (1780), i. 245; d'Holbach, *Morale universelle*, ii. 199 and iii. 50; Millar, *Observations*, 111–12; Démeunier, *L'Esprit*, i. 275.

[65] *Histoire philosophique* (1780), i. 216; Lough, *Essays*, 187, 189.

[66] *Histoire philosophique* (1780), ii. 199 n.; d'Holbach, *Morale universelle*, ii. 199.

render the Chinese particularly resistant to becoming enlightened. 'Comment enseigner la sagesse à celui qui s'estime le seul sage?'[67] If one compares Confucius with Sidney or Montesquieu, avers the 1780 edition, what does one find? Little that need impress.[68] What the continuing hold of Confucianism really proved is that the Chinese languished hopelessly trapped in antiquated modes of thought reinforced by their script. The homage paid to Confucius to whom 'l'on rend un culte, et que l'on a surnommé le *roi des Lettres*', showed the Chinese still felt a need to appear to respect virtue and talent even though they were now devoid of both.[69] Most of what the missionaries had rendered accessible of the writings of Confucius and his disciple Mencius in the West consisted of 'maximes communes et triviales' in no way rivalling Greek philosophy. Worse, Confucius' and Mencius' writings, despite being admired by 'quelques modernes' like Voltaire, were thoroughly 'favorables au despotisme, c'est-à-dire, au plus injuste des gouvernements', as well as overblown paternal authority and the tyranny of husbands, things the Chinese unfortunately confused with 'une autorité raisonnable'.

If marriage was a trap for women everywhere, it was doubly so in China. Chinese tradition, d'Holbach had discovered, also favours polygamy, paternal arrangement of marriage, and generally male tyranny over women: 'enfin ils n'ont pour objet que de faire des esclaves.'[70] This theme of ruthless subordination of women was further echoed by Démeunier whose view of China in his *L'Esprit des usages et des coutumes*, of 1776, projects a comparably negative perspective, adding that the binding and crushing of women's feet capped this female servility.[71] Mainstream Enlightenment had less distance to retreat. Only Voltaire had praised nearly everything, but even he had all along acknowledged that the Chinese were two centuries behind the West in science. Moreover, his views on social hierarchy and the scope of Enlightenment being what they were, it was no great problem for him to acknowledge that the Chinese common people had been abandoned by the mandarins to credulity and superstition.[72] Voltaire showed no interest in the absence of nobility and feudal privilege, ignored the earlier radicals' admiration for Chinese fondness for resistance when weighed down by high taxes or food shortage, and was a professed admirer of the Manchu emperors ruling China since 1648. This last contrasted sharply with the view of the *Histoire* in its 1780 version which was distinctly scornful of the Manchus.[73]

In the 1770s, Voltaire remained the most consistent eulogist of China and the Chinese, rendering 'des déistes de tous les lettrés chinois' and stressing the role of

---

[67] D'Holbach, *Morale universelle*, i. 243; Naquin and Rawski, *Chinese Society*, 38–9, 108.

[68] *Histoire philosophique* (1780), i. 245.

[69] D'Holbach, *Morale universelle*, ii. 198–9.

[70] Ibid. ii. 199 n. and iii. 50; Naquin and Rawski, *Chinese Society*, 92.

[71] Démeunier, *L'Esprit*, i. 120–1, 228, 245.

[72] Voltaire, *Philosophie de l'histoire*, 115, 118.

[73] Bénot, *Diderot*, 174.

reason, reason-based morality, and respect for justice in their civilization.[74] But in this respect he had become wholly isolated. For mainstream Enlightenment, the question of the condition of China's common people was always marginal. Turgot conceded that reason, science, and philosophy had made impressive progress in ancient and medieval China but argued, much like Hume, that in recent centuries the desultory, static character of Chinese society and the mandarins' reverence for tradition had sapped all creativity and dynamism.[75] 'The accounts of all travelers, inconsistent in many other respects, agree', held Smith, 'in the low wages of labour, and in the difficulty which a labourer finds in bringing up a family in China. If by digging the ground a whole day he can get what will purchase a small quantity of rice in the evening he is contented.' 'The poverty of the lower ranks of people in China', he concludes, 'far surpasses that of the most beggarly nations in Europe.'[76]

The *détracteurs*, radical or moderate, claiming China was no model for humanity now concurred in depicting the Chinese as poor, credulous, and devoid of positive moral qualities—a people slavish, timid, and vile.[77] Feller, pronouncing the Chinese 'un peuple profondément corrompu', in 1782, cheerfully cites Raynal as his authority.[78] This was indeed a remarkable reversal of the pre-1750 position. The *Histoire's* summons to the enlightened to come more effectively to grips with the reality of the Far East represented a formidable challenge, especially to readers and the thoughtful. The call to acquire more knowledge of the Eastern peoples, and enter into a real dialogue with the savants of the East, presented all kinds of obstacles and hindrances, political, cultural, and psychological. Nevertheless, there are signs that the men of the Enlightenment in Asia both understood and responded to the challenge and, to some extent, succeeded in initiating a more genuine dialogue with the philosophy, science, and religion of east Asia, a development evident in India and also, to a degree, Japan.

3. ENLIGHTENMENT IN ASIA: THE CASE OF JAPAN

Contacts between Japan and the West were exiguous and difficult. Due to the long-established policy of cultural seclusion imposed on Japan, even its high bureaucracy, by the shogunate, and the accompanying prohibition on Japanese travelling abroad, as well as tight restrictions on the movements and contacts of the Dutch trading community at Deshima, in the Bay of Nagasaki, Japan was shrouded in mystery, a society hard to learn about to an even greater degree than China. Nevertheless, a brief

---

[74] Voltaire, *Philosophie de l'histoire*, 115–18; Nonnotte, *Dictionnaire philosophique*, 85.
[75] Manuel, *Prophets*, 25; Manuel, *Utopian Thought*, 469.
[76] Smith, *Wealth of Nations*, i. 75; Winch, 'Scottish Political Economy', 453.
[77] *Histoire philosophique* (1780), i. 232.
[78] [Feller], *Journal historique* (1782), 238.

period of partial easing of the long-standing restrictions in the second quarter of the eighteenth century, led to an incipient cultural encounter between Japan and the West culminating in the 1770s and early 1780s that was to have far-reaching consequences for both sides.

Like China, Japan was a bitterly contested case, the ground for this controversy having, once again, been staked out by Bayle especially with his idea—subsequently popularized by the *Encyclopédie*—that an enlightened 'way of philosophy' was embedded in Japanese as in Chinese culture. This idea encouraged a growing curiosity about Japan among the *philosophes* matched, from the 1720s onwards, on the Japanese side, by some easing of the long-standing ban on importing and translating European books. The latter was connected with the growing importance in the eighteenth century of the Dutch trading factory at Nagasaki, the smallest of the Dutch establishments in the Far East, with a mere dozen or so resident personnel, but one swollen each year for some weeks by the arrival of the permitted two vessels. Situated on the tiny island of Deshima, in the Bay of Nagasaki, linked to the city by a bridge, this precarious outpost developed into a key conduit not only for trade but also books, scientific instruments, information, and ideas passing in and out of the country.

Slowly, Europeans began to learn about Japan and the Japanese to learn about the West. Two long articles about Japan in volume viii of the *Encyclopédie*, 'Japon', by Jaucourt, and 'Japonois, philosophie des', by Diderot, together with several closely linked entries on aspects of Japanese religion apparently by d'Holbach,[79] set the scene for the developments of the 1770s and 1780s by presenting an image of Japan as a stable, formidable, and praiseworthy society by no means so different in social and moral aspirations from the West as Europeans had been led to suppose. If Japan's location and shape excite the attention of geographers, remarked de Jaucourt, that country is even worthier of the philosopher's attention. 'This astonishing people', the only nation in Asia never conquered by outsiders, was clearly exceptionally homogeneous, the Japanese being a people somewhat resembling the English in their insular pride (and in being a nation among whom suicide was prevalent), insularity being the chief peculiarity of both these two 'extrémités de notre hémisphère'.[80] The Enlightenment ideology pervading these texts stressed the common humanity of the Japanese and Europeans, their basic similarity, and their relevance to each other. 'Human nature', avers Jaucourt, established numerous resemblances between the Japanese and 'us'. They continue to practice sorcery 'which we had for such a long time'; their superstitions, pilgrimages, sacrifices, and cults resembled those of the Europeans and, most importantly, their idea of morality is practically the same, except that they lay more stress on sparing animals, which by no means reflects badly on them.[81] What Jaucourt and Diderot found most remarkable for the philosopher was the impressive progress of Confucianism in Japanese culture and the way it

---

[79] Lough, *Essays*, 174–84.
[80] De Jaucourt, art. 'Japon', in Diderot and d'Alembert (eds.), *Encyclopédie*, viii. 453.
[81] De Jaucourt, art. 'Japon', in Diderot and d'Alembert (eds.), *Encyclopédie*, viii. 454.

combined with native cultural traditions in the sect the *Encyclopédie* calls *Sendosi-vistes* or those who direct themselves according to the *sicuto* or way of philosophy.[82]

While Europe might have overtaken Japan in recent times, the Japanese, like the peoples of the orient more generally, had formerly been 'bien supérieurs' to Euro-peans in all the arts of the mind and hands.[83] The Japanese were even more industrious than the Chinese, averred the *Histoire* in 1770, while in gardens, orch-ards, wealth, and architectural splendour their land ceded nothing to China.[84] Diderot, citing Bayle and Brucker, urged readers to share his high opinion of the Japanese and view them as an essential part of the wider fabric of humanity. Shintoism counts among the main religious sects of Japan, and Shintoism is idolatry; but idolatry is the first step 'de l'esprit humain' in the natural history of religion, and hence part of the process leading men to rational thought.[85] In origin, Shintoism Diderot pronounced a primitive form of deism acknowledging a supreme being and the soul's immortality embedded in a substratum of superstition and idolatry.[86]

Refined by Confucianism, the Japanese 'way of philosophy' Diderot held to be an excellent philosophical cult 'sans religion'. Its chief principle was that men should practise virtue as virtue alone renders men as happy as our nature permits. The wicked, held this sect, have enough to complain of in this world and have no need of being threatened with retribution in the next. The Japanese require of men that they be virtuous because man is reasonable and neither a stone nor a beast. Their extreme hostility towards Christianity is mentioned only in passing. The ethics of the 'Sendosivistes ou philosophes Japonais' reduce to four or five main points, the first being to know how to align one's conduct with virtue and the second, the principle of *gi*, requiring us to render justice to all men. Japanese sages, having rejected metem-psychosis, instead postulated a universal world soul animating everything, from which everything emanates and to which everything returns.[87] But where elite culture was rational, Japanese popular religion, by contrast, emerges in the *Encyclo-pédie* and the *Histoire* as something appalling: 'c'est le fanatisme le plus affreux.'[88] Characteristic of human history generally and deeply emblematic of Japan's in particular was the age-old, still unresolved battle between reason buttressed by science and scholarship and the dark power of ignorance, credulity, and priestly ambition. Here, it was especially 'les vrais principes de la morale de Confucius' that had played a positive role and those of Confucius' mythical Japanese disciple, 'Moosi'—very likely this was just a misprint for 'Kosi', the Japanese for Confucius—whose books, Diderot remarks, enjoyed great authority in Japan.[89]

---

[82] Diderot, art. 'Japonois, philosophie des', ibid. viii. 457.   [83] Ibid.
[84] *Histoire philosophique* (1770), i. 102.
[85] Diderot, 'Japonois, philosophie des', in Diderot and d'Alembert (eds.), *Encyclopédie*, viii. 456.
[86] *Histoire philosophique* (1780), i. 256.
[87] Diderot, 'Japonois, philosophie des', in Diderot and d'Alembert (eds.), *Encyclopédie*, viii. 457–8; Lough, *Essays*, 182.
[88] *Histoire philosophique* (1780), i. 261–2.
[89] I owe this observation to M. Powers; Diderot, 'Japanois, philosophie des', *Encyclopédie*, viii. 457–8.

For their part, the Japanese viewed the West through the prism of Confucianism, Neo-Confucianism, and, to a lesser extent, the Dutch. The eighteenth century was a period in which leading scholars, such as Motoori Norinaga (1730–1801), re-examining Japan's own history, ancient myths, Buddhist traditions, and the idea of Japan's 'ancient way', developed a conception of national learning, or *Koku-gaku* (National Studies), modifying the former China-centredness of Japanese culture, advancing a less monolithic conception of knowledge and tradition. The resulting tension between Confucianism and 'nativism' opened the door, to an extent at least, to study of the West.[90] It was a cultural shift beginning in the 1720s and 1730s, at a time when the VOC and its trade were still at their height, before the rise of British hegemony in India. The long-lived Shogun Yoshimune (shogun: 1716–45), supposing Holland was the chief Western centre of astronomy, medicine, and other sciences, in 1739 ordered the imperial librarian, Aoki Bunzo (1698–1769), later an expert Hollandologist and author of a treatise on the use of sweet potatoes in times of rice shortage, and the court physician, Genjo Noro, to learn Dutch. In 1745, he permitted the Japanese interpreters, at Nagasaki, to obtain and use Dutch books.[91]

The first two microscopes arrived in Japan, as presents for the shogun, on two different Dutch vessels, in 1746–7. The first five Dutch paintings known to have reached Japan, two flower still-lifes, two portraits, and a sleeping Venus, arrived in 1739.[92] From the 1750s, Dutch, French, and Latin dictionaries for the Deshima college of interpreters began arriving regularly along with a trickle of Western books. By the 1770s, an unbroken stream of telescopes, microscopes, magnifying glasses, thermometers, books, almanacs, clocks, surgical instruments, and exotic animals and plants were reaching Japan. The college of Dutch interpreters, meanwhile, had grown into a substantial body, according to Thunberg, comprising by the mid 1770s forty to fifty scholars.[93] The future Uppsala professor visiting the East Indies in connection with his scientific researches after nearly three years in South Africa spent several years serving as a VOC surgeon and became an expert on Japan. The college's main function was to assist the Dutch merchants and accountants on Deshima with their trade and contracts. But the head Japanese interpreters were also eminent scholars eager, notes Thunberg, to acquire Dutch books especially about medicine and natural history.[94] These they studied carefully, becoming adept at understanding and retaining their contents. With the resident Europeans, these men intensively discussed natural history, medicine, herbs, geology, and maps.

Thunberg spent a year and a half in Japan in the VOC's service, from August 1775 to December 1776.[95] Son of a Lutheran minister and amongst the foremost figures of Sweden's later Enlightenment, in the Japanese he believed he had found a people truly capable of sharing in the budding global Enlightenment as he understood it. He too, though, having spent years in Leiden and at Paris, was distinctly unimpressed

---

[90] Nosco, 'Place of China', 39–40, 42.   [91] Maclean, 'Introduction of Books', 10.
[92] Ibid. 12.   [93] Ibid. 18; Feenstra Kuiper, *Japan*, 221–2; Kragh, *Natur, Nytte*, 87.
[94] Thunberg, *Reise*, iii. 24.   [95] Sörlin and Fagerstedt, *Linné och hans apostlar*, 184–5, 193.

with their scientific knowledge: 'the sciences in general fall infinitely short, in Japan, of that exalted pre-eminence they have attained in Europe.' Medicine here 'neither has attained, nor is it likely it ever will, any degree of eminence'.[96] Whilst at Edo (Tokyo), the Japanese capital, in the summer of 1776, he conducted several seminars on medicine, physics, natural history, and botany with the court physicians and astronomers, several of whom knew enough Dutch to act as an effective bridge for intellectual contact between Japan and the West.[97] The Japanese, he observed, were especially drawn to natural history and astronomy despite possessing only such basic principles as they had acquired from the Dutch, otherwise knowing 'nothing about anatomy or circulation of the blood'.[98] Meanwhile, he strove to acquire Japanese, something officially forbidden by the shogunate. He toiled using an old Portuguese–Japanese dictionary one of the interpreters (after repeated requests) secretly provided. Though he found the language exceedingly difficult, he made some progress, later publishing a brief twenty-six-page glossary of Japanese terms in his account of his scientific travels published originally in Swedish, and, in 1791, appearing as his *Reise durch einen Theil von Europa, Afrika und Asien, hauptsächlich in Japan* (4 vols., Berlin, 1792).[99]

Astounded by the magnificence of the temples at Kyoto (Miyako), what especially captivated Thunberg was the variety and splendour of Japan's gardens and flora. Discussing medicine and herbs, and collecting botanical specimens as well as classifying in Linnaean terms a large proportion of Japan's trees and shrubs, Thunberg established a lasting interaction with Japanese scholars. With two of those with whom he became familiar, Katsuragawa Hoshu (1751–1809) and Nakagawa Jun'an, he remained in contact even after returning to Sweden: they sent him botanical specimens, he sent them medical books.[100] He was especially proud of having taught the Japanese to use *eau mercurielle* as a cure for venereal diseases, maladies originally brought to Japan seemingly by the Dutch.[101] Passionate about botany, he was also the first European to dispatch from Japan (besides Java and Ceylon) numerous botanical specimens. He also sent temperature measurements to the Societeit van Wetenschappen, at Haarlem, and other scientific data. The results of his botanical research in Japan he subsequently collected in his *Flora Japonica* (1784). Much additional information about Japan and Japanese culture, and the Japanese language, as well as about the Dutch in Ceylon and Java (and at the Cape), appeared in his account of his travels. After returning to Sweden, via Holland, in 1779, he was appointed to a chair at Uppsala, to which university he later bequeathed his vast collection of Japanese and other natural history specimens.

Thunberg toured Japan, after seeing Batavia, at a critical moment of relative openness. The so-called 'first surgeon' at Deshima, the head of the factory (*Opperhoofd*),

---

[96] Thunberg, *Travels*, iv. 55.   [97] Thunberg, *Le Japon*, 131, 140.   [98] Ibid. 142.
[99] Thunberg, *Reise*, iii. 26–7, 214, 216–42.   [100] Thunberg, *Le Japon*, 2, 34.
[101] Maclean, 'Introduction of Books', 19; Opstall, 'Dutchmen and Japanese', 116; Sörlin and Fagerstedt, *Linné och hans apostlar*, 194.

and one or two assistants, were, indeed, the only Dutch in a position to learn anything about the country and its politics and culture, their main opportunity for doing so being the annual trip required to the palace in Edo which, with its 1.3 million inhabitants, was at the time considered the largest city in the world, to show obeisance to the shogun and express profuse thanks for favours received. This annual ritual, sometimes lasting as long as three months, occurred in the spring and early summer, precisely the best season for botanists to examine Japan's astounding trees and shrubs, and included lengthy stays at the special 'Dutch inns' or lodgings at Osaka and Kyoto, precisely where the finest, most carefully cultivated gardens in Japan were to be seen.[102]

The other prominent Western scholar in this incipient and short-lived East–West Enlightenment in Japan was Isaac Titsingh (1745–1812), scion of an Amsterdam regent family who took up an administrative position at Batavia in 1766 and already knew everything to be learnt about Japan from the only available recent reference materials—the *Encyclopédie* and the *Histoire philosophique*, on being dispatched to Nagasaki, as *Opperhoofd* (director) of the Dutch trading factory, in 1779. Like Thunberg, Titsingh was shocked by how little interest most of his colleagues at Batavia, and among the Dutch merchant community at Deshima, took in Japanese culture and learning, and in Japan's flora and natural history.[103] He spent slightly over four years in the country before leaving for the last time in November 1784, a period long enough to master the language to an unprecedented level and acquire a fair knowledge of the country, much of which was completely new to Europeans. Though Thunberg laid the foundation, Titsingh was arguably the first enlightener to engage seriously in dialogue with Japan, and the West's first fully-fledged Japanologist. While spending most of his stay confined to Nagasaki, there too he developed productive ties with the local cultural elite.[104] Besides two lengthy excursions into the interior to the court at Edo, in 1780 and 1782, he made several shorter trips to Osaka.

A land of over twenty million inhabitants, or roughly equivalent at the time to France, Japan was a source of immense fascination to Thunberg, Titsingh, and the tiny group of Westerners at Nagasaki, Batavia, and Malacca infected with their enthusiasm and they learned a great deal, quickly. The commonplace that 'China and Japan were hardly known at all' to the Enlightenment West hence actually requires serious qualification.[105] The temporary, partial easing of Japan's hitherto strict isolation in the 1770s and 1780s continued for some years mainly because the tenth shogun, Ieharu (ruled 1780–6), had a chief minister, Tanuma Okitsugu, who personally took an interest in learning about the West and, in particular, wished to discover how Japan could benefit from Western science and techniques. Briefly, the long-standing tight restrictions imposed on the tiny resident Dutch colony's

---

[102] Sörlin and Fagerstedt, *Linné och hans apostlar*, 193–4.
[103] Thunberg, *Le Japon*, 164; Proust, 'Quelques dictionnaires hollandais', 19.
[104] Lequin, *Isaac Titsingh*, 57.
[105] Withers, *Placing*, 93.

movements, as well as temporarily resident seamen and soldiers, all concentrated on a single street, on Deshima, were relaxed. While the governor of Nagasaki was supposed not to engage in face-to-face contacts with the Dutch community, Titsingh's particular ally, the liberal-minded governor, under Ieharu, Kuze Tango-no-kami, entered into an intense dialogue with him through one of the interpreters, Namura Naosaburo.[106]

Study of the West in eighteenth-century Japan was called *Rangaku* (short for *Oranda-gaku*, or Holland-knowledge) and during the time of Titsingh's stay this was a branch of learning central to Japanese elite culture and actively encouraged by the authorities in Edo, albeit it remained confined to a tiny group of interpreters and Dutch-language experts constituting a close-knit college in Nagasaki, and a few other highly placed *Rangakusha*, or Holland-experts based mainly at court. Officially, the point of studying *Rangaku* was to learn about obviously useful aspects of Western culture, in particular medicine, astronomy, and botany, but very soon, interest reached beyond these to other topics. The result was a cultural clash between innovation and tradition in the form of a conflict between *Rangaku* and Neo-Confucianism. The incursion of Western scientific and cultural concepts in Japan, including Copernican heliocentrism and various other, for the Japanese, highly novel ideas, proved decidedly unsettling.

Deshima's first surgeon, or 'opper-chirurgijn', was one of the very few Dutch officials based in Japan in the later eighteenth century disposing of something like a professional scientific library. One of these officers, Thomas Neegers, who died on Deshima in January 1778, shortly after succeeding Thunberg in the post, left an interesting inventory of his books which included not only works on surgery, anatomy, and pharmacology but also a copy of Bernard Nieuwentijd's *Regt gebruyk der Wereld-beschouwing*, the first printed work principally concerned with Spinoza and Spinozism known to have reached Japanese soil, a significant fact even if Neegers kept his thoughts about it to himself. A second copy of this core work of Dutch physico-theology that surfaced in Japan belonged to an official who died on the voyage from Batavia to Nagasaki, in July 1778, while a third cropped up among the books of a German bookkeeper who died on Deshima in 1782. Dutch physico-theological philosophy, including systematic refutation of Spinoza, by the 1770s evidently permeated the Dutch cultural milieu at Deshima.[107]

Medicine was the *primum mobile* of this incipient Dutch–Japanese Enlightenment. Another of Neegers's books was a copy of Johann Adam Kulmus's *Anatomische Tabellen*, a German work crucially significant in Japanese medical history as the court physician, Ryotaku Maeno (1722–1803), having learnt Dutch (from Aoki Bunzo) and the rudiments of European medicine, grew convinced, particularly after examining the corpse of an executed Japanese woman, in March 1771, that

---

[106] Lequin, *Isaac Titsingh*, 67; Opstall, 'Dutchmen and Japanese', 115–16.
[107] Maclean, 'Introduction of Books', 35–7.

the Chinese-Japanese accounts of the vital organs were less accurate than European accounts. He accordingly initiated the translation of Kulmus's book into Japanese, assisted by a team of four or five other scholars, including the noted Confucianist and *Rangakusha* Sugita Genpaku (1733–1817), a scholar who trained many students in his academy at Edo. Their rendering appeared under the title *Katai Shinsko*, in five volumes, in 1773 or 1774.[108] Maeno also translated several other Dutch works.

This unique cultural dialogue was enthusiastically pushed forward by Titsingh who made a point of giving his Japanese friends 'the best' European books, 'particularly on natural history, botany, physick and surgery', generating an appreciation among the Japanese to which Titsingh afterwards acknowledged himself 'indebted', he assured an English correspondent, 'for what I have collected [concerning Japan]'. Observing 'my eagerness for instruction, they were delighted with it and have never hesitated to provide me with such books and information as they deemed the most adequate to the purpose'.[109] Engagement with Japanese scholars and study of Japan in turn stimulated more enlightened reading and discussion among the leaders of the Deshima Dutch community. Among the best of several notable Dutch libraries in Japan late in the century was that of the *Opperhoofd* Gijsbert Hemmy who died on Deshima in 1800. He had brought many dozens of books with him including a complete set of Buffon's *Histoire naturelle* in twenty-one volumes, Musschenbroek's *Beginselen der Natuur*, several English works, and an account of Surinam.

To this cultural *rapprochement*, Tanuma Okitsugu eventually encountered intense opposition from a rigidly conservative court clique. The murder of his son, also a member of the council of state, in May 1784 was followed by his own overthrow, in 1786, and then a general reaction, including the banishment of Kuze, an event that broadly arrested Japan's encounter with the Enlightenment. For his role in the dialogue between Kuze and Titsingh, the interpreter Namura Naosaburo was executed. However, the interruption proved less than total. Titsingh's circle of Japanese friends, or learned Rangakusha, persevered only now strictly in private, the ablest, like Namura Motojiro (1729–88) and Yoshio Kozaemon (1724–1800), doing so as professional interpreters, or else, like Thunberg's friend Katsugawa Hoshu, whose family had for generations served at court, Nakagawa Jun'an (1739–86), another friend of Thunberg, and, at Miyako, Ogino Gengai (1737–1806), as the shogun's chief physicians. Katsurgawa Hoshu, like Nakagawa Jun'an, had learnt much of what he knew about Western medicine, including the technique of blood-letting which he apparently thought beneficial in a wide range of conditions, from Thunberg.[110]

Several district governors remained supportive, including Titsingh's other close ally and friend in Japan, Kutsuki Oki-no-Kami Masatsuna, *Daimyo* [lord] of Fukuchiyama in Tamba, a nobleman who learnt Dutch from the interpreter Yoshio Kozaemon and paid for the instruction in Dutch of the scribe Otsuki Gentaku (1757–1827). The latter became a student, in both Dutch and medicine, of Sugita

---

[108] Ibid. 34–5; Nosco, 'Place of China', 42, 45. [109] Lequin, *Isaac Titsingh*, 71.
[110] Feenstra Kuiper, *Japan*, 264–5.

Gempaku and Ryotaku Maeno, and eventually one of the most famous of the Japanese Hollandologists, in 1788 completing a key Japanese text *Rangaku kaitei* [Guide to Hollandology]. Otsuki enjoyed dressing up as a Dutchman and, from 1794, took to giving a Dutch-style new year's party for colleagues, an illustration of which survives.[111] Another friend was Shimazu Shigehide (1745–1833), governor of Satsuma (Kagoshima, in South Kyushu), likewise an 'enlightened' *érudit* intensely interested in everything Dutch who spoke the language fluently.

The relative openness facilitating Titsingh's contacts and research would perhaps have been impossible without a basis in Enlightenment philosophy as well as science. Titsingh's interests were wide, covering all the sciences, geography, and also philosophy, as we see from his *Discours philosophique*, composed in December 1779, a few months after arriving in Japan. Here, he includes a brief summary of Copernican astronomy, pronouncing our earth but 'a small part of the universe', and expounding for the benefit of another high imperial official with whom he conversed, the treasurer, Gotoo Soozajemon Sama, his intensely deistic world-view. The document probably does not mark the actual debut of East–West Enlightenment philosophical dialogue in Japan, but is incontrovertible evidence that an incipient philosophical dialogue between the Dutch and Japanese existed. A believer in a 'First Being' who created the world and men, Titsingh tried to formulate what he saw as the core 'natural theology' of all religions. Central to his thought was the idea that every people and individual venerates the First Being by obeying the laws of his or her land, and complying with their duties towards their fellow men, irrespective of what faith they profess, a universalism holding that all would be saved after death.[112]

His sharing the *Encyclopédie*'s and *Histoire*'s sympathy for Japanese thought and his antipathy to Christianity emerges from several features, especially his negative view of all theology based on revelation and detestation of 'priestcraft'. Priests had mostly played a harmful role in history, and, in particular, fomented political instability and strife, provoking wars and diverting men from true morality. Instead of directing piety and morality towards 'het algemeen nut' [the common good] of society, theologians mostly endeavour to forge segregated confessional factions for self-promoting reasons, forming parties of adherents among the ignorant and deceiving people into believing the Almighty confides his wishes and bestows favours mainly through them. Immersed in Diderot's article 'Japonois, philosophie des', in the eighth volume of the *Encyclopédie*, and d'Holbach's articles on Japanese religion, Titsingh citing Locke, Leibniz, and Wolff in his *Discours* clearly believed European and Japanese intellectual development are closely related.

Separating theology from morality and deprecating priestcraft, Titsingh adopted something of Diderot's and d'Holbach's evolutionary historical perspective. It is this radical tendency that enabled him to contemplate in a philosophical spirit aspects of Japanese values most opposite to those of Europe. An expression of disgust he found

---

[111] Opstall, 'Dutchmen and Japanese', 120–1.   [112] Ibid. 85–6, 88, 91.

in a European book, at the prevalence of homosexuality in Japan, he answered, in a manuscript note penned during his visit to the Chinese court, in 1794–5, remarking in a neutral tone that this inclination was so 'general that a great many from Emperor down to domestic servants are given to it' and that it was entirely usual among the princes and district governors.[113] Valentijn had already noted that homosexuality seemed more prevalent in Japan than anywhere else in Asia. The practice seemed indeed to be more widespread in Japan than China, adds Titsingh, the Japanese being quite open about this.

The most fundamental feature of Titsingh's enlightened creed is his concept of the equality and brotherhood of the great minds of the East and West, men who have grasped the unity of man and the universe, the nature of man's duties, and overriding rightness and centrality of a socially grounded, as opposed to faith-grounded, morality. The great men of humanity he lists as 'Teikwo, Woosin Gonggen Sama, Taiko Gongensama, Koosi [i.e. Confucius (551–479 BC)], Leibnits, Neuton, Lokke, Wolf [i.e. Christian Wolff] en anderen, die in haar leeven, door groote daden en kundigheeden, tot eere van het eerste Weesen, en tot wellust van hunnen even-menschen verstrekken [and others who in life, through great deeds and plying scientific knowledge tended to the honour of the First Being and the well-being of their fellow men]'.[114] The Japanese Titsingh here refers to are the thirteenth-century poet Fujiwara no Teika (1162–1241), the fifteenth, legendary Japanese emperor, Ojin (200–310) (Woosin Gonggen Sama), and legendary warlord Taiko Toyotomi Hideyoshi (1536–98).

This first forging of a Dutch–Japanese cultural symbiosis continued in corres-pondence between Masatsuna and Titsingh after the latter left Japan, in 1784, a correspondence that has no parallel in the whole history of the Dutch engagement with Japan from 1600 to 1853. Masatsuna, immensely learned in everything con-cerning his own society, nurtured a special interest in plants and herbs, foreign geography, numismatics, languages, and natural philosophy and eagerly sought books enabling him to learn about India and Africa as well as Europe. Titsingh sent him texts on all these subjects as well as dictionaries Dutch, French, and Latin and several works on coins. Latin had for some time interested Japan's Holland experts as the books brought to Japan by the VOC contained numerous Latin terms and expressions. By the 1780s, however, French had become even more desirable and Dutch–French dictionaries were, of imported items, among the most prized by Japanese scholars.[115]

A notable feature of Titsingh's correspondence with Masatsuna is his expressions of hope that in Japan popular superstition and error would recede sufficiently to allow Enlightenment to advance and flourish also there. He complained in particular that his highly placed friends, and the Japanese generally, were prevented from

---

[113] Titsingh, *Private Correspondence*, i, pp. xxxii–xxxiii.
[114] Quoted ibid. 92.   [115] Proust, 'Quelques dictionnaires hollandais', 20.

visiting foreign lands. Writing from Batavia, in June 1785, he communicated his hope that, on coming to power, the crown prince, due to his better education, might somehow become convinced of the usefulness of interaction between his people and foreigners and ameliorate things to the point that it would become possible for them to travel. A people so cultured, admirable, and suited for the sciences would, perhaps, now finally emerge from its isolation and share 'in de algmeene voordeelen van het menschdom' [in the universal benefits of mankind].[116] In this respect, Titsingh's hopes were, of course, entirely frustrated. Yet, for a few years a remarkable cultural interchange occurred and the example stands today as a true expression of the Enlightenment's uniqueness, greatness, and indispensability to humanity.

A report about Masatsuna and the Japanese circle of Hollandologists was sent to Batavia, presumably by Titsingh, that was subsequently remitted to Holland. In the issue of the *Rotterdamsche Courant* of 27 November 1784, shortly prior to Titsingh's departure from Japan, appeared an article, sent from Batavia with other letters from Nagasaki, announcing that the foremost men of Japan were now eagerly learning Dutch in order to read the best Dutch books, especially about botany and herbs. The governor of Tamba (Kutsuki Masatsuna) was reported to be translating the *Katechismus der Natuur* (4 vols., Amsterdam, 1777–9), the chief work of Johannes Florentius Martinet (1729–95), the foremost late eighteenth-century Dutch work of physico-theology countering Spinozism, materialism, and radical ideas. The first volume of Martinet's *Katechismus* had reached Titsingh only shortly after his arrival in Japan and appears to have figured prominently in his debate with the Japanese.[117] Evocatively, in the fifth part of Martinet's *History of the World*, of 1784, Masatsuna, governor of Tamba, is declared the most prominent of the Japanese scholars at present enthused with Dutch and Western studies.[118]

---

[116] Lequin, *Isaac Titsingh*, 98–9.   [117] Ibid. 104.   [118] Ibid. 108.

21

India and the Two Enlightenments

1. RADICAL CRITIQUE OF THE BRITISH RAJ

In Enlightenment Europe and Asia, debate about India, for political, economic, and strategic but also philosophical reasons, was intense. During the Seven Years War (1756–63), Britain's triumph over her opponents, European and local, was swift and spectacular, indeed so far-reaching as to usher in a whole new era in global history. Enlighteners needed to come to terms with, explain, and evaluate India's dramatic transformation and integrate it whether in a positive or negative fashion into their world vision. For moderate enlighteners defending the basic principle of empire, India was a key case. On the other hand, those building a radical general critique of colonialism, a philosophical tradition reaching back to Bayle and Lahontan and culminating in the *Histoire philosophique* and writings of Du Perron, Démeunier, Dohm, Haafner, Volney, and Condorcet,[1] found in the Indian context much evidence supporting their systematically damning conclusions.

In India, as Voltaire put it in 1774, good fortune followed the British everywhere.[2] By the mid 1760s, England had 8,200 white troops and 60,000 sepoys deployed in the sub-continent, according to the *Histoire*, dominating all Bengal, the Coromandel coast, and the Carnatic and ensuring a dominant role in Indian politics. The perception of general oppression in India itself was nothing new. Rather, from Montesquieu onwards, a heavy emphasis on the horrors of 'oriental despotism', along with the idea that 'le gouvernement despotique' had been usual in India for millennia, was a prevailing assumption common to mainstream and radical viewpoints. But Europe's reading public now encountered two diametrically different ways of explaining the transformed, post-1763 Indian situation stemming partly from the clash of vying interests but also from deeply troubling moral and philosophical concerns. According to radical critics, Britain introduced only new and harsher forms of exploitation and her hegemony, backed by unprecedented military force, not only filled the princes of northern and southern India alike with fear, jealousy, and aversion, but weighed mercilessly on the downtrodden and poor.[3]

---

[1] Starobinski, *Remède*, 33–4; Goggi, 'Diderot et le concept', 363–4.
[2] [Voltaire], *Fragmens*, 217.　　[3] *Histoire philosophique* (1770), ii. 137–8.

Those championing the British Raj granted that much was wrong in India but insisted on the opportunity for a truly civilizing agent to transform the continent into a more orderly, secure, and better-governed entity.

Before and after the decisive British victory at Plassey in 1757, the chief obstacle to the British Company's political and economic ascendancy in northern India was the nawab of Bengal, a despot who strove tenaciously to defend his interests and those of his flourishing governing elite and merchant class. He could only hope to block British ambitions and equip himself for such a struggle with the aid of both the indigenous merchants and the French and Dutch. For the embittered relations between the British and the nawabs of Bengal, in particular Shujauddin Khan (1727–39) and his successor Alivardi Khan (1740–56), immediately prior to the 1757 'revolution', stemmed from deep-seated, irresolvable quarrels over trade, influence, and long-established trading privileges which the English, in the nawab's view, continually overstepped and abused. These extremely bitter disputes especially concerned access to markets, resources, and supplies and, from 1748, extended to English insistence on searching vessels belonging to other nations, including Armenian and Muslim as well as Dutch craft navigating the great Bengal estuaries and rivers with the aim of preventing both local merchants and the Dutch carrying for the French.

The last independent nawab of Bengal, Siraj-ud-Daula khan (1756–7), quarrelled still more bitterly with the British over their 'privileges', and what he considered their ceaseless encroachments and presumption, leading to all-out war and the ensuing 'revolution' of India. Having taken the English fort at Casimbazaar in June 1756, Siraj-ud-Daula attacked the British headquarters in Calcutta with 32,000 men.[4] As events in Bengal unrolled toward their dramatic climax, the Dutch *directeur* at Hugli, Adriaen Bisdom, with only a small force at his disposal but at the cost of antagonizing both sides, both demanding he side with them, remained neutral. The nawab succeeded in capturing the English fort which he then plundered and wrecked, locking up seventy-one captured British in the notorious 'Black Hole of Calcutta', 'over which', as Karl Marx later put it, 'the English hypocrites' 'have been making so much sham scandal to this day'.[5] But in January 1757, a fresh British force, under Clive, shipped up from Madras, reoccupied Calcutta and, in early 1757, forced the nawab, now informally in alliance with the Dutch and formally with the French, to retreat deep into the interior. After plundering Hugli, Clive set siege to the French headquarters, Fort Orléans, at Chandernagore, which was also bombarded by naval warships dragged up the Hugli river. Chandernagore surrendered in March 1757, demoralizing the French and Dutch throughout India.[6] Four months later, Colonel Clive won his climactic victory over Siraj-ud-Daula at Plassey (23 June

---

[4] Brissot, *Tableau*, 206–13; Gijsberti Hodenpijl, 'Handhaving', 266.
[5] Marx, *Notes*, 81.
[6] [Voltaire], *Fragmens*, 74–5, 137; Brissot, *Tableau*, 214, 218.

1757), capturing his opponent, as Voltaire noted, much as Cortes had captured Montezuma and by this means paralysing the government of an entire empire.[7]

As governor of Calcutta, Clive, about whom Voltaire was far more complimentary than 'Raynal', ordered the dethroning of Siraj-ud-Daula who was murdered soon afterwards. A subordinate prince, Mir Jaffir, who had betrayed his predecessor by deserting to the British before the great battle, was now fêted and made nawab under 'la protection des Anglais', as Voltaire expressed it. Mir Jaffir, plainly, was just a tool for the British Company's interests: a package of extremely one-sided commercial, fiscal, and purchasing privileges, aimed no less at the Muslims and Armenians than the Dutch and French, supplemented by additional territorial rights, was proclaimed and then rigidly enforced throughout Bengal by the Company's troops, as well as on all Dutch, Muslim, Armenian, and other foreign shipping approaching its shores. Local governors and numerous other former underlings of the nawab and his court were replaced.

Outright supremacy in Bengal was nearly achieved but not quite. Mir Jaffa and his successor still had control of their revenues and deputy governors and some semblance of sovereignty. A last attempt to block British hegemony in Bengal by stiffening the nawab with a countervailing military presence occurred in 1759. The 'Dutch of Bengal', as a contemporary account put it, 'seeing the uses which on all hands were made of Moguls and Nabobs in this distracted state of the country, from the superiority of European discipline, formed in their turn the design of trying their fortune in the same way'. A secret plan for military intervention, sent from Hugli to Batavia, stressed the immediate danger that a drastically weakened nawab would soon enable the English to seize outright and absolute control. With the English Company heavily engaged fighting the French on the Coromandel coast, the Dutch *gouverneur-generaal*, Mossel, dispatched a military force from Batavia large enough potentially to lever the balance back. Under this 'well concerted but badly executed plan, a formidable body of European and Malay troops, with seven ships, were, towards the end of the year 1759, imported into Bengal'.[8] As the troops, not expecting to be attacked, began disembarking some distance up river, a British force, on Clive's orders, taking them by surprise, attacked immediately and after several hours of fierce fighting thoroughly routed them and, as Marx puts it, threw 'them back into their boats'.

The 'revolution' of India involved an unprecedented shift in political, cultural, and legal relations between European and Asiatic society, signifying not just British predominance over all northern India but eventual British domination of Asia generally. It was a 'revolution' that precipitated huge changes in world trade and profoundly altered the power balance between the main European colonial empires, as well as crucially affected enlightened debate. The Portuguese, based at Goa, though nominally Britain's allies, lost no less heavily from the ensuing changes than the rest.

---

[7] [Voltaire], *Fragmens*, 216.   [8] Marx, *Notes*, 82; Bolts, *Considerations*, 41.

They were made to feel not just British hostility to their continued presence but, the viceroy at Goa complained to Lisbon, wholly detrimental effects to their trade.[9] And it all happened with extraordinary speed. It had not been until the 1730s that British power and trade in India began to outstrip Dutch power and trade in India, Dutch commerce still amounting to roughly three-quarters of the volume of the British India trade in the mid 1750s.[10] French power in India had looked particularly formidable during the century's second quarter and down to 1757, the Compagnie des Indes' annual dividends rising from 100 to 150 *livres* between 1722 and 1745 with the share price rising proportionately. In 1746, the French, under Dupleix, even briefly captured Madras. The clashes of the late 1740s trimmed the dividend back to 70 *livres* by 1749; but the French company had seemingly recovered its position by the mid 1750s, formidably challenging Britain for primacy during the opening phases of the Seven Years War. British arms won no major successes on sea or land until 1757. The French and Dutch collapses had been both sudden and unexpected. After beating the French in the field and overrunning their outlying posts, the British captured the French headquarters, at Pondicherry, in January 1761, deporting the white community *en masse* back to Europe and demolishing the town itself.[11]

But it was not clear, though, even after 1759, that Britain had finally secured an unchallengeable ascendancy over India's princes, power structures, and resources. It is often supposed that crushing the French-backed nawab of Bengal at Plassey was so decisive as to render British dominance of the sub-continent subsequently undisputed. But actually the prospect of a counter-coup of Indian princes and European powers against Britain remained a real one, infusing politics and culture with a constant tension until the 1790s. After 1763 as before, India's indigenous princes and merchants had nowhere else to look but to the French and Dutch as a realistic counterweight to British hegemony, especially in southern India where the Dutch remained strongly entrenched in their coastal enclaves but also in Bengal. On south-east India's Coromandel coast, the Dutch were still the chief trading power for the moment due to the centrality of this area's cotton exports in their inter-Asian trade, especially with the Moluccas, Java, and Makassar where Coromandel cottons were exchanged for the pepper, spices, rice, and sugar imported annually into southern India from Batavia. In 1770, noted the *Histoire*, Dutch exports from south-east India, chiefly Negapatnam, still slightly outstripped British exports, with 4,700 bales (of which 1,500 to other parts of Asia) as against 4,200 bales of cotton goods exported by the English company.

For decades after 1757, British hegemony remained incomplete and vulnerable. By 1759, the English East India Company from its base at Madras certainly held 'dans les fers le Coromandel', as the *Histoire* expressed it, 'comme ils y tiennent le Bengale' [held Coromandel in shackles as they hold Bengal].[12] It is true that on south-west

---

[9] *Cartas de Manuel de Saldanha*, 51–2, 168.
[10] Ibid. 43; Arasaratnam, 'Dutch East India Company', 326, 346; Chaudhury, *From Prosperity*, 41.
[11] *Histoire philosophique* (1780), ii. 477, 491–2.   [12] *Histoire philosophique* (1770), i. 334.

India's Malabar coast, since around 1720, the previously dominant Dutch had lost their former predominance. But the Dutch could not easily evacuate the great fortresses they still retained in southern India as these would then be occupied by the British or French, or recovered by the Portuguese, who would then doubtless impose their own trading monopolies on Malabar and southern Coromandel. Abandoning their Indian fortresses would irreparably harm Dutch commerce with Asia overall, argued the VOC's senior officials, and expose Dutch Ceylon to attack.[13] Thus the Dutch retained their bases at Cochin, Cranganore, and Cannanore and, if they could no longer manipulate local princes or curb British activity in the area,[14] they could collude with the French who had repeatedly succeeded in forming alliances with southern Indian princes and continued to do so, enabling Indian princes to build sometimes formidable coalitions against Britain's growing ascendancy.

Franco-Dutch strategic thinking, like that of the princes, was concerned with preserving a balance of the European powers and trying to prevent outright British control. Unlike the princes, the Dutch, French, and Portuguese were not interested in preserving Indian autonomy, princely independence, and the integrity of Indian culture per se. Nevertheless, the quest for a strategic balance, even if intended only to secure as large a share of India's trade as possible, depended on shoring up princely and merchant autonomy against the British. This, Dutch and French officials recognized, was the only way of preventing total British hegemony and, with it, the end of any kind of equilibrium among the commercial powers. Although hardly designed to resist a large force equipped with heavy artillery, having houses all around close to the walls, the Dutch complex at Hugli-Chinsura, contemporary paintings show, was nevertheless an impressive symbol of the continuing Dutch presence in Bengal, remaining one of the chief European settlements in India for several decades.[15] Political intrigue in Bengal as in southern India remained intense, and although the British were openly challenged by Indian princes only in the south and then only sporadically, in the north too they were ceaselessly opposed more guardedly. It was Clive's and his successors' 'constant aim to exclude the French from every possible chance of getting a footing', recalled a senior British colonial official, 'in that part of India where they might be supposed, to have retained some connection in consequence of their former possession'.[16] The British strove likewise further to squeeze Dutch, Portuguese, and Danish as well as the Armenian activity; but nowhere, as yet, were they wholly successful.

Indian princes opposing the British Raj did so on many levels, in their commercial arrangements with indigenous and Armenian merchants as well as the French and Dutch. Most famously, it was Hyder Ali (c.1722–82), nawab of Mysore, described in 1781 as a prince of 'much ambition and enterprise, ever in alliance with the

[13] Ibid. 520; Das Gupta, *Malabar*, 27, 30–3, 43, 79; Schrikker, *British and Dutch*, 39, 51.
[14] Chaudhuri and Israel, 'East India Companies', 429.
[15] Gijsberti Hodenpijl, 'Handhaving', 260; Jacobs, *Koopman in Azië*, 83–5.
[16] MS BL IOL E/1/71, fo. 462: 'Letter from Robert Palk'.

French, who treated [British] offers of peace and friendship with marked indifference and neglect', who fought Britain's ascendancy on both the Malabar and Coromandel coasts.[17] In 1772, the Marquis de Chastellux, discussing the future of French influence in India, claimed British dominance could still be prevented, and a more natural and equitable balance between Indians and Europeans restored, through indigenous alliances and French assistance bolstering Dutch military intervention.[18] In the years 1780–2, a powerful French force, prepared at Mauritius, reached Indian waters in alliance with the Dutch and several indigenous princes. It failed to capture Madras. But it did win a string of naval engagements off the tip of India and clearly showed Britain's hold on India was not yet to be taken for granted.

It was this background of continuing international rivalry, and, after 1782, further attempts by Indian princes, including Hyder's son Tipu, to build alliances with the French and Dutch, that fixed the basic framework of Enlightenment debate about India.[19] The so-called Third Mysore War (1789–92) caused Gibbon, whose income from East India stock was threatened, to remark, late in 1791: 'our affairs in that country seem in a very ticklish situation.'[20] At the heart of the struggle was the huge, disproportionate, value of Europe's procurement of silks, cottons, calicoes, and other products from the sub-continent. With China and Java, India shared a dramatically lower level of manufacturing costs compared to Europe, a difference most conspicuous in textile production. Labourers' wages, explained Adam Smith,

will there purchase a smaller quantity of food; and as the money price of food is much lower in India than in Europe, the money price of labour is there lower upon a double account; upon account both of the small quantity of food which it will purchase, and of the low price of that food. But in countries of equal art and industry, the money price of the greater part of manufactures will be in proportion to the money price of labour; and in manufacturing art and industry, China and Hindostan, though inferior, seem not to be much inferior to any part of Europe. The money price of the greater part of manufactures, therefore, will naturally be much lower in those great empires than it is anywhere in Europe.[21]

In Bengal, furthermore, this general factor was further accentuated. The region's unusually dense population, agricultural fertility, abundance of skilled labour, and low costs of production stemming from relative cheapness and availability of raw materials, especially cotton yarn and silk thread, and of rice, generated an unparalleled competitiveness and productivity in cottons, calicoes, and silks. The global significance of this was then further enhanced by cheap and easy transportation via the vast river network which was invaluable also for irrigation purposes and maintaining high levels of rice output.[22] And besides all this, there accrued in the village textile workshops a remarkable fund of ancient and newer handicraft technique. With unwearying industry and a few paltry tools, observed a Danish report of 1789,

[17] MS BL IOL E/1/71, fos. 461ᵛ–2.   [18] Chastellux, *De la félicité publique*, ii. 164–5.
[19] Haafner, *Reize*, ii. 277; Travers, 'Imperial Revolutions', 159.   [20] Gibbon, *Memoirs*, 452.
[21] Smith, *Wealth of Nations*, i. 217.   [22] Ibid. ii. 266–7; Chaudhury, *From Prosperity*, 132–8.

the innumerable densely inhabited textile villages of Bengal produced the 'prettyist and finest cloths without the use of machines' one could find.[23]

The regime of the Bengal nawabs, it was clear by the early 1760s, was paralysed not only at court but also at many intermediate levels. After only a relatively short transition period from 1757 to 1765, Clive and his associates, loudly complaining of 'oriental despotism' and depravity, ended nominal indigenous princely rule in Bengal and established a pattern of more direct control sometimes designated the system of 'double government'. The nawab was forced formally to assign the *diwan*, or responsibility for Bengal's taxes, to the British. In May 1768, the Company began officially to 'ban all European and Armenian merchants from carrying on trade in Bengal, Bihar and Orissa', or exporting goods from there, issuing orders that 'all such merchandize should be seized and confiscated'.[24] Finally, in 1772, the new governor of British Calcutta, Warren Hastings (governor of Bengal: 1772–85), arrested the Indian deputy governors of the areas around Calcutta on charges of corruptly hoarding rice supplies, initiating the direct British administration that ensued.

'Every intermediate power', reported Hastings to London, in March 1773, 'is removed and the sovereignty of the country wholly and absolutely vested in the Company.'[25] British sway in Bengal enabled the Company to dominate both the river systems of northern India and the largest and most profitable textile resource in Asia, drawing goods off ever more profitably from the population. While neither the nawab nor the French or Dutch concerned themselves overly with the interests of the textile-producing villages or the Indian and Armenian merchants trading in silks and calicoes, nevertheless, their efforts to preserve themselves necessarily involved shielding the groups under them to an extent. Prior to 1757, 'the weavers manufactured their goods freely and without oppression', as it was put in 1772, and it 'was then a common practice for reputable families of the *Tanty*, or weaver caste, to apply their own capitals in manufacturing goods which they sold freely on their own accounts'.[26] Indigenous princely rule and a strong French and Dutch presence remained the only way, also in the future, of restoring their prosperity and freedom.

When the British became 'maîtres de cette riche contrée', as the *Histoire* puts it, the quantity of cotton exports from Bengal increased vigorously while the value of receipts entering Bengal, in exchange, fell drastically. The fact itself was undisputed by Enlightenment writers and philosophers, as it is by historians today, but the precise significance of this was very variously interpreted. One could perhaps explain the large drop in returns while output and exports rose in terms of the 'conquerors' now differently settling a large part of the bill using revenues collected within Bengal in the name of the nawab. Alternatively, one could explain it in terms of the imposition of a harsh new system of oppression. With a monopoly of force, the

---

[23] Chaudhury, *From Prosperity*, 133.
[24] Bolts, *Considerations*, 199, 206; Abbattista, 'Empire', 481.
[25] Quoted in Ahmed, 'Orientalism', 194; Travers, 'Ideology', 11–12, 17.
[26] Bolts, *Considerations*, 194.

Company was able to wrest every branch of the Bengal trade from the natives and Armenians as well as the Dutch and French, reducing the operations of Indian merchants throughout the sub-continent.[27] Even the surplus rice crop available for the cities came under British control while both indigenous shipping from eastern Indian shores and the previously flourishing seaborne commerce of Gujarat, through Surat, contracted markedly.[28] Especially heavy losers were the local indigenous traders and textile weavers of Bengal. For the local populace, according to some, the 'revolution' spelt disaster and ruin, through the loss of their former economic autonomy. The indigenous merchant community dominating the Bengal silk trade until the 1760s were rapidly replaced by local agents, or *compradors*, wholly subservient to the new rulers.

In short, Bengal's relatively prosperous condition around 1750 deteriorated after 1757, the region undergoing a process of impoverishment affecting the Bengali village artisan especially.[29] For daring to sell their products on their own initiative, recorded Willem Bolts (1735–1808), a Dutch-born official with long experience of Bengal, weavers were 'frequently seized and imprisoned, confined in irons, fined considerable sums of money, flogged', and brutalized by the Company's agents. As for the winders of raw silk, called *nagaads*, 'this last class of workmen were pursued with such rigour during Lord Clive's late government in Bengal', with a view to boosting returns on the Company's investments in raw silk, 'that the most sacred laws of society were atrociously violated; for it was a common thing for the Company's *sepoys* to be sent by force of arms to break open the houses of the Armenian merchants established at Sydabad (who have from time immemorial been largely concerned in the silk trade) and forcibly take the *Nagaads* from their work and carry them away to the English factory'.[30] The *nagaads* were treated 'with such injustice that instances have been known of their cutting off their thumbs to prevent their being forced to wind silk'.[31]

Production and processing of silks, calicoes, and opium in the hinterland were now controlled by the Company, as was transportation, storage, and export.[32] As Company sway over the local economy intensified, huge fortunes were amassed, not least by Clive himself. Such massive personal balances accrued to the latter that he had to devise new methods of repatriating private wealth to Britain, and, from 1765, figured among the first to purchase diamonds in large quantity, as a means of transferring vast sums from India, most of his diamonds being sold in London to the Jewish merchant Yehiel Prager.[33] He was widely emulated by others including Hastings. Indeed, so great was the demand for diamonds by Company officials

[27] Chaudhury, *From Prosperity*, 334–5; Kanta Ray, 'Indian Society', 514–17.
[28] Kanta Ray, 'Indian Society', 514–17; Habib, 'Eighteenth Century', 104.
[29] *Histoire philosophique* (1780), ii. 240–1; Stuurman, *Uitvinding*, 297–8.
[30] Bolts, *Considerations*, 195; Chaudhury, 'Asian Merchants', 320.
[31] Bolts, *Considerations*, 194–5.
[32] Datta, 'Agrarian Economy', 422.
[33] Yogev, *Diamonds and Coral*, 172, 177, 255.

during the early phase of colonial domination that the mines were rapidly depleted, output in southern India declining markedly from the 1780s onwards.[34]

The sharply contested implications of these developments were not slow in spreading to the philosophical arena. Voltaire recognized at once what was at stake. He had always insisted on the superiority of British ideas, institutions, toleration, and science, and in his account of recent developments in India claimed the British, despite some mishaps, should be admired and praised for their competence, skill, and constructive attitude, especially the religious toleration and legal procedures they introduced, not criticized as brutal conquerors and rapacious marauders. The tendency of the moderate Enlightenment and missionaries to eulogize British hegemony in India was eventually to become a defining feature of attitudes towards European expansion in Asia more generally. The moderate mainstream often inclined to theories of racial superiority and European, especially British, superiority in civilization and religion over a supposedly debased culture plunged in despotism. This was the usual method of explaining and justifying colonial rule and economic control.

In the 1760s, a previously indirect, remote relationship between Europeans and the weaver-artisans of Bengal, with the power of the local princes intervening, was transformed into direct subordination of a large proportion of the Bengal textile villages to Company control, ensuring British direction of practically all sectors of the economy. Not unnaturally, continental commentators, whether or not they had ever been to India, often described this transition in a manner highly unflattering to the British. Almodóvar, echoing the *Histoire*, designated the British conquest of Bengal as a 'revolución prodigiosa' forging a 'methodical tyranny' in place of Indian 'arbitrary authority', establishing crushing taxes and systematic oppression, in fact 'altering and corrupting all sources of confidence and public happiness'.[35] The tyranny Britain imposed on Bengal in the 1760s, held Almodóvar, a catastrophe for India, was a human disaster on an enormous scale. However, before long, many British commentators too grew harshly critical. If the *Histoire* judged 'cette révolution dans le commerce de Bengal' a plundering of its prosperity and draining of its wealth out of the country by substituting for the pre-1763 system approximating to free trade a harshly extractive system maintained by force and rigidly applied, Adam Smith's analysis was not very different. 'The great fortunes so suddenly and so easily acquired in Bengal and the other British settlements in the East Indies', he argued, 'may satisfy us that, as the wages of labour are very low, so the profits of [capital] stock are very high in those ruined countries.'[36] The East India Company he accused of compressing Bengal's trade into an exclusive monopoly system likely to prove 'as completely destructive as that of the Dutch'.[37]

---

[34] Ibid. 123, 323.
[35] 'Malo de Luque' [Almodóvar], *Historia política*, ii. 206–9; Paquette, 'Enlightened Narratives', 70.
[36] Smith, *Wealth of Nations*, i. 99.
[37] Ibid. ii. 22; Ahmed, 'Orientalism', 192, 194.

Bengal's subjection transformed trade relations among the European powers not just in India but throughout Asia and beyond. From around 1770, Company management of Bengal's opium exports generated a marked increase in British commerce with Malacca and the Malay Peninsula, the English rapidly replacing the Dutch as the main suppliers of the drug.[38] Opium in this way became instrumental in British commercial expansion in south-east Asia as it did later in China. The drain on Bengal was a system of extraction closely linked to other branches of Britain's growing world trade primacy. Much of the export of calicoes and cottons was destined for the African market, to be exchanged for slaves or, in the rougher qualities, to the New World, to clothe slaves. Around a quarter of all British exports to Africa during the eighteenth century consisted of Indian textile products.[39]

The political, legal, and moral effects of the acquisition of Bengal to many looked as disastrous as the economic effects. 'The difference between the genius of the British constitution which protects and governs North America, and that of the mercantile company which oppresses and domineers in the East Indies [i.e. India]', averred Smith in 1776, 'cannot perhaps be better illustrated than by the different state of those countries.'[40] No starker contrast could be drawn, held Bolts, between British society and British 'liberty' and the realities of the regime imposed by the East India Company in India under the auspices of Parliament. A brilliant linguist who had lived in England since the age of 14 and, afterwards, in Lisbon (where he experienced the earthquake of 1755), Bolts entered the Company's service in 1759, quickly acquiring Bengali to add to his English, French, Portuguese, and Dutch, and within a few years established a profitable business of his own while simultaneously acting as a senior Company judicial official in Calcutta. Intriguing with the Dutch at Hugli-Chinsurah, however, in 1768 led to his disgrace and deportation.[41] Henceforth, he allied with Dutch, French, and, after visiting Vienna in 1774, Austrian interests. His tirades against British power in India, though a form of vengeance on the Company by spreading adverse publicity, had a lasting effect on enlightened opinion and public debate. His *Considerations on India Affairs; Particularly respecting the Present State of Bengal and its Dependencies* (1772), published after his return to London to seek redress in the courts, was widely noticed in England and on the Continent where it appeared in Holland in a French translation, *L'État civil et commerçant de Bengale* (1775), by Jean-Nicolas Démeunier, an acquaintance of Diderot from the Franche-Comté and later leader in the French Revolution.[42]

Bolt's thesis was that the legal proprieties and standards applied in Britain itself had been totally disregarded in India. The British dominions in Asia, he contended, 'like the distant provinces during the decline of [the Roman] empire, have been abandoned, as lawful prey, to every species of peculators; insomuch that many of the servants of the Company, after exhibiting such scenes of barbarity as can scarcely be

---

[38] Smith, *Wealth of Nations*, ii. 22; Reid, 'A New Phase', 62–3; Trocki, 'Chinese Pioneering', 98–9.
[39] Habib, 'Eighteenth Century', 110.   [40] Smith, *Wealth of Nations*.
[41] Hallward, *William Bolts*, 5, 65–7, 82.   [42] Diderot, *Corr.* xiv. 196 n. 7.

paralleled in the history of any country, have returned to England loaded with wealth'.[43] 'Monopolies of all kinds are in their natures unavoidably pernicious but an absolute government of monopolists', he insisted, 'such as that of Bengal in fact is, must of all be the most dreadful.'[44] If Parliament continued to permit a situation in which Company employees 'by a subversion of the rights of mankind, in the unrestrained exercise of every species of violence and injustice, are thus suffered to monopolize, not only the manufactures but the manufacturers of Bengal', it was plain the 'consequences cannot prove other than beggary and ruin to those provinces'.[45]

Bolts's proofs that the 'true principles of British law and the constitution were not being observed' helped unleash a tremendous debate, some, particularly abroad, denouncing British misconduct in India as such, others discrediting the Company with a view to seeing it replaced with something better. Edmund Burke, who was of Irish birth and fiercely critical of how Ireland was being misgoverned in the interests of a tiny minority, at the majority's expense, waxed particularly indignant at the deficiencies of the sway Britain was imposing on India but essentially on the ground the charter conceded by Parliament was being subverted. Much preoccupied from the late 1770s with what seemed to him a political and moral disgrace, an 'absolute Conquest putting an end to all Laws, Rights and Privileges', he proved relentless in denouncing the new order in India but based his criticism entirely on Parliament's lax supervision of the East India Company's charter.[46] The Company, he urged in Parliament, in 1783, had systematically violated every article of the charter Parliament had bestowed when entrusting India's government into its hands. With British rule as such or the legality of Parliament laying down a charter by which the Company should administer India, Burke had no complaint. What was unacceptable was the lack of integrity, proper standards, and conformity to the principles of British law that had prevailed hitherto, as well as the fact that honest Britons trying to investigate the Company's servants' misdeeds in India had been uniformly decried, discredited, and 'ruined'. 'If the city of London had the means and will of destroying an empire, and of cruelly oppressing and tyrannizing over millions of men as good as themselves, the charter of the city of London should prove no sanction to such tyranny and such oppression. Charters are kept, when their purposes are maintained: they are violated, when the privilege is supported against its end and its object.'[47]

As the 1780s progressed, Burke became ever gloomier about the state of India and even suggested on occasion that if the British were unable to govern the country in a decent and orderly fashion they should give it up. But his position still differed from the far more fundamental critique if not of Bolts then of the *Histoire* and other radical onlookers. The *Histoire*'s scathing analysis was followed by the writings of

---

[43] Bolts, *Considerations*, 'Preface' p. v; Travers, 'Ideology', 16.
[44] Bolts, *Considerations*, 'Preface' p. vi; Abbattista, 'Empire', 484–5; Buchan, *Adam Smith*, 173 n. 56.
[45] Bolts, *Considerations*, 207.
[46] Burke, *Pre-Revolutionary Writings*, 272; Burke, *On Empire, Liberty*, 282–5.
[47] Burke, *On Empire, Liberty*, 367; Lock, *Edmund Burke*, ii. 32–8; Pitts, *Turn to Empire*, 64, 70.

Abraham-Hyacinthe Anquetil Du Perron (1731–1805), the researcher of the Parsees and first European translator of the Zend-Avesta, a deep and bitter critic of European misconduct in India. His intervention was followed by other works broadening the radical critique, including the *Lotgevallen op eene reize van Madras over Tranquebar naar het eiland Ceylon* by the Halle-born Jacob Gottfried Haafner (1755–1809), certainly the fiercest of all critics of Dutch and French as well as British colonialism writing in Dutch.[48]

An admirer of Rousseau, Haafner styled himself someone who respects 'all men of whatever colour, nation and religion they may be, as my fellow men and brothers' and a 'deadly enemy of all despotism'.[49] Believing the Hindus far outstripped in virtue the handful of whites tyrannizing over them in India, he thought them justified in scorning the Europeans morally.[50] Foe of all prejudice, superstition, and tyranny, who spent most of the 1770s working at the Dutch trading posts in Bengal, he became a free burgher at Negapatnam, in 1779, where he subsequently witnessed at first hand—and loudly denounced—the ruthless British onslaught on the last remaining Dutch enclaves in southern India when these were overrun during the Fourth Anglo-Dutch War (1780–4). As these strongholds fell, the walls of the fortresses were demolished with explosives on the pattern of the earlier demolitions of Louisbourg, in Nova Scotia, and Pondicherry.[51] After a spell as a British prisoner, Haafner travelled widely in both India and Ceylon and then lived for a time in Calcutta where he resumed studying Indian culture and history, before returning to Holland in 1787.

Vegetarianism and the refined, gentle moral outlook of Hinduism, he held, much like Anquetil Du Perron and Herder who was also inclined to regard ancient Indian culture as 'pure and lofty' as well as praise the Brahmans for the ensuring the continuity of Hindu culture, had contributed to rendering the Hindus gentle, passive, and easily exploited, enabling the Europeans in India with their prejudices, ignorance, and arrogant lust for domination to domineer to an even greater extent than they were inclined to do in any case.[52] The despotic commercial and fiscal regulations imposed by the British in Bengal had caused the growing poverty and misery of the area, argued Haafner, for these stripped the populace of their natural right to the produce of their land and to use and dispose of it as they saw fit.[53] Europeans mostly disdained Asiatics, something that lacked all justification in his eyes, being merely fruit of a false consciousness and religious bigotry. Both Protestant

---

[48] Haafner, *Reize*, i, preface pp. vii–viii.
[49] Haafner, *Onderzoek*,167–9; Haafner, *Reize*, i. 46–7 and ii. 298–9; Zonneveld, 'Echte antikoloniaal', 25–6.
[50] Haafner, *Onderzoek*, 158–60, 167.
[51] Zonneveld, 'Echte antikoloniaal', 21; Velde, 'Orientalist', 91; Schrikker, *British and Dutch*, 95–6.
[52] Haafner, *Reize*, i. 239, 350, 366–7, and ii. 162–3, 166; Anquetil Du Perron, *Législation orientale*, préface pp. 1–II; Germana, 'Herder's India', 130–1.
[53] Haafner, *Onderzoek*, 164.

and Catholic missionary activity he considered tools for subjecting native popula-tions to external control and depriving them of their resources and freedom. No other enlightener was so comprehensively scathing about the missionaries—and Christianity Protestant and Catholic, generally—not only in India, but South Africa, Surinam, China, and Japan as well.[54]

Indian culture was indeed vitiated by credulity and superstition. But these were just as deeply rooted in European society. What could be crasser than the blindness of allegedly enlightened Europeans enthusing over Swedenborg, Gassner, Cagliostro, Mesmer, and other ridiculous mystiques and irrationality of every kind?[55] What broader licence for faith-healers, charlatans, and impostors of every sort could man concoct? No radical writer stressed more than Haafner the illegitimacy and negative effect of European rule and pretensions on indigenous populations whether in Asia or the New World.[56] 'Yes, the discovery of the two Indies by the Europeans is the greatest misfortune that could have happened to these lands.'[57] For destructive impact, the British conquest of Bengal and the Carnatic, he maintained, was the eighteenth century's answer to the Spanish Conquest of Mexico and Peru. So despotic was the British Raj, he wrongly predicted, that its sway must, before long, provoke a general Hindu revolt of such massive proportions as to overthrow British rule.[58]

2. ADMINISTRATION AND LAW IN BRITISH INDIA

The most chilling instance of Company tyranny, held its critics, was the callousness of its handling of the great famine of 1769–70. This disastrous rice shortage began due to drought, away to the north-west, in Bihar. It grew steadily worse through two harvest failures, culminating in possibly the most catastrophic famine in recorded history. Whether or not, as some believed, there were really reserve rice stores in Bengal's cities locked in the Company's warehouses and ships, countless desperate refugees streamed into Calcutta, begging for help at the Company's doors where they were turned away empty-handed. Great numbers died in the streets. Country roads and the Ganges were covered with corpses; lurid reports reached Europe, speaking of hordes of dogs, pigs, vultures, and jackals devouring the dead. Even Adam Smith, usually apt to insist that 'popular fear of engrossing or forestalling may be compared to the popular terrors and suspicions of witchcraft' and highly sceptical about claims that dearth is ever caused by hoarding,[59] acknowledged that the calamity was greatly aggravated by Company mismanagement, albeit more due to incompetence than

---

[54] Haafner, *Reize*, i. 239; Haafner, *Onderzoek*, 6, 10; Zonneveld, 'Echte antikoloniaal', 28.
[55] Haafner, *Reize*, i, preface p. vii and pp. 71–2.   [56] Ibid. i. 348–9.
[57] Ibid. i. 349–50 and ii. 170–1.   [58] Haafner, *Onderzoek*, 163–5.
[59] Smith, *Wealth of Nations*, ii. 111.

rapacity. 'The drought in Bengal, a few years ago,' he commented in 1776, 'might probably have occasioned a very great dearth.' But it was 'some improper regulations, some injudicious restraints imposed by the servants of the East India Company upon the rice trade', that did most to convert 'that dearth into a famine'.[60]

The great Bengal famine of 1769–70, like the earlier Lisbon earthquake, came to the notice of all Europe and long remained a notorious catastrophe that helped propagate the radical critique of colonial rule.[61] The great achievements of the British in philosophy, science, and statecraft had evidently failed, remarked Brissot de Warville in 1777, to make them 'plus humains que leurs voisins'. How could they justify allowing such deprivation and misery, no less than three million Bengalese expiring of hunger while they themselves continued to dine well, disposing of abundant supplies?[62] The figure of three million deaths from starvation, a considerable portion of Bengal's population, reported by the *Histoire*, and afterwards Brissot and, in Dutch and German, by Haafner and Wekhrlin,[63] staggered many Europeans but was actually an underestimate. Far more, possibly ten million, actually perished. Hastings acknowledged, reporting to London in November 1772, that around a third of Bengal's inhabitants had been lost.

The scale of the mortality seemed incredible. But for the thinking person, averred the *Histoire*, the crucial questions were what led the Company's officials to be so negligent in their attitude to the starving millions and how does one explain the supine attitude of the indigenous population in the face of such callous indifference? The English were efficient enough at storing supplies adequate for their own use in magazines that no one attacked; meanwhile, they made no effort to supply the unfortunate population as the price of rice quadrupled and then reached six times its normal level.[64] Rampant corruption and oppression, and neglect of all higher moral principles, presented a 'revolting contrast' to the standards of government at home. This was something radical *philosophes* felt they could explain: 'masters without rivals in an empire where they were really just traders it was hardly likely the English would not abuse their power.'[65] Most remarkable of all, held Diderot, was the docility of the populace in the face of such arrogant insensitivity. No spontaneous fury, no attacks on the Europeans' grain stores or their houses, no assassinations or violent demonstrations. The starving simply abandoned themselves to despair, quietly awaiting death.[66] Would not the English have done more to alleviate the crisis, and not remained complacently in their well-guarded quarters, had they more reason to fear the violent protest one would expect from Europeans were bread prices to rise to such levels?[67]

[60] Smith, *Wealth of Nations*. ii. 103. [61] Arnold, 'Hunger', 87.
[62] Brissot, *Lettres philosophiques*, 28; Haafner, *Onderzoek*, 164, 228–9, 234, 236–7, 258.
[63] *Histoire philosophique* (1780), ii. 245; Wekhrlin, *Graue Ungeheuer*, 1 (1784), 300–4; Kanta Ray, 'Indian Society', 514.
[64] *Histoire philosophique* (1780), ii. 242–3; Travers, 'Ideology', 18.
[65] *Histoire philosophique* (1780), ii. 249–51; Ahmed, 'Orientalism', 169.
[66] *Histoire philosophique* (1780), ii. 245–6.
[67] Ibid. ii. 246–7; Wekhrlin, *Graue Ungeheuer*, 1 (1784), 304.

The human disaster clearly stemmed in part from the fact that political and military control lay with an organization only loosely regulated by Parliament and originally intended for commerce, a trading organization supervised by gentry who were themselves an interested party in the Company's operations. 'Of all political tyrannies', declared Bolts, 'the Aristocratic is worst, having ever been found, from experience, the most partial and oppressive. And of all aristocracies perhaps a trading one is least endurable, from being most likely to abuse power; as was frequently verified in ancient times and in later ages has been practically exemplified in Venice and Genoa.'[68] If the Company's 'trading spirit renders them very bad sovereigns, the spirit of sovereignty seems to have rendered them equally bad traders'.[69] By the 1770s, the Company, increasingly geared for war and maintaining ever larger garrisons, hovered on the verge of bankruptcy.

Smith denounced the Company as a greedy and destructive monopoly wreaking havoc on India's economy and inhabitants, an organization like the VOC that had everywhere wasted and perverted economic life in the areas under its control. Yet, in his view, like Burke's, it was not empire as such which erred but these commercial monopolies, unwise parliamentary resolutions, and outmoded and restrictive mercantilism.[70] Precisely proper imperial regulation was what could save the day. Wide-ranging changes and improvements were urgently needed as was already acknowledged by the British Parliament's Regulating Act of 1773 and India Act of 1774, bringing the Indian acquisitions to an extent under direct British government control. Burke, Smith, and many others proceeded from a deep conviction that Parliament needed to go further and ensure that the empire rested on the strengths of British law, traditions, and government.

Those justifying colonial expansion as a national asset and positive civilizing force conceived of empire as something that could powerfully stimulate economic development both at home and in Asia while providing security, orderly government, and legal stability. The 1774 India Act is sometimes held to have ended the most rapacious, chaotic phase of the 'revolution' in India. But the measures of the early 1770s did not in fact do much to curb what in 1783 Burke continued to denounce as 'an oppressive, irregular, capricious, unsteady, rapacious, and peculating despotism', emanating from charter-government over India 'without any fixed maxim, principle or rule of proceeding'.[71] The efforts afoot to correct the mistakes of the past and place the Indian administration on a more orderly footing, it was increasingly recognized, could only succeed by laying down firmer principles and training a whole new class of colonial officers and administrators with a knowledge of Indian and of local languages adequate to the scale of the task. Somehow British laws and local laws and practices had to be brought into an effective working partnership.

---

[68] Bolts, *Considerations*, 209.
[69] Smith, *Wealth of Nations*, ii. 406.
[70] Pitts, *Turn to Empire*, 55–7; Buchan, *Adam Smith*, 135; Marshall, 'Britain', 585.
[71] Burke, *Empire, Liberty*, 345; Gibbons, *Edmund Burke*, 121, 204; Metcalf, *Ideologies*, 18–19.

In 1772, Hastings issued a directive that was to have far-reaching implications for the further development of law, administration, and social structure in British India. 'In all suits regarding inheritance, marriage, caste, and other religious usages or institutions, the laws of the Koran with respect to the Mohammedans and those of the Shaster with respect to the Gentoos shall invariably be adhered to.' Hastings's edict consolidated the British policy of scrupulous non-interference in the 'personal laws' of its Indian subjects for over a century and half.[72] This crucial principle of non-interference in large areas of law, particularly surrounding religious and marriage-related matters, if sometimes rather selectively applied, meant that no comprehensive civil code, whilst this approach remained in force, could ever be envisaged or developed under colonial rule. Group, paternal, and religious rights in this way became the first-order level of law rather than individual rights and equality. Tradition, existing structures of authority, and family authority were reinforced.

The British not only needed to learn more about the Indians to rule them effectively, it seemed, but saw advantage in finding indigenous allies and winning the allegiance of learned Indians. This meant engaging seriously with Indian thought and culture, a process that in turn came to be seen as an effective means of enhancing the legitimacy of British rule. There was especially an urgent need for knowledgeable, reliable legal officials and translators in the courts. In 1781, Hastings established in Calcutta a Company-sponsored Muslim *madrasa* which soon had some forty boarding students (some hailing from as far away as Kashmir and Gujarat), and some ninety students in all, paid for by the Indian government. This was the first British-sponsored educational institution in northern India.[73] It had a head and three 'underteachers' and was undoubtedly intended to prove useful as an administrative tool, the motive for setting it up being the hope of seeing its graduates employed in the courts, though it is unclear whether any of its graduates were actually so employed in the early years.

From the early 1770s, study of Sanskrit also began to be encouraged by the colonial administration. What scope did such a framework allow for a wide-ranging reform tendency at work within the new Indian empire? The celebrated example of Sir William Jones indicates that there was some. The colonial state did eventually show some interest in developing a coherent, unified code with regard to the criminal law and an increased willingness to intervene where it was a question of what it regarded as reprehensible community mores, including those pertaining to the 'woman question' such as child marriage, *sati* (widow burning), the prohibition of widow remarriage, widow maintenance, and other issues that had never been problems in traditional Indian culture but were viewed as serious social problems by colonial administrators. But these were usually deemed necessary exceptions rather than reflecting any general strategy of the administration.[74]

---

[72] Metcalf, *Ideologies*, 25–6; Sharifi, 'Semi-autonomous Judge', 62.
[73] Cohn, *Colonialism*, 47; Gabriel, 'Learned Communities', 109.
[74] Chakrabarty, *Provincializing*, 118, 122.

By far the greatest as well as intellectually most impressive of the Enlightenment minds in British India, Jones, author of the *Grammar of the Persian Language* (1771), *Al Sirajiyyah: or, the Mohammedan Law of Inheritance* (1792), the *Institutes of Hindu Law or, The Ordinances of Menu* (1794), and *A Digest of Hindu Law* (1797), had been schooled at Harrow and early on developed a strong antipathy to tyranny, arrogance, and injustice.[75] At Oxford, during the mid 1760s, he astounded the dons with his precocity in Arabic and Persian. His preface to the *Persian Grammar* stands out for the eloquence and cogency of its plea for the study of Eastern languages and literatures. Jones was equally a defender of the value and profundity of Eastern philosophy (a cause in which he had something in common with Voltaire whom, in 1770, whilst travelling in Europe, he had once unsuccessfully attempted to visit at his lakeside retreat of Ferney).[76]

Jones arrived in India, as senior judge in Calcutta, in 1783, without any intention of learning Sanskrit to add to his Arabic and Persian. But he quickly became dissatisfied with the Company's inefficient administration and the deficiencies of the justice being administered. Although the Asiatic Society of Calcutta, which he set up in January 1784 for English savants and bibliophiles residing in the area, was initially more concerned with promoting historical, geographical, and legal studies than practical improvements, this changed as he became increasingly impatient with the failure of various schemes to translate Hindu law digests and codes into Persian and recognized the impossibility of administering justice efficiently in India using Persian alone. Anxious above all to improve the standard and efficiency of justice administration, he became convinced that there was an urgent need for British civil servants in India to learn Sanskrit and other modern Indian languages and to explore, preserve, and translate ancient Sanskrit poetry and medical, mathematical, and philosophical literature on the one hand for their intrinsic value and, on the other, as an instrument for understanding and elucidating Hindu law.

Collecting information about Indian learned men, Jones found a native scholar, Ramalocama, at Nadia, in 1785, who was not a Brahman and hence lacked the 'priestly pride, with which his [Brahmanic] pupils in general abound', and set out to master Sanskrit himself with his aid.[77] By 1787, he had not only advanced quite far in the study of Sanskrit but formulated his famous thesis of Sanskrit's close affinity with ancient Greek, Latin, and Persian, his hypothesis of a common Indo-European linguistic and ethnic ancestor stem, and conviction that ancient Indian religion and myths stood close to those of Egypt, Greece, China, and Rome.[78] He laboured tirelessly on his great plan for systematizing, translating, and explaining the essentials of Hindu law and institutions, an undertaking that culminated in his famous posthumous digest *Institutes of Hindu Law* (1794). As the British governor-general

---

[75] Cannon, *Life and Mind*, 5, 9; Ahmed, 'Orientalism', 170, 186–7.
[76] Cannon, *Life and Mind*, 26–7.
[77] Ibid. 229–31; Cohn, *Colonialism*, 28–9.
[78] Stroumsa, *New Science*, 158.

and the Court of Directors saw it, this was all part of a project to deepen and strengthen the reach of British imperial rule in India as, equally, was his work to introduce into government service scholarly Brahmans and pundits whose confidence he had won. Meanwhile, the prestige of Sanskrit and Persian and their literatures were enhanced as his view that Greek, Persian, and Sanskrit were related became increasingly influential and known.

Particularly in accord with the Company's expansionist and aggressive way of seeing its own hegemony in India was the fact that Jones's approach was useful for tying Indian society into a closer subordination to the Company. Evidently, the Hindu past was politically and culturally relevant to the present. Hastings promoted the idea that the British could win the support of the Hindu Brahmans by showing that they were far more useful to them and their authority than had been the Mughal rulers who, as devout Muslims, had been hostile to the Hindu priesthood.[79] While Hindu thought was disfigured, as Voltaire and others saw it, by a surfeit of superstition, the Brahmans had since an early date not only impressively explored astronomy and mathematics, but also penetrated to the profoundest truths of natural theology and moral philosophy, having always clearly postulated a supreme God, Creator and *conservateur* of the world, who was unquestionably a providential deity 'rémunérateur, punisseur et miséricordieux' towards men. This sustained the moral order while, at the same time, Hindu gentleness and passivity was a constant aid to imperial sway over the population. The ancient Brahmans having developed a philosophy of resignation and apathy, stressed Voltaire, this had become one of the chief causes not just of India's subjection to others but of India's generally wretched plight.[80]

As the matter appeared to Jones himself, extending the grip of the Raj was not the main aim of his Sanskrit and Hindu studies. His overriding motive, rather, was to uncover the basic principles and coherence of Hindu law which he thought of as a once-existing fixed body of codes and digests, in order to cleanse the corpus of Indian law of subsequent accretions freeing the indigenous population from (and British judges in India from dependence on) what he saw as the venality and corruption of modern Hindu and Muslim scholars, interpreters, and spokesmen. The administration of law under the British crown in India he sought to render consistent with what he thought of as 'pure' Hindu and Muslim law, providing firm guidelines so that the pandits, Brahmans, and Indian 'lawyers' could no longer deceive and 'deal out Hindoo law as they please'.[81] The effect, though, was to enlist Hindu and Islamic law to the service of the Company's administration, revenue collection, and property law, all incorporated into a new bureaucratic enlightened despotism in Asia.[82]

Jones, then, no less than Anquetil Du Perron, was remarkable for towering scholarship combined with powerful reforming inclinations. An open supporter of

---

[79] Cohn, *Colonialism*, 45; Metcalf, *Ideologies*, 9–10.

[80] Voltaire, *Philosophie de l'histoire*, 109; [Voltaire], *Fragmens*, 39–40, 140–1, 143, 148–50, 164–5, 173.

[81] [Voltaire], *Fragmens*, 30; Metcalf, *Ideologies*, 12–13, 23; Dirks, *Castes of Mind*, 34.

[82] Ahmed, 'Orientalism', 173–4, 186–8, 200; Travers, 'Imperial Revolutions', 149.

the American cause and someone praised by Richard Price as 'a zealous and decided Whig', impressive for the 'excellence of his public principles',[83] he did not doubt the British constitution required amending, in particular to lessen the monarchical and aristocratic dimensions in favour of a strengthened and more genuinely representative assembly.[84] It was never his view that there was any inherent superiority in British rule, civilization, or religion and it was his firm conviction that European hegemony in Asia was something temporary that needed to be subject to vigorous criticism and made as responsible as possible.[85] Yet, there was also a sense in which Jones's reforming inclinations were trapped within the imperial system in which he worked. The uses to which his work was put tended merely to reinforce indigenous subordination and structures of hierarchy while extending English case law for regulating the colonial elite. Brissot saw the transplanting of the British legal system to India as a tragedy because British law was not organized on the basis of fundamental principles of a kind that could have rescued Indian society from what he saw as its degradation. What was needed, in his view, was 'l'esprit philosophique', the advance of 'la raison universelle, de cette raison qui n'a pour guide qu'un ordre invariable prescrit par la nature des choses'.[86]

Others sympathized with and supported Jones at least as regards the need to understand Indian languages so as to systematize and effectively administer Indian law and institutions, and precisely such a symbiosis of British power and Hindu as well as Muslim law slowly emerged. In 1789, the orientalist Jonathan Duncan (1756–1811), resident in the Hindu centre of Banaras, later governor of Bombay and with Jones a founding member of the Asiatic Society, resolved to use a revenue surplus to found at Banaras a 'Hindoo college or academy for the preservation and cultivation of the laws, literature and religion at this center of their faith and common resort of their tribes'.[87] Duncan sought to impress the local population 'by our exceeding in our attention towards them and their systems, the care shown even by their own native princes'. Though libraries and texts were not considered a vehicle for preservation of tradition in the Hindu concept of learning, Duncan's scheme was to establish a library that would collect, preserve, and study manuscripts at the expense of the British government, though the teachers and students themselves would have to acquire and correct the necessary manuscripts to build up the library. The function of the new college of Sarasvati Bhawan was explicitly the 'preservation of Hindu law and the production of officials knowledgeable in these laws, able to assist British judges in the courts'. Established in a house near the resident's abode, the college opened in 1791. Kashinath Pandit who had compiled a Sanskrit dictionary for Jones and assisted Duncan as a pandit of the court became the first head teacher. The professors except for one were all Brahmans.

---

[83] Stuurman, 'Cosmopolitan Egalitarianism', 126.   [84] Ibid. 110–11.
[85] Ibid., p. xvii.   [86] Brissot, *Tableau*, 58.
[87] Gabriel, 'Learned Communities', 118–20; Cohn, *Colonialism*, 47–8.

The College's progress was noted with approval by the Court of Directors, in March 1792, as 'an institution founded expressly to promote the study of the laws and religion must be extremely flattering to their prejudices and lend greatly to conciliate their minds towards the British government'. But quite apart from political considerations, 'so long as we profess to govern the Hindoos by their own laws, it is essentially necessary that the study of them should be encouraged lest people should suffer through the ignorance of the expounders of them'. Top students were soon given jobs as court pandits. Significantly, it was almost exactly simultaneous with the advent of a meaningful reformism within the British Indian administration that Dutch enlightened reformism reached its peak in Ceylon. There, particularly under Governor Willem Jacob van de Graeff (governor: 1785–94), efforts similarly pivoted on creating a better relationship between administration and native population by extending regular supervision both in a geographical and administrative sense and developing and improving the administration of the law.[88]

However, such studies and the officially directed application of Hindu and Muslim law also created a formidable and growing barrier between Enlightenment values and the legal and cultural system being upheld. A strong supporter of the policy of leaving Muslim legal structures intact, for which he was later sternly rebuked by the Utilitarian writer James Mill, Jones in effect materially helped further the Company's policy of leaving indigenous family, caste, and societal law and mores essentially unchanged.[89] His reforming inclinations, being boxed within the imperial system in which he worked, created a philosophical and moral quandary that no one could overlook. Jones, Duncan, and other reformers were undoubtedly deeply troubled by aspects of the caste system, as well as the institution of child-marriage, the taboo on widows, and other traditional features of Indian society, including, of course, 'thuggery'. But the cultural mechanism they helped establish proved inherently incapable of tackling those traditional practices violating the radically enlightened principles of individual liberty, human rights, and equality.

The rift between the divergent Enlightenment blocs hence not only involved sharply contrasting views of the legitimacy and status of British, Dutch, French, and Portuguese colonial rule, but encompassed an irresolvable disagreement over the role of religion and tradition in law, and in family and gender relations in Asian societies besides the general problem of individual liberty and social hierarchy in religiously ordered societies. All shades of enlightened thought saw something disturbingly wrong in the relationship between the post-1772 British colonial administration and the Indian population proposing wide-ranging changes. But unlike its radical rival, officially sanctioned moderate Enlightenment remained vulnerable to the charge that it was justifying and protecting not just national imperial sway over Asian populations that were defenceless, powerless, and impoverished but also local social hierarchies and religious systems based on ancient tradition and notions of

---

[88] Schrikker, *British and Dutch*, 52–3, 93, 95, 100.   [89] Dirks, *Castes of Mind*, 32–3, 35.

caste. By doing so, they were protecting inherently oppressive patterns of privilege and servitude, much as in eastern Europe and Russia the systems of Montesquieu and Voltaire proved useful to local elites seeking to retain serfdom.

Jones's insistence on the profundity of ancient Indian philosophy contributed to his feud with Anquetil Du Perron over the latter's *Zend-Avesta, ouvrage de Zoroastre* (1771). Anquetil, another ardent admirer of ancient India, though critical also of French and Dutch colonialism, was implacably hostile to British sway in India. His path-breaking translation of the *Zend-Avesta* was accompanied by a long commentary that provoked Jones's ire not just by seeming to him not to do justice to Zoroaster's thought but to be marred by misplaced invective against British rule in India and unjustified disparagement of Oxford and Cambridge scholars.[90] The most learned of radically enlightened critics of the British Raj, Anquetil was also, apart from Haafner, the most hostile. A Parisian of Jansenist background who had studied Hebrew and Arabic at the Sorbonne, the surviving inventory of his library shows that he was intensely fascinated by Islam, Judaism, and all manner of fringe sects—Quakers, Moravian Brethren, and Swedenborgists—but also a reader of Spinoza, Toland, Bayle, Lahontan, Boulainvilliers, and Weishaupt. By the early 1780s, he was also a declared foe of the French nobility. He later became a zealous supporter of the Revolution.[91]

Intoxicated as a young scholar with the dream of uncovering the philosophical foundation of ancient Persia, Anquetil at the age of 23, in 1754, set out for India resolved to acquire ancient Persian and Sanskrit. After arriving by sea at Pondicherry, in 1755, he spent three years working his way overland across the sub-continent to Surat. After painstakingly studying for a further three with the Zoroastian scholar Dastur Sorabjee Kumana (d. 1773), he felt up to the immense task of translating the Zend-Avesta while turning his attention also to the ancient Indian Vedic texts. Returning to Paris, in 1762, with a large cache of experience and 180 Sanskrit and Persian manuscripts that he deposited in the Bibliothèque du Roi, he finally published his translation, firmly placing Zoroaster and Zoroastrianism in Europe's consciousness, in 1771. Jones's response, his *Lettre à Monsieur A- du P-* (1771), entirely missing its importance and originality, denounced it as brazen 'imposture', a forgery couched in bombastic prose, a stance from which he subsequently refused to budge. Herder, by contrast, was immensely impressed.[92]

In France, Du Perron's writings became a key resource for the wider critique of colonialism as it was evolving in India. In his *Législation orientale* (1778) and *Historical and Geographical Research on India* (1786), Anquetil Du Perron (who also had Bolts's book in his library) further developed the existing radical critique with numerous additional insights and learned perspectives. Like the *Histoire*—and

---

[90] [Jones], *Lettre*, 24–5; Cannon, *Life and Mind*, 42–3.
[91] *Catalogue des livres de M. A. H. Anquetil-Duperron*, 27–9, 61, 120, 142, 235–6; Kieffer, *Anquetil-Duperron*, 29–31, 36–7.
[92] App, 'William Jones's', 6; Germana, 'Herder's India', 125, 131.

Herder who similarly sympathized with the Asian (and New World) victims of arrogant European marauders[93]—he sought to counter Montesquieu's powerfully influential vision of oriental despotism as innate and climatically determined, a notion permeating the ideology of the officers around Clive and Hastings and serving as an constant prop to all manner of justifications of European hegemony in the East. The *Histoire* grants that despotic government 'est malheureusement celui de toute l'Inde', but like Anquetil was extremely dubious as to whether this was something innate, as Montesquieu maintained, inherent in the spirit of Indian custom and tradition, the natural state of affairs in the Indian sub-continent. Like Diderot, he saw it rather as the outcome of a complex structure of imposture, exploitation, and oppression depriving the people of what was rightfully theirs.[94]

Contemporary India excited among the radical *philosophes* a bitter-sweet mixture of compassion and contempt, of fascination tinged with growing disdain. On the one hand, the remarkable legacy of ancient India was emerging from obscurity, India being recognized as the very birthplace of civilization, or at least one of its main original sources. Among Anquetil's crucial contributions was his clear demonstration, using translations of Mughal legal documents, that Indian society and princely authority, both Muslim and Hindu, was not just based on the rule of law but a complex legacy of legal principles and regulation by courts that had degenerated over time and was now being extensively flouted, even, he maintained, completely dismantled by the princes and especially by the British.[95] It was princely rule and the particular structure of despotism in India that had rendered European control inevitable, in Anquetil's view, echoing Boulanger and d'Holbach in the *Recherches sur l'origine du despotisme oriental*. Repeatedly attacking Montesquieu, he saw the current situation as the culmination of a long process of deteriorating circumstances for most of the people.[96] Like the materialists, he saw this process as something driven by the totality of nature and subject to laws that nature obeys 'invariablement'. The entire physical world 'nous présente une suite de révolutions qui dépendent d'un ordre constant'.[97] Montesquieu's vision of a lawless realm of absolute despotism in reality existed nowhere in Asia, in fact was a complete literary fantasy. In every land, men conduct their affairs under law and specifically their own laws. Study of the history, culture, revelations, and languages of Asia by Europeans, he concluded, is no mere academic speciality but something offering perspectives essential to any basic study of man and especially for grounding the essential rights of man, or as Anquetil, rediscoverer of Zoroastrianism as a noble form of monotheism, expressed it, 'et surtout à assurer les droits imprescriptibles de l'humanité'.[98]

---

[93] Germana, 'Herder's India', 127–8.
[94] *Histoire philosophique* (1770), i. 336; Abbattista, 'Empire', 486; Stuurman, *Uitvinding*, 306–7.
[95] Stuurman, 'Cosmopolitan Egalitarianism', 268–9; Pagden, 'Immobility', 56.
[96] Anquetil Du Perron, *Zend-Avesta*, i, 'Discours préliminaire' pp. cxvii–cxix; Anquetil Du Perron, *Législation orientale*, 1–5, 9–10, 13, 43, 186.
[97] Anquetil Du Perron, *Législation orientale*, p. vii; Stuurman, *Uitvinding*, 306–7; Stroumsa, *New Science*, 101–2.
[98] Anquetil Du Perron, *Législation orientale*, 180–1; App, *Orientalism*, 365.

Had the 'revolution' in India been positive for society, averred the radical enlighteners who composed the *Histoire philosophique*'s first version, in 1770, claiming to be *philosophes* who sought the good of the entire human race and to be indifferent to national quarrels and national advantage, they would have disregarded the use of military and naval force, usurpations, and deceptions with which the British gained their ascendancy and gladly focused only on the desirable effects of their rule and the changes they introduced. But how could any objective observer deny that the outcome, however lucrative for the Company and its senior officers, had been totally disastrous for India's people?[99] The British empire was not the main enemy of humanity but it presented a formidable obstacle. 'Cette puissance orgueilleuse', as Cerisier expressed it in 1778, intent on securing a 'universal monarchy' over the commerce, navigation, and seas of the world, had, as part of this scheme, established 'un despotisme si révoltant' in 'Hindustan' that they committed there more cruelties 'que les espagnols dans le Nouveau monde'.[100]

But why were the people so readily tyrannized over? If there is anywhere on the face of the globe where men should be equal, proposed Helvétius's disciple Delisle de Sales, it should be the fertile lands of northern India watered by the Ganges and Indus. For there the rice that nourishes men and the cotton that clothes them spring from the ground with hardly any effort. Yet, precisely here, he intoned, echoing the *Histoire*, oppression and inequality prevail most and not just owing to foreign domination. It was due above all to the princes and caste system of India where the people since time immemorial are victims of superstition and thoroughly divided into a 'multitude de castes'.[101]

While Radical Enlightenment exhorted respect for the Indians as men and, like the mainstream, sought to elevate the dignity of Indian civilization and achievement in the past, it simultaneously sought an explanation for the abject subservience of modern Indian society not only or primarily to British oppression, but still more in the country's cultural, social, and intellectual traditions. This further widened the gap between the alleged greatness of ancient India and miserable condition of contemporary Indian society. What a difference, exclaimed Helvétius, in 1772, between present-day India and that India once renowned and cited as the cradle of the arts and sciences.[102] The scorn in which present-day Indian society was held in Europe was a proof, he suggested, of the contempt in which every and any society comes to be held if it succumbs, as the Indians had, to credulity, self-abnegation, indolence, and indifference to reputation and renown.

Yet, stressing credulity implied the seeds of modern India's degradation were to be found in the distant past, that there were features to be deplored in ancient India too, and especially Hindu proliferation of sects and the Brahmans' love of meaningless 'metaphysics' and grip over the people's religious imagination.[103] The quintessential

---

[99] *Histoire philosophique* (1770), i. 358.   [100] Cerisier, *Observations impartiales* (Kn. 19191), 47.
[101] Delisle de Sales, *Philosophie de la nature*, vi. 237.   [102] Helvétius, *De l'homme*, ii. 802.
[103] *Histoire philosophique* (1770), i. 32–4, 40.

flaw, held Delisle, was ignorance laying a basis for absurd beliefs that could then be utilized to buttress the most insidious social hierarchies. As nature and good fortune had blessed India with great fertility, and the ease with which India's climate, soil, and resources supply all men's needs, the philosopher needs to discover the source of the 'barbarous inequality' that had eventually over time concentrated all wealth, privilege, and power in a tiny segment of society leaving poverty, infamy, and wretchedness the portion of the uncomprehending majority. 'Quelle est la cause de cet étrange délire?' The answer is identical to that perpetuating the misfortune of all peoples on earth, held the *Histoire*—error allied to superstition underpinning a totally perverse moral and hence also social and political order. This was the key to understanding the miserable state of the human condition and how the shackles of general servitude that everywhere characterized Man's condition were kept in place, sustaining an edifice of oppression and misery that only 'philosophy' is powerful enough to overthrow.

One particular caste invented by the 'fanaticism' of the Brahmans, held Delisle, especially deserved to be 'vengée par les philosophes': that of the Pariahs. That ancient ruler of Hindostan under whom Indian society's division into castes began, being urged to divide society by his priests, published an edict forbidding consumption of cow's meat under the severest penalties. Those who refused to obey, explains Delisle, citing footnotes in Anquetil Du Perron's edition of the *Zend-Vesta*, were then proclaimed abominable and untouchable.[104] It was the descendants of these 'untouchables' who formed the caste of Pariahs in his day. Those unfortunate enough to be born into this caste are given all the vilest and lowest tasks, such as cleaning latrines and burying the dead. If an untouchable even touches a member of another caste, the latter has the right to kill him or her on the spot.

Degradation rooted in superstition, however, extended much further. The 'Pulchies' of Malabar, he adds, echoing the *Histoire*, suffer degradation still more insulting to human reason than that afflicting the Pariahs.[105] Custom and law forbid them huts on the ground so that they must live in large nests constructed in trees. Europeans, he notes, sometimes become indignant on seeing such vile indignity heaped on humans born under the same sky as others, with the same bodily organs and intelligence. Catholic apologists suggest the Indian caste system, like Egyptian animal-worship and inter-communal strife between Sunni and Shia Muslims, proves there is nothing especially divisive about Christianity.[106] But have Europeans any right to portray themselves in a favourable light while pouring scorn on the caste-obsessed oppressors of the Pariahs and 'Pulchies'? Europe has always trodden the black race under. Spain has long been devoted to religious persecution. From the Vatican's dark, superstitious entrails have crept a thousand sinister conspiracies against groups of all sorts—Albigensians, Vaudois, Protestants, Jews, and, of course, the *philosophes*.

---

[104] Delisle de Sales, *Philosophie de la nature*, vi. 238; Kieffer, *Anquetil-Duperron*, 259.
[105] *Histoire philosophique* (1770), i. 34; Delisle de Sales, *Philosophie de la nature*, vi. 238.
[106] Bergier, *Apologie*, ii. 136–7.

By the 1780s, the message of critics such as Diderot, Deleyre, Bolts, Delisle, Haafner, Anquetil, Démeunier, and Brissot, recycled through the *Histoire* and other radical texts, had become integral to the emerging democratic revolutionary ideology of the day. Ruthless rivalry between European powers had not only made conflict and war overseas inevitable but brought indigenous populations under a brutal, alien sway.[107] Who could have imagined, asks Diderot in the *Histoire*, that British rule in Bengal would prove so oppressive that the inhabitants would actually look back with regret and nostalgia on the pre-1757 'despotisme de leurs anciens maîtres'?[108] India, held Diderot, was a land where 'le despotisme et le fanatisme' had long prevailed but where conditions for the common people had now drastically deteriorated. When Lord Clive returned from India weighed down with gold and his 'crimes' no one supposed the wretched Indians would ever regret his departure; but they did. The subsequent trial of Warren Hastings, commented Mirabeau, proved the 'barbarian' Clive was less adept in the arts of rapacity and tyranny than his pitiless successors. Under these, extortion reached such a pitch of refinement as to dwarf everything previously seen.[109]

The full-blown critique of British power in India not only became a central strand of the Radical Enlightenment but had an impact also on some later Enlightenment thinkers less willing to accept the basic premises and wider conclusions of radical thought. 'Under pretext of establishing factories in Hindostan, affirmed Kant, in 1795, all the 'commercial nations of Europe' and not only the British, had 'carried thither foreign troops, and by their means oppressed the natives, excited wars among the different states of that vast country; spread famine, rebellion, perfidy, and the whole deluge of evils that afflict mankind, among them'.[110] It was the rivalry of the European nations and absence of a proper rule of law that had wreaked the havoc. Chiefly at fault, it seemed to him, was the whole system of 'armed trade', the entire structure of European diplomacy, competition, and warfare.

In Britain too reaction to excesses, linked to the impact of the *Histoire* and Bolts, was vigorous and forceful. It developed for a time into one of the first stirrings of modern humanitarianism to be organized as a distinct pressure-group in the public sphere.[111] To an extent literate public opinion in this instance was prodded by the Radical Enlightenment into sharpening its own social and moral awareness. But the essential question remained: was the moral and political disorder in India simply a question of the Company failing to meet standards set by Parliament and British law or was the colonial system itself reprehensible?

For years, Burke laboured, tirelessly reiterating his impassioned plea for Parliament to do more 'for the redress of these abuses' in India. The 'moderate' critique

---

[107] Anquetil-Duperron, *Zend-Avesta*, i, 'Discours préliminaire' pp. cxiv–cxv.
[108] *Histoire philosophique* (1770), i. 89–90; Rebejkow, 'Notes', 475; Abbattista, 'Empire', 486–7, 494.
[109] Mirabeau, *Aux Bataves*, 188.
[110] Kant, *Perpetual Peace*, 72–3; Muthu, *Enlightenment*, 196.
[111] Irvine, 'Abbé Raynal', 565–6.

lost all momentum, however, during the protracted and controversial trial for corruption between 1788 and 1795 of India's first governor-general, Warren Hastings. A major national spectacle to begin with, by the early 1790s the British public, increasingly absorbed in the struggle with France, had lost all appetite for pursuing misdemeanours by high officers in Asia and forgotten former worries. Shelving its temporary apprehensions about colonial rule, it became steadily more self-congratulatory about its power in India.[112] In the years around 1790, strikingly, in India as elsewhere moderate mainstream Enlightenment everywhere crumbled away as a viable choice in politics and social theory as in philosophy. By the early 1790s, the remaining choice was between two extremes: imperial pride, apt to deploy racial and religious categories to justify new hierarchies of control, and Radical Enlightenment.

Diderot, Anquetil, Delisle, Jones, Haafner, Brissot, and all Enlightenment thought about India assumed that for the peoples of India to function as societies, or a society based on anything resembling social justice and equity, '"reason" had to prevail', as Chakrabarty expressed it, 'over all that was " irrational" and "superstitious" among its population. In their eyes the people steeped in ancient religion were as much responsible for their own misery as the princes and the colonizers.[113] Undoubtedly, they saw their "superstitious" contemporaries in India as examples of an earlier type, as human examples of the principle of anachronism.'[114] Yet, we should remember also that they envisaged the progress of reason as embedded in and growing out of Indian religions, philosophy, and law no less than the culture of Europe and tried to theorize a reality in which what India and Europe shared ultimately mattered more than what was different between them. They were the first in the West to grasp that neither philosophically nor morally could Europe justifiably claim that India was intrinsically subordinate, or that India should be subject to any religion, creed, or social vision placing Europeans in a position of superiority. They were the first to see that India and Europe are merely parts of a single reality, single humanity, and single world.[115]

Brissot predicted that the kind of legal order the British were introducing could not bring India out of the degradation into which it had sunk. India must eventually undergo a great revolution, he predicted, one that would throw off the colonial oppression Britain had, ruthlessly imposed, a revolution which in some ways he dreaded since it would, he thought, inevitably cause rivers of blood to flow. But India, he thought, in 1784 when he published his *Tableau de la situation actuelle des Anglois dans les Indes orientales* (Paris, 1784), had not yet sufficiently developed a sense of what he termed 'liberté universelle' to react fully against the mass 'd'usurpations et d'injustices' to which the people were being subjected or to grasp what kind of revolution was needed.[116]

---

[112] Marshall, 'Britain', 583–4.   [113] Imbruglia, 'Indignation', 168–9.
[114] Chakrabarty, *Provincializing*, 237–8.   [115] Ahmed, 'Orientalism', 167–8.
[116] Brissot, *Tableau*, 10–11.

22

Russia's Greeks, Poles, and Serfs

1. RUSSIA'S 'LIBERATION OF GREECE' (1769–1772)

On learning, in June 1770, that the Greeks of the Morea had risen in response to the arrival of Catherine the Great's war fleet, Voltaire, waxing positively fervent, cheerfully designated her crusade against the Ottoman Porte, in plain defiance of the facts, consummately 'philosophique'. Her troops had landed in the Peloponnese, she wrote that month, and, together with local Greek insurgents wishing to recover their liberty, seized several towns, including Calamata and, after a battle at Mistras, occupied the nearby site of ancient Sparta: 'voilà la Grèce au point de redevenir libre.' She admitted her great excitement, albeit modern Greece, she reminded him, was far from being what it had once been.[1] Her war against the Turks, he replied, 'est sans contredit la plus belle manœuvre qu'on ait fait depuis deux mille ans' and of paramount importance. He would give everything he had in the world to see her imperial majesty seated on the sultan's sofa in Constantinople. The immortal Catherine would soon turn that vile Turkish 'prison' into 'le lieu le plus délicieux de la terre'.[2]

Developing this strange politico-cultural fantasy further, over the next weeks and months, Voltaire emerged as perhaps the pre-eminent enthusiast for Greek Independence, or rather the liberation under Russian protection of greater Greece including Constantinople, of the eighteenth century. Yet in his mind this liberation was entirely detached from any wider libertarian programme, or set of values, something justified purely by Greece's ancient cultural superiority and classical splendour though fired also with a dash of crude *turcophobie* that sat awkwardly with his wider political stance and oft stated cosmopolitanism.[3] A week later, proclaiming his deistic goals, he urged Catherine to return 'aux pauvres Grecs' their ancient Jupiter, Mars, and Venus as Greece had only been great under those pagan gods. By what fatal development the Greeks had become completely stupefied after becoming Christians he did not know; but he hoped this calamity could now be reversed for all mankind's sake: 'j'espère que tout Chrétiens qu'ils sont ils ranimeront leur courage sous vos drapeaux'. Repeatedly admonishing her to wrest all Greece

---

[1] Catherine to Voltaire, 7 June 1770, in Voltaire, *Corr.* xxxvi. 237–8.
[2] Voltaire to Catherine, 4 July 1770, ibid. xxxvi. 309.
[3] Mortier, *Le Cœur*, 143.

from the Turks, Constantinople and much of Asia minor included,[4] from early on in the conflict, he began worrying that Catherine and her court were really more interested in annexing the Crimea, Moldavia, Wallachia, and other territories from the Turks and Tartars than liberating greater Greece.

Styling himself 'le vieil hermite des Alpes', Voltaire pronounced the numerous French and other commentators vehemently opposing Catherine's expansionist drive southwards profoundly mistaken. Such misguided commentators must be people devoid of any desire to learn Greek: for should Catherine take Constantinople she would doubtless establish 'une belle académie grecque'. Poets would compose a *Catheriniade*, modern Phidiases would cover Greece with her image, and the Ottoman empire's collapse would be recounted everywhere in Greek. Athens would become one of Russia's principal regional and cultural capitals, 'la langue grecque deviendrait la langue universelle'.[5] These words were penned shortly before Rousseau composed his *Considérations* on the government of Poland, recommending a strengthening of Polish national identity and urgent reforms to save that land from the Russians, and a few days after Mably completed his *Du gouvernement et des lois de Pologne* (1770), where he likewise summons the Poles to save themselves from Russian tyranny and expansionism before it was too late.

Before writing this book Mably had held a series of discussions with visiting Polish nobles, discussing how Poland could be saved from the ascendancy the Russian crown had imposed 'impérieusement', as he put it, on the Poles.[6] To do this the Polish nobility must first emancipate and reform themselves on the basis of *la philosophie*, sweeping away the old *misérables études* from their universities, their present scholasticism and theology, he believed, being 'plus dangereuses que l'ignorance'. Next they must change their constitution fundamentally, base it on universal principles, and make it more genuinely republican. Ultimately, in more favourable circumstances the reformers must emancipate the serfs and make the Poles a free people.[7] In the future, Poland should be a crowned republic with a strong assembly (without the notorious *liberum veto* enabling any individual noble to block any measure) and a very limited hereditary constitutional monarch like the doge of Venice, or Sweden's monarch during the Swedish age of liberty.[8] Many things were wrong with the British constitution in Mably's opinion but none was worse than leaving control of the use of the nation's revenues in the hands of the king.[9] France, added Mably, was encouraging the Turks to resist Catherine's aggression and would surely support Poland's resistance and renovation too. Rousseau's recipe was very different: he chiefly stressed tradition, the people's feelings, and the national factor. What above all the Poles must do is impress on every Pole an indelible sense of Polish

[4] Voltaire to Catherine, 13 July 1770, in Voltaire, *Corr*, xxxvi. 328.
[5] Voltaire to Catherine, 14 Sept. 1770, ibid. xxxvi. 441–2.
[6] Mably, *Du gouvernement et des lois*, 58.
[7] Ibid. 8–9, 30–2, 86–7, 104; Wright, *Classical Republican*, 167–8.
[8] Mably, *Du gouvernement et des lois*, 52, 57–8.
[9] Ibid. 70, 278.

identity and withdraw into themselves relying on their own agriculture to sustain their economy.[10]

Mably detested Voltaire and, apart from Jaucourt, maintained few links with the Diderot circle. 'A jealous, irascible spirit', according to Gibbon who clashed with him at a dinner in Paris in 1777, shortly after Mably returned from the only long trip he ever made outside of France—to Poland; Mably revenged himself by reviewing Gibbon's *Decline and Fall* unfavourably. But he counted as one of Europe's leading authorities alike on ancient and modern politics and hugely contributed to the emergence of a powerful non-Rousseauiste democratic republican tendency in the late eighteenth century.[11] In contrast to Rousseau, it was especially his insistence that 'philosophy', and particularly social theory, moral philosophy, and politics—which he rated far more important aspects of 'philosophy' for men than metaphysics—that distinguished his erudite republicanism.[12] Study of politics, insisted Mably, has a deadly serious purpose, namely to work 'efficacement au Bonheur de la société', which in turn is possible only by first discovering the 'principes fondamentaux de la politique' which in turn requires close study of ancient Greek politics and philosophy.[13] He agreed with Helvétius and d'Holbach that the quest for happiness individual and collective underlies both moral and political philosophy but criticized their moral thought as altogether too libertarian and lax. There is no easier way for a prince to corrupt his people, he agreed with Rousseau (while harshly criticizing his rejection of 'philosophy', erudition, and reason), than foment ease, luxury, pleasures while *la mollesse*; poverty and a simple, austere morality are what buttress a successful democratic republic.[14] Hence, a strong civic cult, Mably also agreed with Rousseau, is essential for a viable republic, excessive toleration and indifferentism, and prevalence of deism, being altogether detrimental. Radical in most respects, Mably diverged from the radical view of toleration and freedom of conscience.[15]

Catherine was the third figure beside Frederick and Joseph at the centre of the Enlightenment debate about 'enlightened despotism'. Among her foremost contributions to the Enlightenment was her conscious effort over many years not just to engage closely with French philosophy and literature but to encourage their propagation, and that of the French language itself, among the Russian nobility. From early on in her reign she took care to ensure the prompt translation, publication, and diffusion in Russian (and at Petersburg and in the Baltic provinces, in German) of many key Enlightenment works and added to this diffusion by personally translating Marmontel's *Bélisaire*. At one stage, she actively planned the translation and publication of Diderot's *Encyclopédie* in its entirety.[16] Regarding the sincerity of her

---

[10] Wright, *Classical Republican*, 170–1; Trousson, *Jean-Jacques Rousseau*, 700–2; Dent, *Rousseau*, 174–9.
[11] Gibbon, *Autobiographies*, 314–15.
[12] Mably, *Phocion*, pp. xxii, 9.
[13] Ibid., pp. xxiii, 14–15, 36.
[14] Ibid.; Mably, *Du gouvernement et des lois*, 65–6, 72–3.
[15] Mably, *Collection*, viii. 407.
[16] Clardy, *Philosophical Ideas*, 12, 16–17; Tsapina, 'Secularization', 339.

commitment to a moderate-style Enlightenment, especially the Enlightenment of her heroes Montesquieu and Voltaire, there can be little doubt; but neither can there be any doubt as to her implacable opposition to the Enlightenment's radical goals.

A common error in perceptions of Catherine is to suppose she was enlightened in the early part of her reign, retreated after the great Pugachev rebellion of 1773, and then repudiated the Enlightenment altogether after 1789. Actually, there was much more consistency in her approach, and that of those close to her, than this schema would suggest. Her close confidante, the Princess Ekatarina Dashkova (1743–1810), with whom she was intimate even before becoming empress, had closely studied Bayle, Montesquieu, Voltaire, the *Encyclopédie*, and Helvétius in her youth. Residing abroad during the 1770s, Dashkova met Voltaire and, in 1770, Raynal, and became acquainted with Diderot who, for a time, conversed with her regularly, in Paris.[17] Her brother Alexander Vorontsov (1741–1805), president of the Petersburg College of Commerce from 1773 to 1793 and subsequently imperial chancellor under Tsar Alexander I, himself a prominent representative of the Russian Enlightenment, studied in Paris for seven years as a youth in the 1760s and knew the *philosophes'* writings intimately. As a diplomat, in London and at The Hague, he corresponded occasionally with Voltaire. From the outset, though, there was an inherent tension between this officially encouraged court Enlightenment, promoting the cult of enlightened despotism and imperial expansion, and the incipient radical tendency, French and Russian, which Catherine, Dashkova, and Vorontsov all came to repudiate in emphatic terms. Already, early on, Dashkova grasped that Helvétius's *De l'esprit* which she read soon after its publication could have serious destabilizing effects in a country like Russia.[18]

In the eyes of the enlightened in France, Germany, and eastern Europe, Catherine stood for a particular kind of Enlightenment, one that represented more than just a eulogy of enlightened despotism. Hers was a political and cultural programme powerfully promoting autocracy and expansionism, both military and colonial, as well as aristocracy (and, eventually, by implication, retention of serfdom). It was a conception Voltaire espoused avidly and—publicly at least—without qualification. 'We are the lay missionaries', he wrote to the empress, in November 1773, 'who preach the cult of Saint Catherine, and can boast that our church is quite universal.'[19] Although he never visited Russia in person and was mildly jealous of Diderot's proximity to the empress in 1773–4, no other *philosophe* remained in such a close relationship as Voltaire to the Russian sovereign over so many years. If he supported, indeed in Russia was accused by some of influencing, her ecclesiastical policy and tolerationist programme, he unreservedly endorsed her conception of 'enlightened despotism', sanctioned her militarism and expansionism, and positively encouraged her massive onslaught on the Ottoman empire known to history as the First Russo-Turkish War (1768–74). Indeed, his backing for her flagrant aggression against the Turks, and especially the plan of her favourite, Count Orlov, who since 1763 had

---

[17] Versini, 'Diderot', 236.   [18] Dashkova, *Mon histoire*, 151–6.
[19] Wolff, *Inventing Eastern Europe*, 232; Dixon, 'Proveshchenie', 236.

dreamt of transforming greater Greece into a reborn independent nation under Russia's protection, is altogether remarkable as the expression of a particular kind of enlightened vision, not least for its complete disregard for the consequences of Russian expansionism in eastern Europe and the Near East. Voltaire dreamt of liberating greater Greece from the Turks, as a path to reviving the creativity and liberty of ancient Greece.[20] It was a commitment that placed the whole package of his socio-cultural ideals in a curiously blinkered, unrealistic light.

In 1764, the election to the Polish throne following the death of August III, rigged by the pro-Russian faction among the Polish nobility, led to the crowning of a Pole, Stanislaw Augustus Poniatowski (1732–98), a former lover of Catherine's, who was expected to be a pliant Russian puppet. Poniatowski, last king (1764–95) of Poland and one of the most remarkable in modern times, roundly praised by Voltaire as an 'homme éclairé' who strove valiantly to solve Poland's chronic problems, was in fact chief promoter of the Polish Enlightenment (albeit he too approved only of an aristocratic Enlightenment, as recommended by Montesquieu), and the initiator of a programme of political reforms, overseen by his chancellor, Andrzej Zamoyski.[21] It was not hard to see how Poland embodied the very antithesis of enlightened values for Voltaire and many other enlighteners, being a land seething with more religious tensions and with a more dominant Catholic Church and nobility, as well as subject peasantry, than probably anywhere else in Europe. Unlike nearly all the rest of Europe, Poland was still a land of witchcraft trials and formal accusations of Jewish ritual murder in the late eighteenth century. Poniatowski, who actively intervened trying to convince his compatriots that the Jews did not murder Christian children or use Christian blood for ritual purposes, and many other Polish enlighteners themselves, regarded their country as exceptionally unenlightened.[22]

Despite turning out to have a mind of his own, Poniatowski faced unrelenting opposition in the Polish parliament, the Sejm, from several bishops indignant over plans to prune back ecclesiastical power, elements of the *szlachta* seeking to keep the aristocracy's monopoly of political rights intact, the Radziwills in Lithuania, and numerous others. From 1767, the country slid into anarchy and civil war in which at local and national level religious differences played a large part. Russia intervened on the pretext of protecting Orthodox and Lutheran towns and localities, as did Prussia. Russian troops arrived to 'prevent civil war' and help restore order in some of the eastern provinces, at which point Voltaire, assisting both Catherine's and Frederick's policies, and the cause of toleration as he saw it, himself intervened with a remarkable 54-page, anonymously published political pamphlet, the *Essai historique et critique sur les dissensions des églises de Pologne* (1767), a tract fiercely critical of both Polish Catholicism and the aristocratic republic, warmly praising Catherine and the Russian troops. The Polish Catholic episcopate, led by the bishop of Cracow and the Jesuits, were chiefly responsible, held Voltaire, for the opposition to King

---

[20] Batalden, *Catherine II's Greek*, 24–5.   [21] Voltaire, *Essai historique*, 44.
[22] Ibid. 48–50; Davies, *God's Playground*, i. 518–19; Butterwick, 'Provincial Preachers', 210.

Stanislaw. They were also chiefly responsible for Poland's miserable condition generally. Not content with persecuting the 'Greeks' (i.e. Orthodox) and Lutherans, the Polish Church constantly persecuted the Reformed and Unitarians as well, indeed actively promoted Catholic intolerance! 'Le *contrains-les d'entrer,* fut employé dans toute sa rigueur.'[23] But whatever else the Russian intervention did, it did little to advance what Voltaire called 'le système de la tolérance': in 1768, the Orthodox peasantry and Cossacks of the south-east rose in revolt, according to some reports, massacring as many as 200,000 Polish Catholics and Jews.

Poland's seemingly hopeless chaos provided a perfect pretext for further intervention. Maria Theresa and especially Frederick, the chief instigator of the partition, profiting from the fact that relatively few Russian troops were available for use in Poland, urged his proposal for a joint Austro-Russian-Prussian hiving off of territory and this was agreed in 1771 (and implemented the following year), becoming known to history as the First Partition of Poland. The Polish commonwealth lost over a quarter of its former territory, nearly half of this annexed by Russia, notably the Belorussian provinces of Polotsk, Vitebsk, Homel, and Mscislaw. The country's remaining population of around ten million (under half of which was Polish-speaking), remained as deeply divided as ever, though, between its four irreconcilable major religious blocs—Catholic, Orthodox, Lutheran, and Jewish. No enthusiast for any church, Voltaire could not resist emphasizing every merit of the 'Greek' Church over that of Rome. He stressed the doctrinal primacy of the Greek Church, that all four Gospels were originally composed in Greek, that the original terminology of Christian theology is Greek, that all significant Church Fathers in the first four centuries were Greek. Nothing, in short, could be more absurd than Rome's claims to primacy over the Greek Church and nothing more tyrannical than the Catholic Church in Poland. Besides its other points of superiority for Voltaire, the Greek Church, unlike that of Rome, never challenges the secular authority's political supremacy and never troubled the Byzantine emperors. The Greek Church had always remained responsibly subordinate to the state. In the vast Russian empire, the Greek Church was 'entièrement dépendante du pouvoir suprême'.[24]

Mably and Voltaire could not have disagreed more about the significance of Catherine's ambitions for humanity and the world, or over Poland-Lithuania and Greece. Mably supported the Confederation of Bar against the Russians, Prussians, Greeks, and Voltaire; Voltaire constantly urged Catherine not to abandon 'ces braves Spartiates' while simultaneously countering Polish Catholic pretensions, informing her in October 1770 that d'Alembert was with him at Ferney and that together they spent their entire time contemplating Greece's forthcoming liberation and loudly execrating the sultan. 'Les Grecs, les Spartiates, ont bien dégénéré', answered Catherine, seeking to sober him a little; it seemed they preferred rapine to 'la liberté'. For several years more the Russo-Turkish conflict dragged on, though it soon emerged

---

[23] Voltaire, *Essai historique*, 25, 44, 48; Batalden, *Catherine II's Greek*, 16; Wright, *Classical Republican*, 165.
[24] Voltaire, *Essai historique*, 6–7, 17–18.

that for all their gains elsewhere, the Russians would lose their footholds in Greece. By the summer of 1771, a distraught Voltaire lamented the prospect that Catherine, after overrunning 'cette Chersonese Taurique [i.e. the Crimea]', might terminate the war without 'liberating' Greece. What will happen, he asked in July 1771, should the Turks regain mastery of 'ma pauvre Grèce'? What will be the fate of the beautiful land of Demosthenes and Sophocles? He would willingly sacrifice Jerusalem to the Muslims; 'ces barbares' are made for the land of Ezekiel. But should the theatre at Athens again become a Turkish kitchen-garden and the Lyceum an Ottoman stable he would grieve infinitely.[25]

Voltaire persisted in dreaming of the rebirth of a greater Greece under Russian tutelage and so did some among the enlightened Petersburg noble elite. It was during the summer of 1771 that the future first major figure of the Russian Radical Enlightenment, Alexander Radishchev (1749–1802), then a 22-year-old student from a wealthy landowning family, studying together with a group of other young Russian noblemen under Catherine's patronage at the university in Leipzig where he had been resident since 1766 (remaining until 1771), but in touch with Russian diplomats in Germany and deeply exhilarated by the news from Greece, translated the pamphlet *Voti dei greci all'Europa Christiana*, a plea for international assistance for the Greek cause and support for Russian intervention, by Prince Anton Ghikas, an Albanian officer on the staff of Count Orlov's brother.[26] If there was scant support in Germany, Austria, or France for Greece's liberation under Catherine's auspices, and Voltaire's enthusiasm remained altogether exceptional, there were certainly Russians, Greeks, and others in south-eastern Europe thrilled by the prospect.

Had Greece, which only seems to know how to recite prayers, acted with courage and vigour, replied Catherine to Voltaire, the Athenian theatre would no longer be a Turkish kitchen-garden nor the Lyceum a stable.[27] But the Greeks had proven incapable of seizing the opportunity. Deeply saddened by the collapse of the Greek revolt, Voltaire nevertheless remained firmly behind Catherine's expansionism in Poland-Lithuania, an aristocratic republic to which he was totally unsympathetic, and the Crimea as well as in the Balkans. In his mind, the mere fact that Catherine claimed to be championing religious toleration and restoring order when claiming protective rights over the Orthodox in Poland and the Balkans, and that she and Frederick were invading a land characterized by bigotry, intolerance, and an all-powerful Church, settled all doubts. This alone, it seemed to him, sufficed to justify her annexing vast stretches of Polish territory and subjecting the rest to a more overweening Russian ascendancy than before.[28]

A year later with the war still in progress but with the Turks back in control of the Peloponnese, Voltaire for the second time reproached Catherine for seeking territory

[25] Voltaire to Catherine, 30 July 1771, in Voltaire, *Corr.* xxxviii. 39; Menant, 'Relations', 214.
[26] McConnell, *Russian Philosophe*, 37–8; Batalden, *Catherine II's Greek*, 18.
[27] Catherine to Voltaire, 25 Aug. 1771, in Voltaire, *Corr.* xxviii. 59.
[28] Gay, *Voltaire's Politics*, 178; Wright, *Classical Republican*, 164–6; Bianchi, *Révoltes aux révolutions*, 133.

in Poland and elsewhere while abandoning her and his dream of making a triumphal tour from Constantinople to Athens 'comme je l'espérais'.[29] He reproached Frederick too for urging the empress to settle with the Ottomans and focus on Poland instead of helping expel 'ces vilains Turcs' from the Bosporus, 'ces ennemis des beaux arts, ces éteigneurs de la belle Grèce'. That Catherine would one day rule over Greece, with Prussia's acquiescence, Voltaire had still not altogether abandoned hope of seeing. Soon she should vigorously renew her war against the Ottomans, he urged Catherine, in February 1773, and this time take Constantinople. Skilled at partitioning territory, he added, alluding to the recent First Partition of Poland (to which he had no objection), she should soon magnificently partition the Turkish empire and finally stage 'l'*Oedipe* de Sophocle dans l'Athènes'.[30]

Among numerous Enlightenment translations appearing at Petersburg, during the war, another remarkable item rendered by Radishchev and this time published by the Petersburg Academy of Sciences after his return to Russia was a key work by Mably. After nearly five years of higher study in Germany, where he along with several other young Russian nobles had become fervent enlighteners, Radishchev in the years 1771–2 had translated Mably's *Observations sur les Grecs* (1749), in its Genevan edition of 1766.[31] The timing and nature of this project clearly had a particular significance. In this work, Mably not only declares revulsion against monarchy and the rise of the republican spirit to be what made Greece great, but plainly implies that only such a 'revolution' can free men from subjection, supine decadence, and lack of public spirit.[32] While it fitted with the mood of euphoria about Greece Catherine sought to foment, Radishchev's fascination for ancient Greece echoing of Mably's exaltation of the ancient Greek republics and democracy was entirely at cross-purposes with Catherine's intentions. Catherine was willing enough simultaneously to stir memories of ancient Greece in enlightened circles while chiefly appealing to the religious fervour of present-day Russians, Greeks, and Ukrainian Orthodox; but it was hardly her goal to exalt republics. Mably by contrast was the first eighteenth-century *philosophe* plainly to affirm that 'revolution' toppling monarchy in favour of republics is the way to free men generally albeit doing so while continually evoking ancient Greece. As he saw it, if the Poles or anyone else wanted to achieve 'great things' in the modern age they must always have the ancient Greek republics in mind. During the early part of her reign and especially during her first war with the Turks, the empress made a point of posing as the rescuer of Greek Orthodoxy and the Greek Church, and it was her support for Orthodoxy that she now chiefly wished to advertise publicly, as this also justified her political and military expansionism in south-eastern Europe and the Near East.[33]

[29] Voltaire to Catherine, 1 Aug. 1772, in Voltaire, *Corr.* xxxix. 12.
[30] Voltaire to Catherine, 13 Feb. 1773, ibid. xxxix. 298.
[31] Thaler, 'Introduction', 6; Madariaga, *Catherine*, 192.
[32] Mably, *Observations*, 11–12, 52–3; Mably, *Du gouvernement et des lois*, 179.
[33] Catherine to Voltaire, 31 May 1770, in Voltaire, *Corr.* xxxvi. 221; Voltaire to Catherine, 4 July 1770, ibid. 309; Venturi, 'Première Crise', 13–14.

Her church policy consciously reaffirmed the Greek origins and traditions of the Russian Orthodox Church, leading to her actively recruiting several Greek scholars and ecclesiastics to serve her in Russia. Support for Orthodoxy in a variety of contexts was part of the price she paid for Church acquiescence in her initial seizure of power, having come to the throne against the background of her husband's murder in circumstances of all too dubious legitimacy. Accordingly, she deliberately surrounded her accession with a show of piety, the Manifesto announcing her assumption of the crown proclaiming defence of Orthodoxy the chief motivation of her *coup d'état*. Equally, she explained her war against the Turks in terms of freeing the Orthodox.[34] If these claims stretched the truth somewhat, her preference for Orthodoxy as against Catholicism (and dislike of Catholic influence in the Ukraine and the Polish borderlands) was real enough. Several (highly illiberal) actions at the start of her reign, such as her confirming the expulsion of the Jews from within the then boundaries of the Russian empire, ordered by the Empress Elizabeth in 1742–3, a measure strongly supported by the Church but untypical of her statecraft more broadly, fitted with this 'Greek' dimension of her imperial strategy.

A crucial link between Russia and the Greek world of the Balkans, we have seen, was Eugenios Voulgaris (1716–1806) who arrived in Petersburg in 1771, as Catherine's librarian and adviser on Greek affairs.[35] He had already intervened in the struggle for Greece under Russian patronage by translating Voltaire's 1767 pamphlet on the 'justice' of Russian intervention in Poland in defence of Orthodoxy into Greek, and publishing it at Leipzig, in 1768, and greatly rejoiced that 'poor suffering Greece' would now revive from the 'heavy yoke' of bondage that had almost destroyed his countrymen's hopes.[36] Fervent admirer of Locke, Newton, and Leibniz, and half ally and half foe of Voltaire whose conception of toleration he could only partly stomach, Voulgaris was both the senior Greek ecclesiastic and foremost Greek enlightener in the Russian empire and, at the same time, an enthusiast for autocracy and empire, the political model in his view best fitting Greek, Russian, and all truly Christian Enlightenment. Voulgaris typified the pre-1790 Greek enlightenment embodying its close synthesis of Greek Orthodoxy with (moderate) enlightened thought.[37] Given the struggle then still in progress in Greece, one might suppose Voulgaris and Radishchev converged in a common zeal for the Greek past and ardour for reviving it, but actually the struggle, for Radishchev, nurtured on Mably, and employed now in a government department dealing with legal issues, including serfdom, meant something completely different than for Voulgaris—as did the Greek past generally and its lessons for Russia. But it was Voulgaris who in his Greek publications supported Catherine's autocracy and expansionism including

---

[34] Pipes, 'Catherine II', 5; Kitromilides, *Orthodox Commonwealth*, essay vi, 11–13.
[35] Henderson, *Revival*, 73–4; Tsapina, 'Secularization', 339; Israel, *Enlightenment Contested*, 322–5.
[36] Batalden, *Catherine II's Greek*, 16–18, 22; Henderson, *Revival*, 69–71.
[37] Kitromilides, 'Enlightenment', 42–3.

(even if in an ambivalent fashion) her toleration policy.[38] From the standpoint of Voulgaris and the Orthodox, and also that of Voltaire—but hardly Mably or Radishchev—something of permanent value was retrieved from the failed offensive in greater Greece. Under the treaty of Kutchuk Kainardji (1774), restoring peace, the Russian ruler secured a vague protectorate over all the Orthodox in the Ottoman empire.[39]

A fiercely republican document, Mably's text celebrates the general revolt against 'monarchy', in favour of democracy and republics, in fifth-century Greece as a great and fundamental 'revolution' in Greek and all human history, something giving the Greeks 'un génie tout nouveau'. Here was a vision well suited to act as a lever to any incipient radical proclivities in Russian society.[40] That it could and did in fact so act in Radishchev's mind, contributing to the budding radical tendency in the Russian context, a tradition that arose first among precisely those Russian nobles educated at German universities at Catherine's expense or else who lived in France and Holland as diplomats, is revealed by Radishchev's footnotes to Mably's text, one of which states that 'despotism is a state most repugnant to human nature', stressing the need to reform the Russian penal code in terms redolent of Helvétius, one of Radishchev's chief heroes, and Beccaria.[41]

Another of the twelve aristocratic Russian students who had been chosen by Catherine to study with Radishchev at Leipzig, also a precursor of the Russian Radical Enlightenment tendency, was Feodor Ushakov, a gifted youth noted for a particular kind of moral fervour who died young and about whom Radishchev later wrote a biography. At Leipzig, the Russians attended the lectures of the philosophers Ernst Platner (1744–1818) and K. F. Hommel (1722–81), an admirer of Beccaria credited with initiating abolition of judicial torture in Saxony. A student essay by him written in 1770 that Radishchev kept shows Ushakov greatly prized Beccaria's views on penal issues and revered Helvétius, the very *philosophe* against whom Princess Dashkova earlier had put herself on her guard. In his account of Ushakov's life published in 1789, Radishchev relates how the two of them first discovered Helvétius's *De l'esprit* which Ushakov was so smitten by he read it through altogether four times. It was by studying Helvétius, affirmed Radishchev, that 'we learned to think'.[42] In their debates and note-taking, Ushakov and Radishchev still had reservations and invoked Platner and 's Gravesande's *Introductio ad Philosophiam* to counter Helvétius's irreligion and materialism. But the seeds of the struggle between radical and moderate enlightenments in the Russian context had been planted through their discovery of Helvétius and deliberations in Leipzig.

[38] Henderson, *Revival*, 72–4.
[39] Zamoyski, *Holy Madness*, 120.
[40] Mably, *Observations sur les Grecs*, 11–12; Wright, *Classical Republican*, 16, 39–40.
[41] Venturi, 'Première Crise', 13; McConnell, *Russian* Philosophe, 49–50.
[42] McConnell, *Russian* Philosophe, 34–5; Clardy, *Philosophical Ideas*, 43–4.

2. DIDEROT'S CLASH WITH CATHERINE

Catherine admired Voltaire and still more Montesquieu whose *Esprit des loix* she read at least five times, and considered her 'bible'. It was a book in Diderot's judgement for which she had far too great an esteem.[43] Likewise, she was attracted to Beccaria and may even have been sincere, early in her reign, in speaking of emancipating the serfs, despite saying nothing about this in her great project of legal reform, the *Nakaz*. But her 'enlightened' aspirations were always strictly bounded. The best proof of her determination to bring Enlightenment to Russia was precisely the celebrated Instruction, or *Nakaz*, that she composed personally in 1765–7 to direct the convention of representatives from the empire's towns and nobility summoned by her to help draw up a definitive and enlightened code of laws. Translated by Voulgaris, it was reissued in Greek in 1771.[44] Though Beccaria figured prominently in the debates, Montesquieu remained her chief guide with some 294 out of the 526 articles of the *Nakaz* featuring phrases or extracts borrowed from *L'Esprit*.[45] Her laying claim to the epithet 'enlightened' was deserved from the moderate standpoint and earned much praise.

She had no wish for Russia to remain an Asiatic 'despotic' state in Montesquieu's sense and strove to equip her empire with the appurtenances of 'intermediary powers', especially in its law courts, judiciary, and legal system, to lend it the air of being 'modéré' in the manner and form intended by Montesquieu. Published in Russian, in 1767, and French in 1769, and freely on sale in Petersburg from 1768, Catherine's 'Instruction', insisting that Russia was a 'European power', provided the basis of the first real public debate in Russian history about law, politics, and public affairs and drew much attention at the time. While Lycurgus and Solon would willingly have signed her work, Voltaire, full of praise after reading it, assured her, they would have been incapable of writing it.[46] Diderot, by contrast, albeit inevitably only in private, severely criticized her text, especially for failing to broach the sensitive issues of serfdom and divorce.

Nor, despite the cynicism of Petersburg's diplomatic community, should the *Nakaz*'s practical importance be underestimated. Even if partly imperial propaganda stemming not from the Legislative Commission's deliberations but her own advisers' proposals, it was still a project of great significance. Predictably, the convention, its delegates drawn from different segments of society (other than the peasantry and clergy), failed to reach any agreed position. But the congress, while clearly revealing the many points of tension and disagreement in Russian society, did provide much useful information and publicity. In Catherine's mind it proved that only a highly centralized 'enlightened despotism' like hers could cut through Russian society's ingrained conservatism and override the pervasive but traditional preferences of

---

[43] Marrese, 'Liberty Postponed', 37 n. 47; Versini, 'Diderot', 232.
[44] Batalden, *Catherine II's Greek*, 17.
[45] Voltaire, *Corr.* xxxix. 15–16; Madariaga, 'Catherine', 292.
[46] Gay, *Voltaire's Politics*, 176; McConnell, *Russian* Philosophe, 43.

most nobles, professionals, and townsfolk for more ordered, entrenched, clearly delimited spheres of privilege, special rights, charters, and influence.[47]

In Russia, the only unified, concerted impulse towards far-reaching social and institutional change emanated from the court itself and the bureaucracy—and not from society. Certainly, in eastern as in central Europe, the picture was one of vast injustice and oppression with innumerable reasons for discontent and, in the eyes of a few, these urgently needed to be addressed. But no amount of grievance and dissatisfaction could in itself supply a conceptual framework capable of generating, justifying, and promoting a comprehensive programme of fundamental reform. This could happen only among the governing circle, at Catherine's side—or alternatively, and potentially more far-reachingly, in the minds of a few ultra-enlightened noblemen like Radishchev or Prince Dimitri Golitsyn, a diplomat long resident in Paris and The Hague and well read, who supplied the Russian material for the *Histoire philosophique*. Mere unarticulated discontent, however great, could neither envisage nor encourage toppling an entire political and social system nor conceive lines along which it might be replaced with something intrinsically different. Only 'philosophy' could do that. Hence, it was Catherine and her ministers, not pressure from elements in Russian society beyond the nobility's highly educated upper crust, which recast the law on an 'enlightened' basis, pruned the Orthodox Church's influence over education, property, and dissent, widened toleration and economic regulation, and extensively reformed the penal code. Several important new laws, reflecting the impact of the *Nakaz*, especially new regulations relating to administration and the penal law, an area where the influence of Helvétius and Beccaria was particularly marked, were duly implemented by the ruler.

These circumstances explain the relevance of the extensive commentary on the *Nakaz* penned by Diderot, seven years after the framing of the Instruction, his *Observations sur l'Instruction de l'Impératrice de Russie* (1774), the first draft of which was completed back in Holland, at The Hague, in August 1774. Before undertaking his only long journey, Diderot had read extensively on Russia and its history and, in the years 1765–7 whilst he was Catherine's ambassador in Paris, been briefed on Russian affairs by Golitsyn, who was so radical-minded he fervently longed to end serfdom in his country, the serfs being a vast segment of society that in Russia were virtually slaves and whom only the nobility had the right to own. Diderot also learnt much from her ambassador in the years 1772—9, Alexander Sergueievitch, Comte Stroganov, and from António Nunes Ribeiro Sanches, a physician of Portuguese Jewish extraction trained at Leiden under Boerhave who had lived many years in Petersburg but been expelled by the Empress Elizabeth due to his Jewish origins. Subsequently settling in Paris, Ribeiro Sanches became friendly with Diderot and d'Holbach.[48] It was partly owing to him, perhaps, that Diderot showed an unusually

---

[47] Madariaga, 'Catherine', 292; Raeff, *Understanding Imperial Russia*, 90–3, 97.
[48] Dulac, 'Discours politique', 35, 38; Versini, 'Diderot', 226, 232.

sympathetic awareness of the chronic difficulties of Jewish society in eastern Europe. He also conferred with other experts. Grimm later recalled, writing to Catherine after Diderot's death, that during the years 1765–7, Golitsyn, Diderot, and the *physiocrate* Le Mercier had convened regularly, sometimes three times a week, to discuss Russian affairs over dinner at which 'this triumvirate' amused themselves reorganizing the entire government of Russia.[49] Conferring with Princess Dashkova in 1770, Diderot raised the serf question with her. A substantial landed proprietress who by the time of her death owned some 5,000 serfs, according to her account, so convincingly did she defend serfdom as appropriate for certain specific contexts such as Russia and the Russian nobility's treatment of their serfs that Diderot had to yield to her arguments.[50]

Aware how easy it would be to irritate or antagonize the empress and how difficult it would be to achieve anything meaningful, Diderot was particularly anxious on reaching Petersburg, in 1773, not to repeat the fiasco of Le Mercier de la Rivière, his *économiste* friend who, in 1767, had gone as a surrogate for himself to assist the empress's deliberations concerning the *Nakaz*. Le Mercier had immediately irritated her, however, by adopting too high a tone and, after six months, been sent home humiliated.[51] Diderot, lodged near the Winter Palace, stayed at her court for five months, over the winter of 1773–4, during which Catherine met him almost daily for lengthy interviews at fixed times. Catherine liked him and was impressed by his intellect and personality but kept him largely to herself, allowing scant opportunity for him to propagate his views more widely at court by participating in formal councils or consultations. The spectacle of a notorious and once imprisoned *philosophe* eccentrically closeted in such intensive discussion with the powerful empress who however kept his reformist views firmly under wraps was so extraordinary as to attract a good deal of (often disapproving) attention, as well as derisive wit, throughout Europe's courts. He was constantly attired in just a plain black outfit which struck some as a sort of challenge to the entire courtly culture around him. He failed to attend learned meetings at the Imperial Academy of Sciences which he virtually boycotted, continually snubbing its permanent secretary, a long-standing foe, Euler. Invited often to dine at the palaces of the high nobility, he made himself thoroughly unpopular there too by making no effort to hide his atheism. Catherine permitted him no influence. Yet after months of daily conferences, she assured Voltaire, writing in January 1774, she remained as dazzled as ever by his eloquence and insight.[52]

Grimm, also at Petersburg at the time, afterwards recalled the completely unceremonious style in which he engaged her in conversation, even grabbing her hand or arm at times, just as if exhorting his companions in the 'synagogue of the Rue Royale'.[53] She indulged him in that. But her subsequently negative response to his

[49] Grimm to Catherine, 19 June 1786, printed in Dulac, 'Discours politique', 51, 56.
[50] Dashkova, *Mon histoire*, 91–3; Marrese, 'Liberty Postponed', 27, 31–2.
[51] Dulac, 'Discours politique', 39; Versini, 'Diderot', 225.
[52] Catherine to Voltaire, 18 Jan. 1774, in Voltaire, *Corr.* xl. 282–3; Naigeon, *Mémoires*, 346.
[53] Dulac, 'Modes', 122; Trousson, *Denis Diderot*, 533.

suggestions, and dismissal of his political and social theories as hopelessly imprac-
tical, fitted a complex, slightly tense intellectual-political dialogue between them
begun long before. Simultaneously, the disharmony, a decade later to erupt into an
open quarrel between Diderot and Grimm, began to show. Both men were affected by
their differences over the question of political reform. Grimm, chiefly concerned to
further his own career in the courts of Europe, and hence to flatter Catherine and
all the 'enlightened despots', began viewing Diderot's increasingly critical attitude
towards Russian society, culture, and institutions, especially the court and nobility,
laws, and Church, less as touchingly naive than a threat to his interests.[54]

Whilst at Petersburg, Diderot constantly admitted his inexperience and 'naivety' in
political matters and 'ignorance' of Russia to the empress, in a flurry of apologetic,
self-belittling notes. He urged her not to take his 'babbling' too seriously as part of
a deliberate tactic, enabling him to speak relatively freely without annoying her. He
ventured few direct criticisms, seeing he would get nowhere if he did, aside from
urging her to move her capital to Moscow, Petersburg being too much at the empire's
edge for the bright torch of Enlightenment to illumine Russia as it should.[55] But in
response to her queries and explanations, he wrote numerous papers on different
topics, over 400 pages of text, only parts of which were actually read or shown to her
at the time.[56] He talked and meditated but did not see much. In the end, he never
went on to Moscow as originally intended and scarcely left the capital at all.

Later, composing his *Observations* after returning, Diderot took good care that she
should not set eyes on his commentary, knowing perfectly well how she would react if
she did. The *Observations* were not in fact addressed to her at all, it emerges from their
lofty, censorious tone but rather to an imagined 'Catherine', a ruler who listens to the
voice of 'reason', meaning that of the radical *philosophe* and Golitsyn, Le Mercier, and
his other allies deliberating Russian reform. He was not ungrateful for her favour, nor
inclined to underestimate her capacity to change things in Russia. But he had found
her fundamentally unsympathetic to his standpoint, unwilling to confront what in his
view and that of his circle were the true priorities. In fact, as he put it unceremoniously
at the time, writing to a friend, he had come to regard her as—though he never
despised her as he did Frederick—'la souveraine la plus despote qu'il y ait en Europe'.[57]

Catherine saw nothing of Diderot's *Observations* until after his death when all
his books and papers, as agreed under their contract, were remitted to Petersburg
by Grimm. When finally she laid eyes on what he wrote after returning from Russia,
she flew into a rage and apparently destroyed the copy she received (Grimm having
wrongly assured her there were no others); at least no version of it was ever found
afterwards in Russia.[58] 'This piece is really babble', she wrote angrily to Grimm.

---

[54] Trousson, *Denis Diderot*, 604–5; Dixon, 'Proveshchenie', 230.

[55] Wolff, *Inventing Eastern Europe*, 226–8.

[56] Dulac, 'Discours politique', 33.

[57] Diderot, *Corr.* xiii. 210, 226, letters of 30 Mar. and 9 Apr. 1774; Versini, 'Diderot', 233; Trousson,
Denis Diderot, 559; Dulac, 'Modes', 130–1.

[58] Diderot, *Political Writings*, 78–9; Jimack, 'Obéissance', 161.

As Diderot never raised such strong objections as formulated here to her face she also pronounced it devious deception. It decisively changed her view of him, though even while in Russia, she complained later, he naively wanted to promote 'impractical theories' and see everything 'overturned'.[59] Known today from two manuscript drafts that survived in France, the text begins by affirming, 'there is no true sovereign except the nation; there can be no true legislator except the people', reiterating the principle he had so daringly stated in his article 'Autorité politique' in the *Encyclopédie*. The people will only sincerely venerate laws they themselves are authors of and where the legal system is their achievement. He insisted on the principle of equality before the law, signalling rejection of enlightened despotism and its underpinning in aristocracy: 'the laws are useless if they do not apply equally to everyone; they are made in vain if there is a single member of society who can infringe them with impunity.'[60] The 'first line of a well-made Code', asserts the next paragraph

should bind the sovereign. It should begin thus: 'We the people and we the sovereign of this people swear conjointly to obey these laws by which we will be equally judged; and if it should happen that we, the sovereign, becoming the enemy of our people, should change them or infringe them, it is just that our people should be released from the oath of loyalty, and that they should pursue us, depose us and even condemn us to death if the case demands it.'[61]

Here, clearly stated, was the principle of the people's right to depose despots who violate the law and the theory of a contract underpinning all legitimate monarchy, acknowledging the people's right to resist 'tyranny' opponents had always deemed implicit in the *Encyclopédie* and that d'Holbach had spelt out the previous year in his *La Politique naturelle* (1773), prompting the Dominican Richard to comment that this conception of popular sovereignty of 'Messieurs nos philosophes modernes' can only produce general revolt and anarchy.[62] Diderot did not send his text to Catherine because his visit there led him finally to reject enlightened despotism, in principle and absolutely, without exception. Henceforth, his war on 'enlightened despotism' was not just a campaign against Frederick. 'The Empress of Russia', he wrote, in his *Observations*, is certainly a despot.' 'Is it her intention to perpetuate the despotism and transfer it to her successors, or to abdicate it?' If she wished to end despotic government in Russia sincerely, then 'her abdication should be formal' and steps taken to find 'the surest way of preventing the re-emergence of despotism'.[63]

Most uncompromising of all was Diderot's paragraph insisting that there must be a law 'requiring the representatives of the nation to assemble every five years to judge whether or not the sovereign has acted in conformity with any law he or she has sworn to uphold, and decide on the punishment if it has been infringed, that is whether to allow the ruler to continue again swearing allegiance to those laws or to

---

[59] Dulac, 'Discours politique', 49–51; Wolff, *Inventing Eastern Europe*, 230.
[60] Diderot, *Political Writings*, 81; Trousson, *Denis Diderot*, 558.
[61] Diderot, *Political Writings*, 81.
[62] Richard, *Défense de la religion*, 256, 263, 268–70.
[63] Diderot, *Political Writings*, 82; Wolff, *Inventing Eastern Europe*, 231.

depose him or her'.[64] To this he adds: 'People, if you have supreme authority over your sovereign, make a Code; if your sovereign has supreme authority over you, abandon your Code. You will be forging chains for yourselves alone.'[65]

Diderot's *Observations sur l'Instruction* were radical politically and socially. 'There is only one way to prevent the abuses of serfdom and its dangers', he maintains: 'abolish serfdom and rule only over free men.'[66] This would not be easy to accomplish in a land where the landowners themselves scarcely understood the disadvantages and abuse the institution gave rise to and where the serfs were so brutalized as to be unaware of the meaning of freedom. Responding to Catherine's Instruction, clause 77, where she says 'it is essential to try to avoid the causes which have so often led to the revolt of serfs against their masters', Diderot remarks: 'there is an excellent way to prevent revolts of serfs against their masters: there should be no serfs.'[67] All labour should earn its proper reward so there should be no legal restrictions either on the freed serf's, or other Russian peasant's, ability to purchase ownership of the soil. In effect, he urged a gradual but unrestricted transfer of land ownership from the crown, Church, and nobility to the peasantry.

Her rule Catherine had closely identified with the Church and the people's faith, added Diderot, bringing throne and altar in a close relation whereas 'the distance between throne and altar can never be too great. Experience in all times and places has shown the danger of the altar resting beside the throne.'[68] Both Montesquieu and Catherine 'had begun their works by invoking God'. Much better, he suggested, would be 'to begin stressing the necessity of the laws' which are the foundation of human happiness' and the contract which is implicit in all societies and the basis of liberty and good government. Both mention 'God' as a matter of policy, assuming government on its own lacks sufficient legitimacy in the people's eyes. But the very need for such a tactic should have alerted them to the nature of the evil and the danger of increasing it.[69] *Philosophes* and priests had, undeniably, both pronounced and written much against each other. But never has the *philosophe* killed priests while the priesthood had killed many *philosophes*; the *philosophe* has killed no kings while the priesthood has killed many kings.[70]

In claiming 'Russia is a European power', meaning *not* Asiatic and hence not 'despotic', Catherine again stood too proximate to Montesquieu for Diderot's taste. 'It matters little', retorted Diderot, who disliked Montesquieu's geographical determinism and aspects of his historicism, 'whether Russia is Asiatic or European. The important point is that it should be great, flourishing and lasting.'[71] The character of a society, its style, *mœurs*, degree of freedom are always the result of legislation and government, Montesquieu was fundamentally wrong about this; the real question is whether government and law 'are good or bad'. Such things are not intrinsically

---

[64] Diderot, *Political Writings*, 82, 152.   [65] Ibid.
[66] Ibid. 126; Strugnell, *Diderot's Politics*, 184–8.
[67] Diderot, *Political Writings*, 127; Marrese, 'Liberty Postponed', 32.
[68] Diderot, *Political Writings*, 83.   [69] Ibid. 83–4.   [70] Ibid. 85.
[71] Ibid.; Wolff, *Inventing Eastern Europe*, 231–2; Strugnell, *Diderot's Politics*, 157–8.

'African or Asiatic or European'. As things stood, one is enslaved in the northernmost climes—the Age of Liberty had just ended in Sweden and in Denmark-Norway Struensee had been overthrown and executed in 1771, not long before—where it is very cold and enslaved in Constantinople 'where it is very hot; but everywhere a people should be educated, free and virtuous'.[72] If what Peter the Great brought to Russia from Europe was 'good in Europe', that does not make Russia European; it means that those benefits should be good everywhere.

Back from Russia, Diderot praised Catherine's good intentions in print but privately insisted on exposing what he saw as the despotic system of government, law, society, and institutions in Russia and the impossibility of the *Nakaz* producing a truly positive result.[73] She had done nothing to diminish 'l'autorité despotique' and could not do so without an enlightened class of advisers and administrators to assist her; and, after her death, the situation would become worse. The commission to reform Russia's laws had merely altered a few names, not changed the oppressive reality.[74] His views were in perfect accord with the highly critical remarks of the 1774 edition of the *Histoire philosophique* which takes Peter the Great to task for reducing Russia to an oppressive tyranny. He had no wish to relax his despotism. If anything he increased it 'et laissa à ses successeurs cette idée atroce et destructive que les sujets ne sont rien et que le souverain est tout'.[75] Overturning Voltaire's entire eulogy of the tsarist structure created by Peter and Catherine, Diderot saw no possibility of a conscious, politically and morally responsible 'third estate' emerging in a land wholly under the heel of an aristocracy and military caste that seemed impervious to becoming 'enlightened' or changing its outlook. Meanwhile, the populace were sunk in the most complete credulity, intolerance, and superstition 'fomentées par un clergé nombreux, plongé dans la crapule et dans l'ignorance'.[76] In serf-ridden lands like Russia, Poland, and Denmark, the nobles and clergy, he thought, like Filangieri later, were the only free men, the rest being 'slaves'.[77]

The fact that an almost general toleration prevailed at St Petersburg except, Diderot noted, that the Jews remained excluded, counted for comparatively little in such a generally dismal context.[78] A deplorable tableau was made worse by the Russians' unattractive habit of considering themselves, rather like the Chinese, the wisest, most sensible people on earth, a 'mad pride' often stiffened by those returning from visiting the rest of Europe.[79] As for the famed St Petersburg Academy of Sciences, created by Peter and supposedly flourishing under Catherine, and the capital's artistic academies, these seemed to Diderot to be no more than a superficial adornment or excrescence. Virtually all their active members were foreigners, mostly Germans, Swiss, and Huguenots, who spoke and wrote in languages the vast majority of Russian-speakers could not understand. The Academy did little to promote

---

[72] Diderot, *Political Writings*, 85.   [73] *Histoire philosophique* (1780), x. 39, 48, 52.
[74] *Histoire philosophique* (1780), x. 49; Versini, 'Diderot', 232–4.
[75] Lortholary, *Mirage russe*, 214.   [76] *Histoire philosophique* (1780), x. 46–7.
[77] Filangieri, *Scienza della legislazione*, ii. 103–4.   [78] *Histoire philosophique* (1780), x. 47.
[79] Ibid. x. 48.

Russian as an enlightened language. Since the savants and artists that belonged to these bodies had no real connection to Russian society were they not 'inutiles et ruineux'?[80]

3. RUSSIA'S 'FIRST RADICAL'

Radical thought, always hostile, tended to harden further toward 'enlightened despotism' with the passage of time and, without doubting the greatness of Peter, to disparage the Russian Enlightenment in particular. The fact that Catherine, while acting on none of the main points Diderot urged her to reform, basked in the reputation of being truly enlightened which Voltaire, the only *philosophe* who never bored her, and her patronage of Diderot, materially enhanced, was noticed by many others besides Diderot and Catherine themselves. Expecting great things from Catherine in the 1760s, Herder became wholly disillusioned just a few years later, seeing her response to Diderot as characteristic of the wider set of tendencies evinced by the tsarina of which he also heartily disapproved.[81] Catherine had no intention of surrendering, or restricting, her autocratic power, and after the great peasant rising known as the Pugachev Revolt (1773–4) abandoned any inclination she may have had to break down the institution of serfdom.

The Pugachev rising was led by a disgruntled Cossack leader proclaiming himself Tsar Peter III—the lost tsar who had supposedly returned to reclaim the throne from his dissolute wife—in which Cossacks, Old Believers, and resistance to conscription, new taxes, and secularization all played a part. The insurrection devastated vast areas, stirring up the peasantry throughout the empire's south-eastern regions, a convulsion in which many manor houses were sacked and torched and over a thousand nobles and their dependants, some 5 per cent of the Russian nobility, slaughtered, bludgeoned by peasants or executed by officers of the rightful 'tsar'. Pugachev, though supposedly married to Catherine, acquired many captured noblewomen for his harem. Although the rebellion's aims were fluid and vague, it was clearly driven by pressure from below aiming to recover autonomy for the Cossacks and end serfdom, redistributing the land to the peasantry. Pugachev's last and most wide-ranging proclamation, of 31 July 1774, a text propagated widely among the villages along the Volga, expressly summons the serfs to rise and kill their masters and take the land.

Deeply shaken, Catherine reacted on many levels, cutting back Cossack autonomy further and reaffirming her commitment to a society of orders with an elaborately defined urban commercial estate and, not least, by systematizing and reinforcing the privileges of the nobility with a series of decrees on the subject. It had long been obvious to her (as it was to Frederick and Joseph) that their alliance with the nobility

---

[80] *Histoire philosophique* (1780), x. 50; Trousson, *Denis Diderot*, 544.
[81] Barnard, *Herder's Social and Political Thought*, 72–3.

and the Church was entirely indispensable to the survival of her, and their, autocracies. She could not abandon her reliance on aristocracy in government, for running the provincial administration, diplomatic service, or the army and navy, and hence saw no alternative but to defend and confirm noble privilege as a linchpin of the social system. This in turn meant shoring up serfdom and the entire hierarchical structure of Russian rural and urban society, including her elaborate system of segregation and disabilities relating to Catholics, Muslim Tartars, and Jews.[82]

Long known as the 'first Russian radical', Radishchev was in fact preceded by Golitsyn and several others, including Narychkin, the young man sent from Petersburg to accompany Diderot from Holland to Petersburg. But Radishchev undoubtedly deserves a special place in the Russian Radical Enlightenment's history. His radicalism originated, we have seen, in his studies at Leipzig and especially the works of Helvétius and Mably. His personal philosophy matured whilst working as a customs official in Petersburg in the early 1780s above all through reading the *Histoire philosophique*. In 1781–2, he eloquently expressed his views in a poem, *Liberty: An Ode*, celebrating the American Revolution, the work marking the commencement of the Russian radical stream in literary form. It included some openly subversive lines though these were not printed until later. Here, he exclaims: 'Your example [i.e. of the Americans] has set a goal for us—we all wish for the same.'[83] The ode's less provocative sections appeared in 1782; and even this sufficed for Catherine to complain to Grimm that Radishchev's views were lies and a 'stab in the back'.[84] Princess Dashkova, uncompromisingly Anglophile, given to Montesquieu, and insistent on enlightened absolutism as the appropriate form for Russia, predicted that Radishchev's views would sooner or later land him in serious trouble.[85] She was right. As early as 1780, Radishchev began composing the eventually celebrated work that led to his subsequent trial and imprisonment, *A Journey from St Petersburg to Moscow* (1790).

Although it is usually assumed *A Journey* was inspired by the French Revolution since it appeared only in 1790, it was actually largely complete by 1788 before the onset of the Revolution.[86] The work for which Radishchev is chiefly famous in reality has the *Histoire philosophique* as its principal source of inspiration.[87] Before having his book privately printed, on his estate, Radishchev submitted the text to the police as required but the censors, assuming it was a mere travel book, failed to notice the implications of his proclaiming that 'every man is born into the world equal to all others' and his echoing Diderot's call for the emancipation of Russia's serfs, a sentiment shared by only a tiny number of Russian aristocrats.[88] The censors ordered

---

[82] Madariaga, *Catherine*, 60, 140; Hufton, *Europe: Privilege*, 173–4.

[83] Thaler, 'Introduction', 8–9; Zamoyski, *Holy Madness*, 20; Bancarel and Goggi, *Raynal*, 299.

[84] Lang, *First Russian Radical*, 113.

[85] Marrese, 'Liberty Postponed', 32–3, 37; Tortarolo, *L'Illuminismo*, 156.

[86] Thaler, 'Introduction', 9–10.

[87] Ibid. 24–5; Lang, *First Russian Radical*, 105; Madariaga, *Catherine*, 194.

[88] Radishchev, *A Journey*, 102.

the removal of some 'undesirable' remarks but the police failed to check that he had actually deleted them before the text went to press.

A Journey confronts the reader with successive harrowing descriptions of social relations in the Russian countryside. 'Nothing is more harmful', avers Radishchev, 'than to see forever before one the partners in slavery, master and slave. On one side there is born conceit, on the other servile fear. There can be no bond between them other than force'. And this narrow bond 'extends its oppressive autocratic power everywhere'. Such are its doleful effects the landowners are not the only oppressors of men or vocal champions of servitude: 'it appears that the spirit of freedom is so dried up in the slaves they not only have no desire to end their sufferings but cannot bear seeing others set free. They love their fetters, if it is possible for man to love his own ruination'. All this emotive and highly subversive passage, Catherine indignantly noted later, in her detailed jottings on Radishchev's text, 'is borrowed for the most part from the Abbé Raynal's book'.[89] She was right.

When Radishchev's book appeared, in 1790, Catherine, whose total opposition to the democratic republican upsurge in France manifested itself as early as the pamphlet wars of 1788, was among the first to read it and, according to a secretary who was present, flew into a rage, denouncing Radishchev as 'a rebel worse than Pugachev'.[90] Given that Radishchev serves up an unprecedented critique of serfdom while, like Diderot, dismissing the Russian empire's apparent stability as a tranquillity based on superstition, directed by an ignorant clergy, this is hardly surprising. He also indicts Peter the Great for imposing the fetters of servitude on the wretched *muzhiks* and diminishing his own 'greatness' by establishing 'despotism' on its present foundations. Only around seventy-five copies had been distributed when Radishchev, perceiving danger, destroyed the rest. Arrested on 30 June 1790, he was interrogated by Catherine's head of secret police. During his imprisonment at Petersburg, Radishchev drew up a statement confessing that Raynal's 'bold expression I considered in excellent taste, and, seeing him universally read, I wanted to imitate his style'.[91] He profusely apologized, assuring the empress of his obedience to 'Her Imperial majesty's most wise laws'. She was not impressed. After thorough investigation and interrogation, he was sentenced to be executed by the Petersburg central criminal court. The death sentence was then confirmed by the Imperial Council of State but, on 4 September 1790, as was then usual with death sentences, Catherine commuted it to ten years' exile at Ilimsk, in Siberia. She also stripped him of his noble status and privileges.

'The purpose of this book', notes Catherine, 'is clear on every page: its author, infected and full of the French madness, is trying in every possible way to break down respect for authority and the authorities and stir up indignation in the people against their superiors and the government.'[92] Not only was he a rebel against authority, but

---

[89] Ibid. 152; Catherine, 'Notes', 259; Bancarel and Goggi, *Raynal*, 295.
[90] Lortholary, *Mirage russe*, 258–9; Thaler, 'Introduction', 11; Clardy, *Philosophical Ideas*, 45.
[91] Clardy, *Philosophical Ideas*, 113.
[92] Catherine, 'Notes', 239; Madariaga, *Catherine*, 193–5.

he rejected the very principle of aristocracy and social hierarchy. 'According to his system (the present French system) all estates are established equal in the name of man and his so-called rights!'[93] Commenting on the passage where Radishchev holds all men are born equal claiming men set up governing authorities over themselves only for their own advantage and security and that 'consequently, wherever being a citizen is not to his advantage, he is not a citizen and whoever seeks to rob him of citizenship's advantages is his enemy', Catherine retorted that he advocates 'principles completely destructive of the laws and that have turned France upside down'. Denouncing his 'calumnies' against the landed magnates and 'everything else established and accepted', she highlighted his 'bewailing the sad fate of the peasants when it cannot be denied our peasants who have good masters are better off than any in the world'.[94] As for his protest at the harsh recruitment system for the army and 'the murder called war': 'what do they want?', she replied, ' to be left defenceless to fall captive to the Turks and Tartars, or be conquered by the Swedes?'[95]

Radishchev did not hesitate to predict a general rising of the serfs. Their future release from servitude being inevitable and 'the more procrastinating and stubborn we have been in loosening their fetters, the more violent they will be in their vengefulness', he urges Russia's landowners to emancipate them now if not for justice's sake then to save themselves. 'Shall we not be brave enough to overcome our prejudice, to suppress our selfishness, to free our brothers from all bonds of slavery, and re-establish the natural equality of all.' To these and other such pleas, Catherine answered that the landed proprietors will certainly not listen as the author himself was clearly aware since, in fact, he puts 'his hopes in a peasant rebellion'.[96] *A Journey* includes, embedded towards the end, the most subversive lines of the ode that he had refrained from publishing in 1782, lines echoing 'Raynal' and Mercier predicting the general overthrow of tyranny: 'everywhere martial hosts will arise, hope will arm all; everyone hastens to wash off his shame in the blood of the crowned tormentor. Everywhere, I see the flash of the sharp sword; death flying about in various forms, hovers over the proud head. Rejoice fettered peoples. The avenging law of nature has brought the king to the block.'[97] This ode, commented Catherine, is plainly 'criminal' and 'manifestly revolutionary', one in which 'tsars are threatened with the block' and 'Cromwell's example cited and praised'.[98] Directing Radishchev's interrogation from a distance, she had specifically instructed her police chief, Sheshkovskii, to discover more about the meaning of this ode.

Radishchev was packed off to Siberia under guard and in chains. Hitherto, Catherine had been remarkably liberal, the most relaxed of any of the 'enlightened despots', about book censorship. But the Radishchev episode, along with a warning

---

[93] Catherine, 'Notes', 242; Lang, *First Russian Radical*, 110.
[94] Radishchev, *A Journey*, 147; Catherine, 'Notes', 243.
[95] Catherine, 'Notes', 240.
[96] Radishchev, *A Journey*, 153–4, 191; Catherine, 'Notes', 247–8.
[97] Radishchev, *A Journey*, 197.
[98] Catherine, 'Notes', 248; McConnell, *Russian Philosophe*, 89–90, 113.

from her governor-general of Moscow that French revolutionary publications were freely available there, changed her mind. She now instituted a systematic censorship of books and bookshops to ensure nothing was available to the Russian reading public opposed to 'religion, decency, and ourselves'.[99] After Catherine's death, in 1797, Radishchev was permitted to return and even resumed work in Petersburg, in the legislative department of the Senate. But he found it hard to readjust and, in 1802, committed suicide.

What remained of his radical legacy? As a physical object, his book was banned and long remained very effectively suppressed. Today only around fifteen of the originally around 600 copies survive.[100] Yet, despite it all, an indelible impression and memory of the work somehow lived on and today it stands as one of the most important publications in Russian history.

---

[99] McConnell, *Russian* Philosophe, 196–7.
[100] Madariaga, *Catherine*, 196.

Part IV

Spinoza Controversies in the Later Enlightenment

23

Rousseau, Spinoza, and the 'General Will'

1. TOWARDS THE MODERN DEMOCRATIC CONCEPTION OF SOVEREIGNTY

Although the notion seems strange to us today, in the 1790s it was usual for those sympathetic to the French Revolution, and also those opposed to it, to speak of it as the realization of modern 'philosophy'. When examined, this perception can be seen to possess considerable cultural and political significance, a significance the modern historiography of the Revolution has totally ignored. What was meant was that modern 'philosophy', considered in all its aspects, entailed a vast mobilization of intellectual and cultural impulses and that it was this intellectual 'revolution' prior to 1788 that drove the vast transformation, political, social, and legal, that Europe and the entire world subsequently experienced. 'The French Revolution', exclaimed the Göttingen professor Lichtenberg in 1789, 'is the accomplishment of philosophy, but what a leap from the *cogito, ergo sum* to the first resounding of *à la Bastille* in the Palais Royal!' [Die französische Revolution das Werk der Philosophie, aber was für ein Sprung von dem *cogito, ergo sum* bis zum ersten Erschallen des *à la Bastille* im Palais Royal!].[1] Given Lichtenberg's approach to scientific and philosophical questions, he clearly intended to say by this that a vast shift to a systematically rational view of reality on many levels was required before human ideals and needs could be visualized, expressed, and legislated for in the manner of 1789.

Thinking in terms of basic human rights was obviously one such dimension; another was the virtual destruction of confessional and theological differences as a meaningful divide between humans. 'It was philosophy', as Spinoza's German biographer, Diez, held in his *Apologie der Duldung und Pressfreiheit* [Apologie for Toleration and Freedom of the Press], of 1781, that discredited and almost destroyed 'intolerance', undermining the whole edifice of bigotry and theological thinking that the churches had laboured for centuries to build up. It was 'philosophy', he declared, that freed men from 'the yoke of Rome' and drove back superstition.[2] Only through 'philosophy' had it become evident that by not believing in the New Testament, of

---

[1] Lichtenberg, *Schriften und Briefe*, i. 708–9; Karthaus, 'Schiller', 211.
[2] Diez, *Apologie*, 82–3.

Christianity, the Jews 'in no way disturb society and that neither does the renegade who doubts the divine character of both testaments'.[3] But perhaps the most important level on which 'philosophy' was thought by such writers to have emancipated man was by redefining the state as an instrument for securing the common good defined as the collective interest of the majority in this world. 'What a development!', exclaimed Wekhrlin, in 1791: the torch of philosophy has finally been taken up in society and the 'rights of reason and of Man' transferred to the sphere of reality. 'The true principles of society have been researched and *aufgeklärt*, 'all founts and canals of human understanding opened and cleaned', and the public understanding has been brought to grasp 'the general good'. In short, the century of the Enlightenment was one in which human life had ceased to be 'the plaything of politics and religion'![4] With the public sphere, freedom of the press, and the Revolution, humanity had become, or so it seemed, briefly, the sphere of 'reason'.

What this fourth part of the volume is designed to accomplish is to survey the great European intellectual controversies of the 1770s and 1780s, in an attempt to see what they can teach us about the relationship of 'philosophy' to the Enlightenment movement more generally on the eve of the Revolution and hence about the relation of philosophy itself to the revolutionary era. It is a sufficiently established fact that requires no input here that during the 1780s, in Germany, philosophical controversy considered as a broad public cultural event revolved to a large extent around the question of Spinoza. Recently, the centrality of Spinoza in philosophical controversy in the 1780s has been demonstrated also for the Netherlands.[5] The leading Dutch thinker of the era, Diderot's sparring partner Hemsterhuis, saw his own philosophical œuvre as an attempt to check the largely subterranean but widespread Spinozist presence in the Netherlands. Several Dutch writers stressed the connection between Spinoza and the new materialism of Diderot and d'Holbach. Cerisier, for example, one of the compilers of the *Leidse ontwerp*, the chief manifesto of the Dutch democrats in the 1780s, observes in his *Tableau de l'histoire générale des Provinces-Unies* (10 vols., Utrecht, 1777–84) that Spinoza's system had now been renewed in the later eighteenth century by 'new Diagoras', as he dubs Diderot, Helvétius, and d'Holbach, who, however, possess 'ni le génie, ni la profondeur et la subtilité de Spinosa'.[6] An admirer of the early Dutch Enlightenment of Spinoza and Bayle, Cerisier also cherished the memory of Balthasar Bekker whose opinions, he notes, despite all the ferocious opposition, in the end 'ont pénétré et même prévalu'.[7]

Since 'philosophy' had now entered the public sphere and the reading societies in Holland, it seemed essential to professional philosophers to steer things, especially among the students, by popularizing 'philosophy' in such a way as to thwart the Spinozist threat. Among the professionals deploying philosophy as a device for solving social and political issues in this way was the German-born anti-Wolffian

---

[3] Diez, *Apologie*, 14.   [4] Wekhrlin, *Paragrafen*, 2 (1791), 108–9.
[5] Krop, 'Dutch *Spinozismusstreit*', 185–211.   [6] Cerisier, *Tableau*, ix. 571.   [7] Ibid. ix. 569.

Johan Frederik Hennert (1733–1813), professor of philosophy at Utrecht, admirer of Hemsterhuis, and a keen reader of German, French, and British philosophical literature.[8] Drawn to Scottish Common Sense, Hennert's translation of and commentary on Beattie's work came out at Utrecht in three volumes in 1791. Harassed by the democrats, during the battle for control of Utrecht university between 1783 and 1786 (though also supported by some of the student body) he was forced to abandon his lecture-room in late 1786 and flee to Germany from whence, however, he returned to his chair, victoriously, after the Patriot defeat and stadholder's 'happy' restoration, in 1787.[9]

In the first volume, published in 1780, of his six-volume *Selected Tractates*, Hennert presented the public with Dutch translations of the two discourses delivered before the Berlin Royal Academy in 1745 and 1746, on Spinoza and Bayle's critique of Spinoza, by de Jariges, one of the foremost mid-eighteenth-century Spinoza commentators, accompanied by his own observations. His account is characterized by a more nuanced view of Spinoza's significance for religion, morality, and society than had hitherto been usual in the Netherlands, plainly shaped by the current controversy in Germany. The philosophical battle surrounding Spinoza was now increasingly urgent, he explains, because more and more people were beginning to realize the enormity of the untruth the preachers had foisted on them in the past, claiming Spinoza is full of contradictions. For, on the contrary, far from being inconsistent Spinoza, in reality, is formidably systematic and incisive. 'No one is known to me', admonishes Hennert, like Jacobi and Rehberg, 'who has more powerfully countered the doctrine of final causes than Spinoza.'[10] Spinoza was also upright and well-meaning, if unworldly. Moreover, Leibniz, argues Hennert, borrowing from Lessing and Mendelssohn, took his doctrine of pre-established harmony from him.[11]

The real danger in the present situation, a recipe for social and cultural disaster, as he saw it, lay in continuing to peddle a false picture among the people, as the preachers had always done in the past. For this meant abandoning Spinoza to the materialists. This was exceedingly dangerous not because the man in the street was likely to read Spinoza—there was little chance of that—but because the most intelligent and erudite individuals would; and when such readers see that the preachers have misled them, students and enquiring minds are prone to go disastrously wrong. Intelligent readers, impressed by Spinoza, are only too apt to suppose Diderot and d'Holbach had correctly anchored their virulent materialism, atheism, and social reformism in Spinozistic positions. He had read most of the French materialist literature of recent years, including all d'Holbach's works, and was convinced this literature is not based on a correct reading of Spinozism.[12] The solution to the problem Spinoza poses for Dutch culture was to convince society Spinoza was not really an atheist or enemy of religion, or even a thinker denying

---

[8] Krop, 'Dutch *Spinozismusstreit*', 193.   [9] Cerisier, *Tableau*, v. 3–4, 7–8.
[10] Hennert, *Uitgeleezene Verhandelingen*, i. 242, 246, 252; Israel, 'Failed Enlightenment', 27.
[11] Hennert, *Uitgeleezene Verhandelingen*, i. 9, 274, 276–7.   [12] Ibid. i. 33–4.

divine providence.[13] Rather, a huge gap separates Spinoza from d'Holbach. Where 'present-day atheists' scorn religion as useless and damaging for morality, politics, and society, Spinoza was really a kind of Socinian showing the 'greatest respect for religion, esteeming the contemplation of God above everything else'.[14] The Spinoza challenge in the Netherlands could best be dealt with by professional philosophers wresting Spinoza out of the hands of the materialists and redefining him as a Socinian and a theist, sympathetic to religion.

What is new in this fourth part of this volume is the observation that these Dutch and German reactions have a broader European relevance and were connected in some respects to responses to materialism also in France and Switzerland, most importantly in the late controversial writings of Voltaire. But first it is necessary to clarify one of the most vitally topical points of controversy relating to Rousseau. The idea that, to live securely and as well as possible, men must unite their efforts so that the absolute right of each individual to do whatever he or she could do in the state of nature is transposed into the absolute power over the whole of the state 'according to the power and will of all at the same time', is a founding principle introduced by Spinoza and common to Spinoza and Rousseau, as well as Diderot and d'Holbach. The consequent requirement to obey the laws of that state that unites the force of all individuals for the common enterprise in this way is shared by all four thinkers and leads directly to the seemingly strange-sounding, paradoxical proposition that whether individuals wish to or not they 'shall be compelled to live according to the precept of reason' [coacti sint ex rationis praescripto vivere], as Spinoza expresses his idea, that is, obey laws made in the name of the collectivity of individual wills and compelled the more, the more the state corresponds to the best and most natural type of state, that is one that is democratic rather than monarchical in character.[15]

Hence, as an alert Spanish scholar has pointed out,[16] one of the most famous—and notorious—of Rousseau's maxims in the *Contrat social*, namely that whoever refuses to obey the general will 'shall be compelled to do so by the whole body' and thereby will 'be forced to be free', is actually not Rousseau's idea at all but derives straight from Spinoza. However, there is an important difference in the way the idea is employed by the two thinkers, a difference destined to have considerable relevance to the ideological struggle between the 'revolution of reason' and the Rousseauist revolution of the will between 1792 and 1794. Where in the *Tractatus Theologico-Politicus* and *Tractatus Politicus*, as in Diderot and d'Holbach, the 'general will' always conforms to and is defined by reason, in Rousseau this is not the case. Where for Spinoza the 'common good', what Diderot calls 'la volonté générale', is by definition inherent in reason and not something defined by being willed, in Rousseau it stems precisely from the people's will.

---

[13] Sassen, *Geschiedenis*, 246–7; Krop, 'Dutch *Spinozismusstreit*', 196–7, 200–1.
[14] Hennert, *Uitgeleezene Verhandelingen*, iii. 508.
[15] Rousseau, *Social Contract*, 195; Spinoza, *Tractatus Politicus*, in Spinoza, *Opera*, iii. 298.
[16] Villaverde, 'Spinoza, Rousseau', 87–8.

It has long been realized by some historians of political thought that the main derivations and affinities in Rousseau's conception of democracy derive from Spinoza rather than the contractual conceptions of Hobbes and Locke.[17] Since his discovery of Spinoza somewhere between 1746 and 1749, either on his own or more likely through his regular group discussions with Diderot and Condillac, Spinoza was fundamental to Rousseau's tool kit. What has been insufficiently stressed by scholars, though, as the same Spanish scholar pointed out not long ago,[18] is that the divergences from common ground between Spinoza and Rousseau, and especially in their rival visions of democracy, are even more crucial than the affinities, something highly relevant not just to the history of modern political thought and crucial for grasping the ideological tensions shaping the Revolution. Both Spinoza and Rousseau maintain that the absolute power of the democratic republic to compel individuals must be consecrated in society and the minds of individuals by a shared moral creed or civic religion. But where Spinoza's creed involves only the principles of equity, justice, and charity and is strictly universalist, tolerant, and anchored in reason, even if couched in terms of a few rituals and teachings for the benefit of the *multitudo* incapable of grasping the dictates of reason, Rousseau's civic religion is anchored in the popular will and at key points is antagonistic to reason as well as to the equality and justice which he too aspires to see ground his 'general will'. Rousseau's 'general will' is particularist, intolerant, and amenable to far-reaching censorship; and it necessarily retains a strong contractual element, rejected by the late Spinoza as well as Diderot and d'Holbach, assisting the transition from what Rousseau conceived as the more natural solitary state to society—this last, the naturalness of the solitary state, being a conception wholly rejected by Spinoza and, following him, by Diderot and d'Holbach consciously invoking Spinoza.[19]

If Rousseau's *volonté générale* shares with Diderot's and d'Holbach's 'general will' the property of grounding both the rights and duties of citizens, it differs from theirs in that, for Rousseau, each nation expresses its own particular will rather than embraces the universal 'general will' proclaimed by the Diderot circle.[20] Rousseau's equality consequently has a localized, particular quality that helps us understand why it is that he nowhere speaks of the oneness of mankind or proclaims the equality of the black and brown peoples with the whites.[21] It also helps explain how the gender factor could differ so dramatically in the two cases, the status of men and women in Rousseau's schema diverging sharply from that in Diderot's. The 'general will' of the Diderot circle, proclaiming justice and equality the sole basis of the 'general will', appeals to constant and absolute principles, and applies to all human society

---

[17] Vernière, *Spinoza*, 477–8; Villaverde, 'Rousseau, lecteur', 118–19; Israel, *Radical Enlightenment*, 719–20.

[18] Villaverde, 'Spinoza, Rousseau', 85, 91–2, 96–100.

[19] Goggi, 'Spinoza contro Rousseau', 139, 141.

[20] Villaverde, 'Spinoza, Rousseau', 179; Williams, *Rousseau's Platonic Enlightenment*, 96, 110; Cohen, *Rousseau*, 69–73.

[21] Sala-Molins, *Le Code noir*, 237–53.

wherever it may be, laying down values supposedly no less valid in primitive than civilized societies.[22] It was equally relevant as a basis for regulating relations between states and peoples and for organizing democracy within nations. At the same time, it fully acknowledged the inevitability of disagreement and clashes between individual and collective interest. Thus, the Radical Enlightenment's conception of general will lacked that emphasis on unanimity and absence of dissent, indeed pressure to eliminate dissent, typical of Rousseau's (and later Robespierre's) rival conception. Hence it also lacks what Hannah Arendt called the curious equation of will and interest on which the whole body of Rousseau's political theory rests'.[23]

Where Rousseau, like Mably—another former friend with whom he later broke[24]—seems positively to approve of the aggressive patriotism of Sparta and Rome, considering outsiders virtual enemies, so that the group's patriotic sentiment and collective creed overrides all other values, Spinoza privileges the universal values enabling men of all kinds to live in peace and harmony together. This vital difference also explains the wide divergence between Rousseau and Radical Enlightenment with respect to ecclesiastical authority and censorship. For Spinoza and the radical tradition (unlike Hobbes and Locke), stripping every church and all priests of their effective authority in law, education, and the state is essential. For any residual power churches and priests retain not only detracts from the absolute power of the democratic republic but is inherently divisive, mobilizing some in society against others, classifying men by their beliefs, and breaking the true collectivity of the democratic republic by creating ranks and usurping quasi-political powers of approving and disapproving of individuals and their behaviour and thoughts. Where the democratic republic is truly absolute in Spinoza's sense, 'no-one shall be obliged to live according to the criteria or will of another individual and each is guaranteed his own liberty of life-style and thought'.[25] Where absolute in Rousseau's sense, individuals must also be forced to live not just in accordance with the law but also contrary to their own ideas and preferences where these conflict with a collective creed sanctioned by tradition and patriotism, an entirely different conception. From this follow in Rousseau's thought many consequences that are entirely foreign to Spinoza and the radical tradition.

It was a rift which extended also to the role of legislation in society. Law for Rousseau has an unimpeachable and sacrosanct quality whereas in Diderot, d'Holbach, and also Condorcet, who uses the phrase 'the common reason', law follows rather from the usefulness of man to man and the idea that legislation must conform to universal philosophical principles or be 'in conformity with reason and truth', as Condorcet put it, in direct opposition to Rousseau; for otherwise, even if binding in some sense, it is blameworthy and morally useless. The principles

---

[22] Riley, 'Rousseau's General Will', 16–18; d'Holbach, *Politique naturelle*, 30–1, 36.
[23] Arendt, *On Revolution*, 72–4; O'Hagan, *Rousseau*, 120–2.
[24] Wright, *Classical Republican*, 103, 121–2.
[25] O'Hagan, *Rousseau*, 93; Spinoza, *Tractatus Theologico-Politicus*, 64.

underpinning the 'general will' must be enacted to guard men against the dangers abounding on every side and to maximize the collective instinct for group security. Legislation must utilize the universal desire for rules to enable individuals fully to enjoy their individual freedom in their own way while minimizing the disruptive effects of appetite, individual passions, and antisocial temperaments.[26]

Diderot, d'Holbach, and Rousseau, then, all drastically redefine what sovereignty is, reconfiguring it in a firmly anti-Hobbesian direction, moving away from sovereignty located in forms, and in the state and especially the monarch, as well as away from Hobbes's overriding concern with safety and stability. Common to these thinkers is a shift to perspectives locating sovereignty in the well-being of the citizenry, and hence in the *volonté générale*. With their sovereign 'general will', all three discard the entire apparatus of Hobbesian and Lockean contractual thinking. There is no longer any contract because the state, for them, and hence the government, is merely the servant and mouthpiece of society, an instrument for securing the common good of the people, a redefining of sovereignty transforming even the constitutional king into basically a citizen himself.[27] With this concept of sovereignty, a whole new rhetoric of citizenship without contract emerges with the consequence that no prince or king can ever justly decide policy or allocate resources, and much less wage war, in his own interest. He can legitimately rule, as d'Holbach puts it, 'uniquement pour ceux de sa nation'.[28]

In Rousseau, as in Diderot, d'Holbach, and Naigeon, the general will has a thoroughly equalizing role: all citizens are equally subject to, and benefit from, its sway: 'every authentic act of the general will, binds or favours all the citizens equally'.[29] In certain respects, though, this *Spinosiste* turn is carried through more radically in Diderot and d'Holbach than Rousseau. For the former were always more emphatic in claiming 'l'équité est à la justice', as Diderot puts it, as cause is to effect, so that the basis of justice, in any republic, cannot be deemed anything other than 'l'équité déclarée'. Therefore, 'l'équité est supérieure à toutes les lois' and the 'general will' must in essence be the same for all humans everywhere. Hence, it should govern international relations as well as any particular society, a conclusion diametrically opposite to Rousseau who was almost as dismissive of the radical notion of an international order, and the quest for world peace, as Voltaire.[30] As d'Holbach later expressed this idea: the human race should be regarded as a 'vaste société à qui la nature impose les mêmes loix', just as any properly organized particular society should impose the same rules equally 'à tous ses membres'.[31] While the general will

---

[26] D'Holbach, *Système social*, 205–8; Baker, *Condorcet*, 230; Goggi, 'Spinoza contro Rousseau', 137–9, 145, 147–8.
[27] D'Holbach, *Politique naturelle*, 112–13, 119, 123, 132–3, 163, 464; Tortarolo, *L'Illuminismo*, 147; O'Hagan, *Rousseau*, 151.
[28] D'Holbach, *Politique naturelle*, 123; Miller, *Rousseau*, 80.
[29] Rousseau, *Social Contract*, 207; Rosenblatt, *Rousseau*, 245–6.
[30] Diderot, 'Droit naturel', in Diderot and d'Alembert (eds.), *Encyclopédie*, v. 116; Einaudi, *Early Rousseau*, 172–4; Hassner, 'Rousseau', 211.
[31] D'Holbach, *Politique naturelle*, 465–6.

in different republics will probably overlap in part, also for Rousseau, it is by no means deemed a single and universal absolute, neither is it something that arises from nature in Diderot's sense.[32] Neither does Rousseau's 'general will' need to conform to justice, or even be particularly sensible. Rather it leaves ample room for bigotry and also, as has been noted, for racism.[33] Rousseau never joins in the attack on black slavery. His 'general will' is more a question of what is willed, of volition: 'a people is always the master to change its laws', urges the *Contrat social*, 'even the best ones; for if it chooses to do itself harm, who has the right to prevent it from doing so?'[34]

These distinctions between the *volonté générale* of the *nouveaux Spinosistes* and Rousseauist doctrine, and more broadly the differences between Spinoza's and Rousseau's visions of democracy, pervade the whole of the ideological struggle that was to commence in France, in 1788, from the outset. Equality in Rousseau's sense of sharing in a particular 'general will' as participants in the republic diverges dramatically from Spinoza's and Diderot's doctrine especially at the point where individuals, for the latter, being infinitely diverse and divergent in their physiological and emotional make-up, are equal in rights and freedom but can never share in a 'general will' of feeling and sentiment that is particular rather than universal.[35] Where Rousseau sets up a polarity, indeed antagonism, between society and nature, and feeling and reason, Spinoza and Diderot strive to bridge these polarities. For Spinoza, Diderot, and d'Holbach *volonté générale* inescapably embodies an absolute ethics that is one, unified, and the same for all men, anchored in society's needs and hence in nature. For Rousseau, conversely, *volonté générale* embodies rather the specific identity of a given body politic that is not, or not so directly, based on any universal ethics and entails an enforced, positive equality rejected as completely fictional by Diderot.[36] This explains why patriotism and national feeling, not least in his recommended constitutions for Corsica and Poland, are so powerfully stressed in Rousseau.[37]

Inculcating a militant patriotism vaunting ancient tradition is, for Rousseau, the most authentic and effective way to teach citizens to be law-abiding, virtuous, and equal, a notion that makes no sense in Spinoza's, Diderot's, or d'Holbach's schema. The latter's universalism governing the goals of all government and law irrevocably separates their 'general will' from Rousseau's, creating two not just distinct but inherently antagonistic models. With monarchical government now stripped of 'contract' as well as the hereditary principle, what has gone before—great legislators, tradition, charters, historical precedents—loses all power to confer legitimacy. Reason, equality, and justice are the exclusive guiding principles to which governments and reigning monarchs must adhere, rulers being subject to these in exactly the same

---

[32] Diderot, 'Droit naturel', in *Encyclopédie*, v. 116; Hulliung, *Autocritique*, 172; Gauthier, *Rousseau*, 60–1.
[33] Sala-Molins, *Code noir*, 248; Buck-Morss, *Hegel and Haiti*, 34.
[34] Rousseau, *Social Contract*, 227; Miller, *Rousseau*, 62; O'Hagan, *Rousseau*, 122.
[35] Imbruglia, 'Indignation', 132–5; Villaverde, 'Spinoza, Rousseau', 97; Kaitaro, *Diderot's Holism*, 194–7.
[36] Miller, *Rousseau*, 62; Wokler, 'Rousseau and his Critics', 190.
[37] Einaudi, *Early Rousseau*, 186; Borghero, 'Sparta', 315; Parker, 'Souveraineté', 31.

way as the rest of the citizenry.[38] However, there were also a few notable points of convergence. In particular, Rousseau's insistence, in the article 'Économie politique', that any legitimate government directed in the interest of the people should have as a major goal that of preventing extreme inequality of wealth from developing. This is characteristic also of the radical *encyclopédistes*.

Precluding the further growth of inequality should be achieved, held Rousseau, not by confiscating wealth from those that possess it but rather by suppressing the ways and means of accumulating riches at the expense of others. Precisely this was also the view of the radical *encyclopédistes*, as also was Rousseau's hostility to the *taille* and other burdens falling especially on the peasantry in France and elsewhere, and his insistence on minimizing the tax burden on rural producers and peasants and shifting as much of the burden as possible onto commerce, finance, and industry, especially the production of non-essential items and items where profitability is particularly high. This tendency, marked in Quesnay's writing, and physiocratic economics more generally, was in fact common to all the *encyclopédistes* as well as Rousseau.[39] Taxes are required to raise revenue for government. But they should be devised as far as possible, held Diderot and Rousseau alike, to work against the continual augmentation of wealth inequality and the progressive subjection to the rich of a 'multitude d'ouvriers et de serviteurs inutiles'.

2. RADICAL ENLIGHTENMENT, REVOLUTION, AND ROUSSEAU'S COUNTER-ENLIGHTENMENT

Among the most powerful and eloquent writers of his century, Rousseau re-emerged as a major rhetorical and intellectual force during the Revolution. This is a historical fact of fundamental importance in its own right. Admittedly, his specifically political works, in particular the *Contrat social*, had considerably less impact on the public before 1789 than his *Émile* and *La Nouvelle Héloïse*. But Rousseauism was a wide-ranging, emotional creed, a cult as much as a doctrine, a set of sentiments above all, emanating from the whole body of his writings rather than just the political works alone. Between 1764 and 1789 there were at least sixteen editions of Rousseau's complete or selected works including the *Contrat social* with roughly another fifteen editions of the *Contrat* on its own, proving Rousseau's most systematic political work did actually enjoy a more substantial diffusion in pre-revolutionary France than is sometimes alleged.[40]

Journalists and commentators prominent in reporting and diffusing the debates and declarations of the French Revolution soon learnt that Rousseau, whether or not

---

[38] D'Holbach, *Politique naturelle*, 124–5.
[39] Rousseau, 'Économie morale et politique', in Diderot and d'Alembert (eds.), *Encyclopédie*, v. 347–8.
[40] Barny, 'Rousseau', 62; Furet, 'Rousseau', 168–9, 175.

acknowledged by name, was the Revolution's most quoted, useful, and constantly fertile fund of slogans, phrases, and reform proposals of all kinds. To those seeking to de-legitimize the privileged orders, the nobility and clergy, and introduce equality and other basic changes, no one proved more serviceable than Rousseau. During the decisive weeks following the fall of the Bastille when the major steps towards social as well as constitutional revolution were taken in France, and when the privileges of the nobility and clergy were abolished, and many future steps projected, the Revolution's leading figures, both in the National Assembly and in leading revolutionary papers and numerous pamphlets, continually invoked Rousseau, albeit far more often tacitly than citing him by name and usually borrowing his phrases out of context. Mirabeau, Sieyès, Volney, Brissot, Rabaud Saint-Étienne, Bailly, all those prominent in the crucial debates of July, August, and September 1789, employed *Rousseauiste* rhetoric, terms, and concepts.

Consequently, the politically most crucial moments of the Revolution were steeped in intensely charged ideological terms carrying a complex baggage of prior philosophical strife and tension. As Montesquieu fell progressively from favour, during the early revolutionary debates, especially after the defeat of the so-called *monarchiens*, in September 1789, being too closely associated with mixed monarchy and with an aristocratic vision of society on the British model,[41] Rousseau came more and more to the fore, his name, more than that of any other thinker, being linked to the concept of popular sovereignty, eulogizing the people and the idea of 'democracy'. However, the 'Rousseau' that loomed so large during 1788–90 as well as during the middle and, then, later stages of the Revolution, and the Robespierriste Terror, was rarely identical to the Rousseau of reality but rather a repackaged and remodelled 'Rousseau' extensively pruned in successive stages.

The aspects of Rousseauism most at odds with radical thought, and *l'esprit philosophique*—the attack on the concept of progress and the sciences, and idealization of the pristine state and state of nature—were largely screened out from the beginning. Other aspects such as the stress on patriotism, disparagement of philosophy, and the primacy of the feelings of the common man were made much of but only in specific, and especially Jacobin, contexts.[42] Yet other features of Rousseau's thought could be used only after drastic revision. Among those most active in projecting Rousseau's image as the pre-eminent inspirer of the Revolution during the Revolution's early stages was the radical-minded revolutionary utopian journalist Mercier who, unsurprisingly, proved to be simultaneously both an ardent admirer and an incisive critic. The radical 'Rousseau' he projected, most notably in his *De J. J. Rousseau considéré comme l'un des premiers auteurs de la Révolution* (Paris, 1791), was designed to promote what he considered the chief principle to be gleaned from Rousseau's œuvre, namely that even the best and most constitutional real 'monarchy' is merely 'un despotisme modéré' and that only a constitution that is 'démocratique' is and can be truly legitimate.[43]

---

[41] Linguet, *Annales politiques*, 16 (1790), 271; Mercier, *De J. J. Rousseau considéré*, i. 168.
[42] Barny, 'Rousseau', 63–4.
[43] Ibid. 55–6; Barny, 'Rousseau', 66–7; Damrosch, *Jean-Jacques Rousseau*, 351.

An aspect of Rousseau's thought that proved especially useful in 1789, and subsequently, was his insistent emphasis on *vertu publique* and eloquence in linking *vertu publique* with a fiery patriotism entirely alien to the radical tradition.[44] During the summer of 1789, especially after the fall of the Bastille on 14 July, as revolutionary agitation and violence acquired a firm grip among the populace of Paris, and the country became increasingly deeply divided with a still powerful aristocratic-clerical bloc rallying behind the throne and remnants of the royal army gathering not far off, near anarchy spread across much of France and the normal workings of the state seemed all but paralysed. In many regions, the peasantry took matters into their own hands and a general breakdown of law and order threatened. At this point leading voices in and outside the National Assembly—Mirabeau, Sieyès, Brissot, Volney, and Condorcet, all ardent disciples of radical thought—found themselves in an emergency requiring forms of rhetoric the radical tradition itself lacked. What the 'revolution of reason' did not have was a steely edge. As Volney emphasized in a speech of 18 September 1789, 'toute puissance publique' was now enfeebled, faltering, and ill assured, the country's courts of justice indecisive, collection of taxes brought to a halt, reconstitution of the country and its constitution by the National Assembly advancing only excruciatingly slowly. To gain a better grip, speed things up, and achieve 'une représentation véritablement nationale' to replace the old Estates' 'représentation vicieuse et contradictoire' what was needed was firmer resolve and more impetus and passion; 'vertu publique' had to be declared a duty for all who loved 'le bien public' and wished to be good citizens.[45]

Vertu publique proved not just a useful slogan but a matter of life and death for the Revolution. Had not Rousseau taught that to enjoy the rights of the citizen without wishing to fulfil the duties is an injustice threatening the entire body politic with ruin?[46] Rousseau could supply that fervour and streak of fanaticism, that stress on the unity and unbreakable harmony of 'virtue', religion, and republicanism that radical thought itself lacked but the Revolution, seemingly, desperately needed. His republican zeal, exaltation of the people, and devotion to *vertu publique*, justifying harsh measures against opponents and dissidents, rendered Rousseau's message indispensable. It was the only way of justifying the use of coercion against those opposing revolutionary change, a process culminating in the frequent explicit invoking of Rousseau by Robespierre and Saint-Just during the Terror of 1793–4.[47]

Other features of Rousseau's thought, however, were not just less amenable but positively inimical to the revolutionary purpose. Most obvious was Rousseau's pessimism about the feasibility of forming a democratic republic in a large country like France.[48] But there were also other crucial drawbacks to using his political thought. Especially problematic from the revolutionary leadership's viewpoint was that his

---

[44] Mercier, *De J. J. Rousseau considéré*, i. 159–60, 165, 171.
[45] PBN 8–LE29–218: 'Motion de M. de Volney député d'Anjou, séance du 18 septembre 1789', 1–2, 4.
[46] Mercier, *De J. J. Rousseau considéré*, i. 165.
[47] Lafrance, 'Idée rousseauiste', 34–5; Guehenno, *Jean-Jacques Rousseau*, ii. 262.
[48] Barny, 'Rousseau', 73.

political writings provided no 'clear and positive constituent power', as Mercier put it, separate from the people and vested in their representatives.[49] A revolution, as the National Assembly of 1789 understood it, is by definition a transformation of institutions in the people's name by a constituent assembly of equal delegates all with same credentials and status (and hence having only one chamber) acting in its collective interest. But Rousseau flatly denies that the people's sovereign power can be thus delegated.[50]

In his *Contrat social*, Rousseau laid down that the *volonté générale* 'cannot be represented' [ne peut point être représentée]. Sieyès called this an 'unfortunate phrase' and asked 'why not'? In fact in a large and complex society with people busy with many different things vital to them, it fits better with the whole tenor of society and movement of things that a few vital specific points in the wishes of each should be dealt with by proxy and by procurators.[51] The whole principle of 'representatives' and representative democracy as espoused by Diderot, d'Holbach, and Naigeon, and also Mably, and adopted as central to their approach by Mirabeau, Sieyès, Condorcet, Volney, Brissot, Paine, Cloots, Maréchal, Mercier, and the Dutch democratic movement in the 1780s, was incompatible with Rousseau and yet fundamental to the Revolution.[52] Furthermore, while Rousseau's *volonté générale* afforded the patriotic zeal that Diderot's and d'Holbach's lacked, it was devoid of the moral universalism, the emphasis on equality of rights and equity as the basis of justice and the moral order, basic to *la philosophie nouvelle*'s political agenda and fundamental to the Revolution.[53] This was a major drawback for the revolutionary leadership because Rousseau's doctrine is altogether unconducive to such an approach, in fact a barrier to any programme of basic and universal human rights, something the Assembly's leaders were strongly committed to from the outset.[54] *The Declaration of the Rights of Man and the Citizen* unquestionably had little or nothing to do with Rousseau; its roots were in philosophy, and especially in radical thought, not in feelings and not in French society. But it was the very basis of the revolutionary outlook and agenda.

But this was not all. For in Rousseau, notes Mercier, there is no clear right of resistance to oppressive government, or affirmation of the people's right to change its government, a message central to the *Histoire philosophique* and the late political thought of Diderot, d'Holbach, Deleyre, Raynal, and Mercier as well as of the revolutionary leadership and indispensable to the ideology of the Revolution.[55] Finally, for radicals it was a decided nuisance that Rousseau limits toleration and, as the concomitant of his intolerance, retains a strong censorship to uphold

---

[49] Mercier, *De J. J. Rousseau considéré*, i. 59–60 and ii. 12–13; Rousseau, *Émile*, 425–7; Bonnerot, 'Louis-Sebastien Mercier', 421; Furet, 'Rousseau', 173.

[50] Barny, 'Rousseau', 73–4; Lafrance, 'Idée rousseauiste', 31–2, 35; Baker, *Condorcet*, 230.

[51] Rousseau, *Social Contract*, 266; Sieyès, *Manuscrits*, 510; Pasquino, *Sieyès*, 43–5.

[52] Mercier, *De J. J. Rousseau considéré*, ii. 12; Mounier, *De l'influence*, 119; Wright, *Classical Republican*, 123.

[53] Mercier, *De J. J. Rousseau considéré*, ii. 32–4; Villaverde, 'Spinoza, Rousseau', 96, 100.

[54] Mercier, *De J. J. Rousseau considéré*, ii. 34; Sa'adah, *Shaping of Liberal Politics*, 193.

[55] Mercier, *De J. J. Rousseau considéré*, i. 60–1 and ii. 3; Bonnerot, 'Louis-Sebastien Mercier', 421–2; Jourdan, 'Le Culte', 58.

'morality' as well as safeguard opinion. 'As the law is the declaration of the general will, the censorship is the declaration of the public judgment.'[56] These distinctly illiberal features of his thought were totally at odds with Diderot, d'Holbach, and the radical agenda and had no place in the 'Revolution of reason', the Revolution that is in its liberal pre-Robespierriste phase, broadly the years 1789–92.

In his influential re-interpretation of the Revolution, François Furet rightly held that there 'is not much of the Social Contract [of Rousseau] in the French Revolution'.[57] But he was quite mistaken in the inferences he drew from this. His conclusion that the revolutionary experience itself, the ebb and flow of politics, the habits and the reflexes of the people, and not books and philosophers were the main determinants in shaping the revolutionary outcome, fails to explain how it was that the essential, guiding principles formulated by the revolutionary leaders in 1788–9 were highly theoretical and uncompromisingly universalist and had even less to do with the traditional reflexes of the *ancien régime* than they had to do with Rousseau. The agenda of 1788–9 obviously had nothing to do with the habits and experiences of the people except insofar as they responded to the summons to rise and establish a new order. Where the agenda sprang from was the thinking of the twenty or thirty *philosophes-révolutionnaires* leading the Revolution in Paris. The correct conclusion, if we are to place the Revolution in its proper perspective, is not Furet's but something else: what the historian and philosopher must focus on are the ideological components accounting for the major differences between Rousseau's republicanism, and subsequently the Robespierriste revolution, on the one hand, and the democratic republicanism of the revolutionary leadership of 1788–92, on the other. This involves exploring the reservations, mistrust, and suspicion of Rousseau everywhere evident in the thought of Sieyès, Mirabeau, Condorcet, Volney, Roederer, Mercier, Cloots, Gorani, and other revolutionary leaders, many or most of whom were publicly or privately highly critical of Rousseau.[58] 'Quoi de plus ridicule', exclaimed Naigeon in 1792, than 'les éloges exagérés' the Revolution's legislators so fulsomely lavished on Rousseau. Content with a mere few scraps of knowledge of political thought, the revolutionary leadership had negligently produced a constitution, parts of which immediately needed adjusting and the rest of which needed to be completely redone 'sur d'autres principes'.[59] But all active, committed *révolutionnaires* rejected Rousseau to a degree; they had to, even if they pretended otherwise. Naigeon remarked, in 1792, that his open hostility to Rousseau would doubtless sound like blasphemy to 'ces fanatiques exclusivement consacrés au culte de Rousseau', abounding among both rank and file and, from 1792 until Robespierre's downfall in August 1794, among the leaders of the 'Revolution of the Will' of 1792–4. But as he saw it, saving the Revolution depended precisely on defeating Rousseau, curbing these *fanatiques*, and upholding the sway of reason.

[56] Rousseau, *Social Contract*, 296; O'Hagan, *Rousseau*, 156–7.
[57] Furet, 'Rousseau', 175–6, 178.
[58] Ibid. 173–4; Baker, *Condorcet*, 230, 243; Williams, *Condorcet and Modernity*, 93, 135, 174, 268.
[59] Naigeon, *Philosophie*, iii. 151.

Via careful selection, the Revolution absorbed large swathes of both Rousseau *and* his radical opponents. But this involved entrenching within the Revolution's democratic republicanism an inherent and irresolvable ideological contradiction, an underlying conflict of ideas that could not easily be resolved without disruption and violence. If there was scant difference between the radical *philosophes* and Rousseau concerning his slogan 'man is born free and yet is everywhere in chains', huge differences lodged in their contrasting notions of what removing the chains, emancipation, and individual liberty involved. Mercier himself perfectly symbolized the dilemmas of those eager to conflate Rousseau with the legacy of radical thought.

Though more of a Rousseau enthusiast during the Revolution than Mirabeau, Sieyès, and the others, he too accepted that there were formidable difficulties, political and intellectual, inherent in Rousseau's thought from the perspective of the revolutionary leadership. Curiously rendered into English under the title *Memoirs of the Year Two Thousand Five Hundred* (London, 1772), his blueprint for utopia utterly extinguishes theology and theologians, separates morality completely from theology, reforms the law along lines specified by Beccaria, and adopts the *Encyclopédie* as the standard textbook in children's education.[60] The revolution he foresaw in 1771 envisaged the coming transformation of human society as chiefly the task of 'philosophy', the 'philosopher' being defined by him, as by Diderot and d'Holbach, as 'that sagacious and virtuous being who desires general happiness, in consequence of those determinate ideas of order and harmony that he entertains'.[61] His vision differed, though, from the Radical Enlightenment of Helvétius, Diderot, and d'Holbach in being fused with strong doses of both sentimentality and fanaticism.

Already in 1771, Mercier fused radical ideas with Rousseauism not least in his assault on theologians and case lawyers whom he saw 'as a kind of vermin preying on society' and in his extraordinary proposals for ridding mankind of what he saw as the contagion of *ancien régime* case law. Fundamental to the coming revolution, predicted Mercier eighteen years before the actual Revolution, would be immense bonfires on which stupendous quantities of theological and at least 'eight hundred thousand volumes of law' would be hurled.[62] The thousands of lawyers plaguing *ancien régime* society were to be ruthlessly eradicated.[63] Among the statues to great men adorning and inspiring his society of the future, he predicted, would be one to Rousseau standing alongside those of Montesquieu, Buffon, and Voltaire.[64]

In the years 1789–92, as a prominent political commentator, and editor of the revolutionary journal *Les Annales patriotiques et littéraires* (1789–97), Mercier contributed to the process of selecting from Rousseau's legacy and adapting Rousseau to the exigencies of the actual Revolution. He remained loyal to the Rousseauist component of his revolutionary creed up to a point.[65] But in doing so he was also

---

[60] Mercier, *Memoirs of the Year*, i. 60–1, 66, 87.　　　[61] Ibid. i. 1.
[62] Ibid. ii. 5; Muthu, *Enlightenment*, 299 n. 25; Thomas, *Slave Trade*, 481.
[63] Mercier, *Memoirs of the Year*, i. 88–90.　　　[64] Ibid. i. 66.
[65] Naigeon, *Philosophie*, iii. 150–1.

forced to list a large number of specific drawbacks and defects. In the end, he was not far from agreeing with Anarcharsis Cloots's ringing judgement of August 1791, in one of the main journals of the revolution, the *Chronique de Paris*, where he speaks of this Rousseau whom we all love 'but whose mistakes, it is true, are as dangerous as his genius is sublime' [mais dont les erreurs, il est vrai, sont aussi dangereuses que son génie est sublime].[66]

[66] Labbé, *Anarcharsis Cloots*, 163–4.

24

Radical Breakthrough

1. D'HOLBACH'S 'BOMBS'

In the book history of the pre-Revolution era, the year 1770 has a special significance as the publication year of the century's two mostly widely read radical works—the *Histoire philosophique* and the *Système de la nature*. Both exerted a powerful influence over the subsequent history of radical ideas, the cultural impact of radical thought, and on the origins of the revolutionary process. But it was the latter that most systematically and incisively summed up the doctrines of *la philosophie moderne*. In a century in which 'la cabale philosophique' raised the standard of irreligion and revolt on all sides, asserted the ex-Jesuit *anti-philosophe* Aimé-Henri Paulian (1722–1802), shortly before the Revolution, this subversive cabal issued its general 'code scandaleux' in 1770 under the title *Système de la nature*.[1]

The two-volume *Système* appeared anonymously and with a false title page declaring 'Mirabaud' the author and 'London' the place of publication, in February 1770. Fréron, like Bergier, at once recognized here the logical summation of the entire corpus of *philosophisme*, the foe he had fought for two decades. The mask of concealment had hitherto never altogether slipped from the visage of *la philosophie*, he asserted in his review in *L'Année littéraire*.[2] Traces of decency and submission to authority had previously restrained all freethinkers. But now 'cette doctrine exécrable' was fully bare-faced with its blasphemous claim there is no God, or ordained authority or morality, and that all is matter and the movement and interests of bodies. This supreme bible of atheism he pronounced a 'ramas de blasphèmes et d'absurdités réchauffé de Spinoza'.[3]

While the police actively suppressed the work from the outset, and many eager persons trying to obtain it in the spring of 1770 were unable to, Bergier already guessed, in February as the furore first erupted and only some 200 copies were yet circulating in Paris, that its impact would be unprecedented.[4] By late March, leaders of opinion ands several courtiers were engrossed. The initial hundreds of copies

---

[1] Paulian, *Véritable Système de la nature*, i, preface p. 1 and p. 179 and ii. 162.
[2] Fréron, *L'Année littéraire* (1770/8), 313.
[3] Ibid. 314; Balcou, *Fréron*, 329–30.
[4] Balcou, *Fréron*, 23; *Mémoires secrets*, v. 67; Deschamps, *Correspondance*, 341, 345, 348, 356.

swiftly became thousands. Banned by the Holy Office, in Rome, in November, what began as the focus of a purely French controversy quickly became European in scope as more and more bans and editions materialized—pirated French editions, Swiss editions, additional Dutch editions, and before long versions printed in Britain and Germany as well.

To Paulian, a professor of physics and mathematics at Avignon, a son of a Protestant minister and convert to Catholicism from Nîmes, author of *Le Véritable Système de la nature* (2 vols., Avignon, 1788), a rebuttal composed a whole two decades after its target, the *Système* seemed chiefly inspired by Diderot's views on biology and science generally. Fusing science and social theory, this work capped all previous efforts to overthrow existing structures of authority, religion, and politics with its thesis that promoting men's worldly happiness is the sole valid criterion in evaluating the legitimacy of laws and government. The work seemed to Paulian and others the very distillation of all that is most contrary to God, faith, piety, and morality found in 'Diderot, Voltaire, Bayle, Spinoza, Hobbes, Epicurus and Lucretius'.[5] A summation based partly on ancient thought, especially Lucretius, and partly on modern ideas, especially 'the Jew Spinoza', 'le premier impie', he wrote, echoing Bayle, who dared present atheism 'd'une manière systématique'.[6] It was a total outrage, adds Paulian, that its authors, veritable 'Apôtres du mensonge', had not been seized and imprisoned.

'Since Spinoza', wrote a high-society army officer, the Baron Antoine-Joseph d'Arcy, to his philosophical friend the Marquis de Voyer, from Paris, in March 1770, 'nothing has appeared so much in favour of atheism.'[7] Fruit of a group effort redacting a long tradition reaching back to Spinoza and Bayle, from the moment it appeared the *Système* was deemed 'le nouveau Code de nos philosophes modernes'.[8] Voltaire read it at once, in the month of its publication, January 1770, and then again, seeing its pivotal significance for *la philosophie* and the future of his cause.[9] From the first, he denounced it as a powerful but defective work grounded on a faulty grasp of science. On him, old and ill though he was, the book had an energizing as well as deeply disconcerting effect. Countless readers, he observed, eight months after its publication and shortly after it was officially banned together with six other texts—mostly by d'Holbach—by the *Parlement*, had already read it. What chiefly troubled him, as always, was not the radical *philosophes'* metaphysics and science as such, from which he was no longer as removed as he had once been, but their proposing to assail God, the devil, rulers, and priests, as he put it in July 1770, all at the same time; and that, in so doing, they were obviously winning the sympathy of many sophisticated readers. By June Bonnet had read it and written to Formey, assuring him that no

---

[5] Paulain, *Véritable Système de la nature*, ii. 162, 271–84, 300, 325, 382.
[6] Ibid. i. 57–60, 263, 335 and ii. 149–50, 325–7.
[7] Deschamps, *Correspondance*, 340.
[8] Paulain, *Véritable Système de la nature*, i, preface pp. ii, xvi–xvii; de Bujando, *Index*, 443.
[9] Voltaire, *Dieu. Réponse*, 4.

more 'infernal' work had ever been published: 'Spinosa n'est rien auprès de l'auteur. Je crains qu'on le refute mal.'[10]

With the furore erupting in the wake of the *Système* the full implications of *la philosophie moderne*'s 'invasion of the republic of letters in France', and what Pidsansat de Mairobert, in the subversive journal *Mémoires secrets*, called the 'revolution it has caused in men's minds', finally emerged.[11] In Paris, the *Système* divided opinion, in fact 'tous les esprits', down the middle, noted Voltaire, as neatly as any minuet at Versailles, some readers deeming it highly damaging, others enthusing over it as a secular revelation.[12] This more or less open schism in enlightened circles manifested itself in an obtrusive manner in France, and soon also Germany, Italy, Holland, and Britain, and eventually became obvious also in Spain, Russia, Scandinavia, and the Americas. Even in Hungary and Poland, by 1789, there were a few isolated voices enthusing over this new philosophy. Voltaire, like d'Alembert and Galiani, was one of those who thought the work far too long and repetitive. Had it been more concise, it would have had 'un effet terrible' though even as it is 'il en fait beaucoup'. Voltaire's correspondence during his last years shows that he viewed the work as the supreme challenge of his philosophical career, something he had to defeat if he was to remain the public figurehead of the *parti philosophique* in any meaningful sense. The rising prestige of *la philosophie nouvelle* in its fully atheist-materialist format menaced his standing in a way that prompted him to review his entire intellectual œuvre both as an intellectual system and public stance. For with this text his intellectual and tactical leadership of the cabal came more than ever into question. Voltaire grew fearful, as Grimm rather brutally expressed it, lest the *Système* overthrow the ritual of Ferney and lest 'le patriarchat ne s'en aille au diable avec lui'.[13]

In composing the *Système*, d'Holbach professed to have based it on *l'expérience*, meaning scientific experiment together with political and social experience. But his and Diderot's was decidedly not the empiricism of Locke so revered by Voltaire, but rather that deriving all intellectual faculties from the capacity to feel and experience envisaging the mind, rooted in nerve fibres, is an integral part of the body.[14] For the rest of his career as a *philosophe*, the atheistic hylozoism of d'Holbach, Diderot, and their disciples linked to democratic republicanism and a generalized assault on monarchy, aristocracy, and the Church was the prime target of Voltaire's opposing efforts not just in his *Questions sur l'Encyclopédie* (1770–1), his last large-scale work, and many letters, but also his *Réponse* to the *Système*, the *Lettres de Memmius* (1771), and the *Histoire de Jenni* (1775), his last philosophical story.[15] D'Holbach's, Diderot's, and Helvétius's ideas, however repugnant and unscientific in the eyes of Voltaire, were incontestably penetrating near and far.

---

[10] *Lettres de Genève*, 788.
[11] *Mémoires secrets*, i. 3; Baker, *Inventing the French Revolution*, 110–11, 187.
[12] Naville, *Paul Thiry d'Holbach*, 111–12; Negroni, *Lectures*, 348.
[13] Monty, *Critique littéraire*, 113–14; Pellerin, 'Diderot, Voltaire', 61.
[14] D'Holbach, *Système de la nature*, 167, 228–37.
[15] Cronk, 'Voltaire (non-)lecteur', 179.

The cultural consequences of such an acrimonious furore, and such a severe crackdown by the Paris police, were bound to be far-ranging. Parents throughout France, declared Bishop Laulannier of Egie, aggrieved by the impact of *le nouveau système philosophique* for society, worried lest their sons be spiritually corrupted through reading such books.[16] The landgrave of Hesse-Cassel received word that the French prelates, seizing the opportunity, were again vehemently denouncing *la philosophie* at every turn while the Paris publishers for the time being had abandoned all thought of reprinting or distributing the *Encyclopédie*.[17] Of all the forbidden books 'condemned to the flames' and creating a great din in Germany in the 1770s, recalled Goethe who read it at Strasbourg, also in 1770, writing years later in his *Dichtung und Wahrheit* (professing to scorn it), it was above all the *Système de la nature*, a work that he read 'out of curiosity', that 'we took in hand'.[18]

'La philosophie', as a system of reforming, enlightened values, had now tilted, perhaps decisively, against the 'moderate' goals of Montesquieu, Voltaire, Turgot, and Hume. In 1770, the 'modern philosophy' effectively graduated from the underground to become a public if still illicit cultural phenomenon of the first order and for the first time since the Seven Years War was again invoked as a cause of current political difficulties. Louis XV's new chief minister, Maupeou, publicly supported by Voltaire (at the price of seriously annoying Choiseul) and to an extent Turgot,[19] tried to deflect the opprobrium stemming from his heavy-handed attempts at political reform onto his *parlementaire* opponents. *Parlementaire* resistance to royal policy, he suggested, in his edict of 27 November 1770, smacked of deliberate subversion aggravated by the corrupting influence of the *philosophes* and their *esprit de système*.[20]

But this was a distinctly risky strategy given that the *parlements* boasted a better record than the royal court as opponents of the *Encyclopédie* and *la philosophie*. Such a tactic was also highly ironic given Diderot's, Helvétius's, and Condorcet's (besides Voltaire's) withering contempt for the *parlements*.[21] All the *philosophes* viewed France's legal aristocracy as more crassly steeped in precedent, legalism, Jansenism, and tradition than anyone else. If Diderot considered Maupeou a scoundrel and a tool of despotism, 'ces infâmes' of the *parlements*, and the *noblesse de robe*, he had long deemed a serious obstacle to human liberty, improvement, and the 'general will', indeed reason itself.[22] That king and ministers were now more actively combating *la philosophie* and intensifying their efforts against 'forbidden' books, struck Voltaire, meanwhile, as a disastrous development. Writing to d'Alembert on 2 November 1770, he styled the *Système* 'un grand mal moral', a book, according to Voltaire, doing immense harm to their cause at Versailles and throughout France, a work read by the

---

[16] Laulannier, *Essais*, 244.   [17] Voltaire, *Corr.* xxxvii. 133.
[18] Pecharroman, *Morals*, 21 n.; Sauter, 'Paul Thiry', 132; Goethe read it again years later, borrowing it for several months in 1812–13 from the Jena university library.
[19] Echeverria, *Maupeou Revolution*, 147–55, 233–4.
[20] Ibid. 53–4, 228, 231–3, 235–7; Gay, *Voltaire's Politics*, 32.
[21] Strugnell, *Diderot's Politics*, 135–6; Spitz, 'Civism to Civility', 118.
[22] Diderot, *Réfutation*, 380; Diderot, *Lettre apologétique*, 157.

ignorant and women besides *savants*.[23] The author, ruining philosophy for ever in the minds of all the magistrates and heads of households, had rendered all 'philosophes exécrables' 'in the eyes of the king and the whole court'.[24] 'Ce maudit *Système de la nature*', he assured d'Alembert in January 1771, a year after first perusing it, had blighted their cause, 'et nous voilà perdus' for a book all sensible people despise.[25] He and his following among the *parti philosophique*, the partisans of Lockean empiricism and Newtonianism, he believed, had suffered a possibly irreversible defeat. Had the book been as good as it was actually bad, its author should still not have published it but thrown it on the fire. His side would never recover from 'cette blessure mortelle'. Even long after, the year 1770 was remembered as a turning point, the *Système de la nature* being what one enthusiastic radical, under Napoleon, called 'le plus beau monument' que la philosophie ait élevé à la raison'.[26]

Philosophically, the rift had long been discernible. But from 1770 it began to exert an unprecedented effect on opinion and the public sphere. Whereas Spinoza had been read by very few, explained the Dutch Sephardic *philosophe* Isaac de Pinto in 1774, at Amsterdam, the modern *philosophes matérialistes* made massive inroads among 'les esprits foibles et demi savants' within a very short time, owing to their deft methods, excellent style, and 'superficial' science. With their 'sophismes' they stripped away the 'greatest consolation' of the wretched whose number is so vast while simultaneously unnerving the affluent by menacing them with 'la perte de leur bonheur'. They caused a deep split. That philosophy had become entwined with social tensions as well as the struggle for political power first became fully manifest to the discerning at this juncture. Even if God does not exist, added (the sceptical) de Pinto, the crime against humanity committed by the *Système*'s authors remains immense given the book's broad socially destabilizing effect.[27]

That there were intelligent men swayed by arguments such as those expounded in the *Système* struck Voltaire and Frederick as perfectly shocking. When the book arrived on Frederick's desk at Potsdam early in 1770, it appeared to him even more odious than the *Essai sur les préjugés* (1770) which he had just angrily refuted. Like Voltaire, the Prussian *roi philosophe* was perturbed less by Diderot's and d'Holbach's atheism (which scarcely bothered him) than the social, political, and educational theses Diderot and d'Holbach drew from their monism. Well practised in calculating political impact, he suggested, some months later, that the *Système*'s author had smashed countless windows and would require no small degree 'de ménagement' to reconcile innumerable discriminating persons revolted by its contents, such as himself, 'avec la philosophie'.[28]

---

[23] Voltaire, *Questions*, iv. 285; Darnton, *Literary Underground*, 141, 199.

[24] Voltaire to d'Alembert, 2 Oct. 1770, in Voltaire, *Corr.* xxxvii. 63; Naville, *Paul Thiry d'Holbach*, 113; Pappas, *Voltaire et d'Alembert*, 119; Baker, *Condorcet*, 28; Garrard, *Rousseau's Counter-Enlightenment*, 27.

[25] Voltaire to d'Alembert, 18 Jan. 1771, in Voltaire, *Corr.* xxxvii. 216; Mortier, *Combats*, 202–3.

[26] See the MS note before the title page in the copy of the 1770 edition of the *Système de la nature* in the library at Corpus Christi College, Oxford.

[27] De Pinto, *Précis des arguments*, 11–12, 14.

[28] Frederick the Great to Voltaire, Berlin, 19 Jan. 1771, in Voltaire, *Corr.* xxxvii. 225.

From the moment d'Holbach began propagating the new democratic republican ideology in the *Système* followed by the publication in March 1770 of the *Essai*, it had become clear to Frederick, as it had not been earlier, what the radical maxim 'toute erreur est nuisible' really meant. Suddenly, he grasped what he, Voltaire, and d'Alembert were up against. Diderot's and d'Holbach's principle that the consent of the governed is the exclusive source of legitimacy in politics underpinning a comprehensive reform package, challenging all commonly accepted and traditional beliefs, and denying outright the possibility of any consolation for the poor in a future life[29] threatened to overturn the whole edifice of *ancien régime* religion, authority, and institutions. Repeating the procedure he had adopted with the *Essai*, Frederick penned a furious reply, denouncing the anonymous author as an 'ennemi des rois' intent on rendering all monarchical government 'odious', a pillar of 'philosophic pride' whose overly optimistic hopes, and hatred of aristocracy, had launched a hopelessly naive quest bound to agitate the people and end in catastrophe.

The anonymous author was wrong to try to enlighten the people and extend to them freedoms and opportunities that come only with education.[30] 'The author' evidently believed the gradual advance of reason, dissipating the people's errors and credulity, is the true engine of human progress.[31] Such a perspective is profoundly mistaken since not only religion and tradition but also superstition and credulity are essential to ordinary people's lives and the maintenance of the moral and social order. Without popular 'superstition' and the Church holding sway over the lower orders, men's beliefs and ignorant prejudices have no firm anchorage and become perilously unstable, ending all deference to authority and rank. Without popular credulity and superstition, kings and aristocracy cannot be secure, and without kings and nobles, there can be no order or discipline, only chaos. Frederick's thesis that it is better not to teach the truth to most men was then scathingly ridiculed by Diderot in private notes on the royal critique. Quite the contrary, retorted Diderot: man's happiness and best interest are undoubtedly founded on truth, 'le fondement de toute vraie morale'.[32]

If the Prussian monarch disagrees why is he bothering to write at all or complain that the *Essai sur les préjugés* is replete with error? What could be more incoherent than claiming the truth is not for men while composing texts to correct the errors of others? And what could be meaner than championing in print the arrogance of holders of age-old coats-of-arms or to speak of the necessity of ignorance, credulity, and superstition which kings, aristocrats, and priests then exploit for their own advantage?[33] If the truth is valueless to humanity, how is it that the successive efforts 'de l'esprit humain' have had some success?[34] After 1770 Diderot always referred to

---

[29] D'Holbach, *Système social*, 201–2; Citton, *L'Envers*, 61.
[30] Beales, 'Philosophical Kingship', 506–7.
[31] D'Holbach, *Système social*, 170–6; Mauzi, *L'Idée du bonheur*, 572.
[32] Diderot, *Pages inédites*, 2.
[33] Ibid. 23.   [34] Ibid. 8; Strugnell, *Diderot's Politics*, 130–4; Lepape, *Diderot*, 365.

Frederick as a 'tyrant' and 'monarque détestable' privately, though in texts for publication, of course, he softened his language.[35] During his trip to Russia across Germany in 1773, in the company of Catherine's enlightened chamberlain Alexis Vassilievitch, a friend of Beccaria, and on returning, again via Leipzig, in 1774, he made a point of bypassing Prussia and boycotting Frederick. It was a calculated snub that Diderot—whom Frederick scornfully dismissed as 'le Spinosiste de Langres'— was one of the few in a position to deliver with impunity, a snub Frederick reacted to by writing in a highly piqued and sarcastic manner on the subject to Voltaire and d'Alembert. The *Histoire philosophique* included a sally against the 'philosophe de *Sans Souci*' by which Frederick was likewise mightily offended and to which he indirectly replied via a riposte published under the name of one of his academicians, the Berlin Huguenot pastor Moulines.[36]

Diderot's blanket rejection of Frederick's and Voltaire's concept of Enlightenment, moreover, was increasingly widely shared. Condorcet, countering Turgot's disdain for Helvétius's last work, likewise refused to accept that truth is just for the few.[37] During the Middle Ages and Renaissance when (according to radical *philosophes*) highly oppressive circumstances prevailed owing to the triumph of 'superstition', Ibn Rushd and, later, the Italian naturalists had had to form hidden networks that alone cultivated reason and 'philosophy', concealing the 'truth' from the majority in conditions where furtive clandestinity was the only way to advance *le prosélytisme philosophique*. But such practices inevitably produce undesirable moral and political consequences. Since 'the chief basis of men's rights' is the natural equality of men, the concealment practised by Ibn Rushd and the Italian naturalists was bound to foment a secret morality and hypocritical politics.[38] Far better that the rift between reason and society's misconstruing of everything should be out in the open.

Frederick, informing Voltaire, in July, that he had now examined the *Système*, found it 'téméraire', and composed a draft rebuttal, expected Voltaire's concurrence.[39] Since kings draw their legitimacy and power solely from society, according to 'the author', they are merely 'ministres de la société', placed at the helm exclusively 'pour son bien'; consequently, subjects 'ought to possess the right of deposing', as it is put in the English version of Frederick's text, 'when they are disgusted with their sovereigns'.[40] No likelier formula for conjuring up upstarts and inciting civil wars, suggested Frederick, could be imagined. The *Système* was truly formidable in being cogent enough, on a first reading, to seduce many readers. Its catastrophic errors concealed 'with great art' are 'not discovered til the book has been several times perused'.[41] Citing the horrendous slaughter caused by the French Wars of Religion,

---

[35] Lepape, *Diderot*, 365; Rebejkow, 'Notes', 473.
[36] Pilati, *Lettere*, 70–1; Versini, 'Diderot', 227.
[37] Condorcet, *Tableau historique*, 268–9.
[38] Ibid. 203–5.
[39] Frederick the Great to Voltaire, Sans Souci, 7 July 1770, in Voltaire, *Corr.* xxxvi. 319–20.
[40] Condorcet, *Tableau historique*, 171–2; d'Holbach, *Système social*, 251.
[41] Voltaire, *Corr.* xxxvi. 147.

Frederick warned of the truly horrific carnage and disorder rebellion against legitimate monarchs all too readily induces.[42]

Incensed by the charge that kings were responsible for the 'ignorance' and even crimes of their subjects, and that royal government sanctioned by priests is 'la véritable source du mal moral', Frederick indignantly denied the existence of 'age-old treaties between monarchs and priests' such as the *Système* conjured up 'by which the former promise to advance the priesthood, in exchange for the priests preaching submission to the people'.[43] 'Nothing is more false, nor has been more ridiculously imagined', he retorted, than the author's 'crude opinion' about this supposed ancient league between monarchs and priests. This, however, was a little too much for Voltaire, who replied that Frederick was correct, of course, that no such conspiracy existed any longer but wrong regarding the past, as there *had* once been such an age-old alliance, the Theodorics and Clovises, for instance, artfully forging their monarchy with the papacy's aid.[44]

The 'prétendus philosophes de nos jours' had no right to undermine popular 'superstition' or provoke general scandal. His opponent, suggested Frederick, 'has almost literally copied the system of fatality exposed by Leibniz [i.e. of Spinoza] and systematically refuted by Wolff'.[45] He would certainly be shown up. Voltaire hastened to express his agreement, calling the king's refutation 'a lesson' for the whole human race: you defend with one arm God's cause and with the other you crush 'la superstition'.[46] What consummate moderation! True Enlightenment is a fight equally against 'atheism' *and* 'superstition'. He urged him to publish his text. But Frederick, while following the controversy over the *Système* almost as obsessively as Voltaire, had no wish to participate publicly, considering himself above such a thing whilst he lived. He preferred not to publish his two critiques also because they were far from orthodox and he preferred not to scandalize his subjects.[47] He was content to circulate his two texts among philosophical associates, especially Voltaire, d'Alembert, and his *académiciens*. Both rebuttals appeared in print only after his death.

While praising Frederick for his polemical skill, Voltaire made no attempt to hide his sombre view of the situation, waxing especially pessimistic in letters to Paris. 'Voilà une guerre civile entre les incrédules', he assured d'Alembert, while in the same missive remarking despondently that Frederick was growing distant, suspicious, and indignant because some *philosophes* 'ne soient pas royalistes'.[48] Meanwhile, the

---

[42] Frederick the Great, *Examen de l'Essai*, 52.

[43] Ibid. 165; d'Holbach, *Système social*, 258–9, 535–43, 559; Richard, *Défense de la religion*, 211, 213–14, 22–3, 231; Mortier, *Combats*, 199.

[44] Mortier, *Combats*, 199; Dupré, *Enlightenment*, 205; Frederick the Great, 'A Critical Examination of the *System of Nature*', 164–5.

[45] Frederick the Great, 'A Critical Examination of the *System of Nature*', 151–2, 155; Citton, *L'Envers*, 86, 175.

[46] Voltaire to Frederick, 27 July 1770, in Voltaire, *Corr.* xxxvi. 355–6.

[47] Frederick to Voltaire, Potsdam, 18 Aug. 1770 and Frederick to Voltaire, Potsdam, 26 Sept. 1770, ibid. xxxvi. 399, 461.

[48] Voltaire to d'Alembert, 27 July 1770, ibid. xxxvi. 354; Mortier, *Combats*, 199.

Système came under the Berlin Royal Academy's scrutiny, its secretary, Formey, figuring among the radical *philosophes'* chief Protestant adversaries. A convinced Wolffian, Formey was deeply shocked by the *Système*,[49] as was Jean Castillon (1704–91), astronomer royal at the Berlin Observatory since 1765, an Italian mathematician from Castiglione, previously at Lausanne and afterwards Utrecht. As the *Système's* author professed to base his system on science, various scientists felt called on to pronounce on his conclusions. Reacting very differently from Lalande, a leading astronomer in Paris and known atheist,[50] Castillon composed a full-length point-by-point rebuttal which, in April 1771, he submitted to the Academy for endorsement. Pronounced 'très-propre à détruire les sophismes de ce dangereux ouvrage' by Formey and the Academy's committee, Castillon's 549-page assault on *philosophisme* was warmly recommended also by the *Journal encyclopédique* and other journals.[51] This ensured semi-official status for the tome and a high international profile, though, at Amsterdam, de Pinto found it, like Bergier's rebuttal, too long-winded, deeming his own 138-page reply better suited to influence opinion.[52]

Another major refutation dismissing Needham's research (and Buffon's experimental confirmation of Needham), findings buttressing the *Système's* biology, was the 500-page *Réflexions philosophiques sur le* Système de la nature (1772) by the Württemberg philosopher Georg-Jonathan von Holland (1742–84). Citing the counter experiments of the Dutch physicist Musschenbroek, this book was considered among the best rebuttals and was enthusiastically praised in Catholic, Protestant, and Jewish circles alike by Paulian, de Pinto, and many others.[53] Yet, Holland too not only materially aided the *Système's* diffusion by quoting extensively from it in French (and concurring with some of its moral opinions), but also initiated the *Système's* wide diffusion in German since a German version appeared at Berne in 1772, preceding by many years a translation of the *Système* itself and, hence, given the great interest in the latter in Germany's courts and universities, and in Switzerland, a text that long remained the principal German-language account of the controversy.

Castillon's and Holland's refutations, like Frederick's and Voltaire's, and those of Bergier and de Pinto, were all vehicles of typically mainstream Enlightenment views. An admirer of Locke and lifelong adherent of Newtonianism, Castillon, like Holland, equally champions Samuel Clarke, whose proof of God's existence and refutation of Spinoza are assailed in the *Système* but defended and drawn on extensively by Holland and Castillon.[54] Where the *Système* tries to demolish Locke's non-material faculties of the mind, Castillon reaffirms Locke's doctrine, arguing that

---

[49] Guyot, *Rayonnement*, 49.   [50] Lalande, 'Second Supplément', 38, 40.

[51] 'Extrait des registres de l'Académie Royale des Sciences et Belles Lettres de Berlin', 18 Apr. 1771, in de Castillon, *Observations*, dedication and preface; Sauter, 'Paul Thiry', 130; Charlier and Morier, *Journal encyclopédique*, 121–2.

[52] De Pinto, *Précis des arguments*, 17–18.

[53] Holland, *Réflexions*, i. 12–13, 18; Paulian, *Véritable Système*, ii. 9, 14, 24, 53–4; Sauter, 'Paul Thiry', 130; Echeverria, *Maupeou Revolution*, 222.

[54] D'Holbach, *Système de la nature*, 443–72; Holland, *Réflexions*, ii. 83–103.

consciousness cannot be inherent in matter. Both Castillon and Holland deny that sensibility is transferable, like movement, from one body to another or can be something integral to matter and hence, potentially, the grounding of thought.[55] Even Lockean revisionists, like Bonnet and Condillac, observes Castillon, despite discarding—ill-advisedly in his opinion—Locke's non-material faculties of the mind, and embracing 'sensationalism', still claimed their sensationalism in no way precludes 'immaterial beings' or the soul's immortality which, indeed, they thought they had demonstrated.[56] Where the *Système* rejects Locke's teaching and Condillac's revisions, embracing one substance, endorsing Newton 'the physicist' but despising Newton 'the philosopher'—Castillon held that 'l'immortel Newton's' proofs of God's existence, of the non-physical character of gravity, and that matter in itself is something 'destituée de toute force' and consequently incapable 'de produire aucun phénomène', remained indispensable to any cogent system. Newton the scientist seemed to him at one with Newton the philosopher.[57]

Condemned from all sides, not infrequently by hardened unbelievers and sceptics, the *Système* nevertheless everywhere captured the limelight. D'Alembert, having studied both the *Système* and Frederick's reply, by July, judged the former too long and dogmatic (his own atheism being of a more sceptical kind) and yet 'un terrible livre' bound to have a vast effect.[58] The astute and cynical Galiani, once among the regulars at d'Holbach's table, reading the *Système* at Naples, in June, recognized at once that it was from the same hand as the *Christianisme dévoilé*. Not realizing, or pretending not to know, whose this was, though, he wrote to d'Holbach deprecating the book for its length, fervour, and excessive emphasis, as he saw it, on the world's miseries.[59] While the *Système*'s style and systematic manner of exposition may have been new, the core ideas, it seemed to all commentators whether they agreed with them or not, derived from elsewhere, the whole thing being concocted from Epicurus, Hobbes, and especially Spinoza and Toland. The *Système* did, though, granted several critics, including Voltaire, expound atheism more cogently and successfully than had Spinoza, a century before.

A radical reply to its detractors, apparently by Naigeon, appeared under the title *Discours préliminaire*, later in 1770, reaffirming d'Holbach's and Diderot's principle that truth alone can procure for men 'un bonheur solide et permanent' and that if the common people are to learn the truth and achieve a *bonheur solide*, this can happen only via a progress of reason engineered by men who venerate the truth above everything since reason alone enables us to distinguish between true and false, real and illusory, useful and damaging.[60] If reason is to promote mankind's

---

[55] Holland, *Réflexions*, i. 22, 127, 169; Castillon, *Observations*, 178–80, 248, 264–5.
[56] Castillon, *Observations*, 68; Bonnet, *Mémoires autobiographiques*, 171–2, 323–4.
[57] D'Holbach, *Système de la nature*, 190–200; Castillon, *Observations*, 422–3; Voltaire, *Dieu. Réponse*, 7–10, 13–14; Camuset, *Principes*, 244.
[58] D'Alembert to Voltaire, Paris, 25 July 1770, in Voltaire, *Corr.* xxxvi. 352.
[59] Galiani, *Correspondance*, i. 180, 203.
[60] [Naigeon?], *Discours préliminaire*, 51.

well-being, society's entire system of morality and education must be purged of the distortions introduced by theologians and 'fanatics' who instead of forming children into 'citoyens humains, magnanimes, vertueux' pervert them instead into opinionated ignoramuses and *dévôts*, fearful, superstitious, and devoid of true morality.[61] Society needed a revolution in its basic educational, moral, social, and political premisses.

2. VOLTAIRE'S LAST ENCOUNTER: BATTLING SPINOZA

From Voltaire's standpoint, the main issue was that so many were privately signalling agreement with the *Système*. This is what he meant by saying that the *Système* would cause 'un mal affreux à la philosophie'.[62] To him, counter-attacking while securing and expanding his alliances seemed crucial. God, he joked, in a letter to Frederick of 20 August 1770, a month before the appearance of the first of his own formal refutations, *Dieu. Réponse de Mr. de Voltaire au* Système de la nature, in any case now had the two least superstitious men in Europe on his side 'ce qui lui devait plaire beaucoup'. Yet he was more than a little troubled by the king's dogmatic insistence on excluding the vast majority from being told the truth. While concurring about the undesirability of enlightening most men, the question of where precisely to draw the line worried Voltaire quite a lot. In his essay *Jusqu'à quel point on doit tromper le peuple* (1771), he pronounced it 'une très grande question' to what degree the common people, nine out of ten parts of humanity, should be treated 'comme des singes'.[63] The *Système* was exerting a vast impact, partly, as he acknowledged, because it is eloquent and includes many excellent passages. But here, he assured Madame Du Deffand in October 1770, precisely because of its power to attract, it resembled the bogus financial schemes of John Law (1673–1729), the Scottish adventurer whose grandiose project for issuing bank-notes crashed sensationally in 1720, causing vast loss, despair, and scandal in France. This new doctrine similarly promised much, including alleviation of the miseries of the poor which it proclaims the outcome of ignorance, deception, and vested interest, while really inflicting immense harm on everybody, especially the high-born and powerful.[64] Worst of all, it blighted the *philosophes'* reputation where it counted most, in select circles. The disaster would affect him less than the rest, though, he added, jocularly, as he expected to die shortly and would soon discover who was right on the soul's immortality—Plato or Spinoza, St Paul or Epictetus, Christianity or Confucianism.

Voltaire's first counter-salvo, he informed Frederick, was an attack on the scientific grounding on which the *Système* is built, the geological-biological systems of de Maillet

---

[61] Ibid. 47, 51.   [62] Naville, *Paul Thiry d'Holbach*, 113.

[63] Mortier, *Le Cœur*, 98; Martin-Haag, *Voltaire*, 143.

[64] Voltaire to Marquise Du Deffand, 21 Oct. 1770, in Voltaire, *Corr.* xxxvii. 40; Naville, *Paul Thiry d'Holbach*, 113.

and Buffon. Both had advanced, ridiculously in Voltaire's view, proto-evolutionist notions, arguing there is no Creator and that nature created itself, among other things postulating that the Pyrenees and the Alps were formed by the sea.[65] These ideas fused with bits of Maupertuis and borrowings from the recent French translation of Lucretius by d'Holbach's assistant and Naigeon's friend La Grange, published under the title *De la nature des choses* (1768), to form a complete system of 'transformism' including the thesis—absurd in Voltaire's eyes—that men evolved from lower, aquatic creatures or, as he put it, were originally porpoises with split tails that evolved into buttocks and legs over time. Especially ludicrous, he suggested, was the author's adapting Needham's conclusion about the spontaneous generation of eels (scorned also by Frederick).[66] At this crucial moment when the *Système* 'fait tant de bruit' in Europe, such propositions, he assured Chancellor Maupeou whose favour he still sought and to whom he sent a copy of his refutation, spelt danger and must be crushed.[67]

Voltaire was especially dismayed by the divided response among the *philosophes* in Paris. Though generating a huge stir among 'les ignorants', he liked to think, and impressing superficial minds high up the social scale, the *Système* was justly angering all sensible people. But this was not quite how it was. In fact, he repeatedly complained how shameful it was so many supposedly discerning readers had embraced 'si vite une opinion si ridicule'. The *Système*'s science is wrong, he insisted, and so is its philosophy. Its author might be more eloquent than Spinoza, yet Spinoza was more cogent in crucial respects, especially, in admitting an 'intelligence' in nature 'à l'exemple de toute l'antiquité', unlike the *Système*'s author who considers intelligence merely an effect of movement and combinations of matter, something in his view—and also, Camuset notes, in Clarke's and Montesquieu's before him—much less plausible.[68] To sustain his attack on transformism and the *Système*'s use of Needham (which Needham himself, then living in France, disavowed),[69] Voltaire cites the experiments and conclusions of the Italian naturalist Spallanzani rejecting all accounts of generation and of nature that, following Spinoza and the *Système*, fail to postulate 'un entendement qui la gouverne'.[70]

It was because the *Système*'s author wished to avoid being designated Spinoza's disciple, Voltaire assured d'Alembert, in late July 1770, that, like Strato, he acknowledges no eternal intelligence immanent in nature. Strato of Lampsacus, third head of Aristotle's academy at Athens (from roughly 287 BC to 269), was the Hellenistic

---

[65] Voltaire, *Questions*, iv. 290–1; Dupré, *Enlightenment*, 37.

[66] Voltaire to Frederick, 20 Aug. 1770, in Voltaire, *Corr.* xxxvi. 406–7; Voltaire, *Dieu. Réponse*, 10, 12, 17; Frederick the Great, 'A Critical Examination of the *System of Nature*', 155.

[67] Voltaire to Frederick, 20 Aug. 1770, and Voltaire to Maupeou, 22 Aug. 1770, in Voltaire, *Corr.* xxxvi. 407, 410.

[68] Voltaire, *Questions*, iv; Voltaire to Grimm, 23 July 1770, in Voltaire, *Corr.* xxxvi. 349; Camuset, *Principes*, 13–14; Mortier, *Combats*, 198.

[69] Deschamps, *Correspondance*, 376.

[70] Voltaire, *Corpus*, iv. 450; Sandrier, *Style philosophique*, 247; Onfray, *Les Ultras*, 230–1.

thinker all but forgotten until Bayle had revived his memory early in the century, considered the closest ancient equivalent to Spinoza and whom Voltaire too appropriates as his literary surrogate for 'Spinoza' and d'Holbach in his *Lettres de Memmius* (1771).[71] This ancient confusion, held Voltaire, inspired Strato to accord intelligence to his dog but refuse it to the maker of all nature's wonders. How ridiculous to derive intelligent creatures from mere motion and matter, things that in themselves possess no intelligence! Writing to the duchess of Choiseul, in October 1770, he specified what he saw as both the chief novelty and prime weakness of the *Système* in its doctrine that mind emerges from inert matter. 'Spinoza ne pensait ainsi', he maintained, attributing a kind of dualism to the latter. Spinoza admits both intelligence and matter 'et par là' his book surpasses the *Système de la nature*.[72]

Throughout late 1770 and 1771, the *Système* remained the chief theme of Voltaire's correspondence. 'Ce maudit *Système de la nature*' has caused irreparable damage, he wrote to Grimm in October, requesting that he extend his greetings to 'Frère Platon' [i.e. Diderot] even if the latter chose not to concede 'intelligence' to God as Spinoza does. Again the deploying of Needham's experiments to underpin hylozoism he, like Frederick, dismissed as 'très antiphilosophique', adding that Spinoza may be less eloquent 'mais il est cent fois plus raisonnable'.[73] In October 1770, he reported to Condorcet and d'Alembert, that de Voyer had sent him in manuscript a refutation of the *Système* by the veteran Spinoza fighter Dom Deschamps claiming 'la nouvelle philosophie' if not crushed would produce 'une révolution horrible'.[74] He agreed entirely. The *nouvelle philosophie* was disastrous. But what he could not reconcile himself to was that 'all' the other *philosophes* were taking the *Système*'s part, concurring with the latter while ignoring the better-grounded propositions of his *Réponse*. In this rebuke, Condorcet, who had originally moved in his orbit but now adhered to a radical standpoint, was included. By thus expressing his pique, Voltaire effectively acknowledged his loss of a presiding position among the *parti philosophique* and all prospect of guiding its direction and strategy.[75]

For months Voltaire kept up a barrage of letters to prince, dukes, countesses, *philosophes*, and *salonnières* all around Europe, denouncing the *Système* and insisting on the harm it was inflicting, always linking the book to the Spinoza debate. Assuring Friedrich Wilhelm, the Prussian crown prince, in Berlin, in January 1771, that the *Système*'s ideas had no sound basis in philosophy or science, he granted it had eloquent passages, but pronounced it absurd to deny the existence of a supreme intelligence in the world. Even Spinoza who knew his geometry is obliged to agree.[76] Spinoza admits 'une intelligence universelle'; indeed, intelligence spread through

---

[71] Voltaire, *Lettres de Memmius*, 443–4; Israel, *Enlightenment Contested*, 445–57.

[72] Naville, *Paul Thiry d'Holbach*, 112; Pomeau, *Religion de Voltaire*, 396.

[73] Voltaire to Grimm, 10 Oct. 1770, in Voltaire, *Corr.* xxxvii. 24.

[74] Naville, *Paul Thiry d'Holbach*, 12; Pecharroman, *Morals*, 20 n.; Robinet, *Dom Deschamps*, 79; Boulad-Ayoub, 'Voltaire', 60.

[75] Baker, *Condorcet*, 28, Mortier, *Combats*, 201.

[76] Voltaire, *Corpus*, iv. 442–3; Naville, *Paul Thiry d'Holbach*, 114.

matter forms the very basis of his system. How does the *Système*'s author propose to answer that? Whether or not this 'intelligence universelle' follows the path of justice is the central question posed by Spinoza's philosophy and, surely, it is both absurd and impertinent to propose 'un Dieu injuste'.[77]

Opponents of all final causes (i.e. the *Spinosistes*) reject teleology outright. But here Spinoza, he wrote to another correspondent, Bernard Joseph Saurin, in November 1770, had always seemed to him more bold than rational: the Spinozists 'ne veulent pas que le soleil soit fait pour les planètes'.[78] The *Système*'s author, argued Voltaire, writing to Delisle de Sales, a minor *philosophe* who had denounced the *Système* as a mere 'jeu de l'imagination',[79] advances only conjectures and proves nothing in a book based on two basic absurdities: first, the chimera that non-thinking matter can produce thought, like a cabbage produces seeds, as he puts it in his marginal notes in his own copy, a *sottise* even Spinoza avoids; and, secondly, that in giving rise to living beings nature 'peut se passer de germes' or elicit them from decomposing inanimate matter.[80] It was to France's eternal shame that *philosophes*, otherwise learned, could embrace such inept theses. But while his counter-offensive became more strident with the passing months, Voltaire also became increasingly worried lest the split among the *philosophes* become an irreparable breach. He had had no choice but to conduct himself as he was doing, he assured Grimm, on 1 November 1770, expecting this to be passed on to Diderot and d'Holbach, and if one weighed his words carefully, it would be seen that his pronouncements need antagonize no one.

Voltaire threw his prestige into the scales against the revolutionary philosophical system summed up by the *Système* while simultaneously rigorously re-examining the basic elements of his own system. This meant intensifying the philosophical quest in which he was already engaged even before the *Système*'s appearance, to deepen and refine his critique of one-substance solutions to the major metaphysical problems, problems he had wrestled with continuously since the 1730s and aired at some length, relying as before on Locke to restrict reason's scope and help negate materialism with scepticism, in *Le Philosophe ignorant* (1766).[81]

The series of Voltaire's late works rejecting atheistic materialism for a modified deistic Newtonianism actually commences with the sixteen-page anonymously published essay *Tout en Dieu* (1769).[82] Denying Hobbes had openly professed atheism or rejected final causes like Spinoza,[83] Voltaire here strives to counter Diderot and d'Holbach, staking out Spinozism as the decisive arena of combat around which

[77] Voltaire to Prussian crown prince, 11 Jan. 1771, in Voltaire, *Corr.* xxxvii. 208.
[78] Voltaire to Bernard Joseph Saurin, 10 Nov. 1770, ibid. xxxvii. 75.
[79] Delisle de Sales, *Philosophie de la nature*, ii. 5–6, 244–5; Vernière, *Spinoza*, 641.
[80] Voltaire to Delisle de Sales, 25 Nov. 1770, in Voltaire, *Corr.* xxxvii. 99; Voltaire, *Lettres de Memmius*, 441; Voltaire, *Corpus*, iv. 441.
[81] Voltaire, *Philosophe ignorant*, 63–7, 72–6; Paganini, 'Scetticismo', 156–7; Paganini, *Introduzione*, 157–9.
[82] [Voltaire], 'Tout en Dieu', 32; Boulad-Ayoub, 'Voltaire', 56–7.
[83] Voltaire, *Questions*, iv. 260; Blom, *Wicked Company*, 93–100.

the pending struggle for the Enlightenment's future would be fought. Here, the strengths and weaknesses of Spinoza, much the foremost modern representative of *l'athéisme philosophique* with which he was at war, became pivotal to the outcome of the 'guerre civile' waged between the *philosophique* unbelievers in Christianity.[84] *Tout en Dieu* (1769), written prior to the *Système*'s appearance, supposedly a 'commentaire sur Malebranche', adopts a light-hearted tone but had a serious message. Acknowledging that he had discarded his former commitment to free will, here Voltaire concedes that critics might well be tempted to attack him for shifting his ground, adducing the same 'objections' against his revised standpoint as he levelled against Spinoza. He parries such objections by arguing that where Spinoza converts God into the 'universality of things', in his own now revised philosophy 'the universality of things emanates from God'. One might still answer, though, he realized, that if God's productions do indeed emanate from him,, they must nevertheless still be in some sense part of him, a conclusion leaving Spinoza intact.[85] The essay is candid, a kind of experiment steering between Newtonian metaphysics, Leibniz, and Spinoza. By 1769, this veteran Lockean of four decades' standing was not just wrestling still with Spinoza's system—something characterizing his philosophical efforts throughout[86]—but striving to transcend it in a new manner, by pruning back natural theology and abandoning not just 'le profond Locke's' miracles, but also his freedom of the will and aspects of his Divinity while still adhering with undiminished fervour to Creation, divine providence, fixity of species, and the divine origin of morality.

That Malebranche and St Paul had actually both stood in closest proximity to Spinoza, Voltaire jocularly remarked, sending d'Alembert a copy in August 1769, hardly anyone hitherto had suspected. Benedict de Spinoza must indeed have been 'un esprit bien conciliant' as everyone, it seems, falls sooner or later despite himself back into 'les idées de ce mauvais juif'.[87] This was more than a flippant remark, d'Alembert realized, since Voltaire is here applying the observation to himself. D'Alembert responded agreeing that the system propagated by their opponents threatened to engulf both Locke and Newtonianism as well as destroy all prospect of an alliance between *la philosophie* and royal courts. He had always supposed that in metaphysics Malebranche and other such 'dreamers' either did not know themselves what their ideas meant or else, underneath, were really 'Spinosistes'; and that Spinoza's thought is, in the end, itself either meaningless or else signifies that matter is the only existing thing and that in matter 'il faut chercher ou supposer la raison de tout'.[88]

---

[84] Ibid. iv. 277–84; Voltaire, *Lettres de Memmius*, 457–8.

[85] [Voltaire], 'Tout en Dieu', 64; Citton, *L'Envers*, 87, 268, 274.

[86] Israel, *Enlightenment Contested*, 90, 766–70.

[87] Voltaire to d'Alembert, 15 Aug. 1769, in Voltaire, *Corr.* xxxv. 160–1; Pappas, *Voltaire et d'Alembert*, 105–6.

[88] Pappas, *Voltaire et d'Alembert*, 106, 109; d'Alembert to Voltaire, 29 Aug. 1769, in Voltaire, *Corr.* xxxv. 183.

Voltaire's battle with the 'Spinosistes modernes', as he calls them, and Spinoza, was much the most vital philosophical encounter of his last years. Spinoza occupies centre-stage in Voltaire's post-1770 thought mainly due to his great alarm at the rapid progress of *la philosophie moderne* but also because he realized he had to adjust some of his own philosophical premisses. The growing number of Diderot's and d'Holbach's disciples, several of whom—Naigeon, Condorcet, Chastellux, Lalande, and La Grange—figure in Voltaire's correspondence, signalled both the extent of his failure and, more generally, in the French context, the collapse of moderate Enlightenment as a viable intellectual-political project. Even d'Alembert, while opposing the social and political strategy of Diderot, Helvétius, and d'Holbach, largely concurred with their metaphysics.

Rejecting freedom of the will involved dangerously narrowing the scope of his natural theology: man is free when he does what he wants; but he is not free, Voltaire now accepted, to will or not will what he desires.[89] He also conceded in a way he had refused to do earlier that the divine power resides in nature itself and that there is no contradiction between the necessity of the divine will and its freedom. All things produced by the divine power are equally subject to the unalterable and eternal laws of nature. Yet still, God and nature remained distinct. On rereading the *Système* again, in its 1771 re-edition, he fought d'Holbach's thesis that matter is unchangeable, eternal, and independent and that there is nothing beyond matter, by insisting that d'Holbach contradicts himself by attributing immutability to a God who changes unceasingly.[90]

Revising his judgements about Spinoza, Voltaire saw that he needed also to show greater respect than in the past for aspects of Bayle. Where earlier he had generally deprecated Bayle, now he praised Bayle but also affirmed the very thing he had previously denied, even in the *Philosophe ignorant*: Bayle *had* after all misunderstood and misrepresented Spinoza. While deriding Montesquieu for his feeble riposte to Bayle's claim that a society of true Christians would be unworkable in a world of non-Christians,[91] Voltaire continued to criticize Bayle for supposing a society of atheists could be viable. Had Bayle been given five or six hundred peasants to govern he would assuredly have proclaimed 'un Dieu rémunérateur et vengeur'.[92] Ordinary folk, contended Voltaire and Frederick, neither could nor should be enlightened and positively needed a strong 'brake' on their unruly passions, something afforded only by faith and the threat of a God who rewards and punishes.[93]

Bayle was mistaken about atheism and, like Diderot and d'Holbach, had neither read Spinoza carefully enough nor reported him accurately. But he would now show that one can breach 'les remparts du Spinosisme' on a side Bayle had neglected to attack.[94] If reworking his general stance led to his lessening his former reliance on

---

[89] Voltaire, *Il faut prendre*, 533.   [90] Voltaire, *Corpus*, iv. 453.
[91] Voltaire, *Questions*, v. 330–2.   [92] Ibid. ii. 287.   [93] Ibid.
[94] Voltaire, *Philosophe ignorant*, 64–5; Voltaire, *Questions*, iii. 59–63, iv. 281, and v. 330–2; Martin-Haag, *Voltaire*, 68.

Newton's and Clarke's physico-theology, his underlying allegiance to the 'argument from design' persisted.[95] Physico-theology, savagely assailed by d'Holbach, had lost something of its former compelling quality, but he still insisted the *Système* fails to weaken 'ce grand argument' of the physico-theologians: that the world is 'un ouvrage qui démontre un ouvrier'.[96] Everywhere in the universe we find signs of 'design', and hence a 'raison agissante'; and that first mover is and can only be God.

Locke too he still defended against d'Holbach's charge that having recognized the absurdity of innate ideas, he had failed to draw the 'immediate and necessary consequences' from his discovery.[97] For Voltaire, Locke's non-material faculties of the mind remained valid and were no mere concession to the theologians. Following Spinoza, d'Holbach urges against Clarke and the theologians that we can have no idea of thought, indeed of intelligence itself, and can derive neither thought nor intelligence cogently, other than as something inherent in the senses. This Voltaire, following Locke and defending Clarke (and Nieuwentijt), rejected. He had abandoned the soul's immortality but not its immateriality. God may have no eyes or nose, he remarks in his marginal notes to d'Holbach's text, but God must think and is the author 'de notre faculté de penser'.[98]

By more openly bracketing *la philosophie moderne* with Spinoza in a way that privately he had done all along, Voltaire was both raising the stakes and highlighting the links between Spinozism and what he regarded as atheistic materialism's pernicious social and political consequences. In his *Questions sur l'Encyclopédie*, the longest philosophical discussion focuses, of course, on Spinoza. There, as also in his thirty-seven-page essay *Il faut prendre un parti, ou le principe d'action* (1772), Voltaire tries to use Spinoza's error in denying the existence of void to prove his 'universal substance' is not a fully cogent concept. In particular, he counters his equating God with nature by showing that Spinoza himself, unlike the crowd 'de ceux qui crient Spinosa, Spinosa' (that is Diderot, d'Holbach, Helvétius, and their followers), recognized the need to postulate in nature a power that is both necessary and 'intelligent'.[99] This admission, he thinks, crucially undermines Spinoza's position: for if nature possesses the power to think how can this infinite, universal being lack the power to make designs? If it makes designs, how can Spinoza's God or nature not have a will? If he has a will, how can Spinoza absolutely deny all 'final causes'? An intelligence destitute of will would be something absurd because this intelligence 'ne servirait à rien'. The great necessary Being, he concludes echoing Leibniz and Wolff, has thus willed 'tout ce qu'il a opéré'.[100]

But if God had really created the cosmos, answered Diderot and d'Holbach, not only would the order of the universe be due to divine providence, so would all the

---

[95] Voltaire, *Questions*, v. 333; Cronk, 'Voltaire (non-)lecteur', 178–9.
[96] Voltaire, *Corpus*, iv. 446–7.
[97] Voltaire, *Questions*, iv. 443.
[98] Ibid. iv. 445; Cronk, 'Voltaire (non-)lecteur', 179, 181.
[99] Voltaire, *Questions*, iv. 278–9.
[100] Ibid. iv. 281–4; Voltaire, *Lettres de Memmius*, 458; Voltaire, *Il faut prendre*, 523.

disorder, violence, malignity, and oppression rendering all worldly existence precarious and frequently wretched and miserable.[101] If the order of the universe proves the omnipotence and intelligence of a divine Creator, then the disorder proves that Creator's feebleness, inconstancy, and unreasonableness. The universe, holds Voltaire, is governed by divine providence and God is just. But if so is this then not a mystery just as obscure as those of the theologians whose 'mystères' deists constantly ridicule? Deists, without saying so, make the 'God' who is the foundation of their natural religion himself the greatest of mysteries. What are his powers and wherein resides his justice? How does he direct the world and rule over humanity? The cruel, unjust way most peoples have been governed proves only that dread of the afterlife has little effect on the perverse. Do not monsters like Tiberius, Caligula, and Nero prove clearly enough the non-existence of a providence 'qui s'intéresse au sort de la race humaine'?[102] The Enlightenment's two wings were now locked in combat philosophically and publicly. While crossing Germany, on his way to Russia, in the late summer of 1773, Diderot stopped off first at Düsseldorf and then Leipzig, not only openly proclaiming his atheistic morality and creed, according to a Swiss pastor who met him in the latter city, 'avec la ferveur d'un visionnaire', but assuring everyone who would listen that Voltaire's philosophy is 'absurde'.[103]

Voltaire refused to accept Diderot's and the others' rejection of divine providence.[104] It was this and especially his tenacious adherence to the Newtonian doctrine that the regularity and organization of the planetary system reveals a combination of mutually interactive laws that must have been concerted by a single intelligence which still most obviously separated him from Spinoza's denial of teleology in nature. We see most evidently in nature that 'dans le grand tout' there is 'une grande intelligence' which Spinoza refuses to concede despite acknowledging (or so Voltaire argued) that mind is separate from matter.[105] Equally, there remained an irreducible collision between Spinozistic ethics as something based exclusively on society's needs and Voltaire's conception that all the religions known in history deliver approximately the same system of virtue and morality and that this single system must have been bequeathed to man by 'l'intelligence suprême', being inherent in the providential order, something man discovers through experience.[106] If the philosophical gap had narrowed, it still remained appreciable while Voltaire's resistance to the political and social consequences ensuing from Diderot's and d'Holbach's stance remained undiminished. Complimenting him on his *Memmius*, in April 1772, the Prussian king hailed this text as a masterpiece in which the most abstruse issues were rendered accessible to busy men of the world. He himself would willingly

---

[101] [D'Holbach], *Le Bon-Sens*, 31–2, 36–7; Dupré, *Enlightenment*, 265–7.
[102] [D'Holbach], *Le Bon-Sens*, 79, 92, 159.
[103] Mortier, *Diderot en Allemagne*, 33–5.
[104] Voltaire, *Corpus*, iv. 445–6; Martin-Haag, *Voltaire*, 69–70, 183.
[105] Voltaire, *Lettres de Memmius*, 442–3.   [106] Ibid. 460–2; Voltaire, *Questions*, iv. 279–80.

subscribe to his standpoint and endorse 'ce symbole de foi philosophique'.[107] Distancing *Voltaireanisme* from the *nouveaux philosophes,* Voltaire in his last decade also noticeably toned down the earlier stridency of his anti-Christian rhetoric.[108]

A curious feature of Voltaire's fixation with Spinoza during the early 1770s was a growing tendency to contrast him favourably with d'Holbach privately while in texts for publication still adhering to his decades-long public outright hostility to Spinoza. Developing his attack on radical thought in letters as well as in *Dieu. Réponse de Mr. de Voltaire au* Système de la nature (1770), *Questions sur l'Encyclopédie* (1770), *Lettres de Memmius* (1771), *Il faut prendre un parti* (1772), and *L'Histoire de Jenni, ou le sage et l'athée* (1775), Voltaire adopts a double procedure.[109] Privately, he mobilized Spinoza against d'Holbach whilst, publicly, redoubling his denunciation of Spinoza and *Spinosistes modernes.* This extraordinary tactic undoubtedly stemmed from realizing that d'Holbach is shallower but also absorbed much more easily than Spinoza.[110] Castillon, at Berlin, was among those misled by Voltaire's here overly subtle intellectual acrobatics. While the philosophical writer of the *Questions* (i.e. Voltaire), affirms Castillon, judges the *Système's* author to be diffuse 'et peu correct',[111] he grants nevertheless that this anonymous author greatly surpasses Spinoza being as eloquent as 'le juif hollandois est sec', equally methodical, more geometrical, and a hundred times clearer.[112]

However, Voltaire was far from thinking d'Holbach surpassed Spinoza, quite the reverse. In a letter to an unknown correspondent of September 1772, he again declares Spinoza too intelligent to disavow 'une intelligence dans la nature', insisting the author of the *Système* reasons less well than Spinoza 'et déclame beaucoup trop'.[113] The double strategy resulted from Spinoza's being read only by *savants* while d'Holbach was being read, as Voltaire put it, by *savants,* the ignorant, and women alike. Some women were certainly reading d'Holbach avidly.[114] The 35-year-old Madame la Marquise de Voyer—a distinctly liberated lady, as she also delighted in d'Argens's erotic philosophical novel *Thérèse philosophe*—was not just 'enchanted' by it but convinced it was 'bon et vrai'.[115] Another who read it in the early 1770s, possibly even before she was 20, was the future Madame Marie-Jeanne Roland (1754–93), destined to preside over the most eminent *philosophique* salon of revolutionary Paris.[116] A confirmed philosophical materialist for a time, after 1776 she merged *philosophisme* with zeal for Rousseau (besides enthusiasm for the American Revolution), her inclination to the principles of Diderot, Raynal, and Helvétius being checked by what she herself confessed was a strong personal, emotional need to believe in the God of deism.[117]

---

[107] Frederick the Great to Voltaire, Sans-Souci, 22 Apr. 1772, in Voltaire, *Corr.* xxxviii. 353.
[108] Pappas, *Voltaire and d'Alembert,* 127–8, 173.   [109] Pearson, *Voltaire Almighty,* 336.
[110] Voltaire, *Questions,* iv. 285.   [111] Castillon, *Observations,* 2, 356.
[112] Ibid. 352; Voltaire, *Questions,* iv. 283–5, 286.
[113] Voltaire to?, 1 Sept. 1772, in Voltaire, *Corr.* xxxviii. 51.   [114] Ibid. iv. 285.
[115] Deschamps, *Correspondance,* 348, 357.   [116] May, *Madame Roland,* 28–39.
[117] Ibid. 59, 69, 115.

In his published writings Voltaire continued depicting Spinoza as an obscure thinker contradicting himself by first denying and then embracing final causes.[118] The *Système* Voltaire ties to Spinoza's alleged confusions as well as tendencies in the *Encyclopédie* from which he sought to distance himself.[119] The open rift between the two enlightenments after 1770 worried Voltaire and d'Alembert. But, as the *anti-philosophes* observed, it also enabled the public to grasp more clearly the nature of the split between the two blocs. Some *philosophes*, notes Barruel in *Les Helviennes*, acknowledge creation whereas the materialists reject it. Some grant 'free will' while others assert fatalism; and some acknowledge a spiritual soul whereas their opponents postulate a material soul in flagrant contradiction of Locke.[120] What all their opponents including Rousseau called 'la philosophie moderne' or 'la nouvelle philosophie', d'Holbach and Diderot labelled simply 'la philosophie' and placed in outright opposition to all theology natural and revealed, which they declared the 'ennemie née de l'expérience', the force ceaselessly opposing the 'bonheur des nations' and 'progrès de l'esprit humain' everywhere buttressing 'superstition' and credulity.

'La philosophie moderne' constitutes for them the sole true basis of knowledge and human happiness, the sole ideology aiming at the good of society as a whole forged on behalf of humanity universally.[121] It was a philosophy for the people that had to be fought for against the people, since it totally overturns the beliefs and assumptions of received thinking. Anyone fighting what is commonly believed—and for his freedom to do so—laments d'Holbach, we have seen, is in the eyes of most a mad, unnatural, or 'de-natured' being who deserves to lose all right to the protection the laws normally afford.

The struggle between Voltaire and the 'synagogue holbachique' continued unabated with the appearance of the *Le Bon-Sens* (1772), published by Marc-Michel Rey in Amsterdam, and banned in France in January 1774 (together with Helvétius's *De l'homme*), followed by further editions in 1772, 1774, 1775, and again in 1792.[122] Voltaire was equally appalled by Helvétius's *De l'homme* which appeared posthumously, in 1773. For besides its intrinsic materialism, this work, the fruit of fifteen years' arduous work, showed how utterly he had failed to detach Helvétius from Diderot and d'Holbach. Causing a fierce outcry on all sides, it was a book to which the response would have caused Helvétius and his wife acute distress, noted Diderot, had he lived even six months after its sensational publication.[123] Diderot, we know, read *De l'homme* in manuscript and subjected it to close criticism well prior to Helvétius's death. By the summer of 1773, he mentions in a letter having read *De l'homme* no less than three times. The next year, he completed his critique of

---

[118] Voltaire, *Questions*, iv. 283–5.
[119] Pappas, *Voltaire and d'Alembert*, 124–6.
[120] Barruel, *Les Helviennes*, ii. 17–29, 158–63, 166–8.
[121] D'Holbach, *Système social*, 562–4; d'Holbach, *Système de la nature*, ii. 398.
[122] Haar, *Jean Meslier*, 51; Negroni, *Lectures*, 350.
[123] Diderot, *Réfutation*, 311, 314–15, 341.

Helvétius's system, the *Réfutation de l'ouvrage d'Helvétius intitulé L'Homme* (1773–4), one of his longest, most interesting late works. There was much in Helvétius's text, he stressed (contrary to what one scholar recently claimed[124]), to be admired. Its 'principles' he rated far above Rousseau's.[125] But while holding there is only one substance,[126] Diderot, like Spinoza, was not the sort of materialist who thinks mental phenomena directly reflect material events. Animals and humans, he agreed, arise from different levels of organization of matter but mental phenomena are not, with him, reducible simply to physical processes like pleasure and pain. He did not agree that the same set of external circumstances, or the same education, necessarily affects one individual in essentially the same way as another. What disturbed him about Helvétius's system was its overly reductive character.

Human motivation, rooted in physical and mental reactions, so directly tied by Helvétius to his principle that pleasure and pain will prove always 'les seuls principes des actions des hommes'—a principle with which Diderot agrees up to a point—becomes a form of hedonism in which all pleasures and pains are purely corporal responses, and morality merely response to rewards which Diderot rejected.[127] 'Rewards alone', as Helvétius' disciple Dragonetti expressed it, 'tie the wayward interest of the individual to the public, and keep the eye of men intent on the general good.'[128] Helvétius himself offered an excellent illustration of the falseness of his thesis that 'pleasure' and 'pain' are the sole basic determinants of human motivation. Rich and blessed with a beautiful wife, he nevertheless preferred to pursue truth and suffer the consequences than spend his time in bed delighting in voluptuous pleasures with her. Were his thesis correct, he would not have sacrificed the prospect of more time in bed with Madame Helvétius, even without knowing as he did that he risked 'her happiness' as well as his own by publishing his book.[129] Foreseeing the persecution ahead, he would have burned the manuscripts of his books instead.

Diderot and d'Holbach agreed with Helvétius that true morality is one and must be identical 'pour tous les habitants de notre globe' and should everywhere underpin the system of laws.[130] Our acquisition of ideas through the senses, as physical, efficient causes, means that physical sensibility, and hence personal interest, is the exclusive source of all justice and morality. Only on this basis can we construct a realistic and convincing ethics of integrity, by which Diderot and Helvétius meant a moral mechanics grounded on the principle that physical sensibility shapes all our ideas. Such principles must secure the maximum degree of freedom possible for each individual consistent with the promotion of the *bien public*.[131] But Helvétius's

[124] Edelstein, *Enlightenment*, 12–13, 124 n. 25.
[125] Diderot, *Réfutation*, 292, 317; Citton, *L'Envers*, 33–2; Besse, 'Observations', 137.
[126] Besse, 'Observations', 137; Diderot, *Rêve d'Alembert*, 306; Kaitaro, *Diderot's Holism*, 137–8, 151.
[127] Diderot, *Réfutation*, 310; Besse, 'Observations', 138.
[128] Dragonetti, *Treatise on Virtues*, 31.
[129] Diderot, *Réfutation*, 310–11, 314–15, 327.
[130] D'Holbach, *Système social*, 71; Diderot, *Supplément*, 178.
[131] Diderot, *Supplément*, 328–9, 340, 386; Hayer, *La Religion vengée*, vii. 17.

approach, accounting physical sensibility 'la cause unique de nos actions' and deriving morality straightforwardly from pursuit of physical 'pleasure', struck them as misleading, especially in supposing upbringing and schooling with their rewards and punishments can effectively determine and direct the moral feelings of individuals.

Completed by 1769, Helvétius had long hesitated to publish his culminating work, deterred by the growing skill of the police in detecting authors' stylistic features and finding complicit scribes, booksellers, and *colporteurs*. The furore over *De l'esprit*, royal disfavour, and the retractions of 1758–9, together with warnings of the severe punishment to follow should he ever again defy the crown by perpetrating anything of the sort, had long weighed on his nerves and depressed him. He never got over it. Preparing his parting salvo was both the consolation and torment of his last years, his culminating act of rebellion. Shortly before his death, in January 1771, he assured a sympathetic jurist at Rouen that the 'prudence' his correspondent praised was not something characteristic of him but learnt from painful experience. A *lettre de cachet* and consignment to the Bastille were not threats to be taken lightly. He remained deeply pessimistic: 'je regarde les lettres comme perdues en France.'[132] He was resolved not to publish, circulate in manuscript, or clandestinely propagate his last book whilst he lived, to shield his wife and himself.[133]

But he also refused to give in. Only a handful of intimates knew of the book's existence. In his last surviving letter, he pronounces his text ready but one he would never bring out whilst he lived, given that 'l'Inquisition est plus sévère ici' than in Spain.[134] Only when his end was near did he move. He died on 26 December 1771, without any confessor being called, surrounded by friends—d'Holbach, Morellet, the explorer Bougainville, and Chastellux who, later, in 1772, delivered the *Éloge* celebrating his life and achievement at the Académie. As he expired, Naigeon and Condorcet both later recalled, arrangements were already in train for publication in Holland. The beautiful Madame Helvétius whom some reckoned 'a nobler soul than he' and who, reportedly, had wanted to sell all 'and take refuge in Holland rather than submit to the shame of recantation', in 1759, was more adamant than any that now was the moment to strike back in the only way she could, against his and her persecutors. In her salon where young materialists like Volney and Cabanis were attracted during the 1780s, her husband's œuvre and, still more, the *Système de la nature* remained foundational texts.[135]

The book, with its preface fiercely critical of the French court, but deliberately flattering to Catherine and Frederick (much to Diderot's displeasure), was secretly printed late in 1772, at The Hague, by the firm of Pierre-Frederic Gosse (1751–1826). The preface, certain to cause outrage in Paris, as in Italy and Spain, claimed the

---

[132] Helvétius to Mercier-Dupaty, 3 Jan. 1771, in *CGdH* iii. 347; Smith, *Bibliography*, 289.
[133] Smith, *Bibliography*, 292–3; Besse, 'Observations', 137–8.
[134] Smith, *Bibliography*, 293; Helvétius to Vincent Louis Dutens, 26 Nov. 1771, in *CGdH* iii. 372.
[135] *CGdH* iii. 386, 393–4; Casanova, *Memoirs*, iii. 280; App, *Orientalism*, 443, 449.

Enlightenment was now shining brightly in northern lands but was ever more overshadowed by 'superstition' and 'despotisme asiatique' in 'the south'.[136] Whilst printing was in progress, a manuscript copy was dispatched to Petersburg by the Russian minister at The Hague, Dimitri Alexeievich, Prince Golitsyn. After examining it, Catherine, in one of her last pro-*philosophique* interventions prior to her complete alienation from radical thought following the Pugachev rebellion, agreed to permit the work's dedication to herself. On its appearance, her extending her patronage over it naturally provoked consternation at Versailles.[137] What further incensed the French envoy at The Hague, the Marquis de Noailles, who suspected that the highly provocative preface had been penned by Diderot, was that the Russian ambassador himself became the book's chief distributor, dispatching copies on all sides, and even obliging the French embassy officially to accept one.

Reporting further to Paris, in September 1773, Noailles confessed to having been wrong to suppose, three years before, that the 'madness' of the *philosophes* had peaked with the *Système*. For with the posthumous publication of Helvétius's *De l'homme* 'that madness' had now attained fresh heights.[138] Diderot, supposedly en route to Petersburg at the time, reported Noailles to Paris, was lodged next to the prince of Orange's library, as Golitsyn's specially honoured guest. Even if he was not the author of the appalling preface, he was certainly propagating equally pernicious sentiments everywhere in Holland.[139] (However, after Diderot returned to Paris, the Utrecht professor Hennert assured Eurler that he had not in fact made much impact in Holland where few people had wished to see him.) Back in Paris, the (atheist) astronomer Lalande noted that Diderot had erred in speaking so freely, his open atheism causing many people to avoid him.[140]

Versailles took such exception to Golitsyn's role that, in October 1773, a formal complaint was lodged at the empress's court. Catherine's foreign affairs minister answered that she had no connection with the offending publication (which was patently untrue) and that, in any case, numerous works offensive to her had appeared in France wholly unhindered by the French crown. Catherine received her own specially bound printed copy in September 1773, along with a letter from Gosse, thanking her for extending her 'protection éclairée' to the project. She was too immersed, however, in the *Histoire philosophique*, she explained to Voltaire, to find time for Helvétius just then.[141] *De l'homme*'s dedication to Catherine doubtless explains its prompt diffusion in Petersburg. Here was a milieu where *De l'esprit* had long been a celebrated work, Princess Dashkova mentions in her memoirs having read the earlier work twice by the time she was 16. *De l'homme* also penetrated in France and southern Europe but far more slowly than in the north. The police, not only in Paris but throughout France, reportedly, suppressed this work 'avec une

[136] Helvétius, *De l'homme*, i, preface 12.
[137] Golitsyn to Alexander Mikhailovich Golitsyn, The Hague, 22 Dec. 1772, in *CGdH* iii. 427–8.
[138] Noailles to d'Aiguillon, The Hague, 14 Sept. 1773, in *CGdH* iii. 449.
[139] Noailles to d'Aiguillon, The Hague, 14 Sept. 1773, ibid. iii. 449–51.
[140] Trousson, *Denis Diderot*, 554.   [141] Catherine to Voltaire, 22 Sept. 1773, in *CGdH* iii. 452.

vigueur incroyable'.[142] Although eagerly sought after in Paris, noted Grimm in his *Correspondance littéraire*, in November 1773, copies remained hard to obtain and there was little likelihood of this changing soon.[143] Nevertheless, by then the text was well known in radical circles. Several associates besides Diderot, including Grimm (who disliked it), had seen and commented on it in manuscript.[144] Turgot and Condorcet had by then both read it and, as usual, disagreed as to its significance, Turgot denouncing what he saw as its lack of logic, taste, and morality; Condorcet judged it a 'good book', though he did not think Helvétius 'un grand génie'.[145]

During 1773, the first edition of this 'ouvrage posthume', some copies including, others lacking, the dedication to Catherine, was followed by a second, third, and fourth all with 'Londres' on the title page.[146] Three more French editions followed the next year. Unusually, for a forthrightly irreligious and radical work, the German rendering appeared just a year after the French, at Breslau in 1774, under the title *Von Menschen, von dessen Geistes-Kräften und von der Erziehung desselben*. The translator, Christian August Wichmann, had also rendered several texts of Restif de La Bretonne into German. Two further French editions appeared in 1775, followed by the English version, *A Treatise on Man* (London, 1777). A second German edition came out in 1785, again at Breslau, while a Danish-Norwegian version, *Om Mennesket*, appeared at Copenhagen in 1788 (second volume in 1791).[147]

De l'homme was a radical bombshell, undermining every principle of existing law, administration, and morality. Voltaire received his copy from Holland, at Ferney, in June 1773 and Frederick his, at Potsdam, in August. Predictably, both strongly disapproved. Even among the radical *philosophes* themselves, some were taken aback by Helvétius's forthrightness against existing structures and authority, seeing his posthumous legacy as too subversive and divisive, a work bound to force men to take sides. What the reactions of Noailles, Turgot, Condorcet, and Diderot had in common was their all seeing that *De l'homme* had deepened the lines of schism. Helvétius's chief fault, Condorcet assured Turgot in December 1773, was that he denounced 'despotism' too bluntly and insistently for the good of the *parti philosophique* and their cause. The universal oppression and misery of peoples 'results', held Helvétius, 'from defective laws and a too unequal division of wealth' [dépend de l'imperfection de leurs loix et du partage trop inégal des richesses].[148] Neither 'despots' who read scarcely anything, nor their accomplices who read still less, might notice. But there was every risk their flatterers and spies who abound everywhere would infer from Helvétius's parting salvo that 'tous les gens d'esprit' were their 'implacable' ennemies. Helvétius's indictment is so plainly aimed at kings,

[142] Grimm, *Corr. littéraire*, iii. 461.   [143] Ibid. iii. 457 n.
[144] Smith, *Bibliography*, 291; Krebs, *Helvétius*, 140–1.
[145] *Correspondance inédite de Condorcet*, 99.
[146] Smith, *Bibliography*, 298–313.
[147] Fromm, *Bibliographie*, iii. 315 and v. 278–9; Smith, *Bibliography*, 333–41.
[148] Helvétius, *De l'homme*, ii. 665–6.

priests, and lawyers, and also nobles and the wealthiest, that one could only conclude that *la philosophie* sought to overturn the existing order.[149]

The essential link between politics and Helvétius's moral theory is that all men individually desire their own pleasure and hence desire to be despots, and hold sway over others, while only the general good can balance the conflicting desires of men by creating a just, equitable, and good government.[150] The supreme enemy of all humanity, consequently, is *le pouvoir arbitraire* together with ignorance which paralyses the republican impulse, reducing peoples to inertia and base submission or 'mollesse'.[151] Hence, only a state formally organized 'to reconcile individual with the general interest' [pour unir l'intérêt particulier à l'intérêt général] in the interest of the whole community,[152] that is a representative democratic republic or genuinely benevolent enlightened despotism (which Helvétius unlike Diderot still considered a possibility), can deliver legitimate, genuinely non-despotic government. Ignorance Helvétius rated the foremost asset of princes, courtiers, and priests. Any magistrate forbidding freedom of the press, the chief antidote to ignorance, opposes moral, legal, and political amelioration itself.[153] The risk in all this was that such a blueprint was bound further to intensify the hostility of Europe's courts and legal elites and stoke up a rising persecution of the 'gens d'esprit'.[154]

Diderot disagreed. He thought *De l'homme* was not blunt enough. What the world needs, he urged, disagreeing with Lalande, Condorcet, and whoever else advised against confrontational tactics, summing up his critique of *De l'homme* in late 1773, is philosophy forthright, unequivocal, and compelling enough to force everyone to take sides, the kind expounded in 'le *Système de la Nature* et plus encore dans *Le Bon Sens*'.[155] The *Système*'s author does not first claim to be an atheist and then pretend to be a deist. His philosophy unfolds clearly and resolutely forming an overarching coherent system. No one can be in doubt about his meaning. He starts by showing 'men are only unhappy because they do not understand nature' [L'homme n'est malheureux que parce qu'il méconnait la Nature], that the world is a sink of misery and oppression owing to ignorance, that human wretchedness is avoidable, and that everything can be changed through Enlightenment.[156]

There was also something distinctly strange, Condorcet agreed with Diderot, though, as well as Turgot, in writing 'si fortement contre le despotisme' while simultaneously pouring incense on the names of Frederick (whom Voltaire had always urged Helvétius to cultivate) and Catherine who Turgot and Condorcet

---

[149] Ibid. ii. 821, 825.
[150] Helvétius, *De l'esprit*, 340, 343, 382; Helvétius, *De l'homme*, ii. 553–5.
[151] Helvétius, *De l'homme*, ii. 527–8, 530, 532–3, 557.
[152] Helvétius, *De l'esprit*, 375; Ladd, 'Helvétius and d'Holbach', 225–6.
[153] Helvétius, *De l'homme*, ii. 797–9.
[154] *Correspondance inédite de Condorcet*, 141.
[155] Diderot, *Réfutation*, 359, 398.
[156] D'Holbach, *Système de la nature*, 165, 548.

both thought had done nothing but harm humanity and whom they supposed Helvétius eulogized simply because she praised his works.[157] Voltaire, for his part, dismissed *De l'homme* as in part tedious and for the rest a mix of the curious and excessively audacious. It was the last that worried him. For some passages read like a re-run of the *Système* in their egalitarianism and attack on social hierarchy and kingship. It was a sally bound to push him still further into a corner especially now that Condorcet too showed a growing fondness for atheism, materialism, and wide-ranging political reform in the spirit of Helvétius, Diderot, and d'Holbach.[158] We are in real peril of finding ourselves like the Apostles, he admonished d'Alembert, in June 1773, that is, followed by a small minority and persecuted by the great majority. Should any powerful men take the time to read *De l'homme*, 'ils ne nous pardonner-ont jamais'. Every such attempt at an all-embracing system, combining materialism with sweeping political, moral, and legal reformism, is both a waste of time and exceedingly dangerous as such schemes are practically never truly coherent. 'Je ne connais que Spinoza', Voltaire summed up, simultaneously lambasting both Helvé-tius and the *Système*, 'qui ait bien raisonné' but he is unreadable.[159] In any case, it is not with metaphysics but truth of fact that one undeceives mankind and advances *la philosophie*.[160]

After 1770, it was impossible to doubt that the aim of Diderot's, Helvétius's and d'Holbach's books was comprehensively to assail the double yoke 'de la puissance spirituelle et temporelle' and eventually to overthrow them, replacing these with a completely new institutional framework.[161] The battle Diderot, d'Holbach, Condor-cet, and Madame Helvétius were fighting had now obviously become a social and political as well as intellectual struggle, hence from this point on Voltaire and d'Alembert could no longer afford to be in any way associated with them. The 'revolution' they envisaged was a universal re-evaluation of all values and hence one of a fundamentally different kind from the much more limited 'revolution' Voltaire and d'Alembert strove for. The former was something altogether more sweeping, dangerous, and difficult but also more of a piece, more obviously and closely tied to their philosophical core doctrines and, it was now clear, something intellectually more attractive if not to most readers then at least to the many who felt aggrieved in the France of the 1770s.

Voltaire took no pleasure in combating his *philosophe* critics, and did his best to exempt Diderot from his sallies. But he also felt tightly constrained by Frederick's ire, the repressive censorship policy of the French court, and the political implications of the publicity accorded to the materialists' views. He thought the *matérialistes* were misguided, and their ideas about creation and the emergence of intelligence in nature

---

[157] Ibid. 148; Desné, 'Voltaire et Helvétius', 405.

[158] Badinter and Badinter, *Condorcet*, 80–4; Baker, *Condorcet*, 34–5; Williams, *Condorcet and Modernity*, 17, 122.

[159] Voltaire to d'Alembert, 16 June 1773, in Voltaire, *Corr.* xl. 24.

[160] Ibid.

[161] [D'Holbach], *Le Bon-Sens*, preface p. vi.

completely wrong, but he also thought that the court at Versailles, Frederick, and society generally were making far too much of the alleged danger posed by 'atheism'. The furore against 'atheism' struck him as an irrational obsession typical of Christians and monarchs rather than a grave problem for deism per se. Why are Christians so dreadfully aroused by the—as he saw it—real but exaggerated harm caused by atheism? A single year of civil war between Caesar and Pompey, he suggested, damaged humanity far more than could 'tous les athées ensemble pendant toute l'éternité'.[162]

Diderot, while dismissing Voltaire's deistic writings as the efforts of an 'esprit faible', hurtful words to which Voltaire alludes in his *Lettres de Memmius*,[163] and remarking, in 1774, that Voltaire today was a mere 'parrot' of the Voltaire of thirty years before,[164] always genuinely appreciated his stupendous literary and philosophical accomplishment. He had no more wish to be dragged into an open fight with Voltaire than did the latter with him. In a letter intended to hold Naigeon in check, of June 1772, he grants that Voltaire's support for Maupeou's policies made him a tool of royal oppression but also sternly reminded his disciple that in the past Voltaire had often intervened to defend the unjustly oppressed and revenge the innocent. Voltaire had lost his grip, urged Naigeon, and become an 'insensé'; but it was this *insensé* who, long before, first introduced Locke's and Newton's philosophies in France, led the assault on popular prejudice, and for decades advocated toleration and liberty of thought. His name is rightly honoured everywhere 'et durera dans tous les siècles'.[165]

Voltaire and Frederick, along with d'Alembert, wished to leave ancient beliefs broadly intact for the majority. But precisely the political character of Voltaire's and d'Alembert's stance, and fear of alienating those monarchs they considered their allies, lent Voltaire's published attacks on the *Système* and more generally on atheism and materialism a contrived appearance in the eyes of some that fed the suspicion, rife among both the *anti-philosophes* and the *coterie d'Holbachique* (and shared by d'Alembert), that privately the patriarch of Ferney's allegiance to Newtonianism and natural theology had slackened but without his being willing to admit this. He had abandoned freedom of the will. Was he fully convinced himself of the existence of God and was his urging more reverence for Locke and Newton not dictated more by deference to monarchs and courts, hence tactical considerations, than anything else? Even his oft-repeated assurances that belief in a Supreme Being and providence are a necessary brake on men's passions, suggested some, was window-dressing not genuine conviction.

Both 'nouveaux philosophes' and *anti-philosophes* whose efforts seemed so often and paradoxically to converge questioned the late Voltaire's sincerity. The Abbé François, in his *Observations*, dedicated to the cardinal-archbishop of Besançon, in 1770, asks whether Voltaire's *Dictionnaire philosophique portatif* genuinely upholds belief in a Supreme Being and the soul's immateriality? Was Voltaire's stance not a

<hr>

[162] Voltaire, *Lettres de Memmius*, 445.   [163] Ibid. 438.   [164] Diderot, *Réfutation*, 362.
[165] Diderot to Naigeon, undated June 1772, in Voltaire, *Corr.* xxxviii. 418.

mere rhetorical façade apt to collapse into materialism when examined, into the 'monstrous' doctrine of 'Strato', Spinoza, and Fréret? To be fair to Voltaire, though, added François, still more damagingly, it was probable that he did believe in God and the soul's immortality, but needing to impose a show of unity on his otherwise hopelessly divided band of 'disciples' (who were mostly atheists and materialists), he felt obliged to finesse his views somewhat and 'whisper in two voices' in order to continue presiding as 'maître' over the *secte nouvelle*.[166] Voltaire professed to champion divine providence. But his use of the term in his late works makes his providence often seem more like a euphemism for the 'necessity' of the *matérialistes*.[167] If he thought he was skirting great difficulties by dispensing with miracles and revelation and accommodating divine providence minimally, it failed to impress either *nouveaux philosophes* or *anti-philosophes*.

3. THE TRIAL OF DELISLE DE SALES (1775–1777)

Another great 'affair', widening the rift and weakening Voltaire's position further, was the furore that erupted in 1775–6 over the curiously hybrid philosophy devised by Jean-Baptiste Isoard Delisle de Sales (1743–1816). Delisle was a gifted former member of the Oratorians from Lyon who taught for some years, for the Oratorians, at Riom and then as a professor of rhetoric at Nantes.[168] In 1768, he had resigned his chair, abandoning academe for the life of a freelance *philosophe* in Paris. His philosophy he presented to the world in his six-volume *De la philosophie de la nature*, the first three volumes of which appeared legally, soon after the *Système de la nature*, in 1770. Delisle, Voltaire was initially pleased to see, proclaimed himself a staunch champion of moderate and providential thought, loudly avowing allegiance to theism, the necessity of 'religion', and the soul's immortality.[169] 'La morale', holds Delisle, in the second volume where he denounces the *Système de la nature*'s author as a *sophiste* and *enthousiaste*,[170] is inconceivable 'sans l'intervention de Dieu' and useless without the soul's immortality.[171] Delisle's declared aim was to champion 'la modération', stiffen royalism, counter subversion, and crush the pernicious systems of 'Spinosa, Bayle, Fréret et La Mettrie'.

Yet attentive readers soon noticed something amiss with his reiterated assurances of 'moderation'. Besides omitting Diderot's and Helvétius's names from his list of adversaries, his magnum opus exhibited various suspicious features. If Condillac's sensationalism, with its explicit rejection of Locke's doctrine of the 'faculties of the

---

[166] François, *Observations*, 158–60.
[167] Stenger, 'Matérialisme de Voltaire', 282.
[168] Helvétius to Delisle de Sales, 10 Nov. 1770, in *CGdH* iii. 341–2.
[169] Delisle de Sales, *Philosophie de la nature*, i. 152–3; Balcou, *Fréron*, 327; Mortier, *Le Cœur*, 21, 381.
[170] Palmieri, *Analisi*, iv. 43–4; Delisle de Sales, *Philosophie de la nature*, i, pp. xl and 119–20, 129.
[171] Delisle de Sales, *Philosophie du bonheur*, i. 19; Delisle de Sales, *Philosophie de la nature*, ii. 9.

soul', was acceptable with due qualification, his definition of nature as 'matter in movement' looked suspect, as did his notion of mind in primitive creatures. More disturbing still was his thesis that there exists only 'one element' in the universe, a claim hard to construe other than as reaffirming Spinoza's single substance. Hardest of all to square with moderation was his insistence that movement is inherent in matter and that matter is not inert, as Newton, Clarke, and Voltaire maintain.[172] In fact, Delisle's God possessed neither intelligence nor benevolence and was identical to the 'Grand Tout'.[173] Furthermore, he openly professed admiration for Diderot's *De l'interprétation de la nature* and *Lettre sur les aveugles*, slighting Voltaire by eulogizing Diderot instead of Locke as the true 'prométhée de la métaphysique'.[174]

In addition he shared Diderot's and the *Histoire philosophique*'s militant social reformism and hostility to race prejudice. If there were black slaves who seemed to acknowledge the natural dominance and higher intelligence of the whites, as some claimed, this was only, Diderot argued, because the whites had instituted and perpetuated their ignorance.[175] In the wake of the *Histoire*, Delisle de Sales likewise expresses fierce indignation at the *sophisme* that blacks are of a lower order of intelligence to whites. He fiercely assails the Jesuit father Pierre-François-Xavier de Charlevoix, who in his four-volume *Histoire de l'Isle Espagnole ou de S. Domingue* (Paris, 1730), or rather 'roman' as Delisle derisively calls it, maintained that all the blacks of Guinea 'naissoient stupides', that most could not count to beyond three, and that their lack of aptitude for social organization legitimized the institution of slavery.[176] This is total calumny, countered Delisle, invented to justify their oppression. In fact, the blacks are gifted and intelligent people.

Admittedly, blacks write no philosophical books like' les citoyens oisifs de votre Grande-Bretagne'; but set them free and give them educators of the calibre of Locke and Newton and more than one African will excel in your universities. However, the first book written by a black will probably be 'un manifeste pour la liberté contre ses tyrans'. Readers could rest assured that he would not be permitted to make the stifled voice of truth heard with impunity: his book will be burnt in all Europe's capitals 'pour s'épargner la peine d'y répondre'.[177] Attempts to justify slavery in secular legal terms were still being made by using statements taken from Grotius and Pufendorf deriving the slave-owners' property right over their slaves from their having been sold to slave-dealers and then their owners. Diderot and his colleagues working on the *Histoire* had been scathing about this argument. So was Delisle. He denounced it as an appalling *sophisme*: by what absurd madness of the human mind could anyone imagine, he asks, 'qu'un homme libre pouvoit se vendre'?[178]

[172] Delisle de Sales, *Philosophie de la nature*, ii. 330–4; Palmieri, *Analisi*, iii. 45 and iv. 43–8; Citton, *L'Envers*, 176, 186, 258.
[173] Barruel, *Les Helviennes*, ii, 167–9.
[174] Delisle de Sales, *Philosophie de la nature*, ii. 330–4; Vernière, *Spinoza*, 398.
[175] *Histoire philosophique* (1780), vi. 203–7.
[176] Delisle de Sales, *Philosophie de la nature*, iv. 191–2.
[177] Ibid. iv. 193.   [178] Ibid. iv. 191.

Delisle made scant attempt to disguise his alignment with the scientific, psychological, and moral ideas of Diderot and Helvétius, and even professed being a disciple of the 'immortal Helvétius' who had conceived the idea of composing 'un code moral pour l'espèce humaine, fondé sur la philosophie de la nature' at the same time as he himself.[179] Helvétius, moreover, had directly or indirectly clearly contributed to the genesis of the book. After publication, he wrote to Delisle in December 1770 warmly approving of it and complimenting him on its 'success'.[180] Although the work aroused hardly any interest initially, attentive readers, including officials of the *Parlement de Paris*, after a time perceived that the much-vaunted 'modération' of this vast and meandering but not uninteresting work was bogus. Far from championing theism and royalism, Delisle was a materialist, sensualist, and *Spinosiste*, a loyal disciple of Helvétius who had done much to encourage him, seeking to pull the wool over everyone's eyes.[181] He later admitted having embraced materialist ideas since around his twentieth year, or 1763. Only his antipathy to d'Holbach, whatever caused it, proved genuine. While neither original nor particularly consistent, he was undeniably erudite (as well as a renowned bibliomaniac whose library by the mid 1770s reportedly boasted 32,000 volumes). He also possessed a more detailed knowledge of the clandestine philosophical literature, readers saw from his footnotes, than practically anyone else. His Achilles heel was a willingness to go to any lengths to become a celebrated *philosophe*.

The universities, Oratorians, and clergy had every reason to consider him a renegade. The legal proceedings against him, a direct 'spin-off' from the controversy over the *Système*, grew from small beginnings into one of the foremost *causes célèbres* of the French eighteenth century. When originally delivered to its appointed censor, in 1769, his text was still far from complete. Delighted by the opening sections denouncing atheism and stating his aim as being to expound only what the Paris *Parlement* called 'des vérités incontestables',[182] the censor fell into the trap of too quickly concluding, from the book's deliberately misleading opening, that Delisle's goal was to affirm God's existence and providence. The polemic against the *Système* the censor took at face value, not noticing that Delisle mainly disparages d'Holbach's prose style, unoriginality, and failure to acknowledge predecessors from whom he had drawn, rather than his actual ideas which, in fact, scarcely differed from Delisle's. The censor therefore approved the first three volumes for 'tacit' permission provided the title page stated 'Londres' or 'Amsterdam' as the place of publication, without realizing the complex, devious character of the work he had approved.

[179] Ibid. i. 5–6, 36, 60, 84, 87, ii. 103, 124, and iii. 379–80.

[180] Helvétius to Delisle de Sales, 20 Dec. 1770, in *CGdH* iii. 342–4: 'je ne suis point étonné de la sensation prodigieuse que fait la *Philosophie de la nature*'; Delisle de Sales, *Philosophie du bonheur*, i, préface pp. vi and 57.

[181] Palmieri, *Analisi*, iv. 43–8; Mauzi, *L'Idée du bonheur*, 118 n.; Benítez, *Face cachée*, 189.

[182] Oxford Bodleian Mason 1.1.142/no. 76: *Sentence du Châtelet qui condamne un livre imprimé en six volumes ayant pour titre: De la Philosophie de la nature* (9 Sept. 1775) (Paris, 1775), 2.

Delisle had obviously reflected much on the *Système* to which his work was less a reply than a competitor.[183] The *Système*'s author, lacking sufficient genius to raise a monument to the truth, had written not 'un ouvrage utile, mais un ouvrage singulier'. He had sought celebrity by publishing 'le livre le plus hardi qui fut sorti de la main des hommes', albeit one that not only reproduces but reinvigorates the 'absurdités' of Spinoza and Fréret.[184] All his main 'opinions extravagantes' his rival had garnered from two principal sources—Spinoza's *Tractatus Theologico-Politicus* and Fréret's *Lettre de Thrasibule*—the mix then being spiced further with some La Mettrie, Bolingbroke, and Shaftesbury.[185] This and the praise he lavishes on Fréret, Boulanger, and other earlier atheists whom he considered the real sources of d'Holbach's thought showed he had no objections to radical ideas as such. In thirty years' time, he predicted, the *Système* would no longer be read by anyone just as in his day most people no longer read 'les rapsodies théologiques' of Spinoza, *Leviathan* of Hobbes, or *Les Trois Imposteurs*. Science, theism, and reason would by that time have overthrown this colossus that today seems as if it is going to crush us: 'et malheur à nous si j'étois un faux prophète.'[186]

What Delisle meant by claiming to have cut the 'Gordian knot', readers gathered, was that there is only one substance 'dans le monde' and that God never departs from the universal laws of nature.[187] Though formally denounced by the Assembly of the Clergy for purveying doctrines incompatible with Christianity, the first rumblings of the furore the book caused blew over and for four years it seemed the affair would remain insignificant.[188] But while initial sales were negligible the work's illicit character and also its attractions as a *anti-philosophique* target gradually emerged more clearly. The plot thickened when the Parisian publishers, replicating the same title pages as originally authorized, published the latter three volumes, in 1773, as if these had been authorized too, when these volumes had not actually been seen by any censor. Reviewing these, in August 1774, Fréron repeated his earlier judgement: the work is devoid of originality, full of contradictions, dangerous to religion, and subversive politically.

In his *De l'esprit*, Helvétius claims sensual pleasure and pain are the sole motor of human motives and only 'contrepoids qui meuvent le monde moral', holding the true science of legislation to consist in using rewards and penalties to unite the individual with the general interest.[189] With this, Delisle entirely concurred. Already in his earlier review, Fréron noted that Delisle's ostensible thesis was Voltairean and deist, but that behind this pretence lurked a reworking of Diderot with an explicit

---

[183] Delisle de Sales, *Philosophie de la nature*, iv. 334–6.

[184] Ibid. iv. 336; Palmieri, *Analisi*, iv. 48.

[185] Delisle de Sales, *Philosophie de la nature*, v. 338.

[186] Ibid. v. 339–40.

[187] Ibid. ii. 181; Reynaud, *Délire*, 62.

[188] Malandain, *Delisle de Sales*, i. 154; Delisle de Sales, *Philosophie de la nature*, i. 119–20.

[189] Helvétius, *De l'esprit*, 328, 340; Ladd, 'Helvétius and d'Holbach', 225.

acknowledgement of the latter's influence on his scientific ideas.[190] In his second review, Fréron also drew attention to the fact that Delisle, in his 'modest way', entertains far-reaching practical as well as theoretical aims, namely to instruct the world's legislators as to how best to reform the entirety of the world's laws which Delisle pronounced 'stupides, féroces, sanguinaires', comprehensively renewing the legal systems of all the peoples on earth. His presumption in usurping the place of kings, ministers, and magistrates, and aspiring to be man's supreme guide, was no mere eccentric feature of this professor's temperament but entirely typical of that astounding lack of modesty, prudence, and understanding characterizing the *philosophique* sect generally.[191]

Had not Helvétius indicted all elites, including the *parlements* whom he accuses of hypocrisy, imposing bad laws, and complicity in immorality and lies?[192] Eager for revenge, certain magistrates saw in Delisle a brazen crypto-radical and self-confessed disciple of Helvétius and Diderot and one who was neither dead nor able to conceal his authorship, but an author uncommonly vulnerable to being used as a stalking-horse for the entire *philosophique* sect. Despite the great mass of radical literature circulating at the time, Delisle was a shrewdly chosen target. Despite his disavowals, he could be easily incriminated as an atheist and *matérialiste*. A former professor who had appended his name to his work and abundantly cited his sources, he presented excellent opportunities for lawyers to implicate his friends and associates and the *parti philosophique* generally. Formal denunciation in the Paris courts, in September 1775, swiftly led to the book's judicial condemnation as 'impious, blasphemous, and seditious', the court ruling that the *Philosophie de la nature* should be publicly lacerated and burnt in the Place de Grève, as an irreligious work, impudently proclaiming the total reform of society via 'une grande révolution qui se prépare' in the minds of the population.[193]

During the interval between his book's condemnation and its public burning, late in 1775, the Abbé Reynaud published a 74-page pamphlet *Le Délire de la nouvelle philosophie*, a particularly virulent *anti-philosophique* outburst devoting particular attention to Delisle's equating God with nature and thesis that God 'n'est pas libre'.[194] If his semi-veiled Spinozism was readily unmasked, so was Delisle's combining Diderot's materialism with a heady dose of legal reformism with a clearly seditious political stance all couched, his assailants granted,[195] in a fiery, penetrating style capable of retaining the reader's attention. A *philosophe* who had furiously insulted the legal and medical professions as well as the clergy, he seemed splendidly qualified to unite in one powerful chorus of condemnation all strands of professional antipathy towards the *la philosophie moderne*. With his bogus gestures of support for theism to screen his atheism, he was even useful against Voltaire. In this way, a

---

[190] Balcou, *Fréron*, 328; Malandain, *Delisle de Sales*, i. 61, 151.
[191] Malandain, *Delisle de Sales*, i. 156–7; Balcou, *Fréron*, 353.
[192] Helvétius, *De l'homme*, ii. 827, 832–3.
[193] Oxford Bodleian Mason 1.1.142/no. 76: *Sentence du Châtelet*, 2.
[194] Reynaud, *Délire*, 53–4, 61–4; Monod, *Pascal à Chateaubriand*, 472.   [195] Reynaud, *Délire*, 3.

third-rate *philosophe* became a major target of the Jansenist-minded judicial authorities. Public destruction of the *philosophe* who wrote that 'La Mettrie n'a guère menti que quand il a nié Dieu'[196] seemingly promised a sure way of soundly thrashing *la philosophie* generally.

Initially, Voltaire, Grimm, and d'Alembert were not unduly concerned. Delisle was viewed by them as of little account and it amused them that an obscure author whose books had sold badly for six years, and gone unnoticed, should suddenly emerge, as Grimm's *Correspondance littéraire* put it, as 'un des plus dangereux suppôts de l'Encyclopédie'.[197] But jocularity soon gave way to grave concern. Early in 1776, it emerged that a concerted campaign was afoot, organized by the *parlements* and 'intolerance of Jansenism', encouraged by the *dévôt* faction at court. The goal was to pursue Delisle ruthlessly in the courts as a way of attacking *la philosophie* generally. The affair developed into an episode (though one generally ignored by modern historians) of such importance that Voltaire, in the closing stages of his career, devoted around seventy letters to it. The legal proceedings and new attack on *la philosophie*, it soon became clear, were part and parcel of a wider campaign on the part of the same mostly Jansenist magistrates hounding Delisle, to secure full restitution of the *parlements* whose powers the crown had recently curtailed, and paralyse the reform edicts issued by Turgot in his capacity as a royal minister in the current administration.[198]

Seeing he was about to be imprisoned, Delisle, in February 1776, appealed to Voltaire for his help. After first gathering more information, from Morellet among others, Voltaire realized that Delisle's predicament menaced the entire *philosophique* movement. Condorcet too became seriously alarmed and flung himself into the affair. Urging d'Alembert to concert the *philosophes'* efforts in Paris, Voltaire dispatched letters in all directions summoning the entire 'church' of the *gens de bien* to mobilize to defend the good cause from the immanent peril posed by the Jansenist-parliamentary court-clerical assault. There were dark warnings of a figurative new St Bartholomew's day 'massacre', only this time one involving slaughter of the *philosophes'* reputation and public standing. Meanwhile, foes of his among the Paris magistrates were attributing to him, Voltaire learnt, a virulent printed anonymous attack on those driving the Delisle trial, entiled *Lettres de l'inquisiteur de Goa*, a tract actually penned by Delisle himself.[199]

Delisle made no attempt to flee but gallantly stood his ground. Arrested and imprisoned, in March 1777, his reward was at last to win some renown and boost his readership. For over six years, lack of sales and proper permission had deterred Delisle's Parisian publishers from bringing out a 'third' (i.e. first full) edition of his work. But now a Dutch publisher, attracted by the uproar and lure of burgeoning

---

[196] Delisle de Sales, *Philosophie de la nature*, iv. 222.
[197] Malandain, *Delisle de Sales*, i. 162.
[198] Ibid. i. 172–3; Delisle de Sales, *Philosophie du bonheur*, i, préface p. ix.
[199] Malandain, *Delisle de Sales*, i. 185; Staum, *Minerva's Message*, 91.

sales, brought out in Holland a timely 'third' edition, in fact the first complete version, explicitly associating it with the deceased Helvétius (whom Delisle publicly acknowledged as his mentor). Rising sales and his constancy in facing his persecutors in court rendered him an international *cause célèbre*, this being the only case during the Enlightenment in which a *philosophe* was formally brought to criminal trial in France for his ideas and publications, a sobering prospect for the other *philosophes*. Finding him guilty of blasphemy and subversion, his judges sentenced him to perpetual banishment from France while also severely reprimanding the original censor and French publishers. This 'abomination est révoltante', protested Marmontel, something worthy of the fourteenth century. 'Le fanatisme', commented Condorcet, having just received his own complete edition of Delisle's work, is more violent than ever in Paris.[200]

Yet, after a promising start from the *dévôt* standpoint, the affair failed to produce the spectacular triumph the *anti-philosophes* and Jansenist magistrates expected. In fact, for the *philosophes'* adversaries it rapidly degenerated into a complete fiasco. Instead of producing an intensified repression of the *incrédules*, Delisle's imprisonment at Châtelet suddenly reversed into an unprecedented triumph for the *philosophes*. Someone had forgotten about or badly miscalculated the sympathies of much of the reading public. For not only did the trial transform Delisle's book into one of the century's greatest best-sellers but, helped by Voltaire's efforts, it made Delisle an international celebrity. During the weeks of his trial, the magistracy effectively lost control of the process of condemnation and retribution. Suddenly, it was their public image instead of his that was pilloried and severely damaged. The magistrates were defeated by what Delisle later called the 'confédération des hommes de bien'. Publicity was becoming an organized force. Flattering messages and soon also congratulations poured in from all sides. Fashionable well-wishers and their lady friends began visiting Delisle in his cell in such numbers the judicial-clerical scheme of vengeance collapsed in derision. Collections were made to provide financial support, the proceeds remitted to the prison along with all manner of presents and baskets of sandwiches, donations that, rather than keep for himself, France's philosophical martyr distributed among the prisoners. The outcry and ridicule surrounding Delisle's formal condemnation and banishment not only astounded and dismayed the *Parlement* but turned into a stunning setback for the *anti-philosophique* forces, Jansenism, and the judicial process.[201]

It became impossible to make an example of Delisle. Swallowing a bitter pill, the *Parlement*, on 14 May 1777, suspended his banishment and granted amnesty. On being triumphantly released from the 'fanatisme atroce et absurde' of the 'Jansenists' of Châtelet, as d'Alembert put it, Delisle at once travelled to Ferney to thank Voltaire in person for his decisive intervention, everywhere publicly thanking the many who had intervened to save him from the clutches of the *dévôts*. At Ferney he

---

[200] Labbé, *Gazette littéraire*, 87.
[201] Delisle de Sales, *Philosophie du bonheur*, i, préface p. ix; Malandain, *Delisle de Sales*, i. 186–8.

ostentatiously remained through the summer of 1777. Subsequently, he continued to enjoy renown and be widely read in France down to the Revolution, an expanded seven-volume edition of his work appearing in 1789 in the midst of the great political upheaval of that year.[202] Yet, despite it all, Delisle's triumph could scarcely be construed as a victory for Voltaire although he had led the chorus that freed him. Rather it was a posthumous triumph for Helvétius, as well as Diderot and radical ideas generally.

If Delisle's 'persecution' ensured brisk sales for his *Philosophie de la nature*, down to the Revolution, it also assisted his and his allies' efforts to unmask the corrupt state of the law and the irrationality of justice under the crown, and generally promote their thesis about the insidious collusion of despotism, lawyers, and priesthood.[203] If both Voltaire and d'Alembert were genuinely delighted by their success in freeing Delisle, their position and their kind of Enlightenment were nevertheless weakened precisely by their success. Since Delisle now needed a position and protector, both warmly recommended him to Frederick, expecting their protégé's erudition would easily secure a post as a librarian in Berlin. But after reading Delisle's book, Frederick was in no mood to comply with requests for solidarity among the *philosophes*. Delisle's text, he answered d'Alembert, brimmed with 'idées chimériques' that might be pardonable in someone who is drunk but not in someone claiming to be a *philosophe*. Delisle he suggested should become a *folliculaire* (copy-editor?) at Amsterdam, or else follow the example of some ex-Jesuits who had become coachmen in Paris: 'il vaut mieux être le premier cocher de l'Europe que le dernier des auteurs.'[204]

Frederick refused to support any writer holding such reformist, egalitarian, and universalist views. The 'peu sistématique' Delisle, he suggested later, writing to Voltaire in January 1778, might do best going to Sweden where the frozen wastes of the north would help cool the ardour of his 'Provençal' blood and he could become 'le plus bel esprit de Stockholm', his universalism converting the Lapps into 'metaphysicians' and refining the habits of the *sauvages* inhabiting the fringes of the polar region.[205] D'Alembert had for some time been growing uneasy at Frederick's increasing coolness towards the Enlightenment in general. The king had not forgiven the *philosophes* for the *Système de la nature*, he lamented, writing to Voltaire early in 1778, whose author had perpetrated the 'grande sottise de réunir contre la philosophie, les princes et les prêtres'. Diderot and d'Holbach, 'très mal à propos selon moi', had effectively wrecked Voltaire's philosophical project and his own by convincing kings and priests of their powerful and enduring interest in working together.[206]

---

[202] *Chronique de Paris*, 43 (5 Oct. 1789), 169.

[203] Darnton, *Corpus*, 144; Darnton, *Forbidden Best-Sellers*, 48–9, 70, 397 n.

[204] Voltaire to Frederick, undated Apr./May 1777 in Voltaire, *Corr.* xliv. 254; Malandain, *Delisle de Sales*, i. 192.

[205] Frederick to Voltaire, Potsdam, 25 Jan. 1778, in Voltaire, *Corr.* xlv. 188.

[206] Granié, *Lettre á M...*, 24; Malandain, *Delisle de Sales*, i. 193.

Marginal intellectually, Delisle nonetheless became a pivotal figure in intellectual history. His book and trial proved the impossibility of bridging Radical Enlightenment and moderate Enlightenment even when literally mixing their two languages together. The Delisle de Sales affair, converging as it did with Turgot's dismissal from government in 1776, and the final illness and death of Voltaire soon afterwards, marked the turn at which the French and general moderate mainstream Enlightenment began its retreat to humiliation and failure. The increasingly reactionary stance of Louis XVI's regime, after 1774, and the deeply ominous Olavide trial in Spain (1776), together with the reaction in Denmark-Norway after 1771, the unwillingness of Frederick any longer, after 1770, to support Enlightenment in any guise, and Catherine's abandonment of her law reforms after the Pugachev rebellion, and her reversion to harsh methods of repression, spelt the effective end, the running into the sands, of Voltaire's and d'Alembert's Enlightenment.

The increasingly reactionary mood in Berlin, Madrid, and Petersburg and more conservative turn at Versailles, following Turgot's downfall, confirmed the impossibility of projecting, justifying, and carrying through any wide-ranging programme of legal and political reform within the existing political and social framework. Extolling moderation sounded worldly-wise, shrewd, and prudent but the moderate Enlightenment, divided between its religious and deist wings, proved completely ineffective in reality. The bankruptcy of Voltaire's and Frederick's Enlightenment became more or less plain for all to see. Delisle de Sales, sensationally tried in 1777 under the *ancien régime* for publishing a text which he himself afterwards admitted assails 'le Despotisme royal dans sa base', subsequently endorsed and ardently supported the principles of the *philosophique* Revolution of 1789–92.

However, like Naigeon, Condorcet, and many others he was subsequently deeply alienated and shocked by the Revolution of the Will of 1793–4 when in his opinion every clause of the *Declaration of the Rights of Man* was torn up and violated. As a result, he reverted to royalist sympathies. On this ground, he was arrested and tried again, in 1794, under what he termed the 'dictature of Robespierre', accused this time of deprecating in print the Jacobins for whom the very word 'philosophie' was anathema and converted, as he put it, into a term of insult and abuse.[207] Yet his good fortune did not desert him. Unlike Condorcet, Brissot, and Cloots, but like Paine, he survived the experience.

---

[207] Delisle de Sales, *Philosophie du bonheur*, i, préface pp. i, viii, l, lv, 9; Staum, *Minerva's Message*, 91, 147.

25

Pantheismusstreit (1780–1787)

1. LESSING'S LEGACY

Besides the Counter-Enlightenment's triumph in Bavaria in 1785–6, and Joseph II's backtracking regarding freedom of expression in Austrian lands from 1786, there were also other indications prior to 1789 that central Europe's general political and cultural constellation was turning against the Enlightenment and highly intolerantly against its radical wing. By the later 1780s, figures such as Forster, Bahrdt, Diez, Dohm, Wekhrlin, Knigge, and Knoblauch saw compelling reasons for anxiety—especially in Prussia, following the accession of Frederick the Great's successor. Neither Protestantism nor Catholicism, as most people seemed to think, was what was direly imperilled by conspiracy and 'despotism', warned Forster, referring to Germany's increasing fixation with conspiracy, secret societies, and organized subversion. The real threat was different. If Europe's crowns felt obliged, once again, to clamp fetters on men's consciences and proclaim confessional allegiance vital to statecraft, then the real menace, he urged, quoting from Lessing's *Nathan der Weise* in the *Berlinische Monatsschrift*, was not to organized religion, but to 'reason, freedom of thought, *Aufklärung* and love of truth'.[1]

On a philosophical level, unmistakable signs of reaction against the *Aufklärung* were manifest also in other responses to Lessing's rich legacy. In his last months, Lessing felt repulsed, deeply frustrated, and isolated at Wolfenbüttel. Health inexorably deteriorating, he finished three culminating works—*Erziehung des Menschen Geschlechts* (Education of the Human Race] (1777), *Ernst und Falk* (1778), and *Nathan der Weise* (1779)—that together formed a passionate and comprehensive challenge to central Europe's accepted cultural and social values. If the first pronounces revelation a form of 'education' imparting to men 'nothing that human reason left to itself could not also arrive at' but instilling it faster and more easily than individuals could acquire it through reason itself, it also relegates revelation to an inferior, narrower status than that of reason while altogether marginalizing ecclesiastical authority.[2] Indeed, all three works illustrate not just the wide impact of his

---

[1] *Berlinische Monatsschrift*, 14 (1789), 547, 553, 578–80; Beiser, *Enlightenment*, 180–1.
[2] Lessing, 'Education', 218.

philosophy on social, cultural, and political criticism but proclaimed the need for a general re-evaluation of all values right across the board.

The great critic, thinker, and dramatist's most masterly and controversial play, *Nathan the Wise* has always been rated among the peaks of classical era German literature and the Enlightenment's foremost pleas for toleration and a more equal, 'enlightened' relationship between Christians, Jews, and Muslims. Set in twelfth-century Jerusalem, the play's centrepiece, the famous parable of the Three Rings, was certainly intended to promote toleration and mutual respect among the three revealed religions—Judaism, Christianity, and Islam. However, the play is less concerned with minimizing differences between faiths, or preaching indifferentism, than promoting the idea that champions of each of the Three Rings cannot know which is the true one but must prove the legitimacy of the faith that each individually adheres to by their actions, by living a life of virtue, devotion, and goodwill. This, to Lessing, is the real meaning of 'true religion'.[3]

That the play also reflects aversion to 'positive religion', something Lessing himself speaks of, is sometimes acknowledged, as is the Spinozistic thrust of Nathan's remarks about miracles and what is commonly believed.[4] But besides promoting toleration and eulogizing reason, the play dramatizes the collision between Enlightened Despotism (symbolized by 'Saladin') allied to conventional religion and what Lessing deemed the Enlightenment's true values. In the encounter between 'Saladin' and Nathan is staged a clash of world-views framed by Lessing's insight that veritable enlightened values and despotism are locked in irresolvable conflict. For all his talk of 'justice' and disapproval of intolerance, 'Saladin' has no real grasp of genuine morality or respect for others and is ultimately motivated, we discover in the opening of the last act, by appetite for power and money. He is a monarch who, for these gains, routinely sacrifices what is best.[5]

Nathan der Weise was first performed in Berlin only in April 1783. At its opening performances, it received a notably cool and suspicious welcome marked by the conspicuous absence of the Jews (who reportedly stayed away out of apprehension). Its tense reception left the meaning of Lessing's legacy even more bitterly contested than before.[6] That for many years the drama proved extremely divisive throughout German-speaking central Europe and also Denmark-Norway where the Danish version was kept off the stage until 1799, and remained highly controversial for decades thereafter, needs to be borne in mind.[7] For Lessing's views collided fundamentally with what was commonly felt, believed, and thought not only among the orthodox but also in official Enlightenment circles.

Admittedly, most took it for granted that not just a great deal, but enough had been accomplished by the *Aufklärung*, thanks to Frederick, Catherine, and Joseph, and that the shift in public and official attitudes had been decisive, beneficial,

---

[3] Schilson, 'Lessing and Theology', 174–5; Forst, *Toleranz*, 405–6.
[4] Lessing, *Gesammelte Werke*, ii. 322, 334–5.
[5] Lessing, *Gesammelte Werke*, ii. 474; Bohnert, 'Enlightenment', 356–8.
[6] Bourel, *Moses Mendelssohn*, 396.   [7] Bohnen, 'Lessing und Dänemark', 306–8.

and sufficient. Was not superstition in full retreat? 'Our present age', commented the town secretary of Quedlinburg in 1784, referring to the spread of toleration in Prussia, 'is rightfully termed *aufgeklärt* [enlightened].'[8] The last witch trials in central Europe, in West Prussia in 1779 and another at Glarus in Switzerland in 1783, provoked outrage among the reading public, swamping the 'Hottentots' of the Glarus town government in derision.[9] Few felt much more was required. If reforms were still needed to right a few obvious defects, it was rare indeed to encounter calls for the entire social, religious, and political fabric to be transformed. Few thought of the social and political system as inherently oppressive and despotic. In this sense, the Radical Enlightenment remained a fringe phenomenon. Yet it was precisely this radical tendency that faced the undoubted fact that central Europe remained a region of wide-ranging religious, ethnic, and gender discrimination, extensive restrictions on individual freedom, serfdom, and vast inequality of status and wealth.

If the *Aufklärung*'s successes were everywhere manifest so were its failures. Toleration was nowhere complete and was less and less so in Prussia, Bavaria, Bohemia, and Austria. The state of education seemed highly unsatisfactory to many. Establishing equality before the law, ending serfdom, and unshackling the press had made only modest progress overall. Social and legal integration of the Jews, ending persecution of homosexuals, unmarried mothers, and the suicidal, and reforming marriage and family law had scarcely begun. Repressing older forms of superstition in rural areas looked successful on the surface; but the fight against irrationality, having reached a certain point, seemed now in retreat. The rise of the new, wildly popular fads— Mesmerism, wonder cures, masonic rituals, Father Hans Joseph Gassner's exorcisms, and secret 'mysteries' characteristic of the 1780s, a trend vigorously encouraged by popular theologians and increasingly noticeable also in high society—were not just fleeting fads of a moment but aspects of a shift in mood fervently supported by a growing army of *Anti-Aufklärer*, a trend capable of accelerating the reversal against the Enlightenment and restoring the sway of 'superstition'. Far from exterminated, the 'Hottentots' of Glarus seemed to be gaining fresh vigour and support with which to bring society more rigorously under the sway of the devout, mysterious, popular, and irrational.

Of course, mainstream Enlightenment voices too, Kant included, were greatly disturbed by this trend. But if one concedes the reality of miracles, averred Carl von Knoblauch (1756–94), a jurist, critic, and ally of Wekhrlin always insisting on the impossibility of wonders and miracles, then one has no answer. Conventional philosophers, Wolffians and Lockeans, could not coherently rule out on purely philosophical grounds belief in any wonders, even werewolves, fairies, and magic.[10] What could they reply to Mesmer and Gassner? The only solution for man's predicament, urged Knoblauch, was a redoubling of effort against belief in supernatural forces, thaumaturgy, wonder-works, exorcism, and, in the case of 'Poland,

---

[8]　*Berlinische Monatsschrift*, 3 (1784), 297.
[9]　Ibid. 3 (1784), 300, 311; [Knoblauch], *Taschenbuch*, 68–74.
[10]　[Knoblauch], *Taschenbuch*, 68–74; Knoblauch, *Ueber Feerey*, 11–12.

Hungary, Silesia, Moravia, Austria and Lorraine', the deep-rooted belief in vampires.[11] In his opinion, there is no magical explanation for anything. Only a philosophy proving the will cannot arbitrarily change real things could stem the craze for wonder cures, mystery, and Gassner and the only philosopher whose philosophy was sufficiently consistent and cogent to block thaumaturgy, he contended, was Spinoza.[12] The author of the *Ethics*, he judged like many in the 1780s, 'was the most consequent of all the philosophers' [der konsequenteste von alle [philosophen] war].[13]

That most, in all social classes, were unwilling to accept that philosophical reason is the universal guide and adamantly refused their far-reaching criticism does not mean the views of Lessing, Herder, Bahrdt, Thorild, Diez, Forster, Weishaupt, Wekhrlin, Knoblauch, Maimon, Cloots, and Dohm and numerous others portraying their social world as inherently oppressive and defective judged from an enlightened perspective were either mistaken or marginal. Rather, it was precisely the public's undiminished belief in incomprehensible forces, it seemed more plausible to argue, that most hampered the general adoption of science, legal science, and social science as the path to a general overhaul of politics, law, and legislation, and ameliorating the human condition.[14] The Gassner and Mesmer enthusiasts Knoblauch accused of manipulating women and the illiterate in particular.[15] If the Counter-Enlightenment of feeling, mystery, and belief was gaining ground, the social critics and educators of the *Aufklärung* felt driven to fight back, raise fresh resources, and deploy 'philosophy' still more robustly in combating what they considered totally pernicious as well as absurd cults of the irrational. The 1780s hence simultaneously witnessed a heightening of enthusiasm allied to mystical fads *and* an escalation of 'philosophy's' war on 'superstition' and credulity. To reverse the tide of fanaticism, sorcery, Gassnerism, and Mesmerism, radical *Aufklärer* strove to convince the more sophisticated, including those professionally engaged in defending faith in wonders, revelations, and miracles (i.e. the theologians), that it was they who were fomenting the burgeoning fervour for wonder-cures and religious zeal.

It was against this backcloth that erupted the greatest of the all central European intellectual controversies of the late eighteenth century, the so-called 'Pantheism struggle' or *Pantheismusstreit* of 1780–90. This was a philosophical drama that dragged on at full intensity for five or six years but still continued to resonate powerfully through the years of the French Revolution when it not only particularly fascinated those, like the young Hegel, Hölderlin, and Schelling, inclined to view the Revolution favourably and place it in a philosophical context, but convinced them that the truly major modern shifts and movements in philosophy had Spinoza as their starting point.[16] Its timing and context explain not just the peculiar intensity and wide ramifications of the great German 'Spinoza controversy', reaching to the

---

[11] Knoblauch, *Taschenbuch*, 19.
[12] Knoblauch, *Euclides Anti-Thaumaturgicus*, 3, 10–11, 17–18.
[13] Ibid. 13.
[14] Knoblauch, *Taschenbuch*, 45, 101–3; Knoblauch, *Euclides Anti-Thaumaturgicus*, 11–12.
[15] Knoblauch, *Taschenbuch*, 44; Knoblauch, *Anti-Taumaturgie*, 39, 41.
[16] Schelling, *Ages of the World*, 105; Pinkard, *Hegel*, 30.

heart of the literary and journalistic, as well as the academic, philosophical, and theological worlds, but help us also to understand how an intellectual quarrel could exert a massive impact on central European cultural life as a whole and on the careers and reputations of so many key figures, ranging from Lessing, Mendelssohn, Goethe, and Herder to Thorild, Jacobi, Rehberg, Wizenmann, Maimon, and Kant.

What was most remarkable about this controversy was that an old fixation, now over a century old, should not only remain undiminished in its power to stir up controversy but continue to provide the chief focus for society's deepest and most disturbing intellectual worries and tensions, bringing what previously had been in large part a hidden obsession, buried in the undergrowth of private thought and debate, fully into the public sphere. As Goethe famously remarked in the middle of the furore, the public dispute about Spinoza and Spinozism that erupted in Berlin, Hamburg, Weimar, Königsberg, and all of Germany in the 1780s, far from being an essentially new development, merely brought to the surface for the first time a tangle of previously concealed intellectual encounters and relations that all the major participants in the public drama had been privately wrestling with for decades, but almost always contending with in the isolation of their private thoughts.[17]

What occurred, affirms Goethe, was a sudden uncovering of concerns that had been entirely integral to German intellectual life and philosophy ever since Leibniz first recognized Spinoza's central importance for every basic question, whether in philosophy, religion, science, or morality, in 1671. Practically everyone involved, including Goethe himself, irrespective of whether they were strongly drawn towards Spinoza's system, like Lessing, Herder, Forster, Lichtenberg, Diez, Wekhrlin, Knoblauch, Thorild, Maimon, and Heydenreich, and a little later Hegel, Schelling, and Hölderlin, whether they favoured some elements in Spinoza but with stronger objections, like Mendelssohn, Rehberg, or Wizenmann, or those who were comprehensively hostile, like the younger Reimarus, Kant, Reinhold, Jacobi, Biester, and Hamann, had privately been immersed in this debate long before 1784–5. Lessing and Mendelssohn were preoccupied with Spinoza from the early 1750s. Hamann, doyen of German Counter-Enlightenment, first closely studied Spinoza, he told his ally Jacobi in November 1784, over twenty years before.[18] Solomon Maimon (1754–1800), foremost Jewish philosopher of the Enlightenment after Mendelssohn, became a convinced 'Spinozist' for some years during his second stay in Berlin (1779–82).

2. THE EARLY STAGES OF THE GERMAN 'SPINOZA CONTROVERSY'

If Gassner and Mesmer were to be swept away, if popular superstition, credulity, ignorance, and enthusiasm were ever to be broadly eradicated from human life, many

---

[17] Zammito, 'Most Hidden', 335–6.   [18] Bayer, 'Spinoza', 319.

obsessions, creeds, and philosophies would totally disappear; but what would replace these? In the 1780s, at the height of the Western Enlightenment, it seemed to some of the acutest minds in Germany that there was only one way of answering this question. 'If the world still exists in some incalculable point in time further on', remarked one of the most admired German scientific intellects of the age, the Göttingen professor Lichtenberg, towards the end of the *Pantheismusstreit*, 'the universal religion will certainly be a modified Spinozism. Reason left entirely to itself leads to nothing else and it is impossible that it should lead to anything else.'[19]

The *Pantheismusstreit* is usually said to have originated in two sets of conversations between an aspiring young author, Friedrich Heinrich Jacobi (1743–1819), and Lessing a few months before the latter's death. However, even before Jacobi entered the scene, others, including Lessing himself, had been debating Spinoza in a manner that if not more open than in the past was considerably more appreciative and positive and, consequently, bound to precipitate a major new Spinozist controversy once this revisionism became more generally known. Actually, rather than Jacobi, it was the later Hanoverian official and conservative writer August Wilhelm Rehberg (1757–1836) who was seemingly the first, in 1779, responding to that year's Berlin Academy prize competition, publicly to assert in a published text that, despite the mountain of academic and ecclesiastical condemnation and scorn heaped on him and his ideas for over a century, if judged from a purely objective, philosophical standpoint, Spinoza is more cogent and 'consequent' than Leibniz, Wolff, or any other major figure competing for primacy in German thought and that since this must become obvious sooner or later, this fact inevitably signified a pending great crisis in philosophy.[20]

In asserting this, Rehberg, a declared Humean sceptic, was not claiming there exists such a thing as a universally valid and impregnable philosophical system. What he meant was that if such a system of metaphysics is conceivable and explicable to us, then Spinoza's system, when fairly compared with the rest, is unquestionably the closest thing to it. In publicly stating this viewpoint, Rehberg, as he himself later noted, preceded Jacobi and the others who subsequently stoked up the furore. But it hardly matters who initiated the public controversy. The same claim about Spinoza's superior consistency was reiterated with increasing frequency in the 1780s by Jacobi, Lichtenberg, Herder, Goethe, Knoblauch, and Rehberg himself, developing 'into a kind of fashion in German philosophy'.[21] However if Jacobi did not precipitate the controversy, he did figure centrally in it and to an extent lent shape to a feud which convulsed the entire German cultural, academic, and intellectual scene and to a greater extent than any other of the second half of the eighteenth century.

Son of an affluent businessman, Jacobi was a minor financial official of the state of Jülich-Berg, with a position leaving ample time for travel and literary and philosophical pursuits. An autodidact of Lutheran background living in a predominantly

---

[19] Lichtenberg, *Werke*, 174.   [20] Rehberg, *Sämtliche Schriften*, i. 7–8; Beiser, *Enlightenment*, 306.
[21] Rehberg, *Sämtliche Schriften*, i. 8; Bourel, *Moses Mendelssohn*, 391.

Catholic milieu, he had spent two years in Geneva (1759–61) acquiring a thorough knowledge of the French and Franco-Swiss Enlightenment and, from around 1761, began seriously studying philosophy. He admired Rousseau but especially Bonnet whose works he knew almost by heart.[22] Having made a special study of Spinoza, a thinker to whom Bonnet evinced fierce antipathy, examining his *Ethics* early in the 1770s in Schmidt's 1744 translation (along with Wolff's refutation), Jacobi considered himself an expert on Spinoza already prior to his encounter with Diderot at his country home near Düsseldorf in 1773.[23] Immersed in the ebb and flow of German intellectual life, Jacobi was also, since 1774, a long-standing acquaintance of Goethe with whom his first intense two-day encounter, near Düsseldorf, as the poet himself recalls in his *Poetry and Truth*, had Spinoza as its central topic.[24] But with Goethe his relationship subsequently soured. Neither Goethe nor Wieland with whom he had worked for a time evidently thought very highly of Jacobi's several novels.

Jacobi first visited Lessing in July 1780, spending several days in his company at Wolfenbüttel whilst on business en route to Hamburg where he was to establish friendly relations with the Reimarus family. Long discussion with the ill and frequently bedridden Lessing presented Jacobi with a unique opportunity to advance his own ambitious philosophico-religious agenda. Like many others, he had immense respect for Lessing. For some time, though, since the latter stages of the *Fragmentenstreit*, he had suspected that Lessing had broken altogether with theism and the entire Leibnizian-Wolffian legacy. On finally meeting him, at Wolfenbüttel, and then Brunswick and Halberstadt, later in 1780, this suspicion was confirmed in a series of conversations in which Lessing confided his private thoughts to him.[25] Nothing further occurred during Lessing's last lingering illness ending with his death on 15 February 1781 or immediately thereafter.[26] But although circumstances obliged him to move slowly, it seems likely that Jacobi deliberately schemed to draw Mendelssohn and other friends of Lessing into a trap from the outset. For he had taken a positive dislike to Mendelssohn and the kind of providential theism he and others of the 'enlightened' circle in Berlin, notably Biester, Eberhard, and Nicolai represented.[27] At some point Jacobi formed a plan to use the 'Spinozist' dimension of his Lessing conversations to exert a wide impact in the German cultural arena with a view to advancing his own particular intellectual strategy and weakening the moderate halfway-house *Aufklärung* that he detested by accusing it of collapsing in the face of—and having an inherent leaning towards—Spinozism.

Jacobi commenced his campaign against the Berlin *Aufklärer* rather subtly, in the summer of 1783, by writing to his own (as well as Lessing's and Mendelssohn's) female friend Elise Reimarus, in Hamburg, confiding to her that Lessing 'in his last days was a decided Spinozist' and urging her to communicate this 'unexpected' and

---

[22] Bourel, *Moses Mendelssohn*, 393–4; Vallée, *Spinoza Conversations*, 98.
[23] Bourel, *Moses Mendelssohn*, 395.   [24] Ibid. 393; di Giovanni, 'Introduction', 52–4.
[25] Strauss, 'Einleitungen', p. xxiii.   [26] Engel, 'Von "Relativ wahr"?', 222, 229.
[27] Christ, 'Johann Georg Hamann', 253; Beiser, 'Enlightenment and Idealism', 26.

disturbing fact to Mendelssohn, a philosopher deeply attached to Lessing who, Jacobi had recently learnt, was preparing a lengthy literary tribute in Lessing's memory. This tribute to Lessing, Mendelssohn informed Herder, in May 1781, he had originally hoped to complete in the summer following Lessing's death. But he had seen little of his friend in recent years and was taken aback by the seizure of their mutual correspondence along with Lessing's papers and philosophical texts by the duke of Brunswick. When the papers were released what he found gave him even more reason to pause for thought. In this way, he got seriously behind with the project (which was never to materialize).

Elise wrote to Mendelssohn, in August 1783, enclosing a copy of Jacobi's letter, and asking what he knew of Lessing's views at the end of his life and how the matter should be handled. Mendelssohn, already uneasy prior to this, due to the distinctly Spinozistic tendency of some of the essays and comments in Lessing's unpublished papers (as he informed Lessing's brother Karl Gotthelf in April 1783),[28] replied in a defensive, apprehensive tone. What does it mean to call Lessing a 'decided Spinozist'? Spinoza's thought evolved in stages. Which of Spinoza's systems did Jacobi think Lessing adhered to: 'the one expounded in his *Tractatus Theologico-Politicus*, the Cartesian system found in his *Principia Philosophiae Cartesianae*, or the one post-humously published in his name by Ludovicus Meyer [i.e. the *Opera Posthuma*, including the *Ethics*]'?[29] If Jacobi had in mind 'the system of Spinoza generally held to be atheistic', Mendelssohn desired to know whether he supposed Lessing had construed that system 'in the way Bayle misunderstood it, or after the manner in which it has been better explained by others'. He conceded, though, that the Lessing–Jacobi dialogue mattered too much to be left unclear in its significance and details.[30]

Mendelssohn faced a serious difficulty. Any publication projecting Lessing as a 'Spinozist' would seriously damage not only his deceased friend's reputation and legacy which had anyway become more vulnerable with the *Fragmentenstreit*, and still more so with the staging of *Nathan the Wise*, but, worse, would prejudice the whole cause of comprehensive toleration in central and northern Europe and with it the position of the Jews. It would also damage his own personal standing since he was the publicly proclaimed chief ally and friend of Lessing and his chief mission in the Enlightenment—serving as a kind of bridge between Judaism and German culture— made him the foremost beneficiary of Lessing's toleration. His own position would thus inevitably be compromised by any discrediting of Lessing's stance as would the whole campaign to attack prejudice, bolster toleration, improve the position of the Jews, and weaken ecclesiastical authority. For these goals could then all be publicly dismissed as disreputable and impious, being 'Spinozistic'.

Discrediting Lessing as a 'Spinozist' would also harm the German Enlightenment and prospects for a central and Eastern Jewish Enlightenment in a more general way,

[28] Goldenbaum, 'Mendelssohns schwierige Beziehung', 306.
[29] Jacobi, *Über die Lehre*, 10.
[30] Vallée, *Spinoza Conversations*, 81; Altmann, *Moses Mendelssohn*, 607–8.

both being crucially dependent on championing divine providence, immortality of the soul, and the integrity of Scripture. Philosophically, his own recently published *Jerusalem, oder über religiöse Macht und Judentum* [Jerusalem; or on Religious Power and Judaism] (1783) had reaffirmed his and his allies' general condemnation and rejection of Spinoza. Although Mendelssohn only refers once to Spinoza by name in that text, it was plain that the whole work constituted a kind of purged *Tractatus Theologico-Politicus* designed to reconcile philosophy with the workings of divine providence, establish toleration and personal religious liberty on firm foundations, while blunting the impact of Spinoza's critique of Scripture.[31] Spinoza had become if not Mendelssohn's own private nemesis then certainly his chief interlocutor while at the same time it was undeniable that sections of *Jerusalem* were intended to refute views of Reimarus publicized by Lessing during the *Fragmentenstreit*, and, hence, by implication, to criticize Lessing too.

Lessing had not only lent publicity to Reimarus' withering critique but broadly accepted his fierce disparagement of the Old Testament text and main personalities. In this respect, the *Fragmentenstreit* had renewed Spinoza's assault on the authority and authenticity of Scripture while simultaneously rendering his hermeneutical arguments better known.[32] Reimarus' and Lessing's standpoint obviously contradicted Mendelssohn's long-standing claim that the Old Testament's doctrines are in perfect accord with reason and teach the rudiments of rational natural theology, including immortality of the soul (a thesis Reimarus and Lessing expressly rejected) as well as the chief points of universal morality. In *Jerusalem*, Mendelssohn abandons his earlier standpoint that the core doctrines of the Hebrew Bible are identical to those of philosophical natural religion, feeling obliged to fall back on the much vaguer tenet that what was revealed to the Israelites by God implies prior awareness of those truths.[33] This posed a severe challenge to Mendelssohn, and the whole relationship of Judaism to the Enlightenment, a challenge made acute by Jacobi's initiative.

All this was worrying enough. But Jacobi's intervention proved unsettling for Mendelssohn and the future of the *Aufklärung* also in another way. Linking Lessing to 'Spinozism' would inevitably cast the *Fragmentenstreit* in a new light and confirm for many readers the reality of that hidden allegiance to irreligion, libertinism, rejection of tradition and religiously based morality, as well as anti-Scripturalism which Goeze and other orthodox adversaries had so loudly denounced. This would vindicate all those disposed to believe that the core of the *Aufklärung* was rejection of religion and religiously based morality, putting an entirely new coloration on the much vaunted friendship of Mendelssohn and Lessing and the, for many, surprising fact that during the *Fragmentenstreit* Lessing was even more hostile to the liberal Neologists, Semler, Teller, and Eberhard, than to orthodox theologians like Goeze.[34]

---

[31] Goetschel, *Spinoza's Modernity*, 137; Crouter, *Friedrich Schleiermacher*, 68–9.
[32] Goetschel, *Spinoza's Modernity*, 196–7.
[33] Ibid. 197; Bourel, *Moses Mendelssohn*, 209, 334; Hess, *Germans, Jews*, 114–16.
[34] Schmidt-Biggemann, *Theodizee*, 150; Goldenbaum, 'Mendelssohns schwierige Beziehung', 304.

In November 1783, Mendelssohn received, via Elise and her brother (who added his own comments), a thirty-six-page letter from Jacobi (slightly varying copies of which subsequently found their way to Herder, Hamann, and Hemsterhuis), enclosing the then still unpublished text of Goethe's *Ode to Prometheus*. The missive contained a detailed word-for-word report of his encounter with the ailing Lessing, a meeting that began, Jacobi explained, with their discussing Goethe's poem, an ode powerfully expressing Goethe's new-found anger and frustration at divine providence's inability to aid the distressed and persecuted, a poem so irreverent it positively appalled Jacobi. Showing the manuscript to Lessing, he had pronounced it 'Spinozist' through and through, assuming it would shock him too and that Lessing would join in condemning irreligion and curbing the growing encroachment of Spinoza's perspectives into German culture.[35] Lessing, however, had answered that 'the point of view the poem expresses is also my own. The orthodox concepts of the divinity are no longer for me; I cannot stand them. "*Hen kai pan*. Ich weiss nichts anders" [One and all! I know nothing else]. This is the tendency in this poem; and I must admit, I like it very much.'

'Then you are', asked Jacobi, 'more or less in agreement with Spinoza?' 'If I am to call myself by anybody's name', answered Lessing, 'then I know none better.'[36] The discussion continued the next day: 'I certainly did not expect to find in you a Spinozist or pantheist', began Jacobi, 'and you put it to me so bluntly! I had come chiefly expecting your help against Spinoza.' When Lessing asked whether he had really studied Spinoza, Jacobi explained that he had, over many years, and believed 'hardly anybody has known him as well as I', to which Lessing reportedly answered: 'es gibt keine andere Philosophie, als die Philosophie des Spinoza' [there is no other philosophy but the philosophy of Spinoza].[37] They then moved on to Leibniz and it emerged that neither Lessing nor Jacobi thought Leibniz had succeeded in refuting Spinoza and that both judged that his determinism did not differ fundamentally from Spinoza's. Since they agreed about this, Lessing urged Jacobi to publish his view of Leibniz's relation to Spinozism, since most 'people still talked about Spinoza as if he were a dead dog',[38] meaning that hitherto it had been usual to pretend that philosophers, theologians, and scientists, and Leibniz and Wolff above all, had conclusively dismissed Spinoza's 'atheism' and fatalism. But where Lessing (and Lichtenberg) considered this absurdly superficial, Jacobi (and Rehberg) condemned it, quite differently, as fatally complacent.

The generally accepted 'dead dog' presumption *was* absurd but, then, to grasp Spinoza accurately requires too much effort for all but a few so that most readers were dependent on what their recognized authorities told them. Since Jacobi continually stressed Spinoza's unparalleled cogency in reasoning, Lessing asked how it was, then, that he himself was not a Spinozist; since he was not, Lessing presumed he

---

[35] Vallée, *Spinoza Conversations*, 7–9, 26; Pätzold, *Spinoza, Aufklärung*, 82.

[36] Jacobi, *Über die Lehre*, 16–17; Herder, *Gott*, 154–5; Goldenbaum, 'Mendelssohn's schwierige Beziehung', 308 n.

[37] Vallée, *Spinoza Conversations*, 9–11; Rohls, 'Herders "Gott"', 273.

[38] Jacobi, *Über die Lehre*, 23–4; Vallée, *Spinoza Conversations*, 90, 93.

must be a thoroughgoing sceptic who 'turned his back on all philosophy'. His intention, explained Jacobi, was to exploit the very consistency and force of Spinoza's arguments—together with the impossibility of accepting his conclusions—to create a wholly new standpoint in philosophy: a 'springboard into faith', a new kind of philosophical dualism to which he was to adhere until his death, monist by reason, Christian in sentiment.[39] Jacobi should forget 'springing into faith', retorted Lessing, and instead embrace Spinozism.

Some modern scholars have construed this as a case of Lessing's playful posturing, indulging his taste for enlivening debates by adopting provocative positions he did not necessarily take seriously, to draw Jacobi out. But practically no one—apart from Mendelssohn, momentarily, in his initial attempt to deflect Jacobi—interpreted Lessing's words thus at the time. Denial that he was a crypto-Spinozist so common among late nineteenth- and twentieth-century scholars is almost wholly a subsequent phenomenon. Not one of the participants in the *Pantheismusstreit* (not even Mendelssohn), however divergent their views in other respects, considered this a real possibility, as there were many reasons for inferring Lessing was indeed a 'Spinozist'. Not even those contemporaries who heartily regretted his Spinozism and who, like Elise, her brother, the younger Reimarus, and Mendelssohn himself, judged it best to heavily qualify it, thought there was any way, in view of his texts, to deny the fact itself. To contemporaries, noted Knoblauch, nothing seemed more obvious than that a thinker like Lessing who sought to explain everything in exclusively this-worldly, natural terms should recognize in Spinoza's thought a philosophical apparatus uniquely well suited to his purposes.[40] As Ernst Cassirer noted, in 1932, the great writer had a much deeper knowledge and understanding of Spinoza than most of his contemporaries and 'toward the end of Lessing's life', it would seem that ' he no longer had any essential objection to the logical necessity and systematic unity of this doctrine', despite adjusting some aspects which he infused with his own powerfully original perspective.[41]

On parting, Jacobi presented Lessing with copies of three works by Hemsterhuis whose reputation in Germany he was promoting. These were the *Lettre sur l'homme et ses rapports* (1772), *Sophie ou de la philosophie* (1778), and *Aristée, ou la divinité* (1779), writings with which Lessing—unlike Herder who had been familiar with Hemsterhuis since 1772 and had translated another of his texts, the *Lettre sur les désirs*, into German, publishing it in the *Teutsche Merkur*, in 1781[42]—was then still unfamiliar. Jacobi and Lessing agreed to resume their discussion shortly. On returning from Hamburg, Jacobi found Lessing so captivated with Hemsterhuis that he spoke of translating the *Aristée* into German. He was baffled, though, by Lessing's insistence that Hemsterhuis's thought is 'pure Spinozism' in a 'beautiful exoteric

---

[39] Vallée, *Spinoza Conversations*, 90, 93; Pätzold, *Spinoza, Aufklärung*, 84–5; Crouter, *Friedrich Schleiermacher*, 78–9.

[40] [Knoblauch], *Taschenbuch*, 66.   [41] Cassirer, *Philosophy*, 190.

[42] Heinz, 'Genuss, Liebe', 434, 437; Verzaal, 'Besuch', 165.

wrap'.[43] 'From what I knew of Hemsterhuis', he protested, 'he was no Spinozist. Diderot himself assured me of this.' Diderot had indeed studied Hemsterhuis at The Hague and was far from considering him a 'Spinosiste'.

Yet Lessing had a point. Hemsterhuis's goal in his early endeavours had been to persuade the Amsterdam silk merchant, banker, regent, and antiquarian much connected with Russia, Baron Theodore de Smeth (1710–72), a close friend and highly cultivated man privately an ardent Spinozist,[44] to abandon this allegiance. Reality in Hemsterhuis forms an essential dualism, albeit body and soul, unlike Descartes's two substances, continually interact. His case against materialism, like that of the Newtonians, chiefly relies on the idea that motion is not innate in matter.[45] It was hence a critique vulnerable to a consistent hylozoic materialism of the kind expounded by Diderot. Furthermore, despite relying on body and soul dualism, Hemsterhuis at the same time saps notions of divine providence and supernatural agency by injecting a certain pantheistic tendency which accounts for Lessing's construing him as a closet 'Spinozist'. De Smeth too had argued that if Hemsterhuis ever ironed out his inconsistencies, he would profess himself a Spinozist. Hemsterhuis adamantly disagreed but failed in his task. In August 1786, he wrote to his regular correspondent, the pious Princess Golitsyn, deeply regretting that his *De l'homme* appeared too late to sway his friend who had died four years before 'tranquillement Spinosiste'.[46]

Hemsteruis combated Spinoza partly for private reasons but also because he was dismayed by his growing penetration of the Dutch intellectual context. 'Les Hollandois ont vécus avec [Spinoza]', he assured Princess Golitsyn in March 1789, having been his disciples, protectors, and admirers, and without any doubt had furnished 'les plus sçavans, les plus rafinés et les plus déterminés Spinozistes qui existent'.[47] Having himself known La Mettrie (whom he despised as a fool)[48] and, in 1773, encountered Diderot and early come to recognize the underlying connection between philosophy and social forces, Hemsterhuis subsequently viewed the unfolding of the democratic movement in the United Provinces in the 1780s with mounting alarm.[49] Fighting Spinoza and repelling egalitarianism and democracy were more closely entwined in Hemsterhuis's outlook than that of almost any other conservative contemporary.

Having recently read and reread Spinoza's *Ethics* several times, Hemsterhuis in his correspondence kept up his attack on Spinoza's thought as the philosophy 'most diametrically opposed to my own'.[50] Diderot whilst in Holland, in 1773–4, had penned extensive notes on Hemsterhuis's *Lettre sur l'homme et ses rapports* (1772)

---

[43] Jacobi, *Über die Lehre*, 36–7; Verzaal, 'Besuch', 172.

[44] H. Moenkemeyer, *François Hemsterhuis* (Boston, 1975), 12–13, 32; Sonderen, 'Passion', 214–15.

[45] Sonderen, 'Passion', 252–3.

[46] Krop, 'Dutch *Spinozismusstreit*', 187.

[47] Hemsterhuis to Princess Golitsyn, 10 Mar. 1789, in Hammacher, 'Hemsterhuis und Spinoza', 38 n.

[48] Hammacher, 'Hemsterhuis und Spinoza', 38.

[49] Loos, 'Politik und Gesellschaft', 451, 453–4, 458.   [50] Krop, 'Dutch *Spinozismusstreit*', 186–7.

dismissing his proof of the essential inertia of matter and immortality of the soul, the two components positioning Hemsterhuis close to Mendelssohn and Reimarus.[51] Hemsterhuis when first drafting his text, argued Lessing, 'was still rather hesitant and it is possible he himself did not fully recognize his own Spinozism; but he is most certainly aware of it now'.[52] Lessing urged Jacobi to reread Hemsterhuis's last texts and he would see. Even where he most categorically holds body and mind to be separate substances, Hemsterhuis constantly hypothesizes, Lessing saw, as to what follows if we concede that matter alone produces every possible modification and individuation within each life-form, to judge whether his claims for creation, spirituality, and inertness of matter really hold, creating structures of thought more cogent than his declared position. In the *Aristée*, Hemsterhuis opposes the 'argument from design' while maintaining the oneness and unity of the universe, providing an anti-Newtonian depiction of gravity as inherent in the material fabric of the universe, and arguing for the relativity of our concepts of 'good' and 'evil'.[53] He was conducting an unending but not very confident dialogue with Spinoza, de Smeth, Diderot, and with himself.

At the same time, Hemsterhuis agreed with the then controversial view of the Utrecht professor Hennert that Spinozism should not be equated with atheism as most commentators maintained.[54] While the principal aim of the *Lettre sur l'homme* is to block Diderot and d'Holbach by showing the honest reader committed to the systematic use of reason that pure reasoning does not arrive 'aux systèmes du matérialisme et du libertinage', he simultaneously undermines his undertaking through the retreats into which he is forced.[55] Lessing's insight was something Jacobi took to heart. In July 1784, he sent Hemsterhuis a long epistle, enclosing a draft dialogue between 'Spinoza 'and 'Jacobi', destroying his friend's system. Spinozism is irrefutable, he insisted, both by his arguments and in general. It was Jacobi who was mistaken, retorted Hemsterhuis, claiming his own doctrine of the soul and of motion fully refutes Spinozism and materialism. Later, in his *Über die Lehre Spinozas*, Jacobi published an imaginary dialogue between 'Spinoza' and the author of the *Aristée*, a hypothetical 'Hemsterhuis' who finally abandons his lifelong struggle against Spinozism, shattered by his seventeenth-century precursor's relentless reasoning.

Meanwhile, to Jacobi, the case made by Mendelssohn and the Berlin *Aufklärung* for theism, providence, and the soul seemed no more compelling than Hemsterhuis's efforts. Anyone who knows anything about Spinoza, he assured Elise (and through her Mendelssohn), knows the Cartesianism expounded in Spinoza's first book has nothing to do with Spinozism. Furthermore, he was astounded Mendelssohn should oppose the *Opera Posthuma* to the *Tractatus Theologico-Politicus* since, far from being in opposition, the two works plainly stand in complete agreement. As for Bayle and

[51] Diderot, *Commentaire*, 131, 135, 137, 139, 151.
[52] Vallée, *Spinoza Conversations*, 100; Verbeek, 'Sensation et matière', 259.
[53] Hemsterhuis, *Aristée*, 13–15, 26, 46–7.
[54] Ibid. 190, 193; Petry, 'Frans Hemsterhuis', 422.
[55] Verbeek, 'Sensation et matière', 251–2.

Leibniz, it was not they who had misunderstood the true character of Spinoza's philosophy. Rather it was 'those others [i.e. Mendelssohn and his friends] who believed they had explained it better who really misunderstood it—that is they twisted it'.[56] At Hamburg, the younger Reimarus, a leading figure in local society, protector and editor of his father's literary legacy, and fervent believer in an intelligent Creator and divinely ordained morality, accepted that Jacobi's account left 'almost no doubt that Lessing had embraced Spinozism'.[57] He himself now remembered utterances from Lessing's own lips that had at the time perplexed him but now made sense following Jacobi's disclosures. Reviling d'Holbach's *Système de la nature* which he had vehemently attacked in his introduction to the 1781 Hamburg edition of his father's *Abhandlungen*, the younger Reimarus concurred with Mendelssohn that the primary threat to German culture now was the rising tide of materialism, though he also believed materialism's advance was being helped by Hume's scepticism. Especially Hume's arguing in his *Dialogues* that it is 'therefore wise in us, to limit all our enquiries to the present [material] world, without looking farther' and that no satisfaction is to be attained by the speculations of metaphysicians 'which so far exceed the narrow bounds of human understanding' seemed to him to assist the materialists.[58]

Elise too accepted that Lessing must have concealed his real opinions from both Mendelssohn and her brother, out of regard for their theistic sensibilities. All this left the trio with a formidable dilemma. His enemies would loudly 'rejoice' at seeing Lessing, toleration, the renewal of German culture, literature, and theatre, and all authentic *Aufklärung* in the German context and the other great causes he had espoused, unmasked and discredited as 'Spinozist'. How could the damage be limited? Reimarus urged Mendelssohn to write a full-length treatise definitively refuting Spinoza by proving God's existence and the soul's immortality. Mendelssohn declined initially, pleading ill health. Possessing both the intellect and the stamina needed for such a crucial intervention, it was the younger Reimarus who should do so. By the spring of 1784, though, Mendelssohn had changed his mind. Gripped by a growing sense of urgency, he set out to compose a full-length treatise against the 'Spinosisten'—his famous *Morgenstunden*.[59]

That Lessing had abandoned the Leibnizian-Wolffian legacy to which he himself had always adhered greatly disturbed Mendelssohn. Reimarus, Elise, and Mendelssohn, moreover, had supposed that their dealings with Jacobi about Lessing would remain confidential and that he would respect what they thought was their common goal to protect Lessing's reputation and literary legacy, besides Mendelssohn's standing as Lessing's closest friend. Jacobi, however, dispatched his Lessing revelations in long letters also to other key figures, in particular sending copies, in November 1783, of Mendelssohn's questions to him, and his responses, to Herder and his group at

---

[56] Jacobi, *Über die Lehre*, 43; Vallée, *Spinoza Conversations*, 104.
[57] Altmann, *Moses Mendelssohn*, 622; Bourel, *Moses Mendelssohn*, 410–11.
[58] Reimarus, 'Vorerrinerung', 4, 17.
[59] Mendelssohn, *An die Freunde Lessings*, 186; Strauss, 'Einleitungen', pp. xxxvi–xxxix.

Weimar.[60] Jacobi, Mendelssohn knew, was basically right about Lessing. But detesting what he now saw to be Jacobi's tactics and objectives, he could scarcely admit Lessing's Spinozism openly, given the consequences. The Leibnizian foundation of natural theology and natural law on which he had based his endeavours (equally threatened by Kant's critique) seemed close to collapse.

Herder, responding to Jacobi in February 1784, wrote that he too had been continuously preoccupied with Spinoza (as well as Leibniz and Shaftesbury) for the last seven years, hence since 1777.[61] On discovering in Lessing an even closer philosophical ally than he had previously supposed he felt only 'joy': for he too judged Spinoza's the only truly cogent philosophy.[62] The Weimar Spinoza debate, long preoccupying especially Herder and Goethe, was intensified by Jacobi's intervention but in no way caused or prompted by it. Herder, who, partly under the stimulus of reading Diderot, d'Argens, and Robinet,[63] had been much interested in the hylozoic aspects of Spinoza since at least 1769, had no doubts as to the accuracy of Jacobi's account: 'Lessing is so presented', he remarked later, 'that I can see and hear him speak.'[64] It is true, though, that at this point, Herder and Goethe began studying Spinoza more intensively than before while Herder also urged Jacobi to reread Spinoza's *Ethics*, examining it now from Herder's perspective. Alarmed by these further setbacks to his campaign to rescue German culture from Spinoza, Jacobi visited Weimar for twelve days in September 1784, expending much time and effort closeted with Herder and Goethe reiterating his fears in the light of his revelations. He could no more believe in a personal, transcendental God, answered Herder, than could Lessing. Goethe concurred, much to Jacobi's disappointment, refusing to accept that Spinoza was either dangerous or an atheist, maintaining rather that he was both 'theissimum' and 'christianissimum'. Subsequently, Goethe habitually referred to Jacobi and his Pietist allies, such as the poet Matthias Claudius (1740–1815), in terms verging on contempt.[65]

Both the metaphysical and ethical content of the *Ethics* greatly appealed to Goethe, inspiring his conception of Spinozism as a kind of quasi-religion and the potential source of a new cult of the aesthetic. He was impressed especially by Spinoza's lofty tranquillity and the notion of love of 'God' being love of nature and, hence, in no way constituting something self-interested, being adoration of a divinity that gives nothing in return so that all interaction between man and God can only be a one-way intellectual or aesthetic love. 'Weimar Spinozism', despite having been an integral part of Weimar classicism since the early years of Goethe's and Herder's collaboration, undoubtedly became more explicit at this juncture, culminating in the Weimar Spinoza debate of 1784–5. This symposium over the winter of 1784–5 involved entire evenings spent on group readings of the *Ethics* in the company of Goethe's lady friend

[60] Altmann, *Moses Mendelssohn*, 629; Rohls, 'Herders "Gott"', 271, 273.
[61] Rohls, 'Herder's "Gott"', 271–2.
[62] Ibid. 272.
[63] Zammito, 'Most Hidden', 365.
[64] Vallée, *Spinoza Conversations*, 16; Goldenbaum, 'Mendelssohns schwierige Beziehung', 300.
[65] Goethe, *Italian Journey*, 399; Rohls, 'Herders "Gott"', 282; Verzaal, 'Besuch', 170–1.

Charlotte von Stein. On Christmas day 1784 (Frau von Stein's birthday), Herder sent her as a present a copy of the Latin version of the *Ethics* from his own library with a request to share it with Goethe, who did indeed study the *Ethics* closely during 1785, despite being much preoccupied with administration at the time.[66] Goethe in his enthusiasm hailed Spinoza as 'our saint', identifying himself with what was in effect a semi-hidden philosophical sect totally at odds with conventional opinion, conventional morality, and the organized Christian religion, though not the essence of 'Christianity' itself as he and Herder understood it.[67] As a clergyman Herder could hardly express himself as directly; but he too no longer believed Jesus was divine or the Son of God, interpreting him, rather, like Lessing, Bahrdt, Goethe, and the Socinians, and much like Spinoza himself, as a specially inspired man.

Herder, judged a proud, all too lofty spirit by Bahrdt,[68] willingly engaged Jacobi in a dialogue about the meaning of the Lessing conversations while also keeping him informed about the Weimar 'Spinoza' evenings. While his philosophical-literary circle had on one level broken with the practice of mentioning Spinoza only 'with shuddering and loathing', they had broken with it only among themselves. In public, they kept up the old pretence of denying that they were 'Spinozists'.[69] It was during one of their evening conversations, he reported, in February 1785, that Goethe dictated to Charlotte his four-page *Studie nach Spinoza*, his most developed set of comments on the philosopher. Herder himself meanwhile laboured on his own book about God where Spinoza, Shaftesbury, and Leibniz, he informed Jacobi, would all be compared. While Mendelssohn was quite correct to claim Bayle had misunderstood Spinoza, Herder thought Spinoza's monism had not yet been adequately interpreted by anyone. He greatly regretted that Lessing had failed to undertake this task. This work occupied his thoughts for ten years before he finally published it, at Gotha, in 1787.

Spinoza's *Ethics* was being intensively studied in Germany at this time and so was the *Tractatus Theologico-Politicus* which Wekhrlin pronounced in *Das graue Ungeheuer*, in 1786, Spinoza's 'best and most useful work'. 'We still have no book', he agreed with Knoblauch, that 'combats prejudice and superstition with more force and emphasis than this treatise'.[70] It seemed so uniquely useful to the radical-minded not just because it advocates toleration, individual liberty, press freedom, and democracy but also because it shows how what they all considered the true morality can be projected into legislation and society. 'Spinoza owing to his undeniable virtues deserved to be placed in the register of saints far more than many a zealot or *Bethbruder* (prayer brother) who would normally owe his canonization to nothing better than fanaticism.'[71] Likewise, Spinoza had explained more compellingly than

---

[66] Boyle, *Goethe*, i. 353; Irmscher, 'Goethe und Herder', 250; Lauermann and Schröder, 'Textgrundlagen', 51; Rohls, 'Herders "Gott"', 271–2.

[67] Rohls, 'Herders "Gott"', 282; Boyle, *Goethe*, i. 352–4.

[68] [Bahrdt], *Kirchen- und Ketzer-Almanach*, 74–6.

[69] Herder, *Gott*, 15.

[70] Wekhrlin, *Graue Ungeheuer*, 8 (1786), 211; Tilgner, *Lesegesellschaften*, 254.

[71] Wekhrlin, *Graue Ungeheuer*, 8 (1786), 211; Lauermann and Schröder, 'Textgrundlagen', 80–1.

any other thinker how it is that in their choices men suppose they possess free will when actually they are determined to seek what they think is in their own best interest to pursue.

Until early 1785, the reading public noticed few indications that a major furore was welling up behind closed doors, and thus had no inkling that here was an affair likely to reconfigure the entire intellectual debate in progress in Germany. But the participants in what hitherto had been a private affair were all acutely conscious of the broadly unsettling implications of the pending public quarrel. The younger Reimarus, borrowing Mendelssohn's copy of Jacobi's text for close study during the early months of 1784, long hesitated over whether or not to intervene publicly, weighing his options especially in the light of the anticipated effect of any given course of action. In his notes to his revised edition of his father's *Abhandlungen*, he had not only denounced the *Système de la nature* but directly linked the philosophical campaign against hylozoism, one-substance doctrine, and the equation of God with nature to the wider struggle to stem the advance of French materialism in north and central Europe.[72] In 1785, this remained his prime concern.

Appalled by Jacobi's claim that on purely philosophical grounds Spinozism is irrefutable whether by Leibniz, Wolff, Hemsterhuis, or Mendelssohn, with the result that it is, therefore, philosophy itself which must be shelved in favour of faith, Reimarus was no more reassured than Mendelssohn by the 'strange' idealism expounded by Kant in his *Critique of Pure Reason* (1781), a book he found impenetrable—Mendelssohn confided in his reply that he could not understand it either. Yet, Kant was clearly gaining ground for his 'critical philosophy'. Over the winter of 1783–4, he had lectured at Königsberg on 'philosophical theology' to what Hamann called 'an astonishing throng' of students. 'Pure reason', held Kant, cannot demonstrate God's existence since our 'positive knowledge' is very limited. 'But our morality has need of the idea of God to give it a basis and emphasis.' Hence, philosophy should not make us more learned but better, wiser, and more upright. 'For if there is a supreme being who can and will make us happy, and if there is another life, then our moral dispositions will thereby receive more strength and nourishment, and our moral conduct will be made firmer.'[73] 'The command to further the highest good', concluded Kant, 'is objectively grounded (in practical reason), and its possibility is likewise itself objectively grounded (in theoretical reason, which has nothing to say against it).'[74] However, identifying this *summum bonum*, or highest good, with God and God's purposes for man, proclaimed Kant, in his 1783–4 lectures, is possible only via his critical philosophy, not 'feeling' alone. The 'moral sense' of the Scots he dismissed as something 'useless' where unsupported by cogent philosophy while he simultaneously opposed the *encyclopédistes'* reason-based notions of morality.[75]

Diderot and others might ridicule faith, and the apparent cogency of their Spinozistic premises might assist propagation of their views, but Kant's system, it

---

[72] J. A. H. Reimarus, 'Vorerinnerung', in Reimarus, *Abhandlungen*, 13–49.
[73] Kant, *Lectures*, 24.
[74] Kant, *Critique of Practical Reason*, 152.　　　[75] Kant, *Groundwork*, 49–50.

seemed to his burgeoning band of disciples and adherents, conclusively rescues not only 'duty', piety, and feeling but also faith and belief in miracles grounding all this on a rock-solid, unchallengeable philosophical foundation.[76] What especially disturbed Reimarus about Kant, given the sudden powerful surge of Spinoza's prestige, Jacobi's claims, and Mendelssohn's anxieties, was the technical difficulty and complexity of the Kantian antidote. He was not persuaded it offered a viable solution.

Most of all, Reimarus was disgusted by the 'impertinent nonsense' he and his sister encountered in a recently published, fifty-six-page booklet on Spinoza's life and teaching, *Benedikt von Spinoza nach Leben und Lehren* (1783), published at Dessau where the local prince was keen to turn his little court into a 'Mecca' of Enlightenment and press freedom was exceptionally liberal.[77] Composed by Heinrich Friedrich Diez (1751–1817),[78] a celebrated bibliophile as well as leading expert on Turcology, Persia, and Zoroastrianism and, for a time (1784–90), Prussian resident in Constantinople, this short biography scarcely bothered to disguise its favourable view of Spinoza and his philosophy. Admirer of Helvétius and ally of Christian Wilhelm von Dohm, another tract by this author published two years earlier, in 1781, had been the first in Germany to proclaim full freedom of thought and the press a fundamental benefit for society and to call for an end to press censorship.[79] It preceded by six years Bahrdt's today better-known *Über Pressefreyheit und deren Gränzen* [On Freedom of the Press] (1787), a text also to a large extent inspired by Spinoza.[80] His new booklet was warmly praised by Wekhrlin: 'not easily can one find in so few pages so many partly unknown truths so freely and bravely stated or with such energy and majesty, as in this short text.'[81] But Diez's espousing Spinoza's doctrine that morality has no basis in nature, indeed no other basis than the well-being of society, so worried her brother, Elise informed Jacobi, that he now felt that Mendelssohn (a colleague and friend of Dohm's) ought wholly conceal the fact of Lessing's Spinozism insofar as the 'sacredness' of the search for truth permits such concealment.[82]

Not content with praising Spinoza's character, as Wekhrlin soon afterwards did also, in *Das graue Ungeheuer*, Diez, who made no secret of his hostility to Christianity, preachers, conventional morality, and received opinion and asserted that true morality is something entirely separate from organized religion, openly condemned Spinoza's detractors. It was amazing, he suggested, that they should wonder that an atheist should live a morally upright life when they seemed perfectly unconcerned that innumerable people who 'are at the same time fervent Christians' lead morally despicable lives.[83] 'Religious zeal so blinds the individual', suggested Diez 'that he

---

[76] Kant, *Lectures*, 154; Reinhold, *Letters*, 53–5; Tavoillot, *Crépuscule*, pp. xxii–xxiii.
[77] Diez, *Benedikt von Spinoza*, title page.
[78] Hammacher and Piske, *Anhang*, 368.
[79] Diez, *Apologie*, 85, 88–9, 93; further on Diez, see Roudaut, 'Ambiguités', 124–5.
[80] Laursen and Van der Zande, 'Introduction', 99–100.
[81] Wehrlin, *Graue Ungeheuer*, 8 (1786), 210.
[82] Diez, *Benedikt von Spinoza*, 31–3, 36–7; Altman, *Moses Mendelssohn*, 631.
[83] Diez, *Apologie*, 86–90; Diez, *Benedikt von Spinoza*, 40–1; Wekhrlin, *Graue Ungeheuer*, 4 (1785), 302–9.

never knows where to stop.'[84] The social and political power of the world's religions was primarily due to two things, 'fear and ignorance of causes', as Wehrlin expressed it in 1786. Hobbes, Boulanger, Fréret, Hume, and Helvétius had all grasped this fully, as had Lucretius in ancient times, but as yet society had not.[85] But how is mankind to forge a moral order underpinning legislation not based on theology and priestly authority? Here Spinoza seemed uniquely relevant to Diez, Wehrlin, and Bahrdt.

Diez's pro-Spinoza stance, Reimarus and Wehrlin noted, was something startlingly novel on the German scene, at least in print. By the 1780s, Germany, compared to Britain, Holland, or Scandinavia, manifested a relatively large array of Spinozist-materialist thinkers and writers, now prepared almost openly to declare their views. A critical mass of such people had formed of a kind bound to provoke deep anxiety. To Reimarus, his sister, and Mendelssohn, moreover, it seemed obvious that Jacobi's revelations about Lessing could only further encourage subversive pens set on undermining the primacy of conventional morality, the existing social order, and political authority. Diez's tract was followed, in 1785, at Leipzig (and again at Prague the following year) by the first German translations of Spinoza's treatise on the *Improvement of the Human Understanding* and *Tractatus Politicus*, the latter styled Spinoza's treatise 'On Aristocracy and Demokratie'.[86] These editions were translated and sympathetically introduced by Schack Hermann Ewald (1745–1824), secretary to Ernst Ludwig II, duke of Saxe-Gotha (ruled: 1772–1804), who being the protector of Weishaupt since his fleeing Ingolstadt and 'one of our most enlightened [aufgeklärtesten] princes and a great lover of astronomy', according to Lichtenberg, in 1785, encouraged such schemes.[87] Ewald, like his prince, whose 'lodge name' was 'Cassiodorus', ranked high among the Illuminati.

Editor of the *Gothaischen gelehrten Zeitung* and a noted translator and Spinoza expert, Ewald subsequently also published as the 'first volume of Spinoza's 'philosophical writings', the *Tractatus Theologico-Politicus* in German translation (for the first time), at 'Gera', in 1787, followed by the *Ethics*, in the second and third volumes of this series (1790 and 1793). The question whether Spinoza was an 'atheist' or not, suggested Ewald in his preface to the 1785 volume, had unfortunately so overshadowed everything else that society had quite forgotten that he has highly important things to say about legislation and the form of the state.[88] His Spinoza translations had the specific aim of encouraging discussion about politics and the best form of state, an announcement that clearly implied that issues of democracy, and the relationship of democracy to aristocracy, were now a perfectly respectable thing for an enlightened people to be discussing.[89] The emphasis in European debate about Spinoza was patently shifting in the texts of Ewald, Diez, Wehrlin, and

---

[84] Diez, *Benedikt von Spinoza*, 41.
[85] Wehrlin, *Graue Ungeheuer*, 8 (1786), 8–9.
[86] Lauermann and Schröder, 'Textgrundlagen', 39–40.
[87] Lichtenberg, *Schriften und Briefe*, iv. 649; Schüttler, *Mitglieder*, 48–50.
[88] Ewald, 'Vorrede', pp. v–vi; Herder, *Gott*, 11 n.; Lauermann and Schröder, 'Textgrundlagen', 39.
[89] Ewald, 'Vorrede', pp. vii–viii.

Bahrdt, from whether it was permissible to read his texts to what exactly were the practical, moral, and political implications of espousing Spinoza's perspectives.

3. MENDELSSOHN, JACOBI, AND THE PUBLIC RIFT

Having resolved after all to take up the challenge of definitively refuting Spinoza, Mendelssohn, announcing his change of plan, set furiously to work.[90] In August 1784, he sent Jacobi a list of objections to Spinoza's metaphysics, headed by the observation, already made by Leibniz and Voltaire, that it is manifestly self-contradictory to allocate God the attribute of thought while denying him 'intellect'. Jacobi's response arrived only in April 1785, in the form of a systematic restatement of Spinoza's system in forty-four theses accompanied by detailed notes. But before receiving this material, Mendelssohn had already gone ahead and published his *Morgenstunden oder Vorlesungen über das Dasein Gottes* (1785), proving God's existence and providence, and combating Spinoza while yet (as he had promised) including no reference to Jacobi's Lessing conversations or correspondence with himself. The specific aims of Mendelssohn's contribution to the *Pantheismusstreit*, as he explained at the time, were to neutralize Spinozism as a system, by demonstrating God's existence and providence while simultaneously arguing that Lessing was a champion of natural religion best classified as a defender of a modified or 'purified Spinozism'.[91] It was a valiant attempt to breathe new life into the Leibnizian-Wolffian legacy and thereby restore stability to the philosophical arena (with the help of a touch of Scottish Common Sense) while defusing the danger in the pending public perception of Lessing as a 'Spinozist'. His treatise was hardly up to date, however, or comprehensive. 'I know that my philosophy is no longer the philosophy of our age', he himself admitted, despairing of effectively appraising the recent contributions of Kant, Platner, Tetens, and Lambert.[92] The intricacies of Kant's critique he could scarcely grasp at all. But his was nonetheless a powerful text driven by his fears at seeing 'natural religion' and the Leibnizian-Wolffian legacy pulverized between Spinozism, on the one hand, and the anti-Enlightenment declamations of Jacobi and the Rosicrucians, on the other. His prime goal, he explains in his preface, and here he was at one with Jacobi, Rehberg, Feder, Kant, and Reimarus, was to check the general drift towards '*Materialismus* that threatens in our time to become so general' while simultaneously resisting the opposite movement in society towards zealotry, irrationality, and Counter-Enlightenment.[93]

How should thinkers respond to the 'allgemeine Umwälzung' [general revolution] in philosophy, as Mendelssohn called it, that now threatened the entire world?

---

[90] Altman, *Moses Mendelssohn*, 632–3.
[91] Mendelssohn, *Morgenstunden*, 114–25; Schmidt-Biggemann, *Theodizee*, 154–5.
[92] Mendelssohn, *Morgenstunden*, 3–4; Crouter, *Friedrich Schleiermacher*, 61–3.
[93] Mendelssohn, *Morgenstunden*, 5; Reimarus, 'Vorerrinerung', 3.

Materialist Spinozism in central Europe posed what was recognized as a universal threat. With a polite nod to Kant, Mendelssohn acknowledged his colleague's superior penetration and insight, but at the same time rather cuttingly observed that the 'all-crushing' Kant had not yet shown the same power to build up new foundations for authority and belief as he had shown in tearing down the old ones.[94] In the *Morgenstunden*, Mendelssohn examines Spinozism from every angle, admitting that it had always had many adherents and 'friends' among contemplative minds but pointing out that it also appealed to zealots and 'enthusiasts', reminding readers of Wachter's 'insight' that Spinozism's origins lay in Cabbalistic mysticism, implying that the two greatest threats of the age, materialism and blind fanaticism, converge in Spinozism.[95]

Mendelssohn in his *Morgenstunden* sought to reformulate the ontological proofs of God's existence and providence, while pre-empting any negative consequences arising from disclosures of Lessing's 'Spinozism', by representing Lessing as the adherent of a 'geläuterte Spinozismus' [purified Spinozism].[96] The text includes a curious dialogue in which 'Lessing' one by one concedes the force of Mendelssohn's proofs of God's existence, beneficence, and providence and the irrefutability of his objections to Spinoza's untreated metaphysics. Reaffirming his stand against undiluted Spinozism he tries to prove—much as Joachim Lange had once done with hostile intent—that 'purified Spinozism' and Lessing's general stance impeccably fitted with the 'Leibnizisch-Wolffischen System'.[97] His book was not a critique of Kant's *Kritik der reinen Vernunft*, a work denying philosophical reason's ability to attain definite knowledge of God or the providential character of his creation. Even so, given the context, Mendelssohn's text was bound to be greeted by many as a much-needed counter-blast to Kant as well as Spinoza.

The crux of Mendelssohn's rebuttal of Spinoza, like those of Leibniz, Wolff, and Voltaire, was his objection to locating thought and intelligence in God without assigning to him will, the power to choose, and intelligent design.[98] 'Without this unifying subject the parts of the whole remain isolated and unattached, always many; only through all-embracing thought can they be united.'[99] Spinoza had erred but remained 'this great man' whose errors are not just reparable using the principle of 'sufficient reason' but, as Lessing had seen, eminently worthy of being corrected to produce great and true philosophy. On concluding, Mendelssohn broaches the questions raised by Jacobi's conversations with Lessing and correspondence with himself. He fought Jacobi by endorsing Lessing and up to a point Spinoza with the claim that 'verfeinerte Pantheismus' [purified Spinozism] can be combined with religion and morality', as Lessing maintains, but only via the Leibnizian principle that

---

[94] Mendelssohn, *Morgenstunden*, 5; Reinhold, *Letters*, 24.
[95] Mendelssohn, *Morgenstunden*, 104; Israel, *Radical Enlightenment*, 649–50.
[96] Rohls, 'Herders "Gott" ', 280.
[97] Heydenreich, *Nature und Gott*, 91–2; Israel, *Radical Enlightenment*, 548.
[98] Mendelssohn, *Morgenstunden*, 107–9, 112.
[99] Ibid. 112; Bourel, *Moses Mendelssohn*, 430–2.

'das einzige vollkommenste Wesen hat sich von Ewigkeit her mit nichts als mit der Betrachtung des Vollkommensten beschäftigen können' [Throughout eternity, the sole most perfect being has been able to concern himself only with contemplating what is most perfect].[100]

Mendelssohn had planned to finalize this last section only after conferring further with Jacobi. However, having failed to make his intentions clear, Jacobi, who had some reason, having heard nothing for months, to suspect Mendelssohn had forgotten his promise not to discuss their dialogue publicly without consulting him prior to publication, rushed to counter any attempt to draw the sting from Lessing's 'Spinozism'.[101] Taking his silence for a breach of faith, Jacobi now published his own account of the Lessing affair, and dialogue with Mendelssohn, under the title *Über die Lehre des Spinoza in Briefen an den Herrn Moses Mendelssohn* (1785), without making further contact with Mendelssohn or the Reimaruses. Besides the correspondence with Mendelssohn and his debate with Hemsterhuis, the book's appendixes included responses to Mendelssohn's objections to his Lessing interpretation and Goethe's thus far still unpublished odes 'Prometheus' and 'Divinity', poems included without having asked the poet's permission.

Jacobi's reply to Mendelssohn appeared almost simultaneously, but just before, the *Morgenstunden*, at Breslau, in September 1785.[102] His was the deeply paradoxical claim that Spinoza is the most cogent of all philosophers and yet also the chief corrupter of the human mind and morality.[103] If with this paradox he could couple proof that Lessing, hitherto the most widely respected figurehead and spokesman of advanced Enlightenment in Germany, deemed Spinozism the only convincing philosophy (as Herder and Goethe, not to mention Lichtenberg, Diez, Ewald, Wehrlin, Knoblauch, Rehberg, Bahrdt, and many others did also), Jacobi would have discredited the Enlightenment generally as well as capsized Mendelssohn's theist and Jewish Enlightenment. He would have raised public awareness of the creeping danger of a broad materialism penetrating German culture by proving that no consequent reader, guided by reason alone, can do other than follow Lessing and Herder, and embrace Spinozism, and that if Spinozism is to be successfully blocked by Christian values then the only way is to reject *Aufklärung* and 'philosophy' altogether. In this fashion, he expected to deliver a devastating blow to enlightened ideals and projects.[104] Spinozism being the necessary outcome of all fully consistent philosophical demonstration and enlightened striving, and yet equivalent to moral ruin and 'atheism', the only morally and culturally responsible option is to reject the Enlightenment *in toto*.

Leibnizio-Wolffianism, argued Jacobi, renewing the arguments of the anti-Wolffian Pietists of the 1720s, reduced to essentials, is no less deterministic than Spinozism and indeed collapses into it, once its inner inconsistencies are removed:

---

[100] Mendelssohn, *Morgenstunden*, 133.
[101] Goldenbaum, 'Mendelssohns schwierige Beziehung', 303.
[102] Rohls, 'Herders "Gott"', 278.
[103] Di Giovanni, 'The First Twenty Years', 423.
[104] Beck, 'From Leibniz to Kant', 30; Franks, 'All or Nothing', 96–9; Neiman, *Unity of Reason*, 148.

the only escape from the philosophical maze, held Jacobi, was his recommended leap of faith. Faith he declared the exclusive basis of all genuine human values, responsibility, and true moral action.[105] He conceded, though, that such a leap was scarcely consonant with the taste of the age. Lessing had refused to take this standpoint seriously, treating it with undisguised irony.[106] But precisely because Spinozism represented the underlying 'philosophy' of the Enlightenment, the 'teaching of a Helvétius, of a Diderot', had achieved the ruinously general penetration that they had. Moral catastrophe and a generalized threat to the entire social order was the inevitable result.[107] Diderot, Helvétius, and the author of the *Système de la nature* were the prime representatives of the materialist 'atheism' of the modern age and plainly intended to destroy religion, morality, and society itself. To this, Jacobi added a further revelation which he had so far withheld. He had asked Lessing whether he had ever tried to convince Mendelssohn of the correctness of his Spinozistic views. He had avoided doing so, answered Lessing, or so Jacobi claimed, except once when he brought the matter up but then quickly retreated, on encountering stern resistance, deeming it best to leave the matters as they were rather than force the issue. Mendelssohn and Lessing may have been friends, announced Jacobi, but Mendelssohn had not enjoyed Lessing's confidence or been at all proximate to him philosophically.[108]

Jacobi's book, no less than Mendelssohn's, had a sensational impact. On its release, Jacobi liberally distributed copies to all key participants—Herder, Goethe, Mendelssohn, and also Hamann, who received three. The book found many eager readers. By late September, Hamann had already gone through it three times, thoroughly approving of everything. Goethe, who also received and read his copy in September, besides being annoyed to find his poem 'Divinity', placed at the beginning of Jacobi's book,[109] was disconcerted to discover that in some copies the poem also appeared under his name which meant that he too, Herder was amused to see, was now firmly bracketed with Lessing as a known, active, and committed 'Spinozist'. Jacobi had arranged for the more obviously offensive of Goethe's two poems, 'Prometheus', a text sternly protesting against the notion of divine providence, to be printed on separate pages (this time without Goethe's name) so that where buyers desired, it could be bound in, while in those principalities where the censorship authorities forbade the poem, it could be omitted without risking seizure of the book itself.[110] Goethe rebuked Jacobi for his conduct only in a private letter, though, preferring to make no public statement.[111]

Kant, meanwhile, profoundly frustrated by the failure of his *Critique* to win the recognition he believed it deserved and by his Göttingen colleagues' habit of

[105] Neiman, *Unity of Reason*, 148; Vallée, *Spinoza Conversations*, 123; Beiser, *German Idealism*, 362.
[106] Strauss, 'Einleitungen', p. xxiv.
[107] Jacobi, *Über die Lehre*, 132; Hammacher and Piske, *Anhang*, 464.
[108] Goetschel, *Spinoza's Modernity*, 170.
[109] Jacobi, *Über die Lehre*, 3.
[110] Mendelssohn, *An die Freunde Lessings*, 191–2; Altman, *Moses Mendelssohn*, 699.
[111] Verzaal, 'Besuch', 170–1.

dismissing his transcendental idealism as an abstruse metaphysics akin to Berkeley's idealism,[112] had long considered materialism the most pernicious threat to German culture and philosophy. Throughout his earlier pre-critical phase as well as in many passages of the *Critique* he conducts a kind of silent war against Spinoza (something modern Kant specialists are often curiously blind to). But since the onset of the *Pantheismusstreit*, he had become additionally agitated, recognizing at once the heightened menace of a reinvigorated Spinozism, both in its pure form and as modified by Herder's revisions, as something eminently capable of disrupting society and destroying the *Aufklärung* itself.[113] In addition, he was more than a little irritated by the public's view of the relationship between himself and Mendelssohn. Word reached him from his chief ally at Halle, Ludwig Heinrich Jakob, that readers there greatly admired the *Morgenstunden* and were jubilant that Mendelssohn had scored a great 'triumph' over Kant (which, however, Mendelssohn laid no claim to having done).[114]

Kant was almost equally exasperated by Mendelssohn's book and Jacobi's, a copy of which also reached him, in September, sent by their common friend Hamann, who hoped he would now join forces with Jacobi against Lessing's legacy, Mendelssohn, and the *Berlinische Monatsschrift*. He encouraged Kant to make some public intervention. The clash between Jacobi and Mendelssohn represented something of a dilemma for Kant. He found his reputation and philosophy directly affected by an affair in which he could not, he felt at first, straightforwardly intervene, since he could not appear to align with Lessing and his now estranged former student Herder; but neither could he align with Jacobi and Hamann, nor indeed Mendelssohn and Reimarus, in the middle. Yet neither could he easily remain silent. The fact that Mendelssohn's book was widely misrepresented as a sally against himself no less than Spinoza was not the only reason Kant eventually allowed himself to be persuaded to enter the affray. If he despised Herder and Jacobi, suspecting the latter of being merely out to make a name for himself and whose book 'was not worth a serious refutation', he assured Marcus Herz,[115] his Jewish disciple (and one of Mendelssohn's closest allies), he was annoyed that his philosophy was being challenged from several different directions at once.

After initially deciding to refute the *Morgenstunden* much to Hamann's and Jakob's delight, an undertaking that became public news on being reported in Ewald's journal, Kant changed his mind, realizing Mendelssohn was primarily assailing Jacobi's claims, not his system.[116] It became clear to him that the public controversy unhelpfully entangled two essentially different questions that needed separating: first, whether Lessing was a 'Spinozist' in Jacobi's sense or a 'purified Spinozist' in Mendelssohn's, a dispute of little interest to him (though reading Jacobi did make

---

[112] Beiser, *German Idealism*, 90–1; Ameriks, *Interpreting*, 135.
[113] Zammito, *Genesis*, 10–12.
[114] Ibid. 232–3; Jakob to Kant, Halle, Kant, *Briefwechsel*, i. 317–18.
[115] Kant to Herz, 7 Apr. 1786, Kant, *Briefwechsel*, i. 323; Zammito, *Genesis*, 235–6.
[116] Kant to Jakob, 26 May 1786, in Kant, *Briefwechsel*, i. 329; Goldenbaum, 'Kants Parteinahme', 176, 184–5.

it appear probable that Lessing inclined to 'atheism'); and, second, and more important, the problem posed for society by the crumbling of every philosophical demonstration of God's being and the consequent growing 'praise and almost deification of the incomprehensible Spinozistic chimera' [die Lobpreisung und fast Vergötterung des unverständlichen Spinozistischen Hirngespinstes] together with what he considered Jacobi's absurd summons to embrace positive religion as the only appropriate solution.[117]

Prior to Kant's intervention, the *Pantheismusstreit* was a three-cornered fight reflecting the splits between Radical Enlightenment, moderate mainstream Enlightenment, and Counter-Enlightenment, with the first and last paradoxically reinforcing as well as attacking each other. Both the latter groups contended that Spinozism was irrefutable, something Kant flatly denied. The last group included Hamman, Jacobi, and Jacobi's gifted young acolyte, the Tübingen-trained Lutheran preacher Thomas Wizenmann (1759–87), at Barmen, someone Jacobi consulted over every step in the drama from the summer of 1783 when the desperately sick Wizenmann stayed with him at Düsseldorf. Expending his last energies wrestling with Spinoza and also Kant's *Kritik*, Wizenmann emerged as one of Jacobi's principal allies.[118] The only answer, held this group, was to relegate philosophy to secondary status, rendering it again subordinate to religious faith. Their solution amounted to a form of Counter-Enlightenment brusquely rejected by Kant who insisted such a standpoint could only encourage superstition, freethinking, and state repression of freedom of thought, expression, and the press.[119]

Equally antagonistic to the first group, the adherents of radical thought, Kant had little sympathy either for those like Mendelssohn, Hemsterhuis, Garve, Tetens, and both the younger Reimarus, claiming philosophy in their manner could counter Spinozism and the tide of French materialism. All of these, in Kant's opinion, were as much in error as the rest having gone entirely the wrong way about demonstrating Spinoza's errors. Christian Garve (1742–98), a leading Berlin *Aufklärer* and advocate of British-style empiricism and the first to review Kant's *Kritik*, was one of those responsible for its initially frosty reception. Garve despised Jacobi's 'incomprehensible return to faith in God with the help of some revelation and tradition' that was 'neither a philosophical creed nor exactly a Christian one either', his treating vital issues in a confusing manner. Like Mendelssohn, he felt Jacobi should have left Lessing out of the whole business and also omitted that 'revolting poem' [of Goethe's]. Equally repelled by Kant's *Kritik*, Garve's solution was to hail Mendelssohn's 'instructive' *Morgenstunden*, praising it for the systematic quality and clarity of its argument and originality, especially his 'notion that all existing things must be known and conceived by some being'.[120]

---

[117] Kant to Biester, 11 June 1786, in Kant, *Briefwechsel*, i. 330–1.
[118] Thomas Wizenmann (ed.), *Von der Goltz*, i. 309–14, 343, 346, 360.
[119] Zammito, *Genesis*, 12–14; Otto, *Studien*, 199.
[120] Beiser, *German Idealism*, 88–9; Ameriks, *Interpreting*, 135; Altmann, *Moses Mendelssohn*, 711.

4. KANT'S INTERVENTION

Kant finally decided to intervene when the classicist Johann Erich Biester (1749–1816), editor of the *Berlinische Monatsschrift*, secretary of the Berlin *Mittwochgesellschaft*, friend of Mendelssohn, and librarian at the royal library in Berlin, wrote in June 1786, urging that from every standpoint it was necessary for him to pronounce on the furore. The real question, he agreed, was whether Jacobi and his allies were justified in asserting that rational knowledge of God and his providence is impossible and that Spinoza's system cannot be overturned philosophically.[121] At a time when fanaticism on the one side and unbridled systematic atheism (of Diderot, Helvétius, and d'Holbach) on the other were both advancing, it was surely incumbent on philosophers of widely acknowledged standing and authority like Kant to guide the public in the proper direction. Biester and Marcus Herz, though, were pressing Kant to intervene in support of Mendelssohn. In fact, Kant produced an essay, *Was heisst: Sich im Denken orientieren?* [What does it Mean: To Orient Oneself in Thinking?], published by the *Berlinische Monatsschrift* in October 1786, distancing himself as much from Mendelssohn as Jacobi, and with such dexterity that he succeeded in interposing himself in Mendelssohn's place as the new arbiter of the middle ground, the 'third force' effectively mediating between Radical and Counter-Enlightenment in the *Pantheismusstreit*. Neutral between Mendelssohn and Jacobi and coolly polite throughout, tactfully styling Jacobi 'an acute author' and Mendelssohn a stalwart seeker after truth, he warned of the 'danger' of enthusiasm and of 'dethroning of reason' while blaming Mendelssohn just as much as Jacobi for causing the confusion by 'arguing dogmatically', using 'pure reason in the field of the supersensible', and thereby opening the door to mindless zeal and perplexity.[122]

Mendelssohn's book Kant pronounced clear, adroit, and as acute an example as could be found of its philosophical genre (which he now pronounced obsolete).[123] For 'all the proofs of the worthy Mendelssohn in his *Morgenstunden*... accomplish nothing by way of demonstration', and since the task he had set himself is impossible for any philosophical system to accomplish, his book is just an exercise in reason overreaching itself and becoming lost in futile and empty metaphysical speculation. Kant's other main objective was to discredit Jacobi's contention 'that the Spinozist concept of God is the only one in agreement with all the principles of reason and must nevertheless be rejected'.[124] If the primacy of properly delimited reason in metaphysical questions is denied, then 'a wide gate is opened to all enthusiasm, superstition and even to atheism'.[125] The contention that Spinoza's conception of God is the only correct outcome of philosophical endeavour was clearly motivated, he suggested, by a desire to debase and discredit philosophy itself. 'Have you thought', he demanded of

---

[121] Altmann, *Moses Mendelssohn*, 750–1.
[122] Kant, 'What Does it Mean?', 4, 7, 11; Kuehn, *Kant*, 306.
[123] Kant, 'What Does it Mean?', 7.
[124] Ibid. 11–12.
[125] Kant, 'What Does it Mean?, 11; Neiman, *Unity of Reason*, 153.

Jacobi and Hamann, 'about what you are doing and where your attacks on reason will lead?' It was a question that echoes also in the preface to the second edition of his *Kritik*, in 1787.[126] Properly delimited reason, he maintained, is the only basis for our concept of God and for pursuing philosophy. Mendelssohn's opponents were jeopardizing 'freedom of thought'. Kant appealed to all embracing enlightened ideals to defend reason and above all that precious freedom. All must be free to adopt their own convictions, but whatever participants in the controversy decided 'do not dispute that prerogative of reason which makes it the highest good on earth, the prerogative of being the final touchstone of truth'.[127] Whoever does so would be unworthy of freedom of thought and expression and would 'surely forfeit it too'.

Kant's raising the spectre of governmental repression was an allusion not just to the crack-down on the Illuminati in Bavaria and growing role of the Rosicrucians but also a recent ban on his own system, at Marburg, where, following attacks on him by his Göttingen opponents Feder and Meiners, his system was judged apt to spread scepticism and morally pernicious.[128] His *Critique*, announced Kant, is the only cogent, effective way to block Spinoza and materialism, and sole correct basis for moral philosophy. The 'supreme principle of morality', he proclaimed in his subsequent *Grundlegung zur Metaphysik der Sitten* [Fundamental Grounds of the Metaphysic of Morals], had now, happily, been discovered. 'In a being which has reason and a will,' he contended, 'nature would have hit upon a very bad arrangement in selecting this creature's reason to carry out its purpose if nature's object were its conservation and welfare, in a word, its happiness.'[129] Such a task would have been much better performed by instinct. But in fact man's 'existence' has a different and nobler end, for which, 'and not for happiness, reason is properly intended'.

Given that reason was imparted to us as a practical faculty and not to secure our conservation or happiness, then 'its true destination must be to produce a will, not merely good as a means to something else, but *good in itself*, and for which reason is absolutely necessary'.[130] It is this 'will' that is the 'supreme good'. With this idea of morality not geared to 'happiness' but duty and his accompanying idea of the 'categorical imperative', Kant believed he was well placed to demonstrate the practical necessity of the doctrines of 'freedom of the will' and divinely given duty, and, hence, of a divine law-giver. Only in this way, held Kant, can God's existence be shown to be something definitely real and indispensable, as inherent in our consciousness of duty and integral to our categorical imperatives. But the validity of such a conclusion depends entirely on embracing his critical system: 'if the ideality of time and space is not adopted', explained Kant, then 'nur allein der Spinozism ubrig bleibt' [nothing remains but Spinozism] where space and time are 'essential determinations of the original being itself', while the things dependent upon it (ourselves, therefore

[126] Kant, 'What Does it Mean?, 12; di Giovanni, 'The First Twenty Years', 426; Beiser, *Enlightenment*, 52.
[127] Kant, 'What Does it Mean ?', 14; Zammito, *Genesis*, 240–1.
[128] Zammito, *Genesis*, 242; Reinhold, *Letters*, 28.
[129] Kant, *Groundwork*, 8–9.
[130] Kant, *Grundlegung*, 12; Guyer, *Kant's System*, 185, 280; Neiman, *Unity of Reason*, 154–5.

included) are not substances but merely accidents inhering in it'.[131] Either one embraces Kantianism, the sole viable middle path between Spinozism and Counter-Enlightenment, or else lapses into Spinozism, on the one side, or, alternatively, sheer unreason, on the other.

For the moment, the situation remained highly unsettling. Kant's *Kritik*, declared his foremost supporter at Halle, Ludwig Heinrich Jakob, in 1786, constituted a true 'Revolution' and imparted to philosophy an entirely new appearance.[132] But the number of professors, students, and others embracing Kant's system and its general level of popularity were still far too limited to resolve the wider contest. The Leibnizian-Wolffian school, Jakob reminded the public, was still the strongest, 'at least in Germany', while *Materialismus*, as Mendelssohn acknowledged, was regrettably still threatening to become 'general'. As long as philosophers use only the kind of arguments levelled by Mendelssohn against Spinoza, then Spinozism would loom ever larger. What was needed was for the universities to abandon the Leibnizian-Wolffian system and convince the public that both the Leibnizian and Spinozist philosophies are untenable 'since they both collapse into an illicit and crude *Dogmatismus*'.[133]

Mendelssohn bore no grudge towards Kant; he was far more distressed to see how Lessing appeared in Jacobi's book and the latter's claiming his lifelong friend had not confided his true opinions to him.[134] In an emotional missive of October 1785, he complained to Kant of Jacobi's shabby conduct in publishing private correspondence 'without having asked for and obtained permission of the correspondents' and his misrepresenting Lessing's opinions and maligning him as a 'declared Spinozist' in a book he considered a 'monstrous' mixture of rationality and zealotry: 'the head is Goethe's, the body Spinoza's, and the feet Lavater's', the last a reference to Johann Caspar Lavater, one of Jacobi's heroes and a prominent Counter-Enlightenment fundamentalist very hostile to Mendelssohn.[135] Despite rapidly declining health, Mendelssohn returned to his desk in a feverish final bout of work, preparing a lengthy supplementary refutation of Jacobi's claims. At all costs, he strove to prevent Lessing, 'the admired defender of theism and rational religion', irredeemably losing his reputation in the eyes of respectable people and being transmuted for ever into a 'Spinozist, atheist and blasphemer'.[136] Admitting Lessing had been attracted to *Pantheismus* in his youth (and this time without hiding Lessing's rejection of Christianity), he again insisted that the mature Lessing professed a 'purified Spinozism', as *Nathan der Weise* attests. Delivering his finished text personally to his publisher in Berlin, on 31 December 1785, in freezing weather, on foot, and too lightly clad, Mendelssohn caught a severe cold, leading to coughing fits, fever, and chronic debilitation. Deeply agitated and upset, he died five days later.

---

[131] Kant, *Gesammelte Schriften*, v. 101–2; Beiser, *German Idealism*, 262.
[132] Jakob, *Prüfung*, preface pp. ii–iii.
[133] Ibid. preface pp. xvii–xix and 189, 191.
[134] Mendelssohn, *An die Freunde Lessings*, 193.
[135] Mendelssohn to Kant, 16 Oct. 1785, in Kant, *Briefwechsel*, i. 297–8; Altman, *Moses Mendelssohn*, 705.
[136] Mendelssohn, *An die Freunde Lessings*, 187.

Mendelssohn's last book, *An die Freunde Lessings* [*To the Friends of Lessing: An Appendix to Mr Jacobi's Correspondence on the Doctrine of Spinoza*], appeared posthumously three weeks later, on 24 January 1786. 'Was Lessing a Spinozist?' Baldly posed, without establishing first what Spinozism is and what it is not, this is a question that makes no sense.[137] Reaffirming his view that Spinozism stands closer to Jewish teaching than the 'orthodox teaching of the Christians', Mendelssohn contended that the degree of 'purification' required to pass from Spinozism to natural religion and theism is less than what is needed to bridge Spinozism and Christianity.[138] 'Thus the report that Lessing was a Spinozist could be for me neither astounding nor alienating.'[139] He provided perhaps the most searching examination of Leibniz's relation to Spinoza that had yet appeared while resuming his assault on undiluted Spinozism as 'atheism' as something detrimental to society, and ultimately incoherent, its one-substance doctrine providing no explanation for the origin of motion. For these remarks, he was criticized for aligning Judaism too closely to Spinozism, by some 'enlightened' Berlin Jews, while the Kantians had no use for his arguments and the radicals rejected them.[140] Mendelssohn, his philosophy, and his general reputation and legacy had, in a most unfortunate fashion, become trapped between Lessing, Kant, and Jacobi. His reputation was never to recover to anything like the level it had attained shortly before.

Despite Hamann's warning he might damage his cause by appearing vengeful, Jacobi relented hardly at all at the spectacle of Mendelssohn's distress and demise. Rather, hearing from Hamann what Mendelssohn had written to Kant, he triumphantly recycled his designation of his book, delighted at being advertised as having 'Spinoza's head, Herder's body and Goethe's feet'! Answering Mendelssohn's rejoinder, he produced his *Wider Mendelssohns Beschuldigungen in dessen Schreiben an die Freunde Lessings* [*Against Mendelssohn's Accusations Concerning the Letters about the Doctrine of Spinoza*] in April 1786. Rejecting Mendelssohn's complaints, he derided his invoking *Nathan der Weise* as evidence of Lessing's theism.[141] One might as well cite Voltaire's plays as evidence that *he* was a Christian. All the evidence drawn from Lessing's writings, he argued (correctly), indicates his Spinozism not least his *Education of the Human Race*, a work Jacobi had long considered incompatible with the providential deist position Lessing supposedly professed before 1780.[142] Lessing merely deployed Christian theism in *Nathan*, retorted Jacobi, as a cover for the play's underlying pantheism and Spinozism.

5. LATER STAGES OF THE *PANTHEISMUSSTREIT*

Herder, meanwhile, was far from dissatisfied with the turn matters were taking. With the uproar gripping the attention of key professional philosophers like Mendelssohn,

---

[137] Mendelssohn, *An die Freunde Lessings*, 186–7.   [138] Ibid. 188–9, 196–7.
[139] Ibid. 189.   [140] *Der entlarvte Moses Mendelssohn*, 5–6, 17, 19.
[141] Jacobi, *Über die Lehre*, 309–11; Jacobi, *Wider Mendelssohns Beschuldingen*, 74–5, 78; Christ, 'Johann Georg Hamann', 256–7.   [142] Jacobi, *Wider Mendelssohns Beschuldingen*, 81.

Kant, and Garve, Spinoza had become not just the chief focus of attention for students and enquiring young scholars but a key shaping factor in cultural life generally. Only good would come, he assured his friend (and Dohm's), the poet Gleim, shortly after Mendelssohn's death, from the furore Jacobi had stirred up. 'Ich bin ein Spinozist', he asserted, 'trotz Lessing und habe mich kindisch gefreut, meinen Bruder im Geist so unvermuthet hier zu finden.' [I am a Spinozist independently of Lessing and have childishly rejoiced to find here, so unexpectedly, my brother in spirit.][143] His main contribution to the public controversy, his booklet *Gott. Einige Gespräche über Spinozas System* (Gotha, 1787), made public at long last his revisionist interpretation of Spinoza. Herder flatly denied Spinoza was an 'atheist' or a 'pantheist', teacher of blind necessity, mocker of religion, or opponent of revelation, and in particular, like Voltaire and Hennert, denied that Spinoza's 'God' lacks intelligence.[144] According to him, there is a meaningful sense in which Spinoza distinguishes between God and the world even though nature flows directly from the being of God, and miracles and providence in the usual senses of these terms are excluded. Cast in the form of a series of five dialogues, his text seeks to dismiss the prevailing view of Spinoza as a century-old distortion and common prejudice for which Bayle's *Dictionnaire* was largely responsible. It was a book that perplexed many, greatly offended his former mentor Hamann, and disgusted Kant, who viewed it as yet another Herderian attack on himself and endorsement of the radical Georg Forster's recent critique, published in the *Teutsche Merkur*, the Jena journal edited by Wieland and Reinhold, in the autumn of 1786, of Kant's racially hierarchical view of anthropology and the origins of humanity.[145]

Since the idea of God constitutes the beginning and end of Spinoza's thought and as all truth and being follow directly from God's eternal being, Spinoza cannot be an 'atheist'. Rather he must be interpreted, held Herder, as a philosophical enthusiast for God since he locates all happiness—and all morality—exclusively in the knowledge and intellectual love of God.[146] Furthermore, Spinoza was right, requiring correction only, in the view of Weimar's church *Generalsuperintendant*, as regards his defective conception of matter and extension for which he had leaned too heavily on Descartes and his denying God purpose. Although Herder's conception of God was not identical to Spinoza's and was tinged with theism, as Rehberg notes in his lengthy review of Herder's work in Wieland's journal *Teutsche Merkur*, late in 1787, it was sufficiently permeated by Spinoza's spirit for him to be counted in this debate consistently with the 'Spinozists'.[147] A splendid re-exposition of Spinoza, salvaging his reputation by denying he was an 'atheist' and demonstrating the unity and beauty of his system, Herder's beautiful prose, declared Rehberg, exuded an admirably gentle, non-polemical tone. He regretted only that Herder remained so hostile

---

[143] Rohls, 'Herders "Gott"', 284.
[144] Herder, *Gott*, 15, 52, 85–6, 116, 127.
[145] Rohls, 'Herders "Gott"', 208; Beiser, *Enlightenment*, 196.
[146] Herder, *Gott*, 53, 87; Rohls, 'Herders "Gott"', 284–5, 287.
[147] Rehberg's review of Herder in Wieland, *Teutsche Merkur* (1787), pp. clxi–clxxi.

towards Kant.[148] Herder's plea for the compatibility of Spinozism with morality greatly pleased him and was strongly recommended by Rehberg (rather remarkably) to young readers.[149]

While Herder's God remains the 'force of all forces', something immanent in the world and not transcendent, the accompanying hints of theism, though highly problematic, likewise pleased others, including Goethe. But precisely this aspect of Herder's vision aroused scepticism and suspicion among hard-core materialists. 'Herder has squared the circle', commented Wehrlin, sarcastically, 'or what is almost the same thing, [manages to] unite Spinozism with religion.'[150] He felt Herder needed reminding that Spinoza's God has neither will, nor intelligence, nor beneficence. This attempt to 'de-Spinoze Spinoza' struck him as unhelpful and dangerous. There was a need to avoid 'unnatural accommodations', fudging, mixing philosophy with theology, and diluting rigorous, sharply defined systems.[151] Nevertheless, however subtly Herder (and the Socinians) might wish to modify Spinoza's conception of God, it was now clear that the whole question of God had been rendered so very uncertain by Lessing, Herder, and Kant that there no longer existed any sound basis, as Wehrlin put it, for condemning Spinoza.[152]

If Kant was furious, Jacobi, too, disliked Herder's intervention. His rejoinder, in the revised edition of his *Über die Lehre des Spinoza* (1789), asserts (not without justification) that Lessing and Herder both strove to bridge two things that cannot be bridged, to assign awareness and intelligence to God, and not to do so, at the same time.[153] Very different was Goethe's reaction. Goethe received his copy of Herder's text during his Italian journey, at Rome, in sweltering weather on his birthday, 28 August 1787. 'It was for me both consoling and refreshing', he assured Herder, 'in this Babel, the mother of so much deception and error' to encounter something so 'pure and beautiful to read and think about', though, of course, Goethe, unlike most others, had heard all this before—directly from Herder's mouth. From private notes jotted a few weeks later, it seems Goethe indeed endorsed Herder's stance, including his efforts to 'refine' Spinoza's conceptions of God and matter in what he took to be a Leibnizian direction.[154]

Together Lessing, Herder, and Goethe had driven a wedge such as central Europe had never witnessed before between Christianity and major currents within high culture. Reviewing Herder's book, Ewald proclaimed it a true cultural revolution and a landmark that Spinoza should thus be publicly defended.[155] The *Pantheismusstreit* proved crucial not just as a kind of ultimate confrontation and reckoning between

[148] Rehberg, *Sämmtliche Schriften*, i. 39–43.
[149] Rehberg's review of Herder in Wieland, *Teutsche Merkur* (1787), pp. clxiii–clxv.
[150] Wehrlin, *Hyperboreische Briefe*, 1 (1788), 40, 43; Otto, *Studien*, 296 n.
[151] Wehrlin, *Hyperboreische Briefe*, 1 (1788), 41.
[152] Wehrlin, *Graue Ungeheuer*, 4 (1785), 311–12.
[153] Ibid. 289; Jacobi, *Schriften*, i. 221–2, 228.
[154] Rohls, 'Herders "Gott"', 288; Boyle, *Goethe*, i. 496–8; Irmscher, 'Goethe und Herder', 252–3.
[155] Otto, *Studien*, 295–6.

the major impulses contesting German philosophy and literature but also for turning philosophy's internal disputes into a public drama and rendering philosophy itself more central to European literature, high culture, and religion. Despite being of pivotal importance in the cultural debates of the day, there was little interference in the *Pantheismus* strife by law courts and princely governments. Forbidding meta-physical speculation about the most fundamental matters, commented Wekhrlin, a critic who both impressed and amused Lichtenberg, had for the moment clearly gone out of fashion among 'enlightened' regimes.[156]

Taking stock in the later 1780s was no easy matter. Publicly, Kant and Kantianism in the end gained most. But in late Enlightenment Germany, interaction between the public and private spheres was tense and fraught with contradiction. There was much resistance to Kant as well as Jacobi and, among many discerning readers, especially adversaries of Counter-Enlightenment unmoved by Kant, Spinoza too registered substantial gains at least for the moment.[157] A vivid instance is a conversation between Lichtenberg, Lavater, and another clergyman at Göttingen in early July 1786. Scarcely had the visiting clergymen sat down than the conversation turned to 'Mendelssohn, Lessing, Jacobi and *Spinozismus*'. For the theologians the furore represented a great crisis in their lives. Immersed in the latest science, Lichtenberg, who ever since first exploring Spinoza many years before always held him to be a 'quite extraordinary' intellect, assured his visitors that a close and deep study of nature, even if only a thousand years on, 'werde endlich auf Spinozismus führe' [will finally lead to Spinozism]. 'The more our knowledge of the world of bodies grows', he assured his visitors, 'the more the borders of the realm of spirits would narrow.' Lessing was entirely right to opt for Spinozism: 'all that exists is one and beyond that there is nothing! *En kai pan, unum et omne.*'[158]

The *Pantheismusstreit* disclosed for all to see, observed Lichtenberg, Bahrdt, Wekhrlin, Ewald, Diez, Herder, Goethe, Rehberg, and others, that Spinoza was by no means so full of contradictions as past generations supposed; the truth rather was the opposite.[159] This was also the opinion, in a different way, of Wizenmann, author of a text whose title translates as *The Results of the Jacobian and Mendelssohnian Philosophy Critically Assessed* (1786), which caused a stir with its forceful refutation of Mendelssohn's arguments and affirmation of the need for a new fideism with which to block the Enlightenment.[160] Spinoza is irrefutable if one adheres to philosophical arguments, held Wizenmann; and what this means is that philosophy cannot guide men and that Christianity's truth is clear to us not from arguments or reasoning but from experience, facts, its inner psychological and moral force. Collaborating closely with Jacobi, Wizenmann wholeheartedly supported his strategy

[156] Wekhrlin, *Graue Ungeheuer*, 10 (1787), 132–3; Lichtenberg, *Schriften und Briefe*, iv. 319–20, 972.
[157] Pinkard, *Hegel*, 31.
[158] Lichtenberg to J. D. Ramberg, Göttingen, 3 July 1786, Lichtenberg, *Schriften*, iv. 678–9.
[159] Wekhrlin, *Graue Ungeheuer*, 4 (1785), 310.
[160] Von der Goltz, *Thomas Wizenmann*, ii. 138, 141, 279; Altmann, *Moses Mendelssohn*, 747–8.

of provoking the maximum possible uproar over Spinoza as the most effective way to block not just materialism but *Aufklärung* itself throughout central Europe.[161]

Wizenmann's strategy was to use theistic arguments like those of Reimarus to destroy 'atheism' and 'atheism' to destroy deism and both to prove that no demonstration of the existence or non-existence of God, or his relationship to the universe, is possible by means of philosophical reason.[162] Like Jacobi, Wizenmann combined a vigorous critique of Kantianism with his rejection of Mendelssohn's 'dogmatism'. He too fiercely resented Kant's describing their stance as a 'complete abdication of reason'. In his powerful 'open letter' to Kant, published in the *Deutsches Museum*, in February 1787, a mere few days before his premature death, Wizenmann insisted that reason on its own cannot coherently ground either Spinoza's or Mendelssohn's position. This outcome authorizes theology to invoke historical evidence with which to anchor revelation and commitment to faith. It was no part of his agenda to maintain, as Kant suggested, that Spinozism is the sole philosophical system fully in accord with all the requirements of reason while yet condemning it as ungodly. His contention, rather, he corrected Kant, was that the Spinozist conception of God and the universe, a system which he thought had long existed before Spinoza, is the most consequent and coherent system of pure speculative reason, something he thought Kant himself was close to conceding—though actually Kant deemed Spinoza's arguments consequent, only formally objecting that his starting premiss, his definition of substance, was entirely arbitrary and hence not consequent.[163]

Wizenmann agreed that Kant's *Kritik* proves that Spinoza's speculative system is invalid and steps outside the bounds of the unalterable limits of human reason, vainly seeking to demonstrate links in the internal chain of existence of things-in-themselves which our reason can in no way do. But Kant seemed unwilling to acknowledge the full implications of the limits on speculative reason he himself had introduced: namely that reason cannot prove the objective reality of God's morally binding laws.[164] Far from colluding in reason's abdication, Wizenmann claimed to have said nothing essentially different from Kant himself, either about reason, Spinoza, or Mendelssohn. His charge against Kant was one of inconsistency and failing to recognize the consequences of his own system. The allegedly 'objective' but in fact 'subjective' reasons Kant offers for belief in God, Wizenmann concludes, are weak while his own and Jacobi's fideism and traditionalism, invoking historical facts, offered a more concrete and objective grounding for Christian commitment. At death's door, the expiring Wizenmann labelled Kant a self-centred 'dogmatist'.

'A need of pure practical reason', Kant remained convinced, 'is based on a duty to make something (the highest good) the object of my will so as to promote it with all my strength. In doing so, I must presuppose its possibility and also its conditions,

---

[161] Otto, *Studien*, 174.

[162] Wizenmann, 'An den Herrn Professor Kant', 284.

[163] Ibid. 286; Kant, *Lectures*, 74–5, 86, 131; Kant, *Critique of Practical Reason*, 107.

[164] Kant, *Critique of Practical Reason*, 151 n.; Wizenmann, 'An den Herrn Professor Kant', 288–9; Otto, *Studien*, 99–201.

which are God, freedom, and immortality; these conditions I am not in a position to prove by my speculative reason, though I cannot disprove them either.'[165] 'God's governance of the world in accordance with moral principles is an assumption without which all morality would break down.'[166] But Jacobi and Wizenmann simply refused to see any significant difference between Kant's moral and social subjectivism and their own position.

Among younger scholars searching for an exit from the impasse gripping German philosophy were several highly charged intellects, among them Fichte, Maimon, and Heydenreich. Maimon was a remarkable autodidact who had emerged from the confines of eastern European Jewish tradition. Harbouring a fierce dislike of 'most of the rabbis' and traditional Jewish learning, he moved from Polish Lithuania via Königsberg and Stettin to Berlin, first coming to grips with modern philosophy by reading Wolff and, in around 1780, meeting Mendelssohn. His subsequent progress was rapid. Studying Locke in German, he translated Mendelssohn's *Morgenstunden* into Hebrew, and quickly mastered the systems of 'Spinoza, Hume and Leibniz'.[167] Before long, he was an expert on Kantianism and, by early 1789, had completed his commentary on Kant's philosophy, *Versuch über die Transcendentalphilosophie*, which he showed to Herz who brought it to Kant's attention, leading to its publication in 1790. Kant acknowledged to Herz, in May 1789, that 'one of the most eminent disciples' he had acquired was this Lithuanian Jewish philosopher who had first studied his *Kritik* in the mid 1780s, shortly after Mendelssohn's death. Even if he was not quite sure what his significance was (Maimon's book was notoriously obscure), Kant realized that this tattered Yiddish-speaking refugee from eastern Europe had somehow become a commentator in the debate about his 'critical philosophy'.[168]

Having escaped from rabbinic 'theocracy' and Talmudic narrowness in Lithuania, and still bitterly railing against what he saw as the dismal 'darkness' and prejudice of both Polish-Lithuanian Catholicism and Judaism, he commenced his odyssey in modern philosophy by composing a critique of Wolff's metaphysics which led him directly to a close study of Spinoza. *Aufklärung* we learn from his autobiography, was for him a vital concern, the dawn of truth after an interminably long night of darkness. In Berlin he conversed regularly with Mendelssohn who to some extent took him under his wing. But the two Jewish thinkers continually returned to the same stumbling-block: Maimon believed the Leibnizian-Wolffian system which Mendelssohn had adapted was a kind of half-way house on the path to Spinozism with Mendelssohn remaining blind, wilfully or unconsciously, to Spinoza's superior coherence.[169] The latter endeavoured to wean Maimon from his Spinozism. It was Maimon's radical enlightenment and reputation as a 'heretic' (and his indulgence in sensual pleasures) that resulted in his expulsion from Berlin, in 1783, and subsequent

---

[165] Kant, *Critique of Practical Reason*, 150.
[166] Kant, *Lectures*, 159.
[167] Maimon, *Lebensgeschichte*, 202; Kuehn, *Kant*, 214, 360.
[168] Buzaglo, *Solomon Maimon*, 1–2.
[169] Maimon, *Lebensgeschichte*, 152, 155–7, 172–3; Melamed, 'Salomon Maimon', 68, 71, 73.

rejection by the Dutch Jewish communities, some months later, and that of Breslau after that. Maimon, meanwhile, remained dissatisfied with both sides in the public controversy. He agreed with Jacobi whose philosophical astuteness he acknowledged that there was an inherent tendency to Spinozism in the positions of Mendelssohn (and Lessing) that they had always refused publicly to acknowledge. But he disapproved of the political motives and manipulation of the public behind Jacobi's resort to public controversy.[170]

Meanwhile, Karl Heinrich Heydenreich (1764–1801) offered a detailed critique of Mendelssohn's concept of a 'purified Spinozism', linking this directly to the Kantian controversy. Heydenreich was a Lutheran pastor's son, teaching through most of the 1780s at Leipzig where, despite being rumoured to be a private 'Spinozist', he was appointed full professor in 1789. In his *Über Mendelssohn's Darstellung des Spinozismus* [Over Mendelssohn's Presentation of Spinozism], of 1787, written after a close rereading of Spinoza's *Opera Posthuma*, he held Mendelssohn was fundamentally mistaken in identifying an underlying convergence between Spinoza and the 'Leibnizisch-Wolffischen System'.[171] Stressing Spinoza's monism and determinism, Heydenreich concurred with Jacobi, Wizenmann, Maimon, and Rehberg that Spinoza's cogent argumentation is impregnable by philosophical means and that Spinoza cannot be 'corrected' in the manner proposed by Mendelssohn. But he also disagreed with them, and Kant, that Leibniz's and Wolff's pre-established harmony is basically monistic and Spinozistic; rather he considered their system essentially dualist, arguing Wolff had been right to deny that Leibniz's parallelism of body and spirit bore any genuine similarity to Spinoza's parallelism.[172]

Jacobi, Wizenmann, and Rehberg were to be thanked for doing more than anyone else to transform Spinoza's image in Europe and convey something of the real spirit of Spinozism to the public.[173] For Heydenreich, as for Rehberg, but unlike Wizenmann, Jacobi's 'leap to faith' and abandonment of philosophy must also be rejected. But where Heydenreich especially diverged from Rehberg, Wizenmann, and Jacobi, leaning towards Herder whose approach toward Spinoza he both praised and criticized (for suggesting that Spinozism contains a residual Cartesian dualism) was in proclaiming a Spinoza who is, after all, compatible with Christianity. Spinoza can be made compatible, he urged, via a theism that cannot be philosophically grounded but is, as Kant held, intrinsic to the human mind and our moral consciousness.[174] Why not synthesize Spinoza and Kant, the two acutest minds of the age, and combine both with a revised Christianity? Heydenreich, who had also studied Boulainvilliers, Orobio de Castro, Lucas, Bredenburg, and Jariges as commentators on Spinoza,[175] certainly had no wish to be straightforwardly labelled a 'Spinozist'. He rejects

---

[170] Melamed, 'Salomon Maimon', 72; Maimon, *Lebensgeschichte*, 166.
[171] Heydenreich, *Natur und Gott*, 90, 93–4, 96–7; Gawoll, 'Karl Heinrich Heydenreich', 409.
[172] Otto, *Studien*, 218–19.
[173] Ibid. 86–7.
[174] Ibid. 221–3; Heydenreich, *Natur und Gott*, i. 193, 210, 216, 220.
[175] Heydenreich, *Natur und Gott*, i, pp. xxi, 85; Herder, *Gott*, 16–17.

Spinoza's denial of creation from nothing as unprovable and his greatest error; Spinoza's denial of the possibility of miracles, he holds, on Kantian grounds, to be something no philosopher can prove.[176] But he devised a way to stress Spinoza's general coherence and cogency without negating this through a 'leap to faith'— precisely by effecting a synthesis of Spinozism with Kantianism, the latter a system he had been closely studying since 1785.[177] Without Kantianism, he warned, there is absolutely no defence against unadulterated Spinozism.[178]

Swayed by Reinhold's *Letters*, Heydenreich emerged during the late 1780s as one of a rapidly swelling following convinced of the irreparable defects of the systems of Mendelssohn, Garve, and traditional philosophy and thoroughly won over by what he called the 'Revolution' of Kantianism. But he continued criticizing those who thought the Kantian 'revolution' meant there was no longer any point in studying the great metaphysical systems of the past from Plato to Herder. His *Natur und Gott nach Spinoza* (1789) was in many ways typical of the closing phase of the *Pantheismusstreit*, offering as it did something like a harmonious resolution. Unlike Kant, but like Maimon—Maimon too had turned to reading Kant in the wake of the controversy and striven to blend Kant with his own earlier Spinozism[179]—Heydenreich combined a new stress on 'practical reason' with continuing efforts to defend and renew Spinoza by emphasizing the latter's internal consistency.[180] He not only argued for a dispassionate, historically researched, and accurate account of Spinoza's life and thought but, unlike Herder, used Kant's system to forge a wholly new relationship between Spinozism and religion.

Where Spinoza's teaching correctly understood permits no reconciliation with any sort of faith or religious authority, for Jacobi, Heydenreich (and others) held one must circumscribe Spinoza's conception of God within its inherent limitations, viewing it, from a Kantian perspective, as something not ultimately irreconcilable with God but possessing its own internal validity and cogency.[181] This corrective was vital because, like Maimon, he was convinced that there is a major contradiction and source of instability in Kant's system. Maimon lacked Heydenreich's concern to redeem religious belief but similarly argued that Spinozism should not be equated with 'atheism'.[182] Even embracing Kant's core distinction between things-in-themselves and our perceptions, one is still obliged to choose between Hume's scepticism or else Spinoza's rational 'dogmatism', if one desires a meaningful philosophical hypothetical design for the world, a framework for encasing our understanding of science, religion, and reality. This has to be Spinoza (as Lichtenberg claimed), for nothing else is internally fully consistent.

---

[176] Heydenreich, *Betrachtungen*, i. 262–4, 268–9, and ii. 191.
[177] Otto, *Studien*, 223; Gawoll, 'Karl Heinrich Heydenreich', 409.
[178] Heydenreich, *Betrachtungen*, ii. 174–5.
[179] Maimon, *Lebensgeschichte*, 201–2; Melamed, 'Salomon Maimon', 73–5.
[180] Heydenreich, *Natur und Gott*, i, pp. iii–iv, xii.
[181] Gawoll, 'Karl Heinrich Heydenreich', 424; Pinkard, *German Philosophy*, 92.
[182] Maimon, *Lebensgeschichte*, 201–2, 217; Melamed, 'Salomon Maimon', 85–6, 94.

In the three years before the French Revolution, the great *Pantheismusstreit,* or more correctly *Spinozismusstreit,* drew not so much to a close but an inconclusive deadlock. Paradoxically, there were three clear but totally incompatible and divergent gainers: Kant, Spinoza (with French materialism hanging on his coat-tails), and German Counter-Enlightenment. All three dramatically gained ground, the last possibly most of all. Mendelssohn and the old cohesion of German university philosophy and culture, hence Leibniz and Wolff, were the losers. All three surviving rival blocs were deeply conscious of the social and political implications of the positions they embraced. These then became more generally obvious once the Revolution began. By late 1789, Jacobi and Rehberg were feverishly immersed in politico-philosophical concerns, linking their antagonism to the Revolution to their rejection of radical thought, while others, among them Herder who was extremely outspoken in supporting the Revolution's basic principles in its early radical, pre-*Rousseauiste* phase, no less ardently championed the Revolution's ideology, linking the latter to radical ideas and Spinoza.[183] One consequence was to foment a distinctly tense atmosphere at court at Weimar. Eventually, the war for and against Spinozism became part of the German ideological struggle over the meaning and significance of the Revolution itself.

[183] Beiser, *Enlightenment,* 149, 215, 307–8; La Vopa, *Fichte,* 101–3, 110.

26

Kant and the Radical Challenge

1. DILEMMAS OF MODERATION

Not only did the *Pantheismusstreit* coincide with, it also clearly exerted a decisive effect on, the general reception of Kant's *Kritik*.[1] The public furore about the status and significance of Spinoza's system ended by massively raising the stock of Kant's, and it was this shift in public perceptions, from 1786, that levered the great breakthrough in his career and transformation in German professional philosophy, a triumph aided in particular by the famous *Briefe über die Kantische Philosophie* [Letters on the Kantian Philosophy] by Karl Leonhard Reinhold (1757–1823), albeit also by many other interventions and publications.[2]

Reinhold was a Viennese ex-Jesuit who, following a religious crisis in 1782, and deep disillusionment with Catholicism—as well as much other traditional thinking—joined the Illuminati under the code-name 'Decius'. Fleeing Austria in November 1783, he took up residence in Jena where, helped by introductions from Sonnenfels and von Born, he established close links with Christoph Martin Wieland (1733–1813), a prominent literary figure and ex-Pietist keenly interested in how the individual outlook can be reshaped by successively adhering to different philosophies and whose Weimar journal, *Die Teutsche Merkur*, Reinhold helped edit. Reinhold formally converted to Protestantism, with Herder administering the rites, and married a daughter of Wieland. Appointed to a chair in philosophy at Jena in 1787, he soon established himself as an exceptionally effective philosophy lecturer, drawing large crowds of students and accomplishing more than anyone apart from Kant himself to make Kantianism the new intellectual driving force in the universities. His initial letters concerning the 'Kantische philosophie' appeared in the *Teutsche Merkur* in August 1786. These, constituting 'arguably the most influential work ever written concerning Kant',[3] were composed at the height of the *Pantheismusstreit* and were in large part a response to the Jacobi–Mendelssohn quarrel.

Reinhold's *Briefe* imparted a powerful boost to Kant's 'critical philosophy' chiefly by ignoring the difficult technical terminology that had previously hampered

---

[1] Kuehn, *Kant*, 326; di Giovanni, 'The First Twenty Years', 423.
[2] Zammito, *Genesis*, 241.
[3] Ameriks, 'Introduction', p. ix.

appreciation of his arguments,[4] and concentrating on persuading the public of the advantages of the new system as a defence of religion, traditional values, and morality and as a weapon against irreligious scepticism. Spinoza's unparalleled cogency in metaphysics and Bible criticism, Reinhold agreed with Jacobi, Wizenmann, Heydenreich, and Rehberg, put him in a category quite different from the other philosophers of the past. The mortal threat to society this posed could only be countered, he maintained, using Kant's demonstration that Spinoza's philosophy is a 'transcendental illusion' and hence morally and religiously illusory. Spinozism he proclaimed the equivalent in metaphysics to what Catholicism is in the sphere of the mysteries: 'the one system that has the most coherence and highest plausibility among all the pseudo-systems of non-belief.'[5] This was another way of saying the materialists and Spinozists were substituting a pseudo-religion for conventional religion and misleading the students and intelligentsia. It had taken over a century of concentrated effort for the profound challenge posed by Spinoza to be finally overcome. This heroic feat, performed for all mankind, was Kant's immortal achievement. Supernatural religion, natural religion, superstition, scepticism, and irreligion along with overstretched metaphysics, Spinozism first and foremost, must now all lapse into ignominy and oblivion to be replaced by 'ethical religion' based on rational faith and 'practical reason'. Not only were Spinozism, materialism, and Hume's 'dogmatic scepticism' finally relegated to the status of untenable 'heresies', announced *Die teutsche Merkur*, in April 1789, but so were all overblown metaphysics and philosophical *Supernaturalismus*, something the old 'school philosophy' had proved incapable of achieving.[6]

Where Mendelssohn, Feder, Garve, and the younger Reimarus had been mildly shocked by the sceptical, seemingly destructive implications of the *Kritik*, Reinhold urged that Kant in fact resolves all our main philosophical difficulties, an achievement he grandly compared to Newton's not just in laying down the ground rules of physics and astronomy but reconfiguring our entire picture of reality and the universe. Far from being yet another disorienting innovation, Kantianism was an unrivalled instrument for reasserting the supremacy of authority, faith, and traditional morality, Reinhold underlined these conservative implications, well before Kant himself stressed them in his *Critique of Practical Reason* (1788).[7] Kant's philosophy purified and freed morality from 'superstition' by anchoring it in practical acceptance of theism based on the postulates of pure 'practical reason', as Kantian terminology expresses it. Proclaiming the first *Kritik* a 'masterpiece of the philosophic spirit' and heavily stressing the distinction between things-in-themselves and reasoning based on representations of things, Reinhold, along with Jakob, at Halle,

---

[4] Pinkard, *German Philosophy*, 96–9; di Giovanni, 'The First Twenty Years', 427; Franks, 'All or Nothing', 102.

[5] Reinhold, *Letters*, 61; Ameriks, 'Introduction', pp. xvi–xvii.

[6] Wieland, *Teutsche Merkur* (Apr. 1789), 26, 33, 40.

[7] Ibid., p. xi.

and Kant's other key allies, proclaimed Germany the new world centre of progress in scholarship, the sciences, and philosophy.[8]

Reinhold, no less than Jacobi or Rehberg, galvanized the German cultural and intellectual scene by splitting the world of thought, culture, and science into three irredeemably divided and warring blocs. Long evident to the discerning, a basic tripartite division in culture now became obvious to everyone. There were the religious orthodox and zealots on one side, a bloc scorned by Reinhold and, in his opinion, totally marginalized by Kant. There were the materialist-Spinozists, rightly loathed by all professing respect for authority, tradition, and religion and capable of being repulsed only by Kant; and, finally, the middle 'Parthey', consisting of two distinct parts. These were, first, the obsolete, increasingly discarded Leibnizian-Wolffian contingent, and, second, the grouping Reinhold pronounced Germany's salvation, the rapidly swelling army of Kantians. Kant's greatest strength, held Reinhold, is that he proves that all attempts to unseat a personal God who knows, watches, judges, rewards, and punishes are just the futile writhing of 'our presumptuous reason' failing to acknowledge its innate inner limitations.[9]

Via Kantianism alone could society and its universities, schools, and churches successfully resist *die neue Philosophie* [the 'modern philosophy'], as Reinhold calls Spinoza-based materialism, using the German form of the current French expression, 'la philosophie nouvelle' (i.e. Spinoza, Diderot, Helvétius, d'Holbach).[10] Reinhold's was a schema that reduced everyone opposed to *die neue Philosophie* who did not embrace Kant to the status of either religious fanatics or obsolete pedants hindering society's most essential task, despite the fact that most university professors, Reinhold himself noted in 1789, persevered in rejecting Kant, and the Leibnizian-Wolffian legacy still boasted countless adherents, including the formidable Eberhard and his *Philosophisches Magazin* (1789–91) at Halle. The effect of Kant's proposed general Reformation of thought, observed Maimon in 1793, was to divide all philosophical Germany into *Kantianer* and *anti-Kantianer*, 'a Revolution' in ideas that within a few years did in fact end the still lingering, residual hegemony of the Leibnizio-Wolffians.[11] During these years, many young thinkers, Heydenreich at 25 in 1789, Fichte at 28 in 1790, Schiller, at 32 in 1791, previously trapped by a painful sense of having to choose between orthodoxy and materialist determinism, underwent an exciting, liberating, and profound change of outlook through conversion to Kantianism.[12]

For all his cool sobriety, Kant's intervention in the *Spinozastreit* impacted powerfully on every level of central European high culture, especially his claim that Man's quest for happiness is inseparable from traditional religion and morality, the moral life depending on belief in God, freedom of the will, and the immortality of the soul.[13]

[8] Kant, *Critique of Pure Reason*, 133–9; Kant, *Critique of Practical Reason*, 5–9; Reinhold, *Letters*, 5–7.
[9] Reinhold, *Letters*, 20–1; Wieland, *Teutsche Merkur* (Weimar, 1787), 3.
[10] Wieland, *Teutsche Merkur* (Apr. 1789), 12–13, 26, 33.
[11] Maimon, *Ueber die Progressen*, 5; Kuehn, *Kant*, 353–5.
[12] Gawoll, 'Karl Heinrich Heydenreich', 409; Breazeale, 'Introduction', 4–6; Beiser, *Schiller*, 41–4.
[13] Kant, *Critique of Pure Reason*, 134–6, 140, 154–7; Kant, *Critique of Practical Reason*, 12, 36–40, 52, 85–90.

Scores of readers, alarmed by the Jacobi–Mendelssohn furore, rejoiced to learn that whatever Lessing's real views, the disturbing questions raised by the *Pantheismusstreit* had been settled in favour of religion, authority, tradition, and conventional thinking. 'The atheism that today more than ever haunts the moral world in the forms of fatalism, materialism and pantheism' Kant had proved to be a spineless monster, 'a chimaera', and done so 'with a vivacity', claimed Reinhold, 'that our modern theologians cannot claim in their unmasking of the devil'.[14] To a reading public inundated with shocking disclosures since the commencement of the *Fragmentenstreit* and unable to make head or tail of Kant's technical vocabulary, this was gratifying news.

Greatly relieved also were numerous readers with no particular interest in Lessing, Mendelssohn, Jacobi, Herder, or Wizenmann but deeply unsettled by the impiety of Voltaire, Rousseau, and Lessing's *Ungenannte* (Reimarus) and who loathed the very name Spinoza. Countless such readers felt vindicated on seeing their beliefs definitively endorsed by the latest triumphs of academic philosophy. According to Heydenreich, Reinhold, and even Jacobi (after a fashion) Kant not only crushed atheism, materialism, and Spinozism, but discredited Voltaire's irreverence and Hume's corrosive scepticism. Since 'philosophy cannot prove that a truly divine revelation has to be general', deism too could now be dismissed as just a poetic myth:[15] Above all, Kant's breakthrough meant the philosophical restoration of Christianity and accepted morality to hegemony over learning, science, and the Enlightenment.

A future life and God's existence were practical reason's 'two articles of faith', announced Reinhold, though in his first *Kritik*, and later, Kant usually speaks of practical reason's three 'postulates'—belief in God's existence, freedom of the will, and immortality of the soul.[16] Society's now once again firmly anchored God-given morality presupposed acceptance of the distinction between body and soul and belief in a judge who dispenses future rewards and punishments. How the assumption of 'freedom of the will' necessarily follows from the concept of 'practical reason' and his general stance Kant had already shown in his *Groundwork of the Metaphysics of Morals* (1785).[17] The core of Kant's achievement in ethics and social theory, then, the central plank of his reconciliation of feeling and piety with speculative thought, was his concept of 'practical reason' distinct from 'pure reason' which, in turn, notes Reinhold, 'makes necessary both the expectation of a future world and the presupposition of a highest principle of moral and natural laws'.[18] Although it was not until 1788 that Kant set out the full implications of his doctrine in the *Kritik der Praktischen Vernunft* [Critique of Practical Reason], by 1785 his conception was already clear from his *Grundlegung* [Groundwork].

---

[14] Reinhold, *Letters*, 21; Heydenreich, *Betrachtungen*, i. 40.
[15] Heydenreich, *Betrachtungen*, ii. 205; Kuehn, *Kant*, 353.
[16] Kant, *Critique of Pure Reason*, 139, 141–4, 150, 155; Kant, *Critique of Judgment*, 301, 311, 321, 325.
[17] Kant, *Groundwork*, 47–8, 53, 57–9.   [18] Reinhold, *Letters*, 65.

Kant sought to restrict the scope of reason with respect to morality and, like the Scots, distance himself from the reason-based utilitarianism of Helvétius and d'Holbach, but did so differently and not quite to the same degree as the Common Sense thinkers and Hume.[19] It is in his *Groundwork* that Kant first explains his later famous doctrine of the 'categorical imperative', postulating a morality completely separate from religious authority (though compatible with it) chiefly anchored, unlike the moral reason of Spinoza and Bayle, in 'duty' and 'feeling' instead of social utility but employing 'practical reason' to extend and justify itself.[20] 'Act', as Kant formulates the principle, 'as if the maxim of your action were to become by your will a universal law of nature.' Its robust innovativeness lay in combining feeling and duty with the 'proven' sovereignty of 'practical reason' over human impulse. Kant's long-standing commitment to teleology and a physico-theology guiding the human collectivity towards its divinely given goals is not directly introduced into his argumentation in the *Groundwork*, but there is little doubt that it is implied there or that his physico-theology strongly re-emerges, albeit as a dimension of 'practical reason' not 'pure reason', in his *Kritik der Urteilskraft* [*Critique of (the Power of) Judgment*] (1790).[21]

By 1789, Kantianism seemed to have achieved an unstoppable momentum. This, his third *Kritik*, sprang directly from the *Pantheismusstreit* and includes a lengthy discussion of Spinoza, and from a Kantian (but by no means from a general) perspective marked the controversy's effective conclusion. While much of this text's second half argues against materialism and deism more generally, it also contains Kant's most explicit assault on Spinoza's system. 'If one accepts the mere mechanism of nature as sufficiently explaining the purposefulness of nature, then one cannot ask why the things in the world exist.' If one accepts 'an idealistic system', such as Spinozism is, for Kant, then one can speak only of the physical possibility of things which are hardly 'ends' in any meaningful sense: 'now one might interpret this form of things as due to chance or blind necessity', but either way the question about final ends is 'baseless'. Spinoza extinguishes all talk of final 'ends'. But if we assume the 'relation of ends in the world to be real and further suppose a particular kind of causality that governs this relation, namely a cause that acts intentionally, then we may not simply stop at the question of why things in the world (organized beings) take this or that form, or are placed by nature in this or that relation with others'.[22] 'Since we already conceive of an intellect which must be regarded as the cause for the possibility of such forms as they really manifest themselves in things in the world, one must also ask about the objective ground that could have determined this productive intellect to have such an effect, which is hence the final end to which such things exist.'[23]

Countering Spinoza's determinism and elimination of all final ends, in his third *Kritik*, Kant affixed his sails more firmly than ever to creation and the mast of divine

[19] Kant, *Groundwork*, 9–10.   [20] Ibid. 12–15, 25–6, 29–31.
[21] Kant, *Critique of Judgment*, 279–92; Wood, *Kant*, 114–17.
[22] Kant, *Critique of Judgment*, 240–1; Guyer, *Kant's System*, 303–5.
[23] Kant, *Critique of Judgment*, 284–6.

purpose and providence and his banner to the campaign against Spinoza. While we lack the possibility of absolutely knowing or understanding the ideas of God and immortality of the soul, we can say that accepting and believing in these concepts constitute the 'conditions of the practical use of our pure reason', that 'they are the conditions of the application of the morally determined will to this object which is given to it *a priori*, namely the *summum bonum*'. In the sphere of morality and social action, although we cannot know and understand God or immortality theoretically, we must assume their possibility and can justify assuming them in that they 'contain no intrinsic impossibility' or contradiction.[24]

If, on the other hand, one keeps to pure, theoretical reason as the foundation, 'like the otherwise so acute Mendelssohn' it is impossible to 'conceive how those who persist in seeing space and time as attributes belonging to the existence of things in themselves can avoid fatalism of actions'.[25] In other words, in the dispute between Mendelssohn and Jacobi, Kant virtually conceded that the latter was right and that, unless one adopts Kant's perspective, philosophy is indeed powerless to defeat Spinoza's arguments. Furthermore, the fight was indeed far from just academic. From a moral and social standpoint, Spinozism was disfigured in Kant's eyes by the gravest objections. His system suppresses all teleology, eliminating every possibility of conceiving of purpose, design, and choice in the universe and the substance which is its grounding; secondly, Spinoza removes all possibility of contingency regarding our actions and how things happen.[26] Spinozism also destroys fixity of species and all meaningful separation between animals and man. With his third *Kritik* Kant 'proved' that Christianity could now be shown, without reference to revelation or theology, to provide a 'conception of the *summum bonum* (the kingdom of God) that alone satisfies the strictest demand of practical reason'.[27]

The advantages of Kant's system for an essentially monarchical-aristocratic society sanctioned by ecclesiastical authority searching for a new kind of moderate Enlightenment moral philosophy based on the divine plan and divine purpose but distinct from morality based on religious authority, on the one hand, and from the quest for human happiness based on equality, the scheme of the radicals, on the other, were instantly apparent. First, the moral order and society itself seemed to have become sturdier and more stable through reinstating the primacy of theology over moral and social life by means of a 'revolution' confined to the mind. 'Among all other European lands,' asserted Reinhold, in 1790, 'Germany is the most disposed towards revolutions of spirit and the least disposed towards political revolutions.'[28] Secondly, the incisiveness and intellectual cogency of the arguments of Spinoza, Bayle, Collins, and other radicals against the existing proofs of God's existence and beneficence, and against the divinely delivered character of morality, could be safely negated without

---

[24] Kant, *Critique of Practical Reason*, 4–5; Guyer, *Kant's System*, 163–4, 314–15.
[25] Kant, *Critique of Practical Reason*, 106; Pätzold, *Spinoza, Aufklärung*, 116.
[26] Guyer, *Kant's System*, 303–4, 312–13.
[27] Kant, *Critique of Practical Reason*, 134–5.   [28] Ibid. 133.

contradicting their specific objections. With regard to their arguments against creation, divine providence, and divinely delivered morality from *consensus gentium* (agreement of the peoples), a principle vigorously but hardly convincingly championed, against Spinoza and Bayle, by Le Clerc and Voltaire, Kant concedes that the radicals are right on a superficial level. The standpoint of Le Clerc and Voltaire is indeed totally wrong as otherwise we should all believe in ghosts and demons.[29] Yet, if philosophy cannot directly defend creation, divine providence, or fixity of species, and hence not social hierarchy either, it can marginalize and circumvent Spinoza, and in Kant's hands need make no concessions to fatality, determinism, evolutionary ideas, or equality.

'Morality', as Kant summed his position up in 1792, 'inevitably leads to religion and, through religion, extends itself to the idea of a mighty moral lawgiver outside the human being whose ultimate goal (in creating the world) determines what can and ought to be the ultimate human end.' Like Siegmund and Alexander Baumgarten, before him, Kant embraces Leibniz's and Wolff's thesis that the 'world created by God' is, as Kant put it, 'the best of all possible worlds', but unlike them and unlike Leibniz, Wolff, and Mendelssohn, denies this is demonstrable by 'pure reason', maintaining instead that our necessary reliance on this doctrine arises rather from 'moral faith' underpinned by 'practical reason' with 'practical reason' proven to be the real basis of the social and moral order, an order effectively buttressed by Kantian critical philosophy alone.[30] With this strategy Kant could powerfully entrench a more traditional stance on moral values than could other enlighteners and reaffirm many essentially theological prohibitions, including that on suicide. His anti-Spinoza stand enabled him to classify as immoral all sexual activities considered forbidden by the churches including fornication, concubinage, prostitution, incest, masturbation, homosexuality, and bestiality.[31] Both Spinoza's conception of reason and socially based morality Kant in his third *Kritik* declares moribund along with his denial of final causes and contingency.[32]

By the end of the 1780s, Kantianism was triumphing everywhere from Copenhagen to Vienna and from Berne to Prague, re-establishing in the wake of the Leibnizian-Wolffian ascendancy the effective hegemony of the centre. But how stable was the Kantian colossus? It was impossible to forget that there was also a third corner to the triangle and not a few officials and government ministers now refusing to espouse the Kantian or any other moderate *Aufklärung* as a viable basis for authority, religion, and an aristocratic order. Both the Austrian court and the German princes in general, observed Reinhold, were now torn, in the aftermath of the 1784–5 Bavarian and Austrian edicts against the Illuminati, between what he called having a 'philosophical eye', recognizing the need for substantial reforms in

[29] Kant, *Lectures*, 39; Kant, *Critique of Judgment*, 237–42.
[30] Kant, *Lectures*, 137–9, 155; Henrich, *Between Kant*, 158–9.
[31] Kant, *Religion within the Boundaries*, 35–6; Hull, *Sexuality, State*, 307; Hösle, *Morals and Politics*, 112.
[32] Kant, *Critique of Judgment*, 235–339; Guyer, *Kant's System*, 304–5.

law, society, and religion, on the one hand, and, on the other, outright repression, rejection of Enlightenment, and the impulse to protect 'the old doctrinal structure of folk religion against all public attack'.[33] Deeply conscious of linkages between philosophical developments on the one hand and, on the other, the wider cultural shifts of his age such as the declining prestige of the Catholic Church, 'the fallen reputation of monasticism in several Catholic states', the rise of toleration and free speech in the Austrian monarchy, and the nagging, incessant talk about abolishing serfdom (in Denmark-Norway, Germany and Austria-Bohemia-Hungary, the German-speaking Baltic Russian provinces, as well as Poland and Russia), Reinhold stands out in retrospect for the clarity with which he perceived all these wider social shifts and related them to the great political events of the age—the American, Dutch, and (after 1789) the French revolutions.

Philosophy, more than anything else, he reminded the reading public, lay at the heart of what he called the present 'shaking' of assumptions, tradition, superstition, beliefs, and practice, a process transforming attitudes and hence, in turn, social reality.[34] By clearing away the presumptions of earlier metaphysics, Kant's 'moral ground of cognition stands firm', as Reinhold put it, 'as the only one that survives testing, giving at once content, coherence, and thoroughgoing determination to the notions that are supplied by ontology, cosmology, and physico-theology for the doctrinal structure of traditional teaching and theology'.[35] Precisely because such ideas as those of the First Cause and the Necessary Being are totally transferred by Kant from the sphere of what is or can be known by pure reason, 'they are elevated above all the counterproofs and doubts to which they were vulnerable' while remaining 'indispensable to the single true ground of cognition and constitute, together with it, well-ordered parts of a single and complete structure that from now until eternity will rest upon unshakable foundations'.[36] Not only had Kant finally rescued for the general public a vigorous physico-theology akin to that of Reimarus but had even expanded physico-theology via his new apparatus of 'moral teleology'.[37] Through Kant, God powerfully re-emerged as not just the maker and governor of the universe, and the Creator of all species including the different varieties of men with their varying characteristics, but also what Kant calls 'the lawgiver of the world in relation to moral laws'.[38]

The collision between Kantianism and Spinozism spanned the entire spectrum of human ideas. Kant's defence, or quasi-defence, of divine purpose and revelation, set against the absolute rejection of the miraculous by the Spinozists, supported his adept manoeuvring and judicious publicity in choosing the best ground for positioning his work as the new chief bulwark of received assumptions and notions, including miracles. The narrow boundaries imposed by his technical categories on what pure reason can and cannot demonstrate, and drastic curtailment of

---

[33] Reinhold, *Letters*, 134.   [34] Ibid. 132–4; Boyle, *Goethe*, ii. 55–6.
[35] Reinhold, *Letters*, 43.   [36] Ibid.   [37] Kant, *Critique of Judgment*, 329–34.
[38] Kant, *Lectures*, 29, 113; Niezen, '*Aufklärung*'s Human Discipline', 182, 184.

metaphysics, turned the reality and nature of miracles into something beyond our knowing or posing questions about while yet obliging us to assume, as a matter of course, that there have been miracles foundational to moral truth. What this means in practice, he explains, adopting an ingenious middle-of-the-road tactic, is that there exist rational human beings who, though not disposed to renounce belief in [miracles], never allow this belief to intervene in practical matters. In theory, they believe there have been and are miracles 'but they avow none in their practical affairs'.[39] Here indeed was finely crafted, consummate moderation—and quintessential Kant.

In assessing the initial general impact of Kant's critical philosophy in central Europe, it is important to stress both its unsettling and reassuring aspects. Many were shocked; but not a few, included many radical-minded, rejoiced to see the still powerful old metaphysics and many exponents of Leibnizio-Wolffian theologico-philosophical general systems so entirely shattered.[40] Assailed alike by Jacobi's supporters and Kant's allies, Reinhold and likewise Jakob, the foremost German translator and interpreter of Hume who also published a vigorous refutation of Mendelssohn's *Morgenstunden*, after the latter's death, Leibnizianism rapidly receded and the dead Mendelssohn, observed Maimon, paid a disproportionate price.[41] But the 'all-crushing' Kant's shoring up of older moral and belief structures was still more remarkable: Kantianism quickly transcended Germany's confessional boundaries as well as, from the late 1780s, penetrated Danish-Norwegian cultural space.[42] Even if diffused more slowly in Catholic Germany and Austria than in the Protestant north, Kantianism was greeted enthusiastically and, again, mainly because philosophy lecturers in South German universities soon judged it the most robust available defence against materialism, determinism, Spinozism, and atheism.[43] The diffusion of Kantianism in the Catholic German-speaking world began just prior to the French Revolution, with the Benedictine Matern Reuss (1751–98), at Würzburg, in Franconia, among the first—already by 1788—to lecture on Kantianism to Catholic students. Intellectually, a parallel bridging process began, slightly earlier, among the Jews of Berlin and Königsberg.

2. CRITIQUING KANT'S CRITICAL PHILOSOPHY

It was in Kantianism, then, that *Aufklärung* and Christianity, reason and faith, were finally and decisively reconciled. But, behind the scenes, the Kantian 'revolution' still left some crucial questions unresolved. Many remained unpersuaded in both the other two corners of the warring triangle. Jacobi, though taken to task by Reinhold

[39] Kant, *Religion within the Boundaries*, 99; Wood, *Kant*, 107–8, 185.
[40] Lichtenberg, *Schriften und Briefe*, iv. 732–3; Kuehn, *Kant*, 355.
[41] Maimon, *Lebensgeschichte*, 166–7; Goldenbaum, 'Mendelssohns schwierige Beziehung', 267–70.
[42] Rørvik, 'Kant-resepsjonen', 236.
[43] Hinske, 'Kant im Auf', 196–8; Hinske, 'Andreas Metz', 303; Boyle, *Goethe*, ii. 55.

for still claiming reliance on reason leads inexorably to fatalism and atheism and failing to grasp the significance of Kant's *Kritik*, fared considerably better in this new context than Mendelssohn and the Leibnizian legacy.[44] In the last stages of the *Pantheismus-streit*, Jacobi succeeded in broadening his attack on Spinozism and Mendelssohn into a general assault on the Enlightenment while simultaneously tying his campaign to Kant's triumphant bandwagon as a means of countering charges of 'enthusiasm' and irrationality. Since Kant and he himself were both pruning back reason's autonomy, Jacobi continually reproached him (and Reinhold) for 'inconsistency', in charging him with misunderstanding, irrationalism, and 'enthusiasm' and not without reason.[45] If denying God's demonstrability and his leap to faith were evidence of 'enthusiasm', then, surely, Kant's *Kritik* stands open to exactly the same charge.[46]

Like Wizenmann, Rehberg, Heydenreich, Maimon, and Fichte,[47] Jacobi genuinely considered his own position closely proximate to Kant's and cited several passages from the latter's writings holding God's existence and the soul's immortality to be only 'morally' certain, ascertainable solely via 'practical reason' as certainties that cannot be demonstrated by pure reason, supporting his claim. Here, Jacobi, like Wizenmann and Rehberg, offered a clear, potentially deadly riposte not just to Mendelssohn but the *Kantianer* as well. Jacobi had (like himself) as good a claim as Kant and Jakob, Rehberg rightly observed, to insist that he was responding to and accommodating as well as partly countering Hume's scepticism.[48] What especially appealed to Jacobi and Rehberg in Hume was his claiming past philosophers, like Descartes and Locke, had postulated a massive gap between evidence based on perception, on the one hand, and belief, on the other, whereas in fact our working suppositions about the world and other people are mostly anchored in assumptions and beliefs rooted in a very limited ground of direct experience and perception rather than direct experience.[49] This feature of Hume, particularly as tempered by Reid who, in Jacobi's eyes, successfully demonstrates the 'reality' of what Hume calls 'belief', a notion Jacobi identifies with his principle 'Glaube', proved especially useful to all who resented the disdainful way Kant's defenders dismissed Jacobi's objections and 'leap into faith'.

In his *David Hume über Glauben, oder Idealismus und Realismus* [David Hume on Faith; or, Idealism and Realism] (Breslau, 1787), Jacobi answers the complaint that he had been too vague in responding to Kant's *kritische Idealismus*, by elaborating the Humean dimension to his thought and explaining Reid's importance.[50] Kant's system, held Jacobi, who read and reread Kant's first critique several times, rests on a dubious dualism, curtailing the scope of reason while simultaneously subordinating

---

[44] Reinhold, *Letters*, 24–6; Goldenbaum, 'Mendelssohns schwierige Beziehung', 24–7, 35, 37.

[45] Jacobi, *Über die Lehre*, 319–22; Vallée, *Spinoza Conversations*, 35; di Giovanni, 'The First Twenty Years', 425.

[46] Altmann, *Moses Mendelssohn*, 750; Neiman, *Unity of Reason*, 152.

[47] Rehberg, *Sämmtliche Schriften*, i. 12–14; Fichte, *Foundations*, 78–80.

[48] Rehberg, *Sämmtliche Schriften*, i. 12–13, 15; Forster, *Kant and Skepticism*, 22–4.

[49] Jacobi, *David Hume*, 33–5; Fogelin, 'Hume's Scepticism', 90–3.

[50] Kuehn, *Kant*, 326.

the evidence of the senses to reason while accusing Jacobi's supporters of belittling 'reason' and preaching simplistic reliance on 'pure faith' which Jacobi rejected as 'sheer misrepresentation'.[51] Kant held that things-in-themselves cause our sensations and are then synthesized by our minds into intuitions. But causality is an a priori condition of all human experience. Hence, for Kant, causality is both fundamental and unknowable or beyond human cognition, our awareness of it being purely empirical, creating a problem which he refuses to acknowledge and that undermines the rest of his argument.[52] Without the assumption of the thing in itself, as Jacobi famously formulated his objection, one cannot enter into the Kantian world-view while yet, with it, one cannot stay within it.[53]

At the same time, by continually praising Kantianism and criticizing Herder, Jacobi managed to win Kant round to an extent and negotiate a working truce. By 1789, Kant was virtually proclaiming Jacobi his ally, suggesting he had denounced Jacobi and his ideas in 1785 only because he was then under massive pressure to discredit Spinozism.[54] He, Jacobi, and Rehberg, he now accepted, formed a kind of common front (with Biester) against Spinozism and materialism. No doubt these shifting alignments within and between the three warring philosophical blocs, Radical Enlightenment, Counter-Enlightenment and Mendelssohnian or alternatively Kantian moderate Enlightenment balancing reason and faith, however fascinating to Wieland and Reinhold, produced more bewilderment than clarity in most onlookers. But while Kant's philosophy exemplifies perfectly the moderate mainstream's endorsement of the basic condition and order of the world, and human society, Kant also maintains that true 'enlightenment' is a process of emancipating oneself from prejudices, from an 'immaturity' that is undesirable and for which one is responsible. But how can a philosophy claiming the universe is based on a divinely decreed order contend that men are responsible for their own immaturity? Hamann, though Kant's loyal friend and loathing Mendelssohn and the Berlin Enlightenment as he did, disagreed on this point in many a discussion at Königsberg, regularly identifying this discrepancy as the 'proton Pseudos', the first and fundamental error in Kant's system, and here perhaps he was right.[55]

Nor was it just on the conservative flank that Kant had left loopholes skilfully exploited by the likes of Jacobi, Wizenmann, and Hamann. On his other flank, too, there were some undeniable weak links. Maimon was another critic of Kant who pivoted his criticism on the difficulty of blocking Hume's scepticism. Pure reason may never produce knowledge of that basic architecture of reality which we would like to possess. Yet we cannot give up the search and must strive for glimpses and, this being so, it is still a challenging problem that Spinoza's system, as Fichte, Reinhold, Heydenreich, Wizenmann, Lichtenberg, Wekhrlin, Knoblauch, Rehberg, and so

[51] Jacobi, *David Hume*, 14–15, 21.
[52] Pinkard, *German Philosophy*, 95–7; Tavoillot, *Crépuscule*, pp. xxvi–xxvii.
[53] Tavoillot, *Crépuscule*, 223; Henrich, *Between Kant*, 76; Rockmore, *Kant*, 172; Wood, *Kant*, 32, 73.
[54] Zammito, *Genesis*, 246–7.   [55] Schmidt, 'What Enlightenment Was', 89; Kuehn, *Kant*, 320.

many others at this time thought, remained much the most compelling.[56] Especially troubling to Maimon was the ungrounded separation of body and soul, and the form and content of physical things, in Kant's metaphysics, and especially the result produced by Kantian epistemology that the form of things is a priori knowledge inherent in human reason while the content of things remains closed to us. The forms of things Kant held to be 'in us a priori' while the content is merely our representation [Vorstellung] of objects always a posteriori. Such a dualistic account of cognition seemed implausible to Maimon who argued that making 'things' and forms correspond, the precondition for true cognition, requires that we accept that mind determines not just the form but also the content of things.[57] Kant had remarked in a letter to Markus Herz, as early as March 1789, that Maimon's approach was 'mit dem Spinozismo … einerlei' [the same thing as Spinozism].[58] Maimon, like Heydenreich, Rehberg, and perhaps even Reinhold, in any case concluded Kant had not finally defeated Spinozism—indeed that his ideas, fundamentally important though they were, needed correcting and when corrected would ultimately produce a new form of Leibnizian dogmatism.

By the early 1790s there were already an appreciable number of ex-Kantians. Maimon had been 'an adherent', he recalled in 1792, 'of all philosophical systems in succession, Peripatetic [in Lithuania], Spinozist, Leibnizian, Kantian, and finally Sceptic'. He had seen something good and true in all of them; but he also detected irresolvable difficulties.[59] The reading public was being shepherded in droves to Kant but had *Auflärung* put down deeper and firmer roots now that it had been reconfigured by Kant? Did Kantianism cohere as a philosophical position and moral system as well as a recipe for social and political reform? Everywhere there were signs that the philosophical battle had not, after all, ended.[60] For Lichtenberg, an admirer and friend of Kant, Kantianism's spectacular successes, however impressive, entirely failed to change his conviction that it was still Spinoza who 'thought the greatest thoughts that had ever come into a human head'.[61] Fichte, who was to be Reinhold's successor at Jena (from 1794), was by 1790 even more impressed with Kant. 'No, great man, you who are of such importance for the human race, your work will not perish! It will bring rich fruits. It will give mankind a fresh impetus; it will bring about a total rebirth of man's first principles, opinions and ways of thinking.'[62] But before long he too detected worrying structural problems in the grand design and especially with the way Kant's 'pure reason' buttresses his crucial concept of 'practical reason'.

Reinhold argued that Spinoza would have been the victor in this the greatest confrontation in history of philosophy were it not for Kant's masterful delimiting but

---

[56] Buzaglo, *Solomon Maimon*, 130–1; Fichte, *Wissenschaftslehre*, 92.
[57] Beiser, *German Idealism*, 249; Fraenkel, 'Maimonides and Spinoza', 217–18; Buzaglo, *Solomon Maimon*, 38, 42.
[58] Fraenkel, 'Maimonides and Spinoza', 232.
[59] Kuehn, *Kant*, 360; Schmidt, 'What Enlightenment Was', 109.
[60] Maimon, *Ueber die Progressen*, 5.
[61] Lichtenberg, *Schriften und Briefe*, i. 697.   [62] Fichte, *Early Philosophical Writings*, 365.

also strengthening of the apparatus of 'pure reason', Spinozism being the 'one system that has the most coherence and highest plausibility among all the pseudo-systems of non-belief'.[63] But Rheinhold was a bafflingly complex, as well as humourless man who would brook no contradiction, an Illuminatus who tended to operate on different levels. Publicly, he presented himself as staunchly moderate mainly perhaps because he saw no alternative but to work with the princely courts and through public opinion. However, underneath, later events suggest, he still nurtured lingering radical tendencies. If he sought to bring the *Aufklärung* into a stable balance with revealed religion as part of the solution to the grave tensions at work both in society and within his own mind, his commitment to Kant later proved less robust than it had initially seemed. Part of the problem was that Kant, like Locke and Hume, had drastically narrowed the scope of pure reason, and far more than they, transformed philosophy into a highly technical subject leaving the content of morality, politics, and social theory broadly outside the sphere of reason's competence. By doing so, Kantianism largely accepted philosophy's subordination to authority, Christian theology, and the existing social order at a moment when authority, theology, and the social order were precisely the things most in question and under attack. The inevitable result was that philosophy, if not completely disarmed as an instrument of reform, was, as we see also in the context of the 'perpetual peace' controversy, severely weakened.[64] Given the many urgent social and political problems weighing on Enlightenment writers, Kantianism ultimately merely added to the list of factors hindering moderate mainstream Enlightenment from engaging effectively with the major political, moral, legal and social problems of the age.

For several years, Reinhold had been entangled with Von Born's curious speculations about ancient Egyptian religion, as well as the Spinozistic tendencies inherent in Illuminism.[65] After 1785, he continued to believe that the origin of the Mosaic law is Egyptian, becoming one of the main proponents of an idea, fundamental to Illuminism, and popular generally in the late eighteenth-century German-speaking world, that the idolatrous, superstitious, and animalistic aspects of ancient Egyptian religion were mere surface froth, a front to assuage the ignorant masses while the real 'Egyptian mysteries', clandestinely preserved by the priesthood, were the first formulation in human history of rationalistic 'natural religion'. Indeed, Reinhold equated Mosaic monotheism with the true 'Egyptian mysteries'. In his study of the Hebrew mysteries, first published in Von Born's journal in Vienna, in 1786, Reinhold followed Toland in equating Moses' monotheism with primitive *Spinozismus*, or *Spinozismus ante Spinozam*, and revived Toland's idea that the core of Moses' true teaching survived as a secret cult behind the formalistic observances of popular Hebrew religion and traditional Judaism.[66]

Was Kantianism, for Reinhold, ultimately just a bridge between truth and what people will accept? In espousing Kant's philosophy and joining forces with Wieland

---

[63] Reinhold, *Letters*, 61; Melamed, 'Salomon Maimon', 76.
[64] Israel, *Revolution of the Mind*, 124–53.
[65] Assmann, *Moses the Egyptian*, 115–25.   [66] Ibid. 117.

at Jena, Reinhold had not deep down rejected Illuminism, Pantheism, and Spinozism as a personal solution for himself, or even for mankind generally, but only relegated these to the sphere of distant insights. In the contemporary crisis which he saw looming, and in which the divisions among Kant's followers seemed to him an alarming dimension, he thought it more urgent for the moment to find a philosophical methodology capable of underpinning a more moderate form of Enlightenment of a sort that could sway the people and the princes. He had been genuinely elated to discover Kant's *Critique*. But subsequently he had had certain doubts. Above all, he saw a need to reconfigure Kant's terminology so as to make his categories clearer and more systematic and in particular to ground the existence of two distinct elements in all representations of objects—form and matter—an enterprise in which he was not very successful.[67]

Kant's reliance on 'practical reason', and the power of judgement to guide moral sense, was likely to prove but a weak instrument in the face of intense moral zeal and religious fervour, especially zeal claiming justification for practising religious and moral intolerance or insisting on the obligation of those with religious or moral authority to impose social discipline rigorously on the majority. Kant had in effect subordinated reason to feeling without saying so, as Jacobi and Fichte grasped, as well as to a purely inner categorical imperative, and this placed him in a trap from which there was no easy exit. It was all very well for Kant imperiously to dismiss Bayle's concept of the 'erring conscience', and hence a key part of his defence of toleration, as an absurdity, as an 'Unding' [non-thing].[68] But he had undeniably diminished reason's power to counter the force of misguided 'moral' imperatives. Reinstating original sin, moreover, which the Spinozists and materialists had laboured so hard to eradicate, only detracted from the ability of his 'practical reason' to check the pretensions of the many forms of puritanism, fanaticism, intolerance, and fundamentalism now welling up in Prussia and Austria alike, let alone in Poland, Hungary, and among Wekhrlin's 'Hottentots of Glarus'. It also turned his categorical imperative with its implication that man can convert himself into a good, and even perhaps into a believing, being through his own efforts into a deep philosophical paradox.[69] 'How it is possible that a naturally evil human being', as Kant himself put it, 'should make himself into a good human being surpasses every concept of ours.'[70]

Kant's system obliged him to reject outright, along with other moderate Enlightenment thinkers, comprehensive freedom of expression and of the press as urged by Spinoza, Diderot, and d'Holbach and, in Germany, latterly, by Lessing, Diez, Bahrdt, and Wekhrlin; indeed, this was something that necessarily followed from the nature of his 'practical reason'. Certainly, Kant reaffirms the Enlightenment's general disapproval of superstition, priestcraft, and overbearing ecclesiastical authority but he simultaneously assigns a positive role to the churches and careful censorship of books

[67] Henrich, *Between Kant*, 134–7.
[68] Kant, 'On the Miscarriage', 27; Hunter, 'Kant's *Religion*', 26; Forst, 'Toleranz', 207–8.
[69] Kant, *Religion within the Boundaries*, 66–70.   [70] Ibid. 66; Wood, 'Rational Theology', 404.

and expression as something useful and necessary to society, in particular for ensuring correct moral and religious attitudes. As he admitted, this then involved some further thorny difficulties. In the case of a theological censor who is also a scholar and worries that eagerness to save souls might cause him unjustly to censor research in biblical criticism and obstruct scholarship, Kant suggests this person should strive to create an internal barrier in his mind between the theological and philosophical spheres being primarily theological where appropriate and scholarly in scholarship's proper sphere. But it was hard to see that any such internal check could be a reliable regulator.[71]

In short, Kant's 'practical reason' had the multiple disadvantage of being a tool easily appropriated by theology and by social forces opposed not just to Radical Enlightenment but to all Enlightenment. Kant was an Enlightenment thinker with a marked republican, if not democratic, tendency who conceived that the progress of reason working through history would drive the progress of legislation and constitutionality, via separation of powers and the cutting back of princely absolutism. The interests of the majority and the ideal of perpetual peace would eventually gain ground driven by the advance of 'reason'. But if, at the same time, it is 'our universal duty to elevate ourselves' to an 'ideal of moral perfection' ultimately fixed and sanctioned by faith and religion then men must, finally, submit to the approval or disapproval of theologians in the sphere of moral action, as Kant's many Catholic admirers quickly (and enthusiastically) grasped, as well as in strictly religious matters; and perhaps even in the sciences and scholarship. Nor was this all. Kantianism incurs yet another major disadvantage with its dry complexity and technical intricacy. For this reinforced the tendency to narrow philosophy's scope, segregating specialists from society generally. By doing so, the *Kantianer* hastened the rise of a fresh kind of pedantry and scholasticism.

'There are some arrogant Kantians', commented Maimon in his autobiography of 1792, 'who believe themselves the sole proprietors of the Critical Philosophy, and therefore dispose of every objection, even where intended not as refutation but as fuller elaboration, by the mere baseless assertion that the author has failed to understand Kant.'[72] Such pedantry and the splits between the academic Kantians were also one of the chief worries bothering Reinhold. For all these reasons, the *Pantheismusstreit* not only bolstered Kantianism but also lent additional weight to Jacobi's, Wizenmann's, Rehberg's, Maimon's, Heydenreich's, and Reinhold's suspicion that the absolute limits Kant imposes on reason, producing a highly technical sphere of 'pure reason' from which he expressly excludes moral knowledge and the moral sense, and hence social theory and legislation as well, far from triumphant breakthrough, as its growing host of adherents alleged, was in reality a colossus with feet of clay.

A further difficulty with Kantianism was that Kant's providential conception of history as adapted to theories about the origin of species and of human origins scarcely worked as an answer to hylozoism, a doctrine Kant condemned outright,

---

[71] Wood, 'Rational Theology', 408–10; Kant, *Religion within the Boundaries*, 36–8.
[72] Maimon, *Autobiography*, 107.

and the Spinozistic idea of nature creating itself. Kant maintained that 'the possibility of living matter cannot even be thought; its concept involves a contradiction, because lifelessness, inertia, constitutes the essential character of matter'.[73] Regarding humanity's universal character and relationship to nature, Kant found himself attacked especially by Herder and the radical ethnographer Georg Forster (1754–94). Much was at stake here as the post-critical Kant, despite his novel devices and strategy, still conceived of God, rather like Crusius and the two Baumgartens, as a kind of monarch over the world, a being external to the world who arranges human history according to a providential plan, even if our reason is unable to determine how providence acts in history in particular cases.[74] A central feature of Kant's vision was his conviction that 'we have sufficient cause for judging man to be, not merely like all organized beings a *natural purpose*, but also the *ultimate purpose* of nature here on earth, in reference to whom all other natural things constitute a system of goals according to fundamental propositions of reason'.[75] Man thus stood, in Kant's eyes, at the apex of the hierarchy of organized beings designed for unknowable purposes by God. Central to Kant's vision is the idea that the designing hand is external to the process.

The battle between Kant and the monists over this question, an integral part of the *Pantheismusstreit*, began in 1784 with the appearance of the first part of Herder's *Ideen zur Philosophie der Geschichte der Menschheit* [Ideas for the Philosophy of the History of Man] (4 vols., 1784–90), where, using the latest research on biology, anthropology, and physiology, Herder first expounded his Spinozism systematically as a general philosophy, eliciting a notably hostile reaction from Kant. Mankind, Herder argued, derives from an evolutionary process whereby organic matter arises from inorganic, and live species evolve towards higher species, leading eventually to the emergence of man who is thus the product of nature rather than a divine Creator. Furthermore, man is here deemed a unitary entity not divided into ranks or races, and without black men being in any way subordinate. Furthermore, man is deemed the creator (not the receiver) of his own culture, morality, and society. Humanity developed gradually from the all-pervasive creative force of nature, the role of a governing providence being now consciously minimized (as also earlier in Vico).[76]

Kant's reviews of the first two volumes of Herder's work, appearing anonymously in the *Allgemeine Literatur-Zeitung*, disputed what Herder claimed was the empirical basis of his theses in physics and biology. His general argument, and especially his all-pervasive creative force in nature, Kant pronounced a wild speculative construct completely beyond the scope of empirical science, nothing but an unsubstantiated metaphysical conjecture.[77] Kant demanded undeviating adherence to strict procedures and parameters of the kind he had laid down for a genuine empiricism in biology and anthropological science. But whose philosophy more genuinely appealed

[73] Kant, *Critique of Judgment*, 242; Guyer, *Kant's System*, 339–40.
[74] Kant, *Lectures*, 156–7; Henrich, *Between Kant*, 103; Wood, *Kant*, 98–100.
[75] Kant, *Critique of Judgment*, 279.
[76] Barnard, *Herder*, 64, 110–11; Zammito, *Genesis*, 180–2.   [77] Zammito, *Genesis*, 184–6, 203–5.

to evidence and experience? Radical and moderate Enlightenment had from the outset always disputed which kind of empiricism is the more authentically experience-based doctrine, Spinoza's monistic reduction of everything to the same set of observable rules as against Locke's dichotomy of reality differentiated into the observable and the unseen.

Kant, who viewed his transcendental idealism as the only coherent alternative to Spinozism, especially abhorred the hylozoic tendency in Herder, his notion that a general generic force in nature could govern the modification and transformation of species.[78] Precisely the weightiest philosophical objection to such reasoning, he held, is that it blocks all teleology, removing all 'purpose' from nature, reopening the door to Spinozism.[79] As part of this bad-tempered dispute, Kant later published an essay in the *Berliner Monatsschrift*, in November 1785, emphasizing his own commitment to fixity of species: 'throughout organic nature, amid all changes of individual creatures', he contended, 'the species maintain themselves unaltered.'[80] With these and similar phrases, Kant reaffirmed his denial of mutation of species, attacking both Herder and Forster who at this point emerged as among the fiercest critics of Kant's biology, anthropology, and social theories. Hylozoism Kant rejected as incompatible not just with the basic dualism of matter and motion, essential to Newtonianism, but also with all teleology and 'argument from design', principles fundamental to his own system and vital also to his insistent distinction between man and the rest of Nature's species.[81]

Just as physical equality among men has as its consequence an equality of rights, commented the German philosopher Tetens in 1777, 'so must likewise physical inequality of types have as its direct consequence a narrowing of moral and legal equality'.[82] By the 1770s, the moral and legal implications of the Enlightenment's internal struggle between advocates of mankind's unity and opponents postulating a hierarchy of races reached its culmination. The radical *philosophes'* sweeping rejection of every kind of racial and confessional hierarchy and fervent belief in the essential unity and equality of all mankind here clashed head-on with Kantianism. Those identifying with the existing order on the basis of moderate Enlightenment principles had in some degree, if only tangentially, to legitimize empire and the dominion of some peoples over others, and for these thinkers racial theory more and more came to provide a means of underpinning more traditional, legalistic, and constitutional arguments. As a rule, the more explicit arguments asserting racial differentiation and innate superiority of some over others became, the more unyielding and emphatic were the resulting justifications of imperial dominion and right to mastery over others.

To Kant's arguments, Forster, a future revolutionary leader and egalitarian publicist who was primarily an ethnographer but housed a good deal of 'philosophy' in his

---

[78] Ibid. 220–1, 224, 239–42; Beiser, *German Idealism*, 262.
[79] Zammito, *Genesis*, 240; Barnard, *Herder*, 65.   [80] Zammito, *Genesis*, 205.
[81] Ibid. 205–9; Kant, *Critique of Practical Reason*, 146, 149–50.
[82] Tetens, *Philosophische Versuche*, ii. 684–5, 687–9.

library, including Helvétius and the 1783 German translation of the *Système de la nature*, besides the main texts relating to the *Pantheismusstreit*,[83] retorted that it was Kant who was re-introducing metaphysical notions into the sphere of empirical science and violating authentic empiricism.[84] Where Kant argued for the separateness of man and fixity of species, Forster throughout insisted on the essential unity of mankind, publicly attacking Kant's standpoint several times, including in the autumn of 1786 in the *Teutsche Merkur*. Kant's position Forster denounced as 'unscientific', charging him with introducing inadmissible theological criteria into a discussion of anthropology and human origins, besides attributing the course of nature to divine providence, and unjustifiably reading purpose and teleology into natural processes. To Forster it was Kant not Herder who was hindering science with unhelpful definitions and categories instead of proceeding empirically.[85]

For Kant, the crucial issue was how to ground a scientific biology while retaining key strands of teleology and providential design.[86] He proceeded by rejecting polygenesis and reverting to Buffon's starting point, namely that mankind constitutes a single species, but replaced the radical *philosophes'* notion of racial differentiation as inessential mutation mechanistically driven through climate and circumstances with an explicitly teleological conception of racial sub-categories deemed permanent and irreversible. Postulating four basic races of humanity, Whites, Blacks, Hindustanic, and Kalmuck, outwardly distinguished by skin colour, he ruled that these could not be considered products of mere chance or mechanistic laws alone but must be thought of as pre-formed by providence, all humans containing certain seeds [Keime] or natural predispositions that developed or were arrested under the stimulus of climatic and other conditions. This 'further development of purposive primary predispositions implanted in the line of descent', as Kant calls them, then results in racial differentiation.[87]

Once racial character emerged, it was fixed, contended Kant, and there could be no further evolutionary change caused by different climatic or other conditions.[88] Once formed, racial characteristics, the intended nature of which was demonstrated, he thought, by the blackness of Africans (whose colour protects them from the hot African sun),[89] are unchangeable. Whichever racial orientation was actualized at the formative point froze the other seeds into quiescence. By combining fixity of species in this way with the idea of modification under climatic stimulus, Kant devised a racial theory typifying his wider strategy of mediating between key elements of opposition in the philosophical and scientific debates of his time as a way of

---

[83] *Verzeichnis der hinterlassenen Bücher von Georg Forster*, 41, 43, 53, 66; Berman, *Enlightenment*, 9, 56–7, 63–4.
[84] Gascoigne, 'German Enlightenment', 152–4; Zammito, *Genesis*, 208–10.
[85] Zammito, *Genesis*, 208–9.
[86] Zammito, *Kant, Herder*, 302.
[87] Kant, 'Use of Teleological Principles', 44; Brown, 'Social Sciences', 1080; Hess, *Germans, Jews*, 49.
[88] Bernasconi, 'Who Invented the Concept', 23; Zammito, *Kant, Herder*, 303–4.
[89] Bernasconi, 'Who Invented the Concept', 26.

transcending and resolving them. The element postulating pre-existing seeds, divinely implanted and formed for purpose in Kant's theory, derived from an innovatory idea introduced into biology and medicine by Haller and Bonnet in the years 1758–62, in particular in the latter's *Considérations sur les corps organisés*.[90]

During the later 1780s, Kant's racial theories were fiercely contested. Herder in the second part of his *Ideen zur Philosophie der Geschichte der Menschheit*, which appeared in August 1785, further developed his theory of cultural relativism while firmly upholding the idea of a universal, single morality and, as part of this, rejecting the notion of race as a system of ranks.[91] Kant replied by reasserting his racial theory in his *Bestimmung des Begriffs einer Menschenrasse*, the following November. In his 1786 essay 'Noch etwas über die Menschenrassen' [Still more about the Human Races], Forster denied the legitimacy of invoking teleology of any kind in science and philosophy and played down the physical and mental differences between whites and other races as much as possible, despite admitting that blacks do appear to be a separate branch of humanity from the rest in the sense that they originated separately and that the blackness of the African's skin is a consequence of climate.[92] Indeed, in this essay Forster included a general table indexing skin colour, arranging all the peoples in the zones from northern Europe to the equator, and from the equator southwards, arguing for proportionate calibration between white and brown and then from brown to black, and then, in the southern hemisphere going back again, in reverse shading, interpreting the whole spectrum as a mechanistically determined response to climate.[93] It was against Forster that Kant further elaborated his race theory in his essay *On the Use of Teleological Principles in Philosophy* (1788). He argues here that the evidence of the skin colour of children resulting from interbreeding between whites and blacks, and whites and Arabs, disproves the rule embodied in Forster's table. For the children simply combine the characteristics of both in a diluted but balanced manner irrespective of the location of their birth.

Equally, Forster's theory was disproved, argued Kant, by the lack of gradations in colour in West Africa where 'nature instead makes a sudden jump from the olive-skinned Arabs or Mauritanians to the blackest Negroes in Senegal' without going through any intermediate rungs and by the fact that none of the racial groups, whites, blacks, yellow-skinned, or east Indian brown, are found indigenously in the New World.[94] Forster's argument was further weakened, and the grounds for distinguishing different races of men strengthened, held Kant, by the evidence of the gypsies, an originally Indian people that persisted in preserving their original skin colour (and other racial traits) with such consistency over the generations that 'no difference would, in all probability, be found between them and those who were born in India'.[95]

---

[90] Ibid. 24; Zammito, *Kant, Herder*, 304–5.   [91] Barnard, *Herder*, 138–43; Wood, *Kant*, 187–8.
[92] Kant, 'Use of Teleological Principles', 44; Gascoigne, 'German Enlightenment', 153; Hess, *Germans, Jews*, 92.
[93] Kant, 'Use of Teleological Principles', 45.
[94] Ibid. 45, 49.   [95] Ibid. 45; Bernasconi, 'Kant', 148.

Lurking behind Forster's opposition to his racial schema, Kant rightly identified a tendency, lacking all basis in any philosophically cogent position, in his opinion, to view all living beings as being bound together in a shifting kinship, a vast natural chain of organic being descending to mosses and lichens, deriving from a single productive process rendering everything living 'part of a system of reproduction descended', in Forster's eyes, 'from a common line of descent'.[96] Acute observers were not slow to recognize the resurgence of the Spinozist tendency here as in numerous other contexts at the time. It was still not respectable to invoke Spinoza explicitly. Rehberg's affirmation in print that Spinozism is undoubtedly the most coherent system of metaphysics that exists but is not 'proven truth but only a perfect work of art which, of its kind, can not be superseded' provoked murmurs and exposed him, as similar remarks had earlier Heydenreich, despite repeated affirmations of Humean scepticism in the first and Kantianism in the latter case, to charges of underhand subversion and 'atheism'.[97]

[96] Kant quoting Forster, ibid. 51; Gascoigne, 'German Enlightenment', 147–8, 171.
[97] Rehberg, *Sämmtliche Schriften*, i. 8.

27

Goethe, Schiller, and the New 'Dutch Revolt' against Spain

1. DRAMA AND POLITICAL PHILOSOPHY

If Kant's 'practical reason' powerfully bolstered moderation and Christian values, he was also a champion of political, social, and educational reform provided that it did not affront authority and the princes. Indeed, the reasons he gives for refusing to justify revolution and preferring compromise, pragmatism, and gradual reform are among the most attractive features of his thought.[1] But the mainstream, Kantian no less than Wolffian, however firm its moderation and benevolence, in late eighteenth-century circumstances was in no position to undertake a wide-ranging reform programme precisely because it could not oppose princely rule. The discussions of the group of enlighteners comprising the Berlin *Mittwochgesellschaft*, or 'Wednesday Society', a society meeting regularly from 1783 to 1798 with the object of combining the efforts of prominent 'enlightened' Prussian officials and key writers, editors, and thinkers such as Biester, Nicolai, and Mendelssohn, only confirmed the impossibility of carrying through comprehensive change from a moderate standpoint.

There was little difficulty in identifying problem areas. Various legal reforms had been introduced since the 1740s, including Frederick's 1765 edict decriminalizing 'fornication' and ending the penalties for irregular sexual liaisons between men and women. But in Prussia, the economy remained under the deadening hand of an old-fashioned mercantilism, fiscalism, and royally enforced commercial monopolies,[2] the nobility remained a separate and excessively militarized caste, direct taxes remained low to 'please the nobility' as radical critics put it,[3] throwing an unjust burden on the rest of society, the serfs remained un-emancipated, the marriage laws antiquated and divorce difficult to obtain, the Jews under a wide range of disabilities, the press under growing restrictions, primary education in a highly unsatisfactory state, and the problems of illegitimacy, infanticide, and male and female vagrancy acute. In Silesia,

---

[1] Ellis, *Kant's Politics*, 82–3, 173–4, 179; Kersting, 'Politics', 359–61.
[2] Mirabeau, *De la monarchie*, i. 166–9, 173–9 and iii. 283–6, 288, 319, 326–9.
[3] Ibid. i. 192.

Frederick, knowing that the 800,000-strong Catholic majority remained secretly loyal to Austria, was careful to leave the clergy's traditional domination over the Catholic majority largely intact, refusing to prune ecclesiastical jurisdiction back.[4] As in Germany and Austria more generally, the difficulty lay not in identifying problems—there was virtual consensus about that—but in agreeing how to tackle the obvious need for profound and wide-ranging reform. During the 1770s and 1780s, those, like Lichtenberg, prone to dismiss the fashionable talk of 'improvements' and 'our greater humanity' in Germany as mere empty lip-service, just a passing fashion, seemed more and more justified.[5]

The Berlin *Mittwochgesellschaft* gathered on the first Wednesday of every month, to hear lectures and discuss their contents in an intense, disciplined manner, and, through its regularity, prestige, and members' eminence, became something of a legend in its own time. If anything could prove Radical Enlightenment superfluous, a wrong-headed extremist underground of little general significance, and set the course for social and legal amelioration in central Europe, it was this remarkable seminar. With its membership fixed at twenty-four, it represented the very cream of the respectable *Aufklärung*. Yet this private circle of the intellectual elite of Prussian high culture and bureaucracy was obliged to refrain from directly addressing the public sphere and even found it necessary to adopt some of the characteristics of a secret society. Such practices were simply necessary in an eighteenth-century monarchy such as Prussia. The *Mittwochgesellschaft* could not evade the need to confine its debates to the secrecy of closed meetings, binding its participants to refrain from discussing details of its deliberations with outsiders.[6] At the same time, it was here that the *Aufklärung* found itself most profoundly split. Rather than demonstrating the moderate Enlightenment's potential to forge a tolerant, stable, and well-organized society, balancing 'reason' against authority, religion, and tradition, in alliance with the power of enlightened despotism, the Berlin's Enlightenment think-tank, the *Mittwochgesellschaft* proved instead the impossibility of concerting any such programme.

The *Mittwochgesellschaft*, however discreet, was in the end unable to bridge the gap between its moderate members and those who sought to steer reform in a more egalitarian and libertarian direction. The moderates included the editors of the *Berlinische Monatsschrift*, Friedrich Gedike, an admirer of Montesquieu's legal and moral relativism,[7] and Biester, champion of amended noble privilege and Protestant hegemony in Prussia. Among the more radically inclined were Dohm, Struensee's younger brother Karl August von Struensee, who took up a financial post in Prussia after returning from Denmark, and Franz von Leuchsenring (1746–1827), a fervent member of the *Illuminatenorden* whose lodge name was 'Leveller' and who, in 1783, had briefly served as tutor to the Prussian crown prince, Friedrich Wilhelm.

---

[4] Mirabeau, *De la monarchie*, i. 354, 364.   [5] Lichtenberg, *Schriften und Briefe*, i. 697.
[6] Hull, *Sexuality, State*, 213; Schmidt, *What is Enlightenment?*, 235.
[7] Schmidt, *What is Enlightenment?*, 242.

Leuchsenring was a rebellious character, expelled from Berlin by royal authority in 1792 for his sympathies with the French Revolution. He moved to Paris and became a Jacobin. Long before that, though, he broke with Goethe and Herder besides other leading *Aufklärer*. The two currents could not work together because one side broadly upheld the existing order while the other was republican and anti-aristocratic in orientation.[8]

That the public sphere and expression of opinion remained shackled in Germany was underlined by the coverage in the papers and journals of the American Revolution. Events in America undoubtedly made a deep impression from the mid 1770s onwards at many levels of society and there was widespread sympathy for it. Yet virtually all forthright expression of opinion in print unreservedly supported the British crown, extolled Britain, and opposed the Revolution, in some cases recycling large extracts drawn from the pamphlets of Isaac de Pinto, the Dutch Sephardic publicist who counted as the most adamant European adversary of the rebel cause in print. Characteristic of the prevailing tone were the professorial pronouncements of the Göttingen professor August Ludwig Schlözer (1735–1809), one of German's leading political commentators, a principled monarchist and leading opponent of the Revolution who was later also a prominent adversary of the Dutch democratic revolution and the post-1789 anti-monarchist tendency in the French Revolution.[9] Having spent many years in his youth as a tutor in Sweden and at St Petersburg, Schlözer was internationally celebrated as a champion of the British way—aristocracy, monarchy, Montesquieu, and moderation.

Admittedly, Göttingen belonged to the electorate of Hanover and one would expect its professors to back Britain. But during the American Revolution, Göttingen set the tone for all Germany. Disagreement with Schlözer occasionally surfaced in the press but the undoubted fact that many people were enthusiastic for the American cause remained veiled as did the widespread revulsion at the princes' hiring out many thousands of trained troops to serve under British command in America. Among known enthusiasts for the American Revolution were several professors, including Forster who taught from 1779 at the college for noble youths, the *Carolinum* at Cassel, and at the *Carolinum* at Brunswick Dohm and Jakob Mauvillon (1743–94), both also opponents of de Pinto.[10] Mauvillon, a future radical member of the Illuminati, later worked with Mirabeau on his important study of the Prussian monarchy published in 1787. Dohm, a closet radical and later member of the Deutsche Union who was to emerge as a leading proponent of popular sovereignty in Germany, published some sharp criticisms of Schlözer's and de Pinto's pro-British arguments while professing not to be defending the rebels albeit mincing words in such a way as plainly to signify that he was. But such hints could be made only in the most muffled fashion, without any statement of democratic, republican, or

---

[8] Ibid. 240; Schüttler, *Mitglieder*, 93.
[9] Van Horn Melton, 'Enlightenment to Revolution', 114, 121–2.
[10] Beiser, *Enlightenment*, 163; Schüttler, *Mitglieder*, 41, 101; Krebs, 'Deutsches Museum', 8.

revolutionary principles, even though Dohm later clearly emerged as an advanced *Aufklärer* with strong egalitarian and democratic sympathies.[11] Even Wekhrlin, despite his enthusiasm for the *Histoire philosophique* and sympathy for the revolt of the Peruvian Incas against Spain, minces his words, refraining from expressing positive support for the American Revolution.[12]

To this pattern there was a conspicuous exception, but one that proves the rule. At the close of the revolutionary war, after Prussia recognized the new United States and was negotiating a trade treaty with American representatives in Holland, there appeared in the *Berlinische Monatsschrift* a long, four-page ode to American freedom signed only with the initials J.F.H.L. This ode, composed by Johann Friedrich Herel (1745–1800), a professor of philology at Erfurt, warmly praised the fighters for American Independence and suggested Britain had received her just deserts for her 'tyrannical conduct and for causing the war'. Furthermore, it boldly averred that the 'tyranny' so gloriously overthrown in America differed little from that prevailing in Europe and in the German states in particular. It was unmistakably an ode not just to American freedom but liberty in general and more than this, echoing Raynal, a eulogy also to 'süsse Gleichheit' [sweet equality] that even ventured to style nobility 'Europens Pest' [Europe's plague].[13] In short, it expressed an unequivocally Radical Enlightenment view of the American Revolution. The response was a violent polemic in the press, largely condemnatory, the sharpest retort issuing from Schlözer who redoubled his efforts in defence not just of Britain but of the principles of monarchy and aristocracy and the system of princely rule in Germany.

From 1776, the question whether the Enlightenment was inherently prone to foment revolutionary awareness and create a social context dangerous to the stability of the social order, monarchy, and the Christian religion lay at the heart of the Enlightenment's self-questioning. Inevitably, such debates estranged the two rival wings of the Enlightenment from each other more and more. Moderate Enlightenment now increasingly stressed the dangers and risks of subversion, Kant always staunchly opposing change by revolution in principle even though he later contradicted himself by speaking forcefully over a period of years in favour of the French Revolution.[14] Radical Enlightenment (usually) disavowed violence but openly embraced the principle of revolution if not necessarily in the sense of a general uprising then certainly in the sense of a general transformation of values, attitudes, and institutions. Among the most widely read tracts presenting the moderate view was one entitled *Über Aufklärung* [On Enlightenment] anonymously published by the Prussian Lutheran pastor Andreas Riem (1749–1807), in early 1788. Riem warned against both the religious and political dangers posed by 'false enlighteners, hotheads who pass their notions off as philosophy, and their mistakes as truth'.[15]

[11] Krebs, 'Deutsches Museum', 2, 6–8, 11; Lichtenberg, *Schriften und Briefe*, iv. 760; Delinière, 'Polémique', 53; Beiser, *Enlightenment*, 350.   [12] Mondot, 'Wekhrlin et la Révolution', 132–4.
[13] Delinière, 'Polémique', 58–9; for the poem, see ibid. 64–7; Krebs, *Helvétius*, 103.
[14] Ellis, *Kant's Politics*, 37, 82, 106–7, 143–4; Kersting, 'Politics', 360.
[15] Riem, 'On Enlightenment', 172.

If Enlightenment means spreading 'the truth' and reason's sway then, like Christ's message, held Riem, an admirer of the Neologists, Teller, Jerusalem, and Spalding, it cannot be extended too far. But in what he calls the widespread 'deception' perverting the true message of the Enlightenment he espied vast danger. In his pamphlet, he cites both the American and Dutch revolutions as blatant instances of mass social and political subversion, disasters ruinous for all mankind not just the Americans and Dutch, catastrophes both caused not by 'enlightened' thinking but false Enlightenment ideas. According to Riem, five years after the revolutionary war ended, the American Revolution was a highly 'destructive political revolution' born of 'deception', practised both in Britain and in America. Had British ministers understood the real position in America better, they would have acted differently. 'If the colonies had acted without deception', they would not now find themselves in an anarchic state maintained with 'weak bonds without any majesty, a state whose constitution is without true inner greatness and without the force that a well-ordered state ruled by a sovereign must have'.[16] 'False' Enlightenment was the source of the rot and direly threatened the whole world.

Likewise, the United Provinces were more stable and happier before 1780, under uncontested Orangist sway. Unfortunately, the democrats had gained the upper hand and won widespread support by employing 'false' philosophy and 'deception'. If the legitimacy and justification of the Dutch Revolt against Philip II, was undeniable, Riem roundly denied the legitimacy of the Dutch democratic movement of the 1780s. 'Was it truth and Enlightenment or foolishness and deception that made [the Netherlands] an object of intrigue, a theater of riot, rebellion and civil war? Had not its unenlightened demagogues led it to the brink of the abyss whence it would have toppled into the depths of the most frenzied anarchy had not the enlightened genius of Prussia rushed to save it?'[17] Astoundingly for us today, for Riem, Prussian military intervention, directed by an absolute monarch, ruthlessly deployed to suppress a democratic movement, represented what was 'enlightened' while the democratic movement embodied wrong philosophy, 'deception', and what is 'unenlightened'.

Prominent conservative officials and professors, such as Möser, Schlözer, and Rehberg, expressed similar viewpoints. For them too, adopting the proper attitude towards the American and Dutch revolutions was a question of differentiating between true and false Enlightenment, though for Rehberg supporting the American, Dutch, and French revolutions was less a question of 'deception' than erroneously projecting 'pure, theoretical reason' into the realm of the political relations where it does not belong.[18] Tradition, the legacy of the past, existing forms, cannot just be negated and swept aside by 'reason'; this is what rendered 'philosophy' of a certain kind exceedingly dangerous. Rehberg, who was to emerge as one of the leading ideological opponents of the French Revolution in Germany in the early 1790s,

---

[16] Ibid. 177.   [17] Ibid.
[18] Rehberg, *Untersuchungen*, i. 8, 17–18, 55; Knudsen, *Justus Möser*, 184–5.

never doubted that the prime cause of what he saw as an overwhelming, unmitigated disaster for all humanity stemmed from wrongly applying pure mathematical-philosophical reason, culminating in Sieyès's famous pamphlet 'What is the Third Estate?' This he styled a 'powerful, shallow, badly written, declamation' based on reasoning out of place, pitiful, and ignorant.[19] The catastrophe that to his mind ensued consisted above all in the destruction of privilege and nobility by the subversive principle of equality.[20] And what was the essential cause of so great a social and political calamity? Who can doubt that it lay in injecting the concept of *volonté générale*, itself a product of a 'philosophical dream' of pure reason leading inexorably, he states, to Spinozism, into the political realm where it is totally out of place.

Culturally significant encounters between the German literary and intellectual elite, the American Revolution, and the Dutch Revolt of 1572 as a discreet surrogate for contemporary revolution and as a key debating and literary topic in the 1780s, were bound to arise in so highly fraught an intellectual context. In his *Tractatus Theologico-Politicus*, Spinoza maintains, mainly for reasons of tact and prudence, that the Dutch Revolt against Philip II of Spain, unlike the English Revolution of the 1640s, was actually not a people's rebellion but a legitimate, justified 'restoring' of the 'freedom of the citizenry' that had been usurped by Charles V and then Philip II of Spain, rulers who, in the Low Countries, were merely counts, not kings, and, consequently, were there nothing but overbearing 'tyrants', seizing what they were not entitled to. Charles V and Philip II had violated the laws by behaving as monarchs in the Netherlands when they were not monarchs. This was a conventional enough explanation in the Dutch Republic of the seventeenth and eighteenth centuries. But in the Germany of the 1780s, this subtle, if deeply ambiguous way of portraying usurpation and tyranny as something wholly distinct from true monarchy provided a rare opportunity for discussing and exploring the meaning of revolution in a public sphere saturated with traditional notions of princely and religious authority, obedience, and aristocratic primacy. It was a safe and clever ploy as Protestant publicists had always agreed in the past that the Dutch Revolt of 1572 was legitimate, even if they usually interpreted it as a religious struggle against the papacy and Inquisition and one that subordinated its incipient democratic tendencies to the supposedly wise, glorious, and devout princely authority of William of Orange.[21]

In this way, the potent myth of the allegedly illegitimate 'tyranny' of Philip II of Spain in the Low Countries and the supposedly praiseworthy and legitimate Dutch Revolt became a surrogate for open debate among German journalists, dramatists, poets, and publicists during and immediately after the American Revolution. The Dutch Revolt provided a respectable vehicle for portraying, considering, and perhaps even exalting popular insurrection against tyranny in the name of 'freedom', law,

---

[19] Rehberg, *Untersuchungen*, i. 88–91, 102.   [20] Ibid. i. 89, 102.
[21] Krebs, 'Deutsches Museum', 3–4.

piety, and the 'constitution'. The pivotal and special ambivalence of the Dutch Revolt in central Europe during these years stemmed from its having welled up from below, engineered by the people but being led by a much celebrated prince. William of Orange headed a rebellion against a Catholic monarch whom even de Pinto, Schlözer, and Riem deemed an unmitigated 'tyrant'.[22] The drama of the Dutch Revolt thus evolved in the German context, not least in the hands of Goethe and Schiller, a uniquely powerful but yet delicate form of politico-cultural mythology permitting consideration of whether or not it offered what Wehrlin claimed was a universally valid model of struggle for freedom and better government.

Writers had to be extremely discreet. The theatres, like the papers, were strictly controlled. Among the regulations of the Vienna Burgtheater, issued in 1778, for example, it was declared 'improper to seek to spread certain libertarian sentiments in monarchical states'.[23] But neither the theatres nor the journals, nor university lecture courses, were normally likely to suppress allusions where these were sufficiently dressed up in unobjectionable historical guises. Dramatizing the Dutch Revolt for the press or the stage thus lent itself peculiarly well to being used as quietly subversive propaganda in that such debate could readily be made to resemble an innocent literary or historicizing exercise, even though all could see that the theme was actually powerfully topical on multiple levels. Essays and plays dealing with the Dutch Revolt hence became an integral part of the contemporary weave of central European Enlightenment culture and politics.

The Dutch Revolt was uniquely topical, tactful, and appropriate but also highly complex and ambiguous, indeed enveloped in contradiction historically, politically, and philosophically. For the princes of Orange, having first led the Revolt and helped found the United Provinces, afterwards, in the eyes of many, including Wehrlin, betrayed both the people and the true Dutch freedom. By establishing a hereditary stadholderate in 1747, and tightening the reins of favouritism, court intrigue, and oligarchy, the mid- and late eighteenth-century stadholders were widely felt to have established a new 'despotism' based on usurpation, illegality, and arrogance. This renewed tyranny blighting the Netherlands culminated, held Wehrlin, after William IV 's death when his widow, Anna of Hanover, daughter of the British king, purposely selected the fat, authoritarian, and highly unpopular Ludwig Ernst, duke of Brunswick, to preside over the Dutch court, army, and patronage machine and, in particular, cement the country's 'subservience' to Britain, coupling aristocratic *anglomanie* with princely authority, corruption, and betrayal of the people, all features at the time with a far-reaching resonance in Germany.[24]

Goethe first drafted his play *Egmont* in 1782 but then abandoned it for some years, despite its being well advanced, worrying lest it might be politically imprudent to complete it in the form in which he originally cast it, with the Patriot commotion

---

[22] Riem, 'On Enlightenment', 177–8; Wehrlin, *Graue Ungeheuer*, 9 (1786), 157–63.
[23] Brandt, *German and Dutch Theatre*, 205.
[24] Wehrlin, *Graue Ungeheuer*, 9 (1786), 341–5; Israel, *Dutch Republic*, 1080–4, 1090–4.

growing in intensity. Only in 1787, following Prussia's suppression of the new Dutch revolution, did Goethe hit on the adroit solution of merging the play's political resonance with a countervailing ethical and emotional message, enabling him to heroicize and draw the public's sympathy to his central character, Egmont, without rendering the latter too obviously an opponent of absolutism, monarchy, and religious authority.[25] Egmont's significance is precisely that it is his superior insight and moral uprightness that inspire him to sacrifice himself in the way that best, and least disruptively, serves the people's interest and unifies the populace against the tyrannical threat they face. Goethe completed his *Egmont* in Italy, during the heat of the Roman summer of 1787, steeped in Herder's latest book and the great German Spinoza controversy whilst hearing of the outbreak of the new revolt in the southern Netherlands, against Joseph II's reforms. This Brabant rebellion too invoked William the Silent and the Revolt of 1572. How strange, remarked Goethe, 'to think that in Brussels at this moment, they are enacting scenes which I wrote twelve years ago'.[26] 'I have never before felt so free in spirit while writing a play', he added, still in Rome some weeks later, and still musing about the *Pantheismusstreit*, 'nor finished one with more scrupulous care'.[27] The play was published a year before the outbreak of the French Revolution, in 1788.

Much engrossed at the same time in working out his botanical theory, Goethe withdrew somewhat into his shell during the weeks he was finishing the piece, avoiding Roman high society: 'the fashion of this world passeth away', he reminded himself, adding that 'my only desire is to follow Spinoza's teaching and concern myself with what is everlasting so as to win eternity for my soul'.[28] These were weeks in which Goethe enthusiastically renewed his commitment to Herder's approach and to the idea that the greatest art, man's greatest masterpieces, are created 'in obedience to the same law as the masterpieces of Nature. Before them, all that is arbitrary and imaginary collapses: there is Necessity, there is God'.[29] In the weeks after completing it, still at Rome, he continued in this deeply contemplative mood, meditating on what divided him and Herder from the likes of Jacobi, Lavater, and Claudius and formulating some naturalistic questions which he and Herder wished to propose to Georg Forster, who was then about to embark on a new transoceanic journey.[30]

A member of the Weimar masonic lodge since 1780, in February 1783 Goethe also joined the Illuminati of which Herder was already a member, albeit still gaining no access to Weishaupt's philosophical texts despite rising to the Order's fairly high grade of 'regent'.[31] It probably never entered his mind that he himself might conspire and act against the princes or the court system and, in any case, he quickly became

25 Ellis, 'Vexed Question', 117, 128; Boyle, *Goethe*, i. 515.
26 Goethe, *Italian Journey*, 360, 362, 365.
27 Ibid. 416.
28 Ibid. 377; Ellis, 'Vexed Question', 128–9.
29 Goethe, *Italian Journey*, 385, 401.
30 Ibid. 401–4; Irmscher, 'Goethe und Herder', l252–6.
31 Mulsow, 'Adam Weishaupt', 28.

disillusioned with the whole business. In fact, he uttered not a word of criticism of the Prussian and British leaders who suppressed the Dutch democratic movement in 1787. Goethe was decidedly no democrat and no revolutionary. Rather he viewed the whole conflict in Holland as a prolonged, unnecessary disturbance. Hearing that the Prussians had invaded the United Provinces and taken Amsterdam, he reported the forceful, largely non-violent suppression of the democrats, in a letter to Herder, as a justified piece of firmness. 'This would be the first engagement in which our century shows itself in all its greatness,' he affirmed, declaring himself a 'child of peace' and one henceforth resolved to 'live in peace with the whole world'. 'Without a sword being drawn, with just a cannon shot or two, the whole affair is over and nobody wants to prolong it.'[32]

But still, as a self-proclaimed Spinozist, enemy of conventional thinking, and scientist, he needed to explore the problem of rebellion against tyranny and the issue of revolution. It is remarkable that both Goethe's *Egmont* and Schiller's *Don Carlos* were completed in the year of the Prussian stifling of the *Patriottenbeweging*, in 1787. In the finished version of Goethe's play, the audience is shown a 'just' revolution, achieved by the 'Netherlanders' represented as a people composed of worthy artisans, shopkeepers, and the like, a revolution in which a despotic monarch is abjured and repudiated. The play shows a people rising indignantly to defend its 'constitution' against monarchical tyranny and its insidious ways, the latter being lent a clearly Herderian resonance. The king's refusal to permit toleration is deemed a clear sign of unacceptable tyranny that justifies revolution. In this way, Goethe creates a 'revolution of the stage' as something morally justifiable and even attractive, just as he had earlier reconfigured suicide, with his *Werther*, a book banned in Saxony when it first appeared and, as we have seen, prohibited in Italy. But while glorifying Egmont, Goethe depicts him not as a foe of monarchy, or leader of the revolution of which he became a symbol, but rather as the victim of a tragedy of politics whose insight into men enables him to combine heroic efforts to restrain popular anger and remain loyal to the king, while yet dying for 'freedom' in a more intensely personal and ambivalent way than would any genuine revolutionary.[33] His beheading is due, moreover, not to harsh royal despotism but the ruthless inhumanity of an overly powerful and errant military commander, Alva.

One of Herder's—and d'Holbach's, Cerisier's, and, later Paape's—favourite themes, the need for different peoples to develop a new kind of international ethics in which they respect and value each other as equals, and take care to avoid war, just as Spinoza's individuals do for the greater mutual security, reciprocal help, and advantages in this world, reverberates in the closing scenes, preceding Egmont's execution. Alva's natural son Ferdinand, denying he is a 'foreigner' to such a man as Egmont and deploring his father's duplicity, expresses admiration for the hero's personality and understanding of what his far-seeing, purely inwardly revolutionary,

---

[32] Goethe, *Italian Journey*, 402–3.
[33] Boyle, *Goethe*, i. 517; Kerry, *Enlightenment Thought*, 59, 61–5.

new ethic promises humanity.[34] Their reconciliation at the close revives the doomed Egmont's faith in humanity, symbolizing the possibility of a renewed international order based on ethics, mutual help, and respect. In Egmont, there are Spinozistic and Herderian dimensions but no anti-monarchical or revolutionary message per se.

Schiller too composed a great drama about Philip II and tyranny slowly and painstakingly, while shifting course through the fraught circumstances of the 1780s. Redrafting his *Don Carlos* again and again, over much of the period from 1783 to 1787, taking far 'too long' by his own admission in writing it, he experienced the utmost difficulty in finishing the play.[35] Again the central character, the marquis of Posa, is 'not a revolutionist', as Carlyle later explained, 'but a prudent though determined improver'.[36] Nevertheless, there were blatantly revolutionary aspects to his role: for while Posa aspires to work with and through the crown if he can, he wants Philip to emancipate mankind, create our world anew—'O give us freedom of thought'—and employ his monarchy's resources for the 'people's good', restoring man's ' lost nobility'. In fact, the improvements Schiller (Posa) seeks are so far-reaching that were his agenda to materialize, it would entail the political, social, and religious transformation of the entire world, a universal revolution but, he hopes, a peaceful one.[37] In this sense Schiller's early creative period as a writer was truly a 'revolutionäre Jugendperiode' [revolutionary youth phase], as Georg Lucacs termed it. For a time, he was strongly inspired by republican ideals and a virtual, if also hesitant, philosophical radical, one who supported the early phases of the French Revolution, repudiating it only from late 1792 as populist authoritarianism took control.[38]

It was on the ground of his sympathy and support that the French National Assembly, on the initiative of the radical playwright Marie-Joseph Chénier, in August 1792, made Schiller an honorary citizen of the republic along with George Washington and Pestalozzi.[39] By the mid 1780s, not unlike Goethe earlier, Schiller had experienced a deep inner crisis concerning religion, composed several poems rejecting the idea of divine providence (in which he had once fervently believed), and converted to a worldly, philosophically 'enlightened' ethics.[40] His favourite teacher at his high school, the Karlschule, in Stuttgart, Jacob Friedrich Abel (1751–1829), was a fervent disciple of Lessing and, from 1787, of Kant, and ardent advocate of philosophy teaching in education. An Illuminist and leading advocate of Enlightenment reform in Württemberg, Abel deeply affected the young poet's imagination, rendering him one of the most erudite as well as philosophically involved of the great writers of the Enlightenment. Already at school, he had read extensively in recent German, French, and British philosophy.[41] His *Don Carlos* (1787) figures among the

---

[34] Kerry, *Enlightenment Thought*, 68–70; Ellis, 'Vexed Question', 128; Boyle, *Goethe*, i. 519.
[35] Schiller, *Briefe über Don Carlos*, 197; Carlyle, *Life*, 76–7; Beiser, *Schiller*, 238.
[36] Carlyle, *Life*, 66.
[37] Schiller, *Don Carlos*, 121–4, 203.   [38] Alt, 'Schiller and Politics', 12–13, 15.
[39] Ibid. 14; Karthaus, 'Schiller', 211.   [40] Beiser, *Schiller*, 31.
[41] Ibid. 16; Schings, *Brüder*, 25–8; Riedel, 'Aufklärung und Macht', 114–15.

greatest dramas in German. Its central figure, Posa, is not just a full-blown republican visionary set on advancing mankind's happiness but also a powerful literary symbol expressing the spirit of what Schiller knew of the Illuminatist leader Knigge whom he met in 1784. Knigge, on bad terms with Goethe whose personal aloofness he detested, reciprocally admired Schiller as 'perhaps the greatest genius of our times'. Posa also represented other committed Illuminati that he knew, including Abel.[42] Like Abel and Knigge, Schiller too supported the American Revolution and Dutch democratic movement of the 1780s.[43]

Ardently opposed to intolerance and political tyranny, Schiller had already expressed loathing of Philip's tyranny, in his rather free translation of Mercier's *Philip II, King of Spain* into German, published in 1786.[44] Yet, from the outset, Schiller also opposed the materialism of Helvétius and d'Holbach, harbouring a growing suspicion of the abstract, and preference for the concrete, traits that later led to his adopting Kantianism as his philosophical creed.[45] Posa 'advocates the cause of truth and justice, and humanity', as Carlyle puts it, with 'glowing eloquence', much as 'Schiller too would have employed in similar circumstances'; but as he worked on *Don Carlos*, Schiller's doubts about the Illuminati and the 'Posa' syndrome inwardly grew. He also needed to adjust his standpoint outwardly, due to the sudden discrediting of the Illuminati and massive suspicion surrounding them, after 1785.

Among the accusations levelled against the Illuminati during and after their suppression, in 1785–7, as we shall see, was the claim that for all their rhetoric of liberty and emancipation, their organization masked a despotic, fanatical leadership excessively inclined (as Posa is to a degree) to intrigue. Precisely this defect Schiller highlights in his freedom-fighter, especially with his remarks on Posa's shortcomings in his *Letters over Don Carlos* (1787), a text he published soon afterwards, in Wieland's *Teutsche Merkur*.[46] From 1786–7 onwards, Schiller's pessimism and scepticism about spreading liberty and Enlightenment via organizations such as secret societies, as well as by revolution, waxed steadily stronger.[47] By the time he completed *Don Carlos*, he had already commenced his retreat from a fully radical stance. The *Letters over Don Carlos* were needed to address the public's considerable bewilderment about the play's meaning. In his letters, Schiller makes no attempt to hide the fact that, whilst writing it, he himself had long agonized over the play's political message, changing his mind several times and in major respects. Neither does he try to mask the ambiguity of his haunting vision, expressing both the nobility and the ruinous idealism of his revolutionary republican who liberates men. Posa's attempt to establish a new and better kind of state and society, on the basis of the loftiest ideals and concepts, fails with disastrous consequences.[48]

[42] Riedel, 'Aufklärung und Macht', 87–9; Borchmeyer, 'Kritik', 367, 376; Hermann, *Knigge*, 68–9, 136–7.
[43] High, *Schillers Rebellionskonzept*, 1–6, 9.
[44] Ibid. 28–30; Alt, 'Schiller and Politics', 19.
[45] Borchmeyer, 'Kritik', 364; Schings, *Brüder*, 145, 187.
[46] Schings, *Brüder*, 92, 101–2; Schiller, *Briefe über Don Carlos*, 233–4; Hermann, *Knigge*, 136.
[47] Borchmeyer, 'Kritik', 367–9; Karthaus, 'Schiller', 217–19.
[48] Schings, *Brüder*, 101, 196; High, *Schillers Rebellionskonzept*, 50–1.

Schiller next set himself the task of writing a narrative history of the Dutch Revolt and at the same time, as Carlyle later aptly put it, interweaving with this narrative the philosophical themes that he believed it raised—'points of polity, and national and individual character', animating the 'whole with that warm sympathy which, in a lover of freedom, this most glorious of her triumphs naturally called forth'.[49] Immersing himself in the sixteenth-century sources, Schiller spent several years engaged in researching the 'Revolution' of 1572, to use his term for it,[50] at Weimar and at Jena where he settled in 1787 and, then, in composing his history of the commencement of the Revolt, entitled *Geschichte des Abfalls der Vereinigten Niederlande von der spanischen Regierung* (1789). Despite initially failing to establish close relations with Goethe, who had then just returned from his Italian journey but who disliked *Don Carlos*, he quickly established amicable relations with Wieland and Herder and got to know Reinhold. Goethe became his close friend only later. While contemplating the 'history of that memorable rebellion which forever severed the United Netherlands from the Spanish crown', he continued to examine closely the proposition that there is a recourse 'against the arrogant usurpations of regal power' and 'plans against the liberty of mankind', namely to rebel and persist in 'heroic perseverance'. Schiller in 1789 still eulogized the Dutch Revolt as expressing 'a spirit of independence', the new 'views of truth' having enabled the insurgents 'to examine the authority of antiquated opinions' and reject received ideas.

It was this that enabled them to rise up heroically and break 'the severe rod of despotism' menacing them, shattering the 'arbitrary power [which] threatened to tear away the foundations of their happiness'.[51] His explicit purpose in writing the history 'of this great revolution' was to 'awaken in the breast of my reader a spirit-stirring consciousness of his own powers'.[52] But, again he remained alive to the very real dangers society risks from leaders who come forward offering to organize revolution. It was fortunate for Schiller's subsequent reputation, notes Carlyle, that Posa's speeches and his account of the Revolt 'were not penned several years later, for his ardent celebration of freedom would then have been imputed to the influence of the French Revolution' and he 'might have been called a Jacobin'; as it was reaction-ary writers denounced him as a conspirator sympathizing with the Illuminati.[53] Briefly, his history was a success, though the first volume goes no further than Alva's arrival in the Low Countries, in 1567. Unsurprisingly in the fraught circum-stances, no second volume ever appeared.

It was on the strength of this work, and largely through Goethe's intercession (Goethe having now befriended him), that Schiller was offered the chair in history at Jena by the duchess of Sachsen-Weimar-Eisenach (1739–1807), in 1789. For some years subsequently, Schiller was primarily a historian and student of philosophy. Commencing the series of lectures that he gave on 'universal history' at Jena in 1789,

---

[49] Carlyle, *Life*, 85.   [50] Schiller, *Briefe über Don Carlos*, 204.
[51] Schiller, *History of the Revolt*, 11.   [52] Ibid. 8–11, 23.
[53] Carlyle, *Life*, 76; Hermann, *Knigge*, 267, 287.

he proclaimed 'the philosophical spirit' the only proper agent for making sense of historical studies and the only way to discover any worthwhile meaning in human history which for him was the history of 'freedom' and the construction of modern sociability.[54] The advance of the 'philosophical spirit' was also what led men to understand the complex reality, including history, shaping our lives, thereby giving rise to the Enlightenment; and that same shaping, ordering agent, philosophical reason, is what educates us to see how the human reality must be reformed and reorganized.[55]

Posa stands for the ageless opponent of tyrants and Inquisitors who extols 'freedom' and seeks to accomplish what Schiller calls an 'allgemeine Duldung und Gewissensfreiheit' [universal toleration and freedom of thought]. Yet, not only his original ardour for Posa's idealism and 'republikanische Freiheit' [republican free-dom],[56] but other early convictions slowly withered, plunging the poet into a deep intellectual crisis rooted in what he envisaged as a clash between reason and feeling that left him in no mood to address students or pursue his academic career at Jena. Having abandoned all notion of the universe being guided by providence, he felt increasingly afflicted by the spectre of materialism and emptiness in the soul.[57] What helped him cope with this personal crisis, and the drama of the collapse of Illuminism, was Kant's idea that wherever 'theoretical reason', reason in the abstract, takes charge the result is a one-sided grasp of reality that easily gets out of hand potentially with tragic circumstances. This became an enduring conviction that turned Schiller more and more away from radical ideas and revolution as a mean-ingful or viable option for men.

The retreat of ignorance and superstition was impressive, explained Schiller, in his *Philosophische Briefe* (1786), but what had occurred was really just 'a half Enlighten-ment' [*Halbe-Aufklärung*], leaving questions of society's core moral values and the role of authority more clouded than ever.[58] From an early point in his career, Schiller veered by turns vigorously and hesitantly towards the Radical Enlightenment until becoming partially disillusioned with the French Revolution late in 1792. But he was never wholehearted about this and remained somewhat ambivalent, significantly, also long afterwards, never fully repudiating the Revolution after 1792. If one considers only philosophical arguments based on reason, he always acknowledged, then radical thought is undoubtedly more coherent than received thinking and officially sanctioned systems. Nevertheless, his heart told him that philosophical reason cannot be the whole story. He did not so much reject radical thought as socially and culturally harmful, as so many did, as qualify it as a 'one-sided and unstable philosophy, all the more dangerous' precisely because it 'blinds our clouded Reason with the appearance of justice, truth and conviction'.[59]

---

[54] Schiller, *Universalhistorische Schriften*, 414–18.   [55] Ibid. 428.
[56] Schiller, *Briefe über Don Carlos*, 196; High, *Schillers Rebellionskonzept*, 27.
[57] Beiser, *Schiller*, 42–4.
[58] Schiller, *Philosophische Briefe*, 29.   [59] Ibid.

3. ART AS THE NEW 'RELIGION'

Goethe professed Spinozism, Schiller eventually Kantianism. But both were in search of ways to exit from the dilemmas they saw, and the tragedy they felt was implicit, in the logic of Revolution. If he still had his difficulties, Kant had at any rate emerged as the great synthesizer of the traditions of British empiricism and European rationalism. Dividing reality and the human condition into totally separate spheres that can never meet or interact—*phenomena* and *noumena*, reason and sensibility, scientific knowledge and moral knowledge—for many proved a cogent way to restore reason's autonomy albeit now within strict limits while reconstituting theology and transforming philosophy into a self-contained specialism ruling only the individual soul that is sensitive and learned while also offering a programme of slow, gradual reform of society and politics. The implications of this for morality, social awareness, and politics were far-reaching. Yet, despite this, as the reactions of Goethe, Herder, and Wieland showed, such a coldly dispassionate, all-encompassing system of dualism along with Kant's ungainly written style ultimately repelled not a few thinkers, artists, and scientists besides students.

At the same time, it was scarcely possible for a Goethe or a Schiller, however troubled by the prospect of revolution, not also to be deeply disturbed by the menace of reaction. The philosophical-emotional crisis these great writers experienced in these years hinged on whether complete estrangement from conventional thinking and tradition must translate into a revolutionary consciousness, or whether there exists, after all, another way to revolutionize the world, an alternative way to reject received values and the thought of the past, creating a new and higher reality not by means of mass action but inwardly, without engaging in outward revolution.

Among those estranged from the values of the society around them, some could see no alternative to combating those values head-on. Besides Wekhrlin, Diez, Dohm, Forster, Weishaupt, Knigge, Thorild, and Herel, these included the Göttingen-trained jurist of lesser noble extraction from Nassau-Dillenburg, prominent also as head of an underground group of opponents of princely authoritarianism at Giessen, Karl von Knoblauch (1756–94). Implacable opponent of despotism and popular credulity who referred to Europe's monarchs (and the Roman emperors before them), as 'Sultane' [sultans], Knoblauch fully embraced Spinozism and hylozoism. An important point for him was the need to dispel any notion that Spinoza's metaphysics involves a fatalism incompatible with the right to resist tyranny.[60] To his mind Spinoza's philosophy was not just something philosophically profound, convincing, and modern but also closely akin to an entire tradition of other 'modern' philosophy—the ideas of Diderot and d'Holbach, philosophers who stood 'close to Spinoza', as his friend Wekhrlin expressed it. In addition, there was Helvétius and other materialist thinkers of high moral calibre whose metaphysical, social, and political

---

[60] Knoblauch, *Taschenbuch*, 63–5; Knoblauch, *Politisch-philosophische Gespräche*, 107–8.

thought, according to Wekhrlin and Knoblauch, 'stands at [Spinozism's] edge constantly apt to being blown on to [Spinoza's] territory by every gust of wind'.[61] Ideas derived from contemplating the creative power of nature, the insight that the laws governing it are always the same and the key to understanding how best to organize human life, seemed to them and others more relevant than Kantianism as a path to reforming society's defects.[62] But recognition that Spinoza infuses the whole tradition of French late Enlightenment materialism and that his moral ideas, politics, and theory of human emotions, 'the affects' which he had tried to turn into a demonstrative science, 'are full of important but little-known truths', as Wekhrlin expressed it in 1787, led to Spinozism being pressed into service as the underpinning of both an outward and inward revolutionary consciousness.

But there was another path. Goethe and Schiller convinced themselves they had found the inward way. What does it mean to strip divine providence from one's view of nature and acknowledge that man's body and soul constitute a single substance? It could signify a re-evaluation of all values taking place entirely within. By this route, Spinoza revived in German-speaking lands also became linked to an aloof, quiescent, politically passive current sharing with the activist revolutionary approach of the 1770s and 1780s a new conception of humanity and total rejection of divine providence and governance of the world, and the *ancien régime*, morally, intellectually, and scientifically, but seeking not a transformation of social and political circumstances but to discover and explore the eternal in nature and man, the universality of morality and oneness of what is best, most lasting, and noblest, especially as manifested in ancient Greece and what today we call Renaissance Italy.

Does the oneness of body and spirit not really mean that the eternal and the transitory, as Schiller expressed the point, however contradictory in appearance, must somehow be unified in what is human and in human life?[63] Instead of sighing over man's ineradicably evil nature, the aware person now had to consider what discarding the old morality, religious disposition, and metaphysical framework really entails for moral, cultural, and spiritual life. Realizing that man does not stand outside of nature, has no supernatural guide or supernaturally given values or laws, and is neither good nor evil in nature, must involve reconstructing one's inner world but not necessarily the world outside. 'Nothing happens in nature, Benedict teaches us, that can be ascribed' as Wekhrlin put it, 'to any defect in nature.'[64] The implications for self-seeking, altruism, abstinence, and monasticism besides eroticism of all kinds including homosexuality were obviously far-reaching. Everything had to be re-examined in a new light.

The 'revolution of the mind, in short', could be an outwardly oriented revolution transforming law, politics, institutions, and morality, hence fomenting a new kind of

---

[61] Wekhrlin, *Graue Ungeheuer*, 4 (178), 298, 303, 309.
[62] Ibid. 11 (1787), 115–17; Knoblauch, *Anti-Taumaturgie*, 15–16, 23.
[63] Schiller, *On the Aesthetic Education*, 67–9, 72; Taylor, *Perspectives*, 22–30.
[64] Wekhrlin, *Graue Ungeheuer*, 11 (1787), 116.

individual as a consequence of political revolution and legal revolution, something the young Fichte, Hegel, Schelling, and Hölderlin were all deeply preoccupied with through the 1790s. But Spinoza could also be taken to heart in a way that detaches his philosophy from social and political concerns, via a 'revolution of the mind and of sensibility' transforming the individual outlook, an artistic, cultural, and moral emancipation separate from social and political concerns, yielding no changes in laws and institutions but instead creatively elevating and inspiring a thinly spread cultural elite composed of the most creative, independent, and sensitive. Spinoza revived could loom democratic and socially reformist or else merely promote Goethe's and Schiller's idea of artistic 'revolution' confined to a tiny group.

Spinoza's doctrine that there are no 'final ends' in the universe, 'that the world considered as a whole, can have no purpose', as Knoblauch expressed it, meant that henceforth meaning and value must be sought in the 'eternal', understood as the highest form, or most sublime expression, of the this-worldly, in man's life in the here and now.[65] The new Spinozists believed they had at last found a philosophy that puts the human condition in its proper perspective, planting in Goethe's and Schiller's minds especially the idea that literary genius, rather than being in receipt of divine inspiration, is poetically and artistically elevated above the common run of things and that it is their special artistic and scientific insight, nurturing men's deepest insights and intuitions, that brings mankind closest to 'God', that is to nature. This orientation lent a special priority to art, literature, and also to aesthetics as a field of philosophy. On meeting Hemsterhuis when the latter visited Weimar with Princess Amalia Golitsyn in 1785, it was not the Dutch thinker's metaphysics but his aesthetic ideas and elitist, aristocratic sensibility that Goethe was keen to learn about, though he was not free to range across the board as Hemsterhuis and the pious princess had made it clear beforehand that they refused to discuss Spinoza and the *Pantheismusstreit*.[66]

The social and political context was a harsh one, everywhere characterized by expanding aristocracy, princely power, and police surveillance, in Vienna, Berlin, Königsberg, Munich, Prague, and Budapest alike. Against this backcloth, a new heightened artistic sensibility offered the artist a tempting escape route to another world, a way to rise above social and political concerns, an exit encouraging cultivation of a strain of cultural Spinozism wholly divorced from the harsh realities of both the revolutionary impulse and the prevailing status quo. If Goethe's Spinozism eschewed materialism linked to egalitarianism and democracy in quest of an exultant nature worship and artistic self-emancipation behind the shield of existing institutions and enlightened despotism, his second stay in Rome, from June 1787 until early 1788, marked the culmination not just of his Italian journey but a kind of inner pilgrimage to reconcile the spiritual, philosophical quest he had embarked on together with Herder and his Weimar friends with his poetic ambitions and efforts

[65] Knoblauch, *Euclides Anti-Thaumaturgicus*, 3, 14, 25–31.   [66] Verzaal, 'Besuch', 168–71, 174.

to forge a new approach to literary and art criticism of a sort that would satisfyingly unite modernity with the classical past.

Goethe professed to have been 'captured' by Spinozism, commented Rehberg who, later in 1809–10, was to lead the critical attack on Goethe's novel *Elective Affinities* (1809), denouncing it for corroding public morals. But he was drawn to Spinozism, he suggested, primarily because Spinoza removes divine governance and final causes. By silencing the gods and banishing intention from the design of everything, Spinoza projects a world that became Goethe's where every existing thing, sexual and suicidal urges included, is autonomously real but yet an expression of the deeper reality of nature, untrammelled by any alleged intrinsic moral status or other metaphysical abstraction of a supposedly higher order. For there is no higher order, for the Spinozist and, for Goethe, nothing external to nature. On the basis of this 'pantheistic immanentism', he constructed a world-view infused with a lofty aesthetic paganism from which religious authority and Christian abstinence are purged while the figure of Jesus is recast as a kind of superior, ultimate man. Where Jacobi, Wizenmann, and Rehberg escaped what the latter called the 'despairing nothingness' of acknowledging the autonomy of things in themselves, by opting for Burke, and Fichte combined inner renewal with radical politics, Goethe and Schiller anchored their thought in a new kind of inner religiosity rooted in artistic sensibility itself.[67]

Goethe travelled in Italy in an elevated mood so remote from the everyday realities of people's lives that 'it seems strange to me', he remarked, 'when I read a newspaper'. This estrangement from everyday reality is doubly paradoxical in his case since he was a leading official in the administration of Saxe-Weimar. In practice, Goethe had thrown in his lot with social and political conservatism and could cultivate his Spinozism exclusively in an aesthetic fashion. His self-immersion in Spinoza helped him devise a new form of abstraction, transforming his vision of art and literature but also alienating him, for all intents and purposes, as much from everyday social reality as any non-immanent metaphysical abstraction could have done. The outward forms of the world, including the social realities of Italy and its nobles, clergy, and peasantry, seemed scarcely to interest him; neither did Italy's politics. 'The form of the world is transitory. I prefer to occupy my mind exclusively with enduring conditions and thus, according to the teachings of *** [i.e. Spinoza], truly procure eternal life for my spirit.' 'Again and again' the *Italienische Reise* reaffirms Goethe's impulse to transcend smallness and find greatness.[68] Plainly he was immersed in a kind of religious quest. His constant urge to contemplate the totality of the arts in all their interconnectedness was connected to a philosophical vision aspiring to universality, harmony, and wholeness emancipated from the ordinary and banal. His second stay in Rome, infused with intense elation, he recollected later as a spiritual rebirth whereby he finally found himself in relation to the world and the art of the past. It was a vision that still found a certain place for politics and especially political

---

[67] Rehberg, *Sämmtliche Schriften*, i. 11–12; Nauen, *Revolution, Idealism*, 5.
[68] Hösle, 'Religion of Art', 6, 12; Tantillo, *Goethe's* Elective Affinities, 12–13.

heroes of the sort he envisaged himself as—men entrusted to soothe and calm the masses, check anarchy, and ensure the social harmony without which there can be no single-minded pursuit of art and the sublime.[69]

Schiller, by the early 1790s powerfully under the influence of a Goethe who reinforced his partial aversion to the politics of revolution and radical reformism, and inspired by Kant, was equally devoted to the pursuit of the sublime through art and equally committed to the idea that it is through the aesthetic that man rises from mere feeling to the meaningfully moral and rational. No doubt he too was tempted to withdraw into the autonomy of the aesthetic. But unlike Goethe he was still strongly inclined to a republican viewpoint; unlike most other German observers he never abandoned his personal commitment to the ideals of the French Revolution. No less resolved than Goethe to search for philosophical renewal,[70] he saw Kant's categories as useful for underpinning the new aesthetic and justifying rejection of some of the radical positions he had himself espoused in the early and mid 1780s. But he still sweepingly rejected the prevailing forms of society, politics, and morality, accusing the mainstream of modern philosophy of vainly trying to legitimize 'an oppression which was formerly authorized by the Church'.[71] This left him in a more complex intellectual and psychological posture than Goethe, strongly attached to the processes of both outward and inward 'revolution'. What Schiller now sought in philosophy was evidence that there is a higher life, open to every individual that involves transcending the merely utilitarian and corporeal, harmonizing bodily reality with man's higher nature, in particular through art, to forge a new kind of spiritual nobility through becoming uplifted via inspiration and virtue.[72] Here he was at one with Goethe, the beauty of high art is the widest and truest approach to unity and harmony in human life and the true equality among men; but neither could he let go of his social and political revolutionary tendency.

---

[69] Tantillo, *Goethe's* Elective Affinities, 12–13; Ellis, 'Vexed Question', 127–9.
[70] Schiller, *On the Aesthetic Education*, 47; Beiser, *Schiller*, 129–33.
[71] Karthaus, 'Schiller', 211–13.
[72] Nauen, *Revolution, Idealism*, 5; Taylor, *Secular Age*, 313, 610, 615.

Part V

Revolution

28

1788–1789

The 'General Revolution' Begins

1. NOBILITY VERSUS THE THIRD ESTATE

If Leibniz had been virtually alone in prophesying the potential of certain new ideas to revolutionize the world during the early Enlightenment,[1] such prophecies surfaced more and more frequently after 1760. According to the Parisian revolutionary journal *Chronique de Paris*, in April 1790, Rousseau, Voltaire, Helvétius, Hume, and Raynal had all predicted the Revolution, issuing prophecies royal ministers had once all mocked but now took very seriously, and no one could dispute that 'Raynal' and Mercier, in particular, had repeatedly predicted a great revolution.[2] Widespread after 1760, expectation that a fundamental revolution was pending that would transform everything fundamentally became positively ubiquitous in France in 1788 and during the tense weeks preceding the Estates-General's convening in 1789.

Later Enlightenment thinkers predicted the advent of a great revolution in the not too distant future precisely because the decades-old war of ideas in progress seemed inherently bound to produce an eventual political and ideological eruption with far-reaching social consequences. To some observers, it appeared that everyone, aware of it or not, was already implicated in some way in a universal tussle over the 'happiness of man', at stake being the survival of the existing social, religious, and political order. We clearly find this awareness, for instance, in the late diary entries of the leading Swiss *Aufklärer* Albrecht von Haller. Languishing at Berne, ill, depressed, addicted to opium, and in his last years distinctly wavering in his formerly solid religious faith, from around 1770 Haller was increasingly disturbed by the books piling up around his bed, especially, his entries show, those of Raynal, Mercier, Helvétius, and d'Holbach.[3]

---

[1] Leibniz, *New Essays*, 463; Hösle, *Morals and Politics*, 588; Israel, *Enlightenment Contested*, 9.
[2] *Chronique de Paris*, 99 (9 Apr. 1790), 393.
[3] Haller, *Tagebuch*, i. 177, 354–6 and ii. 15, 116, 208–10.

Haller was deeply preoccupied with the impact of these men, 'die neuen Philoso-phen' [i.e. the 'philosophes modernes' or the 'modern philosophers']. Once a banned, suppressed, barely perceptible underground they were now, he realized, permeating Europe and the wider world with such vigour as to change the general cultural landscape: their ideas, he feared, might well, one day, become hegemonic, the dominant way of thinking. If they did, his world would be hurled upside down and become 'inhabited by prejudice-free philosophers, with religion banished'.[4] Should this happen, 'it is, I believe, sufficiently proven that the new philosophy will prove the downfall of social life'. As every individual will make his or her own worldly happiness their goal in this new society, all individuals will compete with the rest resulting in the total dissolution of social bonds and that state of war of all against all of which Hobbes was the first to speak 'and that will not cease until faith gives rise to peace'.[5]

There would be no revolutionary menace had enlightened thought not begun to merge in some way since the 1750s and 1760s, in Paris especially, with artisan resentment, popular anticlericalism, and political discontent. But this fusion was occurring.[6] *Die moderne Philosophie* is a philosophical campaign the inner logic of which leads directly to revolution, averred Haller, and then to disaster and social breakdown. 'When once a philosophical rabble, an army trained in the secrets [of modern philosophy], realizes it is stronger than the individual prince or general, this proud discovery will powerfully manifest itself.' 'Our struggle with the freethinkers is not a purely theoretical struggle', therefore, but rather a 'war between Good and Evil, between the happiness of the world and its misery'.[7] The only way to fend off catastrophe was to fight harder, which in the Helvetic Confederation meant that the cantons, headed by Berne where he himself sat in the Great Council, must repress *die moderne Philosophie* more resolutely and render their subjects firmer in both religion and obedience by countering its doctrines more vigorously and systematic-ally—in the schools and churches as well as books.[8]

The role of the press, slogans, and popular reactions in shaping the early stages of the Revolution is recorded in some detail and roughly the same terms by numerous local and national journals of the years 1780–90 so that it is possible to gain a fairly detailed grasp of this crucial last phase of the cultural and social mechanics of concept infusion that during 1788–9 evolved into what was now a full-fledged Radical Enlightenment revolutionary discourse. This was the culminating phase of that process of intellectual (and cultural) diffusion that forged the Revolution. Censorship effectively ground to a halt in France in 1788, the result being a spec-tacular, unprecedented expansion of political and controversial publications. Over 1,500 pamphlets appeared between May and December 1788 and over 2,600 in the first four months of 1789 before the convening of the Estates-General. In France,

---

[4] Haller, *Tagebuch*, ii. 327, 350.   [5] Ibid. ii. 331.   [6] Garrioch, *Making*, 192.
[7] Haller, *Tagebuch*, ii. 329, 350–1.   [8] Ibid. ii. 351.

nothing like it had been seen before.[9] The most important feature of this cultural transformation, and the one most blatantly ignored by conventional historiography of the French Revolution, is the emphasis everywhere on 'philosophy' and the 'philosophique' in both positive and negative evaluations of the projected 'revolution'. This raises serious questions about the way historians typically explain the Revolution's causes.

Of course, when seeking to explain the French Revolution, one must be clear as to what question one is trying to answer. If one wishes to know why the *ancien régime* monarchy broke down in 1789, the answer certainly lies principally in France's strategic and financial problems. By 1787, desperate and on the verge of collapse, the French court found itself without the resources to support the role that it had always aspired to play in recent centuries in international, maritime, and colonial affairs. Continually worsted by Britain and Prussia since 1750, most recently in the Dutch political crisis of 1787 when 'by virtue of the right of brigands', as Gorani expressed it, the new king of Prussia, egged on by the British Prime Minister, Pitt, invaded the Dutch Republic and crushed the Dutch democratic revolution whose leaders were allied to France, the French court found itself in a deeply humiliating predicament at home, internationally, and overseas.[10] Financially ruined by the recent further ballooning of what had already earlier, by the 1760s, become an unprecedented and crippling royal debt, its prestige shattered by vast colonial losses and other failures, the crown had to admit there was no solution to its chronic and now inescapable financial and political failure other than to reorganize and rationalize the state in the only way that would yield substantial increases in revenues and enhancement of resources. This was by persuading France's privileged elites to abandon some or all of their fiscal exemptions and contribute more extensively to the power of the state. This was the beginning of the breakdown of the *ancien régime*.

France's elites were willing enough to surrender, or rather exchange, some of their privileges and immunities—provided they remained privileged elites, with their legal and honorific status confirmed, and provided that in return, they shared more directly henceforth, politically and administratively, in the exercise of royal power. A gravely weakened nominal monarchy was by 1788 on the verge of being reactivated as an aristocratic state. But if we ask how and why this attempted political reorganization rapidly shifted from a programme of fiscal and political reform designed to recast the dominance of three entrenched privileged elites—nobility, clergy, and judiciary—into a drive to emasculate the crown and obliterate these elites, substituting for *ancien régime* France a unitary state based on the principle of equality, universal human rights, and democracy underpinned by freedom of thought, expression, and the press, then the issue is quite different. There is only one major formative factor and only one cogent answer—the Radical Enlightenment; everything else is entirely secondary. All suggestions that the bourgeoisie was rising, or that

---

[9] Popkin, *Revolutionary News*, 25–6; Garrioch, *Making*, 183.
[10] Gorani, *Recherches*, ii. 176; Israel, 'Failed Enlightenment', 36–42.

particular sectors in the population had become economically or socially more influential during the course of the eighteenth century, or that slow-moving cultural processes had changed basic assumptions, are not just largely speculative but altogether unfounded, having neither any convincing inner logic nor any applicability either to the detail of events or the rhetoric of revolutionary discourse. If we scrutinize the facts alone we receive clear guidance. Searching for the influence of businessmen, merchants, men with strong enterprise concerns within the revolutionary process whether inside or outside what in 1789 became the National Assembly, research comes up with very little. The entrepreneurial class concerned with business, markets, and the widening of opportunities for profit clearly had practically nothing to do with the Revolution. Artisans and peasants by contrast played a large part—but only indirectly and secondarily (and often anarchically), in reacting to the Revolution once set in motion. Plainly, the initiative was seized by a tiny group that was socially entirely unrepresentative—a remarkable fact.

The proposed compromise between crown and privilege entailed the three socially dominant elites—nobles, clergy, and *parlementaires* (high legal officials)—exchanging most of their fiscal and proprietary privileges for reinforced legal and honorific privileges combined with enhanced local and national political influence. At first, these elites looked well placed to dominate local and provincial affairs on the envisaged new basis. France's domestic situation was highly volatile; but its legal and institutional structure vigorous and powerfully developed. Certainly, bread prices were rising and the urban and rural population in many places restless and discontented. But this was nothing new; and, besides, popular discontent, events were to prove, could without much difficulty be shepherded and manipulated in all sorts of directions and on behalf of even the most contradictory causes. There was little on the surface that spelt dire peril for France's traditional elites and the institutional framework they presided over.

During 1786, the king's controller-general, Calonne, presented his ambitious plans for reforming the state finances and local government as well as establishing new mechanisms of consultation between court and provinces. Opposition, as expected, came mainly from the *Parlement* of Paris which had a long history of obstructing royal efforts at reform as well as opposing royal measures against Jansenism. To outflank the *Parlement*'s obstructionism, Calonne advised the king to convene an Assembly of Notables, theoretically representing all the privileged elites together with the Commons, or Third Estate, but actually dominated by the nobility and higher clergy. But the plan failed. Despite alarm at the scale of the royal debt, now put at 113 million *livres*, the Assembly failed to underwrite Calonne's plans. Recalcitrant nobles and clergy had little difficulty in securing the backing of the Paris plebs. In April 1787, Louis replaced Calonne with a leading opposition figure, Loménie de Brienne, archbishop of Toulouse. Somewhat predictably, as nothing else suggested itself, the archbishop reproduced, while altering a few details, basically the same reform package as his predecessor. He also began implementing the reforms in the hope of strengthening his hand.

In provinces without provincial estates where the right to consent to taxation had long since been ceded to the crown (the *pays d'élections*), Loménie instituted regional assemblies with standing committees dominated by the three elites to work with the crown's *intendants*, to get them to share in the fiscal administration, including regulation of the grain trade and tax collection. These assemblies consisted partly of local dignitaries nominated by the crown and partly local notables co-opted by their colleagues. Next, with the Assembly of Notables and *Parlement* of Paris still refusing to cooperate, the former was dissolved. But judicial and aristocratic recalcitrance persisted unyieldingly. The *parlements* especially were experienced in such confrontations and in the ensuing clash easily won the backing not just of the nobility and clergy but in many cities also the common people. Politically, the crown was everywhere outflanked. At this point, nobility, clergy, and *parlementaires*, spurred by the Paris *Parlement*, urged a convening of the Estates-General (which had not met since 1614) as a way out of the impasse that would also consolidate the privileged elites' capture of France's administration, fiscal machinery, and political process.[11]

Revealingly, it was precisely in provinces such as Brittany and the Dauphiné where the hierarchical traditions of the provincial estates, local *parlements*, and noble precedence, and in the latter case also residual serfdom, persisted most, that popular opposition to royal policy was most pronounced. The French Revolution was one in which the force of popular anger and sentiment was always instrumentally crucial, even in 1788, but a largely inarticulate force surging first this way and then that, mostly blind to the play of interests and highly volatile. At Rennes and Grenoble, the provincial capitals of Brittany and the Dauphiné, popular demonstrations at this point erupted in defence of privilege, the old constitution, and the *parlements*. A particularly violent tumult backing the local *parlement* and estates occurred in Grenoble on 7 June 1788. In all provinces, the united cry was one of no consent to new taxes prior to the convening of the Estates-General.

The king had little choice but to yield. With the people demanding respect for precedent, privilege, and the *parlements*, in August, the convening of the Estates-General was announced for 1 May 1789. For nine months, both in Paris and the provinces, preparations for the gathering henceforth dominated politics. There was much discussion of old precedents and charters. It soon emerged, however, that something wholly unexpected and unprecedented was occurring: in the summer of 1788 the main struggle suddenly transformed itself from one between crown and privileged elites into one between the latter demanding the Estates-General's traditional format ensuring nobility and clergy together commanded twice the Third Estate's voting power and a tiny group of newcomers on the scene, mostly literary men and professional intellectuals, wanting privilege curbed and a doubling of the Third Estate's representation to ensure parity of voting power with the privileged

---

[11] Mounier, *De l'influence*, 27.

orders (and, in practice, overall superiority as a minority of clergy and nobility backed these demands).

Here in embryo, in this campaign to overturn the legal ascendancy of privilege, was a revolution. All kinds of local clubs and reading societies that had flourished for some years, in some cases decades, in the cities became actively involved in the movement for the 'doubling' of Third Estate representation. Among Third Estate spokesmen, the foremost opinion-shaping instrument turned out to be the suddenly burgeoning local press. The legalities, history, precedent, and experience all promised nobility, clergy, and *parlementaires* an impregnable ascendancy. They had local structures of influence, tradition, and all the charters on their side, and to begin with popular support as well. But as preparations for the Estates-General progressed during 1788, rank and past practice, it emerged, were no longer so decisive as in the past in shaping attitudes. Rather the 'doubling' of representation became a formal demand, and as the situation developed in late 1788, it became clear neither tradition nor any institutional body, nor received thinking, were driving developments but something previously never seen or heard of: the welling up of a militantly anti-aristocratic and anticlerical discourse roundly denouncing privilege, nobility, clerical influence, and the *parlements*.

This shift, already noticeable in the spring and summer of 1788, marks the real beginning of the Revolution which truly began, remarks Jean-Paul Rabaut Saint-Étienne (1743–93), one of the early leaders, not with the convening of the Estates-General in 1789 as most later supposed, but during the months of agitation and persuasion preceding, especially the summer and autumn of 1788 when 'a great number of writers' set to work influencing elements of the Third Estate, diffusing texts everywhere reminding the people of their 'rights', 'ses droits'.[12] Radical Enlightenment rhetoric began to saturate the public arena in speeches and newspaper articles emanating from all sides. This uncompromising, increasingly strident ideological assault on the *ancien régime* social and cultural world was concerted by a relatively small number of publicists, journalists, and discontented nobles. But what counted was not their numbers but their ideological cohesion and access to their audience. They seized the attention of the urban public deploying—as far as most people were concerned—an entirely unheard of new rhetoric of equality, democracy, and *volonté générale*.

Only radical ideas could have done this work. The legitimacy of the existing order had in the past always been both effectively and plausibly upheld by appealing to law, history, and tradition and to divine will. The *anti-philosophes*, here as so often, put their finger on the underlying issue in dispute. Inequality of condition and status and the mutual dependence of men, held Chaudon, is 'un dessein marqué de la Providence, un ordre légitime auquel tout homme doit se soumettre' [a design marked out by providence to which all men should submit].[13] One either

---

[12] Rabaut Saint-Étienne, *Précis historique*, 24, 56–7; Stone, *Genesis*, 214–16.
[13] Chaudon, *Dictionnaire anti-philosophique*, i. 324.

acknowledged the validity of the existing social order or one stood out as an obdurate rebel against it. In Christian theology, it is in matters of faith, in spiritual status, the *anti-philosophes* reminded readers, that men are equal, not in worldly condition. Christian *philosophes* firmly acknowledged this; deists and the irreligious might acknowledge it too. Only those proclaiming a universal egalitarianism sought to overturn it, something impossible without a novel metaphysics to back it up. Here was a dimension of reality that no pragmatism or middle of the road position could evade. Philosophy either acquiesced or rebelled, splitting the Enlightenment fundamentally.

In Brittany, the contest between the 700–800 local nobles entitled to appear in the local estates and the Third Estate's spokesmen, especially over whether the Breton delegations to the Estates-General should accept 'equality in repartition of taxes' and agree to prune the *noblesse de robe*'s privileges, was particularly turbulent. Against the journalists, the *Parlement* of Rennes, 'perhaps the most ignorant of the thirteen [judicial] senates of France', according to one local periodical, lent the three privileged orders unstinting support.[14] What was at issue was the primacy in Breton society of privilege, precedent, charters, ennobled magistracy, clergy, and tradition, indeed the very principle of a society of ranks sanctioned by ecclesiastical authority. Especially active in stirring up opposition to this formidable edifice was Volney's journal *La Sentinelle du peuple*, based in Rennes, which, by December 1788, was openly summoning the Third Estate to reject uncompromisingly all proposals and pretensions of the *privilégiés*.[15] This energetic young orientalist and zealous disciple of Helvétius and d'Holbach, projecting radical ideas in the most strident terms, sought to mobilize dissatisfaction against the privileged orders and succeeded.

The very first issue of this revolutionary paper denounced the Estates of Brittany as entities 'illégales et abusives', demanding that superfluous ecclesiastical properties revert to the nation. In subsequent issues, Volney openly incites the Breton people to defy nobility, clergy, and *parlementaires* by refusing to permit voting by orders in the forthcoming Estates-General. The 'public interest' is essentially the interest of the people and Bretons must ensure they are not the last to move 'dans la révolution qui entraine maintenant toute la France'.[16] Already publicly mocking the British constitution where a king is supposed to hold an entire people in the balance, by December 1788, Volney was loudly admonishing his countrymen that 'tous les hommes naissent égaux'.[17] The Breton nobility he compared to a sickly old aristocratic lady, needing intensive nursing by her underlings (the clergy and *parlementaires*) and huge amounts of medicine to prop her up, her imminent and inevitable demise being sure to transform everything for the better.

---

[14] Linguet, *Annales*, 15 (1788–9), 431–4, 436 and 16 (1789–90), 272.
[15] Volney, *Œuvres*, i. 32, 35, 41, 46, 57, 64–5.
[16] Volney, *Sentinelle du peuple*, 1. 6–7, 3. 16, 18, 4. 7; Doyle, *Aristocracy*, 173.
[17] BL 911 c. 3/5 Lettre de M. C. F. de Volney à M. le Comte de S., 14, 17.

The uproar over the proposals for doubling the representation of the Third Estate, and impassioned speeches urging the nobility in various localities to merge with the Third Estate, was, to an extent, a product of pre-revolutionary political or social conditions. But the terms in which Third Estate opposition to the privileged orders was orchestrated most definitely were not. Rather, the emerging discourse of protest amounted to a complete rupture with the past. In 1788, many key commentators and publicists—Volney, Mirabeau, Sieyès, Le Chapelier, and Condorcet among them—refused to concede any legitimacy or constitutional standing to the Estates-General as a historically defined form of assembly, demanding instead sweeping reforms before acknowledging its legitimacy.[18]

When the Assembly of Notables reconvened, as part of the preparations, in November 1788, the crown formally proposed 'doubling' the Third Estate's representation and adoption of a system of proportionality between electors and Third Estate representatives so that each representative represented a certain number of voters. Ministers proposed these changes in the Estates-General's structure and procedure, rendering the Assembly more representative by strengthening the Third Estate, in the hope of lessening tension and counter-balancing the influence of the privileged. But the king's ministers had no wish to end separate deliberation and voting among the orders. Politically as well as socially, France remained a society of orders and, in theory, at least, nobility and clergy could still overrule the Third Estate. Over the next months the crown continued to pursue what royal ministers considered a tactful, even-handed strategy, allowing some enhancement of the Third Estate's status and prospective role while retaining safeguards designed to ensure the continued division of society into ranks and the ultimate primacy of privilege.

Delegates to the Estates-General had in the past been expressly mandated to support or oppose particular proposals and in 1788–9 too, before the Estates convened, matters proceeded along traditional lines. Representatives to the Estates were deemed to represent specific orders in specific localities not individuals or citizens. *Cahiers de doléances* supposedly expressing local opinion in the parishes were drawn up in all the localities of France to bind and direct the delegates. This accorded with precedent and, under more normal circumstances, would have reinforced the privileged elites' predominance since local meetings in the bailiwicks were organized, chaired, and notarized in practice by nobles, notables, and lawyers, with nobles and clergy also holding their own separate gatherings. This time, though, matters proceeded differently due to the tide of unremitting oppositional rhetoric surging up in the clubs and literary societies, and local press, backed by growing unrest in the countryside and streets spurred by that year's disastrous grain harvest. Highly articulate and literate 'Patriot' committees entrusted with overseeing the elections for representatives of the Third Estate formed in voting localities across France. Dominated by men of the clubs, these commissions ensured election of

---

[18] Baker, *Condorcet*, 248–60, 266; Williams, *Condorcet and Modernity*, 252.

delegates often militantly antagonistic to the system of orders and the pre-eminence of 'aristocrats' and priests. In this way, infiltrating the electoral committees and selection of the Third Estate representatives, radical thought for the first time gained direct entry to the political arena.

2. THE REVOLUTION'S SECOND PHASE

The Revolution's second phase began in late April 1789 with the Third Estate's 600 elected deputies gathered at Versailles refusing the royal agenda and procedural proposals as to how the three estates would vote. At this point, in both the Estates-General and at court, a divisive discourse began to be heard, introduced earlier in the 1780s in Switzerland and Holland, labelling the opposed blocs *Aristocrates* and *Démocrates*.[19] The Third Estate's deputies, historians have often remarked, included no peasants, artisans, or labourers. This is perfectly true. But as constituted at Versailles, in 1789, and especially with respect to its leadership, the Third Estate featured no businessmen, bankers, shopkeepers, merchants, landowners, workshop-owners, or other members of other major occupation groups characteristic of 'bourgeois', middle-class life either. Nothing could be more ill founded than to suppose, as some still do,[20] that there existed a 'revolutionary class' in society in 1789 that can meaningfully be designated 'bourgeois' in terms of either social position or class consciousness.

Edmund Burke, who from the outset was perfectly horrified by the social make-up of the Assembly, particularly what he regarded as the shocking lack of landowners, big property owners, men of rank, and high-ranking churchmen, was acutely conscious of the staggeringly high proportion of minor lawyers in the body. But he makes no mention of the almost equally striking and significant lack of lawyers among what emerged as the leading group—except for the case of the rival faction headed by Jean-Joseph Mounier (1758–1806), a senior lawyer from Grenoble, a grouping important and powerful but which turned out, we shall see, to be an *anti-philosophique* clique.[21]

Leaving aside the Mounier group, the Third Estate's leadership were mostly journalists, editors, literary men, intellectuals. Among the foremost were the *philosophe*, historian, and political commentator Mirabeau—rejected by his own order, the nobility, but elected at Aix-en-Provence by the Third Estate—the *philosophe*-journalist Volney, fresh from combat in Rennes, the astronomer Bailly, Antoine Pierre Barnave (1761–93), a highly talented orator from the Dauphiné doubly unrepresentative in being, like Rabaut, a Protestant as well as an intellectual,[22]

---

[19] Sabatier, *Journal politique*, 1 (1790) 41–2.   [20] Hunt, *Politics, Culture and Class*, 176–7.
[21] Burke, *Reflections*, 36–40; Marmontel, *Mémoires*, iii. 178–9.
[22] Mounier, *De l'influence*, 69–70.

and the Abbé Sieyès, a retiring personality of bookish disposition full of enmity, as Madame de Staël later noted, for the aristocracy. Despite the amazingly high proportion of lawyers among the rank and file, only one or two, like Barnave and Le Chapelier, figured among the leading clique and these were altogether untypical. Experience in law evidently counted for little. These 'philosophes du Tiers' as opponents derisively called them, assumed the lead in rejecting the designation 'the Third Estate' as unacceptable and insultingly redolent of 'slaves', 'helots', and 'negroes'. They repudiated the whole terminology of the past, refusing usage of the term 'orders' in their chamber's deliberations. By redefining the nobility and clergy as 'classes privilégiées' instead of the higher orders, they took the offensive from the start, introducing a deliberately provocative rhetoric precluding all possibility of preserving political privileges for the nobility and clergy. They simply refused to countenance a higher status for any social class as they did any curbs on press freedom, liberty of thought, or religious toleration.[23]

Sieyès's three historic tracts appeared between November 1788 and January 1789, before the convening of the Estates-General. Especially the first, the *Essai sur les privilèges*, and last, his renowned *Qu'est-ce que le Tiers-État'* (January 1789), brilliantly captured the mood, phraseology, and *philosophique* terminology of the moment, especially the journalistic campaign of 1788. They affected the course and especially the rhetoric of the Revolution. But they were based on ideas he formulated in the early 1770s, that 'liberty in general' is what most favours the pursuit of individual happiness in society and that the chief foes of liberty are the particular 'liberties' of privilege, charters, and special rights,[24] the defined status *ancien régime* societies accord aristocrats, ecclesiastics, and judicial elites. Sieyès's speeches and tracts were based on extracts taken from a range of thinkers, a feature typical of the speeches in the Estates-General in 1789 as, earlier, of the speeches in the clubs and societies of 1788. His stunning success the good *abbé* owed in large part to being a *philosophe*-politician and lifelong addict of materialist epistemology and metaphysics.

Sieyès rejected the views of Montesquieu and Rousseau. But Montesquieu nevertheless figured prominently as one of the *grandes authorités* constantly cited during the early stages of the revolutionary ferment just as he had in the Genevan and Dutch revolutions of the 1780s. Only after a certain point did the *Esprit des loix* fall from favour among the Third Estate's leaders, observed Simon-Henri Linguet, editor of the *Annales politiques, civiles et littéraires*, a journal previously published in Brussels but transferred to Paris with the advent of a free press, in 1788. Montesquieu receded, he explained, looking back, the following year, along with the last shreds of sympathy for the nobility for which that book provided the intellectual 'arsenal'. As the principles of equality and democracy more and more established their ascendancy,

---

[23] Sabatier, *Journal politique*, 1 (1790), i, 42; Mounier, *De l'influence*, 86, 110; de Staël, *Considérations*, 203–4.
[24] Sieyès, *Manuscrits*, 361.

Montesquieu gave way to Rousseau and Mably, the authors from whom deputies, journalists, and orators were 'able to pillage the most ideas' to spice their speeches and pronouncements though they rarely acknowledged their names.[25]

The passive revolt of May, with the Third Estate's refusing to permit verification of credentials separately from the other two orders, insisting on a collective procedure rendering all votes equal, was tentative, almost timid, initially, but resolute. As the weeks passed, Third Estate resolve to defy privilege and the king was stiffened by mounting *philosophique* rhetoric at the privileged orders' expense. In a speech delivered on 8 May, Volney, impatient at the prevailing hesitation, reminded his colleagues that 'the classes who live by abuse' were determined to permit no real change. Self-interested obstinacy explained their strategy, and the Third Estate should base theirs on an equally unsentimental grasp of reality. Formal minutes should be kept, more formality in speaking adopted with less freedom to interrupt, and, above all, their lingering 'metaphysical' deference to precedent eschewed. The past should no longer inhibit Assembly speakers from pronouncing such forthright terms as 'constitution', 'chamber', and 'deputies' in their speeches.[26] What was needed was a total political change with all precedent cast aside. Volney called on the Assembly immediately to drop all vestiges of an un-philosophical attitude and immediately forget every category of the past. Slowly but surely, newly coined terminology, completely irreconcilable with the traditional usages and procedures of the Estates-General, was adopted.

Quiet non-cooperation in May was followed by open revolt in June. Inviting members of the other two chambers to join them in a joint verification of all representatives of the nation, Third Estate deputies were joined by a few clerical and noble defectors. The resulting enlarged Commons, quite illegally and contrary to all precedent, declared itself the 'National Assembly', on 17 June, after which more of the clergy went over as did around a third of the nobility. Most nobles, however, and the higher clergy refused to acknowledge the new body. But, lacking any lead from the court, they offered no outright resistance to the proceedings. It was left to the king to respond. On 20 June 1789, the Assembly were shut out of the hall where they met on the king's orders. Armed guards appeared. It seemed the crown would now stand firm and halt the budding revolution in its tracks. But the show of royal firmness quickly evaporated. Convening instead in the Tennis Court and spurred on by Jean Sylvain Bailly, astronomer, member of three academies, son of the keeper of the king's pictures, and a *philosophe*, formerly a protégé of Buffon, friendly with Diderot, the deputies took the famous Tennis Court oath, later immortalized in a stirring painting by Jacques Louis David, vowing 'never to separate' until the constitution was satisfactorily recast.

---

[25] Linguet, *Annales*, 16 (1790), 271; Sabatier, *Journal politique*, 1 (1790) 42; Rétat, '1789: Montesquieu', 74–5.

[26] Volney, *Discours prononcé dans la Chambre* (8 May 1789), 2, 4.

Surrounded by groups of noble and clerical opponents of the incipient Revolution, the king replied with a compromise declaration read out in the Assembly on 23 June, conceding many points in dispute, including an end to fiscal immunities for the privileged, but rejecting the proposals emphatically rejected by the notables, especially abolition of honorary privileges and an end to voting by orders in the Estates-General. Led by Mirabeau, Bailly, and Sieyès, the National Assembly rejected the royal compromise. The deadlock that ensued was serious and tension rose. A week later, it was the court, though, that backed down. Louis acknowledged the new body, summoning the recalcitrant rump of nobility and clergy to rejoin the rest of what was now officially recognized by king and court as the National Assembly. The Revolution was fully under way.

The resistance of the *privilégiés* and tentativeness of the Third Estate's response, observed Volney, in his speech of 8 May, had 'filled Paris with false rumours and calumny'. By proceeding slowly the *philosophes-révolutionnaires* risked being accused of betraying their charge. A feeling of urgency, their sense of being driven by the people to spur on their less ideologically inclined majority, intensified during the summer due to a combination of court and noble intrigue. By early July 1789 Paris was extraordinarily tense. Since the Assembly's leadership was bolstered by the groundswell of support in the streets and cafes of Paris, the way this support was rallied was crucial. Paris may have abounded with resentful personalities bearing grudges. But so does any capital at any time. Far more important is that the leading agitators, Brissot and Condorcet among them, were, in the words of the conservative *anti-philosophe* Sabatier, themselves *philosophes* while their following were those Sabatier derisively dismissed as 'demi-philosophes', those echoing Mirabeau, Sieyès, Volney, Bailly, Condorcet, and Brissot, in the streets, popular 'philosophers' and demagogues now so implacably fired up against noble birth and priesthood as to have become 'esprits extrêmes'. The very word *noblesse* sufficed to drive these types into such fury, he alleged, as could easily precipitate a 'Saint Barthélémi philosophique'.[27]

As royal regiments were brought up and what were interpreted by the Revolution's supporters as moves to engineer a counter-revolution by military force unfolded in the wings, an armed rising occurred in Paris, on 12 July, demonstrating crowds being joined by troops of the Garde Française (the palace guard). The organizing committee of the movement which then assumed responsibility for the capital at once instituted a National Guard to patrol the streets. On 14 July, a mob of artisans, shopkeepers, and journeymen stormed the Bastille, massacring the governor and part of the garrison amid scenes of graphic violence. Confused and dismayed, the king yet again caved in. Remaining at Versailles, he dismissed the regiments summoned by his principal advisers and relatives to re-impose his authority. It was an unprecedented situation.

---

[27] Sabatier, *Journal politique*, 1 (1790), 47; McMahon, *Enemies*, 65.

3. BOOKS AND REVOLUTION

The Revolution's leaders, noted royalist and other critics, both in the Assembly and in Paris, were a mere tiny, wholly unrepresentative group, representing no established segment of society. Who were the Revolution's leaders? The hard-core revolutionaries were just 'des philosophes' and 'demi-philosophes'. This was absolutely true. The power and privileges of the king, nobility, and clergy as well as of the *parlements* were arrested by men uttering *philosophique* rhetoric who had become masters of the country despite having no standing or position in *ancien régime* terms, doing so as representatives of discontented townsmen. Their hegemony solidified because their rhetoric more powerfully voiced the people's frustration and desire for change than did anyone or anything else but was inherently extremely precarious from first to last.

It was an extraordinary, unheard-of situation. These men would soon discover, admonished opponents, that breaking all the bonds of the past as they proposed is totally impossible without living in 'un monde de philosophes'.[28] The Assembly's leaders had not yet learned, warned experienced observers, that, human imperfections being what they are, the presiding clique could not possibly succeed. These *philosophes* had forgotten about the need for dependence and subordination and about human greed, duplicity, and villainy. Perhaps they had; but for the moment they held the reins. The power of ideology to shape revolutions has been shown often enough in the nineteenth and twentieth centuries. But the question of how exactly the *philosophes-révolutionnaires* of 1789 accomplished what they did with a considerable measure of popular support, given that the common people did not read their books and would scarcely have understood them had they tried, remains.[29] But it was not the books of the *philosophes* that precipitated philosophy's breakthrough. The popular Revolution of 1789, as Sabatier, Mounier, and others saw it in 1789–90, was chiefly inspired by smaller, cheaper, and simpler texts, summaries, and excerpts the *philosophes* instigated, and especially the revolutionary journals, extracts pasted together 'et que le peuple a fort bien saisis'.[30] Among other examples, Sabatier cited a 'disgusting' paraphrase of a few lines of the *Contrat social*, the brochure *L'Orateur aux États-Généraux* that penetrated 'incroyablement parmi le petit-peuple', winning support among persons completely incapable of reading the *Contrat social* itself.

The Revolution stemmed from discontent swept up in a catch-all of *philosophique* rhetoric by a mass of minor and hack journalists diffused through society, using the press, concepts contained in the books of a few great writers recycled, debased, and brought down to the level of the common people. There was plenty of Rousseau mixed into the potent concoction undoing the entire institutional and legal framework of the French monarchy; but also much Mably, 'Raynal', Helvétius, Mirabeau, Brissot, Sieyès, Volney, and Condorcet. But the essential point is that the revolutionary *philosophes* leading opinion in Paris and the National Assembly were themselves

---

[28] Sabatier, *Journal politique*, 1. 119–20.
[29] Ibid. 1. 121.   [30] Ibid.

chiefly shaped by books and philosophy and were by and large not *Rousseauistes*, or, at least, as in Brissot's case, not pure *Rousseauistes*. Rather, as time would show more clearly, they were essentially heirs to the Radical Enlightenment.

A materialist *philosophe* since at least 1770, Sieyès was a hardened ideologue who excluded all faith, theology, metaphysics, spirituality, and miracles from his thought, something historians' curious and completely misplaced concern with aligning him with Locke has tended to obscure.[31] Even if it is true, as has been claimed, that the striking affinities in his thought with Spinoza's system are completely 'fortuitous and vague',[32] none of these are at all surprising given his thorough immersion in more recent radical thought. About Locke, Sieyès says absolutely nothing. He greatly admired Condillac; but Condillac was not his political guide. His main set of notes on philosophy, or 'Grand Cahier métaphysique', dates from around 1770 and analyses the ideas of Helvétius, Condillac, and Bonnet on mental processes and on evidence in exhaustive detail while also displaying an (in France) unusual degree of familiarity with Leibniz and Wolff as well as other early and later Enlightenment thinkers. His key doctrine, locating him close to Helvétius and Diderot, was that man has as his principal goal the desire to be happy and that 'toute son activité se porte à lui procurer le bonheur'.[33] What he called the 'true social order' must be based on a clear grasp of what this means for the individual's relationship to society. The 'true social order' was indeed something the world had not yet seen. The interest of all the individuals making up society must be deemed equal, his undeviating rejection of the prescriptions of Montesquieu being rooted in explicit dislike of his relativism and respect for privilege. Loathing nobility and class stratification, Sieyès also notably avoided the eulogizing of ancient Sparta and Rome so beloved by Mably and Rousseau, these to him being models entangled in slavery and irrelevant to his project.

What caused the Revolution, asked Rabaut de Saint-Étienne, a Huguenot from Nîmes guillotined during the Terror? It was caused, he explained, by ideas circulated beforehand containing 'all the germs of the Revolution', completely new ideas expressed in the writings of the *philosophes* assailing the *préjugés* of the age thereby creating a context breeding a school of 'hommes supérieurs' whose writings diffused on all sides 'une foule de vérités utiles'.[34] Voltaire had perhaps started the process by fighting for liberty of thought and expression. But those that followed went further, the *philosophes* suffering severe persecution, some being publicly condemned by the *parlements*, others dispatched to the Bastille. Nevertheless, through their efforts 'the truth' began to penetrate everywhere. Their books saturated every part of the kingdom and 'entered houses of all kinds', until finally, by 1788, France's 'inquisition' of thought, worn out by its burgeoning task, ground completely to a halt. The de facto liberty of the press secured in 1788 was the first step in the Revolution. It was these heroes of thought who then, in their turn, generated 'une multitude de

---

[31] Thompson, *French Revolution*, 29; Quiviger, 'Sieyès', 128–9, 134.
[32] Forsyth, *Reason*, 38.   [33] Ibid. 141–2.   [34] Sieyès, *Préliminaire*, 37.

disciples', forging a bench of critical opinion, a new kind of reading public that finally assumed the role of a collective tribunal judging kings and ministers. Such an informed, enlightened tribunal of opinion was unknown to the ancients, he added, because they lacked printing.[35]

It was through instructive reading that the public outlook was transformed and men learnt to examine questions of government and politics. In particular, the *Encyclopédie*, by bringing all the sciences together in a single compilation, held Rabaut, had created a basis for discussing politics, economics, and state finances. Rousseau too exerted a huge impact, expounding advanced political principle in his *Contrat social* which afterwards rallied all the 'bons esprits'. Next, 'Raynal' thundered against all 'les tyrannies', denouncing despotism, breaking the old bonds, unmasking every form of political and religious hypocrisy, denouncing every yoke, making contemporaries share his 'indignation contre les tyrans'.[36] We have not forgotten the effect of the *Histoire philosophique* in France, he declared in 1792. Next came the great agitation of 1788 provoked above all by the pamphlets of the *philosophes'* innumerable disciples. Rabaut Saint-Étienne himself figured among these together with Sieyès, Volney, Mirabeau, Mounier, Condorcet, Barnave, and many others. It was in 1788 that the ideas of Mably, Rousseau, and Raynal, he observed, came to permeate every debate. Paris especially was the 'foyer' of Enlightenment discourse; and it was not just the Revolution's foyer but an active power in its own right and one, suggested Mounier, that swept Rabaut, Barnave, Bailly, and many another from their instinctive moderation to positions more radical than initially intended.[37]

The revolutionary leadership in 1789 were to be found partly in the National Assembly, partly in the Paris commune or city government, and partly editing the new revolutionary press. Louis-Pierre Manuel (1751–93), former tutor to the children of a Paris banker, cast into the Bastille as a young man for his *Essais historiques* (1783), and after the Bastille's fall a prominent leader of the Paris commune, was another who did not doubt that France was reborn in the years immediately prior to 1788, emancipating herself after centuries of oppression, thanks to 'la philosophie', and that it was this that drove the Revolution. The pens of Rousseau, Mably, and Raynal, in particular, accomplished more in the first stages of the Revolution, he contended, than the swords of the revolutionary militias. It was 'philosophy' that proved and established the people's 'rights' demonstrating that all France's existing laws were born of 'prejudice' and 'ignorance' while those 'we lack are those made by nature and reason'.[38] The nobility endlessly cite charters, titles, and privilege, he remarked jubilantly, in June 1789, but now in vain. Suddenly, everyone grasps that this is all nonsense. Precisely the principle of general equality taught by 'philosophy' revealed to the people that they possessed natural rights and that these rights must

---

[35] Ibid. 7–9; Rabaut Saint-Étienne, *Précis historique*, 19–20.
[36] Rabaut Saint-Étienne, *Précis historique*, 22–3.
[37] Ibid. 23–4; Mounier, *De l'influence*, 100–3.
[38] Manuel, *Lettres... recueillies*, 1–4, 7, 15, 20.

ground the new order. The revolution that 'la philosophie préparait, mais qu'elle n'espérait pas encore', made by a people enlightened by 'les Montesquieu, les Rousseau, Voltaire, Mably et Raynal', would, moreover, also sway other peoples and ultimately forge a new international order based on peace to replace the old one that for so long rendered our world 'the cake of kings'.[39] 'Voilà pourtant les miracles de la philosophie!' Ideologically speaking, furthermore, the new France had no borders and the Revolution would certainly spread: Raynal, who through his *Histoire* prepared 'tant de conquêtes à la philosophie', had, or so he believed, authorized the revolutionary French to proclaim 'comme Louis XIV, il n'y a plus de Pyrénées'.[40]

Everywhere, local assemblies and reading circles divided into factions supporting or opposing the new ideas, the context where everyone, held Rabaut, saw the Revolution incipiently emerging.[41] Paris abounded in 'hommes instruits', men who understood these ideas and to whose unprecedented form of power the royal government remained completely blind, being unable to grasp the nature of their ascendancy and incapable of checking it. Another who stressed the vital role of this intellectual subversion transforming France before and during 1788 was Diderot's disciple Naigeon. An ardent supporter of the Revolution of reason based on the Declaration of the Rights of Man of 1789,[42] he later also emerged as inflexibly opposed to the fanatical extremism and anti-intellectualism of Marat and Robespierre which, in his view, as of so many others, afterwards tragically perverted and destroyed the true message and values of both the Revolution and the Enlightenment. The downfall of the old order and government, held Naigeon, in 1790, resulted from a process that became irreversible and insuperable once diffusion of new revolutionary ideas proceeded beyond a certain point and spread through all social classes. The surge of ideas made the rapid conquest of 'liberty' possible. It was the 'philosophes', representatives of a 'reason' tempered by experience, who showed the way and who 'formed', he says, both the Assemblée Nationale itself and, more importantly, the guiding attitudes and awareness of the Assemblée Nationale driving the Revolution.[43] By 1790, the *ancien régime* 'gothic building' was utterly in ruins; but the Revolution would not be complete, he warned, until freedom of thought, expression, and the press were fully secure, the numbers and wealth of the clergy drastically curtailed, and until religious authority had been so completely emasculated that whether a man was a Christian, Jew, deist, or idolater no longer mattered and the 'true faithful' came to be identified exclusively with the 'good citizens'.[44] Only by obliterating royal, ecclesiastical, aristocratic, and *parlementaire* power, something only partially accomplished by 1790, could government effectively uphold the basic rights of men on the basis of 'justice envers tous' without which no truly legitimate authority is conceivable or possible.[45]

---

[39] Manuel, *Lettres . . . recueillies*, 22, 91.   [40] Ibid. 102; Whaley, *Radicals*, 13–14, 51–2.
[41] Rabaut Saint-Étienne, *Précis historique*, 58, 62–4; Doyle, *Origins*, 146.
[42] Naigeon, *Adresse à l'Assemblée Nationale*, 81–3, 86.
[43] Ibid. 9.   [44] Ibid. 41–2, 53, 71, 77.   [45] Ibid. 113, 122.

Freedom of the press turned out to be the most potent of the principles introduced by *la philosophie* in 1788. In a state that is free, enlightened, and where the 'droits sacrés de l'homme et du citoyen' are embraced, as Naigeon explained it, everyone may say and publish whatever they please, and precisely this freedom is indispensable to discovering the truth, something that serves the interest of all. Where Montesquieu, Helvétius, d'Alembert, and Buffon mumbled and minced their words about many matters through fear of the theologians, 'ce nouvel ordre de choses si désiré et si inattendu' recognizing 'la superstition' as the worst and most dangerous of human weaknesses could at last overpower the enemies of reason by means of this powerful weapon.[46] Everyone was speaking of Rousseau, Voltaire, Mably, Raynal, Montesquieu, and Helvétius. In his *Philosophie ancienne et moderne* (Paris, 1791), Naigeon would remind readers that Diderot, whom he here designates 'mon intime ami', the bravest of the *philosophes* and most resolute in combating 'la superstition', the thinker to whom his own intellectual and political evolution owed most, was also a figure to whom the Revolution owed an immense debt. His personal task in the Revolution was to complete Diderot's work and edit his papers.[47] Diderot's large contribution to the *philosophie moderne* making Revolution was not something most people had much awareness of as it had operated chiefly through multi-authored compilations like the *Encyclopédie* and the *Histoire philosophique* and anonymously published clandestine publications. But Diderot's ideas, Naigeon reminded them, were not only closely linked to the Revolution's ideology politically and philosophically but still relevant for resolving the dilemmas and difficulties 'auxquels la Révolution a donné lieu'.[48]

According to Naigeon, Rousseau's influence should be resisted and this was one of the main areas where Diderot could be useful. Citing a passage where Diderot contradicts Rousseau's conception of popular sovereignty, he urged the need to ensure a democratic executive respects the citizenry's wishes and representations in general but also to equip it to reject popular pressures and demands in specified circumstances. Here a midway position was desirable. Rules should be adopted, Diderot suggested, to the effect that petitions signed by more than a given number of citizens must always be considered, discussed, and responded to while petitions signed by fewer than the stipulated number of citizens should not, that is, could legally be ignored. Especially helpful was Diderot's effort to create a genuine balance between an executive arm not permitted to become too confident of its power and the caprices of a volatile, impressionable, and ignorant people. Popular opinion pressures those in government and may often be changeable and ill considered; yet it remains the opinion of the people: 'quelque fou soit le peuple, il est toujours le maître.'[49] But it should be master within defined limits.

---

[46] Naigeon, *Adresse à l'Assemblée Nationale*, 100–2; Pellerin, 'Naigeon', 30, 32.
[47] Naigeon, *Philosophie*, ii, pp. viii, xxiii–xxv.
[48] Staum, *Cabanis*, 29, 91.
[49] Naigeon, *Philosophie*, ii. 221–2.

At the outset, Mirabeau, Sieyès, and the rest of the leading group of *philosophes-révolutionnaires* sought to widen freedom of expression, undermine privilege, and promote the principle of equality. But there was another, more moderate reforming faction among the Third Estate, equally convinced *la philosophie moderne* was driving events, who aimed to steer in a different direction. Mounier was a moderate monarchist who in fact heartily detested *la philosophie moderne* while readily acknowledging that it was the most powerful agent steering revolutionary developments. He headed a grouping that sought a very different kind of revolution. In his *Considérations sur les gouvernements et principalement sur celui qui convient à la France* (Paris, 1789), he passionately pleaded with his fellow Third Estate representatives in the Estates to discard the precepts of the *philosophes* that so many of them seemed determined to follow, or rather those disagreeing with his hero, Montesquieu. The *philosophes* had often been justified in attacking popular *préjugés*. But their obsession with wrong thinking, ignorance, and error had led them to overstep bounds they ought to have respected.

By prioritizing ideas over experience, the *philosophes* had gone politically astray, imitating Plato in creating republics that could never exist outside their heads, introducing 'd'erreurs méprisables' while neglecting better, more upright principles.[50] The overriding danger now, urged Mounier, was that 'philosophy' would usher in 'la tyrannie démocratique', a trap that could only be prevented while still securing a measure of reform by following the British model. What was needed was mixed monarchy and an upper chamber composed of peers and bishops. His opponents complained that not everything about Britain was perfect. But English zeal for their constitution, their unshakable belief in its superiority over everything else, even if it blinds them to undeniable defects, was nevertheless invaluable for it ensured they abided by the dictates of experience eschewing *la philosophie*.[51] The Assemblée should emulate Britain and ground France's new constitution on experience, monarchy, and aristocracy, turning their backs on *philosophique* notions. Mounier's challenge to *la philosophie nouvelle* from the standpoint of 'moderation' was a powerful one. But by October 1789 it had been completely shattered.

[50] Mounier, *Considérations*, 18, 32, 35.
[51] Ibid. 51; Baker, *Inventing the French Revolution*, 258–61.

29

The Diffusion

1. PUBLISHERS, BOOKSELLERS, AND *COLPORTEURS*

How did the furtive participants in the world of clandestine philosophy of the decades before 1750 evolve into the leadership of the Assemblée Nationale of 1789? Where the 'nouveaux philosophes' had earlier constituted a murky underworld confined to hidden corners, asserted the best-selling *anti-philosophe* Caraccioli in 1765, their world had now become a veritable 'contagion' spreading in the towns and countryside and emanating also from Europe's courts. They complain of tyranny. 'Quelle tyrannie n'exercent-ils pas eux-mêmes sur les esprits en voulant que tout le monde soit de leur avis.'[1] One might perhaps be surprised by Caraccioli's reference to courts. But there can be no doubt that Europe's royal and princely courts, diplomatic services, nobilities, and, in Paris, the high-society salons, figured among the chief conduits of radical ideas.

Several cultural historians have rightly stressed that the salons, like the courtly culture of the time, were above all a social 'space', an arena for a kind of sociability in which literary concerns, wit, and sophistication were cultivated together with good taste, aristocratic demeanour, and dress fashion, and where there was little serious engagement with *philosophique* ideas. The salons as a cultural space—leaving aside the two specialized 'philosophique' salons, those of Helvétius and d'Holbach, which obviously form a separate case—were much less novel, recent research suggests, than social historians have been prone to assume. In reality there were no particularly new 'social spaces' apart from freemasonry, and however important socially these 'spaces' including the Paris salons were, none of them seemingly mattered much as agents generating and formulating, as opposed to diffusing, fundamentally new ideas. It is true then that the salons 'dictated polite patterns of behaviour' but completely wrong, it turns out, to suppose they set the 'intellectual agenda'. Regarding the latter, they were just, incidentally, at times, a passive amplifier.[2]

Most participants in the salons, including nearly all the lady *salonnières* presiding over these bodies, showed scant interest in 'philosophy'. But their salons were useful

---

[1] Caraccioli, *Cri de la vérité*, 329, 340.
[2] Lilti, *Le Monde*, 69, 135–6, 216; Jones, *Great Nation*, 178.

conduits within France and internationally where the few who were interested could expand their contacts, knowledge, and channels of communication. The Swedish court and diplomatic nobility, for example, were as avid as any in Europe for the literary sophistication of the Paris salons. In the main, what they sought and wished to demonstrate there were elegant manners, fashionable demeanour, easy familiarity with French literature, social standing, and wit; for the most part, they could not have been less interested in philosophy if they tried. But this does not apply to all. There was always also a Count Gustav Philip Creutz, Swedish ambassador in Paris for seventeen years, a regular presence at the salons, and someone who knew Diderot, d'Holbach, Raynal, and Grimm personally. He had a copy of the *Traité des trois imposteurs* in his library and continually sent quantities of French philosophical texts back to Sweden, for himself, his friends, and also the crown prince. He was used to hearing the most daring opinions expressed. When the crown prince, Gustaf, visiting Paris in 1770–1, met Creutz's best friend among the Paris literary circle, the academician Marmontel, he was amazed, he reported to his mother the queen, to find that he was the most fanatical republican imaginable.[3]

If far too much stress has been placed by social historians on the role of salons, the same is true of freemasonry. Freemasonry was certainly a novel as well as important socio-cultural phenomenon in the eighteenth century, but, again, not one of much significance for the generation and formulation of basic new ideas. Diderot, aware perhaps that Palissot, Fréron, and others of his enemies were keen masons, heartily despised freemasonry as did several other leading radical figures, including Condorcet, Mirabeau, and Lessing, who all became more and more scornful of a movement they saw as based on the search for status, love of ceremony, fashion, conventional thinking, and ignorance.[4] In one of his most important pre-revolutionary works, *De la monarchie prussienne* (1787), the future revolutionary leader Mirabeau denounces freemasonry in the most emphatic terms for failing to promote any worthwhile ideals, its constant splits and divisions, and being inundated with fools, charlatans, and *fripons*. 'Les vrais principes et la révolution désirée' [true principles and the desired revolution], Mirabeau assured readers in 1787, could be diffused only slowly, gently, and precisely without the *fripons* being able to take over and ruin the process, by courageously writing the 'great truths' and boldly publishing them in books and pamphlets: this is the 'palladium du bonheur de l'humanité'.[5]

Mirabeau scorned freemasonry and insisted on the primacy of books and reading and so did most other observers commenting on the process of the 'revolution of the mind'. Sabatier de Castres, who defected to the ranks of *anti-philosophie* after briefly belonging to the *parti philosophique* himself, later claimed to have written to his former philosophical mentor Helvétius clearly predicting the French Revolution as early as July 1766. Save for a miracle, Sabatier assured Helvétius in his 'letter', it was

---

[3] Wolff, 'Swedish Aristocracy', 263–4.

[4] Mirabeau, *De la monarchie*, v. 67–72, 100–3; Lepape, *Diderot*, 283–4.

[5] Mirabeau, *De la monarchie*, v. 102.

inevitable that the 'torrent de l'esprit philosophique' must, before the century's end, cause the 'fall of the clergy, collapse of the throne, and ruin of the great landowners'.[6] Three things made this certain in his opinion: the (since the 1740s) wide, rapid diffusion of radical thought, the force of its arguments, and its all too obvious social usefulness to resentful and scheming people. Warnings of the sort complaining that 'l'esprit philosophique' was becoming what Sabatier de Castres termed a 'dominant' force in society, rare in the 1760s, became distinctly more common after 1770. Within a few years, rapid diffusion transformed the Radical Enlightenment from a clandestine network largely hidden from view to the principal challenge, advancing though books and reading, to the existing order.

Various cultural mechanisms helped diffuse radical ideas widely during the three decades prior to the Revolution. Besides illicit printed literature, the mass of *anti-philosophie*, and the Paris high-society salons, there were the condemnatory edicts of *parlements*, priestly training in the seminaries, and often remarkably detailed ecclesiastical (and academic) indictments assailing *la philosophie moderne* as a scourge destroying religion, morality, and social hierarchy.[7] Most crucial of all was the impact of the new ideas on long-standing grievances and gross inequalities that could be potentially alleviated, if only psychologically at first, by adopting radical interpretations reconfiguring familiar and ancient forms of subordination as newly conceived forms of malign, culpable 'oppression' and 'tyranny'. Ambition, resentment, and fashion doubtless played a great part in the French as in all revolutions. The role of personal rancour in shaping the pre- and post-1789 careers of Mirabeau, Sieyès, Volney, Condorcet, Brissot, and virtually every other significant revolutionary leader of whatever stripe is obvious. What needs explaining is not the special usefulness of radical ideas to potential leaders of protest movements who by the 1780s were expressly seeking to trigger 'la révolution désirée' for this is self-explanatory, but the actual diffusion of radical thought, the process whereby it became an established rhetoric, an ideology at hand, ready for use as a powerful political tool, and here the answer lies in the further expansion and institutionalization of the court and official Enlightenment widening the channels of diffusion enabling the illicit process to accelerate.

A pre-eminent example of a structural change assisting corrosion of traditional values and attitudes was the network of provincial academies set up after 1750 expressly to stimulate public debate, maintain libraries and reading-rooms, and provide access for the public, and also offer prizes for exceptional essays on topical questions as well as generally promote mainstream thinking. Such academies, of which there were around thirty-five in France by 1789, and their reading-rooms, functioned as locally active clubs where moderate, radical and *Rousseauiste* visions of society, law reform, politics, economics, and morality competed for attention.[8] In this way, *la philosophie moderne*, *anti-philosophie*, and a militant Rousseauism

---

[6] Sabatier to 'Helvétius', Paris, 15 July 1766, in Sabatier, *Apologie*, 125–36.
[7] Caraccioli, *Cri de la vérité*, 120–1.   [8] Mackrell, *Attack*, 105–6; Doyle, *Origins*, 79.

presented themselves and were all widely adapted to specific social and political issues. But it was a milieu in which depth of knowledge and understanding was often less evident than superficiality, adroitness in deploying incisive maxims and pithy quotations drawn from *la philosophie*. In the 1780s, Brissot, Marat, and Robespierre—for some years an active member of the academy at Arras—figured among the regular competitors in academy debates, essay competitions, and election intrigues, all displaying skill at giving speeches on current issues in the light of Rousseau, Montesquieu, and Voltaire. Without ostensible knowledge of the writings of such authors no one counted for much in these circles. 'Philosophy' had become the entrance ticket to the arena of political debate.

Robespierre was elected a member of the Académie of Arras in 1784, the same year as winning second prize in the Metz Académie's competition for an essay on monarchy.[9] For several years he was a fully active member of the Arras academy and, by 1786, its president. This means his encounter with *la philosophie* reached back some way but need not mean he necessarily drew inspiration in any positive way from its message. Indeed, Robespierre was regularly singled out precisely for the shallowness of his grasp of philosophical ideas. 'He was never a learned man', noted another revolutionary leader, Roederer, in 1794, 'nothing remained to him from his sterile studies at college, any more than from his practice at the Bar. While working on subjects proposed for prizes by provincial academies, he acquired ideas that were more philanthropic than philosophical.'[10] No doubt Robespierre was not alone in responding to the 'torrent' of *l'esprit philosophique* in a sullen, basically uncomprehending, anti-intellectual manner. Deep down he hated *la philosophie* and so did many others. But as his background confirms, there was no such thing as a revolutionary leader whose revolutionary stance was not decisively shaped, even if only superficially, by *philosophique* ideas; and who was not trained in debating basically new principles or, for whom such debates were not the admission pass to the clubs and politics.

Another anti-intellectual revolutionary leader with no sympathy whatever for the true radical outlook was the Swiss-born Jean-Paul Marat (1744–93), a slightly more erudite *Rousseauiste* than Robespierre who published his first violently anti-monarchical political work, in England (in English), at the age of 31, in 1774. Admittedly, no one could be less *philosophique*. Nevertheless, early on he loudly professed his veneration for Montesquieu and Rousseau, entering academy competitions, mostly unsuccessfully, at Berne, Bordeaux, and other places. He was to initiate his Paris newspaper, *L'Ami du peuple*, one of the most militantly demagogic and denunciatory of the Revolution, in September 1789, becoming the idol of the Paris mob. Thoroughly despised by Condorcet and the rest of the Paris Académie des Sciences as an *anti-philosophique* charlatan and unyielding Mesmerist, he too nevertheless experimented extensively (like all the others) with both mainstream and

---

[9] Whaley, *Radicals*, 2, 15; Scurr, *Fatal Purity*, 40–5, 61.   [10] Roederer, *Spirit*, 129.

Radical Enlightenment ideas for the indispensable purposes of self-advertisement and advancing his career. Before 1789, Marat was quite eager to highlight his oft-proclaimed enthusiasm for Montesquieu's political and social conservatism, something about which later he lapsed quiet.

With some aspects of the *philosophes'* case Marat had no quarrel. It had always been the job of the priestly class, he agrees, at the outset of his *De l'homme* (3 vols., Amsterdam, 1775), to blind the human race in their own interest 'et de prêcher au nom des Dieux l'ignorance et l'erreur', propagating a thousand absurd stories about man and his destiny. He agreed also that during the eighteenth century, a 'revolution' had removed the 'bandage that superstition held over men's eyes', meaning that a 'revolution' in thinking brought about by the *philosophes* commencing with Locke and culminating in Newton, Voltaire, and the incomparable Montesquieu, the young Marat states, had indeed transformed the arena.[11] But Marat, much of whose work from 1774 onwards brimmed over with a peculiarly harsh, vengeful, and unphilo-sophical rhetoric, was far less inclined than Sieyès, Mirabeau, Brissot, Condorcet, Volney, or Cloots to identify with the *philosophes* (other than Rousseau and Montesquieu) or agree that they had found the right answers. Indeed, a feature unique to him was his unyielding insistence that the *philosophes* (other than Rousseau) had failed to find the answers. *La philosophie*, according to him, had altogether failed to proclaim 'les grands principes'.[12] For the populist Marat (again like the others), it went without saying that the illiterate and semi-illiterate mass of people whom he was one day to manipulate more skilfully than any other revolutionary leader grasped nothing at all about society, morality, or the nature of man and had to be firmly led by leaders who did understand the *grands principes*. But neither did the *philosophes*. The crucial point for him was that the true principles were grasped by only a very few with special insight, otherwise 'la connoissance de l'homme est entièrement ignorée'.[13] By 1775, Marat was already an inflexible ideologue of a peculiar kind who basically rejected the Radical Enlightenment, dismissing it as corrupt, 'atheistic', too much concerned with philosophy and reason and unwilling to acknowledge the primacy in man of his powerful, stirring 'soul'.

Marat's answer to those scornful of his Mesmerist creed—that man consists of two totally separate substances, body and soul—was that they should immediately stop reading his books as his ideas are not for them.[14] Like Robespierre, he especially detested *philosophes* claiming man's soul is material and that mind arises from sensibility and sensations. Dismissing Buffon as a crude materialist, Helvétius as a *sophiste*, and the materialist *philosophes'* conclusions generally as 'vaines déclam-ations', he held the will is free, that 'l'entendement est donc toujours subordonné à la volonté dans la raison', and that sentiment which is what counts, far from contrary to 'reason', is something into which reason is subsumed.[15] The sole writer of the century

---

[11] Marat, *De l'homme*, i, préface pp. vi–xiv.   [12] Ibid. i, préface pp. xv–xx.
[13] Ibid. i, préface p. xxii.   [14] Ibid. i, 1, 13–14, 225.
[15] Ibid. i. 208, 225, 251, 310–11 and ii. 77, 237, 256–7.

altogether glorious in his eyes was Rousseau who by attacking 'reason', repudiating the *philosophes*, and demonstrating truth lies in men's feelings displayed an eloquence, nobility of soul, and force no other contemporary thinker rivalled: 'sublime Rousseau...prête moi cette force, cette noblesse, cette chaleur d'expression qui étonne, qui'enflamme, qui ravit et qui fait l'âme de tes écrits précieux.'[16]

But whether one focuses on genuinely radical theorists like Sieyès, Mirabeau, Condorcet, Cloots, Brissot, or Volney, or pseudo-*philosophe* anti-intellectuals like Marat and Robespierre, whether one considers true defenders of basic human rights or violent demagogues, highly principled leaders or charlatans, genuine democrats or murderous impostors, nothing about the French Revolution as a general renewal of law, legislation, and society, or its causes, can be understood without beginning with the philosophical controversies raging before, during, and after all its main stages— the very thing that historians and philosophers over the last century have collectively avoided doing. It has proved an astoundingly universal and utterly unfortunate mistake.

The principal diffusion mechanism, throughout, just as Mirabeau stated, was undoubtedly the book and the book trade, phenomena providing excellent evidence for historians and the best objective tests by which to ascertain what texts had the greatest impact during the critical phase of rapid diffusion. Among the foremost contributions made by book history to our understanding of both Enlightenment and the French Revolution in recent years is the clear confirmation it provides of the wide penetration of radical literature via a plurality of channels from the 1750s especially. It has long been known that Rousseau's *Contrat social* did not circulate widely before 1789, except in Switzerland where it was often read (albeit mostly for local reasons), though nor should one understate the book's reach—it was in fact known to many readers.[17] The broader message of the book-historical evidence, though, seems not to have been properly absorbed by historians or philosophers: for if traditional historiography, prior to the rise of book history as a force in cultural studies, massively underestimated the penetration of French society by the major radical works in French, precisely in this vital respect book history itself has failed fully to take stock of its own findings.

Rousseau was always central; what is wrong with existing interpretations of the Revolution is the assumption that he had few real rivals for the political and moral soul of the Revolution, an assumption completely untenable since the 1980s, with the emergence of more specific detail about the clandestine book trade in France. This evidence proves beyond any question that the *Système de la nature* and numerous other major radical political works including others by d'Holbach (even though no one knew at the time he was their author) had a wider, more sustained diffusion than Rousseau's political writings. The sales impact of the *Contrat social* which appeared only in two regular and nine pirated editions in the years 1762–3 and then enjoyed

---

[16] Marat, *De l'homme*, ii. 378–9.   [17] Darnton, *Forbidden Best-Sellers*, 67.

just one further reprint before the Revolution, in 1772,[18] was relatively modest compared with that of the prime radical works. Along with the *Système*, the most widely known everywhere in the Atlantic world, as well as the hardest-hitting, was the *Histoire philosophique* generally attributed to 'Raynal'. Also vigorously diffused were Helvétius's *De l'esprit* and *De l'homme* and the works of Mably. Radical Enlightenment in other words, once an invisible underground, had by the mid 1770s become France's best-selling and most widely diffused oppositional literature about society and politics.

Admittedly Rousseau's *Émile* diffused far more widely than the *Contrat social*, passing through twenty-two separate editions before the Revolution, and *Émile* did play a notable part in the emergence of revolutionary ideology. But it was prized primarily for exalting ordinary feeling against 'reason' and for its ideas about education and promoting natural religion rather than any specifically political or social message. Demand for other, more notorious forbidden books, like the *Système* or the *Histoire philosophique*, far outstripped anything by Rousseau while, likewise, the reading public's interest in Helvétius's *De l'esprit* (1758), a much earlier work but one whose sales notably 'held up', as Darnton put it, 'until the 1780s, eclipsed by far demand for *Émile*.[19] If these findings surprised historians and philosophers, and judging by the continuing bias towards overemphasizing the role of Rousseau's writings and ideas in the making of revolutionary democratic republicanism, have by no means yet been fully digested, there is no reason why they should surprise anyone. All the evidence about illicit books in France prior to 1789 incontrovertibly demonstrates the very wide and astoundingly rapid penetration of printed clandestine philosophical literature. This impact was then intensified by other vehicles of diffusion—the rhetoric of *anti-philosophie*, salons, academies, official and academic condemnations, and seminary training in refuting radical concepts.

And besides all this there was yet another key cultural mechanism at work. Much of the Radical Enlightenment's greatest diffusion from the 1750s onwards was achieved indirectly rather than by openly materialist writings, by widely selling compendia such as the *Encyclopédie*, and reviews and summaries in other works. The one factor that did clearly recede by comparison with the first half of the eighteenth century was the clandestine manuscripts so crucial to the diffusion of Radical Enlightenment before 1750. What in the early eighteenth century was a marginal cultural phenomenon, reaching only a few hundreds, via illicit manuscripts and furtive discussion, had by the 1770s and 1780s become an unstoppable torrent inundating French provincial society and the capital, penetrating all sections of literate urban society. The *Système de la nature* passed through at least thirteen editions in French between 1770 and 1781 and is listed third in the famous checklist, assembled by Darnton, of best-selling forbidden books in France during the two decades prior to 1789. It ranks second in terms of orders placed by French booksellers

---

[18] Tatin-Gourier, '1762–1789, *Émile* et le *Contrat social*', 110–12.
[19] Darnton, *Forbidden Best-Sellers*, 67.

with the key Swiss supplier, the Société Typographique de Neuchâtel, out of 720 books listed.[20]

The *Système* ranked among the four or five books most in demand, the book-historical data show, among readers in such widely dispersed provincial towns as Nancy, Montpellier, Lyon, and Rouen, and not just initially but continuously through the 1770s and 1780s. At Lyon, d'Holbach's *Système* easily topped the list of forbidden works supplied during this period from Neufchâtel by five of the most prominent booksellers;[21] and while several other radical works, such as Mirabeau's *Essai sur le despotisme*, Helvétius's *De l'esprit*, and other writings of d'Holbach including the *Christianisme dévoilé* and *Contagion sacrée*, were also notably in demand, as were the *Œuvres* of La Mettrie, no other large, major text attained half the level of sales of the *Système*.[22] In Lorraine, the picture was similar, the *Système* outstripping every other serious work apart from Le Mercier's equally radical *l'An 2440*, selling notably faster than other best-selling radical books like Helvétius's *De l'homme* and Raynal's *Histoire philosophique*.[23] Even so, the high profile of the *Histoire* in the duchy with fifty-seven copies, Helvétius's *De l'homme* (40), and d'Holbach's *Système social* (37), which went through at least five French editions down to 1788,[24] illustrates the penetration of a considerable range of radical works also on France's eastern border.[25]

In the ancient and remote town of Loudun, in western Poitou, a single *libraire*, Malherbe, made thirty-two orders to the Société in Neufchâtel between September 1772 and November 1779 in which 117 illicit publications figured. Of these 117, the *Système* not only topped the list among works 'philosophical' in any serious sense but ranked fourth on the overall best-selling list with 167 copies. This far outstripped other notorious clandestine works like the *Histoire philosophique* (55), d'Argens's *Lettres chinoises* (54), d'Holbach's *Christianisme dévoilé* (52), d'Holbach's *La Contagion sacrée* (51), and d'Holbach's *Histoire critique de Jésus-Christ* (28), though all appeared within the top quarter.[26] Still more striking is the evidence for deliveries from the Neufchâtel Société to regular *colporteurs* in France. Third in size on this list of illegal works of all kinds supplied by *libraires* to the street pedlars, the *Système* with 700 copies, and sixth most requested, the *Histoire* with 510 copies, despite being large, complex, and highly sophisticated intellectual works easily eclipsed d'Holbach's *Christianisme dévoilé* (220), d'Holbach's *Bon-Sens* (194), and more salacious, best-selling items like the *École des filles* (185) and *Thérèse philosophe* (331). Indeed the *Système* eclipsed all other major illegal works in France apart from the *Histoire*.[27]

[20] Darnton, *Corpus*, 171–2, 194; Vercruysse, *Bibliographie*, 1770, sections A6, A7, A8, A9, and 1771, A1, 1774, A5, 1775, A5, A6, 1777, A4, 1780, A1 and A2, 1781, A1 and A2.

[21] Darnton, *Corpus*, 220, 223; Darnton, *Forbidden Best-Sellers*, 26, 28, 48–9, 63, 402.

[22] Darnton, *Forbidden Best-Sellers*, 223.

[23] Ibid. 222–3.

[24] Ibid. 173–4; Vercruysse, *Bibliographie*, 1773, A4, A5, A6, 1774, A6 and 1788, E2.

[25] De Bujando, *Index*, 444; Darnton, *Corpus*, 42.

[26] Darnton, *Corpus*, 216–17.   [27] Ibid. 227–8.

Even so, notable local oscillations in the pattern stand out. The main specialist book-seller retailing illicit literature at Rennes, Blouet, placed eleven orders with the Société between October 1772 and September 1776 for copies of 120 forbidden works in which four other works of d'Holbach—the *Bon-Sens, Histoire critique de Jésus-Christ, Le Christianisme dévoilé,* and the *Théologie portative*—besides *Thérèse philosophe* all outstripped the *Système*. At La Rochelle, the firm of Pavie placed fourteen orders between March 1772 and March 1784, in which requests for Mirabeau's *Essai* and d'Holbach's *Théologie portative* outstripped the *Système*.[28] But all evidence for provincial France, as also for Paris, without exception, confirms that d'Holbach achieved a greater degree of penetration than any other radical writer and not only via his *Système* but also a whole spectrum of other works. The proof is conclusive also that other radical authors such as Helvétius, Raynal, Diderot, d'Argens, Mercier, Mirabeau, Mably, Brissot, and the main reviser of *Le Militaire philosophe*, Naigeon, penetrated deeply everywhere.

An uncommonly fierce anti-religious work supposedly published 'à Londres', in 1768, *Le Militaire philosophe*, had by 1776 been reissued in at least four other editions.[29] Naigeon, besides being a notable anti-Rousseauist radical author in his own right, was a key functionary in the wider mechanism of the diffusion of Radical Enlightenment and not least the *Système*. An expert in the forbidden philosophical manuscripts at quite a young age, researching originals, authors, and variants, it is doubtless this which first brought him to Diderot's attention leading to his being brought into the inner circle of the *encyclopédistes*. It was also Diderot, in or around 1765, who first introduced him to d'Holbach. A well-known connoisseur of the Parisian art scene and artists with a taste for classical authors but little of d'Holbach's appetite for science or economics, he was also, we have seen, the author of the key entry 'Unitaires'—judged 'terrible' (tremendous) by Voltaire—in the *Encyclopédie*.[30] Among his later projects was his collaboration with the tutor of d'Holbach's children, La Grange (1738–75), in preparing a special (and luxurious) edition of Lucretius (1768) and another of Seneca, left incomplete when La Grange died in 1775 and finally published with the encouragement of both Diderot and d'Holbach in 1778.[31] A declared atheist, Naigeon headed the team of assistants labouring in the engine-room, so to speak, of d'Holbach's 'synagogue'. Methodical and exact, Diderot and d'Holbach both came to rely on him to an unusual extent, the former naming him his literary executor and the latter remaining his intimate collaborator throughout his last years. In 1789, along with Deleyre and Madame Helvétius, Naigeon became an ardent *révolutionnaire*.

With the help of his younger brother, likewise a professed atheist, Naigeon organized the checking, stylistic correction (to remove Germanisms), and transcription of d'Holbach's manuscripts (to render them unidentifiable by his hand). He also

---

[28] Ibid. 219–20.   [29] Ibid. 121–2; Vercruysse, *Bibliographie*, 24, 26, B2.
[30] Voltaire to Damilaville, 12 Mar. 1766, in Voltaire, *Corr.* xxx. 133; Vercruysse, *Bibliographie*, 19.
[31] Wickwar, *Baron d'Holbach*, 105; Naville, *Paul Thiry d'Holbach*, 98.

arranged their clandestine smuggling from the 'boulangerie de Grandval', d'Holbach's country house where d'Holbach held innumerable discussions and joint reading sessions with Diderot, to the northern border town of Sedan where Naigeon's brother held an official post and could relatively easily arrange transportation, unnoticed, across the border to Liège where an agent of Marc-Michel Rey forwarded the manuscripts to Amsterdam.[32] Printed in very large print-runs, on good paper, they were distributed from Amsterdam to France, Germany, and Switzerland and on such a large scale that this must have been with the collusion of elements of the city government in return for his undertaking to export the great bulk of the supply abroad.[33] Well practised in the requisite techniques, Rey personally managed the delicate business of smuggling illicit book consignments into France. Due to Naigeon's and Rey's elaborate precautions, d'Holbach himself may have known relatively little about the production and distribution processes. He might indeed initially have heard of the impact of 'his bombs' prior to acquiring his own personal copies of his texts, through hearing accounts of their arrival, infiltration, and effect narrated at his own dinner table (where he made no open admission to being their author and where most guests either did not know, or could only guess, that he wrote them).

D'Holbach's regular salon, Morellet's *Memoires* and other evidence indicates, actually comprised two different circles, a small inner group headed by Diderot, Naigeon, and Deleyre, all close, active participants in the baron's ruminations and compositions, and an outer group composed of around ten intimates not directly involved in producing his works but who, Morellet avers, knew without any doubt—though they never discussed the matter with each other until after his death—that d'Holbach authored the *Système* and a whole barrage of other radical works. These were besides himself Saint-Lambert, Marmontel, Suard, Roux, Darcet, Raynal, Helvétius, and Chastellux.[34] Jean-Baptiste Suard was a conservative journalist, admirer of Voltaire, associate of Raynal, and intimate of Montesquieu during the latter's last days. Jean Darcet, from Douazit in the Landes, like Suard and Deleyre, introduced to *la philosophie* by the elderly Montesquieu, was a leading chemist and member of the Académie des Sciences. The Bordelais Augustin Roux, also a dogmatic atheist, notes Morellet, had likewise been close to the elderly Montesquieu.[35]

D'Holbach's Thursday and Sunday dinners were attended usually by between ten and twenty persons, not infrequently including one or more eminent foreign guests, such as Franklin, Hume, or Wilkes, and most frequently, Galiani. This necessitated discretion at all times. The regular outer circle did not directly collude in preparing radical clandestine works for the press, though it is conceivable that one or two at least, especially Saint-Lambert, were more implicated than Morellet realized. Most of them lacked precise knowledge of how d'Holbach's sensationally subversive illegal

---

[32] Sauter, 'Paul Thiry', 127.
[33] Vercruysse, *Bibliographie*, 19; de Booy, 'L'Abbé Coger', 186.
[34] Wickwar, *Baron d'Holbach*, 90; Boulad-Ayoub, 'Introduction', 8–9, 11.
[35] Shackleton, *Montesquieu*, 390–1.

works were redacted and distributed.[36] But they kept d'Holbach's secret, remaining loyal to him over many years, unstintingly contributing to 'la conversation la plus libre, la plus animée et la plus instructive qui fût jamais',[37] helping turn his regular dinners into a kind of private institute, primed by his money, good taste, and fine wines, for the propagation of international revolutionary egalitarian ideology established under the nose of the court in the heart of Paris.

No one, least of all the Inquisition in Rome who prohibited the work in November 1770, supposed the *Système* was really the work of 'Mirabaud'. In France, a large monetary reward was publicly offered, in October 1770, noted the duke of Württemberg approvingly, for information leading to the author's arrest. But the substantial reward offered had no effect, despite the fact that all along every connoisseur of literary and philosophical activity in Paris and some further afield, observed Fréron, knew the author's identity. Even Fréron, remarkably, never mentions the 'Antichrist de la Rue Royale', d'Holbach, by name.[38] In 1782, the Utrecht professor Hennert assured Dutch readers that 'Mirabaud' was not the author and that the *Système social* (1773) and *Morale universelle* (1776) were certainly by the same hand as the *Système*, the three works together constituting the 'atheist Bible'. He too knew the author's identity but averred: 'I will not make the real author's name known whilst he is still living.'

D'Holbach's authorship was an open secret in Holland which no one wished publicly to divulge.[39] The inevitable consequence was a profusion of rumour everywhere as to who exactly the author and collaborators were. For years, the *Système* was advertised as being (and in Britain, Holland, Italy, and Germany was often assumed to be) by Helvétius.[40] The 1774 'London' edition includes a portrait of Helvétius facing the title page while the *Compendio del Sistema della natura* appearing at Venice, in 1798 or the 'anno primo della Libertà italiana' [first year of Italian liberty], still attributes the work to Helvétius. Many contemporaries suggested it was the work of a consortium of *esprits forts*.[41] Gradually, it became the received view that the *Système* had been composed 'by a society', as the English radical John Jebb put it, 'of the most eminent French unbelievers'.[42] In a way, this was correct for while d'Holbach was the principal author, the 'bible' of French atheistic materialism *was* the product of team effort and years of close discussion, though Diderot himself seems to have contributed much more to the discussion stage than the actual writing. Naigeon helped finalize the text, as probably did one or two others, but most of it was certainly d'Holbach's. The *Système* was not infrequently also attributed to Diderot, something rendering him decidedly nervous during his last years.[43] Many pages of

[36] Morellet, *Mémoires*, i. 132–3, 138–9.   [37] Ibid. i. 133.
[38] Balcou, *Fréron*, 367; Robinet, *Dom Deschamps*, 71.
[39] Hennert, *Uitgeleezene vehandelingen*, iii. 427, 472, 481, 483.
[40] Diderot, *Corr.* x. 84; Smith, *Bibliography*, 364, 375.
[41] *La France littéraire*, iv (supplement 2nd part), 199; *Index Librorum Prohibitorum* (1786), 284; *Mémoires secrets*, vi. 264; Palmieri, *Analisi*, i. 51, 129.
[42] Jebb, *The Works*, ii. 162.   [43] Diderot, *Corr.* x. 25, 96 n.; Pellerin, 'Naigeon', 31–2.

the *Système* reveal the stamp of Diderot's style of thought and writing, noted Grimm, in 1788, though modern scholars have never been able to agree whether his input was considerable or not. Only in the later 1780s did rumour begin to stabilize around d'Holbach as main author, in collaboration with Diderot or Naigeon.[44] In any case, largely conceived in the course of their discussions, the *Système* was seemingly ready as early as 1766–7, but then held back from publication for several years.[45]

For such a large, complex, and anonymous work to achieve the astonishingly sustained as well as profound impact it did, in so many countries, with nothing certain known about its author, is an extraordinary, even perhaps unique, phenomenon. Not until 1821, or over half a century later, was the writer's real name positively revealed to the reading public. But what chiefly matters historically and philosophically is its unparalleled propagation and impact. Bergier, announcing his intention of writing a full-scale refutation, recognized at once, in early February 1770, that this book with its seemingly cogent arguments, vigorous and eloquent style, and 'tirades' against received thinking worthy for power and eloquence of Demosthenes, wholly surpassed every other challenge and would become the very 'code' of the militant *philosophes*. He was under no illusions as to what the *anti-philosophes* were up against. Not only was this book insidious, well written, and well printed; it was expounded with passion and ingenuity, and was in every way formidably systematic: 'c'est le livre', in short, 'le plus hardi et le plus terrible qui ait été fait depuis la Création du monde'.[46]

The underground culture of advertising, distributing, and reading illicit works, with the *Histoire philosophique* and the *Système* heading the list, developed over several decades. France, Switzerland, the Low Countries, Britain, Milan, and Germany, especially Berlin and the Rhine valley, formed a kind of inner circuit permitting rapid and large-scale diffusion of radical works. Most of the rest of Europe, including Scandinavia, Ireland, Spain, Italy, and outer Germany, then formed a kind of intermediate circuit, after which came an outer circuit consisting of North America, Russia, Spanish America, Brazil, eastern Europe, Batavia, and the Dutch network in Asia where diffusion was slower and more sporadic but in the end also far-reaching. Italy and Spain were lands where ecclesiastical supervision of society and culture was still tight but also, partly for that reason, a context where social, cultural, and religious tensions were opening up a large potential space for radical thought. Politically fragmented, Italy was a land of elaborate book censorship and close control of debate and individual expression where one needed to watch one's step. Spending several months at Rome in 1786, Goethe felt obliged to use a false name lest the notoriety of his novel *Werther*, denounced by the Lutheran Church in Saxony in 1774 for appearing to glorify suicide, should create difficulties for him

---

[44] Vercruysse, *Bicentaire*, 9–11.
[45] Ibid. 225, 228, 230 n. 24, 235–7.
[46] Quoted in Charbonnel, 'Réquisitoire de Séguier', 15; Albertan-Coppola, *L'Abbé*, 161–2.

in Italy. The Italian version had been publicly condemned and even years later, in 1782, a batch of copies was publicly burned by the archbishop of Milan.[47]

Yet Italy also featured bizarre disparities and shifts of policy aggravated by long-standing political fragmentation. Censorship, often heavy-handed, was also patchy and strikingly inconsistent, encouraging the expansion of a lively clandestine network of readers and hidden connoisseurs of clandestine literature. Florence was one centre of this under-the-counter culture of book-buying and distribution and of Italy's 'société sécrète de hardis penseurs', as one late eighteenth-century French radical source termed it, a place where many examined modern philosophical works.[48] Illicit books, banned by the Church but also by the princes of Tuscany, Piedmont, and Naples and the Venetian Republic, the latter an aristocratic preserve where plebeians were less free than anywhere else,[49] according to contemporary commentators, could nevertheless fairly easily be procured, especially through Livorno.[50] In fact, a substantial, organized trade in clandestine literature arose. While Parisians were quick to complain about the Inquisition in Italy, wrote Alessandro Verri to his brother Pietro from Paris, in October 1766, official interference with the book trade seemed to him to be more systematic in France than Italy.[51] Galiani, writing to d'Holbach, requesting a copy of de Pauw's banned *Recherches philosophiques*, from Paris, in July 1770, remarked that no precautions need be taken as, at that time, there were no official searches of books imported into Naples.[52]

Clandestine importing of radical writings was encouraged by the failure of Italy's domestic publishing industry to produce anything intellectually or politically challenging in a society with many sophisticated readers, especially at the princely courts and among the nobility and Venetian patriciate.[53] To cater to such readers, a highly customized market evolved specializing in the clandestine advertising and procurement of French materialist books. Among the chief suppliers during the 1760s and 1770s was the Jewish merchant Moseh Beniamino Foà, owner of two bookshops in the duchy of Modena, at the time among the more liberal of the smaller Italian principalities, and official purveyor of foreign literature to the duke. Like much other evidence, Foà's catalogues show that French rather than British, German, or other works heavily dominated the Italian official and unofficial Enlightenment alike. Importing his supplies from Amsterdam, Frankfurt, and France, mostly via Livorno, Foà also supplied books to the neighbouring ducal library at Parma directed by the famous librarian Paciudi. Among his regular customers were several residing at considerable distances away, including Beccaria at Milan.[54]

[47] Braida, 'Censure', 96; Delpiano, *Governo*, 153–4.
[48] Delpiano, *Governo*, 84–5; Maréchal and Grasset, *Costumes civils*, ii. 70.
[49] Braida, 'Censure', 75.
[50] Balsamo, 'Gli ebrei nell'editoria', 57–8.
[51] Braida, 'Censure', 86 n.
[52] Galiani to d'Holbach, Naples, 21 July 1770, in Galiani, *Correspondance*, i. 203.
[53] Maréchal and Grasset, *Costumes civils*, ii. 75, 77, 80.
[54] Balsamo, 'Gli ebrei nell'editoria', 60.

Among social elites, in at least a small liberal Italian state like Modena, booksellers could even discreetly advertise *libri proibiti* just as the Société Typographique de Neuchâtel, among others, did in France. Officially banned titles of Voltaire, Rousseau, and Hume, works generally not prohibited throughout the rest of Europe but which, in practice, circulated in Italy without too much difficulty under the counter, they readily sold. But they offered also a spectrum of more illicit and actively repressed writings, of Boulanger, Fréret, d'Argens, d'Holbach, Raynal, and Mably, besides Pilati, Gorani, and later Filangieri, works subject to automatic seizure in the Venetian Republic and Piedmont as well as the Papal States. The original French version of the *Encyclopédie* was also offered by Foà alongside the less seditious (but also banned) Lucca version. Available in Italy's great princely libraries such books could readily be consulted by anyone of any standing. It was not until 1792, astonishingly, that Modena's ducal librarian was instructed to refuse access to texts expounding the democratic principles of the French Revolution. Until then, everything the duke purchased, including all the more notorious titles, remained more or less accessible to visiting readers.[55]

Meanwhile, the Netherlands where the largest quantity of printed clandestine philosophy was actually produced presents a most instructive contrast with both Italy and France. Here too book censorship constituted a formidable obstacle to the diffusion of clandestine books and ideas even if the real impetus behind book censorship there came less from the rather clumsy, ramshackle supervisory apparatus of the provincial and city governments than the force of popular aversion to freethinking and 'godlessness' and universal unwillingness of booksellers to deal in such matter except to trusted customers and furtively. As Diderot expressed it after living for some months in The Hague in 1784, the Dutch people 'soit bigot' and was definitely more devout and 'superstitious' than in France. More specifically, the Dutch nation as a people were, far more than the French, 'ennemie de la philosophie et de la liberté de penser en matière de religion'. Indeed, 'le matérialisme y est en horreur', and whatever Holland's importance as an export centre for radical books, the distribution of 'livres impies' in the streets and cafés of Dutch cities was more widely frowned on than in France or Italy.

Among the common people as well as in polite society, 'les incrédules' were both less common and 'more hated'.[56] The degree to which homosexuals were hounded in the Netherlands remained unparalleled. Yet, for all its faults in radical eyes, the United Provinces, due to its republican, libertarian past, still remained potentially 'la patrie de tous les amis de la liberté',[57] the place in Europe where literacy and reading had spread widest, where kings and aristocracy counted for least, the laboratory where one could see the rise of universal prosperity and the makings and stirrings of democracy emerging. Helvétius, bitterly resentful of the persecution he faced, felt that it was to the constitutions of the English and Dutch that Europe

[55] Balsamo, 'Gli ebrei nell'editoria', 62.
[56] Diderot, 'Voyage de Hollande', 428; Trousson, *Denis Diderot*, 518.
[57] Diderot, 'Voyage de Hollande', 406.

owed whatever vestiges remained of liberty. Otherwise, the yoke of despotism would be total. Every good citizen, hence, 'doit donc s'intéresser à la liberté de ces deux peuples'.[58]

For all these reasons the Dutch Republic constitutes a crucial case in the history of the diffusion of the Radical Enlightenment. The old notion once prevalent that the Dutch Enlightenment was an essentially unified, 'national', moderate, and Christian Enlightenment very different from that evolving in France, for example, looked correct as long as one examined only the official surface of things. Without question, the Dutch enlightened societies of the 1770s were heavily fortified against radical ideas which, indeed, it was one of their prime purposes to combat, a tendency reinforced by their close relationship with the city governments and local church councils.[59] On the surface the picture was one of harmony. The mistake that was made by historians was not to realize that Dutch culture was heavily bifurcated into respectable and unrespectable sectors and that the Dutch cities and universities were the scene of a flourishing forbidden freethinking underground no less than they were the scene of a flourishing if equally hidden and persecuted homosexual underground.

Radical Enlightenment in the Netherlands, however important its political dimension in the history of the Patriot movement in the 1780s, in its more philosophical anti-religious aspect remained confined to a persecuted, repressed, and (possibly) small as well as intensely resented counter-culture within Dutch culture. Compared to France, Italy, and most of Germany, the Netherlands may have been a land of toleration in religion and political commentary, but the prevailing attitudes of Dutch society in the late 1770s impressed Carl Friedrich Bahrdt, no less than Diderot, as exceptionally narrow and rigid. As part of this there was noticeably more blanket, uncompromising opposition to Semler and the German Neologs in Holland than in Germany.[60] Diderot also noted that for private buyers forbidden books were generally harder to procure in Holland than in France and other evidence confirms that clandestine works were nowhere sold openly but remained a strictly furtive, clandestine trade.[61]

This stuffiness reflected a deep-seated polarization powerfully at work behind the shutters. Only after some weeks in Amsterdam did Bahrdt discover that, despite appearances, not everyone was addicted to conventional thinking, churchgoing, and being conformist; there were, after all, some 'philosophers' in Holland. The bigotry and intolerance of popular culture were indeed so obtrusive as to prevent the ordinary person, in his view, from recognizing true moral worth or uprightness. Even the worthiest, most philanthropic individuals were mere 'rubbish in the eyes of the typical Dutchman' where of the wrong confession.[62] The prevailing mentality was rigidly confessional and anti-intellectual and this philistinism was further intensified by the peculiar bleakness of the Amsterdam coffee-houses which, as Diderot also

---

[58] Helvétius, *De l'homme*, i. 437.   [59] Mijnhardt, *Tot heil van 't Menschdom*, 91–3, 372–5.
[60] Eijnatten, *Liberty and Concord*, 338–9, 345.
[61] Ibid. 314–15; Diderot, 'Voyage de Hollande', 112.   [62] Bahrdt, *Geschichte*, iii. 271–5.

noted, were an exclusively male preserve, without women being present, where the atmosphere was so laden with tobacco smoke, complained Bahrdt, that customers could not see three paces ahead let alone read, think, or discuss elevated topics.

Only by chance did Bahrdt discover the existence of an Amsterdam 'Friday' club of about fifty genuinely enlightened men convening weekly to discuss 'philosophy' and new literary publications. A freethinking son of the famous Leiden professor of Arabic Johannes Jacobus Schultens (1716–78) came personally to escort him to his first meeting, expressing deep resentment that in Amsterdam 'intelligent men dwell as quietly and isolated as if they must conceal their own existence lest they be unmasked as men of understanding and be persecuted'.[63] At the first meeting Bahrdt attended, he was cordially received but also, he says, carefully questioned to make sure he really was the implacable adversary of ordinary thinking, conventional prejudices, bigotry, and *Priesterdespotismus* he claimed to be. He was impressed by the Amsterdam freethinking underground but at the same time grasped that this 'temple of reason', impressive though it was, was condemned to remain tragically opposite to the general tone of Dutch life. The true 'philosophical' fraternity in the Dutch Republic, much like the Spinozist urban and student fraternity in the late seventeenth century, formed an elaborate underground culture of hidden networks, socially and psychologically as well as intellectually segregated from mainstream society. But this very repression and isolation, the bitter hostility that surrounded them, rendered this philosophical 'hard-core' more bitter and resentful against prevailing assumptions and prejudices even than the radical-minded elsewhere.

Afterwards, Bahrdt also visited the older Schultens, a scholar of secret Unitarian tendency, from whom he heard a harrowing account of his lifelong struggle in Arabic studies and theology.[64] Professor Schultens too had had to conceal much from those about him, especially the theologians. His impressive library later auctioned in Leiden, in 1780, contained not only everything relating to Arabic studies and Bible hermeneutics, including numerous works by Semler and other Neologists, but also practically everything by and about Spinoza in Dutch, Latin, and French and all the major works of the French Radical Enlightenment including the *Système de la nature*, *Le Bons-Sens*, the *Système social*, and many other works of d'Holbach, Helvétius, and Boulanger. Both Schultens apparently had a detailed knowledge of radical thought and both seemingly sympathized with it to a considerable extent. But they had had to keep their views under wraps. In fact, it was impossible, the Patriot-minded professor Frederik Adolf van der Marck (1719–1800), a 'left Wolffian' in philosophy, observed, to hold certain positions in science and philosophy, to speak of the unchanging laws of nature governing the universe, play down revelation and miracles, or suggest non-Christians could be morally admirable, as he had with his doctrine of the 'pius naturalista', without being publicly accused of being 'Spinozist' and menaced with being ousted from one's position, as he had been from Groningen.

---

[63] Bahrdt, *Geschichte*, iii. 280–2.   [64] Ibid. iii. 294–6; Eijnatten, *Concord and Liberty*, 97.

Van der Marck was dismissed from his professorship by the stadholder in 1773, vividly illustrating the Dutch churches', and public's, paranoid obsession with 'Spinozism' and its stifling role in intellectual life and in politics. Accused of 'Spinozism', his dismissal was supposedly for unacceptable religious heterodoxy. But as both Van der Capellen and later Mirabeau noted this was merely a pretext. The real reason for Van der Marck's dismissal was because he had been inspiring students with the sentiments of liberty while the stadholder, as Mirabeau put it, preferred 'qu'on lui forme des esclaves'.[65] When restored to academe by the Patriots in Deventer, in 1783, Van der Marck duly published one of the resounding pro-Patriot pamphlets of the decade, asserting that the Creator of nature had 'established absolute equality and perfect liberty for mankind and has ordained that whosoever violates these rights is in a state of sedition with God's lawful society'; he urged everyone to defend these rights against oppressors whoever they might be.[66]

The official Dutch Enlightenment was uncompromising in its opposition to radical ideas; but the inevitable result in an enlightened age was to nurture a larger and larger underground of clandestine 'Spinozists'.[67] One can dispute whether there actually was 'a closing of the Dutch mind' during the Enlightenment beginning in the early eighteenth century,[68] or whether what was actually happening was slightly different, namely a continuation of the bifurcation of Dutch intellectual culture typical already in the late seventeenth century, with mainstream Dutch Enlightenment remaining neither more nor less rigid than a hundred years earlier in its outright rejection of naturalism, libertinism, and anti-scripturalism but changing in two other respects: it became on the one hand internally more flexible and tolerant of other Protestant confessions such as Lutheranism and Anabaptism; and, on the other, reacted against French cultural dominance of courtly and aristocratic culture shifting toward what has been aptly called 'an anti-cosmopolitan and more inward-looking mentality'.[69]

In France, rigour in suppressing forbidden books tended to ebb and flow with political circumstances and the mood at court. A particularly sustained crack-down followed Le Breton's arrest, in 1765, and the appearance of the illegally printed volumes completing the *Encyclopédie*. Though able to spend lavishly on prohibited books, Helvétius repeatedly complained about this growing repression in his correspondence. Writing to Voltaire, in January 1767, he despaired of obtaining a copy of the clandestine compilation *Recueil nécessaire* ('Leipzig' [Geneva], 1766), published by Cramer, at Geneva: whatever price one offered 'on ne peut l'avoir'. Contraband tobacco sellers, he observed, were these days much bolder in Paris than contraband booksellers, a clear sign the crack-down was succeeded in intimidating the *colporteurs*. Here, he wrote despondently, they speak only of hanging 'les colporteurs' and

---

[65] Mirabeau, *Aux Bataves*, 132–3; [Van der Capellen], *Aan het Volk*, 46.

[66] Schama, *Patriots and Liberators*, 69–70.

[67] Israel, 'Failed Enlightenment', 28.

[68] For this point of view, see Mijnhardt, 'Urbanization', 173–5.

[69] Ibid. 175; Israel, *Dutch Republic*, 1041, 1048–50.

burning 'les auteurs'.[70] The spirit of Lisbon had subsumed Paris and daily he expected to witness an *auto-da-fé*.

The heightened repressive atmosphere in France intensified the retaliatory shock of the *Système* appearing as it did, in February 1770, at the peak of an unprecedented flow of printed radical literature. Among the stream of texts appearing more or less simultaneously were d'Holbach's *Essai sur les préjugés* ('Londres', 1770) supposedly by D.M [i.e. Du Marsais], but today attributed to d'Holbach, with amendations by Naigeon,[71] a text that incensed Frederick but Voltaire dismissed as full of 'verbiage sans esprit' and not worth reading (although this did not prevent his attempting to discover, through d'Alembert, who wrote it). Was the miscreant Diderot, Damilaville, or, possibly, Helvétius?[72] After the *Système* came the *Examen impartial des principales religions du monde* (1770) by d'Holbach, the *Recueil philosophique* (1770), short texts by d'Holbach, Boulanger, Du Marsais, Diderot, and Hume edited by Naigeon; the *Tableau des saints, ou Examen de l'esprit ... des personnages que le christianisme révère et propose pour modèles* (1770), *L'Esprit du judaïsme* (1770), a devastating attack on the Jewish and Christian priesthoods, and *Israel vengé* (1770), based on the Spanish of Orobio de Castro edited by d'Holbach.[73] These were followed by more works of Mably,[74] and then the *Le Bon-Sens ou idées naturelles opposées aux idées surnaturelles* ('Londres' [Amsterdam], 1772), plainly penned, remarked Voltaire, by someone altogether lacking 'de bon sens', besides *La Politique naturelle* ('Londres' [Amsterdam], 1773), the path-breaking *Système social* ('Londres' [Amsterdam], 1773), the *Éthocratie, ou le gouvernement fondé sur la morale* (1776), and, finally, *La Morale universelle* (1776).

The response to such an unprecedented challenge was a further wave of repression. At the French clergy's annual General Assembly, early in 1770, an epoch-making declaration was issued, denouncing the collaboration of the Church's enemies and foes of the state. Faith being the foundation of the people's fidelity, the assembly proclaimed the new clandestine philosophy society's foremost adversary, condemning nine recent underground philosophical works by name.[75] Funds were voted to support Catholic apologists ready to devote their pens to combating the *Système*, especially Bergier who was now relieved of his pastoral duties as a canon in Paris and assigned a pension enabling him to devote himself fully to compiling what Naigeon later styled his 'recueil complet' of all the pious frauds and *sophismes* theologians had devised over eighteen centuries in defence of Christianity.[76] Following the Assembly's resolutions, on 20 August the prelates published a pastoral *avertissement* 'Sur les dangers de l'incrédulité', denouncing in particular the *Système* and Helvétius's

[70] Helvétius to Voltaire, *CGdH* iii. 273.
[71] Mori, 'Du Marsais philosophe', 186–7; Vercruysse, *Bibliographie*, infra.
[72] Voltaire to Frederick, 8 June 1770, in Voltaire, *Corr.* xxxvi. 239.
[73] Conlon, *Siècle des Lumières*, xvi. 120.
[74] *Mémoires secrets*, viii. 287.
[75] *CGdH* iii. 335–7; Paulian, *Véritable Système*, i. 196; Chopelin-Blanc, *De l'apologétique*, 119, 122.
[76] *Mémoires secrets*, v. 132; Deschamps, *Correspondance*, 435; Everdell, *Christian Apologetics*, 128.

De l'esprit, a directive reissued in their dioceses. So alarmed were the bishops they went in delegation to remonstrate with the king.

The *Parlement* of Paris, meanwhile, powerfully declaimed against this growing subversion by books. After a powerful *réquisitoire* by Chancellor Antoine Louis Séguier (1726–92), *avocat général* of the *Parlement* since 1755 and long-standing foe of Diderot and the radical *philosophes*, dated 18 August 1770, the *Parlement* had the *Système* publicly lacerated and burnt on 21 August 1770, together with *La Contagion sacrée*, 'Fréret's *Examen critique des apologistes*, *Le Christianisme dévoilé*, the *Discours sur les miracles de J.C.*, and other works proclaimed 'impies, blasphématoires et séditieux'.[77] Séguier's indictment, a text reissued in Italian, at Florence, the following year, proclaims a plot or 'confederation' of seditious authors working in all genres—poetry, history, novels, eloquence, and even in dictionaries as well as philosophical works—'contre la religion et le gouvernement', a 'ligue criminelle' designed 'to destroy the intimate harmony between the social orders' maintained by religion which had always existed between the Church's doctrine and the political laws of society. Everything had become 'infected' and even the theatres were now helping spread 'ces maximes pernicieuses'. There had arisen 'parmi nous', declared Séguier, 'une secte impie et audacieuse' that dressed up the false wisdom it peddled under the pretentious and undeserved name of 'la philosophie'. With one hand this sect of self-styled philosophers strove to overthrow the throne and, with the other, the altars. A 'revolution' was being engineered; and Europe's kingdoms were feeling their 'antiques fondemens' being shaken by principles all the more dangerous because ostensibly concerned with advancing humanity's happiness—'d'autant plus dangereux qu'ils paroissoient tendre au bonheur de l'humanité'.[78]

Séguier also drew attention to the widening readership for works like the *Système*. As it had matured in France since the late seventeenth century, over three or four generations, radical thought constituted a philosophy claiming the happiness of peoples and individuals is the first law of politics and social theory and that peoples have both the power and right to replace their government whenever they choose with one better attuned to the majority's interests.[79] Such pretensions were exerting an appeal. No sooner do such books appear in the capital than they are diffused through the provinces, and according to Séguier (as well as Voltaire) being read by women as well as men. Once the prerogative of the better off, these books were now penetrating into the ateliers and attics 'et jusque sous les chaumières', a paradoxical claim given that, through his text, Séguier himself was alerting a wide public to what was most subversive in the text, citing verbatim several especially challenging passages.[80] This deliberate appeal to the lower orders Séguier declared a grave social, intellectual, religious, and political menace: 'le peuple étoit pauvre, mais consolé; il

---

[77] *Réquisitoire sur lequel est intervenu l'arrêt du Parlement du 18 août 1770* (Paris, 1770), 1–3; *Mémoires secrets*, v. 154–5; Vercruysse, *Bicentaire*, 24.

[78] Séguier, *Réquisitoire* (1770), 2–3; Delpiano, *Governo*, 226 n. 49; Israel, 'Equality', 132.

[79] Séguier, *Réquisitoire* (1770), 17–18.   [80] Ibid.; Wickwar, *Baron d'Holbach*, 87.

est maintenant accablé de ses travaux et de ses doutes.' [the people were poor but had their consolation; but now they are overwhelmed by their labour and their doubts.][81] The judicial authorities were starting to apprehend that intellectual sedition on such a scale could perhaps mobilize social unrest.

The social 'revolution' implicit in Radical Enlightenment's diffusion was both emphatically alleged by the authorities and Church and intended by the radical underground itself. The Paris *Parlement*'s decree of 10 January 1774, condemning *Le Bons Sens* and Helvétius's *De l'homme* to be publicly burnt, equally invokes what the judiciary now considered the most dangerous aspect of the phenomenon—diffusion among the lower orders—especially deploring the popular style of *Le Bon Sens* (1772), a kind of 'catechism', the edict notes, of all the most 'monstrous consequences' of that 'depot of lies and horrors', the *Système de la nature*. It was obviously deliberately aimed at the uneducated and specifically at undermining their beliefs.[82] While the 'contagion' manifestly comprised dozens of works, a torrent gushing forth on all sides, the decree identifies the *Système* as the doctrinal core. The latter was a text comprehensively rejecting the proofs of God's existence composed by 'Clarke, Descartes, Malebranche et Newton' while simultaneously undermining the political order and monarchy. Most scandalous of works, the *Système* crowned all the efforts of which impiety is 'coupable envers l'état et la religion'.[83]

Fréron agreed that the situation had become so dire as to require a much more vigorous royal repression. He too urged the king personally to take charge of the fight, much as in the late 1750s *anti-philosophes* had implored the dauphin to. One could only hope, admonished Fréron in his *L'Année littéraire*, that the court was now so indignant at the *philosophes'* flagrant excesses as finally to be ready to take the most drastic action. Just as history records that Louis XIV imperiously crushed the Protestant 'menace', so, it would surely one day commemorate his great-grandson's intervention to crush the audacity of a 'cabale de lettrés' whose progress threatened the entire overthrow of religion. With thanks and profound relief future chronicles would record how His Most Christian Majesty, sword in hand, 'gloriously exterminated' *la philosophie* itself.[84]

Voltaire, meanwhile, was scarcely any less alarmed by the rising social and political challenge. If he had no precise knowledge of how this torrent of radical literature, and its ruthless diffusion, was organized, he knew perfectly well where the books were printed and from where they issued around France, Germany, Italy, and Switzerland. The operation centred on Holland and especially the Amsterdam printing shop of Marc-Michel Rey where production of the *Système*'s first edition was complete by November 1769.[85] Rey's literary editor, Allamand, answered Voltaire's repeated complaints by assuring him that this latest mass of irreligious *brochures* would

---

[81] Séguier, *Réquisitoire* (1770), 6.
[82] Oxford Bodley, Mason 48: *Recueil d'arrêts* no. 5, 'Arrest de la Cour du Parlement qui condamné deux libelles intitulés, l'un Le Bons Sens, l'autre, De l'homme', 10 Jan. 1774, 2.
[83] Ibid. 6–9.　　　　[84] Balcou, *Fréron*, 367.　　　　[85] Vercruysse, *Bicentaire*, 23.

have no more effect on society than those of Toland and Tindal earlier. But Toland and Tindal, retorted Voltaire, in June 1771, were scarcely known outside Britain whereas, owing to changes Enlightenment had wrought in the meantime, this new literature was perused everywhere from the Scandinavian glaciers to Venice. One finds no statesman today 'qui ne pense en philosophe'. What Europe had undergone since Toland's day was 'une plus grande révolution' even than the Reformation of the sixteenth century.[86] In pursuing such reasonable principles as toleration and enlightenment, the human race had endured seven long centuries 'de sottises et d'horreurs'; now, thankfully, the 'revolution' had arrived but his radical opponents were spoiling it all.[87]

No one doubted that a 'revolution' of the mind had occurred and was occurring. But the intellectual revolution generated by the spread of *la philosophie nouvelle* and the burgeoning in the lodgings, cafés, and reading-rooms of this 'secte impie' was not ending with toleration and the retreat of superstition but was manifestly pregnant with the promise or, as Voltaire and Frederick saw it, threat of social and political 'revolution' and here they were at one with the *parlements*. In the decree of the Paris *Parlement* preceding the public burning of the second edition of 1776 of *La Théologie portative*—another popularly oriented radical atheistic catechism injected into society by d'Holbach and Naigeon—*la fausse philosophie* is accounted an underground movement appearing to have no other object than to prepare 'in the shadows, and bring about suddenly, a revolution in belief, in government and in morality' [n'être occupé qu'à préparer dans les ténèbres et à opérer tout à coup une révolution dans la croyance, dans le government et dans les mœurs].[88]

Police, bishops, and *Parlement* pursued the *Système* and other recent clandestine philosophical publications in the early and mid 1770s with unprecedented vigour. Among other consequences, the backlash produced a further crack-down on the *Encyclopédie*. A leading publisher, Charles-Josephe Pankoucke, who, in Diderot's opinion, treated his employees shoddily, had earlier, in 1769, bought the publishing rights from Le Breton, David, Durand, and Briasson and planned, together with the Genevan consortium led by Cramer which had a one-third interest in the venture, to reissue the *Encyclopédie* in France with tacit permission. Although Diderot always hoped to see an improved edition materialize one day, he refused to edit for Pankoucke. The project proceeded, hence, without him. But Pankoucke's timing proved unfortunate. The first three volumes of his *Encyclopédie* appeared almost simultaneously with the *Système*, in 1770. Practically the entire stock of 6,000 copies was impounded at the Bastille and Pankoucke briefly imprisoned there.[89]

This latest setback to the Paris *Encyclopédie* encouraged de Felice—the Italian editor denounced by Voltaire as an *imposteur* and *apostat*—to press on with the aid

---

[86] Voltaire to Allamand, 17 June 1771, in Voltaire, *Corr.* xxxvii. 438–9.

[87] Voltaire, *Histoire de Jenni*, 101–2, 108–10, and notes by Brumfitt and Gerard Davis, 142–5.

[88] Oxford Bodley, Mason 48: *Recueil d'arrêts* no. 11: *Arrest de la Cour du Parlement qui condamne une brochure intitulée:* Théologie portative (Paris, 1776), 2.

[89] Guyot, *Rayonnement*, 59–60; Darnton, *Business*, 29–30, 46–9.

of several prominent Swiss savants, notably Bonnet, Haller (who reworked all entries on physiology and medicine), and Alexandre-César Chavannes, professor of theology at Lausanne, with his purged and redone rival version, preserving the *Encyclopédie*'s original articles only where judged religiously and philosophically acceptable from a Reformed standpoint. This rival Swiss Protestant *anti-encyclopédiste Encyclopédie* of Yverdon, while retaining most of the anti-Catholic insinuation of the original, otherwise converted radical ideas throughout into enlightened Calvinist ones. 'Personne la lit', sneered Voltaire, in August 1771, with six volumes of the Swiss version available, 'mais on l'achète.'[90] By 1775–6 all forty-two volumes of the 'Encyclopédie d'Yverdon' were in the bookshops. This was in no sense Diderot's undertaking but a hostile competitor designed to supplant it. If it fought intolerance and obscurantism, it also mounted from a firmly moderate Enlightenment standpoint stinging attacks on the dangerous 'absurdities' of the author of the *Système de la nature* and generally on 'l'orgueil philosophique' which it too judged a general plague and the prime motor of sedition driven by 'le Spinozisme des philosophistes anciens et modernes'.[91]

Yet, in Switzerland too, radical concepts were gaining ground. The *Système* penetrated deeply, finding many readers, a few of whom, Gorani among them, were clearly highly sympathetic to d'Holbach's message. Corresponding with his former mentor Beccaria, at Milan, in March 1771, from Vaud, in the canton of Berne, he inquired whether the *Système* was circulating as vigorously in Italy as around Berne and whether it was being debated and making proselytes as on Swiss soil.[92] A prominent French *érudit* with many contacts in Italy then passing through and brave enough to praise the book was the Parisian astronomer Joseph-Jérome Lalande who also counted among the most notorious atheists in Paris. Later a fierce foe of Robespierre and the Rousseauist tendency in the Revolution. Lalande eulogized the book with such ardour during his Swiss trip, reported Gorani, that he provoked quarrels with several preachers.[93] The Swiss furore surrounding the *Système* culminated in August 1771 when a fresh edition appeared at Neufchâtel. The outcry stirred by local Reformed ministers resulted in the book being publicly burnt and its Swiss publisher, Frederic-Samuel Ostervald, one of the Société Typographique's two directors and a *philosophe intrépide*, according to Voltaire, being publicly disgraced and stripped of command of the civic militia, accused of reproducing this acme of all irreligion for profit. While Voltaire resented this text, he could not help becoming incensed whenever intolerant preachers orchestrated persecution of authors. He appealed to Frederick to intervene but the king, implacably hostile to the *Système*, refused, claiming Neufchâtel, though technically under the Prussian crown, enjoyed special freedoms.[94]

[90] Voltaire to d'Alembert, 19 Aug. 1771, in Voltaire, *Corr.* xxxviii. 55–6.
[91] Guyot, *Rayonnement*, 60, 68, 98, 101.
[92] Gorani to Beccaria, Nyon, 12 Mar. 1771, in Voltaire, *Corr.* xxxvii. 303–4.
[93] Ibid. 304; Findlen, 'Forgotten Newtonian', 314.
[94] Voltaire, *Corr.* xxviii. 55–6; Darnton, *Forbidden Best-Sellers*, 54.

D'Alembert, meanwhile, though privately no more objecting to d'Holbach's meta-physics than Lalande or Gorani, was as worried as Voltaire and Frederick. Being as much an atheist as Diderot, he privately demurred from Voltaire's scathing attack in his *Letters of Memmius* on the 'Stratonism' of Diderot and d'Holbach, albeit almost imperceptibly, as Voltaire himself notes, by saying not a word about it in their intensive correspondence.[95] But he desperately feared the consequences of the radical challenge to kings and their courts and especially their core thesis that kings and priests are eternal allies against the majority's interests. With Voltaire, he became increasingly *royaliste* during 1770s, distancing himself still further from the *coterie d'Holbachique* and Diderot, with whom he now no longer had any contact.[96] Naigeon severely took him to task privately for his timidity and hypocrisy in pretending to frown on irreligion; and, after 1789, also publicly reproached him.[97]

Meanwhile, Swedish and Russian noblemen were not the only aristocrats playing an active role in propagating radical ideas. Especially where it was impossible to print anything of a radical nature and difficult and dangerous to attempt to smuggle in books by ordinary methods, the securest way of diffusing radical ideas was to import books in an ambassador's bags or those of a great nobleman. In Spain and Portugal, the aristocracy were almost the only social sector where Enlightenment ideas had penetrated to any extent and here the Inquisition archives provide valuable details about the mechanics of the process. When the author Bernardo Iriarte (1735–1814) was denounced to the Inquisition, at the age of 39, in 1774, by one of his brothers, a Dominican friar, accusing him of deriding religion and speaking disrespectfully of the clergy, some interesting facts came to light.[98] Bernardo was found after investigation to belong to a far-flung freethinking aristocratic network accustomed to inform one another about illicit literature and regularly obtaining and reading the works of prohibited authors such as Voltaire, Rousseau, Diderot, Helvétius, d'Holbach, and Raynal. Iriarte's denunciation was supported by another friar, Fray Diego de Cisneros, who was the librarian at the Escorial. He informed the Inquisitors that none other than the Spanish ambassador at Rome, Don José Nicolas de Azara, a nobleman widely considered a hardened freethinker (and who read d'Holbach's *Système* in 1771), had written to Bernardo, warmly recommending Voltaire's *Dictionnaire philosophique* as something sure to please him. Iriarte was found guilty of impiety, being a *materialista*, and helping foment in Spain an underground cult of Voltaire. He was sentenced to lengthy confinement, indoctrin-ation, and confiscation of all his possessions, though the sentence, apparently, was never carried out.[99]

---

[95] Voltaire to d'Alembert, 27 Sept. 1771, in Voltaire, *Corr.* xxxviii. 136, 156.
[96] Pappas, *Voltaire and d'Alembert*, 116–17, 126 n.
[97] Naigeon, *Philosophie*, iii. 240.
[98] Lafarga, *Voltaire en España*, 66, 207.
[99] Ibid. 66–7; Defourneaux, *L'Inquisition espagnole*, 151; Sánchez-Blanco Parody, *Europa*, 246–7.

2. *ANTI-PHILOSOPHIE* AND THE DIFFUSION OF RADICAL LITERATURE

Several French *anti-philosophes* won renown outside the francophone world through translations of their refutations which were permitted to circulate freely and were often collected in seminary libraries, despite containing extensive quotes from radical texts and surveys of radical literature. *Anti-philosophie* in translation combated but at the same time served to advertise further afield the very threat being countered, a role enhanced by their appearing more accessibly and usually more rapidly than the radical works they denounced. The German version of the *Système* appeared only in 1783 (reissued in 1791), thirteen years after the French original,[100] while d'Holbach's *Système social* translated as *System der bürgerlichen Gesellschaft*, and *Le Bon-Sens* (*Die gesunde Vernunft oder die übernatürlichen Begriffe im Widerspruche mit den natürlichen*), were published only in 1788,[101] in the former case sixteen years after the original. Both Jamin's *Pensées théologiques* (1768), published at Mannheim, in the rendering of Father Hemmer, confessor to the elector of the Palatinate, as *Theologische Gedanken über die Irrthümer dieser Zeit* (Mannheim, 1770), and Nonnotte's *Dictionnaire philosophique de la religion* (4 vols., Liège, 1772) issuing at Augsburg in 1775 (and 1777), appeared in German within two years of the original. Nonnotte's *Dictionnaire*, successful in French, came out in two different Italian versions, at Florence and Venice, in 1773, and in Spanish and German not long after. Besides German, Jamin's *Pensées* was reissued repeatedly in Italian, under the title *Pensieri teologici*, rendered by the Franciscan Father Luigi da Missaglia, working from the fourth French edition (Brussels, 1773). The third Italian edition appeared at Venice in 1783.[102]

With this material, any reader in France, Italy, Germany, Spain, Portugal, or the Austrian Netherlands could keep abreast of the Radical Enlightenment. Nonnotte's *Les Erreurs de Voltaire* (1762) passed through no less than six French editions in its first eight years and fifteen French impressions altogether down to 1823. It reappeared in a Spanish version prepared by Fray Pedro Rodríguez Morzo in 1771, an Italian version (1773), and four German editions between 1768 and 1781, the last in Pressburg.[103] Nonnotte was honoured with a papal brief congratulating him for his efforts against the *philosophes*, in April 1768, acknowledgement which clearly encouraged the lively diffusion of his *Gli errori di Voltaire*, the Italian rendering of his attack on Voltaire, a version that reached its third edition, at Venice, in 1778.[104] Besides Nonnotte, Jamin, and Bergier, widely translated *anti-philosophes* included also Chaudon, Carracioli, de Genlis, and Feller.[105]

---

[100] Fromm, *Bibliographie*, vi. 373; Vercruysse, *Bibliographie*, 1783, no. E1.
[101] Vercruysse, *Bibliographie*, 1788, nos. E1 and E2; Fromm, *Bibliographie*, vi. 373.
[102] Jamin, *Pensieri teologici*, preface.
[103] Fromm, *Bibliographie*, v. 38; Pomeau, *Religion de Voltaire*, 344; Lafarga, *Voltaire en España*, 109; Pearson, *Voltaire Almighty*, 311.
[104] Rotta, 'Voltaire in Italia', 429.   [105] Fromm, *Bibliographie*, iii. 380.

Table 3. Early translations of key works of *antiphilosophie*

Author	Title	First French edn.	Italian	German	Spanish	Portug.	Russian
Bergier	*Apologie*	1769	1774 (V)	1786			
Bergier	*Déisme réfuté*	1768	1769, 1773 (V)	1779 (Vi)	1777	1775	1787
Bergier	*Examen*	1771	1772 (V)	1788 (F)			
Chaudon	*Dictionnaire*	1767			1793		
Feller	*Catéchisme philosophique*	(1773)		1781 (A)			
Gauchat	*Lettres critiques*		1783–7 (11 vols.) (R)				
Jamin	*Pensées théologiques*	1768	1782 (M)	1770 (Ma), 1775	1778		
Masson des Granges	*Philosophe moderne*	1759	1769 (Lu)	—	—		
Nonnotte	*Dictionnaire*	1772	1774 (V)	1775 (A)			
Nonnotte	*Erreurs de Voltaire*	1762	1773 (Fl.), 1774 (V), 1778 (V)	1768 (F), 1773 (F), 1781 (Pr)	1771, 1772		1793
Paulian	*Dictionnaire*	1770	1774 (V)				

Notes: A = Augsburg; F = Frankfurt; Fl = Florence; Lu = Lucca; Pr = Pressburg; V = Venice; Vi = Vienna; Ma = Mannheim.

In Catholic central Europe, as in Italy and Spain, translated *anti-philosophique* literature opened up a whole new philosophical panorama. In Germany, by mid-century, there was a well-established genre of anti-atheist and anti-deist literature. But it did not address the philosophical challenge as such. The Gotha Protestant preacher Johann Caspar Löwe's *Introduction to the Religious Conflicts with the Deists* (1752), for instance, attacks 'naturalists' and 'pantheists' from a theological standpoint, much as theologians had earlier combated Jews, Muslims, and heretics. He especially combats the naturalists' disparagement of Scripture while praising Locke for respecting Scripture.[106] German readers are warned against d'Argens's *Lettres juives* (1738) and Diderot's *Pensées philosophiques* (1746), 'one of the most poisonous libels against Christianity',[107] but his counter-attack focuses mainly on the Bible criticism of Edelmann, Bayle, Spinoza, Toland, and Collins. While he also rebuts Spinoza's arguments against the conceivability of miracles in chapter 6 of the *Tractatus Theologico-Politicus*,[108] Löwe provides little detail about recent philosophical developments. But by the early 1770s, such responses seemed inadequate. It was no longer anti-scripturalism in the first place that constituted the threat but the new philosophy.

The German version of Nonnotte's *Dictionnaire philosophique*, published at Augburg in 1775 (reissued in German in 1783, 1790, 1804, and 1810), in its preface

---

[106] Löwe, *Dogmatische und moralische*, preface, 3; Otto, *Studien*, 169–70.
[107] Löwe, *Dogmatische und moralische*, 19.   [108] Ibid. 249–50.

includes the Latin text of Clement XIV's congratulatory letter, dated Rome, 27 October 1772. Scorned by Voltaire as 'le plus ignorant des prédicateurs',[109] Nonnotte was eulogized by the pope for his comprehensive assault on the *philosophes*. 'The philosophical spirit', complains the German translator, had gained so much ground in southern as well as northern Germany by 1775, that 'nowadays one speaks about nothing but philosophy'. The impact of 'l'esprit philosophique', moreover, represented a serious menace in Germany as elsewhere. Were this fashion confined to 'the true philosophical spirit', philosophy that combines reason with faith, limiting reason's scope and upholding both religious values and ecclesiastical authority, it would pose no problem. But materialism was gaining ground and it was this that necessitated rendering into German what seemed to him Nonnotte's devastating rebuttal of French materialist thought and publications.[110]

The wrong kind of 'philosophical spirit', the sort admitting only reason as man's guide, is here dismissed as a 'madness full of pride' now penetrating everywhere in German-speaking Europe, overcoming that spirit of submission that respects authority and piously subordinates everything to theology's dominion. The moral, social, and political implications were such that materialist philosophy's advance, in both the original and translation, was dragging Germany into a cultural predicament graver in his view than any his homeland had ever experienced. 'The invasions of the northern barbarians, the Goths, Huns, and Wends, had wrought vast devastation, assuredly, but yet this havoc amounted to less than today 'die ansteckende Seuche des philosophischen Geistes schadet' [the raging epidemic of the philosophical spirit causes harm]. Far from remaining confined to the ranks of the learned, this fatal zeal for philosophy was even powerfully invading 'die Frauenzimmer' [women's circles]. The ideas projected by the *Système de la nature* and *Militaire philosophe* negated all religion, morals, and everything else most vital in society, ideas whose 'unholy progress' was proceeding with disconcerting speed.[111]

The Mercedenarian friar and court preacher Rodríguez Morzo, who also translated Guyon's attack on Voltaire, prepared several Spanish translations of works by Nonnotte in 1769–72. The influx of undesirable ideas into Spain, he claimed, constituted a giant intellectual conspiracy to destroy the Catholic religion and overturn monarchy by preaching universal toleration and the principles of the *Encyclopédie*. The originators of this global conspiracy were 'Espinoza [i.e. Spinoza], Hobbes and Bayle'; the current heads were Voltaire, Helvétius, and Rousseau.[112] When in 1777, the Spanish translation of Nicolas-Sylvestre Bergier's refutation of deism appeared under the title *El deismo refutado por si mismo*, its translator, another friar, Nicolas de Aquino, hailed Bergier as one of the greatest champions of Catholicism against the

[109] Voltaire, *Questions*, ix. 211–12.

[110] 'Vorrede des Uebersetzers', in Nonnotte, *Philosophisches Lexicon*, i, p. ix; Fromm, *Bibliographie*, v. 37.

[111] 'Vorrede des Uebersetzers', in Nonnotte, *Philosophisches Lexicon*, i, pp. xx, xxii, xxx, lxxxv.

[112] Herrero, *Orígenes*, 40–3; Sánchez-Blanco, *Absolutismo*, 228–9.

tolerantismo and *la impiedad* of the *philosophes*, maintaining that toleration is something the true Christian must oppose by every means possible, even violence if need be.[113] The names of 'Bayle, Montesquieu, Volter, Helvecio, Rousseau and others', complained Aquino, were being heard far too often in Spain.

Anti-philosophie, in short, was one of the chief factors promoting the spread of radical ideas in Europe and soon also North America, Spanish America, and Brazil. In assembling 'all the proofs which establish the truth of religion', as Madame de Genlis put it, *anti-philosophes* consciously provided 'the salutary but revolting detail of all the extravagant and pernicious principles which modern philosophy has renewed and propagated within the last thirty or forty years'. Madame de Genlis quotes extensively from d'Holbach, Helvétius, Diderot, Condorcet, and Morelly as well as the *Histoire*, throughout her *La Religion considérée comme l'unique base de bonheur et de la véritable philosophie* (1787), a work expressly intended, astoundingly, for the instruction of children especially those 'of his Most serene Highness the Duke of Orleans, and his Highness the Duke of Chartres, to whom the manuscript was read a few months after his first communion', in 1786.[114] De Genlis explains many salient theses of 'modern philosophy', being aware of 'no work upon this important subject, within the reach of the capacity of young people of both sexes. It was what was wanting in the system of education which made me determine to print this essay, which perhaps may be useful, because there exists no other of the kind.' However perverse her logic, her book then promptly reappeared in English, German, and other languages.

Nor was this all; even if one accepts Sabatier de Castres's claim that the works of Bergier and others were mainly read by *séminaristes*, there were many thousands of those and these were being exposed not just to the exact formulations and wording of many key radical theses but also to the *anti-philosophes'* extensive and sometimes laborious replies which did not always sound particularly convincing. In this way, seminaries for training priests became a regular route by which radical ideas and knowledge of democratic and egalitarian books were diffused in Spain, Portugal, Italy, and also Catholic Germany and Austria, a region which, in 1774, according to the Italian enlightener Pilati, who knew Austria well, was 'infinitely' less enlightened than Protestant Germany and where the seminaries remained a crucial cultural agent.[115] Many seminarists, according to Sabatier, were corrupted precisely by the numerous tedious and pedantic works of *anti-philosophie* where they found the theses of Spinoza and the radical tradition exhaustively refuted but were more struck not infrequently by the 'faiblesse des réponses' of Catholic apologists than the force of their pious 'objections'.[116]

As heads of colleges, professors, and librarians, *anti-philosophes* could hardly avoid themselves becoming regular customers for prohibited radical publications,

---

[113] Ibid. 177; Herrero, *Orígenes*, 49–50.
[114] Genlis, *Religion*, i, author's preface pp. vii–viii; McMahon, *Enemies*, 30.
[115] Pilati, *Lettere*, 43.   [116] Sabatier de Castres, *Apologie*, 120–1.

purchasing clandestine works in some quantity which, in turn, meant that the theological colleges in some cases themselves became significant centres for acquiring and studying this literature, and hence for its diffusion. *Anti-philosophie*, then, was also to a considerable extent a self-fulfilling prophecy both through its books and its role in seminary teaching. Those entrusted with training young men studying for the priesthood faced a growing need themselves to learn more about radical ideas in order to be able to train students to repel them effectively. As professional polemicists fighting radical arguments *anti-philosophes* needed a competent knowledge not just of the foremost seditious works but of the whole range of clandestine philosophical literature. A few, like Maleville and Bergier, became genuine connoisseurs of the genre, experts on the origins, development, and scope of the phenomenon.

Needing the books required to train their students in how to counter radical ideas, the seminaries developed into a conduit of cultural diffusion through education of priests. Two prominent opponents of the *philosophes* during the 1760s and 1770s, figuring among those d'Alembert called *la canaille sorbonique*, were the Abbé Ambroise Riballier (1712–85), secretary of the theology faculty at the Sorbonne and principal of the Collège Mazarin, and François Marie Coger (1723–80), one of its professors. Coger, celebrated for his attack on Marmontel's *Bélisaire*, was publicly rebuked by Voltaire, in 1767, for his intolerance and *libelle calomnieux* against Marmontel, reportedly penned under Riballier's dictation.[117] It was also Coger who set as an essay prize title at the university, in 1772, the question whether anything was more offensive to God and to kings than what 'is today called philosophy' and who set university students the question whether *la philosophie* is any less the enemy of monarchs than of God.[118] Amid the avalanche of anti-theological works cascading onto their heads from Holland, remarked d'Alembert—citing '*La Théologie portative* [d'Holbach], *l'Esprit du clergé*, *les Prêtres démasqués*, *le Militaire philosophe* [Naigeon], le *Tableau de l'esprit humain*, etc., etc.'—religion's besieged defenders had brought forth 'le feldmaréchal Riballier qui y commande' and such doughty officers as his 'colonel of Hussars', Coger, who could be expected to fight to the last.[119]

Riballier and Coger, like Bergier, were under no illusions as to the character of the challenge they faced, or their need in combating it for copies of the titles they lambasted. In a surviving letter, sent from Paris to Marc-Michel Rey in Amsterdam, of March 1770, precisely when the storm over the *Système de la nature* in France first erupted, Coger requests two copies each of no less than a dozen other illicit works and 'surtout trois exemplaires du livre intitulé *Système de la nature*'. Of the others, eight—*Le Christianisme dévoilé* (1766), *Essai sur les préjugés* (1770), *La Contagion sacrée* (1768), *L'Enfer détruit* (1769), *Théologie portative* (1768), *Lettres à Eugénie* (1768), *De la cruauté religieuse* (1768) and *De l'imposture sacerdotale* (1767)—were

---

[117] Marmontel, *Mémoires*, ii. 283; Voltaire, *Corr.* xxxii. 228–9.
[118] *Correspondance inédite de Condorcet*, 122; Condorcet, *Œuvres*, v. 332 and x. 84.
[119] De Booy, 'L'Abbé Coger', 184.

also from d'Holbach's pen or d'Holbach revised by Naigeon. Rey was asked to address the packages 'À Monsieur Riballier Grand-Maître du Collège des Quatre Nations', at Paris.

Rey, however, finding Coger's precautions inadequate, suggested a different method. Coger should arrange a 'tacit permission' to receive illicit books from abroad, from the Paris chief of police; Rey's packages could then be addressed 'à Monsieur De Sartines Lieutenant de police à Paris', with the books wrapped in inner packaging within the outer boxes, addressed to 'Grand-Maître Riballier, at the Collège Mazarin'. There was now nothing to fear, responded Coger, delighted with this procedure, 'ni pour vous ni pour nous'.[120] The consignment arrived safely but included only one copy of the *Système* that was damaged. Later, in January 1771, the college authorities needed more clandestine literature. This time, Coger again ordered several copies of the *Système* besides other works. This box too arrived via the Paris chief of police.

The reasons why *anti-philosophique* works were being extensively translated and diffused, and in the case of Canada and parts of the Caribbean, in the 1770s, distributed in French outside Europe, are clear. *La philosophie moderne* was seen to be undermining religion, morals, and monarchy together with the rest of the social order. Church and state therefore tried to fight the threat jointly by mobilizing the loyal Christian majority. This sense of being in the midst of a gigantic struggle grew more marked specifically in the 1770s and 1780s. The French bishops concerted this public campaign against this dire new threat because the 'troupe de séditieux' casting France into such turmoil were no less culpable before the tribunals of men than before the Lord. God forbids men to revolt under any pretext against the sovereigns he himself has given them 'et leur fait un devoir rigoureux de l'obéissance envers eux'.[121] The impassioned attack on the *Système* penned by the Abbé Richard, a fervent future counter-revolutionary eventually executed by the Jacobins, concludes by summoning all loyal Catholics to rally around throne and altar and stand as a united people sworn to combat the horrifying new spectre of *la philosophie moderne*: 'Venez donc, o François, venez tous vous rassembler autour du trône du meilleur comme du plus Chrétien des rois, sous la houlette de vos pasteurs'—and fight.[122] Psychologically, the war of crown and altar against the Revolution had already begun in the 1770s.

---

[120] Ibid. 190.   [121] Richard, *Défense de la religion*, preface pp. xlix–xlv.
[122] Ibid., préface p. xlv; McMahon, *Enemies*, 28.

30

'Philosophy' as a Maker of Revolutions

1. D'HOLBACH'S POLITICS

Most at all social levels in late eighteenth-century Europe undoubtedly accepted the legitimacy and rightness of the existing order. It was what they were used to and it was sanctioned by the churches. The world and everything in it were created by God; and the social order was divinely sanctioned. According to the many strongly influenced by the ideas of Leibniz and Christian Wolff in Germany, Scandinavia, and Russia, God had ordered the world in the best way possible. Yet by the 1770s, there were also an appreciable body of informed and aware individuals inclined—or driven by mounting difficulties—to grant the prime radical premiss, namely that the entire existing social order was one of chronic disorder, exploitation, dependence, and deprivation and hence one that hardly seemed to be divinely ordained.

Once the basic premiss was granted, the rest followed almost of itself. What remedy can there possibly be, asked d'Holbach, in 1773, for 'la dépravation générale des sociétés' where so many powerful factors combine to perpetuate the prevailing disorder and misery?[1] There is only one way to cure such a massive edifice of ills: abolish the whole corrupt system of rank, privilege, and prejudice and replace it with a more equitable society; and only one way to undertake such a task, namely to attack 'error' and proclaim 'the truth'. 'If error is the exclusive source of all the evil on earth', if men are only vicious, intolerant, oppressed, and poor because they have totally wrong ideas about 'their happiness' and about everything else, contended d'Holbach, then it can only be by fighting wrong ideas with courage and resolution, by showing men their true interests and proclaiming 'des idées saines', that society's ills can be tackled. Unlike Diderot and d'Holbach, Helvétius never reached the point of explicitly rejecting monarchy in principle. But he too understood that to change the basic categories and re-allocate advantages and opportunities more fairly and rationally for a better order of human happiness, one must first change the legal basis of society, and before this could be done society's moral ideas had to be placed on a new basis.

---

[1] D'Holbach, *Système social*, 551–2; d'Holbach, *Système de la nature*, ii. 61–6.

When society's defects are structural and deep and chiefly rooted in veneration for rank, faith, credulity, trust in authority, and above all ignorance, then philosophy is not just the most apt but the only agent potent enough to precipitate a rapid, all-encompassing revolution. Re-educating the public, accordingly, seemed to the radical enlighteners the crucial path towards renewing society in a more just and reasonable way, their ultimate aim being to forge a system of legislation and institutions binding the particular interest to the public interest and 'establishing virtue on the advantage of each individual'.[2] But such an aim was unattainable, they all realized, without a prior political revolution, the best outcome of which in large countries like France, Helvétius thought, would be a federal republic or else a league of around twenty small republics linked together for mutual defence. Once suitable forms of government and good laws were in place, these will naturally direct all the citizenry to the general good while leaving each individual free to follow the innate tendency of his or her own personal quest for their particular happiness.[3]

There is thus a definite sense in which the radical *philosophes* were more than just 'chefs de parti', as Rousseau called them,[4] seeking to change opinion. They were also deliberate, conscious revolutionaries albeit not in the sense of being planners of revolutionary action but rather as ideologues preparing the ground for revolution. Furthermore, the revolution they prepared was something which, before the rise of radical ideas, was completely inconceivable as well as unprecedented. In a sense, Burke was right to say of the revolutionary leaders of 1789 that they 'despise experience as the wisdom of unlettered men; and as for the rest, they have wrought under-ground a mine that will blow up at one grand explosion, all examples of antiquity, all precedents, charters, and acts of parliament.'[5] What he did not explain, and what modern historiography has failed to explain, is how such an ideology could capture France in 1789 and where it came from. He did not see that it had long, complex, and specific intellectual and social roots reaching back to 1650.

What d'Holbach called 'the enemies of human reason', defenders of royal absolutism and privilege, and the clergy, daily denounced the *philosophes* as subversives, rebels, 'des factieux', enemies of all authority. To this Diderot and d'Holbach replied very differently from Voltaire who always denied that his kind of *philosophe* was subversive at all—and from his point of view rightly. To them it was rather the 'tyrants'—kings, aristocrats, and priests and their supporters—who were the 'true rebels'; for it is they who foment misery and oppression, provoking the honest and well intentioned to retaliate against the sway they illegitimately usurp. It was those who ruled in *ancien régime* society who rendered established authority 'détestable' obliging good men to 'contemplate its ruin'. To flatter despots, burn incense to tyranny, endorse those—courtiers, magistrates, and priests—who make it their business to destroy the common good, is not righteous submission to legitimate

---

[2] Helvétius, *De l'homme*, ii. 767–8.   [3] Ibid. ii. 774; Helvétius, *Notes*, 1, 115.
[4] Rousseau, *Rêveries*, 31.   [5] Burke, *Reflections*, 49.

authority but betrayal of one's fellow men and country, complicity in the outrages everywhere committed against the human race.[6]

Real treason is not subversion of the existing order but rather such allegedly 'pious' conduct and veneration of ancient charters as sanctions the sway of princes, aristocrats, and priests, without regard for the social and moral havoc wrought on all sides by them and their functionaries. It is despotism, answered *la philosophie moderne*, buttressed by credulity and superstition, that mobilizes the more aware to the point that they feel compelled to fight back and, even though most men understand neither why nor how they are cheated, impels most or some, eventually, to rise and effect the ruin of the existing order. If it is true that society is rendered unhappy, oppressed, and wretched by obsolete ways of thinking, popular piety, and a morality obscure, monkish, and fanatical, then it is to those public-spirited thinkers opposing such beliefs, held Helvétius, that men owe the prospect of replacing this stunted, superstitious, immoral framework with a 'morality clear, healthy and based on Man's basic needs'.[7]

Seeking to correct what d'Holbach calls the 'negligence', perversity, and 'peu de sagesse', of the teachers and 'guides' of men,[8] combating those responsible for filling the world with prejudice, error, and bad laws and institutions, Radical Enlightenment from the 1770s came to be heavily infused with political revolutionary expectations and denunciations of 'tyranny'. Its self-proclaimed task was to instigate a wider intellectual and moral revolution designed to render society and individuals happier. The crucial connection was the conviction continually propagated since the 1750s by Diderot and the *coterie d'Holbachique*, that intellectual and moral revolution is impossible without a political revolution to clear the way and that, equally, a thoroughgoing reform of law and political institutions is impossible without the intellectual and moral revolution they advocated. 'Morality lacks force', as d'Holbach put it in 1773, 'if political reality does not back it up while politics is unsteady and goes wrong if it is not supported and aided by virtue.'[9]

This radical ideology forged by Diderot, d'Holbach, and Helvétius in the 1770s and 1780s had a long history. Originating in the 1650s, it emerged from being a hidden, illicit underground a century later with the widely noticed political articles in the *Encyclopédie*, the by then already highly politicized war of ideas waged by the radical *philosophes* against *ancien régime* institutions rapidly gaining momentum. From the 1760s arose a growing stream of underground, and increasingly political radical works such as the posthumous political masterpiece of Nicolas-Antoine Boulanger, the *Recherches sur l'origine du despotisme oriental*, in 1761, edited by d'Holbach, a work aiming to show how and why, for most of man's recorded history, society had been dominated by forms of theocracy, followed by divine right monarchy, systems of power that entirely trampled on personal liberty and individual

---

[6] D'Holbach, *Système social*, 554–5; Helvétius, *De l'homme*, ii. 777.
[7] Helvétius, *De l'homme*, ii. 922–3.
[8] D'Holbach, *Système social*, 19.   [9] Ibid. 22, 208–10, 247.

rights and dignity. Boulanger too, it was recalled in 1789, had no less than Rousseau, Voltaire, Helvétius, Mercier, and Raynal proved an inspired 'prophet'. He too was among those who in 1789–90 were taken to have predicted the great revolution produced by the progress of knowledge working gradually on *la raison publique* and slowly but inexorably revealing to men the 'true good of society'.[10]

Boulanger's book was followed by d'Holbach's celebrated article 'Représentants' for the *Encyclopédie* penned in or around 1763—a stepping-stone in the development of a democratic revolutionary ideology with its dismissal of all claims of the nobility, judicial elite, and clergy to speak in the name of peoples[11]—a piece with significant input from Diderot.[12] This marked the start of the campaign for 'representative democracy' later to culminate in Sieyès's, Mirabeau's, Brissot's, and Volney's contributions in the revolutionary debates of 1789–92.[13] The pace then quickened with d'Holbach's publishing Boulanger's *L'Antiquité dévoilée* around 1766 and especially after 1770, with d'Holbach's *Système*. After 1770, radical thought swelled into the torrent penetrating everywhere in the 1770s and 1780s with the openly egalitarian, democratic, and anti-colonial writings of the late Diderot, Raynal, d'Holbach, Helvétius, and Mably soon supplemented by further powerfully subversive works by Mirabeau, Brissot, Cerisier, Cloots, Sieyès, Condorcet, Forster, Paine, Godwin, Priestley, Barlow, and the rest.

Diderot, d'Holbach, and Helvétius, then, stood at the intellectual helm of a late eighteenth-century Radical Enlightenment that in the 1770s and 1780s prepared the ground and set the direction for the ideology of the 'Revolution of reason'. This does not mean, though, that earlier sources of radical thought were simply forgotten. There continued to be other and prior sources of inspiration for the radical wing during the revolutionary upheavals in and after 1789, as emerges from the intellectual backgrounds and careers of such hardened atheistic revolutionary democrats as Naigeon, Cloots, and Maréchal. Like Maréchal, Cloots, no admirer of the d'Holbach circle, drew as much or more in developing his anti-Rousseauist naturalism on older materialist sources such as Meslier, Fréret, Collins, and Bayle, as from Diderot or d'Holbach.[14]

D'Holbach in his *Essai sur les préjugés* (1770) and *Système social* (1773) identifies two great 'powers' that had combined to block the path to the benefits society ought to confer on all men equally, namely religion and government. Government had worked against the majority's interests by dividing men according to status, confession, and wealth and seeking the happiness of those who dominate at the expense of

---

[10] *Chronique de Paris*, 30 (22 Sept. 1789), 119 and ibid. 2/99 (9 Apr. 1790), 393; Delisle de Sales, *Philosophie du bonheur*, i, p. liii; Lichtenberg, *Schriften und Briefe*, i. 707i.

[11] D'Holbach, 'Représentans', in Diderot and d'Alembert (eds.), *Encyclopédie*, xiv. 143–6; Mackrell, *Attack*, 42.

[12] Lough, *Essays*, 121, 135–7, 226; Proust, *Diderot*, 120; Tortarolo, *L'Illuminismo*, 137.

[13] Pasquino, *Sieyès* 35–52.

[14] Labbé, *Anacharsis Cloots*, 67, 98–9, 119–20, 166, 215, 235; Mortier, *Anacharsis Cloots*, 56, 421, 198.

the rest. Harmonizing the interests of all under the protection of the law was a duty so imperfectly performed by society in his day that some 'penseurs découragés' (i.e. Rousseau) had concluded life in society is actually 'contrary to the nature of man' and that the wisest course is to renounce society. But Rousseau's vision, he and Diderot, like Gorani or Mary Wollstonecraft later, pronounced a fundamentally misconceived and immoral course.[15] Men have not degenerated in society, it is just that their reason has not yet developed sufficiently for them properly to take advantage of it. 'La corruption des peuples', as d'Holbach calls this phenomenon, or 'the present corrupt state of society', as Wollstonecraft called it in 1792, was the necessary consequence of powerful causes conspiring to blind nations and hold men back in an eternal infancy; and, she added, 'to enslave women by cramping their understandings'.[16]

The moral and social transformation of man (and woman), held this new ideology, the general improvement of society on a new basis, can arise only by carrying further the universal revolution driven by *la philosophie* and that this struggle for reason announces a struggle forced on those capable of enlightenment by what Diderot and d'Holbach deemed the truly brutal, destructive, and savage ignorance of men 'and those who govern'.[17] 'Une politique aveugle' guided by interests entirely contrary to those of society does not permit men to become enlightened either about their own rights, or their true duties, or the true ends of the association that it continually subverts.[18] It was an ideology totally incompatible with the social, political, and educational conservatism of Montesquieu, Hume Voltaire, Burke, Ferguson, and Smith. Even such supposedly 'enlightened' despots as Frederick and Catherine would eventually have to be pushed aside. As for rank, privilege, entails, and aristocratic fiscal exemptions, to them these contradicted every principle of equity, justice, and morality and the 'general will' itself. All distinction of orders, privilege, and forms of legal discrimination, proclaimed d'Holbach, preceding Mirabeau, Sieyès, and Priestley by some years, must be abolished.[19] Dare then Oh Europe, intoned d'Holbach, in 1770, at the close of his *L'Esprit du judaïsme*, to shake off the intolerable yoke of prejudice that afflicts you. Strive to perfect your governments, correct your laws, reform all the abuses, reorganize morality, and shut your eyes for ever to the 'vaines chimères' that have for so many centuries served only to retard true science and divert you from the path to happiness.[20]

The pre-eminent problem in politics, as Diderot and d'Holbach understood it, was to prevent the subjects of government becoming the prey of vested interests and those who govern.[21] Precisely this was the problem the National Assembly, or rather its

---

[15] D'Holbach, *Essai*, 26–8, 53; d'Holbach, *Système social*, 210, 221–2; Tortarolo, *L'Illuminismo*, 146.
[16] D'Holbach, *Système social*, 222; Wollstonecraft, *Vindication of the Rights of Woman*, 93.
[17] D'Holbach, *Système social*, 69–70; Dulac, 'Modes', 123, 128–9.
[18] D'Holbach, *Système social*, 232–3.
[19] D'Holbach, *Politique naturelle*, 119–21.
[20] D'Holbach, *L'Esprit du judaïsme*, 117.
[21] D'Holbach, *Politique naturelle*, 80–1; d'Holbach, *Système social*, 276.

steering group, the constitutional committee, set itself as it embarked on its pro-gramme of fundamental reform in 1789. Diderot, d'Holbach, and later Sieyès, Mirabeau, Brissot, Volney, Condorcet, Cloots, and other leading spokesmen of the Revolution rejected the British constitutional model just as completely and abso-lutely as did Rousseau. They had no disagreement with him there. But, unlike Rousseau, neither did they think the solution to society's difficulties and ending the corruption of politics lay in Athenian-style direct democracy. The dismal failure of the ancient democracies of classical Greece as analysed by Boulanger in his *Recherches* convinced many that direct democracy was incapable of not reverting to theocracy—a form crasser and worse than anything else in radical eyes—due to the people's seemingly ineradicable veneration for religious leaders and willingness to assign them the chief role in public affairs.[22]

Since the common people cannot escape the sway of theology, priestcraft, and vested interests on their own, precisely because they are the people and understand nothing of history, politics, morality, science, or religion, Boulanger's analysis, and d'Holbach's and Diderot's endorsement of it, strengthened the thesis that humanity must trust in a genuine democracy's elected representatives. Diderot, d'Holbach, Sieyès, Condorcet, Brissot, Mirabeau, Mably, and Volney, like the Dutch democratic Patriots of the mid 1780s, such as Schimmelpenninck, Paulus, Cerisier, and Vreede, simultaneously wanted all to be equally free in the sense of enjoying equal protection under the law and equal liberty to pursue their own goals, happiness, and ambitions, while refusing to accept this need involve the direct participation of all in the business of law-making and government, on the model of the ancient democracies.

Scorning the credulity, ignorance, and bigotry of the man in the street, direct democracy seemed to them, no less than Kant, an impossible 'chimère', an invitation to tumult, licence, and ruin, something irreconcilable with the ' general will', social stability, and 'totally incompatible with our nature'.[23] How then can democracy and equality be securely grounded on justice and truly enlightened ideas? Rejecting direct or 'simple democracy', as Paine called it, the early architects of the philosophical democratic revolution, in Holland as in France and Britain, flatly rejecting Rous-seau's exhortations, sought an alternative solution to the problem of how to organize a stable, effective democracy. Their chosen political tool was that of democratically elected representation as a means of both democratizing and lending proper direc-tion to republics, representation held in a new kind of balance between authority to legislate and accountability to the electorate. It was a concept clearly sketched by Diderot, d'Holbach, and their Parisian 'synagogue' in 1763 for the article 'Représen-tants' which subsequently figured prominently in the work of d'Holbach and Mably and constitutes one of the principal differences between what we might call mainline radical republican ideology in the 1760s and 1770s and Rousseau's republican

---

[22] [Boulanger-d'Holbach], *Recherches sur l'origine*, i. 248, 251–2, 255, 258.
[23] D'Holbach, *Système social*, 268–9; d'Holbach, *Politique naturelle*, 65–7, 172, 430–1.

deviationism with its very different conception of the 'general will'.[24] For it remained one of Rousseau's cardinal doctrines that popular sovereignty being unlimited is something that cannot be delegated and that representatives must therefore always be supervised and strictly mandated by their constituents.[25]

This cataloguing of the 'erreurs' of Rousseau in constitutional matters is a crucial feature of the early stages of the French Revolution, as well as of the reaction to Robespierre and the Terror in the mid 1790s, that has long remained insufficiently acknowledged. Declared admirers of Rousseau figured prominently and abundantly in the Revolution. But so did many, including some of his admirers, who recognized that aspects of Rousseau's thought worked directly against the system of representation, free press, and open public debate advocated by the leadership in 1789, theses that needed countering in the sort of democratic republic based on equality proclaimed by radical thought. Many radical ideologues had, like Cloots and Gorani, once been fervent admirers of Rousseau but well before 1789 publicly rejected his legacy in politics and right across the board. At the point he emerged as one of the Revolution's leading journalists in 1790, Cloots was a materialist anti-deist, famous for his universalism and hostility to religion, who opposed all Rousseau's ideas in ethics, education, and general philosophy no less than in politics.[26]

Rousseau's conception remained very much alive behind the scenes, though, and the ideological struggle between the *Rousseauiste* revolution of popular will, sentiment, undivided popular sovereignty, and what the ordinary person (supposedly) thinks, and the radical *philosophes'* revolution of 'reason' and *l'esprit philosophique*— a clash later to culminate in the Terror—was plainly in evidence from July 1789 onwards. There even appeared a novel in 1789 entitled *J. J. Rousseau à l'Assemblée Nationale* in which an imagined 'Rousseau' participates in person in the Assembly's debates. 'Rousseau', recognizing that certain leaders of opinion are exploiting the cachet of his name without following his prescriptions, berates Sieyès, a leading exponent of the doctrine of representation, and Brissot, another critic of direct democracy, for advocating 'le pouvoir constituent', urging delegation, and not eliciting enough input from the people.[27] Rousseau's republican legacy in a word was one d'Holbach, Diderot, Helvétius, Mably, Brissot, and Sieyès, like Paulus and all the leading Dutch Patriot spokesmen, essentially opposed.

2. REPRESENTATIVE DEMOCRACY

Mirabeau and Sieyès, furthermore, like d'Holbach, Diderot, and Mably, denied their model, as compared with Rousseau's, entailed any loss of collective or individual

---

[24] Miller, *Rousseau*, 64, 80, 116–18, 120; Wright, *Classical Republican*, 123.
[25] Baker, 'Representation', 478–80, 484–5.   [26] Labbé, *Anarcharsis Cloots*, 105–6, 164, 168, 235–6.
[27] *Chronique de Paris*, 106 (7 Dec. 1789), 421; Baker, 'Representation', 485–90.

liberty. Sovereign in appearance, the common people in a direct democracy are in reality the slaves of 'perverse demagogues' who manipulate and flatter them. This was precisely the charge radical thinkers later levelled against Marat and Robespierre who, to exponents of radical thought, and Naigeon and Cloots most of all, were despicable Mesmerists, rabble-rousers, and unphilosophical quasi-religious fanatics. As the people cannot grasp what genuine liberty is, their rule in a direct democracy can be harsher than that of the worst tyrant. Direct democracy is inherently bad since liberty without reason is of little value in itself: 'the history of most republics', held d'Holbach, 'offers the unending and revolting picture of nations bathed by anarchy in their own blood.' The only way the 'general will' can be consistently expressed and acted on in society is if the people's 'représentants' are those 'citizens' best qualified to evaluate society's condition, needs, and rights. 'Il faut des talents, des lumières, de la probité pour parler au nom d'une nation; il faut être lié d'intérêts avec elle, pour la représenter fidèlement.'[28] Representative democracy was the key to making the Revolution.

Undeviating advocacy of representative democracy balancing authority against accountability, then, was the characteristic ideal of the Revolution of reason flowing from the Radical Enlightenment. The revolutionary character of the summons to transform government on an egalitarian and democratic basis, whether in its Genevan, French, Dutch, British—or Wolfe Tone's Irish, or Barlow's or Palmer's American—version, was from the 1760s onwards manifested in gradually louder calls for democratic elections participated in by the whole citizenry, with the hereditary and aristocratic principles eradicated. The elections were to choose qualified deputies empowered to rule who could also be regularly petitioned, held to account, and changed by further elections and a variety of other means. It was a model approximating more closely to what we would today call democracy than any system of representation by 'estates' such as lingered still in parts of eighteenth-century Europe. The great difference between representation according to the traditional 'estates' model and the new conception of 'assemblée nationale', or 'senate', propounded by radical *philosophes*, Dutch democrats, and American Founding Fathers, was the elimination of hereditary or privileged access together with the inalienable right to convene regularly or whenever the representatives saw fit, combined with control of the state revenues to ensure these were spent 'to serve the true needs of the state' and not wasted by popular acclaim or used by a king to corrupt the 'representatives of the people' as in Britain, or sustain, as d'Holbach put it, 'la splendeur et la vanité d'une cour'.[29]

The Assemblée Nationale, to use d'Holbach's term for this new representative gathering, would also be empowered to establish regional assemblies and, last and most crucial of all, would control the armed forces. This assembly could never be dissolved by a monarch but could be by the people whenever it no longer faithfully

---

[28] D'Holbach, *Politique naturelle*, 166–9, 275; d'Holbach, *Éthocratie*, 601–2; Mably, *Doutes*, 230–74.
[29] D'Holbach, *Politique naturelle*, 109–10, 166–7, 169; d'Holbach, *Système social*, 276–80.

performed its task of legislating and governing in the 'public interest'. Meanwhile, for as long as this Assemblée Nationale does represent 'the general will' faithfully, it will always be justified in employing force to suppress ambitious cliques, royal pretenders, demagogues, and would-be dictators seeking to violate the 'general will' and manipulate the people. If every individual of our species has 'the right' to defend himself against aggression, contended d'Holbach, by what strange jurisprudence do apologists for monarchy, oligarchy, and churches deny to entire nations the right to resist their tyranny?[30]

If neither the hereditary principle, nor high office, nor royal favour qualifies individuals for election to the Assemblée Nationale, what does? Those who 'naturally' have the right to represent the nation, urged Diderot, d'Holbach, and their following, are those 'citizens' best informed about its affairs, needs, and rights, and hence 'les plus intéressés à la félicité publique'. They should be chosen via regular supervised 'élections' in which no intrigue or corruption intervenes.[31] Essential also is that they should include—contrary to contemporary British practice—no persons salaried or pensioned by the crown. This is precisely what the Revolution sought to accomplish in 1789–90 through the efforts of Sieyès, Mirabeau, Condorcet, Volney, and the rest. To those questioning whether the people would choose the best informed and intentioned, d'Holbach answered optimistically 'that the people rarely makes mistakes about the character of citizens which it scrutinizes'.[32] Provided corrupt practices are eradicated, Diderot, d'Holbach, and their following expected the deputies chosen would be 'enlightened, honest, and virtuous'. Here indeed was the radical wing's Achilles heel as Marat and Robespierre were amply to demonstrate. This same blueprint for democracy was widely taken up by the Dutch *Patriotten* in the 1780s and 1790s, the key Patriot ideologues—Schimmelpeninck, Paulus, Cerisier, Vreede, and Paape all emulating their French counterparts in rejecting 'mixed monarchy' and the British model and proclaiming 'equality', democracy, and representation by the most enlightened, their guiding principles.[33]

Burke, referring to Britain, rather confidently asserted that 'we are not converts of Rousseau; we are not the disciples of Voltaire; Helvétius has made no progress among us. Atheists are not our preachers; madmen are not our lawgivers.'[34] But this was not entirely correct. In his *Reflections on the Revolution in France*, published in November 1790, Burke remarks, referring to France: 'I hear on all hands that a cabal, calling itself philosophic, receives the glory of many of the late proceedings; and that their opinions and systems are the true actuating spirit of all of them.' This was absolutely right. But when he went on to say: 'I have heard of no party in England, literary or political, at any time, known by such a description,' he was patently oversimplifying.[35] If the materialism of Jebb and Priestley owed much to the *Système*

[30] D'Holbach, *Système social*, 285; d'Holbach, *Politique naturelle*, 112–14.
[31] D'Holbach, *Politique naturelle*, 167–8; d'Holbach, *Éthocratie*, 601–2.
[32] D'Holbach, *Politique naturelle*, 169.   [33] Schimmelpenninck, *Verhandeling*, 35–6, 50–1.
[34] Burke, *Reflections*, 73.   [35] Ibid. 76.

de la nature by their own admission, Godwin too clearly states in the preface to his *Political Justice*, a work begun in 1791, that the initial impulse to his thought came from the *Système* as well as other French materialist works.[36] The cry for representative democracy was in fact loudly taken up also in Britain and Ireland by Paine, Jebb, Godwin, Wollstonecraft, Bentham, Turner, Barlow, Tone and their followers as well as Price and Priestley. 'By ingrafting representation upon democracy', wrote Paine, in 1791, 'we arrive at a system of government capable of embracing and confederating all the various interests and every extent of territory and population; and that also with advantages as much superior to hereditary government, as the republic of literature is to hereditary literature.'[37]

John Jebb, after 1775 one of the most important English constitutional, legal, and university reformers, studied the *Système de la nature* even before Priestley, in 1771–2, taking careful notes and agreeing with much that he read. Jebb agreed with d'Holbach especially in moral philosophy, affirming that that author had 'expressed my idea of the religion of nature so far as relates to our duty to our neighbour', only where the French writer 'conceives this to be the voice of nature, I only differ from him in thinking it is the voice of God'.[38] Like Priestley, Jebb, who had read other recent French works, including Marmontel's *Bélisaire*, felt there was a need to purge what most thought of as Christianity of its extensive irrational baggage. For him too, matter is an active not a passive substance and any soundly based materialist conception of the mind leaves no room for traditional Christian notions of the soul or freedom of the will. In 1777, in the preface to his *Disquisitions Relating to Matter and Spirit* (London, 1777), Priestley acknowledged that until a few years before, he, like so many others, had unquestioningly believed 'that man had a soul distinct from his body' and believed this 'soul to be a substance so intirely distinct from matter, as to have no property in common with it'. Only via 'a slow and laborious investigation' that was both personal and yet part of a wider process characteristic of his time, had he been able to free himself from this together with many other 'vulgar prejudices, and to reject many gross corruptions, as I now deem them'. From his new standpoint, arguing for the materiality of the human soul, it seemed 'unaccountable in Mr Locke that having acknowledged, as he does, that there is no clear evidence of two substances in man' he yet resolutely continued to think 'it more probable' that the faculty of thinking 'inhered in a different substance' from the body, namely an immaterial soul.[39]

For while Locke had seen that there was 'no real inconsistency between the known properties of the body, and those that have generally been referred to the mind', he had not concluded, as a true philosopher ought to have done, in Priestley's view, 'that the whole substance of man, that which supports all his powers and properties, was

---

[36] Locke, *Fantasy*, 19, 339–40; Philip, *Godwin's Political Justice*, 39–40, 42, 45–8.
[37] Paine, *Rights of Man*, 180.
[38] Jebb, *The Works*, ii. 167–8; Page, 'Liberty', 224; Page, *John Jebb*, 100; Sonnenscher, *Sans-Culottes*, 381–2.
[39] Priestley, *Disquisitions*, 31.

one uniform substance' and that, hence, man does not consist 'of two substances' as most philosophers and divines insist but only of one.[40] Moreover, there were more British (and American) materialists and atheists than met the eye. Atheists, as Matthew Turner, a prominent surgeon and chemistry lecturer, central figure in the Liverpool Enlightenment and another prominent radical—and unusually a declared atheist (who learnt his atheism from the French materialists)—complained, in 1781, had good reason to fear severe persecution in England; and more perhaps from the populace than the law. In other kinds of philosophical dispute, the vanquished feared only disappointment. But in arguing for atheism any opponent of Britain's 'religionists', whether victor or vanquished in the debate, he answered Priestley's *Letters to a Philosophical Unbeliever* (1780), must 'dread, beside ecclesiastical censure, the scourges, chains and pillories of the courts of law'.[41] In fact, from the late 1770s until after 1800 and beyond, the split between Radical Enlightenment and moderate mainstream was as sharp and clear in Britain as on the Continent and just as evident in provincial cities such as Liverpool as in London or Dublin.[42]

In Germany, the response is generally held to have been weaker. Yet, there too there were strong echoes of the same revolutionary ideology, and not only in the writings of radical spokesmen like Forster, Wekhrlin, Knigge, and Knoblauch. Kant, as he did increasingly during the years of the French Revolution, perceived a need for substantial concessions to the radical standpoint, albeit introducing as well a subtle and ingenious exit clause enabling him to retain princely absolutism by differentiating between the legislative power that must eventually be republican and democratic and the executive power which, in his opinion, could and should be kept monarchical. Only the legislative power, he maintained, must reflect the 'general will'; this would suffice to bestow on the state a true republican spirit, furthering the needs and interests of everyone on an equal basis. 'Republicanism', in his view, is the political principle according to which the executive power (the government) is separated from the legislative. Despotism is where the legislator executes his own laws, so that the private will of the chief is substituted for the will of the public.[43] Here was a device enabling Kant to reject democracy as a form of despotism while fusing central European enlightened absolutism, or forms of it, with representation and republicanism.

Besides representation based on democratic elections, radical enlighteners deemed liberty of thought and expression ['de parler et d'écrire'] vital to the spread of knowledge needed by society, especially as a 'powerful dike against the plots and intrigues of tyranny' and to counteract religious fervour and veneration for priests deemed by them a constant threat to everyone.[44] According to radical thinkers, contrary again to Rousseau but here also Mably, no particular religion should be favoured by the state and the semi-toleration currently prevailing in countries like

---

[40] Priestley, *Disquisitions*, 32, 73, 218–20.   [41] Turner, *Answer . . . a Philosophical Unbeliever*, 60.
[42] Fitzpatrick, 'Enlightenment', 131, 135, 137, 143.   [43] Kant, *Project*, 13, 17–18, 20.
[44] D'Holbach, *Système social*, 281–2.

England, the American colonies, and Holland needed to be converted into a full toleration that did not discriminate against those refusing the sovereign's faith or belonging to theoretically proscribed groups like the Unitarians. The late eighteenth-century practice in European states and America of granting formal or informal toleration while still subjecting all or some religious minorities to disabilities and marks of inferiority was, they thought, not just inherently unjust but totally incompatible with the 'general will'. There is nothing 'de plus contraire à l'humanité, à la justice, à la sociabilité parfaite' than a religion claiming to 'possess the exclusive approbation of heaven'.[45] Such claims should never be acquiesced in by legislatures or executives; rather such churches should be proclaimed enemies of the liberty of man.

It is 'liberty', held Diderot and d'Holbach, that ennobles man, raises his soul, inspires his generosity and love of the 'bien public'. But what they and later radical thinkers, like Paine and Wollstonecraft, meant by this was the 'philosophical' principle of liberty, not the liberties enshrined in countless ancient laws, codes, and digests. Since, according to the radical *philosophes*, only equity, reason, and liberty can ground just constitutional principles, rational laws, and upright government, nothing is more ridiculous than the tradition of venerating ancient charters and privileges and basing everything on remote precedent, as the English do when pronouncing the Magna Carta the foundation of their liberty, this being an 'obscure and crude charter', according to d'Holbach and Wollstonecraft, extorted from a despotic king many centuries ago by a handful of unruly barons at a moment of weakness.[46] Charters and case law are irrelevant and, worse, detrimental to large parts of society; universal principles are what count, held the radical enlighteners, the job of government being to procure for all its citizens true justice, security, and liberty, goals which have nothing to do with particular 'rights' or medieval 'liberties'.[47]

Diderot and d'Holbach knew well enough that political revolution spells fearful and bloody upheaval.[48] Even so, averred d'Holbach, six years before the outbreak of the American Revolution, the English, Dutch, and Swiss, in the sixteenth and seventeenth centuries, had, through revolutionary violence, manifestly gained in the end. These nations threw off first the papal yoke and afterwards that of monarchy. Some object that the English, Dutch, and Swiss accomplished this only by violence, 'par des troubles et des révolutions'. To this d'Holbach answered that it is rather the 'esprit tyrannique et persécution des princes', 'fanatisme' of priests, and ambition of nobles that caused such troubles; and, besides, the violence and killing would have been less had the people been more enlightened. Through revolutionary violence, these peoples manifestly gained in the end. Temporary troubles are more beneficial than permanently languishing under tyranny in circumstances where the people's rights are continually trampled upon. In such circumstances, revolt is justified.[49]

---

[45] Ibid. 282; Cassirer, *Philosophy*, 134. [46] D'Holbach, *Système social*, 428–30.
[47] D'Holbach, *Politique naturelle*, 85; Paine, *Rights of Man*, 220–1.
[48] Diderot, *Essai sur les règnes*, i. 120.
[49] d'Holbach, *Essai*, 53; d'Holbach, *Politique naturelle*, 156–60.

This is one of several passages where d'Holbach, while condemning individual and small-group sedition, offers a qualified but clear justification for mass armed resistance to tyrannical government. D'Holbach and Diderot, while condemning irresponsible violence, did justify mass armed resistance to tyranny where led by responsible leaders. It was a facet of their thought that outraged Voltaire and was abjured by Kant for whom resistance to despotic power is never justified.[50]

The revaluation of all values the radical *philosophes* demanded, and in which Sieyès and Mirabeau followed so closely, did not, however, as it seemed in the early and mid 1770s, necessarily entail mass violence and popular insurrection.[51] Their doctrine was intrinsically revolutionary more in the post-Cartesian sense of involving a drastic shift in perspective, values, social theory, law, administrative practice, court culture, and education than in the sense of unleashing violent insurgency. Indeed, Diderot and d'Holbach, while vehemently inveighing against monarchy, aristocracy, and priestcraft, and rendering direct democracy suspect, also warn of the dangers of revolution and especially the ease with which a revolution can miscarry, repeating Spinoza's strictures, in the *Tractatus Theologico-Politicus*, against violent uprisings and against the English Revolution of the 1640s in particular: for all too often a tyrant executed or expelled is replaced 'par un nouveau tyran, souvent plus implacable et plus méchant que le premier'.[52] Hence 'revolution' is only justifiable when intended to lead to a new order, liberty being not a favour but a right that unwilling princes must be compelled to concede.

What is important is not the violent toppling of the *ancien régime* but its replacement by a new order of equality and democracy. They had shown that an enlightened despot was inherently incapable of doing this. But a contrite constitutional monarch who surrenders most of his power to the National Assembly? Eager to avoid turmoil and bloodshed, d'Holbach, in his *La Morale universelle* (3 vols., Amsterdam, 1776), calls on the newly enthroned Louis XVI to reject his predecessors' ways, break the fetters of despotism, institute true justice, and scrap the mass of obscure, outmoded and barbaric law to become 'le RESTAURATEUR d'une nation illustre, le réformateur de ses mœurs, le créateur de sa félicité'.[53] This was no threat, just an impassioned plea to establish a 'legitimate liberty' beneficial to the ruler and his subjects alike. The radical *philosophes*, in 1789 no less than earlier, hoped the revolutionary transformation they envisaged could be achieved not with 'convulsions dangereuses' and regicide, the thought of which appalled d'Holbach, but 'à l'aide de la vérité' and by the agency of philosophy itself.[54] Royally directed but fundamental reform could perhaps in the end transform society fundamentally, he urged; the voice of reason 'n'est ni séditieuse ni sanguinaire'.[55]

---

[50] Kant, *Project*, 67–8.   [51] Tortarolo, *L'Illuminismo*, 147.
[52] Ibid. 260; d'Holbach, *Essai*, 63; Jimack, 'Obéissance', 162.
[53] D'Holbach, *Morale universelle*, ii. 31–2.
[54] D'Holbach, *Système social*, 261.   [55] Ibid. 261.

No incendiaries advocating armed revolt as such, the radical *philosophes* also knew that their Enlightenment could not succeed without first undertaking a universal moral and political revolution and that re-educating peoples, as Sieyès also noted in 1777, is much harder to accomplish than re-educating individuals.[56] In theory, revolutionizing social attitudes might take the form of a smooth and gentle transition powered by 'une heureuse révolution dans les idées' that somehow leads to elites and royal courts being persuaded and becoming contrite. But experience suggested otherwise—that the Revolution they foresaw would be forced to resort to 'cruel' and violent methods. But gentle or violent, whatever the format the coming 'General revolution' assumed, the essential point when explaining and interpreting it was that its origin lay in 'la révolution de la philosophie' as the journal *Révolutions de Paris* termed the process. The essence of the French Revolution of 1788–92 and 1794–1800 was the common people being exhorted to heed and act on what the radical *philosophes* and *philosophes-révolutionnaires* saw as the truth concerning social reality, morality, and religion and defined as 'their rights'.[57] As Burke commented, against 'these rights of men' there can be 'no prescription, against these no agreement is binding: these admit no temperament, and no compromise: anything withheld from their full demand is so much of fraud and injustice.'[58]

[56] Sieyès, *Manuscrits*, 249.   [57] Baker, 'Revolution', 57.   [58] Burke, *Reflections*, 49.

31

Aufklärung and the Secret Societies (1776–1792)

1. 'REVOLUTION' AND THE SECRET SOCIETIES

Briefly, as progress towards toleration and a freer press, law reform, and a stronger public sphere looked cumulative and real, a distinct note of optimism pervaded enlightened circles during the 1770s and early 1780s in Germany. Lessing's publication of the Reimarus fragments could be considered the start of a new era, demonstrating the possibilities offered by more open debate and growing freedom of the press. From 1785, by contrast, the outlook appeared increasingly ominous. 'We must hurry', urged Wehrlin, in 1787, as this fleeting moment already seemed to be passing, 'to accelerate as much as possible the revolution in the human spirit that a good use of press freedom can set in motion.'[1] At this point, the crumbling of old certainties and of orthodoxy was matched, as elsewhere, by an accelerated diffusion of radical thought, a phenomenon conspicuous in the reading clubs and university life, and at court, and frequently warned against by the Neologs, but evident most glaringly in the ideological struggle erupting after 1770 within the body of central European freemasonry.

Yet, before 1785 too, central Europe in the age of the American, Dutch, and Swiss revolutions also offered many grounds for pessimism, a feeling that to break the fetters of princely rule and church authority more was needed than just books, public debate, and controversy. The outcome of the *Fragmentenstreit* itself was depressing, not least for Lessing. Public debate turned out to be something the princes could still swiftly abort. America only exacerbated matters by exalting new ideals for society and individual freedom while simultaneously offering fresh proofs of how completely Germany remained in thrall to princely absolutism, a contrast rendered painfully obvious by the far more open debate about the American Revolution unfolding simultaneously in the Dutch press. In Germany, princes rigorously constrained discussion and opinion, permitting no open support for the insurgents or their principles, or direct criticism of Britain's imperial policy. 'La Germania tutta',

---

[1] Wehrlin, *Hyperboreische Briefe*, 1 (1787), 301, 303–4.

commented Pilati, in the mid 1770s, 'non e che una prigione di vilissimi schiavi' [The whole of Germany is nothing but a prison of vile slaves].[2]

The same message seemed to be conveyed by developments in Scandinavia. One of the most sweeping, resolute attempts to reform European society from the top downwards on a libertarian basis, marginalizing many vested interests, was in the joint kingdom of Denmark-Norway under the ascendancy of the country's soon notorious German chief minister, the king's former physician, Johann Friedrich Struensee (1737–72). His was a wide-ranging attempt at comprehensive change dramatically defeated by conservative elements at the Danish court and by entrenched opposition among the nobility and clergy and in society. One of the most effective weapons in the campaign against Struensee was popular aversion to atheism and in particular using the press to stoke up an outcry against a radical reformism the clergy condemned as godless, libertine, contrary to tradition, and inspired by Spinoza.

The most important and radical of his many reforms (qualified afterwards but not fully reversed by Danish conservatism until 1799) was his introduction, having persuaded the king to agree, by royal proclamation of 4 September 1770, of unrestricted liberty of the press throughout Denmark and its dependent territories (Norway, Schleswig-Holstein, Greenland, Iceland, the Faeroes, and the Danish Antilles) on grounds for which he had been arguing for many years. Essentially, these were that comprehensive freedom of thought and expression can only benefit society, promote the 'common good' of all the kingdom's inhabitants, and encourage scholarship and science, impartial search for truth inevitably suffering from any kind of censorship of publications, the latter being something that can only hinder advancement of the 'allgemeine Wohl und wahre Beste ihrer Mitbürger' [general good and true interest of their fellow citizens].[3]

In this way, Denmark-Norway became the first country in the world to proclaim unrestricted freedom of the press extending to religion and politics as well as everything else, a fundamental principle of an enlightened society—making freedom of the press a fundamental, universal right and something benefiting humankind both collectively and individually.[4] Britain and the Dutch Republic had long been regarded as countries where the press enjoyed greater freedom than was available elsewhere. Yet, no more than Prussia had either actually proclaimed 'freedom of the press' a positive social and political principle and basic 'right'; and in practice both maintained restrictions and proscribed certain opinions. Nor did public or academic debates in western Europe concerning censorship, and liberty of expression generally, favour an unrestricted freedom of the press. Moderate mainstream Enlightenment broadly rejected full freedom of the press as unacceptable, something propounded only by impious writers like Spinoza, Toland, and Collins.

---

[2] Pilati, *Lettere*, 120–1.   [3] Winkle, *Struensee*, 81–7; Laursen, 'Spinoza in Denmark', 190–1, 195.
[4] Laursen, 'Spinoza in Denmark', 190–1.

Struensee's edict went far beyond the somewhat half-hearted measures previously adopted in Berlin and Stockholm or any publicly enunciated principle in Britain or Holland. As with Diez and Bahrdt in Germany later, Struensee's advocacy of an unlimited freedom of the press sprang directly from his wider radical opinions which derived in particular from French materialist writings, especially Helvétius.[5] Both at court and in the country there was intense opposition to Struensee's reforms in general and his unprecedented press law in particular. His new freedoms were immediately attacked by many of the products of the newly freed press. One pamphlet, the *Alvorliger Betragtninger over den almindelige Tilstand* [Serious Observations on the Common Condition], of 1771, denounced what it regarded as the excessive extent of the new freedoms and negative impact of certain kinds of 'philosophy', while also insisting its protest derived from an 'enlightened' standpoint. It entirely approved of the 'Christian' philosophy of thinkers like 'Grotius, Pufendorf, Leibniz, Wolff, Locke, Newton, Boyle, Boerhaave, Haller, Hoffmann, Sulzer', thinkers who grasped the working of nature correctly and not in the manner of the materialists. But respectable philosophy like this was now under siege in Denmark-Norway. Earlier, Vanini's and Bruno's attacks on 'true religion', occurring in 'dark times', had had little effect on the Danish people. But very different was the situation that had now developed, under the mask of 'philosophy' and science, rooted in the writings and ideas of 'Tindal, Spinoza, Collins, and Bolingbroke'.[6]

One or two of the Danish tracts of 1770–1, however, were by no means wholly unsympathetic to the radical standpoint. Another tract considering the impact of 'philosophy' was *En Grønlaendes Beskrivelse over Kiøbenhavn* [A Greenlander's Description of Copenhagen], which condemned the small group of persons now to be found in Copenhagen who had 'torn themselves from and denied all religion' and believed the world has existed as it is since all eternity. These, the tract states, take as their inspiration and model a Dutch Jew by the name of Spinoza who in a thick, tedious book of metaphysical Latin tries 'to prove that all of nature is only one substance and that all Nature's parts are only just so many modifications of it, so that all that one sees in the whole of nature, is equally as divine, as royal and grand, so that the writer and his pen are equally important, both alike modifications of nature's whole'.[7] This strange doctrine is irreligious and subversive. Nevertheless, even though these Danish Spinozists recognized no sin or punishment for sin, this tract was sufficiently honest to point out, by and large 'they live better and show more charity than the rest [of society] who pretend to be true to and follow their heaven-sent book [the Bible]', their irreproachable morality being 'something which they have in common with their originator [i.e. Spinoza]'.[8]

The vast majority of the tracts, though, were altogether condemnatory. The Danes were becoming lost in a madhouse garden of ideas 'from which no one could find

---

[5] Münter, *Bekehrungsgeschichte*, 10; Glebe-Møller, *Struensees vej*, 13–14.
[6] *Alvorlige Betragtninger*, 16; Laursen, 'Spinoza in Denmark', 196.
[7] *En Grønlaendes Beskrivelse*, 5.   [8] Ibid.

the exit'.[9] One contribution colourfully complained of the vast number of opinions about everything proliferating since the introduction of 'freedom of the press', conjuring up the nightmarish vision of a immense square crammed with a vast and stinking heap of writings on every imaginable topic, financial writings, 'project writings', and also 'Machiavellian, Spinozistic writings of which there were a great many and from which the stink was so dreadful' that the author could not bear it.[10] *Ole Smedesvends Begraedelse over Rissengrød* [Ole Smedesvends Complaint over Rice Porridge] lamented the 'Dutch Jew who was supposed to be learned but wanted people to believe that the world had made itself', which is absurd and as much a lie as if the tract's author had tried to make people believe that his doors could lock themselves: 'this fellow was called Spinach or Spinos'.[11] Among his followers was a 'French fool' named La Mettrie.

Some of the pamphlets openly attacked Struensee as a destroyer of morality and religion and a man devoid of morality, the *Nye Prove af Skriven-Frihed* openly styling the chief minister the new 'Haman'.[12] This was literature addressed to a wide public and designed for popular consumption. It is therefore a clear indication of the penetration of Spinoza's name and ideas into popular discussion and the backlash against Spinozistic as well as other irreligious influences. According to the *Grønlandske Professors . . . Betragtninger over Maanen* [Greenlander Professor's Observations about the Moon] Spinoza 'negtede al Guddom' [denied all form of Divinity],[13] a charge purposely designed to discredit Struensee. That Spinoza was being cited in the Danish popular press as the subversive thinker par excellence and far more than Voltaire, Rousseau, Hobbes, or Locke might surprise readers relying on traditional accounts of the Enlightenment but is far from surprising in the light of the actual controversies of the years around 1770. All the polemicists understood that philosophy lay behind the great political and social changes being introduced in Denmark-Norway and that the way to destroy Struensee was to tie him to Spinoza and materialism.

Having virtually no power base apart from the favour of a by now half-demented king, his authority (and the queen's reputation—Struensee was her lover) rapidly withered. Following an aristocratic coup in the capital, in January 1772, he was arrested together with the queen, during a ball at Christiansborg Castle, stripped of his offices, and arraigned for high treason. The king would have liked to save Struensee but so powerful was the backlash that this proved impossible. Struensee's arrest only further intensified the vilification descending on his head from all sides. A German-language pamphlet appearing shortly after his downfall denounced him as a 'naturalist born out of Spinoza's school', an atheist and lust-maddened sensualist

---

[9] *Anekdoten eines reisenden Russsen*, A3ᵛ.

[10] *Luxdorphs Samling af Trykke-frihedens Skrifter*, xv, no. 6, 14.

[11] Ibid. xv, no. 9, 7; Laursen, 'Spinoza in Denmark', 198.

[12] *Luxdorphs Samling af Trykke-frihedens Skrifter*, xiv, no. 2, 14; Holm, *Nogle Hovedtraek*, 59, 76.

[13] Holm, *Nogle Hovedtraek*, 199; *Luxdorphs Samling af Trykke-frihedens Skrifter*, xv, no. 21, 6.

who utterly scorned the true God and had thoroughly corrupted the court. Found guilty of treason, irreligion, and immorality, he was sentenced to judicial mutilation prior to execution. On 28 April 1772, together with his accomplice Brandt, he was publicly condemned, had his hands cut off, and was then beheaded; their corpses were drawn and quartered, this being all still accepted penal procedure in much of Europe for such 'crimes'. Most of his reforms were either cancelled or watered down.

The Struensee episode proved both how difficult and how unlikely was a programme of sweeping change from the top. Not long afterwards, waging war in America, Britain fully exploited the tight grip of the princes over the German states. In exchange for subsidies, in 1775–6 the Landgrave of Hesse-Cassel, Friedrich II (ruled: 1760–85), a convert to Catholicism who had subjected his territory's diet to almost complete subservience, while gagging all criticism at home, sent most of his army to bolster Britain in North America. By the war's end he had dispatched a grand total of 18,970 men across the Atlantic, over half the total number of more than 30,000 German troops sent, collecting huge sums for his court treasury little of which was used to compensate the families of the nearly 5,000 Hessians who perished, or 4,400 wounded, or those that deserted and never returned. Complaints about neglected farms, rising vagrancy and illegitimacy, fatherless families, abandoned wives, and other signs of social dislocation, with the strain of recruitment and rigorous taxation, stoked up behind-the-scenes, unpublished criticism of the landgrave to unprecedented levels.[14]

And Hesse-Cassel was just the worst case. Generally, a widening sense of resentment pervading the country, a growing awareness of oppression, was unquestionably the chief social and psychological impulse behind the secret societies promoting the underground spread of radical *Aufklärung* from the late 1770s. Modern historians warn of the danger of exaggerating the impact of this phenomenon and, from the 1790s, there undoubtedly was much exaggeration. The French Revolution and spread of revolutionary ideas in Europe, it became a commonplace to allege, had been concocted and put into effect by a vast network of conspiracy plied since the 1770s by insidious secret societies.[15] The idea that the radical wing of freemasonry, or freemasonry itself, was the root from which the French Revolution arose, evolved into a powerful myth, enthusiastically espoused by reactionary groups like the Order of the Rosicrucians. Later, it persisted as a potent mythology among segments of the Catholic Church, and finally, in the early twentieth century, in the fevered minds of Fascist, Falangist, and Nazi propagandists.

But this obsessive exaggeration and misrepresentation does not alter the fact that there really was a network of radical conspiracy stretching across central Europe from Copenhagen to Budapest and, while less potent and sensational than reactionary mythology would have it, it did exert a certain political and cultural impact.

---

[14] Taylor, *Indentured to Liberty*, 40–1, 44–5, 103.
[15] [Grolmann], *Kritische Geschichte*, 60, 64–6, 84; [Grolmann], *Neuesten Arbeiten*, 'Vorrede', pp. x–xi; Jacob, *Living the Enlightenment*, 9–13.

The deeply fragmented, diffuse, problematic character of freemasonry provoked an increasingly critical attitude on the part of radical-minded intellectuals accusing masonry of degenerating into a more and more corrupt edifice of pretence, deceit, and imposture. This view, paralleling the wider critique of German society, was vividly expressed by Lessing in one of the most socially engaged of his late works, *Ernst und Falk. Gespräche für Freymäurer* [Ernst and Falk: Conversations for Freemasons], a set of dialogues about freemasonry published in two stages (1778–80). It exerted a strong impression not least on Adam Weishaupt, the Bavarian founder of the secret order of the Illuminati.[16]

Lessing himself had joined the freemasons in Hamburg, in 1771, but soon become disillusioned, in particular by what he perceived as the wide gap between masonic ideals and practice. In the first three of his dialogues about freemasonry's glaring defects, published at Göttingen in 1778, he expands on the essential aims of the Enlightenment, as he saw it, and freemasonry's failure genuinely to pursue any enlightened course. In doing so, he offers one of the most brilliant of all short summaries of the Radical Enlightenment's goals. Even in the best possible political constitution men can devise, three basic limitations, he declares, can never be wholly eradicated—religious divisions, national divisions, and class divisions. Absolute universalism, absolute cosmopolitanism, and absolute equality of wealth are unattainable.[17] Given this law of the human condition, the best cultural milieu, and the best political constitution, must always be whatever most effectually minimizes all three: national, religious, and class antagonism.[18] It is this that should define every enlightened person's approach. Political constitutions exist not to be venerated for their own sake but purely as a means to an end, namely maximization of human happiness. Judging by the right criteria shows us that while 'there are many political constitutions and some are better than others, many are highly defective and obviously at odds with their intention; and the best one has perhaps still to be invented.'[19]

Minimizing religious, national, and class rifts, held Lessing, should be the undeviating aim of all freemasonry. But, alas, masonry nowhere pursued its three prime objectives in reality. Rather it forsook genuinely enlightened ideals for everything that obfuscates them—empty conviviality, silly rituals, deference to authority. It was all a bogus show. Practically nothing the lodges did, the sad truth was, suggested it was even partly their objective 'to redress, through itself and in itself, that division between people' commonly considered 'a necessary consequence of the state and of states in general'. Given they excluded from their ranks Jews and men of the lower classes, the freemasons were clearly incapable of the most elementary steps, being unwilling even to admit 'to their order every worthy man of the right disposition, irrespective of nationality, religion and social class'.[20] Most lodges in Habsburg lands,

---

[16] Weishaupt, *Nachtrag*, 86; Vierhaus, 'Aufklärung', 130–1.   [17] Weishaupt, *Nachtrag*, 195.
[18] Ibid. 193–6.   [19] Lessing, *Ernst und Falk*, 192.   [20] Ibid. 200–1.

especially in Hungary and the southern Netherlands, furthermore, staunchly opposed Joseph's reforms.

To this, Mirabeau caustically added, in 1787, that the lodges were notoriously vulnerable to all kinds of occultism, charlatans and faith-healers and, while collecting considerable amounts in entrance fees, their membership never knew what they did with the money aside from the sizable sums allocated for entertaining.[21] The masonic lodges Mirabeau deemed primarily a path for vulgar mystification, popularizing notions, and silliness of every sort to rise up into refined society.[22] Masonry represented a major and very widespread new sphere of sociability and *mondanité*, certainly, but one which reflected rather than sought to challenge privilege and the social system of the day. Fostering sociability really did nothing more than highlight long-existing contradictions and the escalating encounter between moderate, radical, and Counter-Enlightenment.[23] It certainly produced no new ideas and gravely disappointed all who did.

The first of what were to become nation-wide reform-oriented underground networks opposing conventional freemasonry, the Illuminati, arose in 1776, the year the American Revolution began, at Ingolstadt, north of Munich. Its founder, Adam Weishaupt (1748–1830), taught at Ingolstadt university. The years 1776–8 saw movements of unrest and tension in several universities, Catholic and Protestant, notably Ingolstadt and Giessen where students began clashing ideologically in local battles and founding small secret societies of contrasting hues.[24] Weishaupt felt driven to found his secret society by the hostility to his enlightened standpoint he everywhere encountered in the Bavarian context. He felt trapped in a deeply inhospitable milieu aggravated by the spreading influence within the university of ex-Jesuits and Rosicrucians fired by the most vehement opposition to Enlightenment ideas, proselytes increasingly busying themselves with recruiting students to what was eventually to prove the highly successful ideology of *Gegenaufklärung* [Counter-Enlightenment].[25]

Weishaupt had been raised, a reserved, taciturn orphan, in a Munich household crammed with Enlightenment texts, by a member of the Bavarian ruling council, Baron Johann Adam Ickstatt (1702–76), a renowned expert on constitutional law who had studied under Wolff at Marburg and was a leading promoter of *Aufklärung* in Bavaria.[26] A curator of Ingolstadt university, Ickstatt was a militant secularist instrumental in transferring the university from Jesuit to lay hands prior to 1773 when the pope dissolved the order. A professor of law since 1772, Weishaupt was well placed to influence students. But, at first, a young professor teaching philosophy

[21] Mirabeau, *De la monarchie*, v. 67–8; Porset, *Mirabeau Franc-Maçon*, 93; Beales, *Joseph II. Against*, 536–7.
[22] Mirabeau, *De la monarchie*, v. 69–72.
[23] Mühlpfordt, 'Europarepublik', 332; Sauter, *Visions*, 40–5.
[24] Van Dülmen, *Geheimbund*, 24–5; Haaser, 'Sonderfall oder Paradigma', 253.
[25] Weishaupt, *Verbesserte System*, 12, 20, 26; McIntosh, *Rose Cross*, 103.
[26] Van Dülmen, *Society*, 38; Fischer, 'Reduktion', 284, 291 n.; Müller, *Universität*, 29, 46.

(based on Feder's texts) and canon law, he gravitated sufficiently close to the ex-Jesuits, briefly, to shock his stepfather. His outlook changed in the mid 1770s, through reading Diderot, Mably, Morelly, and especially Helvétius and d'Holbach.[27] What later became the order of the Illuminati was originally just a tiny student society, unconnected with freemasonry, called the 'League of the *Perfektibilisten*'.[28] From the late 1770s, though, the Illuminati began infiltrating Munich masonic circles, drawing in some court officials.

Weishaupt is a clear instance of radical philosophical influence generating a broad social and political awareness followed by active, organizational radicalism. A deep aversion to Catholicism and dread of Jesuit influence reviving, reinforced by a firm conviction that the Bavarian common people were more bigoted and militantly devout than ordinary folk elsewhere, persuaded him that the people were dangerous as well as incapable of seeing how they were being deceived. The notion that Bavarians were exceptionally bigoted was nothing new, being widely propagated at the time not only by radical-minded publicists like Wekhrlin but also conservative Protestant spokesmen like Schlözer.[29] But Weishaupt's war against popular obscurantism, and repudiation of occultism, mysticism, and spiritualism, particular defects as he saw it of Bavarian freemasonry, took a strange form, being hidden and conspiratorial. He loathed but also recognized the uses of mystique in establishing an effective, wide-ranging movement. Though his organization was always anchored (without most participants knowing this) in radical ideas, as a general strategy Weishaupt was by no means opposed to working through the commonplace, including masonic lodges and princely authority. Ardently anti-Jesuit, his secretiveness and penchant for assuming the goal justifies the means struck some as basically a secularized version of the perverted mentality of his detested foe, and hence a comparable form of power-seeking and imposture.[30] He was later accused of spreading republican and democratic ideas in society silently, furtively, imperceptibly, without violence, *à la Jésuite*.[31]

Where a prince proved an energetic reformer, or at least zealous for masonry, the enlightened should, urged Weishaupt, collaborate with him. But, secretly, he was convinced there could be no place for princely authority in his utopian society of the future. Freemasonry to Weishaupt no less than Lessing, Herder, Wekhrlin, or Mirabeau, or his future chief ally Adolf, Freiherr von Knigge (1752–96), had betrayed the Enlightenment and, in reality, aided despotism. Meanwhile Herder too defined the true goal of Enlightenment as being to expand freedom and humanity, freedom meaning individual autonomy based on reason, and was sharply critical of

---

[27] Van Dülmen, *Geheimbund*, 26; Müller, *Universität*, 103–4.
[28] Van Dülmen, *Society*, 105; Fischer, 'Reduktion', 286; McIntosh, *Rose Cross*, 102–3; Mulsow, 'Vernünftige Metamorphosis', 252; Mulsow, 'Adam Weishaupt', 34.
[29] Weishaupt, *Kurze Rechtfertigung*, 68; Schaich, *Staat und Öffentlichkeit*, 103–6.
[30] Weishaupt, *Kurze Rechtfertigung*, 23–4; Van Horn Melton, *Rise*, 268.
[31] Weishaupt, *Anrede*, 179; [Grolmann], *Kritische Geschichte*, 57, 65–6, 80; McIntosh, *Rose Cross*, 105.

masonry.[32] Lessing further developed his critique of masonry in the closing fourth and fifth parts of *Ernst und Falk* but was prevented from publishing these by his employer, the duke of Brunswick-Wolfenbüttel. This was explained later by Knigge who became friendly with the now sick and reclusive Lessing, in Wolfenbüttel, in 1778.[33] The duke, though not unsympathetic to Lessing personally, and later himself brought into the *Illuminatenorden* by Knigge, wished to protect his reputation among the princes and standing among the Strict Observance freemasons.[34] As head of the latter, he figured among the most prominent princely enthusiasts for masonry, especially its mystical side, while caring little for enlightenment. (On this ground, a disdainful Herder designated him 'Hohepriester des Nichts' [highpriest of nothing].) The duke, resenting Lessing's belittling the movement, forbade him to continue his critique.[35] Lessing, however, Knigge later stated, showed the suppressed fourth and fifth dialogues 'to several friends who, presumably without his permission, made copies of them'. By a curious chance, one of these came into his own possession. Regretting that 'so many splendid truths should remain unpublished', he had the manuscript clandestinely printed, at Frankfurt, in 1780, making no mention as to whether he had Lessing's permission to do so (presumably he had).[36]

The preface to the latter part of *Ernst und Falk*, scathingly dismissing the 'fantasies' of so many freemasons who go off in pursuit of the most ridiculous things—alchemy, conjuring up spirits, everything which has nothing to do with the true 'quest for reality'—was written by Knigge. For all too many, despite the verbal support of some masons 'for the American cause in Europe', 'childish antics', had replaced pursuit of truth and Enlightenment. The great principles of equality and toleration were being betrayed especially by excluding the Jews—towards whom Knigge, like Lessing, projected an unusually benevolent attitude. Excluding Jews and Socinians, freemasonry generally nurtured hostility to full toleration, deism, and philosophy also. What could be more ridiculous, asked Knigge, than German masons' habit of construing 'irrespective of religion' to mean acceptance exclusively of those 'belonging to one of the three recognized confessions [Lutheranism, Catholicism, and Calvinism] publicly tolerated in the Holy Roman Empire'?[37]

Lessing's critique was taken to heart by the radically enlightened generally, especially Weishaupt and Knigge.[38] Freemasonry was a corrupt institution, they no less than Wekhrlin and Mirabeau complained, besotted with 'theosophy' and mysticism while spending on charity, supposedly its foremost object, amounted to not one tenth of its spending on banquets, ceremonies, and 'illuminated' evenings.[39]

[32] Reill, 'Enlightenment', 287–8.
[33] Hermann, *Knigge*, 90.
[34] Lessing, *Ernst und Falk*, 202; Knigge to Weishaupt, Frankfurt, 13 Jan. 1781, in *Korrespondenz des Illuminatenordens*, i. 213–14; Schings, *Brüder*, 57.
[35] Van Dülmen, *Geheimbund*, 66.
[36] Lessing, *Ernst und Falk*, 202; [Grolmann], *Kritische Geschichte*, 76.
[37] Lessing, *Ernst und Falk*, 207; Hermann, *Knigge*, 101–3.
[38] Weishaupt, *Anrede*, 191–4; Weishaupt, *Nachtrag*, 116–17.
[39] Wekhrlin, *Graue Ungeheuer*, 3 (1784–5), 125–6.

This absurd 'mystagomanie' was closely related, they thought, to the growing enthusiasm on all sides for the most senseless 'mysteries', spiritualism, and exorcism.[40] The reason masons never reveal their secrets, suggested one detractor, was that they did not have any. As the *Illuminatenorden* spread, the masonic lodges particularly of Ingolstadt, Munich, Eichstätt, Vienna, Mainz, Bonn, Neuwied, and Aachen fell largely into the hands of Illuminati, a direct consequence of which, in line with Weishaupt's ideas, was a marked lessening in banquets, ceremonies, and ritual.[41] Later, the league also penetrated at Weimar, Gotha, Jena, and Leipzig, though in Protestant Germany it consisted mostly of tiny groups and at Gotha and Weimar at least had no real radical edge. At Weimar, where Goethe and Herder too joined, the organization may have been mainly intended as a means of keeping an eye on the movement's activities on behalf of the prince.[42] In any case, under Goethe's and Carl August's supervision, it remained politically innocuous.

Besides Carl August of Weimar and the duke of Braunschweig, other princes joined, including Duke Ernst of Saxe-Gotha. Enlightenment in Weishaupt's and Knigge's, as in Herder's, Lessing's, and Mirabeau's, estimation was a re-evaluation of all values affecting everyone, including the princely courts, the entirety of society. One objective was to foment a more comprehensive toleration and this was why the Count von Neuwied, whose house had long presided over the most religiously tolerant fragment of Germany, was at one point suggested as a possible presiding head for the movement as a whole.[43] Equality was another fundamental principle. Emancipating the serfs, according to Mirabeau, was one of the Illuminati's foremost goals.[44] Weishaupt's was a movement dedicated to bringing humanity back to what he conceived as resembling man's original blissful state of equality and freedom, considered by him the optimal human condition, but this process of recovering man's birthright would occur only under the best political constitution.[45] Unlike masonry which viewed its lodges as autonomous bodies, the Illuminati thought in terms of an integrated network pursuing common aims even though the order's objectives remained veiled from most initiates—both rank and file and the princes and courtiers who joined.

Jesus was viewed by Weishaupt and Knigge, much as by Lessing and Bahrdt, as a great moral teacher and leader, the 'liberator of his people and all human kind', the supreme prophet of the 'doctrine of reason'.[46] Real Christianity, unlike what most people mean by religion, taught equality, toleration, peace, and love.[47] Like Spinoza, Radicati, and many radical thinkers before them, they maintained that Christ's true

---

[40] Ibid. 3 (1784–5), 259.
[41] Van Dülmen, *Society*, 115.
[42] Van Dülmen, *Geheimbund*, 72; Wilson, 'Enlightenment's Alliance', 375–7.
[43] Van Dülmen, *Society*, 115.
[44] Mirabeau, *De la monarchie*, v. 98–100.
[45] McIntosh, *Rose Cross*, 104.
[46] Ibid.; Weishaupt, *Anrede*, 185–90; Knigge to Zwack, 20 Jan. 1783, in Van Dülmen, *Dokumente*, 290–1.
[47] Weishaupt, *Apologie*, 103–4, 106.

teaching had nothing to do with the dogma, hierarchy, and absurd miracles churches had filled people's heads with since the Apostles and that 'unser grösser Meister Jesus' [our great master, Jesus] and his adherents had originally embraced equality of goods and the principle of equality generally. Christ's real purpose, according to Weishaupt and his close followers, had been 'allgemeine Freyheit und Gleichheit unter den Menschen ohne alle Revolution einzuführen' [to introduce general freedom and equality among men without any [violent] revolution].[48] This too was Weishaupt's aim. Aware most of humanity is addicted to mystifying religion, Weishaupt and Knigge acknowledged the need, though, to calm the anxieties of those worried by the growth of irreligion.

There really existed, then, an underground current secretly promoting what Weishaupt called 'a *Weltreformation* [world reformation] of the hitherto prevailing religious and political constitution', meaning eliminating princes, priests, and serfdom and replacing these with the principles of freedom, toleration, and 'general equality' besides substituting for conventional Christianity a purely 'philosophical religion'.[49] Some historians claim the Illuminati were not really radical at all as they had no plans to attack existing governments and nurtured no cult of revolutionary violence. This is true but beside the point, which is the decisive role of radical ideas in forging late eighteenth-century revolutionary consciousness.[50] Secret societies undoubtedly did take the initiative in propagating egalitarian, republican, and materialist ideas and preparing the way for 'einer allgemeinen Religions- und Staats-Umwalzung' [a general overturning of religion and the state]. This is what enabled the Counter-Enlightenment's dishonourable slanderers, pasquille-writers, and 'reputation murderers', as Wekhrlin put it, deliberately to spread a poisonous atmosphere, ruthlessly twisting the truth by alleging a degree of dishonesty, treasonable intent, and violent and murderous designs that had no basis in reality.[51]

While the league of the Illuminati kept its hidden 'highest mysteries' a profound secret, it eventually emerged that these were simply 'das Weihauptische System'— Weishaupt's philosophical ideas. Contemporary observers, including the ultra-reactionary court official and freemason Ludwig Adolf Christian von Grolmann (1741–1809), who subsequently published one of the best-known collections of secret documents of *Illuminatismus, Die neuesten Arbeiten des Spartacus und des Philo* (1793), later revealed that the order's highest grades were, in effect, just a veiled vehicle for propagating materialist and atheistic ideas and that the 'highest mysteries' of the so-called *Philosophengrad* [philosophers' grade] embedded nothing other than what Grolmann terms *Spinozismus* [Spinozism], and the 'Spinozistic *Grundsätze*' [basic principles] that everything that exists is matter, that God and the universe are one, that all organized religion is political deception devised by ambitious men.[52]

---

[48] [Grolmann], *Kritische Geschichte*, 26–7, 29–30, 32–3; [Grolmann], *Neuesten Arbeiten*, 53, 56, 74.
[49] Weishaupt, *Anrede*, 170–2; [Grolmann], *Neuesten Arbeiten*, preface, p. vii.
[50] Wilson, 'Enlightenment's Alliance', 374.
[51] Wekhrlin, *Graue Ungeheuer*, 3 (1784–5), 123–4.
[52] [Grolmann], *Kritische Geschichte*, 79; Mulsow, 'Adam Weishaupt', 30; Riedel, 'Aufklärung', 112–13.

Although the spectre invoked by the likes of Grolmann was overblown and paranoid, the documents he and others published were authentic and his character-ization of Weishaupt and the order's other leaders as deeply subversive materialists not inaccurate. The Illuminati were not a violent organization or actively subversive politically. But they were conspiratorial and at leadership level, from the outset, uncompromisingly radical in their ideas. During the late 1770s, we learn from Weishaupt's correspondence, he was inspired chiefly by d'Holbach's *Système de la nature, Politique naturelle,* and *Système social* and also Helvétius's *De l'esprit* and *De l'homme*.[53] These were the works on which he based his reform programme. In a letter dating from 1777–8, he also saw an urgent need to render d'Holbach's *Morale universelle* into German, though no such translation actually appeared until many years later.[54]

If, beginning in the 1760s, Helvétius's philosophy represented a considerable force in Germany, as in Italy and Russia, and remained so throughout the 1770s and 1780s, it was d'Holbach's writings that exercised the strongest pull on Weishaupt and precisely during the years of the *Illuminatenorden*'s greatest penetration, albeit Helvétius's and d'Holbach's legacies were at this time not clearly distinguishable owing to d'Holbach's subterfuges and the curious preface introducing the German translation of the *Système de la nature,* the *System der Natur, oder von den Gesetzen der physischen und moralischen Welt,* in 1783, pronouncing Helvétius the probable author of this sensational text. Another radical work, loudly denouncing the world's twin evils of 'superstition' and 'tyranny', published in German whilst Illuminism was at its height, at Dessau, in 1783, was Deleyre's *Tableau,* under the title *Gemälde von Europa aus dem Französischen des Abts Raynal übersezt von E.W.v.R.* (Ewald?), a publication eagerly greeted by the brilliant young Spinozist orientalist Diez.[55]

The *Système*'s German translator, Christian Ludwig Paalzow (1753–1824), was a 30-year-old Halle-trained Berlin jurist, experienced in translating from French, thoroughly familiar with Voltaire and Montesquieu, who had figured earlier among the many radical-minded eagerly supporting Lessing in the *Fragmentenstreit,* in particular by attacking Michaelis and Semler.[56] A propagator also of Fréret's reputation, Paalzow notes in his anonymous 'translator's preface' that 'this famous *Système*' was certainly not by 'Mirabaud', as the original version pretends. 'If it is not by Helvétius himself, the book is at any rate fashioned on the principles of this remarkable French philosopher.'[57] For publishing *De l'esprit* in 1758 under his own name Helvétius had paid a heavy price. But the posthumous consequence, reinforced by *De l'homme*'s appearance under his name, was that the new ideology of equality, materialism, secular morality, and emancipation, in Germany and Habsburg central

---

[53] Weishaupt (Spartacus) to Zwack, 5 Mar. 1778, in Van Dülmen, *Dokumente,* 220; *Korrespondenz des Illuminatenordens,* i. 32; Schings, *Brüder,* 145 n.; Riedel, 'Aufklärung', 113.

[54] Weishaupt to Zwack, 25 Aug. 1778, *Korrespondenz des Illuminatenordens,* i. 84.

[55] [Deleyre], *Gemälde von Europa,* 'Vorbericht' pp. iii–iv.

[56] Hess, *Germans, Jews,* 172, 190–1.

[57] [Paalzow], 'Vorbericht', in [d'Holbach], *System der Natur,* p. vi; Schröder, *Ursprünge,* 510–11.

Europe as in Italy and Russia, came to be more closely linked with him than any other writer.

Paalzow urged readers to study the controversy surrounding the *Système*, directing their attention to the relevant publications of Priestley, Reimarus, Jerusalem, Platner, and Isaac de Pinto.[58] Some objected to the *Système*'s materialism, suspecting it of propagating atheism, granted Paalzow, but no one could fail to be impressed by the author's zeal for *die Rechte der Menschheit* [the rights of humanity] and his high regard for morality, and these were precisely the qualities that attracted the Illuminati leadership. Besides, held Paalzow, citing Priestley's positive opinion of it, the book was not really 'atheistic' given its intense moral fervour.[59] Later, Paalzow also published German renderings of d'Holbach's *Système social* (Altona, 1795) and the *Contagion sacrée* (1796) besides other radical works.

2. WEISHAUPT'S 'GENERAL REFORMATION OF THE WORLD'

Radical Enlightenment was now rapidly insinuating itself into a quasi-masonic underground pledged to avoid violence but whose secret general plan, *le grand œuvre*, was to spread 'general enlightenment' in the world, overthrow superstition and *Despotismus*, emancipate the serfs, and replace princely rule and the churches with what the order's secret documents called a 'general equality' and a 'better' religion than Christianity. 'Ce projet', in Mirabeau's words, 'étoit beau, noble, grand, mais on a manqué de prudence dans son exécution.'[60] *Illuminaten* entering the higher grades were taught that the 'philosophic' history of mankind is essentially that of *Despotismus* and *Freyheit* [freedom] in ceaseless conflict and that within society the chief allies of *Despotismus* in this cosmic struggle for humanity's future are ignorance, priestcraft, and superstition.[61] 'Die Freyheit hat den Despotismus zur Welt gebracht', urged Weishaupt, 'und der Despotismus fürht wider zur Freyheit' [Freedom brought despotism into the world, and despotism leads men once again to freedom].[62] The ultimate aim of his conspiracy was to introduce an 'allgemeine und dauerhafte Freyheit' [general and lasting freedom] in which 'reason is the only law-book of mankind'.[63]

Weishaupt's key conception 'Despotismus', meaning monarchy, aristocracy, serfdom, priestcraft, and *ancien régime* institutions generally, and use of 'slavery' to describe humanity's condition, were more redolent of d'Holbach, Diderot, and

---

[58] [Paalzow], 'Vorbericht', in [d'Holbach], *System der Natur*, p. x.
[59] [Paalzow], 'Vorbericht', vi–viii.
[60] Mirabeau, *De la monarchie*, v. 100.
[61] [Grolman], *Neuesten Arbeiten*, 17, 23–4, 37; Weishaupt, *Anrede*, 172.
[62] Weishaupt, *Anrede*, 172.
[63] [Grolman], *Kritische Geschichte*, 27–8, 47, 49–51; [Grolman], *Neuesten Arbeiten*, 34, 37, 46–7.

Helvétius than Rousseau as was his idea of a universal morality and set of human rights taught by reason being 'ein allgemeines Recht' [a universal right] to which all other law, morality, and institutions should be subject.[64] Especially typical of d'Holbach is Weishaupt's replacing divine providence with Nature and reason as the two overriding factors in his 'philosophical history of mankind'.[65] Weishaupt, or 'Spartacus' to give him his clandestine code-name, was gripped, in classic radical fashion, by the notion that man's supreme enemy on earth is man himself and that it is owing to our wrong ideas and ignorance that men eke out their existence plunged in 'persecution, slavery and oppression where despotism, intolerance, and wars of religion, foment St Bartholomew's night massacres and Sicilian Vespers'.[66] The central principle of *das Weihauptische System* was his thesis that happiness is not just for the few but for all and that to achieve general emancipation from superstition and oppression universal enlightenment is the crucial step.

Likewise characteristic of d'Holbach is Weishaupt's conception of 'die bevorstehende Revolution des menschlichen Geistes' [the immanent revolution of the human spirit] by which mankind will revert to equality and freedom as something engineered by *Aufklärung*, the only force strong enough to bring it about.[67] *Aufklärung*, held the *Illuminatenorden*'s leadership, is the sole effective engine of human progress, by which they, like d'Holbach and Diderot, meant not Voltaire's or Kant's limited Enlightenment, but a 'diffused universal Enlightenment' changing all men's outlook and religious views fundamentally. So great was the power of superstition among the general population that for most of humanity das *Reich der Venunft* [the kingdom of reason], the power to conduct one's life as an independent being, will always remain a mere dream, an impossibility, without carefully concerted sustained intervention.[68] Even where enlightenment is achieved, men will still require 'secret philosophy schools' to serve as a permanent 'Archiv der Natur und der menschlichen Rechte' [archive of nature and of human rights], to explain, judge, and guide.[69] For whether men live under a *Democratie* or despotic rule is ultimately a question of the people's values and morality, the level of which, something uplifted only by combating ignorance, the people cannot elevate on their own.[70]

'Whoever wishes to introduce general freedom, spreads general Enlightenment,' intoned Weishaupt, explaining that true Enlightenment does not mean knowledge of words or categories but of things. *Aufklärung* 'is not knowledge of abstract, speculative, theoretical sciences, which inflate the mind, and do nothing to improve the heart',[71] but the gradual eradication of priests and kings together with the entire

---

[64] Weishaupt, *Anrede*, 174–6, 183.
[65] Ibid. 178–9; Fehn, 'Moralische Unschuld', 214, 216–17.
[66] Weishaupt, *Über die Schrecken des Todes*, 26.
[67] Weishaupt, *Anrede*, 179, 192–3; Fehn, 'Moralische Unschuld', 209–12.
[68] [Grolmann], *Neuesten Arbeiten*, 40–1, 46; Fischer, 'Reduktion', 292.
[69] [Grolmann], *Neuesten Arbeiten*, 37–8, 47, 69.
[70] Ibid. 49; Schings, *Brüder*, 167; Weishaupt, *Anrede*, 179.
[71] Weishaupt, *Anrede*, 183.

ideology of priestcraft, monarchy, and aristocracy. He was particularly critical in defining *Aufklärung* of what he considered the narrow, petty, word-spinning definitions usually favoured in Catholic central Europe. True *Aufklärung* cannot be *Wort-sondern-Sachen Kenntnis* [words without knowledge of realities]. It must be a universal transformation especially of social and political realities.[72] *Aufklärung* is about transforming social and moral reality. Accordingly, he bracketed false, unenlightened 'learning' together with the mainstream Enlightenment as one of the four chief pillars, with political oppression, social subordination, and false religion, underpinning tyranny, superstition, and ignorance.[73] Enlightening some to keep others in error makes power, he argued, and furthers subjection; only *Aufklärung* to enlighten all generates freedom: only 'Aufklärung um andere wieder aufzuklären, giebt Freyheit'.[74]

It was Weishaupt's joining the principal Munich masonic lodge, in 1777, and adopting an elaborate secret constitution, dividing his members according to a complex system of classes and degrees, that enabled him to consolidate his organization as a clandestine network embedded within freemasonry and vastly expand his organization. While fiercely critical of the wider masonic movement and disdainful of masonic ritual, the order nevertheless remained inextricably entwined with freemasonry, developing rather like a parasitic plant, using the parent body as a source of sustenance and recruits and instrument for propagating its ideology. At first the Illuminati spread slowly, remaining rather localized, having only nineteen members in March 1778 and still only forty-five, mostly in Munich and Ingolstadt, in mid 1779.[75] Munich, first and the largest of the *Illuminaten* circles, at its height, in 1784, counted some 300 members and was the group most often accused of being riddled with 'materialism'.[76]

While they graduated from grade to grade, so that the organization was hierarchical in a sense, membership was based on the principle of equality. However much camouflaged and unknown even to its own membership, by adopting a strategy of infiltrating members into prominent positions in the German courts and seeking to recruit highly placed officials, the Illuminati signalled their ambition of transforming society from top to bottom. Growth accelerated from 1779, and especially 1782, following the disastrous failure of German freemasonry's general congress, that year, to reconcile the warring factions in their midst at Wilhelmsbad.[77] The Wilhelmsbad fiasco and its irresolvable splits revealed for all to see just how incoherent, intellectually void, and directionless freemasonry really was.[78] At that point, droves of disillusioned masons, demanding something more purposeful, joined the Illuminati.

---

[72] [Grolmann], *Neuesten Arbeiten*, 46–7, 50–1.   [73] Ibid. 119–20.
[74] Ibid. 46; Weishaupt, *Anrede*, 183.   [75] Von Dülmen, *Geheimbund*, 28–9, 31.
[76] Wehrlin, *Graue Ungeheuer*, 3 (1784–5), 131, 134 and 4 (1785), 351; Schüttler, *Mitglieder*, 215–19; Schaich, *Staat und Öffentlichkeit*, 46, 49.
[77] Mounier, *De l'influence*, 176; Schaich, *Staat und Öffentlichkeit*, 45–6.
[78] *Korrespondenz des Illuminatenordens*, i, p. xix; Wilson, *Geheimräte*, 189.

The league spread more in Protestant than Catholic Germany in the early 1780s, due to the efforts of two key organizers, Knigge, who brought around 500 persons into the movement, and the humbly born translator and musician Johann Joachim Christoph Bode (1730–93). Son of a prominent official at Hanover, utterly scornful of the 'foolishness' of freemasonry and the Strict Observance in particular, Knigge was active in the order from 1780.[79] Bode, a linguist and French teacher, one of those recruited by Knigge, became the main organizer in Thuringia, including Weimar where he recruited Goethe and Herder.[80] At Stuttgart, the organization's hub was the elite secondary school, or Karlschule, which Schiller attended until 1780 and where over a dozen professors and students became members.[81] At its height, around 1785, the order had a membership in Germany and Austria of around 2,500.[82]

Universal enlightenment, held the Illuminati, is the answer to humanity's problems and the only answer. The point of the *Illuminatenorden*, for Knigge (who generally dispensed with the aristocratic predicate 'von' styling himself plain Herr Knigge), was to advance without violent revolution a general 'Weltreformation' [world reformation], two main aspects of which, as with Weishaupt, were eradication of princes and replacing conventional Christianity with the 'religion of reason'.[83] Knigge cherished the same books as Weishaupt, citing Raynal's *Histoire philosophique* as a particular favourite.[84] He was also fond of Rousseau,[85] though, and liked theosophy and creating a mysterious pseudo-religion incorporating more mysteries and trappings into the culture of the Illuminati, a penchant reflected not least in a draft creed circulated, in 1784, among those consulted about the forming of the highest grades of the order, the *Philosophen* and *Docenten* grades. Politically more skilful and better connected than Weishaupt, behind the scenes he was a declared democrat and, after 1789, one of the French Revolution's most active supporters in Germany. An enthusiast for French philosophical literature generally, he later translated into German the second part of Rousseau's *Confessions* (1790) and Boulanger's *Despotisme oriental* edited by d'Holbach, which he published at Altona in 1794, entitled *Über den Ursprung des Despotismus, besonders in den Morgenländern*.

Of all his 'colonies' in northern Germany, Knigge considered the lodge in the little principality of Neuwied (Claudiopolis) the most active and truest to the cause.[86] But 'Philo', to give Knigge his secret code-name, was closely linked to many courts including that of Hesse-Cassel, indeed was a man of considerable influence throughout the empire. For this reason, Grolmann and others considered him more 'dangerous' than Weishaupt. It was Knigge, acknowledged Weishaupt, who brought in the

[79] Schings, *Brüder*, 56–7; Stammen, 'Adolf Freiherr von Knigge', 84–5.
[80] Stammen, 'Adolf Freiherr von Knigge', 69; Hermann, *Knigge*, 117.
[81] Riedel, 'Aufklärung', 113–14.
[82] Mulsow, 'Adam Weishaupt', 28; McIntosh, *Rose Cross*, 94–5, 97; Hermann, *Knigge*, 114.
[83] [Grolmann], *Neuesten Arbeiten*, 5, 34, 40, 46; [Grolmann], *Kritische Geschichte*, 27–8, 53, 64, 74–5, 80–2.
[84] Knigge to Weishaupt, Frankfurt, 5 July 1781, in *Korrespondenz des Illuminatenordens*, i. 336.
[85] Knigge to Weishaupt, Frankfurt, 13 Jan. 1781, ibid. i. 218.
[86] Ibid. 293.

large numbers in Protestant states and demonstrated the need scrupulously to mask the society's ultimate aims if prominent men, including princes, were to join. Both men pursued a large and varied membership, agreeing that to broaden the movement effectively one could not debar those only mildly enlightened or who remained attached to tradition and religion.[87]

Precisely due to the multi-tiered system of organization and ideology Weishaupt and Knigge developed, the Illuminati never acquired anything like a unified ideological-philosophical programme known to and supported by the rank and file. The league looked coherent in organization, and extended impressively across both Catholic and Protestant parts of Germany, making it appear, briefly at least, rather formidable. Weishaupt's movement was indeed the most extensive and remarkable subversive organization in Europe prior to 1789. In response to its growth, reactionary Rosicrucians, ex-Jesuits, and mystical freemasons, groups consciously opposing Enlightenment and defending the social order, Christian morality, and faith, instigated a sustained campaign against them. From the outset, the league remained deeply fragmented organizationally and intellectually, and this could hardly have been otherwise as the documents and statements of aims shown to newcomers and novitiates in the lower 'Minerval' 'grades' of the movement provided no indication of the true aims of Weishaupt and the other *Areopagiten*, as the order's radical leaders were called.

Key figures were deeply shocked when they began to suspect. A central figure in the order's internal splits, and an Illuminatus who had earlier, in the mid 1770s, particularly influenced Weishaupt's own formation, was the Göttingen philosopher Johann Georg Heinrich Feder (1740–1821), who entered the order in 1782. A Lockean empiricist continually urging Weishaupt to stick to a moderate course, proclaiming that 'moderata durant' [moderate things last],[88] Feder evinced a growing antipathy to both radical thought and the inflated theosophy of Knigge. Before long, a distinct Göttingen faction emerged, led by Feder and his close associate Christoph Meiners, likewise a Lockean empiricist and conservative ally of the court totally opposed to radical goals. If Weishaupt greatly prided himself, as he admitted in a private letter of 1782, that a humble Ingolstadt professor like himself should become the leader and 'teacher' of famous professors at Göttingen like Feder and Meiners, the latter never regarded him as in any way their 'teacher'.[89] Rather, the 'naive' Weishaupt, complained Knigge, in January 1783, disrupted things, causing 'our best people in Göttingen' to have second thoughts about belonging to the order, by prematurely recommending 'the writings of Boulanger' (i.e. d'Holbach's *Le Christianisme dévoilé*).[90]

---

[87] Knigge, *Philos endliche Erklärung*, 352.
[88] [Grolmann], *Kritische Geschichte*, 36; Mulsow, 'Adam Weishaupt', 34.
[89] Mounier, *De l'influence*, 210; Van Dülmen, *Dokumente*, 262.
[90] Knigge to Zwack, Jan. 1783, in Van Dülmen, *Dokumente*, 310–11.

Knigge made a special trip to Göttingen and supposed he had saved the situation, mollifying the professors and dispelling their shock. Here, though, events were to prove, he was mistaken. Radical materialism combined in Weishaupt's mind with hatred of 'despotism' and the thesis that naturalist truth had always been cultivated by an 'enlightened' underground which had, since remote times, shrouded its secret knowledge in 'mysteries', a concept powerfully influenced by Boulanger and Herder.[91] Feder loathed such speculative theories and strove to reconfigure the order as something free from materialism no less than mysteries, pseudo-religion, and masonic hocus-pocus. Meiners reacted equally angrily to Weishaupt's 'system' when fully revealed in draft texts intended to define the creed of the highest grades circulated by Weishaupt among the inner circle in 1784.

Some, however, proved more susceptible to Weishaupt's 'naturalistische Prose-lytenmacherei' or radical proselytizing. Franz Dietrich, Freiherr von Ditfurth (1738–1813), jurist and anticlerical master of the masonic lodge and head Illuminist at Wetzlar, a personage not afraid 'of the boldest propositions', showed real eagerness at least for a time to embrace Weishaupt's concept of Enlightenment. Inducted into the order by Knigge in May 1781 under the code-name 'Minos', he immediately ordered all the books Weishaupt urged him to read, including d'Holbach's *Système social* and Raynal's *Histoire philosophique*. Reading the latter with 'warm ardour', Ditfurth implored Weishaupt to recommend more books of the kind, both for himself and the local 'brothers',[92] though later he was to prove less of a democrat than his protégé Bahrdt, whom he groomed for the role of clandestine organizer from 1781.[93]

All initiates in the first grade really knew of the movement was that it was devoted to advancing *Aufklärung*. Similarly, the organization's official publicity surrounding new lodges or *Minervalkirchen* [Minerval churches] made clear only that the organization sought to promote *Aufklärung*.[94] Princes and high officials recruited into the movement were shown only documents containing no hint of the thoroughgoing political and religious transformation Weishaupt envisaged.[95] The stated common objective in the lower grades was to eradicate intolerance, confessional thinking, dogmatism, and deference to priests and cultivate independent critical thinking, freedom of thought, and general toleration; this was the order's programme of 'education'.[96] Most members proceeded no further than the second grade and hence discovered nothing more of the order's philosophy. Second-grade members, constituting a regular learned society, imbibed ancient history, science, economy, and some specifically philosophical texts.[97]

---

[91] Mulsow, 'Adam Weishaupt', 45–54.
[92] Ditfurth to Weishaupt, 5 Nov. and 27 Dec. 1781, in *Korrespondenz des Illuminatenordens*, i. 415, 433.
[93] Mühlpfordt, 'Europarepublik', 325–7.
[94] Schings, *Brüder*, 30–1.
[95] [Grolmann], *Kritische Geschichte*, 65–6, 70, 80.
[96] Van Dülmen, *Society*, 110, 112–13; Riedel, 'Aufklärung', 110–12.
[97] Van Dülmen, *Geheimbund*, 36–7.

So heavy was the emphasis on 'Enlightenment' readings, furthermore, that membership was confined in practice to academics, students, librarians, courtiers, and officials, the very highly educated. Hence, not only was there no place for peasants and artisans but none for merchants, shopkeepers, and businessmen either.[98] This matters because Marxist historians have often claimed the revolutionary consciousness of the late eighteenth century stemmed from changing economic forces and was a 'bourgeois consciousness'. But the true 'bourgeois consciousness' as a rule remained wholly antagonistic to radical thought. What the order of the Illuminati shows is that the budding revolutionary consciousness derived from intellectual leaders reacting to social, political, and cultural conditions. But only in the third grade, that of the 'Mysteries', did elements of moral, social, and political theory concocted by Weishaupt from d'Holbach's *Système social*, *Politique naturelle*, and *Système de la nature* and from Helvétius's works feature in the educational programme.[99] Only when a member of the grade of Mysteries entered the inner circle of the ruling *Areopagiten* was the order's reformist agenda fully revealed.[100] The movement was heavily didactic and erudite and yet, at the same time, a secret political organization, secrecy being essential not only to its activity but very survival. Its regions and locations as well as members' names appeared in its correspondence and documents only in code, with Bavaria as 'Griechenland' [Greece], Swabia 'Panonia', Ingolstadt 'Ephesus', and Munich 'Athens', Vienna being 'Rome', Mannheim 'Thessalonica', Jena, 'Syracuse', Weimar 'Hieropolis', and Göttingen 'Andrus'. If Weishaupt was styled 'Spartacus' and Knigge 'Philo', Feder was 'Marcus Aurelius', Herder 'Damasio', and Bode 'Aemelius'.[101]

In terms of principle not much divided Weishaupt and Knigge. Yet, from 1782 they fought each other in an increasingly bitter feud with Bode aligning with Weishaupt, their disagreements stemming from differences of style and an irreconcilable personal antipathy.[102] Where the 'Protestant', Knigge, liked ceremonies Weishaupt, 'a Catholic', scorned the ceremonial side.[103] Weishaupt had a 'fine mind and was a deep thinker', granted Knigge, 'something all the more admirable in that he had had to cultivate it amid the obstacles of a stupid Catholic education'.[104] But 'Philo' detested 'Spartacus' 'Jesuitischen Charakter' [Jesuitical character] and found him far too domineering.[105] The people, suggested an embittered Knigge, after their final

[98] Van Dülmen, *Society*, 115–17; Schaich, *Staat und Öffentlichkeit*, 47–51.
[99] Van Dülmen, *Geheimbund*, 37; Müller, *Universität*, 266; Krebs, *Helvétius*, 364–5.
[100] [Grolmann], *Kritische Geschichte*, 76, 80–2.
[101] Van Dülmen, *Dokumente*, 248, 253, 255, 260, 267; Mulsow, 'Adam Weishaupt', 34, 37; McIntosh, *Rose Cross*, 105.
[102] [Grolmann], *Kritische Geschichte*, 27–8, 32, 47, 57; Stammen, 'Adolf Freiherr von Knigge', 71.
[103] [Grolmann], *Kritische Geschichte*, 15–17.
[104] Ibid. 342.
[105] [Grolmann], *Kritische Geschichte*, 40, 57; Van Dülmen, *Dokumente*, 288, 305; Van Dülmen, *Geheimbund*, 71; Schings, *Brüder*, 173.

break, would find themselves beneath a severer yoke than ever were they to come under Weishaupt's rule, far worse than under the Jesuits.[106]

In February 1784, at meetings chaired by Goethe partly at his house at Weimar, Knigge defended himself against Weishaupt's accusations before Bode, Herder, and Duke Ernst but failed to rally the Weimar group to his support.[107] The quarrel only intensified thereafter until, finally, Knigge was expelled, albeit signing a paper saying he was resigning voluntarily.[108] Shortly afterwards, he joined another secret society, Bahrdt's Deutsche Union. Defending himself, in *Philos endliche Erklärung* (1788), Knigge identified the root of the split and the *Illuminatenorden*'s failure in its secretive, hierarchical structure, the cause, he—and others, Herder among them—believed, of a fatal contradiction between the movement's proclaimed espousal of freedom and *Aufklärung* and inner tendency to authoritarianism in practice.[109]

Complete absence of intellectual convergence at the top ensured the speedy collapse of the *Illuminatenorden* during the years 1785–7. But if the internal clash between moderate and Radical Enlightenment guaranteed the league's swift disintegration, it was the wider clash between Enlightenment and *Gegenaufklärung* in Bavaria and Austria, culminating in the mid 1780s, which precipitated the official suppression and persecution of the society. Chronic incoherence in the ranks rendered success impossible and ensured the almost complete dissolution of the league in the years 1785–7. The order's remnants were then left to mutate into the successor leagues of the Weimar Illuminati and the more coherently radical Deutsche Union.

3. BAVARIA'S COUNTER-ENLIGHTENMENT

There was good reason, held Weishaupt, why fiercely Catholic lands like Bavaria, steeped as they were in bigotry and narrowness, nurtured more adherents of *Naturalismus* than other regions.[110] While the *Gold- und Rosenkreuz* accused the Illuminati of attempting to take over German freemasonry and subvert German society more generally with radical ideas, the Illuminati alleged (and feared) that this was precisely what the Rosicrucians, who attracted many conservatively inclined figures of a previously moderate enlightened background,[111] aspired to do in reverse. The close linkage of Weishaupt's Illuminism with Helvétius and the *Système de la nature* contributed directly to the movement's downfall.

---

[106] [Grolmann], *Kritische Geschichte*, 57; Van Dülmen, *Dokumente*, 310; Van Dülmen, *Society*, 107–9; Stammen, 'Adolf Freiherr von Knigge', 75, 80; McIntosh, *Rose Cross*, 106–7.
[107] Schings, *Brüder*, 91–2; Hermann, *Knigge*, 119.
[108] Erker and Siebers, 'Das Bahrdt-Pasquill', in Goldenbaum, *Appell*, ii. 917.
[109] Knigge, *Philos endliche Erklärung*, 343, 358–9; Schings, *Brüder*, 174; Wilson, *Geheimräte*, 196–8.
[110] Weishaupt, *Nachtrag*, 10.
[111] Sauter, *Visions*, 26–9, 31, 39–42.

An official of the Bavarian regime, Karl von Eckartshausen (1752–1803), had briefly joined the Illuminati in Munich until he realized the movement's secret philosophy focused on explaining everything in terms of reason, something totally unpalatable to his strongly mystical streak. He immediately defected, becoming one of Weishaupt's most implacable foes. Eckartshausen denounced not the Enlightenment as such, but the 'falsche Aufklärer' [false enlighteners], thinkers like Helvétius and the *Système*'s author who, in his view, were poisoning young people's minds with a vision of philosophy that rejects religion as 'superstition'. Materialism and atheism, he went so far as to declare in his attack on radical thought, are much worse for society than war or a plague.[112] Many agreed. Karl Theodor, the Bavarian elector, alarmed by reports of conspiracy submitted by defectors from the league, especially Eckartshausen, his court archivist, decided to act.[113] In June 1784, he issued a first, relatively mild edict prohibiting secret societies without naming the Illuminati as such. In this way, observed Wekhrlin, who declared the banning of Bayle at Ingolstadt a 'scandalous blot on the *Aufklärung* in Bavaria', as did the leading Austrian Illuminatus, Ignaz Edler von Born (1742–91), in two articles denouncing the measures being taken against the Bavarian Illuminati,[114] Bavaria sank under 'all the curses of stupidity and barbarism, into intellectual emptiness, uncertainty, tyranny, despair and slavery'.[115]

The elector's first edict produced only a further wave of protests from clergy and some professors: the Illuminati were evading the restrictions and secretly planned to destroy princely authority and religion via assassination, suicide, and sodomy.[116] Further measures were urged and, in March 1785, Karl Theodor obliged with a much harsher edict, condemning the freemasons and Illuminati 'as traitorous and hostile to religion'. Forewarned, Weishaupt escaped arrest, fleeing the electorate which he was never to see again. Other Illuminati were arrested, though, or expelled from their posts, among them an Ingolstadt philosophy professor, Agustin Schelle (1742–1805), a former Benedictine who moved to Salzburg where he became university librarian.[117] Another of those arrested was an army officer, Ferdinand Maximilian von Meggenhofen (1761–90), a law graduate of Ingolstadt and disciple of Weishaupt, eager to transform Bavarians into 'enlightened and upright citizens' through 'philosophy' and now regimental auditor at Burghausen. His home was searched and papers seized. Brought to Munich, he was interrogated for two days. Found to be 'corrupted by philosophy' and maintaining undesirable contacts, he was stripped of his position and sentenced to confinement and vigorous Catholic re-education in state custody in a Franciscan friary.[118]

---

[112] Eckartshausen, *Ueber Religion, Freydenkerey*, 53–4, 58.
[113] McIntosh, *Rose Cross*, 108–9; Schaich, *Staat und Öffentlichkeit*, 174, 259, 321.
[114] Wekhrlin, *Graue Ungeheuer*, 4 (1785), 169; Schaich, *Staat und Öffentlichkeit*, 245–6.
[115] Wekhrlin, *Graue Ungeheuer*, 4 (1785), 176.
[116] Wekhrlin, *Graue Ungeheuer*, 7 (1786), 7–10.
[117] Schüttler, *Mitglieder*, 134.
[118] Ibid. 102; Wekhrlin, *Graue Ungeheuer*, 'Beilage', 12, 14, 26, 73; Mounier, *De l'influence*, 220 n.

Another Bavarian Illuminatus arrested was the Ingolstadt university librarian and town school inspector Anton Drexl (1753–1830). Likewise an enthusiast for *Aufklärung* and disciple of Weishaupt, Drexl had presided over a reading circle debating current philosophical 'Gegenstände' [circumstances] and issues of key enlightened journals, like the *Berlinische Monatsschrift*. 'Many of the happiest hours of my life', admitted this erudite priest, 'I owe to this small circle of studious young friends.'[119] After the Ingolstadt lodge dissolved, Drexl had remained in touch with Weishaupt and visited him at Regensburg. Summoned to appear before the university rector, he was interrogated about his contacts and reading *conventicula*. Dismissed for 'Naturalismus und Irreligion', amid a barrage of hostile propaganda,[120] he fled to Italy, becoming lecturer in Greek at Pavia and later librarian at Brescia.

The Bavarian public were readily persuaded that the Illuminati were not just a 'sect of impertinent philosophers' but atheists, criminals, and enemies of society. Public opinion fully supported their being hounded and suppressed.[121] With this, the power of a strident, highly repressive *Gegenaufklärung* to sweep not just radical but all Enlightenment from the scene for the first time became fully manifest. Radical enlighteners were the immediate target of the witch-hunt; but all enlighteners were threatened by the Counter-Enlightenment mood.

The crack-down in Bavaria in 1785–6 was more than a regional event. The court at Munich, backed by the clergy, persecuted anyone, professors, students, army officers, or whoever, suspected of maintaining contact with other members of the order. This was the start of the European Counter-Enlightenment as a concerted, officially sponsored political movement. From Bavaria, repression spread to the other German Catholic principalities. Following the Bavarian lead, the archbishop-electors at Bonn and at Mainz where there was an active Illuminist cell that included Anton Joseph Dorsch (1758–1819), a philosopher and radical enlightener later to figure among the foremost German Jacobins, issued their own edicts banning secret societies and tightening censorship.[122] What Weishaupt's sympathizers called the 'campaign of calumny by an implacable cabale' to persecute 'the friends of virtue and the truth' by claiming he had preached 'irreligion, atheism, regicide, assassination and propagated principles the most contrary that there are to those of good morality', swiftly became a political instrument more potent than Illuminism ever was. According to Weishaupt, it aimed at 'extinguishing the flame of reason, and holding society under the despotism of the most shameful ignorance', and in any case won a stunning victory.[123] Supported by ordinary folk 'who always resist new ideas' and were fired up with bigotry, as Weishaupt put it, this aggressive new creed successfully demonized

---

[119] Wekhrlin, *Graue Ungeheuer*, 7 (1786), 117–19; Schaich, *Staat und Öffentlichkeit*, 54, 218–20.
[120] Wekhrlin, *Graue Ungeheuer*, 7 (1786), 122–32; Schüttler, *Mitglieder*, 42–3; Müller, *Universität*, 236.
[121] *Beilage zum grauen Ungeheuer von Wekhrlin*, 9, 76.
[122] Blanning, *Reform*, 272–3, 276; Van Dülmen, *Geheimbund*, 92–3.
[123] Weishaupt, *Über die Schrecken des Todes*, 'avant-propos du traducteur'.

Aufklärung as moral pollution plotting the overthrow of religion, tradition, and morality by penetrating society via secret societies.[124]

Repression of the Illuminati in Bavaria marked the start of a general reaction following Frederick the Great's death, in 1786. A potent mythology had been forged of the rightness of authority and of the admirable piety and loyalty of the common people infused with tradition and boundless hatred of philosophical subversives which would one day form part of the seed-bed of extreme authoritarianism in central Europe. Besides religious bigotry, the rhetoric of denunciation, observed Wekhrlin in 1785, particularly exploited the language of narrow *Patriotismus* and chauvinism with most of the public wholly failing to perceive how such mindless, self-defeating loyalism buttressed courtly, aristocratic, and priestly 'despotism'.[125] No less dismaying for the radical-minded, there was no effective counter-barrage to the tide of calumny and vituperation, though at Vienna, where Joseph's initial reaction was merely to forbid all publications on the subject, for or against, his presumed support afforded some hope he would intervene to counter anti-Illuminist propaganda.[126]

Among the most ardent supporters of the emperor's reform programme, the Illuminati enjoyed a degree of favour at court in Vienna—until 1785 at least. Several of the ousted professors from Bavaria fled to Austria where initially they were welcomed by Joseph's minister of education Van Swieten, and assigned alternative academic posts.[127] It was not long, though, before Illuminism found itself under a shadow in Austria too. The Vienna Illuminati, owing to Born's leadership and energy often called the 'Bornianern', had positively flourished during the early 1780s. But they faced bitter opposition within the masonic movement from both court-oriented moderates and hard-line Counter-Enlightenment *Rosenkreuzer*. Mozart, who joined the Viennese masonic movement late in 1784, entered a lodge more specifically Catholic in orientation than that presided over by Born. Nevertheless, he seems to have counted among Born's admirers and composed the cantata 'Der Mauerfreude' ['The Mason's Joy'], for tenor and male chorus K.471, a work first performed in April 1785, in his honour.[128] Mozart, in any case, was a regularly attending masonic 'brother' and, while the point remains disputed, the evidence suggests that, like the young Beethoven at Bonn, he gravitated toward the Illuminati rather than the moderates or (as has also been claimed), the Rosicrucians.[129]

Never particularly sympathetic towards freemasonry, by 1785 Joseph had grown positively hostile, influenced in part by the tide of negative propaganda

[124] Wekhrlin, *Graue Ungeheuer*, 1 (1784), 257, 264–5 and 2 (1784), 139 and 6 (1786), 207–10; Weishaupt, *Nachtrag*, 9–12, 40–1, 44–6.
[125] Wekhrlin, *Graue Ungeheuer*, 3 (1784–5) 121–4 and 4 (1785), 365–6.
[126] Ibid. 3 (1784–5), 143, 148–9.
[127] Wangermann, *From Joseph II*, 48.
[128] Solomon, *Mozart*, 326–8; Till, *Mozart*, 122–4, Van Dülmen, *Geheimbund*, 321.
[129] Van Dülmen, *Geheimbund*, 326–8

denouncing Illuminism but also realizing, like Frederick, that Illuminism at heart was anti-monarchical.[130] The imperial edict or *Freimaurerpatent* of December 1785 reduced the number of Viennese lodges and required detailed membership lists, placing masonic activity firmly under police surveillance, as well as seeking to curb the influence of the Rosicrucians and other reactionary mystery-mongers proclaiming faith, alchemical doctrines, and Templar legends, these groups being among those who most staunchly opposed Joseph's ecclesiastical and educational reforms.[131]

The 1785 reform of Austrian freemasonry by which Joseph sought to get a firm grip over the movement, a reform vigorously supported by Born but highly unwelcome to Sonnenfels and most of the Austrian masons, effectively blighted both the moderate grouping and the Illuminati. In 1786, Born, deeply dismayed, resigned from all masonic activity, he and Sonnenfels accusing each other of betraying the movement. The edict led to Illuminism being entirely dissolved in Vienna by the summer of 1786 and also caused a steep decline in Austrian freemasonry generally.[132]

Weishaupt himself, meanwhile, migrated, in August 1787, to the 'enlightened' court of Gotha. Gotha and Weimar refused to hand the leader of the *Illuminaten* over to the Bavarian elector who complained loudly of his presence in Thuringia. Briefly, the duke of Saxe-Weimar considered assigning Weishaupt a chair at Jena where Reinhold was recruited, in 1787, and Schiller in 1788. There were lengthy discussions with Bode and other local leaders of the Illuminati. But the duke hesitated, as did his cultural adviser, Goethe, because, as they told Bode, they had reservations about Weishaupt's philosophy and personality. Before long, as more information about him came to light, all thought of appointing him lapsed.[133] Bode, as Schiller noted, at this point decisively broke with Weishaupt, seeking to renew and revive Illuminism on a regional and moderate basis, excluding Weishaupt and radical ideas.[134] Reconfiguring the league on a new basis seemed a distinct possibility. If Herder had become thoroughly disillusioned with all the secret societies some years earlier,[135] as by 1788–9 had Goethe too,[136] Bode, who considered the 'anarchy' dividing the *Aufklärung* to be chiefly the work of ex-Jesuits, did much to spread alarm at the risk of a Jesuit-inspired *Gegenaufklärung*,[137] and was not without some support, Schiller during his first years in Weimar and Jena, in the mid 1780s, being among those attracted to his ideas and leadership.

[130] Beales, *Enlightenment and Reform*, 102–3; Beales, *Joseph II. Against*, 541, 543.
[131] [Grolmann], *Kritische Geschichte*, 67–8; Van Dülmen, *Geheimbund*, 87–9; Reinalter, 'Ignaz von Born', 364–6, 369; Solomon, *Mozart*, 322–3.
[132] Reinalter, 'Ignaz von Born', 372; I am also indebted here to the current research of Dr Tristan Coignard.
[133] Wilson, *Geheimräte*, 128; Mulsow, 'Adam Weishaupt', 27–30, 66.
[134] Schings, *Brüder*, 140, 143.   [135] Wilson, *Geheimräte*, 191–3.
[136] Ibid. 142–4.   [137] Ibid. 164.

4. THE DEUTSCHE UNION

Publication of the *Illuminatenorden*'s secret documents, in 1787, a notable event, as Jacobi stressed at the time, had the effect of discrediting the league in the eyes of the public as something irreligious, immoral, atheistic, and criminal. Counter-Enlightenment in Germany proved a severe blow not just to the radical tendency and leadership of the remaining secret leagues but to the Enlightenment broadly, radical and moderate. A sinister new slogan, the *Despotismus der Aufklärung* [despotism of the Enlightenment], invaded Germany's cultural landscape that was to remain a key theme of Counter-Enlightenment through the nineteenth and early twentieth centuries and still today features among the main pretensions of Postmodernism.[138] Among the traumatized leadership of the remaining secret leagues, the repression commencing in Munich in 1785–6 looked in retrospect like the commencement of the *Aufklärung*'s general collapse in central Europe and the final triumph of bigotry, repression, anti-intellectualism, anti-Semitism, injustice, and *Jesuitismus*.

The formerly lively Stuttgart cell had already dissolved in 1785 and in other regions Illuminism disappeared completely.[139] But in philosophical circles at Jena and Göttingen where Feder and Meiners, like Bode and Reinhold, sought to re-establish and reform the Illuminati as a movement of 'moderate' thought and goals in no way hostile to princely authority, the movement persisted for a time.[140] Weishaupt himself joined the efforts to regroup on a new basis, in a book published in 1787 confessing that he had indeed sought to rid Germany of princes and aristocracy but had now been converted to more sensible and moderate views. Now, he declared, he aimed merely at equality before the law, a 'Gleichheit der Rechte', renouncing all thought of social equality and elimination of princes.[141] But Weishaupt by 1787 was a discredited, marginalized figure and soon ceased all activity as an apologist for the order, though some suspected he might still be involved behind the scenes with the league's principal radical successor organization, the Deutsche Union.[142]

Moderation had some success. But still there were rifts. Students and professors throughout Germany, observed Weishaupt, were now reassessing their philosophical positions, carefully examining Kantianism, on the one side, and its counterpart, pantheism-Spinozism, on the other, a process pushing some towards more moderate positions and others towards materialism.[143] Bahrdt, who originally became a freemason in England in 1777 and who had had some connection with the Illuminati since the early 1780s, emerged in 1783 as the founder, chief organizer, and archivist of a smaller, still more secretive, and by no means exclusively northern competitor and successor organization, the Deutsche Union der Zweiundzwanziger [German Union of the Twenty-Two], the number referring to the original membership of Bahrdt's

[138] Wilson, *Geheimräte*, 164–5, 172–3, 178.   [139] Ibid. 96–7.
[140] Schings, *Brüder*, 130; Wilson, *Geheimräte*, 142.   [141] Weishaupt, *Nachtrag*, 87–8.
[142] [Grolmann], *Kritische Geschichte*, 82–3.   [143] Ibid. 126–7.

secret lodge, in Halle.[144] A secret society, 'of the writing and reading community', it spread in no small part through the channel of local reading societies.[145] The original model of the literary societies, or *Lesegesellschaften*, had been established by Gottsched at Leipzig in the 1750s. They were open groupings in which men of the middling strata mixed with nobles and academics and which by the 1770s had become major (and among the least court-oriented) vehicles for advancing *Aufklärung* in central Europe.[146] They maintained up-to-date libraries, often linked to local publishers and booksellers, and collectively subscribed to journals. The *Lesegesellschaft* in Trier, for example, in 1783 rented four rooms in the house of a local bookbinder, the rooms being used respectively as spaces for reading, writing, debating, and shelving books.[147] Among the most notable and most clearly linked with radical tendencies, as well as suspect, by 1789, was the literary society at Mainz. Several key academics had joined who later became democratic activists, among them Dorsch and Georg Forster.[148]

In early 1782, the Mainz society even attempted to place in its meeting-room a bust of Raynal which it had had prepared (with the latter's permission). The archbishop-elector's prohibition on their doing so was one of those small symbolic victories over *la philosophie* that Feller's ultra-reactionary *Journal historique et littéraire*, a journal later banned for political trouble-making by both Vienna and Mainz, gleefully reported.[149] After 1789, this club became irrevocably split between its rival moderate (i.e. pro-noble and pro-ecclesiastical) and democratic wings. At Bonn, the reading society was known to have been closely linked to the local secret cell of the Illuminati; but there were also certainly others of the kind.[150] Such societies, though overwhelmingly deferential in tone, and in their publicizing activities, were nevertheless also a platform for debating Enlightenment issues and notably helped spread political consciousness in Germany during the years of the American Revolution, and subsequently. It was within these societies, mostly in academic centres such as Mainz, Giessen, Jena, Halle, and Marburg, that the Radical Enlightenment chiefly spread during the 1780s, a tendency rendering them all to an extent a focus of suspicion, princely, ecclesiastical, and popular. The Marburg society, another radical focus, is known to have supplied no less than six members (from a total membership of slightly over 100) to the Deutsche Union.[151]

---

[144] [Grolmann], *Kritische Geschichte*, 83; Bahrdt, *Geschichte*, i. 3–5 and ii. 37; Erker and Siebers, 'Das Bahrdt-Pasquill', in Goldenbaum, *Appell*, ii. 911; Mühlpfordt, 'Bahrdts Weg', 998, 1001.

[145] Mühlpfordt, 'Europarepublik', 326–7.

[146] Ibid. 338; Van Dülmen, *Society*, 46; Haug, 'Bedeutung', 306–7.

[147] Blanning, *Reform*, 202; Tilgner, *Lesegesellschaften*, 20–3.

[148] Tilgner, *Lesegesellschaften*, 37, 110, 367; Blanning, *Reform*, 196–202; Gascoyne, 'German Enlightenment', 159, 163.

[149] [Feller], *Journal historique* (1782), 'Extrait d'une lettre de Mainz' (16 May 1782); Blanning, *Reform*, 203–4.

[150] Tilgner, *Lesegesellschaften*, 109–110.

[151] Haug, 'Bedeutung', 304–7.

Some, like Georg Forster's father, begged Bahrdt not to persist with his underground venture in such a menacing, unfavourable climate; others, though, could see little alternative in such a bleak context as the late 1780s.[152] Among the most active members of the Deutsche Union assisting Bahrdt were Degenhard Pott, a freethinking Leipzig publisher, and Knigge, now at Hanover.[153] Given the organization's concentration in university cities, students, curiously, amounted to only a relatively small proportion of the membership, at most around 10 per cent of the total.[154] A larger group—well over a hundred of them, many Prussian and Austrian—were the court and provincial officials and jurists.[155] There was also a strong contingent of around forty physicians. Almost entirely absent, once again, were artisans, business people, manufacturers, and financiers. Such people played little part in the spread of Radical Enlightenment.

Its ideological and intellectual purity, the Deutsche Union's social composition shows, mattered more to Bahrdt than any capacity for conspiracy and subversive political action. This conformed to his conviction that 'reason' can be society's sole guide to what is true when 'infallible' which means, since even the wisest make mistakes, that perfecting human reason is possible only within a context where freely seeking truth evolves through debate as a sustained group activity, 'the collective and concordant reason of cultured humanity [being] in no way subject to error in matters that depend wholly upon reason'.[156] Only collective reason is a reliable guide to what matters in human life, including 'the restoration of the rights of mankind with regard to the free use of reason' and the other freedoms attainable only via 'secret work against hierarchical despotism, the oldest and only genuine goal of all true freemasonry'.[157]

The Deutsche Union pursued its goals by 'advancing the Enlightenment' and promoting the reading and awareness of enlightened texts.[158] 'Philosophy', contended Bahrdt, is the sole active and reliable antidote to the ill effects of error, superstition, and 'positive religion' which buttress all *Despotismus*. Bahrdt's ultimate aim was to carry Enlightenment right into the homes of the common people.[159] *Aufklärung* in the case of a professor and in that of the day labourer, in his eyes, is and has to be seen to be the same. Only through a victory of this kind can there be more genuine morality in the world, less strife and denunciation, and can there be a society in which men are more knowledgeable, upright, and fortunate. But the professors and officials forming the movement's backbone still needed to settle the quarrel between the theists and atheists, resolve the question that is whether an intelligent divine providence governs the world proclaiming the true moral order as so many, headed by 'Father Arouet at Ferney' [Voltaire], as Wehrlin ironically put it, maintained, or whether, after all, 'Spinoza und die Seinigen' [Spinoza and his people] are

---

[152] Mühlpfordt, 'Europarepublik', 328.   [153] Ibid. 329, 334, 340.   [154] Ibid. 349.
[155] Ibid. 348–9.   [156] Bahrdt, *Würdigung*, 10, 12, 16; Bahrdt, *Freedom*, 119, 167.
[157] Bahrdt, *Geschichte*, ii. 39; Haug, 'Bedeutung', 300.   [158] Bahrdt, *Geschichte*, ii. 38–9.
[159] Mühlpfordt, 'Bahrdts Weg', 999.

right. If the latter, this would mean that 'in the laws of nature and morality one seeks in vain for *Endursachen* [final causes]'. The evidence of terrible famines, earthquakes, and human disasters caused by natural events of every kind persuaded Wekhrlin, Diez, Knoblauch, and many others that in fact it must be the *Spinozisten* who are right.[160]

A prominent 'discreet radical', promoter of a free press, social reformer, and member of the Union was Christian Wilhelm Dohm (1751–1820), a pastor's son from Lemgo, professor, and since 1779 Prussian official who sought not just to emancipate the Jews but 'improve' them and integrate them successfully into German society through re-education and using the resources of the Enlightenment state.

The Deutsche Union was a secret society pursuing aims less concealed from its own membership than had the Illuminati. The leadership consisted of 'declared, honest naturalists and atheists' for whom masonic rituals and paraphernalia existed mainly for the benefit of novitiates. The society's proclaimed ultimate aim was the 'dethroning of moral despotism, the unchaining of humanity from superstition and the raising of reason to the magistrate's chair for judging all truth' [der letzte Zweck der Union ist Entthroning des moralischen Despotismus, Entfesselung der Menschheit von Aberglauben und Erhebung der Vernunft auf den Richterstuhl aller Wahrheit].[161] To its several hundred members the society's broad aims were revealed in a general manifesto or 'Plan der Deutschen Union', prepared in 1786, circulated in an improved form late in 1787 and followed, in September 1788, by the 'Secret Plan' of the Deutsche Union.[162] For Bahrdt, as for Weishaupt and Knigge, it was not just Christianity that was at fault, but all 'positive religion', all forms of revelation subjecting reason to faith. Nature, he held, is an infinite chain of physical cause and effect governed by the unalterable laws of Nature alone; meanwhile, most men are oppressed and miserable, and only a process of universal Enlightenment can break the chain of error and *Despotismus* rendering men wretched.[163]

Like the Illuminati earlier, the Deutsche Union made a particular point of recruiting district postmasters since these were especially well placed to keep the organization's communications secure.[164] During 1788, organizing the Deutsche Union was practically Bahrdt's sole activity, taking up all his time and entailing a huge postal bill.[165] Recruiting and maintaining contact with the membership involved a considerable work-load. Merely introducing young persons to 'our secrets' is not enough to 'eradicate the original sins of love of princes and patriotism'. Intellectual emancipation requires long study and reflection to erase 'groundless, cowardly people's duties' from students' minds.[166] Closely linked to local reading societies, academic life, administration, justice, medicine, and the postal system, the Deutsche

---

[160] Wekhrlin, *Hyperboreische Briefe*, 3 (1788), 41–2.
[161] Bahrdt, *Geschichte*, i. 168, 184–5 and ii. 42; Bahrdt, *Würdigung*, 3, 6–7; Mühlpfordt, 'Bahrdts Weg', 1001. [162] Mühlpfordt, 'Europarepublik', 328.
[163] Bahrdt, *Würdigung*, 6–7, 27, 42–5, 62, 107, 121; Bahrdt, *Geschichte*, i. 106, 127.
[164] Mühlpfordt, 'Europarepublik', 341; Bahrdt, *Geschichte*, ii. 43–4.
[165] Bahrdt, *Geschichte*, ii. 30.   [166] Wekhrlin, *Graue Ungeheuer*, 3 (1785), 250, 257.

Union was designed to be much more tightly unified and effective than its predecessor. Though the general tone was even more academic and literary than before, the
Deutsche Union was a more emphatically republican movement than the Illuminati,
insiders often attributing Weishaupt's failure to an insufficiently discerning admission of young men. More exacting scrutiny was called for and, this time, more
coherently than with the Illuminati, princes and state ministers were expressly
excluded.[167] However, the organization was not directly hostile to princely governments as such, styling itself rather a league dedicated to the 'Aufklärung der Menschheit und Dethroniserung des Aberglaubens und des Fanatismus' [enlightenment of
mankind and dethroning of superstition and fanaticism].[168]

Membership expanded from 230 in late 1787 to around 600 by 1789, including
eleven university professors. A quarter of the 1789 membership resided in Austrian
territory, mostly Vienna where Von Born joined and a Swabian Protestant publisher
of clandestine books, Georg Philipp Wucherer (1734–1805), a respected bookseller
with a wide-ranging clientele but also promoter of and dealer in forbidden philosophical literature, figured among the most enterprising members and its ablest
recruiter.[169] Wucherer, it is clear, had strong grievances against Joseph's regime,
believing it despotic, censorious, and grudging in implementing its own tolerationist
policy.[170] The method of opposing Joseph's 'enlightened despotism' was to import
and distribute forbidden books and tracts attacking especially enlightened despotism, the pope, and Jesuits. From 1786 Wucherer formed a close link with Bahrdt for
the importing and propagation of radical and democratic literature, much of it work
by Bahrdt himself.[171]

Like the Illuminati, the organization conceived of itself as the reverse of 'Fanatismus', as applying reason to mankind's earthly happiness.[172] Believing in miracles and
revelation in Bahrdt's view can never achieve anything useful for men, being just
building-blocks for *Priestertirannei* [priestly tyranny].[173] Revealed religions only
divide men, concealing the true nature of social relations. Because Christianity
condemns to damnation those who lack faith in incomprehensible mysteries, from
the late 1770s Bahrdt rejected it as an immoral and objectionable faith, a foe of
universal moral values. Its great fault is that it teaches ordinary folk that faith not
morality is the path to salvation whereas reason shows the reverse is the truth.[174] For
these reasons, he denounced credulity as worse than atheism and 'positive religion' as
the 'destroyer of reason and all *Aufklärung*'.[175] Organized religion in his eyes was a bar
to moral conduct, hindrance to the sciences, and the chief cause of *Intoleranz* and
Menschenhass [hatred of man] in the world.[176] 'Er hat alle Arten des despotismus
geschaffen und erhalten' [It has forged and maintained every kind of despotism].[177]

---

[167] Bahrdt, *Geschichte*, ii. 43; Mühlpfordt, 'Europarepublik', 328–9, 355.
[168] Hermann, *Knigge*, 145; Winter, 'Georg Philipp Wucherer', 60.
[169] Winter, 'Georg Philipp Wucherer', 59–60.   [170] Ibid. 2, 17–18.   [171] Ibid. 28.
[172] Mühlpfordt, 'Europarepublik', 329.   [173] Bahrdt, *Würdigung*, 70–83.
[174] Ibid. 96–7, 167–8.   [175] Ibid. 132–3, 136, 147.   [176] Ibid. 149–50.   [177] Ibid. 149.

Luther's and Calvin's Reformation had entirely failed to do its job. While church hierarchy and tyrannizing over consciences along with endless error stemming from 'blind faith in positive religion' had been cut back, the source of the rot, 'den blinden Glauben selbst' [blind faith itself], remained intact along with ecclesiastical courts and censorship instead of pope and bishops.[178] A new Reformation was needed to establish man's most precious possessions, *Toleranz und Gewissensfreiheit* [toleration and freedom of conscience]. His stance toward Christianity being much influenced by Lessing's, all *Naturalisten* and *Atheisten* were admitted to Bahrdt's organization but mockery of Christ and Christianity was forbidden. Reimarus' thesis that Christ was just an ambitious schemer had gained ground, it distressed him to see, via the *Fragmentenstreit*, further widening the rift between the 'philosophers' and 'the Christians', a quarred actually based on a complete misapprehension. If his former conviction that Jesus' teaching somehow reflects divine inspiration had died in that controversy, Lessing's arguments had helped him integrate Christ centrally into the history of human thought as had discussion with Eberhard, who in 1772 had published an apology for Socrates virtually equating his teaching with that of the true Jesus: 'Herr Eberhard convinced me Christ put forward no essential precept that Socrates had not likewise taught.'[179]

What Bahrdt called 'my *Aufklärung*'—his unreserved espousal of reason—led him to view Jesus not as a messenger sent by God, but no more, nor less, than a particularly gifted moral thinker imbued with the basic doctrines of Greek philosophy garnered in Palestine, he presumed, from Greek-speaking Jews. Jesus' inspiration, men must accept, was not a divinely inspired phenomenon. But he still hoped, like Lessing, to prevent an irrevocable split between those estranged from Christianity and those embracing the name of 'Christian'. Bahrdt burned with desire to present Jesus to the world, as he put it, in this new and 'advantageous' light, clearing his reputation of both dreadful slurs sullying his name in the Germany of the 1780s—the 'superstitious' notion of a wonder-worker and expounder of the supernatural, on the one hand, and, on the other, Reimarus' politically ambitious leader of a sect.[180]

Disillusion with freemasonry, Bahrdt records, had helped him realize that to change the world and establish his new religion, Jesus must have formed an underground sect, a kind of secret society on the model of masonry and the Illuminati, to advance the cause of truth against the intolerance and false doctrines taught by the Jewish and later 'Christian' priesthood.[181] This idea was the key to a true grasp of Christian history and underlay his new conviction that his views simultaneously represented the 'true' Christian position, and the 'true' philosophical position, in contradistinction to the doctrines of both the Protestant and Catholic churches, on the one hand, and of the materialist philosophers and Spinozists as well as Kantians and other theistic philosophers on the other.

---

[178] Ibid. 227–8, 232. [179] Bahrdt, *Geschichte*, iv. 112–15; Eijnatten, *Liberty and Concord*, 360.
[180] Bahrdt, *Geschichte*, iv. 124–5. [181] Ibid. iv. 126; Schmidt, *What is Enlightenment?*, 8.

The location of the Deutsche Union's headquarters (Halle) supposedly remained a closely guarded secret. However, like the Illuminati, the Union had different grades of members, now reduced to three of which the third grade, the names of whose members were unknown to those in the lower grades, constituted the leadership.[182] Its membership ramified from Halle to Leipzig, Hanover, Vienna, Frankfurt, Giessen, and Marburg. Outside Prussia, Hesse, the Palatinate, and Vienna were particular centres of strength.[183] In Viennese government circles, opinion varied about how seriously to take the reports of a new revolutionary conspiracy in a tighter, more unified guise than the Illuminati. Joseph saw no immediate threat but others viewed this new phenomenon in a more sinister light.[184] In Vienna, Wucherer reportedly recruited 111 new members, often customers for his books, within a year, including some based as far afield as Budapest, Prague, Galicia, and Transylvania.[185] It was Wucherer that had suggested to Bahrdt that he publish his tract on press freedom in Vienna. Increasingly, his activities attracted the attention of Count Pergen's police and, eventually, the emperor himself. Arrested for selling copies of a forbidden work, *Die Gesunde Vernunft*, his premises were searched, his large stock of illicit literature seized and destroyed, and a commission set up to investigate his network further. Heavily fined, Wucherer was expelled from the monarchy.[186]

5. PRUSSIA'S COUNTER-ENLIGHTENMENT

From an 'enlightened' perspective, German society presented some impressive bright spots but also some decidedly dark patches, indeed a powerful resurgence of superstition and 'enthusiasm'. The cultural and intellectual state of Germany, immediately prior to the outbreak of the Revolution in France, thus illustrated with particular vividness the mixed and confused picture of late Enlightenment Europe, a deadlock between the rule of reason and that of unreason. How is it, asked Wekhrlin, that the 'barometer' of science and learning (he admitted that the arts were a different matter) stands always lowest where religious orthodoxy—Catholic or Protestant—is strongest? By no means was he referring only to lands where, in his view, the light of reason was practically extinguished such as Catholic Italy, Spain, and Poland, the last performing particularly poorly on his 'philosophical map of Europe' in 1779. He also meant Denmark-Norway and 'half of Germany' which he considered comparably sunk in unscientific, unknowing, and uncomprehending 'darkness'.[187]

---

[182] Bahrdt, *Geschichte*, i. 134–5 and ii. 55, 57.   [183] Ibid ii. 41.
[184] Beales, *Enlightenment and Reform*, 103.
[185] Ibid. 328, 340, 343, 348; Winter, 'Georg Philipp Wucherer', 64; Bernard, *Limits*, 57–8.
[186] Bernard, *Limits*, 57–60; Wangermann, *From Joseph II*, 40–2; Laursen and Van der Zande, 'Introduction', 101–2.
[187] Wekhrlin, *Chronologen*, 1 (1779), 9–10; Tilgner, *Lesegesellschaften*, 253.

With admirable lack of bias, Wekhrlin cites Catholic Bavaria, Lutheran Württemberg, Catholic Westphalia, and the mainly Protestant *Reichstädten* (Imperial Free Cities), including Hamburg, Lübeck, Nuremberg, and Frankfurt, as bastions of confessional prejudice, credulity, and ignorance, strongholds of unenlightened attitudes.[188] While 'modern' philosophy teaches that man's happiness—that of the majority not the few, and the general well-being—and not that of vested interests, should be the 'Zweck des Staats' [the aim of the state], and of politics and society itself, declared Wekhrlin in his *Hyperboreische Briefe*, these proud city republics try to keep everything tradition-bound, based on prejudice, corrupt, and dependent on purchase, with family connection and favour crucial to all success whether office-holding, obtaining justice, or simply in plying one's business, leaving the citizenry no choice but continually to bribe and flatter burgomasters, civic officials, and their allies.[189] How ironic that the common folk should so detest the 'philosophers' seeking to rescue humanity from its 'tyrants'! But ironic or not, the less educated were successfully being mobilized against the *Aufklärung*.[190]

Most smaller principalities were less dismal from an enlightened perspective. But Prussia and Austria were now shackling the press and curbing freedom of thought as well as blighting society and men's happiness, as always, by maintaining armies as large as the state's resources could support. Militarism and large standing armies, held Knoblauch in his *Politisch-philosophische Gespräche* of 1789, cast a dark shadow over Germany and had become the principal device for keeping the citizenry yoked to despotism: 'without possessing a numerous standing military force, our "sultans" could never—since the time of "Ludwig dem Burgerfeind" [Louis enemy of the citizenry] whom flatterers call "Louis le Grand" [i.e. Louis XIV]—have conducted themselves in the despotic manner they have.'[191] Struensee's overthrow in Denmark by courtiers backed by Frederick, suppression of the 1782 Genevan revolution, the Bavarian reaction, the crushing of the Dutch democratic movement in 1787, rebellions against Joseph in Brabant and Hungary, were all bound further to intensify radical conspiracy and subversion. And this subversion spread just as in France the 'esprit public', as Wekhrlin termed it, established not only what he called 'true freedom of thought', but had by 1788 created more opportunity for expression of the truth than mankind had ever before witnessed.[192]

Religious toleration might have made great strides in Prussia, Austria, Bohemia, and other regions in the decades 1760–89. The building of Catholic churches in such once solidly Lutheran Prussian towns as Ruppin, Bernau, Greifenburg, and Pyriz where there had previously been no organized Catholic worship the *Berlinische Monatsschrift* in 1784 described as a kind of modish rivalry, each aspiring to appear

---

[188] Wekhrlin, *Graue Ungeheuer*, 3 (1784–5), 107.
[189] Wekhrlin, *Hyperboreische Briefe*, 3 (1788), 88–9.
[190] Ibid. 3 (1788), 121–3.
[191] Knoblauch, *Politisch-philosophische Gespräche*, 61.
[192] Wekhrlin, *Hyperboreische Briefe*, 3 (1788), 37.

more 'enlightened' than the next and all spurred by local officials and garrison commanders requiring chapels for Catholic army contingents.[193] However, with the spread of Catholic worship came larger Catholic communities and a growing fear that the confessional unity and stability of Prussian society was eroding. The consequent anxieties then in turn reinforced the growing atmosphere of suspicion and obsession with conspiracy theories typical of both Protestant and Catholic Germany in the 1780s. Protestant commentators became increasingly alarmed by signs of a shifting balance in mixed Protestant–Catholic cities such as Breslau (Wrocław) and Danzig (Gdańsk), with book-sellers reporting huge increases in sales of Catholic prayer-books, often supposedly to wavering 'Protestants'. Biester was one who deliberately fomented this anxiety, attributing the exploding demand for Catholic pious literature in Prussia to Catholic secret societies and 'Jesuits' tacitly permitted to run clandestine schools.[194] Despite hitherto being one of Germany's foremost vehicles of (moderate) *Aufklärung*, and one supposedly dedicated to spreading freedom of thought, the *Berlinische Monatsschrift* became the first journal to insist on a connection between subversive Catholic 'secret societies' in Prussia and the rapid spread of the Catholic presence.[195]

A former pupil of Michaelis at Göttingen, Biester not only denounced Catholic 'secret societies' but spoke of the insidious 'inclination to wondrous mysteries' they foment among the people, deliberately using enlightened rhetoric to intensify growing tensions and justify mobilizing prejudice.[196] Protestant obsessions with 'Jesuit' influence and the *Rosenkreuzer* were attended by alarming talk of their influence spreading from Bavaria to Vienna, Prague, and other centres. Despite the wariness of Joseph and his ministers, Catholic 'secret societies' were reportedly at work everywhere, threatening central Europe's confessional stability, simultaneously undermining while also exploiting toleration and free thought with the aim of re-introducing the untrammelled sway of priestcraft. The secret society of the 'true Catholic brothers' in Vienna, reportedly, was particularly energetic in urging Protestants to reunite with the Catholic Church.[197] Moderate *Aufklärer* in Prussia in the early and mid 1780s as well as conservatives appear to have been even more worried about Catholic 'secret societies' than radical Illuminati. But at the courts paranoia about 'secret societies' of every sort fed political suspicion of all underground networks.[198]

Where radical enlighteners during the 1780s chiefly feared a general repression of press freedom, majority opinion continually complained of excessive press freedom, the presumption of minorities, and abuse of toleration.[199] In his *On the Freedom of*

---

[193] *Berlinische Monatsschrift*, 3 (1784), 181.
[194] Ibid. 7 (1786), 436–57; Wieland, *Teutsche Merkur* (1786), 275–8; Eijnatten, *Liberty and Concord*, 333.
[195] *Berlinische Monatsschrift*, 7 (1786) 447 and 8 (1786), 44–67; Laursen, *Politics*, 216, 227.
[196] *Berlinische Monatsschrift*, 8 (1786), 65.
[197] Wieland, *Teutsche Merkur* (1786), 271.
[198] Ibid. (1786), 99, 108–13.
[199] *Berlinische Monatsschrift*, 3 (1784), 312; Sauter, *Visions*, 79–82.

the Press (1787), cast in the form of a passionate appeal to Joseph and the new Prussian monarch, Friedrich Wilhelm, Bahrdt made no attempt to disguise the fact that in central Europe the independent-minded constituted what he called 'a very small public'.[200] Freedom of thought in Germany in the 1780s, held Forster, now back from Vilna and based at Mainz, remained little more than a 'pious wish'.[201] Ardent admirer of Lessing, he rebuked Biester in his own journal for feeding alarmism about the alleged Catholic threat, accusing him of encouraging readers to think in confessional terms when he should be teaching them to think independently, judge religion on the basis of reason, and escape from the appalling history of priestly tutelage and confessional deadlock. By 1787–8, the situation in central Europe generally seemed to the radical-minded less promising than deeply ominous. The revolts of the Genevans against their patrician oligarchy and Wallachians against their landowning aristocracy proved perhaps, suggested Wekhrlin, that not all peoples are so benighted as blindly to follow nobles, patricians, and priests, like the bigoted Flemish and Hungarians. How is it that an ignorant people inured to 'slavery' like the Wallachians suddenly resolves to rise and free itself from oppression?[202] However that may be, in 'civilized' lands the radical philosophical underground seemed the only way forward.

The new Prussian king, Friedrich Wilhelm II (reigned: 1786–97), widely considered an intellectual mediocrity and thoroughgoing reactionary (scorned by Frederick) who disliked Neologist theology and even the relatively tolerant attitudes of moderate enlighteners like Biester and Gedike, let alone the radical fraternity, a personage drawn to Christian mysticism since the early 1780s, openly embraced Counter-Enlightenment. His ministers, especially his most trusted adviser Johann Christoph von Wöllner (1732–1800), who sympathized with the Rosicrucians, were basically reactionary even if the latter also endorsed some moderate Enlightenment attitudes. Wöllner and Friedrich Wilhelm were reportedly preparing stringent new press laws to control dissent and establish what Wekhrlin termed a new kind of 'Spanish Inquisition'.[203] Certainly, Wöllner aimed to reverse the shift toward freedom of thought across a wide front and ensure there was no chance that *Publizität* and relative freedom of the press generated what Wekhrlin called a true 'revolution of the human spirit in Germany'.

To the relief of most preachers, the new Prussian censorship law, the so-called *Edict on Religion*, published in July 1788, though not in all respects as reactionary as sometimes alleged, confirming formal toleration for Jews and other religious minorities, for example, did appreciably strengthen censorship and press restrictions, tighten links between the crown and the two officially sponsored churches (Reformed and Lutheran), and decree dismissal of preachers and professors judged unsound in doctrine. Principally aimed at the spread of Socinianism, Unitarianism, and deism within the major tolerated confessions, this edict accused Socinian-minded pastors of

---

[200] Bahrdt, *Freedom*, 109.   [201] *Berlinische Monatsschrift*, 14 (1789), 571.
[202] Wekhrlin, *Graue Ungeheuer*, 3 (1784–5), 184–5.
[203] Wekhrlin, *Hyperboreische Briefe*, 2 (1788), 12–13.

perniciously undermining the mysteries and dogmas of religion. Ominously for the future, moreover, the measure was endorsed by numerous moderates who regarded themselves as 'enlightened' including Neologists such as Semler.[204]

Fomenting the clandestine Radical Enlightenment in these circumstances meant following a difficult, risky, and defiant path. Under the edict, several writers were quickly muzzled by official pressure, including Bahrdt and August Cranz (1737–1801), a radical journalist known for his hostility to 'superstition' religious and political, admiration for Mendelssohn, and advocacy of Jewish equality who staunchly opposed all ecclesiastical authority (including that of the rabbis).[205] It was apparently a temporary secretary with access to Bahrdt's papers, supplied by Pott, who denounced him to the authorities, leading to his arrest in April 1789. At the same moment he was found to be the author of the caustic satire *Das Religions-Edikt. Ein Lustspiel* [The Decree on Religion, a Comedy] (1788), an anonymously published piece ridiculing Wöllner's decree. If Bahrdt drew any consolation from his piece being clandestinely reprinted soon afterwards and read by many,[206] his misdemeanours in the eyes of the crown resulted in his being harshly dealt with. Overseen by Wöllner, he was interrogated, tried, and, in April 1789, condemned and sentenced to imprisonment at Magdeburg.[207]

One of Friedrich Wilhelm's aims was to counter irreligion by weakening Neology and strengthening the conservative clergy within the main Prussian churches and universities.[208] By pruning back liberal theology and toleration, from 1787, royal policy shifted the focus from the half-hidden rift within the Enlightenment to the much more public and obvious split between those for and against *Aufklärung* as such. A second key aim was to crush the secret societies. In a missive to the elector of Saxony of October 1789, the king denounced the Deutsche Union as an insidious attempt to revive Illuminism which he and the Bavarian elector considered irreligious, treasonable, and dangerous. The Saxon court, Prussia demanded, should also take energetic action and, in particular, arrest suspected members at the Leipzig Fair, one of the order's main channels of communication. The chief principles [*Grundsätze*] of this radical underground, according to Prussia's ministers, were: to abolish the Christian religion (and all other religions); detach subjects from their oaths of loyalty to their princes; under the pretext of 'Rechte der Menschheit' [rights of humanity], teach all manner of *Extravaganzen* opposed to each state's established laws and institutions for the maintenance of social order; and, finally, advance these goals justifying every means, even the most perverse and criminal.[209]

[204] Hunter, 'Kant's *Religion*', 11, 22; Sauter, *Visions*, 43–5, 54, 56, 89.
[205] Wekhrlin, *Hyperboreische Briefe*, 2 (1788), 12–14; Altmann, *Moses Mendelssohn*, 511–12; Schmidt, *What is Enlightenment?*, 8–10.
[206] Van der Wall, 'Religie en Verlichting', 27, 411.
[207] Bahrdt, *Geschichte*, i. 46, 132; Mühlpfordt, 'Bahrdts Weg', 1003–5.
[208] Kuehn, *Kant*, 339; Sorkin, *Religious Enlightenment*, 162.
[209] Friedrich Wilhelm of Prussia to elector of Saxony, Berlin, 3 Oct. 1789, in Van Dülmen, *Dokumente*, 410–11; Mühlpfordt, 'Europarepublik', 341.

If the *Rosenkreuzer* had wrought a potent myth conjuring up a vast international conspiracy in which French atheistic materialism, freemasonry, and irreligion coalesce into a stupendous war-machine assailing the existing order, their foes, ensconced in their taverns and university reading circles, retaliated with an equally potent rival conspiracy theory depicting mystical-irrational secret societies (the *Rosenkreuzer*) spearheading the massed ranks of popular bigotry, unenlightened obscurantism, and absolutist court intrigue, all joining forces to form a gigantic coalition to obliterate all *Aufklärung*, indeed 'reason' itself, along with the hopes, rights, and the true interest of all mankind.[210] Mirror images of each other, feverish and overblown, both were nonetheless also firmly anchored in the realities of the central European culture, politics, and society. All passionate exponents of *Aufklärung*, even the most moderate, found themselves in difficulties from 1787. Kant, Königsberg University's rector at the time of the king's accession, had been obliged to preside at inauguration ceremonies at the university marking the coronation in September 1786.[211] A philosophy such as his, denying any possibility of objective proofs of God's existence and the miraculous, must, he realized, become suspect to the new censorship authorities and attract official disapproval.[212]

Amid this embattled atmosphere, the outbreak of the French Revolution acted like a clarion call for the likes of Dohm, Wekhrlin, Knoblauch, Knigge, Dorsch, Schiller, and Forster, as well as liberal Neologs like Eberhard and also some of the moderate fraternity, including Kant. A moment of great excitement for a few, it suddenly seemed the setbacks and pessimism of the last few years had been brooded over excessively and could now be forgotten with humanity's sudden great leap forwards at hand. It became possible to imagine, if only briefly, that all the goals of the Radical Enlightenment were almost within men's grasp, after all. Despite the crack-down at home, more broadly all could now glimpse what Wekhrlin called the dawn of 'true religion', the only, eternal, and universal 'religion', 'der Religion der Natur', and envisage a new dawn with mankind soon dwelling happily in a released, emancipated world of press freedom, freedom of thought, and democratic republics—'das Reich der Philosophie und der Toleranz' [the kingdom of philosophy and toleration] seemed near.[213]

With the drama of the Revolution and the ideological struggles it entailed, the question of the Illuminati receded but was by no means wholly forgotten. Rather, it lingered in various contexts and playing a notable part in the broadening attack on the 'modern philosophy' during the 1790s also in Britain and the United States. The American radical Eliahu Palmer, disciple of Paine, Barlow, d'Holbach, Condorcet, and Volney, powerfully retorted in his *Principles of Nature* (New York, 1801), remarking:

---

[210] Vierhaus, 'Aufklärung', 115–16, 133–4; Kuehn, *Kant*, 320.
[211] Kuehn, *Kant*, 315.
[212] Ibid.; Wood, *Kant*, 17–18.
[213] Wekhrlin, *Hyperboreische Briefe*, 5 (1789), 187–9.

The Illuminati in Europe have been represented as a vicious combination of persons whose object was the destruction of all the governments and all the religions of the world. If the enemies of philosophy in that part of the globe, mean by governments the corrupt monarchies of the earth, and by religion, popular superstition, founded upon the idea of a supposed mysterious intercourse between beings of the earth, and celestial powers, then they are right in this respect, for these are the governments and religions against which reason and philosophy ought to direct their energies; but if by government, they mean a system of genuine republicanism founded upon equal rights of man—and by religion the idea of simple Theism, and the immortality of moral virtue, then their assertions are false, and their productions a calumny against reason and the rites of human nature; the plain truth of the case is, that those who oppose philosophy and bestow upon it harsh and malignant epithets, are interested in keeping up a privileged system of plunder and robbery, which makes nine-tenths of the human race absolute slaves to support the other tenth in indolence, extravagance, pride and luxury.[214]

Among the most notable American radical voices, Palmer went further than Paine in his critique of Christianity. But he never had the impact of Paine whose *Age of Reason* may have provoked an unprecedented chorus of denunciation in America but was nevertheless reprinted eighteen times in no less than five American cities between 1794 and 1796.[215] Paine, Barlow, Palmer, and other American radicals were for several years convinced that 'reason' was on the verge of triumphing, that the 'power of thought has become vastly impulsive', suddenly and not only in France, Switzerland, Italy, Holland, and Germany but also Britain and America, and that reactionary governments and churches, unable to restrain it, were being overwhelmed. However, their confidence that radical thought would soon 'subvert the thrones of civil despots' and destroy 'this pretended intercourse with heaven, that has subverted every thing rational upon earth', [216] turned out to be distinctly premature.

---

[214] Palmer, *Principles*, 160–1.   [215] Jacoby, *Freethinkers*, 58.   [216] Palmer, *Principles*, 160.

32

Small-State Revolutions in the 1780s

1. THE GENEVA REVOLUTION OF 1782: DEMOCRATS VERSUS 'ARISTOCRATS'

The Dutch democratic revolution of the 1780s together with that decade's several small state revolutions helped shape the intellectual horizons of the leaders of the 'General Revolution' of 1788–92 and 1794–1800. Throughout Europe by 1780 existed a widely diffused, revolutionary awareness philosophically based in part but also drawing inspiration from the American and Dutch revolutions. Also, 'some of the republics of Switzerland' were considered instructive examples, as Van der Capellen put it, of how peoples could elect their own representatives on a broad suffrage in a responsible and disciplined manner.[1] Although most Swiss thought of their republics in a particularist, traditional, and non-ideological light, the small Swiss revolutions of the 1780s were followed by democratic ideologues and *philosophes* in Britain and Europe with intense interest.

Republican idealization of the thirteen republics of the Swiss Confederation has a long history reaching back to Machiavelli.[2] Eulogized for the rustic simplicity of their morals and politics by Machiavelli, Mably, and Rousseau alike, the Swiss cantons were also viewed by Rousseau, notably in his 'Projet' for a constitution for Corsica of 1765, as a didactic model for others, a concrete case demonstrating the logic of his own political theory. For Rousseau, the Swiss republics were an invaluable counter-example to both absolutist France and mixed-monarchy England.[3] In the days when all the Swiss had been poor and men more equal, the cantons had been militarily and politically formidable and even the French king avoided entanglements with them. Unfortunately, held Rousseau—but also Mably (and some others)—many Swiss cantons had fallen victim to corruption, luxury, and moral decay, with the undermining of wholesome agriculture by the vitiating effects of commerce and luxury.[4] This applied, held Rousseau, especially to Fribourg and Berne, republics where

---

[1] Van der Capellen, *Aan het Volk*, 36.
[2] Kapossy, 'Neo-Roman Republicanism', 229–30.
[3] Rousseau, *Projet*, 141; Rousseau, *Gouvernement de Pologne*, 226–7, 232–3; Wright, *Classical Republican*, 181, 184.
[4] Rousseau, *Projet*, 110, 126; Rousseau, *Lettres écrites*, ii. 42.

inequality had become marked. Meanwhile, ranged against this egalitarian perspective there was another and opposite Enlightenment perspective shared by Hume, Gibbon, and several German writers. Gibbon, who opposed both the American and French revolutions, was a deeply conservative spirit who, especially whilst at his beloved retreat at Lausanne, proved a stout defender of the Swiss oligarchies against the revolutionary tendencies at work in Switzerland.[5] Like Hume and Meiners, he thought the Bernese oligarchy in many ways admirable: 'while the aristocracy of Berne protects the happiness,' he wrote later, 'it is superfluous to inquire whether it be founded in the rights of man.'[6]

Provided oppression was restrained by a strong sense of duty and propriety, agreed the Göttingen savant Meiners, author of the *Briefe über die Schweiz* (4 vols., Berlin, 1784–90), an opponent of German radical thought in general and Georg Forster in particular, inequality and oligarchy are not malign. In Berne, as in the other Swiss republics, the peasantry were entirely free of servile obligations and dues. Moreover, if Berne was an outright oligarchy of around eighty families dominated by rural landowners and undeniably the most aristocratic of the Swiss republics, it was also, held Meiners, the best governed and most prosperous, indeed 'one of the most perfect aristocracies, and perhaps the most perfect that has ever been seen in reality'. Berne he considered to be wisely administered, flourishing—despite what he admitted was the dilapidated state of its subject territory of Vaud and Lausanne—and offering a far ampler freedom of speech and thought than Venice while, at the same time, championing strict morals and exercising rigorous censorship, substantial added benefits in his opinion.[7] It was not for his political opinions that Berne rightly expelled Rousseau, in 1762, he argued but for his heterodox religious opinions.[8]

If Berne, where Haller became a member of the governing council in 1745 and remained prominent in public business until 1773, exemplified the wealthy but tranquil, uncontested aristocratic republic, the poor Swiss republics represented for Rousseau and his admirers the very acme of political wisdom and republican virtue. Unfortunately though, from Rousseau's standpoint, nearly all the Swiss republics, whether Catholic like Lucerne and Fribourg or Protestant like Zurich and Schaffhausen, had in fact evolved constitutionally more and more in an oligarchic direction especially during and since the period 1680–1713, emulating Berne which since its conquest of the Vaud had tended to lead the way in this general process of oligarchization.[9] Even so, Rousseau's thought also provided a device—through his important distinction between sovereignty and government—whereby the authority of the Genevan 'Small Council' [*Petit Conseil*], as established under the key compromise

[5] Gibbon, *Memoirs*, 236, 273–4, 276, 288.
[6] Ibid. 215.
[7] Meiners, *Briefe*, i. 119, 122, 163; Carhart, *Science*, 13, 22, 255.
[8] Rousseau, *Confessions*, 495, 541–2; Rousseau, *Gouvernement de Pologne*, 222; Rousseau, *Lettres écrites*, ii. 42.
[9] Kapossy, 'Neo-Roman Republicanism', 235.

settlement of 1738, and the other oligarchic regimes could to an extent be cogently defended.[10]

Berne was unusual in manifesting little internal organized opposition (except in Vaud) to the ruling aristocracy. Both in Zurich where there was more manufacturing and stronger guilds and Lucerne where there had been little economic change, society was both more stratified and politically divided. Meiners suggested that where Berne was 'eine demokratische Aristokratie', Zurich was 'eine aristokratische Demokratie'.[11] In any case, all the prosperous, more urbanized republics had become increasingly hierarchical and 'aristocratic' in character while manufacturing, finance, wealth, and oligarchy had in turn made the Swiss more dependent on the outside world, that is divided and weak, so that in the contemporary setting, all Switzerland trembled, as Rousseau put it, if the king of France even frowned.[12] Yet Swiss rustic vigour and virtue were not wholly moribund, especially not in the rural cantons, and nor was the true republican spirit. It was on this basis that Rousseau advised the Corsicans (and others) to stay as poor and as equal as possible.

Besides these commentators, reference should be made to Bahrdt and Wekhrlin, who had both toured and lived for periods in Switzerland and begun as great enthusiasts for the Swiss context but later become deeply disillusioned by personal experiences there. Wekhrlin, writing in 1787 and much taken with Raynal and the *Histoire philosophique*, was a materialist eagerly looking forward to what he saw as the future age of 'happiness of peoples', 'virtuous regimes', 'human freedom', and 'harmony of the laws'. All the aristocratic republics were thoroughly despicable in his view, with Venice, which he visited in 1767, the most oppressive, oligarchic, and distrustful of its citizens of all. Expelled from Augsburg, in 1777, and Nördlingen, in 1778, Wekhrlin considered the German Imperial Free Cities almost equally stiflingly oligarchic and reprehensible. Augsburg he viewed as an especially contemptible polity as it provided no genuine toleration or freedom of speech or the press at all, but was a place devoid of all Enlightenment where the citizenry were locked into an absurdly rigid set of elaborate compromises between an equally bigoted Lutheranism and Catholicism, every senatorial decision and appointment being obsessively weighed in terms of Lutheran–Catholic parity.[13]

Wekhrlin, convinced 'philosophy' is mankind's chief hope in politics and morality alike but, unlike Mably, Rousseau, and Meiners, believing the Swiss cantons every bit as narrow and defective as the German and Italian city republics, accounted Berne, with its flourishing bookshops and book trade, marginally more enlightened than the rest. For 'ignorance' and 'enslaving human reason', as well as poverty, in his estimation, there was nothing worse than precisely the poor Swiss republics eulogized by

---

[10] Rousseau, *Lettres écrites*, i. 238–40; Brooke, 'Revisiting', 80–1; Whatmore, 'Rousseau', 411, 413.
[11] Meiners, *Briefe*, i. 164–7 and iii. 62.
[12] Rousseau, *Projet*, 122.
[13] [Wekhrlin], *Reise durch Ober-Deutschland*, 67–8; Mondot, 'Wekhrlin et la Revolution', 128, 130.

Rousseau, especially Glarus and Söldthurn.[14] Owing to his scathing published criticism of the thirteen Swiss republics generally, and his journal's blistering attack on the bigotry and obsession with witches of Glarus in particular, Wekhrlin was declared persona non grata by the Swiss Confederation and placed under a special ban.

Connoisseurs of political ideas had become accustomed to see Switzerland as a kind of laboratory of republican politics in theory and practice and this that country continued to be down to the 1790s. Especially, the Genevan revolution of 1782 fascinatingly played out in miniature many of the key themes of the revolutionary era more generally. Like Berne, Geneva was a city republic, controlled by a small, entrenched, and wealthy oligarchy. Also like Berne, Geneva until the 1750s enjoyed a considerable reputation among the enlightened—fomented by Voltaire and d'Alembert, as well as Rousseau, as a paragon of toleration, crypto-Unitarianism, and good sense governed in the interest of the whole. The yawning gap between myth and reality had begun to become painfully obvious, however, to both outsiders and the native citizenry by the late 1750s. The magistrates controlling the *Petit Conseil* and the governing committees, many began to see, actually represented only their own vested interests while the much vaunted sovereignty of the citizenry with political rights, supposedly represented in the 'General Council', proved chimerical.

Moderate *philosophes* like d'Alembert and Voltaire—and also Rousseau in this respect—had forged a poignant myth of Geneva, which the *Encyclopédie* helped promote, as a haven of *la liberté*, toleration, deism, and republican well-being.[15] It was a mythology kept alive by some and later reinforced in German-speaking Europe by Meiners's eloquent eulogy of Berne, which, though in many ways wide of the mark, obstinately persisted. The problem with this whole construction was that their enthusiasm (or wishful thinking) and, in Meiners's case, religious and ethnic bigotry supported an excessively narrow distribution of political power, something to which Rousseau, if not Voltaire or d'Alembert, strenuously objected. The citizenry of Geneva and Berne in reality enjoyed neither religious freedom, nor freedom of thought, nor freedom of the press, additional limitations on liberty to which Rousseau and Meiners in principle offered little objection.[16] The same was true of Geneva's stringent religiously directed policing of sexual activity. Far from condemning this, both Rousseau and Meiners endorsed it. Indeed, Meiners attributed Geneva's growing divisions and troubles in the eighteenth century to the loosening of the rigid moral code imposed after the Reformation and the clergy's waning grip over behaviour, marriage, and family life which he deplored. Divorce, he thought, had become too easy to obtain.[17]

---

[14] Wekhrlin, *Graue Ungeheuer*, 10 (1787), 194; Wekhrlin, *Hyperboreische Briefe*, 1 (1788), 88–94; Böhm, *Ludwig Wekhrlin*, 23, 130.

[15] Meiners, *Briefe*, ii. 203.

[16] Ibid. ii. 222; Leigh, 'Le "Contrat social"', 104–6.

[17] Meiners, *Briefe*, ii. 220–5.

Geneva's population of around 25,000 actually consisted of three groups each with a sharply differentiated legal status. The lowest, constituting around three-quarters of the population, included numerous Huguenot immigrants who arrived after 1685 and also Savoyards and others all alike excluded from representation even in the General Council. The oligarchy of wealthy old-established families controlling the 'Small Council' while denying the majority, the lowest stratum, any rights whatsoever also resented the pretensions of the bourgeois middling group while constantly striving to extend its grip over legislation and taxation and reinforce 'aristocracy' as a way of subordinating the whole to their own particular interests.[18] The *Petit Conseil* of the 1750s, according to the French resident, was opposed outright, on one side by a democratic faction aiming to transform Geneva's entire institutional framework and, on the other, by the 'moderates', mostly pragmatic businessmen, shopkeepers, and merchants who cared nothing for principle and aimed for a businesslike compromise between the upper and middle strata, leaving the rest as they were.

Hence, much as at Zurich, not only the patrician oligarchy but also the middling group aligned more with Montesquieu when invoking philosophical authority than Rousseau.[19] Ever since defending the city's distinctive character and traditions in his *Lettre à d'Alembert* (1757) Rousseau had been a celebrated and popular figure in Geneva. But since the central aim of Rousseau's *Contrat social* appeared to be helping the Genevan citizenry 'regain' their rights by mastering the *Petit Conseil* the latter promptly banned it as a dangerous, subversive work, more thoroughly suppressing it than any other government.[20] Rousseau's texts in this way became part of the fabric of Swiss politics. Vernet and other Genevan conservatives exploited the opportunity afforded by the book's local suppression to pronounce certain well-known democratic opponents of the regime complicit in its composition and distribution, notably a close friend of Rousseau's in Paris, Toussaint-Pierre Lenieps, a jeweller-goldsmith banished from Geneva in 1731.[21] Furthermore, while there was some support among Geneva's population for Rousseau's republican principles, there was even more aversion to the unchristian, deistic tendency in *Émile*. This book appeared in the early summer of 1762, at almost at the same moment as the *Contrat social*, and was likewise immediately condemned by the *Petit Conseil*, this time as destructive of 'the Christian religion and all Revelation', albeit again chiefly for political reasons, using the pretext of religion. This was done on the advice of one of the city's most learned men, its *procureur-général* and a long-standing, fervent advocate of moderate Enlightenment, Jean-Robert Tronchin.[22] At Geneva, in June 1762 the *Contrat social*

---

[18] Leigh, 'Le "Contrat social"', 105; Rosenblatt, *Rousseau and Geneva*, 152.
[19] Whatmore, 'Venturi', 444.
[20] Rousseau, *Lettres écrites*, i. 240.
[21] [Tronchin], *Lettres*, 11; Whatmore, 'Rousseau', 402, 409.
[22] Whatmore, 'Rousseau', 271; Trousson, *Jean-Jacques Rousseau*, 524–5; Rosenblatt, *Rousseau and Geneva*, 269–70.

and *Émile* were both publicly condemned, 'shredded and burned by the public executioner before the gates of the city hall'.[23]

Subsequently, secret orders were issued for Rousseau's arrest and trial (here against Tronchin's advice) should he set foot in the city ever again. Hence, at Geneva, Berne, and throughout Switzerland, the fund of local sympathy for his democratic republican ideals was largely negated by a combination of disapproval for his religious views and fear of his anti-oligarchic proclivities. Geneva's expulsion of Rousseau and shredding of his books was by no means something the Swiss Enlightenment as a whole broadly disapproved of. On the contrary, Bonnet was confident Berne would follow Geneva's example and strongly recommended its doing so. Berne, with the explicit approval of Haller and Bonnet, did subsequently suppress both *Émile* and the *Contrat social*,[24] and for good measure, in July 1762, expelled Rousseau in person from its territory (he was then at Yverdon). Somewhat to Haller's and Bonnet's annoyance, his second expulsion from a Swiss republic was opposed by some Bernese citizens. 'Je suis surpris', wrote Bonnet to Haller from Geneva, that Rousseau 'ait un grand parti à Berne': he was undoubtedly an enemy of the Bernese oligarchy 'et s'il en était le maître, votre aristocratie serait bientôt changé en pure démocratie'.[25] Bonnet and Haller promoted a Protestant and anti-materialist Enlightenment in Switzerland and also an oligarchic, anti-democratic Enlightenment; and the two things were ideologically closely linked just as were materialism and democracy in *la nouvelle philosophie*. Bonnet's pupil the physicist and geologist Horace Bénédict de Saussure (1740–99), professor at Geneva's university for over a quarter of century (1762–86), backed democracy in 1782, briefly; but on seeing what was entailed changed his mind, afterwards becoming an ardent supporter of the aristocratic faction.[26]

Expelled from Bernese jurisdiction, Rousseau migrated to the nearby (theoretically Prussian) principality of Neuchâtel, settling in the village of Môtiers. No admirer of Frederick, Rousseau found himself obliged, like Edelmann earlier and Bahrdt later, to request the king's permission to stay. His continuing literary and philosophical foray into the tense Genevan politics of the early 1760s, meanwhile, was also vigorously countered by Voltaire who for the time being still regarded his friends among the aristocratic oligarchy, including Tronchin, as his natural allies.[27] Voltaire unquestionably strove to damage Rousseau's standing with the Genevan reading public, his 1762 tract *Idées républicaines* containing a stinging attack on the *Contrat social* which he denounced for its contradictions and 'ignorance présomptueuse'.[28] He was also suspected by Rousseau of instigating his expulsion from his native city. Such suspicions contributed to Rousseau's decision, in May 1763, to abjure 'for ever' his citizenship of Geneva, describing this as the ultimate sacrifice of one who had deeply revered and loved the name of 'Genevan'.[29] Voltaire agreed with Rousseau that to

[23] Rosenblatt, *Rousseau and Geneva*, 269–70; Whatmore, 'Rousseau', 387; Trousson, *Jean-Jacques Rousseau*, 524–7.   [24] Trousson, *Jean-Jacques Rousseau*, 531; Maissen, *Geburt*, 584.
[25] Trousson, *Jean-Jacques Rousseau*, 532.   [26] Meiners, *Briefe*, ii. 200.
[27] Gay, *Voltaire's Politics*, 196; Palmer, *Age*, i. 131–2.   [28] [Voltaire], 'Idées républicaines', 547–9.
[29] [Tronchin], *Lettres*, 8–9; Trousson, *Jean-Jacques Rousseau*, 559–60.

work well republics should be small; but thought his idea that they must also be poor perfectly absurd. 'Our government', at Geneva, he pointed out, was 'un gouverne-ment mêlé de démocratie et d'aristocratie' and included some very rich persons as well as poor.[30] Rousseau's ideas about direct democracy and the primacy of large assemblies of the people over fixed organs of government he considered a mixture of the absurd and the dangerous.

Rousseau voluntarily cancelled his citizenship. But his supporters in Geneva, some forty of them, organized a protest petition eventually signed by some 700 citizens which they submitted to the *Petit Conseil*, accusing the magistracy of tyrannical abuse of power and violating Geneva's constitution by persecuting their city's celebrated *philosophe*.[31] Tronchin at this point intervened with his *Lettres écrites de la campagne* (1763), denouncing Rousseau's books as subversive of Church and state and claiming the *Petit Conseil* had actually observed the constitution to the letter. Where Rous-seau's defenders claimed he had not attacked the core of Christian teaching, Tronchin answered that he had rejected both prophecy and miracles.[32] Making no attempt to deny that Geneva's institutions were wholly controlled by a tiny group estimated at twenty-five leading families,[33] Tronchin argued that freedom in a republic is best preserved by a firm division of powers and scrupulous respect for precedent and the law. In these respects the *Petit Conseil* was irreproachable whilst the misguided citizens protesting on Rousseau's behalf, and bringing such sweeping accusations against the magistracy, were damaging the republic's reputation, stability, and international status.[34]

To this Rousseau replied with his *Lettres écrites de la montagne*, composed in a mountain valley near Neuchâtel between October 1763 and May 1764. Published at Amsterdam by Marc Michel Rey soon afterwards, this text appeared in the Geneva bookshops in December 1764. Rousseau, defending the *Contrat social* and *Émile*, here reaffirms the need for shared religious dogmas but makes no concession to either the Reformed or any other Christian standpoint, styling the Geneva pastors intolerant and arrogant. Admitting he had indeed had Geneva and other Swiss small states in mind when composing the *Contrat social* and repeating his argument that the 'general will' is indivisible, he expounded what he saw as the process by which pristine democracy gradually dissolves in all societies into systems of government by fewer and fewer and until finally absolute monarchy evolves, an inexorable, thoroughly reprehensible process tantamount to destroying the state and reducing the mass of the citizenry to slavery.

All Geneva, noted Voltaire, was thrown into bitter strife. Rousseau had his supporters; but most Genevans at that time were against him. The text was also interpreted by both local opinion and Mably and Rousseau's *encyclopédiste* foes as an

---

[30] [Voltaire], 'Idées républicaines', 548.
[31] [Brissot], *Philadelphien*, 23–4.
[32] [Tronchin], *Lettres*, 11–12.
[33] Ibid. 111; [Brissot], *Philadelphien*, 24; Miller, *Rousseau*, 85–7.
[34] [Tronchin], *Lettres*, 12, 85, 100, 113.

attempt to subvert the *Petit Conseil*'s oligarchic rule. Rousseau himself records that the explosive reaction to his text in Geneva was mainly negative and that he was widely denounced as a *séditieux* and *incendiaire*, the uproar continuing for many months well into 1765. Even his and Voltaire's publisher, Cramer, regarded him 'comme l'ennemi de ma patrie'.[35] Rousseau having earlier sought to discredit Voltaire by publicizing his alleged authorship of the notoriously and virulently anti-Christian clandestine text the *Sermon des cinquante*, Voltaire seized the opportunity to retaliate by publishing an 'anonymous' pamphlet, *Le Sentiment des citoyens*, lambasting Rousseau's sedition and accusing him of moral depravity and abandoning his five children as foundlings. Where Rousseau thought his *Lettres* breathed the pure spirit of 'stoic resignation', Diderot too took the view that Rousseau here is again merely seeking revenge, sowing discord, and complaining excessively.[36] Following weeks of hesitation due to the deep divisions in the city, and only after hearing Rousseau's *Lettres* had been publicly burned at The Hague and Paris, the *Petit Conseil*, supported by Voltaire, officially banned the text in Geneva. It was suppressed soon afterwards also in Berne.[37]

Meanwhile, Neuchâtel pastors likewise condemned his writings as impious and petitioned for Rousseau's expulsion from Neuchâtel too. Stirred by the local clergy, more and more Neuchâtelois began harassing him. On 6 September 1765, after a hostile sermon in the village church, stones were thrown through his windows. He hastily departed Môtiers, spending his last weeks in Switzerland, in the autumn of 1765, in a retreat on the Île de Saint Pierre in the middle of Lake Brienne. Shortly afterwards, expelled from Neuchâtel and definitively re-expelled from Berne, he departed Switzerland, that 'murderous land', for ever.

But by this point, Voltaire had had second thoughts about the *parti aristocratique*. He had not forgotten their reaction to d'Alembert's article 'Genève' and his reservations were soon turned to antipathy by the burning of his own locally printed and anonymously published *Dictionnaire philosophique portatif*, at the request of the Reformed consistory, in August 1764. As he studied more of Geneva's history and constitution he also began to worry lest he become excessively drawn into the bitter and perhaps irresolvable political fray. Concluding that Geneva's patricians were too censorious, too close to the consistory, and had proceeded unjustly in suppressing his own books and even perhaps Rousseau's, he chose this moment to sell his house, Les Délices, on the city's edge, purchased a decade earlier (with Tronchin's help), and, in April 1765, took up residence on his newly acquired estate with its imposing chateau at Ferney, a half-hour's coach ride from the city—but on the French side of the border. This afforded some semblance of neutrality amid Geneva's political storms while the patricians continued visiting him (and his theatre and dining room), in droves and Geneva's political deadlock continued unabated.

[35] Trousson, *Jean-Jacques Rousseau*, 583–9.
[36] Rousseau, *Confessions*, 521–2; Diderot to Grimm, undated, Dec. 1774, in Diderot, *Corr.* iv. 308.
[37] [Brissot], *Philadelphien*, 24; *DJJR* 522; Whatmore, 'Rousseau', 388.

Receiving numerous visitors from the city and hearing its various divisions explained from all angles, and more and more disliking the secrecy, narrowness, selfishness, and rigidity of the patricians (and their upholding a thoroughly Calvinist and puritanical sexual code), he decided a *philosophe* had no choice in Geneva but to steer a middle course between the patriciate and those urging some widening of the competence of the General Council.[38] From late 1765 onwards, Voltaire regularly intervened discreetly as a behind-the-scenes supporter of the *Représentants*, as the middle-class opposition were known, while simultaneously remaining in contact with patrician leaders, peppering his discourse with profuse protestations of neutrality. A number of formal political discussions with both factions present were held at Ferney. But this failed to prevent the friction between the *Petit Conseil* and the 'General Council' steadily intensifying. The latter routinely refused to approve the nominations of office-holders presented by the former while the *Petit Conseil* equally obdurately refused to recognize any right of veto over its appointments and officers vested in the General Council.

Voltaire's tract *Idées républicaines* (1765) is a quintessentially moderate document in which Rousseau's *Contrat social* is roundly assailed but neither democracy nor republicanism are espoused as general principles. Instead, much emphasis is placed on constitutionality and the rule of law and 'tolerance' pronounced 'as necessary in politics as in religion'.[39] Neither Genevans nor other humans are faced by an outright choice between aristocracy and democracy. Rather the best constitutions, like the British, combine aristocracy and democracy.[40] At Geneva, the moderate reformers could now claim to have both Voltaire and Montesquieu solidly, and Rousseau partially, on their side. After a certain point, in January 1766, the *Petit Conseil* concluded it had no alternative but to offer concessions. To keep these to a minimum, it formally requested the French crown, Berne, and Zurich to arbitrate, accusing the opposition of trying to institute a 'pure démocratie', though the protesters disclaimed any such intention.[41] The deadlock ended for the time being with the compromise 'Edict of 1768', forged approximately along the lines Voltaire and others had been urging for some years, confirming the basic profile of the existing constitution but granting the General Council broader rights in the annual process of appointing the city's syndics and magistrates and extended its power to submit representations from below, while also slightly enlarging the pool of oligarchs from which office-holders could be chosen and creating a mechanism, involving the General Council, for creating new patricians.[42]

The constitutional commission eventually completed its task and published the draft of the proposed new code in April 1779. The *Petit Conseil* flatly rejected it.

[38] Gay, *Voltaire's Politics*, 204, 206.
[39] Voltaire, *Political Writings*, 195, 199, 211.
[40] Ibid. 202–5; Gay, *Enlightenment*, ii. 464.
[41] [Brissot], *Philadelphien*, 25; Whatmore, 'Venturi', 442; Maissen, *Geburt*, 441–2.
[42] Gay, *Voltaire's Politics*, 213–14, 231.

Virulent rhetorical exchanges followed leading to angry incidents and a power struggle that brought the opposition briefly into control. At this point, Geneva issued her famous edict of 10 February 1781 admitting all the disenfranchised male house-holders to full rights of citizenry and equality before the law.[43] With the anti-aristocratic party moving toward a full-scale democratic takeover, the *Petit Conseil*, by thirteen votes to eleven, brought ninety-eight new men onto the Great Council.[44] The patriciate recovered control of the *Petit Conseil*, revoked the decree extending the rights of citizenry, and halted the democratization process. Both sides appealed to the guaranteeing powers. The deadlock was finally broken in early April 1782 when the 'revolution' of Geneva proper began with angry crowds of shopkeepers and workmen yelling against the old *politique aristocratique* seizing control of the city by force of arms. Overwhelming the militia, they occupied the town gates, squares, arms depots, and town hall. This time, both councils were purged of 'aristocrates', forty-three *grandes perruques* being held more or less as prisoners in their homes.[45]

A *commission de sûreté* was set up to maintain order, headed by Étienne Clavière and Jean-Antoine Duroveray, the people's liberation from 'tyranny' was celebrated, and, to crowd applause, it was announced that work on a thorough revision of the constitution had begun. All natives born in the city whose families had been there for three generations were proclaimed full citizens. However, the neighbouring cantons of Berne and Zurich, thoroughly alarmed, refused to recognize the new government. The Bernese oligarchy, having entirely sympathized with Britain against the American Revolution,[46] disapproved of the Genevan revolution too. In a declaration of 12 May, Berne and Zurich jointly condemned the coup as contrary to Geneva's laws and constitution and formally protested at the arrests. Both this and a subsequent ultimatum from Berne alone were rejected.[47] At this point, Louis XVI's chief minister, Vergennes, decided to intervene militarily to suppress the democratic movement (as Prussia was to do, five years later, in the Netherlands). Vergennes made this decision despite France at this point being in formal alliance with the American rebels against Britain and virtual alliance with the Dutch democrats against the House of Orange. Condemning the 'oppression' occasioned in Geneva by subversives moved by 'les idées de la démocratie absolue', France mobilized against the Genevan revolution.[48]

The propaganda war between the two sides spilled over into the international French-language press, both sides trying to drum up support for and against the democratic republican tendency. In Holland the anti-Orangist Patriots backed the democrats and the stadholder's party the patrician oligarchy. Among the latter, curiously, was Manzon's *Courrier du Bas-Rhin* whose earlier republican sympathies

---

[43] Gay, *Voltaire's Politics*, 37–8; Blamires, *French Revolution*, 120–1.
[44] Blamires, *French Revolution*, 122; Benetruy, *L'Atelier*, 17–18, 22–3.
[45] [Feller], *Journal historique* (1782), 358–60; Meiners, *Briefe*, ii. 203.
[46] Dippel, *Germany*, 221.
[47] [Feller], *Journal historique* (1782), 200–2, 283; Kapossy, 'Neo-Roman Republicanism', 237.
[48] [Feller], *Journal historique* (1782), 285–6.

and pro-Pilati stance of the late 1760s had by this time given way to hostility to the American rebels and robust support for crowns, princely authority, and the status quo.[49] The contradiction between France's support for the movements in America and Holland and for the *parti aristocratique* in Switzerland was much commented on and highlighted by radical publicists like Mirabeau and also Brissot who visited Geneva at this point to study its revolutionary awareness, new constitution, and debates.[50] The latter could scarcely have arrived at a better moment, he noted afterwards, 'pour connaître toute l'énergie de l'esprit républicain'.[51]

Neither Berne nor Zurich wished France to extend her leverage in Switzerland and, in the end, only Berne, despite her long republican tradition and her notorious xenophobia, joined the French and Savoyard invasion force. Paralysed by internal divisions, Zurich remained neutral.[52] Alone among the Swiss cantons, sprawling Berne with its French-speaking appendages of Lausanne and Fribourg, where there was considerable unrest and support for the Genevans, directly intervened in the struggle. To Brissot, Mirabeau, and the radical fringe, Bernese intervention seemed an even more glaring but instructive contradiction than that suffusing French policy.[53] Berne's judges and lawyers as well as her 'aristocrats' were roundly accused by Brissot and Mirabeau of betraying the Helvetic Confederation and their own republic and its liberty and wholly isolating the Bernese within Switzerland.[54] Hints of broader Swiss criticism of Geneva's, Berne's, and Zurich's *parti aristocratique*, and signs of agitation in Fribourg, heartened radical opinion generally. The considerable European impact of the Genevan revolution, and simultaneous protests against the Augsburg patriciate, demonstrated, suggested Wekhrlin later, in 1785, that not all peoples are so entirely sunk in ignorance as blindly to submit to their nobles, patricians, and priests; the desire to be free of oppression was a stronger force among some of Europe's people than many thought.[55]

All Europe watched in fascination as 12,000 French, Savoyard, and Bernese troops set siege to the armed democratic faction in Geneva. According to both Meiners and Brissot (who at this point left for Neuchâtel), most of the populace laboured as if inspired at preparing the defences and strengthening the walls, showing a remarkable willingness to fight.[56] The concerted Franco-Savoyard-Bernese encirclement of Geneva's Revolution, Brissot noted, many attributed to the apprehensions 'l'esprit philosophique' had by now aroused in the minds of sovereigns and oligarchies everywhere. Not only conservatives but most middle-of-the-road Genevan patriots, businessmen and lawyers alike, aghast at Geneva's predicament, likewise blamed their

[49] Beermann, *Zeitung*, 434–5.
[50] Dumont, *Souvenirs de Mirabeau*, 7; [Brissot], *Philadelphien*, 47, 193.
[51] [Brissot], *Philadelphien*, 50–1; de Luna, 'Dean Street Style', 167.
[52] [Feller], *Journal historique* (1782), 200–1; Lerner, 'Radical Elements', 304, 306.
[53] [Brissot], *Philadelphien*, 51, 143, 181, 220; Mirabeau, *Lettres*, i. 184–5.
[54] Meiners, *Briefe*, i. 236–7; Soetard, 'L'Émile', 17.
[55] Wekhrlin, *Graue Ungeheuer*, 3 (1784–5), 184–5, 187.
[56] Meiners, *Briefe*, ii. 206; [Brissot], *Philadelphien*, 49.

precarious situation on misplaced 'enthousiasme de la philosophie'.[57] Others chiefly blamed Berne for blindly supporting the *parti aristocratique* instead of pursuing the path of compromise. In any case, there was no way of resisting for long. After three weeks, the revolutionary committee, headed by Clavière, Duroveray, and a brother of Marat, decided to surrender to prevent serious bloodshed. But they did so without informing the populace beforehand, capitulating and then departing by boat at night before the besiegers entered the city.

Geneva was occupied by foreign troops and the *parti aristocratique* restored to power. The former constitution was reinstated, all new laws were revoked, and full authority returned to the *Petit Conseil*. All printing and public expression were placed under strict censorship, clubs and societies were banned, and the civic militia thoroughly purged. A package of restrictive decrees, known as the Edict of Pacification, including a drastic reduction in the powers of the Great Council, was introduced and what Brissot called 'le tableau le plus complet du despotisme' imposed. According to Meiners, who arrived six weeks after the fall of the democratic regime, Geneva experienced a complete truncation of her normal social and cultural life, despite the restored regime's efforts to promote theatrical performances as a diversion from politics. All other forms of gathering apart from church congregations were forbidden.[58] Twenty-one revolutionary leaders, including Duroveray and Clavière, were formally banished, though besides these other prominent men, some 500 political outcasts in total fled the city.[59] Including family members around 2,000 persons left. In the Netherlands, the defeat, deeply distressing for the democrats, resonated for months in polemical exchanges between Cerisier's radical republican *Politique hollandois* and Manzon's (since 1781) increasingly anti-democratic *Courrier du Bas-Rhin*.[60]

Unsurprisingly, suppression of the revolution, or what democrats called 'l'exécrable liberticide' perpetrated by Geneva's 'aristocrates', failed to end either the underlying political struggle or the resentment stirred by *l'esprit philosophique* which Brissot clearly identified as the main engine of the new revolutionary awareness. The exiles denounced what they called 'la nouvelle aristocratie de Genève' as a usurping elite treating their fellow citizens as a conquered people who proceeded with their tyrannical suppression of the people's 'rights' by hardening their hearts on seeing the suppressed fury on the faces of their co-citizens every day.[61] And, despite their military and political superiority, the *aristocrates* clearly did fear fresh turmoil quite possibly soon should the French crown, for whatever reason, become less able or willing to help. Formally banished from the republic, in June 1782, shortly before Britain finally recognized American Independence, the exiles, led by Clavière and

[57] Brissot, *De la vérité*, 257.

[58] Meiners, *Briefe*, ii. 199–200; Quastana, *Pensée politique*, 358.

[59] [Brissot], *Philadelphien*, 73, 75–6; *Réclamation des Genevois Patriotes*, preface p. v; Whatmore, 'Neither Masters', 76–7.

[60] Beermann, *Zeitung*, 436–8.

[61] *Réclamation des Genevois Patriotes*, preface pp. iii–iv.

Duroveray, many of them the authors of the compromise of 1768, migrated initially to Neuchâtel.[62]

There they were joined among others by Mirabeau and Brissot. Like Brissot, Mirabeau was keen to make himself an expert on the Genevan revolution and the ideology of democracy just as he afterwards made himself an expert on the Prussian monarchy. He even ventured to send Vergennes a manuscript memorandum explaining and defending the democratic revolution and the conduct of the exiles.[63] As the presence of the revolutionaries was clearly inciting unrest elsewhere in Switzerland, Prussia eventually agreed to intervene in support of the Bernese authorities and Genevan *aristocrates*, and in the autumn of 1782, Frederick expelled the entire dissident group from Neuchâtel. After interludes in England and Ireland where, on 30 July 1784, some of the exiles inaugurated what they hoped would be the new colony of La Nouvelle Genève, at Waterford,[64] the exiled group mostly settled in Paris where their leaders lost no time in resuming collaboration with Mirabeau and Brissot, publicists who more and more spoke of the need to combine 'la philosophie' with political action to democratize society as well as reform Europe's laws, end black slavery, emancipate the Jews, and generally emancipate mankind.[65] The first concrete collaboration between Brissot and Clavière—who were to be guillotined together by the *Robespierristes* in 1793—was their jointly written *Le Philadelphien à Genève* ('Dublin' [Paris?], 1783), a work vigorously lambasting the 'despotism' imposed on Geneva by France.[66]

A revolution favourable to the people, based on philosophical principles, was being prepared in the reading-rooms of Europe, declared Brissot and Clavière in another text they published jointly, in 1787, and there could be no doubt that this process would be accelerated by the impact of the Revolution in America as well as developments in the Low Countries and France.[67] In this way, the beginnings of the expatriate, intellectual revolutionary diaspora soon to be swollen by fleeing Dutch Patriots came into being, linking in an unprecedented fashion Paris, Switzerland, the Low Countries, London, Ireland, and, soon, also radical circles in Germany. The publicity they organized contributed to the build-up of a revolutionary consciousness in western Europe generally and helps explain why the aristocratic counter-coup of 1782 made so acutely an unfavourable impression on a great many contemporaries, including Price and Godwin, in England.

In Paris, the democratic faction's leaders, headed by Clavière, Duroveray, and Étienne Dumont, the latter privately sceptical about radical republicanism and 'la philosophie' but a talented editor who became one of Mirabeau's speech-writers as

---

[62] [Brissot], *Philadelphien*, 52, 56, 75, 147; Blamires, *French Revolution*, 140.

[63] Quastana, *Pensée politique*, 352–3.

[64] [Feller], *Journal historique* (1784), 58.

[65] Benetruy, *L'Atelier*, 38–9, 44; Livesey, *Making Democracy*, 29–31, 61.

[66] Livesey, *Making Democracy*, 31.

[67] Clavière and Brissot, *De la France*, preface p. xxvii; de Luna, 'Dean Street Style', 167–8.

well as, later, co-editor of his revolutionary journal *Le Courrier de Provence*, became full-time professional democratic agitators. Clavière befriended not only Brissot and Mirabeau but also Delisle de Sales. In this way, the 'violent persecution' unleashed against the revolutionary faction by Geneva's *parti aristocratique* ultimately turned against the latter and, Brissot suggested, also damaged Berne and the courts of France and Savoy which, blind to their own true interests, had so blatantly made themselves the tools of 'aristocratic' reaction against the people's manifest rights and interests.[68]

Geneva was a relatively small city but yet became a key emotional symbol, throughout Europe, for 'les peuples libres' and those aspiring to become free through the years prior to 1789.[69] A trans-European war of words stemmed from the Genevan revolution that was especially intense in Switzerland but raged also in Germany, France, and the Netherlands where the exiles told their story in various journals, depicting the Genevan counter-coup in the most emphatically negative terms.[70] The Genevan *parti aristocratique* answered by tightening its links with Berlin and London and feeding its own propaganda to the pro-Orangist press. The spread of the idea that the 'Aristokraten' had overthrown the Genevan republic with the help of neighbouring princes and opposed all peoples everywhere lent added impetus to Dutch Patriot adoption of 'anti-aristocratic' rhetoric in the mid 1780s which, in turn, helps explain the stunning impact and pivotal role of 'anti-aristocratic' rhetoric and ideology deployed by Mirabeau, Brissot, Clavière, and other radical ideologues in France during 1788 and the months prior to the gathering of the States-General in 1789.

It seemingly required only a slight further weakening of the French monarchy's faltering grip and the revolution would be back in full flow in Geneva, Fribourg, Neuchâtel, Berne, and Zurich. The hold of the *parti aristocratique* over Geneva and Berne looked distinctly precarious by the mid and late 1780s. In March 1789 erupted another 'revolution' in Geneva resulting in a compromise obliging the 'aristocrates' to abandon some of the *pouvoirs usurpés* secured with French help in 1782, though the exiled leaders failed, as yet, to return or recover their former positions and dominance.[71] Publication (in London) later in 1789 of the two-volume *Révolutions de Genève* encouraged the incipiently revolutionary leaders and journals in Paris to acknowledge the Genevan revolution as their forerunner in raising the central principles and questions of the 'General Revolution'. While the Swiss movement had been temporarily checked, the unfinished business of Geneva could be expected to be put right shortly when France had firmly established her own liberty, by a new French intervention—this time anti-*aristocratique*.[72]

All the oligarchic Swiss republics took fright over developments in France during 1788–9. According to Gorani, then residing at Nyon in the canton of Berne, both Berne and Geneva were convulsed with frantic political debates by the summer

[68] Livesey, *Making Democracy*, 147.   [69] *Réclamation des Genevois Patriotes*, preface p. xiii.
[70] 'Demofilus', *Zakboek*, 49.   [71] Dumont, *Souvenirs de Mirabeau*, 41.
[72] *Chronique de Paris*, 2/87 (28 Mar. 1790), 345–7.

of 1789.[73] Sporting the French revolutionary cockade became common though banned in several cantons; and in some, including Fribourg, a ban was introduced also on importing French journals except for anti-revolutionary publications. At Berne, the ruling clique, hoping to mollify the citizenry, widened somewhat the category of families whence members of the great council and executive council could be drawn. But none of this halted the democratic agitation, spurred by a propaganda campaign orchestrated from Paris.[74] After the *Declaration of the Rights of Man*, in Paris, in August 1789, Genevan democrats began formally urging the Paris National Assembly to declare that the Genevan oligarchy had violated the exiles' natural rights and repudiate the three-power guarantee, announcing France no longer opposed the return of the exiles of 1782.[75]

On 28 December 1789, Brissot, now a leading revolutionary journalist in Paris, implored the French National Assembly, in his journal *Le Patriote français*, to put right the crime committed against the Genevan exiles. The French crown had put Geneva in chains; France must now break those chains. In fact, France should now declare herself 'la protectrice des républiques opprimées' everywhere. On the 29 December 1789, the National Assembly debated Geneva, Volney and Mirabeau opening the debate with the most scathing attacks on the aristocratic patriciate. Volney's denunciation of the Genevan 'aristocrates' as 'la tyrannie la plus affreuse' so impressed the assembly the text was published.[76] By December 1789, it seemed just a matter of time before Geneva's oligarchy was overthrown, the revolutionary regime of 1781–2 restored, and the General Revolution spread to Berne and further into Switzerland. 'Many individuals, and some communities', admitted Gibbon, then at Lausanne, 'appear to be infected with the Gallic phrenzy, the wild theories of equal and boundless freedom; but I trust that the body of the people will be faithful to their sovereign and to themselves.' In any case, so convinced was he that any revolt whether successful or not in Switzerland 'would equally terminate in the ruin of the country' that the first sounding of 'a rebel drum would be the signal of my immediate departure'.[77] Greatly alarmed that the 'fanatic missionaries of sedition have scattered the seeds of discontent' among the Swiss, Gibbon concurred more and more in Burke's political creed.[78]

2. AACHEN, LIÈGE, AND THE AUSTRIAN NETHERLANDS

Geneva, Berne, and Zurich were cantons where the bourgeoisie had made considerable progress. But the part of western continental Europe where commerce and

---

[73] Catalano, 'Alcune lettere', 151–3.
[74] Brissot, *Patriote français*, 237 (2 Apr. 1790), 4; Fontana, *Venise et la Révolution*, 452.
[75] Brissot, *Patriote français*, 29 (29 Aug. 1789), 4–5.
[76] Ibid. 142 (28 Dec. 1789), 4, and 145 (31 Dec. 1789), 1–2.
[77] Gibbon, *Memoirs*, 215.   [78] Gibbon, *Autobiographies*, 342.

industry advanced most in the eighteenth century and bourgeois prosperity and resources most dramatically expanded was the southern Netherlands. The Brabant-Flemish revolution of 1787–90, consequently, offers a most interesting object lesson for social scientists and historians regarding the role of social forces, especially as this region with slightly over three million inhabitants (including the independent prince-bishopric of Liège), in 1780, was the scene of the most reactionary counter-revolution witnessed in Europe down to 1790. Home of the most economically mature commercial-industrial class in continental Europe, the land where business was strongest was simultaneously culturally, politically, and intellectually the most reactionary. It would be hard to find a clearer disproof of Marxist ideology than the Brabantine counter-revolution of 1787–90. Nowhere else in continental Europe was industry and trade more strongly developed and dynamic; nowhere else was the bourgeoisie so avid for precedent, privileges, charters, aristocracy, religion, and clergy.

Admittedly, there were radical democratic tendencies too, a recent flurry of pamphlets in Dutch and French appealing to disaffected segments of the citizenry, seeking to coax these to life. But such elements agitated largely around the fringes—West Flanders, Aachen, and Liège. In most of Brabant and Flanders, the radical tendency was weak and unrepresentative despite the crushing of the Dutch demo-cratic movement in 1787, bringing many Dutch political exiles to Antwerp, Brussels, and other cities where they lent their support to Joseph's reforms as well as the local democratic tendency. Gerrit Paape spent many months in Antwerp. Pieter Vreede (1750–1837), a Leiden manufacturer as well as Patriot leader, transferred his textile workshop, employing eighty workers, to Lier where he established a Protestant congregation under the terms of the 1781 Toleration, permission subsequently abrogated, locally, in 1789, with the further progress of the rebellion against the Josephine reforms. Its intolerance and staunchly Catholic character together with its zeal for the old constitution and charters filled the Dutch Patriot exiles with horror, despair, and indignation.[79]

By contrast, the insurrections in Augsburg and Aachen (Aix-la-Chapelle) in 1785–6 affronted urban oligarchies entrenched within an array of privileges acknow-ledged by the emperor. By 1786, Aachen, a city where the cell of Illuminati in the early 1780s, the surviving lists show, was larger than in Berlin, Hamburg, or Dresden and in whose code it was designated 'Gaza', was prey to two warring factions, leading to pitched brawls in taverns and streets.[80] After an infuriated mob wielding sticks and words stormed the city hall, severely injuring several of the city's 'senators', the local imperial circle—chiefly the three neighbouring princes, among whom, as duke of Cleves, figured the Prussian monarch—felt obliged to send commissioners and troops to restore order. Their original design in May 1787 was merely to correct a few 'abuses' in the existing constitution.[81] But as the months passed and the disorder

[79] Dhondt, 'Conservatieve Brabantse ontwenteling', 425–7.   [80] Schüttler, *Mitglieder*, 197.
[81] [Dohm], *Plan d'une constitution*, pp. xix–xxi, xxiii.

showed little sign of abating, and as the mounting uproar in the neighbouring Austrian Netherlands and France gathered momentum, the Prussian delegate—who happened to be Dohm—left with a remarkably free hand by Berlin, found himself able to propose more sweeping changes.

Dohm instigated the scrapping of more and more of the old Aachen constitution and, with the spectacle in France unfolding before his eyes, eventually, in April 1790, drew up an entirely new draft constitution, going so far as to remove virtually all reference to charters and traditional privileges and proclaiming 'all the citizens are equal' and possessing equal rights in voting and standing for civic office. The effect was to sow even sharper divisions than before, most people being readily swayed against this attack on tradition. From the viewpoint of the Aachen oligarchy and neighbouring princes, a further drawback of the new constitution was that, with the Revolution in France now in full swing, French publicists began claiming Dohm's principles had been inspired by the French National Assembly and that despite concessions to local 'préjugés populaires' and dealing with a people 'infinitely less enlightened' than the French, he had espoused an approach enlightened, 'vraiment démocratique', and essentially that of their Revolution.[82] The clash between tradition and *la philosophie* in this way fuelled an irresolvable crisis.

Concerted opposition to Joseph's reforms, meanwhile, attained significant proportions throughout Brabant, Flanders, and Hainault. Local opinion opposed especially his toleration decree, marriage reform law (1782), abolition of pious confraternities, closing of some monasteries (1783), sweeping changes to guild regulations, and reform of Louvain (Leuven) university. The rebellion began as a vigorous movement of protest, headed by a Brussels lawyer, Hendrik van der Noot (1731–1827), commissioned by the States of Brabant to formulate their legal objections to the reforms. By the summer of 1787, the ambitious Van der Noot, busily intriguing in Paris, London, and Berlin, was already being dubbed 'le Franklin des Pays-Bas', an epithet to which Georg Forster, who was in Brussels when Van der Noot's supporters took over the city, in 1789, roundly objected as it seemed obvious from any enlightened or libertarian perspective that he in no way deserved it.[83] The basic charge against Joseph's measures was that they overturned a centuries-old constitution and charters of privileges. Support for the protests was broad-based. But it was the solidly anti-reform fervour of the middle-class population of Antwerp and Brussels, the world of trade and business, that most astounded and shocked both the radical-minded and the imperial authorities.

A lively pamphlet war ignited, with Xavier de Feller, the *anti-philosophe* editor of the *Journal historique et littéraire*, helping stir popular sentiment to the utmost against Josephism, *la philosophie*—routinely blamed by Feller for causing the revolutionary upsurge in the world—and Enlightenment generally.[84] Another of the Counter-Revolution's spiritual leaders, and equally tenacious as an adversary of

---

[82] Ibid., pp. xxvii, xxxi, 26, 30.   [83] Gorman, *America and Belgium*, 184–7.
[84] [Feller], *Journal historique* (1784), 107–8, and (1792), 21–6.

enlightened ideas and reform, was the ultramontane bishop of Antwerp, Jacob Wellens (1726–84), a former professor of philosophy and theology at Leuven and a hero of the Antwerp middle class.[85] Hence, Counter-Enlightenment set to work to legitimize the Brabant protest movement and vilify the reformism it so strenuously opposed.[86] By June 1787, Van der Noot was mobilizing opposition also among the Brussels guilds and in the autumn the capital witnessed a series of rowdy disturbances.

The Austrian Netherlands 'revolution' arose out of a sustained campaign of obstruction by the States of Brabant, Flanders, and Hainault which even suspended routine fiscal collection for the monarch. It was plainly instigated by prelates, lower clergy, and nobles as well as office-holders, magistrates, and guilds. The priests and nobility, commented the English radical novelist Robert Bage, 'were the prime movers of throwing off the yoke of tyranny; and they would undoubtedly have produced a liberty that would have delighted the soul of Mr Burke and all good bishops'.[87] Yet, despite this and the early involvement, from 1786, of Louvain's students in sustained anti-government agitation encouraged by the clergy,[88] in one crucial respect, the Belgian Revolution of 1787–90 was highly advanced, indeed could justly claim to be manifestly more 'advanced' than the revolutions in Holland and France. For no other revolutionary movement of the 1780s matched that in Brabant-Flanders as a true people's movement. It was overwhelmingly popular, the others were not to the same degree. Following Joseph's decision, in June 1789, in the face of Brabant's resistance to revoke the province's constitutional privileges, popular indignation reached boiling point.[89] The insurrection proper was precipitated by a small-scale invasion by a rebel force of some 3,000 volunteers drawn from all over the southern Netherlands, under Van der Noot who had been in exile in the United Provinces, as the stadholder's guest, over the previous year. Its spectacular impact, however, accrued from a simultaneous armed rising in Brussels, led by Jean-François Vonck (1743–92). In Brussels, Antwerp, and other cities, it was the guild members, shopkeepers, artisans, and labourers, and, in the countryside, the villagers, who practically from the start imposed their will on the course of the insurrection, to an extent seen nowhere else. They rose on all sides. Except in Luxembourg where the Walloon half of the duchy, to the surprise of some, proved less sympathetic to the rebellion than the German half, the Austrian garrison was driven into a handful of large fortresses.

The eruption at Brussels both fascinated and baffled radical opinion. Would the Brussels rising, asked the journal *Révolutions de Paris* in late August 1789, prove an 'heureuse révolution', anti-aristocratic and anti-ecclesiastical on the Dutch, Swiss,

[85] Vanysacker, 'Verlicht ultramontaan', 97, 101–2.
[86] Ibid. 112; Heirwegh, 'La Fin', 472; Polasky, 'Success', 414–15.
[87] [Bage], *Man as he is*, iv. 126–7.
[88] Hebeis, *Karl Anton von Martini*, 94–5.
[89] Doyle, *Oxford History*, 162; Kossmann, *Lage Landen*, i. 59; Roegiers and Van Sas, 'Revolutie', 233.

and French model? Soon afterwards, the same journal pronounced Brabant, like Holland and Switzerland, the scene of vast political turmoil.[90] Most ironic was the political rhetoric employed by one of the foremost European manifestos of the decade, the *Manifeste du peuple brabançon* (1789). This widely distributed text summoning the common people to resist, resoundingly stressed popular sovereignty and the people's right to take up arms to curb 'tyrants' defying the people's will, more so perhaps than any text of the Dutch Patriots. But what is most astounding is that its author, Van der Noot, shamelessly borrowed its ringing phrases without saying so from an uncompromisingly radical source, cheerfully pilfering entire passages from d'Holbach's *Politique naturelle* (1773). He did so highly selectively, however, justifying popular rebellion on behalf not of the people, general welfare, or basic human rights but ecclesiastical and aristocratic privilege and restoring Brabant's historic 'liberties'.[91]

The radical democratic wing, led by Vonck, weakly represented in Brabant, had some support in the Ostend area and was strong in Liège, headquarters of a vigorous anticlerical movement. This undercurrent in Liège had been noted since at least the early 1780s for vocal support for the American Revolution and enthusiasm for Raynal, several editions of whose *Histoire* were published there. In Liège, it was the fashion, complained Feller, predicting serious trouble ahead, to mock whoever adhered to the principles of 'obedience and order'. The rising 'insolence philosophique' Feller detected in Liège in the early 1780s was something he thought boded ill for the future of the local princely-ecclesiastical regime. The 'enlightened' Prince-Bishop François-Charles de Velbruck (ruled: 1772–84), who had no time for Feller's Counter-Enlightenment views, had not only protected Raynal but founded a public library, school for midwives, and literary society, and even tried to reduce the fiscal privileges of the Liégeois nobility and clergy. The citizens of Boston, Feller admonished him, having in the 1760s with great deference erected a statue to George III, only ten years later dragged the same statue through the streets mutilated 'de la manière la plus ignominieuse'.[92]

In Liège, tension had been building since Velbruck's death, in 1784, when the new prince-bishop chosen by the disaffected cathedral canons, Constantijn Franciscus van Hoensbroeck (ruled: 1784–92), began trying to reverse his predecessor's policies and appropriated the right to nominate half the magistracies in the city government as a way of strengthening princely-ecclesiastical control. Van Hoensbroeck concurred entirely with Feller and Wellens; but precisely his ultramontane strategy exploded in his face. A territory where, according to Dohm, two-thirds of the land belonged to the Church and the clergy were 'almost entirely' exempt from taxation, the prince-bishopric belonged, like Aachen, to the Holy Roman Empire and was

---

[90] [Prudhomme and Tournon], *Révolutions de Paris*, 6 (16/22 Aug. 1789), 45, and 7 (22/8 Aug. 1789), 45.
[91] Roegiers and Van Sas, 'Revolutie', 232; Polasky, 'Success', 416–17; Heirwegh, 'La Fin', 477–8.
[92] Droixhe, 'Raynal à Liège', 216–18.

much entwined with the politics of north-west Germany. In August 1789, a local revolution erupted in Liège, most observers interpreting this as just a symptom of the 'contagion' spreading from Paris, without pausing to consider the local causes. Van Hoensbroeck was bloodlessly overthrown, insurgents avowing the principles of liberty and equality seized his palace, militia, and government.[93] On 26 August 1789, the prince-bishop fled to Trier.

The Austrians intervened and briefly expelled the pro-French revolutionaries, but before long, it was the Austrians who were ousted. A striking characteristic of the Liège rising was a sweeping refusal from the outset to discuss charters and precedent of any sort: 'all privilege', observed Dohm, approvingly, historic rights, and precedent were rejected from the outset in favour of *la volonté générale* and the 'Rights of Man' expressed as philosophical principles.[94] The equality of all citizens was declared and numerous ecclesiastical privileges and exemptions abolished. The Liège democratic revolution lasted a year and a half until Prussian troops, ten battalions equipped with artillery, occupied the bishopric in December 1789. Prussia's new king wished to prevent the further spread of revolutionary democratic agitation and restore Liège's ancient 'constitution' precisely as he had restored the stadholderate in Holland.[95] But disagreements with Van Hoensbroeck led, in the spring of 1790, to the Prussians evacuating and the Patriots resuming control.

After weeks of confused fighting in many places, the Brabant rebellion gained the upper hand throughout the southern Netherlands. In November 1789, by which time the Austrians had lost Mons and most of the Walloon area, an enthusiastic Brissot, observing the scene from Paris, summoned the insurgents to declare their independence adopting the American Revolution as their model.[96] By December, the Austrians were cleared from the entire southern Netherlands apart from the fortified city of Luxembourg and by early January volunteers were gathering from Ghent, Brussels, and across the Austrian Netherlands for an attack on that citadel.[97] The rebel triumph seemed to echo the American Revolution, but more particularly conjured up resonances of 1572 and the revolt against Philip II of Spain.[98] The 'revolution' culminated in the convening of the southern Netherlands Estates-General in January 1790.[99] The expected declaration of independence of briefly the United States of Belgium duly materialized. But this was a venture opposed by Britain and the United Provinces, powers objecting partly to the people taking matters into their own hands but mainly withholding recognition because, as an independent entity, the country hardly seemed capable of serving as a reliable barrier to France.

---

[93] Droixhe, 'Raynal à Liège', 478; Fontana, *Venise et la Révolution*, 326, 364; Houtman-De Smedt, 'Het prinsbisdom', 420.
[94] Houtman-De Smedt, 'Het prinsbisdom', 420; Dohm, *Exposé de la Révolution*, 19–22, 29.
[95] Fontana, *Venise et la Révolution*, 364–5.
[96] Brissot, *Patriote français*, 94 (10 Nov. 1789), 3.
[97] *Chronique de Paris*, 2/12 (12 Jan. 1790), 47.
[98] Dhont, 'Conservatieve Brabantse ontwenteling', 435–6; Israel, *Dutch Republic*, 1117.
[99] *Chronique de Paris*, 2/34 (4 Feb. 1790), 137.

Their texts show that the south Netherlands revolutionaries were to an extent infused by the American example. But it was only the most conservative reading of that Revolution that appealed, justifying rebellion where provoked by royal infringement of historic rights and privileges. The Brabant revolution of 1789–90 genuinely sought independence but did so postulating a federal solution preserving all the historic privileges of the provinces, towns, nobility, and Church. The main institutional bodies, the provincial States of Brabant, Flanders, and Hainault, the Estates-General, and city governments, eventually split, moreover, between defenders of privilege, magistracies, and ecclesiastical property, led by Van der Noot, and the radical democratic fringe, allied with France, proclaiming 'liberty and equality'. Apart from at Liège such enlightened persons were to be found, according to Paape, mainly in Ostend, Bruges, and Ghent where some aspired to 'acknowledge Man's true rights' and 'erect true freedom on its throne'.[100] For some weeks this bitter tussle, symbolized (ironically) by Van der Noot's adherents openly associating themselves with the Estates-General of 1572—and William the Silent's legacy—by sporting Orange cockades, and thereby also openly aligning with the Orangists in the north, reverberated across Europe.

At a theoretical-constitutional level the argument was about whether sovereignty lay with the people or was vested in the States; on a practical level, the question was whether and how to widen representation in the Estates-General. The question was settled, however, not by arguments or constitutional factions but by vigorous intervention of the people, peasants as well as the urban populace of Brabant, especially in Brussels.[101] Although it was the common people, particularly the Brussels guilds, that drove the revolution, the States of Brabant ruled that sovereignty rested in the States; and it was this view, with fervent popular acclaim, even in Austrian Limburg where grievances against nobility and clergy were sharper than elsewhere, that prevailed.[102] All this, held Condorcet, a democrat and a *philosophe* convinced the ignorance of the masses constituted the chief danger to liberty, showed just how easily the people can be manipulated to act directly contrary to their own best interest.[103]

The French revolutionary journals, of course, backed Vonck against Van der Noot, as did the exiled radical Dutch Patriots. A full-scale ideological war had set in, pitting the Belgian Revolution against the Genevan, Liège, Aachen, Dutch, and French revolutions. Where the Dutch Patriots supported what Brissot termed 'le parti démocratique du Brabant', Dutch Orangists and the court at The Hague supported Van der Noot, intending thereby to entrench the 'parti aristocratique' in power.[104] The Brussels-based revolution being a movement against enlightened ideas and a

[100] Ibid. p. iv, dedication 11; Paape, *Hollandsche wijsgeer in Braband*, iv. 75–7.
[101] Dhont, 'Conservatieve Brabantse ontwenteling', 441–2; Doyle, *Oxford History*, 162–3.
[102] Heirwegh, 'La Fin', 481; Polasky, 'Success', 420–1.
[103] Condorcet, *Œuvres*, ix. 173; Baker, *Condorcet*, 269.
[104] Brissot, *Patriote français*, 156 (11 Jan. 1790), 4; Paape, *Zaak der verdrukte Hollandsche Patriotten*, 2–4, 9.

reforming emperor, it was a movement, in Paape's view, inevitably opposed by all 'reason-loving democrats' and men of the Enlightenment.[105] These backed the emperor, explained Paape, as any enlightened person must scorn the 'stupid', priest-ridden, so-called 'Patriottismus' of the southern Brabanders, consisting solely of yearning for 'the old constitution' and 'pure fanaticism which the artful priesthood knows how to cultivate'. *Brabantsch Patriottismus* he reckoned the most popular but also the stupidest, basest, most despicable kind of rebellion conceivable.[106]

The *Vonckisten* were too weak to hope for success. Collapsing first in Brussels where, in their anger, the shopkeepers and artisans pillaged the homes of leading Vonckists, almost everywhere they were unable to stand their ground. Defeated in the clashes of March, Vonck and his main adherents had, by May 1790, been forced to flee, mostly joining the foreign liberation movement in exile in France alongside the Dutch Patriots. Crushed at home, the Belgian democratic movement nevertheless remained formidable because Vonckist expatriates in France with their Paris committee, the Comité des Belges et Liégeois Unis, still drew significant support from Liège and coastal Flanders, and counted on powerful backing from the National Assembly.[107] Van der Noot and his followers were roundly denounced by Brissot's *Le Patriote français* and other Paris journals for deceiving 'the people'.[108] Only Linguet's *Annales politiques, civiles, et littéraires*, a periodical with Belgian ties and less anticlerical than the other pro-Revolution journals (though equally hostile to the *parlements*), defended the Brabantine movement.[109] Brissot's hostility and that of other French revolutionary commentators provoked a stern rebuke from Van der Noot's chief ideologue, Van Eupen, published in Brussels in January 1790: 'our people' laugh with 'Christian' zeal at the 'folie philosophique' [philosophic madness] inspiring the revolutionary leadership in Paris. To this Brissot replied that the partisans of *la liberté française* were far from wanting to destroy the Christian religion. What they condemned was the 'criminal abuse' of religion by the priesthood and the appalling ignorance they fomented, the unjustified vast wealth of the clergy, and its prodigious influence over the people.[110]

The disdain of Dutch Patriots and Parisian revolutionists, needless to say, had scant effect on opinion in the southern Netherlands. Fomented by the press and encouraged by priests, huge massed rallies of armed artisans and shopkeepers, summoned by the guilds and supported by the peasantry, denounced the Vonckists as agents of toleration, irreligious ideas, and the 'philosophie de ce siècle'.[111] In March 1790, with virtually the whole country in open revolt, massed rallies

---

[105] Rosendaal, *Bataven!*, 72–4; Paape, *Hollandsche wijsgeer in Braband*, iv. 140, 168, 202–3; Popkin, *News and Politics*, 192–3.
[106] Paape, *Hollandsche wijsgeer in Braband*, iv. 140, 168, 202–3.
[107] Polasky, 'Success', 418.
[108] Brissot, *Patriote français*, 325 (29 June 1790), 3.
[109] Linguet, *Annales politiques*, 17 (1790), 28–9, 31, 289–96.
[110] Ibid. 162 (17 Jan. 1790), 3–4.
[111] Kossmann, *Lage Landen*, i. 62; Polasky, 'Success', 418.

publicly denouncing toleration, Joseph, and the Enlightenment, reached their crescendo in Brussels. With its open hostility to toleration and Enlightenment, the southern Netherlands revolution closely resembled the outlook of the anti-Patriot Orangist mobs rampant in the United Provinces, except the latter were Protestant zealots and the former Catholic. It resembled too the reaction that developed in western France (Brittany, Anjou, and the Lower Loire), during the wars of the Vendée, from 1792, in favour of religion against revolutionary democracy, and the uncompromising loyalism of the popular chauvinist-royalist, anti-revolutionary 'King and Church' mobs in Britain.

The revolution in the Austrian Netherlands thus developed into an outright denial of the principles of 1789 and direct contradiction of the Swiss, Dutch, German, and French democratic revolutions. If some members of the States of Flanders admired aspects of the American Revolution and publicly subscribed to Démeunier's study of the American state constitutions published at Ghent in 1790, there was little support for equality or democracy.[112] Gerrit Paape, by 1789, after two years of exile in Flanders, viewed the traditionalist revolt of the Brabant Patriots as implying total opposition to the enlightened ideas and democratic values of what he terms 'philosophische Patriottismus'. In the southern Netherlands, 'superstition and stupidity sit on the throne: everybody kneels before these and the forces of Hell are invoked against those seeking to render these poor mortals wiser and better. Leave them just as they are, humanity-loving Joseph! Make no more efforts to further their happiness; no punishment could be severer than that; already, they run in their thousands into the arms of slavery.'[113] For, according to the democrats, the legal and administrative reforms Joseph had attempted to introduce were sorely needed, as was his attempt to dissolve some monasteries and relieve the land of 'an unbelievable number of idlers and spongers'.[114] But the people opposed his reforms! 'The spirit of Brabant Patriotism', concluded Paape, 'however much in conflict with men's true interests, sound reason and the true Rights of Man [de waare Rechten van den Mensch], pervades the common folk, dominates all limited understandings and directs all who are zealous for religion.'[115] Accusing the Catholic clergy of being the true authors of the Brabant uprising, and horrified by the Brabant Patriots' subservience to the Church, aristocracy, and the old constitution, Paape urged all true *Patriotten* to support the *royalisten*.

Gerrit Paape who, early in 1788, published his *De Hollandsche wijsgeer in Braband* [Dutch philosopher in Brabant] emerged not just as one of the most unsympathetic observers of the Brabant revolution, but also among the most insistent on the need for genuine democratic revolutions dedicated to furthering what he called 'the happiness and freedom of peoples', something he argued which is not and cannot

---

[112] Démeunier, *L'Amérique indépendante*, 1, list of subscribers; Gorman, *America and Belgium*, 254–5.
[113] Paape, *Hollandsche wijsgeer in Braband*, iv. 114, 116.
[114] Ibid. i. 15, 16–18, 51–3, 71.
[115] Ibid. iv. 75.

be made by the people but only by 'philosophy'. How could a real democratic movement be generated in the Austrian Netherlands moving along similar lines to the revolutions in the Dutch Republic and France? Of the Patriots in exile, no other declared so insistently that 'philosophy' was the sole active agent capable of eventually reforming south Netherlands society. That human beings eke out their lives mostly immersed in contradiction, false loyalties, and credulity, he suggested, is the saddest of circumstances. Flanders and Brabant demonstrated what no one capable of interpreting social facts correctly could deny, that 'philosophy' alone, and the spread of wisdom and science that generates it, held out any promise of the sort of general reformation of society capable of delivering a better order and enabling individuals to break free of the shackles binding them, so as to lead happier lives.[116] As 'reason is natural' in man, what Brussels and Antwerp proved, in Paape's opinion, was that 'reason' can be suppressed but only by going about it assiduously with great art and cunning for centuries, as the Catholic clergy had in the southern Netherlands.

Despite strong popular support, the Brabant 'revolution' was never secure. The threat of being overrun by French revolutionaries allied to Vonckists, Genevan exiles, and Dutch *Patriotten* was such that by early 1792, the provincial States, including the nobility, resolved to surrender their newly won, nowhere recognized independence; reaffirming their loyalty to Vienna, they agreed to resume cooperation with the new emperor, on a compromise basis. Following complex negotiations and increasingly profuse assertions of their adoration of monarchy, the States voted him the taxes they had refused his brother in exchange for full restoration of privileges, ecclesiastical property, and historic 'rights'.[117]

---

[116] Paape, *Hollandsche wijsgeer in Vrankrijk*, 142–3.
[117] *Venise et la Révolution*, 717–18; Roegiers and Van Sas, 'Revolutie', 235.

33

The Dutch Democratic Revolution of the 1780s

1. HOW TO MAKE DEMOCRACY

The American Revolution was not the only major Western democratic republican revolution to precede the French Revolution. Though largely forgotten by modern international historiography, the Dutch democratic revolution of the 1780s too is of surpassing significance for the history of modernity in the West. In America, explained William Godwin, early in 1787, 'a valuable experiment is now carrying on for the vindication of the character of republicanism; and it is extremely to be desired, that it may have a happy and a favourable issue. But the experiment in Holland is little less entitled to our attention; and it is by no means accompanied with the same degree of uncertainty and hazard.'[1] Erroneously, as it turned out, he thought the Dutch venture the more certain to succeed.

By early 1787, Europe's first ever popularly acclaimed democratic republic seemed virtually secured. Community councils and people's committees had arisen all over the United Provinces and largely taken over control of the country from the stadholder and traditional urban oligarchies. 'In a word, the banner of liberty that is now unfurled from the walls of Utrecht', declared Godwin, 'demands the benediction of every friend to mankind, and the cause of the democracy of Holland needs only be to be understood, in order to its being consecrated to perpetual veneration.' The Dutch context indeed looked crucial for what the radical-minded, like Godwin, seemed to promise the rest of Europe and the world: 'thus a new republic of the purest kind is about to spring up in Europe and the flame of liberty which was first excited in America, and has since communicated itself in a manner more or less perfect to so many other countries, bids fair for the production of consequences, not less extensive than salutary.'[2]

Elie Luzac (1721–96), pillar of the moderate Enlightenment in the Netherlands, and a champion of the Orangist cause, was equally inclined to regard the Patriot

---

[1] [Godwin], *History of the Internal Affairs*, 342–3.
[2] Ibid. 344–5; Locke, *Fantasy*, 26; St Clair, *The Godwins*, 40.

revolution of the 1780s as a movement seeking to replace the Dutch *ancien régime* with the new principles of equality, individual liberty and freedom of the press and to see the change as a product of 'philosophy'; and he too viewed it as essentially an international rather than specifically national phenomenon. Only he considered this as a development generally disastrous for the political and moral order.[3] A key question for the historian today is how far Luzac, who combined admiration for Wolffianism as interpreted by Formey with an intense attachment to Locke, was right to see modern 'philosophy', that is materialist philosophy forged in France, as the primary shaping factor behind the foremost European democratic upsurge prior to the French Revolution.

The most striking feature of the *Patriottenbeweging* is what has been termed 'the energy with which relatively broad sections of the population began to discuss political issues and political principles'; even in remote villages and small towns ordinary people for the first time began to discuss politics in terms of abstract political principles and enlightened values.[4] This marked a huge transition in European history even if much of this discussion was neither original nor very sophisticated. At the same time, rejection of aristocracy and monarchy became explicit, emphatic, and uncompromising among a certain segment of publicists. For the ideological shift in the Netherlands in the mid 1780s was simultaneously a transition from a debate among entrenched elites to a debate among the public and a shift from justification by historical precedent and statute to justification by 'philosophy',[5] as part of which leading publicists encouraged Catholics and dissenters to criticize the shortcomings of the Dutch Revolt when examined with a 'philosophical' eye.[6]

Diderot, in his 'Voyage de Hollande' of 1773–4 and contributions to the *Histoire philosophique*, berated the Dutch for betraying the legacy of their Revolt and permitting their republic to degenerate into a form of government 'presque aristocratique' wholly inappropriate for the kind of society it had once been. Like Pilati, Mirabeau, and others, Diderot emphasized the ever more pervasive threat to liberty posed, as he saw it, by the stadholderate and Orangist court intrigues, echoing the worries of Dutch republicans at the time concerning the marriage in Berlin, in October 1767, of the prince of Orange, Willem V, to Princess Sophia Wilhelmina of Prussia, Frederick the Great's niece, and sister to the next in line to the Prussian throne. For this marriage, avidly sought by the stadholder, the republican-minded saw as a major potential threat to the 'bonheur général' of the people, strengthening the House of Orange and, via the duchy of Cleves, the westernmost part of Prussia directly adjoining the Netherlands geographically, providing an easy bridge for Prussian troops to enter the Republic.[7] Prussia had no strategic interests in common with

[3] Velema, 'Verlichting', 49, 51–2.

[4] Kossmann, '1787: The Collapse', 7.

[5] Leeb, *Ideological Origins*, 226; Velema, 'Jonathan Israel', 152, 154, 156; Israel, 'Toleration, Spinoza's "Realism"', 164–6.

[6] Klein, *Patriots republikanisme*, 256–8.

[7] Diderot, 'Voyage de Hollande', 390–1; Velema, *Republicans*, 17, 19–21.

the Republic, indeed no interests in common with the Dutch of any sort; yet dynastic links and court intrigue were now in a position decisively to shape affairs in the Netherlands.

The true interest of the Dutch was to stay as close as they could to a 'pure démocratie' and this they had failed to do.[8] By supporting the Orangist cause in the revolution of 1747–8 and expanding the stadholder's power, the common people had, in Diderot's eyes, forsaken the values their forefathers fought for. They were preparing for their country's reversion to monarchy, aristocracy, and subservience to Prussia and Britain, basely permitting their society with its celebrated freedoms to fall again under the 'joug du pouvoir arbitraire', a charge later regurgitated, in February 1784, almost word for word by the Amsterdam lawyer Irhoven van Dam, one of the most radical of the Dutch Patriot writers.[9] The bones of their ancestors were crying out, protested Diderot, asking whether they had reddened the seas with their blood for the princes of Orange.[10]

Diderot was right both about the overall prosperity of Holland and the exceptional spread of its wealth across society. 'Holland, in proportion to the extent of the land and the number of its inhabitants', noted Adam Smith, in 1776, was 'by far the richest country in Europe',[11] even though it had lost much of its economic dynamism by 1780 and was saddled with a failed colonial system. It was also the most highly literate society in the world. Diderot got to know his main counterfoil, Hemsterhuis, probably at the Russian envoy, Prince Golitsyn, residence at the centre of The Hague where he lodged through most of his stay. Hemsterhuis asked Diderot to respond to his latest book and Diderot produced detailed marginal notes rejecting all his moral and metaphysical arguments, eventually amounting virtually to a small book in reply.[12] Neither thinker then or subsequently yielded any ground. While liking his person and respecting his integrity, Hemsterhuis rejected Diderot's philosophy and loathed his (and the *Histoire philosophique*'s) interpretation of Dutch history, society, and culture.[13]

Later, in the early 1780s, he set out his own political views in his *Réflexions sur la République des Provinces-Unies*, acknowledging that republics have their advantages but also seeing great danger in taking man as the measure in politics and legislation. Diderot was idealizing society and the individual in a manner liable to prove disastrous. Hemsterhuis did not believe democracy can nurture either a stable or free republic.[14] Individuals are created by a great and wise God but society is the work of imperfect and short-sighted men.[15] In a republic like the United Provinces, a hereditary monarchical element was required, in Hemsterhuis's view, to lend stability and buttress the social hierarchy. Morality is not something that can be formed by

---

[8] Diderot, 'Voyage de Hollande', 391; Strugnell, *Diderot's Politics*, 190–1.
[9] Irhoven van Dam, *Courier*, 1/48 (17 Feb. 1784), 189.
[10] Dulac, 'Modes', 132.   [11] Smith, *Wealth of Nations*, i. 379.
[12] Diderot, *Commentaire*, 5–6.   [13] Trousson, *Denis Diderot*, 519.
[14] Loos, 'Politik und Gesellschaft', 464.   [15] Ibid. 461.

society. In the rising tide of the Dutch, French, and American democratic movements, Hemsterhuis saw scant promise of future well-being or true renewal. What
especially distressed him was the hatred and fanaticism that during the 1780s seemed
to spur both sides in the Dutch struggle on to ever greater strife and confrontation.
The local victories of the new democratic civic militia, or *free corps*, in Amsterdam
and elsewhere by the mid 1780s presaged, he thought, only crass demagoguery. Many
Patriotten seemed willing to achieve their ends through violence, something that
appalled him. He was much relieved, in 1787, when the Prussian troops marched in
to crush the agitation and ideological fermentation and restore the stadholderate.

Prior to 1784–5, the ideology of the *Patriottenbeweging* was only to a limited extent
a product of Enlightenment thought. Its language and ideology were still chiefly
drawn from the past, justification being sought in terms of what were claimed to be
the true principles of the Revolt against Spain and episodes of the Republic's
seventeenth-century history, especially the so-called First Stadholderless period
(1650–72) when the country was run in a self-consciously republican, anti-Orangist
mode by Johan de Witt and the Holland regents. In *Aan het Volk van Nederland*, the
electrifying booklet of September 1781 with which Joan Derk Van der Capellen
(1741–84) started the Patriot movement, there was only one truly novel element:
the elevation of the 'people', in a far more emphatic way than in the past, as the chief
source of legitimacy in politics.

The limited role of Enlightenment concepts in the pre-1784 ideology of the
Patriottenbeweging is clearly illustrated by the most substantial Patriot publication
of the movement's opening phase, the two-volume *Grondwettige Herstelling* [Con-
stitutional Restoration] of 1784. This work, published anonymously, was compiled
by several leading Patriots, including Van der Capellen. Claiming the Republic's
institutions were in a state of dangerous decay, needing urgent, thoroughgoing
remedial action, it urges the 'people' to undertake this restoration with the help of
the civic militias and the 'good regents'. The basic elements of this restoration were
still primarily those of the existing commonwealth, those of the Revolt against Spain
and Union of Utrecht which, according to these authors, had always been a *Volksregeering* [popular government].[16] Arming the respectable citizenry to resemble the
American militias was proclaimed the right way to compel the stadholder and
provincial States to respect the ordinary burgher's rights while simultaneously
keeping the ignorant and undisciplined mob in order.[17] The work's arguments and
justifications were anchored in precedent and alleged privileges secured in the past.
The *Grondwettige Herstelling* advocates the sovereignty of the people in general terms
but continued to envisage future Dutch government functioning on the basis of
existing, historically grounded institutions, with a reformed regent elite remaining in
charge.

[16] Gobbers, *Rousseau in Holland*, 224; Leeb, *Ideological Origins*, 205–6.
[17] Leeb, *Ideological Origins*, 189–92.

Even this much, though, elicited a fierce reaction from conservative circles. Incensed by the *Grondwettige Herstelling*, the Leiden professor Adriaan Kluit, an Orangist and prominent opponent of democracy and, later, human rights doctrines, published a hard-hitting reply, entitled 'The sovereignty of the States of Holland defended against the modern doctrine of people's government' (1785).[18] The whole point about the Republic's constitution, held Kluit, is that sovereignty does not lie with the people. The 'pernicious philosophy' spread about by the likes of Rousseau, Paine, and Price holding that the people are the true sovereign is totally rejected in favour of what Kluit considered the invaluable insights of Grotius, Pufendorf, Coccejus, Huber, Thomasius, and other theorists who stress the strictly institutional character of sovereignty.[19] In his *Academische Redevoering* published at Leiden in 1787, Kluit was bitterly to lament what he decried as the pervasive, insidious, and thoroughly dangerous influence of Rousseau, Raynal, Mably, Price, and 'the Americans' in the Dutch Republic.[20]

Traditional perspectives receded during the mid 1780s. The early Patriot revival of traditional, historically based Dutch republicanism gave way from 1784 to a 'philosophical republicanism' based on the idea of representative democracy. It was not just the 'despotism or unbearable rule of a hateful aristocracy, but equally', as Irhoven van Dam put it, 'the unruliness of an unlimited and incorrectly instituted democracy that we must avoid'.[21] It was a rhetoric that penetrated widely and became part not so much of popular awareness but of that of the active leadership imbued with enthusiasm for the American Revolution. It was a discourse chiefly forged, though, by paper editors and other leaders of opinion, hardened ideologues such as Paulus, Schimmelpenninck, Irhoven van Dam, Paape, Vreede, Cerisier, and Fijnje drawing their principles from French 'philosophy' and also from British radical thought— Paine, Price, and Priestley—rather than from American example or constitutions.[22]

Those who adopted an Orangist, pro-British attitude adhered to an anti-democratic rationale of the type developed by Luzac, Van Goens, de Pinto, Kluit, and Hemsterhuis and, with time, mostly retreated from their former enlightened commitments. For Orangism was intensely conservative in its aims and increasingly hard to reconcile with any species of reformism. This became especially apparent after the Patriot defeat in 1787, when the stadholder took to relying on three main strategies to consolidate his triumph—popular Orangism, the Orangist court bureaucracy, and close alliance with Britain and Prussia. The 'sound philosophy of the Patriots' William V defeated, according to Paape, by mobilizing the uneducated mob, bribing office-holders with favours, and plying a 'Machiavellian statecraft' subservient to London, all three the methods of an unscrupulous, oligarchic, and aristocratic court politics.[23]

---

[18] Palmer, *Age*, i. 331; Klein, *Patriots republikanisme*, 208–9.
[19] Klein, *Patriots republikanisme*, 47, 209; Kluit, *Academische Redevoering*, 27–8.
[20] Kluit, *Academische Redevoering*, 90 n., 93 n.; Van der Wall, 'Geen natie', 50; Van Vliet, *Elie Luzac*, 399–400.
[21] Irhoven van Dam, *Courier*, 1 /17 (31 Oct. 1783), 65.
[22] Velema, 'Anti-monarchism', 24–5.
[23] Ibid. 35, 102, 113–18.

Admittedly, neither side was anything like a monolithic bloc. Most popular support for the *Patriotten* was scarcely more intellectually aware or Enlightenment oriented than popular Orangism. Most Patriot sympathizers, according to Paape, supported the Patriot leaders only because *Patriottismus* was a protest movement decrying the stadholder and urban regents, and in the case of the many non-Reformed people supporting the *Patriottenbeweging*, also against the Reformed Church. Many supported it simply because it was a campaign against the high bureaucracy and *gens en place*, the 'Aristocraaten',[24] or because it promised equal rights to Catholics and Protestant dissenters. But whether they supported the movement for this or that reason, or opposed Patriot ideology altogether, as the least literate sections of the urban population generally did, few grasped how Patriot principles and priorities came together to form an intellectual system. The conventional *Patriottismus* of the fatherland-loving masses, stressed Paape, was a 'fantastic thing', containing so many internal 'contradictions and strange, unexpected and false conclusions' that it was quite impossible to describe it as a coherent set of ideas. Like all modern revolutionary ideologies, Dutch democratic sentiment in the 1780s and 1790s should be studied as a social movement insofar as it was widely diffused and politically potent but on a second level as an intellectual phenomenon specific, coherent, and precise among a small group of leaders and journalists. Those who edited the opposition newssheets, and delivered the principal speeches at its meetings, were those who developed its core ideas.

There is no contradiction, therefore, in describing the Dutch democratic revolutionary movement of the 1780s as a mass movement among which advanced Enlightenment ideas had barely diffused among the rank and file while, at the same time, treating it as a highly sophisticated and abstract philosophical system rooted in complex arguments and debates—often in French, Latin, English, or German rather than Dutch—fully accessible only to a tiny number of persons. In this respect, French revolutionary ideology as it erupted in 1788–9 was not very different; the bulk of its supporters had little gasp of its meaning or intellectual content. All modern revolutionary movements based on complex ideologies have, in this regard, been alike. Like major technological changes, a modern ideology can have a profound significance for millions by answering to powerful social pressures and needs, while, at the same time, being understood and fully absorbed by only a tiny handful.

Paape's perspective, much like Irhoven's, accorded a crucial role in society and politics to the 'wijsgeer', the 'philosopher', 'philosophy' being one of the most vital terms of their discourse. The aim of 'philosophy' was to combine the advancement of individual happiness with pursuing 'the happiness and freedom of the peoples'. If Nature created man 'with the aim of leading him to the height of all happiness', the

---

[24] Paape, *Onverbloemde geschiedenis*, 37, 45–6, 51.

true philosophy or *la philosophie moderne* teaches the philosopher to gear his life to the happiness of the people and balance self-interest against the general interest, repudiating all superstition, striving for a society 'waar het algemeen welzijn de wet steld' [where the general well-being lays down the law].[25] Unlike Irhoven, Paape provides no more than the barest hint as to the intellectual sources of 'philosophy', but this is because its intellectual origins are less important to him than its cogency and practical, social orientation, hence its relevance to concrete problems. Among the works conducive to humanity's enlightenment, he lists Locke's political treatises, Montesquieu's *L'Esprit des loix*, and Rousseau's *Contrat social*, a work in which 'humanity discovered its own worth and every citizen read with rapture that he was free and equal with all other mortals'.[26] Mably he thought came among the foremost for having 'vigorously and earnestly rebuked the French for their weaknesses and shortcomings, and summoned them to seek' what he calls, using a Dutch Golden Age term, 'de ware Vrijheid' [the true freedom].[27]

Radiating from Utrecht, by 1785, the Patriot movement had become sufficiently broad-based and democratic in discourse to be fairly termed the world's first modern, ideologically based, democratic revolutionary movement. The 'Leidse Ontwerp' [Leiden Draft], was the first recognizably democratic draft constitution for the United Provinces. It was composed by out-and-out republicans—Wybo Fijnje (1750–1809), Pieter Vreede, Schimmelpenninck, and Cerisier—and intensively debated (but not formally adopted) in October 1785 by the first general convention of representatives of Holland's new burgher militias.[28] This document, calling for 'eene waare representative Democratie' [a true representative democracy], flatly denies the States-General were sovereign, claiming that the regents were merely 'representatives' of the people and that the citizenry's basic rights rested not on precedent but on 'reason'.[29] 'True republican freedom' now meant that laws must have the people's consent. The *Ontwerp* reflects the rapid forging of Europe's new democratic rhetoric and in spreading the use of the new rhetoric of 'anti-aristocracy' used earlier in Switzerland but not yet widely adopted elsewhere. Proclaiming 'freedom' an inalienable 'right' of the citizens, despite its having in practice been continually infringed not just by the stadholder but by his accomplices, an 'illegal aristocratic cabal', the *Ontwerp* denounces 'domineering aristocrats' as the people's main enemy.[30] This useful term, 'de Aristocratie', comprised the prince's entourage, all Orangist regents, high office-holders associated with the court, and also the VOC directors; in fact the entire ruling elite were collectively labelled 'Aristokraten' and foes of the people.[31]

---

[25] Paape, *Hollandsche wijsgeer in Braband*, iv. 45–6; Paape, *Mijne vrolijke wijsgeerte*, 11–12; Altena, 'Ondankbaar vaderland', 168–80. [26] Paape, *Mijn Tegenwoordig Vaderland*, ii. 137–8.

[27] Ibid. iii. 138.

[28] Van Sas, 'Patriot Revolution'; Rosendaal, *Bataven!*, 518–19, 110; Klein, *Patriots republikanisme*, 250–2. [29] *Ontwerp om de Republiek*, 15, 49, 62–8; 'Demofilus', *Zakboek*, 20–1.

[30] *Ontwerp om de Republiek*, 33, 62–8.

[31] Ibid. 35, 47, 61; 'Demofilus', *Zakboek*, 21, 35–6, 40–51; Irhoven van Dam, *Courier*, 2/9 (1 Oct. 1784), 35, and 2/16 (26 Oct. 1784), 61.

Cerisier, Fijnje, Vreede, Irhoven van Dam, and also Paape all figured prominently among those responsible for this polarizing new discourse.[32] The fiercest 'anti-aristocratic' tract, entitled *De Adel* (1786), published under the pseudonym 'Anonimus Belga', was the work of Petrus de Wakker van Zon (1758–1818), a close ally of Irhoven. Partly influenced by Rousseau, it mounts an uncompromising attack on the principle as well as consequences of 'aristocracy'.[33]

Abhorring the mistakes of the past, leading Patriot publicists, most emphatically Irhoven, the fondest of quoting Raynal (and Diderot) as well as Mably, Cerisier, Priestley, and Price, deemed tradition and Dutch history useless as guides for making a true democratic republic and recapturing the people's rights and freedom. Only 'philosophy' can lead men to 'love of man and the people's liberty'.[34] In Irhoven, already in 1783, we find the concept 'onweesgerige' [unphilosophical] being used to mean undemocratic, intolerant, and allied with monarchy, aristocracy, and the clergy and the notion, prompted by Mably, that if the citizens are only shown 'the path of truth they will follow it without repugnance'.[35] Among the principal leaders, 'true Patriotism', or as Paape later called it, 'philosophische Patriottismus', began to emerge in 1782–3. Its principal claims were ones no amount of precedent-seeking and searching in constitutional history could substantiate, explicable only in terms of Enlightenment concepts.

First, there was the principle that the prime legitimizing principle in society and politics should always be 'het algemeen belang' [the common good] understood in a purely secular sense to mean the interest of the majority, all being deemed equal. Secondly, there was the call to abolish all 'bad laws and customs, and especially those shown to be bad not only by reason and sound understanding but also experience', a criterion which for 'philosophical' Patriots meant abolishing practically the entire existing structure of law. Thirdly, there was a need for a broader, more genuine toleration. Fourthly, there was the new discourse of *anti-Aristocratie*, consciously arousing popular antagonism against entrenched elites, both 'autocrat and the aristocrat', that is against not just the stadholder but all the ruling elite and the *gens en place*, the beneficiaries of the existing system, the demolition of which was deemed essential to securing the people's freedom. Nothing was judged more crucial than this new ideology if the democrats were to prevent the 'aristocracy', whose designs were judged wholly incompatible with 'civil liberty', and preachers, groups both skilled at deceiving the ignorant ordinary burgher, regaining their ascendancy.[36]

The key ideologues, Paulus, Paape, Irhoven, Schimmelpeninck, Fijnje, Vreede, and Cerisier followed 'the great Rousseau', Mably, Paine, Priestley, and Price, in

---

[32] 'Demofilus', *Zakboek*, 12, 21, 27, 31, 35–6; Klein, *Patriots republikanisme*, 232–6, 251.
[33] Gobbers, *Rousseau in Holland*, 231, 234, 242; Rosendaal, *Bataven!*, 248; Velema, *Republicans*, 110–11.
[34] Irhhoven van Dam, *Courier*, 1/79 (4 June 1784), 313; Paape, *Leven van zijne Doorluchtigste*, 167–8.
[35] Irhhoven van Dam, *Courier*, 1/19 (7 Nov. 1783), 78, and 1/24 (5 Nov. 1783), 93.
[36] Paape, *Aristocraat en de Burger*, 9, 23, 53, 55; Israel, 'Gerrit Paape', 21.

upholding 'equality' as the foremost principle of an enlightened politics and were frequently critical, like all radical writers, of British 'mixed monarchy'.[37] Equally, Dutch Patriot ideologues concurred in rejecting Montesquieu's principle that different forms of government fit different societies according to their particular 'mœurs'; indeed, towards Montesquieu there was a growing aversion among some Patriot publicists, reflecting the great Frenchman's antipathy towards the Republic, preference for constitutional monarchy, accommodation of aristocracy, and praise of Britain, all of which lent themselves more readily to Luzac's, Kluit's, and Hemsterhuis's perspectives than democratic ideology.[38] Even so, Montesquieu remained basic fare for all and was as frequently discussed in Patriot texts as Rousseau, Mably, Raynal, Priestley, and Price.

Rutger Jan Schimmelpenninck (1761–1825), a gifted young lawyer of Mennonite background, from Deventer, was a well-read Patriot theorist who later became the last Grand Pensionary of the Batavian Republic (1805–6). In 1784, he published, first in Latin and then, the following year, in Dutch, his intensely republican *Verhandeling over eene wel ingerichte volksregeering* [Treatise Concerning a Well-Constituted People's Regime], a text using both French and British radical republican theory but with the former predominating.[39] His guiding idea is that representative democracy, through regular elections, is the correct way to extend democratic principles to medium-sized and large countries, or complex societies with a federal tradition, such as the United Provinces. This doctrine, unsurprisingly, was taken up by Schimmelpenninck in the context of criticism of Rousseau with a degree of insistence almost unparalleled in the Europe of the mid 1780s.[40]

Schimmelpenninck admired Machiavelli, and through Dutch translations was familiar with the constitutions of the new American states. But the main theoretical influences on his democratic ideology derived from Rousseau, Mably, Montesquieu, Diderot, and Raynal.[41] He translates and highlights Rousseau's claim in the *Contrat social* that the 'sovereign power of the people cannot be represented for the same reason that it cannot be alienated'; but, like Paulus later, rejects this, along with Price's and Priestley's somewhat equivocal qualifications of it, insisting on the distinction between *opperste magt* (majestas) [sovereign power] 'and the *opperste bewind* (summum imperium)' [executive power]. He agrees the people's sovereign power can never be alienated, much less irrevocably surrendered, but insists the executive power can be entrusted to delegates chosen from among the people provided this is done through the mechanism of democratic elections.[42] The ruling assembly should not proclaim laws in the name of the assembly itself, like the British Parliament, but in the name of the people as a whole. The power to frame laws must

---

[37] Schimmelpenninck, *Verhandeling*, 35–6, 50–1.
[38] Velema, 'Elie Luzac and the Two Dutch Revolutions', 143–4; Van Vliet, *Elie Luzac*, 337–9.
[39] Leeb, *Ideological Origins*, 182 n.; Klein, *Patriots republikanisme*, 193.
[40] Schimmelpenninck, *Verhandeling*, 4–5.
[41] Kluit, *Akademische Redevoering*, 90 n., 93 n.
[42] Schimmelpenninck, *Verhandeling*, 6–7, 35; Klein, *Patriots republikanisme*, 222.

be entrusted to an elected assembly; but the power and right to make laws ultimately rests not with the assembly but the people, and representatives cannot legitimately retain power against the people's will.

The power to proclaim laws in the name of the people derives, he argues, not from any contract or agreement between society and the executive but from the agreement each burgher has made with his fellow citizens by which he promises to subordinate his own to the common will of his fellow citizens.[43] Quoting from Dutch translations of the constitutions of Pennsylvania, Georgia, South Carolina, Massachusetts, New York, and also Mably's analysis of these, Schimmelpenninck considers how best to organize democratic elections for legislative assemblies. Should the voting, as some think, be secret in order to protect the individual's freedom? He thinks so but others argue, he notes citing a passage of Mably, that by stipulating an open declaration of votes, individuals will be less likely to vote according to personal whims or biases, or opt for unsuitable candidates.[44]

Schimmelpenninck's doctrine that democratic republicanism is the most natural, rational, and fitting form of government for humans was supported by both invoking and criticizing Rousseau and citing Raynal, Diderot, and Mably.[45] Crucial to this kind of democratic republic, he argues, is that the citizenry should possess sufficient awareness of politics 'to be able to judge fittingly over the *gemeenebest* [common good]'. 'Those who have sunk into poverty' must be excluded from electing high office-holders, he argues, as they can easily be corrupted and 'also out of fear of their all too great ignorance'. However, he urged granting the suffrage to all who are householders or owned any land. 'One should assert as a firm rule that the level of ownership of property required for eligibility to vote should be so moderate that only the lowest stratum of the common people is excluded while those of the people who are of middling standing should be given the right to vote.'[46]

The revolutionary democratic movement in the Netherlands reached its climax during the spring and summer of 1787. After a faction of the old Amsterdam regents tried and failed to concert with the stadholder and mobilize Orangist mobs against the Patriots there, the Patriot clubs organized a huge popular demonstration that filled Dam square and adopted a petition demanding a purge of the city government. This was followed by a local coup bringing Amsterdam under firm Patriot control. At Rotterdam, Paulus and his supporters seized the town hall, in August, while Fijnje and Paape led the coup that secured Delft. Leiden, Dordrecht, and other towns similarly fell into Patriot hands. On the other hand, at Arnhem, Zutphen, and elsewhere in the east, Orangists tightened their grip and the Free Corps were vigorously suppressed. All the provinces remained deeply divided and despite vigorous support for both opposing factions there was also uncertainty, drift, and pessimism.

---

[43] Schimmelpenninck, *Verhandeling*, 7–8.   [44] Ibid. 12–13.
[45] Ibid. 54–5.   [46] Ibid. 22.

2. LIBERATION MOVEMENT IN EXILE

By the summer of 1787 the country was openly divided, clearly on the brink of civil war, albeit the Orangists lacked the resources to halt the democratic revolution on their own. The new Prussian monarch, Friedrich Wilhelm II (1786–97), meanwhile, a declared foe of all Enlightenment and the stadholder's brother-in-law, decided to intervene. When his sister Wilhelmina was detained by the Gouda Free Corps near Schoonhoven, in June 1787, he declared the incident an insult to the House of Hohenzollern and began amassing troops. To hold France back, Britain threatened to go to war in support of Prussia and the stadholder. In September 1787, a Prussian army of 26,000 men invaded marching in two columns towards The Hague and Amsterdam. The Patriot revolution simply disintegrated without significant resistance. The prince of Orange returned to The Hague in triumph, his restoration accompanied by a barrage of anti-Patriot theorizing, in which prominently featured Kluit's *Academische Redevoering over het misbruik van 't algemeen Staatsrecht* (Leiden, 1787) loudly denouncing equality, democratic ideas, and democracy as a sure recipe for anarchy.[47]

Hemsterhuis's relief at the Anglo-Prussian suppression of the democratic movement was certainly shared by many Dutchmen. On 8 March 1788, the prince's birthday was celebrated as never before, jubilant crowds expressing their joy with illuminations, street decorations, fireworks, music, and dancing at the defeat and scattering of the democratic party.[48] Sporting orange emblems and denouncing Patriot emblems became *de rigueur* for everyone wishing to avoid being beaten up or thrown into a canal. Equally, though, many deeply resented what had happened. To stifle opposition and protest, a full-scale counter-revolution was put in motion for the first time in Europe, something of crucial importance both for its symbolism and ideological significance and because, perhaps more than any other factor, this explains the scale of the Patriot flight to France and Flanders.

The Dutch press was placed under new restrictions, political meetings forbidden, and the Free Corps and Patriot clubs dissolved. The city councils were subjected to a thorough purge of Patriot sympathizers far more extensive than the Orangists had carried out in 1672–3 or 1747–8.[49] The old-style militia companies, purged of anti-Orangists, were restored. Likewise, all the universities were purged.[50] For months there was also considerable continuing disorder with Orangist mobs—and sometimes Prussian troops—attacking and pillaging homes of leading Patriots, especially in Rotterdam, Amsterdam, and the Hague, but also elsewhere.[51] Known Patriot sympathizers were still being affronted in the streets months after the invasion. This and court-initiated legal proceedings against Patriot leaders caused a large number, several thousand Patriots, fearing for their safety, families, and property,

---

[47] Kluit, *Academische Redevoering*, 32, 44–5, 76–9.   [48] Ibid. 455.
[49] Ibid. 62–3; Rosendaal, *Bataven!*, 47–8.   [50] Van Eijnatten, *Opklaring*, 16.
[51] Rosendaal, *Bataven!*, 44–6, 543; Rosendaal, *Nederlandse Revolutie*, 56–60.

to cross into the Austrian Netherlands. This vigorous reaction was certainly a major factor sustaining the democratic movement in exile after 1787. So many were stripped of their positions and status, so many shocked by the scale of the repression, that Orangism for many discredited itself through a process of overreach, a tactical error counter-revolution and Counter-Enlightenment repeated many times subsequently.

The *Patriottenbeweging*'s collapse was spectacular. But so was the Patriot exodus and setback to French prestige. Despite the country's financial crisis, part of the ministry at Versailles, led by the naval minister, the Marquis de Castries, a protégé of Marie Antoinette, viewed the Dutch debacle as so serious a setback for France that restoring the Patriot alliance and rendering it militarily effective by land, sea, and in the colonial sphere came to be considered by these ministers the monarchy's foremost concern abroad.[52] No sooner were they established in France and Flanders than the Patriots began to revive their activities. Aided by Mirabeau and La Fayette, Cerisier, who settled in Paris in October 1787, and other Patriot leaders in France obtained financial support for the refugee community and other concessions. Cerisier resumed his journalistic career and, early in 1788, joined Brissot, Condorcet, Clavière, and Mirabeau in the society Les Amis des Noirs.[53] Assisted in settling their families, the refugees were also granted full freedom of religious practice by a royal edict issued at Versailles in November 1787, the exiles being assigned several churches in Dunkirk and nearby places besides legal recognition for their marriages and property.[54] Where the Republic had become a client state of Britain and Prussia, the Dutch democratic revolution in this way became a client of the French absolutist crown during the last two years of its existence (1787–9).[55]

Predictably, Patriot ideology gained in intensity in exile. 'When one looks', Paape later remarked, after returning to Holland following the Batavian Revolution of 1795, 'at the matter with hindsight, one can say that by pursuing the *Patriotten*, and forcing them to flee, the Prince of Orange merely sent them to the high school of *Patriotismus* and revolution.'[56] In exile, they hoped for their eventual return and in the meantime willingly allied with the democratic cause elsewhere, basking in the moral support of French and British radicals like Mirabeau, Paine, and Godwin. Despite being riddled with feuds caused by personal animosities, differences over whom to blame for the disaster of 1787, and quarrels over scarce financial resources, the Patriot colonies in France succeeded in establishing entrenched democratic revolutionary cells. At Saint-Omer, a group headed by Valckenaer emerged as a particularly lively and, after 1789, pro-revolutionary formation that eventually affiliated with the Jacobin club in Paris.[57] At Brussels, from 1789, Irhoven and others actively colluded with the French revolutionaries in secret.

[52] Price, *Preserving the Monarchy*, 67–8, 214.
[53] Rosendaal, *Bataven!*, 242; Rosendaal, *Nederlandse Revolutie*, 76, 82, 186–7.
[54] Paape, *Hollandsche wijsgeer in Braband*, i. 54–5, 61.
[55] Palmer, *Age*, i. 340.
[56] Quoted in Altena, 'Ondankbaar vaderland', 180.
[57] Gobbers, *Rousseau in Holland*, 240; Rosendaal, *Bataven!*, 583.

As matters turned out, this embryonic liberation movement in exile was to have highly significant implications for the further diffusion of *la philosophie* and democratic revolutionary ideology, as well as for the prospects for the wider democratic revolution in Europe. According to Mirabeau, who compiled the famous protest counter-blast *Aux Bataves sur le stadholderat* (1788) with a team of associate writers, notably Cerisier, Brissot, and Dumont-Pigalle, and which reappeared almost at once in a Dutch translation, prepared at Antwerp by Paape, all Europe's peoples mourned the Patriot defeat. Only Europe's princely courts rejoiced in the stadholder's restoration. Whatever the truth of that, Mirabeau, Brissot, and Cerisier were right to stress the French and wider European significance of the exodus of several thousand politically highly motivated refugees who had lost all for the moment but had every intention of regaining their possessions, standing, and influence and teaching their persecutors a lesson.

In 1787–8, Mirabeau's main object was to integrate the cause of the Dutch Patriots, as he had earlier that of the Geneva revolutionaries of 1782, into that of the French democratic ideologues which he now proclaimed the general cause of humanity. The suppression of the *Patriottenbeweging*, styled by Mirabeau in *Aux Bataves* an 'odieuse révolution', had, he predicted, little chance of succeeding in the long run. The Patriots had stumbled 'dans la cause de l'humanité, de la raison, de la justice' but they were not beaten yet and would never be.[58] Praising Van der Capellen in particular, Mirabeau in this way joined hands ideologically with the Patriot publicists in a booklet that was reissued several times and had a greater European impact than any text of the Dutch Patriots themselves. 'Tous les hommes sont nés libres et égaux.'[59] Men being equal and free by the intention of nature, they are further rendered equal by the primitive avowal underlying all societies; for in constituting a primitive society each individual equally gives up the same portion of his own liberty. But this reduced liberty will soon disappear entirely in societies where men fail to make freedom and equality the continual object of their efforts. Government is instituted for the happiness of the people and the people has the inalienable and absolute right to reform, correct, or totally change its government 'lorsque son bonheur l'exige'.[60] In fact, a people cannot conserve a free government except via constant and firm adherence to the rules of justice, moderation, virtue, economy, 'et par un recours fréquent à ses principes fondamentaux' where necessary by force of arms.[61]

Denunciation of Britain at this point emerged as a key component of both Dutch and French revolutionary democratic ideology. The English were culpable for their oppression of others, their systematic 'brigandage' around the world, being a nation that persecutes 'la liberté' everywhere as if it were a rival. Thankfully, that people's 'féroce patriotisme' was counterbalanced by the 'sublime philanthropie' of a few

---

[58] Mirabeau, *Aux Bataves*, 2. [59] Ibid. 117; Rosendaal, *Bataven!*, 245; Velema, *Republicans*, 21.
[60] Mirabeau, *Aux Bataves*, 120. [61] Ibid. 127; Rosendaal, *Bataven!*, 244.

exceptional men, meaning Paine, Priestley, Price, and so forth. Mirabeau admired the 'illustrious citizens' of Britain, among whom, in the past, he had included Burke whose sentiments regarding America and India, he, like Cloots, had once approved. But Burke had taken anything but a supportive position with regard to the late 'revolution' in Holland. It is not for us, he advised his countrymen, to research into the legality of the government of this or that country. For the English it is enough 'de faire triompher le parti le plus favorable à nos intérêts'.[62] This Mirabeau considered abhorrent. Britain was no model for others. How can civil and political liberty be presided over by a hereditary monarch who distributes offices and pensions, by a hereditary nobility endowed with 'de grands privilèges', or a septennial Parliament to which non-existent towns are represented whilst many large towns are excluded? The British consider their institutions are the finest in the world. But what do they offer other nations? Despite the successes which have dazzled it, such a nation 'est plus digne de pitié que d'envie'.[63] When one thinks how Montesquieu and other philo- sophers have lauded the English constitution, deeming it 'le plus parfait modèle de la liberté civile et politique', exclaimed Mirabeau, one can only sigh for the human race.[64]

With the outbreak of 'a philosophical revolution',[65] as Paape terms it, in France, in 1789, the spirits of the Dutch Patriot exiles began to rise. Fortunately for Europe, exclaimed Paape, 'and to the honour of sound reasoning', the French took matters firmly in hand, resuming the fight against the sinister trinity of superstition, ignor- ance, and prejudice designed to deny peoples their happiness. What could be more impressive or pleasing than a land 'where the true freedom, sound philosophy, and the real good of the people is desired, supported and defended with the most perfect agreement'.[66] The French Paape and his colleagues came to see as 'a people that really dared render itself free and institute philosophical laws'. France, he wrote in 1790, was definitely a country where, 'judging by their writings and pronouncements', 'philosophy' had advanced further than among the Dutch or Flemish, a land where the preachers do not declaim so loudly 'tegen de gezonde Wijsgeerte' [against sound philosophy].[67]

[62] Mirabeau, *Aux Bataves*, 189.   [63] Ibid. 106.   [64] Ibid. 184–5, 211; Stone, *Genesis*, 143.
[65] Paape, *Mijn Tegenwoordig Vaderland*, iii. 161.   [66] Ibid. i. 2–3.
[67] Paape, *Hollandsche wijsgeer in Vrankrijk*, 261–2.

34

The French Revolution

From 'Philosophy' to Basic Human Rights (1788–1790)

1. FROM THE BASTILLE TO THE KING'S RETURN TO PARIS (JULY–OCTOBER 1789)

In a vote on 18 June, after a fiery three-day debate of deep significance, the Third Estate of the French Estates-General transformed itself into the 'National Assembly', at Sieyès's suggestion, by 491 votes to 90. This transformation which, under the terms of their commissions, the deputies had no right to vote for at all, and was rightly dubbed a 'usurpation' of power by Marmontel, entailed more than just a change of name and merging of three orders. No longer were the deputies mandated by or answerable to particular groups, vested interests, or defined entities. Henceforth, delegates were no longer representing particular communities, classes, or localities but were simply individual representatives of a people all deemed equal and equal in rights so that the representatives simply represented the *volonté générale* as a whole, a conception totally at odds with all known precedent, an obvious product of 'philosophie' justified in particular by Sieyès.[1]

This amounted to a thoroughgoing transformation in the nature of representation itself, from the *ancien régime* model to the Diderot–d'Holbachian model rooted in the (Spinozistic) principle—contrary to Hobbes—of natural freedom and equality carrying over into and being reconfigured in society. The effect, noted Marmontel, was virtually to create 'une démocratie armée', an armed democracy sporting a fig-leaf of monarchy, run by a tiny clique, 'la faction républicaine', led by Mirabeau and Sieyès who were in effect a new kind of 'corps aristocratique' only one of 'philosophy' instead of one of birth, pedigree, wealth, or social status.

For the moment, the Assembly remained at Versailles, still acknowledging the king's veto in theory while an emergency committee took over the administration of

---

[1] Marmontel, *Mémoires*, iii. 213, 228; Halevi, 'Révolution constituante', 74–5, 81.

Paris. But no one knew whether the king and court had genuinely acquiesced in the changes thus far or were merely engaging in a tactical deception in preparation for a counter-coup. Several royal regiments were brought up to the city's environs. If the much rumoured royalist conspiracy was real (probably the king had no intention of bombarding Paris), it was poorly executed. But Mirabeau and the National Assembly were certainly deeply alarmed by 8 July and Paris so tense the situation degenerated into the storming of the Bastille on the 14th. Immediately afterwards, the contingents of the royal army lately brought up withdrew, demoralized, from the scene. The king entered Paris in person, on 17 July, with a small entourage of officers and, in an extraordinary ceremony interpreted by most as one of 'contrition', participated in a deeply symbolic official consecration of the Bastille's storming as a liberation from 'despotism'.[2] Reconciling himself to the changes in Paris, Louis approved the replacement of royal troops with the new city militia (National Guard) and appointment of Bailly as the new mayor while the astronomer warmly welcomed the king, pinning a tricolour cockade to his hat. From this point on Louis was deeply distrusted by a great many, and by no means only hard-core revolutionaries.

Jean-Sylvain Bailly (1736–93), a well-meaning but rather timid man, according to Mounier, was a *philosophe* much resented by Mesmer enthusiasts for his part in the Académie des Sciences' condemnation of Mesmerism as superstitious and un-philosophical.[3] An ally of Delisle de Sales (who delivered a public homage to him, after the Terror, in 1796), and former protégé of Buffon, as an enlightener he enjoyed a European reputation, though Catherine the Great, having earlier authorized presentation to him, via Grimm, of a splendid honorific medal portraying her, on hearing of his new role as revolutionary leader waxed so indignant she immediately cancelled the award. The first academician since Fontenelle simultaneously (from 1784) to belong to the Académie Française, Académie des Inscriptions, and Académie des Sciences, Bailly was a long-standing critic of the *ancien régime* and privilege, albeit no outright republican but a reforming monarchist swept along (eventually to his downfall) by popular acclaim.[4]

The Bastille's fall was followed by weeks of widespread rural unrest in several regions, involving attacks on noble chateaux and, in some areas, extensive murder and pillage. According to the Venetian ambassador, reporting to Venice on 17 August, by then around fifty noble chateaux had been pillaged, some torched, in the Dauphiné alone.[5] The Assembly repeatedly expressed outrage over the violence and dismay at the anarchic conditions. But, as one observer put it, having established itself as the voice of government through the people, the Assembly had no way of controlling the people and especially not the peasants.[6] The violence and

---

[2] Hardman, *Louis XVI*, 105–8; Lüsebrink and Reichardt, *Bastille*, 39, 46.

[3] Bergasse, *Considérations*, 19, 27.

[4] 'Vie de Sylvain Bailly', in Bailly, *Œuvres posthumes*, pp. xii–xiii, xxxi, xlii–xliii; Mounier, *De l'influence*, 103–4; Lortholary, *Mirage russe*, 259.

[5] Fontana, *Venise et la Révolution*, 320.

[6] Dumont, *Souvenirs de Mirabeau*, 94–5.

accompanying outbreak of panic prompted the first wave of noble emigration. Many nobles from affected areas including a considerable batch of famous families—the Condés, Contis, Polignac, and Breteuil from the environs of the capital—departed for the eastern frontier.[7]

But it was not the rural violence but the Bastille's fall, withdrawal of royal troops, and emergence of an orchestrated revolutionary press and street campaign in Paris that were the levers of the basic shift of power from crown to National Assembly and to the opinion-formers in Paris closely tied to the dominant clique in the Assembly. Economic conditions, meanwhile, dramatically deteriorated, especially in Paris where the shortages and high cost of food grew worse as the months passed, owing precisely to the flight of thousands of noblemen and their families and the consequent redundancy of tens of thousands of domestics, cooks, coachmen, tailors, and servants. The city's foremost industry, the luxury trades, came to a virtual standstill. Widening hardship then in turn intensified the combined air of desperation and expectancy.

But unemployment and shortages notwithstanding, the general mood in the cities remained broadly euphoric. Most former procedures, practices, and fixed boundaries rapidly lost all meaning and crumbled away. The result was a 'revolution' of the press, theatre, and culture generally, the espousal of complete press freedom being a topic much discussed in the Assembly in late July.[8] In this heady atmosphere, just a few days after the Bastille's fall, Louis-Marie Prudhomme and Antoine Tournon set up their soon famous illustrated revolutionary journal, the *Révolutions de Paris*. Other enterprising editors rapidly followed suit, setting up a whole array of new journals, Brissot inaugurating his *Le Patriote français* on 28 July. Its main aim, he declared, was to spread the enlightened ideas or 'Lumières' needed to 'prepare a nation to receive a free constitution'. A key journalist and local politician rallying opinion in 1789, Brissot rapidly turned his paper into a major vehicle of radical influence in Paris.[9]

The psychological impact of the Bastille and its aftermath had, as is well known, a profound influence on the course of the Revolution and cultural life of the nation. Much less well known is its equally profound intellectual and ideological impact. For these events forced a basic and soon irrevocable split between the rival wings of the Enlightenment in their attitude to the Revolution. There were noticeable differences of emphasis already before July 1789. Yet, until then, enlightened opinion, noted the Abbé Morellet, had remained fairly broadly united: liberty, toleration, 'l'horreur du despotisme et de la superstition, le désir dé voir réformer les abus' had long been, after all, common ground for all enlighteners ranging from Voltaire to liberal monarchists and *parlementaires* like Mounier and Portalis.[10] All this changed in

[7] Furet, *Revolutionary France*, 69.
[8] Brissot, *Patriote français*, 1 (28 July 1789), 1; Granié, *L'Assemblée*, 61; Andries, 'Imprimeurs', 248.
[9] [Prudhomme and Tournon], *Révolutions de Paris*, 8 (29 Aug./4 Sept. 1789), 26; de Luna, 'Dean Street Style', 172, 176.
[10] Morellet, *Mémoires*, i. 381.

July, however, as emotions ran high and the issue of equality became more central. Where Naigeon (with whom Morellet had bitterly clashed in the past) was among the 'most zealous partisans' of equality and the early Revolution, a fervent *révolutionnaire*, as he expressed it later himself,[11] conservative sceptics like Morellet and Suard, nurturing aristocratic and moderate royalist views, began quietly opposing the popular cause. So did Marmontel who rapidly recoiled from the sweeping changes proposed. These men rejected the Revolution on principle and soon felt obliged to withdraw from earnest conversation with their former friends into a brooding silence.[12]

Five days after the storming the Bastille, the Paris theatre world began to seethe with its own internal drama. The noted young playwright and publicist Marie-Joseph Chénier, an energetic and able demagogue, brother of the poet André Chénier, appealed to the Comédie Française's actors to stage his newly completed and extremely daring anti-monarchical play *Charles IX*, a drama designed to prove royal censorship had now lapsed completely and, in particular, inspire hatred of 'les préjugés, le fanaticisme et la tyrannie' as well as of civil war.[13] Most of the actors, accustomed to royal censorship and being directed by the court, not playwrights or the public, refused. Chénier then began to agitate publicly, his friends even interrupting an evening performance at the Théâtre Français demanding that *Charles IX* be staged for the public good. He was backed by both the *Révolutions de Paris* and *Le Patriote français*, creating a furore that soon led to the new municipality intervening. The result was that the play was performed against the wishes of the theatre personnel and actors, on 4 November 1789, with Mirabeau and Danton, among others, attending. It ran for several months over the winter of 1789–90, inaugurating a fresh era in theatre history characterized (until Napoleon) by a whole new rhetoric of revolutionary values and close alignment with 'philosophy'.[14]

Among Madame Helvétius's circle gathering regularly at her mansion in the village of Auteuil-Passy situated between the Seine and the Bois de Boulogne, the drama played itself out in microcosm. Among her household and salon, her particular favourite, Cabanis, was closely linked not only with Mirabeau but, according to Morellet, also several other deputies 'des plus violens'. Cabanis and the rest supported, indeed positively exulted over, the peasant risings and attacks on noble property. Those who were most euphoric were those *réformateurs* driven by *l'ambition démocratique* to embrace radical positions—Morellet names in particular Sieyès, Volney, and the aphorist Nicolas Chamfort (1741–94), an ardent anti-aristocrat close to Mirabeau and neighbour of Madame Helvétius, member of the Académie

[11] Naigeon, *Lettre du citoyen*, 2, 7.
[12] Garat, *Mémoires historiques*, ii. 315, 354, 365–6; Pellerin, 'Naigeon', 32; Mortier, 'Les Héritiers', 457–9.
[13] Schama, *Citizens*, 495; Friedland, *Political Actors*, 260–9.
[14] [Prudhomme and Tournon], *Révolutions de Paris*, 5 (16/22 Aug. 1789), 26; Brissot, *Patriote français*, 19 (18 Aug. 1789), 1; Lichtenberg, *Schriften und Briefe*, i. 700; Graczyk, 'Théâtre', 399.

Française since 1781 as well as associate of the *philosophes*, an enthusiast for the principles of the Revolution who, in October 1789, actively supported the legislative assault on church property. Chamfort likewise held Sieyès in high esteem and, when not airing his zeal for sweeping change in the cafés, stands, and corridors of the Palais Royal, figured prominently at Auteuil.[15]

Cabanis, in whose native region, the Bas-Limousin, serious disorder had broken out, found himself nearby on the day of the Bastille and at Versailles the next, passionately conferring with comrades, especially Volney and Garat. Dominique-Joseph Garat (1749–1833), who came from near Bayonne, was another typical *philosophe-révolutionnaire*, one of those generating the 'Revolution of reason' who drew a sharp and explicit distinction between Rousseau's *volonté générale* which he totally rejected and representative democracy in the mould of Diderot and d'Holbach which he and his associates embraced.[16] Not long afterwards, Cabanis joined Mirabeau's team of researchers, journalists, and speech-writers. Cabanis, Garat, and Madame Helvétius, and others of her entourage, were convinced of the truth, recalled Morellet later, of the early July rumours warning that king and princes were actively conspiring to cannonade Paris, reduce the capital to submission, and throttle the Revolution. Over such burning questions during the summer of 1789 the heirs of the *philosophes* irrevocably split.

By August, Morellet, horrified by the loss of the clergy's tithes and the nobles' privileges, openly repudiated the Revolution, breaking permanently with Madame Helvétius who, instead of staying neutral between the conflicting viewpoints as he implored, sided with Cabanis, Volney, Chamfort, and Mirabeau against himself.[17] Particularly galling for 'moderates', many of whom became more and more emphatically Anglophile in this heady atmosphere, was the promise, central to the constitutional rhetoric of Sieyès, Mirabeau, Volney, and Roederer, reports Dumont, to improve on England's performance and put matters right where the English and Americans, allegedly, had got them wrong.[18] Such talk was characteristic also of Brissot, Condorcet, Garat, and other spokesmen and publicists outside the Assembly but well placed to influence opinion in Paris via the municipality, clubs, and press pressure. The dominant group in the *philosophe-révolutionnaire* leadership wanted no vestiges of authentic monarchical power and influence in the new constitution and were really all veiled democratic republicans, wanting no constitutionally defined aristocratic, *parlementaire*, urban oligarchic, or ecclesiastical roles either. Condorcet urged that the pending new constitution should be ratified by the whole citizenry and publicly urged elimination of the principles of aristocracy and privilege. He also recommended setting up representative bodies for rural

---

[15] Marmontel, *Mémoires*, iii. 185, 187; Staum, *Cabanis*, 122–3; Arnauld, *Chamfort*, 151–2, 162–3, 166–75.
[16] Garat, *Mémoires historiques*, i. 195–7.
[17] Morellet, *Mémoires*, i. 387–8; Rials, *Déclaration*, 125.
[18] Dumont, *Souvenirs de Mirabeau*, 108.

communities to counterbalance the towns without permitting the formation of any kind of new landowning elite.[19]

The king had lost much ground politically and was never trusted again. He acquiesced for the most part but could not avoid showing his aversion to the revolutionary changes around him. Most of all he detested the 'metaphysical and philosophical government' and its manners, symbols, and uniforms he saw emerging everywhere,[20] and the vastly ambitious constitutional proposals, the founding documents of the Revolution, drawn up at Versailles at this juncture by the Assembly. Three crucial decrees especially stand out: the general abolition of feudal privileges of 4 August, Declaration of Rights of 27 August, and the edict on the royal veto. These resolutions framed in a few weeks after the Bastille were not the work of rioting peasants or the unemployed. Neither had they anything to do with merchants or business and not much with France's lawyers. Legal experience was irrelevant to an astounding extent. Sieyès's ally Pierre-Louis Roederer (1754–1835) was the only figure among the revolutionary leadership of 1789 with family links in business or industry but even he preferred spending his time reading rather than in commerce. These great changes were delivered not by business, finance, or lawyers but by intellectual leaders and journalists wholly unconnected with business and only marginally connected with the law, a small steering group orchestrating the majority in the National Assembly and Paris municipality through committees, clubs, papers, and street demonstrations.

That most of the Assembly had reached the point where no past or existing charter, institution, law, or precedent any longer looked valid was something without precedent in history and left foreign envoys in Paris aghast. It was one thing for Sieyès, 'perhaps the most resolutely philosophical of the major political actors of the French Revolution', to proclaim in print in November 1788 that all privileges are by definition an affront to the rights of the 'non-privilégiés'—the majority—urging their immediate extinction as something required by 'la philosophie', having already demanded this also in his *Que-ce que le Tiers État*?[21] But it was quite another for the National Assembly, willingly, confusedly, or unwillingly, to espouse such an unheard-of principle. Bad laws had corrupted society, urged Sieyès, and conspired 'contre la multitude'. Morals and the laws were all wrongly constituted.[22] This was the language of the radical *philosophes*. What was revolutionary and astounding was that the Assembly agreed.

Such radically enlightened resolutions were driven in part, of course, by fear and, for the rest, by the small *philosophique* minority mobilizing the Paris plebs against opponents in the Assembly. This was done by rallying opinion in the cafés around the Palais Royal, launching rumours, and mobilizing support in the streets. Although

[19] *Chronique de Paris*, 30 (22 Sept. 1789), 117; Mounier, *De l'influence*, 123.
[20] Harman, *Louis XVI*, 110.
[21] Sieyès, *Essai*, 5; Sieyès, *Qu'est-ce que le Tiers*, 175–6, 179–80; Sewell, *Rhetoric*, 28.
[22] Sieyès, *Essai*, 3, 9–10; Baker, 'Reason and Revolution', 86–7.

they were known to be a relatively small minority, nevertheless the 'parti de philosophie' in the Assembly achieved a powerful ascendancy over its proceedings,
especially by forming committees and dominating the debating clubs and reading
societies both in Paris and provincial centres.[23] On 4 August 1789, a majority of the
Assembly, including nobles and clergy, panicked by the attacks on aristocratic
chateaux in the provinces and news that the violence was spreading, voted in
principle to abolish all feudal dues and serfdom in France and suppress all provincial
privileges. Abolished also were many other noble 'rights', including hunting 'rights',
privileged access to military and civil posts, and special status before the law.
All remaining 'rights' were to be gradually eliminated by purchase. In one of
'philosophy's' greatest coups, all citizens, without distinction of birth, were proclaimed eligible for the first time in the world's history for all posts, positions, and
dignities. The entire system of status, exemptions, and special fiscal privileges,
including ecclesiastical immunities, thus came to an end. Sieyès's great principle
(drawn from Diderot), that all privileges are by the nature of things 'injustes, odieux,
et contradictoires à la fin suprême de toute société politique',[24] became the motive
spring of the Revolution.

Over the next week, it was further agreed that venality of judicial offices, a long
tradition in France, should end, all remaining vestiges of seigneurial jurisdiction be
quashed, and the ecclesiastical tithe suppressed without compensation.[25] Following
the 4 August decrees, the ancient privileges of the guilds and guild masters also
lapsed. The Assembly's minority of doctrinaire egalitarian virtual democrats, headed
by Mirabeau, Sieyès, and the group later known as the *Feuillants*, around Barnave,
pushed these momentous edicts through, taking advantage of the intimidated
state of the more conservative representatives and temporary paralysis of vested
interests.[26] Rather farcically in the circumstances, the Assembly, at the suggestion
of Trophime-Gérard Lally-Tolendal (1751–1830), eloquent orator, liberal noble, and
admirer of Voltaire, eager to retrieve what he could of the *ancien régime*, at the same
time awarded Louis XVI the title of 'Restaurateur de la Liberté Française', while the
archbishop of Paris sanctioned a special Te Deum to give thanks to the divinity for
the end of feudalism.[27]

Obliteration of feudalism came—at least in theory—as if in an instant, recorded
Bailly. The Assembly did more for the people in a few hours than the wisest, most
enlightened nations 'n'ont fait en plusieurs siècles'.[28] Nothing better proves that
government draws its power from public opinion, commented Brissot, than the
dramatic course of the Revolution in Paris.[29] Philosophy did the work and won

[23] [Prudhomme and Tournon], *Révolutions de Paris*, 5 (9/15 Aug. 1789), 27–9; Marmontel, *Mémoires*,
iii. 195; La Gorce, *Histoire religieuse*, i. 215–16; Whaley, *Radicals*, 22.

[24] Sieyès, *Essai*, 5; Forsyth, *Reason*, 64–8, 72–8.

[25] Mirabeau, *Courrier de Provence*, 23 (3/5 Aug. 1789), 24–8.

[26] Mackrell, *Attack*, 173–4; Sonnenscher, *Sans-Culottes*, 305.

[27] Bailly, *Mémoires*, ii. 266; Marmontel. *Mémoires*, iii. 308; Fontana, *Venise et la Révolution*, 320.

[28] Bailly, *Mémoires*, ii. 216.   [29] Brissot, *Patriote français*, 10 (7 Aug. 1789), 3.

over the public and no one, however prominent, could impede its progress or soften its impact. Even Sieyès, who attacked privilege and separate orders of society more incisively than anyone, could not. Construing the *ancien régime* as a product of 'l'empire de l'aristocratie, qui en France dispose de tout', he had long inveighed against the 'feudal' superstition that 'avilit encore la plupart des esprits'.[30] But he had always focused on the nobility without giving much thought to the clergy, though here too he favoured far-reaching reform reducing the ecclesiastical estate from a separate order to a much weakened and humbler professional grouping of salaried state servants. But he opposed one particular aspect of the proposed reforms— proceeding without compensation in abolishing tithes—considering this an unjustified despoliation of the clergy. This was his only caveat regarding the radical changes he did so much to initiate. But even this caused astonishment and outrage among sections of the Assembly, some deputies construing his reluctance as that of a priest unable to set aside his own group's special interest. Afterwards, while remaining a prominent figure in the Assembly, he never again possessed quite the same preeminence he enjoyed until early August.[31]

This effectively transferred command of the 'philosophical' steering group for the moment to Mirabeau, enabling him to broaden still further the attack on privilege, as he did in a fiery speech on 13 August. The deputies had legislated on the subject of 'priestly aristocrats', 'judicial aristocrats', and 'aristocrats' of the nobility, but not, as yet, on 'l'aristocratie municipale', the sitting oligarchies in the city councils. It was just as essential, held Mirabeau and Volney, to reform the municipalities, countering 'la corruption de l'aristocratie et du despotisme' in city government, as to eliminate other kinds of 'aristocracy'. Mirabeau and Volney urged the need to enlarge the councils, render them elective, representative, and accountable on a basis ensuring those elected would be men of talent and experience. The resulting decree stipulated that henceforth there must be the same ratio of municipal officers to population in all the municipalities and all must represent equivalent constituencies.[32] In Paris, the new city council of 300 represented sixty equal 'districts' into which the city was now divided, each having five representatives. To head the *assemblée* of Paris was an executive of sixty chosen by the 300. The districts also all had their own local committees representing local opinion. It was an arrangement designed to strengthen the people's voice which had the effect of according Paris a stronger say than anyone could foresee.

The next momentous step was the *Declaration of the Rights of Man and the Citizen*. In the historical literature, historians usually at this point hasten to reassure readers that most deputies knew nothing about, and had no interest in, 'philosophy'. This is true but also irrelevant as the *Declaration* was not made by 'most deputies', any more

---

[30] Sieyès, *Qu'est-ce que le Tiers*, 32; Baker, 'Reason and Revolution', 87; Sewell, *Rhetoric*, 58–63.
[31] Bailly, *Mémoires*, ii. 255–6, 275; Sewell, *Rhetoric*, 131–6.
[32] *Journal des décrets*, 5/10 (1789), 26; Brissot, *Patriote français*, 17 (15 Aug. 1789), 2, 5, and 18 (17 Aug. 1789), 1–3.

than by lawyers, businessmen, or public opinion. As with the other key edicts of 1789, it was framed via arduous debate by a tiny steering group of leading spokesmen, supported by journals like the *Révolutions de Paris*, Brissot's paper, and Mirabeau's *Courrier*, all of which were saturated in the philosophical terminology of the Radical Enlightenment judging the Rights of Man something established by *la philosophie*, not anyone's laws or charters, or any religion, and hence 'éternels, inaliénables, imprescriptibles'.[33] Contrary to what is sometimes claimed, France's existing culture of law and legal thinking had no input whatever.[34] It is quite wrong to suggest that there was any trace of legal discourse or experience in the debates which were exclusively *philosophique* in character and in the decisive closing stages led by Mirabeau and Sieyès, with Brissot and Condorcet actively participating via the Paris municipality, Condorcet being the latter's envoy to the Assembly at Versailles.[35] Condorcet had formulated his own first draft of a Declaration in June, having advocated the need for a philosophical Declaration of the inalienable 'rights' of Man well before 1788.[36] Other draft versions followed during early and mid August intensifying what since late July had developed into a complex and heated debate over the entire question of human rights and what it means to declare men to be born free and equal. Certainly, many and perhaps most deputies disliked the 'philosophy'; others were reluctant to pass any declaration before the terms of the future constitution itself had been agreed.

Hammered out in committee after numerous revisions and compromises, in which Sieyès and Mirabeau took the lead, the French *Declaration* was the product of debate at a high intellectual level. The American declaration, acknowledged Mirabeau, had set a crucial example, but he also criticized it. Since ignorance and 'error' were the chief reasons why basic human rights had been for so long trampled on everywhere what was really needed was a 'déclaration raisonnée', something clearer, more abstract and philosophical; something invoking 'plus hautement la raison' than the American declaration which had been written behind closed doors by a tiny committee. In the enlightened age in which they were living it especially behove France to present to the universe a new model, 'un code de raison et sagesse qui soit admiré et imité par les autres nations'.[37] Condorcet was even more dissatisfied with the American declaration and especially the Virginia state declaration of rights (1776) and those of six other American states he had studied, especially disliking their provision of taxes to support churches.

To the exasperation of many, the discussion continued for a whole month, turning the Assembly's debating chamber into what one observer called a Sorbonne student

---

[33] Mirabeau, *Courrier de Provence*, 22 (1/3 Aug. 1789), 13; [Prudhomme and Tournon], *Révolutions de Paris*, 6 (16/22 Aug. 1789), 36–7 and 7 (22/7 Aug. 1789), 38–41.

[34] Guilhaumou, *L'Avènement*, 120–2.

[35] Bailly, *Mémoires*, ii. 211; Dumont, *Souvenirs de Mirabeau*, 96–7; Williams, *Condorcet and Modernity*, 28–9; Baker, *Condorcet*, 265–8.

[36] Baker, *Condorcet*, 265.

[37] Dumont, *Souvenirs de Mirabeau*, 15–16; Baker, *Inventing the French Revolution*, 263–4.

class. For Sieyès, it was a key principle that all public authority and powers without exception 'sont une émanation de la volonté générale'.[38] His reasoning, as so often in his and Roederer's case, pivoted on the (Spinozist, unHobbesian) doctrine that on establishing society, men do not surrender their natural liberty and 'rights' but rather secure them on an equal basis protecting the weak from the strong and precluding all institutionalized subordination no matter how many royal edicts and charters claim the contrary.[39] Every citizen has a right equally to the common advantages that arise from the state of society, each seeking happiness in his own way. Sieyès's draft found many supporters but not enough to decide the issue. Rather the entire process became increasingly bogged down in disputes over words and 'metaphysical' battles. Sieyès's text, with its thirty-two articles reiterating that the law 'ne peut être que l'expression de la volonté générale', a will expressed by a body of representatives chosen for a 'short time' by the citizenry,[40] though acceptable in principle to Brissot, Rabaut de Saint-Étienne, another of the steering group, and the *Révolutions de Paris*, was also criticized by them as too long, too much of a 'thèse philosophique', 'trop métaphysique', and beyond most people's grasp.[41]

Others had much stronger objections. Marat both at the time and also later, after establishing his paper, protested against the 'spéculations métaphysiques' dominating the discussion, arguing for more direct democracy, wanting everything to be brought down to the level of the ordinary reader.[42] Lally-Tollendal, urging that all 'metaphysical ideas' be cast aside, thought the declaration should be based not on *la philosophie* or popular will but the English Bill of Rights of 1689, this being embedded in experience and social hierarchy. Like Lally-Tollendal, Mounier sought to subordinate every concession that had to be made to equality and democracy as much as possible to positive 'liberties' and laws. For most deputies, though, minimizing the philosophy and emulating Britain had the insuperable drawback of following a model that relied on supposed 'ancient rights and liberties' and was essentially aristocratic. Thwarted here, Lally and Mounier subsequently supported La Fayette's short, unpretentious, and relatively non-*philosophique*, American-style draft (in which Jefferson apparently had a hand).[43]

Until mid August rival leading texts from more than twenty different submissions were considered, the main contest being between Sieyès and Mounier. From 14 August, however, the debate took a different direction when, on the intervention of Démeunier, yet another *philosophe-révolutionnaire*, an anthropologist, writer on the Indies, and secretary to a count, a new committee was formed from which the authors of the twenty drafts under discussion were excluded, to fuse the best elements

[38] Sieyès, *Préliminaire*, 6–8.
[39] Ibid. 15; [Prudhomme and Tournon], *Révolutions de Paris*, 6 (16/22 Aug. 1789), 36.
[40] Sieyès, *Préliminaire*, 20, article no. xxvi.
[41] Brissot, *Patriote français*, 21 (20 Aug. 1789), 1; Rabaut de Saint-Étienne, *Projet*, pp. iv–v.
[42] Marat, *L'Ami du peuple*, 1: 1; Rials, *Déclaration*, 189–90.
[43] Mirabeau, *Courrier de Provence*, 29 (18/19 Aug. 1789), 7–8; Edelstein, *Terror*, 194.

of the versions into a final draft.[44] With Démeunier's backing, Mirabeau was able to seize the initiative in the proceedings. Assisted by his regular editorial team—the Swiss exiles, Duroveray, Clavière, and Dumont—Mirabeau captured the very essence of the Radical Enlightenment with his formula that the legislative and executive powers of government exist solely 'pour l'avantage de ceux qui sont gouvernés' and not for the advantage of those that govern. Mirabeau held that a people shaped by antisocial institutions and weaned on prejudices is incapable of adjusting to 'des principes philosophiques' in all their fullness and requires something simpler than Sieyès's draft.[45] His draft differed from that of Sieyès in some respects, especially in being much shorter and less systematic, but fundamentally was no less *philosophique,* something that disgusted Dumont who admired England and increasingly disliked his boss's philosophy. He later dismissed the *Déclaration* as a ridiculous 'mosaïque de prétendus droits éternels qui n'avaient jamais existé'.[46]

Typical of Mirabeau's doctrine and among his phrases adopted into the *Declaration*'s final version was his holding ignorance and 'le mépris des droits naturels inaliénables et sacrés des hommes' to be the cause of the misfortunes of peoples. Sieyès meanwhile produced a second, shorter draft but one that again built its doctrine of rights on a conception of human nature linked to popular sovereignty and the protective role of the state. Welcomed as more incisive than his first and more coherent than rival versions, this draft also met opposition on some points. The deputies bickered furiously over the precise terms. 'Philosophy' won many skirmishes but by no means all, being defeated not least over Articles 10 and 11 dealing with freedom of expression and religion, key clauses provoking fierce exchanges in the Assembly especially between the clergy and those Brissot designated followers of a 'philosophy' of gentleness and toleration. Vigorous demands for God's name and the Decalogue to figure in the preamble were hotly debated but rejected with Volney among those most vigorously opposed.[47] Equally, those demanding explicit recognition of the Catholic Church as the public church failed to get their way. But Mirabeau could not secure unqualified recognition of the liberty and equality of all religious cults that the radical leadership urged.[48] Dragging the Assembly's majority towards consistently 'philosophique' positions proved impossible. What some today and then consider explicit references to Rousseau but were actually standard references to *la philosophie moderne* were deleted, except from Article 6 opening with the doctrine that the 'law is the expression of the general will'.[49]

---

[44] Rials, *Déclaration*, 197–202.

[45] Ibid. 206.

[46] Dumont, *Souvenirs de Mirabeau*, 97; Baker, *Inventing the French Revolution*, 263–4, 272–3; Blamires, *French Revolution*, 144.

[47] [Prudhomme and Tournon], *Révolutions de Paris*, 6 (16/22 Aug. 1789), 36; Rials, *Déclaration*, 219, 226.

[48] [Prudhomme and Tournon], *Révolutions de Paris*, 7 (23/7 Aug. 1789), 38–41; *Mirabeau à la tribune*, i. 44–6.

[49] Mirabeau, *Courrier de Provence*, 30 (20/1 Aug. 1789), 16; Hunt, *Inventing Human Rights*, 221.

The final version of Article 11 adopts Mirabeau's phrase affirming the 'free communication of ideas and opinions is one of the most precious rights of man'. But his and Volney's efforts to ensure the law could never restrain freedom to speak, write, and print were overruled (rather ominously for the future). The final compromise version cobbled together in late August adds the proviso (also in Article 10) that with the freedom accorded the individual 'accepts responsibility for any abuse of this liberty set by the law'.[50] Everyone understood what this meant. Mirabeau publicly registered his 'pain' that the Assembly, instead of embracing unqualified toleration and stifling the germ of intolerance altogether, had, as it were, placed that 'germ' in reserve, keeping open the possibility of restoring the Church's authority at some later point, and this in a declaration of basic human rights. The addendum to the article, he pointed out, flagrantly contradicts Article 3 stating that nobody may 'exercise authority that does not emanate expressly from the nation'.[51] He and his colleagues were also defeated in the clashes over press freedom, being forced to concede the continued banning of 'mauvais livres'.[52]

Having mostly backed Mirabeau and Volney in these clashes, Brissot's *Patriote français* finally came out, albeit with some reservations, in favour of the revised Mirabeau draft. Agreement was little by little secured around his revisions. In one crucial vote, on 20 August, 620 deputies voted for Mirabeau's version, 220 for Sieyès's second draft, and, and despite Lally-Tolendal's eloquent pleas to the assembly to forsake 'philosophy', only 45 for that of La Fayette.[53] After several days more wrangling over several articles *The Declaration of the Rights of Man and the Citizen* was finally proclaimed on 27 August, its ringing phrases owing something to the American example but most to radical *philosophique* literature. The Assembly's *Declaration* clearly envisaged society's renewal on a completely fresh basis, not one supposedly inherent in the nation's legal past (as with the American declaration), something to be more exactly defined by the forthcoming constitution. Where the American declaration spoke of unalienable rights as something inherent in 'our constitution' and 'our laws' that had been infringed by the 'present king of Great Britain' but not necessarily past ones, the French declaration spoke of wholly natural rights that needed to be enshrined in laws yet to be made. Mirabeau, Condorcet, and Volney undoubtedly felt the Assembly had in some degree 'disfigured' the *Declaration*.[54] All the same, the final outcome was a stunning success for the *philosophes-révolutionnaires*. For the first time in history, freedom of thought and expression for everyone was enshrined as a basic principle and right of enlightened and morally justified human society, the very bedrock of democratic modernity was in place.

[50] Mirabeau, *Courrier de Provence*, 31 (22/3 Aug. 1789), 1, 40–5; Aston, *Religion*, 128.
[51] Mirabeau, *Courrier de Provence*, 31 (22/3 Aug. 1789), 44, 46; ibid. 32 (24/5 August 1789), 3; Forst, *Toleranz*, 452.
[52] Aston, *Religion*, 128.
[53] Mirabeau, *Courrier de Provence*, 22 (21 Aug. 1789), 2; Hunt, *Inventing Human Rights*, 16, 21, 220.
[54] Mirabeau, *Courrier de Provence*, 32 (24/5 August 1789), 1–3; Condorcet, *Œuvres*, ix. 166–8.

On precisely this ground, the *Declaration* was full-frontally attacked in France and right across Europe. Its basic principles were contradicted and condemned by Pope Pius VI in 1791.[55] But much liberal, moderate enlightened opinion criticized it severely too, Madame de Staël, for instance, later dismissed it as too apt for 'dangerous interpretation'.[56] A famous champion of toleration in France and prominent lawyer, Jean-Étienne Portalis (1746–1807), considered the *Declaration* a disaster, a device for fomenting despotism and totally contrary to every tradition of French law, fomenting 'idées bien exagérées de liberté et d'égalité'.[57] Abroad, the first to denounce its principles publicly, publishing in the *Berlinische Monatsschrift*, with Biester's encouragement, was Justus Möser who at this point opened up a remarkable split in German thought and culture no less than between German and French 'philosophy'.[58] Men are truly equal, retorted Möser, denouncing the Assembly's abolition of feudal rights and jurisdiction, only in a Christian sense, spiritually. Nowhere are they or should they be considered equal in worldly status or civil rights.

Several commentators, including Eberhard, in his *Philosophisches Magazin*, disagreed, endorsing the concept of fundamental human rights based on equality and freedom of expression both as a general principle and as expressed in the French *Declaration*.[59] An even more robust reply to Möser, 'Gibt es wirklich Rechte der Menschheit?'[Are there really Human Rights?], appeared in Eberhard's *Philosophisches Magazin*, composed by the ardent Spinozist Knoblauch.[60] 'The great inequality of force [among men] and consequent insecurity among the weak this creates,' he argued, reiterating a key Spinozist argument, 'drives people to form a state whose force, resulting from the uniting of many individual capacities and individual interests, then becomes a purposely directed power' providing security and stability for all 'and protecting the weak against the usurpations of the strong'.[61] Equality not only exists but is a universal principle, the most crucial of all political and legal concepts. What do not exist, retorted Knoblauch, are 'rights' conceived as concessions granted as privileges by rulers, lawyers, priests, or any authority. Human rights exist everywhere, universally and without reference to any authority.

Passage of the *Declaration*, a manifesto totally incompatible with an *ancien régime* society of orders, spurred the social ferment in the country imparting a new impulse to the revolutionary *esprit* as a reforming force also in other contexts. At its first meeting since the Bastille's fall, on 23 August 1789, the Société des Amis des Noirs, with Condorcet presiding, underlined the challenge implicit in the *Declaration*, issuing a public summons for an immediate end to the slave trade and for existing

[55] Rials, *Déclaration*, 21–6; Taylor, *Secular Age*, 413–14, 570.
[56] De Staël, *Considerations*, 184.
[57] Portalis, *De l'usage*, ii. 387.
[58] Möser, 'Ueber das Recht der Menschheit', *Berlinische Monatsschrift*, 18 (July–Dec. 1790), 396–401, 499–506; Knudsen, *Justus Möser*, 168–71; Godechot, *Counter-Revolution*, 108.
[59] Eberhard, *Philosophisches Magazin*, 3 (1790/1), 377–96; Dippel, *Germany*, 166.
[60] Knoblauch, 'Gibt es wirklich Rechte der Menschheit?', *Philosophisches Magazin*, 4 (1791/2), 424–46.
[61] Ibid. 441–2.

slaves to be treated better, a summons reissued in Canada by the *Gazette de Montréal*, edited by Fleury Mesplet (1734–94), a printer, originally from Lyon, with marked radical leanings, the first real representative of radical ideas in Canada, and a journalist who had propagandized on behalf of the American rebels in Canada in 1774–6, and been imprisoned by the British.[62] In Canada, there were around 300 black slaves at the time and the French landowners, with the agreement of the British authorities, were solidly in favour of retaining black slavery.

As yet, there could be no immediate end to slavery itself, explained the Société, because existing slaves were not yet sufficiently 'mature'. They needed first to be prepared for their emancipation but emancipation must come.[63] Further declarations issued by Condorcet, as president, in late November and early December, rebutted hostile rumours spread by Caribbean planters, claiming the society's supposedly ill-considered intentions would recklessly foment chaos in the colonies. The society would first end the slave trade and only later seek to abolish slavery itself, something it intended to do in stages to avoid ruining the colonies economically. Meanwhile, the first priority was to ensure the free blacks and mulattos of Martinique, Guadaloupe, Saint-Domingue, and the other Caribbean colonies secured representation with their own deputies in the National Assembly.[64] There was in fact a small group of mulattos already in Paris who in the early weeks of 1790 were encouraged to organize and invoke the 'droits de l'humanité' precisely by the heads of the group of Assembly deputies accused by moderates and conservatives of being driven by 'la philosophie' or what one commentator called the 'devouring zeal' of a *philosophie théorique* completely ignorant of the realities of the Caribbean.[65]

Emancipating the slaves in the French West Indies was still some way off, but already in the late summer and autumn of 1789 erupted a major, widely publicized debate engendering furious splits within the Assembly due to the strength of commercial interest in Nantes and Bordeaux and the countervailing efforts of the Caribbean planters. A mediocre novel entitled *Le Nègre comme il y a peu de blancs* appeared at this point, the *Chronique de Paris* commenting, in October 1789, that the author aimed to help transform the way people think about blacks, inculcate love and esteem for them, and restore their virtues to them in the eyes of whites. These aims the *Chronique* pronounced excellent, echoing what 'des philosophes éloquens et sensibles' have said in defence of the blacks.[66] Another text, a play about a fictional conspiracy of blacks and Indians to expel the English from Barbados and emancipate the slaves, entitled *Les Esclaves*, reviewed in January 1790, was again pronounced dismal literature but infused by admirable ideals plainly inspired by the *Histoire philosophique*. The piece also proved that, under the new freedom of the theatre, the

[62] Lagrave, *Fleury Mesplet*, 350–2.
[63] Brissot, *Patriote français*, 24 (24 Aug. 1789), 4; Thomas, *Slave Trade*, 520.
[64] Brissot, *Patriote français*, 115 (1 Dec. 1789), 4, and 117 (3 Dec. 1789), 2.
[65] Granié, *L'Assemblée*, 120.
[66] *Chronique de Paris*, 1/48 (10 Oct. 1789), 234.

Paris stage no longer served the cause of 'corruption' but rather that of 'la réforma-tion publique'.[67] In Paris, reportedly, in early March 1790, the French aristocratic exiles seeking refuge in Berne and other Swiss oligarchies drew more hope and consolation from the Assembly's and Paris press's fierce divisions over black eman-cipation than anything else.[68] Certain 'aristocrats' were reportedly delighted at the prospect that the Assembly would soon emancipate the blacks, as this, they thought, would infallibly cause the French colonies to secede, Bordeaux and Nantes to revolt, civil war to ensue, and the Revolution finally to be crushed.

Part of the *Declaration*'s purpose, plainly, was to provide prior justification for a forthcoming constitution drawing legitimacy from abstract principles alone and not any existing laws, charters, or constitution. Should the steering group succeed with their constitutional plans nothing would remain of a society of orders. The Assembly bloc most vigorously opposing their scheme were the so-called *parti anglais*, led by Mounier and Lally-Tolendal, the first 'a serious dry politician' who detested 'abstract propositions', according to Gibbon (he dined with both of them agreeably at Lau-sanne, later that year, after they fled revolutionary France), the latter 'an amiable man of the world and a poet'.[69] They advocated a constitutional monarchy organized on bi-cameral lines with a royal veto over legislation and the king free to choose his ministers, as in England. This group were forever invoking Montesquieu, the phil-osopher most often attacked by Sieyès, and enjoyed extensive support in the Assem-bly until their decisive defeats in September. Among their allies was Nicolas Bergasse (1750–1832), a famous enemy of *la philosophie moderne* scorned by Cloots as an admirer of Mesmer as well as ardent Rousseauiste.[70] The climax of the struggle between the *parti anglais* and the 'party of philosophy', as Roederer termed the leading group, centred around the issues of the royal veto and bi-cameralism.

Mounier and Bergasse strongly advocated bi-cameralism, Bergasse having publicly argued for a two-chamber system since before the Estates-General's convening, although he preferred a non-aristocratic upper chamber while Mounier eulogized Britain's House of Lords, deeming it the indispensable intermediary between crown and Commons. Mounier urged France to emulate Britain also in this respect even though, he added derisively, a hereditary chamber at first glance shocks 'les notions philosophiques'.[71] But that, he contended, was precisely its strength, the French people and their representatives being far too attentive to *philosophes* with imprac-tical notions leading to fundamentally wrong decisions and damagingly discrediting the once immensely prestigious British constitutional, legal, and social model. It was of paramount importance that the French learn to turn their backs on 'philosophy'

---

[67] Ibid. 2/15 (15 Jan. 1790), 57.
[68] Ibid. 2/69 (10 Mar. 1790), 274.
[69] Gibbon, *Memoirs*, 237.
[70] Bergasse, *Considérations*, 19; Mortier, *Anarcharsis Cloots*, 157, 186; Pasquino, 'Nicolas Bergasse', 81–2.
[71] *Chronique de Paris*, 9 (1 Sept. 1789), 33; *Lettre à Monsieur Raynal* (Mar. 1789), 4, 11.

and espouse political wisdom born of experience.[72] Self-proclaimed champion of 'moderation', Mounier, unlike Brissot, Volney, and Mirabeau, also eulogized the American state constitutions which, he thought, sensibly followed British practice except for Pennsylvania, the (then) constitution of which with its single chamber he dismissed as forged 'par des idées trop abstraites et métaphysiques'.[73]

Mounier demanded a British-style mixed monarchy with clear separation of powers,[74] underpinned by Montesquieu's doctrines; but his arguments stood little chance of winning politically since they pivoted on handing back to the nobility a share in power they had long possessed but had now already lost.[75] Though influential and powerfully backed by moderate Enlightenment opinion abroad, most obviously Schlözer at Göttingen,[76] the *monarchiens* were quickly routed in the Assembly. Already in his tracts of 1788, Sieyès dismisses admiration of the English constitution as a crass state of mind appealing to those who disdain 'la philosophie' and like waffling about 'experience' but which actually served only the interests of the crown and nobility.[77] Britain's constitution could hardly sustain impartial examination on the basis 'du véritable ordre politique', being the product of mere contingency and circumstances. The Assembly alone reflects the will of the nation, the task of the executive, he argued, being to carry out not obstruct the people's will. Sieyès remained adamant in deriving his principles from recent *philosophique* (and physiocratic) literature as a rational guide, deeming this wholly superior to history, foreign models, or experience.[78]

Condorcet, in fact, did favour a bi-cameral arrangement, provided the upper house did not resemble the House of Lords but consisted of 'hommes éclairés' distinguished for intellectual abilities and with only a limited veto over the main Assembly's resolutions.[79] A large majority, though, followed Sieyès and Mirabeau in rejecting bi-cameralist solutions. On 10 September 1789, the Assembly voted by 849 to 89 votes that the new constitution should stipulate one assembly, not two.[80] Meanwhile, the royal veto was also considered indispensable in a veritable mixed monarchy by the 'parti anglais' and here support for moderate thinking was strong. The *monarchiens* urged an absolute veto. Barnave favoured the so-called 'sanction limitée' or suspensive—in effect temporary—veto and this became the cry of the majority.[81] On 15 September, the suspensive veto passed by 673 votes to 352 with Sieyès and Rabaut among the latter.[82] The royal veto debate stands out as among the most crucial episodes of the early part of the Revolution for being the first

---

[72] Mounier, *Considérations*, 44–6; Schama, *Citizens*, 443.
[73] Mounier, *Considérations*, 42; Baker, *Inventing the French Revolution*, 260, 281–2.
[74] Mounier, *Considérations*, 23, 28; Mounier, *De l'influence*, 5.
[75] Sieyès, *Qu'est-ce que le Tiers*, 96; Furet, *Revolutionary France*, 76; Pasquino, *Sieyès*, 27.
[76] Van Horn Melton, 'Enlightenment to Revolution', 121–2.
[77] Sieyès, *Qu'est-ce que le Tiers*, 96–7; Quiviger, 'Sieyès', 134; Doyle, *Aristocracy*, 219.
[78] Forsyth, *Reason*, 21.   [79] *Chronique de Paris*, 10 (2 Sept. 1789), 37–8.
[80] Ibid. 19 (11 Sept. 1789), 75.   [81] Ibid. 2: 331–2.   [82] Doyle, *Oxford History*, 120.

'constitutional' controversy in which the Paris populace not only took more than a passive interest but reversed a decision of the Assembly.[83]

Sieyès working with Brissot, editor of the *Patriote français* and one of the chief stirrers of political emotion in Paris, was firmly against allowing any form of veto to remain in the king's hands, and this position was vigorously supported in Paris. The *Révolutions de Paris* recounts how Brissot and other organizers of Paris political opinion orchestrated outside pressure on the *Assemblée* against those (including Mirabeau) trying to preserve an element of effective monarchy by retaining a royal *véto suspensif* over legislation.[84] The way to drive the Revolution forward, urged Brissot, Chénier, and other key publicists outside, was to advance the cause of *la philosophie* as a form of external pressure exploiting to the full the possibilities offered by liberty of thought, speech, the press, theatre, clubs, and the right to gather and demonstrate. In 1789–90, these men publicly judged everything good or bad not on the basis of precedent, experience, interest, or religion but solely according to whether or not it was 'vraiment philosophique'. The success of this strategy forced liberal, anti-aristocratic clergy seeking to ally with the democrats in the Assembly to adopt their terminology, hoping it was a coherent stance. They too now openly proclaimed, as the Abbé Fauchet notably did in his *Second Discours sur la liberté française* delivered at the church of Sainte Marguerite, Faubourg Saint Antoine, on 31 August 1789, that true religion is that which is fully reconciled and united with *la philosophie*.[85]

A very common error among historians interpreting the veto episode, repeated by Furet and Baker, is that in insisting on the unitary character of sovereignty, repeating the phrase 'volonté générale', and appealing to Parisians to intervene in the debate, the leaders of the Assembly minority and newspaper editors supporting them were following or using the doctrines of Rousseau. Furet in fact gets everything doubly confused by also suggesting that the stress on the unity of sovereignty was an unfortunate carry-over of the pre-1789 absolutist, monarchical mentality.[86] In reality, nothing was carried over from before 1789 and Sieyès was always inflexibly anti-Rousseauist as well as anti-absolutist; and Brissot frequently was. In trumpeting their *volonté générale*, they, like Mirabeau, were simply following the radical tendency, the term being a collage of Rousseau, Mably, Raynal, Diderot, d'Holbach, and Helvétius. The Assembly minority that followed them consisted of a tiny batch of *philosophes-révolutionnaires* and a wider coalition merely recognizing that the royal veto's keenest supporters were exactly the same persons who had most obstinately resisted merging the three orders into one single assembly, in June, and supported monarchy and aristocracy in some degree throughout.

[83] Ibid. 120–1; Dumont, *Souvenirs de Mirabeau*, 101, 104; Bailly, *Mémoires*, ii. 326–7, 345.
[84] [Prudhomme and Tournon], *Révolutions de Paris*, 8 (29 Aug./4 Sept. 1789), 25–6.
[85] *Chronique de Paris*, 29 (21 Sept. 1789), 113; Dawson, *Gods of Revolution*, 57, 68.
[86] Furet, *Revolutionary France*, 76–8; Baker, *Inventing the French Revolution*, 274.

What is true, though, is that in mobilizing popular pressure against the majority, the Assembly minority established a dangerous precedent and momentarily found themselves aligned with Marat's new paper, *L'Ami du peuple*. A new note of illiberal extremism, extraneous to the proceedings thus far, was introduced by this new revolutionary paper first established in mid September. Denouncing the 'criminal project' of 'les classes privilégiées' in terms of unparalleled stridency, Marat demanded the 'aristocratic party' be eliminated altogether from the Assembly.[87] He was right, granted the minority faction around Sieyès, to attack the 'corrupt faction' of *monarchiens* seeking to dominate the Assembly but should do so 'avec modération'. This, complained Marat, was like putting a soldier on trial for fighting his hardest against perfidious enemies.[88] In his issue of 28 September 1789, he broadened his denunciation to the bankers and financiers 'who build their fortunes on the ruin of others'.[89] His relentless militancy, populism, and anti-intellectualism concocted what became a regular complaint in certain quarters, that the revolutionary leadership were insincere in proclaiming their egalitarian principles. Bailly and others he denounced for presenting themselves as 'bons patriotes' whilst actually seeking connections and pensions at court.[90] Annoyance at Marat's setting himself up as a public censor, fiery verbal assaults on individuals, and inciting fear with his unrelenting denunciations of secret betrayals and court *pensionnaires*, and repeated calls for purges of the Assembly and its committees, provoked efforts to obstruct publication of his journal.[91]

These failed thanks to the intervention of Brissot among others and freedom of the press continued (until the autumn of 1792); Madame de Staël's claim that the years 1789–91 in France were a time when French society was 'allowed, freely and unequivocally, the liberty of the press', though challenged by some historians, broadly held true.[92] But the difficulty of containing virulent, uncompromising, and divisive extremism and the predominance at crucial moments of the Paris streets proved irresolvable. Slowly, support grew for Marat's view that it is not 'philosophy' but the people's will and direct popular sovereignty that constitutes the true criterion of legitimacy. 'It is public opinion alone that can make laws,' insisted sympathizers later prominent in the Jacobin Club.[93] Marat's hectoring, with its unrelenting stress on 'morality', 'virtue', and the ordinary man's feelings, created a powerful underlying tension that would one day be exploited by the *Robespierristes* to derail the Revolution of Reason as a whole.

---

[87] Marat, *L'Ami du peuple*, 12 (22 Sept. 1789), 107–8, and 13 (23 Sept. 1789), 114–15; Sa'adah, *Shaping of Liberal Politics*, 119.

[88] Marat, *L'Ami du peuple*, 13 (23 Sept. 1789), 114; Baczko, 'The Terror', 24.

[89] Marat, *L'Ami du peuple*, 20 (28 Sept. 1789), 170–1.

[90] Ibid. 20 (29 Sept. 1789), 174; Dawson, *Gods of Revolution*, 64–5.

[91] Marat, *L'Ami du peuple*, 19 (28 Sept. 1789), 165–6; Baczko, 'The Terror', 31–2; Guilhamou, *L'Avènement*, 135–6; Andries, 'Imprimeurs', 252.

[92] De Staël, *Considerations*, 194; Walton, *Policing*, 5–6; Whaley, *Radicals*, 28.

[93] Chisick, 'Intellectual Profile', 122–4.

The first major exponent of an overriding popular sovereignty in the spirit of Rousseau, Marat, was also the first unrelenting critic of the principle of representation crucial to the 'party of philosophy'. If his temperament and background explain his harsh militancy, ideas contributed too especially his long-standing fervour for the 'sublime Rousseau'.[94] If scholars have noted how sharply Sieyès diverges from and criticizes Rousseau on everything concerning representation and popular sovereignty, it is doubtful whether historians have generally taken sufficient note of this.[95] Replacing 'la philosophie' with unrelenting emphasis on popular sovereignty, ordinary men's feelings, and 'virtue', Marat insisted, like Danton and Robespierre later, that the people's representatives must be made to defer to the people's will. With Marat's *L'Ami du peuple*, a new tone of intolerance as well as a harshly dictatorial tendency reared its head.[96] The main Girondin charge against Marat, later, during the power struggles of 1792, was precisely his inciting the populace to take the law into their own hands.

Marat's supporters claimed to be more genuine egalitarians than the current leadership most of whom, like Condorcet, Volney, Sieyès, Bailly, Le Chapelier, and Cloots, more or less openly disdained the multitude for their ignorance and addiction to 'superstition'. Marat's chief objection to materialist accounts of the mind was that to him they seemed incapable of explaining the passions, the quest for 'glory', and power of sentiment in man. Helvétius would never succeed in making the passions and reason contrary principles, argued Marat, nor in opposing one to the other.[97] The materialism and sensationalism of Helvétius, Diderot, and Sieyès he believed quite incompatible with 'virtue' and the popular will as it prioritizes knowledge and understanding. This subordination of reason to popular will and feeling is what especially distinguished his and the *Robespierristes*' 'Revolution of the Will' from the Revolution of Reason of the Radical Enlightenment. For Marat, understanding remains always subordinate to the will and where reason is something fixed the popular will is free.

Late in September 1789, precipitated partly by the arrival of the prestigious Flanders regiment at Versailles, rumour again had it that the 'parti aristocratique' was attempting a *contre-révolution* to regain power and stifle the *volonté générale* by using the military. Anger surged. Whether or not Louis was really contemplating a military coup, some of those close to him certainly were. Furthermore he was resisting full acquiescence in the August edicts. All royal resistance (and support for the veto) ended with the celebrated march of 5 October. The marchers, formed from groups gathering first in the public gardens and squares of Paris, eventually totalling some 30,000 female and male citizens, many hungry women carrying home-made pikes and other makeshift weapons, marched on Versailles to get bread, thoroughly aroused by reports that the evening before, at Versailles, banqueting

---

[94] Marat, *De l'homme*, i, preface pp. xiv–xv, xix, 174, 207–8, 310, and ii. 256, 378–9.
[95] Forsyth, *Reason*, 59–63; Pasquino, *Sieyès*, 45, 78–9.
[96] Mortier, *Combats*, 336; Baker, *Condorcet*, 316.   [97] Marat, *De l'homme*, i. 251, 310.

officers had trampled tricolour cockades under foot, vowing to stamp out the Revolution. The crowds attacked and dispersed the guards, several whom were killed, and occupied the palace. The by now extraordinarily unpopular queen was fortunate to escape being cut to pieces herself. The crowds also invaded the Assembly's meeting-hall. Order was belatedly restored by the National Guard. The next day the royal family was brought to Paris accompanied by an immense procession amounting perhaps to 60,000.

Welcoming the royal family to the city, Bailly delivered a famous speech setting the seal on an event which finally paralysed conservative elements in the Assembly and encouraged what the *Chronique de Paris* called 'la généreuse minorité', that is the *philosophique* group dominating the Assembly, to feel more secure, being powerfully backed and sustained by 'toute la force populaire'.[98] To Gibbon, watching closely from Lausanne, this outcome seemed totally disastrous: 'their king brought a captive to Paris after his palace had been stained with the blood of his guards; the nobles in exile, the clergy plundered in a way which strikes at the root of all property; the capital an independent republic; the union of the provinces dissolved; the flames of discord kindled by the worst of men (in that light I consider Mirabeau;) and the honestest of the Assembly, a set of wild visionaries (like our Dr Price,) who gravely debate, and dream about the establishment of pure and perfect democracy of five-and-twenty millions, the virtues of the golden age, and the primitive rights and equality of mankind, which would lead, in fair reasoning, to an equal partition of lands and money'.[99] He was right up to a point and especially insofar as the Paris populace were now in a position to act as 'self-appointed watch-dogs', as it has been put, of the Revolution.[100]

Popular intimidation of the court during the October days also meant intimidation of that part (the majority) of the National Assembly, comprising liberal aristocrats, clergy, pragmatists, and *monarchiens*, opposing the universalist, egalitarian constitutional proposals of Sieyès, Mirabeau, Volney, and the steering group. Indeed, at this point a number of key deputies, Mounier and the archbishop of Paris among them, utterly dismayed and cowed, withdrew from the Assembly altogether.[101] Resigning from the Assembly's *comité de constitution*, Bergasse withdrew into obscurity; one of the few *monarchiens* to survive the Terror, he later became an ultra-conservative.[102] Lally-Tolendal left for Switzerland, Mounier for his native Dauphiné. Montesquieu had been definitively defeated. Yet, the fact that the revolutionary leadership owed their power to the people's backing, by no means implies they pursued a programme desired, or even imagined, by the Paris populace. Rather they used their popular mandate to pursue their own course. Although they were and

---

[98] *Chronique de Paris*, 1/45 (7 Oct. 1789), 177–8; Hunt, *Politics, Culture and Class*, 58–9.

[99] Gibbon, *Memoirs*, 236.

[100] Doyle, *Oxford History*, 123.

[101] Granié, *L'Assemblée*, 87; Arnauld, *Chamfort*, 169–70; Aston, *Religion*, 132.

[102] Pasquino, 'Nicolas Bergasse', 81.

were known to be a minority in terms of opinion, yet they commanded a majority of votes and continued to dominate, not least by forming standing committees and by late 1789 formal debating clubs, both in Paris and in provincial centres.[103] Mirabeau, meanwhile, inclined to radical positions on most issues but having wanted the veto, remained for a time as popular as ever, the populace assuming he was against the veto just as they were. The multitude was much perturbed by rumours he was in danger or had been wounded. Nevertheless, through his unexpected persistence in arguing the king should be the symbol of the *volonté générale* and should possess a veto, siding here with Lally-Tollendal, he ended by damaging his own standing much as Sieyès had earlier.[104]

The crucial backing that enabled the minority to succeed, emanating as it did chiefly from the Parisian cafés, streets, and journals, encouraged talk elsewhere in the country of 'Paris' exerting an undue influence on the Assembly and national politics. This was dismissed by the pro-leadership Parisian press as a way of stirring up fears and jealousy, as Brissot put it, in the provinces against the capital. Among both defeated moderates and conservatives, the Paris mob were bitterly blamed, however, less for becoming 'watch-dogs' which they were only potentially than for allowing themselves to be shepherded by upstart publicists, journalists, and self-proclaimed shapers of opinion to act against the king, in support of the Assembly's most radical faction.[105] Installed in the Louvre, king and queen were now virtual 'hostages', recorded the Venetian envoy, living the next tumultuous months in an isolation resembling custody while the Assembly, occupying new quarters in the Tuileries, consolidated its grip despite the capital's economic distress daily intensifying. At one point, the Venetian envoy, deriding the Paris artisans for their apparent subservience to a handful of intellectuals, and continually echoing their slogans and principles, remarked: 'these *philosophes* who are not even able to read have not yet learnt that philosophy has always been poor.'[106]

As the Revolution continued in the autumn of 1789, there was no let-up in the pace of fundamental change on the basis of principle. In late October, the Assembly decreed that in meetings of municipalities and civic public gatherings in all the provinces of France no 'distinction by orders' was ever again to be allowed, this being wholly 'contraire aux principes établis par l'Assemblée Nationale'.[107] On 2 November, following Mirabeau's recommendation, the Assembly by 568 votes to 346 placed all church lands and property at the nation's disposal, clearing the way for the sale of church lands projected in December.[108] Here again, this was in no sense a

[103] [Prudhomme and Tournon], *Révolutions de Paris*, 5 (9/15 Aug. 1789), 27–9; Marmontel, *Mémoires*, iii. 195; La Gorce, *Histoire religieuse*, i. 215–16.

[104] La Gorce, *Histoire religieuse*, i. 215–16; Dumont, *Souvenirs de Mirabeau*, 102–3; Luttrell, *Mirabeau*, 124–5, 151–2; Hont, *Jealousy*, 482–89.

[105] Godineau, *Women of Paris*, 99–100; Mortier, *Anarcharsis Cloots*, 186.

[106] Fontana, *Venise et la Révolution*, 405.

[107] *Chronique de Paris*, 1/65 (27 Oct. 1789).   [108] Kennedy, *Cultural History*, 146.

measure prompted by popular demand. It derived rather straight from the principles of the Assembly's steering group. Later in November, the Assembly announced it had in principle decided to abolish the privileges and physical boundaries of the ancient provinces—Normandy, Brittany, Provence, Languedoc, and so forth—these being of very different sizes and disparate in traditions, privileges, and rank and hence hardly befitting the new order. To replace them the Assembly planned 'departments' of equal size and status. As with the other great revolutionary innovations, this scheme, advocated by Rabaut and Mirabeau in particular, had been carefully worked out in *philosophique* principle beforehand, notably by Condorcet. The goal was to obtain that 'equality of influence that belongs essentially to every individual'.[109]

Revolutionary changes followed month by month. In late February 1790 the Assembly debated draft proposals to eliminate all remaining vestiges of the 'feudal regime', the first article of which reads: 'toutes les distinctions honorifiques, de supériorité et puissance résultants du régime féodal sont abolies'; the second article confirmed the end of all forms of servile obligation. Despite considerable opposition in the Assembly itself, special rights of inheritance by primogeniture were also suppressed. How can privilege, blindness, and pride, as the *Chronique de Paris* explained the situation, be permitted to continue 'in a century in which *la philosophie* presents the light of truth to all eyes'?[110] Its answer was they could not. If to our ears the way the opposing factions were designated might seem to imply a struggle between social classes, it would be wrong to infer this. Opposition in the Assembly was fomented by 'aristocrates'. But this category, it emerges, referred to mainly ideological standpoints, not social class. Both the *Révolutions de Paris* and the *Chronique de Paris* defined 'les aristocrates' not as a social category but as all those who live 'from abuse and have an interest in maintaining the old order of things'.[111]

Nothing could be clearer than that an uncompromising ideology of equality, anti-aristocracy, democracy, and freedom of expression had become entrenched at the outset in the Assembly and Paris press, and dominated subsequently until late 1792. Relentless decrying of 'aristocrates' contributed as much to the Revolution, commented the *Révolutions de Paris*, in November, as the *cocarde*. A good government, held the radical *philosophes*, is one where legislation and the law-makers eschew all theological criteria (no matter how many people consider them sacred), ensuring through laws and institutional structures that education, individual interest, and society's moral values 'concourir', to the general good, 'au bien général', as Helvétius expressed it, meaning the worldly well-being of the majority.[112] Since prevalence of rank and privilege, inequality of wealth and status, and the sway of monarchy, law elites, and ecclesiastical authority were then the foremost feature of European societies, as well as of Canada and Spanish America and to a lesser degree also of

---

[109] *Chronique de Paris*, 1/86 (17 Nov. 1789), 341–2, 352; Condorcet, *Œuvres*, ix. 363, 395–7.
[110] Condorcet, *Œuvres*, ix. 363, 395–7; Corno, 'La Loi révolutionnaire', 66.
[111] *Chronique de Paris*, 1/91 (22 Nov. 1789), 370; Rétat, '1789: Montesquieu', 76–7.
[112] Helvétius, *De l'homme*, ii. 917.

the United States, no one applying the radical *philosophes*' criterion of what makes good government could avoid their highly disconcerting conclusion that, therefore, no good governments existed before 1789 and that only a vigorous turn towards 'la philosophie moderne' could demonstrate what a good government and set of social values looks like.

The main revolutionary journals in 1789 deliberately fostered not just liberty of the press and debate but also the diffusion of extracts of the work of the *philosophes* 'of the first order', Mably, Condillac, Boulanger, Raynal-Diderot, Paine, and d'Holbach as well as Rousseau and Voltaire, so that everything 'de plus philosophique' concerning the origin of societies, the nature of diverse kinds of government, the laws, 'sur le droit public', moral principles, religion, and philosophy should become familiar to more readers and especially young people.[113] As the foremost questions in 1789 seized the attention 'de toutes les classes', it was of great relevance that society should be provided with new 'fixed principles' anchored in deep and thorough consideration of eminent writings of 'philosophy' from prior to the Revolution. 'Quelle reconnaissance ne devons nous pas' to men who braved the Bastille to tell us the truth? It was the *philosophes* who first revealed the real character of the institutions of 'our servitude' and prepared the downfall which Frenchmen had now had the great good fortune to witness of the previous odious system. 'Gloire à ces écrivains immortels!', intoned the *Chronique de Paris*. May their principles become the principles of everyone: 'que leurs idées circulent, et forment l'esprit public; que leurs ouvrages soient entre les mains de tous les bons citoyens.'[114]

From July 1789 an accelerated diffusion of radical ideas proceeded on all sides and in many ways. By the late summer of 1789 all sorts of writers, artists, and organizations, Parisian and provincial, had joined in the work of propagation. Learning that the civic guard at Besançon had agreed to establish at its own expense a 'reading room for the soldiers of the garrison', to enable them better to understand their interests and duties as citizens and participants in the Revolution, the *Chronique de Paris*, in February 1790, called for this example to be widely emulated.[115] The foremost public advocate of freedom of the theatre, the younger Chénier, fiercely attacked France's traditional theatre censorship in three devastating pamphlets, while simultaneously propagating egalitarian and anti-monarchical attitudes as he did also with his later play *Henri VIII*. The theatre, he urged listeners, in a speech of April 1790, was a 'powerful means' of public instruction capable of greatly accelerating the advance of *la philosophie* and the truth. 'La raison universelle', he announced triumphantly, 'marche à pas de géant' [universal reason progresses with giant steps].[116]

It was the *philosophes*, he urged the newly revolutionized public, in his best-known pamphlet, in early July 1789 (though not released until late August), who had taught

---

[113] *Chronique de Paris*, 46 (Oct. 1789), 181.   [114] Ibid.; McMahon, *Enemies*, 67–9.
[115] *Chronique de Paris*, 2/56 (25 Feb. 1790), 222.
[116] Ibid. 2/105 (15 Apr. 1790), 418; Friedland, *Political Actors*, 261.

his generation to think, leading them as if by the hand towards the truth: 'eux seuls ont préparé la Révolution qui commence.'[117] Philosophy's principal heroes, according to Chénier, were 'Voltaire, Montesquieu, Rousseau, d'Alembert, Diderot, Mably, Raynal, and Helvétius'.[118] They had served society during their lives and it was they who, from the tomb, now led the French Revolution. How did 'la philosophie moderne' evolve from the writings of the *philosophes* first into a formidable force and then to a near dominant position in society? Through their writings, their example, and through society's mounting persecution of them. Chénier stresses the unwitting contribution of the bishops who for years campaigned from the pulpit, issuing pastoral circulars denouncing *la philosophie* and its 'doctrine abominable' as the source of all France's ills. The episcopate's efforts were then amply seconded by what he called the 'tyrannie continuelle exercée par les parlements contre les écrits philosophiques', the *parlements* trying to combat 'philosophy' in every way possible.[119] If 'philosophy' in recent decades had permeated the French provinces, appeared in the royal council, entrenched itself in aristocratic homes, if men had finally become reasonable in many respects, the citizens of 1789 owed it all, held Chénier, to those hounded before 1788 not just by the crown but by all branches of authority.

So basic and far-reaching was the change in public thinking, in Paris especially, that the 'philosophique' perspective soon extended also (or even) to attitudes towards women, monks, and Jews as well as the *parlements*. What these four disparate topics had in common was that they all involved proposals for basic change that had nothing to do with the people's preferences or habits. Rather, the proposals to suppress the religious orders, emancipate the Jews, and reform the laws of marriage encountered incomprehension, broadly unsympathetic responses, and a degree of resistance and could be expedited with little more ease than ending black slavery. Nevertheless, the strides taken 1789–90 were unprecedented and impressive. Eliminating the dowry system and introducing civil divorce were things 'enlightened men' had long pressed for, stressed Démeunier, back in 1776.[120] 'Philosophy', he wrote then, as Brissot likewise stressed in his *Lettres philosophiques sur Saint Paul* (1783), requires every enlightened nation to have a comprehensive divorce law because enlightened societies should refuse to chain together 'irrévocablement' husbands and wives who make each other unhappy.[121] Yet before 1789 only Diderot, d'Holbach, Démeunier, and a few other radical *philosophes* were urging this. Portalis and other moderate enlightened opponents of the Revolution might have been right that by 1787, following partial toleration of Protestantism, the French crown, bowing to those, like himself, moved by 'l'esprit philosophique' in what he saw as its positive format and urging more toleration, had virtually introduced a form of civil marriage;

---

[117] Chénier, *Dénonciation des Inquisiteurs*, 45–6. [118] Ibid. 41.
[119] Ibid. 30–1; *Chronique de Paris*, 1/28 (20 Sept. 1789), 110. [120] Démeunier, *L'Esprit*, i. 77–133.
[121] Ibid. i. 229; Brissot, *Lettres philosophiques*, 116, 119–21.

but it was not until the summer of 1789 that civil divorce for all and eliminating dowries as well as civil marriage for the first time began to be widely contemplated and discussed and Olympe de Gouges (1745–93), the herald of woman's emancipation in France, began rallying support in the circles around Condorcet and Brissot for the principle of woman's liberation.[122]

Manifestly, urged the *Chronique de Paris*, the Revolution would have 'une grande influence' on the lives of women in France. The obvious injustice of laws that 'reduce women to the condition of slaves', compelling a mistreated wife to remain under the despotic sway of her husband (unless able to prove her life was in danger), had to be eliminated.[123] But progress was excruciatingly slow. If to radical *philosophes*, civil divorce had long seemed the only answer to 'le despotisme marital', it was not until early 1790 that 'l'opinion publique', according to the radical-minded, began to edge in a positive direction, aided by radical *philosophe*-politicians like Condorcet and Brissot and leading feminists, like Olympe de Gouges and Etta Palm (1743–99). Awareness of the ills caused by indissolubility of marriage became sufficiently widespread for the Assembly to take more heed. It was not until 20 September 1792, though, that the Assembly could muster enough votes to institute civil divorce, pronouncing incompatibility of temperament and a range of other circumstances just and adequate grounds for ending marriages. Under Robespierre, however, and in line with the Rousseauiste preferences of some Jacobins, the position of women deteriorated again in the public sphere and in practice if not in law.[124]

Dissolution of the monasteries likewise proved slow work. Even though 'the great question' of whether or not the religious orders were useful had long before been decided 'par le philosophe et par la raison', commented Mirabeau's *Courrier de Provence*, in late September 1789, the question was still being furiously debated in the Assembly and its committees.[125] Where the higher clergy and nobility and their supporters, remarked the *Chronique de Paris*, after some especially sharp exchanges, found nothing but impiety and blasphemy in the proposals for abolition, the Assembly's 'bons esprits' could see nothing but truth and justification.[126] Among the rank and file of delegates, the Assembly's non-*philosophique* majority could always rally appreciable support for resisting radical proposals. As long as moderates and conservatives dominated the Assembly's *comité ecclésiastique* which featured two bishops and six or seven other members preferring bishops to *philosophes*, drastic changes could in theory be blocked.[127] Their problem was that it was the 'bons

[122] Portalis, *De l'usage*, 226; Hesse, *Other Enlightenment*, 46, 52, 81.
[123] *Chronique de Paris*, 2/35 (4 Feb. 1790), 137; Godineau, *Women of Paris*, 37–9; Corno, 'La Loi révolutionnaire', 62, 65.
[124] Corno, 'La Loi révolutionnaire', 67; Hunt, *Inventing Human Rights*, 63; Kates, *Cercle Social*, 120–4; Scott, *Only Paradoxes*, 40–50.
[125] Mirabeau, *Courrier de Provence*, 47 (28/30 Sept. 1789), 5–6.
[126] *Chronique de Paris*, 2/44 and 45 (13 and 14 Feb. 1790), 175, 179; McMahon, *Enemies*, 71; Aston, *Religion*, 134–5.
[127] La Gorce, *Histoire religieuse*, i. 200.

esprits' who were best able to exert pressure from outside. The *comité*s members were gradually worn down. Although many or most deputies backed the Abbé Gregoire's warning that it would be impolitic and dangerous to abolish the orders completely, such objections were thrust aside in a series of stormy debates between December 1789 and March 1790. On 13 February, all the regular orders except those primarily devoted to educational or charitable work were formally dissolved. Under this measure, the Assembly's *comité ecclésiastique* sent out at the beginning of March questionnaires to all the monasteries and convents, male and female, in France requiring details of the rule and purpose of each establishment and numbers and ages of all occupants. Most complied promptly enough. In the Assembly, meanwhile, how precisely to proceed remained an unresolved and divisive issue through March and beyond.[128]

In April 1790, there were renewed attempts by 'moderates' and clergy, backed by several provinces, to persuade the Assembly to declare the Catholic faith the public religion in France and sole church enjoying public status and support, guaranteeing its diocesan structure and endorsing its subordination to the papacy. The 'moderates' intrinsically had the edge in such a clash. The vast majority of Frenchmen were still devout. Yet, somehow, they were again overruled, prompting an outraged minority of 289 deputies publicly to protest.[129] The revolutionary leadership did intend to keep the Catholic Church in France as an *église d'état*, but wished to reduce it to a much weaker, more subordinate, and less privileged condition than most deputies wanted. To the leadership weakening the Church's grip on the populace and clearing the way for many other projected reforms seemed essential for political, moral, educational, and legislative reasons, and not least to divert resources to the public from the Church and secure civil divorce. Equally, the wide religious toleration recently achieved could hardly be considered secure without massively diminishing the clergy's influence. The age of ignorance is over, proclaimed the *Chronique de Paris*, assuring readers that it was to 'la philosophie' that men owed the fact that they now viewed matters with 'sentiments plus doux et plus humains' than those prevailing in the past.[130] Cloots, yet another of the Revolution's outstanding journalists and orators who, from March 1790, gained a considerable following through his articles in the *Chronique de Paris*, besides being *philosophique* and fiercely anti-Rousseauiste was vehemently anticlerical and opposed to retaining any established, public church as was virtually the whole leadership.

If there was no longer a royally proclaimed, publicly imposed faith, it was hoped that from a public standpoint it would hardly matter any longer to what creed anyone belonged. As far as the public sphere was concerned, the only creed now truly legitimate was 'le patriotisme éclairé'.[131] On 24 December 1789, the Assembly

---

[128] *Chronique de Paris*, 2/5 (5 Jan. 1790), 17; Fontana, *Venise et la Révolution*, 392, 394.
[129] Fontana, *Venise et la Révolution*, 410, 414; La Gorce, *Histoire religieuse*, i. 167, 194.
[130] *Chronique de Paris*, 2/74 (15 Mar. 1790), 293; Fontana, *Venise et la Révolution*, 410.
[131] *Chronique de Paris*, 2/25 (25 Jan. 1790), 98.

issued a decree that proved especially shocking to the papacy and many Catholics, expressly admitting non-Catholics to all judicial, civil, and military functions, posts, and positions, forbidding requirement anywhere in France of any conditions of eligibility for posts other than the purely secular criteria specified by the constitution. Citizenship henceforth was available to anyone from abroad ready to swear allegiance to state and constitution. Even a 'Negro, Turk, or idolater', scoffed the Venetian envoy, or 'the Salé corsairs, can become representatives of the nation or cabinet ministers of France'! Officially, Catholicism had lost all bearing on one's social and civil status. All this had very wide implications.

Talk of emancipating the Jews, from October onwards, met with so much resistance and was so unpopular that it had to be shelved for a time. Yet the Assembly, noted the Venetian envoy, would scarcely be consistent with its own principles should it long continue to exclude the Jews from the Rights of Man.[132] He was right. Despite vigorous opposition in the Assembly and near total lack of popular support for the measure, full emancipation of the more affluent, educated, and Westernized but small Sephardic community passed on 28 January 1790 by 374 votes to 224. After this, it was only a matter of time before the much larger Ashkenazic community received equality of rights as citizens, though it was not until September 1791 that this passed.[133]

Among the Revolution's most welcome and positive achievements, remarked Naigeon, in 1791, was the total destruction of the *parlements* or high judicial courts of France, projected in August 1789, decreed by the National Assembly in November, and finalized in March 1790.[134] The Revolution and the people, agreed the *Chronique de Paris* in December 1789, had no more bitter, committed, or active enemies than the *parlements*.[135] Paine's ally, the American radical Barlow, yet another convinced the 'General Revolution' had been initiated 'by philosophers', denounced France's *parlementaire* 'judiciary nobility', in 1792, as 'a set of men who purchase the privilege of being the professional enemies of the people, of selling their decisions to the rich, and distributing individual oppression; hence the source of those draconian codes of criminal jurisprudence which enshrine the idol property in a bloody sanctuary, and teach the modern European, that his life is of less value than the shoes on his feet.'[136] Like most other fundamental reform initiatives including the abolition of feudal privilege and emancipation of the Jews, liquidating the *parlements* and with them the entire existing legal structure of France was wholly unconnected both with France's traditions and with popular sentiment, being a rallying point, as the *Révolutions de Paris* noted, only for a particular minority in the *Assemblée*.

[132] *Journal des décrets*, 5/10: 12–14; Fontana, *Venise et la Révolution*, 371–2.
[133] Doyle, *Oxford History*, 411; Aston, *Religion*, 252–4.
[134] Naigeon, *Philosophie*, ii. 224–5; *Journal des décrets*, 5/3: 7–8; Fontana, *Venise et la Révolution*, 404.
[135] *Chronique de Paris*, 1/110 (11 Dec. 1789), 437.
[136] Barlow, *Advice*, 6.

2. IDEAS AND THE REVOLUTIONARY LEADERSHIP

We now see why no adequate framework for interpreting the French Revolution is possible without going diametrically against the main trends in the recent historiography and focusing centrally on the question of *la philosophie moderne*. As Necker, Louis XVI's chief minister in 1789 and someone well placed to know, expressed it, the common people had nothing to do with the Revolution viewed as a set of basic changes as such, and enclosed within the narrow circle of their habitual thoughts would have presented the crown with no great challenge, had not the royal financial crisis raised fiscal pressure to the point that popular exasperation reached fever pitch. Even then, nothing remotely resembling the Revolution could have occurred had not *l'esprit philosophique* captured this dissatisfaction and every day extended its conquests, favouring 'toutes les insurrections contre les idées reçues et contre les vérités communes'. For decades preceding the Revolution, explained Necker (whose ultra-royalist enemies accused him of being a secret republican and betraying the king, of being tarred by *la philosophie moderne* too), *l'esprit philosophique* first ruined all sense of duty by assailing religion and then, by reworking the principles of morality and politics, broke all constraints, substituting an exaggerated notion of liberty for the wisdom of limits, and fomenting the confusion spread by the idea of equality in place of the 'prudentes gradations dont l'ordre social se compose'.[137] He was careful though to avoid accusing particular *philosophes* of having a part in what he considered the greatest disaster in history. Remarkably, the only philosopher he cites by name as being responsible for modern *esprit philosophique* as a revolutionary force was Spinoza.

Portalis, by contrast, while agreeing that *l'esprit philosophique* alone caused the Revolution, preferred to say that it was a certain kind that was responsible rather than *esprit de philosophie* as such. Today's historian casting an eye over the pamphlets stirring up the agitation in France in 1788 is readily persuaded of the correctness of Necker's and Portalis's analysis. Society was not created for the happiness of the few or the misery of the majority, thundered the tract entitled *Vérités philosophiques et patriotiques* of late 1788, rather the will of each individual must be subjected to the *volonté générale* and this common will must equally work for the happiness of each individual member and that of all in general. A highly complex conception totally at odds with most received ideas, this perspective sprang from an inevitably complex intellectual development reaching back, underground, over many decades. The forthcoming Estates-General of the kingdom, contends this pamphlet, must be an assembly of the entire nation on the basis of the *volonté générale*.[138] It is not God, the Church, any prophet, precedent, or tradition that decreed this, explains this text, but rather 'this eternal reason that regulates the universe'. This text while extolling 'eternal reason' unequivocally invokes the coming 'révolution'.

---

[137] Necker, *De la Révolution françoise*, i. 14.   [138] *Vérités philosophiques et patriotiques*, 16–17.

What would a pamphlet published in 1788 mean by the pending 'revolution'? It meant the ending of 'error' and 'slavery' with the aid of 'philosophy', replacing the existing legal framework with upright morality and good laws, the true sources of man's happiness and prosperity. In the *Réflexions d'un philosophe Breton*, of 20 December 1788, the Breton people are summoned by the 'philosopher' to recover 'their rights' by breaking the 'humiliating chains' of slavery the nobility and clergy had everywhere heaped on the Third Estate. These 'rapacious' orders are here denounced by 'philosophy' not for transgressing some charter or overstepping precedent, or abrogating alleged historic privileges, but for appropriating 'all the advantages of society' for themselves.[139] Over the winter of 1788–9, Mirabeau, earlier a virtual outcast, on the eve of the convening of the Estates suddenly made an unforgettable impact, especially with Third Estate voters in Marseille and Aix-en-Provence, by denouncing the 'despotism of the two privileged orders, linking his name with that of Raynal, calling for *la volonté générale* to be the only basis of law', and for bread prices to be regulated. At the price of provoking formal protests from the courts of Vienna, Berlin, and Dresden, owing to the unheard-of audacity of his criticism of monarchs, the ideological stance the most prominent figure to emerge from southern France adopted in 1788 was simply that to which he had broadly adhered throughout the 1780s.[140]

The emerging leaders of Third Estate opinion already thought and clearly proclaimed in 1788 that the clergy's authority is nothing, nobility is illicit, rapacious, and superfluous, and that all existing laws and authority without exception need replacing on the basis of philosophical principles. Brissot played a notable part in defeating the royal veto in September 1789 by proclaiming *philosophique* principles, but he had already outlined how he thought the coming Revolution would operate as far back as 1782. By displaying ingenuity and constancy in his writings, the *philosophe* can conquer 'l'opinion publique' and 'l'opinion publique' could in a short time 'prove stronger than kings and command the entire universe'. Philosophy would make the Revolution he predicted; and the prediction proved correct.

One might object that the weight of the modern historiography goes completely against such notions and that no modern historian of the Revolution pronounces *la philosophie moderne* the main cause of the Revolution. But if it is correct that contemporary explanations practically always identify *la philosophie moderne* as the principal factor as they do, then the objection needs to be carefully examined. It would not be the only instance where whole generations of scholars have been misled by paying more attention to modern theories and fashions and what their colleagues maintain than to contemporary reports and analyses. Anyway, it is undeniable that contemporary explanations of the Revolution down to 1800 and subsequently

---

[139] *Réflexions d'un philosophe Breton*, 1, 3 6.
[140] BL 910.c.16/7 *Lettre d'un citoyen de Marseille*, 7, 16; BL 910 c. 16/10, pp. 45–6, 47–8; Garat, 'Jugement', pp. vii–viii; Fontana, *Venise et la Révolution*, 263; Schama, *Citizens*, 342–5.

invariably stress chiefly what Feller, in 1784, called the 'ravages' caused by the astonishing progress of 'l'épidémie philosophique' and that the prevailing consensus about this continued subsequently for decades. If modern historians' habit of ignoring all this is total it is still possible that the basis for it is nothing more than an unconsciously tacit collective assumption.

The constant stress on the role of 'la philosophie' and the need for major decisions to be 'philosophique' constitutes a whole discourse we no longer comprehend and it is easy to see how it might simply be set aside by social and political historians with a shrug of the shoulders as not meaningful. The constant stress on *la philosophie* indeed makes no sense at all to the modern mind not immersed in the language of the Enlightenment. If this is the explanation, then what we are really dealing with is a gigantic historical delusion, an unshakeable assumption that unspecified social changes caused the Revolution when patently social, cultural, economic, and political changes did nothing of the sort, a misconception wrongly separating Enlightenment from revolution that urgently needs clearing away. For it is unalterable fact that, in 1788–9 and in the 1790s, 'philosophy' was everywhere and overwhelmingly deemed the mainspring of the Revolution in a way that nothing else was, and for excellent reasons: because the *philosophes modernes* alone proclaimed 'equality' the exclusive correct and legitimate moral and legal principle for determining relations among men, establishing basic human rights, and reconstituting politics, institutions, social relations, marriage, and the law. These unanswerable grounds for proclaiming 'philosophy' the cause of the Revolution, moreover, remain just as valid and unimpeachable today.

Sieyès's close ally Roederer, defending the Revolution in his *De la philosophie moderne, et de la part qu'elle a eue à la Révolution française* (1799), rightly emphasized, replying to Antoine, Comte de Rivarol's well-known critique published at Hamburg in 1797, that their quarrel was not about whether *la philosophie moderne* was the chief cause of the Revolution, for practically every knowledgeable and commentator (apart from Mounier) agreed about this, but rather about exactly what *la philosophie* taught and what its justifications were.[141] Only *la philosophie moderne* sought to banish religion, held Rivarol, and only by attacking religion could the Revolution introduce such sweeping and, in his view, ruinous changes as ensued. For the Revolution's countless opponents, equality was an artificial, concocted, destructive, and illicit concept spawned either by irreligion or, as with Portalis and Gibbon, 'abstract propositions' wildly adopted. For Sieyès and Roederer, by contrast, equality was genuinely something carried over from the state of nature into society under government. What made it necessary to proclaim the *Declaration of the Rights of Man and the Citizen* throwing the state behind the principle of basic human rights was the pre-existing inequality of means and wealth in society. Unless one wants government by vested interests at the expense of the weak, government that further oppresses most and enriches the strong, the state must intervene on

---

[141] Roederer, *De la philosophie*, 6–7.

behalf of the deprived while keeping a watchful eye over the whole citizenry to 'garantir à tous la plénitude de leurs droits' [guarantee to all the plenitude of their rights].[142]

No historical account of the Revolution can be in any way adequate without explaining how exactly egalitarian, democratic, and anti-ecclesiastical ideas, the principles of the Radical Enlightenment, shaped the Revolution from 1788 onwards, commencing well before the Estates-General met. Without placing *la philosophie moderne* centre-stage there is no way of explaining the Revolution's main character-istics and goals or how it became so fundamentally different in its core concerns from the American and Belgian revolutions of 1776 and 1789. It is only by acknowledging the 'revolution that had occurred long before 1789 in ideas', in Roederer's words, that one can understand why the Revolution was not just a political revolution but also a 'financial, military, civil, moral and religious revolution'.[143] Feller and the *anti-philosophes*, for all their loathing of the Revolution, were close to the mark in identifying its essential cause in an underground network attempting to turn into reality what to him was a catastrophic 'illusion' implacably directed against throne and altar alike, evolving over half a century prior to 1789 which he calls 'l'empire du philosophisme'.[144] It was a construct created by a group of extraordinary writers who impressed all classes of the population with their wit and sarcasms, devising, in his eyes, a whole new language which by a deft combination of force, wit, and obscurity rendered their ideas 'sublime' to the people. This conspiracy began in the 1740s by stealing the idea of a general encyclopedia from the English and turning it an engine of subversion and impiety. The main conspirators, 'parasites' lounging in cafés, gradually insinuated, flattered, and mocked their way to domination of the acad-emies and positions of great power. Among their most effective weapons, suggested Feller, was their appeal to women, especially young and pretty women susceptible to fine phrases, elegant turns of speech, witticisms, and subtle and not so subtle erotic hints and suggestions.

Even Mounier, the major exception, implacable foe of all ideological politics, someone admiring only English pragmatism and the sole prominent contemporary explicitly denying the Revolution could be attributed 'aux philosophes modernes', conspicuously failed to find good arguments for his stance. Just as commentators often exaggerated freemasonry's role in the Revolution, and that of the *Illuminés*,[145] he argued in 1801, so, equally, considering 'modern philosophy' the Revolution's principal cause however general was just a vast misconception, an easy substitute for explaining causes too various and complex to be captured in a phrase. By continually stressing 'philosophy's' role contemporaries were fuelling a bogus explanation readily grasped by superficial minds, but no more valid really, he maintained, than attrib-uting the Revolution to freemasons. Already, as leader of the *monarchiens* in the

---

142 Roederer, *De la philosophie*, 7.
143 Ibid. 23; Roederer, *Spirit*, 9–13, 18.
144 [Feller], *Journal historique* (1792), 22–3.
145 Mounier, *De l'influence*, 6–7, 22; Portalis, *De l'usage*, 373–89.

Assembly in 1789, Mounier loudly complained about the universal tendency, ever since 1787, to claim the agitation gripping France stemmed from a gigantic 'philosophique' conspiracy. The claim is disproved, he contended, by its ridiculously lumping together Voltaire, the 'committee' around d'Holbach, the society for the abolition of slavery led by Brissot and Condorcet, the *philosophes économistes*, admirers of England like himself, disciples of Rousseau who regarded the English 'comme des esclaves', and, most absurd of all, Montesquieu who recommended moderate monarchy with aristocracy and intermediary powers.[146] Here Mounier was right, of course: lumping Montesquieu, Voltaire, and Rousseau with the circle meeting at d'Holbach's *is* total nonsense. But that proves only that the revolutionary leadership that defeated him politically in 1789 could not have been inspired primarily by more than one or two of these strands.

Actually, Mounier's alternative account fails to explain anything about the Revolution as such. It was actually the king's advisers, he urges, who overthrew the existing order by antagonizing the nobility, clergy, *parlementaires*, peasantry, and townsfolk all at the same time. But the instances he cites explain only the king's failure to retain power. How France came into the hands of a group aiming to discredit, demolish, and replace every aspect of the legal and institutional structure of the *ancien régime*, composing a *Declaration of the Rights of Man*, imposing a universal doctrine of equality and anti-aristocracy, ending feudal privilege, changing the entire administrative and legal system, ending ecclesiastical authority, emancipating the Jews, proclaiming the universal suppression of black slavery, introducing divorce and fundamentally changing the laws of marriage to lessen subordination of women to men, emancipating all the citizenry in theory including even the blacks and mulattos in the colonies, seeking to do all this from the very outset, he does not even begin to explain.

Mounier's thesis relies on the financial crisis, people's hatred of taxes, excessive influence of the *parlements*, the arrogance of the aristocracy, Louis's incompetence, and above all, the factor he stressed most, the king's advisers' unwillingness to compromise. By trying to turn France into an absolute monarchy, they had precipitated the Revolution. They could not accept that France, monarchical in appearance, was 'aristocratique en réalité', or permit some admixture of a democratic tint to the monarchy in the interest of 'moderation'.[147] Their surpassing sin was their failure to emulate Britain. But here and in his insistence on the need for aristocratic primacy in society he was manifestly carried away by his own biases, *angliciste* ardour and anti-intellectualism. There had always been taxes, dithering kings, and obdurate *parlementaires* or their equivalents and citing these explains little about the Revolution as such and least of all why and how he failed to lead it.

Mounier aside, then, practically everyone agreed the clique of orators, editors, and journalists goading the National Assembly into embracing the democratic

---

[146] Mounier, *De l'influence*, 33–6.   [147] Ibid. 25–8, 98.

Revolution of 1788–92 and leading the Paris commune were what Jean-François de La Harpe (1739–1803), once a *philosophe* himself but, by 1794, one of their bitterest enemies, called *la secte philosophique*.

Neither was there any great change, in or after 1788, in the way these men's ideas cohered in an interlocking system of principles all solidly based, according to Roederer, on empiricism and science moulded, as Sieyès continually reiterated, by *la philosophie*.[148] They were not dogmatic and inflexible. Their positions evolved; but already long before 1788, they contended that France needed a wholly new kind of government with an Assemblée Nationale eliminating all privilege and established on the basis of equality with 'reason' the exclusive criterion of legitimacy in law and politics, as all men have the same 'rights'. The division of representative assemblies into three orders—nobility, clergy, and Third Estate—they had long rejected outright as they had Montesquieu and those of his disciples advocating separation of powers, 'institutions aristocratiques', and the British model.[149] The 'philosophy' on which they drew was the entire radical tradition reaching back to the middle of the seventeenth century, especially as mediated and amplified by Boulanger, Diderot, Helvétius, d'Holbach, Raynal, Mably, and (more marginally, mostly) Rousseau.

The 'revolution was made in men's minds and habits', averred Roederer, 'before it was made into law'.[150] A 'Revolution of ideas' was urgently needed, agreed Garat, and actually occurred from the 1740s down to 1789. That 'revolution' had to come first to pave the way for the 'revolution of events', of which it was the motor and shaping force.[151] Doubtless there was also a resentful underclass of writers, Darnton's celebrated 'Grub Street', previously unsuccessful and comprising comparatively mediocre minds like those of Louis-Marie Prudhomme and Antoine Tournon, editors of the *Révolutions de Paris*. But what made them important was not resentment or any disposition to mete out 'a crude revolutionary justice', toppling the old establishment.[152] Nor was the *Révolutions de Paris* a 'transforming synthesis of many themes associated with prerevolutionary uses' of the term 'revolution'. What it was was a heavily illustrated Sunday paper depicting stirring crowd scenes designed to foment revolutionary awareness among the barely literate besides the literate,[153] furiously propagating a comprehensive, intellectually coherent, devastatingly critical and sophisticated ideology driven by one key concept, namely that 'philosophy' is the sole transformative agent ready and able to sweep away the old regime and forge the new order.

Far more important than grudges or the literary sociology of Grub Street is the fact that the Revolution's Prudhommes and Tournons viewed all prior human history as

---

[148] Roederer, *De la philosophie*, 2–3; Forsyth, *Reason*, 10, 18–19; Pasquino, *Sieyès*, 17–19, 169.
[149] Marmontel, *Mémoires*, iii. 296; Condorcet, 'Essai sur la constitution', in *Œuvres*, viii. 187–8, 230–1 and 'Sentiments d'un républicain', in *Œuvres*, ix. 130–1, 132–3, 135–6.
[150] Roederer, *Spirit*, 5.
[151] Garat, *Mémoires historiques*, ii. 230, 315.
[152] Darnton, *Literary Underground*, 38.
[153] Baker, *Inventing the French Revolution*, 223; Thompson, *French Revolution*, 112.

'the history of despotism', conceiving this 'despotism' supposedly dominating all prior human history as oppression not just political but also legal, moral, religious, and aristocratic—the latter dubbed by them 'le despotisme féodal'—all cemented together by universal ignorance, superstition, religious credulity, and prejudice. In short, they used to great effect a particular ideology of a special type which was cohesive and systematic and had a complex intellectual provenance. Abolishing the power of the nobility, clergy, municipal oligarchies, *parlements*, plantation owners, universities, foreign princes, and much else was the clearly stated goal of Prudhomme and Tournon from the outset. They set out to create a new society and politics based on a 'Declaration of the Rights of Man', guided by 'la philosophie' and, they occasionally add, the example of the American Revolution.[154] What matters for today's historians and philosophers of the Revolution are certainly not grudges, Grub Street, the ambiguities of our Postmodernists, or Chartier's vague, unconscious social tendencies but their overriding guiding vision, the fact that they launched their illustrated Sunday totally convinced in July 1789 that political and 'feudal' despotism prevailed universally throughout the world due to human ignorance and an alliance of kings and priests which philosophy alone can overthrow.[155] Crucial too is their claim that even though oppression was ubiquitous and the ultimate cause of revolutions, there had not been any real revolutions so far as it requires 'les lumières de la raison' to create the awareness, plans, and conditions without which revolution in their sense is inconceivable.

Some peoples in history, grants the *Révolutions de Paris*, had recovered 'their rights' through revolt 'avant le règne de la philosophie' [before the reign of philosophy]. But this can only happen in a fragmented, hesitant, unnecessarily violent, vengeful, incomplete manner if not guided by 'la pacifique opération de la philosophie'. The more philosophy presides, the less violent and disruptive, and the more complete and successful, the ensuing revolution will be. It is to be hoped, for everyone's sake, they affirmed, that *la philosophie* will outweigh hatred and resentment during the present Revolution's further course.[156] As they understood it, a real revolution needs not only to be made but also consolidated and maintained. Only 'philosophy', they contend, can prevent the French sliding back under 'slavery', and the provinces failing to follow the lead given by Paris. Without 'philosophy' mankind cannot establish well-designed political constitutions or 'les droits sacrés de l'humanité' or counter the very real danger of rural disorder and the despotism of the common people [le despotisme du peuple].[157] 'O mes concitoyens!', intoned their journal, 'n'oubliez pas que l'ignorance est la mère des erreurs; chassez de vous l'ignorance, et je réponds de votre liberté.'[158] Here was an ideology bound to turn

[154] [Prudhomme and Tournon], *Révolutions de Paris*, i, 'introduction', 17, 35, 47.
[155] Ibid., 'introduction', 1–3, 6.
[156] Ibid. 17; Baker, *Inventing the French Revolution*, 219.
[157] [Prudhomme and Tournon], *Révolutions de Paris*, 5 (9/15 Aug. 1789), 12–14, and 6 (16/22 Aug. 1789), 1–4.
[158] Ibid. 3 (26 July/1 Aug. 1789), 14.

the pre-1788 clash between Rousseau and *la philosophie moderne* into a bloody battlefield.

'La philosophie', explained Roederer in 1799, had not in 1789 and 1792 been something enclosed in the books of the thinkers; rather it emanated from them 'like light emanates from the sun'.[159] However, what he termed 'les disciples de la philosophie moderne', Sieyès, Mirabeau, Volney, Condorcet, Le Chapelier, Brissot, and their allies, including himself, had failed to retain control of the Revolution and, from the summer of 1793, been ousted by the faction headed by Robespierre, the Jacobin element proclaiming direct democracy and the will of the people, the feelings of the common man, the Revolution's true inspiration and values. It was at that point, following a bitter power struggle involving a fundamental change of direction, a complete reconstitution of the basic values of the Revolution, that the rights of man were overthrown, freedom of the press and expression ended, and the Terror began. But the royalists and *anti-philosophes* of the day, Roederer was convinced, like Paine and Naigeon, were totally unjustified in laying this catastrophic outcome at the door of *la philosophie*. The Robespierre debacle, held Roederer and the other surviving *philosophes-révolutionnaires*, after 1794, was all the fault of the ignorant and misguided. Robespierre was nothing but 'le détracteur de la philosophie, l'ennemi des philosophes', and the revenger of the 'divinity', a total fanatic, an 'esprit religieux', as Cloots—one of those he sent to the guillotine—called him, convinced 'atheism' was the cause of all he rejected. Philosophy made the Revolution; the people, in its ignorance, misled by demagogues and rendered ferocious by famine and civil war, made the Terror.[160]

What is the 'philosophy' that shaped the Revolution? asked La Harpe, in 1797. Where Fontenelle, Montesquieu, Buffon, d'Alembert, and Condillac were true philosophers, in his opinion, and should be fully exonerated of responsibility having had nothing to do with the catastrophe, those he labelled false philosophers and *sophistes*—Diderot, Raynal, Rousseau, Voltaire, and Helvétius—were the Revolution's true 'artisans', the 'first and most powerful movers of this ghastly *bouleversement*'.[161] La Harpe, like Portalis, and Roederer, and journalists such as Prudhomme and Tournon, envisaged *la philosophie moderne* as a complex, cumulative corpus of ideas and attitudes reaching back many decades. But where La Harpe located the revolutionary potential of *la secte philosophique* in the fact that it had evolved under oppression and in conspiracy attracting all vain and resentful spirits opposed to the existing order, being the best device available for expressing passionate resentment of authority and religion,[162] the Revolution's supporters saw it as the path to universal emancipation.

Many *philosophes*, held Roederer, Brissot, Prudhomme, and Tournon, had contributed to making the Revolution, among them d'Argenson, Montesquieu,

---

[159] Roederer, *De la philosophie*, 41.
[161] La Harpe, *Philosophie*, i. 107–8.
[160] Ibid. 37–8, 41–2; Roederer, *Spirit*, 82–8.
[162] Ibid. i. 126.

Rousseau, Raynal, and Voltaire. Brissot also deeply admired Bayle, Boulanger, and Helvétius. They qualified their choices of names, however, with some significant remarks distinguishing the various contributions. Voltaire mattered chiefly for his peerless literary skill and relentless ridiculing of old-established prejudices; for the rest he was a friend of kings and aristocrats. Brissot was especially caustic about Voltaire whom he considered no friend of the people.[163] Montesquieu seasoned the collective philosophical recipe with 'salt and energy' but one must remember that this great man fell into 'des erreurs' regarding social status and 'corporations' having the misfortune to be both a nobleman himself and also a *parlementaire* (to Prud-homme and Tournon something equally reprehensible).[164] Rousseau, by contrast, had taught readers to think about 'les droits des hommes'. But more important still was 'Raynal', 'armé d'une plume de fer', who had, unlike the others, directly attacked tyranny.[165] Many also stressed Mably's contribution.

What was Rousseau's role in this revolution of the mind? Mirabeau disparaged Montesquieu and celebrated Rousseau for his great role in the making of the Revolution just a few days after the Bastille's Fall, in July 1789, in his paper the *Courrier de Provence*.[166] One should never speak of liberty and the Revolution without paying homage to 'cet immortel vengeur de la nature humaine'.[167] Among the 'truths' expounded by Rousseau pronounced truly *philosophique* by Mirabeau was his idea that the social state can only be advantageous to men if they all own something and no one owns too much.[168] Yet, there was also much contradiction between this veneration for Rousseau and the prevailing enthusiasm for 'philosophy', for proceeding 'under the banner of reason'. Above all there was tension between the Rousseauist claim that it is 'feeling', 'le sens moral', that guides man and emphatic commitment to what Brissot calls 'l'esprit philosophique', tension hard to resolve even in his own mind let alone in reality.[169] But when obliged to choose, as in Geneva in 1782, Brissot condemned the narrow patriotism he encountered there and had also witnessed in England, and especially the kind of uncompromising republicanism that makes men put their country before all other considerations. He expressly rejected this for that kind of 'philosophy' that seeks to 'répandre la liberté par tout l'univers', a universalism typical of the *Révolutions de Paris* and all radical thought.[170]

This split between the cosmopolitanism of the *parti de philosophie*, taken to its furthest extreme by Gorani and Cloots, and the narrow patriotism and xenophobia of Robespierre, Saint-Just, and one section of the *Jacobins* was yet another aspect of the continuing tussle between the Revolution of Reason and the Revolution

---

[163] Brissot, *Patriote français*, 145 (31 Dec. 1789), 4.
[164] Roederer, *De la philosophie*, 24; [Prudhomme and Tournon], *Révolutions de Paris*, i. 35.
[165] [Prudhomme and Tournon], *Révolutions de Paris*, i. 35; Mounier, *De l'influence*, 125.
[166] Brissot, *Patriote français*, 1 (28 July 1789), 382.
[167] Mirabeau, *Courrier de Provence*, 20 (14/27 July 1789), 20.
[168] Ibid. 28 (17/18 Aug. 1789), 1–2.
[169] Brissot, *De la vérité*, 109–12, 178, 185, 196–7, 212, 216–17.
[170] Ibid. 253, 257–8.

of the Will; and the xenophobia of the latter justified itself by citing Rousseau whereas opposing xenophobia involved criticizing Rousseau.[171] Militant chauvinism during Robespierre's ascendancy was further intensified by becoming closely linked, again following Rousseau, to rejection of atheism as unpatriotic and contrary to 'virtue'.[172] The institutionalized Rousseauism of the Jacobins as the militant opposite to the anti-Rousseauism of Mirabeau, Sieyès, Brissot, Cloots, Volney, Condorcet, and so forth, in short, lies at the very heart of the struggle for control of the Revolution.

3. *PHILOSOPHES* AGAINST THE REVOLUTION

The precarious hold of the 'parti de philosophie' over the Assembly helps explain why there was so much talk in 1789, and for decades afterwards, of a 'philosophic' conspiracy perpetrated by a mere handful of *philosophes* enabling them to capture the Assembly. The 'conspiracy' paradigm may have been exaggerated and perhaps, as Roederer put it, 'petty', but it was effective propaganda. The vast majority had no desire to be led by 'philosophy'. Furthermore, the *anti-philosophes* rightly maintained that what enabled the Assembly to be captured by 'philosophy' was a kind of manipulation even if it was less intrigue and conspiracy than speeches and informed opinion goading the lukewarm further than they would otherwise have gone, pressure boosted by street demonstrations, the Parisian press, and anxiety over rural violence. If many spoke of a conspiracy, Gorani emphasized the role of the clubs. But however one explains it, the irreducible fact was that a small minority in the Assembly succeeded in overcoming the majority's inertia, reluctance, 'passions', and interests.[173]

Forming clubs was in part a political and partly a wider social and cultural phenomenon. The Parisian and provincial societies, clubs, and committees proved to be key amplifiers for debates, and rallying points for proposals generated by the Assembly. Condorcet, for example, became a major figure in the policy debates at the heart of the Revolution mainly through his pre-eminent roles in the Société de 1789 and the Paris commune's Comité des Vingt-Quatre of which he became president in December 1789. Everywhere, new clubs sprang up and old societies expanded. Science and mathematics, for the moment, were all but forgotten. Great scientists like Condorcet, Bailly, and Lalande, reported Gorani, from Paris, in September 1790, now spent their entire time discussing laws and politics. The clubs also served as an advanced school in high-level revolutionary philosophy for foreigners like Gorani, Cloots, and later Paine desiring to become part of the Revolution and through whose correspondence abroad the Revolution fed directly into the thought world of leading

---

[171] Cobb, *The French*, 178–9.   [172] Culoma, *Religion civile*, 189–93.
[173] Chénier, *Dénonciation des Inquisiteurs*, 3; McMahon, *Enemies*, 66.

intellectual figures and prominent professors in Italy, Germany, Switzerland, and the Netherlands.[174]

Meanwhile, the Assembly majority that was less than enthusiastic for the full revolutionary programme could most effectively retaliate by citing Montesquieu and, more sporadically, Locke, Hume, Newton, and Voltaire. Given the split within the circle of Madame Helvétius and the defection of Morellet, it is not hard to see how it came about by August 1789 that just as there was a formidable array of *philosophes* supporting the Revolution there was another formidable list ranged against.[175] It was mostly those who had all along supported moderate rather than radical enlightened positions who, like Morellet and Marmontel, reacted very differently from Naigeon, Deleyre, Mirabeau, Brissot, Maréchal, Cloots, Démeunier, Volney, or Condorcet, becoming thoroughly alienated already in the summer of 1789. More joined them during the period of free press and expression, before the Jacobin takeover. But there were also one or two *philosophes* earlier associated with radical positions who became alienated once they saw what was involved and here the key defection—and much the most discussed—was that of Raynal.

Ill feeling between the Assembly's rival factions remained intense throughout. In 1789, the factions regularly disparaged each other as 'aristocrates' for conservatives, the *parti anglais* for the *monarchiens, parti ecclésiastique* for the clergy, and as 'enragés' for *philosophique* reformers. Given this embattled context, it was easy for an anonymous open letter to the National Assembly, or 'diatribe perfide' against the people, as Brissot branded it, dated 'Marseille, 10 December 1789', supposedly written by Raynal and read out in the National Assembly on 5 January 1790, to prove uncommonly contentious. This occurred just a few days after publication of the French translation of Price's strongly pro-Revolution *Discourse on the Love of our Country*, of 4 November 1789, a text much applauded by Brissot. The open letter from 'Raynal' was a text expressing firm opposition to all the basic principles of the Revolution and, as such, besides evoking widespread disbelief that Raynal was really its author, caused deep consternation in the Paris cafés, the Assembly, and among the public alike.[176]

A towering representative of 'idées philosophiques' in 1788, Raynal, like Mirabeau, had been recommended by many in Marseille to represent the city in opposing the nobility's and clergy's separate status and fiscal privileges in the Estates-General.[177] Indeed, he was actually elected to the Estates-General but resigned his seat citing

---

[174] Gorani to Slop, Paris, 14 Sept. 1790 in Catalano, 'Alcune lettere', 157; Williams, *Condorcet and Modernity*, 29; Doyle, *Oxford History*, 142.

[175] See, for instance, the assertion that 'aucun élève des "philosophes", aucun ancien encyclopédiste n'a joué dans la Révolution un rôle aussi éminent que l'Abbé Grégoire ou l'évêque Fauchet, que des religieux défroqués comme Fouché, et surtout que Stanislas Fréron, fils du grand ennemi de Voltaire et redoutable épurateur du midi royaliste', Mortier, 'Les Héritiers', 460–1; Goulemot, 'Penseurs', 83.

[176] Brissot, *Patriote français*, 152 (7 Jan. 1790), 3–4.

[177] BL 910.c.16/7 'Lettre d'un citoyen de Marseille ... sur M. de Mirabeau et l'Abbé Raynal', 1–2, 45–6.

old age. Through 1789 he was continually identified as one of the foremost philosophical prophets of the Revolution and someone who condemned royal absolutism, affirming the advantages of a democratic republic in which people make the laws through their representatives.[178] Brissot's ally Pierre-Louis Manuel figured among the many acclaiming Raynal, together with Rousseau, one of the 'pères de la révolution'.[179] A pamphlet published in the summer of 1789 asserting the advantages of the democratic republic as against monarchy, styling itself a 'conversation' between Raynal and Linguet while praising the National Guard of Paris, has 'Raynal' articulating several key phrases denouncing royal absolutism today known to have been penned by Diderot.[180]

How could one persuade oneself, asked the *Chronique de Paris* in January 1790, that a writer who denounced the conspiracy of kings against their peoples with such vigour should at the very moment his most ardent hopes were being realized, and a great nation was breaking its shackles, embrace 'the most feeble and pusillanimous principles'? 'Raynal's' purported objections to the principle of equality were here dismissed as totally absurd in the eyes of 'la philosophie et de la raison'.[181] For the time being, most supporters of the Revolution simply assumed the text was supposititious and that Raynal had not repudiated his former views. But in fact, showing great courage, according to Mounier, the real Raynal *had* set himself against the Revolution; and all doubts on this score were finally dispelled by his more famous open letter, attacking the Revolution, read to the Assembly on 31 May 1791.

He had been filled with joy by the *Declaration of Rights*, he assured the Assembly in this key text, but complained bitterly about the anarchic state of the country, infractions of individual liberty, and dominant role of the clubs which was such, he thought, as to suborn any form of proper government by subordinating the Assembly's majority to a network of highly articulate cliques outside.[182] It was an intervention that caused widespread dismay. The chorus of scorn and denunciation poured on Raynal's head, as a consequence, marks one of the supreme moments of the philosophical drama infusing and shaping the Revolution. In subsequent years, other former admirers of the *philosophes*, like La Harpe, seeing the direction matters were taking, repudiated not just the Revolution but also *la philosophie*, holding the latter responsible for the crimes of the former. But nothing of the sort had yet occurred in the public sphere and no other defection from the ranks of the 'party of philosophy' was to have so great an impact or be so keenly resented.[183] The new open letter provoked a massive chorus of condemnation and derision, Marie-Joseph

[178] *Conversation entre Messieurs Raynal et Linguet*, 3, 11, 31, 40; Bancarel and Goggi, *Raynal*, 27.
[179] Manuel, *Lettres...recueillies*, 91, 178; de Luna, 'Dean Street Style', 179.
[180] *Conversation entre Messieurs Raynal et Linguet*, 46, 50; Bancarel and Goggi, *Raynal*, 414.
[181] *Chronique de Paris*, 2/30 (30 Jan. 1790), 117.
[182] Raynal, *Adresse* (31 May 1791), 6–7, 15; Livesey, *Making Democracy*, 63–5; Bancarel and Goggi, *Raynal*, 421–7.
[183] Mounier, *De l'influence*, 125; Mortier, 'Les Héritiers', 456, 459 n.; McMahon, *Enemies*, 119–20.

Chénier, Cloots, and others openly denouncing Raynal as a traitor, impostor, and charlatan.

But denouncing him was not enough: it had to be shown that he was not the true author of the ideas associated with his name. The public had been Raynal's innocent 'dupe' for decades, contended the anonymous *T. G. Raynal démasqué, ou Lettres sur la vie et les ouvrages de cet écrivain* (1791), and no one should be surprised. For it was not Raynal, but really Diderot, Deleyre, Pechméja, Guibert, de Kniphausen, d'Holbach, and La Grange, the translator of Lucretius, who were the true authors of the *Histoire philosophique*.[184] Several still living persons, including Bailly, the public was assured, could attest to the truth of this and that the famous passage denouncing black slavery was really penned by the deceased Jean Pechméja, not Raynal.[185] Bailly is there cited as one who knew Diderot at the time he worked on the *Histoire*, and had scrupulously kept his secret thus far but could attest that his hand lay behind more than twenty long sections. Raynal had had no right to claim the credit for the *Histoire*. Several writers, reportedly, had considered exposing his fraudulent conduct years before, following the appearance of the 1780 version, but refrained in view of the hue and cry against him. Actually, it had suited Raynal to flee France at that time and subsequently stay away for years as he was unable any longer to look the veritable authors of that great and prophetic work in the face.[186]

Unlike Diderot and other participants in the venture, Raynal had not even been a true supporter of the American Revolution, charged his critics, and his inadequate, unenthusiastic account of that episode in the *Histoire* had rightly been attacked and discredited by Paine and Mazzei.[187] The controversy touched a very raw nerve. Not only were the vast majority of France's population unfamiliar with, and unsympathetic to, what became the goals of the Revolution, in 1789, but even most of the National Assembly consisted of what have aptly been termed 'reluctant revolutionaries' needing constant prodding to get them to acquiesce in 'notions philosophiques'. They did so often only when sufficiently unnerved by the Paris mob or rural peasants or pressured by the clubs. Plainly, it was *not* ideas on their own which did the work of carrying the Revolution forward. The Paris street crowds and clubs were decisive.[188] Any suggestion that the leadership had adopted the wrong basic principles, muddling their 'notions philosophiques', was bound to be disastrous publicity. Hence the strength of the reaction to Raynal's intervention. Most delicate of all, Raynal in his open letter while affirming like everyone else that the *révolutionnaires* were chiefly inspired by *la philosophie* had had the gall to affirm that, therefore, all the resulting misfortunes of France were the consequence 'de la philosophie' which should now be repudiated. Given that 'la philosophie' had first begun to carry real weight with public opinion precisely owing to the *Histoire* what greater fraud, hypocrisy, and irony could there possibly be than this?[189]

---

[184] [G. T.] *Raynal démasqué*, 6; Labbé, *Anarcharsis Cloots*, 165; Mortier, *Anarcharsis Cloots*, 212–13.
[185] [G. T.] *Raynal démasqué*, 6, 16–17.
[186] Ibid. 6–7; Mortier, *Anarcharsis Cloots*, 169–70.   [187] Mortier, *Anarcharsis Cloots*, 23–9.
[188] Mackrell, *Attack*, 174, 178–82.   [189] Ibid. 49–50; Fontana, *Venise et la Révolution*, 568.

35

Epilogue

1789 as an Intellectual Revolution

1. THE 'GENERAL REVOLUTION' AS A GLOBAL PROCESS

The argument of this third part of our general history of the Enlightenment has focused on the 'revolution of the mind', a dramatic shift in the balance between moderate and radical enlightened thought which was, in turn, the chief cause of the 'General Revolution' of the late eighteenth century. This 'General Revolution' rooted in radical ideas was a transatlantic phenomenon, an inherent part of the American Revolution and the late eighteenth-century Creole opposition to the royal regime in Spanish America as well as of the Swiss and Dutch democratic movements of the 1780s and 1790s and growing critique of the existing social and institutional order in Britain together with the French Revolution's ideology of freedom and 'basic rights' prior to the rise of Robespierre. Nothing could be more mistaken than to suppose the 'human rights' of 1789 were deeply bound up with 'state and nation'.[1] The Radical Enlightenment's Human Rights constituted, rather, an unqualified moral universalism.

The reader will now see why it is that the current habit among many historians of distinguishing between 'philosophical' and 'social' interpretations of the Enlightenment is a giant delusion. There is no such thing as a non-philosophical account of the Enlightenment and could not possibly be. Such a thing would be a complete contradiction in terms. The fact is that one can understand nothing at all about the Enlightenment without exploring its intellectual and ideological divisions and basing one's interpretation on these. What is true is that in the past there have been 'philosophical' accounts of the Enlightenment that make no effort to explain the interaction of social forces, and beyond these general history, with intellectual factors in shaping the Enlightenment's 'philosophical' history. Intellectual accounts of the Enlightenment that focus just on the evolution of ideas are fundamentally unsatisfactory, truncated, and methodologically wrongly conceived. They are also useless for explaining the relationship of the Enlightenment to revolution. Any account of the

---

[1] Moyn, *Last Utopia*, 20, 25–6.

Enlightenment that is satisfactory must be both intellectual and social history, ideas studied in socio-economic and political context. There is simply no way round this basic desideratum.

That the French Revolution was caused by 'philosophy' was affirmed by Lichtenberg and by many other German, Italian, Dutch, and French commentators in 1789 and during the 1790s. The new revolutionary consciousness generated a powerful revulsion against 'aristocracy', traditional ideas, and ecclesiastical authority and also 'enlightened despotism' and forms of absolutism assuming a superficial veneer of Enlightenment, such as evolved in Portugal and Brazil under Pombal's dictatorial rule, and in Russia, Austria, Spain, and Prussia. Revolution then, in turn, became a motor driving the wider dissemination of radical ideas. Like 'philosophy' and 'aristocracy', both the word and concept 'tyranny' fundamentally changed its meaning in Western high culture after 1770. Earlier, tyranny signified legally unrestrained rule that violated long-accepted constitutional procedures, laws, privileges, and legally defined rights, especially of nobles, churchmen, and other favoured persons and institutions. 'Tyranny' in Diderot, Helvétius, Mably, Raynal, Condorcet, and d'Holbach, as well as Price, Priestley, and Paine, by contrast, encompassed all rule irrespective of whether formally legitimate or illegitimate when not grounded, as d'Holbach puts it, 'on the advantages procured for those on whom it is exercised'.

According to older notions, absolute monarchs were free to act however they pleased provided they respected the fundamental laws and accepted religious beliefs. Under the new dispensation, no government was entitled to do anything at all other than what best served the good of society as a whole, this being 'la loi primitive et fondamentale' nature imposes on all those who govern men.[2] Henceforth, nobility, privileges, hereditary office-holding, dynastic pride, venality of office, granting trade monopolies, court splendour, fine gardens, empire-building, religious discrimination, book censorship, foreign wars not motivated by self-defence, and subsidizing churches is by definition all 'tyranny', detracting from the people's happiness and 'la liberté'.[3] 'Tyranny' had become whatever hampers the advance of liberty, democracy, and equality. 'Government on the old system', Paine summed up, 'is an assumption of power, for the aggrandizement of itself; on the new, a delegation of power, for the common benefit of society.'[4] This was indeed a vast cultural shift engineered by radical ideas, and one implying an integrated revolution at once social, moral, educational, religious, and political.

Another aspect of 'tyranny' that in the past no one would have dubbed 'tyranny', or deemed corruption perpetrated by royal courts, was the quest for honours, titles, pedigrees, and privileges. In *ancien régime* society, nobles, diplomats, office-holders, merchants, financiers, lawyers, and army officers all strove, often at huge expense, such is the effect of prejudice and a wrong conception of society and morality, in d'Holbach's view, to obtain 'such baubles', wasting their energies, time, and fortunes

---

[2] D'Holbach, *Système social*, 240–7; d'Holbach, *Morale universelle*, ii. 24, 44.
[3] D'Holbach, *Morale universelle*, i. 146–52.   [4] Paine, *Rights of Man*, 171.

on this pointless and addictive pursuit, continually shepherding their families into the same vain obsession goaded by false pride, fashions, and the presumption of the rich.[5] The grandiloquent titles and privileges princes bestow not only foster a public cult of vanity and affectation but, worse, confer tangible rewards on the most adept, often the wealthiest, at obtaining favour—these rewards were prestige, preferential treatment, exemptions, and position, all things thinking persons consider inherently unjust and socially divisive, indeed the root of ostentation, presumption, and jealousy besides ridiculous family feuds over precedence.

Under the *ancien régime*, almost everywhere 'le souverain est tout, sa nation n'est rien'.[6] Royal and princely courts foment 'tyranny' by creating a cultural milieu organized for flattery, servility, affectation, and hypocrisy. Tyranny is continually reinforced by the self-interest of court sycophants since flattering rulers' and grandees' vanity is what chiefly prompts them to increase exactions on the populace, and blinds them to the drawbacks of doing so, exacerbating their despotic sway and raising minions' remuneration.[7] Little of this truly redounds to the prince's advantage, in the end, since it provokes sullenness and resistance. Hence, 'le flatteur' is really the worst enemy of peoples and kings alike.[8] The worst tyrants, contends d'Holbach, were the most flattered. Life under oppression is the rule almost everywhere; and, yet, revolt is rare because peoples let themselves become downtrodden, adjust to, and become habituated to slavery. Princes ensure this outcome by harnessing ignorance, indolence, and religion to bolster whatever people are used to. The world is full of slaves 'assez lâches pour aimer leurs chaînes, assez fous pour en rire, assez bas pour s'en glorifier'.[9] The worst despotisms such as those of Spain and Naples abase everyone and produce only 'des esclaves découragés, ou des bandits audacieux qui infestent les pays'.[10] To overthrow 'despotism', the entire human reality must be transformed which can only be done by eradicating people's existing beliefs and attitudes, something impossible for the masses and totally unacceptable to monarchs, aristocrats, and clergy. Hence, 'philosophy' is the only possible engine of a 'General Revolution' such as d'Holbach, Diderot, Raynal, Helvétius, or Paine, Barlow, or Palmer, or Wekhrlin, Diez, Bahrdt, Knoblauch, and Weishaupt, envisaged.

Against this backdrop it was impossible that the revolutionary leaders of 1789 should confine their sights to the remaking of France only. Until a narrow patriotism and xenophobic stress on the nation set in under Robespierre, it was inconceivable that the Revolution's intellectual leadership would not, from an early stage, clash violently with the pretensions of 'enlightened despotism' including the legacies of Frederick and Joseph even though France was still technically a monarchy, not a republic, during the years 1789–92. To the evident consternation of the *Berlinische Monatsschrift*, three pre-eminent revolutionary makers of opinion, Condorcet,

---

[5] D'Holbach, *Morale universelle*, i. 163–4.　[6] D'Holbach, *Système social*, 332.
[7] D'Holbach, *Morale universelle*, i. 205–6.　[8] Ibid. i. 206.
[9] D'Holbach, *Système social*, 334–6; Lichtenberg, *Schriften und Briefe*, i. 811.
[10] D'Holbach, *Morale universelle*, i. 215 n.

Isaac-Réné Le Chapelier (1754–94), one of the most active members of the National Assembly's constitutional committee, and the orientalist and publicist Charles de Peyssonel (1727–99), publicly proclaimed Frederick in a published article 'le Néron du Nord' whom 'base adulation' honoured with the name of *philosophe* and by doing so deeply insulted *la philosophie*. Frederick, suggested Condorcet, Le Chapelier, and Peyssonel, had received the epithet 'the Great' for no better reason than having fought twenty-six battles, causing more death and injury than all Europe's other 'tyrants' put together.[11] Such statements were bound to intensify the backlash against the Revolution and against 'philosophy' in Berlin, Vienna, Petersburg, Madrid, and Lisbon alike, underlining more and more the final, irredeemable collapse of Voltaire's Enlightenment and that of Genovesi, Hume, the Verris, Sonnenfels, and Turgot.

This 'revolution of the mind' transforming the Western world between 1760 and 1789 was unquestionably among the greatest, most decisive shifts in humanity's history, and the change in the status and capacity of the radical tendency was obvious to moderate Enlightenment, *anti-philosophes*, and Counter-Enlightenment alike. In the age of Hobbes, Spinoza, and Bayle, and for decades subsequently, it had been common for opponents to attack the radical underground for their 'atheism' and materialism comparing them to those they considered atheists in the ancient world, the implication being that their views were outmoded, something Christian apologists had demolished many centuries before. But by the early 1770s the tone had changed and the writings of those denouncing radical ideas began to reflect an acute anxiety. The defenders of the religious and moral order suddenly understood themselves to be combating something entirely new and rapidly gaining momentum. One should on no account confuse 'les athées modernes, et ceux du temps passé', was the new maxim: these were now obviously two entirely different things.[12] The struggle was no longer confined to a quarrel about God's existence, goodness, miracles, providence, and revelation. What was now at stake was the entire moral, social, political, cultural, and sexual order, threatened by militant reformers and anticlericals who, whether atheists or Unitarians, were unafraid, unlike the unbelievers of earlier times, to preach their creed from the roof-tops challenging the whole of existing society.

It may be that the revolutionaries were never likely to succeed. Most people, even in France, always opposed their principles and objectives. Lichtenberg, a Spinozist privately but not one who thought the public arena was susceptible to such principles, remarked that while the 'political democrats' of the French Revolution undoubtedly based themselves upon the 'monarchy of reason' and cogently championed democracy, they had nevertheless gone wrong: 'try to rule the world with a god whom Reason alone has enthroned, and you will soon find that it cannot be done.'[13] Many had seen this much earlier. 'That kings are the servants of the people, to be obeyed, resisted, deposed or punished, as the public conveniency may require',

---

[11] *Berlinische Monatsschrift*, 16 (July–Dec. 1790), 44–50.
[12] Holland, *Réflexions*, ii. 234.   [13] Stern, *Lichtenberg*, 238–40.

affirmed Adam Smith, in 1759, 'is the doctrine of reason and philosophy; but it is not the doctrine of nature'.[14] It was not what most people feel. But this in turn posed an insuperable obstacle for the moderate Enlightenment. As Smith's remark implies, it was difficult to defeat the revolutionaries on purely intellectual grounds. Tradition is a very powerful force in human life but not one readily defended on enlightened grounds even invoking Hume's scepticism.

It was precisely their insistence that reason is man's sole guide in ordering society and morality which pushed the Radical Enlightenment inexorably towards democratic republicanism, and, equally, the contrary claim that the moral and social order rests on tradition and hierarchy that tilted the moderate mainstream more and more against 'reason and philosophy' and towards precedent and sentiment as the prime defence of monarchy, nobility, and ecclesiastical authority. In the end this destroyed the moderate Enlightenment, handing the initiative to outright reaction and Counter-Enlightenment, on the one hand, and the revolutionary underground on the other. 'I perceive, from the whole tenor of your *Reflections*', Wollstonecraft rebuked Burke, in 1790, 'that you have a mortal antipathy to reason' and believe that men should rely not on reason but sentiment which should lead them to 'reverence the rust of antiquity, and term the unnatural customs which ignorance and mistaken self-interest have consolidated, the sage fruit of experience'.[15] She was right. There were perhaps inherent inconsistencies in the Radical Enlightenment too. Burke could with some justice ridicule 'those democratists, who, when they are not on their guard, treat the humbler part of the community with the greatest contempt, whilst at the same time, they pretend to make them the depositories of all power'.[16] But such inconsistencies were nowhere near so fundamental as those of the mainstream.

One kind of Enlightenment, anchored in Spinoza originally and in the view of Voltaire, and many others, still so anchored in the late eighteenth century (despite the efforts of a growing number of scholars today to deny this), was inherently revolutionary; its counterpart, on the moderate side, inherently anti-revolutionary and inclined to ally with religious authority and tradition as well as monarchy and aristocracy. Christianity undeviatingly supports monarchy, insisted the Sorbonne-trained Dominican philosophy professor from Lorraine Dom Charles-Louis Richard (1711–94), in 1775, and teaches obedience to authority and, above all, that political power comes directly from God. *La philosophie moderne*, on the other hand, to which it stands in outright opposition, teaches that the exclusive basis of sovereign authority lies in the advantages rulers afford their subjects, and hence that they lose all rights and legitimacy the instant they violate 'les devoirs de l'équité'. This contradicts all precedent, religion, and existing law. Worse, he added, when the author of the *La Politique naturelle* (d'Holbach) speaks of 'un despotisme odieux et abusif' he plainly means by this nothing other than 'Christian monarchy'.[17]

---

[14] Smith, *Theory*, 115.   [15] Wollstonecraft, *Vindication of the Rights of Men*, 8.
[16] Burke, *Reflections*, 47.
[17] Richard, *Défense de la religion*, 137–8; McMahon, *Enemies*, 17, 28–30.

That radical thought by its very nature creates the likelihood of a general revolution is clearly prognosticated in the works of many later eighteenth-century writers. When denouncing despots and despotism, it is against kings and monarchy itself, protested Richard, that the author of *La Politique naturelle* hurls his rage, monarchs he depicts as 'des sources fatales de la corruption publique', the destruction 'de tout bonheur, de toute vertu'. Everyone loyal to monarchs he designates miserable slaves without the courage to reclaim their 'droits, et de demander, les armes à la main, le bonheur qui leur est dû'.[18] Bishop Jean-Georges Le Franc de Pompignan (1715–90), later archbishop of Vienne, and one of the clergy's representatives in 1789, published lengthy pastoral 'instructions' to his flock, as early as 1763 and 1766, and more later, admonishing everyone against the new heretical sect driven by 'ce nouveau caractère de l'esprit philosophique' which with its 'esprit anti-royaliste et républicain', its principle that sovereignty lies with the people, its comprehensive *tolérantisme*, and proclaiming philosophical reason man's chief guide in life, diverges from all previously known heresies by fundamentally threatening the Church's primacy, theology, and religion and the entire social order. *La philosophie nouvelle* was a general 'revolt' against authority ecclesiastical and monarchical alike.[19] *Anti-philosophes* no less than their foes, the radical *philosophes*, grasped that the diffusion in France of the ideas of Diderot, d'Holbach, Helvétius, and Condorcet and, by the later 1770s, the numerous body of authors of the second-rank—Mirabeau, Cerisier, Brissot, Sieyès, Delisle de Sales, Naigeon, Mercier, Cloots, Volney, Garat, Démeunier—spelt a total 'revolution' in politics and social thought no less than in religion, metaphysics, and morality.

The true spirit of our so-called *philosophes modernes*, concluded Charles-Louis Richard, in 1775, a year prior to the outbreak of the American Revolution, is an 'esprit de sédition, de révolte, de ligue universelle contre les souverains qui régissent le monde'. Tremble, then, he summoned those holding the sceptres of monarchy, tremble on your thrones! For if one is to believe these *philosophes*, all your subjects would arm themselves against you, 'pour vous detrôner à leur gré, si leur bien-être l'exigeroit'. They announce such doctrines even though God strictly forbids peoples to oppose injustices done to them by those who govern, commanding them to suffer despotic rule patiently and without murmur and especially without protest or rebellion. For to revolt 'c'est résister à l'ordre de Dieu et s'attirer sa condamnation'.[20] All loyal Frenchmen Dom Richard called to rally around the throne, to help the best, wisest, and most Christian of kings, Louis XVI, resist the excesses of this 'troupe de séditieux' equally culpable before God and men.[21] The bishops, happily, were acting vigorously at the highest levels to rally all France to fight the poisonous teachings of the *nouveaux philosophes*.

---

[18] Richard, *Défense de la religion*, 163, 183–4, 193, 211.
[19] Le Franc de Pompignon, *Instruction pastorale*, 2–3, 20, 201–2; Marmontel, *Mémoires*, iii. 217.
[20] Richard, *Défense de la religion*, 183–4.
[21] Ibid., preface pp. xliv–xlv and 26–7.

The great strength of the moderate Enlightenment was its dominance of the middle ground, its forging a judicious balance between 'reason' and 'tradition' and between science and religion, and ability to command the support of princes and churchmen. Every liberal government, church, academy, university, and judicial institution battled for moderate against Radical Enlightenment. But moderate Enlightenment in the end proved unable to deliver the goods where it counted most— in securing the social, moral, and institutional reforms many saw a need for, reforms required to ease deep-seated social tensions. By the late 1780s, it had become obvious that an Enlightenment seeking to engineer change via 'le pouvoir' in the manner Voltaire advocated could not obtain a comprehensive toleration, or wide-ranging legal reform, or end serfdom or ecclesiastical privilege, or curb the nobility's predominance, or reform marriage.

On its own, moderate Enlightenment could not abolish organized discrimination against religious minorities, institute freedom of the press, halt persecution of homosexuals, or emancipate the blacks of the New World. Rather, what leverage it possessed was further trimmed back after 1770, as princes, reacting to the escalating diffusion of radical ideas and then the Revolution, increasingly cracked down on 'philosophy' and democratic voices and publications. By the early 1790s, there was hardly any elbow room left between royalist reaction in alliance with Counter-Enlightenment, on the one hand, and a revolutionary ideology of equality, individual liberty, freedom of expression, and materialist metaphysics, sworn to evict kings and empower peoples, on the other. Despite the widespread support it still commanded in some quarters, moderate mainstream Enlightenment everywhere receded as a feasible strategy in the world of the 1790s—and not least in Britain, being no longer anywhere a viable political option.

Diderot's claim in the *Histoire philosophique* that 'la révolution qui s'est faite dans les esprits' was now about to change the world had been proved right. He was right that the revolution in ideas in Europe and the Americas that occurred between 1750 and 1789 was simultaneously a social, emotional, and an intellectual process. There would have been no social basis for Radical Enlightenment and Radical Enlightenment could have had no importance without vast inequality, economic deprivation, and oppression. But the natural indignation stemming from injustice, oppression, and misery was nothing new and on its own insufficient to precipitate meaningful change. Among nations just as among individuals, contends the *Histoire*, body and soul operate on each other interacting dialectically. Physical needs and philosophical ideas are ultimately inseparable. This is why Enlightenment and revolutionary social change must ultimately be viewed as inseparable parts of a single process: as the Diderot circle put it 'le peuple entraîne les philosophes, et les philosophes mènent le peuple'.[22]

---

[22] *Histoire philosophique* (1780), x. 437.

2. COMMEMORATING THE REVOLUTIONARY ENLIGHTENMENT'S HEROES

It may be that there had been greater geniuses and even more perfect orators than Mirabeau, commented Garat in 1792, but no one had put eloquence to work more powerfully to convert into political action and laws 'les hautes pensées de la Philosophie; et ce talent le plus utile de tous au monde, il l'a déployé dans la révolution d'un empire accoutumé à donner des modèles à l'Europe'.[23] Within the context of 'General Revolution' as understood by the 'parti de philosophie', it was natural to view Mirabeau as the epitome of a new kind of hero to replace the corrupt, outmoded heroes of tradition, religion, classical learning, and court romances. It was consequently natural too that he should have been both one of the inventors and one of the first objects of a new kind of public cult, a revolutionary cult that came to be thoroughly blighted, however, by the triumph of Robespierre and his faction among the Jacobins.

The three days of public mourning to mark the death of Benjamin Franklin, decreed by the National Assembly, at Mirabeau's suggestion, on 11 June 1790 marks the start of the cult of honouring the Enlightenment and 'General Revolution's' great men, the heroes who brought about humanity's emancipation. It was Mirabeau's death, though, in April 1791, that led to a crystallizing of earlier proposals to formalize the political and cultural cult of the heroes who inspired and showed how to carry out the Revolution. Already more than a year earlier, in March 1790, Cloots had proposed that Voltaire's ashes be brought to Paris and specially honoured. For many months there had also been talk of the need to erect a public statue to Rousseau. Meanwhile, there was a general feeling that something more integrated and grander was needed. In April 1791, finally, an ambitious plan was laid before the Paris commune: Sainte-Geneviève, one of the largest buildings in Paris, the reconstruction of which had been taken up by Louis XV personally in 1764 with a view to ensuring its status as one of the most visually impressive churches in the kingdom, should be turned instead into a vast temple of human glory somewhat akin to Westminster Abbey in London.

A 'Panthéon' to receive the tombs of the 'great men of the Revolution' and those who had prepared the way for it through their writings was duly decreed. The deceased Mirabeau, amid great solemnity, almost royal pomp, arriving amidst a vast procession in which walked almost all the 1,200 deputies of the National Assembly, on 4 April 1791, became the first public hero to repose there under the resounding inscription: 'Aux grands hommes, la Patrie reconnaissante'. A great commemorative event, this was the first time anyone other than a king or a saint had ever been publicly projected on such a scale in France let alone celebrated for writings, oratory, law-making, and political achievements.[24] But while only Marat, in

---

[23] Garat, 'Jugement', p. xi.
[24] Fontana, *Venise et la Révolution*, 538; de Staël, *Considerations*, 267; Scurr, *Fatal Purity*, 130–1.

his paper *L'Ami du peuple*, violently protested at the honouring of Mirabeau (whom he denounced as a 'traitor'), from the very outset, the venture encountered the thorniest difficulties. Some had to do with disputes over how to organize competition among artists from which to select those commissioned to sculpt the busts of great men and related projects. Other problems ran deeper, having more to do with the concept itself.

There was immediate disagreement, predictably, over 'la panthéonisation' of Voltaire. One of the greatest writers and thinkers of his age, he had indisputably introduced vast changes in thought and literature. But did this flatterer of kings and courtiers deserve the esteem of humanity and those presiding over the Revolution? Voltaire, Brissot's paper, *Le Patriote français*, reminded readers in January 1790, had desired and obtained a chateau complete with dependants and vassals: 'Voltaire étoit plus poète que politique et les poètes aiment les despotes', a sentiment with which Robespierre wholeheartedly agreed.[25] His *panthéonisation* was eventually pushed through but only over considerable opposition, and it was not until 11 July that Voltaire's remains were brought in an impressive ceremonial procession, directed by the supreme revolutionary master of ceremonies, the artist David, to lie at Mirabeau's side.[26] The great church of Saint-Geneviève in Paris, exclaimed Feller indignantly in his journal, had now become the shrine of the 'carcasses' of Mirabeau and Voltaire, the new 'divinities' of the Parisian rabble who were manipulated on a daily basis by scoundrels 'et débauchés, c'est à dire les dévôts de la philosophie'.[27]

From the outset, predictably, there was virtual unanimity in the Assembly regarding Rousseau. Having agreed to install Mirabeau and Voltaire in the Panthéon, it was inconceivable that Rousseau should not follow as swiftly as could be managed. But here another kind of difficulty intervened. In his last testament, Rousseau stipulated that in conformity with his love of solitariness and retreat from society, he should be buried not in the city he loathed but in perfect solitude. There was no denying that his existing rather elaborate tomb, near Montmorency, a place that constantly drew crowds of devotees, corresponded well enough to his last wishes. Consequently, both transferring Rousseau's remains and installing the official bust originally planned had to be indefinitely postponed.

Meanwhile, no one recommended placing Diderot or d'Holbach in the Panthéon either before or after 1791, the real nature of their contributions being scarcely known to the public. It was more or less only the *parti de philosophie* itself that knew of it. Nevertheless, when Naigeon addressed the National Assembly on the subject of freedom of thought and liberty of the press, in his famous speech of February 1790, reminding them that it was the *philosophes* who had prepared and constructed the 'reason' embodied in the Assembly, and the legacy of the *philosophes* that should 'today second the efforts of this Assembly', it was obvious he was not

[25] *Le Patriote français*, 145 (21 Jan. 1790), 4.
[26] Thompson, *French Revolution*, 197, 218; Jones, *Great Nation*, 530; Jourdan, 'Le Culte', 60–1.
[27] [Feller], *Journal historique* (1792), 149.

referring to Voltaire or Rousseau, both of whom he detested, but rather Diderot and d'Holbach.[28] It matters not at all, he added, trying vainly to raise the status of the atheists and materialists, whether men are 'Jews, Christians, idolaters, deists or atheists', it was the true heroes who should be honoured and the true 'saints sont les bons citoyens'.[29] Helvétius did have a certain heroic status in the Revolution down to 1792 but this, seemingly, was insufficient to get him into the Panthéon and, anyhow, did not last.

On 5 December 1792, Robespierre denounced the now discredited Mirabeau in the Jacobin club and the Jacobins pulled down and smashed to pieces Mirabeau's bust along with that of Helvétius who had hitherto presided over all their meetings, the latter being pronounced by Robespierre an unbeliever and treacherous persecutor of Jean-Jacques. Both busts were trampled under foot.[30] At the Panthéon, nothing further occurred until after the onset of Robespierre's ascendancy and the Terror. But by that time all the *philosophes* ranged against Rousseau were being denounced by Robespierre as atheists undermining 'virtue', and as 'charlatans ambitieux', as he put it in a famous tirade in May 1794: they pretended to denounce despotism and yet received pensions from despots, an allusion to Diderot's arrangement with Catherine.[31] At the same time, the Revolution's official cult of Rousseau had assumed such proportions under Jacobin auspices that it had become impossible to lay him beside anyone else. The foremost hindrance to the Panthéon project during the Terror was that the Jacobin leadership viewed all Rousseau's philosophical opponents as inadmissible and considered Rousseau himself so totally above Voltaire, Mirabeau, and everyone else except Marat who, however, earlier had been almost alone in publicly repudiating the consecration of Mirabeau and Voltaire, that it seemed to the new ruling clique inappropriate to continue with the original schema. Under the circumstances, neither Rousseau nor Marat (to whom Robespierre had never been close) could be installed. Rather the great Genevan's statue should stand supreme, alone, and elsewhere.[32]

As the *Robespierriste* Jacobins gained ground, the Revolution of Reason receded. From late 1792 Chénier's revolutionary plays and pleas for freedom of the theatre were proscribed. Gorani abandoned his formerly passionate faith in the Revolution at the end of 1792.[33] Tom Paine, proclaimed an honorary French citizen in August 1792 and member of the National Convention in September, soon clashed with Marat and then participated in the failed Girondin attempt to impeach him. 'Had this Revolution been conducted consistently with its principles', he wrote to Jefferson, in April 1793, 'there was once a good prospect of extending liberty throughout the

[28] Naigeon, *Adresse à l'Assemblée*, 9; Pellerin, 'Naigeon', 29.
[29] Naigeon, *Adresse à l'Assemblée*, 53.
[30] Scurr, *Fatal Purity*, 218; Culoma, *Religion civile*, 191.
[31] On 18 Floreal of the Year 2 (7 May 1794), see Roederer, *De la philosophie*, 36; Culoma, *Religion civile*, 233, 254; Mortier, 'Les Héritiers', 461.
[32] Jourdan, 'Le Culte', 68–9; Scurr, *Fatal Purity*, 248–9.
[33] Catalano, 'Alcune lettere', 148.

greatest part of Europe; but now I relinquish that hope.'[34] But the authentic democratic republicanism of the early Revolution, still powerfully voiced and pressed for by Brissot, Condorcet, Paine, and many others in the spring of 1793, among them Deleyre who had been appointed a deputy to the Convention for the Gironde in 1792 and was one of the most active anti-*Robespierriste* reformers of this embattled phase of the Revolution, notably with his efforts to widen and consolidate toleration by introducing non-denominational hymns into primary school education,[35] was not finally crushed by the *Robespierristes* until the purges of the democratic radicals in the summer and autumn of 1793 and the arrests began of a great many innocent persons, frequently followed by their execution.

On his death, shortly after his final discussion with d'Holbach on 31 July 1784, Diderot received a Christian burial in the Chapel of the Virgin in the parish church of Saint-Roch, in Paris. During the Revolution, the tombs at Saint-Roch were violated and the remains thrown into a common ditch. With Robespierre's ascendancy, atheism and materialism were loudly condemned and Diderot virtually blacklisted. The disciples of Diderot, d'Holbach, and Helvétius, ardent supporters of the Revolution prior to the Terror albeit staunch foes of Rousseau, were now officially proscribed as enemies of the Revolution through the period from June 1793 to Robespierre's downfall on 27 July 1794.[36] Naigeon, who admitted afterwards being among the most zealous *révolutionnaires* in 1789 and 1790, remained a fervent defender of the Revolution until Robespierre's ascendancy but, like Paine and Roederer, regarded the band of Rousseauist fanatics now running the country as the destroyers of the Revolution, betraying its basic principles—free expression, free press, and individual liberty in favour of a monstrous tyranny constructed on Rousseau's 'general will'.[37] When Robespierre's ascendancy began, Naigeon withdrew into seclusion at Sedan, refusing to betray anyone to the Jacobins.

The Terror accompanied what Roederer afterwards termed 'l'anathème lancé par Robespierre contre la philosophie'.[38] It was a full-blooded Counter-Enlightenment. Condorcet was outlawed and sentenced to confiscation of his possessions in October 1793, Brissot guillotined on 31 October, Pierre-Louis Manuel following a fortnight later. Olympe de Gouges was guillotined on 3 and Bailly on 12 November. In December, Tom Paine, 'the most violent of the American democrats' in Madame de Staël's words, in whose eyes the 'principles of the Revolution, which philosophy had first diffused', were 'departed from, and philosophy itself rejected' by the *Robespierristes*, was first expelled from the Convention and then arrested and imprisoned. Already months before, he had become entirely convinced that the Jacobin government was a tyranny 'without either principle or authority'. Left in his cell, the

---

[34] Quoted ibid. 242–3.
[35] Culoma, *Religion civile*, 195, 240.
[36] Roederer, *De la philosophie*, 36–7; Mortier, *Le Cœur*, 456–7.
[37] BL R 643/6 *Lettre du citoyen Naigeon*, 6 Germinal, an 5, pp. 2, 4.
[38] Roederer, *De la philosophie*, 37.

United States government made remarkably little effort to extricate him.[39] He was fortunate to survive. Gorani fled to Switzerland. Cloots, symbol of the Revolution's internationalism and the Revolution of Reason, expelled from the Jacobin club for cosmopolitanism and atheism in early December, was arrested at the same time as Paine and guillotined soon afterwards.[40]

Rousseau's unitary notion of *volonté générale* and stress on the ordinary man's conscience against 'philosophy' and reason powerfully infused the ideology of both Robespierre and Saint-Just, the former's closest ally during the Terror.[41] However much perverted in detail, Rousseau was indeed the unique inspiration of what Robespierre insisted was the people's Revolution, that of 'virtue', not a revolution of *philosophes*. But after Robespierre's execution on 28 July 1794 and that of those who had colluded in setting aside the democratic republican constitution, freedom of the press, cosmopolitanism, and toleration of atheism, the Revolution swung back behind *la philosophie moderne*, recognizing this as the Revolution's true inspiration and chief identifying and integrating tool.[42] Those believing the Terror followed naturally from the Revolution of 1789, as royalists, *anti-philosophes*, and unsympathetic foreign observers frequently did, could not have been more mistaken. The official view during the later stages of the Revolution of Reason (1794–1802) was actually correct: namely, that 'la Terreur', as Roederer put it, was a full 'contre-révolution, et non une suite ou un complément de la Révolution', it was in every respect a complete and bloody tyranny 'et non un abus ou un accès de la liberté'.[43]

Among the charges levelled against Robespierre, after Thermidor, and among the Revolution's finer ironies, was the accusation that 'jealousy' had prevented his fittingly honouring Rousseau in the Panthéon. Mirabeau's remains, after months of contention over whether or not to evict them, were finally removed on 21 September 1794, a few weeks after Robespierre's execution, while those of Marat, hero of the populist Jacobins but of whom Robespierre was jealous, and whose installation in the Panthéon he had opposed, were installed, albeit not for long. After Thermidor, the new revolutionary leadership soon recalled that Rousseau opposed representative democracy, held that a free people should not be governed by 'représentants', and that a true republic works only in a small society. His status, accordingly, receded as that of Condorcet, Volney, Sieyès, Roederer, Cloots, and others, Diderot included, revived.[44] Deleyre, in enforced inactivity during the Terror, re-emerged after Robespierre's downfall as an active reformer,[45] as did Sieyès, Roederer, and other leaders of the revolutions of 1789 and 1792. At the same time, the publications of all these reappeared in the bookshops. Condorcet's works were republished. Naigeon, restored

---

[39] De Staël, *Considerations*, 339; Foner, *Tom Paine*, 240, 244; Jacoby, *Freethinkers*, 41.
[40] Culoma, *Religion civile*, 191.
[41] On the militancy of Saint-Just's Rousseauism, see Hampson, *Saint-Just*, 70–2, 106–8.
[42] Livesey, *Making Democracy*, 64–5.
[43] Roederer, *De la philosophie*, 29.
[44] Jourdan, 'Le Culte', 69–70.
[45] Mortier and Trouson, *Dictionnaire*, 131.

to favour, resumed editing and publishing more of Diderot's thus far inedited work for which purpose he received a subsidy from the Directory in 1795.[46] Even so, the Thermidorans had no intentions of denying Rousseau what they agreed was his rightful place in the Panthéon. After three and half years of delays, Rousseau's remains were finally deposited in the Panthéon on 11 October 1794, under the words: 'íci repose l'homme de la nature et de la vérité'.

This revival of the *philosophes'* standing, meanwhile, accompanied a sharp reaction against the populist cult of Marat. An anti-Jacobin pamphlet in the form of a 'great dispute' in the Panthéon between the shades of 'Marat' and 'Rousseau' appeared in Paris, in 1795, in which 'Marat' denounces 'Rousseau' for supposing reason and law were the correct weapons to employ against the Revolution's enemies. The pamphlet claims the real Rousseau would have been horrified by Marat's inhuman ferocity and disgusted by Robespierre's obsession with conspiracies.[47] In February 1795, after numerous busts of Marat had been smashed all over Paris and beyond, and barely five months after being laid to rest there, he was unceremoniously removed from the Panthéon. A new rule was introduced: that no one could henceforth be installed less than ten years after their demise.[48] Henceforth, the Panthéon symbolized more than anything else the irresolvable splits dividing both the Enlightenment and Revolution. In a final twist of irony, in 1804, the Panthéon, a veritable well of dispute throughout, was de-secularized by Napoleon, and pompously reinstated as a Catholic church. In 1821, during the Restoration, the remains of Voltaire and Rousseau were quietly removed and relocated out of sight in a subterranean cavern beneath the church.

The 'revolution of the mind' engineered by the Radical Enlightenment during the last three decades of the eighteenth century involved a revaluation of all values that was political, social, and moral as well as philosophical. Everything exalted or despised in the past was set in a new light. The entire legacy of established and religiously approved learning and thought of past centuries, everything the universities represented, was, in a fundamental sense, de-legitimized as a corpus. 'But only momentarily. The Revolution was defeated. But for many perspicacious onlookers this meant that the entire rhetoric of public life, respectable society and academe had withdrawn into a generally suffused false light, a false consciousness of kings, aristocracy and church authority dominating the early nineteenth century. Nothing else so clearly proves to me how things stand in the scholarly world,' remarked Lichtenberg in 1790, than the fact that Spinoza was so long considered to be a wicked good-for-nothing and his views are held to be 'dangerous'.[49] By this he meant that it had become obvious to any intelligent, honourable, and erudite person that Spinozism was the most cogent among the philosophies but nevertheless remained an outcast. Hopelessly wrong and distorted judgements, he thought, had long been

---

[46] Ibid. 338; Livesey, *Making Democracy*, 66.
[47] BL 645 a 42/23: *Grande Dispute au Panthéon*, 8–10, 14.
[48] Doyle, *Oxford History*, 287.
[49] Lichtenberg, *Schriften und Briefe*, i. 730.

the usual thing in academic as in political and religious life and still were. Could this be changed? Probably not, he thought; as in the past, ignorance, credulity, and tyranny would continue to cast everything in a false light.

According to d'Holbach, only the Enlightenment's redoubled efforts can combat error, dissipating the thick mist that had always prevented sovereigns and peoples, teachers and pupils, writers and readers, paying proper attention 'aux objets les plus intéressants pour eux'.[50] No doubt certain 'penseurs découragés', meaning Voltaire, Frederick, Hume, and Turgot, try to convince men that it is useless to suppose philosophy can 'éclairer tout un peuple'. Neither philosophy nor the principles of true morality can be grasped by the multitude.[51] But to render a nation 'reasonable', retorts d'Holbach, it is not necessary that all citizens should be savants or profound philosophers: 'il suffit qu'elle soit gouvernée par des gens de bien.' What the Enlightenment had discovered about society, politics, and man's happiness could be bestowed on whole societies without most people understanding the deepest principles involved. Are not technology and all the sciences an analogy, these too being far beyond the capacity of most men but nevertheless universally utilized to the great benefit of all? Even the most ignorant regularly employ techniques based on principles utterly beyond their comprehension, the original discovery of which required the highest genius.[52] Likewise, the basis of true wisdom is hard to discover and, once found, fully grasped by few, but true wisdom can nevertheless easily be put to use by a well-intentioned government and an open society. *La philosophie* is beyond most people's grasp but even so it can transform everyone's life for the better bringing great benefits.

Radical Enlightenment was a philosophical revolution that created the possibility of a new kind of 'république Européenne', and a new kind of world based on equality, democracy, individual liberty, and freedom of expression and the press. The Enlightenment, both moderate and radical together, constituted a great revolution in the history of mankind. It was a revolution on many levels and in all spheres of human activity which then, in turn, was very closely linked to the revolutionary wave that transformed both sides of the Atlantic politically between 1775 and 1820. Historians frequently find themselves obliged to muse somewhat on the nature of causality, and these two linked phenomena compel such musing perhaps even more than most other historical changes. These two closely linked 'revolutions', the Enlightenment and the political revolutions that followed, obviously had an enormous number of causes and these of many kinds. Some of these were essential conditions, like the invention of printing and the expansion of publishing and the reading public in the eighteenth century; some were highly contingent but nevertheless decisive, like the French royal financial crisis of the 1780s. We would appear here to be as remote from what one historian has called 'the seductive simplicity of monocausality' as one could possibly find oneself. We must also bear in mind, when we consider the timing

---

[50] D'Holbach, *Morale universelle*, ii. 210.   [51] Ibid. ii. 210.   [52] Ibid. ii. 211.

of the French Revolution, that sometimes dramatic major new historical developments arise from a large number of small and often random changes which accumulate and create a critical threshold leading to a fundamental reconfiguration of the general context—innumerable small causes piling up and driving a crucial shift that need not, consequently, be substantially the outcome of any 'big' cause. And yet in the case of the French Revolution, however numerous the causes that shaped its general context, it seems clear that there loomed in fact one particular 'big' cause which had no rivals whatsoever when it came to carving out the specific legislation, constitutional principles, new institutions, and the transformed rhetoric of politics— and that is the Radical Enlightenment.

A process was set in train in the late eighteenth century, a democratic enlightenment based on liberty, equality, and the 'general good', which was then arrested by kings, aristocracy, and Robespierre's Counter-Enlightenment and driven back, but which resumed after a fashion in the post-Second World War era. Many scholars argue that at the end of the eighteenth century the hopes of the enlighteners were blighted by the contradictions within the Enlightenment.[53] Another way of looking at the Radical Enlightenment's defeat is to see it as a temporary and partial setback mainly due to the power of Counter-Enlightenment, faith, and vested interests. In 1789, it seemed to be possible to drive a powerful wedge between the conservatism of ignorance and the conservatism of landownership and money so that the two no longer mutually reinforce each other. It did not happen. But in response to today's fundamentalism, anti-secularism, Neo-Burkeanism, Postmodernism, and blatant unwillingness to clamp down on powerful vested interests, it is at least conceivable that the universalism and social democracy of radical thought might advance again and this time drive the wedge home harder. There are few grounds for optimism. Yet, it is intriguing to think that the programme of the radical *philosophes* could perhaps be completed yet.

---

[53] Gillespie, *Theological Origins*, 276.

Bibliography

Primary

ADAMS, JOHN, *Novanglus; or, A History of the Dispute with America* (Boston, 1774).

—— *Thoughts on Government applicable to the present State of the American Colonies* (Philadelphia, 1776).

—— *The Works of John Adams, Second President of the United States* (10 vols., Boston, 1850–6).

D'ALEMBERT, J. LE ROND, *Discours préliminaire* in vol. i (1751) of the *Encyclopédie*, pp. i–xlv.

—— *Essai sur les élémens de philosophie ou sur les principes des connoissances humaines* (1759), in *Mélanges*, iv. 1–298.

—— *Mélanges de littérature, d'histoire et de philosophie* (2 vols., Berlin, 1753).

—— *Mélanges de littérature, d'histoire et de philosophie* (5 vols., Amsterdam, 1770).

—— *Œuvres complètes* (5 vols., repr. Geneva, 1967).

ALFIERI, VITTORIO, *Memoirs*, anonymous translation of 1810, rev. E. R.Vincent (London, 1961).

[ALLAMAND, J. N. S.], *Pensées anti-philosophiques* (The Hague, 1751).

ALMODÓVAR, DUQUE DE [EDUARDO MALO DE LUQUE], *Historia política de los establecimientos ultramarinos de las naciones europeas* (5 vols., Madrid, 1784–90).

—— *Década epistolar sobre el estado de las letras de Francia* (Madrid, 1780).

Anekdoten eines reisenden Russen über die Staatsverfassung, Sitten und Gebräuche der Dänen (Lübeck, 1771), in CRL *Luxdorphs Samling*, xiii.

[Anon.], *Recueil nécessaire* ('à Leipsik', 1765).

ANQUETIL DU PERRON, A. H., *Zend-Avesta: ouvrage de Zoroastre* (2 vols. in 3 parts, Paris, 1771).

—— *Législation orientale* (Amsterdam, 1778).

—— *Catalogue des livres de M. A. H. Anquetil-Duperron* (Paris, 1805).

Apocalypse de Chiokoyhikoy, chef des Iroquois, sauvages du nord de l'Amérique ('à Philadelphie' [Montreal?], 1777).

Archivo [del General Francisco de] Miranda, ed. V. Dávila (14 vols., Caracas, 1929–33).

D'ARGENS, JEAN-BAPTISTE DE BOYER, MARQUIS, *Lettres chinoises, ou Correspondance philosophique, historique et critique* (5 vols., The Hague, 1739–40).

—— *Lettres juives ou Correspondance philosophique, historique et critique entre un Juif voiageur en differens états de l'Europe et ses correspondans en divers endroits* (1738; 2nd edn., 6 vols, The Hague, 1742).

—— *Mémoires secrets de la République des Lettres ou Le Théâtre de la vérité* (7 vols., Amsterdam, 1744).

[D'ARGENSON, MARQUIS], *Journal et mémoires du marquis d'Argenson* (9 vols., Paris, 1859–67).

ARNOLD, M. (ed.), *Edmund Burke: Irish Affairs* (London, 1988).

As cartas de Manuel de Saldanha... Vice-Rei da India (1758–65) (Lisbon, 1984).

AUDREIN, YVES, *Apologie de la religion contre les prétendus philosophes* (Paris, 1797).

*Avis au public sur le troisième volume de l'*Encyclopédie (n.p., n.d.). (BL)

BACOT, GERRIT JACOB, *Beordeelende Verhandeling omtrent eenige stellingen in de* Algemeen Republiek *van Anarcharsis Cloots*, in Cloots, *Algemeene Republiek*, 155–256. (HKB)

[BAGE, ROBERT], *Man as he is: A Novel in Four Volumes* (4 vols., London, 1792).

BAHRDT, CARL FRIEDRICH, *Geschichte seines Lebens, seiner Meinungen und Schicksale* (4 vols., Frankfurt, 1790).

—— *System der moralischen Religion* (2 vols., Berlin, 1787).

—— *On Freedom of the Press and its Limits* (1787), in J. Ch. Laursen and J. van der Zande (eds.), *Early French and German Defenses of Freedom of the Press* (Leiden, 2003), 92–172.

—— *Würdigung der natürlichen Religion und des Naturalismus in Beziehung auf Staat und Menschenrechte* (Halle, 1791).

[——], *Kirchen- und Ketzer-Almanach aufs Jahr 1781* ('Häresiopel', n.d. [1781]).

BAILLY, JEAN SYLVAIN, *Mémoires de Bailly, avec une notice sur sa vie, des notes et des éclaircissements historiques* (3 vols., Paris, 1821–2).

—— *Œuvres posthumes* (Paris, 1810).

BAQUÍJANO Y CARRILLO, JOSÉ, 'Elogio al Virrey Jauregui', in M. Maticorena Estrada (ed.), *Colección documental de la Independencia del Perú*, 1: *Los ideológos*, vol. iii: *José Baquíjano y Carrillo* (Lima, 1976), 65–95.

BARLOW, JOEL, *A Letter to the National Convention of France on the Defects in the Constitution of 1791* (London, 1792).

—— *Advice to the Privileged Orders in the Several States of Europe* (2 vols., New York, 1792–4).

BARRUEL, ABBÉ AUGUSTE, *Les Helviennes, ou Lettres provinciales philosophiques* (1781–8; 5 vols., 7th edn., Paris, 1830).

[BASEDOW, JOHANN BERNHARD], *Eine Urkunde des Jahrs 1780 von der neuen Gefahr des Christenthums durch die scheinbare Semlersche Vertheidigung* (Dessau, 1780).

BAUMGARTEN, SIEGMUND JACOB, *Nachrichten einer Hallischen Bibliothek* (8 vols., 1748–51).

—— *Geschichte der Religionspartheyen* (1754), ed. J. S. Semler (Halle, 1766).

BEATTIE, JAMES, *An Essay on the Nature and Immutability of Truth; in Opposition to Sophistry and Scepticism* (Edinburgh, 1770).

—— *Elements of Moral Science* (1790–3; 2 vols., repr. New York, 1977).

BEAUMONT, CHRISTOPHE DE, *Mandement de Monseigneur l'Archevêque de Paris portant condamnation d'un livre qui a pour titre, De l'esprit* (Paris, 1758).

BECCARIA, CESARE, *On Crimes and Punishments* (1764), ed. R. Bellamy (Cambridge, 1995).

—— 'Pensieri sopra la barbarie e coltura delle nazioni e su lo stato selvaggio dell'uomo', in Venturi (ed.), *Riformatori Lombardi*, 106–12.

Bedenkingen en Bezwaren door de weleerwaarde Classis van Rechtzinnighuizen (n.p., 1772). (Kn. 19003)

[BELGRADO, JACOPO], *Dall'esistenza nel nostro mondo d'una sola spezie d'esseri ragionevoli e liberi s'arguisce l'esistenza di Dio* (Udine, 1782).

BENTHAM, JEREMY, *A Fragment on Government*, ed. J. H. Burns and H. L. A. Hart (Cambridge, 1988).

—— *The Influence of Natural Religion on the Temporal Happiness of Mankind*, ed. D. McKown (1822; New York, 2003).

BERGASSE, NICOLAS, *Considérations sur le magnétisme animal ou sur la théorie du monde et des êtres organisés* (The Hague, 1784).

BERGIER, ABBÉ NICOLAS-SYLVESTRE, *Le Déisme réfuté par lui-même; ou Examen des principes d'incrédulité répandus dans les divers ouvrages de M. Rousseau* (2nd edn., Paris, 1766).

—— *Deism Self-Refuted; Or an Examination of the Principles of Infidelity* (n.p., 1775).

—— *Grands Hommes vengés, ou Examen des jugements portés par M. de Voltaire, et par quelques autres philosophes, sur plusieurs hommes célèbres* (2 vols., Paris, 1769).

—— *Apologie de la religion chrétienne* (1769; 2nd edn., 2 vols., Paris, 1770).

—— *Examen du matérialisme ou Réfutation du* Système de la nature (2 vols., Paris, 1771).

Bericht van den Prof Van Goens rakende de recensie van zyne vertaling van de Verhandeling van Mozes Mendelszoon, over het Verhevene en Naïve in de fraye wetenschappen (Utrecht, 1775). (Kn. 19107)

Berlinische Monatsschrift, ed. F. Gedike and J. E. Biester (Berlin, 1783–96).

[BERNARD, F.], *Analyse de l'*Histoire philosophique et politique... dans les deux Indes (Leiden, 1775).

[BERTRAND, DOMINIQUE], *Lettre à Monsieur l'Abbé Raynal (17 Mars 1789)* (Marseille, 1789).

BERTRAND, ÉLIE, *Mémoires historiques et physiques sur les tremblemens de terre* (The Hague, 1757).

BILFINGER, GEORG BERHARD, *De Harmonia Animi et Corporis Humani Maxime Praestabilita* (1725; 3rd edn., Tübingen, 1741; repr. Hildesheim, 1984).

BOLTS, WILLEM, *Considerations on Indian Affairs* (2nd edn., London, 1772).

[BONCERF, CLAUDE-JOSEPH], *Le Vrai Philosophe, ou l'usage de la philosophie relativement à la société civile* (1757; Amsterdam, 1766).

BONNET, CHARLES, *Mémoires autobiographiques*, ed. R. Savioz (Paris, 1948).

BOULANGER, NICOLAS-ANTOINE, *L'Antiquité dévoilée par ses usages* (3 vols., Amsterdam, 1777).

[—— and HOLBACH, BARON D', PAUL-HENRI THIRY], *Recherches sur l'origine du despotisme oriental*, ouvrage posthume de Mr. B.I.D.P.E.C. ('Londres' [Amsterdam?], [1762]).

[—— ——], *Examen critique de la vie et des ouvrages de Saint Paul avec une dissertation sur Saint Pierre* ('Londres' [Amsterdam], 1770).

[BOULLIER, DAVID RENAUD], *Lettres critiques sur les* Lettres philosophiques *de Mr. Voltaire par rapport à notre âme* (n.p., 1753).

Brief aan de Heeren van der Nederlandsche Bibliotheek, by J.A.R.L.C.P.S.R. (Groningen, 1775). (Kn. 19113)

[BRISSOT DE WARVILLE, JACQUES-PIERRE], *Recherches philosophiques sur le droit de propriété considéré dans la nature* (1780; repr. Paris, n.d.).

—— *Bibliothèque philosophique du législateur* (10 vols., 'Berlin', 1782).

—— *Lettres philosophiques sur Saint Paul, sur sa doctrine, politique, morale et religieuse, et sur plusieurs points de la religion chrétienne, considérés politiquement* (Neuchâtel, 1783).

—— *Le Philadelphien à Genève, ou Lettres d'un Américain sur la dernière Révolution de Genève* ('Dublin' [Amsterdam?], 1783).

—— *Correspondance universelle sur ce qui intéresse le bonheur de l'homme et de la société* ('Londres' [Neuchâtel], 1783).

—— *Tableau de la situation actuelle des Anglois dans les Indes Orientales* (Paris, 1784).

—— *Lettre à l'empereur sur l'atrocité des supplices qu'il a substitués comme adoucissement à la peine de mort* (Brussels, 1787).

—— *New Travels in the United States of America* (1788), ed. D. Echeverria (Cambridge, Mass., 1964).

—— *Le Patriote français: Journal libre, impartial et national* (journal: Paris, 1789–93).

—— *De la vérité, ou Méditations sur les moyens de parvenir à la vérité dans toutes les connoissances humaines* (Neuchâtel, 1782).

BUFFON, GEORGE-LOUIS LECLERC DE, *Histoire des animaux* (1749), and other extracts from *L'Histoire naturelle*, vol. ii, repr. in Condillac, *Traité des animaux*, ed. M. Malherbe (Paris, 2004), 216–35.

—— 'Époques de la nature', ed. P. Flourens, in P. Flourens, *Des manuscrits de Buffon* (Paris, 1860), 79–124.

BURKE, EDMUND, *A Vindication of Natural Society* (1756), in *The Works of the Right Honourable Edmund Burke* (6 vols., London, 1815), i. 1–80.

—— *Pre-Revolutionary Writings*, ed. Ian Harris (Cambridge, 1993).

—— 'On Empire', in *Liberty and Reform: Speeches and Letters*, ed. D. Bromwich (New Haven, 2000).

—— *Reflections on the Revolution in France* (1790), ed. F. M. Turner (New Haven, 2003).

CABARRÚS, FRANCISCO, 'Discurso sobre la libertad de comercio concedido por S.M. a la América Meridional', *Memorias de la Sociedad Económica de Madrid*, iii (Madrid, 1787), 282–94.

[CADALSO, JOSÉ DE], *Defensa de la nación española contra la Carta Persiana LXXVIII de Montesquieu* (1772), ed. G. Mercadier (Toulouse, 1970).

CAMPBELL, GEORGE, *A Dissertation on Miracles* (Edinburgh, 1762).

CAMPOMANES, PEDRO RODRÍGUEZ DE, CONDE DE, *Discurso sobre el fomento de la industria popular* (5 vols., Madrid, 1774).

CAMUSET, JOSEPH NICOLAS, *Principes contre l'incrédulité à l'occasion du* Système de la nature (Paris, 1771).

'Candidus', *Plain Truth: Addressed to the Inhabitants of America, Containing Remarks on a Late Pamphlet, Intitled* Common Sense (2nd edn., Philadelphia, 1776).

CAPELLEN, JOAN DERK VAN DER, *Aan het Volk van Nederland* (1781), ed. H. L. Zwitzer (Amsterdam, 1987).

CARACCIOLI, LUIGI ANTONIO, MARQUESE DI, *Le Langage de la raison* (Paris, 1764).

—— *La Religion de l'honnête homme* (Paris, 1766).

—— *Voyage de la raison en Europe*, in *Voyages imaginaires, songes et visions* (Amsterdam, 1788).

—— *Le Cri de la vérité contre la séduction du siècle* (Paris, 1765).

CARLYLE, THOMAS, *The Life of Friedrich Schiller* (2nd edn., London, 1845).

Cartas e outros obras selectas do Marquêz de Pombal ministro e secretario d'estado do senhor El-Rei D. Jose I (3 vols. Lisbon, 1820–4).

CASANOVA, JACQUES, *The Memoirs of Jacques Casanova de Seingault*, trans. A. Machen (6 vols., New York, 1959).

CASTIGLIONI, LUIGI, *Lettere dalla Francia (1784)*, ed. P. Bernardini and D. Lucci (Novi Ligure, 2009).

CASTILLON, M. J. DE, *Observations sur le livre intitulé* Système de la nature (Berlin, 1771).

Catalogus Librorum Rejectorum per Consessum Censurae (Vienna, 1754), and continuations (1755, 1756, 1757).

CATHERINE THE GREAT OF RUSSIA, 'Notes' on Radishchev, *A Journey*, 239–49.

CAVEIRAC, ABBÉ JEAN NOVI DE, *L'Accord de la religion et de l'humanité sur l'intolérance* (n.p., 1762).

Censure de la Faculté de Théologie de Paris contre un livre qui a pour titre Histoire philosophique et politique … *par G. T. Raynal* (Paris, 1782).

CERISIER, ANTOINE-MARIE, *Ontwerp om de Republiek door eene heilzaame vereeniging der belangen … gelukkig … te maaken* (known as the *Leidse Ontwerp*) (Leiden, 1785). (Kn. 21045)

—— *Observations impartiales d'un vrai Hollandois à ses compatriotes* (n.p., 1778). (Kn. 19191)

—— *Tableau de l'histoire générale des Provinces-Unies* (10 vols., Utrecht, 1777–84).

—— (ed.), *Le Politique hollandais* (journal: Leiden, 1781–3).

CEVALLOS, JOSEPH, *Respuesta a la carta de... D. Fray Miguel de San Josef... sobre varios escritos acerca del Terremoto* (Seville, 1757). (BL)

CEVALLOS, FRAY FERNANDO DE, *Juicio final de Voltaire*, ed. Leon Carboñero y Sol (1778; 2 vols., Seville, 1856).

—— *Insania o las demencias de los filósofos confundidas* (Madrid, 1878).

CHASTELLUX, FRANÇOIS JEAN, MARQUIS DE, *De la félicité publique* (2 vols., Amsterdam, 1772).

—— *Discours sur les avantages ou désavantages qui résultent pour l'Europe de la découverte de l'Amérique* ('à Londres' [Paris?], 1787), repr. in H. J. Lüsebrink and A. Mussard (eds.), *Avantages et désavantages de los découverte de l'Amérique* (Saint-Étienne, 1994).

CHAUDON, DOM LOUIS MAYEUL, *Dictionnaire anti-philosophique* (2 vols., Avignon, 1769).

CHAUMEIX, ABRAHAM-JOSEPH, *Préjugés légitimes et réfutation de l'*Encyclopédie *avec un examen critique du livre* De l'esprit (6 vols., 'Bruxelles', 1758–9).

CHÉNIER, MARIE-JOSEPH DE, *Dénonciation des inquisiteurs de la pensée* (25 Aug. 1789; Paris, 1789).

Le Christianisme dévoilé ou Examen des principes et des effets de la religion chrétienne (London, 1756).

La Chronique de Paris (journal appearing from August 1789 to August 1793), ed. Louis-Pierre Manuel, Rabaut Saint-Etienne, Cloots, et al.

CLAVIÈRE, ÉTIENNE, and BRISSOT, J. P., *De la France et des États-Unis ou De l'importance de la Révolution de l'Amérique pour le bonheur de la France* ('Londres', 1787).

CLAVIJERO, FRANCISCO XAVIER, *Storia antica del Messico* (4 vols., Cesena, 1780).

CLOOTS, ANARCHARSIS, *Vœux d'un Gallophile* (Amsterdam, 1786).

—— *De Algemeene Republiek of Aanspraak aan de ombrengers der dwingelanden* (Dunkirk, 1792).

[——], *La Certitude des preuves du mahométisme ou Réfutation de l'examen des apologistes de la religion Mahométane par Ali-Gier Ber, Alfaki* ('Londres' [Amsterdam?], 1780).

[——] [B.d.C.d.V.d.G], *Lettre sur les juifs à un ecclésiastique des mes amis* (Berlin, 1783).

CONDILLAC, ÉTIENNE BONNOT DE, *Essay on the Origin of Human Knowledge* (1746; Cambridge, 2001).

—— *Traité des systèmes* (1749; Paris, 1991).

—— *Traité des animaux* (1755), ed. M. Malherbe (Paris, 2004).

CONDORCET, JEAN-ANTOINE-NICOLAS DE CARITAT, MARQUIS DE, *Œuvres complètes*, ed. L. S. Caritat et al. (21 vols., Brunswick and Paris, 1804).

—— 'Vie de Voltaire', vol. vi of *Œuvres*.

—— *Réflexions sur l'esclavage des nègres* in *Œuvres*, xi. 83–198.

—— *Réflexions sur la Révolution de 1688, et celle du 10 août 1792* (n.p., n.d. [Paris], 1792).

—— *Tableau historique des progrès de l'esprit humain: projets, esquisse, fragments et notes (1772–1794)*, ed. J. P. Schandeler and P. Crépel (Paris, 2004).

—— *Ce que les citoyens ont droit d'attendre de leurs représentans* (speech of 7 Aug. 1791) (Paris, 1791).

—— *Esquisse d'un tableau historique des progrès de l'esprit humain*, ed. A. Pons (Paris, 1988).

Conversation entre Messieurs Raynal et Linguet sur la nature et les avantages des divers gouvernements (Brussels, 1789).

Copia de huma carta escrita pelo Padre Guardian do real Convento de Maquinés, e vice-prefeito dos santos Missoens, que nas partes da Barberia conserve a religiosa provincia de São Diogo dos RR. PP. Franciscanos Descalcos (Lisbon, 1756).

CORAM, ROBERT, *Political Inquiries: To which is Added a Plan for the General Establishment of Schools throughout the United States* (Wilmington, Del., 1791).

Correspondance inédite de Condorcet et de Turgot, 1770–1779, ed. Ch. Henry (Paris, 1888).

[COSTE D'ARNOBAT, CHARLES-PIERRE], M.L.C., *Le Philosophe ami de tout le monde, ou Conseils désintéressés aux littérateurs* ('Sophopolis' [Paris?], 1760).

Coup d'œil sur la Grande Bretagne ('Londres', 1776). (BL 8009 e 21/20)

COYER, ABBÉ, *La nobleza comerciante* (Madrid, 1781).

[CRILLON, LOUIS ATHANASE DES BALBES DE BERTON DE], *Mémoires philosophiques du Baron de *****, Chamberlain de sa Majesté l'Impératrice reine* (2 vols., 'Vienne en Autriche', 1777–8).

CRUSIUS, CHRISTIAN AUGUST, *Anweisung vernünftig zu leben, Darinnen nach Erklärung der Natur des menschlichen Willens die natürlichen Pflichten und allgemeinen Klugheitslehren im richtigen Zusammenhange vorgetragen werden* (1744; 3rd edn., Leipzig, 1767).

—— *Gründliche Belehrung vom Aberglauben zur Aufklärung des Unterschiedes zwischen Religion und Aberglauben* (1755), trans from Latin by Christian Fr. Pezold (Leipzig, 1767).

—— *Kurzer Begriff der Moraltheologie, oder nähere Erklärung der practischen Lehren des Christentums* (2 vols., Leipzig, 1772).

—— *Einleitung in die Wahre und vollständige Cosmologie* (Leipzig, 1774).

DAUBE, L. J. J., 'Discours preliminaire' and 'Précis historique de la vie de Dumarsais', in d'Holbach, *Essai sur les préjugés* (2 vols., Paris, l'an 1 (1791–2)), i, pp. i–xxxviii.

DAMNATIO et Prohibitio Operis in Plures Tomos Distribuiti, Cujus est Titulus, Encyclopédie (Rome, 3 Sept. 1759).

DASHKOVA, PRINCESS E. R., *Mon histoire: mémoires d'une femme de lettres russe à l'époque des lumières*, ed. A. Woronzoff-Dashkoff (Paris, 1999).

DAVID, ou L'Histoire de l'homme selon le cœur de Dieu, in Paul-Henri Thiry d'Holbach, *L'Esprit du judaïsme*, ed. J. P. Jackson (Paris, 2010), 119–53.

DE FELICE, FORTUNATO BARTOLOMEO (ed.), *Encyclopédie, ou Dictionnaire universel raisonné des connoissances humaines* (58 vols., Yverdon, 1770–80).

—— *Code de l'humanité ou législation universelle naturelle, civile et politique* (13 vols., Yverdon, 1778).

DELEYRE, ALEXANDRE, *L'Esprit de Saint-Evremont par l'auteur du Génie de Montesquieu* (Amsterdam, 1761).

—— *Tableau de l'Europe, pour servir de supplément à l'Histoire philosophique... des deux Indes* ('Amsterdam' [Maastricht?], 1774).

[——], *Gemälde von Europa aus dem Französischen des Abts Raynal übersezt* von E.W.v.R. (Dessau and Leipzig, 1783).

DELISLE DE SALES, JEAN-BAPTISTE, *De la philosophie de la nature ou traité de morale pour l'espèce humaine* (1770; 6 vols., 'à Londres' [Amsterdam], 1777).

—— *De la philosophie du bonheur* (2 vols., Paris, 1797).

DÉMEUNIER, JEAN-NICOLAS, *L'Esprit des usages et des coutumes des différents peuples* (3 vols., 'Londres' [Paris], 1776).

—— *L'Amérique indépendante, ou les différentes constitutions des treize provinces, qui se sont érigées en républiques sous le nom d'États-Unis de l'Amérique* (3 vols., Ghent, 1790).

'Demofilus' [PIETER VREEDE?], *Zakboek van Neerlands Volk, voor Patriotten, Antipatrioten, Aristokraten en Prinsgezinden* (Dordrecht, 1785).

DESCHAMPS, LÉGER-MARIE, *Correspondance générale*, ed. B. Delhaume (Paris, 2006).

—— *Lettres sur l'esprit du siècle* ('Londres', 1769), repr. in Deschamps, *Correspondance*, ed. Delhaume, 1161–87.

—— *La Voix de la raison contre la raison du temps, et particulièrement contre celle de l'auteur du* Système de la nature ('Bruxelles', 1770), in *Correspondance*, ed. Delaume, 1189–235.

Deutsches Museum, ed. H. Ch. Boie and Christian Wilhelm von Dohm (journal: Leipzig, 1776–88).

DIDEROT, DENIS, *Œuvres*, ed. Laurent Versini (4 vols., Paris, 1994).

—— *Œuvres complètes de Diderot*, ed. J. Assézat and M. Tourneux (20 vols., Paris, 1875–7).

—— *Œuvres complètes*, ed. R. Lewinter (15 vols., Paris, 1969–73).

—— *Œuvres philosophiques*, ed. P. Vernière (Paris, 1990).

—— *Correspondance*, ed. G. Roth and J. Varloot (15 vols., Paris, 1955–70).

—— *Pensées philosophiques*, in Diderot, *Œuvres philosophiques* (Paris, 1990), 9–55.

—— *Le Rêve d'Alembert*, in Diderot, *Œuvres philosophiques*, ed. Verniere, 249–385.

—— *De l'interprétation de la nature* (1753), in *Œuvres complètes*, ed. Assézat and Tourneux, ü. 1–63.

—— *Le Neveu de Rameau*, ed. Jean-Pol Caput (Paris, 1972).

—— *Pages inédites contre un tyran*, ed. Franco Venturi (n.p., 1937).

—— *Political Writings*, trans. and ed. J. H. Mason and Robert Wokler (Cambridge, 1992).

—— *Commentaire sur Hemsterhuis*, ed. G. May, in F. Hemsterhuis, *Lettre sur l'homme* (New Haven, 1964), 44–513.

—— *Principes de politique des souverains* (1775), in *Œuvres complètes*, ed. Assézat and Tourneux, ii. 459–502.

—— *Supplément au voyage de Bougainville*, ed. A. Adam (Paris, 1972).

—— 'Don Pablo Olavidès: précis historique rédigé sur des mémoires fournis à M. Diderot par un espagnol (1782)', in *Œuvres complètes*, ed. Assézat and Tourneux, vi. 467–72.

—— *Apologie de l'abbé Galiani* (1770), in Diderot, *Apologies*, ed. M. Barrillon (Marseille, 1998), 63–133.

—— *Fragments échappés du portefeuille d'un philosophe*, in *Œuvres completes*, ed. Assézat and Tourneux, vi. 444–57.

—— *Lettre apologétique de l'abbé Raynal à M. Grimm* (1781), in Diderot, *Apologies*, ed. M. Barrillon (Marseille, 1998), 135–58.

—— *Essai sur le règnes de Claude et de Néron et sur les mœurs et les écrits de Senèque* (2 vols., 'Londres' [Amsterdam?], 1782).

—— *Réfutation suivie de l'ouvrage d'Helvétius intitulé* L'Homme, in Diderot, *Œuvres complètes*, ed. Assézat and Tourneux, ii. 275–456.

—— 'Voyage de Hollande' (1774), in *Œuvres complètes*, ed. Assézat and Tourneux, xvii. 365–471.

—— and DAUBENTON, LOUIS-JEAN-MARIE, 'Animal', in Diderot and d'Alembert (eds.), *Encyclopédie*, i. 468–74.

—— and D'ALEMBERT, JEAN LE ROND, *Encyclopédie ou Dictionnaire raisonné des sciences, des arts et des métiers* (17 vols., Paris, Geneva, and Neuchâtel, 1751–72).

DIEZ, HEINRICH FRIEDRICH, *Apologie der Duldung und Pressfreiheit* (n.p. [Dessau?], 1781).

—— *Benedikt von Spinoza nach Leben und Lehren* (Dessau, 1783).

DRAGONETTI, GIACINTO, *A Treatise on Virtues and Rewards* (London, 1769).

DOHM, CHRISTIAN WILHELM VON, *Geschichte der Engländer und Franzosen im östlichen Indien* (Leipzig, 1776).

—— *Denkwürdigkeiten meiner Zeit oder Beiträge zur Geschichte vom letzten Viertel des achtzehnten und vom Anfang des neunzehnten Jahrhunderts (1778 bis 1806)* (4 vols., Lemgo-Hannover, 1814).

—— *Exposé de la Révolution de Liège en 1789* (Liège, 1790).

—— *Plan d'une nouvelle constitution de la ville d' Aix-la-Chapelle* (Liège, 1791).

DORAT, CLAUDE-JOSEPH, 'Avis aux sages du siècle MM. Voltaire et Rousseau' (n.p., 1767).

[DUBUISSON, P. U.], *Lettres critiques et politiques sur les colonies... addressés à G. T. Raynal* (Geneva, 1785).

DUMONT, ÉTIENNE, *Souvenirs de Mirabeau*, ed. J. Benetruy (Paris, 1951).

DWIGHT, TIMOTHY, *The Triumph of Infidelity: A Poem* (n.p., 1788).

ECKHARTSHAUSEN, CARL VON, *Ueber Religion, Freydenkerey und Aufklärung* (1785; Munich, 1786).

EDELMANN, JOHANN CHRISTIAN, *Moses mit aufgedeckten Angesichte* (3 vols., 'Freyburg' [i.e. Berleburg], 1740).

EDWARDS, JONATHAN, *The Religious Affections* (1746; Edinburgh, 2001).

—— *The Freedom of the Will* (1753; Morgan, Pa., 1996).

Der entlarvte Moses Mendelssohn oder völlige Ausklärung des räthselhaften Todverdrusses des M. Mendelssohn über die Bekanntmachung des Lessingschen Atheismus von Jacobi ('Amsterdam' [Berlin?], 1786).

[D.J.C.], *España triunfante en el actual siglo filosófico* (Madrid, 1786).

Esprit de Guillaume-Thomas Raynal: recueil également nécessaire à ceux qui commandent et à ceux qui obéissent (2 vols., 'Londres' [Paris?], 1782). (PBN)

Estatutos para la Sociedad Económica de los Amigos del Pais de León (Madrid, 1783).

Estatutos para la Sociedad Económica de los Amigos del Pays de... Tenerife (Madrid, 1779).

Estratto della letteratura europea, ed. Fortunato Bartolomeo de Felice (journal: Berne, 1758–62; Yverdon, 1762–6).

L'Europa letteraria: Giornale (journal: Vicenza, 1768–73).

EWALD, SCHACK HERMANN, 'Vorrede' to Benedikt von Spinoza, *Zwey Abhandlungen über die Kultur des menschlichen Verstandes und über die Aristokratie und Demokratie* (Leipzig, 1785), pp. i–viii.

Exposé des droits des colonies britanniques pour justifier le projet de leur indépendance (Amsterdam, 1776). (Kn. 19118)

FEDER, JOHANN GEORG HEINRICH, *Grundriss der philosophischen Wissenschaften nebst der Geschichte zum Gebrauch seiner Zuhörer* (1767; 2nd edn., Coburg, 1769).

—— *Logik und Metaphysik* (Frankfurt, 1793).

[FELLER, FRANCOIS XAVIER DE, SJ], 'Flexier de Reval', *Catéchisme philosophique, ou recueil d'observations propres à défendre la religion chrétienne contre ses ennemis* (1772; Liège-Brussels, 1773).

—— *Journal historique et littéraire* (journal: Luxembourg-Liège, 1773–94).

FERGUSON, ADAM, *An Essay on the History of Civil Society* (Edinburgh, 1767).

—— *Institutes of Moral Philosophy for the Use of Students in the College of Edinburgh* (Edinburgh, 1773; repr. Garland, New York, 1978).

—— *Remarks on a Pamphlet Lately Published by Dr Price, Entitled* Observations on the Nature of Civil Liberty (London, 1776).

—— *Principles of Moral and Political Science* (2 vols., Edinburgh, 1792; repr. 1978).

FICHTE, J. G., *Early Philosophical Writings*, trans. and ed. D. Breazeale (Ithaca, NY, 1988).

—— *Foundations of Transcendental Philosophy (Wissenschaftslehre)*, ed. D. Breazeale (Ithaca, NY, 1992).

FILANGIERI, GAETANO, *La scienza della legislazione*, critical edn. ed. A. Trampus (7 vols., Venice, 2003–4).

FINESTRAD, JOAQUIN DE, *El vasallo instruido en el estado del Nuevo Reino de Granada y en sus respectivas obligaciones* (1789; Bogotá, 2000).

FINETTI, GIOVANNI FRANCESCO, *Apologia del genere umano accusato d'essere stato una volta bestia* (Venice, 1768).

FONTANA, A. ET AL. (eds.), *Venise et la Révolution française: les 470 dépêches des ambassadeurs de Venise au Doge 1786–1795* (Paris, 1997).

FORKERT, J. G. 'Vorbericht des Übersetzers', to Helvétius, *Discurs über den Geist des Menschen* (Leipzig-Liegniz, 1760).

FORNER, JUAN PABLO, *Discursos filosóficos sobre el hombre* (Madrid, 1787).

—— *Preservativo contra el atheismo* (Seville, 1795).

[FORSSKÅL, PETER], *Tankar om Borgerliga Friheten* (Stockholm, 1759).

Fortgesetzte Sammlung von Alten und Neuen Theologischen Sachen, Büchern, Urkunden, Controversien, Leipzig periodical. (GUB)

FOUCAULT, MICHEL, *Discipline and Punish: The Birth of the Prison*, trans A. Sheridan (1975; new edn., New York, 1995).

[FOUGERAT DE MONTBRON, JEAN-LOUIS], *Préservatif contre l'Anglomanie* ('a Minorque' [Paris?], 1757).

La France littéraire (4 vols., Paris, 1769–78).

[FRANÇOIS, LAURENT], *Preuves de la religion de Jésus-Christ, contre les Spinosistes et Déistes* (4 vols., Paris, 1751).

—— *Observations sur la* Philosophie de l'histoire *et le* Dictionnaire philosophique (2 vols., Paris, 1770).

FRANKLIN, BENJAMIN, *The Papers*, ed. L.W. Labaree et al. (37 vols. so far; New Haven, 1959–).

FREDERICK THE GREAT, KING OF PRUSSIA, *Examen de l'Essai sur les préjugés* ('Londres' [Berlin], 1770).

—— 'A Critical Examination of the *System of Nature*', in the *Posthumous Works of Frederic II, King of Prussia*, trans. Th. Holcroft, vol. v (London, 1789), 147–75.

FRÉRON, ÉLIE CATHERINE, *Lettres sur quelques écrits de ce tems* ('à Londres', [Paris], 1752–4). (BL)

—— *L'Année littéraire, ou Suite des lettres sur quelques écrits de ce temps* (292 vols., Paris, 1755–90).

Freye doch unmassgebliche Gedancken und Errinnerungen über die bisherigen Streit-Schrifften wieder den Herrn Edelmann... vorgeleget von einigen unpartheyischen Liebhabern der reinen Wahrheit (n.p., 1747).

GALANTI, GIUSEPPE MARIA, *Descrizione geografica e politica delle Sicilie* (Naples, 5 vols., 1786–1794).

GALIANI, ABBÉ FERNANDO, *Dialogues sur le commerce des blés* (1770; Paris, 1984).

—— *Correspondance avec Madame d'Épinay... Diderot... d'Holbach* etc., ed. L. Perey and G. Maugrat (2 vols., Paris, 1881; repr. 2005).

GARAT, DOMINIQUE-JOSEPH, *Mémoires historiques sur la vie de M. Suard, sur ses écrits, et sur le XVIIIe siècle* (2 vols., Paris, 1820).

GARAT, DOMINIQUE-JOSEPH, 'Jugement de R. Mirabeau', in *Mirabeau à la Tribune, ou Choix des meilleurs discours de cet orateur* (2 vols., Paris, 1796), i, pp. iii–xii.

GARDINI, ANTON MARIA, *Verità di teologia naturale . . . contro gli atei, deisti e materialisti, e specialmente contro l'opera intitolata* Le Bon Sens (1774; new edn., Padua, 1778).

GAUCHAT, GABRIEL, *Lettres critiques, ou Analyse et réfutation de divers écrits modernes contre la religion* (19 vols., Paris, 1755–63).

GENLIS, STÉPHANIE FÉLICITÉ, Comtesse de, *Religion Considered as the Only Basis of Happiness and True Philosophy* (2 vols., Dublin, 1787).

GENOVESI, ANTONIO, *Discorso sopra il vero fine delle lettere e delle scienze* (1753), in F. Venturi (ed.), *Illuminati italiani*, vol. v (Milan, 1965), 84–131.

—— *Elementa Metaphysicae* (4th edn., 5 vols., Naples, 1760).

—— *Elementorum Artis Logicocriticae Libri V* (1745; 4th edn., Naples, 1759).

—— *Lettere filosofiche ad un amico provinciale* (2 vols., Naples, 1759).

—— *Lezioni di commercio o sia d'economia civile* (2 vols., Bassano, 1769).

—— *Note* to the *Spirito delle leggi del signore di Montesquieu* (4 vols., Naples, 1777).

—— *Delle scienze metafisiche per gli giovanetti* (Naples, 1767).

GIBBON, EDWARD, *The Autobiographies*, ed. J. Murray (London, 1896).

—— *Memoirs of my Life and Writings* (Keele, 1994).

Giornale de' letterati (journal: Pisa, 1771–96).

GLOBIG, ERNST VON, and HUSTER, J. G., *Abhandlung von der Criminal-Gesetzgebung* (Bern, 1782).

GODWIN, WILLIAM, *An Enquiry Concerning Political Justice and its Influence on General Virtue and Happiness* (2 vols., London, 1793).

[———], *History of the Internal Affairs of the United Provinces from the Year 1780, to the Commencement of Hostilities in June 1787* (London, 1787).

GOETHE, JOHANN WOLFGANG, *Italian Journey* [1786–8], trans. W. H. Auden and E. Mayer (Harmondsworth, 1970).

GORANI, COUNT GIUSEPPE, *Il vero dispotismo* ('Londra' [i.e. Geneva], 1770).

—— *Recherches sur la science du gouvernement* (1786; trans. of 2nd edn., 2 vols., Paris, 1792).

—— *Mémoires secrets et critiques des cours, des gouvernemens, et des mœurs des principaux états de l'Italie* (3 vols., Paris, 1793).

—— *Le Memorie* (4 vols., Milan, 1936–42).

[GORDON, THOMAS], *A Letter of Consolation and Counsel to the Good People of England . . . Occasion'd by the Late Earthquakes* (London, 1750).

GORDON, WILLIAM, *The History of the Rise, Progress and Establishment, of the Independence of the United States of America* (2 vols., London, 1788).

GOTTSCHED, JOHANN CHRISTOPH, 'Vorrede' to trans. by J. G. Forkert of Helvétius, *Discurs* (Leipzig-Liegniz, 1760).

GRAFFIGNY, FRANÇOISE DE, *Lettres d'une Péruvienne*, ed. J. Mallinson (Oxford, 2002).

GRANADOS Y GÁLVEZ, JOSÉ JOAQUIN, *Tardes Americanas* (1778; Mexico City, 1987).

Grande Dispute au Panthéon entre Marat et Jean-Jacques Rousseau (Paris, 1795), BL 645 a 42/23.

GRANIÉ, PIERRE, *Lettre à M . . . sur la philosophie dans ses rapports avec notre gouvernement* (Paris, 1802).

—— *De l'Assemblée constituante de France* (Paris, 1797).

GRIFFET, HENRI, *L'Insuffisance de la religion naturelle* (2 vols., Liège, 1770).

[GRIFFINI, MICHELANGELO], *Brevi riflessioni di Eufrasio Lisimaco su il libro* Riforma d'Italia (Bologna, 1773).

GRIMM, FRIEDRICH MELCHIOR VON, *Correspondance littéraire, philosophique et critique*, ed. M. Tourneux (16 vols., Paris, 1877–82).

GROLMAN, LUDWIG ADOLF CHRISTIAN VON, *Die neuesten Arbeiten des Spartacus und Philo in dem Illuminaten-orden jetzt zum erstenmal gedruckt* (n.p. [Frankfurt-am-Main], 1793).

—— *Kritische Geschichte der Illuminaten-Grade* (n.p. [Frankfurt-am-Main], 1793).

[GUYON, ABBÉ C. M.], *L'Oracle des nouveaux philosophes* (Berne, 1759).

HAAFNER, J., *Onderzoek naar het nut der Zendelingen en Zendeling-Genootschappen* in *Verhandelingen raakende den Natuurlyken en Geopenbaarden Godsdienst uitgegeven door Teyler's Genootschap*, xxi (Haarlem, 1807).

—— *Reize in eenen palanquin of lotgevallen en merkwaardig aantekeningen op eene reize langs de kusten Orixa en Choromandel* (2 vols., Amsterdam, 1808).

HALLER, ALBRECHT VON, *Tagebuch seiner Beobachtungen über Schriftsteller und über sich selbst* (2 vols., Berne, 1787).

HAMILTON, ALEXANDER, MADISON, JAMES, and JAY, JOHN, *The Federalist*, ed. T. Ball (Cambridge, 2003).

HANSSEN, P., *Anmerckungen über Johann Christian Edelmanns Irrthümer* (Lübeck, 1745).

HARENBERG, JOHANN CH., *Die gerettete Religion, oder gründliche Wiederlegung des Glaubens-bekentnisses* [von...] *Johann Christian Edelmann* (Brunswick, 1747).

[HATZFELD, JOHANN CONRAD FRANZ VON]: pseud- 'Veridicus Nassauensis', *La Découverte de la vérité et le monde détrompé à l'égard de la philosophie* (The Hague, 1745). (ARH)

HAYER, JEAN-NICOLAS-HUBERT, *La Religion vengée ou réfutation des auteurs impies dédiée à Monseigneur le Dauphin* (21 vols., Paris, 1757–63).

HELVÉTIUS, CLAUDE-ADRIEN, *Réflexions sur l'homme et autres textes*, ed. Jean-Pierre Jackson (Paris, 2006).

—— *De l'esprit* (Paris, 1758; repr. 1988).

—— *Le Bonheur: poème, en six chants* ('Londres' [Amsterdam], 1772).

—— *De l'homme: De ses facultés intellectuelles et de son éducation* (1773; repr. 2 vols., Paris, 1989).

—— *Correspondance générale*, ed. A. Dainard et al. (3 vols., Toronto, 1981–91).

—— *Notes de la main d'Helvétius publiées d'après un manuscrit inédit*, ed. A. Keim (Paris, 1907).

HEMSTERHUIS, FRANS, *Wijsgerige werken*, ed. M. J. Petry (Budel, 2001).

—— *Œuvres philosophiques*, ed. L. S. P. Meyboom (3 vols., Hildesheim, 1972).

—— *Aristée, ou de la Divinité*, in Hemsterhuis, *Œuvres*, ed. Meyboom, ii. 6–76.

—— *Lettre sur l'homme et ses rapports* (1772; New Haven, 1964).

HENNERT, JOHAN FREDERIK, 'Over den aart der wijsgeerte van Spinoza', in J. H. Hennert (ed.), *Uitgeleezene verhandelingen over de wysgeerte en fraaje letteren getrokken uit de werken der Koninglyken Akademie te Berlin* (6 vols., Utrecht, 1780–4). (HKB i. 1–40)

—— 'Derde verhandeling over de wijsgeerte van Spinoza', in *Uitgeleezene verhandelingen*, i. 176–281.

—— 'Het Spinozismus vergeleeken met de gevoelens van Malebranche, Berkeley en der Kabbalistische wysgeeren', in *Uitgeleezene verhandelingen*, i. 282–326.

—— 'Vertoog over het hedendaagsch Atheismus', in *Uitgeleezene verhandelingen*, iii. 404–509.

—— 'Over de natuur van het zedelijk gevoel', in *Uitgeleezene verhandelingen*, iv. 340–407.

HERDER, JOHANN GOTTFRIED, *Selected Early Works, 1764–1767*, ed. E. A. Menze and K. Menges (University Park, Pa., 1992).

—— *Gott. Einige Gespräche über Spinoza's System* (1787; 2nd edn., Gotha, 1800).

—— *Ideen zur Philosophie der Geschichte der Menschheit* (4 vols., Riga, 1785).

—— *Philosophical Writings*, ed. M. N. Forster (Cambridge, 2002).

—— *Another Philosophy of History* (1774), ed. I. D. Evrigenis and D. Pellerin (Indianapolis, 2004).

—— 'How Philosophy can Become more Universal and Useful for the Benefit of the People (1765)', in Forster (ed.), Herder, *Philosophical Writings*, 3–29.

HEYDENREICH, KARL HEINRICH, *Natur und Gott nach Spinoza* (Leipzig, 1789).

—— *Betrachtungen über die Philosophie der natürlichen Religion* (Leipzig, 1790).

—— *Encyclopädische Einleitung in das Studium der Philosophie nach den Bedürfnissen unsers Zeitalters* (Leipzig, 1793).

Histoire de l'Académie Royale des Sciences (95 vols., Paris, 1702–97).

Histoire philosophique et politique des établissemens et du commerce des Européens dans les deux Indes by Raynal, Diderot, Deleyre, etc. (6 vols., Amsterdam, 1770).

Histoire philosophique et politique des établissemens et du commerce des Européens dans les deux Indes (6 vols., Amsterdam, 1774).

Histoire philosophique et politique des établissemens et du commerce des Européens dans les deux Indes (10 vols., Geneva, 1780).

HOLBACH, BARON D', PAUL-HENRI THIRY, *Le Christianisme dévoilé ou, Examen des principes et des effets de la religion chrétienne* (repr. Paris, 2006).

—— *La Contagion sacrée ou, Histoire naturelle de la superstition* (1768; repr. Paris, 2006).

—— *Lettres à Eugénie ou, Préservatif contre les préjugés* (1768; repr. Paris, 2007).

—— *Essai sur les préjugés ou, De l'influence des opinions sur les mœurs et sur le bonheur des hommes* ('Londres' [Amsterdam], 1770).

—— *Système de la nature, ou Des loix du monde physique et du monde moral* (2 vols., 'Londres' [Amsterdam], 1770), repr. in d'Holbach, *Œuvres philosophiques complètes*, ed. Jean-Pierre Jackson (Paris, 2000), ii. 162–643.

—— *Histoire critique de Jésus-Christ, ou, Analyse raisonnée des Évangiles* (n.p. [Amsterdam], 1770), in d'Holbach, *Œuvres philosophiques complètes*, ed. Jean-Pierre Jackson (Paris, 2000), ii. 645–815.

—— *La Politique naturelle, ou Discours sur les vrais principes du gouvernement* (1773; repr. Paris, 1998).

—— *Système social, ou Principes naturels de la morale et de la politique* (1773; repr. Paris, 1994).

—— *Le Bon-Sens du Curé Jean Meslier suivi de son Testament* ('Londres' [Amsterdam, 1772; repr. of the edn. of 'Bruxelles, 1829', Hildesheim, 1970).

—— *La Morale universelle, ou, Les Devoirs de l'homme fondés sur sa nature* (3 vols., Amsterdam, 1776).

—— *Éthocratie ou Le Gouvernement fondé sur la morale* (Amsterdam, 1776), in d'Holbach, *Œuvres philosophiques complètes*, vol. iii, ed. Jean-Pierre Jackson (Paris, 2000), 590–707.

—— *Catalogue des livres de la bibliothèque de feu M. le Baron d'Holbach* (Paris, 1789).

HOLLAND, GEORG JONATHAN, *Réflexions philosophiques sur le* Système de la nature (1772; 2 vols., Paris, 1773).

HUME, DAVID, *Treatise of Human Nature* (1739; Buffalo, NY, 1992).

—— 'Of Superstition and Enthusiasm' (1741), in *Hume on Religion*, ed. R. Wolheim (1963; London, 1971).

—— *Essays Moral, Political and Literary*, ed. E. F. Miller (1741; Indianapolis, 1985).

—— *Dialogues Concerning Natural Religion*, in *Hume on Religion*, ed. R. Wolheim, 99–204.

—— *An Enquiry Concerning Human Understanding* (1748), ed. E. Steinberg (2nd edn., Indianapolis, 1993).

—— *An Enquiry Concerning the Principles of Morals* (1751), ed. T. L. Beauchamp (Oxford, 1998).

—— *The Natural History of Religion* (1757), in David Hume, *Principal Writings on Religion*, ed. J. C. A. Gaskin (Oxford, 1993), 134–93.

—— *The History of England from the Invasion of Julius Caesar to the Revolution of 1688* (6 vols., Indianapolis, 1983).

—— *Letters*, ed. J. Y. T. Greig (2 vols., Oxford, 1969).

—— *Life and Correspondence of David Hume*, ed. J. H. Burton (2 vols., Edinburgh, 1846).

[I.L.V.M.C.E.], *Die Neue Offenbahrung über das Evangelium St Harenbergs* (Leipzig, 1748).

L'Impie démasqué, ou Remontrance aux écrivains incrédules ('Londres' [Paris?], 1773).

Index Librorum Prohibitorum Pii Sexti Jussu Editus (Rome, 1786). (BL)

Índice último de los libros prohibidos y mandados expurgar para todos los reynos y señorios del católico rey de las Españas (Madrid, 1790).

[INGLIS, CHARLES], *The True Interest of America Impartially Stated* (New York, 1776).

IRHOVEN VAN DAM, WILHELMUS VAN, *Courier van Europa* (journal: Amsterdam, 1783–5).

JACOBI, FRIEDRICH HEINRICH, *The Main Philosophical Writings*, trans. G. di Giovanni (Montreal, 1994).

—— *Schriften zum Spinozastreit*, ed. K. Hammacher and I. Piske (2 vols., Hamburg, 1998).

—— *Über die Lehre des Spinoza in Briefen an den Herrn Moses Mendelssohn* (1785), in Jacobi, *Schriften*, i, part 1, pp. 1–146.

—— *Wider Mendelssohns Beschuldigungen betreffende die Briefe über die Lehre des Spinoza* (Leipzig, 1786).

—— *David Hume über den Glauben, oder Idealismus und Realismus* (Breslau, 1787).

JAKOB, LUDWIG HEINRICH, *Kritische Anfangsgründe zu einer allgemeinen Metaphysik* (Halle, 1788).

—— *Prüfung der Mendelssohnischen Morgenstunden oder aller spekulativen Beweise für des Daseyn Gottes* (Leipzig, 1786).

JAMIN, PÈRE NICOLAS, *Pensées théologiques relatives aux erreurs du temps* (1768; Riom, 1798).

JEBB, JOHN, *The Works Theological, Medical, Political and Miscellaneous* (3 vols., London, 1787).

JONES, WILLIAM, *Lettre à Monsieur A…Du P…dans laquelle est compris l'examen de sa traduction des livres attribués à Zoroastre* (London, 1771).

—— *A Discourse on the Institution of a Society for Enquiring into the History, Civil and Natural, the Antiquities, Arts, Sciences and Literature of Asia* (delivered at Calcutta 15 Jan. 1784).

—— *A Grammar of the Persian Language* (7th edn., London, 1809).

Journal des décrets de l'Assemblée Nationale, ed. François-Jerôme Riffard de Saint Martin (5 vols., Paris, 1789–91).

Journal encyclopédique, ed. P. Rousseau (304 vols., Liège–Bouillon, 1756–93).

Journal étranger, ed. A. F. Prévost, E. C. Fréron, A. Delyre, et al (45 vols., Paris, 1754–62).

JOVELLANOS, GASPAR MELCHOR DE, *Obras en prosa* (Madrid, 2003).

Justification de la résistance des colonies américaines aux oppressions du gouvernment britanni-que ('Londres', 1776). (Kn. 19120)

KAMES, LORD, HENRY HOME, *Essays on the Principles of Morality and Natural Religion* (1751).

—— *Six Sketches on the History of Man* (Philadelphia, 1776).

—— *Elements of Criticism*, ed. P. Jones (6th edn., 2 vols., Indianapolis, 2005).

KANT, IMMANUEL, *Gesammelte Schriften*, edn. of the Königlich Preussischen Akademie der Wissenschaften (35 vols., Berlin, 1902–97).

—— *Critique of Practical Reason*, trans. L. White Beck (3rd edn., London, 1993).

—— *Was ist Aufklärung? Ausgewählte kleine Schriften*, ed. H. D. Brandt (Hamburg, 1999).

—— *Religion within the Boundaries of Mere Reason*, ed. A. Wood and G. di Giovanni (Cambridge, 1998).

—— 'What does it Mean to Orient Oneself in Thinking?', in Kant, *Religion within the Boundaries*, 3–14.

—— 'On the Use of Teleological Principles in Philosophy' (1788), in R. Bernasconi (ed.), *Race* (Oxford, 2001), 37–56.

—— *Lectures on Metaphysics*, ed. K. Ameriks (1997; repr. Cambridge, 2001).

—— *Toward Perpetual Peace: A Philosophical Sketch*, in Immanuel Kant, *Toward Perpetual Peace and Other Writings on Politics, Peace, and History*, ed. P. Kleingeld (New Haven, 2006), 67–109.

—— *Groundwork of the Metaphysics of Morals*, ed. M. Gregor (Cambridge, 1997).

—— *Critique of Judgment*, trans. J. H. Bernard (New York, 1951).

—— *Nova Dilucidatio*, in Kant, *Theoretical Philosophy*.

—— *Der einzig mögliche Beweisgrund zu einer Demonstration des Daseins Gottes* (1763), English trans. in Kant, *Theoretical Philosophy*, 107–201.

—— *Briefwechsel*, ed. H. E. Fischer (3 vols., Munich, 1912).

—— *Theoretical Philosophy, 1755–1770*, trans. and ed. D. Walford (Cambridge, 1992).

—— 'On the Miscarriage of All Philosophical Trials in Theodicy' (1791), trans. G. di Giovanni, in Kant, *Religion and Rational Theology*, ed. A. Wood (Cambridge, 1996), 19–38.

—— *Critique of Pure Reason*, trans. N. Kemp Smith (New York, 1965).

KLUIT, ADRIAAN, *Academische redevoering over het misbruik van 't algemeen staatsrecht* (Leiden, 1787).

KNIGGE, ADOLPH, FREIHERR VON, [Philo], *Philos endliche Erklärung und Antwort* (1788), in Van Dülmen, *Dokumente*, 341–61.

KNOBLAUCH, CARL VON, *Politisch-philosophische Gespräche* (Berlin, 1792).

—— *Euclides Anti-Thaumaturgicus, oder demonstrantiver Beweis von der Unmöglichkeit hyperphysischer Begebenheiten* ('Germanien', 1791).

—— *Taschenbuch für Aufklärer und Nichtaufklärer auf das Jahr 1791* (Berlin, 1790).

—— *Ueber Feerey. Auch ein Beitrag zu den Theorien des Wunderbaren* (Berlin, 1791).

[——]*Anti-Taumaturgie, oder die Bezweiflung der Wunder* ('Loretto', 1790).

Die Korrespondenz des Illuminatenordens, i: *1776–1781*, ed. R. Markner, M. Neugebauer-Wöl, and H. Schüttler (Tübingen, 2005).

[LA BEAUMELLE, LAURENT A. DE] L.B.L.D.A., *L'Asiatique tolérant* ('Paris' [Amsterdam], 1748). (AUB)

—— *Suite de la défense de L'Esprit des loix* (1751; repr. Geneva, 1753). (IAS)

LA HARPE, JEAN FRANÇOIS DE, *L'Aléthophile ou l'Ami de la vérité* (Amsterdam, 1758). (BL)

—— *Philosophie du dix-huitième siècle* (2 vols., Paris, 1818).

LALANDE, JÉROME, *Voyage en Italie contenant l'histoire et les anecdotes les plus singulières de l'Italie* (2nd edn., Paris, 1786).

—— 'Second Supplément au Dictionnaire des athées' (1805), in Sylvain Maréchal, *Dictionnaire des athées anciens et modernes* (2nd edn., Brussels, 1833).

LAMOURETTE, ADRIEN, *Pensées sur la philosophie de l'incrédulité* (Paris, 1786).

LARDIZÁBAL Y URIBE, MANUEL DE, *Discurso sobre las penas contrahido a las leyes criminales de España para facilitar su reforma* (Madrid, 1782).

[LAULANNIER, MICHEL DE], *Essais sur la religion chrétienne, et sur le système des philosophes modernes* (Paris, 1770).

LE FRANC DE POMPIGNON, JEAN-GEORGES, *Questions diverses sur l'incrédulité* (3rd edn., Paris, 1757).

—— *Instruction pastorale de Monseigneur l'Évêque du Puy sur l'hérésie: pour servir de suite à celle du même prélat sur la prétendue philosophie des incrédules modernes* (Puy, 1766).

LE FRANC DE POMPIGNAN, JEAN-JACQUES, 'Discours de réception', in *Lumières voilées: œuvres choisies d'un magistrat du XVIIIe siècle*, ed. Th. E. Braun and G. Robichez (Saint-Étienne, 2007), 222–32.

LEIBNIZ, G. W., *New Essays on Human Understanding*, ed. P. Remnant and J. Bennett (Cambridge, 2nd edn., 1997).

LESSING, EPHRAIM GOTTHOLD, *Gesammelte Werke*, ed. P. Rilla (10 vols., Berlin, 1954–8).

—— *Philosophical and Theological Writings*, trans. and ed. H. B. Nisbet (Cambridge, 2005).

—— *Ernst und Falk*, in Lessing, *Philosophical and Theological Writings*, ed. Nisbet, 184–216.

—— *Briefe*, ed. H. Kiesel, in G. E. Lessing, *Werke und Briefe*, ed. W. Barner (3 vols., Frankfurt, 1987).

—— *Anti-Goeze*, in Lessing, *Werke in drei Banden*, ed. H. G. Göpfert (Munich, 1982), iii. 477–546.

—— 'The Education of the Human Race' (1777–89), in Lessing, *Philosophical and Theological Writings*, ed. Nisbet, 217–40.

Lettre au R. P. Berthier sur le matérialisme, printed as an appendix to Claude-Adrien Helvétius, *De l'esprit* (3 vols., The Hague, 1759), iii. 1–34.

Lettre d'un professeur en théologie d'une université protestante à M. d'Alembert (Strasbourg, 1759).

Lettres de Genève (1741–1793) à Jean Henri Samuel Formey, ed. A. Bandelier and F. S. Eigeldinger (Paris, 2010).

Lettre sur l'invasion des Provinces Unies à M. Le Comte Mirabeau, et sa réponse (Brussels, 1787).

LICHTENBERG, GEORG CHRISTOPH, *Werke* (Hamburg, 1967).

—— *Schriften und Briefe*, ed. W. Promies (6 vols., Munich, 1968).

LINGUET, SIMON NICOLAS HENRI, *Annales politiques, civiles et littéraires* (19 vols., Brussels, 1777–92; repr. 1970).

LLANO ZAPATA, JOSÉ EUSEBIO, *Memorias históricas, físicas, críticas, apologéticas de la América meridional* (Lima, 2005).

LORENZANA Y BUTRÓN, FRANCISCO ANTONIO, *Cartas pastorales y edictos* (Mexico City, 1770).

LÖWE, JOHANN CASPAR, *Dogmatische und moralische Einleitung in die Religions-Streitigkeiten mit den Deisten* (Frankfurt, 1752).

Luxdorphs samling af trykke-frihedens skrifter (collection of printed pamphlets dating from 1770–3 in 25 volumes housed in the Royal Library, Copenhagen).

LUZAC, ELIE, *Hollands rijkdom behelzende den oorsprong van den koophandel, en van de magt van desen staat* (3 vols., Leiden, 1780).

—— (ed.), *Bibliothèque impartiale* (journal: Leiden, 1750–8).

MABLY, GABRIEL BONNOT DE, *Collection complète des œuvres de l'Abbé de Mably* (15 vols., Paris, 'l'an III de la République' [1794/5]).

—— *Observations sur l'histoire de la Grèce* (Geneva, 1766).

—— *Entretiens de Phocion sur le rapport de la morale avec la politique* (Amsterdam, 1767).

—— *Observations sur le gouvernement et les lois des États-Unis d'Amérique* (1783), in *Collection complète*, viii. 337–85.

—— *Du gouvernement et des lois de Pologne* (1770), in *Collection*, viii. 1–336.

—— *Doutes proposés aux philosophes économistes sur l'ordre naturel et essentiel des sociétés politiques* (The Hague, 1768).

MCKENNA, THEOBALD, *An Essay on Parliamentary Reform, and on the Evils Likely to Ensue, from a Republican Constitution, in Ireland* (Dublin, 1793).

MAIMON, SOLOMON, *Ueber die Progressen der Philosophie* (Berlin, 1793).

—— *Lebensgeschichte*, ed. K. Ph. Moritz (Frankfurt, 1984).

—— *Essay on Transcendental Philosophy* (1790), ed. and trans. N. Midgley (London, 2010).

MALESHERBES, CHRÉTIEN GUILLAUME DE LAMOIGNON DE, *Mémoires sur la librairie et sur la liberté de la presse* (Chapel Hill, NC, 1979).

MALEVILLE, GUILLAUME, *La Religion naturelle et la révélée établie sur les principes de la vraie philosophie* (6 vols., Paris, 1756–8).

[MANUEL, PIERRE-LOUIS], *Lettres sur la Révolution, recueillies par un ami de la Constitution* (Paris, 1792).

MARAT, JEAN-PAUL, *De l'homme, ou, des principes des loix de l'influence de l'âme sur le corps, et du corps sur l'âme* (3 vols., n.p., 1775).

MARCK, F. A. VAN DER, *Over de liefde tot het Vaderland te bestuuren overeenkomstig met de redelijke en gezellige natuur der menschen* (Deventer, 1783).

—— *Bedenkingen en bezwaren... uit name van de weleerwaarde classis van Groningen... tegen de academische lessen van mr Frederik Adolph van der Marck* (Groningen, 1782).

MARÉCHAL, PIERRE-SYLVAIN DE, *Catéchisme du Curé Meslier* (n.p. [Paris], 1790).

—— *Dictionnaire des athées anciens et modernes* (Brussels, 1833).

—— *Fragmens d'un poème moral sur Dieu* ('a Atheopolos' [Paris?], 1781).

—— *Apologues modernes, à l'usage du dauphin, premières leçons du fils ainé du roi* ('Bruxelles' [Paris?], 1788).

—— *Dictionnaire des honnêtes gens* (Paris, 1791).

—— (with Jacques Grasset de Saint-Sauveur), *Costumes civils actuels de tous les peuples connus* (1784; 2nd edn., 4 vols., Paris, 1788).

MARIANO CORICHE, CRISTOBAL, *Oración vindicativa del honor de las letras y de los literatos* (Puebla de los Angeles, 1763).

MARIN, MICHEL-ANGE, *Le Baron Van-Hesden, ou la république des incrédules* (5 vols., Toulouse, 1762). (IAS)

MARMONTEL, JEAN-FRANÇOIS, *Bélisaire* (Paris, 1767).

—— *The Incas: Or, The Destruction of the Empire of Peru* (2 vols., London, 1777).

—— *Mémoires*, ed. M. Tourneux (3 vols., Paris, 1891).

MARTINET, J. F., *Katechismus der Natuur* (4 vols., 5th edn., Amsterdam, 1782–9).

[MASSON DES GRANGES, DANIEL LE] Abbé M.D.G., *Le Philosophe moderne, ou l'incrédule condamné au tribunal de sa raison* (Paris, 1759).

MATICORENA ESTRADA, MIGUEL (ed.), *Colección documental de la Independencia del Perú*, ser. 1 vol. iii: *José Baquíjano y Carrillo* (Lima, 1976).

MAUPERTUIS, PIERRE-LOUIS M. DE, *Œuvres de Mr de Maupertuis* (new edn., 4 vols., Lyon, 1756).

——'Essai de philosophie morale', in *Œuvres*, i. 171–252.

MAYÁNS Y SISCAR, GREGORIO, *Idea del nuevo método que se puede practicar em la enseñanza de las universidades de España* (1767), in Peset and Peset, *Gregorio Mayans*, 179–351.

MEINERS, CHRISTOPH, *Briefe über die Schweiz* (4 vols., Berlin, 1784–90).

—— *Ueber die Natur der Völker im südlichen Asien auf den ostindischen und Südsee-Inseln*, *Göttingisches historisches Magazin*, 7 (1790), 258–306.

—— *Historische vergleichung der Sitten, und Verfassungen der Gesetze, und Gewerbe, des Handels und der Religion, der Wissenschaften, und Lehranstalten des Mittelalters mit denen unsers Jahrhunderts* (3 vols., Hanover, 1793).

Mémoires authentiques et interéssans ou histoire des comtes Struensee et Brandt (Copenhagen, 1789).

Mémoires secrets pour servir à l'histoire de la république des Lettres en France depuis MDCCLXII jusqu'à nos jours, ed. Mathieu-François de Mairobert et al. (36 vols., 'à Londres', 1780–9).

Memorial literario, instructivo y curioso de la Corte de Madrid (journal: Madrid, 1784–91).

MENDELSSOHN, MOSES, *Gesammelte Schriften*, ed. I. Elbogen et al. (Berlin, 1929–38).

—— *Philosophical Writings*, ed. D. O. Dahlstrom (Cambridge, 1997).

—— *Gesammelte Schriften Jubiläumsausgabe*, ed. F.Bamberger, A. Altmann, et al. (24 vols. thus far, Stuttgart, 1971–).

—— *Morgenstunden oder Vorlesungen über des Daseyn Gottes*, in Mendelssohn, *Gesammelte Schriften*, iii, part 2, pp. 1–175.

—— *An die Freunde Lessings* (1786), in Mendelssohn, *Gesammelte Schriften*, iii, part 2, 177–218.

MERCIER, LOUIS SEBASTIEN, *De J. J. Rousseau considéré comme l'un du premiers auteurs de la Révolution* (2 vols., Paris, 1791).

[——] *Memoirs of the Year Two Thousand Five Hundred*, trans. W. Hooper (London, 1772).

MEYER, JOHANN, *Die Närrische Welt in ihrer Narrheit, Oder endeckte Quellen der Atheisterey und Freydenckerey* (Breslau, 1752). (GUB)

MILLAR, JOHN, *Observations Concerning the Distinction of Ranks in Society* (London, 1771).

[MIRABEAU, GABRIEL-HONORÉ], *Des lettres de cachet et des prisons d'état* (1778; 2 vols., 'Hambourg', 1782).

—— *Essai sur le despotisme* (1775; n.p., 3rd edn. 1792).

—— *Considérations sur l'ordre de Cincinnatus* ('Londres' [Amsterdam?], 1784).

—— *Avis aux Hessois et autres peuples de l'Allemagne, vendus par leurs princes à l'Angleterre* (1777; 3rd edn., Paris, 1792).

—— *Aux Bataves sur le stathouderat* (n.p. [Amsterdam?], 1788).

—— *De la monarchie prussienne sous Frédéric le Grand* (6 vols., 'Londres', 1788).

—— *Mirabeau à la tribune, ou Choix des meilleurs discours de cet orateur* (2 vols., Paris, 1796).

MIRANDA, FRANCISCO DE, *Diario de viaje a Estados Unidos* (1783–4; Santiago, Chile, 1998).

MONIGLIA, TOMMASO VINCENZO, *Dissertazione contro i Fatalisti* (2 vols., Lucca, 1744).

—— *Dissertazione contro i materialisti e altri increduli* (2 vols., Padua, 1750).

MONTESQUIEU, CHARLES DE SECONDAT, BARON DE, *Œuvres complètes*, ed. D. Oster (Paris, 1964).

MOREAU, JOSEPH-NICOLAS, *Nouveau Mémoire pour servir à l'histoire des Cacouacs* (Amsterdam, 1757).

—— *L'Observateur hollandois* (5 vols., The Hague, 1755–9).

MORELLET, ABBÉ ANDRÉ, *Lettres*, ed. D. Medlin et al. (3 vols., Oxford, 1991–6).

—— *Mémoires sur le dix-huitième siècle et sur la Révolution française* (2 vols., Paris, 1822).

[——] *Mémoire pour servir à la béatification d'Abraham Chaumeix, illustre anti-philosophe de nos jours*, in *Œuvres philosophiques de Mr D...* (6 vols., Amsterdam, 1772), vol. i.

—— *Essai sur le cœur humain, ou principes naturels de l'éducation* (Paris, 1745).

[——] *Préface de la Comédie des philosophes* (Paris, 1760).

[MORELLY], *Code de la nature, ou le véritable Esprit de ses loix* ([Amsterdam?], 1755).

MOSHEIM, J. L., *Versuch einer unparteiischen und gründlichen Ketzergeschichte* (1746; 2 vols., Hildesheim, 1998).

MOUNIER, JEAN-JOSEPH, *Considérations sur les gouvernemens et principalement sur celui qui convient à la France* (Versailles, 1789).

—— *De l'influence attribuée aux philosophes aux franc-maçons et aux Illuminés sur la Révolution de la France* (Tübingen, 1801).

MUÑOZ, JUAN BAUTISTA, *Historia del Nuevo Mundo*, vol. i (Madrid, 1793).

MÜNTER, BALTHASAR, *Theologiae Naturalis Polemicae Specimen Exhibens Historiam et Refutationem Systematis illius quod a Benedicto de Spinoza Nomen Habet* (n.p., 1758). (GUB)

—— *Bekehrungsgeschichte des vormaligen Grafen und Königlichen Dänischen Geheimen Cabinetsministers Johann Friedrich Struensee* (Copenhagen, 1772).

MUTIS, JOSÉ CELESTINO, *Elementos de filosofía natural* (1764), in *Pensamiento científico y filosófico de José Celestino Mutis*, ed. G. Hernández de Alba (Bogotá, 1982), 43–68.

—— *Sustentación del sistema heliocéntrico de Copérnico* (1773), in *Pensamiento científico y filosófico de José Celestino Mutis*, ed. G. Hernández de Alba (Bogotá, 1982), 69–91.

NAIGEON, JACQUES-ANDRÉ, 'Lettre sur la mort de M. le Baron d'Holbach', in Naville, *Paul Thiry d'Holbach*, 452–5.

—— *Adresse à l'Assemblée Nationale sur la liberté des opinions* (Paris, 1790).

—— *Encyclopédie méthodique: philosophie ancienne et moderne* (3 vols., Paris, 1791).

—— *Mémoires historiques et philosophiques sur la vie et les ouvrages de Denis Diderot* (repr. Geneva, 1970).

—— *Lettre du Citoyen Naigeon habitant de Sedan, à ses concitoyens*, Sedan, le 6 Germinal, an 5 (n.p., 1797) (BL pamphlet R 643/6).

[——?], *Discours préliminaire* (1770), printed as appendix to Vercruysse, *Bicentaire*, 39–56.

—— and d'HOLBACH, PAUL-HENRI THIRY (eds.), *Le Militaire philosophe, ou Difficultés sur la religion proposées au père Malebranche*, ed. Jean-Pierre Jakcson (Paris, 2008).

NECKER, JACQUES, *De l'importance des opinions religieuses* ('Londres' [Paris], 1788).

—— *De la Révolution françoise* (4 vols., n.p., 1796).

Neuer Zeitungen von Gelehrten Sachen, Leipzig periodical (1718–84).

NIEUHOFF, BERNARD, *Over Spinozisme* (Harderwijk, 1799).

NONNOTTE, ABBÉ CLAUDE ADRIEN, *Dictionnaire philosophique de la religion* (Liège-Brussels, 1773).

—— *Philosophisches Lexicon der Religion* (Augsburg, 1777).

Notice des écrits les plus célèbres, tant imprimés que manuscrits, qui favorisent l'incrédulité, ou dont la lecture est dangereuse aux esprits foibles (c.1744), *La Lecture clandestine*, 2 (1993), ii. 178–92.

Nouvelle Bibliothèque germanique, ed. J. H. S. Formey (Amsterdam, 1746–60).

Nouvelles Observations sur la seconde lettre de Mr de Pinto à l'occasion des troubles de l'Amérique septentrionale ('Londres', 1776). (Kn. 19125)

Nuix, Juan, *Reflexiones imparciales sobre la humanidad de los españoles en las Indias, contra los pretendidos filósofos y políticos* (Madrid, 1782).

O terremoto de 1755: Testemunhos britânicos (Lisbon, 1990).

Observations d'un homme impartial sur la lettre de Mr [De Pinto] *à Mr S.B.* ('Londres', 1776). (Kn. 191223) (HKB)

Olavide, Pablo de, 'Plan de reforma para la Universidad de Sevilla', appendix in Marchena Fernández, *Tiempo ilustrado.*

—— *El Evangelio en triunfo o historia de un filósofo desengañado* (1797; 3rd edn., 2 vols., Madrid, 1799).

Ontwerp om de Republiek door eene heilzaame vereeniging der belangen van regent en burger van binnen gelukkig en van buiten gedugt te maaken, ed. Wybo Fijnje et al. (Leiden, 1785). (Kn. 21045) (HKB)

[Oswald, James], *An Appeal to Common Sense in Behalf of Religion* (2 vols., Edinburgh, 1766).

[Paalzow, Christian Ludwig], 'Vorbericht des Uebersetzers', in [d'Holbach], *System der Natur, oder von der Gesetzen der physischen und moralischen Welt* (Frankfurt, 1783), pp. i–x.

Paape, Gerrit, *De Aristocraat en de Burger* (Rotterdam, 1785). (Kn. 21046)

—— *De Hollandsche wijsgeer in Braband* (4 vols., Antwerp-Dordrecht, 1788–90).

—— *De Hollandsche wijsgeer in Vrankrijk* (Dordrecht, 1790).

—— *De Zaak der verdrukte Hollandsche Patriotten voor de vierschaar der Menschlijkheid gebragt* (Dunkirk, 1790).

—— *Mijn vrolijke wijsgeerte in mijne ballingschap* (Dordrecht, 1792).

—— *Mijn Tegenwoordig Vaderland of wijsgeerige geschiedenis van Vrankrijk* (3 vols., Dordrecht, 1792).

—— *De onverbloemde geschiedenis van het Bataafsch Patriottismus* (Delft, 1798).

[——], *Het Leven van zijne Doorluchtigste Hoogheid Willem de Vijfden ... bijgenaamd de Bederver van zijn Vaderland* (Dunkirk, 1791).

Pagano, Franceso Mario, *Saggi politici de' principi, progessi e decadenza delle società* (2 vols., Naples, 1791–2).

Paine, Thomas, *Common Sense* (Edinburgh, 1776).

—— *The American Crisis*, nos. 1 to 3 (Philadephia, 1777).

—— *Rights of Man* (1790), ed. E. Foner (New York, 1985).

—— *Letter Addressed to the Abbé Raynal on the Affairs of North America* (Philadelphia, 1782).

—— *The Age of Reason, Part the First* (London, 1796).

Palacio y Viana, Josef de, *Defensa de los puntos más interesantes a la religión acometidos por los incrédulos* (Madrid, 1788).

Palissot de Montenoy, Charles, *Petites Lettres sur de grands philosophes* (1757), in *Œuvres complètes de M. Palisso*t (Paris, 1809), i. 269–316.

—— *Lettres de M. de Voltaire à M. Palissot, avec les réponses* (Geneva, 1760).

Palmer, Eliahu, *Principles of Nature or, A Development of the Moral Causes of Happiness and Misery Among the Human Species* (New York, 1801).

PALMIERI, GIUSEPPE, *Riflessioni sulla pubblica felicità relativamente al regno di Napoli* (Naples, 1787).

PALMIERI, VINCENZO, *Analisi ragionata de' sistemi e de' fondamente dell'ateismo e dell'incredulità* (8 vols., Genova, 1811).

PAULIAN, AIME-HENRI, *Le Véritable Système de la nature* (2 vols., Avignon, 1788).

PAULUS, PIETER, *Vrage: In welken zin kunnen de menschen gezegd worden gelyk te zyn?* (1793; 4th edn., Haarlem, 1794). (HKB)

PAUW, CORNELIS DE, *Recherches philosophiques sur les Américains* (2 vols., 'Londres', 1770).

PEREIRA DE FIGUEIREDO, ANTÓNIO, *A Narrative of the Earthquake of Lisbon* (London, 1756).

PERNETY, ANTOINE-JOSEPH, DOM, *Dissertation sur l'Amérique et les Américains contre les* Recherches philosophiques (Berlin, 1770).

[PETIT, ÉMILIEN], *Observations sur plusieurs assertions, extraites littéralement de l'*Histoire philosophique des... deux Indes (Amsterdam, 1776).

PICHON, THOMAS-JEAN, *La Raison triomphante des nouveautés ou, Essai sur les mœurs et l'incrédulité* (Paris, 1756).

PILATI, CARLANTONIO, *Ragionamenti intorno alla legge naturale e civile* (1764; Venice, 1766).

—— *Di una riforma d'Italia* (1767; 2nd edn., 'Villafranca' [Venice], 1770). (BL)

—— *Lettere di un viaggiatore filosofo*, ed. G. Pagliero (Bergamo, 1990).

PINTO, ISAAC DE, *Précis des arguments contre les matérialistes* (The Hague, 1740). (BL)

—— *Letters on the American Troubles* (London, 1776). (BL)

—— *Réponse de Mr. I. de Pinto aux observations d'un homme impartial, sur sa lettre à Mr S.B., docteur en médicine à Kingston dans la Jamaïque* (The Hague, 1776). (BL)

—— *Second Lettre de Mr de Pinto à l'occasion des troubles des colonies, contenant des réflexions politiques* (The Hague, 1776). (Kn. 19124) (HKB)

[——], *Lettre de Mr*** [I. de Pinto] à Mr S.B... au sujet des troubles qui agitent actuellement toute l'Amérique Septentrionale* (The Hague, 1776). (Kn. 19122) (HKB)

PIQUER, ANDRÉS, *Discurso sobre la aplicación de la philosophía a los assuntos de religión para la juventud española* (Madrid, 1757).

—— *Lógica moderna o arte de hallar la verdad y perfeccionar la razón* (Valencia, 1747).

PLATNER, ERNST, *Philosophische Aphorismen* (2 vols., Leipzig, 1776–82).

PLOUQUET, GODFROY, *Dissertatio de materialismo* (Tübingen, 1751).

PLUQUET, THE ABBÉ FRANÇOIS, *Examen du fatalisme* (3 vols., Paris, 1757).

[POLIER DE BOTTENS, GEORGES], *Pensées chrétiennes mises en parallèle, ou en opposition avec les* Pensées philosophiques (Rouen, 1747). (HKB)

PORTALIS, J. E. M., *De l'usage et de l'abus de l'esprit philosophique durant le XVIIIe siècle* (1798; new edn., Paris, 2007).

POSADA, E., and IBAÑEZ, P. M. (eds.), *Relaciones de mando: Memorias presentados por los gobernantes del Nuevo Reino de Granada* (Bogotá, 1910).

PRATJE, J. H., *Historische Nachrichten von Joh. Chr. Edelmanns, eines berüchtigten Religionspötters* (Hamburg, 1755).

Préface de la Comédie des philosophes (Paris, 1760). (Oxford Bod. 257 o 27 (7))

PRICE, RICHARD, *Observations on the Importance of the American Revolution and the Means of Making it a Benefit to the World* (London, 1785).

—— *A Discourse on the Love of our Country* (2nd edn., London, 1789).

—— *Political Writings*, ed. D. O. Thomas (Cambridge, 1991).

Priestley, Joseph, *An Essay on the First Principles of Government and on the Nature of Political, Civil and Religious Liberty* (Dublin, 1768).

—— *The History and Present State of Electricity* (2nd edn., London, 1769).

—— *Autobiography* (Bath, 1970).

—— *An Examination of Dr. Reid's Inquiry into the Human Mind on the Principles of Common Sense* (London, 1774).

—— *Disquisitions Relating to Matter and Spirit* (1777; New York, Garland repr., 1976).

—— *The Doctrine of Philosophical Necessity Illustrated* (1777; New York, Garland repr., 1976).

—— *An History of the Corruptions of Christianity* (2 vols., Birmingham, 1782).

—— *Letters to the Right Honourable Edmund Burke* (Birmingham, 1791).

Proby, W. C., *Modern Philosophy and Barbarism* (London, n.d. [1794?]).

Propositiones Extractae ex Libro cui Titulus De l'esprit des loix (Geneva, 1750).

[Prudhomme, Louis-Marie, and Tournon, A.], *Révolutions de Paris* (journal: Paris, 1789–90).

Rabaut de Saint-Étienne, J. P., *Précis historique de la Révolution française* (Paris, 1792).

—— *Projet du préliminaire de la Constitution françoise* (Versailles, 1789).

Radishchev, Alexander Nikolaevich, *A Journey from St Petersburg to Moscow* (Cambridge, Mass., 1958).

Raynal, Guillaume Thomas François, *A Philosophical and Political History of the British Settlements and Trade in North America* (2 vols., Edinburgh, 1776).

—— *Révolution de l'Amérique* ('Londres', 1781).

—— *The Revolution of America* (London, 1781).

—— *Histoire philosophique*, see *Histoire philosophique*.

—— *Adresse de Guillaume-Thomas Raynal remue par lui-même à M. le président le 31 mai 1791, et lue à l'Assemblée le même jour* (Paris, 1791).

[G. T.] Raynal démasqué, ou Lettres sur la vie et les ouvrages de cet écrivain (Paris, 1791).

Réclamation des Genevois patriotes établis à Londres (Paris, 1789).

Redondo, Patricio, *En boca cerrada no entra mosca: carta al corresponsal del Censor* (n.p., n.d. [Madrid?], 1788).

Réflexions d'un Franciscain sur les trois volumes de l'Encyclopédie ('Berlin' [Paris], 1754).

Rehberg, August Wilhelm, *Sämmtliche Schriften* (4 vols., Hanover, 1828–9).

—— *Untersuchungen über die französische Revolution* (2 vols., Hanover, 1793).

Reid, Thomas, *The Works, now Fully Collected with Selections from his Unpublished Letters*, ed. W. Hamilton (2 vols., Edinburgh, 1872).

Reimarus, Hermann Samuel, *Apologie oder Schützschrift für die vernünftigen Verehrer Gottes*, ed. G. Alexander (2 vols., Frankfurt, 1972).

—— *Allgemeine Betrachtungen über die Triebe der Thiere* (Göttingen, 1982).

—— *Die vornehmsten Wahrheiten der natürlichen Religion* (2 vols., Göttingen, 1985).

—— *Kleine gelehrte Schriften*, ed. W. Schmidt-Biggemann (Göttingen, 1994).

—— *Abhandlungen von den vornehmsten Wahrheiten der natürlichen Religion* (5th edn., Hamburg, 1781).

Reimarus, Johann Albrecht Heinrich, 'Vorerrinerung von dem Daseyn Gottes und der menschlichen Seele', preface to Hermann Samuel Reimarus, *Abhandlungen von den vornehmsten Wahrheiten* (5th edn., Hamburg, 1781), 1–46.

Reinhold, Karl Leonhard, *Letters on the Kantian Philosophy*, ed. Karl Ameriks (Cambridge, 2005).

Réplique au Second Discours d'un soi-disant Bon-Hollandais à ses compatriotes par l'auteur de la Réponse au Premier Discours (Leiden, 1779). (Kn. 19248)

*Réponse à la Censure de la Faculté de Théologie de Paris contre l'*Histoire philosophique... des deux Indes ('Londres' [Paris?], 1782). (PBN)

REYNAUD, ABBÉ MARC-ANTOINE, *Le Délire de la nouvelle philosophie ou errata du livre intitulé* La Philosophie de la nature (Paris, 1775).

RICHARD, CH. LOUIS, *La Défense de la religion, de la morale... et de la société* (Paris, 1775). (HKB)

RIEM, ANDREAS, 'On Enlightenment', in James Schmidt (ed.), *What is Enlightenment?* (Berkeley and Los Angeles, 1996), 168–87.

ROBERTSON, WILLIAM, *The History of America* (4th edn., London, 1783).

ROCHE, JUAN LUIS, *Relación y observaciones phýsicas-mathemáticas, y morales sobre el general terremoto... de este año de 1755* (Puerto de Santa Maria, 1756).

ROEDERER, PIERRE LOUIS, *The Spirit of the Revolution of 1789*, ed. M. Forsyth (Aldershot, 1989).

—— *De la philosophie moderne, et de la part qu'elle a eue à la Révolution française* (Paris, 1799).

ROUBAUD, P. J. A., *Le Politique indien, ou Considérations sur les colonies des Indes Orientales* (Amsterdam, 1768). (BL)

ROUSSEAU, JEAN-JACQUES, *Discours sur les sciences et les arts*, ed. J. Roger (1971; repr. Paris, 1992).

—— *The Social Contract and Discourses*, ed. G. D. H. Cole, J. H. Brumfitt, J. C. Hall, and P. D. Jimack (repr. London, 1993).

—— *A Discourse on the Origin of Inequality*, in Rousseau, *The Social Contract and Discourses*, ed. Cole et al., 31–126.

—— 'Lettre à Voltaire', 18 Aug. 1756, in Rousseau, *Œuvres complètes* (25 vols., Paris, 1826), xx. 307–33.

—— *Lettre à M. d'Alembert sur son article 'Genève'* (1758), ed. M. Launay (Paris, 1967).

—— *Émile* (1762), trans. B. Foxley (Everyman edn. repr. London, 1969).

—— *Lettres écrites de la montagne* (2 vols., Amsterdam, 1764).

—— *Rousseau Judge of Jean-Jacques: Dialogues*, in *The Collected Writings of Rousseau*, ed. R. D. Masters and C. Kelly, vol. i (Hanover, NH, 1990).

—— *The Confessions*, trans. and ed. Chrstopher Kelly (Hanover, NH, 1995).

—— *Considerations sur le gouvernement de Pologne*, in Rousseau, *Discours sur l'économie politique*, ed. Barbara de Negroni (Paris, 1990), 161–309.

—— *Projet de constitution pour la Corse*, in Rousseau, *Discours sur l'économie politique*, ed. Barbara de Negroni (Paris, 1990), 101–60.

—— *Les Rêveries du promeneur solitaire* (1782), ed. H. Roddier (Paris, 1960).

—— *Essai sur l'origine des langues*, ed. J. Starobinski (Paris, 1990).

RUSH, BENJAMIN, *The Autobiography of Benjamin Rush*, ed. G.W. Corner (Princeton, 1948).

[——], *An Address to the Inhabitants of the British Settlements on the Slavery of the Negroes in America* (2nd edn., Philadelphia, 1773).

SAAVEDRA Y SANGRONIS, DON FRANCISCO ARIAS DE, *Memorias inéditas de un ministro ilustrado* (Seville, 1992).

SABATIER DE CASTRES, M., *Journal politique national des États-Généraux et de la Révolution de 1789* (Paris, 1789–99).

—— *Apologie de Spinosa et du Spinosisme contre les athées, les incrédules et contre les théologiens scolastiques platoniciens* (2nd edn., Paris, 1810).

SAINT-CYR, ABBÉ GIRY DE, *Catéchisme et décisions de cas de conscience à l'usage des Cacouacs* ('Cacopolis' [Paris], 1758).

SAINT-LAMBERT, JEAN-FRANÇOIS DE, *Contes américains* (Exeter, 1997).

—— *Essai sur la vie et les ouvrages d'Helvétius*, in Helvétius, *Réflexions sur l'homme*, ed. Jean-Pierre Jackson (Paris, 2006), 5–45.

SCHELLING, F. W. J., *System of Transcendental Idealism* (1800; Charlottesville, Va., 1978).

—— *Philosophy and Religion* (1804), trans. K. Ottmann (Putnam, Conn., 2010).

—— *The Ages of the World*, ed. J. M. Wirth (Albany, NY, 2000).

SCHILLER, FRIEDRICH VON, *Philosophische Briefe* (1786), ed. A. Holthusen (Hamburg, 1937).

—— *Don Carlos, Infante of Spain*, trans. Ch. Passage (New York, 1959).

—— *History of the Revolt of the Netherlands*, trans. A. J. W. Morrison (New York, 1847).

—— *Universalhistorische Schriften* (1789–92), in Otto Dann (ed.), *Friedrich Schiller, Historische Schriften und Erzählungen*, i (Frankfurt, 2000), 409–510.

—— *On the Aesthetic Education of Man* (1794), trans. R. Snell (Mineola, NY, 2004).

—— *Briefe über Don Carlos*, in Friedrich Schiller, *Don Carlos*, ed. G. Fricke (Munich, 1965), 195–234.

SCHIMMELPENNINCK, R. J., *Verhandeling over eene wel ingerigte volksregeering* (Leiden, 1785).

SEMLER, JOHANN SALOMO, *Beantwortung der Fragmente eines Ungenannten* (Halle, 1779).

—— *Lebensbeschreibung von ihm selbst abgefasst* (2 vols., Halle, 1781–2).

SIEYÈS, ABBÉ EMMANUEL-JOSEPH, *Essai sur les privilèges* (1788; new edn., n.p. [Paris], 1789).

—— *Qu'est-ce que le Tiers Etat?* (1788; 3rd edn., Paris, 1789).

—— *Préliminaire de la Constitution française* (Paris, 1789).

—— *Des manuscrits de Sieyès 1773–1799*, ed. Christine Fauré (Paris, 1999).

SMITH, ADAM, *Essays on Philosophical Subjects*, ed. W. P. D. Wightman and J. C. Bryce (Oxford, 1980).

—— *The Theory of Moral Sentiments* (1759), ed. D. D. Raphael and A. L. Macfie (Oxford, 1976).

—— *An Inquiry into the Nature and Causes of the Wealth of Nations*, ed. J. E. Thorold Rogers (2 vols., 2nd edn., Oxford, 1880).

SONNENFELS, JOSEPH VON, *Der Mann ohne Vorurtheil* (8 vols., Vienna, 1765–73).

—— *Über die Abschaffung der Tortur* (Zurich, 1775).

—— *Politische Abhandlungen* (Vienna, 1777).

SPINOZA, BENEDICT DE, *Opera*, ed. Carl Gebhardt (4 vols., Heidelberg, 1925).

—— *The Letters*, trans. S. Shirley (Indianapolis, 1995).

—— *Korte Geschriften*, ed. F. Akkerman et al. (Amsterdam, 1982).

—— *Briefwisseling*, ed. F. Akkerman et al. (Amsterdam, 1992).

—— *Tractatus Theologico-Politicus* (Gebhardt edn. 1925), trans. S. Shirley (Leiden, 1989).

—— *Tractatus Politicus*, in *Spinoza: The Political Works*, ed. A. G. Wernham (Oxford, 1958).

—— *Collected Works*, ed. E. Curley (1 vol. so far, Princeton, 1985).

—— *The Ethics*, in *Collected Works*, ed. Curley, i. 408–617.

SPIRITI, MARQUESE GIUSEPPE, *Riflessioni economico-politiche d'un cittadino relative alle due provincie di Calabria* (Naples, 1793).

STAËL, ANNE-LOUISE-GERMAINE, MADAME DE, *Letters on the Works of J. J. Rousseau* (London, 1789).

Staël, Anne-Louise-Germaine, Madame de, *Considerations on the Principal Events of the French Revolution*, ed. Aurelian Craiutu (Indianapolis, 2008).

Steinbart, Gotthilf Samuel, *Philosophische Unterhaltungen zur weitere Aufklärung der Glückseligkeitslehre* (1782).

Stenger, Gerhardt (ed.), *L'Affaire des Cacouacs: trois pamphlets contre les philosophes des Lumières* (Saint-Étienne, 2004).

Suplemento al Índice expurgatorio del año de 1790 (Madrid, 1805).

Tetens, Johann Nicolas, *Philosophische Versuche über die menschliche Natur und ihre Entwicklung* (2 vols., Leipzig, 1777).

Thorild, Thomas, *Samlade Skrifter*, ed. S. Arvidson (12 vols., Stockholm-Lund, 1933–97).

—— *Dissertationes*. (GrUB Ab 938 'ex biblioteca academica')

[——], *The Sermon of Sermons on the Impiety of Priests and the Fall of Religion* (London, 1789). (GrUB)

Thunberg, Carl Peter, *Reise durch einen Theil von Europa, Afrika und Asien, hauptsächlich in Japan in den Jahren 1770 bis 1779* (Berlin, 1792).

—— *Travels in Europe, Africa and Asia Made between the Years 1770 and 1779* (4 vols., London, 1795).

—— *Le Japon du XVIIIe siècle*, trans. L. Langlès (Paris, 1966).

Titsingh, Isaac, *The Private Correspondence, 1785–1811*, ed. F. Lequin (2 vols., Leiden, 1990–2).

Tone, Theobald Wolfe, *An Address to the People of Ireland* (Belfast, 1796).

[Tronchin, Jean-Robert], *Lettres écrites de la campagne* (Geneva, 1765).

Turgot, Anne-Robert-Jacques, Baron de l'Aulne, 'Réflexions sur les *Pensées philosophiques* de Diderot' (1746), in *Œuvres*, ed. G. Schelle (5 vols., Paris, 1913), i. 87–97.

—— *Reflections on the Formation and Distribution of Wealth*, trans. K. Jupp (London, 1999).

—— *Recherches sur les causes des progrès et de la décadence des sciences et des arts ou Réflexions sur l'histoire des progrès de l'esprit humain*, in *Œuvres*, ed. G. Schelle (5 vols., Paris, 1913), i. 116–42.

—— *Discours sur les avantages que l'établissement du christianisme a procurés au genre humain* (1750), in *Œuvres*, ed. G. Schelle (5 vols., Paris, 1913), i. 194–214.

—— *Tableau philosophique des progrès successifs de l'esprit humain* (1750), in *Œuvres*, ed. G. Schelle (5 vols., Paris, 1913), i. 214–35.

—— *Plan de deux discours sur l'histoire universelle* (c.1751), in *Œuvres*, ed. G. Schelle (5 vols., Paris, 1913), i. 275–323.

—— *Reflections on the Formation and Distribution of Wealth* (1766; London, 1793).

Turner, Matthew, *Answer to Dr Priestley's Letters to a Philosophical Unbeliever* (London, 1782).

Valentijn, François, *Oud ende Nieuw Oostindien*, IV part ii: *Zaken van den Godsdienst op het Eyland Java* (Amsterdam, 1726).

Vallée, G., *The Spinoza Conversations between Lessing and Jacobi* (Lanham, Md., 1988).

Valsecchi, Antonio, *Ritrati e vite letterarie e paralleli di G. J. Rousseau, del sig. di Voltaire, di Obbes, e di Spinosa, e vita di Pietro Bayle* (Venice, 1816).

Vandeul, Madame de, *Mémoires pour servir à l'histoire de la vie et des ouvrages de Diderot*, in Diderot, *Œuvres complètes*, ed. Assezat, i, pp. xxix–lxviii.

Van Dülmen, R. (ed.), *Dokumente*, in Van Dülmen, *Geheimbund*, 147–422.

Van Imhoff, Gustaf Willem, *Consideratien over den tegenwoordigen staat van de Nederlandsche Oost Indische Maatschappij* (1741), *BTLVNI* 66 (1912), 445–621.

Varela y Ulloa, Pedro de, 'Discurso preliminar' to Nuix, *Reflexiones imparciales.*

Venturi, Franco (ed.), 'Storia e dibattiti in Italia e Europa', documentary appendix to Cesare Beccaria, *Dei delitti e delle pene* (ed.) Franco Venturi (1965; repr. Turin, 1994), 110–660.

Vergani, Paolo, *Traité de la peine de mort* (Paris, 1782).

Vernet, Jacob, *Lettres critiques d'un voyageur anglois sur l'Article 'Genêve' du* Dictionnaire encyclopédique (1761; 3rd edn., Utrecht?, 1766).

Verri, Pietro, *Meditazioni sulla felicità* (1763), ed. G. Francioni (Como, 1996).

—— *Discorsi sull'indole del piacere e del dolore, sulla felicità; e sulla economia politica* (Milan, 1781).

Verzeichnis der hinterlassenen Bücher von Georg Forster welche den 4 September 1797 zu Mainz auf der sogenannten Bursch öffentlich versteigert werden sollen (Mainz, 1797).

Volney, Constantin François, *Voyage en Syrie et en Égypte* (2 vols., Paris, 1787).

—— *Extrait d'un ouvrage imprimé à Rennes intitulé* La Sentinelle du peuple (Paris, 1789).

—— *Discours prononcé dans la Chambre du Tiers-État* (8 May 1789) (Paris, 1789).

—— *Œuvres* (2 vols., Paris, 1989).

Voltaire, François-Marie Arouet de, *Œuvres complètes de Voltaire*, ed. Louis Moland (46 vols., Paris, 1877–85).

—— *Correspondence and Related Documents*, ed. Th. Besterman (51 vols., Toronto, 1968–77).

—— [Abbé Bazin], *La Philosophie de l'histoire* (n.p., 1765).

—— *Dieu: réponse de Mr de Voltaire au* Système de la nature (Château de Ferney, 1770).

—— *Questions sur l'Encyclopédie par des amateurs* (9 vols., n.p., 1770).

—— *The Complete Works of Voltaire* (The Voltaire Foundation), vol. xv (Oxford, 1992).

—— *Il faut prendre un parti ou le principe d'action: diatribe* (1772), in *Œuvres complètes de Voltaire*, new edn. xxviii (mélanges no. vii) (Paris, 1879), 517–54.

—— *Essai historique et critique sur les dissensions des Églises de Pologne* ('Basle' [Geneva?], 1767).

—— *Essai sur les mœurs et l'esprit des nations*, ed. R. Pomeau (2 vols., Paris, 1963).

—— *Extrait des sentiments de Jean Meslier*, in *Œuvres complètes*, xliii. 254–327.

—— *Traité sur la tolérance*, ed. R. Pomeau (Paris, 1989).

—— *Dictionnaire philosophique*, ed. Chr. Mervaud (2 vols., Oxford, 1994).

—— *Homélies prononcées à Londres en 1765 dans une assemblée particulière*, in *Œuvres complètes*, xliii. 331–417.

—— *Le Philosophe ignorant* (1766), ed. J. L. Carr (London, 1965).

—— *Lettres à son altesse M. le Prince de Brunsvick* (1767), in *Œuvres complètes*, xliv.

—— *De la paix perpétuelle par le docteur Goodheart* (1769), in *Œuvres complètes*, xxviii. 403–28.

—— *Histoire du parlement de Paris* (1769).

—— *Lettres de Memmius à Ciceron* (1771), in *Œuvres complètes*, xxviii. 437–63.

—— *Notes de M. de Morza sur les systèmes* (1772), in *Œuvres complètes*, xvi. 248–76.

—— *Mémoires pour servir à la vie de M. de Voltaire écrits par lui-même*, vol. ii of Condorcet, *Vie de Voltaire* (London, 1791).

—— *Corpus des notes marginales de Voltaire*, ed. Inna Gorbatov et al. (6 vols. thus far, Petersburg–Berlin–Oxford, 1983–).

—— *Political Writings*, ed. D. Williams (Cambridge, 1994).

[——]'Idées républicaines, par un citoyen de Genève' (1762), in *Œuvres complètes de Voltaire*, ed. Ch. Lahure (Paris, 1860), xviii. 544–56.

—— *Lettre d'un Quakre à Jean-George Le Franc de Pompignon* (n.p. [Geneva?], 1763).

VOLTAIRE, FRANÇOIS-MARIE AROUET DE, 'Tout en Dieu: Commentaire sur Mallebranche', in Voltaire, *L'Évangile du jour contenant*.

—— *Paix perpetuelle... Tout en Dieu...* ('Londres' [Amsterdam], 1769), 54–70.

—— *Fragmens sur l'Inde... et sur plusieurs autres sujets* ('Londres', 1774).

—— 'Poème sur le désastre de Lisbonne en 1755, ou, Examen de cet axiome: tout est bien', in Voltaire, *Œuvres complètes* (1877), viii. 390–401.

—— *Histoire de Jenni*, in Voltaire, *L'Ingénu and Histoire de Jenni*, ed. J. H. Brumfitt and M. I. Gerard Davis (new edn., London, 1992), 59–112.

VREEDE, PIETER, *Waermond en Vryhart: Gesprek over de Vryheid der Nederlandren; en den aert der waere Vryheid* ('Holland', 1783). (Kn. 20400) (HKB)

—— *Beoordeelend en ophelderend verslag van de Verhandeling over de Vryheid* (Arnhem, 1783). (Kn. 2045) (HKB)

[——], *Zakboek van Neerlands Volk, voor Patriotten, Antipatriotten, Aristokraten en Prinsgezinden* (Dordrecht, 1785). (Kn. 21041) (HKB)

Waarschouwing der Reede, tegen het geschrift getytelt Vriend-Broederlyke vermaaning en Raad geeving aan de Hessische en andere Duitsche Hulpbenden (Amsterdam, 1777). (Kn. 19150)

WEISHAUPT, ADAM, *Anrede an die neu aufzunehmenden Illuminatos dirigentes* (1782), in Van Dülmen, *Geheimbund*, 166–94.

—— *Apologie der Illuminaten* (Frankfurt and Leipzig, 1786).

—— *Das Verbesserte System der Illuminaten* (n.p., 1787).

—— *Kurze Rechtfertigung meiner Absichten* (Frankfurt-Leipzig, 1787).

—— *Über die Schrecken des Todes- eine philosophische Rede* (Nuremberg, 1786).

—— *Nachtrag zur Rechtfertigung meiner Absichten* (Frankfurt, 1787).

WEKHRLIN, WILHELM LUDWIG, *Chronologen* (periodical: 12 vols., Frankfurt-Nuremberg, 1779–84).

—— *Das graue Ungeheuer* (periodical: 31 vols., Nuremberg, 1784–7).

—— *Hyperboreische Briefe* (periodical: 6 vols., Nuremberg, 1788–90).

—— *Paragrafen* (periodical: Nuremberg, 1790–2).

[——], 'Anselmus Rabiosus', in *Reise durch Ober-Deutschland* (Salzburg-Leipzig, 1778).

WESLEY, JOHN, *Serious Thoughts Occasioned by the Late Earthquake at Lisbon* (6th edn., London, 1756).

WIELAND, CHRISTOPH MARTIN (ed.), *Der Teutsche Merkur* (journal: 1773–90).

WITHERSPOON, JOHN, *Lectures on Moral Philosophy*, ed. V. L. Collins (Princeton, 1912).

WIZENMANN, Th., 'An den Herrn Professor Kant von dem Verfasser der *Resultate*' (1787), in Tavoillot, *Le Crépuscule des Lumières* (French trans.), 282–307.

—— *Thomas Wizenmann, der Freund Friedrich Heinrich Jacobi's in Mittheilungen aus seiner Briewechsel und handschriftlichen Nachlasse*, ed. A. von der Goltz (2 vols., Gotha, 1859).

—— *Die Resultate der Jacobischen und Mendelsohnschen Philosophie; kritisch untersucht* (Leipzig, 1786).

WOLFF, CHRISTIAN, *De Differentia Nexus Rerum Sapientis et Fatalis Necessitas* (Halle, 1724).

—— *Natürliche Gottesgelahrheit nach beweisender Lehrart* (6 vols., Halle, 1742).

—— *Der vernünffigen Gedancken von Gott, der Welt und der Seele des Menschen, auch allen Dingen überhaupt* (1724; new edn., Frankfurt, 1733).

WOLLSTONECRAFT, MARY, *A Vindication of the Rights of Woman* (1792), in M. Wollstonecraft, *Political Writings*, ed. J. Todd (London, 1993).

—— *A Vindication of the Rights of Men*, in Mary Wollstonecraft, *Political Writings*, ed. J. Todd (London, 1993), 1–65.

ZABUESNIG, JOHANN CHRISTOPH VON, *Historische und kritische Nachrichten von dem Leben und den Schriften des Herrn von Voltaire und anderer Neuphilosophen unserer Zeiten* (Augsburg, 1777).

Secondary

ABBATTISTA, G., 'Empire, Liberty and the Rule of Difference: European Debates on British Colonialism' (18th century), *European Review of History*, 13 (2006), 473–98.

ADAMS, L., *Coyer and the Enlightenment*, SVEC 122 (Paris, 1974).

ADDY, G. M., *The Enlightenment in the University of Salamanca* (Durham, NC, 1966).

ADELMAN, J., 'The Rites of Statehood', *HAHR* 90 (2010), 391–422.

—— *Sovereignty and Revolution in the Iberian Atlantic* (Princeton, 2006).

AGUILAR PIÑAL, FRANCISCO, *La Sevilla de Olavide* (Seville, 1995).

AHMED, SIRAJ, 'The Theater of the Civilized Self: Edmund Burke and the East India Trials', repr. in I. Hampsher-Monk, *Edmund Burke* (Farnham, 2009), 137–64.

—— 'Orientalism and the Permanent Fix of War', in D. Carey and L. Festa (eds.), *Postcolonial Enlightenment* (Oxford, 2009), 167–203.

AHNERT, TH., 'Newtonianism in Early Enlightenment Germany, c.1720 to 1750', *SHPhSc* 35 (2004), 471–91.

—— 'The Soul, Natural Religion and Moral Philosophy in the Scottish Enlightenment', *Eighteenth-Century Thought*, 2 (2004), 233–53.

ALBERTAN-COPPOLA, S., *L'Abbé Nicolas-Sylvestre Bergier (1718–1790)* (Paris, 2010).

ALBERTONE, M. (ed.), *Il repubblicanesimo moderno* (Naples, 2006).

—— 'Thomas Jefferson and French Economic Thought', in Albertone and de Francesco (eds.), *Rethinking*, 123–46.

—— and de Francesco, A. (eds.), *Rethinking the Atlantic World: Europe and America in the Age of Democratic Revolutions* (Basingstoke, 2009).

ALBRECHT, W., *Gotthold Ephraim Lessing* (Stuttgart, 1997).

ALEXANDER, GERHARD, 'Einleitung' to Hermann Samuel Reimarus, *Apologie oder Schutzschrift für die vernünftigen Verehrer Gottes*, ed. G. Alexander (2 vols., Frankfurt, 1972).

ALLEN, R. C., 'David Hartley's New Words for Action: "Automatic" and "Decomplex"', *Enlightenment and Dissent*, 20 (2001), 1–22.

ALT, PETER-ANDRÉ, 'Schiller and Politics', Reeks Burgerhartlezingen Werkgroep 18e eeuw (Utrecht, 2009).

ALTENA, PETER, 'Een "Oude Hellenbroeksman" en de Radicale Verlichting', *GWN* 5 (1994), 139–67.

—— '"O Ondankbaar vaderland": Gerrit Paape en de "vebeterende" ballingschap', *De Achttiende Eeuw*, 38 (2006), 168–80.

—— 'De autobografie van een delfts patriot: Over *Mijne vrolijke wijsbegeerte in mijne ballingschap* (1792) van Gerrit Paape', in Spektator, *Tijdschrift voor Nederlandistik*, 19 (1990), 11–34.

ALTMAN, ALEXANDER, *Moses Mendelssohn: A Biographical Study* (London, 1973).

ALVARES DE MORALES, A., *La ilustración y la reforma de la universidad en la España del siglo XVIII* (1971; 3rd edn., Madrid, 1985).

AMIDSEN, ASSER, *Til nytte og fornøjelse: Johann Friedrich Struensee (1737–1772)* (Copenhagen, 2002).

AMERIKS, KARL, 'Introduction' to Reinhold, *Letters*, pp. ix–xxxv.

—— *Interpreting Kant's* Critiques (Oxford, 2005).

AMOH, Y., 'Ferguson's Views on the American and French Revolutions', in Heath and Merolle (eds.), *Adam Ferguson*, 73–86.

AMUNÁTEGUI, MIGUEL LUIS, *Los precursores de la independencia de Chile* (3 vols., Santiago, 1909).

ANDERSON, M. S., 'The Italian Reformers', in Scott (ed.), *Enlightened Absolutism*, 55–74.

ANDRÈS, B., *La Conquête des lettres au Québec (1759–99)* (Montreal, 2007).

ANDRIES, L., 'Les Imprimeurs-libraires parisiens et la liberté de la presse (1789–95)', *DHS* 21 (1989), 247–61.

ANES, GONZALO, *El siglo de las Luces* (Madrid, 2001).

ANSART, G., 'From Voltaire to Raynal and Diderot's *Histoire des deux Indes*', in A. Craiutu and J. C. Isaacs (eds.), *America through European Eyes* (University Park, Pa., 2009), 71–89.

APP, URS, 'William Jones's Ancient Theology', *Sino-Platonic Papers*, 191 (July 2009).

—— *The Birth of Orientalism* (Philadelphia, 2010).

ARASARATNAM, S., 'Monopoly and Free Trade in Dutch-Asian Commercial Policy', *Journal of Southeast Asian Studies*, 4 (1973), 1–15.

—— 'The Dutch East India Company and its Coromandel Trade, 1700–1740', *BTLVNI* 123 (1967), 325–46.

ARATO, FRANCO, 'Savants, philosophes, journalistes: l'Italie des dictionnaires encyclopédiques', *DHS* 38 (2006), 69–82.

ARAUJO COSTA, LUIS, 'Las influencias de Huet sobre Forner', *Revista de literatura*, 8 (1953), 307–18.

ARBOLEDA, LUIS CARLOS, and SOTO ARANGO, D., 'Introducción de una cultura newtoniana en las universidades del virreinato de la Nueva Granada', in C. A. Lertora Mendoza (ed.), *Newton en America* (Buenos Aires, 1995), 29–66.

ARENDT, HANNAH, *On Revolution* (New York, 1963).

ARKUSH, A., *Moses Mendelssohn and the Enlightenment* (Albany, NY, 1994).

ARMITAGE, DAVID, *The Ideological Origins of the British Empire* (Cambridge, 2000).

—— and Subrahmanyam, S. (eds.), *The Age of Revolutions in Global Context* (Basingstoke, 2010).

ARNAUD, CLAUDE, *Chamfort: A Biography* (Chicago, 1992).

ARNOLD, D., 'Hunger in the Garden of Plenty: The Bengal Famine of 1770', in Johns (ed.), *Dreadful Visitations*, 81–111.

ARTIGAS-MENANT, G., *Du secret des clandestins à la propagande voltairienne* (Paris, 2001).

ASSMANN, JAN, *Moses the Egyptian* (Cambridge, Mass., 1997).

ASTIGARRAGA GOENAGA, JESÚS, 'Political Economy and Legislation: The Great Success of Filangieri's *Scienza della legislazione* in Spain (1780–1839)', *Nuevo Mundo mundos nuevos, coloquios 2006* (on-line publication posted 18 Mar. 2006).

—— 'I traduttori spagnoli di Filangieri e il risveglio del dibattito costituzionale (1780–1839)', in A. Trampus (ed.), *Diritti e costituzione* (Bologna, 2005), 231–90.

ASTON, NIGEL, *Religion and Revolution in France, 1780–1804* (Washington, DC, 2000).

BACZKO, BRONISLAW, 'The Terror before the Terror? Conditions of Possibility, Logic of Realization', in K. M. Baker (ed.), *The Terror*, vol. iv of *The French Revolution and the Creation of Modern Political Culture* (Oxford, 1994), 19–38.

BADINTER, E., and BADINTER, R., *Condorcet: un intellectuel en politique* (Paris, 1988).

BAILYN, BERNARD, *The Ideological Origins of the American Revolution* (Cambridge, Mass., 1992).

BAKER, K. M., *Condorcet: From Natural Philosophy to Social Mathematics* (Chicago, 1975).

—— 'Representation', in Baker (ed.), *Political Culture*, i. 469–92.

—— 'Revolution', in Lucas (ed.), *Political Culture*, 41–62.

—— *Inventing the French Revolution* (Cambridge, 1990).

—— 'Reason and Revolution: Political Consciousness and Ideological Invention at the End of the Old Regime', in R. Bienvenu and M. Feingold (eds.), *In the Presence of the Past: Essays in Honor of Frank Manuel* (Amsterdam, 1991), 79–91.

—— (ed.), *The Political Culture of the Old Regime*, vol. i of *The French Revolution and the Creation of Modern Political Culture* (4 vols., Oxford, 1987).

—— and REILL, P. H. (eds.), *What's Left of Enlightenment?* (Stanford, Calif., 2001).

BALÀSZ, PETER, 'Le Matérialisme athée d'un "Jacobin" hongrois', *La Lettre clandestine*, 17 (2009), 326–47.

BALCOU, JEAN, *Fréron contre les philosophes* (Geneva, 1975).

BALDI, MARIALUISA, *David Hume nel settecento italiano* (Florence, 1983).

BALLSTADT, KURT, *Diderot: Natural Philosopher* (Oxford, 2008).

BALSAMO, LUIGI, 'Gli ebrei nell'editoria nel commercio librario in Italia nel '600 e '700, in *Italia Judaica: Atti del III Convegno internazionale Tel Aviv 15–20 giugno 1986* (Rome, 1989), 49–80.

BANCAREL, G., 'Éléments de la stratégie éditoriale de Raynal', in Bancarel and Goggi (eds.), *Raynal*, 121–41.

—— and GOGGI, G. (eds.), *Raynal de la polémique à l'histoire* (Oxford, 2000).

BARBER, W. H., 'Le Newton de Voltaire', in de Gandt (ed.), *Cirey*, 115–25.

BARIDON, M., 'Les Concepts de nature humaine et de perfectibilité dans l'historiographie des Lumières de Fontenelle à Condorcet', *L'Histoire au dix-huitième siècle: Centre Aixois d'Études et de Recherches sur le XVIIIème Siècle* (Aix-en-Provence, 1980), 353–74.

BARNARD, F. M., *Herder on Nationality, Humanity and History* (Montreal, 2003).

—— *Herder's Social and Political Thought* (Oxford, 1965).

BARNY, R., 'Montesquieu patriote?', *DHS* 21 (1989), 83–96.

—— 'Jean-Jacques Rousseau dans la Révolution', *Dix-Huitième Siècle*, 6 (1974), 59–98.

BARRIÈRE, PIERRE, *La Vie intellectuelle en Périgord (1550–1800)* (Bordeaux, 1936).

BARRIO GOZALO, MAXIMILIANO, 'Iglesia y religiosidad', in Luigi di Rosa et al. (eds.), *Spagna e Mezzogiorno d'Italia nell'età della transizione* (2 vols., Naples, 1997), ii. 241–79.

BARTLETT, R. C., *The Idea of Enlightenment: A Post-mortem Study* (Toronto, 2001).

BARTON, H. A., *Northern Arcadia: Foreign Travellers in Scandinavia, 1765–1815* (Carbondale, Ill., 1998).

BASSNETT, S., 'Faith, Doubt, Aid and Prayer: The Lisbon Earthquake of 1755 Revisited', *European Review*, 14 (2006), 321–8.

BATALDEN, S. K., *Catherine II's Greek Prelate: Eugenios Voulgaris in Russia, 1771–1806* (New York, 1982).

BAYER, OSWALD, 'Spinoza im Gespräch zwischen Hamann und Jacobi', in E. Schürmann (ed.), *Spinoza im Deutschland des achtzehnten Jahrhunderts* (Stuttgart, 2002), 319–25.

BEALES, DEREK, 'Was Joseph II an Enlightened Despot?', in R. Robinson and E. Timms (eds.), *The Austrian Enlightenment* (Edinburgh, 1991), 1–21.

BEALES, DEREK, 'Social Forces and Enlightened Policies', in H. Scott (ed.), *Enlightened Absolutism* (Basingstoke, 1990), 37–53.

—— *Enlightenment and Reform in Eighteenth-Century Europe* (London, 2005).

—— *Joseph II: In the Shadow of Maria Theresa 1741–1780* (Cambridge, 1987).

—— *Joseph II: Against the World 1780–1790* (Cambridge, 2009).

—— *Prosperity and Plunder: European Catholic Monasteries in the Age of Revolution (1650–1815)* (Cambridge, 2003).

—— 'Philosophic Kingship and Enlightened Despotism', in *CHEPTh* 497–524.

BECK, L. W., 'From Leibniz to Kant', in R. C. Solomon and K. M. Higgins (eds.), *The Age of German Idealism* (London, 1993), 5–39.

BEERMANN, M., *Zeitung zwischen Profit und Politik: Der* Courrier du Bas-Rhin *(1767–1810)* (Leipzig, 1996).

BEESON, D., *Maupertuis: An Intellectual Biography* (Oxford, 1992).

BEISER, F. C., *The Sovereignty of Reason* (Princeton, 1996).

—— *Schiller as Philosopher: A Re-examination* (Oxford, 2005).

—— *Enlightenment, Revolution and Romanticism: The Genesis of Modern German Political Thought (1790–1800)* (Cambridge, Mass., 1992).

—— *German Idealism: The Struggle against Subjectivism, 1781–1801* (Cambridge, Mass., 2002).

—— 'The Enlightenment and Idealism', in Karl Ameriks (ed.), *The Cambridge Companion to German Idealism* (Cambridge, 2000), 18–36.

BELAVAL, YVON, *Études sur Diderot* (Paris, 2003).

BELIN, J. P., *Le Commerce des livres prohibés à Paris de 1750 à 1789* (Paris, 1913).

BELL, D. A., *The Cult of the Nation in France: Inventing Nationalism, 1680–1800* (Cambridge. Mass., 2001).

BELL, DAVID, *Spinoza in Germany from 1670 to the Age of Goethe* (London, 1984).

BELLAMY, R., 'Introduction', to Beccaria, *On Crimes and Punishments*, ed. Bellamy.

BENETRUY, J., *L'Atelier de Mirabeau* (Paris, 1962).

BENHAMOU, P., 'La Diffusion de *L'Histoire des deux Indes* en Amérique (1770–1820)', in Bancarel and Goggi (eds.), *Raynal*, 301–12.

BENÍTEZ, MIGUEL, *La Face cachée des Lumières* (Paris, 1996).

BÉNOT, YVES, *Diderot: de l'athéisme à l'anticolonialisme* (Paris, 1970; 1981).

—— 'Diderot, Raynal et le mot "colonie"', in France and Strugnell (eds.), *Diderot*, 140–52.

—— 'Y a-t-il une morale matérialiste?', in Fink and Stenger (eds.), *Être matérialiste*, 81–91.

BENREKASSA, G., 'Mœurs', in *HPSGF* 15/18: 159–205.

BERGHAHN, K. L., 'Lessing the Critic: Polemics as Enlightenment', in Fischer and Fox (eds.), *A Companion*, 67–87.

BERMAN, R. A., *Enlightenment or Empire: Colonial Discourse in German Culture* (Lincoln, Nebr., 1998).

BERNARD, P. P., *The Limits of Enlightenment: Joseph II and the Law* (Urbana, Ill., 1979).

BERNASCONI, R., 'Kant as an Unfamiliar Source of Racism', in J. K. Ward and T. L. Lott (eds.), *Philosophers on Race* (Oxford, 2002), 145–66.

—— 'Who Invented the Concept of Race? Kant's Role in the Enlightenment Construction of Race', in R. Bernasconi (ed.), *Race* (Oxford, 2001), 11–36.

BERRY, C. J., *Social Theory of the Scottish Enlightenment* (Edinburgh, 1997).

—— 'Lusty Women and Loose Imagination', *HPTh* 24 (2003), 415–33.

Berselli Ambri, Paola, *L'opera di Montesquieu nel settecento italiano* (Florence, 1960).

Bertelli, Sergio, *Erudizione e storia in Lodovico Antonio Muratori* (Naples, 1960).

Berti, Francesco, 'Modello britannico, modello americano e antidispotismo', in A. Trampus (ed.), *Diritti e constituzione: l'opera di Gaetano Filangieri e la sua fortuna europea* (Bologna, 2005), 19–60.

Berti, Silvia, 'Repubblicanesimo e illuminismo radicale nella storiografia di Franco Venturi', in M. Albertone (ed.), *Il repubblicanesimo moderno* (Naples, 2006), 157–86.

Besse, Guy, 'Observations sur la réfutation d'Helvétius par Diderot', *Diderot Studies*, 6 (1964), 29–45.

Bianchi, Serge, *Des révoltes aux révolutions: Europe, Russie, Amérique (1770–1802)* (Rennes, 2004).

Bingham, A. J., 'The Abbé Bergier: An Eighteenth-Century Catholic Apologist', *Modern Language Review*, 54 (1959), 337–50.

Birn, R., 'The French-Language Press and the *Encyclopédie*, 1750–1759', *SVEC* 55 (1967), 263–86.

Blamires, Cyprian, 'Beccaria et l'Angleterre', in Porret (ed.), *Beccaria*, 69–81.

—— *The French Revolution and the Creation of Benthamism* (Basingstoke, 2008).

Blanning, T. C. W., *The Culture of Power and the Power of Culture: Old Regime Europe* (Oxford, 2002).

—— *The French Revolution in Germany* (Oxford, 1983).

—— *Reform and Revolution in Mainz, 1743–1803* (Cambridge, 1974).

—— 'Frederick the Great and Enlightened Absolutism', in Scott (ed.), *Enlightened Absolutism*, 265–88.

Bloch, O., 'L'Héritage libertin dans le matérialisme des Lumières', *DHS* 24 (1992), 73–82.

Blom, Philipp, Encyclopédie: *The Triumph of Reason in an Unreasonable Age* (London, 2004).

—— *Enlightening the World: Encyclopédie, the Book That Changed the Course of History* (New York, 2005).

—— *A Wicked Company: The Forgotten Radicalism of the European Enlightenment* (New York, 2010).

Blussé, Leonard, *Strange Company: Chinese Settlers, Mestizo Women and the Dutch in VOC Batavia* (Dordrecht, 1986).

Boehart, W., 'Hermann Samuel Reimarus in der "Gelehrten Republik" des 18. Jahrhunderts: Fragen nach den Grenzen einer "bürgerlichen" Aufklärung', in D. Fratzke and W. Albrecht (eds.), *Lessing zur Jahrtausendwende: Rückblicke und Ausblicke*, 40. Kamenzer Lessing-Tage (Kamenz, 2001), 127–40.

Boes, Maria, '"Dishonourable" Youth, Guilds and the Changed World View of Sex, Illegitimacy and Women in Late-Sixteenth-Century Germany', *Continuity and Change*, 18 (2003), 345–72.

—— 'Women and the Penal System in Frankfurt am Main, 1562–1696', *Criminal Justice History*, 13 (1992), 61–73.

Böhm, G., *Ludwig Wekhrlin (1739–1792): Ein Publizistenleben des achtzehnten Jahrhunderts* (Munich, 1893).

Bohnen, Klaus, 'Lessing und Dänemark', in W. Barner and M. Reh (eds.), *Nation und Gelehrtenrepublik: Lessing im europäischen Zusammenhang* (Sonderband, Lessing Yearbook) (Munich, 1984), 305–14.

Bohnert, Christiane, 'Enlightenment and Despotism: Two Worlds in Lessing's *Nathan the Wise*', in Wilson and Holub (eds.), *Impure Reason*, 344–63.

BONGIE, L. L., *David Hume: Prophet of the Counter-Revolution* (1965; 2nd edn., Indianapolis, 2000).

BONNEROT, OLIVIER-HENRI, 'Louis-Sebastien Mercier: lecteur et éditeur de Jean-Jacques Rousseau', in R. Thiéry (ed.), *Rousseau, l'Émile et la Révolution* (Paris, 1992), 415–23.

BONWICK, COLIN, *The American Revolution* (Basingstoke, 1991).

BORCHMEYER, DIETER, 'Kritik der Aufklärung im Geiste der Aufklärung: Friedrich Schiller', in Jochen Schmidt (ed.), *Aufklärung und Gegenaufklärung in der europäischen Literatur: Philosophie und Politik von der Antike bis zur Gegenwart* (Darmstadt, 1989), 361–76.

BORDOLI, ROBERTO, *L'Illuminismo di Dio: alle origini della mentalità liberale* (Florence, 2004).

—— 'A proposito di Spinoza, d'Illuminismo e d'origini della modernità', *GCFI* 88 (2009), 631–42.

BORGHERO, CARLO, 'Sparta tra storia e utopia: Il significativo e la funzione del mito di Sparta nel pensiero di Jean-Jacques Rousseau', in G. Solinas (ed.), *Saggi sull'Illuminismo* (Cagliari, 1973), 254–318.

BORRELLI, GIAN FRANCO, 'Hobbes e la teoria moderna della democrazia', *Trimestre*, 24 (1991), 243–63.

BOULAD-AYOUB, J., 'Voltaire et Frédéric II, critiques du *Système de la nature*', in Boulad-Ayoub (ed.), *Paul Henri Thiry, Baron d'Holbach*, 39–66.

—— (ed.), *Paul Henri Thiry, Baron d'Holbach: Épistémologie et politique au XVIIIe siècle, Corpus*, 22/23 (Paris, 1992).

—— 'Introduction: d'Holbach, le maître d'hôtel de la philosophie', special d'Holbach issue *Corpus*, 22/23 (1992), 7–11.

BOURDIN, JEAN-CLAUDE, *Diderot: le matérialisme* (Paris, 1998).

BOUREL, D., *Moses Mendelssohn: la naisssance du judaïsme moderne* (Paris, 2004).

BOYLE, NICHOLAS, *Goethe: The Poet and the Age*, i: *The Poetry of Desire (1749–1790)* (Oxford, 1991).

BRADLEY, J. E., and VAN KLEY, D. (eds.), *Religion and Politics in Enlightenment Europe* (Notre Dame, Ind., 2001).

BRAIDA, L., 'Censure et circulation du livre en Italie au XVIIIe siècle', *JMEH* 3 (2005), 81–99.

BRAMANI, L., *Mozart massone e revoluzionario* (Milan, 2005).

BRANDT, G. W., *German and Dutch Theatre, 1600–1848* (Cambridge, 1993).

BRAUN, TH. E. D., 'Diderot, the Ghost of Bayle', *Diderot Studies*, 27 (1998), 45–55.

—— 'Voltaire et Le Franc de Pompignan: Poetic Reactions to the Lisbon Earthquake', in Braun and RADNER (eds.), *The Lisbon Earthquake*, 145–55.

—— and Radner, J. B. (eds.), *The Lisbon Earthquake of 1755: Representations and Reactions, SVEC* 2005: 2 (Oxford, 2005).

BREAZALE, D., 'Introduction' to J. G. Fichte, *Early Philosophical Writings* (Ithaca, NY, 1988), 1–49.

BREÑA, ROBERTO, *El primer liberalismo español y los procesos de emancipación de América, 1808–1824* (Mexico City, 2006).

BROADIE, ALEXANDER, *The Scottish Enlightenment* (Edinburgh, 2001).

—— (ed.), *The Cambridge Companion to the Scottish Enlightenment* (Cambridge, 2003).

BROOKE, CHRISTOPHER, 'Locke en particulier...: Revisiting the Relationship between Locke and Rousseau', in C. Miqueu and M. Chamie (eds.), *Locke's Political Liberty* (Oxford, 2009), 69–82.

BROOKS HOLIFIELD, E., *Theology in America: Christian Thought from the Age of the Puritans to the Civil War* (New Haven, 2003).

BROT, M., 'La Collaboration de Saint-Lambert à *l'Histoire des deux Indes*', in Bancarel and Goggi (eds.), *Raynal*, 99–108.

BROWN, ROBERT, 'Social Sciences', *CHEPh* 2: 1069–105.

BROWNING, J. D., 'Cornelis de Pauw and Exiled Jesuits', *Eighteenth-Century Studies*, 11 (1978), 289–307.

BRUIJN, J. R., and LUCASSEN, J. (eds.), *Op de schepen der Oost-Indische Compagnie* (Groningen, 1980).

BRUMFIELD, W. C., *A History of Russian Architecture* (Cambridge, 1993).

BRUNHOUSE, R. L., *The Counter-Revolution in Pennsylvania, 1776–1790* (Harrisburg, Pa., 1942).

BUCHAN, JAMES, *Adam Smith and the Pursuit of Perfect Liberty* (London, 2006).

BUCKLE, STEPHEN, *Hume's Enlightenment Tract* (Oxford, 2001).

BUCKLEY, M. J., *At the Origins of Modern Atheism* (New Haven, 1987).

BUCK-MORSS, S., *Hegel and Haiti* (Pittsburgh, 2009).

BUIJS, PETER, *De eeuw van het geluk* (Hilversum, 2007).

BUJANDO, J. M. DE, *Index Librorum Prohibitorum, 1600–1966* (Montreal, 2002).

BUNGE, WIEP VAN, 'Rationaliteit en Verlichting', *De Achttiende Eeuw*, 32 (2000), 145–64.

—— KROP, HENRI ET AL. (eds.), *The Dictionary of Seventeenth and Eighteenth-Century Dutch Philosophers* (2 vols., Bristol, 2003).

BURGESS, G., and FESTENSTEIN, M. (eds.), *English Radicalism 1550–1850* (Cambridge, 2007).

BURSON, J. D., 'The Crystallization of Counter-Enlightenment and Philosophe Identities', *Church History*, 77 (2008), 955–1002.

—— *The Rise and Fall of Theological Enlightenment* (Notre Dame, Ind., 2010).

BURUMA, IAN, *Taming the Gods: Religion and Democracy on Three Continents* (Princeton, 2010).

BUSNELLI, MANLIO, *Diderot et l'Italie* (1925; repr. Geneva, 1970).

BUTTERWICK, R., 'Provincial Preachers in Late Eighteenth-Century Poland-Lithuania', in Butterwick et al. (eds.), *Peripheries*, 201–29.

—— DAVIES, S., and Sánchez Espinosa, G. (eds.), *Peripheries of the Enlightenment* (Oxford, 2008).

BUZAGLO, M., *Solomon Maimon: Monism, Skepticism, and Mathematics* (Pittsburgh, 2002).

CAFFIERO, M., 'Gli Ebrei avvelenatori dei cristiani: una polemica nella Roma del Settecento', in D. Balani et al. (eds.), *Dall'origne dei Lumi alla Rivoluzione: scritti in onore di Luciano Guerci e Giusepe Ricuperati* (Rome, 2008), 105–23.

CAMPBELL, P. R., 'The Origins of the French Revolution in Focus', in Campbell (ed.), *Origins*, 1–34.

—— (ed.), *The Origins of the French Revolution* (Basingstoke, 2006).

CAÑIZARES-ESGUERRA, JORGE, *How to Write the History of the New World: Histories, Epistemologies and Identities in the Eighteenth-Century Atlantic World* (Stanford, Calif., 2001).

—— *Nature, Empire and Nation: Explorations of the History of Science in the Iberian World* (Stanford, Calif., 2006).

CANNON, G., *The Life and Mind of Oriental Jones* (Cambridge, 1990).

CANOVAN, M., 'Paternalistic Liberalism: Joseph Priestley on Rank and Inequality', *Enlightenment and Dissent*, 2 (1983), 23–37.

CANZIANI, GUIDO (ed.), *Filosofia e religione nella letteratura clandestina: secoli XVII e XVIII* (Milan, 1994).

CAPRA, CARLO, *I progressi della ragione: vita di Pietro Verri* (Bologna, 2002).

—— 'Alle origini del moderatismo e del Giacobinismo in Lombardia: Pietro Verri e Pietro Custodi', *Studi historici*, 30 (1989), 873–90.

—— 'Habsburg Italy in the Age of Reform', *Journal of Modern Italian Studies*, 10 (2005), 218–33.

—— '"L'opinione regina del mondo": Percorsi dell'evoluzione politica e intellectuale di Pietro Verri', in Santato (ed.), *Letteratura italiana*, 111–31.

CARBONERO Y SOL, LEÓN, *Índice de los libros prohibidos por el Santo Oficio de la Inquisición Española* (Madrid, 1873).

CARDENAS ACOSTA, PABLO, *El movimiento comunal de 1781 en el Nuevo Reino de Granada* (1960; 2nd edn., 2 vols., Bogotá, 1980).

CAREY, D., and FESTA, L. (eds.), *Postcolonial Enlightenment: Eighteenth-Century Colonialism and Postcolonial Theory* (Oxford, 2009).

CARHART, M., *The Science of Culture in Enlightenment Germany* (Cambridge, Mass., 2007).

—— and ROBERTSON, JOHN, 'The Enlightenments of J. G. A. Pocock', *Storia della storiografia*, 39 (2001), 123–51.

CARPANETTO, DINO, and RICUPERATI, GIUSEPPE, *Italy in the Age of Reason, 1685–1789* (London, 1987).

—— —— 'Voltaire, la lumière et la théorie de la connaissance', in Kölving and Mervaud (eds.), *Voltaire et ses combats*, i. 39–45.

CARRIÓN CARAVEDO, U., 'La soberanía en Baquíjano y Carrillo', in A. Castro (ed.), *Filosofía y sociedad en el Perú* (Lima, 2003), 63–74.

CARSON, P., 'The British Raj and the Awakening of the Evangelical Conscience', in B. Stanley (ed.), *Christian Missions and the Enlightenment* (Grand Rapids, Mich., 2001), 45–70.

CASALINI, B., 'L'Esprit di Montesquieu negli Stati Uniti durante la seconda metà del XVIII secolo', in D. Felice (ed.), *Montesquieu e i suoi interpreti* (2 vols., Pisa, 2005), i. 325–55.

CASSIRER, ERNST, *The Philosophy of the Enlightenment* (1932; Princeton, 1979).

CASTRO, AUGUSTO, *La filosofía entre nosotros: cinco siglos de filosofía en el Perú* (Lima, 2009).

CELARESU, M., 'Searching for a "Middle Class"? Francesco Mario Pagano and the Public for Reform in Late Eighteenth-Century Naples', in Paquette (ed.), *Enlightened Reform*, 63–82.

CENSER, J. R., *Prelude to Power: The Parisian Radical Press, 1789–1791* (Baltimore, 1976).

CHAKRABARTY, DIPESH, *Provincializing Europe* (2000; Princeton, new edn., 2008).

CHADWICK, OWEN, *The Popes and the European Revolution* (Oxford, 1981).

CHAPPUIS, PIERRE, 'Joseph Gorani et la Suisse', *Schweizerische Zeitschrift für Geschichte*, 2 (1952), 363–85.

CHARBONNEL, P. 'Le Réquisitoire de Séguier', in Boulad-Ayoub (ed.), *Paul Henri Thiry, Baron d'Holbach*, 15–37.

CHARLIER, G., 'Diderot et la Hollande', *Revue de littérature comparée*, 22 (1947), 190–229.

—— and Mortier, R., *Le Journal encyclopédique (1756–1793)* (Paris, 1952).

CHARRAK, ANDRÉ, *Empiricisme et métaphysique: L'Essai sur l'origine des connaissances humaines de Condillac* (Paris, 2003).

CHARTIER, ROGER, *Les Origines culturelles de la Révolution française* (Paris, 1990).

CHAUDHURI, K. N., and ISRAEL, J. I., 'The English and Dutch East India Companies and the Glorious Revolution of 1688–9', in J. I. Israel (ed.), *The Anglo-Dutch Moment* (Cambridge, 1991), 407–38.

CHAUDHURY, SUSHIL, *From Prosperity to Decline: Eighteenth-Century Bengal* (Delhi, 1995).

—— 'The Asian Merchants and Companies in Bengal's Export Trade', in S. Chaudhury and M. Morineau (eds.), *Merchants, Companies and Trade* (Cambridge, 1999), 300–20.

CHAUSSINAND-NOGARET, GUY, *The French Nobility in the Eighteenth Century* (Cambridge, 1985).

CHERNI, A., *Diderot: l'ordre et le devenir* (Geneva, 2002).

CHIARAMONTE, JOSÉ CARLOS, *La Ilustración en el Río de la Plata: cultura eclesiástica y cultura laica durante el Virreinato* (Buenos Aires, 2007).

CHING, J., and OXTOBY, G., *Discovering China: European Interpretations in the Enlightenment* (Rochester, 1992).

CHISICK, H., 'Interpreting the Enlightenment', *European Legacy*, 13 (2008), 35–57.

—— 'An Intellectual Profile of a Jacobin Activist: Dufourny de Villiers (1789–1796)', in Christine Adams et al. (eds.), *Visions and Revisions of Eighteenth-Century France* (University Park, Pa., 1997), 105–33.

CHOPELIN-BLANC, C., *De l'apologétique à l'Église constitutionelle: Adrien Lamourette (1742–1794)* (Paris, 2009).

CHORLEY, PATRICK, *Oil, Silk and Enlightenment* (Naples, 1965).

CHOUILLET, ANNE-MARIE (ed.), *Les Ennemis de Diderot* (Paris, 1993).

CHOUILLET, JACQUES, 'La Politique de Diderot entre la société démocratique et l'état hiérarchisé', in A. Mango (ed.), *Diderot: il politico, il filosofo, lo scrittore* (Milan, 1986), 23–37.

CHRIST, KURT, 'Johann Georg Hamann (1730–1788): Eine Portraitskizze', in R. Knoll (ed.), *Johann Georg Hamann 1730–1788. Quellen und Forschungen* (Bonn, 1988), 233–76.

CHRISTIAENS, W., and EVERS, M., *Patriotse illusies in Amsterdam en Harderwijk* (Hilversum, 2002).

CHUKWUDI EZE, E., *Race and the Enlightenment* (Oxford, 1997).

CIAPPARA, FRANS, *Enlightenment and Reform in Malta 1740–1798* (Malta, 2006).

CITTON, YVES., *L'Envers de la liberté: l'invention d'un imaginaire spinoziste dans la France des Lumières* (Paris, 2006).

—— 'À quoi servent les Lumières radicales?', *Lumières*, 13 (2009), 135–56.

CLARDY, J. V., *The Philosophical Ideas of Alexander Radishchev* (London, 1964).

CLARK, H. C., *Compass of Society: Commerce and Absolutism in Old Regime France* (Lanham, Md., 2007).

CLARK, J. C. D., 'Eighteenth-Century Social History', *Historical Journal*, 27 (1984), 773–88.

CLAVERIE, E., 'La Naissance d'une forme politique: l'affaire du Chevalier de La Barre', in Ph. Roussin (ed.), *Critique et affaires de blasphème à l'époque des Lumières* (Paris, 1998).

CLÉMENT, JEAN-PIERRE, 'La expedición botánica al Perú de Ruiz, Pavón y Dombey (1777–88)', in Kohut and Rose (eds.), *Formación*, 129–59.

—— and RODRÍGUEZ NOZAL, R., 'L'Espagne, apothicaire de l'Europe', *Bulletin hispanique*, 98 (1996), 137–59.

COBB, RICHARD, *The French and their Revolution* (New York, 1998).

COHEN, H., 'Diderot and the Image of China in Eighteenth-Century France', *SVEC* 242 (Oxford, 1986), 219–32.

COHEN, JOSHUA, *Rousseau: A Free Commuity of Equals* (Oxford, 2010).

COHN, B. S., *Colonialism and its Forms of Knowledge: The British in India* (Princeton, 1996).

COLLEY, LINDA, *Britons: Forging the Nation 1707–1837* (New Haven, 1992).

COMTE-SPONVILLE, A., 'La Mettrie: Un "Spinoza moderne"?', in O. Bloch, *Spinoza au XVIIIe siècle* (Paris, 1990), 133–50.

CONLON, PIERRE, *Le Siècle des Lumières: bibliographie chronologique (1700–1789)* (24 vols. Geneva, 1983–2007).

CONTINISIO, CH., 'Governing the Passions: Sketches on Lodovico Antonio Muratori's Moral Philosophy', *HEI* 32 (2006), 367–84.

CORNO, PHILIPPE, 'La loi révolutionnaire du divorce et ses représentations théâtrales', *DHS* 41 (2009), 61–77.

COTTRET, M., *Jansénismes et Lumières: pour un autre XVIIIe siècle* (Paris, 1998).

COULET, HENRI, 'Présentation' to *Pygmalions des Lumières* (Paris, 1998).

COURTNEY, C. P., 'Les Métamorphoses d'un best-seller: *L'Histoire des deux Indes* de 1770 à 1820', in Bancarel and Goggi (eds.), *Raynal*, 109–20.

CRAMPE-CRASNABET, M., 'Les Articles AME dans l'*Encyclopédie*', *RDE* 25 (1998), 91–9.

CRIAUTU, AURELIAN, *Liberalism under Siege* (Lanham, Md., 2003).

CRISTANI, GIOVANNI, *D'Holbach e le rivoluzioni del globo* (Florence, 2003).

CRONK, NICHOLAS, 'Voltaire (non-)lecteur de Nieuwentijt', *Revue Voltaire*, 7 (2007), 169–81.

CROUTER, R., *Friedrich Schleiermacher between Enlightenment and Romanticism* (Cambridge, 2005).

CULOMA, M., *La Religion civile de Rousseau à Robespierre* (Paris, 2010).

CUNEO, T., 'Reid's Moral Philosophy', in Cuneou and van Woudenberg (eds.), *Cambridge Companion to Thomas Reid*, 289–312.

—— and VAN WOUDENBERG, R. (eds.), *The Cambridge Companion to Thomas Reid* (Cambridge, 2004).

DABHOIWALA, F., 'Lust and Liberty', *Past and Present*, 207 (May 2010), 89–179.

DAGEN, JEAN, *L'Histoire de l'esprit humain dans la pensée française de Fontenelle à Condorcet* (Paris, 1977).

DAHLBERG, L., 'The Habermasian Public Sphere: Taking Difference Seriously?', *Theory and Society*, 24 (2005), 111–36.

DAKIN, D., *Turgot and the Ancien Régime in France* (New York, 1980).

DAMROSCH, LEO, *Jean-Jacques Rousseau: Restless Genius* (Boston, 2005).

D'ANCONA, ALESSANDRO, 'Federico il Grande e gli Italiani', in d'Ancona, *Memorie e documenti di storia italiana dei secoli XVIII e XIX* (Florence, 1913), 3–162.

DARNTON, ROBERT, *Mesmerism and the End of the Enlightenment in France* (Cambridge, Mass., 1968).

—— *The Business of Enlightenment* (Cambridge, Mass., 1979).

—— *The Literary Underground of the Old Regime* (Cambridge, Mass., 1982).

—— *The Forbidden Best-Sellers of Pre-Revolutionary France* (London, 1996).

—— 'Two Paths through the Social History of Ideas', in T. Haydn Mason, *The Darnton Debate: Books and Revolution in the Eighteenth Century* (Oxford, 1998), 251–94.

—— 'Bohemians before Bohemianism', KB Lecture 3 (Wassenaar, 2006).

—— *The Great Cat Massacre and Other Episodes of French Cultural History* (New York, 1984).

—— *The Corpus of Clandestine Literature in France, 1769–1789* (New York, 1995).

DARWALL, S., 'Hume and the Invention of Utilitarianism', in Stewart and Wright (eds.), *Hume*, 58–82.

—— 'Norm and Normativity', in *CHEPh* ii. 987–1025.

DAS GUPTA, A., *Malabar in Asian Trade, 1740–1800* (Cambridge, 1967).

DATTA, RAJAT, 'The Agrarian Economy', in P. J. Marshall (ed.), *The Eighteenth Century in Indian History: Evolution or Revolution?* (New Delhi, 2003), 405–56.

DAVIDSON, IAN, *Voltaire in Exile: The Last Years, 1753–78* (New York, 2004).

DAVIDSON, NICHOLAS, 'Toleration in Enlightenment Italy', in O. P. Grell and Roy Porter (eds.), *Toleration in Enlightenment Europe* (Cambridge, 2000), 230–49.

DAVIES, N., *God's Playground: A History of Poland* (2 vols., New York, 1982).

DAVIES, S., 'L'Irlande et les Lumières', *DHS* 30 (1998), 17–35.

DAVIS, D. B., 'New Sidelights on Early Antislavery Radicalism', *William and Mary Quarterly*, 3rd ser. 28 (1971), 585–94.

—— *The Problem of Slavery in the Age of Revolution, 1770–1823* (New York, 1999).

DAVIS, J. A., 'The Napoleonic Era in Southern Italy: An Ambiguous Legacy?', *Proceedings of the British Academy*, 80 (1993), 133–48.

DAVIS, M. T. (ed.), *Radicalism and Revolution in Britain, 1775–1848* (Basingstoke, 2000).

DAVISON, R., *Diderot et Galiani: étude d'une amitié philosophique* (Oxford, 1985).

DAWSON, CHRISTOPHER, *The Gods of Revolution* (New York, 1972).

DE BOOY, J. TH., 'La Traduction française de *Di una riforma d'Italia* di Pilati di Tassulo', *SVEC* 12 (1960), 29–42.

—— 'L'Abbé Coger, dit *Coge Pecus* lecteur de Voltaire et de d'Holbach', *SVEC* 18 (1961), 183–96.

DEFOURNEAUX, M., *L'Inquisition espagnole et les livres français au XVIIIe siècle* (Paris, 1963).

DE FRANCESCO, A., 'How not to Finish a Revolution', in Imbruglia (ed.), *Naples*, 167–82.

DE GANDT, F. (ed.), *Cirey dans la vie intellectuelle: la réception de Newton en France* (Oxford, 2001).

DELANEY, J., *Rousseau and the Ethics of Virtue* (London, 2006).

DE LANGE, M. H., 'John Toland en Hermann Samuel Reimarus over de wonderen in het Oude Testament', *Nederlands Theologisch Tijdschrift*, 46 (1992), 1–9.

D'ELIA, D. J., *Benjamin Rush: Philosopher of the American Revolution* (Philadelphia, 1974).

DELINIÈRE, JEAN, 'Polémique à propos d'un poème à la gloire de la liberté de l'Amérique', in Krebs and Moes (eds.), *Révolution Américaine*, 53–67.

DEL NEGRO, PIERO, 'Rappresentazioni della guerra in Italia tra Illuminismo e Romanticismo', in G. Santato (ed.), *Letteratura italiana e cultura europea tra Illuminismo et romanticismo* (Geneva, 2003), 133–60.

DELPIANO, PATRIZIA, *Il governo della lettura: chiesa e libri nell'Italia del Settecento* (Bologna, 2007).

DE LUNA, F., 'The Dean Street Style of Revolution: J. P. Brissot, jeune philosophe', *FHS* 17 (1991), 159–90.

DE MAS, ENRICO, *Montesquieu, Genovesi e le edizioni italiani della* Spirito delle leggi (Florence, 1971).

DENEYS-TUNNEY, A., *Un autre Jean-Jacques Rousseau* (Paris, 2010).

DENT, NICHOLAS, *Rousseau* (Abingdon, 2005).

DE POORTERE, M., *Les Idées philosophiques et littéraires de Mme de Staël et de Mme de Genlis* (New York, 2004).

DESNÉ, ROLAND, 'Voltaire et Helvétius', in Ch. Mervaud and S. Menant (eds.), *Le Siècle de Voltaire: Hommage à René Pomeau* (2 vols., Oxford, 1987), i. 403–15.

DESTAIN, CH., 'Chamfort et Rousseau', in L'Aminot (ed.), *Politique et révolution*, 79–89.

DE VRIESE, M., *Beschaven! Letterkundige genootschappen in Nederland, 1750–1800* (Nijmegen, 2001).

DHONDT, LUC, 'De conservatieve Brabantse ontwenteling van 1789 en het proces van revolutie en contrarevolutie in de Zuidelijke Nederlanden tussen 1780 en 1830', *Tijdschrift voor Geschiedenis*, 102 (1989), 422–50.

DICKINSON, H. T., ' "The Friends of America": British Sympathy with the American Revolution', in Davis (ed.), *Radicalism*, 1–29.

DICKSON, P. G. M., 'Joseph II's Reshaping of the Austrian Church', *Historical Journal*, 26 (1993), 89–114.

DI GIOVANNI, GEORGE, 'Introduction' to Jacobi, *Main Philosophical Writings*, 3–167.

—— 'The First Twenty Years of Critique', in Guyer (ed.), *Cambridge Companion to Kant*, 417–48.

DI MITRI, G. L., 'The History of Linnaeism in the Kingdom of Naples', in M. Beretta and A. Tosi (eds.), *Linnaeus in Italy: The Spread of a Revolution in Science* (Sagamore Beach, Mass., 2007), 271–91.

DIOGUARDI, GIANFRANCO, *Attualità dell'Illuminismo milanese* (Palermo, 1998).

DIOP, D., 'L'Anonymat dans les articles politiques de l'*Encyclopédie*', *La Lettre clandestine*, 8 (1999), 102–.

DIPPEL, HORST, *Germany and the American Revolution* (Chapel Hill, NC, 1977).

DIRKS, N. B., *Castes of Mind: Colonialism and the Making of Modern India* (Princeton, 2001).

DIXON, S., 'Proveshchenie', in Butterwick et al. (eds.), *Peripheries*, 229–49.

DOMENECH, JACQUES, *L'Éthique des Lumières* (Paris, 1989).

—— 'Éthique et révolution: le sentiment, de l'*Émile* aux *Fragments politiques*', in R. Thiéry (ed.), *Rousseau, l'Émile et la Révolution* (Paris, 1992), 37–42.

DOMMANGET, M., *Sylvain Maréchal: l'égalitaire, 'l'homme sans Dieu'* (Paris, 1950).

DONATO, C., 'Réfutation ou réconciliation? Fortunato Bartolomeo de Felice critique des *Préjugés légitimes contre l'*Encyclopédie', in Chouillet (ed.), *Ennemis*, 101–12.

DONNELLY, F. K., 'Joseph Towers and the Collapse of Rational Dissent', *Enlightenment and Dissent*, 6 (1987), 31–8.

DONNERT, ERICH (ed.), *Europa in der frühen Neuzeit: Festschrift für Günter Mühlpfordt*, vol. ii (Cologne, 1997).

DORIGNY, MARCEL, 'The Abbé Gregoire and the *Société des Amis des Noirs*', in Jeremy Popkin and Richard Popkin (eds.), *The Abbé Grégoire and his World* (Dordrecht, 2000), 27–39.

DOYLE, WILLIAM, *Oxford History of the French Revolution* (Oxford, 1989).

—— *Origins of the French Revolution* (1980; 2nd edn. Oxford, 1989).

—— *The Old European Order, 1660–1800* (Oxford, 1992).

—— *The Aristocracy and its Enemies in the Age of Revolution* (Oxford, 2009).

DROIXHE, DANIEL, 'Raynal à Liège', in H. J. Lüsebrink and M. Tietz (eds.), *Lectures de Raynal*, L'Histoire des deux Indes *en Europe et en Amérique au XVIIIe siècle* (Oxford, 1991), 205–33.

DUCHESNAU, F., 'Condillac critique de Locke', *International Studies in Philosophy* (Turin), 6 (1974), 77–98.

DUCHET, MICHELE, *Diderot et l'*Histoire des deux Indes *ou l'écriture fragmentaire* (Paris, 1978).

DUFLO, COLAS, *Diderot philosophe* (Paris, 2003).

—— 'Diderot and the Publicizing of Censorship', in M. Laerke (ed.), *The Use of Censorship in the Enlightenment* (Leiden, 2009), 121–35.

DULAC, GEORGES, 'Les Modes d'intervention de Diderot en politique', in France and Strugnell (eds.), *Diderot*, 121–39.

—— 'Le Discours politique de Pétersbourg', *RDE* 1 (1986), 32–58.

DUNN, JOHN, *Setting the People Free: The Story of Democracy* (London, 2005).

Dupré, Louis, *The Enlightenment and the Intellectual Foundations of Modern Culture* (New Haven, 2004).

Dziembowski, E., 'La Défense du modèle anglais pendant la guerre de Sept Ans', in Kölving and Mervaud (eds.), *Voltaire et ses combats*, i. 89–97.

Eames, B., 'Baron d'Holbach's Library', *Australian Journal of French Studies*, 28 (1991), 249–53.

Echeverria, D., *The Maupeou Revolution* (Baton Rouge, La., 1985).

Edelstein, Dan, *The Terror of Natural Right* (Chicago, 2009).

—— *The Enlightenment: A Genealogy* (Chicago, 2010).

Ehrard, Jean, *L'Idée de nature en France dans la première moitié du XVIIIe siècle* (Geneva, 1981).

—— 'Voltaire vu par Montesquieu', in Kölving and Mervaud (eds.), *Voltaire et ses combats*, ii. 939–51.

—— *L'Esprit des mots: Montesquieu en lui-même et parmi les siens* (Geneva, 1998).

Eijnatten, Joris van, *Liberty and Concord in the United Provinces: Religious Toleration and the Public in the Eighteenth-Century Netherlands* (Leiden, 2003).

—— 'Opklaring, opwekking en behoud: Religieus conservatisme in Nederland, 1780–1840', *GWN* 10 (1999), 9–24.

Einaudi, Mario, *The Early Rousseau* (Ithaca, NY, 1967).

Ellery, E., *Brissot de Warville: A Study in the History of the French Revolution* (Poughkeepsie, NY, 1915).

Elliott, J. I., *Empires of the Atlantic World* (New Haven, 2006).

Ellis, E., *Kant's Politics: Provisional Theory for an Uncertain World* (New Haven, 2005).

Ellis, J. M., 'The Vexed Question of Egmont's Political Judgment', in C. P. Magill et al. (eds.), *Tradition and Creation* (Leeds, 1978), 116–30.

Emerson, R. L., *Essays on David Hume, Medical Men and the Scottish Enlightenment* (Farnham, 2009).

Enciso Recio, Luis Miguel, 'La divulgación de los saberes', in Luigi da Rosa et al. (eds.), *Spagna e Mezzogiorno d'Italia nell'etá della transizione (1650–1760)* (2 vols., Naples, 1997), ii. 281–355.

Engel, E. J., 'Von "Relativ wahr?" zu: Relativ falsch—Jacobis Eingeständnis', in Schurmann et al. (eds.), *Spinoza im Deutschland*, 221–49.

Engels, Hans-Werner, 'Carl Friedrich Cramers Hamburger Freunde feiern ein Freheitsfest', in Schütt (ed.), *Ein Mann von Feuer und Talenten*, 177–208.

Erker, B., and Siebers, W., 'Das Bahrdt-Pasquill', in U. Goldenbaum (ed.), *Appell an das Publikum: Die öffentliche Debatte in der deutschen Aufklärung, 1687–1796* (2 vols., Berlin, 2004), ii. 897–939.

Escobar Villegas, Juan Camilo, and Maya Salazar, A. Leon, 'Otras "luces" sobre la temprana historia política de Colombia, 1780–1850: Gaetano Filangieri y "La ruta de Nápoles a las Indias Occidentales"', *Co-herencia*, 4 (2006), 79–111.

Etienvre, F., 'Traducción y renovación cultural a mediados del siglo XVIII en España', in P. Fernández Albaladejo (ed.), *Fénix de España: modernidad y cultura propria en la España del siglo XVIII (1737–1766)* (Madrid, 2006), 93–117.

Evans, R. J., 'Joseph II and Nationality in the Habsburg Lands', in Scott (ed.), *Enlightened Absolutism*, 209–19.

—— 'Maria Theresa and Hungary', in Scott (ed.), *Enlightened Absolutism*, 189–207.

EVERDELL, W. R., *Christian Apologetics in France, 1730–1790* (Lewiston, NY, 1987).

FACCARELLO, G., ' "Nil repente!" Galiani and Necker on Economic Reforms', *European Journal of the History of Economic Thought*, 1 (1994), 519–50.

FARR, J., ' "So vile and miserable an estate": The Problem of Slavery in Locke's Political Thought', *Political Theory*, 14 (1987), 263–89.

—— 'Locke, Natural Law and New World Slavery', in C. Miqueu and M. Chamie (eds.), *Locke's Political Liberty* (Oxford, 2009), 165–88.

FEENSTRA KUIPER, J., *Japan en de buiten wereld in de achttiende eeuw* (The Hague, 1921).

FEHN, ERNST-OTTO, 'Moralische Unschuld oder politische Bewusstheit? Thesen zur Illuminatischen Ideologie und ihrer Rezeption', in Reinalter (ed.), *Der Illuminatenorden*, 207–26.

FEINER, SHMUEL, *The Jewish Enlightenment* (Philadelphia, 2002).

FEOLA, RAFFAELE, *Dall'Illuminismo all restaurazione* (Naples, 1977).

FERGUSON, MOIRA, 'Mary Wollstonecraft and the Problematic of Slavery', in M. J. Falco (ed.), *Feminist Interpretations of Mary Wollstonecraft* (University Park, Pa., 1996), 125–49.

FERGUSON, R. A., *The American Enlightenment, 1750–1820* (Cambridge, Mass., 1994).

FERRONE, VINCENZO, *I profeti dell'illuminismo* (1989; 2nd edn., Bari, 2000).

—— *La società giusta ed equa: repubblicanesimo e diritti dell'uomo in Gaetano Filangieri* (Rome, 2003).

—— *Una scienza per l'uomo* (Turin, 2007).

—— *Lezioni illuministiche* (Bari, 2010).

—— 'Il problema dei selvaggi nell'illuminismo italiano', *Studi storici*, 27 (1986), 149–71.

FICHERA, GIUSEPPE, *Il Deismo critico di Voltaire* (Catania, 1993).

FINGER, OTTO, 'Der Kampf Karl von Knoblauchs gegen den religiösen Aberglauben', in G. Stiehler (ed.), *Beiträge zur Geschichte des vormarxistischen Materialismus* (Berlin, 1961), 255–97.

FINDLEN, PAULA, 'A Forgotten Newtonian: Women and Science in the Italian Provinces', in William Clark et al. (eds.), *The Sciences in Enlightened Europe* (Chicago, 1999), 313–49.

FINK, B., and STENGER, G. (eds.), *Être matérialiste à l'âge des lumières* (Paris, 1999).

FIRODE, A., 'Locke et les philosophes français', in de Gandt (ed.), *Cirey*, 7–72.

FISCH, JÖRG, *Hollands Ruhm in Asien* (Stuttgart, 1986).

FISCHER, NORBERT, 'Reduktion der Religion auf Moral?', in N. Fischer (ed.), *Kant und der Katholizismus* (Fribourg, 2005), 282–302.

FISHER, J. R., *Bourbon Peru, 1780–1824* (Liverpool, 2003).

FITZPATRICK, M., 'Enlightenment in Late-Eighteenth-Century Liverpool', in Butterwick et al. (eds.), *Peripheries*, 119–44.

FLORES GALINDO, ALBERTO, 'República sin ciudadanos', *Fronteras: Revista del Centro de Investigaciones de Historia Colonial* (Bogotá), 1 (1997), 13–33.

FLYGT, STEN GUNNAR, *The Notorious Dr Bahrdt* (Nashville, 1963).

FOGELIN, R. J., 'Hume's Scepticism', in Norton (ed.), *Cambridge Companion to Hume*, 90–116.

—— *A Defense of Hume on Miracles* (Princeton, 2003).

FOLKERTS, HEINZ, *Die Bedeutung französicher Denker des 18. Jahrhunderts für die Herausbildung eines Freiheitsbewusstseins in Spaniens südamerikanischen Kolonien* (Würzburg, 1969).

FONER, ERIC, *Tom Paine and Revolutionary America* (1976; rev. edn., 2005).

—— *The Story of American Freedom* (New York, 1999).

FONTIUS, M., 'Critique', in R. Reichardt and E. Schmitt (eds.), *HPSGF* 5: 7–26.

FORCE, PIERRE, 'Helvétius as an Epicurean Political Theorist', in Leddy and Livschitz (eds.), *Epicurus*, 105–18.

FORST, RAINER, *Toleranz im Konflikt* (Frankfurt, 2003).

—— 'Toleranz, Glaube und Vernunft. Bayle und Kant im Vergleich', in H. F. Klemme (ed.), *Kant und die Zukunft der europäischen Aufklärung* (Berlin, 2009), 183–209.

FORSTER, M. N., *Kant and Skepticism* (Princeton, 2008).

FÖRSTER, WOLFGANG (ed.), *Aufklärung in Berlin* (Berlin, 1989).

FORSYTH, M., *Reason and Revolution: The Political Thought of the Abbé Sieyès* (Leicester, 1987).

FOSSATI, W. J., 'Maximum Influence from Minimum Abilities: La Mettrie and Radical Materialism', in B. Sweetman (ed.), *The Failure of Modernism* (Mishawaka, Ind., 1999), 45–57.

FRAENKEL, CARLOS, 'Maimonides and Spinoza as Sources for Maimon's Solution of the "problem quid juris" in Kant's Theory of Knowledge', *Kant-Studien*, C (2009), 212–40.

FRANCE, P., and STRUGNELL, A. (eds.), *Diderot: les dernières années, 1770–84* (Edinburgh, 1985).

FRANÇOIS-PRIMO, JEAN, *La Jeunesse de Brissot* (Paris, 1932).

FRANCOVICH, G., *La filosofía en Bolivia* (Sucre, 1945).

FRÅNGSMYR, TORE, *Wolffianismens genombrott i Uppsala* (Uppsala 1972).

FRANKS, PAUL, 'All or Nothing: Systematicity and Nihilism in Jacobi, Reinhold, and Maimon', in Ameriks (ed.), *The Cambridge Companion to German Idealism*, 95–116.

FRASCA-SPADA, M., and KAIL, P. J. E. (eds.), *Impressions of Hume* (Oxford, 2005).

FRESCO, M. F., 'He *was* Greek, this Frisian Socrates', in Fresco et al. (eds.), *Frans Hemsterhuis*, 93–149.

—— 'Hemsterhuis und seine Stellungnahme zu Spinoza', in *Mededelingen vanwege het Spinozahuis*, 85 (Delft, 2003), 3–32.

—— GEERAEDTS, L., and HAMMACHER, K. (eds.), *Frans Hemsterhuis (1721–1790): Sources, Philosophy and Reception* (Munster, 1995).

FREUD, H. H., 'Palissot and Les Philosophes', *Diderot Studies*, 9 (1967).

FREUND, GERHARD, 'Ein Trojaner: Lessings Reimarus-Fragmente als Anfrage an die zeitgenössische Theologie', in Steiger (ed.), *500 Jahre Theologie in Hamburg*, 133–52.

FRIEDLAND, P., *Political Actors: Representative Bodies and Theatricality in the Age of the French Revolution* (Ithaca, NY, 2002).

FROIDCOURT, GEORGES DE, *L'Abbé Raynal au pays de Liège* (Liège, 1946).

FROMM, H., *Bibliographie deutscher Übersetzungen aus dem Französischen 1700–1948* (6 vols., Baden-Baden, 1950–3).

FROST, J. W., *A Perfect Freedom: Religious Liberty in Pennsylvania* (University Park, Pa., 1990).

FURET, FRANÇOIS, *Interpreting the French Revolution* (Cambridge, 1978).

—— *Revolutionary France, 1770–1880* (1988; Oxford, 1995).

—— 'Rousseau and the French Revolution', in C. Orwin and N. Tarcov (eds.), *The Legacy of Rousseau* (Chicago, 1997), 168–82.

—— and OZOUF, M., 'Deux légitimations historiques de la société française au XVIIIe siècle: Mably et Boulainvilliers', in *L'Histoire au dix-huitième siècle* (Aix-en-Provence, 1980), 233–49.

GAASTRA, F. S., *De Geschiedenis van de VOC* (Zutphen, 1991).

—— 'De VOC en EIC in Bengalen aan de vooravond van de Vierde Engelse Oorlog (1780–1784)', *Tijdschrift voor Zeegeschiedenis*, 20 (2001), 24–35.

GABRIEL, RUTH, 'Learned Communities and British Educational Experiments in North India, 1780–1830' (University of Virginia, Ph.D. thesis, 1979).

GALLIANI, R., 'Mably et Voltaire', *DHS* 3 (1971), 181–94.

GALLOP, G., 'Ideology and the English Jacobins', *Enlightenment and Dissent*, 5 (1986), 3–20.

GARBER, DANIEL, *Leibniz: Body, Substance, Monad* (Oxford, 2009).

GARGETT, G., 'Jacob Vernet: Theologian and Anti-*philosophe*', *BJECS* 16 (1993), 35–52.

GARNOT, B., 'Les Peines corporelles en Bourgogne au XVIIIe siècle', in Porret (ed.), *Beccaria*, 215–22.

GARRARD, G., *Rousseau's Counter-Enlightenment* (Albany, NY, 2003).

GARRAWAY, D., *The Libertine Colony: Creolization in the Early French Caribbean* (Durham, 2005).

GARRETT, A., 'Human Nature', in *CHEPh* i. 160–233.

—— 'Anthropology: The "Original" of Human Nature', in Broadie (ed.), *Cambridge Companion to the Scottish Enlightenment*, 79–93.

GARRETT, DON, 'Should Hume have been a Transcendental Idealist?', in D. Garber and B. Longuenesse (eds.), *Kant and the Early Moderns* (Princeton, 2008), 193–208.

GARRIOCH, D., *The Making of Revolutionary Paris* (Berkeley and Los Angeles, 2002).

GÄRTNER, JOHANNES, *Das* Journal Étranger *und seine Bedeutung für die Verbreitung deutscher Literatur in Frankreich* (1905; repr. Geneva, 1971).

GASCOIGNE, J., *Cambridge in the Age of Enlightenment* (Cambridge, 1989).

—— 'The German Enlightenment and the Pacific', in L. Woff and M. Cipolloni (eds.), *The Anthropology of the Enlightenment* (Stanford, Calif., 2007), 141–71.

—— 'Anglican Latitudinarianism, Rational Dissent and Political Radicalism in the Late Eighteenth Century', in K. Haakonssen (ed.), *Enlightenment and Religion* (Cambridge, 1996), 219–40.

GASKIN, J. C. A., *Hume's Philosophy of Religion* (1978; Basingstoke, 1988).

—— 'Hume on Religion', in Norton (ed.), *Cambridge Companion to Hume*, 313–44.

GAUCHET, M., *The Disenchantment of the World: A Political History of Religion* (new edn., Princeton, 1999).

GAUTHIER, DAVID, *Rousseau: The Sentiment of Existence* (Cambridge, 2006).

GAWOLL, HANS-JÜRGEN, 'Karl Heinrich Heydenreich: Spinozismus als Metaphysik und Vernunftglaube', in Schürmann et al. (eds.), *Spinoza im Deutschland*, 407–28.

GAY, PETER, *The Enlightenment: An Interpretation: The Rise of Modern Paganism* (1966; New York, 1977).

—— *The Enlightenment: An Interpretation: The Science of Freedom* (1969; New York, 1977).

—— *Voltaire's Politics: The Poet as Realist* (Princeton, 1959).

GAYOT, G., 'War die französische Freimauererei des 18. Jahrhunderts eine Schule der Gleichheit?', in H. E. Bödecker and E. François, *Aufklärung und Politik* (Leipzig, 1996), 235–48.

GEFFARTH, R. D., *Religion und arkane Hierarchie: der Orden der Gold- und Rosenkreuzer* (Leiden, 2007).

GEGENHEIMER, A. F., *William Smith: Educator and Churchman, 1727–1803* (Philadelphia, 1943).

GERMANA, N. A., 'Herder's India', in L. Wolff and M. Cipolloni (eds.), *The Anthropology of the Enlightenment* (Stanford, Calif., 2007), 119–37.

GERRISH, B. A., 'Natural and Revealed Religion', in *CHEPh* ii. 641–65.

GEUNA, MARCO, 'Republicanism and Commercial Society in the Scottish Enlightenment', in Martin Van Gelderen and Quentin Skinner (eds.), *Republicanism: A Shared European Heritage* (2 vols., Cambridge, 2002), ii. 177–95.

GHACHEM, M. W., 'Montesquieu in the Caribbean', *Historical Reflections/Réflexions historiques*, 25 (1995), 183–210.

GHIBAUDI, SILVIA ROTA, *La fortuna di Rousseau in Italia (1750–1815)* (Turin, 1961).

GIBBONS, LUKE, *Edmund Burke and Ireland* (Cambridge, 2003).

GIBBS, F. W., *Joseph Priestley: Adventurer in Science and Champion of Truth* (London, 1965).

GIBSON, CHARLES, *The Aztecs under Spanish Rule* (Stanford, Calif., 1964).

GIJSBERTI HODENPIJL, A. K. A., 'De handhaving der neutraliteit van de Nederlandsche loge te Houghly', *BTLNI* 76 (1920), 258–83.

GILLEY, SH., 'Christianity and Enlightenment: An Historical Survey', *HEI* 1 (1981), 103–21.

GILLESPIE, M. A., *The Theological Origins of Modernity* (Chicago, 2009).

GILLISPIE, CH. C., *Science and Polity in France* (Princeton, 1980).

GLAUSSER, W., 'Three Approaches to Locke and the Slave Trade', *JHI* 51: 199–216.

GLEBE-MØLLER, JENS, *Struensees vej til skafottet* (Copenhagen, 2007).

GOBBERS, WALTER, *Jean-Jacques Rousseau in Holland (c.1760–c.1810)* (Ghent, 1963).

GODECHOT, J., *France and the Atlantic Revolution of the Eighteenth Century* (London, 1971).

—— *The Counter-Revolution: Doctrine and Action, 1789–1804* (1961; English edn. Princeton, 1961).

GODINEAU, D., *The Women of Paris and their French Revolution* (Berkeley, CA., 1998).

GODMAN, P., *Die geheime Inquisition: Aus den verbotenen Archiven des Vatikans* (Munich, 2001).

GOETSCHEL, W., *Spinoza's Modernity* (Madison, 2004).

GOGGI, GIANLUIGI, 'Diderot-Raynal e Filangieri: un studio di fonti', *Giornale storico della letteratura italiana*, 153 (1976), 387–418.

—— 'Ancora su Diderot-Raynal e Filangieri e su altre fonti della *Scienza della legislazione*', *La Rassegna della letteratura italiana*, 84 (1980), 112–60.

—— 'Spinoza contro Rousseau: un commento ad alcuni passi di Diderot e di d'Holbach', *Annali di Ca' Foscari*, 25 (1986), 133–59.

—— 'Les *Fragments politiques* de 1772', in G. Dulac and J. Varloot (eds.), *Éditer Diderot*, *SVEC* no. 254 (Oxford, 1988), 427–62.

—— 'Diderot e l'"Histoire des deux Indes": riflessioni sulla storia', *Studi francesi*, 76 (1982), 32–43.

—— 'Diderot et le concept de civilisation', *Dix-Huitième Siècle* 29 (1997), 353–73.

—— 'Autour du voyage de Raynal en Angleterre et en Hollande', in Bancarel and Goggi (eds.), *Raynal*, 371–425.

GOLDENBAUM, URSULA, 'Der "Berolinismus": Die preussische Hauptstadt als ein Zentrum geistiger Kommunikation in Deutschland', in Forster (ed.), *Aufklärung in Berlin*, 339–62.

—— 'Die philosophische Methodendiskussion des 17. Jahrhunderts in ihrer Bedeutung für den Modernisierungsschub in der Historiographie', in W. Küttler et al. (eds.), *Geschichtsdiskurs*, ii: *Anfänge modernen historischen Denkens* (Frankfurt, 1994), 148–61.

—— 'Kants Parteinahme für Mendelssohn im Spinoza-Streit 1786', in Rolf-Peter Horstmann et al. (eds.), *Kant und die Berliner Aufklärung: Akten des IX Kant-Kongresses* (Berlin, 2001), v. 176–85.

—— 'Mendelssohns schwierige Beziehung zu Spinoza', in Schürmann et al. (eds.), *Spinoza im Deutschland*, 265–317.

—— 'Beziehungen der jungen Berliner Zeitungsschreiber Mylius und Lessing zu französischen Aufklärern', in U. Goldenbaum and A. Kosenina (eds.), *Berliner Aufklärung*, i (Hanover, 1999), 69–100.

GOLDENBAUM, URSULA, 'Einführung' to J. J. Rousseau, *Abhandlung von dem Ursprung der Ungleichheit unter den Menschen*, German trans. by M. Mendelssohn (Weimar, 2000), 1–63.

—— *Appell an das Publikum: Die öffentliche Debatte in der deutschen Aufklärung 1687–1796* (2 vols., Berlin, 2004).

—— 'Friedrich II und die Berliner Aufklärung', in G. Lottes and I. D'Aprile (eds.), *Hofkultur und aufgeklärte Öffentlichkeit* (Berlin, 2006), 123–40.

GOLDIE, MARK, and WOKLER, R. (eds.), *The Cambridge History of Eighteenth-Century Political Thought* (Cambridge, 2006).

GOLDMANN, LUCIEN, *The Philosophy of the Enlightenment*, trans. H. Maas (Cambridge, Mass., 1968).

GONZÁLEZ BUENO, ANTONIO, 'Plantas y luces: la botánica de la Ilustración en la América hispana', in Kohut and Rose (eds.), *Formación*, 107–28.

GONZÁLEZ FEIJÓO, JOSÉ A., *El pensamientio ético-político de B. J. Feijóo* (Oviedo, 1991).

GONZÁLEZ SÁNCHEZ, CARLOS ALBERTO 'Libros europeos en las Indias del siglo XVIII', in Kohut and Rose (eds.), *Formación*, 337–65.

GOODELL, E., *The Noble Philosopher: Condorcet and the Enlightenment* (Buffalo, NY, 1994).

GOODMAN, ALBERT, *The Friends of Liberty: The English Democratic Movement in the Age of the French Revolution* (London, 1979).

GOODMAN, D., *The Republic of Letters* (New York, 1994).

GORDON, DANIEL, 'The Great Enlightenment Massacre', in Mason (ed.), *The Darnton Debate*, 129–56.

—— *Postmodernism and the Enlightenment: New Perspectives in Eighteenth-Century French Intellectual History* (New York, 2001).

GORDON, D. H., and TORREY, N. L., *The Censoring of Diderot's* Encyclopédie *and the Re-established Text* (New York, 1947).

GORMAN, TH. K., *America and Belgium: A Study of the Influence of the United States on the Belgian Revolution of 1789–90* (London, 1925).

GOUHIER, HENRI, *Rousseau et Voltaire: Portraits dans deux miroirs* (Paris, 1983).

GOULEMOT, JEAN-MARIE, 'Ces penseurs n'ont compris rien à la Revolution', in *Le Point Hors-série*, 26 (March/April 2010), 82–3.

GOUREVITCH, V., 'The Religious Thought', in Riley (ed.), *Cambridge Companion to Rousseau*, 193–246.

GRACZYK, A., 'Le Théâtre de la Révolution', *DHS* 21 (1989), 395–410.

GRANT, JAMES, *John Adams: Party of One* (New York, 2005).

GRENBY, M. O., *The Anti-Jacobin Novel: British Conservatism and the French Revolution* (Cambridge, 2001).

GRINDE, D. A., 'The Historical Background', in R. Griffin and D. A. Grinde, *Apocalypse de Chiokoyhikoy* (Quebec, 1997), 168–205.

GROENEWEGEN, P., *Eighteenth-Century Economics: Turgot, Beccaria and Smith and their Contemporaries* (London, 2002).

GROSCLAUDE, PIERRE, *Malesherbes: témoin et l'interprète de son temps* (Paris, 1961).

GROSS, H., *Rome in the Age of Enlightenment* (Cambridge, 1990).

GROSSMAN, M., *The Philosophy of Helvétius* (New York, 1926).

GROSSMANN, W., *Johann Christian Edelmann: From Orthodoxy to Enlightenment* (The Hague, 1976).

GRÜNDER, KARLFRIED, and SCHMIDT-BIGGEMANN, W. (eds.), *Spinoza in der Frühzeit seiner religiösen Wirkung* (Heidelberg, 1984).

GUEHENNO, JEAN, *Jean-Jacques Rousseau* (2 vols., London, 1966).

GUÉROULT, MARTIAL, *Histoire de l'histoire de la philosophie* (Paris, 1984).

GUILHAUMOU, JACQUES, *L'Avènement des porte-parole de la république (1789–1792)* (Paris, 1998).

GULLICK, J. M., *Indigenous Political Systems of Western Malaya* (London, 1958).

—— *History of Selangor* (Singapore, 1960).

GUMBRECHT, H., and REICHARDT, R., 'Philosophe, philosophie', *HPSGF* iii. 7–82.

GUROVICH, GIANCARLO, *F. M. Grimm: un intellettuale nell'epoca dei Lumi* (Udine, 1983).

GUYER, PAUL, *Kant's System of Nature and Freedom: Selected Essays* (Oxford, 2005).

—— (ed.), *The Cambridge Companion to Kant* (Cambridge, 1992).

GUYOT, CHARLY, *Le Rayonnement de l'Encyclopédie en Suisse française* (Neuchatel, 1955).

HAAKONSSEN, KNUD, 'The Structure of Hume's Political Theory', in Norton (ed.), *Cambridge Companion to Hume*, 182–221.

—— 'Natural Jurisprudence and the Theory of Justice', in Broadie (ed.), *Scottish Enlightenment*, 205–21.

—— (ed.), *The Cambridge History of Eighteenth-Century Philosophy* (2 vols., Cambridge, 2006).

HAAR, JOHANN, *Jean Meslier und die Beziehungen von Voltaire und Holbach zu ihm* (Hamburg, 1928).

HAASER, ROLF, 'Sonderfall oder Paradigma? Karl Friedrich Bahrdt und das Verhältniss von Spätaufklärung und Gegenaufklärung in der hessisch-darmstädtischen Universitätsstadt Giessen', in Donnert (ed.), *Europa*, ii. 247–85.

HABAKKUK, J., *Marriage, Debt, and the Estates System: English Landownership, 1650–1950* (Oxford, 1994).

HABIB, IRFAN, 'The Eighteenth Century in Indian Economic History', in Marshall (ed.), *Eighteenth Century in Indian History*, 100–19.

HAECHLER, JEAN, *L'Encyclopédie de Diderot et de ... Jaucourt* (Paris, 1995).

—— *L'Encyclopédie: Les Combats et les hommes* (Paris, 1998).

HALÉVI, R., 'La Révolution constituante: les ambiguïtés politiques', in Lucas (ed.), *Political Culture*, 69–85.

HALÉVY, ÉLIE, *The Growth of Philosophic Radicalism* (Boston, 1955).

HALLWARD, N. L., *William Bolts: A Dutch Adventurer under John Company* (Cambridge, 1920).

HAMILTON, G. H., *The Art and Architecture of Russia* (2nd edn., Harmondsworth, 1975).

HAMMACHER, KLAUS, 'Hemsterhuis und Jacobi', in Fresco et al. (eds.), *Frans Hemsterhuis*, 491–525.

—— 'Hemsterhuis und Spinoza', in *Mededelingen vanwege het Spinozahuis*, lxxxv (Delft, 2003), 3–43.

—— and PISKE, IRMGARD-MARIA (eds.), *Anhang* to Jacobi, *Schriften zum Spinozastreit*, ii. 361–601.

HAMMERSLEY, R., 'Jean-Paul Marat's *The Chains of Slavery* in Britain and France, 1774–1833', *Historical Journal*, 48 (2005), 641–60.

HAMPSHER-MONK, I., 'British Radicalism and the Anti-Jacobins', in *CHEPTh* 660–87.

—— 'On not Inventing the English Revolution', in Burgess and Festenstein (eds.), *English Radicalism*, 135–56.

—— 'Edmund Burke's Changing Justification for Intervention', repr. in I. Hampsher-Monk (ed.), *Edmund Burke* (Farnham, 2009), 343–78.

998   Bibliography

HAMPSHER-MONK, I., 'Edmund Burke and Empire', in D. Kelly, Lineages of Empire (Oxford, 2009), 117–36.
HAMPSON, N., The Enlightenment (Harmondsworth, 1968).
—— A Social History of the French Revolution (1963; new edn., London, 1966).
—— Saint-Just (Oxford, 1991).
HAMPTON, JOHN, Nicolas-Antoine Boulanger et la science de son temps (Geneva, 1955).
HANOU, A. J., 'Verlichte vrijheid', in E. O. G. Haitsma Mulier and W. R. E. Velema (eds.), Vrijheid: een geschiedenis van de vijftiende tot de twintigste eeuw (Amsterdam, 1999), 187–211.
—— Nederlandse literatuur van de Verlichting (1670–1830) (Nijmegen, 2002).
HARDMAN, J., Louis XVI: The Silent King (London, 2000).
HARGRAVES, N., 'Beyond the Savage Character', in L. Wolff and M. Cipolloni (eds.), The Anthropology of the Enlightenment (Stanford, Calif., 2007), 103–18.
HARRIS, J. A., 'The Epicurean in Hume', in Leddy and Livschitz (eds.), Epicurus, 161–81.
—— 'Hume's Four Essays on Happiness and their Place in the Move from Morals to Politics', in E. Mazza and E. Ronchetti (eds.), New Essays on David Hume (Milan, 2007), 223–35.
HASSNER, PIERRE, 'Rousseau and the Theory and Practice of International Relations', in C. Orwin and N. Tarcov (eds.), The Legacy of Rousseau (Chicago, 1997), 200–19.
HAUBEN, P. J., 'White Legend against Black: Nationalism and Enlightenment in a Spanish Context', The Americas, 34 (1977), 1–19.
HAUG, CHRISTINE, 'Die Bedeutung der radikal-demokratischen Korrespondenzgesellschaft "Deutsche Union" für die Entstehung von Lesegesellschaften in Oberhessen im ausgehenden 18. Jahrhundert', in Donnert (ed.), Europa, 299–322.
HAVINGA, J. Ch. A., Les Nouvelles ecclésiastiques dans leur lutte contre l'esprit philosophique (Amersfoort, 1925).
HEATH, E., and MEROLLE, V. (eds.), Adam Ferguson: History, Progress and Human Nature (London, 2008).
HEBEIS, MICHAEL, Karl Anton von Martini (1726–1800): Leben und Werk (Frankfurt, 1996).
HEINRICH, GERDA, 'Die Debatte um "bürgerliche Verbesserung der Juden" 1781–1794', in Goldenbaum (ed.), Appell, ii. 813–87.
HEINZ, MARION, 'Genuss, Liebe und Erkenntnis: Zur frühen Hemsterhuis-Rezeption Herders', in Fresco et al. (eds.), Frans Hemsterhuis, 433–44.
HEIRWEGH, JEAN-JACQUES, 'La Fin de l'Ancien Régime et les révolutions', in H. Hasquin (ed.), La Belgique autrichienne 1713–1794 (Brussels, 1987).
HEMMING, T. D., FREEMAN, E., and MEAKING, D. (eds.), The Secular City: Studies in the Enlightenment (Exeter, 1994).
HENDERSON, G. P., The Revival of Greek Thought 1620–1830 (Albany, NY, 1970).
HENRICH, DIETER, Between Kant and Hegel: Lectures on German Idealism (Cambridge, Mass., 2003).
HERMANN, INGO, Knigge: Die Biografie (Berlin, 2007).
HERR, RICHARD, The Eighteenth-Century Revolution in Spain (Princeton, 1958).
HERRERO, JAVIER, Los orígenes del pensamiento reaccionario español (Madrid, 1971).
HESS, JONATHAN, Germans, Jews and the Claims of Modernity (New Haven, 2002).
HESSE, CARLA, The Other Enlightenment: How French Women became Modern (Princeton, 2001).
HEYBERGER, B., GARCÍA-ARENAL, M. ET AL. (eds.), L'Islam visto da Occidente (Genoa, 2009).
HIEBERT, E. N., 'The Integration of Revealed Religion and Scientific Materialism in the Thought of Joseph Priestley', in L. Kieft and B. R. Willeford (eds.), Joseph Priestley: Scientist, Theologian and Metaphysician (Lewisburg, Pa., 1980), 27–61.

High, J. L., *Schillers Rebellionskonzept und die französische Revolution* (Lewiston, NY, 2004).

Himmelfarb, G., 'Two Enlightenments: A Contrast in Social Ethics', *Proceedings of the British Academy*, 117 (2001), 297–324.

—— *Roads to Modernity* (New York, 2004).

Hinske, Norbert, 'Kant im Auf und Ab der katholischen Kantrezeption: Zu den Anfängen des katholischen Frühkantianismus und seinen philosophischen Impulsen', in Fischer (ed.), *Kant und der Katholizismus*, 189–205.

—— 'Andreas Metz (1767–1839): Zur Kontinuität des katholischen Frühkantianismus', in Fischer (ed.), *Kant und der Katholizismus*, 303–14.

Hobohm, Hans-Christoph, 'Le Progrès de l'*Encyclopédie*: la censure face au discours encyclopédique', in Mass and Knabe (eds.), *L'Encyclopédie*, 69–96.

Höffe, Otfried, *Kant's Cosmopolitan Theory of Law and Peace* (2001; English trans. Cambridge, 2003).

Holenstein, A., Maissen, Th., and Praak, M. (eds.), *The Republican Alternative: The Netherlands and Switzerland Compared* (Amsterdam, 2008).

Holm, Edvard, *Nogle hovedtraek af Trykkefrihedstidens historie, 1770–1773* (Copenhagen, 1888).

Holmes, R., *Coleridge: Early Visions* (London, 1989).

Hont, Istvan, *Jealousy of Trade* (Cambridge, Mass., 2005).

Hope, Nicholas, *German and Scandinavian Protestantism 1700 to 1918* (Oxford, 1995).

Hope Mason, John, 'Materialism and History: Diderot and the *Histoire des deux Indes*', *European Review of History*, 3 (1996), 151–60.

—— 'Portrait de l'auteur accompagné d'un fantôme: *L'Essai sur les règnes de Claude et de Néron*', in France and Strugnell (eds.), *Diderot*, 43–61.

Horkheimer, Max, and Adorno, Theodor W., *Dialectic of Enlightenment* (New York, 2000).

Horowitz, I. L., *Claude Helvétius: Philosopher of Democracy and Enlightenment* (New York, 1954).

Hösle, Vittorio, 'Philosophy and the Interpretation of the Bible', *Internationale Zeitschrift für Philosophie*, 2 (1992), 181–210.

—— *Philosophiegeschichte und objektiver Idealismus* (Munich, 1996).

—— *Objective Idealism, Ethics and Politics* (Notre Dame, Ind., 1998).

—— *Morals and Politics* (Notre Dame, Ind., 2004).

—— 'Religion of Art, Self-Mythicization and the Function of the Church Year in Goethe's *Italienische Reise*', *Religion and Literature*, 38 (2006), 1–25.

Houtman-De Smedt, H., 'Het prinsbisdom luik, 1581–1787', in Ivo Schöffer et al. (eds.), *De Lage Landen van 1500 tot 1780* (1978; Amsterdam, 1991), 409–24.

Hsia, Adrian, 'Euro-Sinica: The Past and Future', *TJEAS* 1 (2004), 17–58.

Hubatsch, Walther, *Frederick the Great: Absolutism and Administration* (London, 1973).

Hufton, O., *Europe: Privilege and Protest (1730–1789)* (1980; Oxford, repr. 2000).

Hull, I. V., *Sexuality, State and Civil Society in Germany, 1700–1815* (Ithaca, NY, 1996).

Hulliung, M., *The Autocritique of Enlightenment: Rousseau and the* Philosophes (Cambridge, Mass., 1994).

Hüning, Dieter, 'Die Grenzen der Toleranz und die Rechtsstellung der Atheisten', in L. Danneberg et al. (eds.), *Säkularisierung in den Wissenschaften seit der Frühen Neuzeit*, ii (Berlin, 2002), 219–73.

HUNT, LYNN, *Politics, Culture and Class in the French Revolution* (Berkeley and Los Angeles, 1984).

—— *Inventing Human Rights: A History* (New York, 2007).

——JACOB, M. C., and MIJNHARDT, W., *The Book that Changed Europe: Picart and Bernard's Religious Ceremonies of the World* (Cambridge, Mass., 2010).

HUNTER, IAN, 'Kant's Religion and Prussian Religious Policy', *Modern Intellectual History*, 2 (2005), 1–27.

—— *The Secularisation of the Confessional State: The Political Thought of Christian Thomasius* (Cambridge, 2007).

HUTCHINGS, K., *Kant, Critique and Politics* (London, 1996).

IBRAHIM, ANNIE, *Diderot: Un matérialiste éclectique* (Paris, 2010).

IHDE, A. J., 'Priestley and Lavoisier', in E. N. Hiebert et al. (eds.), *Joseph Priestley: Scientist, Theologian, and Metaphysician* (London, 1980), 62–91.

IMBRUGLIA, GIROLAMO, *L'Invenzione del Paraguay* (Naples, 1983).

—— 'Two Principles of Despotism', *History of European Ideas*, 34 (2008), 490–9.

—— 'Due opposte letture napoletane dell'*Esprit des lois*', in D. Felice (ed.), *Montesquieu e i suoi interpreti* (2 vols., Pisa, 2005), i. 191–210.

—— 'Indignation et droits de l'homme chez le dernier Diderot', in G. Goggi and D. Kahn (eds.), *L'Édition du dernier Diderot* (Paris, 2007), 125–76.

—— 'Enlightenment in Eighteenth-Century Naples', in Imbruglia (ed.), *Naples*, 70–94.

—— 'Utopia e repubblicanesimo: un'opposizione illuministica', in Albertone (ed.), *Repubblicanesimo moderno*, 347–68.

—— 'Diderot storico e la Spagna di fine Settecento', in D. Balani et al. (eds.), *Dall'origine dei Lumi alla Rivoluzione: scritti in onore di Luciano Guerci e Giuseppe Ricuperati* (Rome, 2008), 227–44.

—— 'Piacere e dolore', in Paganini and Tortarolo (eds.), *Illuminismo*, 168–81.

—— (ed.), *Naples in the Eighteenth Century* (Cambridge, 2000).

IRMSCHER, HANS DIETRICH, 'Goethe und Herder—eine schwierige Freundschaft', in M. Kessler and V. Leppin (eds.), *Johann Gottfried Herder: Aspekte seines Lebenswerkes* (Berlin, 2005), 233–70.

IRVINE, D. D., 'The Abbé Raynal and British Humanitarianism', *JMH* 3 (1931), 564–77.

ISRAEL, JONATHAN I., *Race, Class and Politics in Colonial Mexico 1610–1670* (Oxford, 1975).

—— *Dutch Primacy in World Trade, 1585–1740* (Oxford, 1989).

—— *The Dutch Republic: Its Rise, Greatness and Fall, 1477–1806* (Oxford, 1995).

—— *Conflicts of Empires* (London, 1997).

—— *European Jewry in the Age of Mercantilism, 1550–1750* (1985; new edn., London, 1998).

—— *Radical Enlightenment: Philosophy and the Making of Modernity* (Oxford, 2001).

—— *Diasporas within a Diaspora: Jews, Crypto-Jews and the World Maritime Empires (1540–1740)* (Leiden, 2002).

—— 'Meyer, Koerbagh and the Radical Enlightenment Critique of Socinianism', *GWN* (2003), 197–210.

—— 'The Intellectual Origins of Modern Democratic Republicanism (1660–1720)', *European Journal of Political Theory*, 3 (2004), 7–36.

—— *Enlightenment Contested: Philosophy, Modernity and the Emancipation of Man 1670–1752* (Oxford, 2006).

—— 'Gerrit Paape, "wijsbegeerte", en de "Algemene Revolutie" van de mensheid', *Parmentier*, 16 (2007), 13–22.

—— 'Admiration of China and Classsical Chinese Thought in the Radical Enlightenment', *TJEAS* 4 (2007), 1–26.

—— '"Failed Enlightenment": Spinoza's Legacy and the Netherlands (1670–1800)', KB Lecture 4 (Wassnaar, NIAS, 2007).

—— 'Bayle's Double Image during the Enlightenment', in Wiep van Bunge and H. Bots (eds.), *Pierre Bayle (1647–1706), le philosophe de Rotterdam* (Leiden, 2008), 135–51.

—— 'French Royal Censorship and the Battle to Suppress the Encyclopédie of Diderot and d'Alembert, 1751–1759', in Laerke (ed.), *Use of Censorship* (Leiden, 2009), 61–74.

—— 'Equality and Inequality in the Late Enlightenment', *De Achttiende-Eeuw*, 41 (2009), 5–22.

—— 'Les "Antiphilosophes" et la diffusion de la philosophie clandestine dans la seconde moitié du XVIIIe siècle', *La Lettre clandestine*, 17 (2009), 73–88.

—— 'Toleration, Spinoza's "Realism" and Patriot Modernity', *De Achttiende Eeuw*, 41 (2009), 159–66.

—— 'Democracy and Equality in the Radical Enlightenment: Revolutionary Ideology before 1789', in Albertone and de Francesco (eds.), *Rethinking*, 46–60.

—— *A Revolution of the Mind: Radical Enlightenment and the Intellectual Origins of Modern Democracy* (Princeton, 2010).

JACKSON, M., 'Anthony Benezet', in Rhoden and Steele (eds.), *Human Tradition*.

JACOB, MARGARET, *Living the Enlightenment: Freemasonry and Politics in Eighteenth-Century Europe* (New York, 1991).

—— *Strangers Nowhere in the World: The Rise of Cosmopolitanism in Early Modern Europe* (Philadelphia, 2006).

—— and MIJNHARDT, WIJNAND (eds.), *The Dutch Republic in the Eighteenth Century* (Ithaca, NY, 1992).

JACOB, OTTO, 'Karl Friedrich Bahrdt im Wandel des Urteils', in Donnert (ed.), *Europa*, ii. 421–30.

JACOBITTI, EDMUND, *Revolutionary Humanism and Historicism in Modern Italy* (New Haven, 1981).

JACOBS, E. M., *Koopman in Azië: De handel van de Verenigde Oost-Indische Compagnie tijdens de 18de eeuw* (Zutphen, 2000).

JACOBY, SUSAN, *Freethinkers: A History of American Secularism* (New York, 2004).

JARRICK, ARNE, *Back to Modern Reason* (1992; Liverpool, 1999).

JAYNE, A., *Jefferson's Declaration of Independence: Origins, Philosophy and Theology* (Lexington, Kan., 1998).

JAYNES, J., and WOODWARD, W., 'In the Shadow of the Enlightenment: Reimarus and his Theory of Drives', *Journal of the History of the Behavioural Sciences*, 10 (1974), 144–59.

JEN-GUO S., CHEN, 'Providence and Progress: The Religious Dimension in Adam Ferguson's Discussion of Civil Society', in Heath and Merolle (eds.), *Adam Ferguson*, 171–86.

JESPERSEN, K. J. V., 'The Rise and Fall of the Danish Nobility, 1600–1800', in H. M. Scott (ed.), *The European Nobilities in the Seventeenth and Eighteenth Centuries*, ii (1995; 2nd edn., 2007), 43–71.

JIMACK, P., 'Obéissance à la loi et révolution dans les dernières œuvres de Diderot', in France and Strugnell (eds.), *Diderot*, 153–68.

—— 'The French Enlightenment 1: Science, Materialism and Determinism', in S. Brown (ed.), *British Philosophy and the Age of Enlightenment* (London, 1996), 228–50.

JOARY, JEAN-PAUL, *Diderot et la matière vivante* (Paris, 1992).

JOHNS, A. (ed.), *Dreadful Visitations: Confronting Natural Catastrophe in the Age of Enlightenment* (New York, 1999).

JOHNSON, H. C., *The Midi in Revolution: A Study of Regional Political Diversity, 1789–1793* (Princeton, 1986).

JOLLEY, NICHOLAS, *Locke: His Philosophical Thought* (Oxford, 1999).

JONARD, N., *L'Italie des Lumières* (Paris, 1996).

JONES, COLIN, *The Great Nation* (New York, 2002).

JOURDAN, A., 'Le Culte de Rousseau sous la Révolution', in L'Aminot (ed.), *Politique et révolution*, 57–77.

JÜRGENS, HANCO, 'Welke Verlichting? Tijdaanduidingen en plaatsbepalingen van een begrip', *De Achttiende Eeuw*, 35 (2003), 28–53.

—— 'Contesting *Enlightenment Contested*: Some Questions', *De Achttiende Eeuw*, 39 (2007), 52–71.

KAFKER, F. A., and KAFKER, S. L., *The Encyclopedists as Individuals* (Oxford, 2006).

KAITARO, TIMO, *Diderot's Holism* (Frankfurt, 1997).

KAMMEN, M., *Colonial New York: A History* (New York, 1975).

KANN, R. A., *A Study in Austrian Intellectual History* (London, 1960).

KANTA RAY, R., 'Indian Society and the Establishment of British Supremacy, 1765–1818', *OHBE* ii. 508–29.

KAPOSSY, BELA, 'Neo-Roman Republicanism and Commercial Society: The Example of Eighteenth-Century Berne', in Van Gelderen and Skinner (eds.), *Republicanism*, ii. 227–47.

KARTHAUS, U., 'Schiller und die Französische Revolution', *Jahrbuch der deutschen Schiller–Gesellschaft*, 32 (1989), 210–39.

KATES, G., *The Cercle Social, the Girondins and the French Revolution* (Princeton, 1985).

KEANE, JOHN, *Tom Paine: A Political Life* (1995; new edn. London, 1996).

KEMPSKI, JÜRGEN VON, 'Hermann Samuel Reimarus als Ethologe', in Hermann Samuel Reimarus, *Allgemeine Betrachtungen über die Triebe der Thiere* (Göttingen, 1982), i. 21–56.

—— 'Spinoza, Reimarus, Bruno Bauer: Drei Paradigmen radikaler Bibelkritik', in *Hermann Samuel Reimarus (1694–1768): Ein 'bekannter Unbekannter' der Aufklärung in Hamburg* (Göttingen, 1973), 96–112.

KENDRICK, T. D., *The Lisbon Earthquake* (London, 1956).

KENNEDY, E., *A Cultural History of the French Revolution* (New Haven, 1989).

—— *Secularism and its Opponents from Augustine to Solzhenitsyn* (New York, 2006).

KERRY, PAUL, *Enlightenment Thought in the Writings of Goethe* (Rochester, NY, 2001).

KERSTING, W., 'Politics, Freedom and Order: Kant's Political Philosophy', in Guyer (ed.), *Cambridge Companion to Kant*, 342–66.

KIDD, COLIN, 'Constitutions and Character in the Eighteenth-Century British World', in P. M. Kitromilides (ed.), *From Republican Polity to National Community* (Oxford, 2003), 40–61.

KIEFFER, JEAN-LUC, *Anquetil-Duperron: L'Inde en France au XVIIIe siècle* (Paris, 1983).

KITROMILIDES, P. M., 'The Enlightenment and the Greek Cultural Tradition', *HEI* 36 (2002), 39–46.

—— *An Orthodox Commonwealth* (Aldershot, 2007).

KLEIN, S. R. E., *Patriots republikanisme: Politieke cultuur in Nederland (1766–1787)* (Amsterdam, 1995).

KLEMME, H. F., 'Skepticism and Common Sense', in Broadie (ed.), *Scottish Enlightenment*, 117–35.

KLOEK, JOOST, and WIJNAND, MIJNHARDT, *1800: Blueprints for a National Community* (Assen, 2004).

KNAAP, G. J., 'Slavery and the Dutch in Southeast Asia', in Oostindie (ed.), *Fifty Years Later*, 193–206.

KNOLL, R., *Johann Georg Hamann, 1730–1788: Quellen und Forschungen* (Bonn, 1988).

KNUDSEN, J. B., *Justus Möser and the German Enlightenment* (Cambridge, 1986).

KNUTTEL, W. P. C., *Verboden boeken in de Republiek der Verenigde Nederlanden* (The Hague, 1914).

KOBUCH, A., *Zensur und Aufklärung in Kursachsen* (Weimar, 1988).

KOCH, G. ADOLF, *Religion of the American Enlightenment* (1933; new edn., New York, 1968).

KOERNER, L., *Linnaeus: Nature and Nation* (Cambridge, Mass., 1999).

KOHUT, KARL, and ROSE, S. V. (eds.), *La formación de la cultura virreinal*, iii: *El siglo XVIII* (Madrid, 2006).

KÖLVING, U., and MERVAUD, CH. (eds.), *Voltaire et ses combats* (2 vols., Oxford, 1997).

KÖNIG, HANS-JOACHIM, 'La rebelión de los Comuneros de Nueva Granada en 1780/1 y la formación de un orgullo proprio neogranadino', in Kohut and Rose (eds.), *Formación*, 255–72.

KONTLER, L., 'What is the (Historians') Enlightenment Today?', *European Review of History*, 13 (2006), 357–71.

KOPITZSCH, F., 'Altona—ein Zentrum der Aufklärung am Rande des dänischen Gesamtstaats', in K. Bohnen and S. A. Jorgensen (eds.), *Der dänische Gesamtstaat* (Tübingen, 1992), 91–118.

KORS, ALAN, *Atheism in France, 1650–1729*, vol. i (Princeton, 1990).

—— 'Skepticism and the Problem of Atheism in Early-Modern France', in G. Paganini et al. (eds.), *Scepticisme, clandestinité et libre pensée* (Paris, 2002), 47–65.

—— (ed.), *Encyclopedia of the Enlightenment* (4 vols., Oxford, 2003).

KOSEKI, T., 'Diderot et le Confucianisme', *RDE* 16 (1994), 125–31.

KOSSMANN, E. H., *De Lage Landen 1780–1980* (2 vols., Amsterdam, 1986).

—— '1787: The Collapse of the Patriot Movement and the Problem of Dutch Decline', The Creighton Trust Lecture 1987 (London, 1987).

KRAGH, HELGE, *Natur, Nytte og Ånd, 1730–1850* (Aarhus, 2005).

KRAUSE, SHARON, 'History and the Human Soul in Montesquieu', *HPTh* 24 (2033), 235–61.

—— 'Despotism in the *Spirit of the Laws*', in D. W. Carrithers et al. (eds.), *Montesquieu's Science of Politics* (Lanham, Md., 2001), 231–71.

KREBS, ROLAND, 'Le "Deutsches Museum" et l'Indépendance américaine', in R. Krebs and J. Moes (eds.), *La Révolution américaine vue par les périodiques de langue allemande (1773–1783)* (Paris, 1992), 1–21.

—— *Helvétius et l'Allemagne ou la tentation du matérialisme* (Paris, 2006).

KROP, HENRI, 'A Dutch *Spinozismusstreit*: The New View of Spinoza at the End of the Eighteenth Century', *LIAS* 32 (2005), 185–211.

KUEHN, MANFRED, *Kant: A Biography* (Cambridge, 2001).

—— *Scottish Common Sense in Germany, 1768–1800* (Montreal, 1987).

KUKLICK, B., *A History of Philosophy in America, 1720–2000* (Oxford, 2001).

LABBÉ, FRANÇOIS, *La Gazette littéraire de Berlin (1764–1792)* (Paris, 2004).

—— *Anarcharsis Cloots, le Prussien francophile* (Paris, 1999).

LADD, E. C., 'Helvétius and d'Holbach: 'La Moralisation de la politique', *JHI* 23 (1962), 221–38.

LAERKE, M., 'Introduction' to M. Laerke (ed.), *The Use of Censorship in the Enlightenment* (Leiden, 2009), 1–21.

LAERKE, M., *Leibniz lecteur de Spinoza: la genèse d'une opposition complexe* (Paris, 2008).

LAFARGA, FRANCISCO, *Voltaire en España (1734–1835)* (Barcelona, 1982).

LAFRANCE, G., 'Idée rousseauiste du droit et le discours Jacobin', in R. Thiéry (ed.), *Rousseau, l''Émile' et la Révolution* (Paris, 1992), 27–36.

LAGIER, RAPHAEL, *Les Races humaines selon Kant* (Paris, 2004).

LA GORCE, PIERRE DE, *Histoire religieuse de la Révolution française* (1912; 5 vols, New York, 1969).

LAGRAVE, JEAN-PAUL DE, *Fleury-Mesplet (1734–1794)* (Montreal, 1985).

LAMB, ROBERT, 'Labour, Contingency, Utility', in Steve Poole (ed.), *John Thelwall: Radical Romantic and Acquitted Felon* (London, 2009), 51–60.

LAMBERT, F., *The Founding Fathers and the Place of Religion in America* (Princeton, 2003).

L'AMINOT, TANGUY, *Politique et révolution chez Jean-Jacques Rousseau*, SVEC 324 (Oxford, 1994).

LANG, D. M., *The First Russian Radical: Alexander Radishchev (1749–1802)* (London, 1959).

LANGFORD, PAUL, *A Polite and Commercial People: England, 1727–1783* (Oxford, 1989).

LAQUEUR, THOMAS, *Solitary Sex: A Cultural History of Masturbation* (New York, 2004).

LARRÈRE, C., 'L'Esprit des lois, tradition et modernité', in Larrère and Volpilhac-Auger (eds.), *1748, l'année*, 141–60.

—— 'Diderot et l'atomisme', in J. Salem (ed.), *L'Atomisme aux XVIIe et XVIIIe siècles* (Paris, 1999), 151–65.

—— 'D'Alembert and Diderot: les mathématiques contre la nature?', *Corpus*, 38 (2001), 75–94.

—— and Volpilhac-Auger, C. (eds.), *1748, l'année de l'Esprit des lois* (Paris, 1999).

LARSEN, S. E., 'The Lisbon Earthquake and the Scientific Turn in Kant's Philosophy', *European Review*, 14 (2006), 359–67.

LASCOUMES, P., 'Beccaria et la formulation d'un ordre public moderne', in Porret (ed.), *Beccaria*, 109–17.

LAUERMANN, M., and SCHRÖDER, M. B., 'Textgrundlagen der deutschen Spinoza-Rezeption im 18. Jahrhundert', in Schürmann et al. (eds.), *Spinoza im Deutschland*, 39–83.

LAURSEN, J. CH., 'Spinoza in Denmark and the Fall of Struensee, 1770–1772', *JHI* 61 (2000), 189–202.

—— 'Censorship in the Nordic Countries, c.1750–1890', *JMEH* 3 (2005), 100–16.

—— *The Politics of Skepticism in the Ancients: Montaigne, Hume and Kant* (Leiden, 1992).

—— and van der Zande, J., 'Introduction' to *Early French and German Defenses of Freedom of the Press* (Leiden, 2003).

LA VOPA, A. J, 'Conceiving a Public: Ideas and Society in Eighteenth-Century Europe', *JMH* 64 (1992), 79–116.

—— 'A New Intellectual History? Jonathan Israel's Enlightenment', *Historical Journal*, 52 (2009), 717–38.

—— *Fichte: The Self and the Calling of Philosophy, 1762–1799* (Cambridge, 2001).

LECA-TSIOMIS, M., *Écrire l'*Encyclopédie: *Diderot: de l'usage des dictionnaires à la grammaire philosophique* (Oxford, 1999).

LEDDY, N., 'ADAM SMITH'S Critique of Enlightenment Epicureanism', in B. Leddy and A. S. Livshitz (eds.), *Epicurus in the Enlightenment* (Oxford, 2009), 183–205.

LEE, THOMAS H. C., 'Post-modernist/Post-colonialist Nationalism and the Historiography of China', *TJEAS* (2004), 89–118.

Leeb, I. L., *The Ideological Origins of the Batavian Revolution* (The Hague, 1973).

Lehmann, W. C., *Henry Home, Lord Kames* (The Hague, 1971).

Lehner, Ulrich, *Kants Vorsehungskonzept auf dem Hintergrund der deutschen Schulphilosophie und -Theologie* (Leiden, 2007).

Leigh, Ralph, 'Le "Contrat Social": œuvre genevoise?', *Annales de la Société Jean-Jacques Rousseau*, 39 (1972/7), 93–111.

Lepape, Pierre, *Diderot* (Paris, 1991).

Lequin, F., *Isaac Titsingh (1745–1812)* (Alphen aan den Rijn, 2002).

Lerner, M. H., 'Radical Elements and Attempted Revolutions in Late-18th-Century Republics', in Holenstein et al. (eds.), *Republican Alternative*, 301–20.

Leroux, Serge, 'Un Dieu rémunérateur et vengeur comme fondement-garantie de la morale', in Kölving and Mervaud (eds.), *Voltaire et ses combats*, i. 739–50.

Le Ru, Véronique, *D'Alembert philosophe* (Paris, 1994).

—— 'L'Aigle à deux têtes de l'*Encyclopédie*: accords et divergences de Diderot et de d'Alembert de 1751 à 1759', *RDE* 26 (1999), 17–26.

Lilti, Antoine, *Le Monde des salons: sociabilité et mondanité à Paris au XVIIIe siècle* (Paris, 2005).

—— 'Sociabilité et mondanité', *FHS* 28 (2005), 415–45.

—— 'Comment écrit-on l'histoire intellectuelle des Lumières?', *Annales*, 64 (2009), 171–206.

Linton, M., 'The Intellectual Origins of the French Revolution', in Campbell (ed.), *Origins*, 139–59.

—— *The Politics of Virtue in Enlightenment France* (Basingstoke, 2001).

Lion, Henri, 'L'Éthocratie de d'Holbach', *Annales révolutionnaires*, 15 (1923), 378–96.

Livesey, James, *Making Democracy in the French Revolution* (Cambridge, Mass., 2001).

Loayza Valda, J., 'La Revolución en Charcas y la Universidad de San Francisco Xavier de Chuquisaca', in *Bicentenario del primer grito de libertad en Hispanoamérica, 25 de Mayo 1809* (Sucre, 2009), 121–30.

Loche, Annamaria, 'Motivi politici ne "La Nouvelle Héloise" di Jean-Jacques Rousseau', *GCFI* 89 (2010), 234–59.

Lock, F. P., *Edmund Burke* (2 vols., Oxford, 1998, 2006).

Locke, D., *A Fantasy of Reason: The Life and Thought of William Godwin* (London, 1980).

Loft, L., 'J.-P. Brissot and the Problem of Jewish Emancipation', *SVEC* 278 (1990), 465–75.

Lomonaco, Fabrizio, 'Barbeyrac e Voltaire dalla virtù della tolleranza al ciritto di libertà religiosa', *Logos* (Università degli Studi di Napoli Federico II), 2/3 (2007/8), 73–93.

Loos, Waltraud, 'Politik und Gesellschaft im Urteil Hemsterhuis in seinen Briefen an Amalia von Gallitzin (1786–1790)', in Fresco et al. (eds.), *Frans Hemsterhuis*, 445–69.

Lortholary, A., *Le Mirage russe en France au XVIIIe siècle* (Paris, 1951).

Lough, John, 'Helvétius and d'Holbach', *Modern Language Review*, 33 (1938), 360–84.

—— *Essays on the* Encyclopédie *of Diderot and d'Alembert* (London, 1968).

Louth, Ch., 'Coleridge und Friedrich Schlegel als Lessing-Leser', in K. Feilchenfeldt et al. (eds.), *Zwischen Aufklärung und Romantik* (Würzburg, 2006), 150–64.

Lucas, Colin (ed.), *The Political Culture of the French Revolution* (Oxford, 1988).

Luciani, Paola, 'Les Répercussions de la propagande philosophique des tragédies de Voltaire en Italie: Mahomet', in Kölving and Mervaud (eds.), *Voltaire et ses combats*, ii. 1501–12.

Luebke, F. C., 'The Origins of Thomas Jefferson's Anti-Clericalism', *Church History*, 30 (1963), 344–56.

LÜSEBRINK, HANS-JÜRGEN, 'Zur Verhüllung und sukzessiven Aufdeckung der Autorschaft Diderots an der *Histoire des deux Indes*', in Heydenreich (ed.), *Denis Diderot*, 107–26.

—— 'Aufgeklärter Humanismus: Philosophisches Engagement am Beispiel der Kontroverse über die "Menschenrassen"', in R. Reichardt and G. Roche (eds.), *Weltbürger, Europäer, Deutscher, Franke: Georg Forster zum 200. Todestag* (Mainz, 1994), 188–95.

—— 'Zensur, Exil und Autoidentität (Diderot, Raynal)', in W. Haefs and Y. G. Mix (eds.), *Zensur im Jahrhundert der Aufklärung* (Göttingen, 2007), 145–56.

—— and Reichardt, R., *The Bastille: A History of a Symbol of Despotism and Freedom* (Durham, NC, 1997).

—— and Tietz, M. (eds.), *Lectures de Raynal: L'Histoire des deux Indes en Europe et en Amérique au XVIIIe siècle* (Oxford, 1991), 205–33.

LUSSU, MARIA LUISA, *Bayle, Holbach e il dibattito sull'ateo virtuoso* (Genoa, 1997).

LUTTRELL, B., *Mirabeau* (Carbondale, Ill., 1990).

LYNCH, A. J., 'Montesquieu and the Ecclesiastical Critics of *l'Esprit des lois*', *JHI* 38 (1977), 487–500.

LYNCH, JOHN, 'Francisco de Miranda: The London Years', in J. Maher (ed.), *Francisco de Miranda: Exile and Enlightenment* (London, 2006).

McCONNELL, ALLEN, *A Russian Philosophe Alexander Radischev (1749–1802)* (The Hague, 1964).

MACÉ, L., 'Les Lumières françaises au tribunal de l'Index et du Saint-Office', *DHS* 34 (2002), 13–25.

McFARLANE, ANTHONY, 'Civil Disorders and Popular Protest in Late Colonial New Granada', *HAHR* 64 (1984), 17–54.

—— 'The American Revolution and the Spanish Monarchy', in S. P. Newman (ed.), *Europe's American Revolution* (Basingstoke, 2006), 26–50.

—— 'Science and Sedition in Spanish America: New Granada in the Age of Revolution, 1776–1810', in S. Manning and P. France (eds.), *Enlightenment and Emancipation* (Cranbury, NJ, 2006), 97–117.

McINTOSH, CHRISTOPHER, *The Rose Cross and the Age of Reason* (Leiden, 1992).

McKENNA, A., 'Recherches sur la philosophie clandestine à l'Âge Classique', in McKenna and Mothu (eds.), *La Philosophie clandestine*, 3–14.

—— and Mothu, Alain (eds.), *La Philosophie clandestine à l'Âge Classique* (Paris, 1997).

MACKRELL, J. Q. C., *The Attack on 'Feudalism' in Eighteenth-Century France* (London, 1973).

MACLEAN, J., 'The Introduction of Books and Scientific Instruments into Japan, 1712–1854', *Japanese Studies in the History of Science*, 13 (1974), 9–68.

McMAHON, D. M., *Enemies of the Enlightenment* (Oxford, 2001).

McMANNERS, J., *Church and Society in Eighteenth-Century France* (2 vols., Oxford, 1998).

MADARIAGA, ISABEL DE, *Catherine the Great* (New Haven, 1990).

MAGRIN, GABRIELE, 'Confutare Montesquieu: la critica di Condorcet', in D. Felice (ed.), *Montesquieu e i suoi interpreti* (2 vols., Pisa, 2005), i. 377–411.

MAIOLANI, D., 'Mably e il repubblicanesimo dei lumi', *Il pensiero politico*, 34 (2001), 73–94.

MAIRE, C., *De la cause de Dieu à la cause de la nation: le Jansénisme au XVIIIe siècle* (Paris, 1998).

—— 'L'Entrée des "Lumières" à l'Index', *RDE* 42 (2007), 108–35.

MAISSEN, THOMAS, *Die Geburt der Republic* (Göttingen, 2006).

MAKREEL, R. A., 'Aesthetics', *CHEPh* i. 516–56.

MALANDAIN, PIERRE, *Delisle de Sales, philosophe de la nature (1741–1816)* (2 vols., Oxford, 1982).

MALHERBE, M., 'Introduction' to Condillac, *Traité des animaux*, 7–106.

MALLINSON, JONATHAN, 'Introduction' to Graffigny, *Lettres*, 1–92.

MANKIN, R., 'Hume et les races humaines', *Corpus*, 57 (2009), 75–100.

MANUEL, F. A., *The Prophets of Paris* (Cambridge, Mass., 1962).

MANUEL, F. E., and Manuel, F. P., *Utopian Thought in the Western World* (Oxford, 1979).

MARCHENA FERNÁNDEZ, Juan, *El tiempo illustrado de Pablo de Olavide* (Seville, 2001).

MARKS, P., *Deconstructing Legitimacy: Viceroys, Merchants and the Military in Late Colonial Peru* (University Park, Pa., 2007).

MARKWORTH, T., *Unsterblichkeit und Identität beim frühen Herder* (Paderborn, 2005).

MARRESE, M. L., 'Liberty Postponed: Princess Dashkova and the Defense of Serfdom', *Transactions of the American Philosophical Society, Humanities* (2006), 23–38.

MARSDEN, GEORGE, *Jonathan Edwards: A Life* (New Haven, 2003).

MARSHALL, P. J., 'The Place of the Seven Years War (1756–63) in the Changing Balance between Britain and the Netherlands in Asia', *Tijdschrift voor zeegeschiedenis*, 20 (2001), 15–23.

—— 'Britain Without America: A Second Empire?', in *OHBE* ii. 576–95.

—— (ed.), *The Eighteenth Century in Indian History* (2003; New Delhi, repr. 2005).

MARTIN-HAAG, E., *Un aspect de la pensée politique de Diderot* (Paris, 1999).

—— *Voltaire: Du Cartésianisme aux Lumières* (Paris, 2002).

MARTINO, ARMANDO DE, *Tra legislatori e interpreti: saggio di storia delle idee giuridiche in Italia meridionale* (Naples, 1979).

MARTINSON, S. D., 'Lessing and the European Enlightenment', in I. B. Fischer and Th. C. Fox (eds.), *A Companion to the Works of Gotthold Ephraim Lessing* (Rochester, NY, 2005), 41–63.

MARX, KARL, *Notes on Indian History (664–1858)* (Moscow, 1947).

MAS GALVAN, CAYETANO, 'Jansenismo y regalismo en el seminario de San Fulgencio de Murcia', *Anales de la Universidad de Alicante: historia moderna*, 2 (1982), 261–74.

MASS, E., and KNABE, P. E. (eds.), *L'Encyclopédie et Diderot* (Cologne, 1985).

MASSEAU, D., *Les Ennemis des philosophes: l'antiphilosophie au temps des Lumières* (Paris, 2000).

MASTELLONE, SALVO, 'Italian Enlightenment and the Swedish Constitution during the Age of Liberty (1719–1772)', in N. Stjernquist (ed.), *The Swedish Riksdag in an International Perspective* (Stockholm, 1989), 112–17.

MATICORENA ESTRADA, M. (ed.), *Colección documental de la Independencia del Peru*, 1: *Los ideologos*, vol. iii: *Jose Baquijano y Carillo* (Lima, 1976).

MATTHEY, CHRISTINE, 'L'Ombre et les Lumières: une vision française de l'Espagne au XVIIIe siècle', *DHS* 40 (2008), 413–30.

MAUZI, R., *L'Idée du bonheur au XVIIIe siècle* (4th edn., Paris, 1969).

MAXWELL, KENNETH, *Essays on Empire and Other Rogues* (London, 2003).

—— 'Pombal, the Paradox of the Enlightenment and Despotism', in H. M. Scott (ed.), *Enlightened Absolutism* (Basingstoke, 1990), 75–118.

MAY, GITA, *Madame Roland and the Age of Revolution* (New York, 1970).

MAY, H. F., *The Enlightenment in America* (1976; new edn., New York, 1978).

—— *The Divided Heart: Essays on Protestantism and the Enlightenment in America* (New York, 1991).

MAZZA, E., 'Hume's "Meek" Philosophy among the Milanese', in Frasca-Spada and Kail (eds.), *Impressions*, 213–43.

MÉCHOULAN, HENRY, POPKIN, R. H., RICUPERATI, G., and SIMONUTTI, L. (eds.), *La formazione storica della alterità: studi di storia della tolleranza nell'età moderna offerti a Antonio Rotondò* (3 vols., Florence, 2001).

MEISSNER, JOCHEN, *Eine Elite im Umbruch: Die Stadtrat von Mexico zwischen kolonialer Ordnung und unabhängigem Staat* (Stuttgart, 1993).

MELAMED, Y., 'Salomon Maimon and the Rise of Spinozism in German Idealism', *JHPh* 42 (2004), 67–96.

MELICA, CLAUDIA (ed.), *Hemsterhuis: A European Philosopher Rediscovered* (Naples, 2005).

MENANT, S., 'Les Relations de Voltaire avec la Russie', in Poussou et al. (eds.), *L'Influence*, 209–15.

MERZ-HORN, S., *Georg Forster (1754–1794): Die Kasseler Jahre* (Kassel, 1984).

MESTRE SANCHIS, ANTONIO, *La Ilustración española* (Madrid, 1998).

—— *Apología crítica de España en el siglo XVIII* (Madrid, 2003).

METCALF, TH. R., *Ideologies of the Raj* (Cambridge, 1995).

MEYNELL, H. A., *Postmodernism and the New Enlightenment* (Washington, DC, 1999).

MICHAEL, M., 'Locke, Religious Toleration and the Limits of Social Contract Theory', *History of Philosophy Quarterly*, 20 (2003), 21–40.

MIDDELFORT, H. C. E., *Exorcism and Enlightenment* (New Haven, 2005).

MIHAILA, I., 'L'*Hylozoïsme* de Diderot', in Fink and Stenger (eds.), *Être matérialiste*, 185–97.

MIJNHARDT, WIJNAND, *Tot heil van't Menschdom: culturele genootschappen in Nederland, 1750–1800* (Amsterdam, 1987).

—— 'The Dutch Enlightenment', in Jacob and Mijnhardt (eds.), *Dutch Republic*, 197–223.

—— *Over de moderniteit van de Nederlandse Republiek* (Utrecht, 2001).

—— 'The Construction of Silence: Religious and Political Radicalism in Dutch History', in Wiep Van Bunge (ed.), *The Early Enlightenment in the Dutch Republic, 1650–1750* (Leiden, 2003), 231–62.

—— 'Urbanization, Culture and the Dutch Origins of the European Enlightenment', *BMGN* 125 (2010), 141–77.

MILLER, JAMES, *Rousseau: Dreamer of Democracy* (New Haven, 1984).

MILTON, J. R. (ed.), *Locke's Moral, Political and Legal Philosophy* (Aldershot, 1999).

MOENKEMEYER, H., *François Hemsterhuis* (Boston, 1975).

MOKYR, JOEL, *Industrialization in the Low Countries, 1795–1850* (New Haven, 1976).

MONDOT, JEAN, 'La Réception de Raynal en Allemagne: L'Exemple de Wekhrlin', in Lüsebrink and Tietz (eds.), *Lectures de Raynal*, 189–204.

—— 'Wekhrlin et la Révolution d'Amérique', in Krebs and Moes (eds.), *Révolution américaine*, 125–36.

—— *Wilhelm Ludwig Wekhrlin. Un publiciste des Lumières* (2 vols., Bordeaux, 1986).

MONOD, A., *De Pascal à Chateaubriand: les défenseurs français du Christianisme de 1670 à 1802* (1916; New York, 1971).

MONTALENTI, G., 'Spallanzani nella polemica fra vitalisti e meccanisti', in Montalenti and Rossi (eds.), *Lazzaro Spallanzani*, 3–17.

—— and Rossi, P. (eds.), *Lazzaro Spallanzani e la biologia del settecento* (Florence, 1982).

MONTY, J. R., *La Critique littéraire de Melchior Grimm* (Geneva, 1961).

MOORE, JAMES, 'Montesquieu and the Scottish Enlightenment', in R. Kingston (ed.), *Montesquieu and his Legacy* (Albany, NY, 2009), 179–95.

—— Mora de Tovar, Gilma, 'El comercio entre Guatemala y Perú y el debate de las bebidas embriagantes', *Fronteras: revista del Centro de Investigaciones de Historia Colonial*, 1 (1997), 93–113.

Morales Padrón, F., 'México y la independencia de Hispanoamérica en 1781 según un comisionado regio: Francisco de Saavedra', *Revista de Indias*, 29 (1969), 335–58.

Moreau, Pierre François (ed.), *Architectures de la raison* (Paris, 1996).

—— and Thomson, A. (eds.), *Matérialisme et passions* (Lyon, 2004).

Morgan, E. S., 'Ezra Stiles and Timothy Dwight', *Proceedings of the Massachusetts Historical Society*, 72 (1963), 101–17.

Mori, G., 'Einleitung' to [Du Marsais], *Die wahre Religion oder die Religionsprüfung* (Stuttgart, 2003), pp. vii–liii.

—— 'Du Marsais philosophe clandestin', in McKenna and Mothu (eds.), *Philosophie clandestine*, 169–92.

—— *Bayle philosophe* (Paris, 1999).

Morin, Robert, 'Diderot, *l'Encyclopédie* et le *Dictionnaire de Trévoux*', *RDL* 7 (1989), 71–121.

Mornay, D., *Les Origines intellectuelles de la Révolution française (1715–1787)* (1933; 6th edn., Paris, 1967).

Mortier, Roland, *Diderot en Allemagne (1750–1850)* (1954; repr. Geneva, 1986).

—— 'Diderot and Penal Law: Objections to Beccaria', in F. Jost (ed.), *Aesthetics and the Literature of Ideas* (Newark, NJ, 1990), 203–13.

—— *Le Cœur et la raison: recueil d'études sur le dix-huitième siècle* (Oxford, 1990).

—— 'Les Héritiers des "philosophes" devant l'expérience révolutionnaire', in Mortier, *Le Cœur*, 454–66.

—— *Anarcharsis Cloots ou l'utopie foudroyée* (n.p., 1995).

—— *Les Combats des Lumières* (Ferney-Voltaire, 2000).

—— *Lumières du XVIIIe siècle* (Athens, 2003).

—— 'Diversités culturelles: Aufklärung allemande—Lumières françaises', in F. Grunert and F. Vollhardt (eds.), *Aufklärung als praktische Philosophie* (Tübingen, 1998), 21–30.

—— and Trouson, Raymond, *Dictionnaire de Diderot* (Paris, 1999).

Mossner, E. C., *The Life of David Hume* (1954; Oxford, 3rd rev. edn. 2001).

Mothu, Alain, 'L'Édition de 1751 des *Opinions des anciens*', *La Lettre clandestine*, 3 (1994), 45–53.

—— 'Les Vanités manuscrites des esprits forts', *La Lettre clandestine*, 6 (1997), 65–9.

—— 'Un curé "Janséniste" lecteur et concepteur de manuscrits clandestins: Guillaume Maleville', *La Lettre clandestine*, 6 (1997), 25–50.

—— 'Un morceau des plus hardis et des plus philosophiques qui aient été faits dans ce pays-ci', *Corpus*, 44 (2003), 35–56.

Motta, Franco, 'Le condanni inquisitoriali della "Scienza della legislazione"', in Trampus (ed.), *Diritti e costituzione*, 291–335.

Moureau, F., 'Du clandestin et de son bon usage au XVIIIe siècle', *La Lettre clandestine*, 6 (1997), 271–83.

Moyn, Samuel, *The Last Utopia: Human Rights in History* (Cambridge, Mass., 2010).

—— 'Mind the Enlightenment', *The Nation* (posted 12 May 2010).

Mühlpfordt, G., 'Bahrdts Weg zum revolutionären Demokratismus', *Zeitschrift für Geschichtswissenschaft*, 29 (1981), 99–1017.

MÜHLPFORDT, G., 'Europarepublik im Duodezformat: Die internationale Geheimgesellschaft "Union"', in Hemut Reinalter (ed.), *Freimauerer und Geheimbünde im 18. Jahrhundert in Mitteleuropa* (Frankfurt, 1983).

MÜLLER, WINFRIED, *Universität und Orden: Die bayerische Landesuniversität Ingolstadt zwischen der Aufhebung des Jesuitenordens und der Säkularisation (1773–1803)* (Berlin, 1986).

MÜLLER-SEIDEL, W., and RIEDEL, W. (eds.), *Die Weimarer Klassik und ihre Geheimbünde* (Würzburg, 2003).

MULSOW, M., *Moderne aus dem Untergrund: Radikale Frühaufklärung in Deutschland, 1680–1720* (Hamburg, 2002).

—— *Freigeister in Gottsched-Kreis: Wolffianismus, studentische Aktivitäten und Religionskritik in Leipzig, 1740–1745* (Göttingen, 2007).

—— 'Adam Weishaupt als Philosoph', in Müller-Seidel and Riedel (eds.), *Weimarer Klassik*, 27–66.

—— 'Vernünftige Metempsychosis. Über Monadenlehre, Esoterik und geheime Aufklärungs-gesellschaften im 18. Jahrhundert', in M. Neugebauer-Wölk (ed.), *Aufklärung und Esoterik* (Hamburg, 1999), 211–73.

MUNCK, THOMAS, 'The Danish Reformers', in Scott (ed.), *Enlightened Absolutism*, 245–63.

MUTHU, SANKAR, *Enlightenment against Empire* (Princeton, 2003).

NADELHAFT, J. J., *The Disorders of War: The Revolution in South Carolina* (Orono, Me., 1981).

NAQUIN, S., and RAWSKI, E., *Chinese Society in the Eighteenth Century* (New Haven, 1987).

NASH, G. B., 'The American Clergy and the French Revolution', *William and Mary Quarterly*, 3rd ser. 22 (1965), 392–412.

—— *The Unknown American Revolution* (London, 2006).

—— 'International Repercussions and Reconsiderations of the American Revolution', in Armitage and Subrahmanyam (eds.), *Age of Revolutions*, 1–19.

—— and Soderlund, J. R., *Freedom by Degrees: Emancipation in Pennsylvania and its After-math* (New York, 1991).

NAUEN, FRANZ GABRIEL, *Revolution, Idealism and Human Freedom: Schelling, Hölderlin and Hegel* (The Hague, 1971).

NAVES, R., *Voltaire et l'Encyclopédie* (Paris, 1938).

NAVILLE, PIERRE, *Paul Thiry d'Holbach et la philosophie scientifique au XVIIIe siècle* (5th edn., Paris, 1943).

NEGRONI, B. DE, 'Le Rôle de la citation de Bayle à Voltaire', *La Lettre clandestine*, 8 (1999), 35–54.

—— *Lectures interdites: le travail des censeurs au XVIIIe siècle (1723–1774)* (Paris, 1995).

NEIMAN, SUSAN, *The Unity of Reason: Rereading Kant* (New York, 1994).

—— *Evil in Modern Thought: An Alternative History of Philosophy* (Princeton, 2002).

NELSON, CRAIG, *Thomas Paine: His Life, his Time and the Birth of Modern Nations* (London, 2006).

NEWMAN, S. P. (ed.), *Europe's American Revolution* (Basingstoke, 2006).

NIEWÖHNER, FR., *Veritas sive varietas: Lessings Toleranzparabel und das Buch des drei Betrügern* (Heidelberg, 1988).

NIEZEN, R., 'The *Aufklärung*'s Human Discipline', *IHR* 19 (2009), 177–96.

NIJENHUIS, I. J. A., *Een joodse philosophe, Isaac de Pinto (1717–1787)* (Amsterdam, 1992).

NISBET, H. B., 'Introduction' to Lessing, *Philosophical and Theological Writings*, 1–22.

Nooijen, A., 'Balthasar Bekker's *Betoverde Weereld* and Freethinking in Germany', in Maire-Hélène Queval (ed.), *Orthodoxie et hétérodoxie* (Saint-Étienne, 2010), 63–74.

Noordenbos, O., 'De eeuw der Verlichting', *De Gids*, 134 (1971), 446–53.

Norton, D. F., 'Hume, Human Nature, and the Foundations of Morality', in Norton (ed.), *Cambridge Companion to Hume*, 148–81.

—— (ed.), *The Cambridge Companion to Hume* (Cambridge, 1993).

—— and Kuehn, M., 'The Foundations of Morality', in *CHEPh* ii. 941–86.

Nosco, P., 'The Place of China in the Construction of Japan's Early Modern World View', *TJEAS* 4 (2007), 49–67.

O'Dea, M., and Whelan, K. (eds.), *Nations and Nationalisms* (Oxford, 1995).

O'Hagan, T., *Rousseau* (London, 1999).

O'Keefe, C. B., *Contemporary Reactions to the Enlightenment (1728–1762)* (Paris, 1974).

Oltra, Joaquín, and Pérez Samper, M. A., *El Conde de Aranda y los Estados Unidos* (Barcelona, 1987).

O'Neill, D., *The Burke–Wollstonecraft Debate* (University Park, Pa., 2007).

Onfray, Michel, *Les Ultras des Lumières* (Paris, 2007).

Oostindie, Gert, 'The Enlightenment, Christianity and the Surinam Slave', *Journal of Caribbean History*, 26 (1992), 147–70.

—— *Fifty Years Later: Antislavery, Capitalism and Modernity in the Dutch Orbit* (Leiden, 1995).

—— 'Same Old Song? Perspectives on Slavery in Surinam and Curacao', in Oostindie (ed.), *Fifty Years Later*, 179–92.

Opstall, M. E. van, 'Dutchmen and Japanese in the Eighteenth Century', in J. van Goor (ed.), *Trading Companies in Asia (1600–1830)* (Utrecht, 1986), 107–26.

O'Shaughnessy, A. J., *An Empire Divided: The American Revolution and the British Caribbean* (Philadelphia, 2000).

Otto, R., *Studien zur Spinozarezeption in Deutschland im 18. Jahrhundert* (Frankfurt, 1994).

Oustinoff, P. C., 'Notes on Diderot's Fortunes in Russia', in O. E. Fellows and N. L. Torrey (eds.), *Diderot Studies* (Syracuse, NY, 1949), 121–42.

Paganini, Gianni, 'Hume et Bayle: Conjonction locale et immatérialité de l'âme', in M. Magdelaine et al. (eds.) *De l'Humanisme aux Lumières: Bayle et le Protestantisme* (Paris, 1996), 701–13.

—— *Introduzione alle filosofie clandestine* (2005; new edn., Rome, 2008).

—— *Filosofie clandestine* (new edn., Rome, 2008).

—— 'Scetticismo et certezza', in G. Paganini and E. Tortarolo (eds.), *Illuminismo: un vademecum* (Turin, 2008), 252–65.

—— 'Hume, Bayle e i "Dialogues Concerning Natural Religion"', *GCFI* 81 (2002), 234–63.

—— Benítez, M., and Dybikowski, J. (eds.), *Scepticisme, clandestinité et libre pensée* (Paris, 2002).

Pagden, Anthony, 'The Effacement of Difference', in G. Prakash (ed.), *After Colonialism: Imperial Histories and Postcolonial Displacements* (Princeton, 1995), 129–52.

—— 'The Immobility of China: Orientalism and Occidentalism in the Enlightenment', in L. Wolff and M. Cipolloni (eds.), *The Anthropology of the Enlightenment* (Stanford, Calif., 2007), 50–64.

Page, Anthony, '"Liberty has an Asylum": John Jebb, British Radicalism and the American Revolution', *History*, 87 (2002), 204–26.

PAGE, ANTHONY, *John Jebb and the Enlightenment Origins of British Radicalism* (Westport, Conn., 2003).

PALMER, R. R., *Catholics and Unbelievers in Eighteenth Century France* (1939; new edn., New York, 1961).

—— *The Age of Democratic Revolution* (2 vols., Princeton, 1959).

PANCALDI, G., *Volta: Science and Culture in the Age of Enlightenment* (Princeton, 2003).

PAPPAS, J. N., *Berthier's* Journal de Trévoux *and the* Philosophes, *SVEC* 3 (Geneva, 1957).

—— 'Voltaire et la guerre civile philosophique', *Revue d'histoire littéraire de la France* (1961), 525–49.

—— *Voltaire and d'Alembert* (Bloomington, Ind., 1962).

—— 'Diderot, d'Alembert et l'*Encyclopédie*', *Diderot Studies*, 4 (1963), 191–208.

PAQUETTE, G., *Enlightened Reform in Southern Europe and its Atlantic Colonies (c.1750–1830)* (Farnham, 2009).

—— *Enlightenment, Governance, and Reform in Spain and its Empire, 1759–1808* (Basingstoke, 2008).

—— 'Enlightened Narratives and Imperial Rivalry in Bourbon Spain', *Eighteenth Century*, 48 (2007), 61–80.

PARIKH, I., 'The Need of the Third World for Humanism', in P. Kurtz and T. J. Madigan (eds.), *Challenges to the Enlightenment: In Defence of Reason and Science* (New York, 1994).

PARKER, NOEL, 'Souveraineté et providence chez Rousseau', in L'Aminot (ed.), *Politique et révolution*, 21–33.

PARKINSON, G. H., 'Philosophy and Logic', in N. Jolley (ed.), *The Cambridge Companion to Leibniz* (Cambridge, 1995), 199–223.

PARMENTER, J. W., 'Dragging Canoe: Chickamauga Cherokee Patriot', in N. L. Rhoden et al. (eds.), *The Human Tradition in the American Revolution* (Wilmington, Del., 2000), 117–37.

PASCAL, JEAN-NOEL, 'Diderot dans le *Dictionnaire anti-philosophique* de Dom Mayeul-Chaudon', in Chouillet (ed.), *Ennemis*, 91–100.

PASQUINO, P., *Sieyès et l'invention de la constitution en France* (Paris, 1998).

—— 'Nicolas Bergasse and Alexander Hamilton', in Albertone and de Francesco (eds.), *Rethinking*, 80–99.

PASTA, RENATO, '*Dei delitti e delle pene* et sa fortune en Italie', in Porret (ed.), *Beccaria*, 119–48.

PÄTZOLD, D., *Spinoza, Aufklärung, Idealismus: Die Substanz der Moderne* (1995; 2nd edn., Assen, 2002).

PAUL, JEAN-MARIE, 'Reimarus et le Curé Meslier: évolution et révolution', in J. Moes and J.-M. Valentin (eds.), *De Lessing à Heine: un siècle de relations littéraires et intellectuelles entre la France et l'Allemagne* (Paris, 1985), 73–91.

PEABODY, S., '*There are no Slaves in France*' (New York, 1996).

PEARSON, R., *Voltaire Almighty* (London, 2005).

PECHARROMAN, O., *Morals, Man and Nature in the Enlightenment: A Study of Baron d'Holbach's Work* (Washington, DC, 1977).

PELLERIN, P., 'Naigeon: une certaine image de Diderot sous la Révolution', *RDE* 29 (2000), 25–44.

—— 'Diderot, Voltaire et le Curé Meslier', in D. Guiragossian Carr (ed.), *Diderot Studies*, 29 (Geneva, 2003), 53–63.

PEPE, LUIGI, 'Les Milieux savants en Italie dans la deuxième moitié du 18e siècle', 40 (2008), 211–28.

PERALTA RUIZ, VICTOR, 'Las tribulaciones de un ilustrado católico: José Eusebio Llano Zapata en Cádiz (1756–1780)', in preliminaries to Llano Zapata, *Memorias* (Lima, 2005), 37–73.

PERINETTI, D., 'Philosophical Reflection on History', *CHEPh* ii. 1107–40.

PERONNET, M., 'Police et religion à la fin du XVIIIe siècle', *AHRF* 200 (1970), 375–97.

—— 'Censure de la Faculté de Théologie contre un livre: l'*Histoire philosophique*', in Bancarel and Goggi (eds.), *Raynal*, 273–85.

PERROT, JEAN-CLAUDE, *Une histoire intellectuelle de l'économie politique* (Paris, 1992).

PESET, M., and PESET, J. L., *Gregorio Mayans y la reforma universitaria* (Valencia, 1975).

PETRY, M. J., *Frans Hemsterhuis: Waarneming en werkelijkheid* (Baarn, 1990).

PHELAN, J. L., *The People and the King: The Comunero Revolution in Colombia, 1781* (Madison, 1978).

PHILIP, M., 'Disconcerting Ideas', in Burgess and Festenstein (eds.), *English Radicalism*, 157–89.

—— *Godwin's Political Justice* (Ithaca, NY, 1986).

PHILLIPSON, N., 'Adam Smith as Civic Moralist', in I. Hont and M. Ignatieff (eds.), *Wealth and Virtue: The Shaping of Political Economy in the Scottish Enlightenment* (Cambridge, 1983), 179–202.

—— *Adam Smith: An Enlightened Life* (London, 2010).

PII, ELUGGERO, 'Republicanism and Commercial Society in Eighteenth-Century Italy', in Van Gelderen and Skinner (eds.), *Republicanism*, ii. 249–74.

PINKARD, T., *German Philosophy, 1760–1860: The Legacy of Idealism* (Cambridge, 2002).

—— *Hegel: A Biography* (Cambridge, 2000).

PIPES, R., 'Catherine II and the Jews', *Soviet Jewish Affairs*, 5 (1975), 3–20.

PITTOCK, M. G. H., 'Historiography', in Broadie (ed.), *Scottish Enlightenment*, 258–79.

PITTS, J., *A Turn to Empire: The Rise of Imperial Liberalism in Britain and France* (Princeton, 2005).

POCOCK, J. G. A., *The Machiavellian Moment* (Princeton, 1975).

—— 'The Dutch Republican Tradition', in Jacob and Mijnhardt (eds.), *Dutch Republic*, 197–223.

—— *Virtue, Commerce and History* (Cambridge, 1985).

—— 'Enlightenment and Counter-Enlightenment, Revolution and Counter-Revolution', *History of Political Thought*, 20 (1999), 125–39.

—— 'Historiography and Enlightenment', *Modern Intellectual History*, 5 (2008), 83–96.

—— *Barbarism and Religion* (5 vols. thus far, Cambridge, 1999–2010).

POIRIER, JEAN-PAUL, *Le Tremblement de terre de Lisbonne* (Paris, 2005).

—— 'The 1755 Lisbon Disaster', *European Review*, 14 (2006), 169–80.

POIRIER, JEAN-PIERRE, *Turgot: laissez-faire et progrès social* (Paris, 1999).

POLASKY, J. L., *Revolution in Brussels, 1787–1793* (Brussels, 1985).

—— 'The Success of a Counter-Revolution in Revolutionary Europe: The Brabant Revolution of 1789', *Tijdschrift voor Geschiedenis*, 103 (1989), 413–21.

POMEAU, RENÉ, *Politique de Voltaire* (Paris, 1963).

—— *La Religion de Voltaire* (Paris, 1969).

POPKIN, J. D., *News and Politics in the Age of Revolution* (Ithaca, NY, 1989).

—— 'Robert Darnton's Alternative (to the) Enlightenment', in Mason (ed.), *The Darnton Debate*, 105–28.

—— 'Dutch Patriots, French Journalists and Declarations of Rights: The *Leidse Ontwerp* of 1785', *Historical Journal*, 38 (1995), 553–65.

—— *You are all Free: The Haitian Revolution and the Abolition of Slavery* (Cambridge, 2010).

POPKIN, J. D., *Revolutionary News: The Press in France, 1789–1799* (Durham, NC, 1990).

—— with Popkin, Richard (eds.), *The Abbé Grégoire and his World* (Dordrecht, 2000).

POPKIN, R. H., 'The Philosophical Basis of Eighteenth-Century Racism', in H. E. Pagliaro (ed.), *Racism in the Eighteenth Century* (Cleveland, 1973).

—— and VANDERJAGT, A. (eds.), *Scepticism and Irreligion in the Seventeenth and Eighteenth Centuries* (Leiden, 1993).

PORRET, MICHEL (ed.), *Beccaria et la culture juridique des Lumières* (Geneva, 1997).

—— (ed.), *Sens des Lumières* (Geneva, 2007).

—— and VOLPILHAC-AUGER, C. (eds.), *Le Temps de Montesquieu: actes du colloque international de Genève (28–31 oct. 1998)* (Geneva, 2002).

PORSET, CHARLES, 'Voltaire et Meslier: état de la question', in Olivier Bloch (ed.), *Le Matérialisme du xviiie siècle et la littérature clandestine* (Paris, 1982), 193–204.

—— 'Position de la philosophie de Voltaire', in Kölving and Mervaud (eds.), *Voltaire et ses combats*, i. 727–3.

—— *Mirabeau Franc-Maçon* (La Rochelle, 1996).

PORTER, ROY, 'The Scientific Revolution: A Spoke in the Wheel?', in R. Porter and M. Teich (eds.), *Revolution in History* (Cambridge, 1986), 290–316.

—— *Enlightenment: Britain and the Creation of the Modern World* (London, 2000).

—— *Flesh in the Age of Reason* (London, 2003).

POSTIGLIOLA, A., *La città della ragione: per una storia filosofica del settecento francese* (Rome, 1992).

POUSSOU, JEAN-PIERRE, MEZIN, A., and PERRET-GENTIL, Y. (eds.), *L'Influence française en Russie au XVIIIe siècle* (Paris, 2004).

POWERS, M. J., *Art and Political Expression in Early China* (New Haven, 1991).

PRICE, M., *Preserving the Monarchy: The Comte de Vergennes, 1774–1787* (Cambridge, 1995).

PROUST, JACQUES, *Diderot et l'Encyclopédie* (1962; Paris, 1995).

—— 'De quelques dictionnaires hollandais ayant servi de relais à l'encyclopédisme européen vers le Japon', *DHS* 38 (2006), 17–37.

PUISAIS, ERIC, 'Deschamps entre Spinoza et Hegel', in E. Puisais (ed.), *Léger-Marie Deschamps, un philosophe entre Lumières et oubli* (Paris, 2001).

QUARFOOD, CHRISTINE, *Condillac, la statue et l'enfant* (Paris, 2002).

QUASTANA, FRANÇOIS, *La Pensée politique de Mirabeau (1771–1789)* (Aix-en Provence, 2007).

QUINTILI, PAOLO, *La Pensée critique de Diderot* (Paris, 2001).

QUIVIGER, PIERRE-YVES, 'Sieyès as a Reader of John Locke', in C. Miqueu and M. Chamie (eds.), *Locke's Political Liberty* (Oxford, 2009), 127–42.

RACHUM, I., 'Revolution': The Entrance of a New World into Western Political Discourse (Lanham, Md., 1999).

RACINE, K., *Francisco de Miranda: A Transatlantic Life in the Age of Revolution* (Wilmington, Del., 2003).

—— 'Love in the Time of Liberation', in J. Maher (ed.), *Francisco de Miranda, Exile and Enlightenment* (London, 2006), 88–115.

—— 'British Cultural and Intellectual Influence in the Spanish American Independence Era', *HAHR* 90 (2010), 423–54.

RAEFF, MARC, *Understanding Imperial Russia* (New York, 1984).

—— *The Well-Ordered Police State* (New Haven, 1983).

RAHE, PAUL A., 'The Book that Never Was: Montesquieu's *Considerations on the Romans* in Historical Context', *HPTh* 26 (2005), 43–89.

—— *Montesquieu and the Logic of Liberty* (New Haven, 2009).

RAMOND, CHARLES, ' "Ne pas rire, mais comprendre": La Réception historique et le sens général du spinozisme', *Kairos: revue de philosophie*, 11 (1998), 97–125.

RAO, A. M., *Il regno di Napoli nel Settecento* (Naples, 1983).

—— 'The Feudal Question, Judicial Systems and the Enlightenment', in Imbruglia (ed.), *Naples*, 95–117.

REBEJKOW, JEAN-CHRISTOPHE, 'Les "Notes sur la réfutation des Dialogues sur le commerce des blés" de Diderot', *Studi francesi*, 39 (1995), 467–77.

REID, A., 'A New Phase of Commercial Expansion in Southeast Asia, 1760–1840', in Reid (ed.), *Last Stand*, 57–81.

—— (ed.), *The Last Stand of Asian Autonomies: Responses to Modernity in the Diverse States of Southeast Asia and Korea, 1750–1900* (Basingstoke, 1997).

REILL, PETER, *The German Enlightenment and the Rise of Historicism* (Berkeley, 1975).

REINALTER, HELMUT (ed.), *Der Illuminatenorden (1776–1785/87)* (Frankfurt, 1997).

—— 'Ignaz Edler von Born und die Illuminaten in Österreich', in Reinalter (ed.), *Der Illuminatenorden*, 351–91.

RENWICK, JOHN, *Marmontel, Voltaire and the* Bélisaire *Affair*, SVEC 121 (Banbury, 1974).

—— 'L'Affaire de Bélisaire', in J. Ehrard (ed.), *De l'Encyclopédie à la Contra-Révolution* (Clermont-Ferrand, 1970), 249–69.

RÉTAT, PIERRE, '1789: Montesquieu aristocrate', *DHS* 21 (1989), 73–82.

REVENTLOW, HENNING GRAF, 'Das Arsenal der Bibelkritik des Reimarus', in *Hermann Samuel Reimarus (1694–1768), 'ein bekannter Unbekannter' der Aufklärung in Hamburg* (Göttingen, 1973), 44–65.

REY, R., 'Diderot à travers la correspondance entre Haller et Bonnet', in Chouillet (ed.), *Ennemis*, 113–26.

RHODEN, N. L., 'William Smith, Philadelphia Minister and Moderate', in Rhoden and Steele (eds.), *Human Tradition*, 61–80.

—— and STEELE, I. K. (eds.), *The Human Tradition in the American Revolution* (Wilmington, Del., 2000).

RIALS, STÉPHANE, *La Déclaration des droits de l'homme et du citoyen* (Paris, 1988).

RICHTER, MELVIN, 'Europe and *The Other* in Eighteenth-Century Thought', *Politisches Denken* (1997), 25–47.

—— 'Competing Concepts and Practices of Comparison in the Political and Social Thought of Eighteenth-Century Europe', *Archiv für Begriffsgeschichte*, 44 (2002), 199–219.

—— 'The Comparative Study of Regimes and Societies', *CHEPTh* 147–71.

RICKEN, U., 'Condillac et le soupçon de matérialisme', in Fink and Stenger (eds.), *Être matérialiste*, 265–74.

RICUPERATI, G., 'La cultura italiana nel secondo settecento europeo', in Santato (ed.), *Letteratura italiana*, 33–64.

—— *Frontiere e limiti della ragione: Dalla crisi della coscienza europea all'Illuminismo* (Turin, 2006).

RIEDEL, WOLFGANG, 'Aufklärung und Macht: Schiller, Abel und die Illuminaten', in Müller-Seidel and Riedel (eds.), *Weimarer Klassik*, 107–25.

RIGOTTI, FRANCESCA, 'Biology and Society in the Age of Enlightenment', *JHI* 47 (1986), 215–33.

RIHS, CHARLES, *Voltaire: recherches sur les origines du matérialisme historique* (Paris, 1962).

—— *Les Philosophes utopistes* (Paris, 1970).

RILEY, P., 'Rousseau's General Will', in R. Wokler (ed.), *Rousseau and Liberty* (Manchester, 1995), 1–28.

—— (ed.), *The Cambridge Companion to Rousseau* (Cambridge, 2001).

RIPLEY, B. R., 'Adams, Burke and Eighteenth-Century Conservatism', *Political Science Quarterly*, 80 (1965), 216–35.

RISCO, ANTONIO, 'Présence de Beccaria dans l'Espagne des Lumières', in M. Porret (ed.), *Beccaria et la culture juridique des Lumières* (Geneva, 1996).

RISKIN, J., *Science in the Age of Sensibility* (Chicago, 2002).

RIVA-AGÜERO, J. DE LA, 'Don José Baquíjano y Carrillo', *Boletín del Museo Bolivariano*, 12 (1929), 453–91.

ROBBINS, CAROLINE, *The Eighteenth-Century Commonwealthman* (Cambridge, Mass., 1961).

—— 'The Lifelong Education of Thomas Paine (1737–1809)', *PAPS* 127 (1983), 135–42.

ROBERTS, J. A. G., 'L'Image de la Chine dans l'*Encyclopédie*', *RDE* 22 (1997), 87–105.

ROBERTS, MICHAEL, *The Age of Liberty: Sweden 1719–1772* (Cambridge, 1986).

ROBERTSON, J., *The Case for the Enlightenment* (Cambridge, 2005).

ROBINET, ANDRÉ, *Dom Deschamps: le maître des maîtres du soupçon* (Paris, 1994).

ROBINS, N. A., *Priest–Indian Conflict in Upper Peru* (Syracuse, NY, 2007).

ROBISCO, NATALIE-BARBARA, *Jean-Jacques Rousseau et la Révolution française* (Paris, 1998).

ROCHE, DANIEL, 'Les Anglais à Paris', in D. Balani et al. (eds.), *Dall'origine dei Lumi alla Rivoluzione: scritti in onore di Luciano Guerci e Giuseppe Ricuperati* (Rome, 2008), 489–512.

—— 'Lumières concrètes: savoirs, pratiques, échanges', in Porret (ed.), *Sens des Lumières*, 91–7.

—— 'Encyclopedias and the Diffusion of Knowledge', in *CHEPTh* 172–94.

ROCKMORE, T., *Kant and Idealism* (New Haven, 2007).

RODRÍGUEZ, JAIME E., *The Independence of Spanish America* (Cambridge, 1998).

RODRÍGUEZ, LAURA, 'The Spanish Riots of 1766', *Past and Present*, 59 (May 1973), 117–46.

RODRÍGUEZ DE ALONSO, JOSEFINA, *Le Siècle des Lumières conté par Francisco de Miranda* (Paris, 1974).

RODRÍGUEZ LÓPEZ-BREA, CARLOS, *Don Luis de Borbón, el cardenal de los liberales (1777–1823)* (Toledo, 2002).

ROE, NICHOLAS, *Wordsworth and Coleridge: The Radical Years* (Oxford, 1988).

ROE, SH. A., 'Voltaire versus Needham', *JHI* 46 (1985), 65–87.

—— *Matter, Life and Generation: 18th-Century Embryology and the Haller–Wolff Debate* (1981; Cambridge, new edn., 2002).

ROEGIERS, J. and VAN SAS, N. C. F., 'Revolutie in Noord en Zuid (1780–1830), in J. C. H. Blom and E. Lamberts (eds.), *Geschiedenis van de Nederlanden* (Rijswijk, 1993).

ROGER, JACQUES, 'Diderot et Buffon en 1749', *Diderot Studies*, 4 (1963), 221–36.

—— *The Life Sciences in Eighteenth-Century French Thought* (1963; Stanford, Calif., 1997).

—— *Buffon: A Life in Natural History* (1989; Ithaca, NY, 1997).

—— *Les Sciences de la vie dans la pensée française au XVIIIe siècle* (1963; new edn., Paris, 1993).

ROGISTER, JOHN, *Louis XV and the Parlement of Paris, 1737–1755* (Cambridge, 1995).

ROHLS, JAN, 'Herders "Gott"', in M. Kessler and V. Leppin (eds.), *Johann Gottfried Herder: Aspekte seines Lebenswerkes* (Berlin, 2005), 271–91.

ROMANI, ROBERTO, 'All Montesquieu's Sons: The Place of *Esprit Général, Caractère National*, and *Mœurs* in French Political Philosophy, 1748–1789', in *SVEC* 362 (Oxford, 1998), 189–235.

RØRVIK, THOR INGE, 'Kant-resepsjonen i Dansk-Norske tidsskrifter', in E. Tjønneland (ed.), *Opplysningens tidsskrifter: Norske og Danske periodiske publikasjoner på 1700-tallet* (Bergen, 2008), 231–46.

ROSA, MARIO, 'Sulla condanna dell'"Esprit des loix" e sulla fortuna di Montesquieu in Italia', *Rivista della chiesa in Italia*, 14 (1960), 411–28.

ROSEN, F., 'Jeremy Bentham's Radicalism', in Burgess and Festenstein (eds.), *English Radicalism*, 217–40.

—— 'Utilitarianism and the Reform of the Criminal Law', in *CHEPTh* 547–72.

ROSENBLATT, H., *Rousseau and Geneva* (Cambridge, 1997).

ROSENDAAL, JOOST, *De Nederlandse Revolutie: Vrijheid, volk en vaderland, 1783–99* (Nijmegen, 2005).

—— *Bataven! Nederlandse vluchtelingen in Frankrijk, 1787–1795* (Nijmegen, 2003).

ROSSIGNOL, MARIE-JEANNE, 'The American Revolution in France', in Newman (ed.), *Europe's American Revolution*, 51–71.

RÖTHLIN, NIKLAUS, 'La *Société économique de Berne* e le débat sur la législation criminelle', in Porret (ed.), *Beccaria*, 169–75.

ROTHSCHILD, E., *Economic Sentiments: Adam Smith, Condorcet, and the Enlightenment* (Cambridge, Mass., 2001).

ROTTA, SALVATORE, 'Voltaire in Italia', *Annali della Scuola Normale Superiore di Pisa*, Lettere, Storia e filosofia ser. II vol. 39 (1970), 387–444.

ROUDAUT, M., 'Ambiguités et limites de la tolérance radicale de l'*Aufklärung*', *Lumières*, 13 (2009), 117–34.

ROUSSEAUX, XAVIER, 'Doctrines criminelles, pratiques pénales et projets politiques: le cas des possessions habsbourgeoises (1750–1790)', in Porret (ed.), *Beccaria*, 223–52.

RUIZ MARTÍNEZ, EDUARDO, *La librería de Nariño y los Derechos del Hombre* (Bogotá, 1990).

RUSSELL, PAUL, *Freedom and Moral Sentiment: Hume's Way of Naturalizing Responsibility* (Oxford, 1995).

SAADA, A., *Inventer Diderot* (Paris, 2003).

SA'ADAH, ANNE, *The Shaping of Liberal Politics in Revolutionary France* (Princeton, 1990).

SAHMLAND, I., 'Georg Forsters Wirken als Freimaurer und Rosenkreuzer', in R. Reichardt and G. Roche (eds.), *Weltbürger, Europäer, Deutscher, Franke: Georg Forster zum 200. Todestag* (Mainz, 1994), 167–95.

SAINEVILLE, C. DE, 'Mably et la censure', *AHRF* 46 (1974), 401–11.

ST CLAIR, WILLIAM, *The Godwins and the Shelleys: A Biography of a Family* (Baltimore, 1989).

SALA-MOLINS, LOUIS, *Le Code noir ou le calvaire de Canaan* (Paris, 1987).

SALAÜN, F., 'Voltaire face aux courants matérialistes de son temps', in Kölving and Mervaud (eds.), *Voltaire et ses combats*, i. 705–18.

—— *L'Ordre des mœurs: essai sur la place du matérialisme dans la société française du XVIIIe siècle (1734–1784)* (Paris, 1996).

SALMON, J. H. M., 'Liberty by Degrees: Raynal and Diderot on the British Constitution', *HPTh* 20 (1999), 87–106.

SÁNCHEZ-BLANCO, FRANCISCO, *El absolutismo y las Luces en el reinado de Carlos III* (Madrid, 2002).

SÁNCHEZ-BLANCO PARODY, FRANCISCO, *Europa y el pensamiento español del siglo XVIII* (Madrid, 1991).

SÁNCHEZ ESPINOSA, GABRIEL, 'An *ilustrado* in his province: Jovellanos in Asturias', in Butterwick (ed.), *Peripheries*, 183–200.

SANDRIER, A., *Le Style philosophique du baron d'Holbach* (Paris, 2004).

SANTATO, GUIDO (ed.), *Letteratura italiana e cultura europea tra Illuminismo e Romanticismo* (Geneva, 2003).

SANTINELLO, GIOVANNI (ed.), *Models of the History of Philosophy* (1991; Dordrecht, 1993).

SANTUCCI, ANTONIO (ed.), *L'età dei Lumi: saggi sulla cultura settecentesca* (Bologna, 1998).

SARRAILH, J., *L'Espagne éclairée dans la seconde moitié du XVIIIe siècle* (Paris, 1954).

SASSEN, F., *Geschiedenis van de wijsbegeerte in Nederland* (Rotterdam, 1959).

SAUGNIEUX, JOEL, *Le Jansénisme espagnol du XVIIIe siècle* (Oviedo, 1975).

SAUL, J. R., *Voltaire's Bastards: The Dictatorship of Reason in the West* (New York, 1993).

SAUTER, H., 'Paul Thiry von Holbach (1723–89)', *Pfälzer Lebensbilder*, 1 (1964), 108–41.

SAUTER, M. J., *Visions of the Enlightenment* (Leiden, 2009).

SCANDELLARI, S., 'La difusión del pensamiento criminal de Gaetano Filangieri en España', *Nuevo Mundo Mundos Nuevos: coloquios 2006* (on-line publication posted 18 Mar. 2006).

SCHAFER, R. J., *The Economic Societies in the Spanish World (1763–1821)* (Syracuse, NY, 1958).

SCHAICH, MICHAEL, *Staat und Öffentlichkeit im Kurfürstentum Bayern der Spätaufklärung* (Munich, 2001).

—— 'A War of Words? Old and New Perspectives on the Enlightenment', *Bulletin of the German Historical Institute, London*, 24 (2002), 29–56.

SCHAMA, SIMON, *Citizens* (London, 1989).

—— *Patriots and Liberators: Revolution in the Netherlands, 1789–1813* (London, 1977).

SCHILSON, ARNO, 'Lessing and Theology', in B. Fischer and Th. C. Fox (eds.), *A Companion to the Works of Gotthold Ephraim Lessing* (Rochester, NY, 2005), 157–83.

SCHINGS, HANS-JÜRGEN, *Die Brüder des Marquis Posa: Schiller und der Geheimbund der Illuminaten* (Tübingen, 1996).

SCHLEICH, THOMAS, *Aufklärung und Revolution* (Stuttgart, 1981).

SCHLENTHER, B. S., 'Religious Faith and Commercial Empire', in *OHBE* ii. 128–50.

SCHMIDT, JAMES, *What is Enlightenment? Eighteenth-Century Answers and Twentieth-Century Questions* (Berkeley and Los Angeles, 1996).

—— 'What Enlightenment was: How Moses Mendelssohn and Immanuel Kant Answered the *Berlinische Monatsschrift*', *Journal of History of Philosophy*, 30 (1992), 77–101.

SCHMIDT, PEER, 'Against "False Philosophy": Bourbon Reforms and Counter-Enlightenment in New Spain (1759–1788)', in R. Piper and P. Schmidt (eds.), *Latin America and the Atlantic World* (Cologne, 2005), 137–56.

—— 'Contra "la falsa filosofia": la Contra-Ilustración y la crítica al reformismo borbónico en la Nueva España', in K. Kohut and S. V. Rose (eds.), *La formación de la cultura virreinal*, iii: *El siglo XVIII* (Madrid, 2006), 231–72.

SCHMIDT-BIGGEMANN, W., *Theodizee und Tatsachen: Das philosophische Profil der deutschen Aufklärung* (Frankfurt, 1988).

—— 'Einleitung' to Herman Samuel Reimarus, *Kleine gelehrte Schriften* (Göttingen, 1994), 9–65.

SCHNEEWIND, J. B., *The Invention of Autonomy: A History of Modern Moral Philosophy* (Cambridge, 1998).

—— 'The Active Powers', in *CHEPh* i. 593–607.

SCHNEIDER, R. A., *Public Life in Toulouse, 1463–1789* (Ithaca, NY, 1989).

SCHOBER, ANGELIKA, 'Diderot als Philosoph', in T. Heydenreich (ed.), *Denis Diderot (1713–1784): Zeit, Werk, Wirkung: Zehn Beiträge* (Erlangen, 1984), 35–42.

SCHOFIELD, R. E., 'Monism, Unitarianism and Phlogiston in Joseph Priestley's Natural Philosophy', *Enlightenment and Dissent*, 19 (2000), 78–90.

—— *The Enlightened Joseph Priestley* (University Park, Pa., 2004).

SCHÖNFELD, M., *The Philosophy of the Young Kant* (Oxford, 2000).

SCHRADER, F. E., 'Aufklärungssoziabilität in Bordeaux', in H. E. Bödecker and E. François, *Aufklärung und Politik* (Leipzig, 1996), 249–74.

SCHRIKKER, A., *British and Dutch Colonial Intervention in Sri Lanka, 1780–1815* (Leiden, 2007).

SCHRÖDER, WINFRIED, *Spinoza in der deutschen Frühaufklärung* (Würzburg, 1987).

—— *Ursprünge des Atheismus: Untersuchungen zur Metaphysik- und Religionskritik des 17. und 18. Jahrhunderts* (Stuttgart, 1998).

SCHULTE, CHRISTOPH, *Die jüdische Aufklärung: Philosophie, Religion, Geschichte* (Munich, 2002).

SCHÜRMANN, E., WASZEK, N., and WEINREICH, F. (eds.), *Spinoza im Deutschland des achtzehnten Jahrhunderts* (Stuttgart, 2002).

SCHÜTT, R., *'Ein Mann von Feuer und Talenten': Leben und Werk von Carl Friedrich Cramer* (Göttingen, 2005).

SCHUTTE, G. J., 'Gereformeerden en de Nederlandse revolutie in de achttiende eeuw', *Tijdschrift voor Geschiedenis*, 102 (1989), 496–516.

—— *De Nederlandse Patriotten en de kolonien* (Groningen, 1974).

SCHÜTTLER, HERMANN, *Die Mitglieder des Illuminatenordens 1776–1787/93* (Munich, 1991).

SCHWARZBACH, B. E., 'Les Clandestins du Père Guillaume Maleville et ses autres lectures hétérodoxes', *La Lettre clandestine*, 10 (2001), 161–82.

SCHWARTZ, STUART B., *All Can be Saved* (New Haven, 2008).

SCOTT, H. M., 'Conclusion: The Continuity of Aristocratic Power', in Scott (ed.), *European Nobilities*, ii. 377–99.

—— 'Reform in the Habsburg Monarchy, 1740–90', in Scott (ed.), *Enlightened Absolutism*, 145–87.

—— (ed.), *Enlightened Absolutism: Reform and Reformers in Later Eighteenth-Century Europe* (Basingstoke, 1990).

—— (ed.), *The European Nobilities in the Seventeenth and Eighteenth Centuries*, vol. ii (1995; 2nd edn., Basingstoke, 2007).

SCOTT, JOAN, *Only Paradoxes to Offer: French Feminists and the Rights of Man* (Cambridge, Mass., 1996).

SCRIBANO, EMANUELA, 'Animismo, origine della religione e interpretazione delle favole da Fontenelle a Voltaire', *Annali dell'Istituto di Filosofia* (Florence), 1 (1979), 237–59.

SCRIVENER, M., 'John Thelwall's Political Ambivolence', in Davis (ed.), *Radicalism*, 69–83.

—— 'Thelwall's Two Plays against Empire', in Poole (ed.), *John Thelwall*, 117–24.

SCURR, RUTH, *Fatal Purity: Robespierre and the French Revolution* (London, 2006).

SEIDLER, M. J., 'The Politics of Self-Preservation', in T. J. Hochstrasser and P. Schröder (eds.), *Early Modern Natural Law Theories* (Dordrecht, 2003), 227–55.

SEIF, U., 'Der missverstandene Montesquieu', *Zeitschrift für neuere Rechtsgeschichte*, 22 (2000), 149–66.

SEIFERT, HANS-ULRICH, 'C'est un pays singulier que celui-ci': d'Argens et l'Allemagne', in Seifert and Seban (eds.), *Marquis d'Argens*, 231–53.

—— and Seban, Jean-Loup (eds.), *Der Marquis d'Argens* (Wiesbaden, 2004).

SEIGEL, JERROLD, *The Idea of the Self: Thought and Experience in Western Europe since the Seventeenth Century* (Cambridge, 2005).

SEMMEL, B., *The Methodist Revolution* (New York, 1973).

SENARCLENS, VANESSA DE, *Montesquieu, historien de Rome* (Geneva, 2003).

SENS, A., 'Dutch Antislavery Attitudes in a Decline-Ridden Society, 1750–1815', in Oostindie (ed.), *Fifty Years Later*, 89–104.

SEWELL, WILLIAM H., *A Rhetoric of Bourgeois Revolution: The Abbe Sieyès and* What is the Third Estate? (Durham, NC, 1994).

SGARD, JEAN, 'Diderot vu par les *Nouvelles ecclésiastiques*', *RDE* 25 (1998), 9–19.

SHACKLETON, ROBERT, *Montesquieu: A Critical Biography* (Oxford, 1961).

SHANK, J. B., *The Newton Wars and the Beginning of the French Enlightenment* (Chicago, 2008).

SHARIFI, MITRA, 'The Semi-Autonomous Judge in Colonial India', *Indian Economic and Social History Review*, 46 (2009), 57–81.

SHARP, JAMES R., 'France and the United States at the End of the Eighteenth Century', in Albertone and de Francesco (eds.), *Rethinking*, 203–18.

SHAW, J., *Miracles in Enlightenment England* (New Haven, 2006).

SHEK BRNARDIĆ, T., 'The Enlightenment in Eastern Europe', *European Review of History*, 13 (2006), 411–35.

SHER, R. B., *The Enlightenment and the Book* (Chicago, 2006).

SHIMADA, RYUTO, *The Intra-Asian Trade in Japanese Copper by the Dutch East India Company during the Eighteenth Century* (Leiden, 2006).

SHKLAR, J. N., 'Jean d'Alembert and the Rehabilitation of History', *JHI* 42 (1981), 643–64.

SHOVLIN, JOHN, *The Political Economy of Virtue* (Ithaca, NY, 2006).

SILBER, K., *Pestalozzi: The Man and his Work* (London, 1960).

SILVA, RENAN, 'Del mecenazgo al vacío: los ilustrados de Nueva Granada como intelectuales modernos', in Kohut and Rose (eds.), *Formación*, 535–58.

SKINNER, A. S., 'David Hume: Principles of Political Economy', in Norton (ed.), *Cambridge Companion to Hume*, 222–54.

SKRZYPEK, MARIAN, 'Le Libertinisme polonais et la littérature clandestine', in McKenna and Mothu (eds.), *Philosophie clandestine*, 509–20.

SKUNKE, MARIE-CHRISTINE, 'Jean-Jacques Rousseau in Swedish Eyes Around 1760', in Butterwick et al. (eds.), *Peripheries*, 87–103.

SLICHER VAN BATH, B. H., *Bevolking en economie in Nieuw Spanje ca. 1570–1800* (Amsterdam, 1981).

SLOAN, D., *The Scottish Enlightenment and the American College Ideal* (New York, 1971).

SMITH, D. W., *Helvétius: A Study in Persecution* (Oxford, 1965).

—— *Bibliography of the Writings of Helvétius* (Ferney-Voltaire, 2001).

SOËTARD, MICHEL, 'L'*Émile*, un livre scellé', in R. Thiery (ed.), *Rousseau, l'Émile et la Révolution* (Paris, 1992), 17–24.

SOLOMON, M., *Mozart: A Life* (2nd edn., New York, 1996).

SONDEREN, P. C., 'Passion and Purity: From Science to Art: Descartes, Spinoza and Hemster-huis', in C. Melica (ed.), *Hemsterhuis: A European Philosopher Rediscovered* (Naples, 2005), 199–216.

SONNENSCHER, M., *Before the Deluge: Public Debt, Inequality, and the Intellectual Origins of the French Revolution* (Princeton, 2007).

—— *Sans-Culottes* (Princeton, 2008).

SORKIN, DAVID, *'Reasonable Belief': The Religious Enlightenment, 1689–1789* (Princeton, 2008).

SÖRLIN, S., 'Science, Empire and Enlightenment', *European Review of History*, 13 (2006), 455–72.

—— and Fagerstedt, O., *Linné och hans apostlar* (Stockholm, 2004).

SOTO ARANGO, DIANA, 'La enseñanza ilustrada en las universidades de América colonial', in D. Soto Arango et al. (eds.), *La Ilustración en América colonial* (Madrid, 1995), 91–119.

SPALDING, A., and SPALDING, P., 'Der rätselhafte Tutor bei Hermann Samuel Reimarus: Begegnung zweier radikaler Aufklärer in Hamburg', *Zeitschrift für Hamburgische Geschichte*, 87 (2001), 49–64.

SPALLANZANI, M., *Immagini di Descartes nell'*Encyclopédie (Bologna, 1990).

SPANG, R. L., 'Paradigms and Paranoia: How Modern is the French Revolution?', *AHR* 108 (2003), 119–47.

SPANGLER, M., 'Science, philosophie et littérature: le polype de Diderot', *RDE* 23 (1997), 89–107.

SPELL, J. R., *Rousseau in the Spanish World before 1833* (Austin, Tex., 1938).

SPITZ, JEAN-FABIEN, 'From Civisim to Civility: D'Holbach's Critique of Republican Virtue', in Van Gelderen and Skinner (eds.), *Republicanism*, ii. 107–22.

SQUADRITO, K., 'Locke and the Dispossession of the American Indian', in Ward and Lott (eds.), *Philosophers on Race*, 101–24.

STALLEY, R. F., 'Reid's Defence of Freedom', in J. Houston (ed.), *Thomas Reid* (Edinburgh, 2004), 29–50.

STAMMEN, THEO, 'Adolf Freiherr von Knigge und die Illuminatenbewegung', in Müller-Seidel and Riedel (eds.), *Weimarer Klassik*, 67–89.

STAROBINSKI, J., *Le Remède dans le mal* (Paris, 1989).

STAUM, M. S., *Minerva's Message: Stabilizing the French Revolution* (Montreal, 1996).

—— *Cabanis: Enlightenment and Medical Philosophy in the French Revolution* (Princeton, 1980).

STEDMAN JONES, G., *An End to Poverty?* (London, 2004).

STEIGER, JOHANN ANSELF, 'Ist es denn ein Wunder? Die aufgeklärte Wunderkritik', in J. A. Steiger (ed.), *500 Jahre Theologie in Hamburg* (Berlin, 2005), 112–30.

STEINBRÜGGE, L., *The Moral Sex: Woman's Nature in the French Enlightenment* (1992; New York, 1995).

STENGER, G., 'Le Matérialisme de Voltaire', in Fink and Stenger (eds.), *Être matérialiste*, 275–85.

—— 'L'Atomisme dans les *Pensées philosophiques*', *DHS* 35 (2003), 75–100.

—— 'La Théorie de la connaissance dans la *Lettre sur les aveugles*', *RDE* 26 (1999), 99–111.

STEPHENSON, R. 'The Coherence of Goethe's Political Outlook', in C. P. Magill et al. (eds.), *Tradition and Creation* (Leeds, 1978), 77–88.

STERN, J. P., *Lichtenberg: A Doctrine of Scattered Occasions* (Bloomington, Ind., 1959).

STEWART, J. B., *Opinion and Reform in Hume's Political Philosophy* (Princeton, 1992).

STEWART, M. A., 'Religion and Rational Theology', in Broadie (ed.), *Scottish Enlightenment*, 31–59.

—— 'Rational Religion and Common Sense', in J. Houston (ed.), *Thomas Reid* (Edinburgh, 2004), 123–59.

—— 'Hume's Historical View of Miracles', in Stewart and Wright (eds.), *Hume*, 171–200.

—— 'Arguments for the Existence of God: The British Debate', in *CHEPh* ii. 710–30.

—— 'Hume's Intellectual Development, 1711–52', in Frasca-Spada and Kail (eds.), *Impressions*, 11–58.

—— and Wright, J. P. (eds.), *Hume and Hume's Connexions* (Edinburgh, 1994).

STIENING, G., 'Zur Bedeutung von Lessings Spinoza-Rezeption', in Schürmann et al. (eds.), *Spinoza im Deutschland*, 193–220.

STONE, BAILEY, *The Genesis of the French Revolution* (Cambridge, 1994).

STRAUSS, LEO, 'Einleitungen' to Mendelssohn, *Gesammelte Schriften*, iii, part 2, pp. xi–cx.

STROUMSA, G. G., *A New Science: The Discovery of Religion in the Age of Reason* (Cambridge, Mass., 2010).

STRUGNELL, A., *Diderot's Politics* (The Hague, 1973).

—— 'La Voix du sage dans *l'Histoire des Deux Indes*', in France and Strugnell (eds.), *Diderot*, 30–42.

—— 'Religion and the Secular City in Raynal's *Histoire des Deux Indes*', in Hemming et al. (eds.), *Secular City*, 179–90.

STUURMAN, SIEP, 'The Canon of the History of Political Thought: Its Critique and a Proposed Alternative', *History and Theory*, 39 (2000), 147–66.

—— 'Pathways to the Enlightenment', *History Workshop Journal*, 54 (2002), 227–35.

—— *François Poulain de La Barre and the Invention of Modern Equality* (Cambridge, Mass., 2004).

—— 'The Voice of Thersites: Reflections on the Origins of the Idea of Equality', *JHI* (2004), 171–89.

—— 'Cosmopolitan Egalitarianism in the Enlightenment: Anquetil Duperron on India and America', *JHI* 68 (2007), 255–78.

—— *De Uitvinding van de mensheid: Korte wereldgeschiedenis van het denken over gelijkheid en cultuurverschil* (Amsterdam, 2009).

SUTCLIFFE, ADAM, *Judaism and Enlightenment* (Cambridge, 2003).

SZABO, FRANZ A. J., *Kaunitz and Enlightened Absolutism, 1753–1780* (Cambridge, 1994).

TAMM, D., 'Beccaria et le climat de réformes dans les pays du Nord', in Porret (ed.), *Beccaria*, 189–94.

TANTILLO, A. O., *Goethe's* Elective Affinities *and the Critics* (Rochester, NY, 2001).

TAPPER, A., 'The Beginnings of Priestley's Materialism', *Enlightenment and Dissent*, 1 (1982), 73–82.

TARANTINO, GIOVANNI, *Lo scrittoio di Anthony Collins* (Milan, 2007).

TARANTO, PASCAL, *Du déisme à l'athéisme: la libre-pensée d'Anthony Collins* (Paris, 2000).

TARIN, R., *Diderot et la Révolution française* (Paris, 2001).

TATIN-GOURIER, JEAN-JACQUES, '1762–1789: Émile et le contrat social', in R. Thiery (ed.), *Rousseau, l'Émile et la Révolution* (Paris, 1992), 109–18.

TAVOILLOT, PIERRE-HENRI, *Le Crépuscule des lumières* (Paris, 1995).

TAYLOR, A., *'Down with the Crown': British Anti-monarchism since 1790* (London, 1999).

TAYLOR, CHARLES, *A Secular Age* (Cambridge, Mass., 2007).

TAYLOR, P. K., *Indentured to Liberty: Peasant Life and the Hessian Military State 1688–1815* (Ithaca, NY, 1994).

TAYLOR, RODNEY, *Perspectives on Spinoza in Works by Schiller, Büchner and C. F. Meyer* (New York, 1995).

TEICH, MIKULÁŠ, 'Bohemia: From Darkness into Light', in R. Porter and M. Teich (eds.), *The Enlightenment in National Context* (Cambridge, 1981), 141–63.

TÉLLEZ ALARCIA, DIEGO, 'Spanish Interpretations of the Lisbon Earthquake between 1755 and 1762', in Braun and Radner (eds), *The Lisbon Earthquake*, 50–65.

TERPSTRA, J. U., *Friedrich Heinrich Jacobis 'Allwill'* (Groningen, 1957).

TERRALL, M., *The Man who Flattened the Earth: Maupertuis and the Sciences* (Chicago, 2002).

THALER, R. P., 'Introduction' to Radischchev, *A Journey*, 1–37.

THOMAS, D. O., 'Introduction' to Richard Price, *Political Writings* (Cambridge, 1991), pp. vii–xxii.

THOMAS, HUGH, *The Slave Trade: The History of the Atlantic Slave Trade 1440–1870* (London, 1997).

THOMAS, WILLIAM, *The Philosophic Radicals* (Oxford, 1979).

THOMPSON, J. M., *The French Revolution* (1943; rev. edn. 1985).

TIETZ, M., 'Diderot und das Spanien der Aufklärung', in S. Jüttner (ed.), *Présence de Diderot: International Kolloquium zum 200. Todesjahr von Diderot an der Universität–G. H. Duisburg* (Frankfurt, 1990), 276–97.

TILGNER, HILMAR, *Lesegesellschaften an Mosel und Mittelrhein im Zeitalter des aufgeklärten Absolutismus* (Stuttgart, 2001).

TILL, NICHOLAS, *Mozart and the Enlightenment* (New York, 1993).

TILLET, E., *La Constitution anglaise: un modèle politique et institutionnel dans la France des Lumières* (Aix-en-Provence, 2001).

TOMÁS Y VALIENTE, FRANCISCO, 'El humanitarianismo ilustrado en España y el Discurso de J. P. Forner sobre la tortura', in L. Berlinguer and F. Colao (eds.), *Illuminismo e dottrine penali* (Milan, 1990), 373–402.

TOPAZIO, V. W., 'Diderot's Supposed Contribution to d'Holbach's Works', *Publications of the Modern Language Association*, 69 (1954), 173–88.

TORREY, N. L., 'Voltaire's Reaction to Diderot', *Proceedings of the Modern Language Association of America*, 50 (1935), 1107–47.

TORTAROLO, EDOARDO, *La ragione sulla Sprea* (Bologna, 1989).

—— *L'Illuminismo* (Rome, 1999).

—— *La ragione interpretata* (Rome, 2003).

TOSCANO, ALBERTO, *Fanaticism: On the Uses of an Idea* (London, 2010).

TRAMPUS, ANTONIO, *I Gesuiti e l'Illuminismo* (Florence, 2000).

—— (ed.), *Diritti e costituzione: l'opera di Gaetano Filangieri e la sua fortuna europea* (Bologna, 2005).

TRAVERS, R., 'Ideology and British Expansion in Bengal, 1757–72', *Journal of Imperial and Commonwealth History*, 33 (2005), 7–27.

—— 'Imperial Revolutions and Global Repercussions', in Armitage and Subrahmanyam (eds.), *Age of Revolutions*, 144–66.

TRIBE, K., 'Cameralism', in *CHEPTh* 525–46.

TROCKI, CARL, 'Chinese Pioneering in Eighteenth-Century Southeast Asia', in Reid (ed.), *Last Stand*, 83–101.

TROOSTENBURG DE BRUYN, C. A. L., *De Hervormde Kerk in Nederlandsch Oost-Indie (1602–1795)* (Arnhem, 1884).

TROUSSON, R., 'Michel-Ange Marin et les *Pensées philosophiques*', *RDE* 13 (1992), 47–55.

—— *Jean-Jacques Rousseau* (Paris, 2003).

—— *Denis Diderot ou le vrai Prométhée* (Paris, 2005).

TRUDEL, M., *L'Influence de Voltaire au Canada* (2 vols., Montreal, n.d.).

TSAPINA, O. A., 'Secularization and Opposition during the Time of Catherine the Great', in Bradley and Van Kley (eds.), *Religion and Politics*, 334–89.

TSUDA, TAKUMI (ed.), *Catalogue des livres de la Bibliothèque de Turgot* (3 vols., Tokyo, 1974).

TULLY, JAMES, 'Rediscovering America: The *Two Treatises* and Aboriginal Rights', in G. A. J. Rogers (ed.), *Locke's Philosophy* (Oxford, 1994), 165–96.

TURCO, LUIGI, 'Moral Sense and the Foundations of Morals', in Broadie (ed.), *Scottish Enlightenment*, 136–56.

UMBACH, M., *Federalism and Enlightenment in Germany, 1740–1806* (London, 2000).

URBANIAK, JAN, 'Polen heft eene nieuwe Constitutie aangenomen!' (forthcoming conference paper given at Olomouc, in March 2010).

UZGALIS, W., 'On Locke and Racism', in Ward and Lott (eds.), *Philosophers on Race*, 81–100.

VAMBOULIS, E., 'La Discussion de l'attraction chez Voltaire', in de Gandt (ed.), *Cirey*, 159–70.

VAN BUNGE, WIEP, *De Nederlandse Republiek: Spinoza en de Radicale Verlichting* (Brussels, 2010).

VAN DER BRUG, P. H., *Malaria en malaise: De VOC in Batavia in de Achttiende Eeuw* (Amsterdam, 1994).

VAN DE VELDE, PAUL, 'The Orientalist, Artist and Writer, J. G. Haafner (1755–1809), Caught between Enlightenment and Romanticism', *Dutch Crossing*, 39 (1989), 88–95.

VAN DÜLMEN, RICHARD, *Der Geheimbund der Illuminaten* (Stuttgart, 1975).

—— *The Society of the Enlightenment* (Cambridge, 1992).

VAN DUZER, CH. H., 'Contribution of the Ideologues to French Revolutionary Thought', *Johns Hopkins University Studies in Historical and Political Science*, 53/4 (Baltimore, 1935), 143–76.

VAN GOOR, J., 'Seapower, Trade and State Formation', in J. van Goor (ed.), *Trading Companies in Asia, 1600–1830* (Utrecht, 1986), 83–106.

VAN HORN MELTON, JAMES, 'From Enlightenment to Revolution: Hertzberg, Schlözer and the Problem of Despotism in the Late Aufklärung', *Central European History*, 12 (1979), 103–23.

—— *The Rise of the Public in Enlightenment Europe* (Cambridge, 2001).

—— 'The Nobility in the Bohemian and Austrian Lands, 1620–1780', in Scott (ed.), *European Nobilities*, 171–208.

VAN KLEY, D. K., *The Damiens Affair and the Unraveling of the Ancien Regime 1750–1770* (Princeton, 1984).

—— *The Religious Origins of the French Revolution* (New Haven, 1996).

—— 'Christianity as Casualty and Chrysalis of Modernity', *AHR* 108 (2003), 1081–104.

—— 'Religion and the Age of "Patriot Reform"', *JMH* 80 (2008), 252–95.

VAN SAS, N. C. F., 'The Patriot Revolution: New Perspectives', in Jacob and Mijnhardt (eds.), *Dutch Republic*, 91–119.

VAN VLIET, R., *Elie Luzac (1721–1796): Boekverkoper van de Verlichting* (Nijmegen, 2005).

VANYSACKER, D., 'Verlicht ultramontaan: Een *contradictio in terminis?*', *De Achttiende Eeuw*, 32 (2000), 97–115.

VELEMA, W. R. E., *Enlightenment and Conservatism in the Dutch Republic: The Political Thought of Elie Luzac (1721–1796)* (Assen, 1993).

—— 'Verlichting in Nederland: het voorbeeld van de politieke theorie', *GWN* 5 (1994), 45–53.

—— *Republicans: Essays on Eighteenth-Century Dutch Political Thought* (Leiden, 2007).

—— *Omstreden oudheid: de Nederlandse achttiende eeuw en de klassieke politiek* (Amsterdam, 2010).

—— 'Jonathan Israel and Dutch Patriotism', *De Achttiende Eeuw*, 41 (2009), 150–8.

—— 'Anti-monarchism in Early Modern Dutch Thought', in Van Gelderen and Skinner (eds.), *Republicanism*, i. 9–25.

—— 'Elie Luzac and Two Dutch Revolutions', in Jacob and Mijnhardt (eds.), *Dutch Republic*, 123–46.

VENTURI, FRANCO, *Jeunesse de Diderot (1713–1753)* (Paris, 1939).

—— *Le origini dell'Enciclopedia* (1946; 3rd edn., Turin, 1977).

—— *L'antichità svelata e l'idea del progreso in N. A. Boulanger (1722–1759)* (Bari, 1947).

—— 'Postille inedite di Voltaire ad alcune opere di Nicolas-Antoine Boulanger e del barone d'Holbach', *Studi francesi*, 5 (1958), 231–40.

—— *Settecento riformatore* (5 vols., Turin, 1969–90).

—— 'La Première Crise de l'ancien régime (1768–1776)', in R. Mortier and H. Hasquin (eds.), *Études sur le XVIIIe siècle*, 7 (1980), 9–24.

—— *Pagine repubblicane* (Turin, 2004).

—— (ed.), *Riformatori Lombardi, Piemontesi e Toscani*, vol. iii of *Illuministi italiani* (Milan, 1958).

VERBEEK, THEO, 'Sensation et matière: Hemsterhuis et le matérialisme', in Fresco et al. (eds.), *Frans Hemsterhuis*, 243–62.

—— 'Spinoza on Natural Rights', *IHR* 17 (2007), 257–75.

VERCRUYSSE, JEROOM, *Bicentaire du* Système de la nature: *textes holbachiens peu connus* (Paris, 1970).

—— *Bibliographie descriptive des écrits du Baron d'Holbach* (Paris, 1971).

VERNIÈRE, PAUL, *Spinoza et la pensée française avant la Révolution* (1954; 2nd edn., 1982).

VERRI, L., 'Legge, potere, diritto', in D. Felice (ed.), *Montesquieu e i suoi interpreti* (2 vols., Pisa, 2005), 357–75.

VERSINI, L., 'Diderot et la Russie', in Poussou et al. (eds.), *L'Influence*, 223–34.

VERZAAL, E., 'Het bezoek van Frans Hemsterhuis bij Goethe te Weimar', *Wijsgerig Perspectief*, 39 (1989), 46–50.

—— 'Der Besuch von Frans Hemsterhuis bei Goethe in Weimar', in J. Eklaar and H. Ester (eds.), *Von Goethe war die Rede* (Amsterdam, 1999), 165–80.

VIERHAUS, RUDOLF, 'Aufklärung und Freimaurerei in Deutschland', in H. Reinalter (ed.), *Freimaurer und Geheimbünde in 18. Jahrhundert in Mitteleuropa* (Frankfurt, 1983), 115–39.

VILLANI, PASQUALE, *Mezzogiorno tra riforme e rivoluzione* (Rome, 1974).

VILLARI, R., 'Antonio Genovesi e la ricerca delle forze motrici dello sviluppo sociale', in D. Balani et al. (eds.), *Dall'origine dei Lumi alla Rivoluzione: scritti in onore di Luciano Guerci e Giuseppe Ricuperati* (Rome, 2008), 605–20.

VILLAVERDE, MARÍA JOSÉ, 'Rousseau, lecteur de Spinoza', *SVEC* 369 (1999), 107–39.

VILLAVERDE, MARÍA JOSÉ, 'Spinoza, Rousseau: dos concepciones de democracia', *Revista de estudios políticos*, 116 (2002), 85–106.

VOCELKA, KARL, 'Enlightenment in the Habsburg Monarchy', in O. P. Grell and R. Porter (eds.), *Toleration in Enlightenment Europe* (Cambridge, 2000), 196–211.

WALKER, CH. F., *Smoldering Ashes: Cuzco and the Creation of Republican Peru, 1780–1840* (Durham, NC, 1999).

—— 'Shaking the Unstable Empire', in Johns (ed.), *Dreadful Visitations*, 113–44.

—— *Shaky Colonialism: The 1746 Earthquake-Tsunami in Lima, Peru* (Durham, NC, 2008).

WALL, ERNESTINE VAN DER, 'Orthodoxy and Scepticism in the Early Dutch Enlightenment', in Popkin and Vanderjagt (eds.), *Scepticism and Irreligion*, 121–41.

—— 'Geen natie van atheisten: Pieter Paulus (1753–1796) over godsdienst en mensenrechten', *Jaarboek der Nederlandse letterkunde* (1997), 45–62.

—— *Socrates in de hemel?* (Hilversum, 2000).

—— 'Religie en Verlichting', in E. Van der Wall and L. Wessels (eds.), *Een veelzijdige verstandhouding: Religie en Verlichting in Nederland 1650–1850* (Nijmegen, 2007), 13–35.

WALTERS, K. S., *Benjamin Franklin and his Gods* (Urbana, Ill., 1999).

WALTON, CHARLES, *Policing Public Opinion in the French Revolution* (New York, 2009).

WANGERMANN, ERNST, *From Joseph II to the Jacobin Trials* (1958; 2nd edn., Oxford, 1969).

—— 'Reform Catholicism and Political Radicalism in the Austrian Enlightenment', in R. Porter and M. Teich (eds.), *The Enlightenment in National Context* (Cambridge, 1981), 127–40.

WARD, J. K., and LOTT, T. L. (eds.), *Philosophers on Race: Critical Essays* (Oxford, 2002).

WARD, LEE, *The Politics of Liberty in England and Revolutionary America* (2004; Cambridge, new edn., 2010).

WARD, W. R., 'Late Jansenism and the Habsburgs', in J. E. Bradley and Dale Van Kley (eds.), *Religion and Politics in Enlightenment Europe* (Notre Dame, Ind., 2001), 154–86.

WARTOFSKY, M. W., 'Diderot and the Development of Materialist Monism', *Diderot Studies*, 2 (1952), 279–329.

WATT, J. R., 'Suicide, Gender and Religion: The Case of Geneva', in J. R. Watt (ed.), *From Sin to Insanity: Suicide in Early Modern Europe* (Ithaca, NY, 2004), 138–57.

WATTS, G. B., 'The Swiss Editions of the *Encyclopédie*', *Harvard Library Bulletin*, 9 (1955), 213–35.

WEBER, D. J., *Bárbaros: Spaniards and their Savages in the Age of Enlightenment* (New Haven, 2005).

WEBER, PETER, 'Mirabeau und die Berliner Aufklärer', in P. Weber, *Literarische und politische Öffentlichkeit: Studien zu Berliner Aufklärung* (Berlin, 2006), 169–82.

—— 'Publizistische Strategien der preussischen Justizreformer 1780–1794', in Goldenbaum (ed.), *Appell*, ii. 729–812.

WEIL, FRANÇOISE, 'L'Impression des tomes VIII à XVII de l'*Encyclopédie*', RDE 1 (1986), 85–93.

WERTHEIM-GIJSE WEENINK, A. H., *Democratische bewegingen in Gelderland, 1672–1795* (Amsterdam, 1973).

WESSELL, L. P., *G. E. Lessing's Theology: A Reinterpretation* (The Hague, 1977).

WHALEY, J., *Religious Toleration and Social Change in Hamburg, 1529–1819* (Cambridge, 1985).

WHALEY, L., *Radicals, Politics and Republicanism in the French Revolution* (Stroud, 2000).

WHATMORE, R., 'Venturi and Republicanism in Eighteenth-Century Geneva', in Albertone (ed.), *Repubblicanesimo moderno*, 431–48.

——'Rousseau and the *Représentants*: The Politics of the *Lettres écrites de la montagne*', *Modern Intellectual History*, 3 (2006), 385–314.

——' "Neither Masters nor Slaves": Small States and Empire in the Long Eighteenth Century', in D. Kelly (ed.), *Lineages of Empire* (Oxford, 2009), 53–81.

WICKWAR, W. H., *Baron d'Holbach: A Prelude to the French Revolution* (1935; repr. New York, 1968).

WIELEMA, M., *The March of the Libertines: Spinozists and the Dutch Reformed Church (1660–1750)* (Hilversum, 2004).

——'Hemsterhuis on Evil: A Rationalist Solution', in Fresco et al. (eds.), *Frans Hemsterhuis*, 365–78.

WILKE, J., 'Die Thematisierung der Französischen Revolution in der deutschen Presse', *Francia*, 22 (1995), 61–98.

——'Spion des Publikums, Sittenrichter und Advokat der Menschheit: Wilhelm Ludwig Wekhrlin (1739–1792)', *Publizistik*, 38 (1993), 322–34.

WILLEY, BASIL, *The Eighteenth-Century Background* (1940; Harmondsworth, 1962).

WILLIAMS, BERNARD, *Truth and Truthfulness* (Princeton, 2002).

WILLIAMS, D., *Condorcet and Modernity* (Cambridge, 2004).

WILLIAMS, D. L., *Rousseau's Platonic Enlightenment* (University Park, Pa., 2007).

WILSON, CATHERINE, 'The Enlightenment Philosopher as Social Critic', *IHR* (2008), 413–25.

WILSON, W. DANIEL, *Geheimräte gegen Geheimbünde: Ein unbekanntes Kapitel der klassisch-romantischen Geschichte Weimars* (Stuttgart, 1991).

——'Der politische Jacobinismus wie er leibt und lebt? Der Illuminatenorden und revolutionäre Ideologie', *Lessing Yearbook*, 25 (1993), 133–84.

——'Enlightenment's Alliance with Power: The Dialectic of Collusion and Opposition in the Literary Elite', in Wilson and Holub (eds.), *Impure Reason*, 364–84.

——and Holub, R. (eds.), *Impure Reason: Dialectic of Enlightenment in Germany* (Detroit, 1993).

WINCH, D., 'Scottish Political Economy', in *CHEPTh* 443–64.

——'Commercial Realities, Republican Principles', in Van Gelderen and Skinner (eds.), *Republicanism*, ii. 293–310.

WINKLE, STEFAN, *Struensee und die Publizistik* (Hamburg, 1982).

——*Die heimlichen Spinozisten in Altona und der Spinozastreit* (Hamburg, 1988).

WINKLER, K. P., 'Perception and Ideas, Judgment', in *CHEPh* i. 234–85.

WINTER, M., 'Georg Philipp Wucherer (1734–1805): Grosshändler und Verleger', *Archiv für Geschichte des Buchwesens*, 37 (1992), 1–98.

WITHERS, CH. W. J., *Placing the Enlightenment* (Chicago, 2007).

WOKLER, ROBERT, *Social Thought of J. J. Rousseau* (New York, 1987).

——'The Enlightenment Project as Betrayed by Modernity', *History of European Ideas*, 24 (1998), 301–13.

——'Rousseau and his Critics on the Fanciful Liberties we have Lost', in R. Wokler (ed.), *Rousseau and Liberty* (Manchester, 1995).

——*Rousseau* (1995; Oxford, new edn., 1996).

WOLFF, CHARLOTTA, 'The Swedish Aristocracy and the French Enlightenment (1740–1780)', *Scandinavian Journal of History*, 30 (2005), 259–70.

WOLFF, L., *Inventing Eastern Europe* ((Stanford, Calif., 1994).
—— *The Enlightenment and the Orthodox World* (Athens, 2001).
WOLHEIM, R., 'Introduction' to R. Wolheim (ed.), *Hume on Religion* (1966; London, 1971), 7–30.
WOLTERSTORFF, N., *Thomas Reid and the Story of Epistemology* (Cambridge, 2001).
—— 'God and Darkness in Reid', in J. Houston (ed.), *Thomas Reid* (Edinburgh, 2004), 77–101.
WOOD, ALLEN, *Kant* (Oxford, 2005).
—— 'Rational Theology, Moral Faith and Religion', in Guyer (ed.), *Cambridge Companion to Kant*, 394–416.
WOOD, GORDON S., *The Radicalism of the American Revolution* (New York, 1993).
—— *The Americanization of Benjamin Franklin* (New York, 2004).
WOOD, P. B., 'Hume, Reid and the Science of the Mind', in Stewart and Wright (eds.), *Hume*, 119–39.
WOOLF, STUART, *A History of Italy 1700–1860* (London, 1979).
WOOTTON, DAVID, 'David Hume "the Historian"', in Norton (ed.), *Cambridge Companion to Hume*, 281–312.
—— 'Helvétius: From Radical Enlightenment to Revolution', *Political Theory*, 28 (2000), 307–36.
—— 'The Republican Tradition: From Commonwealth to Common Sense', in D. Wootton (ed.), *Republicanism, Liberty and Commercial Society 1649–1776* (Stanford, Calif., 1994), 1–44.
WORRALL, D., *Theatric Revolution: Drama, Censorship and Romantic Subcultures 1773–1832* (Oxford, 2006).
WRIGHT, J. K., *A Classical Republican in Eighteenth-Century France: The Political Thought of Mably* (Stanford, Calif., 1997).
—— 'The Idea of a Republican Constitution in Old Regime France', in Van Gelderen and Skinner (eds.), *Republicanism*, i. 289–306.
YENNAH, R., 'Rousseau et la Révolution', in L'Aminot (ed.), *Politique et révolution*, 35–47.
YOGEV, G., *Diamonds and Coral: Anglo-Dutch Jews and Eighteenth-Century Trade* (Leicester, 1978).
YOUNG, DAVID, 'Despotism and the Road to Freedom: Cesare Beccaria and Eighteenth-Century Lombardy', *SECC* 13 (1984), 271–9.
YOUNG, J. C., *Colonial Desire: Hybridity in Theory, Culture and Race* (London, 1995).
ZAGORIN, P., *How the Idea of Religious Toleration Came to the West* (Princeton, 2003).
ZAKAI, A., *Jonathan Edwards' Philosophy of History* (Princeton, 2003).
—— *Jonathan Edwards' Philosophy of Nature* (London, 2010).
ZAMBELLI, P., *La formazione filosofica di Antonio Genovesi* (Naples, 1972).
ZAMMITO, J. H., *The Genesis of Kant's Critique of Judgment* (Chicago, 1992).
—— *Kant, Herder and the Birth of Anthropology* (London, 2002).
—— '"The Most Hidden Conditions of Men of the First Rank": The Pantheist Current in Eighteenth-Century Germany "Uncovered" by the Spinoza Controversy', *Eighteenth-Century Thought*, 1 (2003), 335–3.
ZAMOYSKI, ADAM, *Holy Madness: Romantics, Patriots and Revolutionaries, 1776–1871* (London, 1999).
ZARETSKY, R., and SCOTT, J. T., *The Philosophers' Quarrel: Rousseau, Hume and the Limits of Human Understanding* (New Haven, 2009).

ZARONE, GIUSEPPE, *Etica e politica nell'utilitarianismo di Cesare Beccaria* (Naples, 1971).

ZEUSKE, M., *Francisco de Miranda und die Entdeckung Europas* (Münster, 1995).

ZONNEVELT, P. VAN, 'Een echte antikoloniaal: Jakob Haafner (1754–1809)', in T. d'Haen and G. Termorshuizen (eds.), *De geest van Multatuli* (Leiden, 1998), 19–29.

ZURBUCHEN, SIMONE, 'Republicanism and Toleration', in Van Gelderen and Skinner (eds.), *Republicanism*, ii. 47–71.

Index